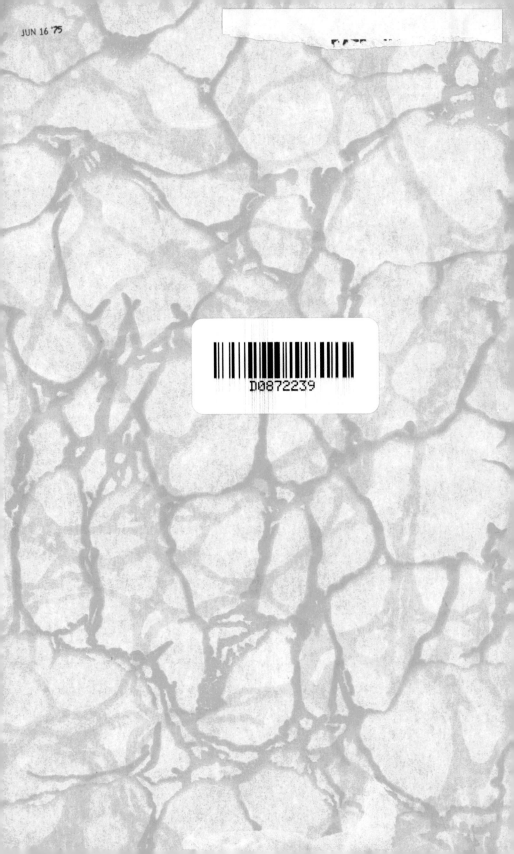

D0872239

# THE OPPOSITION PRESS
# OF THE
# FEDERALIST PERIOD

# The Opposition Press

# of the Federalist Period

## Donald H. Stewart

STATE UNIVERSITY OF NEW YORK PRESS
ALBANY

PUBLISHED BY STATE UNIVERSITY OF NEW YORK PRESS
THURLOW TERRACE, ALBANY, NEW YORK 12201

© 1969 BY THE RESEARCH FOUNDATION OF STATE UNIVERSITY
OF NEW YORK, ALBANY, NEW YORK. ALL RIGHTS RESERVED

STANDARD BOOK NUMBER 87395-042-9
LIBRARY OF CONGRESS CATALOG CARD NUMBER 69-11319
MANUFACTURED IN THE UNITED STATES OF AMERICA
DESIGNER: RHODA C. CURLEY

*To my Mother and the memory of my Father*

# CONTENTS

# CONTENTS

# PREFACE

Within the framework of the American constitutional system the creation of a political party of major importance is an exceedingly difficult task. Local issues alone will not suffice, and even the desire to capture public offices has limitations as a cohesive force. For the past hundred years, new parties have rarely achieved genuine significance in Presidential elections, and many such organizations had only a brief existence. How, then, did it happen that Thomas Jefferson and his associates were able to fashion, in so brief a period and out of apparent nothingness, a party that soon became dominant and that has ever since remained a potent political force?

Jefferson, Madison, and John Beckley were obviously master organizers, and manifold issues were at hand to be exploited. But more than the coincidence of able politicians and numerous issues is required to explain the phenomenon. My thesis is that much of the credit for Jeffersonian achievements at the polls may be attributed to the skillful presentation and use of propaganda (employing that word in its broadest sense). Newspapers in that era were indubitably the most effective instruments for such an endeavor; consequently they have been made the subject of this study.

"Propaganda" is a term that has been much overworked during the last few decades. Use of the word itself is kept to a minimum in the following pages. Yet in considering what

ix

the Democratic-Republicans were attempting to do, I have interpreted it (as does the Institute for Propaganda Analysis) to cover any expression of opinion or activity that I believed was deliberately meant to influence the views or actions of others toward predetermined goals. Clearly, such a definition is a sweeping one, and this study demonstrates that Jeffersonians conducted their operations on the widest possible front. Except in the most obvious cases, I made no effort to distinguish truth from falsehood in the numerous items consulted and utilized. In many instances that task would have been all but insuperable, for the details of many day-to-day happenings were sometimes reported incompletely in the press or have been lost with the passage of time. Moreover, the verity or falsity of opinions as such is a matter scarcely susceptible to judgment.

About 550 papers, some of them dailies, were published in the twelve-year period covered by my research, and copies of nearly that many are extant. To claim to have read every word in every issue of all these would be palpably preposterous. But I did examine copies of nearly all these newspapers and devoted special consideration to the ones that manifested a Republican or undetermined position. I therefore believe the following study provides an adequate delineation of the chief measures of attack and defense, of the rhetoric and reason employed, of the way Republican editors reacted to both favorable and unfavorable quirks of fate, and of which appeals were most widely used.

Inasmuch as newspapers intrinsically are descriptive of their age, a descriptive approach has been utilized herein. To organize the material posed considerable difficulties. After considering several methods, I finally decided to use a topical arrangement of the arguments and—wherever feasible—to follow a chronological sequence within each broad topic. While this meant that various *types* of appeals might be found widely dispersed throughout the volume, it afforded a rather logical order and a continuity that seemed obtainable in no other fashion.

To capture accurately and to convey something of the spirit of the times, articles have frequently been paraphrased and quotations liberally employed. Unless otherwise noted, pertinent passages from the newspapers have been reprinted textually without change of spelling, punctuation, or accentuation. It is hoped that these passages, as well as the study itself, may prove of value to anyone wishing to know more about America's press during the nation's formative years under its then recently adopted Constitution.

One more word seems in order. Few figures in American history have excited more controversy than have Jefferson and Hamilton. Each leader is difficult to evaluate objectively. I hold considerable admiration for both, albeit largely for different reasons. It is not my intention, however, to be an apologist for either. Of necessity, the following pages set forth a predominantly Republican picture of the contest between the objectives of the two men. In reading this work one should ever keep in mind that there was also a Federalist version.

Many years have elapsed since this study began as a doctoral dissertation. Inevitably, a project of this nature must owe a great deal to many persons, and over the years my indebtedness has become indeed great and widespread. Even so, a number of specific acknowledgments are clearly requisite.

To the late Professor Charles J. Ritchey of Drake University and to Professor Ralph A. Brown of the State University College at Cortland, New York, special gratitude is due. The former, both as mentor and colleague, suggested organizational changes while this work was in its early stages, helped me devise and use a process for microfilming many of the newspapers at a time when that practice was still comparatively new, and aided both directly and indirectly in countless ways. The latter first called my attention to the possibilities of this as a subject for research and provided the benefit of his encouragement and constructive criticism on several occasions.

Professor William B. Bjornstad, also of Drake, and Professor Kathleen Moore, of Union College (Barbourville, Kentucky), read drafts of certain chapters and made valuable suggestions. Mrs. Miriam Asher and Mrs. Virginia Lawrence both, while at Union College, checked various items. Professor Eugene P. Link, now of State University College at Plattsburgh, New York, provided valuable information and aid, particularly in matters relevant to his own study on the Democratic Societies. Anyone dealing with journalism in the early years of the United States is perforce beholden to the late Clarence S. Brigham's monumental *History and Bibliography of American Newspapers, 1690–1820*. While Director of the American Antiquarian Society, Worcester, Massachusetts, Mr. Brigham offered keen interest and kindness far beyond conventional courtesy in making available the full resources of the Society's superb collection of early American newspapers. Miss Mary Brown, of the Society's library, was also most helpful in locating specific papers and in making it possible for me to work with a minimum of interruptions. Charles H. Sullivan, of the National Archives, supplied information concerning Oliver Wolcott. Emanuel Bilz, of Santa Monica, California, spent many hours assisting me in translating a sizeable portion of the news items that were in German.

Gratitude is also due to Columbia University, for the grant of a traveling fellowship enabling me to visit most of the forty-five libraries noted in the appendix. My profound thanks go also to numerous staff workers at these libraries for competently and cheerfully complying with requests that must at times have seemed to them needless or inane.

Among those who were my professors while I was at Columbia, appreciation is herewith particularly expressed for the helpful suggestions of the late Professor Evarts B. Greene; to Professor Dumas Malone (now emeritus at the University of Virginia) for his interest and unfailing courtesy, despite my demands upon his time and talents; to Professor Henry Steele Commager (now of Amherst College) for his gracious encouragement; and to Dr. John A. Krout for the stimulation and experience gained from his seminar courses, as well as for his friendly patience and counsel at many points.

The author would be inexcusably remiss without making special acknowledgment to Professor Julian P. Boyd, editor of Princeton's *The Papers of Thomas Jefferson*, whose careful scholarship and generous comments aided immeasurably in the latter stages of writing this volume. Appreciation is likewise tendered to the State University of New York Press and its director, Norman S. Mangouni, for producing this publication, and to Mrs. Nancy Sharlet, who has been simultaneously understanding and painstaking in editing it.

A number of typists labored meticulously and diligently that deadlines might be met; the efforts of Mrs. Paul Helmick, Mrs. John Fehrs, Mrs. Warren Caughey, and Miss Josephine Kiernan merit specific attention. Particular indebtedness is owing to my sister-in-law, Harriet Lindee Stewart, who patiently and capably deciphered many of the notes to put them in readable preliminary form. Bert Balthis, of Winfield, Illinois, demonstrated both his friendship and his capabilities as a research assistant when he traveled with me for several of the many months in which material for this work was originally accumulated. To all of the foregoing, and to others unmentioned, go the writer's heartiest thanks.

My mother and father, Mr. and Mrs. F. H. Stewart, read much of the early drafts, made beneficial observations, and relieved me of many other burdens while this project was under way. Any attempt to express adequately my thanks to them would be futile. Last but clearly not least, endless gratitude is proffered to my wife, Joann Evans Stewart, who had the courage to marry me when this effort was yet in the state of an unfinished dissertation. Without her inspiration and assistance, to say nothing of shouldering more than her share of the responsibilities of raising a growing family, it is difficult to imagine how this work could have reached completion.

D. H. S.

Cortland, New York
February, 1969

# The Opposition Press
## of the
## Federalist Period

# I
## NEWSPAPERS AND THEIR ROLE

The newspapers were to blame. Virtually everyone said so. Thomas Jefferson would not have been elected, nor John Adams defeated, in 1800 without them. On this point both Federalists and Republicans [1] agreed. Jefferson and his lieutenants credited the press with his victory, while Federalist chiefs and journals alike berated opposition newspapers for sweeping that party from office.[2] Accordingly, it is surprising that scholars, politicians, and propagandists have paid so little attention to the instrumentality by which (if contemporaries were correct) in eleven short years, and apparently almost out of thin air, a successful opposition political party was created. Before six or seven of those years had passed, the party so formed was a potent political force; in approximately a decade it had become dominant.

The American press has been historically an object of fluctuating brilliance and significance. Prior to the eighteenth century its beginnings in the English settlements were in job printing for pamphlets, official publications, and occasional tracts or handbills. The settlements were too small to support newspapers as such. Indeed, the earliest "newspapers" to emerge were essentially bulletin boards for their communities, containing little of what today would be classified as news. And since comments about political affairs tended to provoke governmental inquiries, printers felt restricted as to what they could

3

publish. Still, something new and entertaining was needed to maintain the interest of readers, and communications from abroad or from other colonies were meager and irregular.

Publishers thus turned to essays (sometimes "lifted" from European sources), verse, intermittent satirical character studies to supplement official notices, or stereotyped accounts of social functions. Eventually, nearly all the colonial secular literature of the first half of the eighteenth century came to appear in the columns of these "newspapers without news." This provided an opportunity for intellectuals to express themselves and to influence popular thought. Reprints from European works could also insinuate ideas that might be suppressed if directly presented, and the widespread republication of such items as *Cato's Letters* in support of representative government helped unify political sentiment in cultures as disparate as those of Charleston and Boston.[3] Soon politicians and would-be manipulators of sentiment began using newspapers, the foundations of which had been so discreetly established. Eminent historians have stressed the essentiality of the role of the press in developing and solidifying anti-British feeling during the Revolutionary period, and it was realized at the time that American independence was as much the product of the newspapers as of the sword.[4]

Despite the unevenness of its influence, the press has almost from its inception in America come consistently to reflect the life and interests of the nation's citizenry. At times it has both molded public opinion and mirrored it. Seldom has it accomplished both functions so completely as in the years immediately following the ratification of the Federal Constitution.

Adoption of that document had convinced most remaining skeptics of the effectiveness of printed propaganda. The famed *Federalist Papers* in themselves may not have carried the New York state convention for approval,[5] but their potency nevertheless was nationally recognized. A majority of newspaper editors had favored the Constitution and were convinced of the part their publications played in achieving its acceptance. Having helped shape the popular mind, they were eager to continue the process. With policies of the new government being formulated, with offices and power to be obtained, it was inevitable that partisanship should develop and that much of it should be expressed in periodical columns.

Yet there is more than this to the story. The dispute with the mother country had led many Americans to examine seriously the nature of government itself. A dialogue was thus set in motion that has continued long after Yorktown. Apart from self-determination, was the chief purpose of the state to preserve order and security or to promote equality and justice? Copious discussion over adoption of the new fundamental law centered around these principles.

During the Revolution the issues of independence and waging war had created a comradeship of arms among Patriots who might differ on such points. This was true even in the haggling Congress, and the government of the Confederation had been relatively powerless to act decisively on these issues. Unlike these organizations, the system established by the Constitution promised sufficient authority to make its control more crucial in implementing principles, in policies, prestige, and patronage. Divergent opinions and accusations of discrimination thus speedily manifested themselves. Before long, factions, which already existed in many states, appeared on the national scene—forming around differences over foreign relations, sectional interests, interpretations of the basic charter, fiscal programs, or the viewpoints of individual leaders. Gradually, with much effort and occasionally circumspect or even painful backing and filling, these factions coalesced into two major groups: those who essentially supported the objectives of the administration under Washington, and those who sought to redirect or replace it. Terminology, as will be shown, was at first both ambiguous and uncertain, but more and more those favoring the general trends initiated were able to appropriate the name of "Federalist," while critics came— less uniformly—to be styled "Republicans" or (by a later era) "Democratic-Republicans."

Headed by Alexander Hamilton, John Adams, John Jay,

and in a sense by the charismatic figure of Washington himself, the Federalists found their following among the national-minded, among those who believed an "energetic" government should consciously further America's industrial and commercial interests, and among traditionalists desiring discipline and stability. Financiers and veterans, property owners and professional men, members of privileged religious groups as well as speculators eyeing opportunities for quick profits, and farmers interested in export markets, saw the Constitution as meaning management from the nation's capital city and hoped to utilize that management to maintain or further their advantage. Fearful of anarchy, favorably disposed toward England (assuredly, in contrast to the terrors of the French Revolution), and inclined toward nativism, these men constituted a "Weight of Talent, Wealth and . . . family interest," in the words of Charles Pinckney. Geographically, their strength was in the trading centers of the country, the North and East, and among the large planters of the South. Yet despite patrician overtones, the Federalists were not exclusively a well-to-do elite; many a shipyard worker or other artisan and numerous small farmers, as well as temporary majorities from states with Revolutionary debts largely undischarged, saw benefits to be derived from the security and power of a strong central authority.[6]

Republicans (often called "Democrats," at least by their adversaries) found themselves following such men as James Madison, Albert Gallatin, Aaron Burr, William Branch Giles, and—eventually and increasingly—Thomas Jefferson. Unconvinced of the need for swift industralization, apprehensive of tyranny, they favored simplicity, frugality, and equality in government and opposed positive official action to promote economic development. In their eyes Hamilton fostered special privileges and threatened agrarian ways. Stressing liberty and the pursuit of happiness, they applauded the humanitarian gains of the French Revolution, envisioned America as a continuing haven for the oppressed of all lands, and desired a government clearly responsive to public opinion. Philosophically, they were inclined to believe in man's perfectibility and were optimistic concerning the future. While most of their chieftains were relatively well educated, even moderately wealthy, their doctrines possessed a broader appeal to town "mechanics" and to farmers generally than did those of their opponents. All parts of the land contained "outs" desirous of supplanting the "ins," but Republican strongholds were primarily in the South and West (particularly where backcountry farming conditions prevailed), though urban workers came to constitute a significant additional base. Alliances between some of the more prominent editors and outstanding leaders of one political faction or the other intensified the rising partisanship. That these ties were often secret or informal, or both, made them none the less influential.

Jefferson himself was a party to some of the most famous of these relationships. Within two weeks after entering upon his duties in New York as Secretary of State he selected John Fenno's *Gazette of the United States* to publish officially the laws of the federal government. Perturbed by the lack of republican sentiment in the temporary capital and by the almost exclusive reliance upon British sources for news, he deliberately chose Fenno's publication after arranging for it to also print extracts from the liberal *Leyden Gazette*. This was done to counterbalance somewhat the dependence upon English informants and to provide opportunity for a less biased view of European happenings; for a time the Secretary himself translated the desired excerpts.[7] By late summer, 1790, Jefferson had named gazettes in five states to print the laws by authority and expressed desire to do likewise in each remaining commonwealth. Because remuneration was involved, this apparently routine duty possessed "considerable political potentialities. . . ."[8]

Following adoption of Hamilton's assumption bill, however, Fenno's sheet proved less willing to carry items critical of a strong central authority, and in 1791 Jefferson turned to egalitarian Benjamin Franklin Bache's struggling Philadelphia *General Advertiser*. As Bache could make his own trans-

7

lations, the Secretary merely furnished him with copies of the *Leyden Gazette,* asserting that he did so through his "desire of seeing a purely republican vehicle of news established between the seat of government and all it's parts." [9]

After Philip Freneau established his *National Gazette,* however, Jefferson saw to it that the journal was regularly supplied with the Dutch wellspring of foreign news. The association here was perhaps the most celebrated of all of Jefferson's connections with the press. Although he always denied ever writing or dictating any political articles for the *National Gazette,* [10] he helped found that organ and was at least indirectly responsible for much that it contained. As he later told Washington, he arranged to have the *Leyden Gazette* systematically sent to the zealous Freneau for use in the latter's paper, [11] and he strove to obtain pecuniary support for the newssheet. [12] The modern-day editors of *The Papers of Thomas Jefferson* assert that all evidence available substantiates the Secretary's assertion that he "never employed a newspaper pseudonym to impugn the character of his opponent," and that he considered such behavior unbecoming a Cabinet member. [13] Yet even the Virginian's most perceptive biographer admits Jefferson's tendency here to protest excessively. [14]

In the absence of definite proof to the contrary, however, Jefferson's disclaimer should be accepted as technically correct, despite the disbelief of Federalists of his day and a number of writers since. [15] To the Secretary, the press in a republic was obligated to provide the news and an opportunity for dissenting opinion. His relationship with Freneau was clearly questionable by twentieth-century standards, and possibly Jefferson may have had qualms about his actions based upon the criteria of his own times. As yet no party leader, he could not have been blind to the advantages of disseminating views according with his own political philosophy—nor unaware that those views at times differed markedly from official policy. The poet-editor, first approached by Madison, was an employee of the department headed by Jefferson in an administration the *National Gazette* was soon vehemently assailing. His annual salary of $250 for services as a translator was a mere pittance, but it was a desirable addition to the income of a struggling editor. Moreover, his post was that of "clerk for foreign languages," although Jefferson was quite aware that Freneau was competent only in French.[16] Correspondence with Madison indicates that the Secretary knew full well Freneau planned to establish an opposition journal and expressed an intent to give him the official printing business for the State Department.[17] The *National Gazette* was given priority in news dispatches coming to the Department; Jefferson solicited subscriptions in its behalf and urged Madison and other friends to write for it. It would have been strange indeed had he not suggested to Freneau at least some broad outlines of policies he expected the paper to follow, and the famed letter to Philip Mazzei later expressed views remarkably similar to those presented in Freneau's publication.[18] Unquestionably, the *National Gazette* reflected Jefferson's opinions "as in a mirror," [19] and in the anti-administration Boston *Independent Chronicle* the Philadelphia paper was commended as "published under the eye of . . . Thomas Jefferson." [20]

Not that Freneau was any man's mere mouthpiece. The ideas he espoused and the phraseology he used were essentially his own.[21] Also, in Jefferson's defense it should be noted that modern concepts of parties and of loyalty in Cabinet members had not yet developed. Presumably, Jefferson thought he had fully as much right—even a duty—to encourage publications designed to promote his political principles as Hamilton had to establish and aid Fenno's *Gazette of the United States* with the object of propagating the Federalist faith.

The *National Gazette* was not the only partisan sheet with which Jefferson had some tie, however tenuous. Still convinced that a national newspaper was indispensable in creating and continuing a Democratic-Republican party, after Freneau had temporarily left the field in 1793 he once more turned to Bache. Renamed the *Aurora* the following year, the old *General Advertiser* had certain advantages as a party organ. Its editor (until his death in 1798 when he was succeeded by Wil-

9

liam Duane) was Franklin's grandson. It too was well written and well printed and located in the national capital. Jefferson subscribed to the *Aurora,* read it regularly, and frequently urged friends to pen articles for it. Although he denied composing anything for publication himself, he corrected manuscripts which he had prodded Madison to prepare, and interviews and correspondence with Bache denote close cooperation. Thus it may be presumed his interest in the journal was more than academic.[22] From 1793 to 1797 Jefferson held no public office, but even after he became Vice-President Federalists taxed him with sponsoring the *Aurora,* and some contended its mysterious knack for uncovering official secrets was owing to his high station.[23] Much later (in fact, after his Presidency) he openly sought contributions to aid Duane, presumably in recognition of the latter's editorial services.[24]

Jefferson's influence was also at least partly responsible for the coming of Samuel Harrison Smith to Washington to found the *National Intelligencer.* An eager libertarian, Smith had earlier edited the Philadelphia *New World* and the *Universal Gazette,* which had financial difficulties like many other papers of the day; when Washington became the capital in 1800, the Vice-President gave the young printer encouragement to found that national party organ he thought to be so necessary.[25] In addition, he financially aided the efforts of James Thomson Callender, most intemperate of all Republican printers. Callender had published several books attacking Adams and edited the Richmond *Examiner;* that Jefferson sent him money in ignorance of his scurrility defies belief. When the vicious printer (embittered by failure to be named Richmond's postmaster) later turned on Jefferson, he charged that the Democratic chieftain had deliberately hired him to slander Federalist leaders—and the then President's explanations were less convincing than admirers could have wished.[26]

Other outstanding Republicans actively helped develop a party press. John Hancock and Samuel Adams promoted circulation of the *National Gazette* in Massachusetts.[27] Madison, Gallatin, and John Beckley assisted Bache and contributed articles for the *Aurora.*[28] New Jersey's leading Jeffersonian sheet, the Newark *Centinel of Freedom,* was run by a brother of the party's political leader in Essex County.[29] Hugh Henry Brackenridge, prominent western Pennsylvania Democrat, brought John Israel to Pittsburgh to print the *Tree of Liberty* to offset the pro-administration *Pittsburgh Gazette.* Israel's paper was published in a building owned by Brackenridge, who wrote many articles for its pages.[30] Edward Livingston, Tench Coxe, John Nicholas, and others attempted to establish another Democratic paper in Philadelphia in 1799, and Jefferson not only sent money himself but pledged $100 each for Monroe and Madison.[31] That project failed, but a group of party leaders did set up *The Press* in Richmond the following year.[32] Uriah Tracy, Senator from Connecticut, reported in the summer of 1800 that the Republicans were founding papers "in almost every town and county in the country." [33]

Federalist politicians also participated (and perhaps pioneered) in subsidizing or founding journals to serve party purposes. Hamilton's arrangements with John Fenno to commence the *Gazette of the United States* in support of the administration are well known. As Freneau pointed out, if his own annual salary of $250 as translating clerk proved that Jefferson controlled the *National Gazette,* Fenno's emolument of $2,500 was ten times as potent in bringing that printer's paper under Hamilton's sway.[34]

Hamilton, Jay, Rufus King, and others also advanced capital to establish the *American Minerva* as an administration spokesman in New York. Noah Webster was persuaded to leave a Hartford law office to edit the paper.[35] When Webster's journal became less partisan, good Republicans gloated over the valedictory of John Mason Williams's New York *Columbian Gazette,* wherein the editor indicated that "a certain political character" (evidently Hamilton) had falsely led him to believe he would receive $5,000 for printing a Federalist newssheet.[36] And at the century's close the former Secretary of the Treasury was among those contributing $1,000 each to set up William Coleman's *New York Evening Post.*[37]

Many editors, subsidized or not, took a positive role in

party organization and electioneering; a few even ran for office. Henry Kammerer of the *Philadelphische Correspondenz* was endorsed for the Pennsylvania Assembly in 1795, and Samuel H. Smith (later of the *New World*) was secretary for a Democratic nominating group in Philadelphia.[38] The Charleston *City Gazette* was published by Peter Freneau (brother of Philip), who was Secretary of State for South Carolina and Jefferson's political manager in the area.[39] Editor Thomas Greenleaf of the New York *Journal* was a sachem of the Tammany Society and was closely associated with the Burr faction in local Democratic-Republican affairs.[40] Bache and other editors were active in the American Philosophical Society, which certain writers believe was the nucleus around which the Jeffersonian party was begun.[41] Numerous publishers opposing the Federalist administration were active in the influential Democratic Societies during the early 1790s.[42] Bache and Eleazer Oswald of the Philadelphia *Independent Gazetteer* both were members of the Corresponding Committee of the key Democratic Society of Pennsylvania, while John Bradford suggested and organized the Democratic Society of Kentucky.[43]

Such ties between publishing and politics afford some measure of the significance of the press of the period. On leaving Washington's Cabinet in 1793 Jefferson was said to have expressed a desire never to see a newspaper again,[44] but such a wish was utterly incompatible with any plan to achieve a change in administrations—and Jefferson realized it. As commentators long ago noted, to American political parties the gazettes were as tools to the mechanic.[45]

Contemporaries were well aware of this power of the press. Travelers from Europe commented on the multiplicity of journals in the United States, of their efficacy in shaping public opinion, and of their indicating that opinion as an infallible barometer.[46] In this country Federalist and Republican writers alike testified to the importance of the gazettes, though some decried their power while others approved. Whereas the sermon of a Federalist minister might condemn the astounding potency and prevalence of "sentiments conveyed in newspapers,"[47] the newspaper column of a "Crazy Jonathan" stressed the advantages of such periodicals. Never in the world had there been a comparable means of communicating knowledge. Newspapers were published with greater frequency and in greater variety than any other form of publication; "Jonathan" estimated that they came into three-fourths of the homes of a "truly free people." It was an article of faith with editors that tyranny had little prospect of subduing a nation where all classes of society had access to a free press.[48]

Whether applauded or deprecated, in reality the press was for each party "the conduit between its leaders and philosophers, and the masses."[49] As might be expected, editors themselves were convinced of the importance of their own roles. Some clearly expressed a philosophy, emphasizing the vital need of a well-informed public in a democracy, and asserted that the political wisdom essential to a sound popular opinion could become prevalent only through periodicals which were generally circulated.[50] Thus, one such newspaper noted approvingly, farmers were enabled to check on the conduct of their representatives.[51] All political institutions, added another, really aimed at keeping people in ignorance in order to suppress freedom, but the discovery of printing—and the newspapers made possible thereby—constituted a death blow at the foundations of despotism.[52] Still a third writer insisted that nothing had contributed more than the gazettes to general enlightenment. They had multiplied enormously during the last few years. No longer were they restricted to the rich and the learned:

> All ranks and descriptions of men, read, study, and endeavor to comprehend the intelligence they convey, and too often adopt the principles they recommend without examination; and act on them as if they were sanctioned by irrefragable authority.

There were dangers in reading only one paper, but even the worst journals tended to convey instruction and to generalize knowledge. A good newspaper performed infinite service among those incapable of thinking for themselves.[53]

What factors explain this surprising influence of the Fourth Estate? The dingy, four-page newssheets of the late eighteenth century lacked such latterday staples as sports sections, pictures, wire reports, and comic strips, yet they possessed intense interest for their readers. Obviously, they faced little competition from other distracting media designed to inform and entertain. Doubtless much of their fascination stemmed from man's innate curiosity and the varied possibilities of unpredictable news which might be presented to gratify it. In the words of a poetically minded editor who perhaps was a bit more candid than modern journalists:

> Here various news we tell, of love and strife,
> Of peace and war, health, sickness, death and life,
> Of loss and gain, of famine and of store,
> Of storms at sea, and travels on the shore,
> Of prodigies, and portents seen in air,
> Of fires, and plagues, and stars with blazing hair,
> Of turns of fortune, changes in the state,
> The falls of fav'rites, projects of the great,
> Of old mismanagements, taxations new,
> *All neither wholly false, nor wholly true.*[54]

Certainly the growing popularity and consequence of these early newspapers was unrelated to their appearance, which was by contemporary standards unprepossessing. Of the more than five hundred different journals published at one time or another during the Federalist administrations,[55] nearly all were somber "single sheets," folded but once and thus limited to four pages. Paper was scarce and of uneven quality; of durable rag content, it was usually rough, inevitably costly, and frequently had a grayish or even bluish cast.[56] Type, set by the individual printer, ran to a variety of sizes, some of which were appreciably smaller than that used in today's classified advertising.[57] Sheepskin bags, or "ink balls," dipped in home-mixed ink were used to spread the fluid as evenly as possible on the set type after it was locked in place; the actual printing was accomplished by placing a sheet of paper on the type, protecting it with a layer of cloth, and using a long handle to force a large wood block down upon the cloth. A strong pull was required to make a satisfactory impression, and competent pressmen considered two hundred pulls an hour as good.[58]

By far the greatest number of gazettes produced in such fashion were printed weekly. In 1790, according to one compilation, the nation had 70 weeklies, 10 semi-weeklies, 3 tri-weeklies and 8 dailies. A similar list ten years later showed 178 weeklies, 29 semi-weeklies, 3 tri-weeklies and 24 dailies.[59] "Daily" meant six days a week, for none of these papers, which appeared exclusively in the larger seaboard cities, was printed on Sunday.[60]

Subscription rates varied widely, though in 1789 the average national cost was estimated at four cents a copy.[61] Even if accurate, this approximation is misleading, for city dailies had a much lower unit cost than did frontier weeklies. Single copies actually ranged in price from three to twelve and one-half cents; dailies cost from five to ten dollars a year, and weeklies and semi-weeklies averaged around three dollars annually.[62] In farming areas produce was often accepted in lieu of cash.[63]

Delivery in towns might be made by the printer's apprentice; rural patrons were served either by mail, usually paying the postage themselves, or by a "postrider" hired by the printer. The latter was paid through an additional charge to subscribers,[64] or by keeping half the sums he could collect. Some publishers rode their own routes, making certain of deliveries and saving the collection fees.[65]

As the federal postal service expanded, many private postriders were supplanted by the regular mails. The development was gradual, but by 1794 branches from the main post road along the coast moved inland.[66] A number of editors were also postmasters [67] and promoted additional mail routes that would aid in circulating their publications. Postal schedules were uncertain, and there were many complaints about irregular mails,[68] but on the whole publishing benefited tremendously. The Post Office Act of 1792 fixed rates on newspapers at one cent each for all deliveries within a radius of one hundred miles and one and one-half cents for all over that distance. "Exchanges" between editors were to be carried free—a privilege of inestimable value to country printers, who were dependent on this means for obtaining all but local news.[69]

This law was only one factor marking the ever-increasing importance of the press. More striking evidence was the rapid multiplication of newspapers. The approximately one hundred American newspapers published in 1790[70] had more than doubled in number a decade later.[71] Even though as many additional ones failed to achieve any lasting financial success, this proliferation is meaningful as well as phenomenal. By 1810 America possessed more journals in proportion to its population than had ever been known anywhere in the world.[72]

Most of these newssheets, and invariably the ones with the greatest circulation, were printed along the Atlantic seaboard and at or near the largest town in their respective commonwealths. Southern journals were only about one-fourth as numerous, in proportion to population, as those of the New England or North Atlantic regions, and few were of the first rank in influence.[73] Figures may be misleadingly low for states such as New Jersey and Delaware because of their proximity to "city" presses,[74] but the significant facts are that the number of newspapers in the nation was rapidly increasing and that more were being published in rural areas.[75]

Statistical data for the newspapers of the period are virtually nonexistent, but of necessity circulations must have been small by modern standards. Composition was by hand, and many papers used but one press. With capable pressmen making about two hundred impressions an hour, there was a definite ceiling on the number of copies that could be printed. Despite reports of sizable circulations in the extraordinary times of the Revolution, 1,800 copies represented from fifteen to thirty hours' labor on a single press, and A. M. Lee questions most claims in excess of that figure.[76] Printshops with additional presses[77] could turn out more, but some of the towns —particularly along the frontier and in the South—were so small that it is difficult to see how they managed to support a journal at all. Yet most of these papers were distributed rather widely in surrounding rural areas and at times proclaimed an extensive circulation.[78]

Even accepting publishers' claims, these figures were not great. The largest newspaper in the nation, with some 4,000 copies, was the Boston *Columbian Centinel*.[79] This was a semiweekly, in one of America's largest cities; the most widely read dailies had far fewer subscribers. William Cobbett's *Porcupine's Gazette* once claimed nearly 3,000[80] but the 1,500 circulation of the Baltimore *Federal Gazette*[81] was as large as most dailies of the period. Even the circulation of the influential *Aurora* was little larger,[82] and the average circulation for daily papers was only about 500.[83] Some weeklies exceeded 1,500 or 2,000 copies, but as late as 1820, a subscription list of 400 was considered good for country printers, although the break-even point was generally considered to be around 600.[84] The national average for all types of papers at the century's close was probably less than 700.[85]

These figures, however, do not reflect the real importance of the journals themselves. Each individual copy was much more widely read than is the case at present. Inns and coffee houses kept files available,[86] and a Federalist complaint was that many Republicans derived their political views from newspapers they read in taverns.[87] The wide exchange of these papers, through the regular postal service or by means of private postriders,[88] also added immeasurably to their influence.

Yet influence does not in itself provide food and clothing. Judging solely by the profusion of these early periodicals, publishing might have been a fairly profitable business, but most evidence indicates the contrary. Many papers proved to be extremely short-lived. Only nine of those being published in 1775 were still in existence thirty-five years later, and but twenty-eight of the eighty-one at the beginning of Washington's administration remained when Jefferson was inaugurated. Fewer than half the journals published before 1821 continued for two years, and only a fourth lasted four years or more.[89] Epidemics, fires, illness, or death compelled cessation of publication in various instances,[90] but for every newspaper failing because of any of these factors six or eight succumbed from financial anemia. A great outlay of capital was not required to publish,[91] but fixed costs were high [92] and revenue most uncertain. Subscriptions were usually the primary source of income,[93] but most printers sent out their papers on at least partial credit, and the difficulties of collection were enormous. More than one paper failed to survive, not because it lacked subscribers, but simply because the subscribers were delinquent in their payments.[94] Some editors were bitter about customers' indifference to their obligations,[95] while others strove to awaken guilty consciences with ingenious appeals. Both cleverness and feeling, for instance, were represented in this notice of the Baltimore *American:*

### SOMETHING IMPORTANT

Never did R. G. HARPER want an appointment—Never did judge CHASE want a fat salary—Never did Mr. ADAMS want to hold his seat—Nor did ever the Republicans want to turn him out of it, more, than at this crisis, the editor of the AMERICAN wants the payment of monies due to him.[96]

Certain publishers, of course, were financially successful,[97] but for each fortunate editor there were numerous others whose poverty forced them to quit the field, and still more who continued printing at considerable sacrifice. Freneau's *National Gazette* was a financial failure.[98] Bache allegedly lost over $2,000 a year on the *Aurora,* despite Federalist charges he was subsidized by French agents,[99] and the *Gazette of the United States* and even *Porcupine's Gazette* ran deficits over considerable periods of time.[100] With some of the nation's best-known papers in such difficulty, the tribulations of smaller journals can only be imagined.[101]

Consequently, most eighteenth-century publishers needed auxiliary sources of income. The majority retailed books and stationery, and all were eager for job printing.[102] So many editors were postmasters that in 1794 it was feared they might discriminate against rival gazettes by withholding important news until they themselves had printed it.[103] With few exceptions, frontier papers were established in the hope of obtaining public printing for the state. Only through newspapers could state or national laws be disseminated in the West, and official publications afforded editors their most dependable revenue.[104]

This widespread reliance upon public printing inevitably had political consequences. Opposition newssheets carried innuendos that Federalist administrations granted or withdrew the publishing of official notices in accordance with printers' party affiliations.[105] No doubt this governmental patronage may have determined the political leanings of some who aspired to it, but it must be recalled that several state governments were Jeffersonian, and in such cases Federalist journals rarely shared in the state printing. Unquestionably, the importance of securing official publishing helped increase the partisanship of the press.[106]

Possibly the press owed some of its significance to America's physical size, which limited means of obtaining information and led people to form their political opinions from the journals they read. Ninety-five per cent of the nation's population was rural and depended primarily upon newspapers for knowledge of governmental affairs.[107] Frontier gazettes were "indispensable" in linking together scattered groups of settlers;[108] they were equally essential in forming and maintaining genuine political parties. Increasing literacy may have led printers to found new periodicals; these in turn added to the general interest in the press. With property qualifications still the rule, papers were read by practically all voters.[109] Some sheets were deliberately priced below cost because of the political influence it was hoped they would exert,[110] and earnest partisans endeavored to circulate party organs at little or no expense.[111]

Moreover, despite their insignificant appearance and modest circulation, papers of the 1790s represented an improvement over those of earlier decades.[112] Noah Webster's statement presenting the initial number of the New York *Minerva* stressed America's literacy and longing for knowledge:

> Newspapers are the most eagerly sought after, and the most generally diffused. In no other country on earth, not even in Great-Britain, are Newspapers so generally circulated among the body of the people, as in America.[113]

To judge from the contents of these publications, readers hungered for information concerning a wide variety of subjects. Many featured items dealt with topics that today would be ignored or regarded only as "filler" material. Most publishers appeared to feel they had an obligation to elevate their readers culturally or morally, as well as to present them with helpful facts and to recount recent occurrences. Thus the owner of the *Vermont Journal* announced that he was printing serially the life of Baron Frederick Tronck at the request of some subscribers but that no important news would be omitted, since he "was fond of making his paper *useful as well as entertaining.*" [114]

Poetry corners adorned the final page of most country journals, and the majority of papers carried two or three humorous "Anecdotes" for diversion. Often these latter had political connotations, as in the Lancaster *Intelligencer's* citation of its arch-rival, the Federalist *Lancaster Journal:*

> 'A *Democratic Member* of our State Legislature, offered to stake his *reputation to a farthing,* on the propriety of a certain measure which he himself had proposed. A Member present, pronounced it *the most equal bet he ever heard of.*' For this jest see *Joe Miller,* page 45; changing the word *'Democratic'* into *'opposition.'* [115]

Subscribers' pens provided a large proportion of the items in these gazettes. Most of the productions discussed political subjects, but they could range from essays on agriculture or metaphysics to doggerel which it was hoped would pass for a poem. Commonly they were signed by a *nom de plume* (such as "A Whig of '75," or "Cato") or by a mere initial. Issues frequently carried the editor's regrets for inability to publish until later the lucubrations of one writer, or for declining the efforts of another. Not all these "Replies to Correspondents" were as blunt as Isaiah Thomas's to "*The Farmer Happy*— We hope he is; but he is no poet." [116] More conventional was the Frankfort *Palladium's* "M. H. is received; but in its present state is too incorrect for publication. An interview with the Author is requested, in order to point out the objectionable parts." [117] Actually, printers almost universally welcomed these contributions,[118] partly because of the ever-present possibility they might be sorely needed to make up for a shortage of news from distant parts.

To the regret of historians, local news was definitely neglected, perhaps in the conviction that common gossip did not merit publication. National and particularly foreign items were regarded as the publisher's most prized stock-in-trade. Even accounts of legal disputes, ship records in seaports, or nearby Indian raids on the frontier [119] were never permitted to overshadow more distant information. Considering available space, greater concern was shown about foreign affairs than is true in other than wartime today. Perhaps as a carry-over from colonial days, Americans possessed "an ardent thirst for novelty, and the general cry was 'What's the news abroad?' " [120] Since sympathy (pro-French or pro-British) came to be a touchstone often determining one's party leanings, these stories played no small part in contributing to Jeffersonian political organizations. Foreign news kept gazettes from being little more than advertising handbills; it flattered subscribers and introduced a cosmopolitan note into rural communities. As one editor romantically put it:

> Who would not give half a guinea to know, exactly as he does his own calf pasture, what is going on every day when he rises, at Smyrna and Amsterdam, and count as easily as he can the stripes of his waistcoat, the armies that are on foot in Europe. . . . To be able to look up with the tail of his eye as far as Russia, and down again with the same glance to the islands of the West Indies, and see all the intermediate space swarming with men and things.[121]

European "intelligence" dominated most journals, those on the frontier perhaps more than in the cities.[122] This was increasingly true as the French Revolution progressed,[123] but Americans were informed on such subjects as the minutes of the House of Commons and the health of the King of Sweden.[124] Such information was from six weeks to six months old, depending on the speed of the trans-Atlantic voyage and the location of the publishing paper, but its age made little difference. Often editors apologized because of a long delay, or expressed impatience for the arrival of ship-borne reports,[125] yet they rarely failed to print any scrap of foreign news, however outdated.

Most of these items were taken from foreign newspapers, letters from abroad to local citizens, and information contributed by incoming sea captains. Often European stories were prefaced by some such statement as:

> Just as our paper was going to press a gentleman politely favored us with the London Evening Star of the 3rd of March, received by the Ship Mary, arrived this morning from Portsmouth, from which we make the following hasty Extracts.[126]

Inland gazettes relied on the newspapers of the seaboard cities for the greater part of their foreign news.[127]

The sources on which American journalists depended for such intelligence often provided incomplete or contradicting information. At times this led to strange inconsistencies. One issue of the *Goshen Repository,* for example, reprinted an item from London to the effect that the Jacobins in France were not yet "sufficiently glutted with the murder of their King" and reported that Marie Antoinette had been torn to pieces before she could be taken to the guillotine; yet four weeks later this same paper asserted that those persons recently arriving in America from the Old World were firm in their belief that "the French will brave their millions of foes and finally triumph in the permanent establishment of the principle—liberty and equality." [128]

All too frequently the erratic and indiscriminate methods of securing news led to the publication of mere rumor. Occasionally an item of questionable validity would be headed "Important—If True," but normally the editor considered he had done his duty if he indicated the source of the story. Thus the *American Herald* printed a report that later proved completely inaccurate:

> We are informed, that a vessel arrived in Cape-Ann last Friday, the Captain of which says, he spoke with a British packet, bound to Halifax in a short passage from England, the commander of which gave him to understand that War was declared by England against Spain.[129]

Not all publishers made serious efforts to check on the veracity of their information even when it was possible to do so. One "PETER PARAGRAPH," quite possibly commenting on the above tale, satirically furnished the nation's printers with a set of

## DIRECTIONS
*How to fill several columns of a NEWS-PAPER.*

Begin *first* with, It is said, it is reported, as we hear, that there is a probability of a war between Spain and England.

*Next day,* We are confidently assured, that a war, &c.

*Third,* There can be no doubt but that a war, &c.

*Fourth,* Preparations in the two kingdoms are so far advanced, that we hourly expect to hear of hostilities having commenced.

*Fifth,* Give your conjectures; tell who it is thought will join us in the war, and why; who had better, and what powers should keep out of the scrape.

*Sixth,* What would be the consequences of the war; first, the immediate consequences; next, the remote.

*Seventh,* Dive into the origin of the war.

*Eighth,* The origin of wars in general and their destructive consequences.

*Ninth,* From undoubted authority we hear that a sloop from —— is arrived at ——, and brings news, that a brig had arrived at ——, that spoke a ship that had been informed by a brig in such an such latitude and longitude, that it was reported hostilities had actually commenced between the powers.

*Tenth,* Doubt your authority.

*Eleventh,* Not even an idea of war. A battle between a few sailors gave rise to the report. Flourish away upon the early and authentic quality of your intelligence.

23

In this manner you can never be at a loss: For, besides what is mentioned above, you may, in the course of the twelve days wonder, introduce from books, extracts much to the purpose,

PETER PARAGRAPH
—Teacher of Politics.[130]

Obvious irony, this, yet the very fact it was written suggests that individual publishers of that day (as well as later ones) were not averse to making a good story out of rather tenuous gossip.

Basically, however, the fountainhead of foreign news was the European newspaper. This handicapped Republican gazettes, for French papers were generally delayed, and American sheets customarily used British journals. Yet from this English information Jeffersonians endeavored to extract anything that might excite sympathy for France and Gallic ideals.[131] As French news grew in importance, those publishers who read French (or knew someone who did) made their own translations of items from that language. The *Journal de Paris* especially was utilized in this fashion; this helped to account for the importance of the *Aurora* and certain other periodicals.[132]

Second only to European intelligence in interest and importance was that stemming from other parts of the United States. This news was of various types, but political items predominated. If newspaper space is any criterion, citizens of the period were far more interested in continental affairs than in the occurrences of their own neighborhoods. That an extremely keen interest in national politics existed is evident from other sources, and near the close of the decade men were being nominated for state offices as well as federal "chiefly because they represented national parties." [133]

As in foreign news, the primary wellspring for national information consisted of extracts from other newspapers. After the Post Office Act of 1792, virtually every editor could draw heavily upon his "exchanges" to furnish the majority of his really newsworthy items.[134] Any failure of the mails inevitably produced loud cries of dismay from country printers so dependent upon them.[135]

Most stories were simply copied verbatim from the papers received; many editors used shears and paste pot more than pen in filling their columns. Infrequently credit was given, or it might be noted that the item came from a "N. Y. Paper," but generally the publisher failed to acknowledge his source. So universal was this practice that it seldom excited comment, although the *National Gazette* once acidly remarked that when an author borrowed from another without giving credit it was labeled "plagiarism," but perhaps "gentlemen of the type" had another name for such an immodest procedure.[136] Few editors were ready to criticize a process that was their main source of news.

No odium was attached to the copying of congressional debates from other gazettes, for this was recognized as necessary if readers of distant journals were to receive anything like accurate descriptions of proceedings at Philadelphia. On the contrary, some of the papers of the capital encouraged republishing of their accounts of sessions and took pride in the wide circulation of such summaries. Bache pledged "himself to those printers who may prefer copying from his paper, that they need never fear giving two sketches of the same speech," and expressed pleasure that his summaries of the debates were reprinted in various parts of the nation. He said while he would be exceedingly gratified to receive credit, "yet the satisfaction of finding a correct statement of congressional proceedings circulated, will amply repay him for his trouble in giving it." [137] The *Aurora* later boasted that it could produce many testimonials of its accuracy and impartiality in this respect, even from Federalist papers.[138]

Andrew Brown, of the Philadelphia *Federal Gazette,* and Bache were among the first to report the speeches in Congress or to employ men for that purpose, although several papers in the capital were doing it before 1800. Brown allegedly offered to put up $1,100 a year for a reporter for the House of Representatives if the debates would be printed first in his paper.[139] Originally this offer was rejected, but the Boston *Independent Chronicle* later stated that it took its synopsis of one of Harrison Gray Otis' speeches

> verbatim from Mr. Brown's paper in Philadelphia; from this paper we usually copy Proceedings of Congress; they have hitherto been very correct—Mr. Brown is the Printer to the House, and employs a person purposely to take down the debates.[140]

Other Philadelphia publications also served as sources, and gazettes in smaller localities copied, or perhaps recopied, accounts given in those of the larger cities.

For the most part these reports of congressional activities were factual accounts consisting of seemingly objective abstracts of speeches given. In any condensation omissions and questions of emphasis inevitably occurred, and there were a few charges of deliberate deletion or addition. The Boston *Columbian Centinel* accused its chief competitor, the *Independent Chronicle,* of falsifying the speeches of two Massachusetts representatives in the debates over Madison's resolutions against British trade in 1794. Admitting the possibility of error, the *Chronicle* denied any deliberate inaccuracy. Bache's paper had been the source, and he had publicly pledged his accounts to be as correct as was humanly possible.[141]

That some of the proceedings of Congress may have been intentionally distorted in an era of perfervid partisanship is quite conceivable, but such falsification does not appear to have been frequent.[142] Presumably the widespread system of exchanges would have readily enabled editors of opposing political faiths to detect and promptly expose flagrantly inaccurate versions of Philadelphia reports.

Items gleaned from other papers and ideas presented as the publisher's own conclusions were not the only sources of information. As one sheet noted, "A man is a ninny, . . . who thinks all the sentiments in a newspaper are those of the Editor thereof." [143] As noted, subscribers' communications were customarily welcomed, and newly founded gazettes invariably requested them. A piece normally would not be published unless the author's name were known to the editor, but almost invariably it was printed under a *nom de plume* if the writer chose. This afforded contributors the security of anonymity, and doubtless allowed the publisher himself to express occasional opinions on some unusually touchy questions in the guise of a correspondent.[144] Possibly, also, certain public figures wrote letters to themselves under assumed names, asking questions they later (speaking as themselves) found it advantageous to answer.[145] In any event, these communications were considered an integral part of most journals. They provided some local news, furnished a rough index of the temper and interests of the community, and helped mold public opinion.

Essays resembling the modern editorial rarely appeared. Usually, publishers' views were almost indistinguishable from subscribers' letters—and may have been disguised as such. At times, though, articles might be found in which "the Printer" ventured to express briefly his own opinion. Bache's *Aurora* was among the earliest gazettes to practice placing unsigned editor's views under the masthead on page two. After Duane took over, pithy two or three-line political comments, obviously reflecting the attitude of the paper's staff, appeared in the same place.[146] But a true editorial section did not yet exist.

Writers—whether editors, politicians, or laymen—for the public prints were excessively fond of figures of speech. Metaphors were most favored. Rare indeed was the politically minded journal that failed to carry some reference to "the federal farm house" or the "ship of state." Allusions to the vital processes of birth and death or citations from the Bible were common. Sometimes entire articles were written in Biblical style, as in this tirade against the alleged aristocratic, speculative, and pro-British tendencies of the Federalists:

> NOW it came to pass in these latter days that many of the people of Columbia forgot the statutes of their fathers, and fell away from the sect called Republicans, and joined themselves with

the monarchists, the hierarchists, and the aristocrats of Britain. [Eventually, however, a great spirit descended upon Abraham, who spoke out,] saying: 'How long, O ye honest but deluded people, will ye suffer yourselves to be blinded, deceived, and betrayed . . . ?'

. . . . And the people went forth on the great day of election and they voted mightily. . . .[147]

Items with an Old Testament flavor perhaps cropped up most frequently in New England, but they were popular in all parts of the country.

Domestic political news was second only to foreign happenings in prominence for the gazettes of the era. At times it was of even greater importance. Any or all of the sources of information about domestic politics might be biased; some were certainly so. Party feeling came to be intense, and more than one historian has spoken of the period as that of the partisan press.[148] Some secondary accounts leave the impression that virtually every journal was rabidly partisan and that those committed to one party printed nothing favorable to the other.[149] Many newspapers, some of them among the most influential, were of that sort. Coarse and impassioned writing in some of the extreme papers gave an unpleasant cast to all the journalism of the decade, but a number of publishers made some effort to be objective. These and others deplored the scurrility and virulence that were to be found in certain prominent publications.

The Poughkeepsie *American Farmer* lauded the objectivity of various Eastern printers who published "for the good of the country":

> By impartiality we mean the method which they adhere to in editting their papers; instead of Printing only in favor of one nation, they publish, as they receive the information, both against France and Great Britain: this conduct discovers the real American.[150]

In Vermont "REFORMATIST" observed that the two great parties were each represented by a number of potent journals. Persons taking only one newspaper, therefore, lacked access to the truth if the paper were partisan; inevitably they would adopt the prejudice to which they were constantly exposed. Dispassion, however, was obtainable if editors would only: (1) suppress, as printers, their own political sentiments; (2) take at least one outstanding paper of each party; and (3) publish an equal measure (qualitatively and quantitatively) of thoughtful and decent items from both sides, avoiding "the squibs, and the rancourous party trash. . . ." Such a procedure would "certainly be highly serviceable to the public." [151]

Not all gazettes proclaiming objectivity actually practiced it. In 1795 the Boston *Columbian Centinel* deleted its motto, "Uninfluenced by party, we aim only to be just," for it was so strongly Federalist that the slogan was a mockery.[152] Editorial neutrality was difficult. A Vermont paper noted that, while it had promised to be *"Open to all parties, and influenced by none,"* it was "not therefore bound to insert indecent ravings against a government which we have established by our own consent." [153]

Some newspapers, both Federalist and Republican, ridiculed impartiality as a dream that was unattainable even if desirable. The pro-Adams *Newark Gazette* found talk of neutrality in politics "curious," and mentioned certain printers who felt they should serve neither party and therefore published what they called "both sides of the question." This practice, it continued, evaded the issue, and such editors were similar to witnesses who inserted prevarications into their testimony to avoid taking a stand for either the plaintiff or the accused. Such folly should not be tolerated: "The times demand decision; there is a right and a wrong, and the printer, who under the specious name of impartiality jumbles both truth and falsehood into the same paper" must either doubt his own judgment in distinguishing between the two or be governed by ulterior motives.[154]

Republican publishers were upon occassion equally positive. An advertisement for James Lyon's projected national magazine (planned as an anthology of the best Jeffersonian articles throughout the country) claimed that people had been misled

29

by the pretended neutrality of printers. For a paper to breathe alternately the spirit of two parties, argued Lyon, was utterly impossible.[155] In Baltimore, the *American* called professed detachment "all delusion; every party will have its *printer,* as well as every sect its preacher. . . ."[156] The New York *American Citizen,* guaranteeing a continuation of Thomas Greenleaf's policies, concurred. If by "impartiality" was meant equal attachment to the principles of aristocracy and those of republicanism, the paper rejected it "as injurious to the best interests of mankind."[157]

A number of gazettes openly announced their political affiliation,[158] and many additional ones disclosed their position by the items they printed. The more extreme publications of this nature (on both sides) had editors who were, in the words of Isaiah Thomas, "destitute at once of the urbanity of gentlemen, the information of scholars, and the principles of virtue."[159] Such intransigents grew to have an undue prominence and unfortunately came to set the tone for the period.

These immoderate editors were—or came to be—adept in practicing various propaganda tricks. In recent years an attempt to classify the types of propaganda appeals identified seven different devices.[160] Impassioned Democratic editors of the 1790s had never heard of these methods as such, yet we shall find that at times they used any or all of them, often extremely skillfully.

The raucous and zealous publications were more arresting and perhaps more influential than their more sober contemporaries. They may have created an impression of American journalism that was not entirely accurate, for many European observers pronounced American newspapers the most scurrilous and profligate in the world. Even some Americans who recognized that a free press constituted one of the greatest bulwarks of popular government also feared its abuses made it one of the most serious threats to democratic processes.[161]

"The papers are overrunning with election essays, squibs, and invectives," cried a journal of the time,[162] and so it appeared to those who perused party mouthpieces of the cities. But it must not be forgotten that even in this "Era of the Partisan Press" numerous gazettes attempted to operate under standards of decency, reasonableness, and impartiality that were similar to those of many of their descendants today. If the party allegiance of many publications was extremely difficult to determine, such statements as that in 1796 "some four-fifths of the newspapers" supported Adams,[163] and "as late as 1804 two-thirds of the leading newspapers of the country were adherents of the Federal cause"[164] are misguiding. Unless the newspaper openly proclaimed its alignment, criteria for establishing either the existence or degree of partisanship are not easily ascertained. Yet it may safely be said that, except for the brief periods of the Whiskey Insurrection and the XYZ Affair (when outspoken criticism of the administration was at a low ebb), after 1791 or 1792 Republican journalism was always a formidable threat to the party in power. The decidedly Federalist papers did outnumber those openly in opposition, but the preponderance was by no means as great as has been alleged, particularly if neutral or near-neutral sheets are evaluated.[165]

Politicians who recalled the potency of the press during earlier controversies were inevitably to turn to the press and to turn *it* to their purposes in the party conflicts that emerged. The precise origin of parties under the new government is not absolutely certain. Unquestionably, the adoption of the Constitution and the effect of early Federalist policies created a genuine central authority. Control of this came to be (as that of Congress under the Articles had not been) worth a full-scale struggle. As a tool for shaping and forging public opinion, newspapers were destined to be used in forming political organizations. The first flickers of party feeling were gradual and did not occur simultaneously in all parts of the nation, though once lit the flames flared rapidly to amazing heights. In 1790 Bache's *General Advertiser* could bemoan the lack of news:

As to domestic politics, no party disputes to raise the printer's drooping spirits; not a legislature sitting to furnish a few columns of debates, not even so much as a piece of private abuse to grace— Zounds, people now have no spirit in them. . . . Not even an accident, not a duel, not a suicide, nor a murder, not so much as a single theft worthy of notice.

O! tempora, O! mores.[166]

Yet already some press opposition to certain Federalist measures was apparent, and before long Bache's "drooping spirits" were to be elevated beyond wildest expectations by his own efforts in party controversy.

# BUSINESSMEN AND SPECULATORS IN THE SADDLE

In New York City on April 30, 1789, George Washington was inaugurated President of the United States. America's new government under the Constitution thus became a reality. Among the admiring throng viewing the ceremony was a young sea captain (also lately come to New York) who would soon become one of the most vocal leaders in the opposition against the Chief Executive. Yet, at the moment Philip Freneau, like the rest of the crowd and the entire nation, appeared full of optimism and good will for the administration whose inception he witnessed.[1] Few regimes ever opened with such seemingly unanimous support, but the picture was to change drastically within a relatively brief time.

Many factors had induced the thirteen states to discard the Articles of Confederation and to form a closer union, but none was stronger than economic ones.[2] It is therefore not surprising that the first glimmerings of displeasure with the fledgling administration were revealed in criticism of its financial policies. Authorities differ as to the issues that gave rise to the nation's first true party organizations;[3] although newspapers that came to oppose the Federalists devoted more space to problems in foreign affairs, the earliest organized discontent with domestic politics was over questions affecting citizens' purses.

As even a cursory examination of revolutions in both En-

33

gland and America will disclose, the pocketbook is a tradition-
ally sensitive point for men of Anglo-Saxon descent. Excessive
governmental costs and taxation without representation have
ever been feared and detested. So it was that within two
months after Washington had assumed office men were grumbling about the salaries proposed for their new public officials.
Complaints about grants and pensions, unnecessary offices, and
the expense of a military establishment followed soon after.[4]

These strictures were, however, as but the first drops
heralding a downpour; the full storm descended with the inception of Alexander Hamilton's famed financial program.
The ambitious first Secretary of the Treasury envisioned establishing the nation's credit through a refunding process
whereby old governmental obligations would be paid off at par,
through assuming the debts of the individual states, by founding a Bank of the United States, and by imposing a tariff and
an excise tax to assure needed revenue for the central authority. Even when Congress created the Treasury Department
some had feared the concentration of power in that agency;
the Secretary might infringe upon the sphere of the House, or
become more influential than the President.[5] Hamilton had
barely entered upon his duties before rumors began circulating
that some serious move was contemplated concerning the national debt.

"A Lieutenant in the Late American Army," petitioning the
President and Congress, recalled that one objective of the
Constitution was "to establish justice." Since he had been compelled by necessity to sell his certificates (compensation for
"long . . . and hazardous services to his country") for one-
eighth their face value, he was disturbed over reports in August, 1789, about the public debt which prophesied burdensome taxation. With all due respect for the nation's honor and
welfare, he hoped he would not have to pay more in taxes to
redeem principal and interest than he had received for the sale
of his government obligations. Nor should he pay more than
one-eighth the taxes of his neighbor who had never held such

bonds. Any other course would violate elemental justice and would eventually produce national poverty and disgrace.[6]

Forebodings about taxes were well founded. The first step in Hamilton's plan called for refunding the nation's indebtedness. Creating national credit and consolidating the debt at a lower rate of interest had patent advantages, and these were emphasized in the press.[7] Some observers, however, recognized the move as initiating a fundamental division among the American people. A New Yorker's letter in the *American Mercury* referred to the Secretary's report as "the first point blank shot" favoring the moneyed interests. While many thought "that the elevation is too high," the funding system would probably be adopted.[8] A few argued the debt could be discharged more speedily by selling public lands, and "A Farmer" urged that a land tax would be preferable to the proposed tariff and excise tax. These would fall daily upon farmers and laborers, while the former would be paid by all holders of real property only once a year.[9]

Foreign and domestic, the nation's indebtedness amounted to over $54,000,000. About one-fifth of this was owed abroad. Most Americans recognized the foreign obligation, although some disliked the high interest rates for the entire new issue and the idea that the new liability could not be entirely liquidated within fifty years.[10] Only a small number agreed with "A Citizen of Philadelphia," that—since foreigners would realize about $8,000,000 profit on some $11,700,000 worth of certificates they had purchased—the notes should be redeemed at about the 2s. 6d. the purchasers paid per pound and the remaining 17s. 6d. distributed among veterans and other supporters of the Revolution.[11]

Refunding the domestic debt was another matter. Virtual repudiation of $100,000,000 of paper money had embittered many, for they thought it hurt worst the workers or widows and orphans.[12] Equity, maintained "A Farmer," demanded redemption of these "Continentals" in gold or silver before compensation of holders of certificates. "A resolution of Congress cannot cancell [*sic*] the obligations of justice." Hamilton's proposal would oppress owners of real property, and depreciation of seventy-five per cent in the value of farmland was predicted. To compound the wrong by turning the difference over to New York speculators was dastardly.[13]

It was gradually realized that certain men had acquired vast quantities of governmental obligations and that original holders were not to benefit from the restoration of public credit. "An Independent Observer" not only criticized the exorbitant duties proposed as an invitation to smuggling but also challenged the doctrine that "a public debt is a public blessing," [14] which had appeared in a New England paper. This was speculators' language; perhaps the editor himself was interested. It was an open secret that anticipation of Hamilton's report had led a handful of insiders in coastal cities to buy up the greatest share of the national obligations.[15]

When Representative James Madison proposed that the Congress distinguish between original security-holders and those (presumably speculators) who had purchased certificates at a later date, opponents of refunding rallied round that idea. Some newspapers approved the proposed change because of popular sympathy for Revolutionary veterans or their widows and orphans. "Thank God," wrote a "Real Soldier," "there lives a Madison to propose justice" for "the poor emaciated soldier, hungry and naked, in many instances now wandering from one extreme part of the country to another. . . ." [16] Despite assertions that wartime suppliers (paid in bonds) often got four times the actual worth of their goods and that many soldiers might have starved had not charitable purchasers given them something for certificates considered virtually worthless,[17] Hamilton's critics praised Madison for defying the speculators.[18] "An Old Soldier" cited Washington's pledge of justice for enlisted veterans,[19] and the *Pennsylvania Gazette* waxed poetic:

'Tax on Tax,' young Belcour cries,
'More imposts and a new excise,
A public debt's a public blessing,

Which 'tis of course a crime to lessen.'
Each day a fresh report he broaches,
That spies and Jews may ride in coaches.
Soldiers and farmers don't despair
Untax'd as yet, are Earth and Air.[20]

Upon Congressional rejection of Madison's "discrimination" plan, lamentations were broadcast:

'Pay the poor soldier!—He's a sot,'
Cries our grave ruler, B[o̱]ud[i̱]not.
'No pity, now, from us he claims,'
In artful accents, echoes Am[e̱]s:
'In war, to heroes let's be just,
In peace we'll write their toils in dust';
A soldiers pay are rags and fame,
A wo[o]den leg—a deathless name.
To Specs, both in and out of Cong,
The four and six per cents belong.[21]

Public faith had never been plighted to sanctify iniquity. By what right did Hamilton discharge the debt to veterans in worthless Western lands and then call for paying certificates in gold, or declare two-thirds of the debt irredeemable with an annual interest of only four per cent? [22]

Others denied that any contract existed between the government and creditors who had obtained certificates by deluding original purchasers. Some congressmen doubted America's ability to pay six per cent interest and thought two per cent was too much for those who had become creditors through speculation.[23] Honest men paid their debts and secured their homes before indulging in extravagances; why should governments not do likewise? Refunding would actually bring heavier direct taxes, for Americans would never drink enough spirits to raise the revenue anticipated from Hamilton's excise.[24] "A Farmer" wrote again, predicting the ruination of the agricultural class. The nation's specie would flow to city speculators and thence abroad for interest payments, leaving farmers unable to borrow for improvements, while trade and manufacturing languished. A few nabobs with huge paper fortunes could purchase entire townships and establish an aristocracy. If Britain could recompense the Tories, surely America could render fair treatment to her most deserving citizens.[25]

Perhaps, hinted "Uncle Toby" darkly, congressmen were motivated by self-interest rather than patriotism. National honor, he continued, was a "prostituted term" when probate judges ordered government certificates sold at auction, often for only one-eighth their face value, or when the British still retained Western posts and Algerines preyed on American commerce.[26] Certainly, a number of officials who held large amounts of securities strongly supported the administration's program. By 1790 only about one-fourth of the holders of government bonds were original purchasers; the rest had acquired theirs at from one-half to one-tenth face value.[27] Funding, together with the assumption of state debts, transformed these governmental obligations into easily negotiable "pure" capital; Elbridge Gerry in 1789 called the Treasury system an almost perfect plan to promote "speculation and peculation in the public funds." [28]

Bitterly denied was Hamilton's assertion that a national debt possessed definite advantages. Opponents of his plan maintained that merely increasing fluid capital added nothing to the nation's productive capacity and so could not diffuse prosperity.[29] Such wealth as England enjoyed, wrote "A Pennsylvanian," came from her conquests and her efforts in the East and West Indies, not an indebtedness that produced only heavy taxes and hordes of bureaucratic officials.[30]

Nor would the funding system serve to reduce the national debt, even gradually. By 1792 it was charged in the *National Gazette* that America's liabilities were increasing.[31] By this time the young man who had watched Washington's inauguration with such high hopes was editing this newspaper, which most severely censured Hamilton's program. The Secretary himself wrote letters attempting to refute the damaging charge.[32] But writers with such significant pseudonyms as "American Farmer" and "Gracchus" retorted that the policy of refunding debts degenerated into a consistent practice that inevitably devitalized every nation that adopted it. England's experience showed the policy meant an endless cycle of additional loans, taxes, and officers—all for the benefit of a privileged few. Foreign speculators were already too influential; guarded from foes by the ocean, and with no need for urgent borrowing, why the overwhelming concern about the firmness of American credit? [33]

In reality that credit was harmed by the mere introduction of Hamilton's report, claimed a Maryland writer. The rise in price of public securities before its issuance indicated that holders had anticipated six per cent interest and gradual retirement of the principal; when the message proposed to limit retirement to two per cent per year and to slightly lower the interest rate, the price of securities had declined.[34] A New Yorker compared those profiting from funding to drones, while "the industrious bee is forced to furnish them with all the honey of its search." [35]

It was begging the question, argued some, to assert that early purchasers of certificates were hurt worse than were original buyers who had alienated their holdings.[36] Madison's plan for "discrimination" was not impractical. No ingenious argument or simulacrum of "national policy" should outweigh common honesty. "Equity" suggested paying only one-half face value to those who could not prove themselves original purchasers of the certificates; the remainder would go to those who *had* been the first creditors, their heirs, or the government itself.[37]

Concerted efforts were made to force congressional reconsideration of Madison's idea. Meetings of original creditors in Connecticut called for formation of county committees and selection of delegates to a state meeting that would work to secure indemnification for losses suffered from depreciation of their certificates.[38] Similar gatherings (like Revolutionary Committees of Correspondence) were requested in Massachusetts.[39] A New Jersey correspondent called on voters to

39

select representatives who would rectify the funding system in order that creditors who had loaned money to the United States would be rewarded rather than penalized.[40]

Supporters of refunding contended it was impossible to discriminate in favor of original holders, but critics held this should not prevent America's best minds from doing everything attainable to afford justice. Hamilton's plan was itself discriminatory—and in favor of foreigners rather than Americans.[41] Funds had not yet been provided for Washington's army, but it was proposed to give eight hundred per cent profit to speculators. The new census could ascertain the names of original lenders and the amounts they had received for their securities, thereby preventing gross profiteering.[42] An attempt was made to incite nationwide petitioning by veterans and first purchasers with this poorly spelled and liberally punctuated appeal by "A Citizen":

> *The Printers throughout the United States, who wish, that justice, and equity may take place in our land and who are friends .to the widow and the o[r]phan, the decriped, and the war worn soldier, and patriot citizen, are requested to republish the foregoing, for which they will have the thanks of thousands.*[43]

These pressure groups favoring Madison's proposal alleged that speculators also (but with less altruism) were organizing to force Congress into further steps favoring current owners of certificates. Philadelphia holders were said to have presented a petition

> to induce Congress to . . . give six per cent. interest on the whole public debt at once. They call themselves *the patriotic victims of the war*—when in truth three-fourths of them are *speculators* who have purchased most of the public paper for less than half its value.

With the obvious desire of arousing congressional ire against such a move, it was noted that these petitioners accused that body of having lost a disposition to do justice once it had acquired the power: "In short, the whole petition is but a round about way of telling Congress they are a nest of scoundrels." [44]

"PHILANTHROPY" bitterly proposed paying members of Congress and administration officials in Continental currency or "Final Settlement notes." By the time the legislators had trusted the United States as long as had the Revolutionary veterans, "they will find out how much Honour and Justice, &c. there is in the plans, they spend five or six dollars per day in disputing about." [45]

Hamilton himself came under fire almost immediately. Flatterers might compare him to Sully and Necker, but those able financiers had curtailed expenses and did not talk of rewarding soldiers and creditors "with *new obligations* and partial equivalents. . . ." [46] Americans needed to retire the debt as quickly as possible—and the people were entitled to regular, factual statements from the Treasury Department giving a true picture of the government's economic status.[47] "Caius" wrote in 1792 that funding would make American indebtedness, rather than *credit,* immortal and predicted the "sinking fund" would be used as security for further borrowing rather than for liquidating federal obligations. He recalled Mirabeau's warning that reliance on credit was a "fatal deception" and maintained that if Americans wished to preserve their liberties they should never fund their public debt.[48]

Charges of chicanery were made at the time the funding bill was passed. Opponents claimed the plan was deviously complex and that congressional delay in taking final action, long after it was apparent that both funding and assumption were to become law, had served to turn millions of dollars over to foreigners or speculators:

> The whole business . . . has been carried on in a manner altogether unbecoming the dignity, and character of a Legislature, possessing the confidence of three millions of people. . . . [For want of knowledge of this overly complicated system] the property of thousands, will . . . be sacrificed to Exchange Alley deceptions. . . . [Even the] WIDOW should be able to comprehend the value of her note, and not be exposed to the artful calculation of some harpy, who is aiming to take advantage of her ignorance. But as the system now stands seven-eighths of the community are unable to fathom its principles.

> This eccentric plan may suit a $M[o]rr[i]s$, but it is a melancholy consideration, that the citizens of these States should be exposed to a set of speculators either in, or out of government. . . .
>
> This is the happy result of a lengthy session: A system of intricates, beneficial to stock-jobbers.—A partial discrimination in favor of foreigners—party debates—and an enormous expenditure of public money by compensations, salaries and pensions.[49]

Representative Fisher Ames of Massachusetts was accused of failing to present to his colleagues in Congress a petition signed by ten thousand old soldiers who opposed the bill. If considered before passage, the petition might have prevented "speculations 'both in and out of Congress.' " [50] A New Jersey writer found it interesting that government paper was deemed of little worth when in the hands of original purchasers but became of almost inestimable value once it was much in the hands of stock-jobbers. Probably never before in history, the writer proposed, had such inequality in property, without any adequate consideration, ever taken place so suddenly—or the basis for an aristocracy so rapidly formed.[51]

Emotional appeals were frequent. In New Hampshire America's "Widows and Orphans" entreated the President and Congress. A "letter" related how, after losing their husbands, they had been forced to part, at trifling sums, with hard-won certificates, in order to buy bread and pay taxes. Now, apparently, they were to be "doomed to deeper poverty" because of "attempts . . . made by interested men, to prevent a just and easy *discrimination* between the original & the present holders." They foresaw themselves compelled to surrender the last mite to redeem property parted with at a discount, "to save ourselves, our children, our honor and chastity, from the assaults and arrests of cruel creditors, hungry lawyers," etc. Congress was asked to spare them future taxation, to restore their lost property, and to keep them from experiencing "all the wretchedness, that human nature can endure." [52]

"Brutus," who was probably Freneau himself, struck some of the most serious blows at Hamilton's program. His series in the *National Gazette* flayed the funding system as a plot to give added weight to the central government and undue influence to the Treasury Department. In violation of the intentions of the framers of the Constitution, the funding program tended to coerce voters to support whatever course Hamilton chose. The nation's plutocrats, handed fifty million dollars, had been combined and strengthened, and the Bank monopoly made them still more dangerous. Refunding mortgaged America's future by pledging payments based on her chief resources, and farmers and merchants would have to pay eternal tribute to rich speculators. At a time when Europe was in upheaval because of taxes, loans, and monopolies for the few, Americans were copying her mistakes and true republicanism was being eroded. Most of those profiting were either foreigners or else associated with the Treasury Department.[53]

Later "Brutus" letters purported to show how this powerful group of funding beneficiaries cooperated in other, often unconstitutional, measures. The host of revenue officers produced by the system tended to aid the public creditors work their arbitrary will upon the people. The *true* friends of the Federal Government were surely not those who encouraged debt and speculation, or tried by peremptory interpretation to convert limited government into an unlimited one. Hamilton and his adherents should take care.[54]

A New Yorker observed that the coming to America of emigrants who wished to escape absolutist governments constituted a tribute to Americans, who should be constant guardians of the rights of man. In words that Andrew Jackson might later have envied:

> Fear not being dubbed ANTI-FED[ERALIST], while ye are *defending* the ARK *of* GOD! The cry is—what can be the reason of this strange and astonishing rise of the American stocks! O that I had but cash—how soon would I have a finger in the pie! etc.— If we should presume to tell those very astonished lookers on, *that this is all the speculators want,* they would be still more *amazed! bitten fingers* has frequently been a literary theme. *Bite the biter* is practiced every day, but this may possibly turn out, bite him who, just entered the biters school, has not yet learned to bite! . . . Without the FUNDING act, and the BANK act, *said*

the high fliers, America would have sunk into the irretrievable abiss of *discredit* and *poverty! Now,* say we, America is rich indeed—for above *twenty* men own stocks in the American bank, and a great proportion of them are *proxies* from Europe! beware of monopoly! it is an unfeeling, unprincipled, sordid passion, and, if not opposed, will monopolise your ALL! [55]

"BELISARIUS" commented that Madison's motion to distinguish between original creditors and speculators was most heatedly denounced by those who would vote themselves twenty shillings for every 2*s*. 6*d*. they possessed of the public debt. These men asked, "Who were the friends of government, and supported its credit?" He noted that they had displayed their confidence in the government by rating its credit at 2*s*. 6*d*. per pound. They had aided original purchasers in time of need, and had asked only seven hundred per cent profit plus forty-eight per cent annual interest. Any who begrudged them these "reasonable expectations," merely to compensate those who had been robbed of most of the value of their certificates or endured years of military hardship without pay, were obviously knaves.[56]

*"A Citizen of Philadelphia"* and "L." denounced the arguments supporting the funding system as "falsehoods." In two short years the nation had been brought to the verge of ruin. Congress should have merely voted the interest on the old debt and then should have bought up and retired the certificates with income from taxes and the sale of public lands. Or money *could* have been borrowed from Europe at four per cent.[57]

In New Jersey at least two congressmen, Elias Boudinot and Jonathan Dayton, were said to have made money as a result of measures they helped pass.[58] Four "speculating attorneys" in Massachusetts, who had been worth only a thousand pounds altogether when the funding process commenced, had interested themselves in politics, acquired perhaps half a million dollars, and were putting on insufferable airs.[59] A relative of Hamilton allegedly had a fortune in the "immaculate funds," with an income from interest "(for which every farm and house in the United States stands mortgaged)" of "THIRTY THOUSAND DOLLARS a year!" The Treasury books should be immediately opened to reveal the names of those dealing in national securities.[60]

Since propaganda value and accuracy are not always synonymous,[61] Hamilton was accused of obtaining a danger-free post in the army and of taking leave two years prior to the Treaty of Paris to engage in speculation and private concerns. Now he opposed any payment to veterans except in the old depreciated paper the army had already received. Washington, who had pledged that a nation rescued by its citizen-soldiers would never leave unpaid the debt of gratitude, was now silent, despite his "pathetic promises." [62]

Many other correspondents urged compensation for Revolutionary veterans. Jefferson's retirement from the State Department disclosed the appalling scarcity of men with the "hearts of 1775." Were all such "entombed in the funding system, the grave of a brave soldiery?" [63] "A Continental Soldier" sardonically added that the servicemen were to be tried as criminals for grave offenses: They had carried on until the Revolution was won, they had demobilized with a *promise* of payment for their services, they had been forced to part with their certificates at great loss (thus injuring public faith and national honor), and they considered it a hardship to work double time in order to earn enough to pay face value to speculators.[64]

A Baltimore wag might call it the *"funny system,"* but only aristocrats could smile. They had reason to be pleased. Rumor had it "that *eight of them* who a few years since were mere Mushrooms" were receiving, for interest, the total taxes of eight states.[65] This pernicious program even determined some congressmen's votes in seating their fellow-members. Thus the House had accepted Henry Latimer, of Delaware, who was expected to support the paper system, and had rejected James Jackson, of Georgia, a known opponent.[66] One New Jersey newspaper urged voting against public creditors campaigning for office,[67] and another journal suggested the government should be denied all power to borrow except in time of direst emergency.[68] The term "speculator" had become an opprobrious epithet in many parts of the nation; villainous false priests had entered the temple of the Union, and were transacting business there with money changers to engage in the general scramble for "loaves and fishes." [69]

In the opinion of Charles A. Beard, Hamiltonian fiscal policies produced virtually all the partisan opposition to Washington's administrations.[70] As this study shows (in its consideration of neutrality, Jay's Treaty, and other questions only indirectly, if at all, related to financial problems), Beard's view needs serious qualification; but the *National Gazette* also considered the funding system the reason for the first definite division into parties. It had robbed veterans and had harmed patriots and the country as a whole. By 1792 one faction clearly approved the national debt; the other opposed it. One felt speculation to be the soul of credit; the other saw it as the evil child of unruly avarice. One party advocated the greatest latitude in construing the Constitution; the other desired a strict interpretation. Events, the journal added, had already shown the soundness of the latter party's views. The Treasury plan had raised up gamblers in securities, scandals against men in high-places, swarms of office-holders like the locusts of Egypt, sudden wealth, and a malignant hatred between country and city people. It had drained dry the natural channels of business, had ruined many individuals, and had created a sinister pressure group of court favorites threatening popular liberties. It was the veritable source of all the nation's ills. Nearly all classes had come to advocate extinguishing the debt, and there had been popular demonstrations against schemes for throwing wealth into the hands of a favored few.[71]

Copies of the strongest articles in Philadelphia papers were sent out into the countryside by critics of the administration.[72] The Newburyport, Mass., *Morning Star* echoed Freneau's cry that European affairs presaged the end of the day of despots everywhere. True Americans would sympathize with free France, and ever "be ready to oppose all adherents to that curse of Mankind, the *Funding System,* that Germ of American Monarchy!" [73] Pusillanimous Federalist foreign policy toward England [74] was motivated by desire to maintain governmental credit, even at the price of American commerce and agriculture. America's phalanx of speculators, including many congressmen, worshipped a new God—the paper they had so unjustly accumulated. They would defend the funding system if it cost our liberties or independence as a nation. [75]

"VALERIUS" denied that the funding system had produced the relatively improved financial situation of 1794. As well credit the war with the Indians, which had also occurred while business improved. Actually, imports now carried fifty per cent taxes, and living costs had sharply increased. It was America's natural advantages, the industry of her people, and the *principles* of the Constitution that had caused prosperity "to arise superior to all the disadvantages resulting from a wretched administration of government." [76] A financial report to the French National Convention in 1796 pointed to America's experience as a warning against refunding there, [77] and in Albany an irreconcilable ordered an inscription for his tombstone:

SPECTATOR!

> Beneath lies Abraham Yates, Jun. who uniformly opposed the Tyranny of Britain; and the corrupt perfidious Establishment of the Funding System; not for his own good, but for the public good.
> He has directed this last testimonial of the sincerity of his apprehensions; that it will prove most injurious to the equal rights of man, and the essential interests of his country. [78]

Late in the decade it was charged that the program had influenced "almost every measure of government" and that it was beginning to enfeeble the nation. [79]

Closely linked to refunding was Hamilton's proposal to have the central government assume the Revolutionary debts incurred by the several states. Taking over these obligations, [80] supporters contended, would further national tranquility. To depend on the individual states might well prove illusory.[81] Some states, however, had done far more to repay their creditors than had others. Virginia, for instance, had discharged most of her debts through land grants. Broadly speaking, the South (except for South Carolina, with a large unpaid debt) opposed the scheme. The Middle Atlantic states were divided, with commercial interests favoring the idea; New England generally approved, and stood to gain thereby.[82]

Arguments were not solely based, however, on the immediate profit or loss to the state concerned. One New Englander, writing on "The Folly of Esau," warned that would-be monarchists saw assuming state debts as a rare temptation. This mess of pottage would destroy the power and independence of the several states. Massachusetts' congressional representatives were only part of a body ten times their number and might readily lose touch with their constituents. The interests of advocates of assumption disclosed that this "bargain" was in reality for their own advancement and profit.[83]

Citizens were admonished that in the long run assumption would bring heavier taxes and probably even a dreaded land tax.[84] It would encourage the states to be extravagant in other matters. It would turn the allegiance of the creditor class entirely to the central government.[85] And that government would be mortgaging itself to the capitalists, whose field for speculative operations would be even further enlarged.[86]

Sectional implications of the proposition were evident, for the device was the "bastard of eastern speculators." This "brat" had been ushered into the world through the obstetric skill of the Secretary of the Treasury. With Congressman Theodore Sedgwick acting as priest, the baby was baptized "Alex—der Assumption"; bruised in "the *violent delivery*," it had been placed in the care of "nurse G[err]y" who was "to bathe the body with *yankey rum*." But, prematurely gloated the *New-York Journal* with elation over the preliminary defeat of assumption, this babe who was to have redeemed the Eastern states from poverty had perished—possibly strangled by Dr. [Isaac] Whippo, or neglected by Granny [Congressman Thomas] Fitzsimons. Appropriately, interment would be in Boston.[87]

Were the "paper nobility" from Philadelphia north to gain control of the certificates of Southern states, a North Carolina paper complained, one section of America would be paying taxes to support a favored class in another. Why should Virginians be taxed, unconstitutionally at that, to help discharge the obligations of Connecticut or Massachusetts? [88]

After a long struggle and an original rejection by the House, the measure was finally incorporated in the funding bill and adopted in July, 1790.[89] But the methods used in obtaining passage were suspect to many. Persistent were rumors of bribery and illegal loans to gain congressional votes.[90] The deal which finally put it across—location of the national capital on the banks of the Potomac in return for Southern votes—was denounced as a "corrupt bargain." [91] Who could have confidence in a government that decided completely unrelated questions by barter? Might not America's most valuable rights be someday similarly traded away? [92] Even friends of assumption were disgusted with the squabbling over the residence of Congress; Philadelphians were said to be ready to furnish their "beds, wives and daughters" to congressmen if they would move the capital to that city.[93]

"A Citizen of America" regarded the plot to locate the capital "on the wild and savage banks of the Potomack" as a trap for Washington's integrity. New Yorkers would be taxed for nearly one-eighth of an enormous assumption, merely to move Congress out of their state. Even Madison had said little on the proposition,[94] which confirmed the old axiom that every man had his price. If assumption were genuinely desirable, it would have been able to stand on its own feet, without deals.[95]

Criticism of the scheme did not cease with its adoption. In the popular mind it was associated with the funding process, which Republicans condemned in its entirety. Federalists might prate of the "spotless . . . Miss Assumption," which

49

the *New-York Journal* had so precipitately reported dead,[96] but their opponents retorted that this supposedly chaste lady had given birth to two illegitimate children, "Philadelphia" (to be the seat of government until 1800) and "Patowmacus," as a result of the seductive promises of a "Mr. Residence." [97] The excise, it was claimed, would have been unnecessary without assumption, since impost duties were adequate to care for the swollen national debt.[98] And why did the cashier for the new Bank of the United States have to be one of the commissioners and draw two salaries for settling the amounts to be assumed for each state? [99] By asserting that the states, as parts of the old government, had really only owed money to each other, Albert Gallatin charged that almost half the total assumed had been done so needlessly. As late as 1797 there were disputes over the proper sums to be given the several states.[100]

Later analyses indicated that about $40,000,000, or one-tenth of the nation's total wealth, accrued to holders of governmental securities through refunding and assumption.[101] More ominous to many was the growing power of Hamilton. His opponents maintained that the House had virtually abdicated in his favor, that he was originating money bills and influencing Congressional debates, and that his hastily prepared and deliberately obscure reports were imposed upon the public despite their sophistries.[102] By administering any plan enacted, he had practically usurped the power to tax.[103]

The creation of a national bank was perceived as the next step in augmenting the Secretary's power. Here opposition was stern and bitter, for banks were largely unknown and considered unnecessary.[104] Those state banks already existing could discharge every legitimate function of a national institution. For a government which for ten years had been unable to pay a third of the interest due on its obligations to acquire part ownership of this new bank stock smacked of immorality. Indubitably, a national bank invaded state's rights. It might drive local banks out of business, and it could deluge the country with paper money which the states were forbidden to issue.

If a bank were indispensable, why supplant the still-existing Bank of North America, created by the Continental Congress?[105]

The strongest argument presented against the Bank was that it was unconstitutional. Power to establish it could not be deduced, by any amount of reasoning, from the Constitution; such monopolies were incompatible with the American concept of government. Federalist arguments during ratification and over the first amendments noted that the Convention had expressly rejected granting powers of incorporation to Congress.[106] A combined funding and banking interest would make the government an agency of oppression to landowners. Yet, despite the concerted opposition of the South and West, the Bank bill became law.[107]

The new act was denounced as offering prospective stockholders better speculative opportunities than were obtainable anywhere in the world.[108] Investors apparently agreed, for shares were over-subscribed within fifteen minutes after being placed on sale. Southerners grumbled that this was another Philadelphia, New York, and Northern venture.[109] The Massachusetts legislature, however, rejected a proposal to buy stock with state funds; conflicts of interest might arise, and the age was already one of mad speculation.[110]

Opposition papers ridiculed or castigated the Bank, as the occasion and their inclinations suggested. Individual ownership presumably was to be limited to thirty shares, but the *Norwich Packet* charged that through fictitious names and rapid traveling a handful of stock-jobbers had monopolized the entire subscription. If the next session of Congress would nullify the entire transaction "the great body of the *People* will say AMEN."[111]

A subscriber advised Editor Bache to sell his press and paper for "bank Scrip" without delay. The stock was "in full gallop," and would "soon be 1000 per cent." Grandfather Franklin's outdated "maxims of prudence, economy, honesty, &c. are too narrow for the policy of this Rising Empire." The whole population could become rich without working, for a nearly almighty Congress could turn every rag of paper into rubies. If taxes were insufficient they could be raised.[112] New Jersey papers sarcastically advocated a "Potato bank." [113] Unsuccessful attempts to found local banks in New York were derided as designed only to aid the paper-gamblers.[114] Stock-jobbers boasted of friendship for the government, but when the fate of the Bank bill had been in doubt there had been predictions of "open and raging war" on Washington if speculators' appetites were disappointed.[115]

The Bank Directors elected in the autumn of 1791 were the same Congressional leaders who had fought to establish the institution. This violated, said "Caius," the constitutional prohibition against congressmen holding any other office during their terms. How could they be impeached if suspected of malfeasance? [116]

In Boston the Bank was accused of neglecting legitimate business while lending freely to speculators and of attempting to influence state elections. Specie was being drained from the city, and it was suggested the legislature should investigate the right of an outside corporation to operate within Massachusetts without permission from the state government. The middle class had more to fear from banks than from an invading army.[117] Nevertheless, to combat the raging speculative tide—or perhaps to profit from it—Bay State Democrats established their own "Union Bank." It was heralded as a great aid to true businessmen, although the "Hamilton junto" tried desperately to block the enterprise, which broke the speculators' monopoly on the local money market.[118]

Assertions of "interested sycophants" that the public had netted $1,000,000 on its shares of Bank stock were labeled "barefaced impudence." Even if true, however, this meant a gain of $5,000,000 on the entire capital—representing the value of a charter which was public property and which had been donated to speculators for one-fifth its worth. Those in government appeared to be men who sold for the people and bought for themselves.[119] Freneau even printed a poem to Washington on the subject:

George, on thy virtues often have I dwelt
And still the theme is grateful to mine ear.
Thy gold let chemists ten times even melt
From dross and base alloy they'll find it clear.

Yet thou'rt a man—although, perhaps, the first,
But man at best is but a being frail;
And since with error human nature's curst,
I marvel not that thou should'st sometimes fail.

That thou hast long and nobly served the state
The nation owns, and freely gives thee thanks.
But, sir, whatever speculators prate,
She gave thee not the power to establish *BANKS*.[120]

To the end of the decade, in Democratic prints Bank investors were classified as "speculators." Often, too, they were portrayed as British agents, or in league with them. With the debt getting into foreign hands, the Bank and even Congress might fall under foreign control.[121] After all, Hamilton himself was a foreigner and an aristocrat.[122]

The vast quantity of Bank notes in circulation had produced inflation, ruining honest merchants and swindling the poor.[123] By late summer of 1799 the yellow fever devastating coastal cities had subsided, but the *"Bank Fever"* raged unabated. It was proving more fatal to men's property than the epidemic ever had to their lives; a new case, with attendant losses, developed almost daily.[124] As long as Bank directors and stockjobbers constituted a considerable portion of Congress, neither national honor nor anything else in America was safe.[125]

Hamilton's program also called for supplementing the Bank and the funding system with a protective tariff. The duty would not only raise revenue, but also further American commerce and industry—or so it was claimed. Many diversified interests sought protection, and petitions from manufacturers flooded Congress soon after that body first met.[126]

Yet sentiment on the proposed tariff was far from unanimous. One correspondent thought it folly that the United States, without even a cutter (let alone a warship), could ex-

pect to collect duties as did England, where people were inured
to them and to the host of officials they entailed. Unaware that
the burden would be passed on to the consumer, the new government at its very outset would estrange by extravagant imposts those merchants who were chiefly responsible for its
existence.[127]

While protection was significant, the primary purpose of
the first tariff of 1789 was to raise revenue; duties were to be
the chief source of governmental income. Madison accordingly
urged speedy passage of a law applying to spring importations. But coastal merchants, who had placed large orders in
Europe in expectation of the tax, fought for delay so that
their goods might arrive duty-free. As a result of the merchants' pressure, the tariff was not approved until July 4 and
did not go into effect until August 1. Most merchants raised
prices in anticipation of the duty, and some men regarded this
trickery as the first in a series of steps by which the government favored those with capital.[128] The *Connecticut Journal*
discouraged formation of local associations, as in Revolutionary times, to enforce the new tariff. Only sycophants would
form such organizations, which could serve no good purpose.
Citizens should "let the laws alone." [129]

Certainly, the revenue program did not suit everyone, and
at times it must have seemed to please nobody. Congress was
implored to go lightly in taxing any form of commerce; if
trade were hurt the whole community suffered.[130] On paper,
increasing tariff duties in 1790 might realize enough to pay the
interest on the debt. In reality, unless somehow stimulated,
American trade could scarcely stand the burden. With assumption and an additional impost, prospects for prosperity were
dim. Congress had placed private and local interests ahead of
the nation's welfare; it was high time "that a change of men
and measures should take Place." [131]

Despite "the puffs of some court writers," commerce was
nearly as handicapped as before the Constitution. Imposts on
foreign vessels were too low to benefit American shipping, and

duties of five to seven per cent were too small to support manufacturing. Lawyers in Congress had taken pains to create an expensive judiciary for their own profession, but they had neglected the country's truly vital problems.[132] Writers could not agree whether foreign ships were being insufficiently discouraged or were driven from American ports, but they thought the revenue inadequate.[133] Cost of collections consumed half the income, and trade labored under duties on duties. "Colbert," who professed to approve of funding and the Bank, could not stomach the revenue laws. They injured commerce, actually increased American dependence on other nations, and ruined small manufacturers. Absolute prohibition of all imports that America could produce herself would be preferable.[134]

Everything considered, the tariff excited less opposition than funding, assumption, the Bank, and the excise, but in 1799 Democrats were still flaying the whole revenue system adopted by the First Congress.[135] Much earlier, in 1792, the *Federal Gazette* had scoffed at administration claims that the benefits of strong public credit were felt the country over. Merchants rejected such an assertion; they were overburdened with added taxes. Farmers petitioned against the excise, and laborers were harmed by the exclusive privileges given manufacturers. Surely, the people at large felt no "benefits," for they complained "loudly and justly of the extravagance and ruinous measures. . . ."[136]

All of Hamilton's program was criticized, but the choicest epithets were saved for those who speculated in paper and land. Land speculation was an old story, but before independence America had known little stock-jobbing. Business corporations had been rare, and most public securities had borne no interest. Following the Revolution conditions began to change. Institutionally managed investments developed. The transition toward impersonal and specialized capitalism was facilitated by joint-stock companies, the public debt, and improved communications between leading businessmen. Popular atti-

*55*

tudes had sufficiently changed so that Americans would accept new business methods, and wartime contractors and financiers were eager to lead new ventures.[137]

Chief among the new type of promoters was William Duer, who had come from England to New York in 1768 to purchase timbers for the British navy. His meteoric rise commenced when he joined the American cause in the Revolution. A delegate to the Continental Congress, Duer achieved considerable wealth late in the war by furnishing supplies under contract to Washington's troops. Secretary of the Treasury Board under the Articles of Confederation, Duer apparently used his position to promote congressional measures favorable to his investments in Ohio lands. Hamilton made him Assistant Secretary of the Treasury in 1789. Duer took the post to further his own interests, keeping his partner (Andrew Craigie) informed on matters affecting governmental funds. A year later he resigned, possibly because of the rising cries of "speculator," but more likely because Treasury Department employees were forbidden to purchase public lands and securities.[138]

Even before his resignation, Duer's reputation as a manipulator had been established. He and his friends had purchased large quantities of certificates before refunding went into effect, and the mere appointment as Assistant Secretary of a man so favorable to investors had helped raise the price of government securities.[139] Early in 1790 accusations were circulating that Hamilton's plans had leaked out, and that a handful of insiders had been able to buy up most of the public paper at a discount. Critics contended congressmen should be required to testify that they were not speculating in government funds.[140]

The speculative craze snowballed, and newspaper criticism, increasing in bitterness, kept pace. In the Biblical style often affected by political writers of the times, one Marylander related the "confessions" of silversmith turned financier. This "Spelterzink" had been an industrious and prosperous craftsman, but he coveted riches and began stock-jobbing. Out of the need and misery of others, he added greatly to his wealth. Yet all his money, gained "from grinding the Faces of the Poor," failed to bring contentment. Gladly would he give it all to free himself from remorse and to gain "that 'Peace of Mind which passeth Understanding.' " [141]

Philosophers were correct, stated the *New Jersey Journal,* in saying the people at large never gained from a war. In Europe the only beneficiaries were contractors; in America, the speculators.[142] Georgians were warned against the trick by which some Maryland legislators authorized that state to accept sums owing to Englishmen. They then paid their debts in Continental currency while it was still legal tender, obtained treasurer's receipts, and left the state saddled with their obligations.[143]

Speculators were blamed for spreading rumors or for distorting foreign news in order to raise or lower security values, as their own interests demanded.[144] Opposition newspapers, trying to combat the hysteria, drew comparisons with John Law's Mississippi failure and with the South Sea Bubble.[145] In Baltimore even reports that criminals were counterfeiting certificates did not cool the fever.[146] So high did its scrip rise that critics held Madison had been justified in demanding a large payment to the government for the Bank's exclusive privileges.[147] The stock was worth nowhere near the then current prices. What goes up must come down, reminded the *General Advertiser,* and so Brother Jonathan had better take care for his pate. Some of the speculators would be speculating in the mad-house ere long.[148]

In the backwoods, the South, and far north in Maine, jobbers scoured the country for governmental notes of state and nation. Trading upon ignorance, lying about the worth of certificates, often they obtained the paper for next to nothing. A writer in the *Pennsylvania Gazette* wanted to know

> What must be the feelings of the widow and orphan, when they find themselves thus defrauded of a great part of their little

all, and that, not unlikely, the earnings of their late husbands and fathers, who died in the service of their country, by these pests of society who ought to be despised? [149]

When cliché experts asserted honesty, industry, and thrift were the surest sources of public and private wealth, "Square Toes" sneered that such might be true for Europe, but not America. He challenged anyone to produce twenty men who had become rich since 1775 through observing these maxims. "British riders, Amsterdam Jews, American tories, and speculating Lawyers, Doctors and Parsons" had not made up to $50,000 a year since 1783 by such methods. There were but a few honest and industrious Americans who had not "ruined themselves by their honesty and industry." [150]

Laws were requested to curb speculation, for no business other than Bank scrip was transacted in leading cities.[151] An English article describing how speculators cooperated to fleece well-meaning investors was reprinted to dissuade people from entering the market.[152] A New York newspaper tried to foil an attempted corner in Bank stock by exhorting its readers not to sell to manipulators.[153] A Maryland paper admonished in poetic form, concluding:

And sure as death all mortals trips,
Thousands will rue their faith in SCRIPS.[154]

Lotteries were viewed as competing with stock-jobbers. Both were on the same business level, and a first prize of $10,000 was worthy of notice even by holders of stock.[155] "An Observer" censured "Scripomania" for the scarcity of specie in circulation. Money had been drained from ordinary channels of trade, and interest rates were fantastically high.[156] No stranger would ever deduce from Americans' behavior that the federal government's entire revenue was drawn from commerce, and all the paper issued based upon it. Yet in the end the nation could be supported only by the industry of her citizens.[157] Hatred and contempt for stock-jobbers was epitomized by "A LOOKER ON," writing about the rumor of a draft for the army after General St. Clair's defeat in Ohio:

> It had such an Effect, that upwards of *Three Hundred* Brokers of the third order left this Town—Those Men are generally known in this and some other Towns, by the Name of Paper-Hunters, or Hamilton's *Rangers*—Within these few days many have returned, having been assured that Congress will not suffer the original public creditors to be injured—But,—If Creatures must be had, the above, with a few of the higher order, are all that Boston can be willing to send to moisten the Western Soil; even then, 'tis doubtful if the Land would be enriched—One Thing is certain, the Public will not be impoverished.[158]

Freneau's *National Gazette* noted caustically that no direct denial had ever appeared against the charges that government officials had profited on the basis of their own measures before those measures had been formally enacted.[159] If they *had* speculated, blazed the *New-York Journal,* the situation clamored for a display of public indignation. If not, then why were the accusations permitted to circulate unanswered? Administration hangers-on only evaded the imputation or descended to suggestions that those warning against corruption were themselves hostile to government.[160] A Maryland social gathering was requested to name the greatest men in Congress, and a wit immediately replied, "the greatest Speculators!!" Where, then, was the security of the people? [161]

For their own profit, congressmen had "combined with brokers and others to gull and trick their uninformed constituents out of their certificates." [162] Fenno's *Gazette of the United States* demanded the names of these representatives, but Freneau compared this demand to the London woman who sued for defamation of character because one man called her a prostitute. She was a prostitute, and everyone knew it, but no one could prove it without self-incrimination. Similarly, the brokers and those who hired fast ships to beat the news of refunding and assumption into areas where certificates might be picked up cheaply would not expose their employers and themselves.[163]

Cries were strong against the First Congress, which had funded the public debt "into the hands of D[uer] and Co. The infamous practices by which this infamous business was effected, begin at last to be developed, and a stain has been discovered . . . upon our national honor, that no time will wipe away." [164] America's free empire was in danger of being disgraced and enslaved, and the nation's most accomplished speculators were

> Those who *speculate* themselves into Congress—then *speculate* upon the public finances till they establish a funding system and a bank—then *speculate* in the funds and the bank till they engross the whole management of them—then speculate upon the people to obtain six dollars per day for labouring *for themselves*—then *speculate* into Congress at the next election and thus *speculate* upon the property and welfare of their country.[165]

The solution, or at least a partial one, was simple enough: see that speculators were not elected to office. The *National Gazette* suggested four criteria for political candidates. They should be men of independent minds and honest principles, friends of liberty and republican government, not office hunters, and "not jobbers in paper." [166] Speculators were up for election "in every district in the Union," and care must be exercised not to vote for any of them.[167]

Apart from rascality, some feared this craze for financial venture would promote an aristocracy in America. One of the inevitable consequences of quick wealth was a thirst for rank and distinction. Many Americans were republicans in name only, and these newly rich often ridiculed the followers of honest and useful occupations.[168] "Archimedes" offered would-be nobles a "plan." Speculators were to be classified according to wealth and grants were to be made by the government on that basis. Titles (such as "the order of the Leech," and "Their Rapacities"), coats of arms, and mottoes were ironically suggested. Such a system had manifest advantages, for it stimulated diligence and ingenuity by offering great rewards to citizens who "so exercised their virtues as to possess themselves of the wealth of the country at the least possible expence." [169]

Jeffersonians noted with satisfaction a "resurrection of the justice" of America in the spring of 1792, when many speculative empires fell with a crash. Duer and his leading associates, Isaac Whippo and Alexander Macomb, went bankrupt, dragging others with them.[170] When he went to jail, resentment against speculators reached fever pitch. The failure set off a general panic, and feelings were heightened by revelations that Duer had been—through bungling agents, he claimed—the sadly inefficient contractor for St. Clair's ill-fated army.[171]

At first those who had been prophesying a collapse were gleeful. "The SPECULATOR" contrasted the situation in New York City with that of only twenty days earlier, when the craze for bank, government, and tontine stock of all sorts had gripped the city. But now the scene was dismally changed, and those who had made thousands at a single bid had reverted to "the painful task of acquiring property by shillings." Since other bankruptcies would follow, he facetiously suggested that "Congress had better assume the debts of Col. D."[172] An "Advertisement Extraordinary" in the *National Gazette* purported to tell of price increases by Philadelphia and New York barbers. Rates for shaving were doubled and for hairdressing quadrupled, because of long faces and hair which was constantly standing on end.[173]

Bitterness soon entered into many comments. New York, center of the paper debacle, was first and hardest hit. "The speculating tribe" there was "sunk into the abyss of inextricable confusion," and yet some members seemed unaware of their awful predicament.[174] So deplorable were conditions that New Yorkers would rather see a house on fire than a speculator enter the city. All business was suspended, and unemployment was the rule, "owing to a set of Swindlers, who ought to be in Simsbury Mines."[175] One of Freneau's harshest poems described the rise and fall of a typical speculator:

> Egg'd on by hope, from town to town he flew
> The soldier's curse pursued him on his way,
> Care in his eye and anguish on his brow
> He seem'd a sea-hawk watching for his prey.

With soothing words the widow's mite he gain'd
With piercing glances watch'd misery's dark abode,
Filch'd paper scraps while yet a scrap remain'd
Bought where he must, and cheated where he cou'd.

Vast loads amass'd of scrip, and god knows what,
Potosi's wealth seemed lodg'd within his clutch—
But wealth has wings (he knew) and instant bought
The prancing steed, gay harness, and gilt coach.

\* \* \* \* \* \* \* \* \* \* \* \*

Three weeks, and more, thus pass'd in airs of state,
The fourth beheld the mighty bubble fail—
And he, who countless millions *own'd* so late
Stopt short—and clos'd his triumphs in a JAIL.[176]

The *National Gazette* and other papers printed a somewhat biased history-prophecy entitled "CHRONOLOGY OF FACTS." This account related how, from 1775–1783, the blood of patriots had established Liberty in America. Between 1783 and 1789 these patriots received two shillings per pound for their services. In 1789–1790, speculators received two pounds per shilling without performing any useful function; they were able to purchase control of many newspapers. During 1790–1791 millions flowed into investors' hands, the glare of wealth was mistaken for prosperity, and the people slept while chains of aristocracy and monarchy were forged for them. Administration measures gave speculators free gifts; there was poverty in the country, luxury in the cities, and corruption and usurpation in national councils. In 1792 the bubble burst. The champions of public faith were revealed as swindlers, and congressmen were detected in speculations. People awakened with the disclosure of $4,000,000 annual tribute to European brokers. By March, 1793, a new era had commenced. A fully alert public purged official posts of stock-jobbers and monarchy-jobbers; effective measures were taken toward paying off the debt. Industry and virtue were established; republicanism was again in fashion. "The people rejoice in their freedom, *and are determined to maintain* it." [177]

Yet the crash did not completely eliminate the danger. In

Massachusetts, where these *"Pests* of Society" still swarmed along the coast, people were exhorted to unite and exclude every "Ranger, Speculator or Swindler" from the new legislature. That body must be free from contamination, for stockjobbers "will sell their country for a Scrip . . . they consider the State as a *Lottery-Office,* and the Rights and Privileges of the People as a *Discount* from their Prizes." [178] A South Carolina grand jury presented speculation there as one of its grievances. Much of the veterans' "hard earnings" had fallen into the hands of a certain class, "some of which" had been Tories during the Revolution.[179] A "NEW GENEALOGY," written in Old Testament fashion, related for Connecticut readers the origin and rise of America's speculation:

> 1. SATAN begat taxation, and taxation begat opposition, and opposition begat the war, and the war begat the old Confederation. 2. And the old Confederation lived four hundred and three score days and begat speculation . . . which is *living to this day,* and *in all probability will live to the age of Methusaleh.* [And so on, until the adoption of the Constitution, which] . . . begat the new Congress. 9. And the new Congress lived five hundred and forty and seven days and begat the funding bill.[180]

Yet the gambling spirit persisted, despite danger and censure. Bank directors in 1793 were advised that merchants, mechanics, and manufacturers were good risks but were cautioned to avoid discounting notes for speculators.[181] One writer hoped the new federal bankruptcy law would relieve honest debtors and still foil those seeking a fortune by defrauding their creditors. Fraudulent bankruptcy was all too common with manipulators, who in the past had fled from one state to another claiming insolvency but taking their creditors' property with them. Duer and his crew were hoping, despite their promises, to pay nothing at all on their debts. Congress should leave no loopholes for such cunning men.[182] Men who owed small sums often languished in prison for long periods, while those in arrears for thousands were released in a short time and even used their imprisonment as a device for evading just demands upon them. Bankruptcy oaths should be taken in

63

open court, to discourage fraudulency. "May the laws," wrote a Massachusetts correspondent, "ever prove mild and lenient to the unfortunate, but a scourge to *Evil*—DUERS." [183]

Isaac Whippo was said to be commanding a Spanish privateer off the Georgia coast in 1797, still plundering the property of his fellow citizens.[184] Candidates for the legislature in North Carolina were asked to swear that they had not been interested in the funding system or in that state's land speculations.[185] Five years after Duer's failure, certain congressmen were charged with secretly withdrawing public funds to speculate in tobacco.[186] Deception and news-rigging were arts of the jobber's trade; the bankruptcy of a Philadelphia broker disclosed sizable sums paid to several Federalist newspaper editors. Administration supporters were challenged to "furnish a single instance of similar corruption in a democratic printer." [187]

Never, said "Phocion," had there been a time when the outcry for money was so great as in 1795. Interest rates had soared, thanks to British seizures of American ships and to speculation, especially by that time, in land. Judges and legislators had practiced jobbing of the grossest sort. Notes in circulation on land ventures exceeded credibility. All principle was lost in the speculative lust, and people should carefully watch their rulers if they wished to keep them honest.[188]

Following the panic of 1792, American speculators turned increasingly to opportunities in land rather than stocks. Land ventures were nothing new, but after the Revolution all restraint seemed cast off. Joint-stock companies in coastal cities purchased huge proprietary tracts, and currency fluctuations plus widespread ignorance concerning the West enhanced opportunities for jobbing. Many men in public office used their official positions to secure favorable grants.[189] A number of Georgians resented the treaty of 1790, described as more unconstitutional than the Boston Port Bill, whereby the United States confirmed the title of the Creek Indians to a wide area. Jobbers and would-be settlers combined to promote settlement of "vacant lands" in that state. Only Georgia's legislature could legally alienate "four-fifths of her territory," and Secretary of War Henry Knox (whose own land operations were far to the northward) was excoriated.[190]

Speculators, especially in military districts, were engrossing immense tracts; it was predicted that, unless legislative grants of wild land were restricted, America would soon find itself with an aristocracy and a peasantry.[191] Frontiersmen were amused by doggerel concerning three men arguing over the composition of the moon. One said it was fog; a second that it was land. The third denied it was land, "For if it was, the jobbers of New York/Would have their patents there, and men at work." [192] Some Eastern opposition to the military campaigns against the Indians in Ohio was based on the conviction that a favored few had obtained lands there from Congress, and were using the army to extirpate the aborigines occupying these holdings. Harmar's and St. Clair's defeats should produce an inquiry exposing this partiality.[193]

The most notorious land deal was the Yazoo scandal, involving the Georgia legislature. In January, 1795, that body sold 35,000,000 acres in the Yazoo River region of present-day Alabama and Mississippi to several companies of speculators for slightly over one cent an acre.[194] It was said that every legislator favoring the sale except one either owned or had been given shares in one or more of the companies,[195] and honest citizens were horrified. If "THE GEORGIA BUSINESS" were not stopped, predicted one, war with both Spain and the Creeks was inevitable, and the national program for the sale of Western public lands would be destroyed. Any officials involved should be ousted immediately.[196]

Bache's *Aurora* called for the impeachment of a Supreme Court Justice said to be implicated.[197] "A FATHER" urged Congress to buy Georgia's backlands at the full price asked by the legislature; the national government would not have to sell at this time, and an expensive and interminable war with the Indians should be avoided at all costs.[198] Resentment in Georgia was so great that nearly every member of the 1796 legislature was pledged to repeal the sale, and Republican James

65

Jackson resigned from the United States Senate to run for governor and lead the fight.[199] Partisan newspapers carried "advertisements" "For the benefit of the Patriotic Association of LAND JOBBERS," describing tracts to be purchased in the moon and assorted planets,[200] and the new legislature rescinded the action of its predecessor. Unfortunately, the purchasers had already managed to dispose of much of the land in question, and bitter controversy ensued for years afterward.[201]

Federalist Senator James Gunn of Georgia allegedly had led in promoting the sale, which had been made plausible by Pinckney's Treaty with Spain in February, 1795. Following the invalidation of the sale, Democrats chortled that the "great gun" had discharged and "wounded many ducks" who were "waddling in the [Exchange] *Alley."* [202] Supposedly Senator Gunn's vote for the Jay Treaty was secured only by promising him that his part in the Georgia manipulation would not be investigated. Here was but another instance in which national welfare had been sacrificed to benefit corrupt speculators, and Gunn should be impeached.[203]

Southern papers bulged with charges and countercharges. The purchasers and those who bought from them claimed the transaction had been made in good faith.[204] Democrats sneered that these were the outcries of "affectionately interested parents" in their children. Except for "the little speculating town of Augusta," nine-tenths of Georgia's population applauded invalidation of the sale.[205] Surely the rest of the country, save for those expecting to profit from the operation, also approved invalidation. Land-jobbing had become a national disgrace, and French and English newspapers warned their readers against American land agents. The collapse of the Georgia venture should serve as "a b[e]acon to warn the good people," and make speculators "shunned as pests to Society." [206] Individuals who had purchased from "Yazooers" were left without recourse, since a state could not be sued, but the rescinders felt the lesson a sound one. A song, "Capt.

KIDD'S successor," as *"addressed to Speculation, by a* DUERITE," well expressed their sentiments:

> I Purchas'd Georgia land as I sail'd, as I sail'd,
> I purchas'd Georgia land as I sail'd.
> I purchas'd Georgia land, made up of rocks and sand;
> But I paid in notes of hand—and I *failed*.[207]

Not long after the annulment Georgia tendered her western lands, including the Yazoo River region, to the federal government, reserving 5,000,000 acres to quiet any claims against the state. Congress accepted, but the matter remained a political football. Federalists favored at least partial reimbursement to the land companies, particularly when damage suits against them by later purchasers were upheld in some states; but the violent opposition of John Randolph and other Republicans blocked such congressional action during Washington's or Adams's administrations.[208]

Yet the madness continued; in 1796 Secretary of State Timothy Pickering wrote "All I am now worth was gained by speculation in land." [209] North Carolina legislators were accused of fraudulent land entries, and Connecticut politicians had speculated in the Western Reserve.[210] The French-language Philadelphia *Courier Français* held that America contained "more sources of corruption than are to be found in any other young nation." [211] Carolinians laughed over a letter from an imprisoned "speculator" to his fellow-jobbers. His tables for calculating speculative profits had been based on the Yazoo or Connecticut Reserve lands, but these shares had dropped to "less than nothing." He would readily point out the errors to anyone who would furnish him with board and washing; the state was already providing his room.[212] The New York *Diary* deplored the buying and selling of millions of acres unseen by purchasers. Speculators should use land in the moon; it would serve their purposes equally well, and earthly tracts could then be settled and actually cultivated.[213]

Questionable land ventures were a potent campaign issue in

1800. Western Pennsylvania Democrats supported John Hamilton for re-election to the state senate; jobbers would be antagonistic, for he had not speculated, and was "friendly to *the settlers* in opposition to *the Companies.*" Independent voters were cautioned against Federalist threats, submitting their ballots "to the scrutiny of a land jobbing inquisition," or being forced from the polls.[214] Federal Judge Addison electioneered for the Federalists in charges to jurors, but for five years, it was said, he and associates had withheld public funds to purchase Western lands at a time when the government was paying eight per cent to borrow money.[215]

A tasty tidbit for the Jeffersonian press was the case of Jonathan Dayton, Speaker of the House of Representatives. Leading New Jersey Federalist, Dayton had been allied with John Cleves Symmes, a New Jersey speculator, and others in the purchase of vast Ohio tracts in 1788. Terms of the original transaction were never fulfilled, but through collusion with the official surveyor and use of military warrants Symmes and Dayton obtained two-sevenths of the area at the rate of one acre for an acre and one-half of actual land. The nation was thus defrauded of over $30,000.[216]

The Symmes Purchase was only one of Dayton's manipulations. As Speaker, in 1798 he had received from the Treasury $33,000 to pay less than $15,000 in salaries to House members. Well over a year later it was discovered that he had used the balance for speculative purposes; Secretary of the Treasury Oliver Wolcott sharply demanded and recovered the money, but without interest.[217] Shortly afterward, Dayton and his partner sued Francis Childs, New York agent for their firm. Eventually the suit was dropped, but not until Childs had shown in court a series of damning letters. Written in 1796 and now published jubilantly in the *American Citizen,* these clearly revealed that Dayton had bought lands that had appreciated in value because of bills he had sponsored in Congress. He had obtained military land warrants on credit in New York for parcels in the Northwest Territory at only one-eighth the price of two dollars an acre which Congress was about to fix. In other communications Dayton predicted legislation in advance for Childs's benefit, and recommended financing political activity in the districts of congressmen who might oppose funds for the Jay Treaty or other measures raising the value of Western lands. Since one letter enjoined Childs to burn the message after reading it, Dayton was obviously aware of the impropriety of his actions.[218]

Thus was unveiled, said the Kentucky *Palladium,* the system by which the Speaker had "enriched himself, while ostensibly serving the public." [219] Dayton's dropping of the case against Childs proved the validity of the letters; every man in public life needed watching, and none should be accorded unquestioning confidence. Profits of the Speaker's land ventures undoubtedly were used to procure the votes for appropriations to carry out the Jay Treaty, and he had used public monies advanced to him for salary disbursements to Representatives in his own business operations.[220] As one writer put it:

> Jonathan Dayton . . . the late speaker of Congress, is notorious from Boston to Georgia. The deeds of other members of Congress were scarcely known beyond the circle of their respective states, but the speculations of this man have rung throughout the western world.[221]

Republican editors had a field day. Timothy Pickering, too, was accused; the *Aurora* filled columns about the Secretary of State, the erstwhile Speaker, and their land dealings.[222] Senator James Ross of Pennsylvania was said to be implicated with Judge Addison in "as flagrant a scene of iniquity as any of Dayton's transactions." [223] An alleged bookkeeping error of a million dollars by Wolcott in a Treasury report laid before Congress was proclaimed an "ILLUSTRATION . . . *of the means by which public money is applied to* SPECULATIONS." [224] It was stressed, also, that nothing said against Dayton had been disproved, or even denied.[225]

The Republican press summarized the plundering of the nation's treasury "by the speculating tribe placed in authority under the Federal Government." The Treasury books themselves disclosed that "the characters who have been revelling upon unaccounted for *millions* of public money . . . are all speculators. . . ." They revealed what credence should be given the professions of those "high toned Federalists," who bellowed about the wonders of America's laws and administration at the very moment they were undermining the Constitution and rifling the federal exchequer.[226] Land ceded by North Carolina to the Union to help discharge the public debt had never been applied to that end, nor would it be until Dayton and his ilk had disposed of their tracts. Effective land sales would increase settlement in the South and West, but Federalists opposed any strengthening of representations from these sections in Congress. Forbidden to occupy their lands because of a specious law purporting to regulate Indian trade, Tennesseans could only hope that the fruits of the Revolution would not be perverted into a system incompatible with true republicanism.[227]

As Speaker, charged these accounts, Dayton seemed to have been even more corrupt than Theodore Sedgwick, though if the latter's original speculations in public funds were considered the race would be close. How far Pickering excelled them both remained yet to be seen, and possibly the *Aurora* would uncover the names of Dayton's accomplices in his effort to absorb nearly 180,000 acres of soldiers' lands. Speculations by public agents and defaulters had become so manifest, said Jeffersonians, that the "old Tories" were reduced to raising "the silly question, where can you find men who will do better?" [228]

The perfectly evident answer was to elect men of Republican principles. This argument proved to be an extremely potent one in the campaign of 1800.

 THE HIGH COST
OF GOVERNMENT

Foes of the administration had other economic issues than
Hamiltonian finance and Daytonian peculations on which to
base their assaults. Then as today, governmental expenses
provided a superb whetstone for sharpening editorial knives.

Priority targets almost since Washington's inauguration
were delays, inefficiency, high salaries, and alleged extravagance. It was predicted in June, 1789, that the recommendations of the First Congress's committee on wages would set
the country aflame. They were resented everywhere, for proposed salaries were twice what they should be, and "inconsistent with every idea . . . of a republican government." [1] Six
dollars a day for senators and representatives was too much,
grumbled the *Boston Gazette*. A three hundred-day session
would cost $270,000. For a newspaper soon so hostile to cer-
tificate holders, its postscript was amusing: "A correspondent
who is a PUBLIC CREDITOR, hopes that the Revenue will
not be *absorbed* by the great Salaries; but that *something* will
be left for those who loaned their Money to Government. . . ." [2]

Clerks, janitorial help, and other governmental employees
were also overpaid. The doorkeeper would earn more than
some state governors—a clear mark of prodigality. [3] Two dollars per diem would have been ample for congressmen, and
$25,000 annually was double what the President would spend.

71

Did Congress have the revenue of China to squander? Comparisons with British official salary scales were inapplicable, since the American federal system duplicated many state and national offices.[4] Mileage allowances far exceeded actual traveling costs, and clergymen's prayers were worth little if priced at five dollars apiece. Even secretaries would become rich and insolent. The government had not been founded for purposes of ostentation, and cries of "anti-federalism" by *"courtwriters"* would not blind people to the fact that these compensations came from their pockets.[5]

Articles defending adequate salaries as attracting abler men or rendering corruption less likely were in a decided minority.[6] To many, the halving of a $40,000 grant for expenses of a treaty with the Indians suggested laxity in appropriations; pay scales probably could also be cut in two.[7] America had never realized any advantage from diplomatic representatives, noted Bostonians; they would only entangle the country in foreign intrigues. If other nations found it advantageous to treat with America, they could send agents over here.[8] Not all New Englanders were so extreme, but many thought federal wages were too high and feared Congress seemed more concerned about living well than getting the job done. Better to save money and redeem the nation's obligations.[9]

High salaries might centralize federal power, thereby weakening state governments.[10] An infant nation should proceed cautiously; unreasonable taxes would be resented, perhaps with fatal consequences. Americans could not, and should not, "imitate the splendour of European establishments. . . ." The states were the best judges of services rendered, and each should pay its own representatives.[11]

Living expenses were estimated at only seven dollars a week; unless representatives were chiefly desirous of making money, it was thought unnecessary to pay them almost that much per day.[12] Congressional inaction and procrastination rendered the pay scales a mockery, especially in a government supposedly founded on principles of simplicity and economy.

One could write a book—appropriately entitled *A Treatise on Trifling*—concerning the various legislative delays.[13] Even the proposed Library of Congress was subjected to philippics. It was absurd, scolded one writer, to see the national legislature disregard great questions of state and argue about books for members' *"amusement* or *instruction."* Had Americans chosen men uninstructed in first principles who required tuition and texts in addition to six dollars daily? New York's circulating library would be much cheaper.[14] The *Boston Gazette* carried a satiric

### ADVERTISEMENT EXTRAORDINARY

Wanted for the SAN SOUCI Society of New-York, a Number of diverting Novels, Romances &c. to amuse the Members, after the fatiguing Business of lolling in their chairs three Hours for the good of the Nation.—As this little snug Party have no Matters of Importance to call their Attention, and being willing to be doing *something* for their Six Dollars per Day, they propose to expend a few Thousand Dollars of the public Money in procuring a Library.—These industrious Gentlemen (who have already been amusing the Publick for four Months) will then be able to spend their Time as becomes Men of Leisure and Independence, in reading Magazines, and other entertaining Publications.—As our Trade is so flourishing, it is expected that it will have further Assistance, by increasing the Impost, which will enable this Robinhood Society to furnish themselves with a large Collection of the most diverting Pamphlets.

N. B. Any Person willing to contract to furnish this private Library, will have good Encouragement, as the Price will not be regarded, the Contractors having the whole Revenue of the States to dispose of for the same.

A Librarian is wanted, who will receive an ample yearly Salary, besides two Dollars per Day, during the Session of the Society.

For further particulars, inquire of the Sub-Doorkeeper.[15]

"Junius" was particularly biting, even among parsimonious New Englanders, on congressional dawdling and waste. Representatives acted as though the Constitution had been adopted for their sole benefit; they must dread returning home to the constituents they had "ROBBED." [16] An outraged

Virginia correspondent asserted the nation had "sunk into a forgetfulness of everything but private interest; . . . and nothing seems to animate us, but the dispute whether Congress shall chase butterflies on the banks of the Hudson or the Potowmac." A resolution introduced in the Massachusetts legislature instructed that state's senators to strive for reductions in salaries and pensions, to aid business and agriculture, and to restore public confidence "in the Wisdom of the Federal Administration." [17]

Urban jealousy may have produced a New York paper's acid comment on the cost of the President's residence in Philadelphia, but thrift motivated its republication in Boston.[18] If forty-five candidates had run for only four congressional seats in New Jersey's last election, governmental salaries assuredly were attractive enough. Perhaps those seeking the "loaves and fishes [rather] than the *publick good"* would crowd out virtuous and patriotic statesmen.[19] And the presentment of a South Carolina grand jury charged that "almost the whole revenue of the country is absorbed" in newly created offices with inflated emoluments.[20]

Military operations against the Western Indians would probably cost the nation the "enormous expense" of over a million dollars for 1792; yet privates in the new regiments would be paid "but *three dollars per month,"* or only half what congressmen received for one day's sitting. Was it an equal government when officials could live in a manner far superior to that of members of the society which supported them? [21] Representatives were urged "to guard against *every possible additional* unnecessary expenditure," [22] and the *National Gazette,* convinced that public funds were being lavished on favorites, called for abolition of the War Department as the only hope for lasting peace with the red men.[23] Complaints about Congress' prodigality and preoccupation with trivialities continued,[24] and Benjamin Bache sardonically gibed that when a representative actually spoke for reducing the great cost of a military establishment it was accounted "the most extraordinary thing imaginable, and so terrific, that it was hoped such a *Monster* would never again make his appearance within the walls of Congress." [25]

Congressional grants and pensions horrified thrifty New Englanders. Washington's drillmaster, Baron von Steuben, was an outrageous example. With $250 salary and $300 for table expenses every month throughout the Revolution, he had been voted a life stipend of $2,500 annually in 1790. In 1785 he had supposedly been voted $7,000 in full payment for his services; individual states had granted him nearly $50,000. Yet now he was in debt again and appealing to Congress for relief.[26] Pressure from the Society of the Cincinnati had doubtless secured his pensions; "OECONOMIAS" called for a published record of the vote in order that citizens would know whom to reelect. Otherwise, Congress would next be voting its own members life-time pensions.[27] Some years later in 1799 it was noted that most of the recipients of such grants were Federalists; clearly, party membership was as important as any contribution to the nation's welfare.[28]

If anything, attacks on the administration's extravagance increased as the decade wore on. Federalist fustian about America's "unexampled prosperity"—with a tremendous debt for which America had difficulty in making interest payments, inflation, British seizures, differences with France, and daily bankruptcies—was only intended to gull the citizenry into maintaining the salaries of overpaid officials. During John Adams' first two years as President, his family received $80,-000 for wages and expenses. If he could not live on $25,000 plus $4,000 building expenses, he should "retire and make way for one that can." [29]

Fully as irritating to Republicans, and deemed unconstitutional as well, was the Federalist practice of using a government official in a special capacity and compensating him for both tasks. Though John Jay was Chief Justice, he was named envoy extraordinary to the Court of St. James. The Secretaries of State and Treasury were made commissioners in 1799 to settle with Georgia the question of lands acquired by Pinckney's Treaty at seven dollars per day, in addition to their annual salaries of $5,000. In 1800 Chief Justice Oliver Ellsworth was also envoy to France, and General McPherson, both a military and a customs officer. Adams' son-in-law, Colonel Smith, undoubtedly would "be squeezed into the first good birth that becomes vacant . . . according to *pappy's* maxim that '*we* must take care of our friends.' " [30]

Thus the proposal of Senator Benjamin Goodhue of Massachusetts to augment congressional salaries in 1800 was roundly berated. Was this the economy Adams had recommended? The United States was borrowing money at eight per cent at a time when at least one congressman had purchased a New England estate out of his wages. No additional labor nor rise in food prices justified the increase.[31] It was significant that "high salaries and high toned politics" were currently fashionable in states hitherto famed for thrift, while "free living" Southerners opposed prodigality. Federalist New Englanders might favor personal frugality, but they were no friends to public economy. That French officials were highly paid (as a list in a pro-administration paper made evident) was irrelevant: "*What have the people of the United States to do with the salaries of French officials?*" The wave of protests apparently prevented any congressional pay increase during this period.[32]

Even though salary increases were denied, congressmen were still accused of wasting funds. Congressman Robert Goodloe Harper, in the *Aurora's* opinion, frittered away in one year nearly $18,000 worth of time in superfluous motions and silly speeches, simply to gratify his vanity. Congress spent three weeks, at $1,000 per day, in preparing an answer to Adams' message. Many bankrupt persons turned Federalist, wrote "Jonathan," because the government provided for them; citizens were burdened to provide for "sycophants, and a clan of idle, lazy fellows who never earned a farthing by their own industry." [33] Treasury clerks sometimes had to wait for their quarterly pay, but Secretary Wolcott could find funds for higher officials who had been off electioneering or for his own vacation in Connecticut. Adams himself spent two-thirds of the year in Quincy; when "great men" were away resting or speculating in public lands, important duties were left to underlings, and "the cock was making free with the horse's corn," for citizens were not getting their money's worth.[34]

Even more legitimate governmental activities seemed exorbitantly costly. Sums expended on the public buildings in the new national capital appalled Republicans. It was asserted the entire House of Representatives could meet in the kitchen of the Executive Mansion, then under construction, with room enough for the Senate in a chimney corner. Where could be found a President "rich enough to buy suitable furniture for such immense apartments?" The more than $2,000,000 to be spent on buildings by 1801 could have been invested in roads or canals. At ten per cent interest, compounded, in fifty years this would mean $256,000,000, whereas the buildings would be worth less than cost.[35]

Governmental palaces encouraged monarchy, and why should existing cities be taxed to construct a rival metropolis? Only the name "Washington" led people to acquiesce in such extravagance.[36] A Southern newspaper carried an ode:

On the FEDERAL CITY

No more attach'd to Delaware streams
　Where fancy breeds majestic dreams,
Another jaunt the fates prepare,
　For Caesar's great Sanhedrin there.

· · · · · · ·

O FEDERAL TOWN! Proud men prepare
　Vast schemes within your ten miles square:
There, high-born dames shall make abode
And poets squeak the birthday ode.

· · · · · ·

O ye, who sit at helm of state
　Your vast designs you broach too late.
Leave the state-ship on rocky grounds,
　And fools to pay for Federal towns![37]

77

President Washington's suggested national university was a "splendid Quixotism." Assuredly America's poor would not benefit, and Newton, Swift, and Franklin had needed no university. The government not only meddled with trade, farming, and what people wore and did; now it wished to extend patronage and regulation to the mind itself.[38] After the First President died, Democratic papers recalled his instructions for a simple funeral and opposed any elaborate monument for him funded by taxes.[39]

The mint, the Jay mission, and especially increased expenditures for the navy, urged by John Adams, were labeled bleeding arteries of waste. Rarely did one see an American coin, and Jay had spent probably $52,000 on his trip to England (although in rebuttal Jay owned to less than one-fourth as much).[40] The frigates authorized in 1797 were called worthless. Unless a navy could at least rival that of any single foreign power, it only invited attacks on American merchant marine. If peace were the primary object of the government, the vessels would only rot.[41] Even if defense of American trade were possible, maintaining a navy would be a burden upon the entire nation and would favor only the commercial interests.[42] Assuming that the United States had actually adopted the theory that a public debt was a public blessing, a navy was ideal; otherwise, insurance would be considerably cheaper.[43] Every British seizure in the West Indies confirmed the futility of such an establishment.[44]

If Congress would only curtail unnecessary expenses, no additional impost would be needed. Federal courts could be suspended for some years; and if Federalist partisans truly believed Holland, Prussia, Spain, and Portugal were virtually French provinces, why not recall American ministers there and save $50,000 annually?[45] An anonymous source in the government expressed to a Philadelphian the wish that the public debt were "in a train of being discharged"; since it had much increased during the last eight years, Americans obviously were not in that train.[46]

Differences with France produced an open break in 1798,

and the *Farmers' Register* heralded the proposal to raise an additional $2,000,000 with the notice:

> IMPORTANT! *Tax on Lands, Houses, and Slaves.* . . . ordinary expenditures of the present year . . . [were estimated at] *six million, nine hundred and twenty-six thousand, four hundred and sixty dollars.* In this estimate the committee have not taken into view the *expences which may be incurred for the military defence of the country.*[47]

Democratic statisticians figured the day of fasting, requested by the President in recognition of the emergency, had wasted some $12,000 in lost labor in Philadelphia alone.[48] Various estimates of the budget appeared as a full page in several Jeffersonian newspapers.[49] Some states branded interest rates above six per cent as usury; thanks to administrative spending, by 1799 the federal government was openly offering eight per cent on a $5,000,000 loan.[50]

The "8% Loan," as it was immediately stigmatized, became an important Democratic whipping-boy. Even Federalists admitted that this, plus a land tax and the cost of an augmented army, was a potent criticism in New England.[51] The *Aurora* thundered the loan was to be used to defray other than military expenses, for which Congress had withheld appropriations. Even a fifteen per cent discount and this exorbitant interest rate produced few buyers, so low was the state of public credit.[52]

Difficulty in floating the loan necessitated the direct tax authorized in 1798. This was even more objectionable. Costs of assessment and collection ate up much of the revenue,[53] and the unrest it produced required added needless expense. Fries' Rebellion allowed Federalists to display the panoply of national power, but order was so quickly restored that the uprising had been obviously exaggerated. Wolcott's report showed the tax had cost $360,000 to collect instead of the estimated $150,000 and had raised but sixty per cent of the predicted $2,000,000.[54]

Washington was scarcely buried before Democrats were citing his admonitions on the necessity of governmental econ-

79

omy.[55] No wonder Jefferson favored a pay-as-you-go policy, or that New England's adherence to such a practice explained that section's past greatness.[56] Britain's example—with unemployment, soup shops, corruption, and an astronomical debt —was nothing others wished to follow.[57]

Federalist expenditures were thus a favorite theme for denunciation, and in the election year of 1800 they were subjected to especial scrutiny. Wolcott had requested House appropriations of $8,162,923.30—and if interest on the debt were added the total would approach $14,000,000. "Compare this," counselled the New London *Bee*,

> with the former expenses of your government, any five or six years ago; and ask yourselves, whether you ought not to make a change in future to administer your affairs, and to call on you for taxes.[58]

Virginia lawyer George Hay asserted that in the ten years prior to December 31, 1799, the United States had received $77,177,274 and had expended $75,015,406.33. But this paper surplus of some $2,161,000 did not give the true picture. Figures for the public debt, which had increased monstrously, were not included—nor were emergency war expenditures. Actually, said Democrats, there would be a deficit of nearly $3,000,000 for the year 1800 alone.[59] A maze of budgetary statistics, frequently conflicting and impossible to reconcile, appeared in various newspapers. Federalists tried to deny any swelling of the debt, or in any event claimed it grew no more rapidly than resources,[60] but critics called this gross deception. Albert Gallatin's *View of the Public Debt and Expenditures of the United States* alleged a debt increase of almost $9,500,000 during the 1790s, not counting assumption. Since June, 1798, war measures alone had cost some $11,500,000 and had diminished the revenue by $1,250,000 besides.[61] Thus, critics noted, Federalist "excess, tyranny and oppressions of almost every degree" had drawn the United States "to the verge of ruin"; measured in Spanish dollars, the addition to the debt "would fill two hundred ninety-five waggons each of one ton weight," or nearly thirty "waggons" a year. They asked:

> Is this the prosperity which has been wrung in our ears from New-Hampshire to Georgia? Is this the result of *that wise administration*, which has been trumpetted about from almost every pulpit in New-England? [62]

An item ironically headed "PUBLIC BLESSING" prophesied an increase of $20,000,000 in America's indebtedness within the four-year period ending in 1802.[63]

In 1789 Washington's Congress had spent only about $900,000 for all governmental operations; Adams' of 1800 appropriated $6,500,000 solely for the army and navy, with borrowings twenty times what they had been a decade earlier. "If we want to return to the best days of Washington's presidency, let us elect Jefferson who was his principal minister in those days," advised "A Pennsylvanian." [64]

The increased appropriations did not indicate increased prosperity, the "unmatched effrontery" of Federalist assertions notwithstanding. Thanks to the break with France, Virginia's income from tobacco in 1799 dropped $700,000. The state's share of the direct tax was nearly half that much, and failure to complete the "8% Loan" would doubtless mean a quadrupling of the tax. This would require the Old Dominion to pay $1,300,000 (and the nation $8,000,000) annually—with tobacco prices only a third of their former value. Cried "A Scots Correspondent," *"Hail Columbia! happy land! Think of your pockets, . . . and pray do not forget to vote for the ticket for the Jefferson electors."* [65] If, as Adams claimed in 1800, revenues were greater, why the additions to taxes and to the national debt? Economy was the very soul of a popular government; no nation could long remain republican "where the public money is lavished on favorites and partisans." [66]

Federalist transactions with the Barbary pirates not only contrasted with the government's gasconading attitude toward

81

France, they demonstrated the administration's idea of fiscal responsibility. We paid ransom for captives and made gifts to the Dey of Algiers. Counting expenses, the treaty with Algiers was scheduled to cost $816,413. In reality, the final expenditure would total more than $1,500,000.[67]

The Gargantuan gullet of the American people was not wide enough, prophesied Callender in the *Virginia Argus,*

> to swallow such absurdities as the Prussian embassy, the Turkish ditto, and six 74 gun ships, and fifteen hundred thousand dollars per annum *pretended* to be sunk upon fighting with fifteen hundred naked northwest savages. Never before did the world hear of such stupendous scenes of corruption, profligacy, and madness.[68]

Tables were published comparing administrative costs in England, France, and the United States; clearly the United States was headed toward a two billion dollar debt like that of Britain unless a change was made.[69] Financially exhausted, America resorted to every species of taxation the fertile imaginations of rulers could suggest—and the public was told this was needed to defray expenses incident to government. This called for an investigation to see that careful management had been practiced. Such an examination would disclose only infamy, and a single spark of the liberty of 1776 should cause citizens to step forward and elect Thomas Jefferson.[70] Desperate Hamiltonians might argue that Jefferson would abolish the funding system, the army, and the navy, but the public would regard this as a recommendation.[71] If money were the sinews of war, it was well indeed that the United States had not declared hostilities against France.[72]

Official expenditures sooner or later mean taxes, which were no more popular then than now. In addition to complaints about the uses to which the money was put and the amounts disbursed, governmental methods for raising revenue were also condemned. Sources of federal income were proposed as soon as Washington had assumed office. Some proposals were facetious, such as a suggested requirement of a bustle for all women, with a five per cent tax on the cork composing it.[73] Hamilton's request for a tariff and excise, however, ended the horseplay. The excise both hindered trade and was inequitable, was the cry. A Boston tobacconist abandoned plans for manufacturing snuff now that it was to be taxed; such imposts would destroy the nation's infant industries. Hamilton did not hesitate to request a tax on tobacco, which fell heavily upon the South; had he proposed one on molasses he would have stirred up resentment in the North and East, the regions on which he depended for congressional support.[74]

Readers were reminded that the First Continental Congress had referred to excises as "the HORROR of ALL FREE STATES," [75] and Philadelphians wanted to "crush this Hydra at birth." [76] A suggested tax on salt was instantly reprobated. It would fall most heavily on fishermen and farmers and might prove to be killing the goose that laid the golden egg.[77]

Most strongly opposed, however, was the excise laid on spirituous liquors. Resolutions against it—particularly from frontier areas, where most farmers distilled whiskey to supplement a scanty income—flooded Congress and the press.[78] The tax (finally fixed at seven cents a gallon, nearly one-third the average retail price) [79] was denounced as outrageously high and as benefiting merchants while penalizing farmers in proportion to their industry. Tax-gathering methods were burdensome, and their cost might exceed the revenue derived.[80] News of a boundary dispute between two Pennsylvania counties was accompanied by a pregnant comment: "The people in that part of the state, hold the excise law in detestation and threaten to oppose the execution of it." [81]

Georgians, holding their peach brandy a "necessary of life . . . in this warm climate," declared the tax would hurt them even more than it would Pennsylvanians. Northern still owners could operate the year round, but Southern planters could make brandy only about two weeks annually, with little or no chance of evading revenue agents. The excuse for the law was the "exigencies of government," but the only exigencies seemed to be the enlargement of the fortunes of certain demagogues and an increase in the power of the Chief Executive.[82]

83

Critics seethed because their petitions against the excise were uniformly forwarded, without action, from Congress to the Secretary of the Treasury. Such cavalier treatment of popular protests was ominous. Already hostility to the tax was so great that Washington, it was rumored, would appoint a day of fasting and prayer for Providence to dispose the citizenry to obedience. Some monarchists, however, doubted God would support their unjust laws. They suggested authorizing the President to use the militia of one state to enforce statutes in another. This would deny the independence of state governments; the fate of the excise would determine whether this nation was governed "by an aristocratic junto or the *people.*" [83]

A series of slashing attacks by "SYDNEY" upon the excise tax law appeared in the *National Gazette*. The impost was a burden put upon the people by a power external to their state governments. As soon as more revenue was needed, it would be extended from spirits to the actual necessities of life. Officers would need obnoxiously augmented powers to enforce it, and lawlessness would probably increase. Some one hundred thousand Pennsylvanians had no way of marketing their grain other than by conversion to whiskey; these people would be paying six times their fair share of any equitable tax measure.[84] Hamilton had perverted the spirit of the Constitution by assuming indirect taxes were excluded from that document's requirement that direct taxes had to fall equally (according to population) upon all sections of the country. Here was but another instance of the ways in which he felt himself bound by no restrictions and "superior to the sovereignty of the Union." [85]

Others found the law partial in many ways. Officers could seize and sell property of those liable to the tax; doubtless they would sell confiscated items to each other at about one-tenth their true value.[86] A "pimping exciseman" might be anywhere, spying on "the private actions of the free citizens," and reducing American yeomen to slaves.[87] "MUM" informed protesters that the excise was sanctioned by the rum and gin distillers of the Northeast; genteel people frowned on such a plebeian drink as whiskey. He sarcastically called objectors unreasonable, for they now had only to drag their grain five or six hundred miles "(which is nothing to a backwoodsman)" to the coast and to barter it there "for the ambrosial juices of the New-England stills." If frontiersmen knew what was good for them, they would hold their tongues and either pay the tax or destroy their stills. The President was expressly empowered to use militia for enforcement, and while Washington would not murder his fellow-citizens for drinking a glass of un-excised whiskey, none could tell what might be the ideas of his successor.[88]

In Germantown, Pennsylvania, citizens tore down the office sign of an exciseman and replaced it with the four quarters of a carrion. This "spirited conduct" was seen as a revival of the mettle of 1775 and a warning against imitating corrupt British principles. Since Congress had ignored the voice of the people, freemen must oppose every individual so lost as to aid in enforcing the measure.[89]

This virtual invitation to insurrection probably helped convince Federalists that Republicans were responsible for the violence that later erupted. Concerned over growing unrest, the administration sent George Clymer, Supervisor General of the Excise for Pennsylvania, into the western part of that state. He was to encourage local agents, use his influence to secure acceptance of the law, and report on conditions in the area. Clymer seemingly was not overly courageous, and Democrats were amused to read of his secrecy and disguises in the Pittsburgh region.[90]

Enforcement of the law rapidly deteriorated. To Western farmers a jug of whiskey was both a universal medium of exchange and one of the few pleasures of life, and they found many features of enforcement intolerable.[91] Meetings began to be held, and moderates such as Gallatin found themselves unable to stem the trend toward open resistance.[92] The dissidents turned from boycotting excisemen to outright intimidation.[93] Collectors' books were destroyed, and resignations were exacted by force or threat. Persons conforming to the law might be tarred and feathered or have their stills "mended" (shot full of holes) by "Tom the Tinker." Rioters were aware of Eastern criticisms of the tax, particularly those in Freneau's newspaper.[94] Democratic Clubs in seaboard cities as well as on the frontier had branded the law inequitable, disruptive, and dangerous to civil liberties.[95] "Liberty Poles," calling for organized opposition to tyranny as in Revolutionary days, were raised in western Pennsylvania, and the Washington, Pennsylvania, Democratic Society demanded an investigation into the conduct of the administration.[96]

Once the "Whiskey Rebellion" was underway, reaction of the Republican press was almost unanimous. Probably foreseeing that they and the Democratic Societies would be charged with inciting insurrection, editors immediately deplored the uprising while continuing to attack the legislation that had produced it.

Violence was a mistake, said Bache's *General Advertiser*. All possible legal means—petitions, votes, amendments—should have been used to obtain repeal of the excise. But the administration must bear some responsibility for the violent reaction. The tax was odious, and conciliatory measures should have been tried.[97] A land tax, the true cost of which could be known, would have been preferable to any indirect levy. Many Democratic Societies condemned unlawful resistance, however, and declared they had advocated repeal only through constitutional means.[98]

The press reported in full the organization of the "rebellion" and the meetings of its delegates at Parkinson's Ferry, Pennsylvania. Resolutions of the delegates condemned taking citizens from their vicinity for trial and appointed committees to appeal to the President, to petition Congress, and to treat with commissioners of the central government. Committee reports and negotiations with the commissioners were also published.[99] Hugh Henry Brackenridge, a leading insurgent, penned a justification of the unrest which was carried in several papers. Resistance was widespread, he said, and enforcement of the excise was impossible so long as western Pennsylvania and Virginia were discriminated against. Washington should use troops to enforce this part of the hated funding system only as a last resort; the real question was not whether militia would march to Pittsburgh, but whether rebels would move on Philadelphia. Brackenridge deplored talk that the disaffected region might appeal to Britain for aid, but asked: "What will not despair produce?" [100]

Already Federalists were charging that the insurrection had been caused by the Democratic Societies. This was "the first *fruits* of [their] blessed *harvest*"; a few sanctimonious resolutions could not quiet the spirit they had deliberately fostered. The *Independent Chronicle* retorted that if the societies were so potent Congress should suspend the writ of habeas corpus and suppress them. In reality, it would be more accurate to describe the revolt as the fruit "of the blessed HARVEST, sown by the 'advocates of the Funding and Bank System.'" [101]

Why should America suffer British violations of neutrality in silence, when the opposition of her own citizens to "an ambitious and financering SECRETARY" should evoke action against them as insurgents? [102] More liberty poles, inscribed *"Liberty, plenty of Whiskey,* and *No Excise,"* were raised, and as violence grew in the *"La Vende[e]* of the United States," there were boasts that green militiamen—or those left of them—would cut a sorry figure retreating to Philadelphia. Marylanders were reluctant to answer the call for militia, and wild rumors abounded of new excises on such things as infant births.[103]

Convinced that force was to be used, Republican papers became concerned with military matters. They reiterated that the law must be obeyed until rescinded, but attacks on the Democratic Societies led Philadelphia publishers to urge members to answer slurs on their loyalty by helping suppress the revolt.[104] Too, the militia could so conduct itself as to show a standing army completely unnecessary.[105] New England newspapers, however, compared the excitement to a baby lamb of "Great cry and little wool." Thirteen thousand troops were more than Washington had commanded during most of the Revolution, and only two thousand soldiers had been required to suppress Shays' eight thousand rebels. Yet the West had reason to be disgruntled. The frontier had been inadequately protected, and the government had provided no real communication with the outside world.[106] Possibly Britain had used the discontent to foment the uprising.[107]

Militiamen would have to endure privation in the field for the benefit of those who had speculated in funding and assumption.[108] Could the President lawfully leave the seat of government, while Congress was in session, to command the expedition? Any accident might prevent him from considering bills passed within the ten days allowed by the Constitution.[109] When Hamilton also rode with the column dispatched to put down the rebellion, a tempest broke. It was an insult to suppose Washington needed an assistant. The Secretary's absence from his post was a dereliction of duty, even though it might have the beneficial effect of convincing Congress "that money bills can be originated without his instrumentality." When he continued with the force after Washington left it, Democrats wrathfully stormed that Hamilton had usurped the functions of the Secretary of War, just as he was trying to usurp everything else.[110]

The insurrection itself evaporated with the appearance of the army; except for inclement weather, the expedition would have been a picnic. Only twenty malcontents were carried back to Philadelphia and paraded there with placards of "Insurgent" on their hats. Two were found guilty of treason; Washington pardoned both in an act which won general favor.[111]

Two important consequences stemmed from the affair. First, the national government had clearly demonstrated both the determination and the strength to enforce its authority.[112] This may have aided the administration politically, but the elections of 1794 did not indicate it. Federalists had now lost the West irretrievably; in many other areas they had more difficult races than ever before, and Republican congressional candidates carried New York City and Philadelphia.[113]

The second result was the decline of the Democratic Societies as such. Little did it benefit the members of the Democratic Society of Pennsylvania to protest that they had said nothing as extreme as the arguments of a reputable minority in Congress. In the popular mind these organizations—originally formed in the early wave of enthusiasm for the French Revolution that swept America—were allied with the insurgents, and this association was confirmed by no less an authority than Washington himself. His November address to Congress charged the revolt had "been fomented by combinations of men" who had disseminated accusations against the government and mentioned "certain self-created societies" that had concertedly condemned the excise.[114]

To Democratic editors this speech had a monarchical ring. Undeniably, the insurrection should have been suppressed. On the other hand, it should never have been provoked—and opposition to the excise had preceded formation of any of the clubs. Kentucky had not paid the discriminatory tax, yet it had not been invaded. Collections in Pennsylvania had been postponed until the precise moment the building of the settlement and fort at Presqu'isle, which had been encouraged by the state as protection from Indians, was suspended on Washington's urgings because he feared it appeared to challenge the British. If anything, evidence indicated that Federalist measures deliberately provoked the revolt to show the power of the administration and the need for a standing army, to discredit political opposition, and to pave the way for monarchy.[115] Although at least one ringleader could not be captured because of popular sympathy for him, the nation generally had uniformly reprobated the unsuccessful uprising.[116]

Objections to tax measures as such were not limited to the excise on whiskey, nor did the Republican press permit them to die with the rebellion. Protests appeared against other excises, and America was compared unfavorably with the Old World in the freeing of industry and commerce from taxation.[117] The tariff was subjected to continued adverse comment. It had been raised three times in the first three years of Washington's term; apparently similar increases could be expected annually. Adam Smith and the existence of Holland proved the superiority of free trade; benefits of a "favorable" trade balance were illusory. The added duties oppressed both importers and consumers. Talk of a federal land tax, which would fall largely on farmers, produced in New Jersey a call for caucuses to rally opposition. In New England, the assertion was made that the land tax would prove permanent after any "emergency" had passed.[118]

As Franco-American relations became more strained, "JUNO" angrily taunted that the nation's heavy tax burden belied Federalist boasts of peace and prosperity. Bankruptcies had "three times doubled," and trade was prostrate while people grubbed for the necessities of life. Excessive taxation, it should be remembered, had led to the American Revolution. If philosophers were correct in asserting the influx of riches corrupted a people, the government, through imposts, was laboring manfully to keep America virtuous.[119] The new stamp tax merely imitated Britain in order to defray the needless expenditures of Congress; it called loudly for resistance and constitutional redress. As *Frothingham's Long Island Herald* put it, in July, 1798: "LOOK OUT! This day the Stamp Act begins its career—God only knows where it will end." [120]

The same month saw Congress lay a direct tax on lands, houses, and slaves to raise $2,000,000. Even before enactment, this measure was vehemently denounced. An assessment on houses, to be determined by counting the number of window panes, would injure health and morals by tempting men to try to reduce their tax by shutting out "the light of the sun and the air of heaven." [121] Federalist spokesmen claimed the national government was in good condition; if so, "why burthen the People with Stamp Duties, Salt Duties, and a LAND TAX?" Some stories had the tax as high as $15,000,000, but twenty times that amount would not pay for a war. Even Federalist Congressman Robert Goodloe Harper had said a land tax should be restored to only in case of hostilities; apparently that calamity was to be visited upon the country.[122]

Federalists minimized the burden of the new taxes,[123] but the Rhode Island legislature asserted that a general property tax, or almost any kind of levy, would be preferable.[124] This land tax required almost four hundred new officials in New York state alone, and Massachusetts citizens were reminded of hardships entailed by a state tax only half as heavy.[125] The burden fell as unfairly as had that of the excise. In Pennsylvania nearly three-fourths the revenue would come from houses, while the landed warmongers virtually escaped payment. City-dwellers claimed both the land tax and the stamp tax were made palatable to much of the country by assurances that the money would come largely from those in the commercial towns. If cities were to bear most of the taxes, they were entitled to additional representation.[126]

Like Jews under the Egyptians, Americans were forced to make bricks without straw to support a military establishment while their commerce was being destroyed. "If the produce of the Land finds no market, how can the Tax be paid?" Parables reiterating the principle of the goose that laid the golden egg were printed, and voters were advised to remedy conditions by electing candidates favoring peace with France. Even the Federalist *Columbian Centinel* confessed a distaste for the land tax because of its similarity to the French salt tax, but its editor was quickly reminded that America had a salt tax as well —and one that had been recently increased.[127]

Jeffersonian editors reluctantly conceded the constitutionality of the tax, but it was so unintelligible even members of Congress were unable to explain it.[128] As long as the several states were assigned quotas, why could not each collect the levy in its customary fashion instead of estimating house values by counting windows?[129] In Massachusetts General William Heath was supported for governor because "WHEN LAND TAXES and HOUSE TAXES are become the resources of Government a FARMER is a very proper person to be placed in the chair of this commonwealth." [130] The first collections were said to have been made in Connecticut because the close alliance there between church and state was expected to subdue all opposition.[131]

Inhabitants of Bucks and Northampton counties in Pennsylvania refused to let their property be appraised. Assessors were robbed of assessment rolls, and women poured scalding water on them from windows being measured. Leader in the resistance was an auctioneer and ex-soldier named John Fries. When some of the molesters were imprisoned, Fries and about 140 armed men released them. Fearful of the consequences, however, the malcontents thereafter did their best to become inconspicuous. Collections then might have proceeded without further difficulty, but Adams on learning of the affair ordered soldiers (March, 1799) in readiness to quell the disturbance. Fries and followers permitted their property to be assessed, but the Secretary of War called on Pennsylvania's governor for eight troops of militia horsemen to move into the zone, along with five hundred regulars. This force left Philadelphia early in April; within a few days it occupied the entire area of resistance, arresting Fries and other leaders.[132]

Federalist newspapers professed to see a sinister link between the unrest and the coincidental arrival at Charleston of two emissaries from the French Directory to this country. Peaceable citizens of the region had been coerced into supporting the insurgents; the matter was more serious than the Whiskey Rebellion "of Gallatin and the other patriots in the mountains". Revolters had spread the outlandish tale that Adams planned to mortgage all Pennsylvania, to decamp to England with the money, and to buy himself a title! [133]

Again Democratic publishers tended to emphasize grounds for the discontent but to deplore the extra-legal activities of the objectors.[134] The disturbance was only a "federal frenzy," which would please England and give American Tories some short-lived glory. Two thousand troops were being ordered out "where an armed opposition does not exist, and where an organized corps of revolters cannot be found."

Even in the Whiskey Rebellion, Washington had not sent in troops so precipitously. Civil power had not yet proved inadequate, but in despotisms one did not attempt to persuade people to obey—"the logic of the bayonet is there the only one employed. . . ." [135]

Some papers accused designing Federalists of inciting and exaggerating this "hot water insurrection." [136] Secretaries Timothy Pickering and James McHenry sought a standing army, and a "revolt" furnished an opportune excuse. The permanent force already ordered raised might develop into the instrument to burden, insult, disgrace, and finally enslave "the late free citizens of America." If the disturbance were serious, reasoned the New York *Argus* (addressing the Cabinet as the *"five-headed directory of America"*), President Adams was subject to impeachment for running off to vacation four hundred miles from the scene of activity. If not, the "bustle and *expense*" of sending in all the varied military units was merely the "noise of party." [137]

In reality harmony had been restored before the troops arrived, and Federalist cries for scourging the uprisers was "advice worthy of Robespierre." Letters from the field, describing the lack of opposition and relating cruelties inflicted on well-meaning but ignorant prisoners, were reprinted. The force, one writer noted, appeared "well calculated to produce rather than prevent discontent"; if kept there until election time, the effect might be opposite to that intended.[138]

Editor Jacob Schneider, of the Democratic *Readinger Adler,* had criticized the behavior of the Lancaster Light Horse troop quartered in Reading. Incensed cavalrymen dragged him to the market-place and gave him a half-dozen lashes while their commander watched. Jeffersonians raged. Here was "order and good government" with a vengeance, verifying every danger prophesied concerning standing armies. That *"self-appointed dictator,* Captain Montgomery" and his "heroic band" had violated the common law of the land fully as much as John Fries, yet they were not even punished.[139] Moreover, Schneider's accusations must have been uncomfortably accurate, since a later attack was made on the translator for his paper by officers of the 2nd U.S. Infantry.[140]

Fries and two accomplices were tried for treason. Justice Samuel Chase, a zealous Federalist, conducted the second trial and delivered such a partisan opinion as to the law before hearing counsel, that the defendants' disgusted lawyers withdrew from the case.[141] The three men were sentenced to hang, but Adams pardoned them. Praising the President's clemency, the *Aurora* expressed "an abhorrence of the whole proceeding." Federal extravagance had given occasion to levy a hated tax, and the wanton conduct of the agents—many of them old Tories—selected for its collection had provoked resistance. Pennsylvania elections of 1799 and 1800 indicated the voters agreed with Editor Duane.[142] Tales of Federalist prodigality received emphasis the country over as each new and heavier tax was enacted.[143]

Extensive governmental borrowing was also consistently denounced. Opponents of the policy argued that obtaining money from abroad, whether for funding or for later measures, tied America to Holland and England, putting the country in debt to foes and at variance with friends.[144] Nearly all America's ready cash was sucked out of agriculture, commerce, and industry and transferred to London and Amsterdam—making Americans liable to foreign influence and monarchical principles. How could France be otherwise than offended, queried the *National Gazette,* when some of the money originally intended to discharge a sacred obligation to that nation had been cruelly withdrawn and thrown into the funding program for speculative purposes? [145]

As early as 1792, $15,000,000 of the public debt was said to be in the hands of Europeans. Grievous it was indeed that nearly four million people "should be taxed for nearly the exclusive benefit of . . . a few foreign brokers" and about two hundred speculators in Eastern cities.[146] During the later crisis with France, an *Aurora* correspondent professed alarm over rumors that Adams would be empowered to float a large loan. The sum probably could not be raised in the United

States, and the only friendly nation was England. Suppose, when the United States applied to "Pitt and Co.," that they followed the administration's example with France in the XYZ Affair and considered it a demand for tribute! [147]

That governmental indebtedness, a target for the Republican press in the 1790s, might have beneficial aspects was considered ridiculous. At the outset of the decade "PLAIN ARGUMENT" penned columns of sarcasm about the supposed advantages of federal obligations. Since the debt inflated land values, each bondholder should be given a certificate for five times the amount due him. By thus voluntarily paying quintuple her liabilities, America would convince everyone that she would pay what she actually owed; national credit would be unquestioned. Other advantages were: (1) the huge debt would be in the hands of forty thousand enthusiastic supporters of the administration, (2) management of the debt would require five thousand additional governmental employees, (3) since nations in debt paid more liberal salaries, some three or four hundred officials might live as princes, (4) if Englishmen came to own much of the debt, Britain would help the administration against any unrest here that might endanger that investment, and (5) assumption would transform "the few remaining supporters of those perishing systems" [the states] into strong advocates of the federal government. Clearly, it behooved Americans to increase the national debt by every means possible.[148]

Others straightforwardly stigmatized the debt as America's greatest danger. In 1791 three-fourths of federal employees were appointed for the sole purpose of collecting the interest upon the debt.[149] Hamilton's proposal that only two per cent of the liability should be redeemed each year indicated his desire for a perpetual obligation.[150] Freneau put some of his fears and resentment into rhyme:

Public debts are public curses
   In soldiers' hands there nothing worse is!
In speculator's hands increasing,
   A public debt's a public blessing.[151]

Washington's recommendation for the sale of public lands to help retire the debt produced rejoicing. "Opinion" prepared an optimistic table and prophecy of changes in America's official attitude:

| | |
|---|---|
| 1789— | Public debt *may* be a public blessing. |
| 1790. | Public debt *is* a public blessing. |
| 1791. | Public debt *is not* a public blessing. |
| 1792 (Jan.) | Public debt *may* become a public evil. |
| 1792 (Nov.) | Public debt *is* a public evil. |
| 1793. | Public debt is among the greatest of public evils. |
| 1794. | It is wonderful that so great a folly of opinion should have ever existed . . . as that a public debt and perpetual taxes, were the means of public liberty and public prosperity. . . .[152] |

An "interested few" were accused of being responsible for the adoption of the outworn principle of a long-range debt, when even the British were talking of abandoning it. Hamilton was perennially suspect, though after his realization that governments perpetually tend to increase their debts he began to talk of avoiding new debts and extinguishing the current one. But it was infinitely easier to mortgage the resources of posterity than to face the inconvenience of immediately heavier taxes. "Camillus" roared "FACTS SPEAK LOUDER THAN WORDS," and insisted the principal measures of the administration since its inception followed "the malign opinion that the present debt is a national blessing." Public funds had been paid out "to succor gamblers in the funds," the result being a neglect of foreign obligations and a move "toward a monied aristocracy." [153]

Since a government's credit rested ultimately on the reputation and integrity of its citizens, the administration could not have established it. Pretending to seek the post of national poet laureate, "Jonathan Pindar" wrote a series of "Probationary Odes," promising Hamilton and other leading Federalists to swear

The nation's debt's a blessing vast,
  Which far and wide its general influence sheds,
From which Pactolian streams descend so fast
  On their—id est—the speculators' heads.

That to increase this blessing and entail
  To future time its influence benign,
New loans from foreign nations cannot fail
  While standing armies clinch the grand design.

That taxes are no burthen to the rich
  That they alone to labor drive the poor—
The lazy rogues would neither plow nor ditch,
  Unless to keep the sheriff from the door.[154]

At the instigation of Jefferson and Madison, Representative William B. Giles of Virginia early in 1793 introduced some resolutions that, it was secretly hoped, might drive Hamilton from the Treasury Department. Critical of allegedly irregular and arbitrary practices, these stressed that for four years Congress had had but a very imperfect knowledge of the nation's revenue or condition of its finances. Now the Executive was called upon to furnish complete reports on the administration's fiscal operations.

The resolutions were adopted without objection, and Hamilton set about preparing the requested data before Congress should adjourn. If he delayed, whispers of skeletons in the Treasury closet might sweep the country during the summer. Working day and night, within a month the Secretary produced some two hundred pages of information covering all phases of his department's activities. The speed in responding and detail of the report amazed everyone and for a time confounded his opponents.[155]

Yet Jeffersonians were not silenced for long. They had not exposed the corruption they anticipated, but Hamilton's evidence, they claimed, disclosed his technical violations of the intent of congressional appropriations. He had applied some of the principal borrowed to interest on the same loans, failed to inform Congress of his proceedings in foreign advances, and

97

borrowed from the Bank of the United States at five per cent when sufficient public money was on deposit there. He had assumed powers entrusted to the President, and his summaries were deliberately complex so that they could not be understood. He should have furnished Congress with regular reports, and those he had provided should not have been published without permission. Doubt was expressed that he truly desired a full and fair investigation.[156]

Proposals to censure Hamilton's irregularities were overwhelmingly rejected by a Federalist House,[157] but Democrats called Hamilton's vindication a "reputed" one only. How could there be a scarcity of cash in the Bank *and* the Treasury *and* among the people, all at the same time? The Treasury reports purported to show over $2,000,000 in Bank and Treasury; why had not some of this been applied on the public debt, the securities of which had fallen slightly below par? Only a few months previously Hamilton himself had requested authorization to purchase six per cent bonds at the market price, "tho' [then] above par." [158]

A year later Republican newspapers still fumed that the Treasury deficit proved the funding system had failed to accomplish its ends. If the war with the Indians were chiefly responsible for the shortage, instead of a Secretary of War "For Heaven's sake let us have a MINISTER OF PEACE." [159] Again in 1795 editors applauded Washington's call for Congress to work out a definite plan for reducing the nation's liabilities: "In no sentiment are the people more united than in the observation of the President 'To prevent the progressive accumulation of debt, which must in the end ultimately endanger all governments.' " [160]

Bache's *General Advertiser* carried a fictional "account of a meeting of the *paper noblemen* of the United States and the *emissaries of the British* government . . . [with] *irredeemable public debt* in the chair. . . ." Among the resolutions passed was:

> Resolved, that it is the *unalienable* right of *stockholders, stockjobbers, bank directors, and speculators, to discuss with* freedom,

*all subjects* of public concern, and that as no other person or persons are seized with this right, as they alone have the genuine interest of the public debt at heart, it being the paramount interest of America, to which all other interests ought to submit.

Alexander Pacificus, Secretary.[161]

A permanent public debt, counselled Oswald's *Independent Gazetteer,* would inevitably destroy popular liberties. It was fully as bad as privileges, monopolies, and excessive salaries—and it accelerated the nation's growing inequalities in wealth. A South Carolinian with a flair for economics emphasized the vast difference between private and public credit. Profit was the goal of one; expense, that of the other. Merchants used credit to gain riches, but it tended to impoverish and ruin governments. A state inevitably alienated some of its revenue to pay for the sum it pledged, hence it was always poorer after borrowing than before. If foreign specie were attracted, it was in much the same fashion as if a portion of the nation's territory were sold; if loans came solely from a state's own citizens, many persons were made poorer to enrich a minority. Taxes had always to be increased to pay the interest and replace the capital. That large quantities of paper currency stimulated business was an *ignis fatuus*. Easily-acquired loans encouraged rash undertakings, and the fruits of industry would pass to idle hands. Soon exporting would cease because goods would be too costly to compete with merchandise of other nations. National bankruptcy would soon be inevitable, accompanied by the loss of popular freedom and even the power of the sovereign. So ran the history of public loans, and the public might judge of the principles on which they were founded.[162]

America might be flourishing like a "green bay tree," said "Citizens of America," but its branches were "too extensive for its roots"; the first heavy storm of war or insurrection might lay it low. No free government could long exist "without an established character for *good faith*." Already America was behind in interest payments, whereas even England kept her pledges in that respect. A great public debt had been the downfall of Athens and the embarrassment of Rome and Byzantium. Speculators might disapprove, but popular opinion would overwhelmingly support measures to discharge the nation's obligations. The citizenry had "too much virtue to leave the extinguishment of the Debt to an innocent posterity." [163]

Democratic jibes uniformly followed news that investors had patriotically assumed portions of new governmental loans. John Fenno's paper might claim all was venal in France; would he could report that all was disinterested in America. The very "patriots" in whose behalf relations with France had become so strained were in 1798 demanding six and eight per cent interest. Most certainly they were not "GIVING" money to the government, or making any appreciable sacrifice! [164]

Late in 1795 a Democrat entered the House who was to prove himself the peer of any Federalist in matters of public finance. Until Albert Gallatin came to Congress, Jeffersonians were somewhat handicapped in opposing the administration's fiscal moves. Now Gallatin, with logic and insight, analyzed voluminous masses of figures, stripped them down to bare essentials, and presented them to public gaze. An opponent of Federalist economic measures since the time of the tax on whiskey, in 1796 he rose in the House to deny the favorite Federalist claim that the public debt was being reduced. Instead, it had grown by some $5,000,000. Representative William Smith of South Carolina retorted that it had been cut $2,000,000. Gallatin's rebuttal was a pamphlet, entitled *A Sketch of the Finances* . . . , which became an economic Bible for Jeffersonian publishers. He showed that the difference in amounts was largely a matter of bookkeeping, that Smith's figures included anticipated income but not anticipated expenditures, that several items (such as the seventy-four-gun frigates and a sizable floating debt due the Bank) had not been incorporated in the administration's totals, and that the sinking fund had not grown as expected.[165]

Thus from 1796 on Republicans could meet statistics with statistics, and gleefully they did so. James T. Callender derided the assertion that America paid only $400,000 interest annually. Including the floating debt, the nation in 1800 owed approximately $90,000,000. At an estimated average interest rate of six per cent, the government paid out $5,400,000 annually, and Virginia's share alone came to $1,080,000.[166] The Richmond *Examiner* gloated over consideration of a second *"eight per cent loan,"* as it had earlier predicted: "Such things may enrich speculators, but the only consequence which the people can hope from them is a greater increase of their taxes." [167]

What good were increased population and expanding production if they did not contribute to reducing the debt? Actually, governmental revenue was declining—from $8,191,237 in 1797 to $7,431,875 in 1799—and total federal obligations were now nearly double the amount Hamilton had originally funded.[168] A Republican Congress had reduced the debt some $3,000,000 in 1796 and 1797, but the Federalist-inspired war crisis had saddled America with an additional $12,000,000 deficit in two years. Commerce, too, was injured; "When such damning facts stare the people in the face, can it be possible that the executive should retain their confidence?" [169]

The total of $8,000,000 borrowed at eight per cent would amount to

> *one hundred sixty waggon loads of coined silver!!* This *monstrous* sum is by no means mentioned with a view to excite opposition of taxes demanded by the federal government; but for the sole purpose of more effectually awakening the people to the consequences of the war measures of the present administration. . . .

In 1796 people had been told it was a choice between Jefferson and war, or Adams and peace. Now that the deception was clear, worthy citizens would "turn their eyes toward the man who really is for peace." [170]

The very arguments over the amount of national indebtedness, urged the *Republican Watch Tower*, should produce demands for regular, clear statements on governmental receipts and expenditures. Since the Treasury's accounting was so complicated that people could not discover America's true financial condition, the paper would be obliged to anyone who could clarify the situation. This Gallatin had done. His *Sketch* proved that, allowing for all funds that could possibly be applied to debt reduction, obligations by 1800 had increased $6,657,319.44. Other reports differed, even from each other. Treasury Secretary Wolcott admitted an increase of one and a half million, while Theodore Sedgwick's Federalist House committee claimed a one million dollar decrease. This indicated a desire to conceal the state of the nation's finances, probably to hide peculation. Careful study would show Gallatin's figures as giving the only accurate picture; at least he did not insult popular intelligence by including future receipts without also allowing for concomitant expenses.[171] To judge from their squirming answers,[172] administration supporters were consistently sensitive on questions of expense and the debt.

These issues were embittered by accompanying accusations of graft, particularly during the last years of the Federalist regime. Hints of corruption appeared as early as 1792 when the *National Gazette* surmised the *"studied obscurity"* of Treasury reports might not be without purpose and charged that some twenty-five Representatives who voted to reject Giles's resolutions against Hamilton had lately transferred their public security holdings to disclaim economic interest in the matter.[173] Like Georgia's "Yazoo representatives," all too many state and national officials were preoccupied with public plunder.[174]

Even Washington was not immune from suspicion and aspersion. Clerk of the House John Beckley taxed him with receiving advances on his salary, and the attacks were widely reprinted.[175] Defenses by Hamilton and Wolcott were jeered. By comparing the First President to a contractor, it was sneered, through analogy it would be possible to advance wages of all government officials for their full terms at the discretion of the Secretary of the Treasury.[176]

James Reynolds' attempt to blackmail Hamilton was at first expected to expose fraud by the "debauched Creole" Hamilton. Apparently Monroe had pledged himself not to reveal the tale of the Secretary's affair with Mrs. Reynolds nor to make public the papers of Reynolds that originally aroused distrust. But the papers were given to Callender, who aired them, and Hamilton felt compelled to publish the entire story. While purportedly clearing him of dishonesty with public funds in this instance, the account furnished the opposition with a delectable and exploitable personal scandal.[177]

In 1797 "ARISTOBULUS" blamed all the country's ills on "the depravity, the error, or the corruption" of its officials.[178] The *Time Piece* found it symbolic that ornaments for a Presidential party represented the Constitution by a sugar cake; certainly it had literally proved so for some Federalist administrators.[179] Contracts for the frigate *Constitution*, along with five others authorized to be constructed against the Algerines, had gone almost exclusively to Federalists. In three years only three of the six vessels had been completed, and, despite decreased labor costs, almost double the appropriation had already been spent.[180]

The prospectus for the *National Magazine* announced that publication's intention to expose malfeasance in office. Personalities would not be emphasized as such, but men who misused public places forfeited any exemption from attacks on their characters. The magazine promised to review the history of the United States and show the

> origin, progress and alarming influence of that system of iniquity, robbery, bribery, and oppression, hypocrisy and injustice, which may be traced from the attempt of Alexander Hamilton to palm off upon the Convention a monarchical constitution, through the corrupted mazes of funding and banking, stock-jobbing, and speculating systems, down to the alien and sedition laws, standing army and navy of the present day.[181]

Similar motives prompted the *Aurora* to print the "BOOK OF JEDEDIAH. Lamentations in the Wilderness." as an "addition" to the Bible. This told of hard-hearted "King Adamant," and the adulterers, toad-eaters, and swindlers who filled his court and defrauded the public.[182] Other items portrayed minor irregularities as indicative of greater corruption. Secretary of State Pickering was accused of pocketing five dollars given him by a traveler for a passport to Europe.[183] The smuggling schooner *Fair Play* was sold for less than the cost of firewood almost a half year after its seizure—and the deputy marshal's bill for safe-keeping and mileage ran to almost twelve times the sum realized! "Through *such* hands pass three-fourths of the revenue of the United States," while Federalists impudently talked of the integrity and ability of public servants.[184]

Charges of corruption became more strident during the election year of 1800. Dayton had not only speculated while he was Speaker; he had used public money to do so. The question fired by the *Aurora* was pointed:

> Jonathan Dayton, . . . do you or do you not hold in your possession thirty thousand dollars, the property of the good people of the United States—which was advanced to you for public uses, but which you have never returned to the proper owners thereof, for more than two years? [185]

Moreover, he was assumed guilty of nepotism and favoritism as well. Over $1,000 monthly went to pay officers (most of them relatives or friends) appointed for the late army in the small borough of Elizabeth, New Jersey, alone. Though containing abler men, larger towns in the area could scarcely get a single commission, so great was Dayton's influence.[186]

"PUBLIC PLUNDER!" screamed the *Aurora* in a succeeding series of articles. Duane claimed access to official Treasury Department records that afforded definite proof of what had long been suspected—a sinister story "of abuse and waste of the public money." [187] Dayton noted an error in the paper's figures and damned its charge as an utter fabrication. Duane retorted that any inaccuracies were the fault of the comptroller or auditor; the comparatively slight error had already been accounted for. No effort to discredit the newspaper could hide the fact that on January 22, 1800, Dayton owed the government at least $18,142.52. The amount, whether or not it had been recently repaid, was relatively unimportant; but that he had kept the money over eighteen months, even after he ceased to be Speaker, showed him unworthy of public confidence. When and how had repayment been made? Would he or Comptroller John Steele ever have made a statement of their accounts "if the LEGAL NECESSITY of making an annual report to Congress, had not COMPELLED them to it?" [188]

Supporting the accuracy of the accusations, insisted Duane's journal, were the frantic efforts of ranking officials to discover the leak. The trunks of Treasury Department clerks had been searched, and employees suspected of republicanism were discharged. Additional disclosures concerning Dayton's speculations in land (noted in Chapter Two) could be proved in court. And if Dayton had exculpated himself, as claimed by the Boston *Mercury*, he had indicted Wolcott, "for between them the money was not *forthcoming* or accounted for in the beginning of the present year." [189]

Wolcott, Pickering, and then others came under the *Aurora*'s fire. At best, Wolcott was culpable for lack of vigilance, but Duane had no desire to portray him at his best. Public funds had to be publicly accounted for, and it was Adams' responsibility to see that his subordinates discharged their duties. An indolent or corrupt Secretary could cost the nation immense sums. Under the current disbursing system, an official paying out public monies could draw out of the Treasury his own salary plus the entire amount appropriated to his office. If he paid out only a portion of the total authorized, over a few years he could accumulate quite a balance of government funds in his hands. A Philadelphia customs collector had died owing the United States $86,322.80, which had to be collected from his estate. If Pickering should die with a $500,000 balance unaccounted for, his heirs just might take advantage of the recent bankruptcy law. Unquestionably, large sums had been withheld from the public coffers at a time the government had been forced to borrow at usurious interest rates.

Returning to Dayton, the books of Joseph Nourse, Treasury Department Register, showed that from March 3, 1797, to July of that year, the Speaker held $8,611.60 that belonged to the government; from July, 1799, to January 22, 1800. he held $90,917.52; and as of June, 1800, he still retained $18,-142.52 of the public's money. Was not this worthy of the people's consideration? [190]

The manner of reporting the Dayton case was typical of Duane's methods. An article entitled, "MORE *of the* BUDGET" a few days later itemized funds Timothy Pickering was alleged to have in his hands and unaccounted for. The source was the same, and in some instances even Treasury warrant numbers were given. Only the amount differed; the Secretary of State had overdrawn his certified and approved expenditures by $501,918.14.[191] That he justified withdrawing $10,-000 for protection of American seamen was "comical." [192] Federalists, the *Aurora* added, could not deny the money had been drawn from the Treasury; their effort to show that Pickering had a trifling credit with the Bank of the United States was irrelevant. The Secretary's bank account could even have been part of the Treasury money he withdrew. The people were entitled to know where their money was—and the Bank itself owed the government more than three million dollars.[193] Wolcott's customs collectors and revenue supervisors held, on January 1, 1800, $532,267.81 of public funds. Two officials in Boston were said to possess $300,000, and one of these was "*a bankrupt*. O rare friends of regular government!" [194]

Wolcott denounced the charges as "unfounded" in *Claypoole's American Daily Advertiser,* but the *Aurora* demanded evidence contradicting its specifically identified Treasury warrants. The Secretary of the Treasury really confessed the truth when he admitted Duane's figures referred to aggregate sums remitted to Cabinet members. By what right did Pickering have any public money over that required for the expense of his own department? Did he get a percentage for services as agent for the various funds (such as supplying stationery to the Northwest and Southwest territories) he administered? [195] "A CITIZEN" expressed surprise that the Treasury accounts had *not* been publicly exhibited, despite Wolcott's claim; admittedly some of them were yet unsettled. Wolcott had not proved Pickering innocent of borrowing huge sums free of interest from the Treasury for possible purposes of speculation. He had exposed a lamentable system of bookkeeping, which failed to mean what it recorded, and definite irregularities in accounts. If the *Aurora*'s balances were in error, it should have been easy enough for Wolcott to show it.[196] Charges this serious, seconded the *American Citizen,* should be expressly and clearly refuted, or people had every right to assume them correct. Correction and punishment seemed called for.[197]

In an effort to clarify its attacks to the laity, the *Aurora* analyzed Treasury bookkeeping and departmental organization. The former was branded deliberately complex and incomprehensible. Wolcott was again twitted over his mistake of a million dollars in reporting to the last session of Congress. Sedgwick's House committee had figured the public debt some millions too low, and Register Joseph Nourse had announced extinguishment of the French debt at a time interest was still being paid to those who had acquired it through a funding operation. Men of ability were needed in these important posts to prevent blunders and defalcations.

Fortunately, *some* persons, even though outside the Treasury Department, knew the proper duties of officials within it. The Comptroller preserved accounts, examined those settled by the Auditor, and countersigned warrants. Functions of the Auditor were to receive and examine accounts, certifying the balances and turning them over, with vouchers, to the Comptroller. The Register recorded all receipts and expenditures, and debited and credited all warrants. The Treasurer handled the money, disbursing it only on proper warrants and obtaining receipts for sums expended. No disbursement could be legally made without the written authority of the Secretary and the Comptroller, and the Register's books showed to whom warrants were made out. The files showed no record that Dayton ever repaid his $18,142.52; either Treasurer Samuel

Meredith had arrogated to himself the functions of both Secretary and Comptroller, or Dayton had lied—or possibly Meredith was implicated in the ex-Speaker's land speculations.[198]

Loan officers, or agents for paying invalid pensions, in certain states were also liable to the United States for sizable amounts. James Ewing of New Jersey owed $4,960.71; William Imlay of Connecticut, $4,279.03, Mathew Clarkson of New York, $10,745.40, and so on.[199] John Stockton of Delaware, owing a mere $2,399.26, denied the *Aurora*'s charge, but the letter he produced from the Comptroller showed him indebted for that amount on the pension fund alone.[200] The "Hamiltonian system" seemed to be (1) to eliminate all those of adverse political views, (2) to control the press through printing contracts, and (3) to give amounts, over and above their annual expenditures, into the hands of loan officers, collectors, etc., under color of legal appropriations, which enabled them if so disposed to use those sums for electioneering purposes.[201]

Writing as "Robert Slender," Freneau jubilantly applauded "Do-Wayne's" [202] efforts. "Oliver has whitewashed Timothy, Dayton has washed himself, and honest Stockton, has told a plain story, proving that the man was honester than he himself suspected." He ironically asked the *Aurora*'s editor why he could not have minded his own business and let money matters alone. Pickering and his successors were advised that if they obtained funds for "SECRET SERVICE MONEY," Duane would never dare investigate—the scheme had been an infallible refuge throughout England's history for thousands of venal officials.[203] A "dialog" between Pickering and a tradesman over the Sedition Law had the Secretary claiming that men entrusted with high office were above suspicion, but the *Aurora* noted the public accounts were the best commentary on that view.[204]

The Baltimore *American*'s "A NEW POLITICAL CRISS-CROSS, *For children six feet high, and upwards,*" was widely popular:

| | |
|---|---|
| The Treasury— | This is the house that Jack built. |
| [$]3,000,000— | This is the malt that lay in the house that Jack built. |
| Tim. Pickering— | This is the *rat* that eat the malt that laid in the house that Jack built. |
| Billy Duane.— | This is the CAT that catch'd the *rat,* that eat the malt that laid in the house that Jack built. |
| *Sedition Law*— | This is the dog that snarl'd at the CAT, that catch'd the rat, . . . |
| *Judge Chase.*— | This is the cow with the crumpled horn, that *chased* the *dog* that snarl'd at the CAT, . . . |
| *Mr. Adams*— | This is the *maiden* all forlorn, that *fed* the cow with a crumpled horn, that. . . . |
| Billy Liston— | This is the man all shaven & shorn that *courted* the *maid*[*en*] all forlorn, that *fed* the *cow* with a crumpled horn, that chased the *dog,* that snarl'd at the CAT that caught the *rat,* that eat the malt that laid in the house that Jack built.[205] |

Interminably the barrage continued. A remark in the *Gazette of the United States* about large perquisites in the State Department's treaty expenses for making presents to the Indians and Algerines was pounced upon by the alert Duane. Earlier he had commented on humiliating bribes America paid at a time when Federalists boasted "not one cent for tribute," but had refrained from specific accusations. Now he demanded to know if Pickering or McHenry *had* received these perquisites, and whether or not Adams knew about it. Was the $50,000 withdrawn as recently as April 18 part of the presents retained? [206]

The *Mirror of the Times* reprinted Duane's "PUBLIC PLUNDER" and called on its subscribers to "READ AND BELIEVE! !" Anticipating Dayton's slur that to say of a story "it originated in the *Aurora*" immediately identified it as false,[207] the *Mirror* said it was almost proverbial with a certain class of men that no truth was to be found in the *Aurora*. Moderate men, however, recognized that none but a fool (which Duane was not) would dare vengeance of the Sedition Law unless he had "Proofs strong as Holy Writ" to support his assertions.[208] Responsibility of public functionaries was the keystone of the Constitution; if the people judged them wrongly, the fault lay with rulers who scorned to furnish them with adequate information. Calling Duane a liar did not clear Dayton; his silence on the real points at issue argued either a contempt for public opinion or a tacit admission of guilt.[209]

Citizens of New Jersey were naturally interested in the vicissitudes of their fellow-Jerseyman Dayton. The *Centinel of Freedom* printed two mordant letters from "JONATHAN CHEATALL," of "Juggle-Borough," to his "Dear Uncle," the former Speaker. The "old cat" of British influence was now out of the bag, "and scarce had this happened when out popped I don't know how many of her *kittens.*" These, continued "Cheatall," included the XYZ kitten, the tub kitten, the eight per cent kitten, the "army-kitten (*later,* dead)," [210] and now the mal-appropriation kitten, which itself had a whole litter of kittens—"the prettiest little creatures you ever saw." Uncle Jonathan had an $18,000 kitten, Cousin Tim [Pickering] another $500,000 kitten, "and a great many more which Mr. Duane says shall be let out in a few days." It was laughable to see the Federalists vainly scramble to keep the old cat and her kittens in the rotten bag. "Cheatall" doubted the rumor that Adams was determined to get rid of the cat and kittens after all the damage they had done, but Democrats were preparing to whip them with a scourge called "public hatred." [211]

A second letter regretted the Senate's failure to suppress that "blackguard paper," the *Aurora.* At any rate, Dayton possessed enough "family spirit" to give Duane a spunky answer. Now, if he could only show when and how he paid $18,000 back into the Treasury, and how he compensated for the use of that and almost five times that sum at a time when the government was paying eight per cent interest, the Cheatall family honor would be safe.[212]

"INTERESTING" was the caption for the story in the

*Genius of Liberty* about the *Aurora's* figures on public money held by Federalist politicians. The statements were documented, and some forty additional disclosures were promised to prove these betrayals no isolated instances.[213] If Duane's charges were false, would not he have waited until Adams and Wolcott left Philadelphia? Would he solicit investigation, and why had Wolcott's feeble, "contradictory, and unintelligible" letter been the only attempt to answer him? The *Mirror of the Times* pledged, if Duane's statements were proved maliciously false, to rejoice in bringing him to justice as a calumniator. Until then it believed *"him entitled to every mark of gratitude which a generous people can bestow."* [214]

The Portsmouth *Republican Ledger* caustically noted that when Edmund Randolph was forced to resign as Secretary of State, his unaccounted-for deficit of $50,000 produced a suit against him. Now there was not even mention of governmental action against his successor for ten times that amount. Randolph, however, was *supposed* to be partial to France, and Pickering was *known* to be an Anglophile.[215]

Thanks to Albert Gallatin's industry, said the Baltimore *American,* the people now had some knowledge of governmental extravagance. As Callender's *Prospect Before Us* (based on Gallatin's *Sketch*) related, $251,987 was listed as expense for the Barbary pirates. Since the known treaties called for annual tributes totalling but about $24,000, unquestionably much of this quarter-million had been "stolen," though it might not be "possible to ascertain the . . . plunderer." This very Pickering had supported all the high-toned measures of government, winked at British impressments, was implicated in William Blount's conspiracy, purloined Republican addresses to the President, substituted his own remarks for Gerry's dispatches, and served as patron for "Porcupine, Fenno and Co." "Yes, it is the same man, and shame to the party that would support him." [216]

No one, Republicans concluded, could be relied upon. At the year's outset the census in North Carolina was allegedly incomplete because the New England census takers, who had received large advances of money, had absconded to Florida.[217] Federalist tobacco inspectors in Georgia were so venal that, rather than lose forty-three and three-quarters cents per hogshead, they passed tobacco so inferior that export trade was being seriously hurt.[218] William Simmons, War Office accountant and brother to a contractor who had made a fortune on public buildings in Washington, was said to be $4,000,000 short on the Treasury books. There were other examples; the picture Democrats painted was one of almost unrelieved graft.[219]

"A Federalist" offered sardonic "advice" to Wolcott. How *could* he write a letter admitting the practice of letting principal officials "slice up the *treasure* of the people, and let them keep it without interest for years together?" Perhaps he could deny his handwriting or something. He should oppose paying public money publicly; adherence to that policy could require secretaries and agents to live within their *salaries,* and splendor would be curtailed. John Jay was an example. On his English mission he had received $52,721 expenses plus his regular pay of $5,000, and there were stories he had been given $18,000 besides. This was during Washington's "reign," and still Democrats cried shame.[220] In promising *Aurora* readers yet further revelations, Duane said:

> We have shown what a public trustworthy citizen JONATHAN DAYTON was. Jonathan and Exterminating TRACY, were the conspicuous members of the famous *star chamber* committee [which condemned Duane for breach of Senatorial privileges]. Jonathan said that the editor owed him a grudge on that account; but surely the editor could not have done him half so great an injury as he did himself, in his *Letters to Childs.* TRACY will no doubt, say, that it is thro' spite we shall have laid before the public, a *whole length picture* of him, as a companion to Dayton. But the public will judge, whether the fault of *committing* it, is greater—we shall certainly give Mr. Tracy's portrait a high colouring, as soon as possible, and from the records of a court of law—we shall shew the great rogues, as a warning to the small.[221]

"Anglo Federal Politics illustrated by Federal Characters" compared Senator Uriah Tracy to the Yazoo Land speculators. A New York mercantile firm had appointed him as lawyer to collect some accounts; when he had done so, it could not collect from him! Even the new Secretary of the Navy was said to be implicated in shady land speculations involving the public purse.[222] Hamilton himself was accused of secretly buying up receipts and due-bills, which resulted from the Revolutionary invasion of Canada, and holding them as demands upon the government. A high official was alleged to have stated if Jefferson were elected the State Department accounts "ought never to be suffered to go into his hands." [223]

Wolcott came in for his full share of attention. He supposedly had said in September, 1800, that Adams "did not deserve a vote for President." [224] The *Aurora* honored him with one of its "full length sketches," [225] predicting his imminent resignation from the office he had *"too long,* unfortunately, administered." His unfathomable Treasury reports and conflicting figures on the debt were a "monstrous suppression of the true state of the financial affairs of the country," and part of "the whole system of the anglo-federal party."

Recapitulating the charges and urging citizens to read Gallatin's book, the *Virginia Argus* raged:

> *Pickering* retained out of only five accounts, half a million of dollars. *Dayton* without even a contingent expense to pay, retained immense balances in his hands; . . . more than TWENTY MILLIONS of dollars, at this moment, lie in the hands of *Loan officers, Collectors, Supervisors, Banks* &c., belonging to the public, and . . . in the book of the account of the War-Office alone above FOUR MILLIONS of dollars, remained to be accounted for when Congress rose! [226]

"Sidney" reminded residents of Bergen County, New Jersey, that their land tax was the heaviest in years. Yet "EIGHT MILLIONS OF DOLLARS," four times the entire direct tax for the nation, had been transferred from the Treasury "into the pockets of certain characters who have been held up to you as the . . . 'saviours of your country!' " [227]

Republican newspapers insisted the only difference between Dayton, Tracy, and "the rest of the *Anglo-federalists* who have made so much money without any visible profession," and three counterfeiters recently apprehended, was that the former were great criminals and the latter little ones. The counterfeiters would probably be put to "sawing marble, because they dealt only [in] dollars by *tens* or *hundreds,* while the other *gang* . . . may be exalted to the places of Governors of the N. Western territory, Senators and federal judges!" Even so, all were members of the same "Idle Society." [228]

"Turn the grafters out!" is an oft-used political cry. But in 1800 it seemed well-documented (Democrats gloated, early in the next year, over two Treasury receipts to Dayton for precisely the amount they had charged he owed),[229] and the emphasis placed thereon was manifest. Incessant reiteration of these accusations must have had its effect in persuading many voters to accept them.

 EUROPEAN NEWS THROUGH
AMERICAN EYES

More even than Federalist economic tactics, foreign relations
proved a divisive element in American political life. Barring
periods of "cold war" or actual hostilities, at no time have
Americans been more keenly aware of what went on in the rest
of the world; that "intelligence from abroad" was viewed the
most important commodity of nearly all editors has already
been noted.[1] External policies of the new nation thus became
automatically a matter of intense interest. Every known move
of the administration was subjected to the closest scrutiny as
to methods, motives, and consequences.

Opposition newspapers left no stone unturned in endeavoring to expose every shortcoming and sinister implication of
Federalist diplomacy.[2] National weakness and the convulsed
world political situation imposed limitations upon the administration that afforded Democratic-Republicans a number of
bases for legitimate dissatisfaction. Critical printers swiftly
made use of these, often enlarging upon them to convert and
to convince their readers.

With the Revolution yet vivid in memory, Americans were
acutely interested in England, which had attempted to "enslave" them, and in France, which had helped win their independence. The old colonial fear of the latter nation [3] had been
largely dissipated by events after 1763, and most people recognized the crucial importance of French aid against Britain.

Lafayette, popularly the ideal Frenchman, had captured American hearts. French travelers and books appeared in ever-increasing numbers; Gallic philosophical ideas were discussed in American newspapers as well as in the debates over framing and adopting the Constitution. As yet France had not pressed strenuously for repayment of her loans, and the United States had with her a commercial treaty expected to enhance American prosperity.

Already gratified by the respect Paris accorded the venerated Franklin and by French accounts praising their country as a standard of freedom and moral perfection, Americans felt especially flattered at the outbreak of the French Revolution only about ten weeks after Washington's inauguration. Bastille Day was celebrated to mark a struggle commenced in imitation of Americans' own; the prison key Lafayette sent to Mount Vernon indicated Gallic acknowledgement of an ideological debt.[4] Events in France were watched with almost paternal pride.

Through the early years of Washington's first term newspapers throughout the land reflected this interest and popular sense of kinship toward France. In Massachusetts, Kentucky, and the Carolinas (to give but illustrations)[5] the press presented detailed and friendly accounts of affairs in the homeland of Lafayette and Rochambeau. Liberty, it was said in Boston, had now "another feather in her cap."[6] John Bradford's *Kentucky Gazette* held every foe of despotism must be interested in this "glorious" turn of events and promised readers extensive coverage. The Winchester *Virginia Gazette* proudly noted that French journals were being published "with the same freedom as in America," and proposed citizens should particularly rejoice to see some of their distinguished old comrades-in-arms prominent in the movement against monarchy. American approval was at first almost universal; even the *Gazette of the United States* acclaimed the uprising as "one of the most glorious objects that can arrest the attention of mankind."[7]

To the public, events in France represented the overthrow

of tyranny—"a lesson to oppressors" in which the nobility solely was at fault. Parisian sentiments represented the cause of all mankind: that of the people against privilege.[8] Progress of the Revolution was followed in papers everywhere;[9] the successive French Constitutions were widely reprinted,[10] and toasts applauding the National Assembly were drunk in all quarters.[11]

War in Europe and the imposing array of powers against France further excited American sympathy for that country. The French cause was now that "of universal Freedom";[12] a Boston paper suggested state funds or public subscriptions to arm a volunteer force for military aid expressing American gratitude, and the idea was widely seconded.[13] Republican printers redoubled their efforts after England joined the Allied coalition. For most of them, hatred of England was more compelling than was attachment to France, although every opportunity for appealing to either motive was exploited.

Popular enthusiasm for French innovations and military victories seemed limitless. The unanimity of sentiment over Gallic successes, argued Freneau, welded America's own solidarity. It proved to the South that Easterners disavowed monarchy and aristocracy and to the East that Southerners were motivated by forces other than selfishness.[14] Supposedly staid New Englanders were as enthusiastic as the rest of the nation in celebrating French triumphs. In Boston a "Civic Feast" commemorated the "rapid succession of victories which attend the arms of the republicans of France," for which "every good citizen" was to be heartily congratulated. Two parades were held, and a huge roasted ox was consumed at the barbecue following. The State House and residence of the French consul were illuminated at night, and a pair of balloons inscribed "LIBERTY and EQUALITY" was raised over Faneuil Hall. A collection was taken to free prisoners in the city's jail, and Oliver's Dock was renamed Liberty Square. The German retreat in 1792 was compared to that of the British from Lexington, and it was hoped that all the world's despots "would continue dancing to the tunes of Ca ira and Yankey-doodle till they can dance no longer." One group "of citizen Mechanicks" added to the song "God save great WASHINGTON" the following stanza:

> Next in my song shall be,
> Guardians of Liberty
>   Gallia's free band;
> O! May their LIBERTY
> Fix'd on EQUALITY
> With LOVE and UNITY
>   Last to the End.[15]

Boston's festival was perhaps the most elaborate, but in other respects it was only typical of the wave of celebrations. Baltimore and New York had demonstrations rivalling that in the Massachusetts capital; the carmagnole was danced in Philadelphia's public square, and there was feasting in Charleston.[16] "Almost every town of note" in America publicly rejoiced, and accounts of the proceedings were widely approved.[17] In communities too small for elaborate fetes, many a drink was downed (as in the cities on other dates) to appropriate sentiments extolling France's struggle to defend its "property, liberty and lives. . . ."[18] A few commented the shades of Warren and Montgomery would be more pleased if the money and food expended in jubilations were sent as aid to France,[19] but this could be construed as showing a still stronger—and more practical—friendship. Certainly, it did not decry the popular enthusiasm.

Sympathy for France became a mania. "Mr." and "Mrs." or "Miss" were replaced by "Citizen" and "Citess" in some columns; the *Boston Gazette* and the *Massachusetts Mercury* hotly disputed the use of "Citess" or "Civess." The Charleston *Columbian Herald* advocated elimination of forms of address such as "reverend" and "your honor." Wearing the French cockade became the vogue, and revolutionary songs were heard everywhere.[20] At least one writer wanted the French language generally introduced in order that English would be superseded.[21] There were toasts to Tom Paine and *The Rights of Man*, and hope was expressed that libertarian zeal would "never subside till arbitrary power is hunted out of the world." A counter-revolution in France was dreaded as a possible stimulus to renewed monarchical efforts in America, and "An Old Soldier" thought Allied military success would enable Britain to renew her claims to America.[22]

Jeffersonian newspapers considered the French constitutions of 1793 and 1795 superior to America's.[23] These documents defined a system of government that immeasurably surpassed England's and in themselves effectively answered Burke's criticisms of the French uprising. He had deplored the revolutionary chaos, but no French commercial house of consequence had failed in over two years. "Happy is that people, whose commerce flourishes in LEDGERS, while it is bewailed in orations." Burke's arguments must have been inspired by pecuniary considerations rather than conviction.[24]

Criticism of any part of the French Revolution was resented. To Adams' charge that its principles were not new, "A French Citizen" retorted that to conceive liberty was nothing, but to act and fight for it was "everything." [25] If biographical sketches attributed human frailties to Danton or Marat, they disclosed "the influence of the champions of monarchy." The National Assembly was not dominated by the mob, for all France approved its actions. Even the *Connecticut Journal* published the London-originated tale that Washington had been offered command of the French forces and might well go to Paris to accept.[26]

The enthusiasm was no short-lived fad; several years elapsed before appreciable hostility toward the changes in France appeared in the public papers.[27] Gradually, however, some disapproval of events in France became more evident. The entry of England into the lists unquestionably led numerous merchants who were dependent upon British imports to question whither active Francophile sympathies might lead them. And the growing fanaticism of the revolutionists shocked many. Newspapers critical of the administration's fiscal policies continued, nonetheless, to ride the wave of popular fervor—both from conviction and, increasingly, from political expediency. As American official policy seemed to veer from friendly interest to neutrality, and then to disapproval of the excesses of the Revolution, nourishing the still widespread empathy for France became ever more not only belief but sound strategy.

When Federalists expressed horror at "bloody French mobs" and condemned the Reign of Terror,[28] Democratic papers commenced a calculated program of justifying those in power in Paris. This practice was consciously pursued throughout the remainder of the decade and must be acknowledged in order to assess the part of foreign relations in the political propaganda of the period. A defense was found for every French action, from Robespierre's Feast of the Supreme Being to the seizures of American ships.[29]

Extreme friends of the French Revolution exulted in the execution of Louis XVI. The pun, "LOUIS CAPET has lost his CAPUT," was copied in a dozen papers.[30] A Philadelphia theater revived the play "Cato," and each evening the cast appeared before the curtain to join in the Marseillaise with the partisan audience.[31] But as a significant number of Americans failed to share their satisfaction and as the administration's attitude toward the Republic progressively cooled, Francophiles expressed surprise, disgust, and anger.

Those reminding Americans of Louis XVI's help against Britain were informed that "THE SACRED CAUSE OF LIBERTY IS AT STAKE," and the King's friends were allied with the foes of France.[32] He no more deserved pity than did Benedict Arnold, whose beheading also "would without doubt touch the feelings of a few paper-made nabobs amongst us, who would sell their country's liberties for a *funding system*." Public demonstrations of sorrow and the "whine of condolence" were but the efforts of aristocrats "to excite the feelings of the ignorant." Why all the concern over a single life, when so little was shown about war's destruction? England's king and parliament, by their unprovoked attack upon France, would probably destroy a hundred thousand men—each with fully as much feeling as had the French ruler. That "the persons of public servants are sacred," irrespective of transgressions, was a "cursed Kings-creed." Treason required desperate remedies, and if the example sobered other rulers it would have been clearly beneficial. Had the King's plot succeeded, some eleven thousand revolutionaries would have been guillotined—and without a trial.[33]

Republicans charged that men who spread stories of other outrages neither believed their own stories nor feared the spread of anarchy; what they dreaded was the end of despotism and loss of their own perquisites. At their worst, the executions of French royalists were far better than the tortures inflicted in the old Bastille by the dead monarch's agents. Aristocrats had provoked the Revolution and were goading it to further extremes; they were the guilty parties for whatever atrocities had taken place. Items recounting the horrors of past massacres by royal personages, compared to which the guillotinings were trivial, began to appear. When it was rumored that minister to France Gouverneur Morris had been slain by Parisians, Democratic extremists insisted—in view of Morris's strongly royalist proclivities—the only surprising thing was that it had not happened earlier. "If he be in reality no more, 'tis hoped that our government will direct the choice of his successor to one who is a friend to LIBERTY and to MAN."[34]

Following the death of Marie Antoinette the tale was told of the famed necklace for which she had pledged eighteen millions, contrary to Louis's wishes, and then refused to pay. For this dishonest extravagance a lady in waiting had been whipped and Cardinal Rohan, ruined. "Now weep ye Britons with tears of a Crocodile; but Americans do not weep."[35] The general disorder had been exaggerated, contended some. French municipal and national legislative bodies continued to transact their business with the utmost decorum, despite reports. So honest had been the mob storming the Tuileries that the jewels seized there had been taken to the National Assembly. Any misdirected French zeal, insisted "Republicanus," was caused by the alternate ascendancy of political leaders;

the whole nation should not be condemned. Real cause of the war against France was her crime of *"social equality."* [36]

American Francophiles found greatest difficulty in answering charges of French hostility to religion. Strict Christians were shocked by the nationalization of the church, sequestration of church lands, persecution of the clergy, and the blasphemous "Festival of Reason." [37] Even in this case, however, the Republican press had its replies. Since it was the *Catholic* Church in France that was being attacked, a deliberate appeal was made to American religious bigotry. In 1791 there was rejoicing that Frenchmen were being converted "from idolators." Why should Federalists be distressed over Popish priests, "who have been always striving to keep the people in ignorance"; did they intend to call "this Romish Church, this Whore of Babylon, the Temple of God"? [38] Sunday had not been abolished in France as a day of religious duties, nor had all religion been outlawed. Quite the contrary; the Republic encouraged every man to worship according to his conscience. In any event, an aristocrat was more of a menace to the world than was an atheist. [39]

News that French armies in 1798 had captured the Pope brought cheers in New York. Clergymen were reminded of their incessant prayers for just such an event, and a Boston paper sarcastically asked if they were not grateful to God for this blessing. Since "Anti-Christ," the world's greatest evil, had been overthrown, American clergymen should not derogate the agency achieving this happy result. [40] Hébert's "Festival" meant nothing; Robespierre's public ceremony acknowledging the Supreme Being was a crushing retort to libels of French irreligion. [41] In any event, American deists and liberals were not so alarmed by Parisian theological ideas as would have been their ancestors a generation or two earlier. To both anti-cleric and philosopher, events in France bade fair "to emancipate the whole world of man, from the yoke of IG-NORANCE, blind BIGOTRY, and the most humiliating BONDAGE." [42]

On the other hand, Democratic journalists invoked piety

when it served their ends. Washington was reported to have publicly asked "GOD *to have the French Republic* in his holy keeping," and "A Consistent Republican" promptly used the "transfer" technique. Those who had abused France should "hang down your heads for shame," now that America's hero had approved the Revolution.[43] Federalists were quick to use epithets of "monsters" and "murderers" about French leaders, but they applauded a group of Massachusetts ladies that had toasted the female assassin of Marat. Apparently, to slay republicans was virtuous and heroic in the eyes of those who blanched at the guillotine, though use of that instrument at its worst had ever been preceded by a trial.[44]

Even the series of French conquests and the rise of Napoleon did little to vary the pattern. The *Independent Chronicle* rejoiced over detection of a royalist plot in France; this nation would always be interested in triumphs of republicanism over monarchism. Banishment of the traitors without trial might bring condemnation from our "pseudo-patriots," but American Whigs had behaved similarly during the war against England—with less provocation. The presence of a large class that had been dependent upon monarchy demanded energetic measures to stifle the hydra of royalty in France.[45]

Before Bonaparte's ascendancy, the friendly press in America had scoffed at the thought of French military dictatorship. Again calling the tune, the *Independent Chronicle* in 1796 predicted that the principles of the Revolution were so firmly entrenched that no form of monarchy or aristocracy, "even though it should be reflected through the mirror of their most EXALTED WARRIOR," was possible. "CA IRA" three years later lauded recent instances of French watchfulness regarding their officials, and "Z" felt the constitution establishing the Consulate would gratify republicans and disappoint all enemies of France.[46]

The *Chronicle* ingeniously sought approval for French governmental changes by denouncing British and Federalist falsehoods about elections in France. This "card-stacking" diverted attention from the actual changes themselves, which doubtless was often its purpose. The "Tories," it was charged, belabored France whatever happened. One time they branded its government an organization of terrorists; the next instant they criticized as arbitrary legislation excluding extremists from office. Actually, Federalists wanted to see radicals in power. Thus they could cry out against "anarchy and riot, and . . . the inadequacy of republican forms of government." [47]

Napoleon's emergence pleased the *"time-serving* federal junto" in the United States, seconded the *Centinel of Freedom,* for these men hoped resulting convulsions would destroy the French Republic. In fact, however, Napoleon had come forward to weed out of the government the secret enemies of republicanism. Had Bonaparte desired to "turn Cromwell" he would have taken advantage of his return in triumph from the spectacular Italian campaign.[48]

Naturally, French victories meant bloodshed, but they were described as nothing compared to the slaughters perpetrated by their foes. Jeffersonian papers particularly berated "Suarrow" [Suvoroff], the Russian general associated with brutal butchery at Ismail and mass atrocities at Warsaw. Jeered were Federalists who called "themselves christians!" and yet eulogized "this worse than savage wretch." Though a bachelor, dispatches mentioned his *son;* this made "Suarrow" a worthy character to lead "the holy work of restoring religion and good order in France," but was perhaps characteristic of the party of Alexander Hamilton. In contrast, Napoleon in his campaigns was said to make every effort to protect women from the soldiery of both sides.[49]

As 1800 approached, it was conceded that France had occupied large areas. But she was magnanimous beyond all conquerors in history in giving nearly complete freedom to peoples she liberated from other rulers. The "ancient *Republics* of Europe" might be sanctimoniously mourned by Adams, but Holland, Genoa, Venice and the others had truly been oligarchies, and France had afforded them more liberty than they had hitherto enjoyed.[50]

Federalist excitement and rage over French seizures of American ships [51] were countered very similarly in a pattern now quite familiar to leading Democratic editors. Customary first procedure was to deny reports of atrocities or captures as complete fabrications, or else to plead for withholding conclusions until all the facts were known. Once the accusation or offense seemed definitely proved (or at times even earlier), the next step was to minimize its objectionable features or belittle its effect.

For instance, stories that France had issued letters of marque and reprisal against American commerce were "BRITISH FUDGE." [52] A reported French massacre of Americans at Curaçao was contradicted by returning sea captains and thus "turns out to be, what every man of sense at first pronounced it, an electioneering story." [53] Alleged French seizures of American estates in Haiti proved to be merely the courts taking custody for probate purposes; judgment should be suspended until a final verdict was reached.[54] "A French Merchant" called the French prohibition of trade in 1793 a "pretended embargo" to prevent exportation of vital necessities; it *must* be only temporary, for France had to encourage exports to further her manufactures. Federalist printers were called "most industrious in collecting and circulating" all possible tales of French spoilations of American commerce; the number of French raids, therefore, was greatly exaggerated.[55] If an attack admittedly occurred, the French vessel mistook the American for an English ship,[56] the seized craft was released (with damages) after merely being detained,[57] or the captors at least behaved with courtesy and gallantry.[58]

A third tack was to show that whatever action France took was only logical; her course was utterly justified, and she merited commendation for surprising self-control under prolonged provocation.[59] It was also argued that French conduct, however regrettable, was incomparably superior to Britain's —and in spoilations of commerce the British had offended both first and far more seriously.[60] The *Time Piece* even observed that the incidents were too trivial to afford a *casus belli;* it was only British property being carried in our bottoms and of little loss to us when seized.[61] In defending French executions, anti-clericalism, and foreign conquests, it was often urged that the benefits derived far outweighed the evils of the action involved, but in cases of seizures this taxed the ingenuity of even the stoutest Francophiles. Some pointed out, however, that French behavior might at least force the administration to be truly neutral instead of perversely pro-British.[62]

The general affection for France during the decade was employed in frequent appeals by Democratic papers to American gratitude. The monetary debt for wartime advances was widely recognized; the *National Gazette* more than once expressed shame at delay in discharging this obligation now that France needed funds. Individual Frenchmen, also, had not been repaid, and even the Dutch loan to America during its struggle with Britain had been secured only through French aid.[63]

More important by far was the realization by many that France's contribution in soldiers and matériel, as well as money, had been decisive in achieving American independence. Republican newspapers therefore railed against any apparent official lack of interest in the fate of France. Americans were not noted as ingrates; how could they remain inactive at the oppression of those who had freed them? Unless they wished to be branded as secret monarchists, it was time to rouse from their seeming lethargy and show themselves the friends of mankind. Protesting against the administration's policy of neutrality, the *Independent Chronicle* lauded France as the "SAVIOUR OF AMERICA," and claimed many American veterans discovered to their sorrow that their greatest wartime compensation consisted of supplies furnished by that nation.[64]

Following suit, other papers were indignant that the interests of "tyrants" and "allies" should be weighed in the same scales; "All the rubbish of law writers is brought forward . . . to prove that ingratitude is a virtue in certain cases." [65] French immigrants were asked to restrain their just resentment

126

at American forgetfulness and the calumnies heaped upon themselves despite their industry and the wealth they had brought to this land. They were reminded of Montesquieu's axiom: "It is noble to make ingrates." [66] If the administration was determined to be unappreciative, added the *Virginia Gazette,* Federalists should be thorough enough to actually aid in the enslavement of those who had sacrificed to set Americans free.[67]

Most spiteful about American "good faith" was the *Aurora's* "A French Privateersman," as late as 1797. In loans and aid, France had paid $300,000,000 for the treaty right to victual and repair ships in United States ports. But the administration by quibbling had denied that right and instead had grasped the hand of "those who were cutting your throats" during the War for Independence. Clearly, "there are no honest people besides you gentlemen and your dear English; and we [French] the veterans of *York*[town] and Newport, we are Brigands." [68] Federalist arguments that it was Louis XVI, not the French people, to whom Americans owed gratitude were only subterfuges designed to evade an obligation. A letter from the dead monarch was cited to show that he later regretted helping America; his youth had been taken advantage of, and his hand had been forced by the *people* of France.[69] Quoting Washington on the ingratitude of republics, the *Aurora* recounted French aid, and bitingly added the First President might well comment, "for he has given as striking an example of ingratitude as ever was exhibited." [70]

Perhaps the best summary of what most Republicans felt should be the American view was given by the mildly Federalist *State Gazette of North Carolina,* in the form of an imaginary conversation among three citizens:

1st— 'Well, what do you think of the French now; . . . ?'
2nd— 'There never was, or ever will be such a people.'
3rd— '. . . I cannot think so. I think as an American, that the American people are second to no people under heaven.'
1st— '. . . What were, or what could have been, the American people without the French?'

2nd— '. . . we owe all we have to them.'

3rd— '. . . if they had not been truly convinced of our true greatness, they never would have taken notice of us.'

2nd— 'But if they had not taken notice of us, what should we be now?'

1st— 'Why, little more than we are at present, the slaves and vassals of Great Britain.' [71]

Basic, as well, to the Jeffersonian position vis-à-vis France was the insistence that her cause was similar to Americans' own. The Democratic press continually campaigned to keep the public aware of this affinity. Dinners, demonstrations, and toasts exulting over French triumphs continued to be the rule to the end of the century. To cite one example, a report of the capture of the Duke of York's army was captioned "GLORI-OUS INTELLIGENCE," [72] and French holidays and anniversaries of the Franco-American alliance were widely celebrated.[73] Even while "harassed by formidable enemies without, and dangerous commotions within," Gallic progress in arts and sciences had been magnificent.[74] "AN OLD WHIG" in 1799 enthusiastically predicted that with "Economy their standard, and the *blood of their Patriots,* their watchword," the French would soon completely overthrow "ALL THEIR ENEMIES." [75]

Continued efforts, too, were made to convince Americans that France's attitude toward the United States was consistently friendly. Early in the decade this belief was apparently taken for granted; as the French Revolution proceeded, reassurance became advisable. Part of a letter from Franklin that stressed France's amicable disposition toward America appeared in 1793. Its widespread publication indicated some attention to the familiar concluding footnote: "(Patriotic printers through the several states are requested to insert the above extract.)" [76] Much was made of Parisian fetes for American holidays, toasts to American leaders, and the ways in which France was following the American example in revolution. Monroe, who succeeded Morris as minister to France, presented an American flag to that nation; it was accorded a post of honor in the chamber of the National Convention. When Adet, minister to the United States, gave this country a French tricolor, Democratic newspapers hailed his action as a symbol of French amity. That Washington consigned this gift to the non-existent National Archives instead of displaying it in Congress disappointed but did not discourage American Francophiles.[77]

Even in 1798, when relations between the two republics were strained to the breaking point, Republicans insisted France at heart was friendly. She did not wish to, she would not, make war on the United States. Stopping or seizure of American ships merely indicated that the French nation would no longer show respect for a flag that had been used as a convenience to her British enemies and a snare to herself.[78]

When England had joined the coalition in 1793 the last vestige of doubt about the justice of the French cause was removed for most Jeffersonians. Here was conclusive proof France was following the American pattern; was she not now fighting their old enemy? It was significant that those Americans crying out most loudly against alleged French excesses were the very ones who had opposed American independence in 1776. More than by any other single issue was men's republicanism tested by their sentiment for France and opposition toward England.[79]

One of the objections raised in Burlington, Vermont, to acceptance of the Jay Treaty was the signature in which George III was styled "King of Great-Britain, FRANCE and Ireland." France had struggled for years against European counterparts of American aristocrats to establish the government Federalist printers had attempted to persuade Americans would never be organized. So stable, moreover, was this government that Federalists and clergymen were doomed to perpetual chagrin if they expected news of a successful counter-revolution.[80] "Tory" gazettes in the United States might sneer at Gallic "dancing masters" and "fencing masters," but French arms assuredly had outclassed the forces of England and the remainder of Europe on the battlefield.[81] When

"Fenno and Co."—"more anxious to mislead than to inform" —dilated on the excessive cost of the new French regime, Democratic papers retorted eleven million Englishmen paid as much in taxes annually as France extracted from twenty-nine million citizens in four years.[82] The "beautiful and simple" plan "of republican education" won approving attention; here was another instance in which America's sister republic showed its true attachment to democratic principles.[83] From 1791 on, articles were printed indicating that freedom of the press, that cornerstone of liberty, was a reality in France but not in England. And when the French Directory at last suppressed certain Paris journals in 1799, American Republicans deplored the necessity for the act but insisted it had come only as the ultimate resort. The papers had openly agitated for a return of royalty, and the Directory was constitutionally bound to preserve the Republic.[84]

Democratic papers invariably stressed the similarities between the French and American causes. More people, urged the *National Gazette* in 1792, should be aware of the importance of the French Revolution as it affected them; a poem entitled "THE AMERICAN'S PRAYER FOR FRANCE" asked God to grant that kings might reign no more.[85] Federalist efforts to demonstrate the French Revolution differed decidedly from the American were met with violent ridicule or hot denunciation. If leading French patriots were dubbed "tyrants" and "usurpers," so had George III styled Washington and Hancock; in times of great urgency, the American revolutionary government too had stretched its powers.[86]

Hostile predictions that the French Republic was tottering only called attention to its strongest features, or to those points at which it most resembled America. For the French legislature to check any unconstitutional proceeding of the executive was "the first principle of a republican government." Unlike those of monarchies, or even America's, France's military system was grounded on economy. Moreover, the French navy was now formidable—"and every man who feels an indignation at the wicked conduct of the British against the citizens of the United States, must pray for their prosperity and success." [87] Even Washington had mentioned the *"noble struggle for freedom"* of that "magnanimous nation," and confessed his great anxiety for its good fortune; clearly he believed the "French revolution was founded on principles similar to our own." [88] Americans could pride themselves that "the Spark of Liberty which began to shine with such lustre in our Western Hemisphere should waft its enlightening Beams to the transatlantic Shores of France . . ." and from thence, it was hoped, over all the world.[89]

Certain economic considerations, as Jeffersonian editors were quick to show, encouraged partiality toward France. Although American exports to England were greater in volume, those to France were more profitable. The United States imported less from the latter nation, and American carrying trade was helped by reshipping much of what was purchased. Opening of the French West Indies in 1793 would augment the advantages of American trade with their mother country, whereas Britain was growing increasingly hostile to American commerce.[90] Toward the close of the century, as a breach with France seemed imminent, numerous efforts were made to point out the disastrous effects of the loss of trade with that nation.[91]

Most compelling reason of all for aiding France, however, was the conviction of many Jeffersonians that the fall of the French Republic would bring a speedy end to American independence. Should this catastrophe befall France, America would have only the honor of "being the last devoured." [92] As Benjamin Franklin wrote Doctor Mather in 1784, the amity of the government in Paris

> is a friendship of the utmost importance to our security, and should be carefully *cultivated*. Britain has not yet well *digested* the loss of its *dominion* over us; and . . . a *breach* between *us and France would infallibly bring the English again upon our backs;* and yet we have some *wild beasts* among our countrymen, who are endeavoring to weaken that connection.[93]

From the first the *National Gazette* had insisted that the fates of the two republics were inseparably linked; from Newport to Charleston and on the frontier rang the cry: "The freedom of this country is not secure until that of France is placed beyond the reach of accident." [94] Democratic Societies recalled the combination of princes that had dismembered the Polish republic. If the alliance of Europe's crowned heads "straining to eradicate even the thought of liberty" should succeed against France, there was

> no doubt but that the craving appetite of despotism will be satisfied with nothing less than American vassalage in some form or another. The interest of absolute power requires that the voice of liberty should be heard no more, and in the event of the overthrow of the French Republic, the United States, then without an ally, may be forced to yield to [a] European confederacy.[95]

Even when tension heightened late in the decade, the *Time Piece* argued there could be no real enmity between France and America; the republican spirit was one of peace and good will, and the two nations were united by a common opposition to monarchy.[96] The entire case was succinctly phrased by the *General Advertiser* in 1794: *"The salvation of America depends on our alliance with France."* [97] Self-interest is ever the strongest of motives, and few Jeffersonian sheets ignored it in engendering pro-French feeling throughout the country.

The typical Republican editor also exploited a sentiment other than that of a popular predisposition for France. Hatred can be an influence as potent as friendship, and England's participation in the war against the French Republic provided the Jeffersonian press with a twofold appeal against Federalist policies. Antipathy for England and all things English played no small part in the clear-cut, all black-and-white picture etched in printer's ink on the pages of scores of Democratic journals.

Reasons for such anti-British sentiment existed in virtually all parts of the nation. Most evident, perhaps, was that from England Americans had wrested their independence. Added to this went all the old resentment bred by supercilious administrators of colonial affairs, repugnant taxes, military excesses, hireling Hessians and Indian massacres; bad feelings still smoldered, and could be easily fanned into flame. Jeffersonian publishers were nothing loath to act as bellows.

Few, perhaps, were as extreme as Thomas Adams of the redoubtable *Independent Chronicle,* who printed a letter alleging that "From the first arrival of our forefathers on the rock at Plymouth, to the present hour, Britain has been inimical to this country." [98] But all Republican editors avidly rehashed the atrocity tales of the American Revolution—especially those dealing with the cruelty and unspeakable conditions aboard British prison ships. If England were America's mother country, she was "an *unnatural parent* indeed" to inflict such horrors upon her children.[99]

Nor were British enormities confined to ships. It was reported their captives on land were allowed but three ounces of salt pork daily and three pounds of bread per week, with leg-irons for the slightest offense. English troops had allegedly destroyed all farmhouses and churches along their line of march in New Jersey, and their conduct in Boston was called an outstanding example of abandoned perfidy. How could America possibly think of allying herself with the nation that had perpetrated the Boston Massacre? [100]

Reiteration of past British inhumanities paved the way for radicals such as "Franklin," whose animosity in a series of letters to the *Independent Gazetteer* frequently exceeded all reason. To him England was "a nation more perfidious than Savages, more sanguinary than tygers, barbarous as Cannibals, and prostituted even to a proverb." [101] Laughable as such accusations might seem in the twentieth century, their very repetition suggests they were not ineffective in arousing anti-British sentiment during the fading years of the eighteenth.

In view of England's abominable record it was small wonder, sneered Jeffersonian writers, that Federalist penmen consistently toned down all references to the late "unnatural war." Even Henry Lee's eulogy on Washington was supposedly regretted because of the memories it evoked.[102] But Democrats did not intend that people should forget; their newssheets recalled all the anniversaries of the Revolution and encouraged every segment of the population to toast "the

Whigs of 1776." [103] From the outset, England had viewed the Union of her former colonies with disfavor. Even the *Gazette of the United States* had commented in 1789 on the "illiberal . . . conduct of Britain towards America," and on the derogatory opinions her citizens expressed about the United States. As recent "provincials" with an inferiority complex, Americans were exasperated by any assumption of British superiority. English malevolence, cried the *Herald of Freedom*, extended from Americans' commerce and manufactures even to their literature. London reviewers jeered at American publications, and their gazettes studiously avoided republishing any favorable extracts from American newspapers. Yet old Tories in the United States were still sufficiently influential to see that American newssheets copied (as in colonial days) every event occurring in England, that much aristocratic "flummery" was perpetuated, and that the health of "Our King" was frequently drunk.[104]

British attitudes—usually contemptuous, often insulting—toward America continued to be galling in many ways. Instead of offering emollients, Democratic papers delighted in pouring salt on the irritations. Various items accentuated the insolence of English sailors in American ports.[105] Ever a gadfly, the *Independent Chronicle* called attention to "British insolence" in referring to Anthony Wayne as "THE REBEL GENERAL" some ten years after independence had been recognized; presumably ideas of reconquest had not yet been abandoned. Correspondents seethed over a succession of affronts, such as flying the American flag reversed and deliberate violations of American neutrality.[106]

Worse still, England persevered in refusing to fulfill the terms of the Treaty of Paris, and the Republican press took full advantage of every opportunity to castigate the British on this point. Washington's administration had scarcely begun when the Winchester *Virginia Gazette* protested indignantly that Lord Dorchester's secretary had advertised western lands within the United States to be given to Loyalists who would settle thereon. Americans should indeed be outraged when they thought of the British fur-trading posts; years after the signing of the treaty, "the flag of a foreign power now exulting waves over the strongest and most advantageously situated fortresses in our country." [107]

Delay in surrendering the forts had occasioned some questions even in England. Rumors of a contemplated agreement in which America would receive some concession for accepting the permanent presence of the Union Jack over the posts involved were roundly condemned. Britain might not intend to ever give up the strongholds (as her recent strengthening of some of them hinted), and her very retention of them might even help prevent American disunity. But Americans should insist upon speedy cession of their rightful territory, without substitutes, or be damned as cowards in the eyes of the world.[108]

Resentment and concern were by no means confined to any one section of the country. A Georgia paper published a warning from Boston that counselled a close watch on British military preparations, which seemed unduly elaborate, for trouble with Spain over Nootka Sound. Continued occupation of American posts encouraged suspicion that, with France too distraught to rescue America again, England might judge the time ripe "to replace the gem" she lost in the American Revolution.[109] Even the stoutly Federalist *Massachusetts Centinel* could, in 1790, become agitated by stories of English encroachments in Maine.[110]

As party lines came to be more sharply drawn, Westerners reproached "city folk" of the Federalist East for their complacency regarding the frontier forts. The *General Advertiser*'s editor was asked to explain "to us simpletons" the meaning of such terms as "duty" and "peace" as used in cities. Americans talked of "peace" and "friendship" with Great Britain, but, if that nation seized Boston, New York, and Philadelphia and placed strong garrisons in them, would the United States still be at peace with her? If England denied Americans' right to the western territories, by the same token she disputed their very independence; both rested on the same

135

treaty.[111] Not only did the British keep the posts; they built new ones. Construction of a fort on the Maumee River in Ohio openly violated the treaty, and when Lord Dorchester in 1794 told hostile Indians that frontier settlements made in Ohio were unauthorized, and that impending war between England and the United States would enable the savages to recover their lands, American resentment knew no limits. Anglophiles scoffed at this report as absurd, but publication later of Edmund Randolph's letter to British Minister George Hammond regarding the presence of English troops in the Indian attack on Fort Recovery proved British aid to the redskins. Increasingly, demands for war appeared in the nation's press.[112]

Examples, historic or current, of English malice furnished an almost inexhaustible supply of ammunition for Democratic prints, but the editors were not content with these alone. Columns not devoted to some outrage (past, present, or predicted) might well carry some scathing criticism of British government or institutions. Scorn was directed at those who imitated English customs or were obsequious to Englishmen. Letter-writers proclaimed themselves humiliated that members of the First Congress should ape even the absurdities of Parliament, such as wearing boots and spurs to sessions. Others resented the adulation paid British naval officers in American ports; if any ostentatious displays of amity were to be made, the recipients should be America's friends, the French.[113]

Criticism of things English became a favorite method of combatting possible British influence in the United States. "Abandoned wretches" prated of England's "excellent" constitution, but truth was that living conditions, civil liberties, and governmental finances in that country were all in a miserable plight.[114] A Birmingham riot revealed inability to maintain law and order, presaging an early return to barbarism. Hanging a woman for stealing to feed her starving children exemplified the "Horrid English Justice" from which Americans had so fortunately freed themselves. British corruption and immorality were common themes. That George III, "best of kings," had to ride in a bomb-proof carriage for protection from "his loyal subjects" occasioned gloating in more than one Democratic column.[115]

For Jeffersonians, England's predicament was the direct result of supporting a king and an aristocracy. They echoed a mariner's toast: "May no crown ever be valued above five shillings in America." [116] No nation, it was claimed, ever had more vultures seeking to live on other persons' earnings, and Britain's government could function only through graft. Biblically minded Yankees could point to the twenty-seventh chapter of Ezekiel and ask if the prophesied fall of the island merchant kingdom of Tyre might not in reality refer to England. Americans had contended against the "wretched system of British politics and finance" in 1776; now, less than a score of years later, it must not become their example.[117]

Federalists pictured France as the "*only* sink . . . of infidelity, selfishness, and abomination," but the *Boston Chronicle* flung back the words of Federalist Timothy Dwight, President of Yale, who in 1781 had described England as possessing all those evils in superlative degree.[118] However beautiful it might be in theory, indisputably her government was inimical to the natural rights of man. "Publicola" and Burke could produce no instance in which even the purest principles were not destroyed by debauched methods. Thank heaven Americans were no longer ruled by a nation where oppressive laws and press gangs held sway, where freedom of the press was openly prostituted, and where ministerial leaders did nothing to assist the most impoverished.[119] Such conditions augured a revolution or ruin.[120]

Any catastrophe might be blamed upon Britain. When Philadelphia was visited by the yellow fever, Bache, who would soon die in the epidemic, insisted "every appearance" indicated the plague was "a present from the English." British agents had blocked attempts to close American ports to vessels from the British West Indies, from whence the disease probably came.[121]

The excessive cost of England's government was another common target for Democratic shafts; exorbitant military expenditures, bribery, and peculation in high places had caused English business to stagnate. A detailed list of Great Britain's wartime disbursements was compiled and offered to the Home Secretary as "Proofs of National Prosperity, which Mr. Dundas may advance to the House of Commons in the next session." [122] Later in the decade, the mounting British national debt was considered evidence of imminent financial chaos; annual expenditures equalled America's most lavish outlay for an entire decade. This country should abjure any example of folly and ambition involving

> a vast standing army and navy: which must be supported by an ambitious, hypocritical hierarchy; by a proud, overbearing nobility; and by an innumerable train of flatterers, parasites, and pensioners —all of whom must be supported by the industry and hard earnings of unfortunate farmers and artisans.[123]

Unhappy Ireland illustrated what would indubitably have been America's lot under continued British rule. If English troops could slaughter innumerable natives of "their own sister country," America's fate would certainly have been no better. The "horrid ferocity" of "George's blood hounds," as the redcoats were called, was broadcast even on the frontier; the "sad conditions of British ruin . . . in Ireland . . . must convince" every thoughtful man of the unwisdom of copying England's monarchical government.[124]

Republicans found insufferably irritating the bland Federalist assumption that the political systems of England and America were fundamentally similar. Sarcastic indeed was the *Columbian Chronicle*'s comparison of the British and American constitutions: Unlike the President, the King could make war, levy soldiers without limit, hire mercenaries and permanently veto any law. The Senate duplicated the House of Lords except that it was an elective body and amenable to law. But for the fact that the House of Representatives was chosen by the people rather than by money, and that it (with the Senate) could enact laws subject to no higher power, the American House was a copy of Commons. With these "and a few other trivial exceptions, the constitutions are amazingly alike." Both governments had three branches, conceded the *Centinel of Liberty,* but actually they were "as unlike, as three men are unlike three asses." [125] Another writer found the resemblance comparable to that of Cheshire cheese and the moon; they had the same form, but differed greatly in substance. England had only the will of a ministry-controlled legislature for a constitution, whereas Americans had a popularly framed fundamental law, with legislators under it responsible to the people. The government of the French Republic was truly much more nearly like our own.[126]

Economic considerations often tended to increase the antipathy toward England. The thought of paying debts due English merchants or Tories irked many Americans—doubtless doubly so if they were among the debtors in question. "A GEORGIAN" grieved that Americans had not realized the freedom for which the Revolution had been waged. During British occupation, fraudulent judgments had been obtained against Georgia property owners, and their lands sold far below true values to satisfy the debts. Now Congress upheld the judgments, even if the lands had been later recovered. If English agents were permitted to accomplish with legal "scraps of paper" all their military might could not do, America's vaunted freedom was meaningless. Since England had violated the peace treaty by withholding both public and private property, some writers would refuse to pay any British claims; others advocated seizing all English property in America in order that citizens could demand an equitable settlement of all disputed questions.[127]

More grating yet were the restrictions placed by Britain upon American trade. Commerce with the British West Indies (open to Americans as colonials) was now limited, and customs fees put American vessels at a disadvantage. Rhode Islanders felt the varying royal commercial instructions constituted a trap laid to destroy commerce. American foreign trade, trumpeted the partisan *Independent Chronicle,* required

139

prompt and serious attention lest England again subjugate the United States.[128]

To indignities and restrictions Britain added intimidation and depredations. Her sea captains and admiralty courts alike seemed intent on robbing America of her ocean vessels.[129] West Indian corsairs and tribunals both were considered agents of the British government. When a ship was released, the event was sufficiently rare that the Jeffersonian press talked of "partial releases" and "THE ARTFUL DESIGNS OF THE ENGLISH MINISTRY." If, as Federalist organs claimed in 1794, England had freed so many captured American craft, why did not these ships return? The fact was that few indeed had been let go, and more had been condemned afterwards.[130]

Intensified was talk of the necessity to defend American trade against spoilations.[131] How could anyone suggest compromise with a nation "black with . . . crimes," when America's "multilated commerce calls loudly for VENGEANCE!"? From Savannah came resolutions protesting against British outrages; in Connecticut England was described as "worse than Sodom"; and a Charleston paper depicted that nation as a nest of pirates.[132] Howls of protest met a suggestion that the United States government reimburse despoiled merchants for losses to the British. The *General Advertiser* found this insulting; it would make the innocent pay for the guilty. Apparently the administration's policy was to

> fleece the American citizens as much as you can, but beware how you touch the consecrated property of his Brittannic majesty's subjects. . . . Are the United States so abundant in resources that they can lavish millions out of their revenue rather than to redress themselves? [133]

Others lashed the proposal as giving "sanction to the most palpable fraud and injustice." [134]

Reassurances were proffered respecting any possible consequences if America took the retaliatory measures called for by Anglophobes. American trade with England was far less crucial than was commonly believed. Contrary to accepted belief,

British merchants did not supply the United States with "immense capital"; its balance of trade with the mother country was unfavorable, and most of its specie came from France. Had not the non-importation agreements of a quarter-century ago disclosed the dependence of England upon her exports to America? [135] In belittling the effects entailed by positive action against what came to be the gravest of tangible grievances against Great Britain, Democratic editors were perhaps taking a calculated risk. Apparently, so great was their hostility, this did not bother them; they could always retort that the principle involved outweighed mere monetary considerations.

Fear and suspicion of England were ineradicably fixed in Republican minds. Apart from the conviction, already noted, that the fall of the French Republic would be followed by America's own,[136] some compared the mother country to Philip of Macedonia and America to the Athenians:

> . . . after he had kept peace with them, by his intrigues, until he had conquered almost all the rest of Greece, and his power grown very great, he then put by the mask, and the unhappy Athenians were dragged into slavery, chiefly by their own negligence.[137]

Actually, insisted "A Federal Republican," not for a single year since they pretended to grant independence had George III or his ministers failed to disturb or infringe upon American sovereignty. Above all nations, Britain must be watched and dreaded lest she regain her ascendancy over the United States.[138]

Thus Revolutionary memories, British scorn, financial loss in judgments and shipping, and fear of reconquest all combined to concoct a potion of abhorrence for all things British. While not universal, this brew of bitter animosity was still widely prevalent among Americans. Hence Democratic editors could continue to dip their pens in it with every assurance that the writings therefrom would have extensive appeal.

# V
## TARGET: AMERICAN FOREIGN POLICY

Conditioned by admiration for anything French and asperity for all things English, Republicans were censorious indeed respecting Federalist management of foreign affairs. No phase of governmental activity encountered more scathing criticism. Inevitably, some errors were made by those shaping or implementing the diplomacy of the new nation; Democratic strategy was to pounce upon all missteps, real or imagined, and magnify them tenfold.

The outbreak of the French Revolution precipitated unparalleled enthusiasm for France, but it did not produce the first attacks upon the administration's conduct of foreign relations. Most earlier assaults arose from the continued irritation against England already noted. Dissatisfaction was rife with the government's inability to secure more favorable conditions for commerce, to end encroachments upon American territory, or to halt Indian depredations on the frontier.

Ever since Burgoyne had employed Indians in 1777, Americans had been convinced that the Indians were at the beck and call of the English, who were therefore held responsible for all Indian atrocities. That the Indian raids were British inspired was a basic tenet of the Democratic-Republican faith; in 1795 the *Aurora* railed that the British still paid savages for the scalps of western settlers. Following the American Revolution both Spain and England had attempted to detach the frontier settlements from the original states and both had joined with Indians in an effort to check American expansion. Thus more than mere suspicion strengthened the popular belief.[1]

Citizens linked continued British possession of the fur-trading posts with the terror of Indian warfare. Hostile "aborigines" were "received, caressed, clothed, fed and armed, for our direct destruction" by English garrisons on America's own soil. Rumors that border forts were being relinquished were untrue; they had been reinforced and enlarged, even though one was a full twelve miles inside Vermont.[2] The "implaccable bloody-minded loyalists" along the Great Lakes had incited the redskins to take up the hatchet and a fleet under construction at Detroit augured active military aid on their behalf.[3]

In only two months the British commissary at Niagara had distributed sixty thousand rations to Indians, and peace with the savages was impossible so long as English traders furnished them with all the equipment of war.[4] It took strength to impress the red men, who would never respect the United States so long as Americans permitted retention of block-houses that should have been surrendered years ago. To send armies against the Indians was futile while British and Spanish garrisons remained to afford them succor and asylum.[5]

Unquestionably, the administration's handling of the Indian problem had been maladroit. Generals Harmar and St. Clair had proved themselves inept in the Northwest Territory, and even General Anthony Wayne was criticized before his victory at Fallen Timbers.[6] Westerners thought treaties such as Washington's with McGillivray's Creeks in 1790 were not only shameful but unrealistic. The Court of St. James still eyed the land for which Americans contended with the Indians; once land was ceded to the savages, England would bargain with them for it and entice dissatisfied American citizens onto what would then be English territory.[7]

In truth, Republican prints castigated the government no matter what its moves. To do nothing or to sue for peace with the natives was pusillanimous.[8] Yet forceful measures against the Indians evoked humanitarian cries that these were doubly unjust when the British were really to blame, demands for campaigns against the British-held posts instead, or fear of a standing army.[9] Had the United States insisted upon surrender of the forts at the outset, held the *Independent Chronicle* late in 1794, all would have been well. The tribes would have then respected Americans and would have been amicably disposed; probably a profitable trade with them could have been developed. But even if the strongholds were at long last to be turned over, English occupation had served its purpose

> by rivetting an implacable hatred against this country, among the . . . Indians, whose revenge will ever be an obstacle to the growth of our western territory, and probably prove destructive to our fur trade, . . . now monopolized by the British.[10]

Letters from military leaders of campaigns against the red men and publication of Lord Dorchester's inflammatory speeches should convince even Federalists that Britain's machinations excited the savages. Agitated Vermonters and settlers in the Genesee region readied themselves for defense, and the former petitioned Washington for permission to carry the war to Quebec.[11]

Canadian boundary squabbles served also to stress the impotence of the federal government. Lands in Maine down to the Schooduck River, under the pretense that it was the intended treaty boundary of 1783, had been claimed by royal officials; jurisdictional conflicts cried for federal remedial action.[12] In the West feeling was high over the administration's inability, or inertia, respecting opening of the Mississippi to American trade. The *Kentucky Gazette* waxed ironical over "the great prowess" of the American government, which had "been laboring incessantly for us since 1783," only to accomplish precisely nothing in the matter.[13]

Yet all these complaints were as muted whispers compared with the ferocity occasioned by Washington's Proclamation of Neutrality regarding the struggle between France and England. The gradual cooling of official sentiment toward the French Republic had for some months received unfavorable remarks from Democrats. Congress was urged to lay aside "national coyness" and to give open assurance to Paris of American sympathy; the *National Gazette* remarked with acerbity the difference between popular enthusiasm for France and the indifference shown her by the administration.[14] With the coming of Anglo-French hostilities, Republican prints had assumed a pro-French commitment was inevitable.

Both Jefferson and Hamilton, however, agreed upon the desirability of remaining aloof from a European conflict, though they differed profoundly as to method. Jefferson thought neutrality might well be worth something in wresting concessions from the belligerents—and, as an astute politician, he did nothing to stifle the widespread clamor for aid to France when he saw how it embarrassed the Federalists. Certainly he opposed Hamilton's view that the United States could consider the treaties of 1778 abrogated because they were inimical to current American interests, because they had been made with the French monarchy rather than the newly created Republic, and because France could not appeal to a defensive alliance since she had first declared war.[15] Nonetheless, a proclamation was issued, April 22, 1793, explaining to all the world that America was at peace and warning citizens to refrain from hostile acts.[16]

There had been two treaties of 1778 with France. One called for reciprocal trade privileges and established certain free ports in the West Indies. It permitted each nation's privateers to take prizes into harbors of the other and prohibited this convenience to the enemies of either. Citizens of each nation were forbidden to serve against the other, and it was agreed no third nation could fit out privateers to be used against either in the ports of the other. This provision, however, did not automatically imply that France could prepare such vessels for use against another country in American ports. The other treaty mutually guaranteed territorial integrity of the two countries and expressly accepted the concepts

146

that food and naval stores were not contraband and that cargoes in neutral ships were neutral. Significantly enough, England had never accepted these last principles, and thus early in its history the United States became involved in the almost insoluble problems concerning contraband of war.[17] Although the United States, as a benevolent neutral, if not an open ally,[18] offered definite advantages to France, this proclamation of neutrality reached her as an unpleasant surprise. It implied that the French would receive no more aid, direct or otherwise, from America than would her enemy.

Jefferson had disliked the proclamation for several reasons. The very pronouncement of a policy of neutrality restricted freedom of action. Worse still, it was an executive decision that infringed upon the congressional right to determine war or peace.[19] Democratic printers shared his disapproval, but in intensified form and largely for other reasons. Freneau was one of the first to cry out. To him, gratitude and interest alike demanded the active American aid intended in the treaties; "The cause of France is the cause of man, and neutrality is desertion." As France's ally, the United States could seize Canada and could aid the English-held islands in the Atlantic to become independent. Commerce would not be hurt, for Americans could *take* British products instead of paying for them. Only those interested in public funds or under British influence, he concluded, approved of neutrality.[20]

A short time later the *National Gazette* carried a series of letters by one signing himself "Veritas." Some have suspected that "Veritas" was Thomas Jefferson, but this almost certainly is incorrect, although the letters undoubtedly reflected his views.[21] The first letter challenged Washington to justify the proclamation on grounds of duty or of interest. A document that abrogated a beneficial treaty and aided a mutual enemy was a national disgrace. It could never be in America's interest to provoke a former ally to war, which was the logical outcome of a broken treaty unless France submitted tamely to injury.[22] A week later the President was accused of being lulled by the "opiate of sycophancy" into failure to consult the popular will. His proclamation usurped the congressional prerogative to make war, and no special session had been called to authorize this. If such a notice were proper, why the delay until England participated in the war against France? That demonstrated either the Anglophile nature or the cowardice of the administration's course, for several other nations had been engaged in hostilities almost a year earlier. The people's first servant should explain his measures and attempt to determine public sentiment at first hand in order not to confuse the "little buzz of the aristocratic few" and the opinions of "some court-satellites" with the general voice of his fellow citizens.[23]

Following this line, the *New Jersey Journal* repeated the Democratic theme that the French cause was that "of Universal Liberty"; while war with Britain should be avoided, America's aristocrats had prompted the proclamation.[24] The *Boston Gazette* refuted the Federalist sophistry that a treaty made with the French king was not binding with the Republic. Americans had no right to prescribe France's government, and compacts were between peoples instead of internally changing administrations. Speculators and Anglophiles should "sing small," because America's spirit vibrated with that of France. Before long, instead of toasting the success of the revolutionaries, Americans would send men and supplies to further the cause of liberty. Aristocrats were warned they would be closely watched to ensure their strict observance of the recently announced principles of neutrality.[25]

The persistent sniping grew into a volley. Whatever its intentions, said critics, the proclamation placed the United States in an ignominious and dangerous position, and, instead of uniting the people, it tended to divide them.[26] The jubilance of old American Tories clearly demonstrated the partiality of the proclamation; efforts were being made to sow jealousy between the French and American republics. Hamilton's damnable funding system was responsible for the whole neutrality program anyway.[27] Only a nation of ingrates would so repay France for her vital help, now, in her own hour of need.

American friendship would become as infamous as "Punic faith." [28]

Federalists found the charge of ingratitude hard to answer. The Boston *Columbian Centinel* presented their best efforts, essentially arguing that past French aid had been dictated exclusively by self-interest. France had tried to restrict American western expansion and was reluctant to grant fishery rights; her loan was a none-too-generous business arrangement. Moreover, the help had come from Louis XVI, not this republic that had executed him. When French leaders, disturbed at sympathy for the deceased monarch, publicized documents revealing the thoroughly selfish motives actuating his court policies, the *Centinel* reprinted them,[29] and comments on American lack of appreciation became less numerous.

But criticisms on other grounds continued. A fable of sheep and wolves, reviving fear of England, was considered applicable. The sheep had entered an alliance with some dogs for protection against the wolves, and peace prevailed until the wolves persuaded the sheep that the dogs were a useless burden. "The dogs were then dismissed and the wolves fell upon the sheep and devoured them." [30]

Treaties, roared Republican editors, were solemn obligations, to be honored despite inconvenience.[31] This Anglophile-inspired virtual abrogation of the alliance was clearly designed to dissolve the ties between America and France; logically, it seemed the first step toward reunion with Great Britain. Even the name "proclamation" was misleading. Proclamations informed people about laws already enacted, but this competely bypassed Congress, though a careless reader might understand it to be a congressional decision. Besides being arbitary, this manifesto catered unwisely to British hostility. English sailors continued daily to seize every ship they could find with property destined for France on board; now they would use the proclamation as justification.[32]

Hesitatingly at first, then with increasing vigor, attacks were made upon Washington himself and his motives in issuing the pronouncement. At first his advisers were blamed, as in the early criticisms of "Veritas." Since the promulgation placed the President in the position of a special pleader, it was obvious that his prudence had "been surprised." Perhaps the British had threatened to behead him if he aided France.[33] A major advantage of republican governments was the opportunity afforded the people to scrutinize measures and to investigate the conduct of public officers. "A CITIZEN" wrote of the need to check "the arrogant and ambitious designes of certain characters," and strip them "of their meretricious covering," implying by innuendo that Washington was such an individual. Popular favor was a mutable thing, as the Chief Executive should well know; at one time he was beloved by all, but now thousands suspected he had discarded those valued principles of republicanism to which he owed most of his fame.[34]

Federalists rushed to the defense. "Civic" inveighed against incendiaries who violated all decency by insulting the head of the nation. The potent pen of "Pacificus" (Hamilton) began a detailed justification of the proclamation and strictures on those who shouted against it. In Hamilton's eyes, the President had every right to issue such a paper, since the Constitution did not forbid it. The treaties of 1778 were no longer binding: France had been motivated by expedience rather than altruism, she had declared war on England and was therefore not fighting defensively, and aid to her would force the United States into war against the world's most powerful coalition.[35]

Effective as some of the Federalist writers were, they did not silence the opposition. At Jefferson's earnest urging, James Madison entered the lists during the summer of 1793, writing as "Helvidius." [36] The *Federalist*, No. 75, which Hamilton himself had written, had denied that a President could render a treaty inoperative. The British idea of royal prerogatives, whence "Pacificus" borrowed his theories, would end all constitutional safeguards. To say France was waging offensive war was sheerest gibberish. And surely anyone holding an official post under the new Constitution of the United

States should be the last person to question the right of a people to change governments!

There was more, much more, but it followed a similar vein. When Federalists challenged the right of the people to question the wisdom of an announced governmental policy, the *National Gazette* made sneering reference to the infallibility of rulers.[37] A pretended letter from a Tory to friends in London lauded Hamilton as the mainstay of the monarchists and praised Washington on his choice of advisers.[38] After the Democratic Societies were formed, their resolutions uniformly condemned the proclamation.[39] And British ministerial orders in June, 1793, for seizure of American ships in the French West Indies, produced strong protest at these "fruits of neutrality."[40]

Several incidents caused Jeffersonian editors to profess doubt that the administration was truly neutral. When John Singleterry and Gideon Henfield, American volunteers, were arrested for taking service on a French privateer, Democrats called the government more tyrannical than any in Europe. Frenchmen had served in the American army prior to the alliance of 1778, and European nations permitted their citizens similar privileges. These men were apprehended solely on the strength of a proclamation; they had violated no law. Were Americans citizens merely *subjects* that could be prevented from exercising their rights without even any legislative action?[41]

> The government of the United States shows a disposition to draw the cords of authority tighter than proper; and it is certainly of the most interesting moment to freemen to keep a watchful eye over some influential characters; a want of attention in a republic is criminal, for it permits opportunity for usurpation.[42]

Sailing from Charleston with the two Americans aboard, the *Citizen Genêt* had captured the English ship *William*. As prize master, Henfield had brought the *William* to Philadelphia, where the two men were seized and tried in a test case. The jury shared the popular feeling for the prisoners, and the Republican press thrilled with satisfaction at their acquittal.

The virtue and independence of American juries were extolled; the verdict established the right of Americans to serve on French privateers, and Henfield immediately re-enlisted.[43] Federalists objected that despite the finding of "not guilty," according to the judge, Henfield had violated America's treaty with England. Charleston writers then rushed to point out that Henfield's service on the privateer was never denied, but that the jury had pronounced it no crime. Americans were entitled, if they so wished, to emigrate and become citizens of other countries; Joel Barlow and Tom Paine had already done so in France. Once Henfield accepted a French commission, he became a French citizen. A number of Americans had been impressed on British ships that fought against France, and some had enlisted after being carried off. Yet no one dreaded a French declaration of war against the United States for that reason.[44]

Still more reprobated was the administration's handling of the *Little Sarah* incident. The vessel involved was a British fourteen-gun brig, which the *General Advertiser* claimed had been armed as a privateer in Philadelphia. Captured by the French and renamed the *Petite Démocrate,* she was taken again to the Pennslyvania city for refitting. In the interim, American neutrality had been proclaimed. When officials tried to disarm the vessel and prevent her sailing as a privateer, "JUBA" acidly commented on the marvelous difference a simple change in title for the same ship could make in the administration's idea of neutral conduct.[45] Secretary of State Jefferson, together with Pennsylvania state officers, tried to persuade Genêt to keep the *Petite Démocrate* in port, but the French minister refused to suspend work on her and ordered her out to sea.[46]

Nor was Philadelphia the only trouble spot along the seacoast. In Georgia one B. Putnam publicly defended the sale of his ship for fitting out as a French privateer. He did not arm the vessel nor intend to sail her, but he intended to do what he could short of war to aid the *"cause of man."* [47] When Joseph Rivers, of Savannah, accepted a French commission he was clapped in jail, and a mob of alleged British sympathizers tarred and feathered one of his close friends. "A GEORGIAN" contended it was high time the Whigs of 1777 checked the lawlessness of the fast-growing British interest in the city. And in South Carolina, Stephen Drayton berated those who arrested him and stoutly defended his right to join the French army.[48]

Almost as famous as the *Little Sarah* episode was the Duplaine affair, in Boston. A United States deputy-marshal attempted to serve a writ on the British ship *Greyhound*, which had been captured (supposedly in American waters) by a French privateer and brought into the harbor as a prize. The French frigate *La Concorde*, also in port, with the connivance of French Vice-consul Anthony Duplaine held the deputy-marshal prisoner for three days while the *Greyhound* put to sea. Duplaine was arrested for interfering with the orders of a federal court, but he claimed the attempted seizure of the prize vessel violated French treaty rights, and was supported by the local Democratic Society.[49] The grand jury, which Federalists claimed was packed with members of the Society, refused to return a true bill against Duplaine (who was relieved of his exequatur by Washington after his release). Republicans howled that the charges against Duplaine had been dismissed, and that to relieve him as consul was both usurpation and violation of the right of jury trial—"an outrage on the most sacred and valuable right of a freeman." [50] Dannery, replacing Duplaine, wrote an undiplomatic protest against the dismissal to Massachusetts Governor Sam Adams; the resulting newspaper controversy was probably rather unfavorable for the Franco-Democratic cause.[51]

In Charleston Republicans kept vigilant watch to prevent possible benefits to British ships through infractions of neutrality. The captain of an English sloop refused to quit loading military supplies aboard his vessel, and members of the Charleston Democratic Society, aided by local militia, forcibly disarmed her.[52]

Yet irate critics of the administration still claimed official-

dom consistently favored the English. "MODERN NEU-
TRALITY; EXEMPLIFIED" was the word when a British
man-of-war was permitted to victual in Boston after the
announcement of its orders to capture American vessels bound
for France.[53] New York militia restored the *Chilcomb* to her
former owners because she had been seized by a French privateer, the *Carmagnole,* which had been fitted out in Delaware, and many New Yorkers were angry. Article 22 of the
French treaty denied to foes of France the privilege of arming
privateers in American ports; if this did not imply granting
the concession to France, it was meaningless. Even if the
*Carmagnole* had transgressed against American neutrality,
the government had no right to forcibly restore her prizes.[54]
France, resenting this gratuitous insult, might take reprisals
against American ships in her waters:

> As we are daily submitting to the most atrocious depredations on
> our trade by the British, and to the most flagrant breaches of the
> treaty of peace, had we not better connive at a few doubtful acts
> of our allies, than rush head-long into a war with them? [55]

The most cogent Democratic argument against England,
however, was the simple and obvious one of British conduct.
French privateers unquestionably flouted American neutrality,
and increasingly they began to prey on American shipping. But
English depredations upon American commerce were claimed
to be far worse.[56] England began seizing American property,
almost wherever it could be found outside neutral territorial
waters, on the theory that it might be bound for France and
therefore contraband.[57] Innumerable vessels were captured in
the West Indies, and seamen and passengers subjected to
every indignity. English behavior was such that a New Jersey
newspaper insisted, notwithstanding the purportedly peaceful
objective of the neutrality proclamation, Americans were actually involved in indirect war with that nation. Never would the
United States have a more auspicious time for open conflict;
Great Britain was fully occupied, and if all American virtue
had not departed, Washington should call a special session to

determine upon retaliation. Only the "paper jobbers," wrote an Albany correspondent, cried "Peace! Peace!" when there was no peace.[58]

Interest in the sea duel between the French *Embuscade* and the British *Boston,* which took place off New York harbor, was intense. The affair commenced with a public challenge and its acceptance; the mere scheduling of the contest produced wagers, toasts, and scuffles in some American communities.[59] Most citizens were delighted by the *Embuscade*'s victory, and an invitation by "A FRENCH OFFICER" to inspect prisoners' conditions aboard that craft convinced Republicans that only the most blind of Anglophile apologists could continue to calumniate the French.[60]

The British Order in Council of November 6, 1793, directing the capture and condemnation of all ships transporting provisions to the enemy's islands or carrying the property of French subjects, was viewed as a stab in the back from the very nation the American proclamation had been designed to benefit. Kept secret for six weeks to snare more victims, this Order, it was claimed, almost delivered the *coup de grâce* to American foreign trade.[61] Democrats saw this as retribution for a policy that had taken every measure to prevent sailings of American-armed French privateers and to restore the prizes of such ships. Yet, the administration placidly ignored English insults and armings in this country. Britons purchased horses at Norfolk for military use while the administration forbade arms to Frenchmen; Bahaman "privateers" preyed upon American trade exclusively. The obvious course was to repay such pirates in kind.[62]

French Minister Edmond Genêt was heartily disgusted with America's acceptance of British insults, and he yearned to see the United States take retaliatory action. Young, handsome, brimming with revolutionary zeal, and possessing a flair for showmanship, Genêt had been accredited to the United States before Washington's neutrality proclamation. Few public figures have ever been subjected to more adulation, attention, and then criticism in such a brief period; yet even today much of his short official career is obscure or controversial.[63]

Contrary winds or (as Jefferson thought) a plan to excite as much attention as possible had caused Genêt to first land in America at Charleston rather than Philadelphia.[64] His overland trip to the capital was thus through what Federalists considered the most disaffected portion of the nation. Following an enthusiastic reception in the South Carolina seaport, he slowly proceeded northward, savoring ovations at nearly every crossroads. Disgruntled over the excise and with a profound antipathy for England, backswoodsmen welcomed the French minister with sufficient fanfare to convince Genêt Americans emphatically disapproved of neutrality. The celebrations for him were such that Jefferson could write gleefully, "All the old spirit of 1776 is rekindling the newspapers from Boston to Charleston," and Genêt's head may have been somewhat turned.[65]

Spurred on by the papers of Freneau and Bache, who suspected the administration of planning a lukewarm reception and who argued that France's emissary should receive a welcome at least equal to that accorded the Creek chieftains during the treaty negotiations of 1790, Philadelphia's Democrats determined to outdo anything seen in Charleston or Baltimore. They decorated the streets and organized a grand ceremony at the ferry landing.[66] Genêt upset the plans by arriving a day early and in a public stagecoach (as befitted a true republican) rather than by ferry. Philadelphians were charmed instead of piqued; the reception and banquet were held next day, with greater crowds and ebullience than the most optimistic Franchophiles had expected. A round of feasts and celebrations commenced that seemed as though it might continue interminably.[67]

Because thousands did honor to Genêt when only three hundred Philadelphia merchants had addressed Washington approving the latter's proclamation, the Frenchman may have been encouraged to think he could override the Chief Executive on the neutrality he found so odious. Almost certainly some Democratic editors furthered this idea, if indeed they and perhaps some anti-administration leaders did not suggest it.[68] Even prior to the French minister's arrival in the capital, newspapers had distinguished between the administration and the populace on this issue. Bostonians were told that the reception tendered "Gennet" would determine America's part in the European conflict and that France sought to learn who her friends and enemies were, for despite

> the paltry contrasted principles which govern particular persons, scattered throughout the several States, it is presumed that every friend to the 'Rights of Man' in America, will constantly feel an *attachment* for their French *Brethren,* and not suffer the *partial* interest of a few Aristocrats, (or rather Tories, whose souls are absorb'd in the funds) to influence our conduct with respect to them. Let it be remembered that Dumourier is contending the cause both of EUROPE AND AMERICA, and GOD grant him success.[69]

Massachusetts Democrats hotly denied that most Americans wanted the President to refuse to acknowledge France's envoy. Such a canard "could only have originated in some *rotten-hearted* fellow that would sell his country to Britain, for a 'funding system.' " Mock concern was expressed in Philadelphia over the huge reception feast. Doubtless the banqueters were now subject to arrest and prosecution. The proclamation had ordered all "citizens, perhaps it meant subjects" to treat belligerents impartially; Henfield and Singleterry had already been incarcerated for displaying their preference, and now an entire host had shed great quantities of wine for the French cause.[70]

A South Carolinian demanded to know if Washington intended to impose martial law upon the nation to ensure absolute conformity. If Americans acted contrary to the treaty of 1783 in taking up arms for France, what was so sacred about a pact that Britain had flouted ever since it was signed? The vast majority of the people scorned "those GREAT POLITICIANS" who pretended to voice the nation's opinion in foreign affairs and resented bowing down before "a wrinkled crippled, blear-eyed old granny" of an England merely because

157

freemen had dared to think as they pleased about the changes taking place in France.[71]

Such statements readily persuaded Genêt that the administration's proclaimed neutrality opposed the popular will. Open demonstrations in his behalf strengthened this view; some felt only the appearance of yellow fever saved Philadelphia from revolt.[72] Soon the minister was acting in a fashion belying his earlier, universally acclaimed statement that France had no desire for American entry into the European conflict.[73] Under his directions privateers were licensed and fitted out in American ports; they took prizes within American waters and sent them into American harbors. Recruiting offices were set up and operated until closed by the authorities.[74] French commissions were given American citizens, and expeditions were formed against Florida and Louisiana. Republicans openly rejoiced in Consul Mangourit's defiance at Charleston of federal orders to release a prize under duress: "Sir, the weight of America, in the scale of the enemies against France will be of little consideration; begin [the use of force] as soon as you please." [75]

These actions, especially offensive because of the contemptuous manner accompanying some of them, turned more moderate Democrats away from the young French minister. Opinions still differ as to whether or not Jefferson used Genêt to embarrass the administration, but by August Jefferson had become convinced that the Girondist was hurting both the cause of France and of democracy in the United States. Genêt himself came to believe Jefferson was treacherously sacrificing him for political purposes, but his later accusations that the Secretary only feigned friendliness for France and that State Department communications lacked only the signature of English minister George Hammond to make them perfectly British, reflected hot-headedness rather than statesmanship.[76] Already his recruiting advertisements were evoking some demands for his recall, and Federalist editors capitalized on such indiscretions as his strictures against Washington for possessing a bust of Louis XVI and his refusal to attend a Society of the

Cincinnati dinner because a French nobleman member was present.[77] His role in the *Little Sarah* episode turned the majority of public opinion definitely against him.

Genêt's unpopularity with white refugees from the racial uprisings in the French West Indies probably hastened his decline in popularity. The bloody Negro and mulatto insurrections in Haiti in 1791 and 1792 turned the world's richest tropical colony into a shambles and provided Francophobes an opportunity to point to the consequences of spreading French revolutionary doctrines.[78] The hundreds of penniless aristocrats who fled to the United States were bitter over Genêt's parsimony in distributing for their benefit the limited funds at his disposal. They demanded expenses for sending representatives to Paris to tell their story to the French government and venomously opposed Genêt's support for similar representation for the Haitians.[79] Genêt was reluctant to use money sorely needed for his western and southern expeditions to help persons critical of France's new regime, but public opinion gave him no choice. He saw to it that the funds he did distribute were widely publicized, but the criticisms—plus a newspaper controversy with a French general who had been unsuccessful in Haiti—further weakened Genêt's position in America.[80]

Democratic leaders might abandon Genêt as his popularity began to wane, but much of the Democratic press could not. In Philadelphia Freneau from the first had championed him, and Bache was his mouthpiece.[81] Having sponsored mass enthusiasm, they felt it their duty—and a necessity—to maintain it if they could. Any other course than defending this symbol of French republicanism against all attacks might have made them appear ridiculous.

Other Republican newspapers followed their lead. "Bold Justice" denied that Genêt had granted commissions or letters of marque; he had merely *delivered* them from the government in Paris. Everything he had done, seconded "A Friend to Liberty," had conformed with the French treaty, which was of mutual advantage to both nations. Criticism of

Genêt resulted from the abusive "efforts of a contemptible party, who were once as much opposed to the revolution of America, as they now are to that of France." Genêt's charities were broadcast; his denials of authorizing recruiting on American soil and his protests of willingness to be sacrificed in the interests of Franco-American understanding were reprinted to revive flagging spirits. Authors of the whispering campaign against him were boldly challenged to make their accusations in the open.[82]

Whispering there had been, but open charges soon followed. Among the first and harshest arraignments was that by one William Wilcocks, who wrote several letters in the New York *Daily Advertiser*. He accused Genêt of being either the dupe of the anti-administration party, or of hatching some as yet obscure plot against America in collusion with restless and designing Southerners.[83] Democratic fury at the writer immediately rose in shrill crescendo. Washington was so revered that criticism of him at this time was perforce cautious, faint, or prefaced with explanations; Wilcocks was an unknown, for whom no holds were barred.

Wilcocks' attack, the Republican papers claimed, was caused by outraged vanity. He had been among the first to congratulate Genêt, but the latter had been too prudent to answer his personal address. Now he was venting his spleen, seeking cheap notoriety which might help launch him on a political career. This was no matter for any individual citizen, let alone a cheap scribbler: ". . . it is not your business to handle the character of the Ambassador of any foreign power whatever. It is offering indignity to the power that sent him, and meddling with its internal affairs." [84] Wilcocks was "impertinent" and "aristocratic"; a "petty fogging lawyer, who was publicly hissed out of a meeting by the citizens of New York." As "a party tool in British pay," when justice was done in America he would either have his tongue torn out or would suffer the guillotine. Only cowards would write such screeds against France when she was struggling for survival; anyway, John Jay and Rufus King were his superiors in the art of character defamation.[85] Months later Wilcocks (still attacking

Democrats) was yet being pictured as an ignoramus, whose very name was a symbol for unreliability.[86]

Some answers to Wilcocks relied on reason rather than invective. "FAIR PLAY," in the *Federal Gazette,* summed up Wilcocks' accusations: Genêt had offended by (1) fitting out privateers, (2) allying himself with the anti-Federal party in this country, (3) voicing open opposition to the dismissal of Duplaine,[87] and (4) threatening to appeal to the American people over Washington's head. In rebuttal it was urged that privateers had been licensed under instructions from France, for which the minister personally should not be blamed; that Genêt had joined no party, but was too polite to refuse civilities from any group; that Washington had acted arbitrarily in dismissing a foreign consul; and that an appeal to the source of power was not reprehensible in a government made by and founded upon the people. Americans had complaints against England fully as serious as any made against Genêt. For respect abroad, the government should treat France, in the days of her political misfortunes, just as it would have treated her in 1778.[88]

Other correspondents insisted Americans had every right to accept commissions from their ally France, though not from her enemies; it was hinted that English recruiting had also taken place. Genêt merited praise, not criticism, for asserting neglected French rights in this country, for opening America's eyes to her true interests, and for emphasizing the fundamental republican principle of a careful watch over the conduct of public officers.[89]

At the time of the *Little Sarah* incident Genêt, irritated by Washington's intention to virtually intern the ship, supposedly said he would carry a protest against the President's policies to the people of the United States. Genêt himself always denied making the statement in that form.[90] The reaction was the same as if he had, and Jefferson and many Republican leaders were convinced the story was true.[91] On August 12, 1793, John Jay and Rufus King—detested by Republicans, but nevertheless men of considerable standing—published a signed statement to the effect that Genêt had said he would make a popular appeal over the head of the Chief Executive. That Genêt was speaking a language other than his native tongue and that he felt himself harassed made no difference; Wilcocks was in his glory, and other Federalist critics of Genêt joined in the cry.[92]

Democrats were taken aback, though not for long. An astute Philadelphian quickly noted that whether or not Genêt had carried his case to the people, King and Jay, by publishing their charges, had not hesitated to do so.[93] Republican writers had earlier demanded more than innuendos against the minister; now they clamored for proof. The Jay-King statement (worded rather peculiarly, in that the two men swore that they had said Genêt made the threat) had been printed in New York, and the *New-York Journal* assumed the lead in the defense of Genêt. "ONE of the PEOPLE," ostensibly to throw light on the alleged offense, asked an interminable series of questions. Who informed Jay and King, and when, that the Girondist made the threat? To whom was it made, and how? Had they discussed the matter with Washington? Did their hatred of Genêt stem from Wilcocks' libels, their detestation for liberty and France, or from what cause?[94]

Various other writers helped create a defensive pattern, similar to those used concerning French Revolutionary and naval excesses. Washington was able to recognize an insult and could care for himself if actually affronted; with confidence in the President, the public would suspend judgment until the facts were known. The men who made the allegation were actually questioning Washington's dignity. Evidence supporting the accusation was patently inadequate; this was only another British-inspired libel against Genêt.[95] A group of Northerners trying to stir up animosity between France and America had magnified a simple expression of a Frenchman into a wonderful tale, while "their dear . . . British friends can plunder, imprison and assault our citizens" without remonstrance from such Anglophiles. Such agitation aimed at her minister would end in drawing the vengeance of France down upon America. No legitimate purpose could be served by all this outcry; supposedly the people were still sovereign, and was the President now so sacred that an appeal to them from his decision must be counted criminal?[96] Genêt had used only the fearless frankness of a republican, but even if indiscreet his conduct was meticulously correct when contrasted with that of Gouverneur Morris, the aristocratic minister to Paris.[97]

Defiant indeed had sounded the Democratic editors, but their relief at an opportunity to deny Jay's charge was evident. Pennsylvania's Secretary of the Commonwealth Alexander J. Dallas, to whom Genêt was supposed to have first uttered his threat, published a statement that the minister had only mentioned appealing to Congress as the representative of the people. This was a very different matter. As had been customary during the American Revolution, foreign ministers were accredited to the Congress of the United States,[98] and the thus accredited Genêt could see no possible impropriety in appealing to that body. Dallas' declaration, and Genêt's own letter on the subject, received the widest publicity;[99] from far off Vermont, Genêt was praised for attempting to "obtain the sense of the American people . . . through their representatives," since in America no man was infallible.[100]

The "refutation" by Dallas produced a communication from Hamilton and Knox supplementing the charges of Jay and King. Genêt had made similar remarks to Pennsylvania's Governor Thomas Mifflin and to Jefferson, it seemed. Heated denials and counter charges followed as the battle continued. Dallas berated Hamilton and Knox for propagating a report as coming from him without any effort to first confirm it with him. If the threats had been made to Jefferson or Mifflin, why had not one of *them* issued the supplementary certificate? The whole affair still rested on hearsay evidence, though it had unquestionably exposed to public gaze the "enemies of France and freedom."[101]

In Boston, "Junius" called for a congressional investigation, and the *Independent Chronicle* reminded its readers that from the first every effort had been exerted to make Genêt's position uncomfortable. Now appeared this artful tale of "an insult to the President," but true Republicans would assume it baseless so long as Washington himself remained silent.[102] Another writer caustically asked if the attacks on Genêt were samples of the "impartial neutrality" the administration had requested. Federalists shrieked about "disrespect," but how about that they themselves had shown for Genêt's high office and for the nation he represented? [103]

Jefferson's own disapproval of Genêt was grounded on his quick perception that public disapprobation for her agent would be twisted to hurt the cause of France herself. Others, too, tried to prevent such a result:

> We see every day in what manner words are [w]rested from their true intent and meaning, merely to serve the political purpose of injuring the French and courting the British. . . . Besides, it is not the cause of one man, that ought to induce us to give up the cause of Liberty, Equality, and the Republic of France; no, it is the principle that we ought to regard, and not men.[104]

An impromptu poem tossed the matter off as of little moment:

> Let aristocrats say how wounded they feel
> On hearing *Genet's* Democratic *appeal.*—
> But true Sons of Freedom their Freaks will deride,
> As founded alone on *Monarchical* Pride.
>
> Tho' *Jay the great judge* and the *Senator King,*
> To join their clamours, their evidence bring,
> Yet Freemen will see how vain's their Attempt,
> And treat it as Freemen, with Sovereign Contempt.[105]

Other writers saw efforts to discredit Genêt as a British plot to separate America and France. One presented a "Balance sheet" showing how the ministry in London evaluated the affair:

## DEBTOR

The United States—to account current with the French minister. 1793, Aug. To one large malignant, and wicked Lie, to divide the friends of France—valued by the British minister at 10,000 l. sterl.                                        10,000

## CREDIT

| | |
|---|---|
| 1793, Aug. By W. Wilcocks, for printing publishing, &c. | 2,000 |
| By my Lord Chief Justice Jay, for mid-wifery and certificate of birth his one-fifth of merit. | 2,000 |
| By Rufus King, do. | 2,000 |
| By the little secretary [Hamilton] for facilities and credit | 500 |
| By the big secretary [Knox] for reports, &c., | 500 |
| By the governor of the woods [Mifflin] for his gracious message | 500 |
| By his Scotch secretary [Dallas?] | 250 |
| And to so much as he may advance to find out the original author | 250 |
| By balance to be hereafter settled by the G[overn-men]t of the U. S. & the French republic | 4,000 [sic] |
| Sterl. | £10,000 |

Errors excepted [106]

Later, still another writer argued the entire controversy had been foisted on the public to distract attention from British outrages and to give "every wretched scribbler" an opportunity "to try his talents at abuse." [107] Publication of Genêt's correspondence was expected to disclose that Jay, Knox, Hamilton and probably Wilcocks had been promised titles of nobility. The old Tories who tried to blacken the reputations of true patriots such as Sam Adams, William Moultrie and George Clinton and counseled supine acquiescence in British aggressions were now planting upon Washington the Judas kiss of fulsome praise. Americans had more to fear from such men "than from half a dozen Genets." [108] From the horrible outcry raised against him, one would think the French minister had assassinated the President. [109]

But the outcry had been raised, and astute Federalists made the most of it. Despite—or perhaps because of—all the published correspondence, most Americans came to believe that Genêt had substantially threatened to carry his case to the people. His instructions to French consuls to respect the American government and his promises to sue Jay and King were reprinted [110] to little avail. As Jefferson had foreseen, administration supporters cleverly used Washington's popularity and Genêt's indiscretions to bolster the government's neutrality program and to lessen the popular sympathy for France. From all parts of the Union came resolutions pledging support to the President's proclamation and condemning Genêt's activities.[111]

Republicans hastily did what they could. Under the aegis of Madison and Monroe, Democratic counter-resolutions to the President appeared in print. Most of these came from the counties of Virginia and were part of a plan to divorce Genêt from the Jeffersonian cause while still repudiating Federalist arguments. Their pattern was almost identical: complete attachment to the Constitution, but fear of direct and indirect attempts to subvert its principles; warm respect and affection for the Chief Executive; a denunciation of monarchy; and a sincere desire for peace, but a fraternal feeling toward France coupled with the deep conviction that her cause was the cause of liberty. On Genêt they either commented that American gratitude to and love for France should in no way be lessened by ambassadorial indiscretions, or quietly announced their support against his detractors.[112] Ever courteous, Washington sent a reply to the earliest of these addresses. Since the reply lauded the republican form of government and reaffirmed Washington's friendship for the French, it was publicized by Democratic printers.[113]

The Federalists, however, had already obtained the advantage, and it was not to be overcome. Jefferson had always been acutely aware of the importance of newspapers, but very possibly the Hamiltonian propaganda success on this issue convinced him of the absolute necessity for an unswervingly Republican press. Be that as it may, from the commencement of charges concerning Genêt's alleged threat to appeal, the French minister became a political liability, rather than an asset, to Republicans.

Recognition of this fact produced at last some variation in Democratic arguments. Genêt's leading defenders stuck by him doggedly and continued to hurl their epithets of "liar" at Jay and those who made similar charges. The report that the minister had tried to raise an army of five thousand Americans in South Carolina appeared also to be

> *something* like a lie! It is therefore, rather to be regretted, that a *certificate* was not obtained upon the occasion from the *chief-justice* of South Carolina, which might have been here recorded with a former one [by Jay, in New York].[114]

It became increasingly evident that the fight was a losing one, and writers veered toward desperate attempts to prove Genêt had been deliberately victimized by Francophobes. His elimination had long been plotted; the alleged threat of an "appeal" was only an excuse for moving against him. At least one correspondent implicated Jefferson. Hamilton and Knox, he claimed, had drawn up and signed a paper on July 9, based on the slightest of proofs, and had sent it to the Secretary of State. Jefferson then formulated the official version and wrote the lengthy diplomatic letter of denunciation against Genêt late in July, though it was not mailed to Morris until August 14. After the debate on this letter, Jay and King affirmed as *fact* what was founded only on *hearsay*. From these "circumstances" the writer deduced that a cabal was formed to get rid of Genêt *before* the sailing of the *Little Sarah;* that Washington had been led into error in the affair, and that there existed in America a "set of men bent upon embroiling us with France." New Yorkers were told the President's influence had been employed to destroy Genêt—with no supporting evidence, Washington's message to Congress had accused the minister of seeking to subvert the government.[115]

In the South, "TOM THUMB" noted that, for all the furor, Genêt's ministry had revealed the dangerous concentration of legislative, executive, and judicial powers in the hands of the President respecting treaties. Most important of all, it had aroused a slumbering populace and, through the Democratic Societies, had checked the rising tide of aristocracy in America.[116] And the stubborn Boston *Chronicle* claimed, if the Girondist were recalled, his departure would compel France's enemies to openly assail France and her principles rather than attempting to discredit the nation through attacks on her representative.[117] Such reasoning, even if tinged with sour grapes, was soon tested. Genêt's recall had been asked of France, and in February, 1794, this young Frenchman who had questioned Americans' interpretation of their own government [118] was replaced with a new minister from Paris.

For a year or two afterward, however, occasional references to Genêt appeared in the public prints. Men who had opposed him, it was asserted, clearly must have approved Robespierre's fanaticism in France, for the two were "political antipodes." Reports that Genêt had been reinstated in Parisian popular favor evoked the comment that people were realizing he suffered "in America for no other reason than his being a firm Republican." [119] Before the arrival of the new minister, Joseph Fauchet, rumors and evidence of his predecessor's schemes to invade Florida were sufficiently recurring to warrant investigation. The Federalist majority in the South Carolina Assembly had a committee probe the tale of men being recruited for the French army there; Colonel Stephen Drayton and others were seized and brought before the body.[120] Drayton argued the investigation was a continuation of the persecution of Genêt, noted that American recruiters had gone to France during the American Revolution, upheld the right of expatriation (if necessary) to further liberty, and attempted to sue the committee for $60,000 damages.[121]

On the frontier, Spain had protested in the autumn of 1793 against Genêt's planned expedition of Kentuckians to force opening of the Mississippi to navigation by attacking Louisiana. Jefferson passed the warning, together with information about the activities of French agents, along to Governor Shelby of Kentucky. Shelby, who sympathized with the conspiracy, did nothing to prevent the expedition even though General George Rogers Clark (with a French commission) was openly calling for enlistments in the force.[122] Western

Democratic Societies, frantic to clear the Mississippi and to spread the ideals of the French Revolution, furnished supplies to Clark and encouraged recruiting.[123] Newspaper items concerning the proposed plan testified to widespread interest. Definite instructions to Shelby to halt the proposed invasion, plus inadequate funds and disapproval of the scheme by the new French minister, ended the project.[124]

But Genêt's most lasting influence was to be found in the rise of the Democratic Societies, so suggestive to Federalists of those in Paris. These were by no means entirely the creation of the French minister, but it is significant that they sprang up almost simultaneously with his arrival and that they uniformly and enthusiastically supported him.[125] They appeared suddenly, and Federalists who had been inclined to smile at popular manifestations of Francophile frenzy began to frown in worry or to protest harshly. Jacobin societies, not unlike these organizations, had come into being just prior to the uprising in France. Their expressed sentiments, such as freedom to examine and discuss the conduct of public servants and open opposition to any forces inimical to the principles of the French Revolution, were not calculated to win them favor in the eyes of the privileged.[126] Clearly, they constituted a political threat of no mean import, and they talked of coordinating their efforts through correspondence committees as had American revolutionaries two decades earlier. Jefferson watched their growth with a keen and benevolent interest; of such material would be compounded his opposition political party.[127]

Many outstanding names were to be found on the membership rolls of these Societies, and administration supporters could not dismiss the groups with a shrug. Even the wild or foolish resolutions of some of the clubs appeared sinister enough at a time in which it seemed possible for almost anything to happen. Charleston's "Jacobin Club" was accorded membership in the original club of Paris; it induced the legislature to pull down Pitt's statue in the city and helped burn Representatives William Smith and Fisher Ames (with Benedict Arnold and the devil) in effigy.[128] Western Pennsylvania members half-hinted that a revolution and a guillotine would bring proper punishment for congressmen with aristocratic leanings who had disgraced the government. Members in Virginia urged amending the Constitution and were acridly critical of Congress.[129] Possibly inhibited by the wave of sentiment against Genêt when he was minister, the societies seemed almost unrestrained after his recall. In spite of their excesses, they created political power for the common people, and whatever part Genêt played in their development constituted his chief contribution to democracy in America.

Joseph Fauchet, the new French minister, fared little better than his predecessor. At first, however, his official reception was a warm one, which turned the *General Advertiser* toward sarcasm. When Genêt arrived, it noted, he had been welcomed with open arms by the people but with bare civility by the government; now the administration demonstrated friendliness, while the populace was not nearly so interested. This governmental inconsistency (nothing was said about the reversal of the public's attitude) smacked of a policy so malefic it must be kept hidden but at least prompted one high official to reconsider his opinion that the French Republic had not many months to live.[130]

Perhaps Fauchet's efforts to arrest Genêt, in accordance with his instructions from the new Jacobin government, turned extreme Republicans against him.[131] Profiting from the Girondist's experience, at the outset the new minister behaved prudently and appeared to be winning the administration's confidence.[132] Gradually, however, he turned for support toward the more radical Republicans, especially after failing to prevent Jay's mission to England. When, like Genêt, he would have protested publicly, Edmund Randolph (Jefferson's successor as Secretary of State) sharply rebuked him; a minister could remonstrate with the executive to whom he was accredited but could never attempt to influence decisions by an appeal to the people.[133]

Eventually Fauchet, too, was replaced, but not before considerable damage had been done the Republican cause. During the Whiskey Rebellion one of his dispatches (No. 10) reporting that uprising to the authorities in Paris fell into the hands of the British. It alluded to Randolph's "precious confessions" in confidential conversation and seemed to hint at a corrupt intrigue between the two. Randolph feared a terrible revolution was brewing; Fauchet inferred a mass uprising against the funding system and the excise, the spineless policy of appeasement respecting Britain, and official unfriendliness toward France. He reported that the government, with British aid, was stirring up the Whiskey Rebellion to strengthen the administration and forestall the coming storm.

Coupled with other letters of Fauchet, revealed later but hinted at in No. 10, it appeared that certain leading Republicans had wavered between support of the administration or joining the revolt. Randolph, who had opposed using force against the rebels, had approached the French minister with "the overture of which I [Fauchet] have given you an account in my No. 6"—a suggestion that four prominent Democrats could avert civil war if Fauchet would "lend them instantly" enough money to protect them from retaliatory British prosecution for debts owing to Englishmen. Without even these details of the proposal, Letter No. 10 and Fauchet's conclusion seemed still more incriminating than was the case. "Thus," he had written, "with some thousands of dollars the Republic could have decided on civil war or peace. Thus the consciences of the pretended patriots of America already have their prices." [134]

Determined to ruin Randolph (regarded as Francophile) and desiring to secure ratification of Jay's Treaty, the British government forwarded the intercepted dispatch through Secretary of the Treasury Wolcott to Washington. The President, suspecting Randolph of seeking bribes, suddenly confronted him with the letter and demanded an explanation. When his verbal reply failed to convince Washington, Randolph resigned and set about preparing a written justification. [135]

Federalists sneered, but it seems clear today that Randolph

was not personally corrupt. Yet to contemporaries the possibility of his having taken French gold was so great that even Washington treated him cavalierly, for Randolph was certainly garrulous and indiscreet.[136] After frantic endeavors and all sorts of frustrations in obtaining corroborating statements and copies of the earlier dispatches from Fauchet, who had been replaced as minister by Pierre Adet and had already left for Newport on his way back to France, Randolph finally published a lengthy pamphlet in the hope of clearing himself.[137]

Once again the Republican press was on the defensive; Fauchet after all was a Frenchman, and Randolph's sympathy for the Gallic nation was becoming more fully recognized. The reasoning in defense of Randolph followed the old pattern, by now quite familiar to all Republican printers, if not their readers. A suspension of judgment was first requested, for unquestionably Randolph would soon explain away the extraordinary letter; he was the victim of a plot by a British junto to force him from office.[138] The ex-Secretary, never dreaming "of the villainous scheme working against him," had been accused without warning. He called for the "other paper" (No. 6) which was mentioned, but this was "kept back," and he resigned solely because the President had lost confidence in him. The details of his futile pursuit of Fauchet were recounted, but even if these papers did not come he would have sufficient proof that he had been maligned and had acted only properly.[139]

Meanwhile Anglophile printers were enjoying themselves hugely. Randolph had disliked the treaty sent home by Jay, and was believed to have almost persuaded Washington to reject it. As the Columbian Centinel put it, anything suggesting scandal concerning Randolph was "too 'precious' a morceau" to be denied Federalist readers. In Connecticut Fauchet's dispatch No. 10 was reprinted with the comment "there is no pretence that it is not genuine." [140] Knowledge of the letter's discovery supposedly led Fauchet to "prudently" flee the country; Randolph was even allegedly involved in a plot to overthrow the United States government.[141] Few editors of Federalist persuasion showed reluctance to assume the former Secretary had been in French pay.

Still adhering to the stereotype they had developed, Democratic writers fought back grimly. They portrayed the whole matter as a red herring to distract attention from the odious treaty with Britain. The English had tried everything else, and now it was a charge of "French secret service money." [142] So cunningly had the scheme been presented, it was alleged, that Washington, until then sharing Randolph's distaste for Jay's Treaty, had become disgusted with the Secretary and had agreed to the ratification in a fit of anger.[143]

Aristocrats were said to fear publication of Randolph's justification—hence the cry that he should wait until he was taxed with committing some misdemeanor,

> but they forget that they have been charging him with high crimes of bribery &c. and have been calling on him to produce his plea, and now he has taken them at their word, they begin to cry *pecavi* —Alas the poor British faction are chop fallen.

Washington had tried hard to keep the Jay Treaty from leaking out; why had he not pledged his Cabinet to secrecy on the Randolph affair also, "until a fair explanation could be given to the world?" Randolph's publication, in addition to exonerating himself, would doubtless expose Federalist perfidy in high places.[144]

After acidulous comments from Noah Webster and Fenno on the sale of the copyright (like "a criminal at Old Bailey selling his carcass to a surgeon"),[145] Randolph finally saw his "Vindication" in print. Though it ran about one hundred pages, several papers carried extensive extracts.[146] For opponents of the administration, it reaffirmed Randolph's republican sentiments of faith in the people and belief in their sovereignty, principles which were anathema to the aristocratic clique the author claimed had come to dominate Washington's administration. The noisome Jay Treaty, forced through by this group, virtually consolidated the British and American

173

governments; Randolph had been eliminated because he nearly succeeded in persuading the President not to sign it. He had been "prejudged" without more than the formality of a surprise accusation, and Pickering had stolen from his files evidence that would have furthered his defense.[147] A letter from Fauchet helped explain Letter No. 10: the French minister had been hiring agents to purchase flour in America, and Randolph had suggested that three or four of these might uncover evidence that England was inciting the Whiskey Rebellion. If English culpability could be shown, the "rebels" would lose support and the United States spared a civil war. The contractors mentioned, however, were in debt to British merchants, and Randolph suggested that an advance on account might protect them from threat of a debtor's prison if they disclosed any intrigue. There had never been, said Fauchet, a suggestion that Randolph himself should get any money. Randolph insisted he had never, without authorization, shown Fauchet any of Jay's instructions and that he had never been bribed or offered himself for a bribe.[148]

Determined Democrats made much of Fauchet's declaration. Randolph had not requested a bribe, nor had he received money for himself or anyone else. Randolph's pamphlet was "a candid appeal to . . . every lover of the truth"; he had filled his public posts honestly and capably. The aristocrats had counted him as one of them, but when they discovered he sympathized with the French Revolution they converted him into a Jacobin and by means of calumny made him the victim of party spirit. Through a "horrible conspiracy" a single man was "made the instrument of faction, to supply the place of argument." [149] The New York *Argus,* which had been ridiculing Hamilton's prolonged efforts as "Camillus" to justify Jay's Treaty, sardonically prophesied that he would now essay a proof that Randolph's pamphlet was "no vindication at all" and that Fauchet's letter was

> conclusive evidence, that every pretended patriot in America had been bribed with French assignats. This new work is [to be] conducted with unusual brevity. It is not to consist of more than

one hundred and thirty numbers, each of which is to occupy only eight columns of a newspaper.—What will not disappointed malice and ambition attempt! [150]

Yet most Americans seemed to believe Randolph guilty. The New York *Herald* printed an abstract of the *Vindication* with the observation that this seemed to be all the ex-Secretary had to say for himself in "this singular affair." [151] Federalists ridiculed the story of the flour contractors; for months afterward "flour merchant" and "wheat contracts" were their synonyms for any thinly disguised charges of graft. [152] For all practical purposes Randolph was disgraced, and the reputations of Fauchet and his nation were tarnished in the eyes of many. [153] The episode undoubtedly rendered much less effective the Frenchman's later conciliatory pamphlet justifying France's cause in the crisis of 1798, [154] and it unquestionably injured the cause of Jeffersonians in America. Not impossible is the thought that because of this scandal Federalists were able to impose the Jay Treaty upon the American people, although it was out of the question to make them like it. [155]

# VI JUSTICE JAY AND HIS TREATY

Interesting it was, and to Republicans retributive, that one of the ringleaders in the "plot" against Genêt soon became the target for the most furious political barrage of the 1790s. All earlier attacks, Democratic or Federalist, were by comparison mere musketry skirmishing. The fire directed upon John Jay was heavy cannonading, and it lasted interminably.

Notwithstanding America's growing difficulties with France, relations with England during the early half of the decade grew ever more strained. Vigilant Republican editors increased the tension at every opportunity—and Britain continued to give more than ample cause for provocation.

This was no new or sudden development. Since the American Revolution, England had refused even to consider a commercial treaty with the United States, and her discrimination and outrages against American shipping constituted a major cause for the Anglophobia that persisted in the United States. "CAUTION," in 1790, accused the mother country of using every means "to distress the American flag"; masters of American vessels entering English ports were warned to have only reliable American hands aboard, for every pressure was being exerted to get seamen to desert their ships. Yankee skippers attempting to recover their men might find their entire crew impressed.[1] Since three-fourths of American imports came from Britain, and that nation (as in colonial days) served as the chief entrepôt for America's exports, England's conduct toward American commerce was of vital concern.[2]

Trade with France had not materially increased since 1783 until the outbreak of war in Europe. There was jubilation, therefore, when the Paris National Convention in 1793 opened all French harbors to neutral vessels. American merchantmen flocked southward to share in the lucrative trade of the French West Indies only to find that England, contending only the exigencies of war had led France to unseal her ports, held this commerce contraband and subject to seizure.[3]

More and more newspaper stories complained of the treatment suffered by American shipping at British hands. "French" privateers (of either side in the West Indian revolts), as well as those claiming to be English, added to American woes by preying on Caribbean commerce. In retaliation against British policy, France began to seize neutral vessels and to confiscate neutral cargoes; by early summer both pro- and anti-administration newspapers were compiling statistics and publishing interviews to "prove" which nation's mistreatment of America was worst. Some papers, ostensibly seeking impartiality, listed spoilations by both nations.[4] Since British men-of-war as well as privateers considered American ships legitimate prey and were more numerous, England's offenses came to seem more flagrant.

In August, 1793, it was noted that for some time past the newssheets had abounded "with accounts of abuses and depredation[s] committed on our trade . . . by the British."[5] Columns, often headed *"British Insolence"* and "MORE OF IT," carried stories of American ships forced to give way before Britishers in West Indies havens, of privateers stopping vessels and insulting or impressing their crews, or of condemnation proceedings.[6] An American captain never knew when his ship might be boarded, baggage broken open and confiscated, passengers searched, and provisions or part of his crew carried off. If some passengers were women, the indignity and indecency of searching was increased and so produced still more choleric Republican accounts. Such instances afforded excellent Anglophobe propaganda, as did stories of the suckling babe who starved to death when a privateer sailed away with its Negro nurse, or the sick passenger who was robbed and treated so brutally he died soon afterward.[7] Possession of a British passport meant nothing to such raiders, and names such as the *Tyger, Phoenix,* and *Penelope* began to have reputations as evil as the craft of Blackbeard or Kidd.

Early in 1794, newspapers told of hundreds of ships (a compilation later listed 698 for this period), with total cargoes worth millions, already condemned or in British hands.[8] Inasmuch as English law made the governor of every separate island colony an admiralty judge, and most of these were deemed ignorant or venal or both, American masters were given no chance. Even Englishmen, noting their home ports "swarming with American vessels . . . brought in by British cruisers," and witnessing the shocking procedure in admiralty cases, began speculating as to how long the United States would suffer it.[9]

In truth, many citizens were no longer disposed to endure. Demands for retaliation appeared even prior to Britain's Order in Council of November 6, 1793, which authorized seizure of neutral ships carrying provisions to or exports from the French West Indies. America had already borne the indignities customarily befalling infant nations; now, strong under the Constitution, it was disgraceful to crouch before those whom Americans had once made cringe. A navy would protect American trade and secure respect for the dishonored flag; despite the expense, every commercial nation needed warships.[10] Outrages on commerce nearly erased any advantages of neutrality, and Britons were warned to "Beware of the vengeance of heaven, and of the resentment of republics." [11]

Such threats apparently were considerably discounted in England, for there was no discernible alteration in that nation's policy. The Order in Council had been ambiguous and was kept secret for some weeks before being made public, but the modification of January 8, 1794, only made more stringent the regulations concerning the taking of all provision ships.[12]

The *New Jersey State Gazette* trumpeted that England's objective was the destruction of American carrying trade in order that it might never compete with her own. A hundred sail had been taken into Barbados by Sir James Jervis; one-hundred-thirty American vessels were reported from St. Eustatius as condemned; almost three hundred ships were held in Jamaica; and American property detained at St. Kitts alone was valued at more than $350,000—all "in violation of every principle of reason, justice, and the laws of nations." [13]

The list of stoppages, insults, and seizures seemed endless. New England papers seemed most concerned,[14] but Democratic journals the country over repeated the stories; even on the frontier there were recountings of the wrongs done America by the mother country.[15] As noted earlier, the injuries were not confined to the sea. Americans were recurrently reminded that England continued to violate the treaty of 1783 by withholding compensation for kidnapped slaves as well as by retention of the western posts.[16] Fully as vicious as direct aggression aimed at American neutral rights was the British-fostered Portuguese-Algerine treaty of 1793, which ended Portugal's naval blocking of the Straits of Gibraltar and (held many) deliberately loosed the Barbary pirates upon America's trans-Atlantic and Mediterranean trade.[17]

Small wonder the seagoing commerce of the United States was dying; sailors were idle and business at a standstill in many a port.[18] British seizures and impressments followed one another so rapidly that (with some exaggeration) half America's sailors were said to be serving aboard English ships, and "A Republican" could ask cynically why Americans had ever made any effort to become free.[19] Understandable was the sharpness of protests against congressional concern over the number of stars and stripes in the flag; this was as absurd as would be a condemned man's worry about the way his hair was combed while his head went under the guillotine.[20]

As conditions worsened, cries for retaliation swelled into a roar. One widely republished article advocated sequestration of British property in the United States, including that claimed by British creditors. The move would convince Great Britain Americans were in earnest, and the money so realized would serve a multifold purpose. It could be used (1) to ransom American captives of the Algerines, for "the Dey is but an Automaton of George the Third," (2) to indemnify owners of ships seized by the "corsairs of Britain and her African allies," and to compensate American seamen for their mistreatment, (3) to deduct the expenses of campaigns against the Indians—"those copper-colored emissaries of the mother country," and (4) to recompense the widows and orphans of massacre victims. The balance could then be sent to Henry Dundas, British Home Minister, to settle with the creditors as best he might.[21]

Perhaps sequestration could be made doubly effective by coupling it with an embargo, for American trade was believed essential to England.[22] An embargo and an alliance with France, from whom Americans could obtain every product then imported from Britain, should bring the English to terms; America possessed "the commercial weapons of war" to accomplish just that end.[23] As Captain Joshua Barney wrote from Kingston, England appeared determined to ruin American commerce, and a boycott seemed to be the only defense.[24]

Cooler heads asked for genuine efforts at negotiation before throwing down the gauntlet to nations following war "*as a trade,*" [25] but others argued that Americans were being driven toward open hostilities and might as well recognize the fact.[26] Some deplored this development but felt it only wisdom to prepare for war; others gladly sounded the call to arms, since the British were already "treating us as enemies." [27]

Resolutions urging action of some sort, especially the placing of the nation in a state of defense, began pouring in on Congress from all quarters.[28] In March, 1794, the alarmed Congress rushed through bills providing for fortifying a number of harbors and creating a navy by ordering construction of six frigates, ostensibly for use against the Algerines. Some Democrats saw these bills as a device to assuage public wrath without offending Britain by demanding reparation,[29] but most newspapers heartily applauded. In New York and Massachusetts it was thought the whim of England would be the law of nations so long as other countries reacted with servility to British audacity.[30] South Carolinians were told Americans should have declared war when France did; Savannah citizens pledged their support in case of conflict; and a toast in North Carolina enthusiastically recommended for George III a suit of American manufacture—tar and feathers.[31]

The popular response clearly proved that Americans' patience had been strained to the breaking point. All classes of citizens—rich and poor, Federalists and Republicans—gladly labored without pay to throw up defenses around America's harbors. Democratic newspapers kept the enthusiasm aglow by giving detailed accounts of the services of volunteer groups.[32]

Fortifications were not enough, however, and time would be required to build the warships. The demand was for something to show England immediately that cowering before her was ended. In January, 1794, Madison had presented to Congress a series of resolutions providing for retaliatory tonnage and tariff duties upon British ships and goods.[33] Interest in these "Commercial Propositions" was intense. Republican newspapers, strongly supporting the measures, subjected the stand of individual congressmen to hawklike scrutiny. Fisher Ames was roundly execrated for labeling the resolutions "stamped French"; Josiah Parker, of Virginia, retorted that every member of the House should be marked either "French" or "English," in order that the public would know where they stood. Democratic readers saw copious extracts of Parker's reply: Had it not been for Gallic aid in the American Revolution, those who now abused France in Congress would have had no opportunity to do so. Notwithstanding Ames's harpings, the resolutions would not provoke England to war, and they would help develop American manufacturing and would decrease dependence on foreign nations.[34]

Samuel Dexter, of Massachusetts, found it singular that

representatives from the commercial states, himself included, should oppose these resolves while those from the South favored them. Dexter's own interest in the public funds was thought sufficient explanation for the paradox. Opposition to the resolutions "may be strange to *him*, but it is not to his *Constituents*. —*We answer all his* arguments and those of Mr. AMES . . . —as the *Vicar of Wakefield* did Miss HAMBOROUGH's, with this difference indeed, the Vicar said FUDGE—We say FUND!!" [35] Town meetings were held, from which the Democratic prints held none who loved their country would absent themselves, for "Our COMMERCE, our HONOR, and our INDEPENDENCE are in danger, and delays will but increase the hazard." [36] Toasts were drunk, letters were published, and the Democratic Societies attempted to mobilize opinion behind Madison's proposals.[37] Impatiently hooted down were Federalist contentions that virtually any form of retaliation would lead to war with Britain. As the most important neutral maritime nation, the best customer for England's manufactures and her largest source of naval supplies, the United States was vital to that country.[38] Moreover, Americans recalled the effectiveness of the pre-Revolutionary non-importation agreements. (That these agreements had been succeeded by armed conflict was conveniently ignored.) England would not even dare insult Americans had not the proclamation of neutrality convinced her of their cowardice.[39]

Surely America could defend its ports against England while the British were at war with France. If England were dependent upon American trade, these measures would bring her around; if not, at least British influence in American commercial cities would be eliminated.[40] Federalists were said to resemble parrots: a short time previously all they could say was "anti-federalism" in answer to any proposal; now if one suggested anything, from encouraging local manufacturing to opening the doors of the Senate, the reply was always, "It will lead to war." [41] Other Republican editors attempted to allay concern about English reprisals with sarcastic articles about

"British might." A military dictionary might be compiled, it was said, just from English communiques in Europe against the French: "*Covering a high road*" was simply preparing to run away, "*changing of position*" meant a complete defeat, etc.[42]

Most Democratic writers disclaimed any desire for war, but many felt if retaliation produced hostilities the conflict would be a just one in which Americans could expect to triumph.[43] And some, such as "CYMON," welcomed the chance to redress grievances; those who could declare for peace, after all England's affronts, were not worthy to be called Americans. We should show the world that "as we claim the rights of Freemen, so do we possess the courage to defend them." [44] Advocates of the Constitution had proclaimed that "*the long arm of the union*" would protect citizens; surely a stronger government and doubled population would make prospects for victory at least as good as they had been in 1775.[45] Great Britain and Spain were the United States' natural enemies; by fighting them Americans could perhaps acquire Canada and Louisiana, open the Mississippi, and end the Indian menace for all time.[46] If, as some said, the British were at the bottom of the Whiskey insurgency, sniffed the *Independent Chronicle,* "will it not be considered a declaration of war against that powerful nation" to suppress the revolt? No doubt "Pacificus" could satisfactorily answer this query.[47]

Certainly negotiation was hopeless, for only fools relied upon Britain's word—and that nation obviously wanted war.[48] Fenno's *Gazette of the United States* ranted of a "faction, inimical to the people" that might involve America in hostilities with England. Bache retorted this was a strange expression indeed for the minority to apply to the majority of the people's representatives in Congress and to the overwhelming majority of the nation's citizens.[49] Apparently those under the blighting influence of the funding system had a different set of interests than did their constituents or the country at large.[50] Only the first of Madison's motions was voted upon and approved in Congress, and Democratic fury

reached a high pitch. After being held up to universal op-
probrium as an "INFERNAL JUNTO," leading opponents
of the scheme were burned in effigy in several cities and in
Charleston with a figure of Benedict Arnold as a fitting companion.[51]

When Madison's resolutions failed of quick adoption, the
cry for an embargo was redoubled. As Bostonians had put it:

> Lay an embargo. Let it be general, and cover every ship in our
> ports save those of our good allies, the French. Then shall we lie
> on our oars and the Algerines of Africa and the Algerines of the
> Indies be disappointed of getting our ships. Then shall we cease
> to feed those who insult us. Then shall we fairly meet the question,
> Are our sailors to be maltreated, our ships plundered, and our flag
> defied with impunity? [52]

Petitions deluged Congress, and those who advocated attempts at prior negotiations by making formal demands on
England for damages and meanwhile preparing for the worst,
were reminded that

> before an answer is received our few remaining merchantmen may
> be in the hands of our *enemies*. . . . Our critical situation de-
> mands *immediate* attention, and the most probable mode of in-
> suring redress for the injuries we have received is by laying on all
> British property in the United States an EMBARGO! [53]

On March 26, 1794, the prohibition on foreign trade
passed by an aroused Congress was declared in effect by the
President. It theoretically applied to all shipping in American
harbors, although reportedly some early ships bound for
France sailed anyway.[54] Public support for the measure was
instantaneous and widespread. In Baltimore, as soon as the
news came, a local committee was organized to ensure enforcement.[55] New York merchants and clerks helped a customs official compel the return of two British ships attempting
to depart from that port, and similar cases occurred in Philadelphia and Charleston.[56] Americans evidently were determined to see that the embargo was effective, and Republican
editors seconded that determination wholeheartedly. Originally laid for thirty days, before it expired the embargo was

extended another thirty. The nation as a whole seemed to approve the idea. Then, on May 25, the restriction was lifted.

A number of reasons compelled the administration to end the embargo. Federal revenue depended almost entirely on customs and tonnage duties, which would be greatly reduced during a prolonged embargo. Southern export trade was gravely hurt, and some American merchants and idle seamen were being hard hit economically. The French fleet had recovered sufficiently so that a total embargo injured France more than it helped her. Moreover, the administration had already taken steps to negotiate with England.[57]

To the masses, ending the embargo seemed like truckling to the British. Town meetings applauded the curb on commerce and mourned its ending.[58] No Anglophile, it was angrily declared, could point to a single instance in which mechanics or idle seamen "arose in a tumultuous manner in opposition to the embargo." [59] New England papers carried an "epitaph" for "that truly virtuous, prudent and heroic veteran GENERAL EMBARGO," who expired after two months of preparation just as he was "on the point of . . . an effective operation." The funeral would be conducted with naval honors; a great merchant fleet would sail from American ports to rendezvous in the British West Indies, where it was "expected that [British] Admiral Jervis will . . . arrange the *liberal procession* agreeably to some 'new instructions' he may receive from his Brittanic Majesty." Burial would be at Jamaica, and "a monument will be erected *at the expence of the United States,* under the direction of the British commanders, with this short inscription,—BRITISH INSOLENCE TRIUMPHANT!! " [60]

Nowhere was resentment higher than in Baltimore, where Democratic writers ironically commented that Congress, "that body of wisdom," had indeed diligently considered "the warm and pressing recommendations from the different states, that prayed a continuance of the embargo." Permitting ships to leave American ports meant only that Americans were supplying their enemy. English naval policy had not varied one iota;

where, then was the reason for lifting the embargo? Readers were urged to petition for its retention.[61]

There were even attempts to continue the embargo on a voluntary basis. Baltimore's "A.B." called on merchants not to send out their ships after the restriction had been lifted, and a group of captains and mates from the same city formed an association to refrain from going to sea "until we can be assured that our flag will be respected." [62] Philadelphia and Wilmington sea captains followed suit, pledging not to leave port for ten days and petitioning Congress to renew the embargo.[63] The mariners of New York, however, valued profits above "patriotism"; the departure of thirty-one vessels in two days from that port ended any hope of concerted action.[64]

Nevertheless, excitement over Madison's "Commercial Propositions" and the embargo convinced administration supporters that something had to be done. Sedgwick offered a plan for raising any army of fifteen thousand men, and the day after the embargo went into effect Dayton proposed calling up eighty thousand militia and sequestering all English debts.[65] Some Republicans looked askance at these proposals, fearing a Federalist trick. Madison suggested the Federalists had used the emergency as an excuse for strengthening the government's power.[66] The *Independent Chronicle* suspected they had been introduced only to refute Jeffersonian charges of British influence, for they were too extreme for adoption. Knowing the country did not want a conflict, the Federalists could with impunity pose as "war-hawks," [67] and cry that Madison's measures did "not go far enough!" [68] Although these suggestions failed of passage, they received considerable support, and a Republican plan to end all trade with Great Britain until the fur trading posts had been surrendered and compensation received for the damages sustained by American commerce at her hands missed adoption only by the single vote of Vice President Adams.[69] Throughout all this, reports of British outrages, coupled with calls for redress or resolutions asking renewal of the embargo, continued to pour in.[70]

War seemed imminent. The "Ghost of Montgomery"

openly called for it as preferable to the current situation.[71] "ARISTOCRAT," in Virginia, presented a supposed "speech to Parliament" by "George III," who praised his navy and its Algerine friends for their depredations by sea, and his "faithful allies," the Indians, for the massacre of thousands by land. What with the influence of British gold in the country, unresisting America was being forced back to her former allegiance.[72]

The administration desperately hoped to avoid war if possible, fearing it would be the undoing of the young nation. Yet some action was required, and it was decided to send an envoy extraordinary to the Court of St. James. After much study, Washington submitted his choice to the Senate, and on April 19, 1794, that body confirmed the nomination of John Jay.

Save Hamilton himself (whom Washington had considered),[73] no selection could have been more obnoxious to American Democrats. Jay was recognized as one of the high priests in the Federalist party. He had led the campaign to smear Genêt. His Supreme Court opinion a year before that American merchants were liable for British debts had elicited fiery responses from the Republican press.[74] The West had a double reason to hate him, for the Jay-Guardoqui agreement of 1786 (fortunately never ratified), seeking commercial concessions in Latin America, would have closed the Mississippi for thirty years to American navigation.[75]

Howls of protest were instantaneous. With the very idea of negotiation without any other action, Americans only humbled themselves before their oppressors. America should first sequester British debts, and *then* negotiate, when she had a good bargaining position.[76] And to entrust the matter to John Jay was the last straw. He had been nominated only to bolster the shaky aristocratic clique that dominated the administration; the purpose was to forestall sequestration and non-intercourse and thus to deliberately thwart the will of a congressional majority.[77]

Jay's past record was against him. Of aristocratic leanings, he was also pro-British, insisted the Democratic Societies.

Had he not already indicated his opinion that Americans were liable for pre-Revolutionary debts due Englishmen, and that Britain's retention of the Western posts was justifiable? [78] Since these views dealt with issues under question, he would hear his own arguments quoted against him; American interests had already been sacrificed before the negotiations had begun.[79] Most reprehensible of all, his appointment while holding the office of Chief Justice of the Supreme Court violated the principle of separation of powers and was probably unconstitutional.

Much was made of this last argument. If the President could use judges on foreign missions, he could sway the judiciary according to his will and make the courts subordinate to the Executive. Judges were not supposed to be assigned any duties other than judicial; in Jay's absence, how could impeachment proceedings against the President be completed, should the need arise? Might Jay himself be impeached for transgressions as an ambassador, and if the Supreme Court already complained of a crowded docket how was it possible to spare him? He would be away almost a year; would he continue to draw his regular salary, and, if so, "on what principle of *justice, of conscience,* or of *law?*" If he did not, it was an admission that his judicial office was thereby vacated, and a reappointment would be needed before he could resume the post. If the United States could dispense with a Chief Justice for a year, the job was a sinecure and should be abolished.[80]

How could the Supreme Court fairly judge a treaty the Chief Justice had helped make? Was America so destitute of talent that no citizen not already in high office could be found who was capable of this mission? [81] Possibly still more basic was the fact that naming *any* such minister took control of American commercial relations out of the hands of Congress and put it under the President and Senate. Treaty-making should never be entrusted to the executive branch without at least the demarcation of general principles by the legislature.[82]

Few diplomatic missions ever commenced under such handicaps. Republicans had no actual knowledge of Hamilton's admission to British minister Hammond that the United States would under no condition join the Scandinavian league of Armed Neutrality. This disclosure, apparently made to assure England of a friendly attitude, deprived Jay of his only diplomatic high card. But many Democrats were already convinced that what they perceived as American meekness and fawning made any prospect of successful negotiation hopeless.[83] Great Britain would do nothing but "laugh at Mr. *Jay*," wrote one.[84] Another had a "dream" showing a Jay returning home with its feathers plucked, and a Southerner refused to consider himself bound by any treaty obtained through an unconstitutionally appointed emissary.[85]

Feeling against Jay as envoy was so intense that news of his selection had barely reached the frontier before a public demonstration against him was held. He was guillotined and burned in effigy in Lexington, Kentucky, because citizens could not forget his former "iniquitous attempt to barter away their most valuable right [navigation of the Mississippi]." Around the neck of the effigy was a copy of Adams' *Defence of the American Constitutions*, on the cover of which had been written in Latin, "Gold bade me write." Democratic editors saw to it that the spectacle was fully publicized.[86]

Representing a young, comparatively weak nation, and with this avowed enmity at home, Jay was expected to solve through talks a number of problems as difficult as ever confronted a single diplomat. Depredations against American shipping continued throughout the period of negotiation.[87] Correspondingly, the "Paper War with England" also persisted without abatement. Britain was branded "our most malicious foe"; the Algerines could be bought off, but only the will of tyrannical masters influenced the British navy. Electing Federalist congressmen was voting for submission to English impositions; demands for a renewed embargo or for sequestration were repeated.[88]

Every scrap of information and every rumor about the mission were ridiculed and condemned by American Francophiles.

Mockery was heaped upon Jay for the bows he made, the dinners he attended, and the attentions he received. Whatever kindness England showed him must be a result either of recent French military successes or of betraying American interests for royal favor and British guineas.[89] The sovereignty of the people was basely prostituted by such acts as kissing the Queen's hand.[90] Other writers ranted against the snail's pace of Jay's progress; in one month he had eaten a dinner and made two bows, and it would be a century before negotiations were completed.[91] By the end of 1794 he had "already got as far as STATU QUO, and there he holds fast! For more than *six hundred* acts of piracy, not *one shilling of restitution money* is yet come over. . . ."[92] England's conduct was Judas-like; why should she continue her outrages upon American commerce if she had the slightest intention of paying for them? Already the British were said to have prepared a counter-claim for prizes taken and brought into American ports by French privateers to offset Jay's stipulations.[93]

However admirable it might seem to later historians, Jay's formal note to Lord Grenville, the Foreign Secretary, on the terms of a treaty contained nothing Democrats found praiseworthy. Its "tone" was humbly supplicating, whereas Jay had been sent to represent American opinion and to demand American rights. If "pusillanimous *appeals*" were all Americans intended to make, they could have saved money by sending a Clerk of the Court to do the work.[94] Moreover, chimed in the *Aurora*, a commercial treaty (as suggested) would hamper and shackle American business. With the revolutionary spirit spreading, world freedom of trade was in the offing, and Americans should not so restrict themselves that it would be impossible to share in it.[95]

"A.," who wrote a series of letters on the mission for the *New-York Journal*, found the note humiliating. After a disgusting exhibition of gross adulation for the British executive, Jay scarcely hinted at matters essential to American interest. The Western posts, compensation for slaves confiscated by the British army, Algerine depredations, aid to the Indians, and repeal of the obnoxious edicts regarding shipping were virtually ignored. True, permission was requested to submit American appeals and claims against judgments of English admiralty courts, but even if Grenville granted this shadow Americans could still be easily denied the substance of compensation. And if George III were as "humane," "just," "magnanimous," etc., as Jay so sickeningly addressed him, "in God's name, what induced the people of this country . . . to separate from him?" [96]

Now it was the Federalists who were stung into asking the public to reserve judgment until the mission's results showed the wisdom of the methods used. Sarcastically they suggested Jay would have doubtless accomplished more if he had followed Genêt's example by fostering opposition to the British government in England.[97] The Republicans were accused of war-mongering, but the *Independent Chronicle* replied by contrasting the programs offered by the two parties as a means of preserving peace. One group advocated only continued appeasement and furnishing the British "with *six million* of *specie,* arising from the American trade"; the other believed that commercial sanctions in the United States would rouse a half million English merchants and manufacturers to urge their government to make concessions.[98]

At the same time Democrats hedged a bit because of the possibility that the treaty obtained might be advantageous. Whatever success Jay had, they held, would come as a result not of his own or Federalist methods, but of French victories or British fear of American economic reprisals.[99] Some Federalists saw any Republican hint of favorable negotiations as part of a deep-laid plot. Bache's *Aurora* could create false expectations prior to publication of the treaty by suggesting the United States had obtained all it had requested. In that way, indication of any shortcomings in the instrument when printed would engender dissatisfaction and a feeling that America had received nothing.[100] No one in America knew the contents of the treaty prior to its actual arrival in March, 1795, and for some time thereafter only Washington and the State Department were in possession of the details. Jay, who had recently been elected governor of New York, was given a reception on his return to Manhattan, but Democratic papers suspected celebration might be premature. Quite evidently, his mission had failed in ending maritime spoilations, for British *"licensed sea robbers"* still took American ships.[101]

As soon as it was learned that a copy of the agreement had reached Philadelphia there were immediate demands for its publication. "Open covenants, openly arrived at" was an expression yet to be coined, but it epitomized the stand of several Republican editors. If ratified, the treaty would be the law of the land; it therefore affected all the people, and to keep its terms secret showed contempt for public opinion.[102] Had the silence been an election trick to aid Jay's gubernatorial chances, or were "Anglomen" trying to "surprize the Senate into a ratification?" [103] Yet even after the Senate was called in special session, the document was not published, and all debate on it was behind closed doors.

Hard-pressed Federalists showed that this procedure had been followed in the case of treaties with the Indians (which had not been made public until ratified and mutually signed), that it permitted elimination of undesirable clauses without arousing popular feeling, and protected the Senate from being swayed by local opinion in Philadelphia.[104] Democrats were unconvinced. To them the only imaginable reason for secrecy was that the treaty was contrary to the popular interest. A pity it could not be kept secret *after* ratification as well; if public opinion were to be flouted, the expression of contempt for it should be as strong as possible.[105] True, the Constitution gave the President and Senate authority to make treaties. But it communicated "no power to hatch these things in darkness. This practice is borrowed *FROM KINGS* and their MINISTERS, and seems to imply a disposition to assimilate our government, if not in theory, at least in practice, to monarchy." The agents of the people should act in conformity to the wishes of their employers; if the senatorial "conclave" in "the secret lodge at Philadelphia" could change Americans' circumstances without consulting popular opinion, then that body, not the people, was sovereign.[106]

Even before the Senate met, long letters in Republican papers began denouncing the treaty. Federalists jeered at the *"second sight"* of the writers,[107] but complaints against the treaty attracted widespread attention. Early in February Republican writers insisted England would not turn over the frontier forts for another two years. "Montgomery" declared it poor business to enter into any agreement "with the satellites of George the third (and I hope the last)," for "POWER, NOT JUSTICE, is the only rule of their conduct." The *Jersey Chronicle* accused Jay of contemptuously exceeding his instructions; he had gone far beyond the questions of restitution for British seizures and of surrender of the Western posts.[108]

Most influential of the pre-ratification attacks were those of "Franklin" in the *Independent Gazetteer*. His letters, running from March until June, were reprinted the country over.[109] Immediately after the treaty's arrival, "Franklin" (probably Alexander J. Dallas) urged citizens to analyze it before it became part of the law of the land, for afterward would be too late.

British newspapers and private letters received from abroad, "Franklin" continued, had divulged the leading points of the treaty. It was safe to assume that its best features (which would be circulated to gain acceptance for the entire document) were already well known. Yet from those portions that had been revealed, no one would ever guess Jay had been sent to negotiate a redress of wrongs. The Western posts would not be turned over for eighteen months, and the spoilations upon American commerce were to be righted by the very men who had sanctioned them and shared in the spoils. In reality, Americans gained nothing by compensatory trading privileges in the West Indies, for merchants there had already petitioned Dundas that American produce was "essential to their existence." There was no guarantee that England's promise respecting the posts would be worth any more eighteen months hence than it had been in 1783, particularly if she were then no longer fighting France. The prescribed mode of presenting American merchants' claims made it impossible to collect any damages, and infractions of the law of nations respecting neutrality were to be settled by a commission two years after the war was over! Denmark and Sweden did not cringingly offer to have *their* differences arising from a war settled *after that war's completion*. Instead, they won £30,000 and a commerce free from interference, while Americans still endured insults and piracies.[110]

The more one considered the treaty, the more dangerous it appeared. Washington's appointment of an envoy just when Congress was considering measures of securing redress excited suspicion; so also did the excessive secrecy surrounding the entire negotiation. Word was that in Great Britain, where the treaty was fully known, there was rejoicing. Since some nation must lose, how could America also be the gainer?[111] The people were grossly deceived in this compact, which obviously conflicted with America's earlier pledge to guarantee the integrity of the French West Indies. With a single stroke of the pen the United States had insulted the nation that was fighting its battles and had shown her the worthlessness of its professions.[112]

When he went to England, Jay had not been empowered (as Washington's message to the Senate showed) to obtain a commercial agreement. Yet though the administration had evaded Genêt's every attempt for a commercial agreement with France, that was exactly what Jay had made with Britain— and no one could contend Americans had obtained "national satisfaction" for the outrages on their commerce. Jay *should* boast of getting the posts, even after eighteen months; for *his* part, he had given them up long ago. Now the United States conspired with tyrants against France. Like people, nations were known by the company they kept; this association with England boded no good.[113]

Great Britain's record of extreme rancor toward America showed that she must have condescended to treat with the

United States only because of French victories, her own necessity, or the expectation of obtaining great advantages. Since her own subjects acknowledged the dependence of the British West Indies upon America, England granted no benefits that could not have been wrested from her through commercial restrictions. Washington had urged Jay's diplomatic appointment on the ground that he would be fresh from the United States, would have knowledge of the popular temper, and would be ready to vindicate American rights. But the American people overwhelmingly approved the French Revolution, while the treaty would replace France with Great Britain as America's most favored nation. It was an integral part of the vast British plot to exterminate freedom from the face of the earth.[114] Certainly the treaty did nothing to help American trade. Robberies and insults had actually increased—so rapidly that soon Americans would have "nothing left for Britons to steal nor no national principle for them to dishonor." Americans had been the dupes of British artifice and perfidy and now stood on the brink of disater:

> Let not a blind devotion to men [such as Washington] plunge you into an abyss of misery! . . . Remember that nations once free like yourselves, have lost their liberty by supineness, and let it not be said of you, that you had energy enough to purchase Freedom, but wanted vigor to preserve it.[115]

The English had defiantly built a dockyard in Norfolk, Virginia, and had permitted no one to enter; they had aided the savages against General Wayne. Yet, Americans talked of a treaty with these "monsters." American faith, like that of Carthage, would soon become proverbial—while the administration continued to "bend the knee to the Caligula of Great Britain!" [116] Claims against England seemed to have been swallowed up in a treaty of friendship and trade agreements, still secret months after its arrival at the capital. The treaty obviously sacrificed France to England, provided no indemnity nor protection to American merchants, and afforded Britain an advantageous position in the United States which would later enable her to reconquer.[117]

"Franklin" was the most potent of the early voices inveigh-
ing against the treaty, but he was not alone. Most of the
others, however, appeared to reiterate his arguments. "An
American" urged that if England could stop American trade
with France she had an equal right to forbid it with any other
country. Non-importation, or Dayton's plan for sequestration,
would have proved a much more potent negotiator than Jay.
For the past two years, England's principal resources had been
in American trade, but she had given way to the insistence of
the Swedes and the Danes on *their* rights as neutrals.[118]

"*A Loser of Three Brigs, with their Cargoes*" suspected
the British must be snickering at a nation so destitute of political talent that it had to take a lawyer, make him Chief Justice,
send him to England as an envoy, and then (while he was still
absent and holding two offices) elect him governor of New
York! Worse yet, his diplomatic efforts had merely obtained a
promise that the English lower tribunals would be open for
American complaints. After being robbed of nearly seven hundred sail by the British, Americans would still be "at the
mercy of their infamous courts"; [119] they had the rare privilege "of appealing to our robbers for redress." Some citizens
may have been cozened by English gold and influence, but unless the treaty were materially in America's favor and in no
way harmed France it should not be ratified. To date, all the
evidence indicated that these conditions were far from being
met.[120]

The *Aurora*'s "Sidney" began a series very much like that
of "Franklin." Americans must shudder at the prospect of
such close association with the nation from which they had so
lately separated. If they made any commercial treaty, it should
be with France, rather than England. France had made a gal-
lant struggle for liberty, her long-term prospects were extremely bright, her government was similar to that of the
United States, and Americans owed her a tremendous debt of
gratitude.[121] In the view of the *Jersey Chronicle* (begun by
Freneau in 1795) every phase of Britain's "Transatlantic
Jurisdiction in America" demonstrated her "barefaced and

197

impudent" violations of international law and her scheme to incite France against America.[122] Obviously, the treaty should be emphatically rejected by the Senate.

Rejected, however, the instrument was not. The protests of "Franklin" and "Sidney" were still being reprinted when the Senate, by the narrowest of margins, approved the document, only suspending one objectionable article and recommending further negotiation on impressment. This action was announced by the *Aurora:*

> The Treaty of Amity and Commerce (as it is called) between the *court* of Great Britain and the executive of the United States was ratified on Wednesday last. This imp of darkness, illegitimately begotten, commanded but the bare constitutional number required for ratification. Of its hostility to our commerce, to the interests of republicanism, and to the great interests of our country, the people will be fully able to judge, when the ratifications shall have been exchanged and it becomes the supreme law of the land, and not an hour sooner.[123]

Thanks largely to its own efforts, the *Aurora* was soon able to prove itself a poor prophet in the matter of public knowledge of the treaty. The Senate had resolved to keep the text secret, but Senator Stevens Thomson Mason of Virginia showed a copy to Bache, who hurriedly published an abstract in the *Aurora*.[124] Mason could then claim he had read the summary and, because of a few inaccuracies, had given his copy to the Republican editor "to correct false impressions." The complete treaty, together with Mason's note, was published on July 1 in a pamphlet which enjoyed phenomenal sales.[125]

Federalists heaped contumely upon Mason for his disclosure. Democrats retorted that Washington had already determined to make the details public and that Federalist Senator Rufus King had previously shown his copy to George Hammond, minister of Great Britain![126] The recriminations and countercharges are immaterial except as examples of propaganda; Bache's publication had made such questions academic.

The lid was off—off this instance of hated senatorial secrecy and also off Democratic resentment. All other matters seemed forgotten, and some citizens who had been inclined to support the administration were swayed by the fury of Republican wrath or by dissatisfaction with the treaty itself. As soon as the Senate's vote became known, statistics were advanced to show that the population of the states whose representatives had unanimously favored the document was 1,779,432, while that of states whose representatives had opposed it was 1,141,361. In reality, therefore, the treaty had received approval of senators from only a bare majority, instead of two-thirds, of the population.[127] Printed references to the "honorable ten" who had opposed ratification became commonplace, and the other senators were said to be returning homeward from Philadelphia with hangdog looks and a furtive air.[128]

For weeks the atmosphere was electric. European travelers found one half the American citizenry almost at the throats of the other half; there seemed countless "Frenchmen" and "Englishmen" to be seen, but rarely an American.[129] One of the most typical and popular of the inflammatory items in the Democratic press originated in the columns of Colonel Eleazer Oswald's *Independent Gazetteer:*

> Died—the 24th day of June last, of a hectic complaint, which she bore with Christian fortitude and resignation, in the nineteenth year of her existence, Mrs. LIBERTY, the ci-devant consort of America. Her tragical exit is generally imputed to a consumptive habit of body, and many are of the opinion that quack Murray's [the British admiral noted for his depredations] empiricism accelerated her death.
>
> Though some may doubt the authenticity of this intelligence, yet she has certainly relapsed into a state of non entity. In the extremity of her paroxysms, she detached J—n J. esq. to the court of Great Britain, to supplicate his most gracious majesty to alleviate her misery, and his gracious majesty, it is thought, has administered a dose of subtile poison to quiet this turbulent jade, that has so often thwarted his ambition.
>
> She is to be publicly interred this day—and aristocrats will fire a FEU DE JOIE over her grave. . . . At this fatal, this awful interment, subjects of America, mourn. Our Independence is not even nominal, and it is easy to presage our return to our former

station in the scale of political depression. We have incurred the vengeance of France and the bitterness of vassalage seems not our ultimate curse; bloodshed may perhaps render our chains more horrible. Our political fears are not visionary, and our only hope is now in heaven. Our sun which rose with awful splendor has sunk in pristine darkness. Farewell thou radiant goddess that once inspired our souls! may we weep on thy tomb till our abject forms are changed to marble.[130]

Where news of the treaty's terms was known, the Fourth of July was observed as a day of sorrow or as an occasion to deride and execrate Jay. To the customary toasts drunk for the holiday were added a number berating him or making obvious puns upon his name. Many of these were reprinted to foster Republican enthusiasm and to demonstrate how universal and deep was resentment against the treaty. One of the most popular "volunteer" toasts was "A perpetual harvest to America; but clip't wings, lame legs, the pip, and an empty crop to all Jays." [131] One newspaper compiled a selection of twenty-five such toasts, and another noted that the glasses drained from one end of the nation to the other seemed to be accompanied by a single "sentiment of the most pointed disapprobation." [132]

In Philadelphia the *Independent Gazetteer* noted that the solemnity of the day and dejection on citizens' faces made the occasion seem more like a recognition of the interment, rather than the birth, of freedom. That evening disclosed, however, that the quiet had been ominous rather than funereal. A day or so before, only the presence of the military had prevented a riotous attack upon a British ship in port.[133] Now the city's ship carpenters paraded through the streets bearing a lighted transparency of John Jay. The life-size figure carried in its right hand a pair of scales, with *"British gold"* greatly outweighing *"American Liberty and Independence"*; in its left hand a copy of the treaty was extended to a grinning group of senators, and out of the image's mouth came the words: *"Come up to my price and I will sell you my country."* Almost silently the procession moved along to the suburb of Kensington, where the display was burned amid the huzzas of the crowd. A Captain Morrell and his light horse, called earlier to guard against disorder, chose this moment to attempt dispersing the assemblage. The troops were stoned and forced to flee, one horseman lost his sword (later advertised and sold for four cents), and next day the spot was marked by a wooden sign: "Morrell's Defeat—Jay Burned, July 4, 1795." [134] A few weeks later a copy of the treaty was publicly burned before the residence of British minister Hammond.[135]

Such activities were only the buffoonery preceding and encouraging serious business. The treaty was not yet in force; perhaps, even if England accepted it with the twelfth article deleted, Washington could be dissuaded from signing the instrument—or, later, the House might be influenced to refuse the funds needed to carry the compact into effect.[136] Real hope in getting the President to withhold his signature lay in convincing him that the majority of Americans opposed the agreement, and this the Democrats speedily attempted to do.

Boston led the way. Bache's pamphlet had reached that city on July 7, and two days later the treaty text began to appear in the *Independent Chronicle*. On the tenth a meeting of over 1,500 citizens in Faneuil Hall unanimously voted condemnation of the pact and appointed a committee to draft an address to the Chief Executive. A set of twenty resolutions opposing the instrument was drawn up, adopted July 13, and sent by express to Philadephia, with a prayer from the *Chronicle* that they might "have the desired effect." [137]

Thanks in large part to the efforts of the Republican press, word of the Boston resolutions spread over the country. Most telling were the charges that the treaty was not in any sense truly reciprocal, that it surrendered American rights under international law and all benefits of neutrality, that it provided no indemnity for Britain's retention of the Western posts or for confiscated slaves, that there was no assurance of compensation for British spoilations, and that acceptance of these conditions would subject Americans to similar impositions from other countries.[138] Federalists protested that the meeting had acted in haste, that it had not studied the treaty or even read it in the gathering, and that the resolutions had been rushed through.[139]

The Boston meeting, however, served as an example to other communities, for a rash of similar meetings and petitions resulted. There had been rumors in New York of a long petition circulated in Philadelphia against the treaty,[140] but word of the actual resolutions from Boston produced action, and a meeting was held on July 18. This tempestuous affair, at which Hamilton was purportedly stoned when he attempted to address the crowd, selected a committee that two days later catalogued twenty-eight reasons for rejecting Jay's effort.[141] Since New York had long been considered a stronghold of "British influence," [142] this protest was in some respects even more effective than the earlier one at Boston. Accounts of these meetings were succeeded by reports of those in Portsmouth, Trenton, Philadelphia, Charleston, Augusta, and other communities; a gigantic petition from New Jersey to the President was widely reprinted, along with resolutions from some of the cities.[143]

In all this, the newspapers had a vital part. Their writers exhorted citizens to express to the Chief Executive their disapproval of "Sir John Jay," their columns carried notices of meetings at which the people's "*all*" was said to be at stake, and some editors labored to secure signatures for the petitions.[144] When the few resolutions (such as those from Flemington, New Jersey, or the New York Chamber of Commerce) approving the treaty appeared, the Republican press discounted or pilloried them. Thus Jeffersonian writers could argue that the leader of the Flemington meeting was an ex-Tory, that the secretary was a young publicity-seeker, and that the opinions expressed were definitely contrary to the prevailing sentiment in New Jersey.[145] Articles lauding ratification were "a species of sleeping drops"; formation of groups favoring the treaty was denounced as efforts by the moneyed interests to palm themselves off as bespeaking the popular will.[146]

Some papers also hoped either to cajole or force Washington into refusing to sign the hated pact. Surely his wisdom and integrity would let him see the evil in the treaty—"thank heaven we have a Washington left to check the growth of British influence." [147] He had not approved the Senate's secrecy and certainly had never ordered Jay to surrender American rights. The envoy, as one rhymster put it, might be a "dupe" whose deeds patriots abhorred, "But cease my Muse —I will not yet despair/Till WASHINGTON, shall his great mind declare." [148]

If the Chief Executive could not be coaxed with pleas or with honey, there were always threats. Mildest of these, so mild that there was no hint of force, were the items or letters that showed how overwhelming was the popular feeling against the treaty. "Disapprobation," said one propagandist, "appears every day to increase . . . [and] in the southern states especially there seems to be but one sentiment concerning it, that of disgust." [149] Citizens of Delaware were drolly said to be very much divided on the question; some wanted to burn Jay and the twenty approving senators in effigy, while the rest favored doing it in person. [150] Presidential approval, insisted other writers, would forment serious domestic discontent, and might precipitate war with France. [151] Yet after seven weeks, notwithstanding all warnings, Washington reluctantly put his name to the document—and over the country the sound and fury seemed redoubled.

In all truth, the treaty had a plethora of defects, as Democratic editors had pointed out. Article after article was placed under the microscope of intensive examination, and almost none escaped extreme criticism. [152] The first section permitted the unconditional return to the United States of all persons proscribed during the Revolution, even though state legislatures had already readmitted all those whom they thought it wise to admit. Another article expressly permitted aliens to hold land in any state, while a third gave the British a virtual monopoly of the fur trade and trade with the Indians, thus opening the way for extensive smuggling. The sixth article called for a commission to fix American debts due English merchants (saying nothing about British infringements) ; such a tribunal was unconstitutional, its majority might be British, and it could tax the United States at pleasure. This last provision metamorphosed restitution for English robberies into an indemnification to British merchants for debts previous to the war. If the debts were just, insisted critics, judgments should be given against individual debtors instead of making the government responsible.[153]

Under the seventh article a commission similar to the one for debts was to determine the damages to be paid by England for her naval depredations. This arrangement made restitution to Americans uncertain and expensive to obtain, while the government was bound to make compensation to Englishmen, on certain fixed principles, for all property taken within American waters or by privateers fitted out in American ports. Articles 23, 24, and 25 tended to make a common cause between the United States and England to distress America's allies the French.[154]

Some articles were especially censured. The ninth (allowing Britons to hold lands in the United States on equal terms with American citizens) would, it was feared, enable English noblemen—or the ministry itself—to control large areas and to introduce a feudal system into America, on the theory that "it is much easier to PURCHASE than to CONQUER." [155] This might well pave the way for the revival of vast claims in several states by heirs of the old proprietors. Refusing aliens the right to hold land had been a consistent policy of Britain; by this treaty she surrendered it only in name while inducing Americans to give it up in actuality.[156]

"Decius" also wrote that the treaty made no pretense of being a contract between equals, for Articles 5 and 14 let British subjects come to America and reside, whereas Americans could go only to British lands in Europe. The fifteenth provision shackled the American government in regulating commerce—a power vested by the Constitution in Congress alone. More iniquitous yet was the seventeenth, which abandoned the principle that "free ships make free goods" and sanctioned British stopping and searching of American vessels on suspicion. The tenth article, prohibiting sequestration of the contracting nations' property, was entirely an English idea. Americans had no property in England, and this clause forfeited their rights on possible retaliation within the limits of international law.[157]

Primary target for Republican invective was the twelfth article, so objectionable that even the Senate had refused to accept it. It prohibited American vessels from carrying to Europe any coffee, cocoa, sugar, molasses, or cotton. Apparently, Jay had been unaware of growing cotton shipments from the South, but Jeffersonians were quick to remind him. The twelfth article would have completely destroyed the cotton market abroad: "I cannot conceive how Mr. Jay could have consented to such an article, the absurdity of it would strike the attention of a school boy." [158] The items specified were worse than contraband, for American ships could not transport them even in peacetime. In return for this surrender Americans could send ships of seventy tons burden to the British West Indies, carrying such items as Britain permitted and returning with goods similar to those her ships could bring here. This "privilege" was so hedged about with restrictions it was of little consequence,[159] and it contrasted poorly with the complete opening of *French* West Indian possessions. Seventy-ton ships were inadequate for transporting lumber to the islands, and so that trade also would be destroyed by the treaty.[160] Though rejected by the Senate, this article was still adduced as evidence of Jay's perfidy. Accompanying it was the thirteenth provision of the treaty, stating that American merchantmen could carry items from the British East Indies only to the United States. This would outlaw the circuitous voyages that constituted seven-eighths of the India trade and force Americans to export specie to pay for oriental goods.[161] If these goods had to be unloaded in the United States before reshipment, it might be that British warehouses would spring up in American ports; ironic indeed would it be if the "respectable class of AMERICAN NEGOTIATORS" were to lose their business to those "acting under the patronage of LLOYD'S COFFEE HOUSE." No wonder Pitt could tell Commons he was not ashamed of this treaty! [162]

"JURICOLA" and other writers insisted the pact was unconstitutional. Rights of aliens to hold land were a matter within the province of the state governments, Jay had been empowered to treat only for an "adjustment of our complaints," and the commercial clauses and appropriations required the consent of the House before they could be legal.[163] Even commercially, the treaty was solely calculated to injure American carrying trade, of which England was intensely jealous, and to foster which had been a major purpose for creating the Constitution. "By this treaty we have surrendered every commercial right as a sovereign nation," declaimed one irate writer.[164] It gave British ships advantages in American ports that American vessels did not enjoy in British ports, and provision of a £3,000 bond was entirely inadequate insurance against English seizures when the value of American cargoes ranged from double to quadruple that amount.[165] "A Philadelphia Merchant" compiled a "balance sheet" for the consideration of "the Hon. The Chamber of Commerce of New-York," with "debits" and "credits" contrasting the actual state of American trade currently with conditions as they would be under the treaty. He was able to list seventeen respects in which American commerce would be seriously hurt.[166]

As "Franklin" had hinted earlier, there was no excuse for England's eighteen-month delay in turning over the Western posts—twelve years after her original pledge to do so. Moreover, if her word on this point had been broken before, Americans had no assurance it would not be broken again.[167] Almost as reprehensible were the treaty's omissions; the great objectives of Jay's mission were as far from realization as ever. No indemnities were specified for British retention of the posts, inciting Indian raids, or encouraging Algerine depredations. Impressments and the carrying off of Negro slaves were not even mentioned. Commerce still had no protection against a paper blockade.[168] All the so-called advantages derived from the pact were only those to which Americans were entitled anyway.[169]

England's designs had not changed since 1775, except that she was now using covenants rather than troops to gain her ends.[170] America had first gained world renown by resisting British wrongs, and now she was officially endorsing them![171] Almost every line in the ratified document showed British influence. And how else could a London paper predict almost the exact Senate vote on the treaty almost two months in advance?[172] There were other sorts of influence than bribery, as was seen when the British warships *Africa* and *Thisbe* visited Boston harbor, no doubt *"Commissioned by our good ally KING GEORGE, kindly to keep watch for us."* [173]

Since the treaty was patently aimed at harming France, Republican editors were positive that the Gallic Republic would take umbrage at the outcome of Jay's mission. Unquestionably, Americans' obsequiousness made them despicable in her eyes; the alliance of 1778 had not allowed the French to take British property out of American ships, yet the British had been given express permission to remove French property. Americans' specific acquiescence in the stopping of France-bound provision ships was the last word in ingratitude, for it made them an accessory to the scheme to starve that nation.[174] An agreement that altered conditions favorably for Great Britain during a war in progress must certainly infuriate her adversaries. Adet had been sent to America to prevent such a treaty; now that he had failed, an armed conflict with France was probable.[175]

Democrats' disappointment was intensified by the changed status of the American minister to Paris. A year before, Jeffersonians had vigorously applauded the selection of James Monroe to succeed Gouverneur Morris and were amused by the rapidity with which Federalists abandoned the idea of Presidential infallibility when appointments were made that they disliked.[176] As a known friend of France, Monroe was expected to cement good relations there, and the Republican press had contrasted his "dignified" and "manly" behavior toward the National Convention with the "pusillanimity" of Jay in London.[177]

Monroe had been well received in Paris, despite some Gallic suspicion concerning Jay's mission to England. As instructed, he had assured the French government (with which he had been forbidden to draft a trade treaty) that Jay's object was not to make a commercial agreement, but only to gain restitution for damages and possession of the Western posts. Now the treaty made Monroe seem either dishonest or the dupe of his own government; France's attitude had perceptibly stiffened, and Monroe's own situation was clearly uncomfortable. Republican editors felt he had been betrayed by the administration and used as an unwitting mask of smiling friendship to cloak American duplicity.[178]

A Pennsylvania writer summed up America's diplomatic predicament: Great Britain's disposition toward the United States was consistently hostile; even if it were possible to convert this into an attitude of sincere friendship, the treaty was *"too high a price to pay for such a chance."* Rejection of the covenant could not be construed as a war-like act, notwithstanding Federalist cries; if England really wished war, she would have no difficulty finding pretexts. On the other hand, ratification was bound to offend France. If the United States were to be forced to fight either England or France, engaging the former would be more advantageous politically and economically and more in line with popular sentiment. At worst, the powerful French army would help the United States, whereas if the war were with France, neither British affection nor aid could be truly relied upon.[179]

Basically, then, arguments against Jay's Treaty followed five major lines: (1) distrust of England and opposition to any compact with her; (2) criticism of the terms of the treaty itself; (3) charges of unconstitutionality in the negotiation, content, and ratification of the instrument; (4) insistence that acceptance would produce retaliation from France; and (5) proof that the popular will overwhelmingly opposed it. Even after Washington had signed the treaty, Jeffersonian newspapers continued to encourage public expressions of opposition and printed countless items demonstrating widespread disgust. When Federalists protested at the first calls for resolutions and petitions, Republicans sneered that doubtless the "monarchists" would also suppress town meetings if they could. *Vox populi* was usually *Vox Dei,* and if the press were forbidden to canvass national feeling on the issue Americans might as well once again become British subjects.[180]

Yet this "canvassing" was no scientifically impartial public opinion poll, nor did Democratic editors intend that it should be. Every effort was made in their columns to stimulate and publicize expressions of views inimical to the treaty. The letters, resolutions, and comments denouncing the pact undoubtedly greatly outnumbered those supporting it, but in Jeffersonian gazettes the disproportion was staggering. Only old Tories and aristocratic Anglomaniacs, it was held, favored the measure, and the clinching argument against the treaty was one look at the faction that favored it.[181]

Articles that defended the treaty were rare indeed, and any pro-treaty argument was held up to scorn. Of sixty New York merchants advocating the covenant, only eighteen were said to have fought with the American forces during the Revolution; the others were recent immigrants or had been lukewarm at best toward independence.[182] Contrasted with the 1,500 who attended Boston's town meeting to condemn the treaty, only 36 out of 150 members of that city's Chamber of Commerce gathered to approve the endorsing resolutions drawn by the organization's "man midwife," Stephen Higginson.[183] "*A Yeoman of the State of Delaware*" was nauseated by the commendatory letter sent Washington by sundry Philadelphia merchants after his signing; either approval or disapproval was meaningless *following* the act. Merchants were but drones living on the fruits of others' industry, anyway, although "*A Yeoman . . .*" sarcastically applauded their "sublime forebearance" in refraining from expressing their opinion prior to the President's decision.[184] Kentucky's Senator Humphrey Marshall, who had voted for the treaty, was only what citizens of that state deserved, for they knew when they elected him "that he possessed a soul incapable of good, and sentiments opposed to every real friend to her interest.[185] Hamilton's "Camillus" letters were derided as lengthy enough "to exhaust the patience of even a pensioner of Britain." [186]

Washington had signed, but still the argument raged. Westerners could laugh at the storm, writing Easterners that the "Whiskey Boys" could quell any insurrection the treaty might stir up; they would "be very happy to repay the visit you made them last season." [187] But interest on the frontier was also high. Kentucky Masons published resolutions attacking the treaty, especially the privileges given British traders, permission to navigate American territorial waters, and the lack of compensation for Indian outrages and retention of the posts.[188] Other frontiersmen found the instrument shameful: Americans had cowered when they should have threatened, and what cause was there for satisfaction that "his majesty *consents*" to conduct himself according to the law of nations? The United States had ceded England "immunities and advantages which no one nation upon earth has a right to demand of another." One day, it was predicted, America would raise her eyelids to see only "the wrecks of our fallen happiness and liberty." [189]

Never since the Revolution had feeling about a political issue been more intense. When only Bache's abstract of the treaty was known, the New York *Argus* sarcastically printed a "petition" to Jay. The "petitioners" asserted their willingness to give up the East India carrying trade, commerce with the West Indies (save for seventy-ton ships), £5,000,000 for prizes taken by French privateers in American waters or fitted out in American ports; to have one-third of American territory and £3,000,000 for debts decided by chance; to be hanged as pirates if they served any nation against Great Britain; to forego any idea of sequestration; and to acquiesce in the detention of American ships and the confiscation of provision cargoes. They assumed, however, at least *one* treaty provision must be "favorable to America," and they requested Jay to divulge it, now that the "remainder" of the pact had been made public.[190] "Benevolus," in New Hampshire, felt the whole matter a deep-laid scheme "to detect the depths of the designs" which the British ministry had upon the United States. Why should Americans treat with any nation about commerce? Trade flourished best when unshackled, and if it were left to itself "our ports would soon be full of foreign vessels." Jay had been sent to demand satisfaction but returned with a treaty; this was "like asking for a fish, and obtaining a serpent." [191]

Some derided the complexity of the instrument. All one needed to know to understand it were nine different codes of law or procedure, plus the occult sciences and three years of English bookkeeping. When a "speculator in certificates" told Pennsylvanians that common people could not comprehend diplomatic terminology, the retort was that truth and honesty should be intelligible even to rustics.[192] Jay could have done infinitely better; Britain's need for American produce and the threat of the Armed Neutrality would have achieved concessions had he shown firmness. Pitt's uncle, according to reports, had earlier avowed that England was ready to accede to any reasonable American demands. As it was, friends of the United States in London considered the covenant disgraceful and its rejection by the Senate, certain.[193] Thomas Pinckney, former minister to London, had been on the verge of obtaining "a very advantageous treaty" before Jay appeared on the scene.[194]

In late July the French-language *New York Gazette Française* could comment that discussion of the treaty was already exciting too much unrest,[195] but for Republican editors there could be no such thing. The mass of critical articles appeared endless. "Hancock," "Valerius," and "Belisarius," all in the *Aurora,* commenced a direct attack upon Washington himself. Infuriated by the realization that the treaty was signed and that the President's influence (proved so potent against Genêt, the Whiskey Rebellion, and the Democratic Societies) would be used in its favor, these three writers discarded all restraint. The letters of each comprised a series, and were uniformly reprinted by such influential organs as the *Jersey Chronicle, Greenleaf's New York Journal,* the *Independent Chronicle,* and the New York *Argus.*[196] "Hancock" protested against the "superciliousness and arrogance" of the administration. Apparently Washington considered the populace as Burke's "swinish multitude," incapable of judging its own interests. He fancied himself "the *grand lama* of this country," to be approached only with superstitious reverence. When he wrote petitioners in Philadelphia that the reasoning advanced in his reply to the Boston resolutions was also applicable in their case, the tone of his message sounded more as if it came from Potsdam rather than Philadelphia.[197] "Belisarius" thought Washington's signature on the treaty proved him to be advancing "the greatest good of the least number possessing the greatest wealth" and ordered him to stop mouthing "further anathemas at the expressions of popular opinion." A score of evils, which he enumerated, could be attributed to the President's administration.[198]

Of the trio, "Valerius" was perhaps most splenetic. Washington's stand that war with England would mean ruin was deliberately spurious; the treaty would be more certainly harmful. So great was England's need for American food and supplies that she would be impotent without them, asserted this editorial strategist. He prated of Washington's "dark schemes of ambition," and claimed to live in fear of usurpation.[199]

Such tactics may have disgusted those who venerated the Chief Executive, but these were not the only voices so raised. "Portius" thought an accurate history of the administration and its uniform supporters would be incalculably enlightening and claimed Washington had retired to private life at the end of the war simply because no public office was great enough to satisfy his longings. In his heart he had opposed American independence.[200] "Sydney," writing for the *Independent Chronicle* that the Jay Treaty "originated in submission, progressed in *secrecy*, and is at last established by *fear*," added his voice to the opposition, as did "Marcus" in the Norfolk *American Gazette*.[201] "ATTICUS," in the *Independent Gazetteer*, contended the President's Revolutionary services were being decked in all their charms to seduce people from the question of his current motives.[202] The *Delaware Gazette*'s "Z." strenuously objected to Washington's statement that public officials should not substitute the views of others for their own; this would deny the entire concept of representation.[203] And the *Aurora*, center of this abuse, carried letters by "Tully" on deception connected with the treaty and by "Pittachus," who argued that Washington's associates in office were in themselves enough to damn him.[204] Other penmen pilloried the President's delay and vacillation in signing the compact, which they characterized as "this child of his dotage."[205] By November "Pittachus" was calling for impeachment, and "A Calm Observer" was making open charges of dishonesty.[206]

Some Democrats believed the treaty was not Jay's so much as it was Hamilton's. He had probably prepared a draft of the monstrous thing before the envoy ever went to England; Jay's letters to Lord Grenville clearly showed Hamilton's influence.[207] Hamilton's letters as "Camillus," which spiritedly defended the treaty in detail, confirmed these suspicions in the minds of many. Essentially, "Camillus" urged, the slaves carried off by British troops during the Revolution were property, just as any other seized by the enemy in wartime, and for the British to return them to their masters after promising them freedom would be evil. Respecting debts due Englishmen, America had actually violated the Treaty of 1783 first. Jay's effort had given Americans the posts and had provided means for obtaining compensation for maritime spoilations; it thus accomplished two out of three major American objectives. Indemnification for the slaves (least important of the three points) could therefore be given up without loss of honor.[208]

In rebuttal, Republicans quickly asserted the peace treaty

clearly intended the slaves to be left behind, and thus Britain had first violated its terms. In the House Madison contended that until Jay's mission, England had openly recognized the justice of American demands.[209] "Brutus" cited figures on fur shipments to show the preserve guaranteed the Hudson's Bay Company was far from being without value as "Camillus" had implied.[210] Others ridiculed the verbosity of "Mr. Hamilton's last effort"; his defense of Jay's Treaty must have been paid for handsomely. Since he was a learned man who knew various kinds of law and all languages except French, "stupid and illiterate Americans" were sardonically warned to quit opposing "The Solomon of the age." One writer indicated that, if the "Camillus" articles contained the same information Hamilton had desired to present to the New York town meeting, his inability to speak there was small loss.[211]

The former Secretary's pen was a potent one, however, and Democratic editors feared it while affecting merriment. Some of their replies, therefore, were serious. One of the best was a series by "Cinna," who capitalized on Jefferson's statement that treaties were superior to state or ordinary Federal laws. The New York trespass act, which Hamilton had called the first breach of the Treaty of 1783, had been passed before that treaty was signed. Since conflicting state legislation was automatically nullified by a treaty, the odium of original violation must still fall on England.[212]

Despite these attempts to find Hamilton responsible for the treaty, Jay remained the favorite whipping-boy of the opposition press. The ferocity, variety, and volume of the attacks upon him defies description. Some writers questioned his ability; others were certain that, however overrated his talents may have been, "he is not so deficient as to have made or signed such a treaty without some [personal] consideration."[213]

At the Philadelphia town meeting on July 10, Congressman Blair McClenachan had said every good citizen would "kick the damned treaty to hell." Federalists scoffed at this almost incoherent intemperance,[214] but the emotion (if one read

Democratic papers) seemed almost universal—except that most people felt the same treatment should be accorded the envoy also. British gold and a treaty were said to comprise the new method for catching Jays. The emissary had become intoxicated on Lord Grenville's wine, or with joy at kissing the Queen's hand, and had forgotten he was an American.[215] If his betrayal of the nation had not been for actual cash, it resulted from his aristocratic predilections or probable interest in Western lands.[216]

In a hundred towns as many fires consumed dummies of the former Chief Justice, and tar and feathers were heatedly recommended for those who opposed burning him in effigy.[217] Some gatherings, while perhaps showing more originality, exceeded the bounds of good taste or even decency. In Rye, New Hampshire, following speeches against the treaty, the people of the parish adjourned to a nearby barnyard,

> where as an effigy of Mr. Jay, they erected a ten-foot RAIL with a pair of Stag's-horns affixed to it, emblematic of his political cuckoldom! They then most copiously saluted the pole with the most *convenient* implements of the yard, after which they stuck it full of pitch-pine knots, set fire to them, and danced round the blaze singing the *Indian war-who[o]p.*[218]

Southern newspapers had heralded the ratification and text of Jay's work with a crude parody of the Yuletide story. A child, named "TREATY of Amity, Commerce and Navigation," was born in Philadelphia on June 24. Readers should note its illustrious parentage and rejoice:

> The Chief Justice being overshadowed by the prolific spirit of his Gracious Majesty, at the Court of St. James, conceived, and wonderful to relate, after about *thirteen months* laborious pregnancy, was happily, by the aid of Senatorial midwifery, delivered of—The long expected embassorial, daplomatic [*sic*], farci-comical Saviour of fifteen FALLEN states![219]

A brash Northern correspondent wrote that Maine residents thought well of the pact, but the Hallowell *Tocsin* quickly retorted that the further east he went "(even to St. Johns and Halifax) the better he will find them [the inhabitants] pleased with the Treaty." [220] *"Jack Mystick"* bluntly asked the public if the treaty were "so advantageous to America, why are the tories of '76 its most zealous advocates?" [221]

Despite Federalist assertions, "treaty fever" was not subsiding. Abhorrence of the document was universal, stated the *Pittsburgh Gazette.* [222] Carolinians demanded that Jay be brought to trial, and in Boston mobs began to terrorize leading Federalists. [223] Richmond hotheads even threatened secession if the treaty "entered into by that damned arch-traitor John Jay and the British tyrant" were put into effect. Virginia was said to be ready for commercial agreements with any state "averse to returning again under the galling yoke of Great Britain." [224] Such talk alarmed the *Delaware Gazette:* "If this detestable instrument is enforced, may we not anticipate the speedy dissolution of the Union?" [225] A Bermudian privateer had been burned in Boston harbor, and news of the treaty was further enraging the people; popular resentment was getting out of hand. [226] But most Republican papers, which had done so much to engender feeling on the subject, boasted that the discontent "appears every day to increase." [227]

Self-styled poets penned lines on the covenant or berated the diplomat responsible for it. A sample or two will indicate both the quality and content of the doggerel:

> Camillus writes—but writes in vain,
>   The treaty is concluded.
> By which the British *all* will gain
>   While *we* are still deluded.
> Sure George the Third will find employ,
>   For one so wise and wary,
> He'll call Camillus *home* with joy
>   And make him *secretary*.

> . . . . . . .

> United to the British crown
>   By treaty firm and binding,
> *Republicans* must knuckle down,
>   For now they're not worth minding.
> Transported with the glorious thought,
>   Each tory then will sing,

'Your freedom's sold—your country's bought!
Huzza for *George our King*.' [228]

A representative verse from "Another New Bow Wow" was
doggerel in truth:

Then J****y J**, a grave dog, was chosen from the kennel;
We took him for a Mastiff—he prov'd to be a Spaniel,
Who never growl'd or barked once, but justice humbly begs sir,
Not getting which, ran home with his tail between his legs, sir,
*Bow* wow wow.[229]

Sometimes these efforts were set to a popular tune in order
that they might be sung in Democratic taverns or beneath
Federalist windows. An example was "Brother Jonathan," to
the air of "Yanky Doodle":

Brother Jonathan, what're you *'bout*
What the nation ails you?
Why with *Treaty* make such *rout!*
'Vow your reason fails, *you*.

CHORUS
Yanky doodle keep it up,
Yanky doodle dandy,
Sure you've had a pow'rful cup
'Lasses mixed with brandy.

You, if *Treaty* is not right
Georgie [Washington] will not sign it;
Til't has teeth it cannot bite
To him then resign it.
Yanky, &c.[230]

Southerners seemed to like "Huzza for Justice Jay," with a
similar chant for a "reply":

A SONG I here present to you,
For which I ask no pay;
We've won the game, I'm told 'tis true
Success to justice Jay.

. . . . . . .

Come fill a bowl, give us a toast,
Then we to Jove will pray,

217

For strength to hold the Western posts
And d—— old justice Jay.

The "answer" followed the same pattern:

A song I here present to you
Or give you back as pay
If game be won the praise is due
To France, not Justice J.

KING W*******N he did send J
To his brother King, Sir
At Grenville's feet to fall and pray
There to disgrace our land, Sir.

The British King is not our friend
Though wishes us to sway;
On British faith we'll not depend,
NO! nor in Justice J.

Then fill a glass, I'll give a toast
And to great Jove will pray,
To keep us firmly on our posts
And guard 'gainst Justice J.[231]

Often the rhymes were coarse, for the age was not solely one of powdered wigs and minuets. One of the more vulgar appeared in the Charleston *South Carolina State* as a

DIALOGUE ON THE TREATY
J—Y

May't please your highness, I John J—Y
Have travell'd all this mighty way,
To inquire if you, good Lord will please,
To suffer me while on my knees,
To shew all others I surpass
In love—by kissing of your——;
As by my 'xtraordinary station,
I represent a certain nation;
I thence conclude, and so may you,
They all would wish to kiss it too;
So please your highness suffer me
To kiss—I wait on bended knee.
[The king refuses, but tells Jay that Grenville may let him; Grenville consents if the United States will swear submission, and Jay swears Americans will pay whatever price is asked.]

GRENVILLE

Jay took the gold, and well content
With getting all for which he went
To Philadelphia bent his way;
Being there arrived, as some folks say,
Strait to the Senate he repairs,
And putting on some pompous airs,
Told of his vast success—then too,
The money from his purse he drew;
At sight of British gold, some few
Indignant view'd, despis'd it too;
But others following natures bent
To worship it on knees they went.
With lavish hand he shares it out,
To those who kneeling round about,
Would swear to obey King George's call,
And give up *COUNTRY, SOUL* and ALL.
Now those who know it to a hair,
Say J— got the biggest share.

CAETERA DESUNT.[232]

Frontiersmen may have lacked time or talent for rhyming, but "The Political CREED of a Western American," copied in several papers, left no doubt as to their sentiments:

I believe that the treaty formed by Jay and the British king is the offspring of a vile aristocratic few who have too long governed in America, and who are enemies to the equality of men, friends to no government but that whose funds they can convert to their private employment.

I do not believe that Hamilton, Jay or King and their minions, are devils incarnate: but I do believe them so filled with pride, and so fattened on the spoils of America, that they abhor every thing which partakes of Democracy, and that they most ardently desire the swinish multitude humbled in dust and ashes.

I believe the period is at hand when the inhabitants of America will cease to admire or approve the conduct of the Federal executive, because they esteem the man who fills the chair of state. . . .

I believe that the political dotage of our good old American chief, has arrived, and that while we record his virtues in letters of gold, we should consign his person to the tender offices due to virtuous age, and transfer him from the chair of state to the chair of domestic ease. . . .

> I do further believe that the period has arrived, when independent Americans ought to mark with infamy, the man who dares trample on the rights of his fellow citizens. . . .[233]

Kentuckians read a "review" of a new play scheduled for the Harrodsburg Theatre. It was the noted burlesque of "Amity, Commerce and Navigation," featuring "Mr. Envoy" and "that much-despised song, 'Give up All for Nothing at All.' " Tickets could be obtained "by producing British gold and coming up to my price." [234] A Virginia punster described a fictitious mob howling for Jay's blood, with threats of what various members would do to him: cooks ready to "*baste* him" or "give him a belly full," a grocer eager to "*pepper* him" and a saddler to "*pummel* him," whores crying "*pox* rot him" and "*Clap* him up," a tobacconist avid to "make him *smoke*" or a gamester to "make his *bones rattle*," and the like. Eventually the vindictive crowd hanged Jay in effigy, following which a poetaster gave his opinion of the treaty "in these coarse but expressive lines:

> I think J——y's treaty is truly a farce,
> Fit only to wipe the national——." [235]

Charleston echoed Chief Justice John Rutledge's statement that the pact had prostituted the dearest rights of freemen and had laid them at the feet of royalty, and in his charge to a Savannah jury a Georgia Supreme Court Justice had labeled the agreement "a pernicious instrument." [236] Banquets were held honoring the "virtuous ten" senators who had opposed ratification.[237] Randolph's belated *Vindication* proclaimed the ex-Secretary's distaste for the document and disclosed that even Washington had been dissatisfied with it.[238] Thus Republicans appealed to resounding names to bolster their contentions.

The agitation boiled endlessly, for Jeffersonian journalists refused to give up the struggle. Bache had witnessed the Boston meeting when he took his pamphlets on the treaty to that city; he returned to Philadelphia to organize a similar one,[239] and this continued to be the attitude of his fellow-editors. If Washington expressed pleasure at a resolution approving his signing, the opposition press vowed he attached more weight to the views of a few hundred stockholders than to the thousands of the "swinish multitude" who had been so presumptuous as to annoy their infallible and omniscient monarch with their gruntings.[240] If this vile instrument was to be "crammed down" the throats of the people, the least the President could do was to furnish his reasons; popular faith in his superior wisdom was not completely boundless.[241]

When John Rutledge publicly joined Charlestonians in excoriating the treaty, horrified Federalists immediately sought to discredit the man so recently nominated by Washington to succeed Jay as Chief Justice. An open letter in the Boston *Columbian Centinel* branded him unfit to sit upon the federal bench because of his opposition to the treaty, and rumors of improper conduct, drunkenness, and mental lapses were circulated by Hamiltonians as reasons for the Senate's refusal to confirm the appointment.[242] Democrats chortled to see the suddenly discovered "insanity" in Washington's nomination, and the Senate's rejection, almost immediately after that body convened in December, marked the first instance of overruling the President in filling a post of any significance. Surely this action directly contravened the Federalist idea of Presidential infallibility, or else Washington had had *"second thoughts,"* and the Chief Executive and Senate were determined to maintain themselves in power.[243] Jefferson thought it tantamount to a Federalist declaration that only treaty advocates and "none but tories hereafter" would be tolerated in governmental posts.[244]

In the midst of all the turmoil news arrived that Thomas Pinckney, formerly minister to London, had concluded a treaty with Spain. Since the latter nation feared trouble with England over the recent Spanish agreement with France, she wanted to secure American neutrality; the treaty was extremely favorable and included the long-sought-for freedom to navigate the Mississippi. Jubilant Republicans pointed out that French influence (thanks to Monroe) had aided Americans in securing this pact and hoped England would be excluded from the rights granted.[245] Pinckney's alleged earlier expression of approbation for Jay's treaty had been questioned by some and viewed charitably by others; after all, for Pinckney to publicly condemn the Chief Justice's work would have been rude.[246] Nevertheless, in many eyes Pinckney was a Federalist who had approved Jay's efforts, and praise of him was somewhat subdued.[247]

Yet the contrast between the two covenants was too great for Democratic propagandists to ignore. On boundaries, definitions of contraband, and restrictions on the rights of search, Pinckney's treaty had advantages that were completely missing from the agreement with England.[248] What sane person could believe that the man whom Jay had superseded made this arrangement with Spain—and in less than two months, after the earlier failure of Jay's extended negotiations to win similar concessions? That Jay's work at London had furthered Pinckney's success was stoutly denied; Hamiltonians were only chagrined that Pinckney had made a good treaty, so unlike their own.[249] Pinckney should have been left in England where he could have done infinitely better than Jay. If still another argument were needed against the latter's treaty, it was supplied with the suggestion that any extension to Britain of Americans' newly won rights to navigate the Mississippi might conflict with Pinckney's compact.[250]

One Pennsylvanian professed to see the British agreement as a divine chastisement for America's love of English gold and her idolatry of Washington and feared lest we become a lost nation similar to the Jews.[251] Others, however, were determined to avert this dire fate. Certain features of the treaty required monetary appropriations before they could be put into effect. The House of Representatives had not yet voted such funds; a powerful appeal was now made to that body to refuse them. That this would be the Democratic strategy was foretold in a comparatively restrained announcement concerning the President's signing:

The British Treaty has become the supreme law of America.—Let it be honored—with a sigh.—Let the freemen of America be firm, and unitedly instruct their representatives seriously to enquire whether it was constitutionally framed, or can be constitutionally executed.—This must be our dernier resort, and if it fails, unpropitious was the hour when America took up the sword against Britain in 1775;—for the little finger of the treaty, is heavier than the body of the stamp act and tea duty.[252]

Still earlier an alert Boston correspondent had pointed out that the Constitution had given Congress *as a whole* the power to regulate commerce and that therefore the House must have some control over commercial instruments.[253]

The lower house of South Carolina's Assembly formally denounced the Jay Treaty as unconstitutional and inimical to the country's interests, calling on Congress to refrain from voting any money to implement the provisions of the odious covenant. Similar petitions came from groups of citizens in New York, North Carolina, and elsewhere.[254] Virginians even proposed constitutional amendments limiting the treaty-making power in order that America might never again be so humiliated.[255] When the government of George III ratified the treaty with the objectionable twelfth article deleted, Republicans knew that the only hope of blocking its enforcement lay in Congress. The *Aurora* protested against Washington's delay in presenting the British ratification to that body; he had promised to submit it to the House upon its arrival but now was showing further contempt for the people and their representatives while awaiting recovery of the ailing Fisher Ames, outstanding Federalist orator.[256]

Resolutions, most of them urging killing this evil agreement, poured in upon the House when that body considered the document in March, 1796.[257] All the past year's arguments were revived and reinforced. "SCIPIO" called on the House to discover who had induced Washington to give Jay commercial powers. That was the "original crime"; the "wretched negotiator" did not know what America produced, and his covenant afforded no security for the sailors who were a chief support of the nation. If the House spurned the treaty, Americans could return to the sound policy of commercial regulations to enforce respect for their shipping; otherwise, the government might as well be handed over to the President and Senate, for a long step toward tyranny would have been realized.[258] A reward of $1,000 was sardonically offered anyone who would invent a plausible lie to aid passage of the appropriations, but would-be takers were warned that "the bugbear of a war . . . is now rather thread-bare," and would "require somewhat of a new dress." [259]

After some weeks of discussion, the House requested Washington to turn over to it all papers relative to the treaty, as had been done with the Senate. Federalist animadversions at this move incensed the Democratic press. When the people were petitioning, it was scathingly noted, they had been told it was Congress's business to examine the treaty; now it was deemed near-treason for even that body to raise questions. In truth, the legislature ever possessed the right to scrutinize the conduct of the President, even where it lacked the power to stay his actions. Hamiltonians operated under the theory that the treaty-making power could swallow all other Constitutional provisions, and it was high time to abolish such ideas.[260] Washington's statement that he would "consider" the matter was unpleasantly compared with Louis XVI's *"Le Roi, s'avisera"* when he intended to deny a request.[261]

Upon Hamilton's advice, the President refused to submit the papers. Since the House had no treaty-making powers, and since treaties made and ratified were part of the law of the land, surrendering the papers would serve no useful purpose unless impeachment proceedings against the President were contemplated.[262] Republican writers professed no surprise, for they contended the administration feared a complete unmasking if the papers were made public. Yet if the House were *obliged* to pass legislation in support of a treaty, then the pact was superior to the Constitution and all laws; going through the form of an appropriation was mere mockery.[263] Samuel Bayard, American agent for prosecuting claims in British admiralty courts under the treaty, had written that England's conduct would be influenced by that of the House; Washington must therefore be wrong to assume that the treaty was fully in effect. There were rumors that the withheld papers themselves showed Lord Grenville regarded ratification as incomplete until the Representatives had concurred.[264] Bache gratingly noted that though Washington's decision "could not be influenced by the voice of the people, he could suffer it to be moulded by the opinion of an ex-Secretary. Thus . . . though he has apparently discharged the nurse, he is still in leading strings."[265]

A House resolution asserted both the power and the duty to consider the expediency of putting into effect any treaty that was not self-executing, particularly when an appropriation was a *sine qua non*. An issue had been created, but despite exultation in Republican gazettes, the advantage was with the administration. Washington did not present the papers to the House, and that body passed on to consideration of the appropriation itself. Once more, interest blazed high. Attempted "usurpation" was the charge; Federalists accused the House, while Democrats asked: "Will you support your representatives in Congress, or put all power in the hands of twenty Senators and the President?"[266]

Seeking to use organized pressure, as he had so successfully done against Genêt, Hamilton mobilized Federalist merchants to prepare petitions calling for passage of the appropriation. But this time the Republicans were ready. "A CALM OBSERVER" branded such petitions a snare to gag the representatives of the people. Were Congress to surrender its checks upon the Executive, it might as well adjourn *sine die,* as completely unnecessary.[267] The very men who had considered it near treason to criticize the House when that body approved the funding system now seemed almost ready to emulate Cromwell's forcible dispersion of the Long Parliament. Only businessmen, "place-men, old Tories and the knights of the funding system" supported the treaty—possibly thirty thousand individuals, nearly all "entirely devoted to the British interest," but to whom Washington showed more respect than he did to the rest of the citizenry. If Americans could suffer this comparative handful to lord it over three and a half million, "they deserve to be bound in all cases whatsoever, by his Columbian Majesty and a few interested senators." [268] Meetings were held and petitions were circulated against the appropriation to counter petitions that favored it. The true question, editorialized the *Independent Chronicle,* was "shall the *people* or the PRESIDENT be the sovereign of the United States?" [269] The public was continually reminded that those who approved the resolutions against accepting the treaty originally had outnumbered those for it by twenty to one. Many of these recent signers had simply been asked by banks, pensioners, and British agents whether they favored peace or war and did not bother to read the resolves approving the appropriations. [270]

Pressure on the House was tremendous. According to Republicans, threats, bribes, and economic coercion were all used; several insurance companies suspended business pending congressional action. The Senate virtually ceased operations and threatened to vote against the pending Algerian and Spanish treaties if the House failed to provide the required funds. There was even talk of dissolving the Union itself. [271] A Vermont correspondent mordantly asked:

> Can you believe it, Mr. Printer? The house of representatives are determined to exercise the right delegated to them by the Constitution, in not providing for the British treaty. What but war, civil and foreign, must be the consequence of such obstinacy; We shall be ruined by these unprincipled men! The underwriters, in hopes of higher premiums, will shut their officers; debtors, to obtain a longer time, will refuse payment; Great-Britain, to fill her coffers, will take every vessel we have; not an Albany sloop will escape—Spain will attack us on the south—England on the north —the Indians on the west, and the fleet of our enemies will deprive us of the miserable consolation of drowning ourselves . . . —our speculators will be ruined, land will fall, stocks will go to the devil—Public and private credit will be at an end—For heaven's sake, Mr. Printer, what is to be done?

A half dozen guillotines should be imported to speedily decapitate "every refactory member of the majority in Congress." Lord Dorchester's proclamation turning over the Western posts was labeled nicely timed "to forward the British treaty." England could not justly quarrel with Americans over interpretation of their own Constitution, and her situation was too desperate for her to attack. Besides, voting the appropriation might well produce a conflict with France. Even if war with England *should* come, what more could she do than incite the Indians, impress American seamen, and take American ships —things she was already doing under the guise of peace? [272]

British conduct had worsened, rather than improved, since Jay had concluded his negotiations. For months Republican columns had teemed with news of new depredations, customarily headed "Fruits of the Treaty of AMITY, COMMERCE, and NAVIGATION." Accounts of these incidents seemed to increase in number in the period just preceding and during the House debates. Britain seemed more than willing to test American patience, and it may be significant that the outrages reported appeared more flagrant.[273]

When the crew of the American schooner *Eliza*—a vessel which seemed consistently to run afoul of the British— resisted a British press gang attempting to board her at anchor in Hispaniola and then withdrew to another American ship nearby, irate Captain Reynolds of the *Harriot* cut the *Eliza* adrift, ruining her canvas and equipment.[274] A Captain Oakes, of H.M.S. *Regulus,* also off Hispaniola, impressed American sailors and even imprisoned briefly the master of one American craft.[275] Stories of seizures and condemnations appeared with sickening frequency.[276]

Few of these tales lost anything in the telling. The brutality of Captain Hugh Pigot, of the British *Success* and later *Hermione,* was blazoned far and wide. Pigot was later killed by mutineers, and even Federalists referred to his "savage barbarity" after he flogged an American captain senseless. Republicans dwelled on the sufferings of impressed Yankee tars under conditions called ten times worse than the slavery of

Algiers.[277] One correspondent expressed amazement at the lack of concern about the sworn statement that *seventy* Americans had been impressed on a British ship. It was almost as though the account had been one of so many pigeons trapped in a net; a nation so lost as to show no resentment over such an injury could expect only more insults from a country that had long proved itself the scourge of the human race. Surely the "blessed TREATY" had *Christianized* America to make her this meek.[278] As a Marylander noted: "Before the treaty American seamen were impressed by the British; since we have been more closely allied, they treat us as friends, sans ceremonie, and press into their service from the Captain down, and the vessel also." [279]

The *Aurora*'s "Sidney" expressed skepticism that England actually planned to abandon the Western posts and suggested the hesitation of the Senate and Washington—as well as the one-sided benefits afforded Britain under the covenant—as reasons for refusing the appropriation.[280] This treaty chained America as Carthage after the Second Punic War; merchants, farmers, and patriots all would suffer from it, and only the lawyers would benefit.[281] When administration stalwarts belittled Albert Gallatin, opponent of the appropriation, on the grounds of his foreign birth, his role in the argument about the excise, and alleged French influence over him, the *Independent Chronicle* retorted with a substitution in the same description of Hamilton for Gallatin and English for French.[282] Writers sneered at the cowardice and inconsistency of Federalist orators who had prated of the "strong arm of the Union" when they earlier advocated adoption of the Constitution and now portrayed America as too weak to fight Britain. Even those Congressmen who supported the appropriation did not defend the treaty as such.[283]

Good Republicans choked with wrath when New England clergymen used their pulpits to urge House passage of the funds. Here in verity was profanation of the temples of religion. This "self-created society" (with ministers of the Gospel as its officers) was far more dangerous than any other; but

George Washington would not condemn it, for it agreed with him. If the iniquitous pact was unconstitutional, Representatives must abide by their solemn oaths, clergy or no clergy.[284]

Conceivably the House might have disallowed the money had it not been for the dramatic appeal of Fisher Ames. Capitalizing upon his illness to proclaim both disinterestedness and a fear that rejection would yet cause him to outlive his country, Ames played on the frontiersmen's need for surrender of the posts, on the fact that a denial would violate a treaty already ratified, and on fear of war with Britain.[285] Astute Democrats might sniff that Ames's logic boiled down to the unpleasant fact that the House (thanks to the Chief Executive's lack of wisdom) was forced to choose between the two evils of war or the treaty,[286] but Ames's speech helped convert the opposition. A vote soon afterward showed that the *"influence of the executive, with that of the hawkers, merchants, and speculators of every kind, has changed the majority of twenty-five* [which had called for the papers on the treaty] *into a minority of three."* [287] Several congressmen discreetly absented themselves from the roll-call, and thus by a slender margin the necessary sums were voted; the Republicans, Hamilton and Jay had accomplished more for Britain than had "George, Howe, Clinton, Carl[e]ton, and Cornwallis combined." [288]

Announcement of the vote did not preclude more Democratic barbs. Gibes appeared about the expense of the treaty: the $80,000 appropriated was only a beginning, and millions would be needed. Future taxpayers were advised to blame not their immediate representatives but those who made such burdens necessary, and extensive publicity was given to the reasoning of those who had voted against the authorization.[289]

Readers hoping for surcease from the summer's heated debate failed to find it in the *Aurora* and *Independent Chronicle;* in 1796 "Paulding" flayed Washington and the treaty as thoroughly as ever had "Decius" and "Valerius" a year earlier. He saw the explanatory article as "a climax of weakness and wickedness" and a complete "libel upon the American character. . . ." Hamilton would have to write a long series of articles indeed to convince Spain that England had the right to navigate the Mississippi and Americans that permission to British traders to enter Indian lands without a permit did not grant a privilege denied to their own citizens or violate American treaties with the savages.[290] Such was "the British cast of our Executive, that neither the faith nor the interests of the nation are cords strong enough to bind the Administration when in collision with the wishes of the British Cabinet." Washington knew full well that England "was aiding the Savages in their murderous warfare," yet he could with arrant hypocrisy "kiss the knife and tomahawk of those bloody assassins" by calling the king "his 'great, good, and dear friend.' " [291]

Once the treaty was unquestionably in effect, Republican arguments followed two major themes. The first stressed French resentment and predicted warranted Gallic reprisals. Monroe's mission to Paris was gross administrative deception, and Washington's earlier delay in signing the treaty had been to postpone as long as possible the day of reckoning.[292] Details of American infractions of the French alliance of 1778 "would cap the climax of baseness, hypocrisy, and perfidy." Americans had failed to defend France's West Indian possessions as promised, denied her privateers permission to arm in the United States while permitting England's to do so, and revoked the French right to sell prizes in America after solemnly assuring the Republic that the Jay Treaty would not adversely affect her privileges. And all this did not win British friendship![293]

Small wonder that in Paris Americans were beginning to be despised and that France—indeed, all of Europe—spoke "a different language" concerning the United States.[294] In view of the former ally's past forbearance, none could justly blame her now for seizing Yankee vessels.[295] The *Paris Rédacteur* was cited in 1798 as branding Jay's pact the root of the differences between France and America, and, throughout the naval hostilities that followed, Democrats consistently blamed the treaty for French insults and attacks. "Illegitimately begotten," this "inexhaustible source of calamity" was responsible for high taxes, centralized government, Federalist clubs, fallen prices, lost commerce and probable war.[296]

The other, somewhat similar, major tack consisted of emphasizing the black results of the agreement itself; evils foreign and domestic were allegedly its progeny. Before President Washington had signed, news of a recent British order to seize French-bound American provision ships was labeled "One of the first Effects of Jay's Treaty." England now had permission to enforce such orders, enabling her to purchase cheaply the food so seized or to require posting bond against proceeding to France; either result would hurt American shippers.[297]

Cleverly did Republican journalists play both ends against the middle. If prospects were for increased trade with England, the products imported would probably ruin American manufacturers; announcement of the impending dissolution of the Paterson, New Jersey, scheme for "useful manufactures" brought gloating "I told you sos." [298] On the other hand, when trade fell off and unemployment came, the treaty again was blamed. Where once twenty mechanics worked "in Boston, when our trade with France was brisk, and before the British Treaty, there is not one now. Everything is falling— and all for what? To please *one* man, or at most a dozen." [299] In the West reports were rife that British land claims allowed under the covenant would dispossess thousands of frontier families.[300]

Business depression and the threat of war, however, were only a taste of the treaty's effects. "Never was a country so suddenly tumbled from the height of prosperity into an abyss of distress from the perverseness of its government. . . ." [301] Falling prices, stagnation in the stock market, and idle shipping were sufficiently evident to bring comment from even Fenno's *Gazette of the United States;* loss of commerce with Europe and the coastal trade in India were supplanted only by "the pernicious traffic of the British nation, which is fast draining us of our specie." Others charged the curses of merchants and sailors would be added to the chorus against "the blessings of the *British Treaty*," which doubtless would bring bankruptcy and war within another year.[302]

Recent cases in English admiralty courts plainly belied assertions that England would surely indemnify American merchants. That country could not even discharge her obligations to her own citizens; all American shippers could expect for their pains was the cost of the trials.[303] Spoilations upon American commerce had amounted to about six million dollars, and nearly three years after the treaty was ratified only $250,000 had been recovered. Of 689 cases involving captured Yankee vessels, but 83 had been decided. Only three-fifths of the decisions had favored Americans, who would not have won that many had luck not been with the United States in the choice of a fifth and deciding commissioner. Talk of realizing claims was a sorry jest.[304]

Heretofore Federalists had gleefully used the threadbare cry of "War!," with England as the "scarecrow," in order to force through their measures, but now France was speaking more sternly. Loss of specie accruing from America's favorable trade balance with her would shake banks and commerce "to the center." Trade with England netted only ten per cent, while that with France had resulted in nearly ten times that profit; worse yet, the British did not pay in specie, but "in navy bills, which the d[evi]l *cannot negociate.*" [305]

Most fertile of all fields for recrimination were the continued British outrages upon American commerce. Soon after Washington's signing, a story captioned *"First Fruits of the Treaty of Amity, Commerce, and Navigation,"* circulated in all parts of the nation. Captain Home of the *Africa* threatened to burn Newport unless he was given a contribution—"a pretty instance of AMITY." Twenty-eight French-bound American provision ships had been detained by the English without even the promised ten per cent compensation—"a pretty instance of COMMERCE." American vessels had been unjustly condemned by British admiralty courts *since* the treaty had been signed—"*a very* pretty instance indeed of

NAVIGATION!!! ha, ha, ha, Blessed be the treaty-makers! —*By their fruits* ye shall know them![306] At the outset of 1796 the *Gazette of Maine* could say that America was "at peace with all nations except Britain."[307]

Republicans insisted that British concessions to Russia in 1797 of what had been refused to the United States clearly proved Americans should have stood firm in their demands. Later they applauded the formation of a league of Armed Neutrality of the North, which would protect freedom of the seas for neutral nations, but the action fixed "an indelible stigma" upon the United States for abandoning that principle.[308]

Impressments were so frequent that a pretended sailor who supposedly had never read the treaty demanded to know if the document left the security of American seamen entirely up to English caprice.[309] The agreement was *"a Sore that will STINK in the Nose of Posterity"* when it permitted Yankee tars to be carried into a slavery worse than that of Algiers.[310] Seizures of ships continued to crowd the columns of Democratic gazettes and seemed to prove irrefutably that instead of negotiation Americans should have resorted to commercial retaliation, as John Adams himself had urged in 1786.[311] Reports of new British regulations and additional duties aimed at American carrying trade received credence,[312]

> Yet our farmers must be loaded with taxes upon taxes for the payment of British demands, while our merchants can scarcely obtain the interest of their money from the English government, which also permits its cruisers to capture our vessels faster than they pay for those already taken, and in the face of a treaty which cost the United States so much *tribute* and sacrifice.[313]

The Richmond *Examiner* noted that Solomon might state there was nothing new under the sun, but that was before the British treaty, "for certainly neither in the world above, nor in the earth beneath, nor in the waters under the earth, was such a negociation ever heard of." So conscious was Washington of Jay's disobedience that he refused to let the House see his instructions to Jay. A continued embargo would have brought

England to her knees; *"When are we going to burn this absurd and ruinous treaty?"* If Jay would only take himself and his covenant back to England, Americans would be infinitely better off. Even during the crisis with France, America's only hope of avoiding war with Britain was to pray for a complete French victory.[314]

When Governor Jay, addressing the New York Assembly on America's troubled relations with France, remarked that national degradation was more calamitous than war, Republicans were swift to seize the opening and criticize him unsparingly. Where, asked the New York *Argus,* was "this *trembling fear of national degradation"* when Jay signed his infamous treaty? "Consistency! O consistency! thou art often forgotten." [315]

Late in 1800, when campaign feelings were high, the Baltimore *American* presented an itemized statement estimating the cost of the treaty:

| | | |
|---|---:|---:|
| Jay's outfit and expences during 14 months—including his chief justice's salary | $ | 50,000 |
| For loss of our trade with France (tobacco states | 5,000,000 | |
| (Provision & lumber states | 3,000,000 | |
| Loss of revenue by non-intercourse act | 1,000,000 | |
| Lost by French captures because of British treaty | 3,000,000 | |
| Claims of British on old debts before the war— if paid | 12,000,000 | |
| Expence of arming merchantmen | 1,000,000 | |
| Cost of navy and repairs | 8,000,000 | |
| Ships built by subscription | 2,000,000 | |
| Expence of army, forts, arsenals, etc. | 12,000,000 | |
| Interest on loans at 6% and 8% | 2,000,000 | |
| | $49,050,000 | |

This sum, incredible for those times, amounted to five-sevenths the original debt incurred during the American Revolution. Such was the "prosperity the Federalists promised us, and for which we endured Stamp Acts and Alien and Sedition laws." Small wonder they had hypocritically pretended to reprobate British violations of the treaty, or were now abandoning the Federal ship "as fast as they can, to save themselves from shipwreck." [316]

How could any American, it was asked, read about the floggings or executions of American sailors at British hands without raging against England? Such martyrs to liberty as Jonathan Robbins [317] would doubtless murmur amid their groans:

> O my country! If the sacrifice of my life will suffice to prove to you the evil effects of that fatal instrument the British treaty, I shall die in peace. But let America never again be disgraced by another sacrifice.[318]

In all this and countless other items printed condemning Jay's pact, Democratic papers only echoed the bitterness of their chieftains. Madison considered the treaty dishonorable and appalling, Freneau regarded it as the greatest iniquity ever visited upon America, and Jefferson classified it as thoroughly "infamous." [319] There is no record at any time throughout the remainder of the decade that either they or their adherents on newspaper staffs ever changed their judgments regarding "that Pandora's box of America" [320] which resulted from Jay's negotiation.

# VII

## PERFIDIOUS ALBION

Fury over Jay's covenant was still mounting when journals reported the stopping of the American packet *Peggy* by the British warship *Africa* in its search for Fauchet, the French minister.[1] Republicans saw the detention and search of an American sloop in American waters, with ink scarce dry on the treaty, as clear proof of English malevolence. Doubtless it resulted from a plot between Thomas Moore, British vice-consul at Newport, and "some traitors in New York"; happily Fauchet had foiled the scheme by disembarking at Stonington and proceeding to Newport overland.[2]

Maddened by Fauchet's escape, the *Africa's* Captain Home exceeded all bounds. His demands upon Rhode Island's Governor Arthur Fenner for protection for his men, release of a British prisoner allegedly held in Newport, and the right to purchase supplies—all under threat of leveling the town with his guns—made superb grist for Democratic propaganda mills.[3] Washington revoked Moore's exequatur for relaying Home's offensive message and ordered Home to depart, but this action was compared to slapping lightly a man on the wrist for committing a felony.[4] The incident was still cited a year later as indicative of both British viciousness and the administration's Anglophile sentiment.[5]

No one ever made the mistake of charging Republicans with pro-British leanings. Whether or not the treaty was blamed, their gazettes continued to print innumerable tales of English depredations upon American trade. Rising tension with France did not divert Republican editors from these tales, for reports of seizures were as common in 1795 and 1796 as earlier. By mid-August in the latter year, Bache had compiled a list of forty-eight such examples of "British amity." [6] Ships were captured by "Bermudian pirates," taken off Sandy Hook, or purportedly condemned by an English judge simply because he hated France.[7] The *Maryland Gazette* told of thirty vessels, for which not a cent of compensation had been received, carried off to British ports.[8] So common were impressments that even cabin boys were not exempt, and a year after the treaty had been signed an estimated two thousand Yankee sailors were serving under duress in England's navy. Corrupt British admiralty courts and brutal sea captains were rewarded, not dismissed.[9] A sad commentary it was on American independence when seamen could not safely sail without a signed protection from a British consul—and even sadder when such documents were torn up as their holders were impressed.[10] American masters tempted to play the Samaritan were reminded of the *Enterprise,* which had rescued passengers and crew of a sinking British transport. The rescuing craft was forced to take those saved on to Barbados, where a judicial attempt was made to condemn it.[11]

American tars had been "knocked down, hand cuffed, flogged and more than half starved to death for refusing to fight under the British flag against the French," while a supine administration contended America was too weak to claim justice. As a consequence, the nation would have "to take what Paddy gave the drum, viz. *a good beating.*" [12] Accounts of detentions, confiscations, impressments, and cruelties followed in endless and dreary succession, even in many smaller newspapers.[13] Lashing at Federalists, infuriated Republicans noted that "The British do not even apologize for their conduct—they leave that dirty work to their dirty tools in this country." [14]

Succeeding years saw little change in this technique of dwelling on British outrages. James Burnes, of Salem, in 1797 re-counted his ordeals aboard the *Majestic* much as had James Rand his on the *Thetis* the previous year.[15] Bad as French depredations might be, those of England were allegedly worse. British ships hovered in American waters, pouncing on merchantmen; the *Readinger Adler* listed five condemned craft under the succinct heading, "Plundering."[16] Demo-cratic papers invariably catalogued English seizures (one issue of the *Independent Chronicle* named twelve),[17] while French transgressions received far less publicity. They charged the Federalist newssheets with practicing the exact reverse of this policy, blazoning French captures "from one end of the conti-nent to the other."[18]

Indeed, the whole situation was sufficiently serious that the *Aurora,* chiefly on the ground of British outrages, proposed a program foreshadowing that of latter-day isolationists. To avoid war, Americans should abrogate the Jay Treaty, subsi-dize domestic manufacturers and use their products only, modify naturalization laws to attract industrious farmers and artisans, recall ships and ambassadors, and revise militia laws to provide an adequate defense.[19] Britons were obviously "determined to give the *coup de grâce* to the American [carry-ing] trade"; with French assistance, given because of the ad-ministration's stupid foreign policy, they were most apt to succeed.[20] Small wonder the United States was undergoing a business depression.[21]

Writers who opposed withdrawing entirely into a shell ap-plauded any stiffening of America's attitude toward Britain, such as the orders issued to resist impressment of naval per-sonnel. Better war than cringing acquiescence.[22] As lists of offenses continued, public meetings in port cities petitioned Congress for countermeasures.[23] Southerners might perhaps be indebted to Captain Cochran's *Thetis* for driving French privateers from the Carolina coast, but they would have been *"more obliged"* had Cochran not taken several American ves-sels and later blockaded Charleston. Apparently he ousted "the French cruizers [*sic*], merely that he might enjoy the *piratical trade to himself."* [24] "Thousands" of "fraternal hugs" could be cited by 1799; only in port could American merchantmen "avoid *disgrace* from our *British friends."* [25] Though the "FRENCH DEPREDATIONS" so blatantly stressed by the Federalist press were more nearly justified, they were far less extensive; insurance statistics were quoted to prove the point.[26] Richard Carter, impressed on board the *Brunswick* in Kingston and immediately flogged, and Ebenezer Giles, who vainly appealed to Commodore Truxtun for redress against an unprovoked beating on the *Daphne* in St. Kitts, became heroes in Democratic households, yet Pickering accepted the word of "honor" of British officers and rejected Yankee complaints.[27] Sarcastically the *Dedham Minerva* dilated upon the kindness and generosity of the "British, God bless them. . . . To prevent our vessels from being captured by the French they bring them into their own ports and store up their cargoes until better days." Perhaps if Americans offered them all their wealth and all their sailors, the British would protect them completely from French depredations.[28]

Even Canadian gazettes reprobated the activities of British West Indian raiders—which was more than the Federalists would do.[29] Yet so gross were English outrages that it was predicted even the administration could not indefinitely ignore them.[30] When Adams said nothing about British transgressions in his speech to Congress, affidavits of seizures or impressments were published to stir his "treacherous memory"[31] Federalists and State Department officials were berated for indicating that American seamen were *"unprincipled lying sailors,"* in preferring British accounts to those of American citizens.[32]

By 1800 more than three thousand Americans were said to be serving under the Union Jack, whereas the few French impressments which might occur were "no doubt by vessels unauthorized by the [Paris] government."[33] The *Augusta Herald* pugnaciously challenged Captain Pellew of the British *Cleopatra* to attempt impressing hands from American frigates; they could make work *for* him, and might even "teach

him propriety of conduct." [34] As stories of "BRITISH ROB-
BERS! AGAIN" continued to accumulate,[35] Democrats
charged that England released American vessels only when the
mere detention of them was too flagrant a breach of international practice for even the sons of Albion to stomach.

Throughout the entire Federalist period, British policy toward American shipping remained a major Republican
issue.[36] Following the Newport incident involving Captain
Home, however, three specific instances transcended all others
in arousing indignation against English maritime aggrava-
tions. The first involved one Isaac Williams, a Connecticut native with a commission on a French privateer that had preyed
on British shipping. Arrested upon his return home and tried
in federal District Court, Williams was found guilty of violating the Jay Treaty. On his claim that he had taken out French
naturalization papers, Chief Justice Ellsworth ruled an American citizen could not expatriate himself; Williams was fined a
thousand dollars and sentenced to four months in jail.[37]

Immediately Republican writers, particularly "MUTIUS"
in the *Virginia Argus* and "Aristogiton" in the Richmond
*Examiner,* castigated Ellsworth. This decision claimed for
federal authorities a power not granted by the Constitution.
Since expatriation had not been expressly denied, it remained
the right of every man and also served as a safety valve
whereby malcontents could relieve their passions without harming their native land. The Williams ruling, sputtered others,
debased "free born Americans to the state of Russian slaves."
That subjects could not change allegiance was an abominable
British doctrine, but perhaps now America would rouse from
the "torpor" produced by "the machinations of an artful and
wicked faction" that aped English conduct.[38]

When naval hostilities with France began in 1798 the administration became concerned over the prospect that American warships might, by resisting all seizures on the high seas,
bring on a war with Britain also. In consequence, official orders forbade armed opposition to the capture of American
merchantmen (even if actually observed) by other than

French vessels.[39] Unaware of these instructions, or blithely ignoring them, Republicans were able to use as a second focus for their strictures the activities of Commodore Thomas Truxtun of the U. S. S. *Constellation*. His ship's officers had been charged with cruelty, and he—for capturing the French *L'Insurgente,* though this had been only his duty—had been offered presents from the British government and people. By such bribes had Arnold been led to betray his country.[40] Then came in swift succession several tales in which Truxtun surrendered impressed Americans to the tender mercies of British naval officers or received evidence of mistreated Yankees and did nothing.[41]

The most inflammatory item was an account by Stephen Fricker, who claimed to be one of several impressed seamen who jumped overboard and swam to the *Constellation* in Port Royal harbor, Jamaica. The next day, Truxtun returned the men, although they carried their "protections" with them, to the ship from which they had escaped and remained to witness their punishment. Widely circulated, the story caused many a Democrat to nod agreement with the New London *Bee* in finding it "perfectly ridiculous to talk of national *independence* or of the glories of our *navy,* when such outrages are committed by persons in public trust." [42]

Far more effective than Truxtun's facilitating British brutality or than the Williams case in stirring popular feeling, however, was the Jonathan Robbins incident. Arrested in Charleston in February, 1799, at the urging of the British consul, Robbins became the Republicans' chief political martyr —even though almost certainly a synthetic one. To England his correct name was Thomas Nash, a British subject and ringleader in a murderous mutiny aboard H. M. S. *Hermione* more than a year earlier. The prisoner denied both the identification and crime, swearing he was Jonathan Robbins, a native of Danbury, Connecticut. With his extradition requested under Article 27 of Jay's Treaty, Nash—or Robbins, for Republican papers never referred to him otherwise—was haled before Judge Thomas Bee of the District Court of South

Carolina. He produced his "protection" as proof he was Robbins, testifying he had been pressed on board the *Hermione* but had taken no part in the mutiny. Other testimony contradicted him on these points. Judge Bee found his asserted American citizenship false, and ruled him probably guilty of the alleged crime. In compliance with a request from Timothy Pickering for Nash's surrender on sufficient evidence, the prisoner was turned over to the British.[43]

Indefeasible allegiance (not an issue in the Robbins incident) and impressment of Americans had long been detestable to those of humanitarian persuasions and to those who insisted upon America's sovereign nationhood. Republican printers, conveniently ignoring the fact that the State Department had refused (on grounds of inadequate evidence) to surrender others accused of complicity in the *Hermione* mutiny, found this opportunity to flay the Federalists and British too inviting to ignore. Robbins claimed to be an American, guiltless of wrongdoing, who, at the administration's orders, had been given to piratical England for vengeance. The next step would be to let Britain punish all violators of the Sedition Act. Surrender of a native-born Yankee sailor violated the Neutrality Proclamation, which had warned citizens against entering the service of any of the belligerent powers.[44]

If Robbins, as a victim of impressment, was a mutineer he was a hero for daring "to deliver himself from such inhuman thralldom,"[45] but Republicans actually said little on this point. To them the crucial question was his citizenship. Without a jury, Judge Bee had relinquished a person who possessed proofs of American nationality and swore he had not changed his allegiance. Thus, it was charged, did Federalists mock American liberty. Papers described the scene: a British vessel waiting in the harbor for the sacrifice, a band of federal soldiers at the courthouse door to conduct the victim, and the arbitrary judge with a letter from the government in his pocket directing the accused to be condemned and handed over. Here was executive interference in judicial processes. Why had Americans rebelled against George III, if not to free themselves from English tyranny? Doubtless Bee had been bribed; at best he was the tool of party. And where was Adams's professed "pity" when he signed Robbins' death warrant? [46]

"A SOUTH-CAROLINA PLANTER" (Charles Pinckney) wrote a widely copied series of articles for the Charleston *City Gazette*. Since Robbins would face a British court martial, the absence of a jury was especially reprehensible; Congress should provide guarantees against future deliveries of fugitives before a true bill had been found against them by a grand jury. The government should ensure a jury trial for these unfortunates and was certainly obligated to be as firm toward British seizures as toward those of the French. [47]

The *Aurora* carried Freneau's impassioned protests against this "momument of national degradation and individual injustice." Adams, Pickering, and Bee had betrayed to his doom a "native of . . . the pious and industrious state of Connecticut." [48] Robbins' alleged mutiny would have been praised had it been against "our *Indian* or *Algerine* allies," chimed in the *Centinel of Freedom*. If the Jay Treaty were to be construed as giving England the right to claim American nationals as hers and to punish them for an act laudable *per se,* American sailors had absolutely no security—even in their own ports. Assuming that the pact furnished adequate authority for Robbins' delivery "to a British Gibbett," executive pressure on Bee to surrender him was unnecessary. Never had such contempt been shown for American national independence and reputation. [49]

Every effort was made to heighten the pathos of Robbins' martyrdom. His "last letter," written on board the vessel carrying him to court martial, was printed to arouse sympathy and resentment. It protested his innocence and Americanism and predicted he would be used as an example. Nothing in his past life made him afraid: "Whatever may be my fate, I will act like a brave American!" His last request was "that you will comfort my unfortunate Parents. You must excuse this scrawl as I am still in irons. Adieu. God bless you. JONATHAN ROBBINS." [50] Possibly, wrote Republicans, the sacrifice of this "unfortunate victim to British ferocity" would direct attention to "the horrid operations of that scandalous instrument, the British treaty, which has laid prostrate in the dust the honor and dignity of our country, and bartered its interests for a mess of pottage." [51]

Robbins was tried, condemned, and hanged despite Democratic lamentations. His American nativity had caused his death; had he been a Prussian or even a Russian he would never have been impressed. An American judge and an English court martial had both swallowed the accusations of "a set of British bullies" against the solemn oath of a citizen of the United States.[52] Before his execution "Robbins" confessed his true name was Nash and that he was an Irishman,[53] but for those who read only Democratic papers this admission might as well never have been made. News of his death was captioned "ALAS! POOR ROBBINS!!!" and accompanied by valedictory poems. The Baltimore *American* started a fund for a monument in his memory, with approving comments from all parts of the nation. No man reading of the case, editorialized the *Centinel of Freedom,* could say "that ROBBINS HAS NOT BEEN MURDERED." [54]

Nash's demise did not still the tumult. For some time at Republican gatherings his memory was toasted and Judge Bee was execrated.[55] As criticism continued, Federalists became more alarmed. Every Jacobin sheet from Savannah to Portsmouth, they groaned, had been filled with column on column of sorrow for this wretch. As Fenno put it, "Sir Jonathan Robbins ranks as first martyr on the democratic calendar!" [56] Belatedly, administration supporters bestirred themselves. They printed Sir Hyde Parker's official report that Nash had "acknowledged himself to be an Irishman" and circulated a statement from the town clerk and four long-time residents of Danbury that they had never known anyone in that town by the name of Robbins.[57]

Democrats were not silenced. They jeered at Federalist ideas of justice that produced inquiries of town clerks concerning a man's birthplace two months after he had been hanged in chains. Sir Hyde's statement was based only on British newspaper accounts, and Connecticut was so completely dominated by Federalist politicians that residents of Danbury could be found who would swear to anything. At the hearing Robbins had shown a certificate of several years' standing that tallied with both his description and handwriting. Even if he were *not* an American, the episode was still a violation of national rights and of the principle that the accused were innocent until proved guilty; it also demonstrated interference of executive agents with the courts.[58]

When Congress met, New York's Representative Edward Livingston called for the papers on the case and introduced resolutions of censure against Adams and Bee. The President sent to the House all pertinent papers, including English minister Liston's request for the prisoner, Pickering's letter to Bee, the Danbury affidavit, and a report from the British consul that Robbins had admitted being Nash.[59] The opposition of John Marshall, then congressman from Virginia, though it won him the name of an enemy to the right of jury trial, achieved rejection of the resolutions—and Adams's gratitude probably led to Marshall's elevation to the Cabinet and Supreme Court.[60]

But the story was still good campaign material, and Jeffersonians used it to the full. The *Virginia Argus* told of a man held earlier in New Jersey on charges of implication in the *Hermione* mutiny, but an order from the President had prevented his surrender to the British. How came it to pass that an "action was criminal in summer *ninety-nine,* which, in summer *ninety-eight* was not worth investigating?"[61] Proof that Robbins was Nash was so flimsy that "the most stupid pettifogger in the country would be ashamed to rest his case" on it. Adams was berated for meddling with the courts and was warned he would soon face the judgment of the electorate.[62] The *Aurora* argued that all nations had common jurisdiction over piracy, the crime with which Robbins was really charged, and that turning him over (without a jury inquest) to summary British naval justice was unconstitutional. Other stories averred that Danbury Federalist partisans had signed Pickering's affidavits, that the town records had been burned during the Revolution, and that people named Robbins lived near (if not in) the community. The continued agitation served its purpose in preserving the incident as a live issue for the campaign in the fall of 1800.[63]

Even aside from such occurrences, Republicans wanted no coalition with England. When the *Gazette of the United States* reported British ships escorting American merchantmen out of reach of hostile French vessels near Haiti, there were sarcastic comments on the happiness America would gain in an alliance with England. "True we shall now and then be involved in a war about the *balance of power;* but that is nothing compared to the benefits we must enjoy under 'British protection.'" Yet Democrats were convinced Britain desired such an alliance and that Jay's treaty did not go far enough to satisfy her. Some Federalists nourished the same hope, but Republican journalists exploded with wrath at any hint of such an "accursed plan." Not even Adams would have the audacity to fly so blatantly in the face of the popular will.[64]

History proved that Britain's allies usually wound up with territory lost and citizens impoverished.[65] The shades of departed Revolutionary patriots were invoked to protest American degeneracy at the mere contemplation of such a partnership. Perhaps the rumor Adams and Liston had signed a defensive-offensive pact was circulated "just to accustom the people to the idea," though its truth was not out of the question.[66] A letter reprinted from the Paris *L'Ami des Lois* caused a flurry in 1799. Attributed to William Cramond, an Englishman living in Philadelphia, it prophesied wide publicity for a trumped-up quarrel between Adams and Liston; even Republicans would be convinced of the President's impartiality and support administration demands for new war measures. The strengthened government would then moderate its "anger" toward Britain, trample Democrats underfoot, and enter the conflict against France. Though Cramond denounced this "forgery," it was charged he had tried to suppress it—and some of his forecasts seemed to be taking place.[67]

Almost as much as maritime seizures, English tariffs discriminated against American carrying trade. Offers to accept provisions in payment for unsettled debts still due British merchants exemplified Britain's low cunning. While Congress studied these obligations, England would both obtain sadly needed foodstuffs and saddle the interest for the debts on America. Moreover, this procedure would weaken the power of any threat of sequestration to coerce her into a cessation of commercial outrages.[68]

Despite protestations of friendship for the United States, the mother country was still hostile even while faced with serious difficulties.[69] Naval mutinies, military defeats, and predictions of a winter so severe Napoleon might be able to cross the frozen Channel were hailed as heralding England's collapse.[70] The cost of the British government continued to be a topic for both animadversion and self-congratulation; one correspondent calculated Albion's debt as equivalent to a half-dollar for every minute since the creation of the world.[71] Brutalities of English justice, cruelty in military triumphs, or the hanging and quartering of the Canadian rebel McLean were but indications of Americans' fate should they ever revert to British control.[72]

News of British repressive measures in Ireland was to Republicans a reminder of what the loss of American liberties could mean. Long-held sympathy for the United Irishmen flared again, and rumors of French invasion of Ireland were eagerly received.[73] The entire decade was one of extremely bitter anti-British feeling among the Irish, and, especially after 1795, emigration to the United States was high.[74] Most of these newcomers were terribly impoverished, a primary factor in Congressional reduction of the cost of naturalization certificates from $20 to $5. Since most Irish immigrants were drawn to the Anglophobe anti-administration party, many Federalists opposed the lowered fee. Young Harrison Gray Otis, speaking in Congress against the reduction, made an unfortunate reference to "a horde of wild Irishmen" that was to haunt him for years. Democrats seized on the expression, re-counted Ireland's sufferings under British misrule, and sug-gested if Otis could eliminate *"the wild English government, in Ireland,"* the "wild Irishmen" could be easily persuaded to remain there. They acidly suggested a missionary project to enlighten the benighted island, headed by Otis because of his "liberality" and "great knowledge of the world." [75]

Republicans insisted Otis did not represent the nation's sen-timent. Most Americans sympathized with and welcomed Irishmen landing on their shores.[76] The ill-fated Irish Insur-rection of 1798 intensified partiality for Ireland and hatred toward Britain. Any French restriction, real or imagined, on individual rights to which "Peter Porcupine" could point was far surpassed by "detestable British tyranny" in Ireland.[77] English policy of *divide et impera* was being tried again rela-tive to Ireland's religion; an attempt to disunite the free peo-ple of America in order to destroy their liberty would be next. The uprising was similar to Americans' own Revolution, with which Hibernians had openly sympathized. When Federalists suggested the time was not propitious for an Irish revolt, Democrats hotly retorted that the Tory Hutchinson had once given Americans similar advice.[78] An alleged wish that "about half a million" Irishmen would be slaughtered by the English in order to settle the vexatious problem was damned for its savagery but deemed typical of "a *true federalist.*" [79] Irish successes were toasted, use of the term "rebel" for them in the Federalist press was resented, and sympathy for the in-surrection was shown in a hundred ways.[80]

Failure of the uprising and the death of its leaders were be-moaned as illustrating Americans' own imminent danger. In all likelihood they were already the dupes of England's emis-saries in America, and doubtless the troublesome activities of William A. Bowles among the Creeks in Florida were British-inspired.[81] Bowles was an almost legendary figure who had appeared amid the Southern Indians in 1788 and 1791. Claim-ing English support, he attempted to persuade the Creeks to abrogate McGillivray's treaty of 1790 with the United States. After delaying the running of the boundary line between the Creek territory and Georgia, he became involved with Spanish authorities. Carried to Spain to be hanged for incendiary activities, he was kept in custody for several years and then was liberated or managed to escape, returning to his former haunts among the Creeks and Cherokees.[82]

In 1799 Bowles proclaimed the State of Muskogee, with himself as "Director General." Commissioners sent from Spain and the United States to settle the Pinckney Treaty boundary line were warned from his territory, three Gulf ports were opened to nations not at war with Muskogee, duties were imposed on imports to the Creeks, and a hundred acres of land were offered to persons placing themselves under his protection.[83] Surprised and defeated by Spanish troops, Bowles and his chiefs fled to the Bahamas, amid Georgians' thanks to their Florida neighbors for ridding them of these "pests to society." [84] Though England denied any support of Bowles, the *Aurora* flatly stated he had commissions and pledges of aid from the British minister. An English officer had been captured with incriminating evidence on him, it was said, and a vessel of the Royal Navy had landed this officer on American shores "with arms, ammunition and adherents." Here was still another proof of British falsehood and enmity.[85]

Greater menace by far than Bowles to many was the influx of British-made goods. Whether it stemmed from deliberate hostility or mere desire to exploit a good market was immaterial; the result was identical. Merchants and mechanics were being ruined by English imports and importers, and specie was slipping away, cried "AMERICANUS" in 1800.[86] It was no new protest. As early as 1791 even the *Columbian Centinel* had commented on England's ridiculous fashions and the even more foolish American crazes. To the British Americans must appear as absurd as Indians.[87] Thrifty New Englanders criticized wearing mourning for the departed, particularly since most of the black cloth came from Britain. Curtailing British importations would keep thousands of dollars within the country and would aid England's opponents more than would fleets or armies. A mere band of crape was a good old custom and more patriotic; Americans imported too many unnecessary items.[88] Yet black apparently continued to be worn at funerals, for articles against the "silly fashion" in imitation of England appeared intermittently for several years.[89]

At the time of Jay's mission there had been calls for a retaliatory boycott on English goods. So dependent was Britain said to be upon America that this would humble her. Indeed, Americans would profit, for England would soon be forced to buy from them on their own terms.[90] The visible agitation shown by British merchants over possible rejection of the appropriation called for in the Jay Treaty reinforced belief that England dared not risk loss of American trade. American prosperity was not dependent upon Europe, and national honor required some response to injuries. A cessation of British imports would answer and involve no risk of war.[91]

But war, with France if not with England, loomed ever larger as a probability. In 1798 "Solon" called for prohibiting the export of precious metals, except to purchase military supplies. Otherwise, in view of the imminent loss of all trade with France and her allies, the United States would be soon doomed to existing again on a paper currency.[92] Next year found Republicans irate over Pitt's new export duty on woolen goods. By buying British products America helped England wage war against freedom, cried a widely reprinted item entitled "THE NOURISHING OF VIPERS." Non-intercourse with France, suggested by some Federalists, would only cost the United States its most valuable customer; that with England would help American industries and would vitiate the pernicious and omnipresent influence of British merchants and agents in the country.[93]

Great Britain was also upbraided for depredations committed by Algerine pirates upon American commerce. Prior to 1793 Portuguese warships had largely confined the activities of these raiders to the western Mediterranean, although there some Yankee seamen had fallen into the clutches of the Dey. When Portugal on England's encouragement made a truce, however, Algerine corsairs immediately entered the Atlantic and commenced preying on American shipping. Respect for Britain's fleet ensured that nation's vessels comparative immunity; since American Atlantic commerce was perhaps second in importance at that time, the Algerines seemed deliberately loosed on it. Ostensibly, the navy created by the United States in 1794 was primarily aimed at these raiders. In the meantime, efforts were made to purchase peace and to ransom American captives.[94]

David Humphreys, minister to Portugal, was sent to Algiers. The horrible conditions he described suffered by American seamen awaiting ransom were another atrocity for which Americans could thank "the British—this terrible scourge has been inflicted by their deep and crooked policy." [95] Rejection of an earlier treaty with the Dey was scolded, and with England held responsible for further outrages Republicans could find nothing Algerian to praise. William Branch Giles informed his constituents that the English-sponsored truce between Portugal and Algiers had been designed to eliminate American commercial competition, petitions to Congress to protect shipping linked the names of Britain and the pirates, and subscriptions were used to raise ransom money for the languishing captives.[96]

A treaty was finally negotiated, but some skepticism was expressed that the Algerines would honor it. Actually, there were delays in raising the required ransom, and the thorny affair continued to generate dissatisfaction throughout the Federalist era.[97] Few acts of the administration, thundered *Frothingham's Long Island Herald,* exhibited "so glaring an evidence of incapacity and a wanton expenditure of the Public Treasure as has the Algerine business from beginning to end." There had been "enormous waste" of the million dollars voted to redeem the captives and to procure peace. The frigates authorized were not yet built in 1797, and the cost so far for three had exceeded the original appropriation for six.[98]

Westerners resented ransoming prisoners of Mediterranean pirates when individuals advancing sums to redeem captives of the Indians were not reimbursed.[99]

When the new Dey of Algiers in 1798 demanded $600,000 as the price of continued peace, the *Independent Chronicle* confidently predicted the sum would be paid, despite administration bluster elsewhere. *" 'Millions for defence but not a cent for tribute'*—boo!" [100] Actually, this amount was not sent, but tribute continued to be paid intermittently to corsairs, furnishing a contrast to the policy respecting France and affording Pickering opportunities for alleged peculation. Bad as they were, such treaties as that concluded with Tunis were held advantageous compared with Jay's British covenant.[101]

England remained the object of Democrats' fear and hatred, and "British influence" was their war cry throughout the 'nineties. President Adams and John Marshall alike later testified to the deadly effectiveness of this Jeffersonian charge.[102] Accusations that England's interests exerted undue weight in American affairs were not novel, but it remained for Freneau's *National Gazette* to organize a campaign around them. When Franco-British hostilities began in 1793, Freneau held Washington's neutrality proclamation actually favored England, for France had a right to expect American help. He then made every effort to demonstrate both the presence and power of British sympathizers in America. Letters, purportedly from Philadelphians to New Yorkers, were published that alleged the majority of residents in coastal cities condemned French conduct and principles. It was hoped such sentiments would before long spread "to the *peasantry* in the interior." If "the glorious, the *royal* cause" prevailed in Europe, "the justly abhorred principles of modern revolutionists" could be erased for all time. The "fuss" of the "swinish populace" at Genêt's arrival should depress no one; the men who counted were still for Britain and many wanted France defeated so they could garner royal appointments and be no longer subjected to the rabble's continual clatter. Perhaps England's seizure of French-bound American vessels would soon restore the United States to British rule.[103] Almost certainly these "epistles" were fabrications, cleverly designed (through the *Gazette*'s widespread circulation) to stir up resentment in the country by their slurs and in the cities by their misrepresentations.

Other papers followed the lead. There were reports that the British ministry was raising £1,000,000 to bribe America's leading men; rumors of French atrocities indicated some less conspicuous figures might have already been hired to do England's bidding.[104] The "infernal practice" of corruption seemed an inevitable concomitant of the English government, and stories were frequent that its minister in Philadelphia was employing it. Washington himself was wealthy enough to be beyond suspicion, but Republicans suspected certain other officials. Some men in high places who had earlier been poor and had detested the British now fawned on them after America had been insulted.[105]

English immigrants and old Tories, many of whom had gravitated to the Federalist party, were naturally suspected of being under British influence. Some Federalists' celebrations of the King's birthday or their open desire for French defeat made obvious their sympathies and lent color to the charge. Freneau's "A NEW POLITICAL CREED" took advantage of this to assert that Federalists held

> The Briton is superior to the American and the American is superior to the Briton, and yet they are equal and the Briton shall govern the American. The Briton while here is commanded to obey the American and yet the American ought to obey the Briton. . . . The American was created for the Briton and the Briton for the American and yet the American shall be a slave to the Briton and the Briton the tyrant of the American.[106]

As Anglophobia became more intense, creditors of the United States grew increasingly alarmed about the possibility of war and its effect upon their investments. The *Independent Chronicle* thus saw George III as more powerful than at the outbreak of the American Revolution, solely because "the

British plan of debt is an idol that some men have set up to worship." [107] The "paper nobility" would not so oppose retaliatory measures if their precious certificates were floating on the ocean under the American flag and England seized them. Would these "mushroom patriots" then prate of "negociation" without taking hostage British property within their reach? Doubtless some of these speculators had "been already negociating" successfully; if their pockets were turned inside out, more than one would be found carrying the image of the King as the object of his worship.[108]

Some later scholars have endorsed these contemporary views, asserting that British Minister Hammond liberally rewarded congressmen and journalists who furthered his ideas.[109] A New York correspondent called for a keen watch on scribblers against the Democratic Societies. If reports were correct, they kept "their runners and horsemen, if not printers, in pay from Georgia to New-Hampshire." Federalist papers were "crammed with paragraphs" calculated to convince the people "that the KING can do no wrong! Thanks to the Gods, not even *igots* [*sic*] can persuade them (the people) that *they are fools, and* that igots alone are wise!" [110] The grand object of the Court of St. James, argued Democrats, was to reestablish British domination in America; Jay's treaty was undoubtedly the first step.

Real and imagined instances of favoritism toward England were seized upon and magnified as proof the administration was Anglophile. The "strict and impartial neutrality" was mocked by British ships being fitted out in Hampton Roads and by agents purchasing cavalry horses in the South—probably under authority of some secret article in the treaty.[111] That Liston could bring a libel suit against Republican printer Thomas Greenleaf did not surprise the *Aurora*. To slander a French minister was unimportant; Genêt had been libeled, but could obtain no redress. Now unlimited venom might be directed at France and her emissaries, but no writer dared call the British *"pirates, robbers, incendiaries,* or *bar-*

*barians.* . . . Ye Jacobin printers, taint not the hem of the garment of the sacred person of his Britannic majesty's minister, or punishment and persecution shall attend you." [112]

When Federalists talked peace, noted a Jersey correspondent, they meant only peace with England; their horror of war quickly evaporated when it appeared France might be the foe.[113] The *Independent Chronicle* continued to call for retaliation against England's "iniquitous Navigation Acts" to convince the mother country she could not with impunity make laws adversely affecting America, and to show French statesmen American government "is not wholly given over to a predominating and overruling *BRITISH INFLUENCE.*" [114]

Speeches by Adams and Wolcott on French outrages were berated as being biased. The President had correctly observed that a "domestic faction" endangered the nation, but it was a *British* faction rather than a French one. No one who talked of "influence" and failed to refer to English spoilations could be objective; justification of England and condemnation of France must be actuated by something beside reason. Reports that Britain had stopped her depredations should not be credited.[115] The entire administration wanted to "cement us to England." So partial was Pickering it was "a problem whether Secretary Timothy is acting in the double character of Secretary of State, and agent to the British interests or not." [116] English naval recruiting offices were opened in New York, raged the *Albany Register*. Had French vessels tried to procure seamen "to wage war against the *hell of despotism,* the country would have rung with the violation of neutral rights" —but these were British offices and had not been closed.[117]

Jeffersonian papers bitingly attacked Adams' silence in late 1797 concerning English seizures, and they pretended bewilderment over his hostility toward Spain and France, "from which the whole beneficial trade of this country arises." [118] Sensitive to criticism of his grandfather, Benjamin Franklin, Bache suspected there was an English-financed plot to discredit the leaders and principles of the American Revolution. Paid Federalist paragraphists were straining every nerve to reduce Americans once more to provincial status; the Boston *Centinel* and at least two New York dailies were said to have been recipients of Pitt's funds.[119] Almost no "event of importance takes place, but we see the preponderancy of *English* influence," fulminated Bostonians, and Philadelphia Republicans smiled because the extraordinary demands upon "the secret service money of the British cabinet" in late 1796 rendered it likely that "New-York jesuits" would find their *"thirty pieces of silver* will not be quarterly paid, with the punctuality promised and expected." [120] Americans should shun all alien pressure, but it was significant that the cry (raised most loudly by those who were Tories in '76) seemed ever directed at France, while some professed patriots even advocated "an alliance with Great Britain, to avoid *foreign* influence!" [121]

No part of the United States, clamored "Aristides" in Kentucky, seemed safe from the ridicule or propaganda of British hirelings. True Americans of '75, hating royalty and gratefully recalling French aid, were designated "anarchists" and "fraternizing ragamuffins, only fit for the guillotine." Happily, Kentuckians were so far "removed from those foul nests of political intrigue, the large commercial cities on the Atlantic shore," they could distinguish between the friends of liberty and those who would trample on it to achieve "wealth . . . and ascendancy." Even Kentuckians, however, were not immune to the barbs of such as the "mercenary Cobbett." [122] Congressman Robert Goodloe Harper of South Carolina was viewed with suspicion for his unusual efforts to entertain the House on a late May afternoon in 1797 after the customary hour of adjournment. Could this "have been owing to the familiar tap on the shoulder which he had received the moment before, from the *British minister* and to the whisper in his ear from the personage?" Certainly "a *familiarity* of this sort at such a crisis . . . must acquit this distinguished prattler from any suspicion of being under FRENCH influence!!" [123]

In the summer of 1797 the press reported Bache's arrest for publishing on July 24 an assertion "that Great Britain distributed in one year, 800,000 dollars secret service money, among the officers of the Federal Government." Pickering would doubtless have received a portion of this sum, sneered the *Chronicle,* were it not that his rancor toward France and Spain made it unnecessary for England to buy his allegiance and that his personal influence in America was non-existent.[124] An advertisement for James Lyon's projected *National Magazine* noted that printing costs in the South were twice that in New England, which explained why Pitt and Liston spent most of their money in the North where it would accomplish more in fostering Anglophile sentiment.[125] Even the German-language *Readinger Adler* vowed: "There existeth a British faction in the country." Peace with the world at large was held impossible while spies and intriguers were "suffered to corrupt our morals and subvert our political tenets." [126]

British secret service money could be spent without an accounting by agents who were similar in language and dress to Americans. British commerce influenced American merchants who traded on English capital and credit. Rural newspapers copied from city papers supported by the advertisements of such merchants, making the circulation of pro-British stories nationwide. For these reasons, coupled with England's hatred and fear of American competition, English influence was more to be dreaded than that of any other nation.[127] The world was witnessing a great struggle between monarchy and freedom. It appeared freedom would triumph in Europe, but (thanks to insidious British propaganda aimed at convincing Americans of French influence and hostility) there was genuine cause to fear the monarchy's success in America.[128]

The "Pulpit, the Press, the Bar and the Theatre propagate *English* rather than *French* Influence," exploded one commentator. Bribery by secret service, a purchased press, an influenced trade, unscrupulous ministers and old Tories composed a hazard to democracy that was growing, rather than decreasing. Anyone who derogated American achievements simply because they were American was foolish or ill-informed; Americans had to their credit many genuine accomplishments in painting, science, and other fields. But the American press dishonored the nation when the "edges of its paper are gilt in London," for England's policy was to discredit popular government.[129]

American Loyalists by 1796 had strangely been paid more than double the sum officially appropriated by the crown as reimbursement for their losses sustained during the Revolution. Was this "royal bounty" an application of former British Secretary of State Hillsborough's old assertion that England was mistaken in trying to coerce Americans when "they could have been bought with their own gold"? It was fortunate indeed that Adams was temporarily absent from the seat of government in 1799 when Britain's General Maitland came over to offer money and ships in exchange for active support.[130]

A table, headed the "fund of British Corruption," of English secret service expenditures was compiled by the Baltimore *American*. Since Jay's treaty this fund consumed from six to eight times what it had in 1784. (Most of the increase came just before the outbreak of the French Revolution, but it was not to Jeffersonians' advantage to stress that point.) British funds allegedly supported Cobbett's ragings, the enlargement of Fenno's paper, and conspiracies by Senator William Blount and Isaac Sweezy.[131]

> How many things can be done in America for £228,000 sterling [the amount presumably scheduled for 1799]. It is considerably above a million dollars. It is much more than all the salaries of all our officers of government, federal and state, and the profits of all our newspaper printers!!! [132]

The Newark *Centinel of Freedom* even combined political propaganda with the dunning of its subscribers. Since its editors had heavy expenses and were "neither supported by *secret service* money" nor sharing in "the loaves and fishes" of federal patronage, they were dependent upon prompt payment of readers' accounts.[133]

Several Democratic gazettes scented danger in granting American military commissions to British officers in the United States who had been put on a half-pay inactive status by the British army. Pitt openly denounced republican principles, and yet the administration was placing his stipendiaries in positions of trust, thereby augmenting British influence. Should Americans permit the incendiaries who burned their property in the 'seventies to become their leaders against France in the 'nineties?[134]

If conceivable, the cry against British influence became intensified as the election of 1800 neared. To Democratic printers "Federalism" was only a misleading term whereby English immigrants, old Tories, and Francophobes hoped to undermine the republican Constitution. "From the indefatigable pains which a British faction take to accomplish this purpose, we are irresistibly impelled to believe that Pitt's GOLD, has a brisk circulation among *them.*"[135] Talk of an English faction seemed an obsession with many Republican editors, as if by sheer reiteration of the charge they hoped to convince readers of its verity. If British minister Liston was noted "lurking" around the House it was implied an attempt had been made to sway Congress. Noah Webster and William Cobbett were publicly labeled "British pensioners." The Richmond *Examiner* listed "the most conspicuous characters [in the administration] . . . who lately sold the independence of their country," alleging them to be hirelings of King George.[136]

A major stroke of fortune for Republicans was an admission by John Adams, who was exasperated by so much Federalist opposition to himself and to peace with France, that a strong pro-English element did indeed exist in America.[137] Democratic editors elatedly announced they now had unimpeachable corroboration; Adams had been minister to England and surely should know British influence when he saw it. He had reportedly informed a Connecticut clergyman that

'Since the last envoys to France were appointed, the Federalists have been the most seditious men in our country. That there is a strong British faction among us headed by Liston and a British Consul (Supposed to be Hamilton at Norfolk) and aided by Fenno, formerly also by Porcupine; which,' said he, 'I have long been combat[t]ing.'[138]

Democrats made the most of the story, coupling it with reportedly similar statements made to Gideon Granger, then a member of the Connecticut Legislature. Adams was said to prefer the election of Jefferson to that of either Pickering or Pinckney, who might be controlled by these Anglophiles.[139]

The charge of being English puppets was ever one which made Federalists squirm. In 1799 Duane's assertions that Pitt's secret service money was being distributed in the United States produced a plaintive protest from Pickering to the President:

> There is in the Aurora of this city an uninterrupted stream of slander on the American government. I enclose the paper of this morning. It is not the first time that the editor has suggested, that you had asserted the influence of the British government in affairs of our own, and insinuated that it was obtained by bribery. The general readers of the Aurora will believe both.[140]

Adams, evidently restive under the criticism, replied that the enclosure was indeed

> imbued with rather more impudence than is common to that paper. Is there any thing evil in the regions of actuality or possibility, that the Aurora has not suggested of me? You may depend upon it, I disdain to attempt a vindication of myself against the lies of the Aurora, as much as any man concerned in the administration of the affairs of the United States. [But, inconsistently,] If Mr. Rawle [to whom Pickering had given the issue for prosecuting Duane if he deemed it libelous] does not think this paper libellous, he is not fit for his office; and if he does not prosecute it, he will not do his duty. The matchless effrontery of this Duane merits the execution of the alien law. I am very willing to try its strength upon him.[141]

Victory of the Republicans in the New York spring election of 1800 left their opponents with the scant satisfaction of asserting that the most influential citizens of Manhattan remained Federalist. To this Republican papers retorted that those with English connections naturally adhered to the Federalist cause, and during the Revolution New York had more Tories than any other city. Now such men as Jonathan Dayton, whom the *Aurora*'s exposé had shown unworthy of trust, headed a party that desired to introduce British customs, forms, and extravagances in the United States.[142]

Democratic editors took Pickering's ties with England for granted. The Baltimore *American* indignantly predicted the recent stopping and questioning of an American merchant fleet under naval convoy would be allowed to sink into oblivion "rather than offend Mr. LISTON, for he and Mr. PICKERING are said to be two of the *best friends* in the world. . . ."[143] Adams' dismissal of Pickering as Secretary of State had embittered the President's supposed friends. They had enthusiastically approved Washington's unexplained recall of Monroe as minister to France, but considered a similar silence regarding Pickering's dismissal little short of criminal. Republicans sneered that the real reason for the ouster was confirmation of Adams' long-held suspicions of British intrigue in the Executive Department.[144] Shortly after Pickering left the Cabinet, the *Genius of Liberty* impugned his patriotism and personal honesty in the same article. It called attention again to the suit by the Comptroller of the Treasury against Randolph for an unexplained shortage in accounts when he left office. Although Pickering's deficiency of $500,000 was tenfold Randolph's, no similar step had been taken against him. The only logical conclusion was that Pickering was shown consideration because of his pro-English sympathies, while Randolph had been prosecuted because of alleged views favorable to France.[145]

Evidence that Federalist leaders were for all practical purposes under English control was, to Republican newssheets, overwhelming. Adams' talk of resisting a pro-British faction told only part of the story. Why had he not taken action against this "party devoted to the British interest"? He himself was almost equally Anglophile in outlook. An English paper favored his reelection as "a well wisher to *Great-Britain*," and he had once defended the British constitution as the world's best. He had accused Hamilton of favoring England and Oxford-trained Charles C. Pinckney of becoming minister to London through English influence.[146] Using the "transfer" technique, Democrats noted that Washington's will deplored educating American youths abroad as fostering extravagance, dissipation, and "PRINCIPLES UNFRIENDLY TO REPUBLICAN GOVERNMENT." To say the First President had Pinckney in mind might be going too far, but indubitably the advice was applicable.[147] Since Adams, Pinckney, and the Hamiltonian group were all tarred with the same stick of British interest, obviously the thing to do was to vote for the only clearly American candidate— Thomas Jefferson.

Administration supporters attempted to answer the indictment. A France that had at times allied herself with tyrants in Spain, Turkey, and Algiers could not consistently excoriate coalition with any monarchy *per se;* self-interest should dominate the foreign policy of any nation. The calumnies spread against American public officials were actuated not by "patriotism" but by ill-concealed jealousy. "Jacobins" had only "flattery and prayers" in reply to French outrages, while they would make hatred of England a public duty. Yet England convoyed American ships across the Atlantic, while France captured them.[148]

Federalist efforts, however, were not successful. Whether the implication was bribery or love of titles, English background or general dislike for popular government, Federalists were incessantly branded Anglophiles and monarchists. Benedict Arnold, it was claimed, could not have suggested improvements upon the arguments they used. Those who most loudly proclaimed the cause of America against France in the 'nineties had been Tories two decades earlier. From first to last, administration policies clearly demonstrated the Federalist penchant for aping all things British.[149] Federalist papers persistently ignored English depredations upon American commerce, though they railed indefatigably against the less serious French offenses.[150] How could John Jay write in 1779 that England was a tottering nation devoid of virtue and wisdom, equal only to plans "of *plunder, conflagration* and *murder"* and twenty years later head a party displaying "gross partiality" for Britain? It was more than symbolic that the leader of Federalist invective, an editor who printed only scurrility about Vice President Jefferson and had condemned Washington's best appointments, was William Cobbett, a British subject. "Typical" Federalist toasts were said to include one to George III and a return to America's former allegiance.[151] So pronounced was this conviction of Anglophile bias and so insistent was Republican propaganda on the point that even in 1801 Governor Jackson of Georgia could pointedly exclaim: "The richest monarch in Europe is too poor to purchase my principles, or to shake my firm adherence to the Constitution of my country." [152]

An occurrence in 1797 demonstrated to Democrats the ubiquitousness of British influence, albeit the incident was not entirely to Democrats' advantage. Spanish Minister de Yrujo had earlier confided to the State Department his fear of a British attack upon Louisiana. Pickering had scoffed at Spanish worries, but conversations with Liston revealed there had been talk of an expedition against Florida and New Orleans to forestall any French effort at occupation. The British diplomat claimed he had refused to approve, for plans involved a land force of frontiersmen and Indians in violation of American neutrality. Nevertheless, Captain John Chisholm, ex-Tory advocate of the scheme, was sent to London to secure authorization for it. Tennessee's Senator William Blount, the former governor of the Southwest Territory who was desperately overextended in land speculations, became interested in the project as a means of enhancing real estate prices. In a letter to James Carey, interpreter to the Cherokee Indians, he prophesied probable materialization of Chisholm's scheme in late 1797 and disclosed his intention to lead the filibustering force.

Carey was enjoined to silence, but, through either indiscretion or a belated sense of loyalty to his government, the attention of the administration was drawn to the matter. Soon the affair was in the papers, and the *Aurora* cried that Liston was involved as a part of England's over-all plot to provoke the United States into war with France and Spain.[153] Pickering then wrote Liston that he possessed definite information of a design to invade Spanish territory and asked for an explanation. In his reply the British minister mentioned no names but admitted knowledge of the plan and of Chisholm's mission to London.[154] On July 3, 1797, Adams sent the relevant papers to Congress, indicating that Senator Blount was implicated in a conspiracy to seize the Spanish possessions for England. Jeffersonian editors were momentarily in a quandary. Though the plot was presumably British, Blount was regarded as a Republican, and Liston had publicly denied approving the scheme. Already Federalists were chortling that one of those immaculates who raved about foreign influence was the first to be proved succumbing to it. Some of them then claimed Blount was under French influence: the story of a British invasion had been trumped up, and he actually intended to go into Louisiana and then call for French protection.[155]

Not for long, however, were Democratic editors non-plussed. Following the *Aurora*'s lead, they held that Blount had forfeited all respect, regardless of his past political leanings. But the real villains were the British minister and those minions of Albion who had bribed and plotted to drag America into war. Blount's letter was captioned *"High* TREASON! *The* EFFECT *of* BRITISH GOLD." Despite Liston's denial, it was thought certain Blount would not have proceeded without English encouragement. Since diplomatic immunity protected the British minister, the United States could know only what *he* chose to reveal. Clearly, however, a conspiracy existed. To preserve even the semblance of honor and neutrality, the administration must demand Liston's recall and refuse to "receive a Minister from his corrupt and corrupting Government until satisfaction be obtained for this attempt to disturb the peace of our country." [156]

Evidence that Britain supported the "black transaction"

265

was undeniable, and effectually contradicted Federalist talk of a "French plot," according to the *Independent Chronicle* in an issue crowded with articles and opinions on the subject:

> A Jacobin plot in favor of *England*. . . . It is an insult to common sense to pretend to it. BLOUNT might have pretended to be a Republican, as JUDAS of old pretended to be a Christian, to betray his friends with the least suspicion—or as RUSSELL now pretends to be an honest Republican.[157]

After seizure of "900 of our vessels" prattle of England's "respect for our *neutrality*" was ridiculous; had Liston actually been concerned over this he would have disclosed the plot of his own volition, instead of first denying it. The time needed to communicate with England, not Liston's opposition, had delayed operation of the scheme.[158]

The *Gazette of the United States* had long accused Democrats of being Francophiles; now it discovered they were supposedly friendly to England. Editor Fenno should "reconcile his solecism." Actually, Blount had been Washington's appointee, and thus his political views were dubious at best. "REPUBLICANS regard not *men*, but measures," and they would instantly condemn any supposed party member discovered in treason. Doubtless an investigation would reveal that Blount was not the only land speculator involved, but irrespective of his character, it was indisputable that "the BRITISH are fomenting divisions within the United States and driving us into a war with Spain." Liston, that "sly agent of British corruption," should be driven from the country "without delay." [159]

In the meantime the House of Representatives voted to impeach Blount, who was then expelled from the Senate on the charge of high misdemeanors. A sergeant at arms was sent to arrest him, but he was released on bail to answer such charges of impeachment as the House might prepare. Blount went into hiding, whereupon Republican papers screamed that his disappearance was only to be expected; Federalists, despite their comments, were only lukewarm in unravelling and punishing a British plot. The original requirement for posting a bond of

$50,000 had been cut to a mere $2,000. Nowhere was the administration's partiality more evident than in its approach to Liston on the matter. Unlike its treatment of Genêt, the administration almost apologized for even bothering the British minister. No doubt Pickering was "extremely hurt by this new instance of British Amity." [160] Blount had written Carey in April. Adams did not divulge the letter until July—and then first to Liston, "A DEEP *and* PRINCIPAL ACCOMPLICE IN THE CRIME!!," rather than to Congress. The only surprise was that Blount himself was not given advance notice of his imminent exposure, for then perhaps all evidence could have been suppressed. Here was "a plain tale of *British bribery,* and American corruption," without a trace of French implication. As "MUSTARD" put it into doggerel:

SMITH, HARPER, OTIS & Gazetteer JOHN,
  WILL WILCOCKS, old NOAH—the President's man,
Had all nos'd a secret, 'Our country was sold,
  A Democrat rabble had finger'd French gold.'

But time circling round has proclaimed them mere ninnies,
  The source of corruption, BLOUNT, L*****, and guineas.
The Democrats too so bespatter'd with stories,
  Are found our true friends—*They* a d—— pack of Tories.[161]

Shortly after Blount's expulsion. Republican journals announced the arrest in New York of a "Doctor Romaine" who was privy to the "plot to involve this Country in War." Said to have been sent by Liston to London for further information, Romaine allegedly bore papers that proved conclusively the minister's part in the plan. Actually, according to these letters, the scheme was only being postponed until next autumn; Liston would have to find money for it, and any British dissatisfaction centered around the small scale of the proposed operation.[162]

When Federalists sneered that efforts were made to distract attention from the fact that Blount was a Democrat, Jeffersonians retorted that probably this scheme of British corruption never would be probed to the bottom, for

> Mr. Blount is a federalist—Dr. Romaine is a federalist—Mr. Pickering is a federalist—Liston is a federalist—the Senate are federalists—the committee of the house of representatives are federalists. On whom then can the people depend, after what they have seen of the conduct of our public officers in this affair? Who will do us justice? [163]

The *Aurora* even hinted that Alexander Hamilton might be implicated, which was reason enough why the matter was not pressed further.[164]

To Federalist accusations that Jefferson had not presided over the expulsion vote on Blount because he favored the culprit, Democrats retorted that he had retired four days *before* the President's communication "on the subject of this *English plot.*" Moreover he had simply been following Adams' custom of withdrawing a few days prior to the close of each session, in order that the Senate might select a president *pro tempore* should any question of succession to the Presidency arise. Had the Virginian been in the chair, Blount's bond would not have been so reduced he could jump bail.[165]

The report of Samuel Sitgreaves' House committee on Blount's activities, with articles of impeachment, stirred interest afresh as the new session of Congress began. Papers devoted nearly their entire issues to the case.[166] Republicans exulted when Captain William Eaton stated Pickering had told him he did not wish to see Great Britain, America's "only friend," discredited in the eyes of the American people. Dr. Romaine's arrest, said Eaton, had unquestionably implicated Liston, but Pickering had reprimanded the captain for his discovery of the incriminating letters. Did this not prove that Federalism meant English gold, English domination, and English interference in American affairs?[167] The New London *Bee* sarcastically congratulated friends "of the upright English administration on the complete exculpation of their minister," and the prudence of the Federalists in demonstrating their brotherhood toward "the only friend we have." Anglophiles still talked of Blount as a Democrat with French accomplices, but Republican writers felt the Sitgreaves Report

so conclusively demonstrated British complicity that it length-
ened aristocratic faces considerably.[168] Impatience was expressed that some convictions were not immediately forthcoming, but Federalists had packed the committee appointed to
conduct Blount's actual impeachment with believers in administrative infallibility.[169]

A year later Blount's trial was still dragging on, and Republican exasperation was complete. If there were no other motive
for praying England's government would be overthrown,

> saving us from the curse of her precedents, that would be a suffi-
> cient one.—We are cursed with the uncertainty of the common
> law, and with the example of her standing army—navy—taxes
> without number, and without end—alien and sedition bills—and
> finally an endless impeachment! [170]

But the conclusion of the proceedings satisfied Democrats no
more than had its duration. By a vote of 14 to 11 the Senate
ruled it lacked jurisdiction in the case of one of its members.
The opposition angrily demanded to know before what tribunal Blount could now be haled. Apparently, certain individuals or crimes were superior to the law—at least if they were
"connected with the *British* minister!" [171]

Before many months other documents appeared to confirm
Republican suspicions of Liston's perfidy. On the person of
one Isaac Sweezy, reputed horsetrader or horsethief in Pennsylvania, were found letters signed by the English diplomat.
These dispatches to a Canadian judge, which were forwarded
to Adams, supposedly showed Liston was attempting to stir
up the Indians and that the administration had pledged assistance to defend Canada if needed. There was also evidence of
the administration's cooperation with Great Britain to provoke France by encouraging Toussaint L'Ouverture's revolt in
Haiti.[172]

Another letter embarrassing Federalists was made available
to Democratic editors by its recipient. In 1785 Adams had
been replaced as minister to England by Thomas Pinckney.
Still smarting over the apparent slight, he had written Tench
Coxe of the Treasury Department in May, 1792, concerning

the matter. His communication (made public by Coxe in 1800) noted "British influence" in America and commented that several members of the Pinckney clan had been suspiciously close to an old English schoolmate, the Duke of Leeds.[173] When the missive appeared in print Pinckney denounced it as either a forgery or based on a misapprehension; whichever the case, it was now being used as an electioneering trick. Coxe retorted that the letter was genuine, that both Thomas and Charles Cotesworth Pinckney knew of its existence at least a year earlier, and that Adams had not denied its authorship. A quondam Federalist dismissed as Commissioner of Revenue in 1797 and probably seeking revenge, Coxe insisted that beginning with Washington's early appointments there had been numerous proofs that the colossus of English domination "bestrode the land." Men in position to know, he continued, had charged Hamilton was an avowed monarchist; now that Adams had suggested British subversion, Hamilton demonstrated the same enmity toward him as toward Jefferson. Most Federalists were devoted to a republican government, but some of their most powerful leaders were not. Coxe claimed to know for a certainty that the British regarded Fenno's newspaper as *"a Gazette of their own."* [174]

Federalists writhed under this onslaught, but Republicans found their responses lame indeed. If Adams knew nothing of the Duke of Leeds' classmates, as the *Washington Federalist* suggested, he never should have written such a letter. That he (like some modern scholars) had confused his Pinckneys brought guffaws; Charles Pinckney was noted for Republicanism, and to imply that Adams had him in mind was an especially odorous red herring. Well did the President know that it was Thomas and Charles Cotesworth Pinckney who had used friendship with the Duke to obtain diplomatic appointments. Never had Democrats made a sharper indictment than had Adams himself in this letter, and when he had charged English pressure he was quite aware of its significance.[175]

Jeffersonian editors were convinced that by purchase, lies,

and misrepresentation, the British had done their best to involve the nation in war with France. They helped applaud Adams' assertion that he would rather fight France for twenty years than pay her a shilling tribute, while they encouraged bribes "to the British, the Algerines, and to every tribe of ban-, ditti, on the western frontier." [176] Bowles's reappearance among the Creeks, English fortifications abuilding at Halifax, naval seizures and trading prohibitions in the Spanish Bay of Honduras, and overgenerous Canadian land offers to entice settlers from the United States were all facets of the many-sided British hostility toward America. The remark of an English commissioner on claims under the Jay Treaty that American independence was only a bargain in return for an unascertained debt to the mother country, conditional upon its payment, and Lord Grenville's haughty treatment of American minister Rufus King, revealed implacable hatred; it was capped by the evil machinations of Great Britain with the "anglo-federal" party in the United States. [177]

*Any* foreign influence was reprehensible, warned Republican gazettes, but such malice made British intrigues to be dreaded as the very devil. English denials meant nothing:

> That the British government will not stick at falsehood is too well known. They deny to this hour the bribery of *Blount:* They deny that a British faction is secretly upheld in the United States: They deny that they expend money in corrupting foreign governments: They deny that they have committed murder, rapine, plunder and desolation in ASIA, AFRICA and AMERICA. But who is there that believes them? [178]

During Washington's administration, Lord Hawkesbury's report to the Privy Council had asserted that "a British party was already formed in America." The hireling abuse of "Peter Porcupine" (Cobbett), "the employment of Americans to discharge British functions in the United States," and the prosecution of the *Aurora's* editor for his account of England's secret service expenditures, all tended toward the same conclusion. So did the remark by Canada's Chief Justice that Britain held that region as a club to keep this nation *"in awe,"* the announcement of Secretary of War McHenry that *"Old Tories"* should be preferred for officers in the standing army, and the selection of English pensioners for posts of trust in the American revenue service and navy.[179]

Unless Americans foreswore such British influence, and speedily, Republicans held that the United States was undone. If they lacked the honor, gratitude, and common sense to perceive that their true interest lay in the success of the French cause, the least Americans should do was to draw "like the Tortoise within our shell," develop their own manufactures, and rely on their own crops and products. Preservation of American national integrity demanded some such action against the mother country's all-enveloping hostility.[180]

 GALLIA AGGRIEVED

If conviction of English iniquity was a cardinal Democratic tenet, so also was confidence in the virtue of the French Republic—the only major power with government and ideals similar to those of America. Republicans dismissed any suggestion of French animosity as Federalist duplicity designed to further the causes of England and monarchy. Any seemingly inimical measures taken by Paris were forced upon her by military necessity or the double-dealing of America's administration. France's reservoir of good will, moreover, was not inexhaustible.

Republican affection for the Gallic Republic and pride in the progress of her arms continued almost unabated to the century's close. So favorable was sentiment generally that most Federalists exercised extreme caution in their references to France until about the time of Adams' inaugural. A Chamber of Commerce dinner might be publicly censured merely because no one had proposed a toast to the success of the French Revolution.[1] In 1796 even the *Minerva*-owned New York *Herald* felt despots had only spread that revolution by attacking it, and their interference in French internal affairs had brought deserved defeat upon themselves. Reports of the Republic's victories were "Glorious News!" Supporters of Adams, no less, proclaimed America's love for France, whose lone struggle for freedom and security against a coalition of

273

tyrants was a greater achievement than that of ancient Rome. Necessity had obliged this peaceful nation to become a military power, and a magnificent one.[2]

Fiercely did Jeffersonians resent the criticism of Paris that gradually became more common. French aid in America's Revolution may not have been entirely altruistic, but it had made independence possible. Federalists had claimed a debt of gratitude was due Louis XVI so long as they thought the French Republic could not last; now they denied it altogether. Once the treaty with France had been broken, administration leaders seemed prepared to go on to any perfidy.[3] Even though Federalists compared France unfavorably with England, Democrats yet maintained "a good friend is far above a bad parent" in value. Trade with France that provided $3,000,000 in cash annually, her evidences of amity, and her goals of reannexing Canada and Louisiana and of recognizing that "free ships make free goods" were beneficial to the United States.[4] The maligned conduct of the emerging Bonaparte was actually as humane as it was uniformly successful, and it was insisted that neither Genêt nor any other French minister had ever tried to involve America in war with England. By late 1797 pro-administration papers were labeled a "COMMON SEWER of defamation against France," packed with fabrications of governmental changes and counter-revolutions in that country.[5]

The frequent reports of Napoleon's death found in Federalist gazettes were a primary butt of Democratic jokes. Tongue in cheek, the *Farmers' Register* assembled a list of eight impossible methods whereby Bonaparte reputedly had died in Egypt; one more and he would have as many lives as a cat. Reports that he had been mortally wounded were no longer news. "Buonaparte has been *mortally* wounded in every engagement since he set foot in Egypt besides having been very often killed." [6] And to the superstitious who believed a series of narrow escapes had truly been the Corsican's lot Jeffersonians suggested the probability of "Providential interposition." Armchair strategists averred the Egyptian expedition showed conclusively that British naval power could not halt French military progress.[7] Yet Republican confidence in Napoleon's integrity was not unqualified, for at least one paper reprinted the constitution establishing the Consulate with the prophetic comment that France must be wearying of a tedious war, for "this begins to have 'an awful squinting towards Monarchy.' "[8]

Some historians have noted that at times certain members of both parties believed they stood to profit from war and that this opinion operated against strict American neutrality during the 'nineties. Resentment against the plundering of American commerce and desire for additional territory alike served as motives, but some Federalists wished to fight France, while some Democrats wished to battle England.[9] In one of its more moderate articles the *Aurora* held American party differences stemmed largely from divergent opinions respecting the French Republic. Federalists thought it doomed to quickly perish; the belief was not criminal in itself, but their administration was seeking to make it come true. Instead of trying to speed the Republic's collapse, and perhaps gain the good will of the monarchy that would replace it, the United States should assume the French government stable and await developments. Americans certainly would resent official efforts to generate conflict with France merely to fulfill a speculative theory.[10]

Yet, though most Republican papers continued to print with praise any favorable news of French success,[11] unwavering support of France was no longer so prevalent as it had been in the days of Genêt. Interpreting the Jay Treaty as antagonistic to her interests, Paris was showing resentment. Somewhat ruefully, Democratic prophets found their predictions of this eventuality being realized; French seizures of American ships began to rival those of the British,[12] and a sterner Gallic diplomatic attitude was clearly perceptible. With Federalists crowing that this development indicated France's true feeling toward America, Jeffersonian "I-told-you-sos" were vehement. The government of the tricolor wished no war with America, insisted "A Citizen" upon the capture of the *Mount Vernon* by the French privateer *Flying Fish*. France was disgusted with Jay's agreement. American shippers could now know what to expect by studying the alliance of 1778 with France; henceforth they could expect the conduct of that nation to parallel what had previously been tolerated from Britain. "Conviction by reason or conversion by the guillotine" was drunk on Independence Day to the friends of the British treaty, along with a toast to the *Flying Fish* and the hope it would take only Anglophiles' vessels. Federalists who for years had justified English outrages should not whimper now about "French persecutions of our commerce." [13] Long had England been jealous of American carrying trade; at last, thanks to Federalist folly, France was helping her cripple American shipping. America's merchant marine was compared to the man with hair half gray and half black who fell in love with two women. One woman pulled out the black hair to make him look older, and the other pulled out the gray hair to make him appear youthful; before long the unfortunate gentleman was bald.[14]

Republicans maintained that, contrary to Federalist ranting, Gallic conduct was conspicuously superior to that of England before the Jay Treaty. France might resent the insults of Federalist provocateurs—but she had not incited Indian raids, nor yet conducted herself so that America had to resort to embargoes, fortifications, and plans for an army of eighty thousand men. Democrats marked the contrast between the courteous conduct when French captures or detentions were made and the contumely bestowed by the British.[15] Moreover, since England had started the policy of depredations, France was forced for her own salvation to fight fire with fire.[16]

Adopting and adapting earlier Federalist tactics, Republicans now played on the fear of armed conflict. France must possess astounding resources, commented the *Aurora* in 1796, to have humbled four powerful nations in but four years' struggle. Accelerated American naval construction would entail added expenses, prognosticated the *Independent Chronicle,* and arming would mean war within six months. "NUMA" actually stressed the parallel reasoning; he suggested that Federalists get out the old files of the *Philadelphia Gazette* and peruse their own past arguments against war with England. The prophesies of lowered farm prices, closure of the Mississippi, increased debt and executive influence, etc., were equally pertinent in 1797. Any such struggle required an alliance, which would threaten American independence and would contradict Washington's valedictory warning as President.[17] Perhaps the administration could send an army "composed of such heroes as make the British faction" against the French by building a bridge across the Atlantic! [18]

The political campaign of 1796 that resulted in Adams' winning the Presidency produced an open attempt by the French Directory to influence the election, for Paris had become convinced of the necessity of securing a Francophile American President. Accordingly, Adet, then French minister to the United States, was instructed to strive for Washington's retirement and a change in administration. In late October Adet sent to the State Department an announcement that his government would henceforth pursue a policy identical to Britain's toward America. French captains would be authorized to capture such vessels as Jay's treaty permitted England to detain and condemn.[19] Such an announcement, presaging as it did an open rupture, could scarcely have genuinely pleased American friends of France. Yet "A Freeholder" later praised "the just and profound policy" of this decree and also defended it for "the compleat refutation it offers to all the calumnies of the British government, and their deluded apologists in this country." [20] Adet's letter was published in the *Aurora*—without the consent of the administration—on the eve of an election so close that the change of a handful of votes in peace-loving Pennsylvania would have made Pinckney Vice President instead of Jefferson.[21]

This publication was closely followed by that of other communications, ostensibly from Adet to Pickering, but rather clearly intended for the public eye. One urged Frenchmen in foreign lands to wear a tricolored cockade if they wished the protection of the Directory, and many Americans followed suit to demonstrate their sympathies.[22] On November 15, the minister broke the news of his recall as evidence of Gallic displeasure with America's course and appealed to America to return to the principle that neutral ships made neutral goods, to honor her earlier treaties with France, and to disavow the British covenant. All these "notes" went simultaneously to Pickering and the *Aurora,* which published a summary of the last one before the State Department could prepare a translation of the original.[23]

Federalist accusations of "electioneering" were immediate and vociferous. Amid cries of "foreign influence," they printed Pickering's reply that chided Adet for publishing his first note. Democrats countered that the note had been written on instructions sent from Paris before Washington's retirement had become known, but this only rendered them vulnerable to the charge that publication had been deliberately withheld until the time of its maximum possible influence in the campaign. Proof of Democratic implication was seen in the Boston *Chronicle*'s report that Adet intended to suspend his functions a week before that worthy himself announced it. Despite their pious denunciations of alien interests in the United States, Republicans had not hesitated to proclaim that Jefferson's election would make possible maintenance of peace with France. Fear of war perhaps caused Pennsylvania to choose thirteen Republican electors, but for the nation as a whole the scheme may have backfired against administration critics.[24]

Adams won the election (so narrowly that Jefferson gained the nation's second-highest office), but the argument raged on. Democrats held the administration's contention that publication of Adet's note insulted national dignity came dangerously near denying Presidential responsibility to the sovereign people. At worst, Adet's message was an honorable warning that the State Department doubtless would have withheld; actually, American merchants deeply appreciated information affecting commerce, regardless of the source from which it came. Over a year later the quasi-war with France was cited as the final answer to the charge that the French minister's recall had been only an electioneering ruse.[25]

Pickering's reply to Adet was sent in the form of instructions to Charles C. Pinckney, new American minister to Paris. The administration's conduct was defended; France owed as much to the United States as *vice versa* in the matter of services rendered, and certainly her representative had no right to make appeals to the people over the head of their government. This document, too, was immediately given to the press, where Jeffersonians had already flayed the Secretary's earlier response to the sterner French policy on American shipping. France, said Republicans, had every reason to censure the administration's conduct; it had abandoned America's position under international law that the flag of a neutral vessel should protect the goods it carried and had even violated the Neutrality Proclamation by justifying British plundering. In case of war with France, commercial retaliation (potentially so effective against England) would be of no avail.[26] Now Pickering's instructions ignored the fact of unofficial French aid long before Burgoyne's surrender and ran counter to Washington's last speech to Congress, which had called for friendship with France.[27]

"WE THE PEOPLE," claiming to be the sovereign power of the nation, called on Congress to investigate the conduct of the Executive Department and to determine the validity of Adet's charges. Assuredly, the breach with France seemed a stain on Washington's public character, and magnanimous conduct could prevent a rupture. France's real crime seemingly lay in becoming a republic; had she remained a monarchy American aristocrats probably would have aided her, or at least would have maintained an honest neutrality.[28]

Republican arguments were not uniform in all quarters of the country. Some papers quoted the Paris *Rédacteur* to deny that France had broken off all diplomatic relations. No amount of personal friction could destroy the common inter-

ests of the two nations; both governments were popularly controlled, and most Frenchmen realized the Jay Treaty contravened American public sentiment. They consequently appealed to time and good sense to end the British yoke and to
erase Francophobe calumnies; French triumphs would up-
root Americans' pusillanimity and disclose their true interests.[29]

Yet, if formal relations between the two republics had not
yet been officially severed, the break appeared not far distant.
To warn France of displeasure at her changing attitude and to
have a representative more accurately reflecting the administration's views, Washington removed Monroe as minister to
Paris and replaced him with Charles Cotesworth Pinckney.
Openly friendly to France, Monroe had been embarrassed by
Jay's treaty, and his understandable lack of enthusiasm in defending that document led Pickering to insist upon his recall.
Pinckney was known as a Federalist of very moderate views,
but it was questionable whether even a Republican would have
been immediately acceptable to the Directory.[30] Democratic
editors, sensing a stiffening attitude toward France, denounced
the shift. Monroe, whose diplomacy had skilfully prevented a
clash at the time of the British treaty, was "obnoxious" to the
State Department because war between the two republics had
been averted.[31]

Pinckney, brother of the former minister to London and
successful envoy to Madrid, spent some time in Paris while
speculation was rife in America as to whether or not he would
be received officially. Since his instructions had been published
in the United States before he had even reached France and
American "court papers" had railed against the Directory,
Republicans predicted he would be rejected. Their gazettes
accused the administration of fomenting war and called for
people to express their sentiments.[32]

Pickering's instructions to Pinckney were a criticism of
Adet and, according to "A CITIZEN," constituted an effort
to create a permanent estrangement. The attempt to prove the
United States was not obligated to France distorted the facts;

America had sought the alliance in 1778, and its terms clearly bound the United States to defend France if attacked by England. There was only Jay's biased word to "prove" that France opposed favorable terms for American independence, and even British sources testified that it could not have been achieved at all without Gallic aid. The French *people* had forced their government to act, and America's debt was to them rather than their king.[33]

French Foreign Minister Delacroix finally refused to receive Pinckney, who removed to Amsterdam and wrote home for instructions. News that Pinckney had left Paris stirred President Adams to action. In one proclamation he named a day of fasting and prayer for the emergency confronting the nation. A second summoned a special session of the Fifth Congress.[34] His speech of May 16, 1797, before that body severely condemned French conduct and drew stinging criticism from virtually every Republican paper in the country.

Until this time, the period since Adams' election had seen an amusing attempt by the Democratic press to wean the new Chief Executive away from at least the extreme wing of the Federalist party. His inaugural address was warmly praised in such sheets as the New York *Argus* and the *Aurora*. It was refreshing, they said, to hear ostentation ridiculed and the fundamental maxim reiterated that sovereign power was vested in the people. Adams' integrity, lack of public display, and expressed desire for peace with France, all showed him a patriot rather than a partisan. As such, Republicans could support him; they were ready to judge men by their conduct rather than by their words, and he had demonstrated he was no tool of Hamilton and the British faction.[35] Even after the call for a special session, it was suggested that Hamilton was endeavoring to prod Adams into some improper, unpopular action that would lead to war. Thus the ex-Secretary could then "contrast the pacific conduct of WASHINGTON to the warlike system of ADAMS" and, despite public detestation of him, could use this as a step toward realizing his dream of becoming President. There would be still more false rumors of hostilities, for Federalists hoped that continual discussion would make an actual declaration of war more palatable when a seasonable time arrived.[36]

This campaign to cozen rather than bludgeon the new President was abandoned with startling suddenness after Congress convened. Adams' address demanded maintenance of national honor, advocating a system of naval defense and general protection for commerce. Republicans immediately remonstrated; this speech was no less than a war-whoop. The administration would at most make only a show of negotiation, for the President was already "convinced" his government had been "*just* and *impartial*" toward France. If he expected the people to be gulled by this address, "he must suppose himself the president of a nation of *Ourang outangs,* instead of men." [37]

Adams, it was claimed, had deceived the people completely. Elected President by only three votes, he had led them to believe he was under the control of no man. Now he had thrown off the mask, and the devilish British cast of his countenance was evident. Since only Congress could declare war, his ravings only disclosed his animosity toward France. Actually, such language might have prevailed against England, before whom America cringed, but France "would indeed be our destroying angel" if provoked to hostilities. Only Providence could help America now.[38]

The President had called France's refusal to recognize Pinckney a denial of a right. But after the administration's deceit she had recalled her own minister to break off intercourse with America; how could she then with dignity receive its envoy? To such a pass had the Jay Treaty brought the country, for, if Adams' effusion were to be relied upon, Americans could expect war with France within four months. In truth, England had violated "that insidious compact" by seizures of men and property, and Americans were no longer obligated to adhere to it. In this way armed conflict could be avoided, despite the frenzied efforts of Federalist leaders and their "hired papers." [39]

If peace were preserved, it would be entirely owing to the

moderation of the House of Representatives and the magnanimity of France, "and not to the mad projects of Pres. Adams." Before the election Federalists had warned that Jefferson's triumph would mean war while Adams was for peace; could there be any more striking proof of baseness and fraud than this cry of "to arms"? Even Washington sent Jay to England when trouble with that country flared; Adams must be in his dotage to contend he spoke for all the people in advocating belligerent steps toward France.[40]

Public meetings had called for further negotiations and had descanted upon the horrors of war. The *Independent Chronicle* computed the cost of a conflict: $5,000,000 in lost trade with Spain, Holland, and France; $1,000,000 for three frigates; $80,000,000 for an army; $5,000,000 for property confiscated in France; and an estimated $50,000,000 that England would demand for "defending our independence." All would be spent in a project that would no more hurt France "than *Don Quixote's* attack on the *wind-mill*." Grass would grow on State Street and on Broadway, fisheries would be ruined, and British troops might even be quartered in Boston again. A domestic revolt was far from impossible.[41] Other writers slyly suggested Federalists knew little of war's hardships but were sounding the alarm to provide jobs for their friends in the newly created army and navy. Would that all anglo-federal blusterers could "be *drafted* to commence the crusade." Paris considered the United States beneath her notice but would fight if challenged. What then "must we think of those *hair-brained* [*sic*] politicians *Dr.* [William L.] Smith, Harper and *young* Otis for trying to frighten France, with six revenue cutters and three frigates which can never be manned!"[42] When *England* violated the peace treaty, retained the Western posts, stirred up Indians and Algerines, and captured nearly a thousand ships worth $5,000,000, administration leaders represented this "immense loss as perfectly trifling when compared with the dire calamities which a war must occasion." Now that France was the potential foe, the same leaders were "warhawks."[43]

Adams' speech produced interminable debate in the House, which did not for three weeks formally deliver its reply. George Nicholas and Albert Gallatin insisted the British treaty had produced the crisis and argued Federalists were deliberately inciting hostilities. Robert G. Harper, earlier a Charleston "Jacobin," now linked Republicans with France, charging Monroe with virtual treason in influencing that country against the United States in the matter of the Jay Treaty.[44] This vilification of the former minister made Harper, as a renegade, a prime object for Democratic barbs. Monroe, defending himself, called on Pickering for specific charges justifying his dismissal and ignored—said Jeffersonians—this Congressional slanderer who had pretended to be a Republican in order to be elected.[45] When Pickering refused an explanation, Monroe denied the President's right to remove at will, and soon published his correspondence with the State Department. He contended he had been deceived concerning Jay's mission and had been named to mislead France on that score. America had continually irritated the Republic since ratification of the vicious treaty, and yet Monroe had been recalled just as more amicable relations were being achieved. This "View" of Monroe's conduct was widely circulated as a counter-irritant to Federalist war-mongering.[46]

The official response of the House included a recommendation for another attempt at conciliation, and then Congress passed measures creating a provisional army, providing for coastal defense and naval armament, and approving the government's borrowing $800,000. The request for further negotiation coincided with executive plans, although Pickering and other extreme Federalists were angered at Adams' selection of the independent Elbridge Gerry to accompany John Marshall and the once-rejected Pinckney.[47]

Many Republicans feared the mission was only a sham intended to delude the public and to pave the way for war, a standing army, and monarchy. When Federalists insisted the three would not make improper sacrifices to France "even if it would be possible they should BE SO INSTRUCTED," the

*Independent Chronicle* retorted administration scribblers must know party plans so well they could promise the envoys would disregard any instructions not suited to "their [own] idea of propriety." Both time and money would be saved if the administration would only honestly acknowledge its faults. Mordant writers suggested the commissioners' instructions be composed of

> The gasconading speech of John Adams, president by *three votes* of the United States, and the puerile and vapouring conceits of *William Smith, L.L.D., Robert Goodloe Harper, quondam member of a democratic society,* and *Harrison Gray Otis, the man with more than one shirt.*[48] Should the ministers be attended by the *pathos* of these gentlemen, and that of the *hero* of the *last ditch,*[49] little doubt can be entertained of the success of their mission, for the bare idea alone of '*throwing our sword into the scale of Great Britain,*' would convulse the executive directory with terror, and oblige them to subscribe to our justice of good faith, and to the infallibility of our virtuous administration.[50]

Yet while they sneered at the mission, Democrats were not averse to using it as an argument against public criticism of France. Administration gazettes were reprimanded for warning against believing false reports of a settlement. Was it criminal to *hope* for an amicable adjustment when negotiation was still possible? Anti-French agitators such as Wilcocks should leave America for despotic Algiers or Britain, and an Independence Day orator who expressed "virulent" sentiments toward France was accused of undermining efforts at conciliation. A "horrid" report from England that French saboteurs had been sent over to fire American seaports demonstrated how mad for war were the Federalists and how the "royalists" took advantage of freedom of the press.[51] Should the envoys be able to adjust differences with France, it was doubtful that officials would "sacrifice their private feelings" and "make reparation where they have injured." Inasmuch as the President and his ministers had produced a critical situation, "from which, we fear, they have neither the wisdom nor prudence" to extricate America, "the only step still in their power to heal the mischief they have done is to *retire* and leave more skil[l]ful and fortunate pilots to save the vessel of state."[52]

Unfortunately, Federalist leaders suffered from the dangerous disease of "Gallophobia." An item in the *Gazette of the United States* urging restoration of a king to the French throne was said to reveal the government's hostility to the Gallic Revolution. The *Aurora* cited the same paper for April 25, 1796, wherein Republican news items were offered as proof that American Francophiles sought war; now Bache urged examination of Fenno's columns to determine which party desired hostilities.[53] Federalists insisted on portraying the Directory as a *faction* and bemoaned discovery of a royalist plot that would have produced the horrors of civil war. Apparently, "our Pharaohs" still wishfully looked for the downfall of the Republic and were ready to "lend a hand to effect it." Such a course made evident the insincerity of Adams' attempts to negotiate.[54]

So many wild versions of the treatment received by the three envoys at French hands were current that the New York *Diary* called on its readers to refrain from forming an opinion until the truth was known:

> The tory faction will endeavour to torture fact, in order to excite our feelings against the cause of liberty and the revolution. We know their baseness and their cunning; we have fully experienced their perfidy and their intrigues: Let us be calm. . . .[55]

It was said that Adet and Fauchet had been named to treat with the trio, and Federalists protested this degraded America. Democrats agreed they might well desire that the envoys meet other men, but Americans had no right to name France's representatives. However, they slyly noted, if the administration had justice on its side it should welcome the appointment of individuals fully familiar with its conduct.[56]

Gradually, more and more skepticism began to be expressed about the possibility of an official French reception of the mission. The *Aurora* reviewed the hostility of Federalist administrations toward Paris; Pickering's "insulting manifesto" and Adams' slurs could scarcely fail to turn Gallic distrust into open enmity. Governor Jay, familiar with diplomatic usages, was said to have once slighted French Minister Adet in New York—which might explain why American representatives were not invited to a celebration in Paris. No honest man could contend Americans had suffered half the loss in maritime depredations from France that they had from England nor that the government had been impartial in its attitude toward the two nations. No one should expect the envoys to be received unless they were instructed to treat upon principles amicable to the Republic. Although the Directory did not wish war, neither would it cringe before the United States.[57]

As clouds blackened on the international horizon, Republican editors, who on Thanksgiving had implored God to baffle the designs of the warmongers, redoubled their efforts to depict the horrors of combat as something to be avoided at almost any cost. England's corruption exemplified the condition to which a conflict with France would reduce the United States; Indian atrocities, an end to immigration, and assorted other evils would be resultant by-products. Until *all* Americans were united by the actual landing of foreign troops on their soil, it was only sensible to "rely on our distance from Europe as promising security against invasion." [58] Letters of "Junius" in Boston insisted a war with France would be "IMPOLITIC, UNJUST, UNGRATEFUL, *and* RUINOUS to AMERICA." Against England Americans had put about forty thousand men in the field, and had won only through French aid; France could raise three million men, backed by sixty ships of the line. Moreover, France was America's best customer. Why not purchase peace, as the administration had done from an Algiers with far less justification for her conduct? True patriots would pray for the success of the peace mission.[59]

Dire indeed were the warnings from the *Chronicle*. Even realization of the Federalist-British hope for restoration of the monarchy in France would not ensure significant changes in French foreign policy. After all, England's system of navigation laws had commenced under Cromwell. The *Centinel* might claim French depredations had caused American commerce to fall off and that tradesmen and artificers would virtually starve unless merchantmen were armed—but if war came, trade would totally disappear, underwriters would lose their premiums, public creditors the value of their securities, and seamen their liberty (through impressment, perhaps on British ships). "Mr. [Benjamin] Russell says *arm* or *starve*—We say, STARVE you will, if you do ARM!" Gazettes "devoted to war, blood and slaughter" did not breathe the sentiments of the people. Did their prating of "national honor" mean medieval knight-errantry, or fair, firm, and frank conduct that was above petty jealousies? The first was not worth worrying about—let alone fighting for—and a war would produce huge expenses and the total loss of trade, besides confrontation with the million-man army that had conquered all Europe.[60]

"Peter Porcupine" and other Federalists remonstrated against this "campaign of fear" and asserted one-eighth of America's five million people could easily overcome the French. *Carey's United States Recorder,* however, was skeptical:

> Without wishing to derogate from the military prowess of the citizens of the United States, it may fairly be doubted, whether one eighth of our population is equal to the *work of death,* in which such numerous hosts of European veterans have failed: but still more may it be doubted, whether that proportion of them would readily embark upon the very pleasant and *satisfactory* plan of annihilating twenty-eight millions of people! [61]

As hostilities seemed increasingly imminent, Jeffersonian papers carried stories of French triumphs and plans to invade England. There were sarcastic references to America's good fortune in aligning with Britain, now that her rising might was all-powerful. One writer noted that England had 92 frigates and America but 3, while France and her allies possessed 255—all favoring freedom of the seas.[62]

The *Aurora* hammered home the cost of a conflict and its

disastrous effect upon an already unstable national credit. Yet callow Robert Goodloe Harper talked of fighting Napoleon as glibly "as if he were only going to dance a minuet with some of his rural sweethearts in the district of ninety-six." Harper claimed the financial expense could be met by a land tax, but a quarter million farmers would be required to pay $160 each to support the army alone—when loss of the French market would lower farm prices. Moreover,

> At the same time, the British countervailing duty, like a cannon ball sweeping off the stump of a man's arm, will just finish the business. We shall hear no more of the disgraces of the American flag, for *that* flag will cease to exist.[63]

Figures on America's export trade were cited by the *Independent Chronicle* to support this position. During the year prior to September, 1797, America shipped three times as much to France, Holland, Spain, and Portugal as to England.[64] War with France could only reduce the United States to Britain's sorry state of bankruptcy and unbearable taxes; obviously Pitt wanted America as "an appendage to his infamous projects, that both may fall together." The British navy could not protect *all* America's ships, even it if would; France's fall would destroy a most profitable customer; and why should Americans arm, or even be taxed, *"for the purpose of protecting* BRITISH MANUFACTURERS?"[65]

Even after Adams had informed Congress (March 19, 1798) that France had rejected the overtures of the peace mission and had warned the nation to prepare for the worst, there were floods of protests against arming American merchantmen.[66] Such a step would inexorably lead to hostilities under the guise of self-protection, for it left the decision of a conflict up to any sea captain rather than the regularly constituted authorities. Perhaps the Chief Executive wished to make a scapegoat of some honest but short-tempered mariner.[67] Bad as they were, despots normally tried to ascertain the wishes of their subjects on important matters—but the President alone had decided the time had come for America to draw her sword in support of a collapsing Britain. Doubtless England had promised ships, supplies, the conquest of Mexico —anything, to get America involved. But experience warned us to beware; without fail, Albion would sacrifice us to secure peace for herself.[68] Adams' message was fatal to amity. It probably ensured discord, ruin, and disunion, for Americans would not endure bloodshed and financial disaster merely to gratify the President's "individual passions." [69] Frontiersmen noted that Britons planned a military loan to the United States at a time when they could "not even pay the interest on what they owe for spoilations on our commerce. . . ." [70]

In 1795 Timothy Pickering had proclaimed American friendship for France and had asserted it was to the interest of the government to maintain peace. Assuredly, the French triumphs in the intervening years made this analysis even more valid in '98.[71] When things had looked blackest with England, the administration had permitted no move such as arming merchant vessels to widen the breach. Arming was so close to war in its consequences that it was "only a play on words to distinguish between them." Not all American ships could be adequately armed, and once hostilities became general America's commerce rather than England's would be the heavy loser. Moreover, the simple exclusion of American trade from the ports of France and her allies would make "a dollar . . . as scarce a commodity as an honest royalist." [72]

Truly, America possessed the right to arm her merchant ships. But the French war and British alliance that would result made arming no more prudent than consulting a quack doctor for a serious illness. The only remedy—admittedly no speedy one—lay in strict adherence to neutrality. Otherwise, should France prevail against England, Americans would be left at the Republic's mercy; or should she make an advantageous peace, they would be bereft of their only ally. To such a pass had they been brought through "the wretched policy of a party, aided by the influence of a few Clergymen, and treating with contempt all the advice of the sober, Patriotic and enlightened part of the community." [73] America's entire trade rested on Washington's proclamation that "free ships should make free goods." How the world would jeer were Americans to declare war against the Franco-Spanish alliance that advocated this principle and to pray for the protection of the British who denied it! [74] Sailors were warned not to serve on armed merchantmen, which had no regular commissions and might be regarded as pirate vessels; Massachusetts congressmen were cautioned to think of French ships sweeping American fishing fleets off the Grand Banks once cannon shots had been exchanged at sea. [75]

In the (by then) accepted tradition, the Jeffersonian press urged meetings and petitions against this fateful step. Other communities were called upon to second the remonstrance of Newark's town-meeting; resolutions of forty Pennsylvania assemblymen condemned arming prior to a declaration of war or endorsing negotiations so long as "any door to reconciliation remains open." If measures *must* be taken, a partial embargo would safeguard American interests and eliminate the danger of triggering an unauthorized war. [76] In the South readers were asked why they should fight to protect British-manufactured articles; in New England arming was branded "the grossest quixotism," enabling Britain to deprive Americans of carrying trade. [77] Exaggerated, no doubt, was the claim that "The yeomanry, from one end of the continent to the other in their LEGAL Town Meetings, are addressing to Congress, not to plunge us into a war, by arming the merchantmen, &c.," but the resolutions were sufficiently numerous that they were alleged to have "already confounded the War-Hawks in Philadelphia." [78]

As yet, asserted many Republicans, Americans did not know against what their commercial vessels would be arming. Failure to receive envoys scarcely constituted a *casus belli*. The "baron of Braintree" (President Adams) had seen the dispatches from Paris, but as yet no one else had. He categorically announced there was no ground for negotiation, while a supine Congress was expected to ratify his will and the people who paid the taxes and did the fighting were refused information. "From the . . . President's address it would appear, that however he may acknowledge a right in the Legislature to *declare* war, he conceives he has that of making it." [79] Demands were heard to know the *real* differences with France and what sincere efforts had been made to alleviate them. [80] The *South Carolina State Gazette* charged Adams and his Cabinet with responsibility for the growing tension and openly suggested they should resign. [81]

Some blamed Cobbett's *Porcupine's Gazette* for Adams' speech. "This prostitute hireling has risen 50 per cent. in imaginary consequence since the '*war whoop*' (as he calls the president's message of Monday) has been delivered," moaned *Carey's United States Recorder*. [82] The President, chimed in the New York *Journal,* withheld information from Congress and the people but offered "FOOD which will be deemed by many hard to digest—*gun-powder* and *red hot balls.*" Predictions were for "warm debate . . . by which the American *people* will see plainly, who are for MONARCHY, and who for a REPUBLIC!" [83]

Insistent calls now came from every quarter for publication of the papers from Paris. With "Porcupine" screaming "the die was cast," surely citizens were entitled to know whether or not war could be averted. [84] All this "mystery" and rumors of French demands for money or for Adams' retirement were only electioneering tricks for the April voting. The President's political future hinged on his favorite scheme of forcing France "to submit to *his* terms," and actually war "would be a mighty fine affair for the chosen few" who would benefit from honors, contracts, and offices. [85]

Impatient at the delay, the *Aurora* found Adams' last message "extremely curious," as was "every piece which comes from his pen." It mentioned the arrival of dispatches but said some time would be required in deciphering; only a strange cipher indeed required a full week without explanation. More likely deletions and changes were being made. Having perceived "the rashness of having formerly printed Pinckney's correspondence," Adams was editing these communications—

or else "they convey some intelligence, which John and his man Timothy are afraid to tell!" [86] Nearly three weeks later, the *Aurora* fumed the stalling demonstrated both the President's doubts as to the popularity of his course and his conviction that he had done wrong. Should he refuse to surrender these papers, "what becomes of his oath of office, of his engagement to lay before Congress . . . *information respecting the State of the Union?*" [87]

The *Albany Register* hoped the House of Representatives would "call for the despatches . . . in a voice too firm to be disregarded." If Adams had it ". . . in his power to lead the country blindfolded into a fruitless and bloody conquest, on the side of the British government, then farewell to the liberties of America." [88] Accordingly, Democrats rejoiced at the congressional request for the correspondence, and the *Chronicle* congratulated the nation on not taking "a step in the dark." [89]

Any exultation, however, was short-lived. The copies of the dispatches Adams sent to Congress on April 3 presented anything but a pretty picture of French diplomacy. With temporary dominance over the peace party in France, a favorable Austrian treaty, financial interest in privateering and a predisposition toward peculation, the Directory decided to continue commercial depredations against America or to charge handsomely for easing the irritation. After treating the envoys contemptuously, Foreign Minister Talleyrand sent them agents who were little better than blackmailers. A bribe of £50,000 to the minister and a loan of $10,000,000 (plus an apology) to France as compensation for Adams' chauvinistic message were demanded before negotiations could commence. Should these be refused, Talleyrand's friends (designated as X, Y, and Z by Pickering in the papers transmitted to Congress) and a lady associate suavely alluded to the fate of recalcitrant European nations and to the strength of the Francophile party in America.[90] To the demand for money before negotiating Pinckney retorted "No! no! not a sixpence!" and American Federalists soon converted this to "Millions for defense, but not one cent for tribute," as a clarion call to arms.

Thunderstruck Republicans had anticipated nothing of this sort. There had been all sorts of rumors, but most of them had associated French unwillingness to treat with American envoys with justified outrage over the administration's conduct. The vague stories of demands for a bribe had either been discounted or viewed as a clever method of uncovering possible corruption among Gallic public officials.[91] Most Jeffersonian prints published the incriminating dispatches without comment,[92] although the *Aurora* weakly noted the documents were "curious on several points," and the *Time Piece* attacked Adams' delay in making them public, intimating that perhaps the "most important papers" had not yet been disclosed.[93]

Whistling in the dark, the *Independent Chronicle* called this revelation "unpleasant, but not alarming." Obviously, the envoys had not been received and American trade had been hurt. Yet the very mention of additional papers proved negotiations were continuing, while malicious Federalists circulated rumors of demands for Adams' resignation and French naval bases in America. Far better to have kept the communications confidential; war-eager Anglophiles were charged (with some reversal of the truth) with compelling publication even when it endangered the envoys and hampered any future discussions. Customary though *douceurs* might be in monarchies, they still came as a surprise in republics. Doubtless American ministers, sarcastically noted the editor, realized the Congress had never permitted private interests to affect even remotely "the action of a single member on a single occasion." Simple justice demanded awaiting Talleyrand's reply; if he acknowledged the envoys' charges 'twas a pity he had not been guillotined, but his Federalist contacts in America may have convinced him America was hostile to France. Fortunately, neither Adams nor the Directory could declare war by themselves—and conceivably this prompt exposure and denunciation of Parisian corruption might actually speed negotiations. Readers were reminded of Blount's disloyalty (which, after all, had been directed toward achieving war rather than peace) and of the stature England would have gained had only Liston come forward to reveal it. Any conflict with France would be of the administration's making, and if peace were to its *interest* this disclosure did not alter the picture in the slightest.[94]

Adams' call for a day of fasting only repeated this old Federalist device to cozen people into feeling the administration's position was morally justifiable. The *Chronicle* scathingly suggested a "Psalm for the Federal Fast":

> YE Federal states combine
>   In solemn Fast and Prayer
> And urge the powers divine
>   To drive us into war
>         With voices strong
>         Each Federalist
>         On pension list
>         Begin the song.

> \* \* \* \* \* \* \*

> Ye Clergy in this day
>   On Politicks discourse
> And when ye rise to pray
>   Both France and Frenchmen curse
>         For you've a right
>         To pray and preach
>         Exhort and teach
>         Mankind to fight.

[The "Funding gentry," the "Well-Born," Federal judges, Wolcott, Pickering, Jay, and George III all join in]

> \* \* \* \* \* \* \*

> Let all the States attend
>   At this his [Adams'] solemn call
> To curse their ancient *friend*
>   And bless our rulers all:
>         For this the day
>         That heart and hand
>         Thro' the whole land
>         For WAR we pray.[95]

The intrigues of "corrupt . . . scoundrels" should "not be suffered to make an irreconcilable breach. . . ." [96] Americans of all factions would instantly unite to repel any foreign aggression, but if the French government *were* implicated in any attempts at bribery in this instance it was only copying England's more secretive practices in a thousand earlier cases. Doubtless the entire story was but another Anglophile trick; even if true, *"unofficial conversation with strangers"* should not be considered adequate grounds for war.[97] "ANTI-MACHIAVEL" found the envoys both unmannerly and guilty of insincerity in pretending to seek a settlement. They had failed to make courtesy calls on Talleyrand, released a story that varied greatly from the French minister's official account, and set up a howl of attempted bribery. The rest of their dispatches dealt only with private conversations that were about as significant as might be the observation of Talleyrand's cook.[98]

Heavy irony was directed at the nebulousness of the entire affair: *"A Major Mount-florence,* told *Gen.* Pinckney, that he had a conversation with Mr. *Ormond"* to the effect that *"probably* persons would be appointed to treat with our commissioners." Then followed Monsieur W., who introduced X, who then paved the way for Y. "To complete the group a *French Lady* is finally introduced, and a *Mr. Beaumarchais.* Upon this vague conversation between . . . persons totally unauthorized by the government of France, an official communication is made to our Executive." Thus America was expected to rise in arms! The indirect methods used by the envoys explained the lack of any official communication from the Directory. Only Talleyrand's proposal even remotely resembled one, and it requested a loan rather than a bribe. The alleged request for a *douceur* of fifty thousand pounds was absurd; the sum might satisfy two swindlers and their French lady, but it was far too small for five Directors. Moreover, if French officials were willing to sell their nation's honor, they knew full well Pitt's ministry would *far* outbid anything America could possibly offer.[99]

Nothing was revealed by the dispatches but "that the present government of France is unfriendly to this country; and what man is so ignorant as not to know that before?" That some French officials were unprincipled, or that a "lady" had impudently asserted the Gallic nation relied upon a party in America to support her interests, constituted no grounds for expending American lives and dollars. Even an *authorized* demand for a bribe would not have altered the American national interest, and war would not restore commercial losses. Actually, France was only responding in kind to the wrongs she had received. If attacked, Americans possessed the same defenses as in '75, but naval conflicts should be left "to those who are fools enough to engage in them." [100]

Bache, Thomas Adams, and Freneau [101] strove valiantly to show that X., Y., and Z. were not agents but enemies of the French government who were attempting to victimize America as well. A Dalmatian named Wiscovich ("W.") had offered to obtain for French officials information concerning the plans of the envoys. President Adams had withheld this news, lest it disclose how the envoys had been duped; yet because "of this threatened rupture with the French, an alien bill is proposed . . . which would disgrace the cabinet of a despot, and which is unequalled in the annals even of Great Britain." [102] But such irenic efforts seemed ineffectual, for nearly all American factions appeared merged in a passion to avenge the national honor.[103]

"Nestor" applauded the patriotism of American youths but called on them to weigh their actions carefully to avoid *all* foreign influence. Harvard students who had brashly notified Adams of their readiness to fight had no comprehension of what they might face; the horrors of a just war were frightful enough.[104]

Jeered indeed was the slogan, "Millions for defense, but not one cent for tribute." "THEOPHRASTUS" sardonically repeated the phrase (liberally festooned with exclamation points), and added:

> Would to God, Mr. Bache, we had thundered it out three years ago when a petty piratical State compelled us to pay . . . one hundred and sixty-two millions three hundred and seventeen thousand eight hundred and thirty-one cents . . . [as a price for Algerine friendship, together with] an annual tribute of fourteen millions four hundred and twenty-five thousand eight hundred

297

and forty-four cent[s], equal to the lawful interest . . . [on] two
hundred and forty millions four hundred and thirty thousand,
seven hundred and thirty-three cents.[105]

Governor Jay might publicly hope that America would "never
pay tribute to any nation whatever," but his memory was conveniently short respecting this annual disbursement to the
paltry despot of Algiers.[106] Two years later there were acid
comments when the Dey of Tunis exposed the emptiness of the
bold Federalist toast by demanding payments for refraining
from attacks upon American shipping.[107] Apparently Americans had a double standard of diplomacy if they were to resent
even the request for a loan by the nation that had actually
given them money during the Revolution.[108]

Once again began the round of petitions and counter-
petitions. Federalist-inspired resolutions (breathing "the pure
fire of patriotism," according to Anglophiles) flooded government offices with praise and promises of support.[109] Seldom
reprinted in Republican newspapers, these documents drew the
fire of Jeffersonian printers. "CITIZENS BEWARE!"
shrieked the *Aurora;* "immaculate friends of government"
were circulating memorials giving blanket endorsement to all
Executive measures and were securing signatures by misrepre-
senting the documents as *"intended merely to prevent a war,*
and keep *peace and harmony at home."* "Orders from the
Hamiltonian Club at head quarters," seconded the *Independent Chronicle,* "have been sent as usual to all the little
branches thro' the States to *electrify* the minds of Americans," and to delude tradesmen into believing that only a show
of unity could avoid a war almost no one wanted.[110] Even so,
Adams must have been chagrined that so few "real Americans" signed these messages of fulsome praise. The New York
Chamber of Commerce described its tribute as coming from
the people, when less than sixty men attended the approving
meeting—and only a dozen of these "were *native Americans,*
and some of them *Tories* in the late war ! ! !" Small wonder
they were ready to take "orders from the Adulterous
Club." [111]

Petitions were not the monopoly of pro-administration forces. When ranking officers of the New Jersey militia wrote Adams commending his course, the men and junior officers of Morris and Essex counties protested the letter did not express their views. Ready to answer any constitutional call to duty, they refused unqualified support to any official. A similar communication to Governor Richard Howell (whose heated reply was branded as splenetic beyond any effort of Porcupine's) denied any unanimity of complete confidence "in the conduct of our President," and asserted that a conciliatory attitude would do far more than a ream of addresses to Adams in uniting the nation.[112] Other resolutions, from all parts of the country, denied that X., Y., and Z. could in any sense be considered entitled to speak for the French government and protested the administration's obviously greater official desire for more friendly relations with England than with France. Surely Americans were sufficiently mature to suspend judgment until the facts were known before taking up arms against friends who had shed blood to defend their lives and property against the British. Kentuckians held that Congress was overly concerned with extending ocean commerce and bemoaned the certain closing of the Mississippi in case of conflict.[113] At William and Mary College some students even burned the President in effigy.[114]

Petitions from the mechanics and yeomanry opposed those signed by "*lawyers, merchants,* children [to pad the list], *refugees, tories,* and Englishmen." Nowhere, it was caustically observed, did Federalists dare call "lawful town meetings on the subject . . . for they know that in such a situation they would infallibly be found a contemptible minority." [115] Nor did Republicans stoop (as alleged) to the despicable Federalist trick of getting foreigners to sign resolutions favoring peace. From Vermont to Georgia the President's speech was denounced, publication of the envoys' papers labeled inflammatory, and opposition expressed toward any course hostile to France.[116] Significant as were America's resources, they could be fully utilized "ONLY IN SELF DEFENSE." The envoys' own memorial to France (which should have been *"published in gold letters"*) had stressed how inimical it was to American interest to become involved in *"the almost boundless ocean of European politics"* to make the United States a mere satellite of a great power.[117]

The American envoys, said "Brutus," had stressed the cords of affection between the two nations and the lack of real cause for enmity and had frankly appealed to French justice and liberality. Yet Adams ignored this in his determination to promote "the alliance he has probably already formed with England." [118] To summarize, the New York *Argus* added:

> No one can avoid contrasting the dignified and decent language of our envoys with the petulant and intemperate invectives of the President—The one is a model of elegant diction and politeness, while the other may be deemed a pattern of bombast and billingsgate—as if intoxicated with the addresses which the spirit of party alone would have inspired, he forgets the important station in which a mistaken opinion of his abilities has placed him, and descends to the lowest abuse against a nation to whom he owes his present greatness, and which has astonished mankind with his victories. He is often times totally unintelligible. Nature, it is certain, never intended him for a writer. He has borrowed some common place phrases from his favorite Porcupine, and these are to be found in all or most of his answers to the addresses. Among these are the following elegant expressions—'the foul abominations of the French revolution'—'chimerical idea of liberty'—'pirates'—'enemies of the human race'—'atheists'—'scoundrels,' &c, &c. It must be recollected that this reviler of the French nation is at 3000 miles distance from the people he is thus abusing. If they pay us a visit, which may be expected next summer, it is hoped he will expose his dear well-*born* \* person to the fire of the sacreligious wretches, and not leave the farmers, (as he and Jay did the last War) to fight the battles of their country. Who can think with patience of the war in which we are engaged by the indiscretion and intemperance of this man?
>
> '\* *Mr. Adams is the son of a country shoemaker, at Braintree— This would not be worth mentioning, if he was not always talking of the advantages of being* well-born.' [119]

"SYDNEY," in the *Farmers' Register,* thought no true American could sign some of the fulsome addresses to the President. At the moment Americans were "a divided people," disinclined toward blind acceptance of executive leadership. If differences with France were not accommodated, she would find Americans united enough, but in the meantime most citizens thought hostile measures were illogical while efforts were still being made to negotiate.[120] At most, echoed the *Argus* and *Aurora,* Americans would be paying a preposterous price to gratify their resentment. If England destroyed republicanism in Europe, she (aided by other despots) would next turn on the United States; if France won she would made Americans pay dearly for their meddling. "Somebody must pay the Piper. Would it not be best therefore to keep out of the scrape?"[121]

Yet Republicans were struggling against a tidal wave of patriotic sentiment. In Philadelphia theaters nightly demands were made for the "President's March" and "Yankee Doodle," while Francophile cries for the "Marseillaise" were hissed down. Joseph Hopkinson wrote the lyrics of "Hail Columbia" to the first-named tune; the song was introduced to a cheering Federalist crowd.[122] Democrats sneered when Hopkinson was named commissioner to the Oneida Indians "as a reward for partisan services,"[123] but a rash of patriotic songs appeared during this period. Congress issued letters of marque in late June, despite warnings this meant war and in the face of cynical suggestions that Americans should ignore *all* treaty obligations and immediately confiscate, without notice, any French property in the country.[124]

Some Republicans urged cessation of opposition to a now-certain conflict in order that the administration could "not complain of being embarrassed in measures of defence," for

> The innocent pleasures of agriculture must be exchanged for rapine and warfare; gaiety of rural industry for the horrors and carnage of battle. Since it is your unhappy lot to be obliged to combat a second time for existence, be on your guard and arm for defence: The consequences of the war be on the heads of your governors, the duty of defence is yours.[125]

Under Aaron Burr, New York Democrats disarmed Federalists by fully cooperating with Hamilton in fortifying the harbor—thereby forestalling accusations of truckling to a foreign foe. In South Carolina, Governor Charles Pinckney spent over seven thousand pounds to purchase arms, and Edward Rutledge headed a fund-raising committee for building a warship.[126]

Others were not so willing to cooperate in preparing defenses against hostilities that they opposed. *Carey's United States Recorder* lamented that even the rumors of war had seriously hurt trade. Farmers were reminded they had earlier been told rejection of Jay's Treaty would produce war and half-crown-per-bushel wheat; it had been accepted, and wheat had dropped from twenty shillings to ten. Now realization of war with France would speedily confer the blessing of half-crown wheat—with a land tax thrown in.[127] Invoking the law of nations would neither capture British fleets nor destroy French armies, urged a petition from Caroline County, Virginia. Should Americans suffer bloodshed and the loss of half their trade to teach Parisians a lesson in "etiquette"? [128]

Some attempted ridicule: the administration abused France because that nation trembled before our epithets. All who failed to draw sword immediately against Gallia were obvious traitors. Taxes and falling prices were immaterial, or at worst would only achieve decisive establishment of two classes—one of wealth and another of a "swinish multitude" of vassals. Benedict Arnold, it was said, had offered his services against France and rejoiced "to hear of so many of his countrymen having shaken off their delusion, as he predicted they would only eighteen years ago." [129]

More serious writers demanded to know how America planned to finance such a struggle. With its securities selling at a thirty per cent discount, the government could scarcely hope to borrow from citizens at six per cent. Foreign loans were out of the question—old creditors would be hostile and England was already hopelessly overburdened.[130] If Federalists would but count the cost of war they would be far less militant, and huge armaments, even in the unlikely event they proved successful, might well produce some future Caesar. In '76 Americans at least had fought for freedom; in '98 they would be warring "to protect the engines of pampered luxury." [131]

Even if one were to concede cause for conflict existed, insisted "AMERICANUS," the nation's empty treasury made a war utterly inexpedient. Impost and tonnage duties would almost completely disappear, and internal revenues would decline. With doubled expenses, he estimated a three years' struggle would find the United States completely penniless, with harbors devastated, countryside ravaged, citizens exhausted, and "FORTY MILLIONS of dollars [further] in debt." France was too remote to fear the United States militarily, destruction of her armies in the United States would not indemnify American losses, and her West Indian possessions were in such a state of anarchy that their conquest would prove a liability. A new "PACIFICUS" concurred in the view that sound policy dictated suspension of intercourse with France, defending the country if attacked, and awaiting the return of justice to the Gallic nation.[132]

Federalists were in no mood to wait. When in early May Philadelphia's young men signed an address pledging support to Adams, "Peter Porcupine" suggested that the document be presented in person by the signatories, each wearing an "American cockade" emblematic of his patriotism. This black ribbon, folded circularly about four inches in diameter and mounted on the left side of the hat, had been worn by the American army during the Revolution.[133] Accordingly, some 1,200 Philadelphians, properly cockaded, presented their memorial to the President—who also wore the insignia as he received them. Within a month towns everywhere boasted wearers of the emblem.[134]

Democrats indignantly attacked this fad. By what right did Cobbett, a foreigner, advocate the cockade, a military badge with which civilians had no business? Surely Republicans would not assume any insignia so open to misconstruction.[135] Feeling on the matter rapidly approached the ridiculous. Federalists charged that, after futilely threatening and coaxing to discredit the decoration, the "French faction" had labeled it "English." Pennsylvania's Governor Mifflin was said to have counseled Republicans to pull it off whenever they saw it. Cobbett argued that "the fate of this city, and perhaps of the whole country" depended on the symbol; he and others saw wearing it as a test of courage, alleging that tap-room bullies gloried in the opportunity for violence by attacking the wearers.[136]

Sarcasm and ridicule were also employed against wearing the emblem. In Baltimore "Another Youth" denied allegations that those refusing to don the black cockade were the nation's enemies. No proper authority had called on citizens to wear the decoration; true Americans considered it merely the mark of a coxcomb. Doubtless the cockade wearers were bold and intrepid, as could be seen from the amazing dexterity, surpassing that of the heroes of antiquity, with which they handled their badges. But would they show the same skill in handling their guns and bayonets when war actually came?[137] "Astrologus" believed wearing the emblem could be accounted for only by the phases of the moon; another writer referred to Uriah Tracy's talk of "a war of extinguishment." Wearing the sable badge perhaps expressed Americans' mourning for the destruction of France.[138] At a Roxbury Independence Day parade a leading Democrat sported a cockade of cow dung, and in New London a citizen ornamented his hat with "an *old continental fifty dollar bill.*"[139]

Red or tri-colored cockades had previously been worn at times to display sympathy for France, as had sprigs of olive to indicate desire for peace, but now some Democrats condemned the entire practice. Since emblems of both parties might now be found among the rioters, the way to restore tranquillity was to prohibit such insignia altogether.[140] Yet despite premature predictions that cockades were going out of fashion, for almost two years the black badge was worn—and subjected to scorn and reprobation from Jeffersonians. Wearers of that insignia ("pretended friends of order") were charged with bullying those with the tricolor emblem, openly shouting "Rule Britannia!," bacchanalian reveling, and general disorderliness.[141] Rejoicing, albeit somewhat inconsistently, in the victory of William Heath for Congress, Boston Republicans commented that some persons with cockades in their hats "had a vote for gen. Heath in their hands." Perhaps votes should be displayed in hats, or cockades deposited at the polls.[142] Other writers compared the decoration to a dog collar in that it identified the wearer's master—and since British imports supplied most of the silk and the dog collars, mad dogs might easily wear the cockades and frenzied Federalists, the collars! [143]

Engrossing as the topic of a political adornment might be, it was still incidental. The real issue was maintenance of peace with France, and to achieve this Republicans relied on their faith in France's sincere desire for peace and on Gerry's efforts to continue negotiations. Federalist belligerence had reached a crescendo, and the Alien and Sedition bills were approaching passage [144] when Bache's *Aurora* reprinted Talleyrand's diplomatic message of March 18 to the American commissioners as evidence Paris wanted no war. The letter (naturally reflecting the French view) filled nearly an entire page of the newspaper. It cited as grievances Jay's Treaty, the almost openly hostile views of the individuals sent to represent the United States at Paris, and even the instructions given the commissioners. Nonetheless, its entire tone was conciliatory.[145]

Furious Federalists denounced this breach of diplomatic confidence. To them Bache was a traitor engaged in seditious correspondence with the Directory. They alleged Talleyrand's letter had appeared in print before even Adams had seen it. Surely this early publication revealed it as designed for popular consumption and proved the presence of secret agents of France in America.[146] Bache made a public deposition that, while he had acquaintances in the French Foreign Office, he was no agent of Talleyrand and that this letter had reached him through a Philadelphian recently returned from Paris. Some Democrats asserted Pickering had already received the communication, but had intended to delay its publication until

after America had been "committed by a declaration of war."
No crime was ever proved against the Jeffersonian editor, but
he was placed under $2,000 bond for criticizing the Presi-
dent.[147]

Republicans also saw Gerry's remaining in France after
Marshall and Pinckney departed as proof war was not inevitable. Gerry (whose political allegiance was changing) was
considered by many to be a Federalist of sorts,[148] but Republicans reasoned that his position enabled him to know the situation in France better than did Anglophile bigots in America.
If the situation were truly hopeless he would not have stayed
on. Adams' instructions had empowered the envoys "jointly
and *severally*" to negotiate; as a philosopher, Gerry was willing to suffer Federalist abuse if a conflict might possibly
thereby be averted. The very epithets hurled at him furnished
clear proof that Hamiltonians feared he might yet reach a settlement. It was indeed curious that Federalists were ready to
fight France for *not* treating with the United States while they
condemned Gerry for attempting to treat with *her*.[149]

Bitterly denounced were Federalist parades and celebrations for Marshall and Pinckney upon their return. They had
completely failed to attain their objective of peace, yet now
they were honored. Conveniently forgetting their own earlier
adulation of Genêt, Republican comments were acid:

> How cheaply is popularity gained at the present day! The Amer-
> icans send a man on a foreign errand; they allow him *nine thousand
> dollars* to fit himself for the mission, and an additional *nine thou-
> sand* per annum during the time he is employed in it; not content
> with paying him thus liberally for his services, they discover a
> propensity to *deify* him when he returns home. No country or
> party ought to indulge this *idolizing* spirit; it is the offspring of
> blind confidence in the many, and of *design* in the few: it has
> already been carried to too great lengths in this country by all
> parties, and should it continue to be indulged, must eventually
> prove the bane of liberty and of public virtue.[150]

Jeffersonian printers joyfully provided space for the letters
of Gerry and Talleyrand, as well as for the former's communications to Adams. These disclosed that Gerry had not

broken with the administration, was not attempting secret dealings with Talleyrand, and merely remained behind to preserve peace if possible. Moreover, he had already requested his passport and had suggested that Adams appoint a new envoy when orders came for his return to America.[151] Talleyrand's messages implied complete ignorance of X., Y., and Z., and breathed an air of injured amity over Pinckney's and Marshall's Francophobe prejudices. The documents thus supported nearly every Democratic argument that had been made.[152] Elated Republicans quoted the Paris *Clef du Cabinet*, which expressed incredulity that the envoys could have been so naive as to have been honestly deceived by "secret negotiators." The incident had all the earmarks of bad faith and a deliberate insult to the Gallic Republic. "DEMOCRITUS" gloated that Gerry's letters to Talleyrand dispelled even the shadow of doubt: "Truth may for awhile be concealed . . . but the day always comes when the clouds of error are dissipated. . . ."[153]

Clearly, the French government considered America partial toward Britain. Save for Gerry, the envoys had seemed reluctant to do anything to further reconciliation and had shown eagerness to find whatever might exasperate. Jeffersonians summed up the situation in this way: (1) There had been no (official) demand for tribute, (2) There was no fear of a French invasion, (3) The only offensive war would be one of America's making, and (4) Nothing had been asked of the United States but a loan equal to that France had made Americans during their Revolution. It was now high time for lovers of liberty and peace to make themselves known.[154]

The *Aurora* made fun of the "great insult" that had been offered to America. Since the administration had seen fit to plunge the country from peace and prosperity to the brink of war and misery, was it any wonder heaven afflicted the nation "from Boston to Philadelphia with pestilence and calamity?" Had Adams in 1782 insulted "the government of Holland when he sought and negociated a loan for the United States?"[155]

Yet when any of Gerry's reports hinted at unfriendliness or venality on Talleyrand's part, there were cries that *"the letter lately communicated by the President . . . as the last from Mr. Gerry was a forgery."* Accusations of censorship and deliberately garbled translations were frequent.[156] At last Talleyrand denied demanding any reparation for Adams' inflammatory message to Congress, or even requesting a loan; he assured Gerry that a new minister would be received. Apparently convinced of the French official's trickery, the lone envoy received a warm welcome on his return to America in early autumn. Democrats scornfully noted that the participation of some Federalists in the reception exposed the duplicity of a war faction that would abuse a man during his absence and coax him in his presence. Every individual with sufficient judgment and resolution to oppose war must anticipate "the resentment of Tories, and the rage of a group . . . who are too lazy to use any industrious means to support themselves, and are seeking a living by *official appointments."* [157]

Democrats remained convinced a conflict with France had long been the ultimate goal of the Hamiltonians. Had not Fenno's *Gazette of the United States* called for a declaration of war to end the pleading for the French cause, even though a few weeks before Federalists had urged arming merchantmen to prevent hostilities? Did not the unseemly haste of Congress in resolving on warlike measures reveal desire for conflict? [158] Senator Uriah Tracy's remark about "a war of extermination" was seized upon to illustrate both the Francophobia and the ethics of the Federalists. Such prohibition of quarter to men, women, and children was urging warfare to a degree never before advocated by a civilized nation. It was hoped *"Exterminator* Tracy" would likewise be willing to sacrifice his wife and child at a nod from his British masters.[159] "An Old Soldier" saw the Federalists as only old Tories in disguise; they attempted to inflame the popular mind toward a war they had no intention of fighting themselves. He professed willingness to risk life and property to defend America and its Constitution, but, when he saw so many enemies to both fomenting hostilities, he doubted the sincerity of their intentions.[160]

When the *Columbian Centinel* trumpeted that a bill was now before the Senate authorizing Adams to direct the navy to capture *all* foreign vessels attacking commerce, the *Aurora* commented stingingly: "(Not quite so fast, Mr. Centinel, only French vessels.)" [161] The departure of a number of Federalist senators from Congress before the end of the session provoked the taunt that their consciences were haunted by the ghosts of departed heroes of '76 who had seen their work undermined.[162]

The falsehoods that found currency in the Federalist press, Republicans charged, demonstrated perfectly the enmity of that party to France and to republican principles. If Federalists condemned France's banishment of General Pichegru for conspiracy without a fair trial, they should remember America had done likewise with Tories during the War for Independence—and had also confiscated their property afterward. Adams himself once confessed revolutions could not "be carried through with milk and honey"; the French Republic had only taken needful precautions against betrayal.[163] But if there were an unsubstantiated rumor of Gallic saboteurs dispatched to set American seaports aflame, Federalist papers printed it. Was an allegedly French-manufactured blaze in Philadelphia to be followed by a massacre of all young men in that area? Such was the story in the Hamiltonian gazettes. Was there likelihood Bonaparte's army might invade America's Western lands? Read about it in Federalist newssheets. If it were possible for man to cause famines, earthquakes, and tornados, these also would doubtless be charged to the French. "What scarecrows will not these *Federal* gentry invent next?" [164]

Reports of a French privateer cruising off New London in May, 1798, constituted "an *abominable* and *malicious* LIE." Combining emotional appeal with an answer to the tale, Democrats insisted no armed vessel had been seen within fifty miles, but that the purpose of circulating such canards was clear:

> They serve to increase the popular clamour against the French; and did they stop here it would be well enough; but a more cruel and serious mischief is produced. They depress the spirit of commerce and discourage seamen from entering into the merchant's service, and create a thousand unnecessary fears and anxieties for the safety of our friends at sea.

Purveyors of these mendacities for party interest gave the impression no ship was safe, thereby inflicting untold apprehension upon weeping mothers and wives. Surely *"women, . . . inexperienced in speculating duplicity, ought . . . to be exempted from this species of undeserved barbarity."* [165]

This last argument was the more interesting because Republicans did not hesitate to use similar stories about the British when they deemed it advantageous. Two weeks earlier, the *Independent Chronicle* stated six French privateers, alert to stop American ships carrying *British* goods, and ten British men-of-war, ready to seize American vessels bound for France or her allies, were hovering off the coast. "A pretty pickle of fish for the United States to digest." [166]

Since Federalists were so notoriously careless with the truth, should not at least some weight be given the French version of the XYZ affair? In the Paris *Amis des Lois* Monsieur Bellamy (the "Y" of the negotiations) admitted seeing the envoys, with Talleyrand's knowledge. But at no time, he swore, was there mention of a 1,200,000 livre *douceur;* the thought that America purchase Batavian securities had been presented "only as his own idea." Bache hoped the disgraceful conduct of the emissaries might have the beneficial effect of rendering every American foreign representative so suspect that the administration could recall them all and save thousands of dollars annually.[167]

Since Gerry had apparently "escaped the wiles of Talleyrand," some Federalists urged that he speak for himself, dubious as "part of his conduct appears." Presumably they expected him now to advocate hostilities, but Gerry gave scant encouragement to those who desired war. He seemingly felt his printed correspondence justified his behavior, believed Pinckney had tried to read sinister motives into the innocent remark of a lady who merely suggested that America might lend money to France in her war as she had lent it to Americans in theirs, and advised Adams to make yet another official overture to secure amity.[168]

Republicans also exhorted the President to appoint another diplomatic envoy. And in the meantime one peace-loving Democrat had determined to act on his own. Dr. George Logan, a wealthy Quaker who believed only tact and sincere friendship were needed to solve difficulties with France, set sail for that country in June, 1798, armed merely with letters of introduction from Jefferson and Governor Thomas McKean of Pennsylvania. Derided by Federalists for his unaccredited effort, Logan found himself portrayed as a champion of peace by Jeffersonians at home and the French press abroad. High French officials received him, and he may have convinced them the American people would unite in any war effort once hostilities actually began.[169] When Federalists denounced him as an intriguer who even promised aid to France in case of an invasion, the Quaker secured from Talleyrand a reiteration of pledges made to Gerry. The next American minister would be received, and, as evidence of good faith, the French embargo was lifted and captured American sailors were freed. With this cruel blow to the warhawks' hope "for contracts, commissions, and commissary ships," the good doctor returned to Philadelphia, convinced of French wishes for peace.[170]

Secretary of State Pickering refused to receive him, since he was not an official agent, and Washington (to whom he turned) apparently treated Logan as a meddling busybody.[171] Adams, however, listened to him, and the Quaker's mission probably reinforced his own conviction that France in reality did not want war. Federalists generally resented Logan's "interference" with the functions of government. The documents he so trustingly brought back were "flimsy," dis-

311

closing no real change in the French position. At least his impudent folly of blaming French detention of American ships on the "insulting conduct" of the Chief Executive proved America was no monarchy; in a monarchy anyone behaving so would "be elevated to a *lamp post*." [172]

Although hailed in the Republican press as the savior of his country from a ruinous conflict, Logan smarted under the charges against him; after being elected to the Pennsylvania Assembly, he published a letter defending himself. He had gone to France, he asserted, as a private citizen without instructions from anyone. Admittedly possessing no official capacity, he had only tried to preserve peace—and he had paid his own expenses.[173] Republicans praised his defense and charged calumniators could not read its "paragraphs without experiencing the crimson of guilt." The only men opposing Logan were "the SPECULATORS . . . the FUNDING GENTRY . . . the CONTRACTORS and AGENTS . . . many BANKRUPTS . . . the IDLE and DISSOLUTE"— the people as a whole should revere him.[174]

Yet in 1799, on Representative Roger Griswold's motion, Congress made it a misdemeanor for any private citizen to carry on his own negotiations in an effort to settle a dispute with a foreign government. Democrats nevertheless continued to quote the Quaker doctor to show the stability and beneficence of the French Republic and insisted that since his mission France's attitude had been infinitely more amicable.[175]

Even so, in late 1798 hope of peace seemed very dim. Despite Republican protests over raising the sword against America's benefactors, Congress had authorized the navy to capture armed French vessels off American coasts and to retake any seized American ships. American frigates had been on the lookout for Gallic privateers, and Stephen Decatur's *Delaware* captured the *Croyable* early in July. According to the *Independent Chronicle,* the "Tories" could not "conceal their joy at having produced an open rupture between the two Republics." [176]

The outbreak of hostilities did not reconcile the Jeffersonian press to the conflict. The nation, it proclaimed, did not want war; otherwise, why should the "British faction" implore Adams to tour the country? Federalists might thank God that three thousand miles of water separated America from France, even though that fact had not been used to the best advantage. After England's failure in the Revolution, "no other power would ever have dared to molest us." [177] "Democriticus" addressed a sarcastic epistle to the *"mild, amiable, gentle, humane and christian"* John Adams on the pleasures and profits of war. Additional offices would be created, admiration would be accorded by an army for its commander-in-chief, and (through heavier taxes) greater industry would come forth from the populace. Since the adoption of the Constitution, Adams by 1800 would have received only $140,000 in compensation from the Treasury; well might he complain of privations endured. Had he not secretly but patriotically ordered Gerry not to treat separately with France, Americans might now have been handicapped by an embarrassing treaty. Since he had pontificated "Delenda est Gallia," Gallia would now be destroyed. [178]

Ten years previously listeners would have scoffed at the idea that America would have closer ties "with her former oppressor, Great Britain, than with her deliverer, France." Why were not the people informed and defense measures taken if war had been declared? Carnage and destruction, informers and a system of terror designed to promote the ends of "the party of 'order and good government' " threatened American popular rights. [179]

Yet a shooting war discomfited Democrats and made their opinions vulnerable to charges of treason. The *Aurora*'s circulation, for example, slumped badly at the time of the XYZ episode, and Bache's death from yellow fever might have ended the paper had William Duane not edited it for his widow. [180] Moderate Republicans counseled national unity during the emergency. Even groups such as the citizens of Woodford County, Kentucky—while deploring the war and the British alliance—proclaimed their willingness to comply with any

313

Congressional demands for the purpose of resisting invasion.[181] Clearly the *Columbian Centinel* exaggerated when it
contended the partisans of France had now been compelled

> to abandon any public defense of her conduct. Even the prostituted
> *Chronicle,* and the venal and hired *Aurora,* which defended her
> most atrocious measures—which changed *their* principles with *her*
> crimes . . . Even these abandoned presses have ceased to support
> her.[182]

Yet it is undeniable that printed justifications of France became for a time less numerous and less vociferous.

Nevertheless, there was no question about Democratic distaste for the conflict. Westerners found Adams' power to raise
armies and money "serious and alarming." They condemned
war with France as "impolitic, unnecessary and *unjust,* inasmuch as the means of reconciliation with that nation have not
been unremittingly and sincerely pursued; hostilities having
been authorized against it by law, while a negotiation was
pending." Assessing the second regular session of the Fifth
Congress, the *Aurora* concluded only "the vigilant and temperate spirit of Republican America" could save the country
"from the voracious jaws of a *mercenary war faction.*" The
presidential message, calling for unity and continued defense
efforts, was perhaps milder than other statements. However,
it still carried "some tincture of gunpowder, . . . and if the
*constitutional matchmen* should be disposed to apply it to the
lighted torch, it would doubtless produce an explosion." [183]

Almost nothing new was added to the argument in ensuing
months. Republicans continued to bombard Adams with requests to continue negotiations, and charges were rife that
Pickering refused to forward these petitions to the President.
Addresses approving an anti-French stand were obviously
products of handpicked groups and contravened popular sentiment.[184] Talleyrand's letters, his promises to Logan, Lafayette's efforts for amity, and a hundred friendly French acts
(such as forwarding captured American scholarly research
data on to a Professor Ebeling in Hamburg and the extensive
mourning at the death of Washington) all proved France's

desire for peace.[185] Federalist fear that Gallia aimed at world dominion was a chimera conjured up to further the *"crusade* against Freedom"; in reality, French "conciliatory conduct" toward America was giving "a very sensible alarm to the British cabinet." [186]

Indubitably both England and France had mistreated Americans, but any impartial review of the situation would demonstrate grievances against Britain were much greater and more threatening to commerce. Even during the last half of 1798, British condemnations of American property exceeded similar French judgments by nearly ten per cent. Truly the *"maternal* hug" (despite treaties) was worse than "the *fraternal* gripe." [187]

Yet official conduct, contended Republicans, continued to favor England. Jay's Treaty had surrendered the immunities of an independent nation. When Britain protested Genêt's issuing commissions, the administration (though Americans had done similarly in France in '76) had meekly requested his recall. It was charged that England was allowed to establish and to police an arsenal and naval repair shop at Norfolk, had recruiting parties in Charleston, and had bribed Senator Blount to commit a warlike act. Although English commissioners had presented a claim for $19,000,000 against America for confiscated property and had postponed paying the $5,000,-000 due American merchants, there was no talk of war. To judge from Federalist howls about the Directory's alleged "douceur," their true motto seemed to be: *"Millions to Pitt, but not a cent to Talleyrand!"* Actually, every French outrage had been first provoked by the United States.[188]

When the *Aurora* charged Representative Samuel Dana of Connecticut had admitted publication of the XYZ papers was intended to provoke a declaration of war by France against America, other papers echoed: "This is not the first time the party have taken off the masque. . . ." [189] The warhawks were rewriting the Bible—in their eyes, Matthew 5:9 *should* read, "Cursed are the peacemakers, for they shall be called the children of the Devil." Scripturally minded Democrats gleefully retorted to a Federalist recruiting plea—"Who is there, who loves his country . . . that will not readily join it and go up to Ramoth Gilead?"—by noting this was the advice of the false prophets who had wrongly assured Ahab of certain success in war. Seemingly the day of false prophets was not yet past.[190]

Assuredly, Republicans could find a surfeit of items in administration newspapers to bolster charges of Francophobia. Sermons berating France were widely published, French privateers were "insolent freebooters," and there were references to the "dark and horrible" plots of the French Directory.[191] Federalist editors had long been accused of being "under the immediate pay of the British government" in seeking to destroy American peace and happiness. It was asserted enlistments and commissions in the army being raised were largely limited to Federalists and old Tories, who would swear allegiance to an individual rather than to the Constitution.[192] Many of these still held a grudge against France for aiding America gain her independence. In the Massachusetts gubernatorial election of 1800, the *Independent Chronicle* called the Essex Junto "seekers of the loaves and fishes . . . who would *starve* in *Peace,* but expect to riot in luxury if *War* should take place." The piety and humanity of Federalism were exemplified by the *Columbian Centinel,* which allegedly had stated "Every friend to American navigation ought to pray as fervently for the continuation of the war in Europe, as an husbandman for rain in a dry season." [193]

Mocking the Federalists, "JEHU" announced he would cancel his subscription to the Washington, Kentucky, *Mirror* if he read any more about peace:

> Who are those crying out peace, peace, when there should be no peace: Disorganizers, Jacobins, Cannibals, Aliens, Seditious vagabonds, Traitors, Sansculottes, Conspirators,—Jefferson, Gallatin, Levingston, Talleyrand, Logan—Avaunt Miscreants, no peace, Navies, Armies, Blood, Carnage, Extermination, War, War, War! [194]

Predictions of a make-believe rupture between Liston and Adams were reprinted, along with apparently undenied allegations that the President had entered into an alliance with the Haitian rebel Toussaint L'Ouverture in order to affront the French Directory. The Lancaster *Intelligencer* rhetorically asked: "Is not *War* the grand object of the *Federal Leaders?*" [195]

Most incredibly stupid about such a war, continued Republicans, was that it was not truly an American quarrel. It was being engendered by British influence and agents in the United States. While Americans should be wary of both England and France, the United States had far more to fear from the former, which would never forgive it for the Revolution. Many Englishmen now lived in the United States who had ostensibly become citizens (and Federalists), but their hearts still belonged to the king. Perfectly logical, therefore, was the parallelism in language between Minister Liston and "the British party in this country." Alert citizens must sense that the public mind was being prepared for an alliance with despotism; Liston's dispatches unveiled Britain's efforts to embroil Americans in her conflict. Yet at the same time she boasted of her friendship, she employed Colonel Alexander McKee to provoke the Shawnee Indians into action against frontiersmen. Anyone denying the danger of British influence on American councils was either inconceivably blind or wilfully wicked.[196]

England was the inveterate enemy of both peace and republicanism; the "conduct of her government is now *the great evil of the world.*" [197] By contrast, France was not dependent upon American produce, purchased more from Americans than she sold to them, and lacked "literary champions" (such as Cobbett), pensioners, and even a French theater in the United States. Total French secret service expenditures were less than one-twentieth British annual disbursements for that purpose.[198] The *Aurora* compiled a lengthy list of instances of "BRITISH INFLUENCE" in America,[199] which assuredly won Duane a place as high as Bache's had been on the Federalist list of undesirable persons.

The cost of a French war would be insupportable. Was the "moral obligation" to declare hostilities of which Federalists ranted simply that "the direct tax may be extended from houses, lands, and slaves, to windows?" [200] Was not the administration compelled to pay eight per cent interest on a new loan for defense when the old rate had been only six per cent? Should citizens be taxed to pay this much interest when they themselves were liable to charges of usury if they charged as much? The exorbitant rate revealed a sorry economic condition; if Americans were forced to pay so much at the start of the conflict, what would be the price later? Unquestionably, Federalists were giving America the "millions for defense" they promised, but the extra two per cent to financiers, added expense accounts, and suspicious land purchases by administration insiders gave cause for wonder about the "tribute." [201]

Poverty and taxes similar to England's were forecast as the result of military operations. Instead of seeing laborers bring home good food to their families, Americans would have British-like poorhouses, where people might, "if honest pride permits them, resort to take a daily meal of *Elimosinary* soup!" [202] Removing eighty thousand men to become soldiers would leave agriculture prostrate. Federalists boasted of America's resources, but the administration itself estimated a deficit of $3,000,000 for the year ending June 30, 1799; at the rate the administration was going, the next four years would see an increase of $20,250,000 in the national debt even if war were somehow averted. Federalists, like Satan tempting Christ, were using the war scare to bolster their party with power and offices. The Baltimore *American* criticized a drive to add $11,000 in contributions to an overly generous governmental appropriation for completion of Fort McHenry:

> Taxed, as the citizens have been, to raise a *navy*, to lay the foundations of a *standing army*, to support a number of useless officers about the government . . . they feel no inclination to give a further opportunity to enable *their servants* to aid their private views, and create dependents to *serve electioneering purposes*, by subscribing to advance such a large sum.[203]

The indirect losses caused by a conflict would be still greater. Loss of the French trade would cripple America much more than doing without that of England. Actually, Britain wished to stifle America's growing industry. At the present rate of progress, two decades would see Americans manufacturing all they now purchased from the mother country, but if they went to war they would be dependent upon her "for forty years yet to come." Already American merchants, hamstrung by astronomical insurance rates and the need for British convoys for their vessels, were being ruined by the late arrival of their goods. Southerners feared falling tobacco prices; hostilities could both hurt Republican producers and make Britain the carrier and warehouse for that crop and cotton. By 1800 prices had dropped from $10 to $3.50 a hundred, but on word of probable peace "tobacco rose at Petersburg to five dollars." An alliance with England would disgracefully abandon the basic neutral doctrine that "free bottoms make free goods" and work irreparable harm to American commerce.[204]

Worse still, more than dollars would be menaced. Nothing Americans could gain from the fray could compensate for lost constitutional principles. Mistrust of the executive power was justified; in every country, in all ages, it was that branch that had "swallowed up the liberties of the people." Philosophers bewildered about perpetual motion should study continual administrative acquisition of authority. Executive dominance had increased in America, and differences with France gave it further opportunity to expand—under a President openly predisposed toward monarchy. It could well be the real cause for alarm was domestic and these foreign crises, merely distractions.[205] Republicans who had urged a navy in 1794 now found fleets instruments of oppression and "a burthen of slavery" upon the people. American trade was a far more potent weapon than any navy, and the militia could repel any invasion, whereas a standing army might be used to trample popular rights into the dust. Preservation of peace and the election of Jeffersonians to public office were the only safeguards for "THE SOVEREIGNTY OF THE PEOPLE."[206]

From an international standpoint, Gallic and American interests were identical, not inimical. The overthrow of France would "insure slavery to man for centuries to come"; it would be only the prelude to the destruction of republicanism in the United States. Never had a nation been "more completely *humbugged* . . . than ours was in the infamous X. Y. and Z. business." In Paris the whole story was "regarded as an imposture. . . ." France had no intention to overrun the United States, although the same could not be said of Great Britain.²⁰⁷ It was folly to ally with England in *any* conflict, for she opposed the American form of government and had openly begun this war to suppress popular rule anywhere. Her tyranny in India exceeded any despot's in France, and if her resources were so great why was she using the United States as a cat's-paw? Britain's plundering of American commerce, treaty or no, clearly demonstrated that no justice could be expected from her.²⁰⁸

To prove their case, Republicans contended America could not possibly win a war against France. Americans were outmatched, unprepared, and their military effort was ludicrously mismanaged. The navy was laughable, as shown by the jests over difficulties of the launching of the frigate *Constitution* back in 1797. When on the ways, as the blocks were knocked out,

> the frigate was left to her own DESTINATION. But alas! SHE PAUSED! . . . She seemed to hesitate, whether it was for the INTEREST of the UNITED STATES, to take her station on the principles [for which] she was fabricated.
> During this consultation of the TIMBERS which composed her, a large body of some of those (FALS[E]LY STILED FEDERALISTS) applied their strength to 'the long pull, the strong pull, and the pull altogether,' and with the assistance of SCREWS, they gave the FRIGATE CONSTITUTION a start, equal to what the same party gave the FEDERAL CONSTITUTION in the adoption of the BRITISH TREATY. She moved in a dignified moderation, under this COMBINED PRESSURE, about 21 feet (equal to the Senators [plus the Vice President] who adopted the Treaty,) but collecting herself, SHE again STOPPED, and fixed herself immovable for this day. . . .
> On board the frigate we observed the CENTINEL MAJOR [209] who had already ANTICIPATED in his paper its

free egress into the water; but as he observes, 'that it will la[u]nch forth into that element which connects the world together as the CONSTITUTION did into the political one,' we are apt to conclude, FROM THE EVENT, that he is an ANTI-FEDERALIST: for he would not suppose that the *FEDERAL CONSTITUTION* was SCREWED into the people; that it was impeded in its progress, for want of system in its arrangement; and that, finally, by mere dint of manoeuvering, it was adopted by the citizens.[210]

All sorts of analogies were drawn. Adams had attended the "launching," and it had been "fondly hoped" the ship

would have been dallied in his arms, as the favorite of his MARINE MAJESTY.

But as the utility of the American Navy, is an important subject of debate, within the DIRECTORY OF THE OCEAN; the propriety of introducing her into this New World, is, at present undecided. It is however suspected, that the WAT[E]RY GODS consider the naval birth of the United States as premature, and feeling the warmest attachment to her interest, and happiness, have thought proper to impede with the most gentle reflections the progress of her pregnancy.[211]

Demands were made to investigate the *"immense expense"* of building the frigate, which allegedly had cost more than the largest vessel in the French fleet. Construction graft led most taxpayers to regard this "marine bauble . . . as a FIRST RATE grievance, thrown on their shoulders for the sole benefit of a few individuals." Doubt was expressed that the ship would ever reach the harbor lighthouse. If the next Congress, inquiring into the cost, did not find "more than one rotten plank in the structure, we shall be much mistaken. The next two ships to be erected, we hear are to be named FRUGAL-ITY and ECONOMY." [212]

After sneering at the launching fiasco, the *Independent Chronicle* turned to more serious implications. America's real strength lay in neither bombast nor a navy, for with but three frigates citizens were only sporting with the nation's valor rather than upholding its dignity. True power resided in commercial prosperity and importance. It was hoped the United

States might become formidable through "internal regulations," and that "the CONSTITUTION [would] be ever supported on its Republican Principles."[213]

Commodore Truxtun, hero of the *Insurgente* affair, was jeered at his resignation over a question of rank. When he resumed his commission, knowing Republicans sniffed, "How sweet are the loaves and fishes!!!"[214] Government offices were regarded as Federalist ends in themselves. Earlier the party had boasted of fifteen thousand applicants for commissions in the new army; the next moment it deplored the torpor that had led but a hundred or so to offer their services in the ranks and called on Washington to revive drooping patriotism by a tour through the land. Who would be the *soldiers* for this swarm of officers to command?[215] Even after the troops were raised, various news stories sneered at the incompetence, political partisanship, and lack of discipline of the units. Companies should each be united by "one of GOODY HARPER'S *clues*," have their heads shaved for identification, and be organized by divisions to be headed by printers noted for loyalty to "the Listonian monarch." Secretary of War Samuel Dexter was derided as "the little Mars of the United States" ordering units on useless troop movements.[216]

Democrats snorted at news that Adams was studying military science. The roll of leaders vanquished by the French could illuminate the subject. Had Americans joined the crusade earlier, they "might have come in for a share of the honors" of Dunkirk, Lodi, Mantua, and other French triumphs. True, Washington was to command the army. But he had retired, a year ago, from *civil* life because of age—an even more compelling factor in "a *military* employment."[217]

This would be an impossible war to wage. As well try to fight China or Russia; America could not come to grips with them, either. Possibly the navy could capture a few French privateersmen—though even that resembled raising an army to hunt squirrels—but in that event, Americans stood to lose their fisheries and a great number of merchantmen in Dutch and Spanish ports. Commercially, America would be ruined, while France could be hurt only slightly. Her government had spent not an additional livre since trouble with America arose at a time when the administration had squandered nearly $30,000,000. This clearly proved Federalist prattle of an invasion was merely intended to foster a permanent army and navy—and also that France realized America's inability to combat her successfully.[218]

Federalists assailed Republican news items emphasizing French prowess, but Jeffersonians retorted it was the duty of the press to provide the truth. Moreover, foes of republicanism had been stressing Britain's strength, whereas the salvation of world freedom depended upon the means and resources of France. The *Aurora,* congratulating itself on helping avert war, related with relish the fate of seventeen governments that had opposed the Gallic Republic. The "partitioners of France have been themselves partitioned." [219]

Those long ago convinced of the presence of a "French party" in the United States regarded these Republican outbursts as treasonable, designed to divide the people and to prevent a firm policy toward Paris. Since France had a unicameral legislature, Democrats decried the Senate and tried to make the House dominant over the President. Frenchmen had their insurrectional clubs and pretended to exclusive patriotism—"the very character assumed by the party in Bache's Greenleaf's and Adam's [*sic*] anarchical papers." [220]

Democrats scoffed at the inconsistencies in Federalist taunts. First they charged Republican editors were bribed with French gold, and then they sneered at the same editors' poverty. France could have no earthly purpose in bribing the American press, for she had already written the United States off "as an ungrateful nation," and had allowed Americans to pursue their own course "with sovereign contempt." Nothing in the character or circumstances of those few printers who (from love of liberty or what should be national gratitude) were attached to the French cause would support charges of bribery by France or anyone else.[221]

Yet the accusations stung; as tension increased, they were

323

heatedly denied. The editors of the Newport *Companion* denounced "scurrilous" reports that they were influenced and aided by French patronage; they were "REAL AMERICANS" who despised "foreign influence of any kind." New York's *Time Piece* demanded proof of French designs upon America and of the claim that a Republican Directory, headed by Jefferson, Madison, Monroe, and Burr, would aid the enemy. Unless evidence were forthcoming,

> the public . . . will pronounce this information to be a mean, wicked, contemptible, perfidious, and royal *lie,* and the authors of it no better than *low, serving knaves* and *cowardly assassins!*

When Noah Webster charged that supposedly respectable New Yorkers were supplying the French "with vessels, arms and ammunition, to commit depredations on our commerce; and are probably interested in the plunder," he was challenged to name names. Doubtless, returned the *Argus,* he really meant those citizens who had invested in British privateers out of Bermuda or the Bahamas.[222]

Nevertheless, attempting to defend a nation with which America was at swords' points perturbed some Jeffersonians. Vermonters denied that a French flag was hoisted along with the Stars and Stripes at Whiting to celebrate Matthew Lyon's release from jail. "An American" defied Federalists to point out anyone desiring America to *"become a department of France,"* or to pay tribute to that country. Republicans would unite in abhorring such an individual. Yet it was senseless to convert former friends into implacable enemies, as "Priests," "War Promoters," and "Tory presses" were trying to do.[223]

A number of Democratic newspapers did oppose the war. When the *Retaliation,* originally taken from the French, was surrendered by Captain Bainbridge to the *Insurgente* and *Volontaire* in November, 1798, the *Independent Chronicle* roundly berated the *Columbian Centinel* for assuming the die had been cast. Actually, with the recapture, "the account is about balanced."

War is so pleasing a topic with our British gentry, that when the Retaliation was first taken, they thought that France would immediately declare War, and now she is retaken, they cry out, that 'War is unavoidable.' But the Messenger of peace Doctor Logan, says to the contrary.[224]

Republican prints castigated the Supreme Court for its decision in *Bass* v. *Tingey,* which held that ever since Congress had declared the French treaty no longer binding (July 7, 1798), "a *qualified and restricted state of war* has existed," and Frenchmen could be legally classified as enemies of the United States. This ruling sabotaged prospects for negotiation, and every judge who voted for it deserved impeachment. It usurped the congressional prerogative of declaring war, and destroyed any chance of indemnification for French seizures of American merchantmen in peacetime.[225]

Even the capture of the French frigate *Insurgente* by Truxtun's *Constellation,* most spectacular exploit of the undeclared naval conflict, was belittled or deprecated in Republican gazettes. America was still not officially at war; Truxtun's ship had been much more heavily armed and had responded to the Frenchman's hail with a broadside, so that any other result would have been disgraceful. Probably French privateers would now be loosed on *all* American trade. Then Americans could berate those responsible for issuing "orders to this effect, in the emphatic language of the poet: 'Curse on their virtues, they have undone their country.' " [226]

Republican editors were convinced Americans had now given France justification for any retaliatory measures. With naval captures and privateering, Americans had become virtual allies of Britain in the West Indies. As late as 1800, Federalists were dared to justify Truxtun's belligerency at a time when America had sent an embassy to France. Such behavior indicated the mission was "a mere hum, to lull the people," and that *"War"* was still "the grand object of the *Federal Leaders."* [227]

Republicans were certain if Hamiltonians could not provoke France into declaring war they intended somehow to coerce Congress to do so. Panic might further this process, and Jeffersonians viewed as premeditated the wave of hysteria against French "conspiracies" that began sweeping the country. Most famous of the so-called plots was the "Tale of the Tubs." According to this story (which Democrats deemed concocted solely to engender Francophobia), four agents of the Directory left Hamburg disguised as immigrants to America. The State Department was informed that they carried documents, concealed in the false bottoms of two tubs on the Charleston-bound *Minerva,* designed to stir up race riots in America. Forewarned, South Carolina officials boarded the vessel upon its arrival and seized four men and a woman, together with some concealed papers.[228] For a time there was considerable excitement, but from the first alert Republicans were skeptical. Only a revelation from on high could have produced discovery of a genuine plot at such a distance. In Albany, where the version had the "agents" themselves hidden in tubs, the Directory was considered too canny to select three mulattoes, a white man and a woman as conspirators—however much Robert Goodloe Harper might imagine a scheme to rouse Southern Negroes.[229]

The full story finally came out. Democrats guffawed that after the accused had been permitted to leave for the West Indies, information clearing them completely had been received. The tubs had actually contained clothing, the men were no plotters, the documents were love-letters, and the woman merely a lady of easy virtue who had pleased someone at the American embassy so well as "to follow him all the way from France . . . for the wages of her service." Federalists were warned they might cry "Wolf" too often. This "Cypher plot" (referring to the "code" of the "dispatches") had "become a *mere Cypher,* notwithstanding the dispatch of a COACH and FOUR to convey the intelligence to the President." [230]

Still more preposterous was the "tailor plot." For weeks some nervous Philadelphians had noted unusual activity at a Spruce Street tailor's shop. About eighty men and women had been busily cutting and sewing what appeared to be uniforms. Since the blue breeches lacked buttons at the knees, they were clearly destined for Frenchmen or Francophiles. Learning from the tailor that a Frenchman had placed the order, an alarmed Federalist seized the uniforms and "conspirators" to forestall a revolt in Philadelphia—only to learn that the suits had been ordered for Toussaint's troops in Haiti. Now, sneered chortling Democrats, the administration was faced with the weighty problem of determining whether or not making blue breeches constituted treason.[231]

There was little to smile at, however, in the tale of the "*Ocean* massacre." Four French privateers, the story went, had boarded Captain Kemp's ship and had murdered everyone except five or six persons who hid in the hold. Federalists insisted all Americans were outraged, but Democrats (conditioned now by tubs and tailors) immediately branded the yarn a fabrication for "election purposes only." The captors were said to have divided the vessel's cargo—"a trifling inconsistency," since it had sailed from New York in ballast. Handbills of this "base invention" were mailed by government officials at the time of spring balloting in Virginia; the obvious intent "was to influence the election." Probably "Mr. Harper could find a clue to this wicked imposture. . . ."[232]

Unfortunately for those who had fabricated the story, the *Ocean* arrived safely in Baltimore, reporting no sign of French privateers on her passage. Yet the account had already spread. Reverend Jedidiah Morse, in his Fast Day sermon at Charlestown, Massachusetts (April 25, 1799), solemnly proclaimed the slaughter of the *Ocean*'s crew as fact. It was but one, he claimed—and other Federalist preachers joined the cry—of a long list of despicable French perpetrations, aimed at the overthrow of all government and all religion.[233] When even Federalist papers were compelled to admit the *Ocean* was safe, other Federalist arguments tended to be discredited.[234]

Another atrocity charged against the French was a supposed gunpowder plot to blow up the President and Congress in Philadelphia.[235] Robert Goodloe Harper even wrote a book on "Clues to Conspiracies," but gratified Democrats noted it failed to sell. In 1800 the French were also blamed for the insurrection of slaves led by a fellow slave, Gabriel, in Virginia. There were stories of alleged Gallic emissaries to American blacks at least as early as the time of Genêt and the Haitian revolt, but here was an actual uprising. Once more Republicans scoffed:

> This is reviving the days of delusion, when *Illuminati, Ocean* &c. were so loudly vociferated through the country, and a house could not be burned, or a horse killed by lightning, but the French were said to be the authors of the mischief. No evil can possibly happen to us but through their agency.[236]

In the South, however, any accusation related to a slave revolt necessitated a considered defense. Democrats reported the tale as gossipy dilation of the confession of one slave who had understood two Frenchmen were concerned; this had been distorted into an argument against France. Another confession stated the slaves intended to invite all the Scottish merchants to a feast after seizing Richmond, but no reasonable man believed these Federalist businessmen were involved. Yet only weak and illiberal individuals could accuse one and acquit the other. Gabriel, it was noted, "to the extreme mortification of many *violent friends of order,*" was hanged without implicating any Jeffersonians.[237]

Without doubt these "plots" in the long run boomeranged against the Federalists, largely because of the Jeffersonian press. Vigilant Republican editors referred to them frequently, thus impugning any new stories and reminding readers of the unreliability of administration favorites. They even hinted "these friends of war" hired saboteurs to create incidents for which France could be blamed.[238] These terrors were being publicized to divert citizens from the "real danger"—the insidious encroachment of the government upon popular liberties.[239]

At first electioneering falsehoods may have seemed advantageous, since the public could not always distinguish fact from fabrication. But Republicans shrewdly utilized the reaction to the series of discredited "atrocities." Linking the unfounded story of the *Ocean* massacre with the Reverend Morse's charges of an Illuminati, they greatly nullified the effect of the latter accusation.[240]

Carefully nurtured by Democratic journalists, the mood of skepticism grew. "Old South" reviewed with relish all the fantastic attempts to scare people into bolstering the tottering walls of Federalism. The "TUB-PLOT" created such universal fright "that every old woman expected to find treason and rebellion wrapt up in a bundle of linnen, and the contents of a *washing-tub* was inspected" in greatest detail. This gave way to the "TAYLOR-PLOT," wherein every clothing shop in Philadelphia was pictured as a rendezvous for the Illuminati and "bands of *wild Irishmen*" seeking to further Napoleon's descent upon America. Next came the "LADY-PLOT," in which a "French *woman* was to set fire to the magazine, and the President, Senate and House of Representatives . . . was to share the fate of King, Lords and Commons under the fatal explosion of Guy Faux [*sic*]." Harper's pamphlet, designed to expose Democratic conspiracies, exposed nothing but that Americans were too sophisticated to purchase his book. After that came the "COCKADE influenza," then charges of "the ILLUMINATI and the destruction of religion"; this was followed by "the LIE of the Ocean massacre," and now Jefferson —who only vindicated freedom of conscience—was traduced as a deist.[241]

Duane in 1800 warned the *Aurora*'s readers to "BE CAUTIOUS FROM EXPERIENCE: The season of election, is, with the enemies of the people's liberties, the season of Deception—BEWARE OF FABRICATED NEWS!" The Pittsburgh *Tree of Liberty* carried a mock advertisement for the "FEDERAL CLUE AND TUB MANUFACTORY," commencing, "Wanted a few *NEW* and *ORIGINAL ALARM TRAPS*." Ingenious liars should inquire of the British consul. Those familiar with the West Indian sea idiom were especially desired, as it would be necessary to murder three or four ships' companies, torture their officers, throw a few ladies overboard, and eat six or eight children. A man who could adapt this sort of thing to fit the Boston or Philadelphia market should "apply to DR. MORSE or PARSON ABERCROMBIE," and a prize was offered for the most novel "and taking lie." [242]

If hostilities with France were truly a *sine qua non* for the Federalist party, Republicans suggested there may well have been a consistent purpose behind these various "plots." Dismay struck many pro-administration figures when they learned their titular chieftain was inclined to give France yet another opportunity to come to terms. First hint of this was seen in Adams' address to the closing session of the Fifth Congress, after fighting had already occurred on the high seas. Whether the President was influenced by Gerry's reports, the conversation with Logan, resentment at the highhandedness of Pickering and other Hamiltonians, or information from William Vans Murray (the minister at the Hague) that the Directory feared an Anglo-American alliance and was thus disposed toward peace, is not known. Irrespective of motivation, his speech in December, 1798, was patently less truculent than earlier utterances. Though put negatively, his assertion that he would never send another envoy to Paris without guarantees of a favorable reception was really an admission of willingness to negotiate. Perhaps recognizing this, Republican editors guardedly approved the speech, predicting "the war faction" would dislike it; "Honestus" even intimated another minister might be sent.[243]

A second communication from Murray conveyed Talleyrand's assurance that an American envoy would be received with respect, with the implication that Murray himself would be *persona grata*. Gratified indeed was the *Aurora* to announce that Adams had secretly recommended Murray's name to the Senate for a new mission to France.[244] Federalist newssheets, apparently lacking Duane's sources of information, refused to credit this report. They quoted Adams' earlier speeches and damned the story as "a mere fabrication" intended to defame the President.[245] Stoutly the *Aurora* stuck to its story. Adams' prudence furthered the belief that, like his predecessor, he had been deceived by dark intriguers within his party. One high Federalist [obviously Hamilton] was universally infamous for wiliness and "shocking depravity." Indiscretion had forced him to seek his ends by devious means; war and military command were to have been the vehicles by which he was to rise to dictatorial power. To him and his friends "hell is not so terrible, as the thought of peace." Now, "under the blind impulse of their passions we hear these minions of this archfiend bellowing forth even against the president whom they have professed so long and so much to adore." [246]

"Better LATE than NEVER!" cried the *Independent Chronicle*, on hearing of the proposed envoy. It rejoiced at the possibility of peace with America's "only friends," though, if Gerry had been permitted to negotiate, "millions would have been saved." That, however, was spilt milk, and America should be able to obtain a new commercial treaty both honorable and advantageous. Adams was applauded for his honest effort for peace; the aristocrats were discomfited and Logan, vindicated. That the President had made the appointment was sufficient proof, in view of his earlier affirmation, that Murray would be received, "whatever the friends of *order,* and of *blessed war* and *confusion,* may say to the contrary." [247]

Some skepticism persisted concerning Adams' sincerity, but Federalist gibes that Republicans were now "disposed to speak civil things of the President" drew the retort that the party of the opposition was interested in "actions rather than men," and it was hoped nothing "of a political nature will clogg [*sic*] the negociation." [248] It was well reservations were made on this latter score, for many Federalists seemed unalterably opposed to peace with France. Their party was sadly divided over the issue, and Jeffersonians keenly felt the crisis would determine whether America would remain a virtuous republic "or become the satellites of the most stern and savage despotism." Numerous Federalists had now separated from the actual *war* party (which might properly be called the British faction), and like Washington (it was said) had expressed disapproval of any but a defensive conflict.[249]

Pickering labored assiduously, Democrats insisted, to convince Americans French peace offers were a decoy; the entire "ESSEX JUNTO" resisted the idea of an olive branch. Efforts to wreck the presidential mission could be thwarted only by electing known peace advocates to public offices. Ministers who affronted "Heaven with their impiety" and bowed "with sycophantic condescension to the nod of a few monied men in their parish" were straining to foil the embassy and to excite people to war. Hamiltonians predicted American envoys would once more be rejected, labeled any instances of French generosity (such as releasing a Yankee ship) "traps," and even attempted to discredit Lafayette as a possible French emissary to America. Clearly, nothing less than "To arms! . . . will suit the purposes of the . . . American beef-eaters who are fed from the public table." [250]

Talleyrand's letters to the Hague, protesting France's sincere desire for peace, were reprinted.[251] When Federalist senators, livid with indignation, told Adams they would refuse confirmation of Murray's appointment, the President agreed to name two additional Federalists and to postpone their departure until assured they would be properly acknowledged. His delay in dispatching them has since been interpreted as a shrewd political move to mobilize public opinon, and while some Democrats were disturbed over his dilatoriness they were insistent in repetitions the commissioners could expect respectful treatment. To the last, Hamiltonians claimed the envoys would not be sent, but in November Jeffersonian readers were assured "from authority not to be questioned," that the frigate *United States* was waiting at Newport to convey them to Le Havre.[252]

Rumors were even abroad that Adams had proposed to resign. Apparently, these originated in a threat he actually made to High Federalist leaders if the Senate completely rejected a second special mission,[253] but Republicans editorially denied the report. This tale was an artifice "calculated to produce effects most injurious to our peace and honor." The office of President was too distinguished, said Democrats (not alluding to the point that a resignation would bring Jefferson into office),[254] to be cast lightly aside at the caprice of others. Adams was morally bound to make every exertion against the war the enemies of the nation were trying so desperately to provoke. By public acts and private addresses to passion, these intriguers had already deferred the mission.

> Alexander Hamilton wishes it to be suspended forever. We do believe that the President will not truckle to such *extra official* interference.—or to the domineering influence of others who would sacrifice him with as little hesitation to their views as *Jonathan Robbins*—we believe the President will be obstinate on this occasion to save his country from foreign war, and his own reputation and his family, from all its evils.

Adams was a man of prudence and character; the issue would show whether constitutionally selected officials should exercise the executive authority, or if that function belonged to "others of whom the constitution is ignorant." [255]

The petulance of "high-toned *federal printers,* on the late appointment of Commissioners to France," ill-accorded with their earlier objections to any questioning of the wisdom of administration measures. Inasmuch as the Anglophile editors were unacquainted with the contents of the relevant dispatches, their persistent reprobation of the mission was veritably "Jacobinical," disrespectful to the President, and indicated no love for peace. To date Adams had meticulously safeguarded both the nation's honor and interests; apprehension that he would sacrifice them now was totally unjustified.[256]

Just as Republicans were disconcerted when shooting started with France, so now did Federalists discover their own predicament over Adams' peace efforts. The *Aurora* charged many of them regarded war as essential to unite their party, yet some Federalist papers supported the President's conciliatory moves.[257] These saw Adams as a helmsman following "the Washington chart," steering the tortuous passage between conflict with England or with France—when such as Pickering would plunge us into war with France and such as Monroe would provoke war with England. Relying on reverence for the First President to secure approval for pacific moves, Democrats stressed that neutrality had been the supreme goal of Washington's statesmanship. One even noted that, without going into the merits of Jay's Treaty, the policy which dictated it had been "unquestionably wise." [258]

It was inevitable that Anglophiles should criticize attempts to treat with France, although Adams seemed surprised at their exertions to imperil negotiations. This group felt Murray "Frenchified" by his residence in Holland. It professed the assurances that he, Oliver Ellsworth, and Governor William Davie of North Carolina would be courteously received were unsatisfactory. To promote an English alliance, Republicans avowed, they circulated the lies of the European writers John Robison, the Abbé Barreul, and others on the Illuminati and Jacobinism. Despite presidential firmness, efforts were continually made to discredit the negotiations and to inflame the popular mind against France. Surely a firm and fair treaty could be as readily made with Paris as with an Indian tribe. Even Adams was cited to the effect that since the new envoys had been sent, many Federalists had been among the most seditious men in the community.[259] They hoped to obtain popular rejection of a treaty if one were achieved, whereas the securing of a settlement—in spite of sneers and predictions of failure—was unquestionably a cause for congratulation. The same group had also plotted to defeat Adams in the election of 1800 and to supplant him with C. C. Pinckney, but there also it was almost certainly doomed to failure.[260]

So it was that Jeffersonian hopes of a Federalist cleavage came to be realized. The faction headed by Hamilton, Cobbett, and Pickering was accused of striving for an offensive-defensive British alliance in 1797, of creating a large standing army to meet a non-existent invasion threat, and of exerting an undue ministerial control over the administration. That Adams had been duped also was small consolation to the people who had to foot the bill. Hamilton's "Essex Junto" desired Pinckney as the next President, but if Hamiltonians could so influence Adams what would they not do with their own creature in office? America's only salvation lay in entrusting the government to Republicans, who all along had "openly borne testimony against the machinations of Hamilton." [261]

With tongue in cheek, the *Raleigh Register* affected disapproval of the power struggle which had "produced lively bickerings among the Federalists." Long had Adams been chagrined by his own party's estimates of his talents. Hamilton had become obnoxious to the President by earlier trying to displace him. According to Republicans, Adams now cast the odium of attachment to Britain's cause upon his rivals, picturing Jefferson as preferable to either Pickering or Pinckney, and charging definite British influence in high Federalist councils.[262] His letter in 1792 claiming Pinckney's appointment as plenipotentiary to England was due to the South Carolinian's Anglophile proclivities had been at first denounced as a forgery in the Federalist press, but Adams later admitted it.[263] Hamilton claimed this letter alone demonstrated Adams' unfitness for the Presidency and challenged him to prove that he (Hamilton) belonged to any British faction. Jeffersonians, excerpting from these letters and pamphlets in their news columns, advertised that these charges and countercharges among Federalists only proved their whole party was tainted with British influence—as Republicans had long insisted.[264]

Proudly these editors claimed credit for the peace that ensued. Should anyone ask *"What good have the Republicans done?,"* the reply was that they had saved the country millions by stopping army enlistments and ending the construction of warships; they had prevented war.[265] Thanks to Adams, Democratic publishers had at long last found an actual diplomatic program of which they could approve—but they had no intention of letting that fact interfere with the election of their own candidate.

 ISSUES SECTIONAL
AND PAROCHIAL

Frequently overshadowed by the battlesmoke over foreign policy were the brushfire clashes arising around purely domestic disputes. Yet questions of especial concern to particular American groups were ever present and often became sufficiently important to call forth major political polemics. At times based ostensibly on appeals other than to party, occasionally even contradictory, the stressing of local irritations or indications of special benefits came increasingly to be used to whip up sentiment against the administration.

One of the earliest such controversies arose over the location of the national capital. Civic and state pride, along with economic considerations, produced a number of aspirants— New York, Philadelphia, Baltimore and some site (perhaps Richmond) in Virginia vied hopefully to be named as the seat of government. Most New Englanders conceded geographical considerations eliminated their section, but they caustically berated the First Congress for the time and money expended on the question.[1]

Baltimoreans feared fixing the permanent capital at either Philadelphia or along the Potomac would threaten their port's booming trade and their ties with the western interior, but Philadelphians were informed the matter of residence was infinitely more than a rivalry between cities. It involved the safety of the entire nation. For thirty years New York had been America's center of Anglomania; Congress there would be subjected to dread British influence. Ties of blood, commerce and affection were still so strong a stranger would "believe himself . . . in . . . some . . . British town." The city was almost contiguous with New England, and it was "well known *these* states have a common interest in many things, totally different from the interest of all the states to the southward of Hudson's river." New York had worked to attach New England to her selfish views and had courted the Southern states by exempting Negroes from tariff duties.[2]

For their part, New Yorkers taxed Philadelphians with threatening the harmony of the Union by endeavoring to force Congress to meet there. That city's treatment of the Pennsylvania legislature aroused fear mob-rule might dominate national law-making. Gothamites set aside pews in their churches for congressmen and allowed them library privileges without charge; they had also spent $50,000 to construct a Federal Hall. Six months after commencement of the ten-year temporary residence period in Philadelphia, two columns headed "THE CONTRAST" demonstrated the superiority of treatment accorded government officials by New York over that by her sister city.[3]

With the decision to fix the permanent site along the Potomac, a Virginia Anti-federalist twitted Manhattanites who had labored for the Constitution in anticipation of governmental edifices in their city. Advantages promised the New York ratifying convention by ardent Federalists may have converted many votes, and now it was too late to repent.[4] The elated Georgetown *Times* carried a letter from "V[a]." to her "dear sisters," "N.E., N.Y., P[a.], and C[onn]." V.'s empty purse and farm in disrepair resulted from helping defend a wide neighborhood when called on for aid. The Potomac was ideally situated for the "central farm house," but V. had tried to avoid even the appearance of prejudice in the matter of location. Yet had God himself picked the site, "I fear, my dear sisters, that influenced by self interest, you would . . . attempt to out-vote Him."[5]

A clearly partisan pattern may be difficult to detect in these effusions of local pride, but the hot resentment of disappointed regions over the assumptionist bargain [6] and the use of the arrangement to secure passage of assumption by moving the capital in an effort to discredit Hamilton's entire financial program seems significant. Republican newspapers in areas where citizens were already disaffected employed the dissatisfaction as an opening wedge in attacking the Federalist administration. On the other hand (as if to stress the sectional nature of the question) the Republican press near the chosen site was within a few years claiming credit for the choice! That the Potomac was chosen as the permanent seat of government was largely Jefferson's work, so it was claimed, and was not determined by Adams' deciding vote; the capital there would be infinitely safer in the Virginian's hands than in those of the gentleman from Massachusetts.[7]

The apportionment of representatives for Congress afforded another fertile field for criticism of the administration. Madison had proposed a fixed ratio of one representative for every 30,000 persons, but most Northern Federalists desired a smaller legislative body. Fisher Ames advocated a 1:40,000 proportion, but his views were not uniformly shared by his Massachusetts constituents. He was called either ignorant or self-opinionated to assert people were "universally satisfied" with the representation assigned them in the original Constitution; the state convention had requested Madison's figure, which Washington also favored. While a smaller body was less costly and more efficient, a larger body would be harder to bribe. If economy were the goal, Congress had only to reduce the salaries of public officials.[8]

Eventually it was learned the 1:30,000 proportion would leave certain large fractions unrepresented in the North, though none in the South. A proposal to provide representation for major fractions was deemed too favorable to Northern states, and finally a ratio of 1:33,000 was determined upon. While Congressional debate was long and furious, public interest seemed comparatively slight. Press comment

339

was not vigorous, though a little later the *National Gazette* frowned on a Federalist proposal to divide the entire country into population districts of 30,000 each. This scheme, Freneau claimed, would afford New England additional representatives at the expense of the Middle and Southern states. Many readers doubtless shared the cynicism of the Philadelphia correspondent who compared apportionment to division "of a basket of hickory nuts among a parcel of Schoolboys—*by scramble*—in which the strongest are sure to get more than their own share." [9]

More interest, and definitely partisan in nature, was demonstrated at the end of the century. The Richmond *Examiner* strongly protested Congressional delay in passing the census bill for 1800; two million people were being deprived of representation. Pennsylvanians swore Federalists postponed the count until population increases in Middle and Southern states would have no effect in the coming election. Militia figures for western Pennsylvania and for Georgia had disclosed "prodigious" growth in those areas. "Thus is Pennsylvania disserved by the vote of [Senator] James Ross Esq. to postpone the census." The cry was echoed by New Jersey Republicans, who accused New England of discrimination. It rankled that Federalist senators had voted to fix the census date so late their constituents were deprived of an additional elector in the autumn voting. Pennsylvania and New York, with sixty per cent more population than in 1790, suffered even more. The "faithless representatives and senators" of the area had surrendered constituents' rights and taxing power "into the hands of New-England." [10]

Thus linked with representation was the question of unequal taxation. At the time of refunding, Hamilton's own report showed nearly seven-tenths of the public debt was held in Pennsylvania, New York, and Massachusetts. Although the power arising from possession of public funds had already left the South, its citizens would still be taxed to pay interest and principal on obligations held elsewhere. Vermonters were told their state paid into the federal Treasury annually some

$58,560 in taxes on salt, tea, whiskey, and imports, receiving in return only $8,200 in salaries and fees. Thus $50,360 left the state each year to pay for Indian wars, governmental salaries, and interest on the public debt. For a handful of people, in "a new and but partially cultivated country," this was "an enormous sum." Citizens should see where their money went and should revise a system that was leading toward British corruption and bankruptcy.[11] In 1798 statistics were cited to show that Kentucky paid more than twice in taxes what she received in disbursements from the central government. The real picture was even more unfair, for Kentuckians paid not only the original duty on imports, but also merchants' and handlers' profits, which Eastern consumers escaped.[12]

Peculiarly oppressive to farmers, and in direct proportion to their distance from a seaport, was the salt tax. True it was that New England fisheries consumed vast quantities of salt, yet a bounty not only exempted fishermen but afforded them opportunity for speculation. Eastern congressmen had insisted upon such a subsidy, though they uniformly supported measures harmful to tobacco and other Southern staples. Fishermen in Marblehead, Massachusetts, allegedly had "proposed to LEND (not to make a present, O God forbid—only to lend!)" Federalist Representative Samuel Sewall of Massachusetts "a few hundred dollars, and to solicit his advice [on] how such a bounty could be obtained." John Randolph noted the $90,000 anticipated revenue from the salt tax equalled the estimated cost of a memorial for George Washington. Surely the man who had requested a simple funeral would never have sanctioned a monument financed by the salt of the poor.[13]

"Brutus" expostulated that Tennesseans bought and sold "to greater disadvantage than any other state in the union," yet harmful federal legislation had cost tobacco raisers alone some $9,000,000 in the last two years. Federalist printers were ignorant of the economic facts of life; what benefited the Eastern states actually operated to hurt the Western. Farmers paid nine-tenths of the cost of a navy to protect commerce in which they had no more interest than in that "of the planets."

If Adams had obtained the appropriations for which he asked, all Tennessee's resources could not have met the demand. Southerners also noted that the administration had laid a direct tax on land and slaves while excepting "stockholders, and men who deal in money, as the inhabitants of the Eastern states do. . . ." [14]

In New England canny Republicans could turn the other side of the picture to their purpose. The growing South and West were depicted as evading their share of the direct tax through Federalist postponement of the census. Each citizen of Connecticut and Rhode Island had to pay four or five times the amount of a Kentuckian or Tennessean, and residents of the Northwest Territory paid nothing at all. A new census would have saved Massachusetts some $40,000, but Federalists considered electoral votes more important than equitable taxes. Anyone seeking to save money for the Eastern states was branded a Jacobin. Thus did Adams treat his "beloved N. England . . . the most loyal, and truly Federal part of his dominions." [15] Clearer evidence could scarcely be found of tailoring arguments for local consumption.

If representation and taxes were disproportionate, so also was the distribution of federal offices. A potent argument in the Middle and Southern states during the campaign of 1796 was simply that Jefferson was not a New Englander. The Secretaries of State and Treasury, ministers to England, Holland, Portugal, Algiers, and Spain, the Vice President, the Chief Justice and an Associate Justice, and a majority of the directors of the Bank of the United States were all from New England. Did voters wish to make Adams Chief Executive so he might "be enabled to give the few remaining places of trust and profit in the Federal government to other New-England-men?" There was reason for New England's Federalism. With a near-monopoly on public offices, it would be strange otherwise.[16]

That territorial settlers were ruled by governments in which they had no voice was reprehensible enough, held the *Aurora*.

342

Yet Adams had multiplied the evil when he sent to Mississippi a governor (Winthrop Sargent) born in his own state.

Massachusetts and Connecticut thus divide the American 'loaves and fishes' between them at a fine rate, and the Senate co-operate as if they all came from those two states. All New England supplies *'the fishes'* which are of the true *Gudgeon* kind, and the other twelve [*sic*] states find *'the loaves.'* It is remarkable, that New Hampshire, Vermont and Rhode Island have never had a permanent national office of any sort or size given to them. The two central New England states, like political cormorants, eat up all the New England Gudgeons.

Federalist papers impudently harped about "the people's own government," when it was "better to call *the United States* *'Braintree and Litchfield'* at once." This "pernicious narrow devotion to local interests" threatened national harmony. Adams' conduct was selfish and "contemptuous of five-sixth of the country." [17]

Again, however, the argument was adjusted to suit the region concerned. Less than a year later the New London *Bee* complained there was not one from Connecticut among the 265 presidential commissions in the army. This was indeed singular for the most Federalist state of all, which had furnished its quota of soldiers in '75. Perchance as old Tories Connecticut's Federalist leaders had no love for danger, or her citizens were passed over because they recognized the danger of standing armies. [18]

A little later, though, even the *Bee* felt compelled to comment on the number of New Englanders in high places. Most important of the few major posts held by men from other regions was the Vice-Presidency, no appointive office, or Jefferson would not be occupying it. A South Carolinian raged that from Adams' selections it would seem "that all virtue and talents" centered in New England. [19]

"New England economy," as noted earlier, [20] became a venomous byword among Democrats in other parts of the nation. Since Washington's term, lamented "A Pennsylvanian," the country had been run by friends of Adams and Charles C. Pinckney. By 1801 nearly $42,000,000 would have been spent, and all important governmental offices virtually surrendered to the states of Connecticut and Massachusetts. In addition to those protested in 1796, the president *pro tem* of the Senate, the Speaker of the House, and several new ministers had been added to the list of officials from those two states. Connecticut was granted several million acres on Lake Erie, even though the state had formally relinquished her claim to the land and had lost two cases in Federal court on the matter. Arrant favoritism, this, for Pennsylvania had been forced to *purchase* her lake frontage. So marked was Senator James Ross's favoritism for the New England commonwealth that he should have run the year before for governor of Connecticut rather than of Pennsylvania. And Adams favored an established church such as the Congregational one in New England, whereas Jefferson (like William Penn) would maintain liberty of conscience.[21]

Jerseymen bemoaned that "a New-England administration" accorded their state but one major federal post, whereas Connecticut had nine. New England's lust for power had cost Thomas Pinckney the Vice-Presidency in 1797; its electors feared he might get a few votes from Jeffersonian electors and be named President over Adams. Hence they threw away their votes, and Jefferson received the second place. In 1800 citizens of the section still attempted to maintain preeminence and had arranged for their Federalist legislatures to choose their presidential electors.[22]

Of sectional interest also was the question of Negro slavery. Here New England Federalists taunted Democrats about their supposed love of equality and liberty while predominately Democratic Southern states exercised "the most abominable tyranny over their fellow-creatures." Since five slaves counted as much as three Northern whites, "No wonder . . . the *Virginia delegation* is as it is. They cannot be called representatives of a *free* people: for many of them are literally the representatives of slaves." [23] Republicans, particularly in the

North, reacted immediately. In one of the earliest counterparts of a modern editorial, the *Independent Chronicle* observed that intransigent partisans had been making deliberate efforts to split the Union over the slavery issue. Regrettable as it was that Connecticut and all states to the South except New Jersey held blacks in bondage, this gave New Englanders no right to insult Southern congressmen and President Washington "with the rest of them." Contemporary Republicans were in no way responsible for a relic of an old monarchical system, which Virginia leaders agreed should be eliminated safely and gradually. Were the unhappy Africans freed at once their condition would probably not be bettered; Federalists could prove the sincerity of their interest in emancipation by sponsoring a five per cent tax on interest from funds and banks, to be used to purchase Negroes under sixteen years of age. Massachusetts' sanctimoniousness did not add to her popularity and conceivably might cost her dearly later on issues vitally affecting her welfare.[24]

Slavery was a degrading reminder of America's old colonial situation, held the *Gazette Française*. There was no ethical justification for it, but true friends of freedom realized that a *gradual* restoration of liberty to Negroes was the most that was desirable or safe. Talk of Southern aristocrats' hatred of the North spread discord, often fomented by those who paid the loudest lip-service to the cause of unity. Federalist critics of slaveowners really assailed Washington and the Constitution; the Virginian was his state's "first slave holder," and the document expressly recognized the institution.[25]

Some Southerners took umbrage at once over Northern criticisms. Agitation for emancipation stemmed first from the sniveling Quakers, said one. These hypocrites did nothing to protest British and Indian barbarities during the Revolution, or to aid in achieving independence, yet now as lawyers and merchants they schemed to destroy the Southern states and to dominate the Union. In every confederation some members gained ascendancy; if the Eastern states intended to weaken the South, emancipation by purchase "would be a great stroke of policy." Any American faction seeking to take away Southern property would meet with stubborn resistance. Little South Carolina had triumphed over Britain's best troops, and she would defend her possessions to the last rather than see them sacrificed to treacherous Quaker "humanity." [26] The *Norfolk Herald* reprinted an item from the Boston *Centinel,* sarcastically entitled "PURE DEMOCRACY," which ridiculed Virginia leaders for prating of freedom and then advertising for runaway slaves. Hotly the *Herald* retorted:

> We can assure our brethren of Boston that we are no less sensible of the blessings of *national Liberty* than they, but that we are by no means such *hot headed* admirers of the RIGHTS OF MAN; as to overturn order and subordination, or hurl into one common heap of *undistinguished equality,* our CHARACTER, Talent, and Property. We leave the *spirited* YANKEES in full possession of such elevated sentiments, but we shall not cease our exertions to rescue from their purloining Captains the property of our countrymen. [27]

Northern Republicans noted that when New York Federalists ordered their slaves to raise a liberty pole in mockery of the Democratic ones, it revealed ownership of slaves was confined to no one party. Moreover, the Negroes attached a sign, "FREEDOM TO AFRICANS," to the pole, disclosing "a manly and rational sentiment which never warmed the breasts of those whom they are made to call masters." [28]

Both parties used sectional arguments which were not consistent nationally. Southern Federalists harped on Jefferson's advocacy of emancipation in an effort to turn slave-owning voters against him. One John T. Mason replied "a more groundless and infamous falsehood never gained circulation" than that Jefferson would liberate all Negroes if elected. Charles Pinckney assured Charlestonians that Jefferson's views on slavery were academic and (on Jefferson's own authority, as the owner of 200 slaves) would not be put into practice. [29] Kentuckian George Nicholas could advocate the personal liberties of freemen and also assert the rights of property, even in the form of slaves. He did not deny the authority of the state legislature to mandate emancipation on fair terms, but he had the privilege of objecting to terms he felt unfair.[30] The keen and often illogical interest in the entire question was displayed in a weird Federalist story in the *Philadelphia Gazette*. Gabriel, leader of the Virginia slave insurrection, was said to be no slave at all, but had confessed to being the noted James Thomson Callender, who incited the revolt to arouse Southerners to the dangers of Federalist antislavery propaganda and thus promote Jefferson's election.[31]

Republicans hastened to use the slavery issue when it appeared to their advantage. They dwelled on the seizure of a slave ship captured in Rhode Island when it was learned the owner was Federalist Congressman John Brown of that state. And when the federal officer sold the vessel at auction, "this good Federalist Christian Mr. Brown . . . bought the ship in for TEN DOLLARS; can anyone blame Mr. Brown for being a good Federalist?" [32]

A few old Antifederalists continued a running fire on the new government from its inception. "ARISTIDES" in 1790 recounted the defects of the Constitution and claimed the administration had kept not a single promise "of the friends of coercive government." If the Massachusetts legislature lacked power to repeal the vote of the ratifying convention, neither could it retract the condition that certain amendments were obligatory. In actuality, ratification was no more sacrosanct than ordinary acts. The legislature could legally repeal any state law except the constitution from which the law-making body itself derived authority.[33]

Federalists were rebuked for creating fissures in the Union that might produce secession. When the *Columbian Centinel* talked of a party in the South jealous of Northerners, Republicans rejoined that this jealousy had not arisen until after Southern congressmen had detected intrigues by Northern members. Only a change in Northern representation could remove suspicion. To return the present Federalist congressmen might well bring more feuds—even dissolution of the Union. The Massachusetts legislature was later stigmatized as disre-

347

spectful to Virginia in refusing to consider an amendment requiring House approval for treaties. Though some persons wanted a divided America to fall prey to England, state legislatures should promote harmony. Proposed amendments should at least be given the consideration common decency demanded. After all, unity was the "great object." [34]

Excitement over Jay's Treaty evoked some threats of a separation of the Northern from the Southern states. In New Hampshire, the *Grafton Minerva,* deprecating such talk, indicated these suggestions of a New York paper occasioned wide discussion and served "to convince the public of the danger of local views, when they prevail over the public interest." Southerners resented references to "violation of national faith" and smarted under inaccurate assertions that they had not done their share in the Revolutionary War.[35]

More serious, in the heat of the close election of 1796, were the letters of "Pelham," contending that sooner or later North and South would part company and that possibly the time had come. Northern states, noted this New Englander, had received no equivalent compensation for permitting Southerners to count three-fifths of their slaves for representation. Logically, Northerners should be able to count the same proportion of their cattle or horses. Had North and South the same political ideals, union would still be preferable to separation, but if New Englanders had to choose between giving up their government or leaving the Southern states, the choice was obvious.[36]

Furious were Republican retorts to "Pelham." Editor Samuel H. Smith of the Philadelphia *New World* said that nowhere but in the United States could such an idea have been printed. Repugnant as was the suggestion, he inserted one of the letters from "Pelham" in his columns because discussion had therapeutic value. "Greene" branded the New Englander's threat a disgrace to "the *elective mode* of creating a Chief Magistrate." It attempted to secure selecting a friend of monarchy, to inflame party spirit, to shake public credit and to produce hatred between the sections. "Friends of *peace,* of *order,* of *property,* and all that is *good* and *valuable* among men, see the knot of *'exclusive federalists'* at length explained by their own fortunate indiscretion." [37]

"A VIRGINIAN" wrote if ever such a dissolution came to pass it would result when Northern demagogues thought the South was no longer necessary to their aggrandizement. If at the same time the Southern states discovered themselves outwitted and on the verge of war with France, their deliverer, a separation might ensue. Happily, "Pelham's" tirade would affect only a handful. Southerners judged British influence responsible for Northern antipathy. Despite feeling over the Jay Treaty and the possibility a Virginian might keep Adams from the presidency, New England would not break away from the Union. She needed Southern trade, and Massachusetts would not forget the aid she had received in 1775.

Emancipating the slaves would be a curse. The blacks were contented and seldom had sufficient industry to maintain families. Republicanism in the North was no purer than that of the South; the freest of ancient republics had slaves. New England's industriousness and temperance were caused by climate and soil, not by a more virtuous disposition. Even Englishmen commented on that section's hypocritical pretense of piety; the South was fully as religious in every true sense. "Pelham" sounded as if he were an old supporter of funding and Jay's Treaty who was offended by any opposition to his pet projects. Northern states need never fear being called upon by the South to aid in suppressing "the expected and perhaps wished for insurrection of her slaves. . . ." Southerners had done their fair share during the Revolution, and had they used their commercial position to bargain for special privileges King George could have easily reconquered the remaining colonies. Separation now could only lead to civil war and probable British intervention.[38]

Representative Samuel Sewall of Massachusetts, faced with opposition to a federal navy, had raved this amounted to depriving trade of national protection. The commercial states might as well *"separate themselves from the Union,* if they are not to be protected by the agricultural part of the country." Would they, demanded the *Independent Chronicle,* put themselves under British protection? "Pelham," that paper sneered, had been advocating disunion, but Federalists did not scruple to mislead the public into believing "that those who opposed their measures on the ground of economy have in view the wicked and dangerous design of *oversetting the government and dissolving the Union.*" So ran "their matchless impudence, as well as detestable hypocrisy." [39]

Shortly afterward "Peter Porcupine" was accused of fomenting civil war, so "the democratic Republicans" might be totally exterminated.[40] When the Virginia and Kentucky Resolutions appeared, the *Independent Chronicle* denied secession was their objective. For years Virginia had endured abuse from New England without any insurrection. These resolutions were the antithesis of disunion; instead of announcing measures for separation, they appealed to her sister states for united action. "OLD SOUTH" pretended amazement that Northern members of Washington's party should directly contravene the principles of his Farewell Address. The First President had urged public economy, had opposed military establishments, and had pleaded for union—yet many Federalist newssheets were agitating for separation of North and South.[41] The oncoming campaign of 1800 generated the following item in several Democratic papers:

> The salvation of the liberties of this country is involved in the approaching election of the people's first servants.—The system which has been hitherto [has been] found so ruinous to the public prosperity and national character, and so closely approaching to the *old road* toward despotism, that nothing but a determined exertion of the public mind on this important occasion can cure or correct it.
>
> The New England party as it is called, has continued to carry all its projects for several years but that of an actual declared war; some members of that party in Congress again talk of a separation of the Union should they not keep the helm at the next presidential election.[42]

"Burleigh" supplanted "Pelham" of four years earlier in the *Connecticut Courant.* His letters asserted Jefferson's election would be followed by dismemberment of the Union. Republicans asked who would effect this separation, for "Burleigh's" own declarations clearly indicated New England would take the step.

> But Burleigh is mistaken. The PEOPLE of America do not desire a division, nor will they suffer it to take place. It is only dreaded by men of weak nerves, and can only be promoted by men under the influence of mistaken or depraved motives.[43]

"Burleigh" wrote of the calamities inevitably resulting from the election of a slaveholding President and predicted the Northern states would probably leave the Union:

> This, an evil of mighty magnitude, is less, far less, than anarchy or slavery. . . . Perhaps the Potomac, the Delaware, or the Hudson, like the Rhine, may part rival, hostile nations, and the shores of one of them be perpetually crimsoned with the blood of the inhabitants.[44]

Republicans pounced on this continuation of "Pelham's" efforts as an open avowal of Federalist designs to force disunion. "LONG JOHN ALLEN," they said, offered only a rehash of absurd and contradictory reasons for secession if Jefferson were victorious. In the South, however, Virginians talked of leaving the Union—and levied new taxes, built an armory, and drilled militia in readiness if Jefferson should be defeated.[45]

Northern Democratic strategy generally was to reassure the faint-hearted that separation was not a real threat. In a letter earlier to the Federalist *Virginia Gazette,* William Branch Giles had denied he favored disunion. True, he had remarked that separation might be preferable to the *perpetuity* of such nefarious measures as a standing army, eight per cent loan, etc., but he confidently anticipated popular correction of these evils by constitutional means. The "paroxysms" of "Burleigh" that predicted a holocaust if French principles suc-

351

ceeded in America were roundly derided. Frenchmen or Republicans had nothing to do with the Gabriel plot or with conspiracies in South Carolina. When one Negro remarked that a certain Federalist had given each of Gabriel's followers five dollars to further the insurrection, reasonable Republicans waited for the accused's defense and accepted his candid explanation. Had the libelee been a Democrat, "all the hireling presses" would have blasted him, and Allen would have found a new argument for dividing the Union.[46]

Even without the vote of Pennsylvania (perhaps to be nullified by disputes in that state's legislature), Jefferson's election was assured. The Federalists so bitterly opposing him were clearly disorganizers. They had made similarly lamentable and groundless prophecies of disunion when John Hancock had been chosen governor of Massachusetts.[47] A Republican triumph would place in office those who put the interest of the country above section, and would strengthen national solidarity.

Throughout the Federalist era there were periodic outcries from citizens who thought their regional interests neglected at the capital. The opposition press during the 'nineties at times deliberately appealed to this disaffection within the area concerned and called attention to it elsewhere. Western Indian depredations afforded frequent opportunities for this type of argument. Frontier complaints found their way even into New England papers early in Washington's administration. Letters told of savage raids, settlers forced to huddle in crowded, dirty forts, and retreats eastward across the mountains, or plans to settle in Spanish territory where protection would be forthcoming. How could a government astound the world by speedy establishment of national credit and fail in the much simpler task of border defense? Kentuckians who had guarded the nation against Britons and Indians during the Revolution were being "pestered with proclamations, which damp the spirit of the people.—It would be well if the gentlemen who live 500 miles out of danger would consider that protection and allegiance are mutable." [48]

Georgians consistently berated Secretary of War Knox for inadequately guarding their frontier. Along with other high administration figures, he was said to be far more interested in a possible British decoration than in protecting American lives. Though war with the Creeks had broken out, only one federal soldier had been provided for every two miles of borderline. Since national officials had ignored the challenge to prove Georgia had provoked the conflict, was the state receiving so little support because of its distance—or the fear that suppressing the savages would excessively further her population growth (and representation)? [49]

The Georgia border had been disputed for years. By the Treaty of Shoulderbone (or Galphinton), in 1785, some Creek chieftains had ceded the state all land east of the Oconee River, but most of the tribal leaders (including the celebrated half-breed "King," Alexander McGillivray) repudiated this agreement and began terrorizing the frontier. The Confederation Congress, desperately wanting peace, made a cursory investigation and invalidated the treaty. Unfortunately, it lacked power either to force Georgia to surrender the disputed land or to suppress the Creek warriors.

The Constitution gave federal officials more power over Indian problems, and Washington was determined to end the desultory warfare. He invited McGillivray, in Spanish pay since American independence had been recognized, to a conference. The Creek and thirty chiefs were warmly received in New York, and a treaty was negotiated without consulting Georgia. For a sum the Indians recognized the Shoulderbone cession, but (notwithstanding Spanish claims to the area) were solemnly guaranteed all lands between the Oconee and the Mississippi. Thanks to America's urgent need for peace in the Southwest while St. Clair campaigned against the Northern Indians, the treaty had some seemingly discreditable aspects. The money paid—especially McGillivray's secret pension—looked, when discovered, suspiciously like tribute. Moreover, the Creek leader was not really detached from his Spanish alliance, as had been hoped.[50]

Georgians promptly denounced the land guarantee unconstitutional, for it gave away a vast territory previously pledged to the state. Moreover, the permanent prohibition on any local agreements modifying the treaty was based on an "act to regulate Indian commerce," of only two years' duration. Little of the proceeds from the sale of appropriated lands would go to Georgia, and only those "possessed of more federalism than foresight" could envisage benefits to the state from the covenant. There were reports McGillivray had been made an American brigadier-general, with permission to import goods duty-free. "God grant that these are suppositions only!," muttered Georgians, for the unconstitutional tariff exemption would enable this "*quondam Spanish Indian*" to undersell American merchants. All liberty would be lost if "*these first stretches* of *power*" were allowed to grow into precedents. Indeed, the treaty was a test to see if the states retained any rights at all.[51]

Anti-administration sentiment was heightened by charges that "our *merciful . . . rulers*" were imitating England's "*horrid policy*" of using savages to keep the Western settlers confined. Settlers on the Tennessee, though proceeding under a lawful act of the Georgia Assembly, were told their undertaking was lawless and they must suffer the consequences—just as British partisans had reasoned earlier. When frontiersmen tried to evade the treaty by placing themselves under the protection of the Chickasaws, it was alleged the central government ordered Governor Blount to urge other Indians to butcher the rascals "who presumed to doubt whether Congress had not justly and legally annihilated all state rights." Talk of humanity and desire to civilize the Creeks was sheer hypocrisy. Congress viewed Western lands as sources of wealth and power and displayed no intention to let Georgia share in the revenue. There was a concerted effort to reduce all the commonwealths to petty corporations dependent upon "the sovereign will and pleasure" of Knox, and even Washington revealed Federalist hostility when he was said to have quipped, "The United States are at peace with all the world, except the state of Georgia." Perhaps the federal government did not even desire peace on the Southwestern frontier. The treaty line had not been drawn over a year later, the commissioners made no serious attempt to run it, and the Creek representatives failed to appear. As long as animosity existed between Indians and Georgians, the Federalist goal of a standing army might easily be attained.[52]

Feeling between state and nation was sharpened by what Georgians considered unwarranted interference in their Congressional election. Since Anthony Wayne had been unseated as representative from Georgia's lower district on charges of stuffing ballot boxes, the only other candidate was entitled to the post. But Federalists had already found James Jackson a thorn in their sides, and Congress refused to seat him. Republicans raged that "the dangerous tendency" of this short cut to aristocracy was a matter affecting all states. Though a communication from Georgia had declared Jackson the state's representative, he was rejected by a sectional and party vote—the first attack on the principle of free elections. Nevertheless, Georgia would make him governor, the highest honor she could bestow, and leave "the junto of Bankers and Speculators and army contractors" to the scorn of history.[53]

The Treaty of New York did not end the Spanish-encouraged Indian raids against Georgia and the Cumberland settlements. American troops could not be spared from the Ohio country until 1793. McGillivray professed inability to restrain the Creeks, and since many of the Indians were known to be friendly the task of distinguishing and punishing the marauders approached impossibility. In an effort to prevent a complete rupture, the administration sent James Seagrove as agent to the Creeks, with instructions to preserve peace and to prevent them from joining the Northern tribes against the United States.

Seagrove distributed corn for famine relief among the Indians, and promised to establish trading houses if they complied with the treaty of 1790. Georgians decried the "Quakerism" of a Congress which donated nine thousand bushels of scarce

355

corn to "these treacherous prowling monsters of the forest."
In the past gifts had always been interpreted as a sign of the
giver's fear and had produced only pillage and murder. Probably Seagrove sought a monopoly of the Indian trade. Small
wonder Georgia's original enthusiasm for the federal Constitution had evaporated! [54]

Despite the commissioner's protests, Georgians continued
to pasture herds and to hunt beyond the Oconee. A Creek
retaliatory raid would have provoked a full-scale war had not
the state lacked money and supplies for the success of General
John Twiggs's militia expedition. Washington held only Congress could declare hostilities, and federal aid for an offensive
was not forthcoming. Fortunately, McGillivray died, and his
successor (plagued by war with the Chickasaws) was more co-
operative. A Creek council finally agreed to observe the New
York pact and offered reparation for the raids.[55]

Many Georgians were far from satisfied. The treaty had
harmed their state, said they, far more than all the devasta-
tions of the British. One D. M'Clusky, arrested for seeking
vengeance upon Indians who had killed his neighbors, called
the central government "a termagent step-mother, always
ready to scourge, but never to protect." Federalist "oppressors" lolled on their couches, "gorging on the fruits of their
various speculations," while "their toadeaters" prated the
administration was infallible. Congress should have sent provisions for the backwoodsmen, asserted others, instead of
lavishing presents on their enemies. On the next expedition,
the militia would not be duped by promises of federal aid; it
was time the people acted for themselves.[56]

When pledged aid was forthcoming, it consisted only of
some arms and enough money to pay two hundred militiamen.
Georgians snorted. No Indians had ever been pacified by
purely defensive tactics, and the authorized force (plus the
handful of federal troops already there) would be lucky to
protect itself. Perhaps this was some deep-laid plot; certainly
it simultaneously proclaimed hostility and advertised helpless-
ness. Federal officers were arrogant, and some were suspected

of keeping men's pay in their own hands for extended periods. Questioned, too, were Seagrove's denials he had ever sold arms to the Creeks or had incited them against the settlers. "That milky policy, humanity, cannot be pled in the present situation," and if Georgians wished to be no longer "a hunting park for the Creek nation" they should look to their own defenses.[57]

Since the federal government had given at least lip-service to the right of self-preservation, "Manlius" beseeched his fellow-citizens to combine and exterminate the Indians. Coexistence was impossible, and contentions that the land belonged to the savages was maudlin sentimentalism; undoubtedly they had taken it from some weaker people. Georgians alone could wipe out the entire Creek nation in fifty days, without cost to the precious Union. "Mentor" seconded this demand for action. Without retaliation, the natives would reason the settlers could not defend themselves. The national government claimed exclusive power to declare war, but the right to engage in it was more fundamental than that of declaration.[58]

So aggressive were Southern pioneers during 1793–1794 that they lost much sympathy nationally. Preliminary negotiations for what came to be Pinckney's Treaty were under way, and America thus discouraged steps against Spain's Indian allies. But frontiersmen were untroubled by considerations of international diplomacy, and bands of Tennesseans marched against the Cherokees and Chickamaugas in defiance of Governor Blount of the Southwest Territory. Georgians' attacks on the Creeks almost ignited an open conflict, and Washington called on Congress for measures to prevent war.[59]

Insisting the state must be represented in any negotiations with the Indians, Georgians derided Seagrove's desperate efforts for peace. The agent was accused of arousing false hopes with reports of an agreement with the Creeks, and his protests against wanton raids by frontiersmen were dismissed as effusions of an uninformed timeserver desiring to support the perfidious "*Knoxonian* treaty." With federal support,

357

Governor George Mathews finally sent General Jared Irwin to compel the return of settlers who were west of the Oconee. The Creeks distrusted troops on their soil, and Georgians demurred that pampered administration officials knew nothing of frontier conditions where settlers seeking redress for murdered relatives were "held up to the general government as a lawless ungovernable banditti." The money wasted treating with the Indians would have been sufficient to conquer them or to extinguish their claims to Georgia's territory. There was no basis for calling out militia against the Oconee settlers, for moving there was not an insurrection.[60]

Another Creek treaty was signed in 1796 at Coleraine, Georgia, partly because of a futile effort by Georgia to get added lands with which to compensate Irwin's soldiers. The Indians ceded no more territory, and the agreement virtually only reaffirmed the Treaty of New York. Nevertheless, General Wayne's victory at Fallen Timbers, a conciliatory federal trading policy toward the Creeks, and the corrupt Yazoo sale which seemed temporarily to remove much of the land in question from free settlement, all helped bring an uneasy peace to the Southwestern frontier.[61]

Sullen Georgians observed "extraordinary exertions" had been made "to quell the [North] Western Indians, whilst those in the Southern department seem rather under the protection of the union than otherwise." The state's commissioners at Coleraine had been pointedly slighted by federal authorities, and the treaty had no right to rescind earlier agreements. Despite a congressional recommendation to compensate the state for surrendered claims, there was a residue of discontent against the administration, which many citizens decided had scant interest in their welfare.[62]

The Oconee was not the only location where governmental Indian policies were excoriated. Treatment of savages in the Ohio region found little approval in Republican papers. The strictures were not consistent—they berated the administration for being too lenient, inhumane, wasteful and inefficient, or having brutal martinets commanding its troops. They varied with the time, place, and prospective audience of the gazette concerned, but they were prolonged and definitely hostile.

America's craven acquiescence in British possession of Western posts prior to Jay's Treaty was rated the basic difficulty. There could be no peace with the Indians so long as English gold and policy were "employed to increase the enmity of these bipeds of the desert against our frontiers." [63] General Harmar's defeat by the Miamis in 1790 bred numerous aminadversions. Destroying some villages and corn did not hide the expedition's losses of almost double those inflicted upon its adversaries. How could a general tax part of his troops with cowardice and still dismiss them "with *honor* and *reputation*"? By his own confession he had marched 1,400 men ten miles a day to take only one Indian prisoner, to lose pack horses through sentries' negligence, to find an already-burned Indian town, and to have two scouting detachments cut to pieces.[64] William Penn had been infinitely wiser; by maintaining peace with the savages he had saved both lives and extra taxes. As long as lazy redskins could steal blankets and rum in time of hostilities or receive them for saying "Brother" during negotiations, Americans would have treaties and wars. Unless the present-giving system were recast, one continually bred the other.[65]

From the West came calls for action. Settlers had purchased their Ohio land in good faith, or had accepted it for past services. Surely Congress would not see them deprived of its use by barbarians "whom the United States can extirpate with a nod." Various attacks were luridly described, omitting none of the victims' groans or the indignities offered the nation. Instead of humbling, General Harmar's expedition had irritated, and instead of quelling a partial war it had caused a general one. People had nowhere but the central government to look for protection of their lives and property.[66]

Yet Eastern journals showed considerable sympathy for the red man. How much humanitarianism was dictated by political considerations or by desire to curtail expenses would be difficult to ascertain, but numerous articles questioned the injustice of the war and decried robbing natives of their land.[67] The Indians must have had some provocation for their murderous attacks; were *their* complaints listed, their conduct might seem only retaliatory. A series of "Queries," asking who would gain the most wealth and power from the war with the Indians in Ohio, and answering *"Our Rulers,"* appeared in several papers. To who would *"lose* the most *blood*—most *money*—and most *honor*—by it?" the reply was "THE PEOPLE." The *Boston Gazette* advocated ending "sanguinary politicks" by giving the Indians representation in Congress or by relinquishing claims to all territory beyond the Ohio.[68]

At best, campaigns against the Indians had been costly and mismanaged. When would the government stop pushing the Indians westward? Was not taking their hunting lands as bad as England's attempt to tax the colonies?[69] A Quaker petition urged pacific measures, and "BRADDOCK" labeled the *Centinel*'s cry that the "strong arm of the Union ought to be outstretched to protect all its citizens," as "the voice of pride and ambition, but not of wisdom and policy." Colonial experience in New England and Pennsylvania proved purchase of Indian territory would have been far more economical than warfare.[70]

The shocking news of General St. Clair's disaster in November of 1791 redoubled the outcry. The expedition should have been easily successful; its disgraceful failure argued either military incompetence or inexcusable ineptitude in the War Department. Republicans insisted upon the first congressional investigating committee, which absolved St. Clair but led Washington to request the General's resignation. Revelations of insufficient preparation for the campaign and of shortages of provisions and medical supplies brought renewed objurgations upon Secretary Knox. The *National Gazette* shrieked "ministerial inefficiency," and there were ugly rumors someone in the Department had profited financially from contracts preceding the fiasco.[71]

Federalists urged a larger regular force for protection, but

Eastern Democrats were fiercely opposed. In addition to standard charges that greedy settlers had provoked attacks by their encroachments, it was argued a standing army would menace popular liberties and multiply taxes. Militia were both less expensive for frontier defense and infinitely superior to regulars in Indian warfare.[72] The cry from the West, however, was for energetic measures, and Republicans there condemned the administration as indifferent or faint-hearted. Hugh Brackenridge and others insisted peace could be made only by first humbling the Indians; afterward, trade might bind them to America's interest. Only the "Six per Cents, &c. and the luke-warm friends to the Government of the Union" opposed prosecution of the war. Thoughtful patriots would execrate an administration allowing the frontiers "to be deserted, and our citizens exposed to the fury" of wilderness raiders. So populous was the West now that unless the Indians were restrained they could live more easily by plunder than by hunting. Even a Philadelphian felt America should follow the European maxim and *"make peace with the sword in hand."* [73]

There was impatience with General Wayne's careful preparations to defeat the Indians. "ARISTIDES" fumed early in 1794 that the moves of "the great Legionary chief" against the savages had been designed only "to amuse the nation and promote the interest of a few." The increased armament actually merely lined the pockets of a small select group; if Easterners had not conspired to check the growth of the West, militia instead of regulars would have been used. Wayne was castigated for unnecessary delays, playing favorites, disorder and discontent among the troops, and duelling and dissatisfaction among his officers. His victory at Fallen Timbers in August, 1794, finally silenced criticism of his generalship. Yet again in 1797 frontiersmen were complaining that their interests were neglected for those of the East. Why should Congress ransom Algerine prisoners captured three thousand miles from home and do nothing to redeem captives taken by the Indians from their own fields? Surely "the agricultural interest, out of which commerce has grown, is entitled to an equal degree . . . of the . . . protection of the federal Government."[74]

Throughout the closing years of the eighteenth century, Westerners showed awareness that the interests of their section frequently conflicted with those of the East. Pittsburgh area voters, for instance, were reminded in 1796 that Jefferson knew the West and would both realize and attempt to help its problems. Every endeavor to delay admission of new states or gerrymander old ones, every effort to limit the westward movement of the frontier, was seen by men of the Ohio Valley as proof of Eastern enmity. Speculators' titles to unoccupied acres were disregarded, rendered prohibitively costly by local land taxes, or circumvented where the ever-growing class of Western lawyers found it possible.[75] Some secondary writers have viewed the struggle between frontier and seacoast as essentially a struggle over land,[76] but the question of power also entered in. Certainly Federalists in the East resisted granting Tennessee statehood because it would aid Jefferson's prospects in 1796.[77] Many frontiersmen thought their coastal kinsmen had abandoned the principles for which the Revolution had been fought—ideals which Kentuckians were determined to maintain unsullied. Westerners regarded the Jay Treaty, high taxes, restricted immigration, strong courts, and national Bank as foisted upon the nation by mercantile interests and resented them accordingly.[78]

Even greater was their choler over Eastern patronizing or ridicule. Items from Federalist newspapers advertised the East's contempt. For example, a clipping from *Porcupine's Gazette* scoffed at a Lexington, Kentucky, meeting against the Sedition Law as a "mob." The meeting had adopted a number of resolutions, one of "which, for sentiment as well as orthography, is unequalled even in the annals of American Democracy."

> Resolved that thar es sufishunt resen too beeleev and wee doe beeleev that our leebeerte es in daingur and wee plege ouerselves too eche other and too ouer cuntery that wee will defende um agents awl unconstetushonal ataks that mey bee made upon um.

No wonder, continued Cobbett, strangers reading these "elegant remarks" deemed all Americans barbarians. In truth Kentuckians appeared "to be just civilized enough to be the tools of faction, and that's all." If more cultured Westerners took umbrage at being compared with savages in every respect except "*sobriety* and *sincerity*," let them show they merited better "by working a reform in the manners of their hordes." [79]

The Reading *Weekly Advertiser* supposedly called George Nicholas a "little indolent drunken lawyer," addressing an unruly "mobility" at a Kentucky county meeting that refused a hearing to an opposing speaker. Congressman George Thacher of Massachusetts saw Westerners as being in "a state of mental darkness"; giving them information was like putting spectacles on a dead man. His remarks were reprinted in order that frontier readers could realize how "this *light* from the *east*" regarded them—almost as disdainfully as the settlers viewed New England politicians.[80]

Frontiersmen bridled at such superciliousness. Since the Virginia and Kentucky Resolutions, the administration probably did not deplore the communication a Philadelphian had sent to Pickering libeling the latter state. But there was "another *Executive,* in whose eyes detraction and malice will always appear [as] criminal . . . as telling *disagreeable truths to any of the Priviledged Order.*" The objectionable letter had reported strenuous efforts being made to mislead the fickle masses; the Lexington resolutions, French spies, trade with a jealous Spain, and a military force raised in defiance of American neutrality all showed Kentucky unreliable as a defensive outpost and revealed it the most disloyal state in the Union. "One of the Unenlightened Mass" retorted that meetings sanctioned by the Constitution and designed to preserve it were no grounds for accusations of revolt. Pickering's Philadelphia correspondent undoubtedly wanted an army sent into the West and expected a command in it. But his slurs could not harm the state:

> KENTUCKY! in vain the *Harpy Claw* is extended over thee—
> *Vulture* seeks to glut his *voracious* appetite in vain.—Entrenched

behind the *Constitution,* thou shalt continue to flourish, in despite of the *blasting eye* of *Northern jealousy*—the base suggestions of designing and sycophantic *Place Hunters,* or the outstretched hand of rapacity, which fain would fatten on thy spoils.[81]

New Jersey's legislature contemptuously dismissed the Kentucky Resolutions without debate, and two assemblymen moved for unanimous rejection on the ground that the propositions were "indecent and insulting" and came from an insignificant part of the country. Republican editors printed the story to whip up local pride, retorting:

> The above indecent and ungentlemanly observations . . . proves the situation in which the people of this western country stand, in the opinion of the water melon, pumpkin and muscle state assembly of New-Jersey; and if they only were acquainted with the sentiments of the legislature of Kentucky, it would be found, that their question for dismission is held more contemptible and insignificant than they could of our resolutions.[82]

The *Herald of Liberty* accused Federalist Philadelphia businessmen of instituting suits for collection from Western traders as a weapon to compel political compliance. It urged forming an association of merchants in western Pennsylvania, Virginia, Kentucky, Tennessee, and the Northwest Territory to boycott the city and requested "Republican printers throughout the above-mentioned states" to publish the suggestion. When Gallatin was criticized for contracting to supply Pennsylvania with two thousand stand of arms, the *Tree of Liberty* irascibly inquired if Federalists objected to seeing anyone else exert effort to defend the Union. Real reasons for the demurring were probably that these arms would go to militia rather than to a standing army, and the money was being spent in the West. Gallatin had brought many industries to the Pittsburgh region, and such measures as this had saved people of the area thousands of dollars.[83]

Political sectionalism was not new. In 1792 anti-administration writers had indicted Federalists as using an "old trick of the artful interested few to sow divisions among the many." Federalists had tried to persuade Yankees that widespread complaints against speculators and self-interested officials issued "merely from a disaffected party in the southern states, and ought consequently in New-England to be disregarded and despised." Local prejudice was bad enough at best, but it would be a dire calamity if a wretched faction could dupe the public into playing off one part of the Union against another. This despicable clique did not permit *itself* to be divided. From the most abject advocate of monarchy to "the puniest retailer of slanders on the friends of republicanism" or the "lowliest huckster of soldiers' certificates," its members clung "together like a hive of bees." [84]

Inasmuch as pure elections were the very "life of Republican governments," only absolute freeholders, promulgated the *New-York Journal* in 1792, should be permitted to vote. "*It is better* and safer *to* disfranchize *ten thousand influenced tenants than fix a permanent and hereditary balance of influence.*" Otherwise,

> scattered interests will not be able to combine, or prevail over the *consolidated aristocracy of the north.* In vain will our government be called a free one, if the dependent creatures of the landed interest can overpower the independent free-holders of the south.

The matter of free and uninfluenced balloting should be agitated in legislative councils. If Southern freeholders were overruled, separation of the Union might be necessary for "the salvation of the southern interest." [85]

Resentment was keen against Connecticut and Massachusetts. A Pomfret, Connecticut, religious convention "of Calvinistic bigots" was sneeringly said to have found an intermediate distance between truth and falsehood. "Like many other new matters in religion and morality, *Connecticut* had the honor of the first discovery." Freneau's "Hezekiah Salem" made New England's pride and lengthy sermons the laughing-stock of subscribers to the *Time-Piece.*[86]

Gross discrimination, especially aimed at Georgia, had occurred in the assumption of state debts, charged malcontents. A Savannah grand jury fumed that no equivalent had ever been received to balance the inequities. South Carolina, Connecticut, and Massachusetts had been given extravagant appointments; New York and Maryland, sums exceeding their debt; Virginia and Pennsylvania, an extra allowance; and Delaware, an outright douceur. Yet Georgia, with the greatest need to protect frontiers and to extinguish Revolutionary claims, got next to nothing.[87]

Hamilton's promotion of the Society for Useful Manufactures in Paterson, New Jersey, was scarified almost as a matter of course. Not only did this group's plan encourage monopoly, aid the few rather than the many, secure special privileges and provide an excuse for added tariffs, but it competed with existing businesses and would attract to Paterson workers and farmers needed elsewhere. Some years later New Englanders hailed the demise of this textile-making project with "HAMILTON'S *Amusement ended, at the Expense of about* ONE MILLION DOLLARS." [88]

Some Southerners felt themselves traduced in Northern journals, and the *Independent Chronicle* suggested a session of Congress be held in Boston. Thus Northerners could see that the conduct of congressmen who had "the courage to speak up for the Rights of Man" was not as black as had been painted. Only America's enemies could speak, as did the "Court Gazettes," that "while Mr. AMES was employing his time in Congress, the Southern members were spending theirs in a BROTHEL." Actually, Ames had done little for his nation; he talked of "England's *'amicable* disposition' " while Americans suffered from British piracies. "Mr. AMES had better *been in a brothel* than where he was"; his constituents would have benefited thereby. If Southern representatives were consistently portrayed as the most abandoned of men, how could a common national sentiment be achieved? America could never become strong by disunion.[89]

A writer ridiculing Federalists furnished "Advice to Candidates for Congress in Con——t." One prerequisite was membership in "some abolition society, gaining admission by the aid of the clergy." New England Democrats tried to counteract anti-Southern prejudice by recapitulating the services of Jefferson, Washington, and Madison, and by quoting Adams on Massachusetts' debt of gratitude to the Virginia delegation in the Continental Congress. Jefferson's contributions, accurate knowledge of both commerce and agriculture, and firmly established republican principles eminently qualified him for the Presidency. Washington had openly reprobated both Northern and Southern distinctions; surely no virtuous elector would show partiality in the matter of a candidate's residence.[90]

Yet the unpleasant fact was that many Americans, even in Washington's own party, continued to differentiate. The Massachusetts Essex Junto regarded Virginia Federalists as little more desirable than semi-Jacobins, and supposedly Federalist congressmen from Georgia and North Carolina consistently voted with Republicans during 1799 and 1800. Hamilton's financial program had intensified sectional differences; by 1795 control of the Bank and national debt was largely concentrated in the North. Massachusetts alone received in interest on federal obligations one-third more than all states south of Pennsylvania put together.[91]

Except in the Tidewater region of South Carolina, Virginia and the states south and west of her were Republican. When rapidly growing New York and Pennsylvania leaned that way, the scales were definitely tilted against Federalism. As fearful Northern Federalists became more critical of the South, Democratic prints in that area made political capital of their strictures. The New York *Minerva*'s fulmination comparing Virginian patriotism and credit to the Punic Faith of old was reprinted in the slave states. Was Editor Webster (whose paper avowed Virginia laws encouraged idleness, vice, and fraud) the same man whose spelling-book advocated uniform pronunciation to help tie the Union more closely together?[92] Two years later the *Aurora* exclaimed that remarks in Congress on the foreign intercourse bill, though they might "pass current in Connecticut," were as coarse as those "of fish women." "The Yankees have become as famous for abuses as they are for their love of Molasses [and rum]!" [93]

There were sectional overtones even when Democratic Representative Matthew Lyon of Vermont spat upon Connecticut's Federalist Representative Roger Griswold after the later questioned his courage. Federalists attempted to expel Lyon, but a two-thirds vote was needed, and Southern Republicans supported the Vermonter. Sarcastically the New York *Journal* noted the millennium was yet distant, for "the Lyon and the Lamb" were still at odds. Despite "the Connecticut bench" and the wasting of $10,000 worth of time in debate, it appeared thirty thousand citizens would not be deprived of representation.[94]

Local pride was roused over such minor matters as geographical descriptions of the nation. One Joseph Scott of Philadelphia proclaimed Noah Webster and Jedidiah Morse were trying to hurt sale of his writings in New England by branding him unfair to Connecticut. Scott denied any unfriendliness; he had merely explained the litigious spirit of the state (already noted by Morse) by want of necessary information. Since all lawsuits originated either in knavery or lack of knowledge in the parties, to deny that Connecticuters possessed insufficient data was in effect calling them knaves— which was worse. Moreover, Morse needed to show other sections some of the respect he demanded for the Nutmeg State. His *Geography* attributed pride and meanness to Pennsylvanians, sloth and ignorance to Marylanders, gambling and drunkenness to Virginians, and total want of religion to North Carolinians. Did he think these people cared nothing for the world's opinion of them? [95]

"MARFARIO" summarized the objectives of Adams' administration: "*To maintain the present party in power* at every risk." An army, new taxes creating additional offices, inflaming the public against France (and indirectly against republicanism) all tended toward that end. And "By excluding aliens they secure for a *longer* time the further preponderancy of population over the southern states." Both the Alien and Sedition Acts were anathema in the West also. With American liberties so threatened in the East, Kentuckians "far removed from the contaminating influence of European politics" would defend peace and liberty and would resist measures clearly destined to harm frontiersmen. The reprehensible Jay Treaty was driving America to war with France, whereas a suspension of all foreign trade would be preferable to hostilities. Eastern rage for wealth would bring conflict; all the West wanted was peace and navigation of the rivers. If individuals wished to risk their ships they should assume the consequences; New England merchants should not compel the people to betray their true interests.[96]

Many coastal dwellers, insisted Westerners, viewed the frontier as the last "asylum from foreign or domestic troubles and from state persecutions." The monarchical maxims taught in arbitrary New England schools would boomerang before long, for upright parents would not send children there. Already Virginians were founding educational institutions upon pure principles of virtue and civil liberty; in a few years these would be the resort of the nation's aspiring youths.[97]

As Jefferson's election in 1800 grew increasingly probable, Republican papers focused on appeals for unity. The people generally, North and South, held essentially similar maxims of government. They possessed identical principles and revered republicanism as it was originally understood in their state and federal constitutions. Northern minds, however, were being poisoned by tales that all Southerners were Antifederalists, engaged in violent plots to overthrow the government. Similar misrepresentations concerning Northerners were made in the South. Thus entire sections had been made jealous of each other because of a well-organized coterie seeking to maintain power.[98]

Democrats everywhere were warned to be alert against the hue and cry designed to deceive and divide them. New England Federalists, seemingly feeling nothing good ever came from Virginia except Washington and tobacco, were laboring to make that impression universal. In the South there were attempts to sway Republican electors toward C. C. Pinckney, on the specious ground that, even though a Federalist, he would devote more attention to Southern problems than would a Virginian or a Northerner. Were this falsehood to succeed in splitting the Republican vote, the next Chief Magistrate would have political principles inimical to France and radically different from those for which Americans had fought the Revolution. Rhode Island Democrats underlined Jefferson's work for religious toleration as in accord with the beliefs of Roger Williams. Since this was so, the Virginian deserved the esteem and votes of the citizens of Providence.[99]

The census of 1800, it was claimed, would inevitably give increased representation to states predominantly Republican. Jeffersonian editors held this eminently desirable, for the interests of all the states (however much they might vary in certain local instances) were essentially identical: to maintain freedom and to preserve the Constitution and representative forms of government. Although Congressional debates sometimes produced irritation between Northern and Southern members, it should always be recalled "that the inhabitants of a country enjoying the blessing of a free government, necessarily possess that political strength, which is the constant scourge of tyrants and the unvariable enemy of despotic power." [100] Unity under the Republican banner could render that evil power utterly impotent.

CLASS AGAINST CLASS

Even more effective than appeals to sectional rivalries by the Republican press were those used to bestir specific socio-economic groups, or—as it customarily went—mass against a class. Such arguments often proved potent the nation over, wherever men had votes.

One of the earliest targets of the charge of being an exclusive clique was the Society of the Cincinnati. Democrats saw this hereditary organization of Revolutionary officers as inevitably leading to a military nobility. To them the scheme doubtless stemmed from Hamilton's fertile imagination and was designed to secure support for the aristocratic faction he headed. European experience showed what a deep and shameless foundation such an order laid for undermining a social and political system. The Society's ever-increasing, inalienable fund was a certain source of power, and it was to Washington's discredit that he had "been deceived in a business of so extreme magnitude." [1]

A pamphlet by Congressman Aedanus Burke of South Carolina early alerted readers to the dangers inherent in the association. As antagonism against the Cincinnati grew, Pennsylvania and Massachusetts passed resolutions against the order, and Rhode Island deprived new members of all citizenship privileges in that state. The Cincinnati then proclaimed its withdrawal of claims to hereditary honor and disavowed any political intentions, but Republicans noted that the fund, meetings, decorations, and other distinctions were retained. Would not these keep class differences alive? Writers applauded the militia officer who, when told at a governor's dinner that one room was set aside for the Cincinnati, withdrew with the barb that he had never before heard of such discrimination between soldiers engaged in the same cause.[2] Bache best expressed the Republican attitude:

> A correspondent is much pleased with the invitation given to the *order* of the Cincinnati to attend at the Governor's, to march in procession to the President's, to congratulate him on his being a year older—It certainly corresponds with the views of the self-created Noblemen of our country to keep up a full measure of consequence. These *Knights* of America, however, discover some little inconsistency; for instead of rejoicing that the *Premier* of their order is advancing towards the grave, they ought rather to mourn that the period is approaching in which the column of their order will be parallel no more,—the order itself slumbering in the dust.[3]

Although scarcely of prime importance then, the Society was still an issue as late as the end of the century. As soon as the Revolution was over, observed the New York *American Citizen,* foes of republican government commenced intriguing against general suffrage and equal rights. This plotting and an attempt to establish a hereditary aristocracy were furthered by creating the Cincinnati. Doubtless most Revolutionary officers were republicans, but some had desired mere separation from England while maintaining a government on similar principles. The Cincinnati, not the Democratic Societies, was the first "self-created organization." It had even hoped to make Washington king but had failed to obtain his approval. A few Republicans had warned of the danger from the first, but at the time every patriot was considered above reproach; not until Hamilton's financial schemes, the French Revolution, and Jay's Treaty did the populace realize the existence of an Anglophile monarchical faction. Talk of reestablishing the association's hereditary provision in 1800 was linked to Congressman Samuel Lyman's reference to the "bold strokes" needed to sustain national supremacy. The Massachusetts politician probably believed this was "one of the strokes that is to destroy all opposition. . . ." [4]

Membership in the Cincinnati was limited to officer veterans, one reason for opposition to the Society. Equally illuminating and fully as irritating was the attitude of many in power toward the common soldier. A half dozen years after the Revolution had officially ended, enlisted men still complained about the pay owed to them. While the obligation had been nominally discharged by issuing certificates, anyone of common understanding could see veterans had "been cheated out of their honest dues, by speculators, sharpers and oppressors." Did the nation believe a twenty-shilling debt was discharged with certificates worth only an eighth as much? Could even Washington's fortitude, which had overcome defeat, adversity, and calumny, endure seeing the pay of impoverished soldiers go into the coffers of parasites? [5] A rhymester in the *American Daily Advertiser* described how the nation had recompensed

## THE AMERICAN SOLDIER

Deep in a vale, a stranger now to arms,
    Too poor to shine in courts, too proud to beg,
He, who once warr'd on Saratoga's plains
    Sits mul[l]ing o'er his fears, and wooden leg.
Remembering still the toils of former days
    To other hands he sees his earnings paid;
*They* share the due reward—*he feeds* on praise,
    Lost in the abyss of want, misfortune['s] shade.
Far, far from domes where splendid tapers glare,
    'Tis his from dear-bought *peace* no wealth to win,
Remov'd alike from courtly cringing squires
    The great man's levee, and the proud man's grin.
Sold are those arms that once on Britons blaz'd,
    When flush'd with conquest to the charge they came,
That power repell'd and *freedom's* fabric rais'd
    She leaves her soldier—*Famine,* and a NAME! [6]

"CINCINNATUS" exploded with a series of lucubrations on the issue. Governments existed only to secure justice for all.

373

At times individual rights must be submerged for the good of the nation, yet when a government able to make restitution failed to do so, "its basis is oppression, and its continuance will be doubtful. . . ." The army had performed its duty; high time the administration followed suit. Why had the President withdrawn his support from the soldiers' cause? Veterans would never have believed that he could spend four years at the helm of government without an effort to obtain compensation for their services. Such neglect and contempt was dangerous; the time might come when troops would be needed again.

> God and the soldier we alike adore
>   Just at the time of danger, not before.
> The danger o'er, both are alike requited,
>   God is forgotten, and the Soldier slighted.

A single expression of sympathy from their old commander would dissipate the clouds shadowing Washington's fame.[7]

Common decency demanded that the depreciated certificates be made good at par—and to the veterans who had been issued them originally. One writer reported to the President that an equestrian tour of New England disclosed 547 ex-Continentals confined in jails of that region. Every one was in prison for debt, having received "no pay of any value" during the war, though nearly sixty per cent had had families while they were in the service. Had not Washington himself told Congress in 1778 that men who had sacrificed so much should not be permitted to fall into indigence and wretchedness? In the South it was asserted former British soldiers had received preference over veterans in political appointments, and there were irate protests against the delays in paying enlisted men who fought against the Indians during the 1790s.[8]

Censured also was the militia system, for it entailed continued military service for some veterans and onerous duty for the nation's youth. In 1790 Secretary of War Knox proposed a more efficient reorganization of the citizen soldiery, and howls of protest ensued. The camps were immoral, families with

numerous children would be unduly burdened, and the requirement of a militia certificate to exercise citizenship rights was
clearly unconstitutional. More inequitable than a head tax,
compulsory military duty would fall with double or treble
effect upon employers with apprentices, and it would hurt
American manufacturing far more than any tariff could ever
help it. The plan would make mechanics and apprentices forever lackeys to "the rich and opulent of America." If slaves
were similarly liable, would Southern planters wish to equip all
slaves with weapons and uniforms and to pay for their every
neglect of duty? Fear of foreign invasion was a chimera. All
that was needed was to arm men well, "discipline them a little,
and they will fight *as occasion requires.*" [9]

Defenders of the system applauded New Yorkers' depreca-
tion of requests from Philadelphia for exemption from "this
school of manliness, heroism and grace," but there were other
problems. Quakers prayed for relief from service and regarded a monetary commutation (to be used for military purposes) as an equal infringement upon their right of conscience.
Southerners, less amenable to rigid regulations than were New
Englanders, also opposed the bill, and the measure never became law in the form hoped for by Knox.[10]

The several states also had internal problems respecting
militia. Georgians petitioned Congress poetically for lands beyond the Oconee promised them for their efforts against the
Creeks. New Hampshire's new militia law was "repugnant to
the Spirit of Freemen," for it excused those with M.A. de-
grees from military service. The aristocratic Connecticut legislature cleverly provided loopholes exempting the wealthy,
whereas the militia existed to protect property and order, and
the rich had the most property to protect. New Jersey citizens
criticized the severity of proposed disciplinary laws and arbitrary authority given ranking officers.[11]

Questions of pay continually plagued state troops also. An
officer in the army against the Whiskey Rebellion complained
in 1795 that six months after the expedition he was still unpaid. Public officials received their salaries regularly; how

375

could they justify this neglect of men whose very limitation of means should entitle them to utmost consideration? Connecti-' cut's Federalist government offered one shilling in specie for each forty shillings in certificates presented to the state comptroller—equivalent to giving veterans only a shilling a month for their enlistments. Would other states be willing to sit in Congress with a commonwealth that had either thus broken faith or confessed bankruptcy? No ex-soldier should accept less than face value plus interest.[12]

Republican journalists accordingly depicted Federalists as unsympathetic toward the common soldier. Worse still, they alleged, this party in power discriminated against agriculture in favor of commerce and industry, seeking to demolish republicanism itself. As is well known, Jefferson firmly believed agriculture to be the most nearly ideal way of life and farmers to be the best citizens. By 1796 he held opposition to Federalism was found primarily among farmers, for husbandmen were sturdy, self-sufficient, and independent. Supporters of the administration were apt to be Anglophiles, speculators, timid souls preferring calm to liberty, or would-be government officials.[13]

Democrats saw Hamilton's entire financial program as aiding the capitalist and merchant at the farmer's expense. Refunding increased America's fluid capital, but meant higher taxes on real property. Assumption was worse, for it burdened the agricultural portions of the nation to benefit others. It was aimed especially at the Southern states, which manufactured little and imported much. In duties alone, Southerners already paid far more per capita to support the federal government than did citizens of the North. Northern speculators had acquired vast amounts of state and national securities; foreigners would follow suit. Thus the property of farmers, laborers, and veterans was being confiscated through taxes to encourage an idle and useless life by a leisure class. Hamilton's Report on Manufactures, speciously arguing that benefits for one section or occupation helped all, was further proof of the Treasury's design to foster manufacturing at the expense of agricultural interests.[14]

In consequence, critics of the administration began to demand more adequate farm representation in government. "Who are the great body of the people?" asked a Vermont "Land Holder." "Are they Lawyers, Physicians, Merchants, Tradesmen? No—they are the respectable Yeomanry. The Yeomanry therefore ought to be represented." [15] Republican papers exhorted farmers to unite in order to select candidates and to secure favorable laws. Some newssheets boldly proclaimed their Physiocratic leanings, as did the Fredericksburg *Republican Citizen* in its motto, "AGRICULTURE IS ABOVE ALL!!" [16]

The excise, too, was odious and unfair to the South. Why should distilling be taxed and other forms of manufacturing encouraged? Small farmers of the interior found their produce not in great demand, the value of their lands up only slightly if at all, and themselves taxed at a rate evidently intended "to render agriculture tributary" to more favored economic activities. The administration's mercantile regulations manifestly harmed agriculture, while the excise and funding laws deprived farmers of the fruits of their honest industry. Nine-tenths of America's population depended upon agriculture for a livelihood. This overwhelming majority demanded no special privileges such as manufacturers were exacting, but Federalists would learn that the farming class was not insensible to this ill treatment. [17]

Republican editors continually exacerbated rural-urban discord. "A FARMER" found American foreign policy incomprehensible double-talk. "City language" papers descanted about peace and friendship with England when that nation still forcibly retained the Western posts. Any treaty with Britain meant only triumph for American capitalistic interests striving to duplicate her system. [18]

While all good citizens desired peace, the Jay mission revealed to Republicans the urgent need for legislative guidelines limiting the treaty-making power of the executive. These negotiations were ostensibly for commercial purposes, and before the terms of the treaty were known it was widely assumed that weightier claims were being postponed in order to secure indemnification for American merchants. Republicans argued that congressmen would not have so abandoned the general interest of the nation for the partial one of those in trade. The New York Chamber of Commerce might record approval of such bargaining; would frontiersmen with lives in constant jeopardy, thanks to "the imbecility or design of government, have assented to such resolutions?" [19]

When the treaty appeared, agricultural spokesmen were among the loudest in protest. For thirteen years, in defiance of their most solemn obligations, the British had kept the Western posts; now America's envoy not only approved what they had done but "gave them two years longer to carry on their schemes with the Indians for exterminating our frontier settlements." Agrarians should not criticize Jay for disregarding spoilations on American ocean commerce—these concerned the great merchants of the Atlantic ports, who seemed to have a good understanding with Britain and had been altogether too successful in propagating her political maxims in the United States.[20]

"CLEON" tried to explain the election victory of a pro-treaty ticket in the city of Philadelphia while a similar slate was overwhelmingly defeated in the surrounding county. The successful urban candidates were supported by British influence, banks, and speculators and had triumphed over an independent list supported by free and uninfluenced voters only. The result demonstrated the characteristics of city voters, now to be represented by men with views inimical to those of their constituents. Residents of Philadelphia County, on the other hand, were chiefly farmers and mechanics who possessed a degree of independence denied them in the Eastern section. High wages, demand for labor, and the Constitutional[21] declaration that all men are free and equal all tended to maintain the worker's independence. The farmer found the fruits of his labor as valuable as specie and could live on his land in self-sufficiency. "He can raise his food, and manufacture his cloathing. In short, who enjoys more real independence than the farmer?" By control of credit or employment the wealthy forced city dwellers to vote their way—and those desiring aristocracy favored Jay's Treaty. If Republicans the nation over could but unite, this evil influencing of voters could be eradicated.[22]

Democratic printers were unimpressed by Washington's proposal to establish boards for encouragement of agriculture. Too often creatures of whims and lies, members of such boards frequently presented medals and premiums to sycophants. Sound promotion of agriculture required freeing farmers from the shackles of penalty and pecuniary reward and taxing them as lightly as possible. Certainly they should not be burdened to support a navy benefiting only commerce. Even China, with twenty times America's population and resources, and well equipped for "agriculture and manufacturing in the fullest extent," kept the balance of trade in her favor by regulations and permitted her commerce to be carried in foreign bottoms. This relieved her people of the need for supporting a navy and largely eliminated expensive treaties and diplomats. With this example, it was folly for young America, possessing fewer than half the number of inhabitants sufficient for agriculture and manufacturing, to have a navy. Taxes on the farmer provided the vast sums for naval expenses, and coastal cities approved because the money taken from tillers of the soil thus circulated among tradesmen of the ports. Voters in 1800 should select a true republican as President, preferably one who was a farmer and therefore "likely to know and pursue a system of policy consistent with the interest and happiness of the people of America. . . ."[23]

A New York paper claimed America's maritime commerce was worth $180,000,000, of which at least one-fourth had been saved from "*the French and other freebooters*" by the navy. A Marylander, however, retorted

> *If this money had been retained in the country and employed in agriculture and manufactures, what immense riches it would have produced to our children, and children's children, without any needing protection from a navy, or fear of the ravages of freebooters.*[24]

379

A Congress that represented only one class would menace popular government; all interests should be proportionately represented. Voters should study political candidates and decide which ones would best serve their interests. Certainly farmers, the bulk of the population, were entitled to adequate representation to safeguard their calling. Federalists had no love for agriculture; once in complete control and supported by a standing army they would impose arbitrary legislation upon the "sloppy farmers" by the bayonet if need be. Only open eyes and wise votes, discounting Federalist promises, could avert such a fate.[25]

On every occasion Jefferson had shown himself a "friend and patron of agriculture." The "mushroom race of speculators" opposing him had acquired wealth without exercising industry and regarded the populace with contempt. Only pretended farmers could advocate a war with France in which agriculture had everything to lose. Most of these "farmers" were more concerned with banks and funds, and their attacks should rally true husbandmen to Jefferson's defense.[26]

The *Aurora* urged residents of Pennsylvania counties to cast ballots for Republican candidates because "most of them are farmers, the occupation of all others that leads most to virtue." "Senex" did his utmost to persuade Massachusetts yeomen Jefferson's views were identical with their own. How else explain the vilification indulged in by his opponents, for were his merits accurately known the state's farmers would have supported him as enthusiastically as they did Hancock on every major issue since '76. As a plantation owner Jefferson opposed a land tax except in time of dire need.[27] Southern writers similarly contended the burden of capitalism fell on agrarian interests, particularly those of the South. Wise governments encouraged farmers as their most valued citizens, but the administration degraded them "to exempt all the *monied interest,* which is by far the largest in the Northern states, and the greatest favorite of the federal party. . . ." Men who voted Federalist indicated readiness to accept even heavier taxes and further degradation.[28]

Unsatisfactory prices for farm produce augmented rural discontent. Weak markets for crops generated Republican newspaper comments. An inept foreign policy had caused tobacco prices to drop; prohibiting commerce with France in 1798 had afforded England a monopoly on American exports, and five-sixths of that nation's tobacco imports was profitably sold to other countries which in turn supplied the French. Since additional restrictions excluded Americans from other harbors, prices fell by two-thirds—for "every hundred weight of tobacco sold in that manner, the difference between THREE *and* ONE-THIRD DOLLARS, *and* TEN DOLLARS, was taken from the pocket of the Virginia planter, and absorbed in that of the British merchant!" [29]

Planters uninterested in enriching tobacco speculators were advised to combine in withholding their produce from the market until prices rose. The British government, so favored by the administration's trading policy, strove to injure American commerce by attempting to raise tobacco in the Indies; America's trade had only whetted England's appetite for greater profits. Her citizens already more than doubled their money on American produce, while thousands of hogsheads piled up in Virginia warehouses. Federalists could call these figures exaggerated, or the result of gross overproduction, but indisputably many Virginians were discontented. Never before had money been so scarce; non-intercourse robbed Virginia of $5,000,000 annually without harming France. Yankee merchants had combined with Britain "to throw the whole profits of the tobacco trade into the hands of the latter, and at the same time to punish the southern states for their democracy." [30]

Although Republicans thus considered themselves aligned (in rural areas, certainly) with agrarian interests, they readily appealed to merchants and manufacturers on occasion. Throughout the nation—particularly so when times were bad —their gazettes pointed to the shortcomings of the administration as an economic agent. Quite early the *National Gazette* cried that the ostensible purpose for strengthening the government in 1787 had been to aid American commerce. Yet the facts, far more impressive than any promises, refuted this view. Congress had passed no truly helpful legislation, British restrictions still operated against the United States, French navigation laws grew injurious because of the administration's omissions and commissions, and governmental policies to date had fostered concentration of wealth under the pernicious doctrine that a public debt was a national blessing.[31]

American commerce was burdened with additional duties to support a disgraceful Indian war in the Ohio country, while foreigners could carry on their trade at the usual rate. Why, queried the irrepressible *Independent Chronicle,* were the American carrying trade neglected and whale fisheries not promoted? Questions by any intelligent Republican would embarrass those officeholders who gorged themselves on the public revenue "while the *industrious Merchant,* is made the PACK-HORSE to dredge and to toil for their maintainence." [32]

The administration's entire foreign policy revolved around trade with Britain, though statistics proved this was neither *"profitable* nor *advantageous"* to America. In 1793 America's unfavorable balance with the mother country ran to nearly $6,000,000, most of it spent on "articles of frippery and fanatical fashions," serving only to furnish employment for some hundred thousand Englishmen. As if to emphasize the administration's diplomatic blindness, it was noted trade with France netted the United States $2,630,307.[33] Actually, the unfavorable balance with England (canceling favorable balances with France, Spain, Holland, and Sweden put together) could be a potent weapon. As Madison suggested, it showed American commerce was vital to Great Britain and put the United States in a position to exert some pressure. Would Federalist belittling of American trade help Jay's mission? America's provision exports to the British West Indies, for example, were essential—not luxury items such as were imported from London. If they were cut off there would be howls of protest from the British. As it was, the combination of

British importations and British depredations upon American commerce had virtually drained the United States of specie except for the silver obtained from "our good allies, the French Republic. . . ." [34]

The "flourishing state" of American trade and industry was among the proudest of Federalist boasts, but Republican papers were openly scornful. New Englanders asked why, if commerce were so secure, one gentleman who blustered to that effect in town meeting received next day a twenty per cent insurance premium for one voyage to the West Indies? Boston's Civic Festival was postponed in 1794 because of distress resulting from embarrassments to American trade. Any increase in American exports had been caused by the European war, most assuredly not by any policy of the administration. A few wealthy speculators were indeed a poor criterion for judging national economic well-being. Actually, depredations seriously hurt American business, and only the ability to reship French West Indian goods to Europe compensated in any way. [35]

Federalists retorted that prices were higher than ever, comparatively few ships had been lost, and exports had increased in value. Yet the country was headed for ruin; did not Democrats say so? [36] This sarcasm failed to divert the opposition press. The *Aurora*'s "SNUB" insisted Jay's Treaty sacrificed the carrying trade on which depended "the subsistence of every SHIP CARPENTER and EVERY TRADESMAN in the United States, and ultimately the value of the produce of the FARMER." And after the treaty was secured American trade was still worse off, for then *both* France and England plundered. [37]

Swedes and Danes had benefited by the administration's ineptness; their vessels carried the French trade that once gave Americans cargoes. Spain, France, Prussia, and Holland had all agreed with America that free ships should make free goods—a principle that would have ranked the United States among the foremost naval powers. Yet the English treaty broke the obligations of neutrality by permitting seizure of enemy property which might be on American ships. "Having

383

been thus unjust, is it reasonable in us to expect uninterrupted enjoyment of neutral rights?"[38]

Cynical Republicans saw daily "proofs" of the *"unparalleled prosperity"* that Washington had reported to Congress. British seizures and impressments continued unabated. Even Federalist Representative William L. Smith of South Carolina had asserted in the House that revenue barely equalled current expenses and that Treasury funds were inadequate for a military establishment. Governmental operations might have ceased had the Bank refused to refund a $6,000,000 debt, and that institution was now "determined not to lend a farthing more." Surely, with the national debt increasing a million dollars a year, the administration could not claim credit for *both* prosperity and wisdom. Had America been prosperous, this mounting indebtedness were obvious folly—unless one assumed as proved the pernicious doctrine that a public debt was a public blessing.[39]

Throughout the 'nineties politicians continued to sing the "celebrated *federal* song" of good times,[40] though Republicans insisted a sober look warned of national calamity. British impressments had so depleted the numbers of mariners that shipping costs had increased enormously. Startled New Englanders noted in 1799 that "a ship's company was hired in *Baltimore* at forty dollars *a month* each common seaman!" And the citizenry paid heavy taxes for a navy, the only real function of which was to defend the carrying trade—plus an army supported until everyone was disgusted, and a near-war with France prevented only by popular disapproval. Adams was confessedly a tryo in political economy, but his comment in 1792 to Tench Coxe that manufacturing could thrive only under a good government must have meant America had lacked one under Washington. Assuredly his own administration had sanctioned measures ruinous to American commerce and industry.[41]

Generally speaking, however, Democrats made their strongest appeals to the common people rather than to business interests. Their papers emphasized the welfare of farmers and laborers. To these should be added the immigrants, of whose importance anti-administration leaders soon became aware. A small but potent German-language press existed during the period, and a few short-lived papers were printed in French. Except for the German papers in southeastern Pennsylvania, these journalistic ventures were confined to the cities, and a number of them remained aloof from partisan politics.[42] The German press had been significant in the Philadelphia area since 1740, although conservative or politically inexperienced farmers in the eastern and central Pennsylvania counties were at first rather inclined to follow Federalist leaders. "Unpartheyische" frequently appeared in the titles of Philadelphia and Baltimore foreign-language papers, and even in these cities such publications often lasted only a few issues.[43]

Nevertheless the Germans were conscious of their common ties, and occasional Republican pleas to other national groups as such suggest that these also must have been. Perhaps one-third of Pennsylvania's population was German, and even in 1788 there was bitter criticism at the scarcity of German names on the congressional ballot. The *Pennsylvania Packet* called for more adequate representation, and Germans (while most of them voted the Federalist ticket) managed to elect Jacob Heister and John Muhlenberg on the opposition slate.[44]

Anti-administration papers in Philadelphia were from the first friendly to those of foreign extraction. Bache was something of a linguist, and his *General Advertiser* frequently carried French advertisements. His friendship with French émigrés and contacts with many Germans and Irishmen soon made his office something of a rallying place for leaders of the city's immigrants.[45] Freneau was of French descent and Duane (while actually born in America) was considered an Irishman. These editors and their colleagues were quick to defend the foreign-born from criticism and in return expected them to vote against Federalists.

When the *Gazette of the United States* asserted abusers of the government merely pretended to be exercising a constitutional right, it added that "a majority of them are persons

385

from other countries who, having lately escaped from bondage, know not how to enjoy liberty." Such a statement was impolitic in a city full of immigrants, and Freneau took advantage of it. "Hear . . . ye *foreigners* from every country and every clime!" sang out his *National Gazette.* "Here is *John Fenno* come all the way from Boston to lodge information . . . that you *foreigners* are a set of rebellious turbulent dogs." All commoners should unite under the standard of Republicanism against such insults as "J—— A[dam]s's printer" in his "court gazette" had hurled at every immigrant.[46] Somewhat later, a Virginia paper announced that "a number of Irish Democrats, resident in Philadelphia" had, because of threats to republicanism, decided to form "a new Volunteer [militia] Company. Any of their countrymen, of true Republican principles, desirous of being enrolled, are requested to attend the next meeting. . . ." [47]

With such candidates as Gallatin and Muhlenberg heading their ticket, Pennsylvania Republicans definitely catered to the foreign-born vote. German-language newspapers emphasized Teutonic names on the list and applauded the brave farmers who "came to the polls knowing how to vote" and cast ballots for Jacob Heister. They encouraged such men to remain steadfast in efforts to redeem the downtrodden, to secure free schools to end poverty and illiteracy, to block a standing army, and to support Thomas Jefferson. Numerous governmental expenditures—the expense of a military establishment, cost of British seizures, and the extravagance of the "unending squanderers" in the administration—were noted in appeals to characteristic German thrift.[48]

Yet not every German-language journal was Republican. The *Readinger Adler* referred to a rival sheet as "Jungmann's English paper," and Federalists in 1797 founded the *Deutsche Porcupein* to further anti-Jacobinism. This would expose

Scandalous French principles . . . particularly, as some of our German papers have withheld, or even endeavored to justify, the barbarities of the French, [and] their incendiary efforts to piracies committed, and still daily committing against our country.[49]

Democratic Germans warned "honest countrymen" not to be deceived by such hypocrisy. "A Friend to his Country" testified that none but stiff old Tories or fashion-loving dumkopfs would resent being called French-minded. Federalists prattled of "Christianity," but Christ Himself would consider the term American-Republican-Frenchman one of honor. Old Tories were stirring once more, like the frozen snake a farmer warmed at his fire and then had returned the kindness by killing one of his children. The freedom of American children was endangered, and high-minded yeomen should be alert. Jungmann called his paper and its ticket "Non-Partisan," but this was patently false. "You Germans, the vote is coming on!" [50]

A supposed Reading post-election "dialog" between "Herman" and "Jacob" revealed that the majority of votes received by Federalist Daniel Clymer had been from those with "powdered hair" (aristocrats) or Germans under the influence of liquor. Substantial Germans repudiated the "Hessian flies" and voted for Heister. "George Well-informed" joined the cry; the Scriptures proclaimed freedom instead of authorizing one man to rule over another. The mere fact that America had no titled aristocracy meant little if some men actually possessed equivalent power. Here, thanks in part to the efforts of German fathers, power was vested in the people. But if German sons slumbered or failed to verify clever aristocratic arguments, their freedom would end. They must show the world Germans were intelligent and not as stupid as the Tories. [51]

German Federalists shouted the struggle was between the present government or none at all and that all Democrats were merely disgruntled. But the *Readinger Adler*, calling Cobbett "the most villainous person . . . ever permitted to remain in these States," still wished him "a sincere and impartial trial" following his reported arrest for criticizing Adams' decision to send another minister to France after the XYZ affair. The *Adler's* editor nevertheless hoped his readers would soon have the pleasant news of the demise of the *Deutsche Porcupein*, already hanging "by a single hair."

Other German papers took umbrage at Federalist name-calling, carried "conversations" about the McKean-Ross gubernatorial contest, and exulted at McKean's victory in 1799.[52]

Other appeals were made to the foreign-born vote as such during the campaign of 1800. New York's Democratic *American Citizen* lauded the German nation. Both philosophers and politicians mistakenly thought it to be naturally lethargic, whereas there was every reason to believe it would soon become a citadel of liberty. German humanitarianism and high intelligence promised it a future as one of the leading republican states in the world. In the Shenandoah Valley one Jacob Koontz "left no stone unturned among his fellow-citizens the Germans" in amassing Republican votes. The Newark *Centinel of Freedom* printed a letter in Dutch by "Democraticus," praising Jefferson for "the Dutch inhabitants of Bergen County." The *Aurora* turned its wrath on a Federalist in "Paddy Brown's paper" who objected to making legislators of foreigners. In Brown's own Ireland, laws were made by English foreigners, the author of the Prussian law code was a Frenchman, and England's royal family was German. One Benjamin Nones taxed Federalists with anti-semitism, and a South Carolina "Citizen JEW" promoted reprinting of Nones' letter in the South.[53]

More effective than ethnic appeals, to judge from their frequency and labored Federalist efforts to answer them, were attempts to sway specific economic classes. Generally Federalists prided themselves on being "men of property," but oftentimes they tried to show an identity of interest between North and South, capitalism and agriculture, or merchant and worker. The country's general prosperity proved that what helped one group aided all. Republicans were enemies of property and order, desiring to appropriate and divide the savings of the thrifty.[54]

In certain areas, however, there was widespread hostility to merchants. Connecticut's "mechanics"[55] objected to the poll tax, from which rich men (and their sons who went to

Yale College) were exempted. A man with twenty times the property of another might easily pay less than twice the total amount of the poorer individual. Petitions denounced this impost as an inequitable burden and a deterrent to manufacturing. A Hartford committee of correspondence was created to work with mechanics elsewhere for its elimination. In Baltimore workers agitated for incorporation of that city in order that people could "regulate their own internal concerns without an interference on the part of the state." "A Mechanic" noted those of an "anti-republican character" opposed the move, though Baltimoreans intended no harm to the state nor advantage over any part of it. The New York *Diary* insisted the mercantilist politicians and aristocratic landholders of that state looked "upon the honest laborer as a distinct animal of an inferior species." [56]

Kentuckians writing on a proposed state constitution argued that farmers and laborers should be equal to barristers and military officers. "WILL WISP" trumpeted that if all just power came from the people it should be kept in their hands. So-called "great men" served only the purpose of drones in a beehive—

> to eat up all the honey as fast as the other bees make it. . . . Let everyone who is for the good of the country keep up the cry against Judges, Lawyers, Generals, Colonels, and all other designing men, and the day will be our own, but my life for it, if we condescend to consider and reason upon the case, we shall remain clod-hoppers forever.[57]

The editors of the Carlisle *Telegraphe* proclaimed that men could as easily serve both God and Mammon as please the haughty while safeguarding the rights of virtuous farmers and honest mechanics. When Philadelphia Federalists boasted their ticket included the county's wealthiest man, Republicans acidly queried if they were making great riches a criterion for citizenship. A similar note was sounded in Boston. On *"Election Day"* a particular group there saw laborers as "a very respectable body of men." Yet this clique viewed workers as of little consequence on other occasions and often ordered them into the kitchen by the servants' entrance. The *Chronicle* told sailors in 1796 that Jefferson aimed to advance both commerce and agriculture if elected. Two years later this paper retorted to Federalist gloating that Republicans were *"men without fortune." "The best riches of a people are ignorance of wealth."* Socrates, Aristides, Epaminondas, Fabricus "and a world of other Republican worthies *were men without fortunes."* [58]

The *Time-Piece* resented reflections on *"half-starved democrats"* who failed to give feasts for President Adams. Despite the jeers of those who had gained from the sacrifices of the Revolution, it should be recalled that *"poverty* is a strong presumption of *honesty."* A state law requiring tallow-chandlers to move their establishments outside New York City by July, 1797, produced howls of protest there. Probably this arrant discrimination against an honest laboring group came because one chandler plied his trade next door to the residence of "pro-Tory Governor" Jay, thus decreasing the rent Jay received for his *"Stone Castle."* The same decree extended to the soap-boiling industry; some muttered that sugar-boilers would also have been evicted had not James Roosevelt, ardent supporter of Jay, been engaged in that activity.[59]

A Connecticut opponent of war with France cried all society could be divided into two classes—those who actually worked and those who

> live on the stock of the community, already produced, not by *their labor,* but obtained by their *art* and *cunning,* or that of their ancestors. These are, for the most part merchants, speculators, priests, lawyers and men employed in the various departments of government.

Pursuing their own interests, this latter class endeavored to put the state in such condition that the earnings of the laborers fell into its hands. Commerce created no wealth; it merely distributed that which agriculture and manufacturing produced. Governmental authority came from the people, who should exercise their right to investigate the current situation and then prevent a ruinous conflict with France.[60]

Republicans denied hostility to equity and honest business enterprise but attacked anything smacking of privilege or property qualification. During debates on the land tax Representative Otis of Massachusetts advocated a lighter burden on the houses of the wealthy, since the rich consumed more and had loyally supported the administration. Democrats scored these arguments as inimical to men of average means. And the Baltimore *American* claimed Maryland property was assessed at one quarter its actual worth, thus making the requirement for the franchise much higher than the state constitution intended.[61]

Irate Bostonians claimed the alleged equality of the tradesman was a farce, even on election day. Aristocrats might pry into his ballot, use sarcasm to discredit his candidates, or threaten him with loss of work if he failed to vote the dictates of his employer. Even a highwayman, after all, only robbed one of his money. Federalists raved about "foreign influence," but "this DOMESTIC INFLUENCE is much more destructive to the liberties of the citizens. . . ." Merchants and lawyers as yet refrained from openly buying votes, but lavishing "exclusive benefits on some, and a pointed neglect toward others, are a species of bribery." If a tradesman fell "a sacrifice to an overbearing mercantile influence," his fellows should "consider the victim as a particular object of support." [62]

Republicans also assailed clerics and practitioners of the law. Lawyers were especially unpopular in New England, where many pettifoggers had since the Revolution collected debts contracted in time of inflation. Boston's bar consisted almost entirely of prominent Federalists; in New York only Burr and the Livingstons were leading attorneys of the opposition point of view. Most common men, from long experience with tax collections, sheriff's sales, disputed land boundaries and titles, costly trials and frequent perversions of justice, distrusted the law and those who fattened on its practice. Training and experience led many lawyers into politics, and the majority of Federalist candidates were usually of that profession.[63]

Democratic editors took full advantage of this circumstance. Counsellors, they avowed, would descend to any depths for "Almighty Mammon"; judges and their courts were agents of anti-Republican persecutions. Congressmen who were also lawyers frequently neglected their duties to plead cases in Philadelphia courts. The *Boston Gazette,* demanding legal reforms in Massachusetts, exclaimed, "It has been a long established maxim that 'A man had better lose his right than go to law.' " One issue of the *General Advertiser* featured "The ATTORNEY'S SOLILOQUY." Apparently reflecting popular sentiment, it commenced: "To cheat or not to cheat, that is the question. . . ." [64]

The very qualities making for brilliant trial lawyers, argued "Justice," disqualified them as judges and legislators. Rhetoric and passion often outweighed logical defects in pleading but were not desirable attributes in public life. Congress might not menace popular liberties, but lawyers did. If their influence over legislative bodies continued, an intolerable aristocracy was inevitable. The chief interests of a state were agriculture, commerce, and industry. All barristers had to do with these constructive pursuits was to "argue the proper owners" out of their property, "and get themselves into possession." [65]

Above all other groups, attorneys were interested in having laws as obscure and complex as possible. American merchants and farmers, thanks to widespread general education, were quite "competent to all the essential business of legislation." They had intimate knowledge of laws' *effects,* which were after all the chief consideration. The pomp and pageantry of judicial processes bade fair to become "equally as ridiculous as the forms and ceremonies of Romish Priests," [66] yet Massachusetts' delegation to the Third Congress comprised "three Merchants, and thirteen Gentlemen of the Long Robe [lawyers or judges] to represent the Farmers, Mechanics and Tradesmen. . . ." "A LAND-HOLDER" in Vermont branded lawyers "a *necessary evil* in society," representing only a certain class. They should be kept "in their proper stations. Make them Governors—make them Judges—make them Generals, if they are properly qualified; but NEVER make them LEGISLATORS." [67]

Connecticuters applauded a Quaker's request to a friend for a document from "one of those *sinful Men* in the flesh called AN ATTORNEY"; an honest barrister was a modern miracle. Jay and his treaty resembled old Tory Governor Thomas Hutchinson and the Stamp Act; both had the support of nine-tenths of the lawyers, each with "their [own] object in view." A minister to London from backward Morocco, noting the quantity of lawyers at Westminster, allegedly commented his country had only two: the Emperor hanged one to preserve the peace and kept the other in chains to prevent his doing mischief.[68]

Attorneys in politics were called narrowly self-interested, inefficient, or corrupt. Those in Georgia's legislature, for purposes of political spoils, had repealed militia commissions and had named two obviously incompetent assemblymen as generals. New Yorkers alleged a convicted judge still sat on a county bench; Jerseymen labeled justices of the peace frequently illiterate, usually drunk or biased, and always politically ambitious. New Englanders called these officials "harpies" and believed lawyers in the national government had been bought off by special interests or were professionally "incapable of acting . . . from the dictates of plain reason." [69]

The whole legal process involved blind reliance on tradition, red tape and delays, and unequal salaries for judges. If reason outweighed precedent in framing the Constitution, Americans should also avoid foreign leading-strings in matters of lesser import. Foreign writers on the laws of nations often disagreed among themselves—further reason for doubting their omniscience. Far better that Americans should profit from experience and rid themselves of the incubus of a national debt and funding system. Boston Democrats saw the new State Circuit Court proposed by "the *order*" as designed to prolong cases even further and to furnish more jobs for the legal fraternity. Apparently lawyers were "determined to absorb every place of honor and profit in the United States." [70]

Burdensome taxes and "the rapacity of *Lawyers*" had produced Shays' Rebellion. Contrary to the slurs of that "*Catholic* and *polite* prelate," David Osgood, the *Independent Chron-*

*icle* had opposed, rather than promoted, the uprising. But the Federalist "Lawyer's interest" finally deprived the newspaper of the state printing. The journal had incurred the enmity of the bar by its political stand and by publishing the letters of "HONESTUS," who "did more towards informing the people, of the baneful tendency of the Lawyers' influence, than any man either in Europe or America." [71]

That courts were partial to Federalists was taken for granted, and Republicans described the bar as "an asylum for fraud, usury, or perfidy." Noting that the last shipment of felons from England to Botany Bay included five attorneys, the Savannah *Columbian Museum* suggested "a small fleet laden with similar merchandize" should set sail from America. The *Aurora* sneered that the Alien and Sedition Acts gave *"lawyers . . .* reason to bless our good administration for their great kindness in providing laws likely to afford them all employment—*as long as the laws* last!" With both pulpit and bench converted into agencies for propagating anti-republican doctrines, a Virginian sarcastically inquired whether the exclusive right of defamation was vested in lawyers by statute, or by common law based on immemorial custom.[72]

Abraham Bishop, leading Connecticut Republican who was himself an attorney, attacked the political hegemony of his fellow barristers. In a New Haven oration he denominated them a highly intelligent and operative aristocracy, holding

> the *ladder of promotion* . . . with as much power and claim of prescription, as the Pope holds the keys of St. Peter; and in these northern states you find lawyers on ev'ry round of it, ascending and descending, as were the Angels of God in the vision of Jacob; though the two classes of characters are upon very different business.[73]

Probably the ebullient Charles Holt most accurately summed up the attitude of New England Republicans toward jurisconsults in public posts. His New London *Bee* reiterated charges of narrowness and contumaciousness, which made Congress as jingling as the Council of Trent. Even the *"staunch federalist"* writer Joseph Dennie questioned the advisability of elevating counsellors to office. Holt noted that all Connecticut's congressional representatives were lawyers and mentioned that profession's unholy alliance with the clergy. Massachusetts Federalists had even elected the Reverend Mr. Cutler "to Congress, as being more suitable to declaim on politics there than to preach them from the pulpit." [74]

"A CITIZEN" asked fellow Georgians to oppose "all persons whose private interest differs from the public good," thus guarding against clergymen and barristers in office. History showed the clergy to be ever supporters of monarchy and oppressors of the poor. Lawyers made constitutions and laws to suit their own purposes and applied them contrary to the public welfare. People who elected either group to office thereby delivered themselves into the hands of their greatest enemies. [75]

Outcries against the clergy in politics were even more vehement and prolonged than those directed at lawyers. The New England parson had long been a prominent figure, and in that section the Revolution had enhanced his reputation. He assumed authority in matters of individual and social behavior, and his influence was a force with which to be reckoned. Congregationalism of the period has been described as more than a theology and a creed; it was a program for society as well. [76]

Since the American Revolution, however, serious threats to clerical supremacy in the Northeast had begun to appear. Many alarmed parsons claimed irreligion, immorality, and skepticism were widespread and increasing. They noticed fewer family prayers, less Bible-reading, and more lenience in observing the Sabbath than in the past. The rationalism preceding and accompanying the French Revolution became ever more diffused. Dedicated Congregationalists, regarding God as father and judge, were repelled by the deistical idea of a Creator who turned over His universe to the operation of natural law. As French standard-bearers seemed to grow increasingly irreligious, many clerics came to associate all revolutionary philosophy with attacks upon the Christian faith.

Also, as men of social (if not financial) standing, preachers tended to sympathize with lawyers and merchants. To the bonds of natural association were now added this conviction that the democratic ideas so freely expressed undermined religion itself, plus the fear that the clergymen's own influence was under fire. When American Republicans labored for disestablishment, and heroes such as Ethan Allen and Tom Paine penned deist tracts, the clergy's worst fears were confirmed. The overwhelming majority of New England preachers thus openly espoused Federalism and branded the tenets of Jefferson's followers "infidelity." [77]

Deism was not entirely new, even in America. Hobbes and Condorcet had appealed to reason, and Locke had argued that, theologically, natural knowledge was more reliable than revelation or miracles. This seemed logically to augur materialism, but presumably the relative popularity of deism in America was primarily stimulated by the French Revolution. In Paris, as in the colonies fifteen years earlier, the overthrow of aristocracy was justified by "the rights of man." Antimonarchical groups in the United States discovered a community of interest with those in France and began to champion the leveling, freethinking concepts emanating from Paris. The Democratic Societies and such papers as the *Vermont Gazette* and Lyon's *Scourge of Aristocracy* helped spread the doctrine. Part of this was a natural reaction against any authority, temporal or spiritual; part was belief in man's perfectibility, in protest at the hopelessness of Calvinistic determinism. Inasmuch as most outstanding deists were Jeffersonians, infidelity and republicanism were seen as concomitant heresies.[78]

Ethan Allen's *Reason the Only Oracle* spurned the "priestly" contention that only a single class was qualified to study and discuss God's will. The hero of Ticonderoga rejected Calvinism's idea of original sin; every tub should stand on its own bottom. He denied that God magically interfered with universal principles such as the law of gravity. The Creator was continually active in the world through nature, which was in a constant state of flux, and He was knowable by man's own reason.[79]

Even more menacing in clerical eyes was Tom Paine's *Age of Reason*. The author of *Common Sense* was assured an American audience; just as he had labored to deliver mankind from political tyranny, so now he claimed to be performing a similar function in the spiritual field. His newest work attacked the doctrine of man's insignificance and challenged supernaturalism in religion. Essentially a popularization of earlier deistic writers, the volume soon replaced Allen's more ponderous tome as the "Bible" of most American freethinkers.[80]

Clerics who had at first applauded the French Revolution as a continuation of America's soon came to insist that the two movements had no similarity. A revolt against religion and morality itself, they felt, had produced criticism of the clergy and increasing demands for toleration. Their resistance, coupled with disabilities suffered by dissenters in most of New England, provided Republicans with the opportunity to charge that bigotry, tyranny, and hypocrisy motivated pastors attempting to preserve "the Standing Order." Congregational predominance made this conflict uniquely acute in New England, but the Episcopal Church was also strongly Federalist wherever found. Most minority sects, resenting establishment, somewhat inclined toward the Republicans.[81]

As early as 1793, however, Vermont's Shaftesbury Association, oldest Baptist body in the state, warned members against "the French influence," and soon Presbyterian and Congregational ministers combined to combat "infidelity and other hurtful errors." Calvinist ministers equating rationalism and deism with atheism often extended their remarks to the governmental philosophies they felt accompanied these evils and openly supported Federalism. Republicans held that clergymen who meddled in public affairs violated the cardinal principle of separation of church and state. Pastors who used religion to cloak selfish ends and interfered in matters beyond their proper province could not expect their position to shield them from criticism. "The church is in danger!" was worse than the shepherd-boy's cry of "Wolf!"—it was sheer hypocrisy.[82]

397

Freneau demanded proof for the *Columbian Centinel's* accusation that his *National Gazette* constantly vilified the clergy and ridiculed religion. Without proof, the slur would be exposed as "only *a dirty attempt to prevent the circulation of the National Gazette* in *the Eastern States.*" And then, inconsistently defiant, he appended a poem virtually asking "What of it?" French clerics had supported the monarchy, and during the American Revolution more than one minister had been Tory. If the editor had made "of religion . . . a sport," why was he not cited "to a *Bishop's court?*" American independence had outlawed inquisitions and religious executions:

> . . . wholesome laws prevent such horrid scenes
> No more afraid of deacons or of deans
> In this new world one joyful hymn we sing
> *That even a Bishop is a harmless thing.*[83]

A few months later the paper commented acidly that while titles were rapidly dying out in the civil world they still flourished in the ecclesiastical one. "To give the title of *Reverend* to *any man, be he who he may,* is not only anti-republican, but blasphemous." Some forms of address were ridiculous; calling a bishop *"Right Reverend"* implied that all other clergymen were *"wrong Reverends."* Freneau denied any true friend to republican government could be hostile to the French Revolution. Numerous preachers, however, agreed with Timothy Dwight that "The touch of France is pollution. Her embrace is death." They held America could expect only turmoil and bloodshed if she accepted infidelity.[84]

Connecticut ministers, it was said, attempted to dictate selection of the state's representatives to Congress. Because one candidate called church government an institution of men and attacked bigotry, "priestcraft" conducted a campaign of personal defamation against him. "MARAT" quoted Scripture: "All that the fleshbook brought up, the priest took for himself; so did they in Shiloh." So also did they in the Connecticut Assembly, where ministers lobbied to influence legislation, and one sat on each side of the Speaker during debate on an ap-

propriation bill they favored. No epithet was too despicable
for a pastor who fattened himself while fleecing his flock or
discriminating against other sects. Republicans opposed a
scheme to turn over proceeds from the sale of lands in the
Western Reserve to schools and churches; at the least all denominations were entitled to share in the fund. Captives of the
Algerian pirates were far more worthy "objects of charity"
than the "already well-fed clergy." [85]

These disparagements of "pulpit drummers" seemed mild
indeed compared to what came later. At Harvard in 1793 the
Reverend David Tappan suggested that French atheistical
thinking endangered America, and next year saw the wide dissemination of both Allen's and Paine's appeals to rationalism.[86] Divines and Federalists flayed the French for calendar
reforms which "abolished the Sabbath." Democratic papers
retorted that those who libeled Frenchmen as immoral and
irreligious secretly wished liberty crushed everywhere. France
favored freedom of conscience, and Robespierre's addresses
and the Festival to the Supreme Being showed deep religious
feeling. Any depravity or skepticism resulted from the civil
and ecclesiastical tyranny under which the French had so long
been suffering.[87]

A sermon of David Osgood at Medford, Massachusetts, on
November 20, 1794, ignited a powder-train. Ostensibly criticizing Governor Sam Adams for ignoring the federal government in his annual Thanksgiving message, Osgood lashed the
Democratic Societies as copies of Paris Jacobin clubs, foment-
ers of the Whiskey Rebellion, and tools of French ministers.
Gallic atheism, he said, was inducing many Americans to for-
sake their faith. Other Federalist preachers in New England
immediately chimed in on this general theme.[88]

Republican press retorts were rapier-swift. Boston minister
John Gardiner was "a ci-devant lawyer," and "the Trinity-
Church Trumpeter" was amusing his congregation with political matters. "A Friend to the Clergy and an Enemy to Ecclesiastical Presumption," along with a host of others, denounced both Osgood's reputation and scholarship. The

"clownish Bishop of Medford" had exhibited conduct unbecoming a Christian and a gentleman; the writers had only contempt for a man who could use his religious position to broadcast such illiberal views. Condemnation of the Democratic
Societies was especially resented, but Republicans insisted Osgood had hurt only himself by his accusations. "On the Constitutional Society [of Boston] their influence has been as small
as though they had been issued in the form of a BULL from
the Chancery of the Pope." [89]

From this time on extremism was the rule. Clergymen grew
increasingly bitter against the French Revolution, which they
had originally applauded. They styled Francophiles "enemies
of their country," as well as "atheists." Osgood's sermon sold
out three editions within two months, though a Republican retorted " 'The Day of Doom' went through thirty, and is now
forgotten." When Washington proclaimed a day of national
thanksgiving in February, 1795, Democrats correctly anticipated more sermons similar to Osgood's. They noted the proclamation cautioned against arrogance and commented that
certain clerics seemed already to have acquired a degree of
this attribute. Hope was expressed that the "Medford
Bishop" would don the unaccustomed garb of humility for the
occasion. Instead Osgood was more violent than before, and
other Federalist churchmen followed suit. By the Fast Day of
April 2, 1795, the *Chronicle* was warning Federalist pastors
to tread warily in statements concerning France. Should the
remarks of a handful of insolent preachers provoke that country into war with the United States, the American people
would be wrathful indeed.[90]

As the Federalist-Congregationalist tie strengthened, Republicans stressed that Massachusetts churchmen who criticized Governor Adams were undermining the state government on which depended their own establishment. A diminu-
tion of state powers could in the long run only weaken a state
church. Since clerics had sold out to the British party, Jeffersonians objected to enforced tithes to support them. "ANTI-
PARSONS" vowed if his town granted more money to its

minister he'd turn Baptist or Universalist, saving his soul and his money as well.[91]

The clergy, asserted Republican writers, had been employed by the Anglo-aristocrats, who could never hope to dominate America without the aid of members of that order who had "defiled their garments." Yet parsons apparently wishing a reestablishment of British authority were warned this would mean their own insignificance. They were furthering "more of the designs of Party than of promoting the Gospel of peace," and they would find "The 'LORDS SPIRITUAL' in England are as desirous to extend *their* influence in the United States as the Lords Temporal." [92]

Boston's *Independent Chronicle* headed the onslaught against the Congregationalist clergy. Seldom since Osgood's sensational sermon, protested "Philanthropus" in 1800, were its issues free from abuse of the ministry. It lashed the "monk of Medford" as ignorant, venal, and overstepping his bounds. It praised those men of God who promulgated the sentiments that had done so much to achieve American independence— "But what energy of genius can conceive, or what language can express our indignation against those servile beings, who worship the BAAL OF DESPOTISM, as the GOD OF THEIR IDOLATRY." The paper declined to print Osgood's Thanksgiving Day sermon in 1795, terming it "so contemptible that it is not even introduced as published at the request of his hearers." [93]

There was good reason for Republican agitation. Indisputably partisan opinions *were* dispensed from the pulpit, and churchmen were New England's most powerful agency in shaping public opinion. Federalists did not yet control the Massachusetts state government in 1795, but some authorities regard the clergy as decisive in making the commonwealth pro-administration after that time.[94]

Nor was Republican anti-clericalism confined to New England. Even before Osgood's sermon, the Reverend James Abercrombie, a Philadelphia Episcopalian, gained notoriety for his pulpit thrusts "against the contagion of French atheism and deism." Accused of bigotry and hostility to the rights of man, the young preacher soon became friendly with William Cobbett; before long he was charged with soliciting subscriptions for *Porcupine's Gazette.* Americans, asserted "AR-BITER," owed gratitude to the France a junto of "dogmatic priests" had damned as irreligious. Regrettably, these "corrupt apostles" wielded a dangerous influence upon the popular mind, for credulous people believed they spoke with divine authority. Writers lambasted John Jay's 1795 Thanksgiving proclamation for New York as the epitome of "whining cant and religious hypocrisy," sufficient to "render him worthy of a cardinal's hat." Virginians held that "king craft, priest craft, and Episcopalian craft are three staunch friends to tryanny. . . . *Episcopalian* and *Aristocrat,* ought to be synonymous terms." [95]

Jay's Treaty exacerbated the bitterness. "American Tories, both clergy and laity" would beg for mercy, it was dourly prophesied, after France had made peace with all her foes save England. If Britain achieved her hidden purpose of an ecclesiastical hierarchy in America (with lands for bishops) preachers would realize that the treaty opponents they now denounced were in truth their best friends. Clerics who had abandoned their republican principles and studied politics more than divinity had forfeited all respect. Unless they reformed, a day of reckoning was at hand.[96]

In early 1796 several Boston pastors helped Federalist merchants prepare and disseminate a circular letter urging passage of the House appropriation to implement Jay's covenant. Republicans warned that this committee misrepresented the sentiments of the town as a whole. If clergymen were to be concerned in this matter at all, every sect should be represented, and when the *"Royal Proclamation"* was read after divine services it should "be set to *solemn music,* as it would add greatly to the serious efficacy of this *new fangled instrument."* A "Modest Address to the Honorable and Reverend Committee to forward Circular Letters" asked why ecclesiastics should pass judgment on the conduct of a congressional majority, and "WHO GAVE YOU THIS EX-CLUSIVE AUTHORITY" to dictate to the community? "SYDNEY," who branded this "as arrogant a letter as ever was wrote by Hutchinson," asserted fear or clerical influence had swayed many signers and ominously stated that since the clergy had been so conspicuous in promoting the treaty "let them now abide the event." The *Aurora* asserted this "scandal to religion" should "be reprobated by every free citizen." Were not these priests profaning the temple? Cramming the treaty "down our throats by a Royal Priestcraft Memorial" was the greatest insult offered Massachusetts freemen since 1775.[97]

Irreligion did exist, and was spreading, some Jeffersonian newspapers confessed. But this development was certainly not the fault of the French Revolution or of democratic principles. The preachers themselves were responsible. Their contumaciousness and interference in politics had made many worthy people disgusted with organized religion. The *Chronicle*'s "A Citizen," opposing state Circuit Courts, flatly asserted that "PRIESTCRAFT SUBSIST BY SPIRITUAL AND LAW-CRAFT BY TEMPORAL DECEPTION." It was noteworthy that a Harvard oration in 1796 mentioned Washington's name a half dozen times, but omitted any reference to a Supreme Being. Clergymen desiring restoration in popular confidence should stick to religion.[98]

Many more of these attacks were made, but all were cut from the same cloth. How could ministers endorsing Christ's "Blessed are the Peace Makers" use Adams' fast day to cultivate hatred against France? Irrespective of sect, thinking men founded their political opinions on their own best judgment; coming to doubt their pastor's views on politics, they would next question them in religion. "If the ministers of the gospel think it any value to enjoy the friendship and affection of their people, they'll avoid political discussion; and a true well-wisher to Christianity hopes they will." [99]

Even the German-language press denounced the alliance between clergy and Federalists. The public could not be perma-

403

nently blind to the fact that ministers who preached of temperance, morality, and equality before God often associated only with moneyed men or dined at "tables of luxury." Desire for wealth and prominence was characteristic of "the voracious lawyer forever seeking whom to devour" and was conspicuous in business, the army, and the pulpit—and it inflated "the lungs of the greedy Priest who for a worldly reward sends forth his hebdomedary bawling against Republicans in the house of God. . . ." Fortunately, enlightened America possessed leaders who both despised aristocracy and were willing to fight it. Federalist casuistry that Democratic machinations endangered church and state only paraphrased the old royal watchword of "Church and King." Those who bolstered an unjustifiable cause by linking it to religion were like ancient criminals who fled to the altar for sanctuary from the law.[100]

As the anti-French frenzy reached new heights, Republicans reiterated their pleas for peace. Quakers were urged to support a Philadelphia petition that dismayed Porcupine's *"warmaking* tory faction" by asking Congress to take all possible steps to avert war. "Tom Bowling" entreated Massachusetts sailors to "think cool[l]y, and not become the dupes of a few landsmen." The nation appeared to have lost its reckoning, and was in danger of running aground. "If the lawyers, and the Chaplins don't help us, the Lord have mercy upon us—they are fit boys for long and dangerous voyages as they are long winded. . . . They can *talk,* and *pray,* even if they can't *fight.* . . ." Preachers, sneered "A Countryman," could afford to speak of war; when it took place they were well out of danger's path.[101]

Republican journals scoffed at Federalists' manifestations of piety as being essentially hypocritical. One Philadelphian, asked if he intended to observe the President's next fast day, answered dryly: "I am not of the opinion that *in Adams' fall, we sinned all."* Bache denied the Constitution gave the President power to proclaim fasts and refused to suspend publication of the *Aurora* in recognition of the day. Prayer and fasting were matters of conscience; any connection between church and state endangered both religious and political freedom and "should be discouraged." "Brattle Street" warned partisan preachers that their parishioners who were "not longing for a *hot dish of Politics* in that Day, may have the opportunity of gratifying *a Christian taste* in some other congregation of the Faithful." [102]

Sanctimonious Federalists who criticized an entertainment for Jefferson that was presented on a Sunday conveniently forgot their own travel or actual political activity on that day. Their vaunted piety seemed missing when recent lists of officers for the navy included no chaplains. Under war's baneful influence soldiers and sailors could threaten religion more "than the *fabulous* Clubs of the Illuminati—and yet it seems our Pulpit Politicians have their eyes so constantly on France, . . . as not to have a moment for casting a Religious look on the omissions and commissions to be found in their own country." [103]

Supporters of the administration, it was alleged, were trying to "stir up a spirit of religious jealousy" by slyly encouraging anti-Catholic prejudice. Centuries-old atrocity stories about Catholics were introduced in their papers, and some Federalists secretly admitted that the Alien Act was intended to operate "against the unfortunate Irish Catholics who have been flying from oppression to the U.S. for four years past." Such methods accorded with the Machiavellian statement of Frederick the Great: "If I can ever once succeed in exasperating a people, on the score of liberty of religion, and persuade them that their religion is in danger, their clergy and nobility, you may rely on them. *I call this bringing heaven and hell on my side.*" [104]

German-speaking Republicans denied that Frenchmen and Democrats were atheists. These groups believed in freedom of thought and wanted to end clerical tyranny, for "where the D[evi]l himself does not want to go, he sends a pr[e a c h]er." Pharisaic parsons often invoked the Creator's name for their own ends. At best they tried to serve both God and Mammon, and if forced to make a choice they (like their English brethren) would choose Mammon.[105]

New England clerics, like other men, should be pleased to

be judged by their conduct, instead of attempting to assume that pretended infallibility they so deplored in the pope. As politicians they cut nearly as sorry a figure "as Thomas Paine does as a Divine"—each lost standing by stepping out of character and pontificating on matters of which he knew little.[106] Yet the *Independent Chronicle* inconsistently recommended that New England preachers study Judge Edmund Pendleton's speech on "the unhappy system which has reduced this country to its present alarming state," and "read it after service to their respective Parishioners." [107]

Republicans growled that such as Osgood, the Reverend Jedidiah Morse, and Yale's President Timothy Dwight had sabotaged Adams' efforts for reconciliation with France by describing that nation as softening America for invasion through circulating deistic works of Paine and Count Constantin de Volney to undermine religion and morality. Freneau now entered the lists against these Federalist champions. Writing for the *Aurora* as "Robert Slender," an ignorant yokel perpetually perturbed over the non-fulfillment of the dire prognostications of his "betters," he penned a series of letters constituting the ablest replies to their arguments. In his "ignorance," "Slender" exposed the fact that Federalists using violence against free speech displayed the selfsame tendencies they condemned in French revolutionaries. Paine's *Age of Reason* would never have been widely read in America had not the ministers themselves "dragged it into publicity." Unlike their "orthodox" fathers, who had feared Catholicism and had attacked the Quebec Act, Federalist parsons berated France for ousting the Catholics and prayed "for the success of . . . the pope, and the re-establishment of the Romish religion." [108]

"BUG" sarcastically informed the Baltimore *American* he had become a good Federalist and hoped to secure a snug berth in the Army or Navy, or, "If we should be so fortunate as to have an established religion," he would "like to take the Gown." Eager to bear witness against the most innocent person to suit the "present virtuous administration," if deemed worthy of ordination he had already prepared the political discourses that were such happy substitutes for sermons. He would be glad to write addresses proving all Frenchmen fools, to help the editors of the *Federal Gazette* "(and God knows they want assistance)" convince the wealthy their interest lay in ruthlessly suppressing their tenants, to aid in convicting Republican printers of capital crimes, or to preach passive obedience and acceptance of monarchy as the only desirable form of government. Surely such accomplishments entitled him to consideration from the party in power.[109]

The effectiveness of the religious issue was attested in Pennsylvania, where Democrats somewhat inconsistently reversed the tables. "Michael Servetus" noted that the state constitutional convention of 1790 had debated belief in God as a qualification for office-holding. There Ross (Federalist gubernatorial candidate in 1799) voted against such a proposal; McKean (the Republican) favored it. Ross, then, was probably a deist; worse yet, he supposedly had expressed the hope that if he were ever so weak as to believe in Christianity he would still have strength to commit suicide. Frantic Federalist denials of Ross's deism showed the charge stung.[110] The New York *Argus* claimed to execrate deism and atheism, but held "where there is *one* infidel among the true *Republicans* of our country, there are *fifty* among those who falsely dub themselves *Federalists.*" Doubtless that party contained as many infidels as there were in France.[111] In the meantime, Kentucky's new constitution reflected the Jeffersonian anti-clerical trend by making clergymen ineligible for the state legislature.[112]

How could Federalists, if their motives were pure, follow a self-confessed adulterer as leader in the cause of religion and morality? In reality they deplored the American Revolution and believed Hamilton was saving the nation from the baneful consequences of the philosophy of equality.[113] When Adams asked, "What was wrong with religion in America?" he should look to his own party; nothing had injured public morals more than selection of Hamilton and Jonathan Dayton for high offices. Installation of these men provided examples of wantonness and avarice to American youth, and clergymen enlisting under such a banner could not possibly restore religion to its position of former esteem.[114]

Dubbing Timothy Dwight "the Connecticut HIGH PRIEST," the New York *Argus* added when a minister of God "becomes the mouth piece of faction, the virulent, illiberal abuser of men of opposite political sentiments to his own, we cannot refrain from decrying the truly bad example which such a man holds forth for his brethren to imitate." Undoubtedly pastors wished an immunity similar to that enjoyed by United States Senators—including the ability to arraign printers and to fine those who dared criticize them.[115]

"TOLERATION" contended Congress should choose chaplains from every religious denomination in Philadelphia. Already attendance in Episcopalian congregations had dropped off alarmingly, and if ministers of other faiths aided the bishop with Congress he would have more time for pastoral duties. Adams also was censured for permitting English prelates to ordain American bishops. This prostrated the government and religion at the feet of King and Parliament; American clergymen could not preach in England, but theirs could be sent over here.[116]

Some feared Methodist Bishop Coke, who had come from England to Delaware, was far more a political than a religious missionary. Had not John Wesley been employed during the Revolution to use his influence among American Methodists, under the mistaken belief that independence meant the ruination of his church in America? Perhaps Coke feared an ending of British influence would divide Methodism, but the example of the prospering Quakers showed this argument fallacious. However, it *was* difficult to understand how any follower of Christ could possibly support English governmental measures, particularly those in Ireland.[117]

Jefferson's own religious beliefs were a major issue in the campaign of 1800. Federalist gazettes delighted in portraying him as a deist or atheist.[118] Nettled Republicans ridiculed assertions that the Virginian had done away with the Sabbath and had introduced the French decade in his own family. Actually, Jefferson supported a church minister in his neighborhood after compulsory tithing had been eliminated. New Englanders disgraced their religion by "constantly canting about it" and by tyrannizing other sects. More than ever before, America needed an enemy of bigotry at the helm.[119]

When "Philan" in the *Palladium* asserted Jefferson's deism rendered him unfit for the Presidency, "A FREEMAN" retorted that he had never expected to see a Kentuckian openly express a preference for Adams. Any good Christian would pick a carpenter for his ability rather than religious belief; the same should be true in selecting officeholders. If Adams were a Unitarian as reported, objections fully as valid as any against his opponent could be raised against him. Historically, many pious rulers had been tyrants, and the unity of priestcraft and statecraft encouraged this tendency. The best authority for the future behavior of any man was his past conduct, not his theological beliefs.[120]

Normally impressive for cool logic, Boston's "Old South" showed the extremes to which partisans were driven. He compared the attacks of the "Essex Junto" and the clergy on Jefferson to those upon Christ by the Jewish Sanhedrin. The Lord's own life thus demonstrated the "dangerous tendency of PRIESTCRAFT." Did America want to end liberty of conscience, and require religious tests for office? Jefferson's own church was Episcopalian; did Federalists expect Baptists, Quakers and Congregationalists to accept *its* infallibility? Even the "religious creed" of this church, however, "was as justly obnoxious to Mr. Jefferson . . . as the Jewish hierarchy was to our savior." [121] Yet Federalists refused to be silenced. The *Gazette of the United States* put it thus:

THE GRAND QUESTION STATED.

At the present solemn moment the only question to be asked by every American is 'Shall I continue in allegiance to
GOD—AND A RELIGIOUS PRESIDENT;
or impiously declare for
JEFFERSON—AND NO GOD!!!' [122]

Reproved by a cleric for criticizing Parson Abercrombie's political preaching, Freneau retorted that if (as recommended) a man should ever follow his minister's judgment, neither Christianity nor Protestantism could ever have been started. And, he added, preachers did not always agree. During the American Revolution the English clergy had been aligned against America's; both groups could not have been correct.[123]

Despite clerical lamentations, religion was still the dominant note in American society. In most of New England even the suspicion of deism or atheism made one almost a pariah. Thus Federalists strove to stigmatize Republicans as irreligious. Fierce rejoinders in the Republican press, plus counterattacks against the clergy, testified to the importance of the accusation—and, to some, lent color to it. Yet notwithstanding all the sermonizing in various gazettes about the importance of other factors, when the Jeffersonian Pittsfield *Sun* recommended John Bacon for Congress it listed as his first qualification that he was a true Christian. The *Hampshire Gazette* sneeringly doubted that anyone had ever heard of a religious Jacobin, but it was noteworthy that anti-clerical New England papers (unlike some Democratic publications in the South) carefully avoided derogating religion itself. Particularly after 1796, when preachers began to attack Jefferson more openly, they ardently seconded the cry of the New York *Temple of Reason* against the "rapacious priesthood"—but they dared not echo the deist sheet's defense of its particular creed.[124]

One of the period's strangest aberrations was the Federalist clergy's fear of an American "Illuminati." A European secret order of that name had been formed in Bavaria in 1776 to oppose despotism and superstition. It soon claimed three thousand members, but a decade later repressive governmental edicts drove it underground. In reality the order virtually disappeared, but Mirabeau (an alleged member) was held to have spread its views in France. Sensational "disclosures" concerning the organization were published just in time to afford

European conservatives a plausible explanation for the upheaval of the French Revolution. Jacobins, Jesuits, Free-
masons and the admittedly anticlerical Illuminati, the theory
ran, were united in a vast world-wide plot to destroy Christianity and all government.[125]

This view was presented by Professor John Robison of the
University of Edinburgh in his *Proofs of a Conspiracy*. It was
"supported" by "evidence" in a volume by the Abbé Augustin
Barruel, a Jesuit priest who had been expelled from France.
The order had never disbanded, they charged; actually, it had
secretly spread over all Europe. Through spies, immorality,
and disseminating propaganda, its leaders had instigated the
French uprising. Treacherous intrigues had honeycombed the
foundations of European governments and made possible
French victories and the United Irish revolt.[126]

Like many clergymen with Federalist inclinations, the Reverend Jedidiah Morse deemed French philosophy the major
cause of irreligion in America. He saw Paris revolutionaries
as unprincipled atheists who intrigued with Republican leaders to subject the United States to their control. On the Fast
Day of May 9, 1798, Morse delivered a sermon in Charlestown with Robison's work as a text. Infidelity was rife, he
said, and branches of the Illuminati existed in America. The
order was attempting to dominate the Masons, the Democratic Societies had been doing its work, and Paine's *Age of
Reason* was an example of its iniquitous efforts.[127]

For some years Yankee liberals had feared Morse's growing influence, stemming from his recently published *American
Geography*. Congregationalist pastor William Bentley and
others opposed him theologically, and this dislike came also to
have a political basis. Some had hoped to lessen his stature by
belittling his *Geography;* now the *Independent Chronicle* demanded substantiation of his accusations made on Fast Day.
Since Robison's book had been excoriated in London magazines, it was insufficient evidence in itself.[128] Morse in reply
quoted British press comments praising Robison, and within
two months other Federalist pastors were reiterating his

charges that the French Revolution was but the first step toward universal anarchy, atheism, and the abolition of private
property.[129]

About this time the *Chronicle* became involved with the sedition trial of publisher Abijah Adams, and temporarily the
brunt of the Republican defense was borne by other newspapers. The Boston journal occasionally mentioned Morse's
"silly tales about the 'illuminati'," but the *Aurora* bluntly
called Robison's book an "absurd collection" almost without
facts. In Hartford the *American Mercury* at first pretended to
take Morse's charges seriously, though it grew violently hostile as the controversy progressed.[130]

Religious taboos and possible involvement of the Masonic
order (to which a number of prominent Federalists belonged)
made the issue more than just a one-party matter. Several administration gazettes carried articles critical of Morse. "Censor" insisted on substantiation for Robison's "evidence," since
his basis for declaring that several chapters of the Illuminati
existed in America was the unsupported assertion of a prejudiced individual in Scotland. "A Friend to Truth" warned
against those who proclaimed, even before its appearance, that
Barruel's volume proved Robison's claim. While in keeping
with supporters of a volume written by a man subject to spells
of insanity, this approval before reading the book was hardly
an indication of sober judgment.[131] Yet even these papers devoted more space to Morse's arguments, while the *Connecticut Courant* and *Porcupine's Gazette* endorsed the charges
from the start.[132]

Morse's attacks continued unabated. His Thanksgiving
Day sermon in 1798 not only linked the illuminati with the
earlier Democratic Clubs, but accused them of sponsoring the
American Society of United Irishmen. The *Chronicle,* denying
the charges, imputed Morse with far greater concern over
Georgia lands than in the New Jerusalem, and with neglecting
his parish to collect absurd fables for political propaganda. If
some of his own parishioners strayed across the river in search
of a more attentive shepherd, no one should be surprised.[133]

An effort to make charges of Illuminism backfire was started by the Reverend John Cosens Ogden of Portsmouth, New Hampshire. Episcopalian but no Federalist, Ogden anonymously penned a pamphlet entitled *A View of the New England Illuminati*. He agreed such an organization against the popular welfare did exist, but asserted it (unlike Robison's description) centered around monthly meetings of the clergy, who conspired with wealthy laymen to perpetuate New England's church-state union. These monthly meetings discussed politics, damned the religiously and politically unorthodox, and opposed toleration in Canada and the rights of man in France. *These* "Illuminati" had only one interest—power. Historically the clergy had dominated New England by eliminating dissenters, restricting education, gaining preferment for their relatives, and shackling the press. Since they had remained aloof from the people and had courted the rich, these groups of Federalist pastors were obviously the true Illuminati in America.[134]

From this time on "Illuminati" was so freely used by both parties that it came to have little meaning. New England Republicans zealously followed Ogden's lead and hurled the odious term back at Federalists with relish. Everyone knew that the Congregationalist pastors and their political friends were highly organized; they therefore constituted the genuine threat to the country. Insistently Jeffersonians demanded Morse's "proof" of any Republican revolutionary order in America.[135]

In his Fast Day sermon, April 25, 1799, the Charlestown preacher finally named names. He accused a Masonic lodge in Virginia, with predominately French and Haitian emigrant membership, of spreading Illuminism's insidious doctrine. Soon it was known that the Wisdom Lodge, of Portsmouth, was the chapter in question.[136]

Retorts were stinging. The *Independent Chronicle* forsook its hitherto almost indifferent contemptuousness to make Morse the object of concentrated attention. If the plot were serious, the parson should have turned over the list of members to President Adams instead of making it into "a nine-penny sermon." Failure to do so made him virtually an accomplice—and his intimate knowledge of the society's proceedings almost suggested he himself belonged. Assuredly this was no trivial charge to be casually tacked on to his second or third political discourse on the subject. Probably it was another "*Ocean* massacre"; at best it showed him as attempting to whip up party feeling—one article in his indictment of the Illuminati. True Americans would preserve a national dignity and would despise the "little trifling tales of a credulous infatuated Priest" who had forfeited any right to be taken seriously. Morse would accomplish far more good by confining himself to writing geography.[137]

Morse's slander of the respectable Masonic fraternity illustrated Federalist bigotry. How could so great and good a man as Washington belong to a society opposing everything for which he stood? The maligned order resented being classed with European subversives. During the American Revolution, Morse had shown hostility to Masonry as well as doubtful patriotism; now Oliver Wolcott had sent him some records stolen from the Portsmouth lodge, and Morse was interpreting them to suit himself.[138]

Somewhat desperately, the Massachusetts minister sought to obtain confirmation for his various accusations. Unfortunately for him, Josiah Parker, Federalist Congressman from Virginia, reported that a number of members of the Wisdom Lodge were Federalists and that no proof existed that the organization inspired any opposition to American institutions.[139] Morse also inquired of Professor Christopher Ebeling, noted German scholar, concerning Robison's reputation; the unwelcome reply indicated Robison's work was derided in Europe and that the Bavarian Illuminati was both nonrevolutionary and defunct. Doubtless smarting from the discrediting of his stories about the *Ocean* and the Wisdom Lodge, Morse failed to publish this letter. But the German had at the same time written to the (Republican) Reverend William Bentley, a Mason, clearly indicating how Morse's questions had been answered.[140]

The *American Mercury* finally demanded to know why Morse had withheld Ebeling's demolition of his fabrications.[141] When the pastor indicated the letter was private, the *Aurora, Bee,* and *Constitutional Telegraphe* published the German professor's communication to Bentley as though it were his reply to Morse and compared the whole affair to the Salem witchcraft delusion. Though Morse had earlier expressed great admiration for Ebeling, he scorned his opinion of Robison. What further evidence was needed that the Federalist party would stop at nothing to gain control of the nation's purses and consciences? Another published letter, from the former head of the Bavarian Illuminati, denied any connection with the French Revolution and insisted his now-defunct society had been organized solely for the pursuit of knowledge. Morse's arguments had evaporated, and his integrity was questioned; these letters effectually silenced him.[142]

Morse may have been quieted, but the Republican press was not. Throughout the campaign of 1800 it used the term "Illuminati" as one of ridicule and contempt. Federalists insisted Illuminists existed, and that their delusion that mankind needed only information rather than government made them stalking-horses for Jacobin extremists. New England Democrats scoffed at the clamor as designed "merely to serve the purposes of party, by defeating the election of Mr. Jefferson as President. . . . Happy for his friends the deception has been detected." [143]

"Pope" Timothy Dwight allegedly shed tears at Pickering's dismissal from Adams' cabinet; clear evidence, this, of the clerico-Federalist alliance. The "true" Illuminati of Connecticut were portrayed as discouraged and depressed over the blasting of their hopes for an ecclesiastical establishment and a hereditary monarch.[144] Even when the name "Illuminati" was not used to reinforce charges of Federalist villainy, Republicans suspected the clergy of aristocratic tendencies. New

415

Jersey's General Assembly of Divines appointed catechists to spread the Gospel among Indians of the frontier and the Jersey coast, but the suspicious *Centinel of Freedom* doubted the purity of motives involved. The "Clergy in all ages have been oppressive when vested with power," and one parson supposedly had admitted that part of the scheme was "to *promote the stability of government.*" [145]

America's British faction had cause for alarm over the coming election, asserted "Bunker Hill." Professing fear for the safety of religion, its "pious clan" of old Tories and "every little pettifogging negociator" was notable for anything but piety. Jesuitical clergymen wrote harangues for fast days just to make money by selling them as sermons and traduced Jefferson and other Republicans at election time. That Federalist papers openly thanked clerics for their aid demonstrated "the dangerous consequences attending a *State Religion.*" Many bitter attacks on Jefferson came from parsons fearing disestablishment would cost them their salaries. In a sense, the election was a referendum on the question of an established religion, and the nation rejected the idea.[146]

Yet where it seemed advantageous the Republican press readily appealed to religious prejudice. Philadelphia papers were waspish about "New-England Toleration" in taxing Baptists and other groups for support of the Congregationalist Church. Jonathan Dayton as Speaker epitomized his party's attitude toward freedom of religion when he ejected orderly Quakers from the House galleries simply for wearing their hats. Occasionally there were criticisms of American Catholics; the *Aurora* expressed surprise that two workers for Emancipation in Ireland should be openly insulted by Irish Catholics in supposedly tolerant Philadelphia.[147]

When a Federalist writer blamed Methodists for a Negro revolt in Virginia and the Carolinas, Democrats appealed to that faith. Sound British, anti-republican doctrine saw every Christian sect other than Parson Abercrombie's (Anglican) church as disorganizers, Jacobins, and rebels. Three-fourths of American Methodist clergymen were said to be Republicans, but Congregationalists favored Adams because they thought he approved "their . . . bigotry, and persecution." [148]

"A FRIEND TO LIBERTY" recorded approvingly a minister's opinion that "there could be no political salvation for this country" unless Jefferson were victorious. Surely a republican people would reject a man who had warred against a sister republic and had declared republicanism could "mean anything," for a proved friend of democracy and the rights of man. The monarchical rumor that Maryland Presbyterians contemplated a religious establishment for themselves was a base canard; virtually every American sect had suffered under church-state arrangements and opposed them in any form. Yet "The society of Illuminati, [which] was begot in New-Jersey College, brought forth in Elizabeth Town, reared in Connecticut, and confirmed in maturity at Yale and Dartmouth," had this as its goal. Its progeny spread subversive opinions and constituted "a virtual establishment which Presbyterians generally resist." Its members controlled education, pillaged the Episcopal Church of property in five Eastern states, obtained large grants from state legislatures, slandered Catholicism as Anti-Christ, supported Federalist terrorization, discriminated against other faiths, and sent proselyters to the New York and Vermont frontiers "to disturb the peace of others." Jefferson, who respected all beliefs and refused to prostitute fast days for political purposes, would check this evil.[149]

Essentially, however, Republicans deplored injecting religion into political campaigns. Charles Pinckney wondered who, eight years ago, would have dreamed such an issue could produce "so much *calumny, detraction* and *fraud?*" Yet, since this sorry condition was the work of a few artful men, its baneful influence might be short-lived. Historically minded Americans realized religion had always been handicapped under the patronage of civil authorities, and that tranquillity and progress depended upon separation of church and state. Never had churches prospered as since the Revolution,[150] and no patriot wished to change this and introduce vicious European hatreds.

417

People should shun false prophets and oppose attempts to control the consciences of others. Citizens had a duty to think for themselves in temporal affairs, while preachers had an equal obligation to remain aloof from politics. Left to itself, true religion was bound to flourish, while partisan clergymen constituted its most dangerous enemy.[151]

# XI

## REPUBLICANISM AND
## THE NATURE OF SOCIETY

Inextricably linked with his attitude respecting the clergy and their religion was the Jeffersonian's entire philosophy of government. Much of this philosophy centered around the American Revolution, to which aspiring politicians appealed as both a touchstone and a guide for future action. Late eighteenth-century Republicans regarded themselves as intellectual and political descendants of John Locke. While Locke was far from being the only political theorist to influence colonial thinking, his fundamental thesis that the people constituted a power superior to any government was the very essence of the Declaration of Independence. So also were his tenets that men's reason should be used to understand God's natural laws and to evaluate human institutions, and that earthly governments represented agreements between the people and their rulers in order to secure benefits for society as a whole.[1]

This social compact theory was not novel, for the Mayflower Compact antedated Locke by more than half a century and Roger Williams preceded him by several decades.[2] But the Englishman (with the help of Newton's logic) systematized such thinking. He also stressed that men gained knowledge solely through experience and began life on a basis of fundamental equality. Thus the dignity of the individual was entitled to respect, and the chief benefit any government could bestow was to guarantee man's "natural rights" to life, property, and liberty. Governments should possess only the authority necessary for this purpose, and their justification depended entirely upon the degree to which man's reason showed they succeeded in achieving the desired end.[3]

Newton and Locke were widely known in America before 1770, and the political writings of Milton, Sidney, Coke, and Harrington commanded respect. Locke's *Essay Concerning Human Understanding* had been used as a text in several colonial colleges, and his *Treatises* on government were frequently quoted. Many Federalists also accepted his ideas, or claimed to, but Republicans found especial reassurance in Locke's position. He taught that the majority could judge by common sense when a government had exceeded its legitimate bounds. His optimism and faith in individualism buttressed the fight against privileged classes and a centralized authority.[4] What is more, his insistence that all knowledge was empirical undergirded the Jeffersonian faith that information and education would ensure a workable and efficient democracy.

American democratic ideas were thus largely shaped by the Anglo-American doctrine that all governments rested on an implied contract to secure "the general good,"[5] and were reinforced by the arguments used to support the cause of the colonies during the War for Independence. The heritage was chiefly a compound of English Whiggism and domestic experience, but there were European Continental influences as well. Just as seventeenth-century discoveries in physics and astronomy had questioned teachings long regarded as immutable truths, so now were societies everywhere placed under the microscope of scientific analysis. Particularly was this true in France, which had idealized the American Revolution and had enshrined Washington and Franklin among her heroes. The scientific discoveries set in motion by Newton and Locke seemed to show there was no end to what men might learn about God's universe and therefore about the Almighty Himself. His will was disclosed indirectly through man's environment, rather than by miracles or inspired documents. Such thinking weakened Biblical authority, for if natural law and divine law were identical, then God was in essence a First Cause—substantially the position taken by those coming to believe in deism. French deists strengthened the growing emphasis on the test of reason in every field and encouraged the concomitant trend toward religious toleration. While reiterating their primary legacy was from the American Revolution, Jeffersonian editors such as Freneau and Bache readily acknowledged an indebtedness also to Gallic philosophers.[6]

Montesquieu's theory of separation of powers was almost universally accepted by American writers. Republicans seconded his contentions that free speech was a safeguard against despotism and that (as most Federalists also agreed) virtue was the only secure basis of a republic.[7] Voltaire's attacks on superstition and fanaticism were applauded by a number of Jeffersonian sympathizers as championing democracy and the separation of church and state. Rousseau went beyond even Locke in emphasizing popular sovereignty. Where the Englishmen held the people's power to alter their government could be exercised only when rights actually had been violated, the French savant believed adjustments should always be possible. In Rousseau's eyes, representatives possessed no discretionary power; they must ever reflect the popular will that was the only supreme and constant authority. While European intellectuals seemed more concerned over liberty to write as they pleased than about political freedom in its broadest sense, American democratic thinkers held the rights of free speech, press, and assembly, together with short terms and frequent rotations in office, were logically necessary to maintain a proper and continuous check upon government.[8]

Although it would be erroneous to overstress French influence—and there is evidence Federalists may have deliberately done so in an effort to discredit Republicans [9]—it has been noted that European deism had considerable influence in America. Gradually Voltaire's deistic ideas, as developed in America, became associated to many with Republicanism in politics, for some leaders saw a distinct relationship between religious superstition and political credulity. This trend was furthered with the writings of Ethan Allen, Elihu Palmer, and above all Tom Paine, whose productions received wide publicity in Democratic gazettes.[10]

Editor Bache denied that Jefferson had described Paine's *Age of Reason* as "the canonical work of political scriptures," but he reprinted the pamphlet to combat the political heresies cropping up in the United States. To Federalists crying "What are the political heresies?," the Philadelphia printer retorted that they were those principles supported by the few contrary to the publicly expressed opinions of the majority. Politically wise American deists, however, hesitated to go as far as did Paine. Like Freneau and Jefferson, they were willing to criticize the clergy, but they stopped short of publicly disavowing revelation in religion.[11]

While as a faith deism failed to win widespread public approval in America, the attacks upon it acquainted many persons with its arguments. Deists believed in the common man and in the importance of education and environment in achieving his improvement. These convictions, plus an insistence upon individual liberty and religious toleration for fully developing man's innate goodness, had a broad appeal.[12]

The prime tenet of Jeffersonian democracy was the fundamental supremacy of the people. The doctrine of natural rights could be used to justify the American Revolution, doubts respecting the authority of the central government during the struggle over adoption of the Constitution, and Republican opposition to Federalism, fully as well as to defend the Glorious Revolution approximately a century earlier. Unlike their opponents, Republicans possessed the optimism and confidence of Locke and the deists respecting human nature. "Government," bluntly proclaimed the *Independent Chronicle,* "is instituted for man, not man for government." [13] Federalists might profess attachment to this concept, but their skeptical adversaries questioned their application of it in actual practice. Even before developing any party organization as such, Republicans, through their editors, always accented the concept as particularly basic. Under even the best of rulers, then, blind obedience was repudiated; a nation was wise to "provide against the worst." Men who advocated excessive power for benevolent administrators were often merely paving the way for tyranny. Public officials were *created* as such by the people, and officials' authority only reflected the inalienable rights and liberties of their creators.[14]

Even more important than the Constitution itself were these popular rights, for it had been to secure them that the Constitution had been drafted. If citizens deemed their frame of government unsatisfactory, they possessed an inherent prerogative to alter or discard it at any time. Only one fixed rule of politics existed for Bache's *General Advertiser:* "A Constitution should always be the work of the People, and framed for the advantage of the governed; every other principle is subordinate. . . ."[15]

Democrats insisted their political position was grounded on the great doctrines for which the Revolution had been fought and urged the administration to return to "first principles." They considered themselves as steadily adhering to the philosophy proclaimed at the time of independence, when liberty had triumphed "with representative government."[16] In the future, they felt, the world would be divided into the two classes of royalists and republicans, and those who opposed the American and French Revolutions came in the former group. Freneau's *National Gazette* revealed this belief in his attacks on the Federalists:

LOST

The DECLARATION of the RIGHTS of the citizens of the United States: Any good patriot of 1775 who should bring the same to light will receive the thanks of his fellow citizens and the blessings of posterity.

N.B. This is a matter of importance to the people of the United States, as there is some reason to fear a total loss of their rights and privileges will speedily follow the loss of the declaration of them.[17]

*"An Old Whig of '76"* was a favorite *nom de plume* in Republican columns. One of these writers stated anyone versed in

political history could see that the so-called Federalists were the direct descendants of the English Tories. Before 1776 governments had benefited the few; now sovereignty was vested in the people, and the existence of bodies politic that were true to "their original principles must necessarily depend on the actual information of all." [18]

During the French crisis, the *Aurora* imported irony from Kentucky in answer to Federalist allegations that some revolutionary philosophers aimed only to inflame popular passions and to undermine authority. Obviously, ran the sarcastic retort, Republicans had lost the original purity of their motives:

> In 1776 you fought against Britain, and for liberty, and now you are unwilling to fight for Britain and John Adams. In 1776 you fought for the right of raising your money as you pleased, and now you are against John Adams raising it for you. In 1776 you fought in principle against parliament imposing sedition bills upon you, and now that your *own* representatives have done it, you murmur. . . . In 1776 you fought for the right of speaking and publishing your sentiments as you pleased, and now that the Congress has determined that it is expedient of your [*sic*] to give up this right . . . instead of submitting like good citizens you seem determined to make greater use of your tongues than ever. These alone, independent of many other proofs which might have been adduced, manifestly shew . . . depravity. . . .[19]

Sarcasm aside, the logical deduction was that the citizens were the best keepers of their own liberties. Seconding Paine and Rousseau, Jeffersonian printers asserted there was in the American Constitution no suggestion

> of a compact between the people on one side, and government on the other. The compact was that of the people with each other to produce and constitute a government. To suppose that any government can be a party in a compact with the whole people, is to suppose it to have existance before it could have a right to exist.

Accordingly, government was not a trade but a trust; it possessed of itself no rights, but only duties.[20] To keep political abuses to a minimum, the interests of public officials should always conform to those of society. "*Salus populi, suprema lex esto,*" should be the motto of every real patriot.[21]

Men who babbled about "loyalty" while trying to stifle popular liberties were indeed the nation's worst enemies. Unreasoning support of governmental measures was no substitute for national freedom and welfare. Any clique that strove to block the popular will must itself be foiled by all patriotic citizens, irrespective of party. Every election day was an acknowledgement that the populace was "the only source from which legitimate authority can flow." [22] Noah Webster was berated for calling American citizens "subjects" simply because they were compelled to obey the laws. This smacked of Hobbes. Since the people shared in framing legislation, it was surely a Federalist solecism to say men could be subject to themselves. Voters should shun candidates who decried equality and should select for office men who were *of* and *like* themselves in order to guard against misrepresentation. Since government officials were public servants, they were entitled to respect, but should not be treated as nobility.[23]

Slowly the name "Democrat," at first applied to Republicans in scorn, came to be defended as a badge of honor. After all, stated one newspaper, did not the name mean a friend of the people? Anticipating Lincoln, this gazette argued that anyone who used the term disparagingly was himself automatically suspect, for "a *democrat* is one who advocates the people's rights, and a government *of* the people, or arising *out of* the people; formed by them, [and]responsible to them. . . ." Only persons holding such beliefs could be accounted true Americans.[24]

If by very definition democracy was government of or by the people, a republic was the means by which they governed through their chosen delegates. No one advocated pure democracy for America, but the principle of representation retained power in the hands of the populace while avoiding that mob rule that soon led to dictatorship.[25] Even John Adams had described this device as the greatest improvement over the ancients in the area of political science. Gazettes cited him as urging that a representative assembly be "an exact portrait of the people at large," and some Republicans followed Rousseau's view that legislators should merely reflect the wishes of their constituents. To them the idea of legislative discretion would remove the essential difference between America's government and that of England. Britons had a hereditary House of Lords, plus the will of a legislature for a constitution—and that will obeyed the nod of a prime minister. Americans possessed a Constitution framed by the people for themselves, and the servants acting under it were given position by the people and were responsible to them.[26]

Hamiltonians to the contrary, the administration was not the same as the people or the Constitution. To Federalist doggerel—

> The people are the government,
> The government the people;
> *Just as the steeple is the church*
> *And eke the church, the steeple.*

the *United States Chronicle* retorted:

> The steeple may be taken down,
> The church may still remain
> But if the church itself's remov'd
> The steeple stands in vain. . . .[27]

Underlining the belief that congressmen were simply agents of their constituents were frequent letters by representatives reporting on their stewardship. Carried in the local papers, these epistles normally were campaign documents for the next election, but they revealed how the congressman voted and indicated his flattering realization that his power derived from the common man.[28] Ultimately, the right of election was basic to all others the citizenry enjoyed. As one journalist put it, electing a person to office did not make him "divinely inspired and none other than God's vicegerent. No—it is not the man, but our right of putting in that man, which is the inestimable gift of Heaven conferred upon us. . . ." Some Republicans even urged that the electorate should not only choose all legislators, but should fix their salaries as well.[29] They contended deputation of power by the people in no sense meant abdication of it; the way to preserve republican government was "by a continued expression of the public will." [30]

However much Federalists berated them, political parties were probably the best means of achieving representation. Yet editors warned voters that mere party labels were no substitute for actual principles.[31] With that qualification, the *American Herald* deemed parties a positive blessing:

> The new Constitution proceeded, in great measure, from them; they are blasts to keep alive the political fire; by them knowledge is disseminated through the states. . . . Legislatures will no longer attempt to govern, without being acquainted with government.[32]

Though at first parties were scornfully referred to as "factions," no less an authority than Franklin had declared them indispensable to liberty. At times opposing those in power might seem dangerous, but on occasion opposition was needful to preserve popular rights. Parties were a means of ensuring careful examination of public measures. This function was vital, "for when investigation ceases, the people become uninterested at *elections* . . . and . . . ignorantly rivet their own chains." [33]

Organized parties, it was hoped, would help prevent an overcentralization in the national government. Republicans dreaded an expansion of federal power fully as much as they did complete legislative discretion. To them the danger was two-fold: the nation might absorb the functions of the states (reducing them to mere provinces), or too much authority might become concentrated in the person of the Executive. Either eventuality, they held, would doom popular liberty.

Essentially, the defense against the first threat consisted of emphasizing states' rights—a course that eventually led to the famous Virginia and Kentucky Resolutions. Before Washington's administration was a year old, printers were calling on James Sullivan, U.S. district judge for New Hampshire, to "RETRACT his TREASONABLE ASSERTION" that the national government was a "consolidation" and that his state was no longer independent. At the time the Constitution was adopted, noted the irate *Independent Chronicle,* not even the warmest Federalist had talked of a consolidated authority. Now there were those who spoke of consolidation as already accomplished, but it could not be achieved unless the state governments were annihilated.[34]

A *good* central authority did not need to be all-powerful. Laws that were supported by popular opinion did not require armed force to execute them. Like Paine, most Republicans considered government a necessary evil. It grew out of man's imperfections and—in that it checked individual liberty—was something of a combination against the people. The *National Gazette* defied history to show a single instance in which government had interfered with civilian occupations without injury. Rulers actually had no more virtue than the ruled, and any surrender of unnecessary authority to the central government was sheer folly.[35]

Official power, asserted the Bennington *Vermont Gazette,* ceaselessly sought to exceed its statutory limitations. To be kept within bounds it must

> be watched with the most jealous eye, by all who are subject to it. . . . A country deserves no love when it ceases to be a country of Liberty. Human beings constitute a country, not a soil in a certain latitude; and an attachment to liberty is the truest loyalty.[36]

By 1798 the ascendancy of the central government had increased alarmingly—Washington had refused to send diplomatic papers to the House, the Jay Treaty had repudiated earlier pledges, Adams had brought the nation to the brink of war with France, and Congress had approved a stamp act. Doubtful interpretations had been used to emasculate local governments, and citizens were advised to guard closely those rights remaining to them.[37] The Pittsfield *Sun* solemnly warned that

> *Political usurpations have, in all ages, been introduced gradually, and under imposing pretences of necessity and public good, been suffered to pass for the moment, as temporary expedients, and then tolerated by an habitual acquiescence, till their strength has at last become too inveterate for resistance or correction.*
> Political encroachments always proceed with an accelerated

momentum. 'The precedent,' says an illustrious author, '—creates another. They soon accumulate and constitute law. What yesterday was fact, today is doctrine. Examples are supposed to justify the most dangerous usurpations; and when they do not suit exactly[,] the defect is supplied by analogy!'[38]

The menace increased proportionately as the national government became stronger. Every lessening of the sovereignty of the states was viewed as a potential threat to their very existence. John Ward Fenno's famous "swan song" allegedly confessed the Federalist goal to be the elimination of the state governments; war with France and a British alliance were to be the means by which this end was to be consumated.[39] It was to avert such a catastrophe that "The TRUE American CREED" of the *Constitutional Telegraphe,* in addition to affirming the unprescriptible rights and basic equality of all men, called for an explicit pledge: "I do believe that . . . every . . . State, within these United States is and of right ought to be free and independant; that every citizen owes to it all imaginable faith and allegiance."[40]

Fully as ominous to Jeffersonian editors was the trend toward an all-powerful Chief Executive. If a President could claim discretionary authority beyond that specifically granted him by the Constitution, where were its limits, and how did it differ from arbitrary power? That an administration was popular only made any transgressions—since they might be tolerated or overlooked—all the more dangerous to the rights of citizens.[41]

Federalist presidential policies of patronage and removal weakened the people's control over their servants in Congress. As early as the time of Jay's Treaty the Philadelphia *Aurora* accused Washington of feeling himself as omnipotent as had the French kings of old. Another Pennsylvania editor reiterated the need for strict construction of the Constitution, recognition of the legitimacy of political opposition, and a minimum of government as the best safeguards against despotism. A Vermont correspondent held that the President should be active in fulfilling the desires of Congress, but passive in exercising the veto or in striving for Executive dominance. It was on the "shoals of the *executive department*" that nearly all peoples in the past had lost their liberties.[42]

Republican editorialists constantly repeated their belief in a government of laws rather than of individuals.[43] Congressmen, too, might exceed their authority, but they were personally known and their position was not so subject to veneration as was the President's. Without a strong legislative body, the development of monarchy was only a question of time. To guard against this possibility, checks and balances had been created. If the House could not refuse appropriations for treaties and official salaries, Congress was "but *the blind instrument of the executive*," and perhaps in practice Americans already were no longer citizens of a republic.[44]

Americans, insisted these writers, were experienced in governing themselves. Surely, then, stated the *Albany Register,* they would discharge their most vital duty, which was to "watch over the sacred trust of LIBERTY" they had won in the Revolution. Freedom was essential to national greatness, for as the *Jersey Journal* summarized: "PEACE is the *life,* LAWS the *body,* and LIBERTY the *soul* of every republican government. . . ."[45]

About Jeffersonian agrarianism much has been written, and in many respects the American farmer did epitomize the party's ideals of liberty and self-sufficiency. Not all Republicans were agrarian in philosophy, however, and some distinct appeals were made to city "mechanics" on the basis that the party opposed privilege and favored unshackled economic opportunity.[46] Yet only the farmer was apt to be virtually independent economically and to be in a position to cast his vote without fear or favor. His very contact with God's world around him afforded him greater understanding than that possessed by many of the most learned men, said some. Agriculture created wealth that was not artificial and made a nation independent of foreign cataclysms or hostility. From it sprang all branches of political economy, and nothing, peremptorily stated the New York *Diary,* merited more "the attention of a wise government."[47]

Commerce presented an opportunity for accumulation of

great wealth in the hands of a few, but agriculture tended toward a more equitable distribution of worldly goods. Classes other than farmers and laborers, darkly affirmed the *Middlesex Gazette,* lived only "by cunning." [48] Jefferson himself believed the preservation of democracy demanded prevention of concentration of vast wealth, elimination of monopoly, and preservation of a cultural homogeneity—all of which could best be accomplished by maintenance of the numerical superiority of small landowners in America.[49] Thirty thousand traders and speculators should never be permitted to "lord it over 3½ millions of their fellow citizens. . . ." Agriculture was the true support of all government; invariably merchants evaded paying their share, "for however high the duties, taxes, &c. are laid on them, the dearer they sell their goods and the less they give for our produce!" [50] The farmer represented the common man of that day, and in him Republicans had great faith. Not for long, in their estimation, would the yeomanry be gulled by catch phrases and party names; the people could "and they will, THINK FOR THEMSELVES." [51]

A few such expressions might be dismissed as simple electioneering, but writers for the Republican press seemed to take seriously their high estimate of the worth of the average citizen. This esteem agreed with the basic doctrine of the sovereignty of the people and the conviction that the judgment of many was in the long run infinitely superior to the caprice of a single individual. Vigorously opposed were suggestions that state legislatures, because of their access to more adequate information, should select presidential electors. This proposal was a prelude to aristocracy, and, said the *American Citizen,*

> the most pernicious libel that was ever promulgated against the people. If the people be not capacitated, to perform the business of election, what political purpose are they competent to? None at all, there is an end to republican government.

It was the obligation of citizens to select the ablest of their fellows to govern them and to return those men to private life "upon discovering that they had imbibed the least taint from their commerce with power." [52]

Unless popular rights were to be lost, citizens had to be ever on the alert against that very government which they themselves had created. Virtuous officials did not expect, or even covet, extreme adultation. The positive duty of the public was to examine constantly the conduct of those in power, for the fact that the people had put them in office did not ensure that they would *always* act for the common welfare. "The action of laws upon public opinion, and the reaction of that opinion upon government, is the criterion, by which to judge of the wisdom, the policy, or the folly of political measures. . . ." [53]

Federalists might cry ignorance or dishonesty, but opposition to unconstitutional measures was not treason. Indeed it was the highest type of loyalty, for suppression of popular opinion presented all the danger of a secret mine that might explode at any moment. The belief that the administration was *always* right was perilously close to the doctrine of papal infallibility or to the monarchical idea that "the king can do no wrong." In consequence, secrecy in public affairs evinced a sinister contempt for the populace. "Whenever a government abounds with . . . mysteries, you may be assured that something is rotten. . . ." If citizens were prevented from expressing their opinions, depraved officials might not adhere to their duties and sincere representatives could not be aware of the public will. Surely no administration under a Constitution that began with "WE THE PEOPLE" could logically resent inquiries into its measures. [54]

A republican government had the public good as its goal and the voice of the people as its guide. However excellent the Constitution, those in power under it were but the trustees for the citizenry—and principals had every right to scrutinize the conduct of their agents. Hamiltonians argued that separation of powers enabled the branches of government to check on each other and thus to protect individual rights, but this dogma was criminal if it precluded other sentinels. In every nation where popular liberties had been violated, the government had been the culprit. Safeguards were needed, and if necessary at all they should be effective against the government, for to establish it as the only "watchman over itself, is perfectly absurd and ridiculous. . . ." [55] Since *"All power flows from the people,"* citizens had the right to interpret and to apply that power. Criticism of those in high places was not blasphemous, for censure should be bestowed where it was merited.[56]

Late in Washington's first term a number of individuals concluded that this watching and criticizing of the people's agents were best accomplished through group action. They thus began to organize the so-called "Democratic Societies," and there is some evidence that newspapers played a significant part in their creation and activities. Almost a year before the earliest known group of this nature appeared, Freneau's *National Gazette* advocated forming such clubs to maintain popular interest in government and to sound the tocsin against governmental encroachments. Unless vigilance were exercised, he asserted, *"what is every man's business soon becomes no man's business."* People under governments were like sleepers on a beach who would be overwhelmed by the incoming tide if not awakened by friendly monitors.[57]

With the editor of the *Philadelphische Correspondenz* as its vice-president, the German Republican Society of Philadelphia was the first of these groups to announce publicly its formation. Its circular letter reasserted the duty of each citizen to assist in a republican government, either by taking part in it or through advice and alertness against possible errors. With education, observation, and expression of opinions, liberty could be preserved. Such a program was particularly called for among immigrants, who needed to learn about America's democratic system. An offer was extended to communicate with similar organizations created elsewhere in order that a united viewpoint might be obtained and expressed.[58]

The idea spread rapidly. Within the next five years, more than forty clubs were established. Their proclamations, carried in the journals, berated inattention by citizens to their rights, voiced friendship for the French Republic together with a conviction that American interests were akin to hers, and announced an intention to study governmental measures solely upon their merits. Only thus could Americans discharge their sacred *"obligation* to secure and transmit to posterity, unsullied and undiminished, the blessings of freedom" gained by the War for Independence.[59]

These groups received every possible notice in the Republican press, which printed frequent accounts of their meetings, toasts, and celebrations.[60] Yet the very nature of the societies made it impossible for them to long maintain any pretense of political impartiality. They rapidly became centers of opposition to Federalist dominance. Some of them barred from membership men with aristocratic leanings, and they uniformly advocated (as essential for protecting popular liberties) frequent rotations in office even within their own organizations.[61] Alleging that certain individuals had been *"royalizing* themselves" in government, these groups set out to check the growth of reactionary tendencies. Charleston's society prevailed upon the city council to discard all honorific titles such as "Judge" and "Senator," and other clubs criticized England, demanded adequate representation for frontier regions, or publicly opposed a third term for President Washington.[62] In some areas they formed the nucleus of political organizations, actively promoting nominations and effectively supporting anti-administration candidates for office. Everywhere they asserted their right to instruct congressmen on pending legislative measures.[63]

Uneasy Federalists who recalled the effectiveness of Committees of Correspondence in 1775 became violently hostile toward the groups. Disorderly, treasonably Francophile, "Genêt-begotten," dangerous to liberty, and desirous of becoming the "tyrants of America," were among the accusations made. The clubs were pictured as extra-legal governments, pressure groups, and agencies weakening respect for all lawful authority.[64]

For a time the societies held their peace and confined themselves to the issues at hand. Then they struck back furiously. A

Maryland Representative had expressed the wish that Congress could move to a place free from the influence of mobs and these clubs. In reply the *General Advertiser* jeered at the "immense" difference between mere citizens and congressmen. Surely every advocate of efficient government would agree,

> and wish Congress to adjourn to some spot, where the insolence and arrogance of the swinish multitude would not disturb the Congressional sanctuary. In some solitary spot, removed beyond the clamour of the people in every shape, they will have a full opportunity to indulge in their sublime meditations, and concert such plans, as will put it out of the power of *mobs* and Democratic societies, and newspapers to interrupt their serenity.[65]

Obtaining freedom was easier than preserving it, observed the Democratic Society of Pennsylvania; ambition had stifled patriotism in many a breast. Those in authority should not shrink from investigation if there were nothing to hide. The New York *Herald* asked, "Should all other societies be tolerated in a free country, and that [alone], whose object is political information, be proscribed?" [66]

It so happened, however, that one target for the societies' criticism had been the excise tax on distilled liquors, and Federalists seized the opportunity to blame the groups for the Whiskey Rebellion of 1794.[67] In reality most of the organizations had deplored that uprising, although they had condemned the excise while calling for rescinding it by constitutional means. Only those of "prostituted principles," stated the Newark group, would accuse the societies of fostering the insurrection. Governments *could* err, and efforts to stifle inquiry into their conduct were as dangerous as armed uprisings against their legitimate operations.[68]

Though the revolt itself was speedily suppressed, the campaign to eradicate the clubs continued. Republicans, already smarting, were understandably indignant when Washington mildly denounced "certain self-created societies" in an address to Congress. Were not, they replied, the Cincinnati, the Chambers of Commerce and even the Constitutional Conven-

435

tion which the President had headed, "self-created"? "A QUAKER" noted that any ban on self-created societies as such would outlaw his own religion.[69]

Most important from a philosophical perspective was the way in which the press defended the constitutional rights of the members of these clubs. Were Americans to be muzzled whenever they chanced to disagree with those in authority? The Philadelphia *Independent Gazetteer* charged the administration with seeking a scapegoat for an unpopular act. Certainly the charges against the societies were ridiculously contradictory. The organizations were said to be secret, yet they were blamed for too much publicity; they were too contemptible to be noticed, yet they had instigated the rebellion; some men called them self-created, and others felt they were the creatures of the French minister Genêt. Only in uniform opposition to freedom of speech and assembly were the Federalists consistent. Actually, numerous members of Eastern organizations had been foremost among those who marched to put down the rebellion. Imperfect the clubs might be, but if they were not unlawful it was despotic to forbid them.[70] In Europe information was scarce and governmental power unlimited, but surely true Americans could not believe that their enlightened fellow-countrymen would embrace error rather than truth.[71]

Despite their valiant retorts, Washington's disapproval and the insurrection itself did sorely hurt the organizations. While Federalist reports of their demise were for the most part premature, their effectiveness gradually diminished.[72] Republicans themselves admitted that several later administrative proposals they considered unwise were pushed through with relative ease because many societies were by that time dormant.[73]

Yet during their lifetime these Democratic Societies exemplified an elemental principle in their party's creed. Public attention was absolutely indispensable to frustrate the designs of those hostile to popular government. With freedom of speech and press, all other liberties would be secure—and even the most virtuous official might "occasionally stand in need of admonition." Unfettered examination of governmental measures, not uncritical adulation, was the best means of ensuring administration of the Constitution according to the objectives that gave it birth.[74]

Tories did not like a free press, explained one journal, but even though subject to abuse it was crucial to the existence of a republic. "The press," ran an advertisement for a proposed South Carolina newspaper, "like a trusty centinel must ever be on the lookout. . . ."[75] An aristocratic court, cautioned the *Vermont Gazette,* possessed countless means of pandering to the passions of human nature and seducing the masses into surrendering their liberties. When dust is thrown into the eyes of the people,

> more especially gold dust, the political ophthalmist must honestly endeavor to clear away the obstruction. It becomes every lover of his country . . . to warn his countrymen of the danger, whenever he observes the smallest encroachment on their rights, and the spirit of the times tending but remotely to despotism.[76]

Let the citizenry judge what should be printed, echoed other gazettes. Freedom was not compatible with silence, which might well be only "THE QUIET OF SUBMISSION." A certain amount of criticism developed statesmanship, and if an administration wished to avert censure it should avoid foolish and vicious actions. Human nature, contended the *Virginia Argus,* was chiefly governed by either hope, fear, or reason. Those in authority who made themselves objects of hope and fear obtained so great an advantage that they might no longer trouble to rule by reason. An election without discussion could be compared to judging a beauty contest while blindfolded.[77]

Federalists, claimed Republican writers, made the grave and perhaps deliberate error of confusing dissent with disloyalty. As long as the administration was not confronted with actual physical resistance, however, it had no legitimate complaint. Newspapers should expose avarice and ruthlessness and should ignore "impudent" insinuations of slander and sedi-

437

tion. Above all, they should "BE NOT INTIMIDATED
. . . by any terrors, from publishing whatever can be warranted" by the law and by the public interest. Parallels were
drawn from English history to show that, whatever the cost,
any threat to the expression of public opinion must be eliminated.[78]

Republicans retained their faith in the ultimate wisdom of
the masses. If the "wisest and best" were correct in so consistently opposing the will of the majority, then citizens were unqualified to exercise the right of election. In that case the farce
of a republican government was best ended posthaste and the
nation returned to an open monarchy. But Democrats had
more confidence than that. Admittedly the people sometimes
made mistakes. Thus laws were occasionally repealed, but the
repeal was the corrective that proved the long-range value of
public opinion.[79]

This faith in the common man was to a considerable extent
reflected in the party's attitude toward the immigrant. Increasingly, the new Americans turned to the Republicans, whose
press customarily treated them as human beings entitled to
respect—and at times more or less openly invited their political support. A number of organizations designed to aid incoming Europeans and to preserve some of the old ties developed
in the 1790s, especially among citizens of Irish, French, or
German extraction. Republicans were prominent in many of
these groups, some of which came to play an active political
role. Republican editors, some immigrants themselves, were
generally insistent upon the right of expatriation as a concomitant of the natural dignity of man. Even from the government's standpoint, expatriation had value as a safety valve for
malcontents; it should apply not only to Europeans, but also
to Americans who wished to alter their allegiance.[80]

Another outgrowth of this confidence in mankind was the
conviction that almost any intelligent patriotic citizen could
adequately fulfill the obligations of public office. All that had
to be ascertained was that he was honest, not too selfishly ambitious, and that he recognized the authority of the people. To

reelect the same individuals interminably, or to draft others from official positions only, constituted an erroneous, embarrassing, and dangerous admission that the nation was barren of men of attainments. The notion of the "indispensable man" was specifically denied; Americans should demonstrate "that there are more persons than one capable of administering our Federal Government." [81]

More important was the fact that frequent change of officials constituted an efficacious preventive against aristocracy or dictatorship. Since every man in power would be a tyrant as far as he dared, it followed that "Rotation in Office is the very Soul of a Republic. . . ." [82] Terms of office should be limited; several papers wished to require annual elections of all representative bodies. [83] Power was intoxicating, and at the end of their terms officials should be returned to equality with their fellow-citizens, that they might be subject to every act they had promulgated while in authority. To retain men in office sheerly from personal attachment or respect savored of monarchy; quite obviously the framers of the Constitution had contemplated changes in governmental posts at regular intervals. Frequent elections were better than artificial checks and balances in averting autocratic government. "When men in office are good moral characters, we revere them; for their great attainments we respect them; for their virtuous exertions we love them; for a denial of our rights we cashier them." [84]

Retaining men in office for long periods would of itself create a sort of aristocracy, for once officials felt themselves assured in office they demanded the perquisites of place. There should be no administrative class of officeholders as such. To believe that an individual might be born a magistrate or governor was absurd, for true believers in democracy were implacably hostile to distinctions among men. [85]

In America the Revolution had largely demolished the old aristocracy, contended polemicists, but Hamilton's financial policies were held to have created a new one that was still more menacing. It was more numerous, was grounded on speculation rather than real wealth, and as yet had no titles to expose it to public observation. Avarice was its only motivation. With no tradition of honor to maintain, it used meaningless phrases (such as "public faith" and "security of property") to sustain debt, fraud, waste, and the domination of five million Americans by a scant thousandth of that number.[86]

That this class which sought to rule the nation did not use the name "nobility" meant nothing. In themselves, names were of little significance. It was the aristocratic principle—that of government by, or privileges for, the select few—that Republicans found objectionable.[87] "SAPIENS" sardonically pretended to urge his fellow countrymen to entrust all their rights to the wealthy. Since they already possessed the most influence and education, the rich obviously had the time and ability to understand governmental measures, while the poor were unable to know the true meaning of liberty. Being wise, the affluent would institute policies that were "most to *their advantage,* and what will benefit them must of course benefit the poor, for without the poor the rich cannot live. . . ." Clearly, Americans could do no better than to ". . . submit to those who have the NEEDFUL!"[88]

Other writers argued, more directly, that no persons barred from voting by property qualifications could properly be called "freemen," however much they might be flattered by the term. Exercise of the franchise ought to be the natural right of every man from whom his country demanded the duty of aiding in her defense. To argue that these men paid no taxes was simply untrue, for they were affected by both the tariff and the excise. If property alone qualified a person for suffrage, why not give the very rich several votes? In truth, any such restrictions were a blow at the Constitution and at basic republicanism, for at the ballot box all men were clearly equal.[89]

Only too frequently the opulent escaped paying their fair share of the taxes, although they received the greatest benefit from government and should therefore pay more to support it. Luxury duties were proposed to discourage ostentation and artificial distinctions. Possibly, advocated some, laws should be enacted to limit the acquisition of money. Under the Federalists, every governmental bondholder crazed for wealth supported administration measures irrespective of their wisdom. As Freneau stated, it was easier for a camel to pass through the needle's eye than for a wealthy man to be a true republican.[90]

Republicanism thus stressed fundamental equality; not only was this a right intrinsic to humanity, but it was indispensable to that economic and social opportunity that made democratic doctrine so appealing to those of modest means and members of minority groups.[91] If true republicanism meant simplicity in style of life, the same was doubly so in government. "Monstrous salaries" were manifestly inappropriate for officials in a society where all citizens were compeers. Not only would the cost of such emoluments prove burdensome, but public servants might thereby be encouraged to feel superior to the people who had placed them in office. Good Republicans desired a plain, rigidly economical government with few trimmings.[92]

Every government, descanted "PHILOLENTHEROG," had two factions. One sought to preserve old fraudulent systems of control, while the other endeavored to bring about true representation. Federalists represented the former group in America. Their success depended upon hoodwinking the majority; they believed armies and sedition laws were needed, possessed no confidence in anyone but themselves, and dreaded any change.[93] Since they lacked faith in the people and had no respect for their rights, any of their policies were suspect—but most dangerous of all in the eyes of many writers was the idea of a standing army. Historically, military forces in being had always tended to further tyranny and to suppress popular liberties. Republicans claimed the power of the sword was more dangerous in an extensive nation than in a small one and held a militia system was quite adequate to preserve state powers and to guarantee independence. A professional force would be composed of vagabonds and hirelings and would provide a convenient tool for any ruthless seeker after power. Republicans insisted a genuine militia, without privileged exemptions and operating as an agency of the states, could be made thoroughly efficient.[94]

The militia had played, Republicans noted with some exaggeration, a valiant part in the Revolution and had responded more than adequately at the time of the Whiskey Rebellion. If true citizens were asked what an untrained rabble could do against disciplined enemy troops, they should simply reply: *"Enquire at Bunker's hill or at the Bastile."* Unwillingness to rely on a militia bespoke a sense of guilt among those in authority and perhaps indicated a wish to defeat the end of the social compact.[95]

Surely a standing army was more costly; the opportunity for loans and taxes was indeed perhaps why Hamiltonians preferred it. And while the "swinish multitude" paid for the cost of a regular military establishment, those same troops could be used to put the people in their place if they got restive. "A Calm Observer" in 1795 listed four Federalist attempts within two years to bring about congressional measures for a larger standing army. These sinisterly demonstrated their obvious belief that rule should be by power rather than "the sacred principles of liberty and republicanism." Democrats detested a navy as expensive, the tool of monarchs, and a "floating hell," but it was not such a threat to the liberties of the entire country. Moreover, it served in the only area in which Americans would probably ever have to face a foreign enemy. Actually, every male citizen should possess some knowledge of the art of land warfare, for a standing army of mercenaries like the Hessians of old was a clear menace to liberty.[96] Nevertheless, Federalist alarms (which Jeffersonians considered patently exaggerated) during the quasi-war with France produced, in 1798, the creation of such a force.

Republicans stigmatized this enlarged body of troops as utterly unnecessary; America's location rendered it secure from invasion, and national policy forbade aggression. Doubtless, they charged, the increased number of troops was intended to enforce the Alien and Sedition Acts. "There is at present," affirmed the *Independent Chronicle,* "as much danger of an invasion from the French, as from the inhabitants of Saturn, and no more. Hence, this enormous body of men can be designed only for *domestic* employment. . . ." [97] The militia constituted the *"natural* and *cheap defense of nations,"* and well-executed drills of such units were seized upon as proof that a mercenary standing force was superfluous.[98]

> Of all the devices which man has devised for the ruin of the species, that of a standing army has been the most fatal to morals and happiness; ever at the command of a frail, a malevolent, or a mad individual, the People whom they are pretendedly to protect, become subjected by these instruments of despotism. . . . When the people are easy and satisfied, the whole country is an army.[99]

With a President already more powerful than England's king, the people had more to fear from an army of regulars than from all the powers of Europe. That officers' commissions went almost exclusively to Federalists suggested this force was to be a political weapon rather than a purely military one. Perhaps the good pay and quarters would make workers for Adams' reelection; in certain localities the troops appeared to be trying to aid that effort by attempted intimidation of Republican printers.[100] After Editor William Duane had been horsewhipped by soldiers for publishing adverse comments about military threats and terrorizing, Jeffersonian writers asked: "Is any citizen safe . . . in resenting an injury which he may receive from a military officer?" [101]

Until the advent of actual war, a standing army was an unmitigated evil. It tended to produce licentiousness, entailed intolerable expenses, and (unless a paralyzing draft were levied) for enlisted men enrolled only scoundrels who would serve for a pittance. Had not the Boston Massacre shown the irritation and inevitable friction resulting from quartering troops among civilians? [102] In lighter vein, it was noted that if the militia were the "Pillars of the Republic," the soldiers of the "Provisional Army" were its "caterpillars." Possibly they could be used to help farmers suppress the Hessian fly.[103]

Shortly after John Randolph referred in the House to the

"ragamuffins" comprising the army, some officers publicly insulted him with intent to provoke a duel. Randolph protested to Adams against infringement of congressional privilege, and though the President ordered an investigation [104] most Democrats considered the incident another sign of the times. When Charles Holt's New London *Bee* told of the lax morality of army life, he was jailed for discouraging recruiting. How long, Republicans asked, would the servants of the people trample upon their masters? [105]

When motions were introduced to disband the military force, some Federalists allegedly admitted the soldiers were wanted "*to keep down internal enemies.*" Probably the government intended to use them to extirpate the faction that Adams had said must be "humbled in dirt and ashes." Certainly administrative henchmen opposed any move to question the constitutionality of (or do away with) the regiments, for Ross's election bill for a legislative committee to pass on Pennsylvania's electoral vote showed they had determined on measures which could only be effected at the point of the bayonet.[106] In May, 1800, however, the additional troops were ordered dismissed, and Republican joy was uncontained. Citizens were congratulated on this triumph of the popular will. Their support for the militia system was solicited in order to demonstrate "that we need not a standing army." In the eyes of Jeffersonians a great danger had temporarily passed.[107]

Defending liberties against attack was, nonetheless, but one phase in preserving them. If popular rights were to endure they must be disseminated and passed on to future generations. Persons unaware of their prerogatives, or of threats to them, might easily lose them beyond recall. To exercise their capacity to decide wisely on public questions the people must be fully informed. Naturally enough, as has been noted, Republican printers considered an unfettered press offered the best method for achieving this goal.[108]

Independent newspapers, they asserted, were not only a safeguard to freedom, but also an honor to the nation in which they were established:

444

For as through prejudice, error, pride, folly and a natural independence of spirit mankind will imbibe and maintain various and opposing opinions, it is only from a fair statement of the arguments on both sides of every subject, that just and solid principles can be deduced.[109]

Secrecy was ever questionable in government, which was why Republicans rejoiced when the Senate had opened its doors to the public and why the sessions and work of Congress should be fully reported. Knowledge benefited both government and populace. The former derived no real advantage from sycophants, for if anything went amiss in public affairs an administration profited by having that fact called to its attention. The best channel for conveying advice to those in power, as well as a safety-valve for pent-up popular emotions, was the newspaper. Only foolish governments or dangerous ones, then, would tax gazettes or so raise postal rates that their circulation was restricted.[110]

There were two methods of governing men—by *compelling* unanimity (which was the Asian and European method), or by having them govern themselves (as did Americans). Ruling was the art of controlling men's passions, "and if you make their reason do it for you, which it always will when enlightened, your work is done to your hand." [111] Ignorance was, so editors not surprisingly insisted, the foundation of aristocracies or of monarchical states. Hence those persons who would hamper the free flow of information were no friends of republicanism. Anyone who sought to compel uniformity of opinion, to stifle inquiry, or to limit freedom of the press was denounced as the most insidious foe of America and her liberties.[112]

Liberty of speech and press, so essential to wisdom and national prosperity, went together hand in hand with security of property. Only tyrants had reason to dread newspapers' "animadversions." "Misrepresentation of public measures is easily overthrown, by representing public measures truly." As long as governments deserved praise, they should have open commendation, ". . . but if they be . . . pernicious, they ought

445

to be publicly detested. The Liberty of the Press is the great bulwark of Freedom." [113]

The enemies of popular rights were fully cognizant of this truism. Thus, when Federalists inaugurated their system of terror by screaming of French invasions and of tubs and of tailors' plots, "and one-third of the alphabet [referring to the XYZ episode] were marched in dire array to affrighten the people" and to mask aristocratic designs,

> that powerful engine[,] the press, was next assailed; its importance to any political measure was too great to leave it unshackled, or to trust to the judgment of its conductors, a free exercise of its rights.

Congress, charged critics of Federalism, permitted Secretary of State Pickering to select the papers he pleased at the salaries he pleased, ostensibly for the printing of the laws—something most editors had previously considered a duty necessary for the information of the people. Pickering's activities riveted certain printers to the cause of the administration, for their incomes would be jeopardized by freedom of inquiry. Meanwhile, the Sedition Act was passed to suppress or intimidate the journals of the opposition. In Baltimore, for instance, the *American* noted that the *Federal Gazette* enjoyed the public printing, while the *Telegraphe* was "timid as a hare"; both refrained from publishing Duane's accusations of corruption in the central government. Apparently the editors thereof were either venal, frightened, or unaware of a newspaper's obligation to present both sides of the questions confronting the public.[114] In truth, the very principles of republicanism needed to be kept perpetually before the people. Each generation must ever recall that the freedom it enjoyed was a fragile trust, purchased with America's best blood, and that its primary duty was to transmit unimpaired to posterity this priceless inheritance.[115]

One other agency for inculcating democratic ideals and information formed an integral part of the Republican litany. The franchise might be men's birthright, but it was meaningless unless those men were enlightened.[116] Convinced of the significance of man's environment and of his capacity for infinite improvement, it was but logical that Republicans should be enthusiasts for public schooling.

As early as 1792 it was noted that the term "republicanism" was being used by many persons of dubious sincerity. They seemed unwilling to concede that

> the great cause of inequality is the difference of education. He that knows much will influence those who know little; and if those who know much are few, and those who know little are many, an aristocracy exists, which nothing but the general diffusion of knowledge can remedy.
>
> When will these men prove their republicanism by passing laws to establish free schools? Let the education of children become a common charge. If a man has property and no children, still he should be taxed to pay for the education of other men's children. The more knowledge, the safer his property. . . .
>
> Every day before this work is begun, is time lost. All other securities of Liberty without this are trifling. Let every state then divide its territory into proper districts, and establish at least one school in each. Make a beginning, and afterwards carry on the good work as fast and as far as possible.[117]

A leading exponent of this concept, until his untimely death in 1796, was Robert Coram, publisher of the Wilmington *Delaware Gazette*. Coram published a pamphlet (1791) urging a *"Plan for the General Establishment of Schools throughout the United States."* He petitioned the Delaware legislature to establish such a system in that state and enlisted the local Democratic Society in the effort. Coram viewed formal learning as a political question; a people intending to govern themselves had to be equipped with knowledge lest they be at the mercy of well-informed elites or fall victim to anarchy. In his eyes only through a general free education could "a pure Republican Government" survive—and at least some of his fellow editors concurred.[118]

Most assuredly all individuals were not, nor should they be, alike. But they were entitled to a like opportunity. Before men could fully realize their potentialities, superstition and ignorance had to be eliminated. Governments should therefore aid education, particularly in political wisdom, so that the people could recognize dark ambition and thwart its schemes.

To achieve such an end, Republican writers maintained that the newspapers were invaluable. They could hammer home the vital fact that freedom was both the sword and the shield of the common man and could expose the fallacies and perils of aristocracy and despotism. They could help inform the public, lead it to the realization that all forms of honest toil were respectable, and discourage both the unquestioning flattery of officialdom and the acquisition of more than moderate wealth.

Yet the press could not successfully perform these tasks by itself alone. Schools open to all should be founded, some for the very purpose of studying matters political. "Nor is the idea of a school for acquiring the nature of laws and government more absurd than of one for acquiring a knowledge of astronomy and mathematics." [119]

Politics was as dependent upon fixed principles as any other science. The New London *Bee* took pride in its student subscribers at distant William and Mary College. It expressed gratification that American youths were concerned with both learning and patriotism, for properly the two were interrelated. When the quest for knowledge was combined with love for "the principles of liberty and justice, education is of primary importance to the state, and the first blessing a citizen can receive." [120] Each generation's achievements would be evaluated by posterity; it therefore stood to reason that children should be educated at common expense. "To make mankind better, is a duty which every man owes to his posterity, to his country, and to his God; and . . . there is but one way to effect this important principle—which is—by incorporating education with government." A nationwide public school system, offering to pupils the best of the world's teachings, would provide the maximum guarantee for the preservation and efficiency of the democratic way of life. Only through information and instruction, available to all classes, could America's first principles be perpetuated.[121]

 CONSTITUTIONAL
GOVERNMENT:
REPUBLICAN
INTERPRETATION

However crucial were the principles of democracy, they did not develop, nor continue to exist, in a political vacuum. In the United States of the 1790s they were expounded and defended, albeit at times with difficulty, under a government established by the Federal Constitution. A favorite Federalist accusation was that the advocates of a number of these concepts were inimical to that Constitution. Repeatedly, and frequently heatedly, Republicans denied the charge. Many of them had striven actively for adoption of the document. Madison, possibly more than any other individual, had been instrumental in bringing it into being. Mere disagreement with those temporarily in power, they pronounced, in no sense betokened hostility to the fundamental law itself.

From the outset, therefore, Republicans had to evolve the philosophy of a loyal opposition. However meritorious was the Constitution, it "and the administration of it are different things." As courts sometimes reversed both law and equity, so, ran the argument, had Federalist officials subverted the Constitution. Through control of the press, abuse of opponents, and promotion of speculation in Congress, the moneyed interests had gained measures contrary to the basic charter and injurious to the general welfare. Calumny and charges of disloyalty were used to divert attention from such actions; true

449

friends of the Constitution would combat these efforts to pervert it.[1]

Actually, the administration itself interpreted that document differently at different times. In dealing with Algiers Washington held himself powerless to make financial contracts without prior legislative consent, yet to Britain he pledged millions of dollars on his own authority. During the negotiations with the Creeks, he sought senatorial advice, yet when Jay went to England the Senate was not even informed a treaty was to be made. If Washington himself were inconsistent, the national charter was plainly dependent upon the whim or design of whatever Chief Executive might be in power.[2]

Republicans were manifestly as loyal to the Constitution as was Hamilton. Had not that worthy once deserted the Convention and since schemed to change the document? His plan for funding the debt, soon monopolized by speculators, was a British-inspired machination to "engage the wealth of the country in the support of the administration." Adams' *Defence of the American Constitutions* was actually an argument for the English system rather than the American. Fortunately, few people were simple enough to regard the Constitution and the administration as identical. This was well, for today's minority might become tomorrow's majority, and thus should not be crucified for its opinions.[3]

Opposition to a good government was deplorable, conceded the *Aurora*. But by the same token so was support of a bad one. When a government became dominated by a faction and tried to destroy popular liberties, criticism was a mark of loyalty to the Constitution. Failure to protest would be criminal indeed.[4] The great Whig principles of the Revolution were recognized in the fundamental law, but a constant check was needed to ensure that the charter was not distorted. Some recipients of the public trust were ready to betray it. Supporters of the administration often displayed hatred for the sovereignty of the citizenry; was *this* loyalty to a document beginning with "We the people?"[5]

Federalism included all who had desired a monarchy in 1787, and in 1800 these men schemed to take election of the President "out of the hands of those in whom it was constitutionally reposed," and discussed abolishing the state constitutions. Officials seeking to weaken the power of the people should be dismissed as soon as possible. Individuals such as "Burleigh," who feared Jefferson might overthrow the Constitution, either forgot the President lacked power to change a single word of that charter or else admitted (as Democrats had always contended) an administration *could* affect its application.[6]

In its inaugural *"Political Confession of Faith,"* the *Republican Ledger* stoutly affirmed its belief "in the American constitutions, that they are congenial to the rights of man and are calculated to secure and defend the same." Stressing that the people could at all times investigate and hold accountable the public officers who served them, it continued: "I believe the administration of a republican form of government ought to correspond with the constitution, without which the bare name of freedom and republicanism 'is like the body without the spirit, *dead,* being alone.' " Many self-styled Federalists actually opposed popular rights, while other Americans who were traduced as Jacobins and disorganizers defended them.[7]

Yet splendid as it was, the Constitution was not perfect. Republicans had led the drive for the first ten amendments, and now some Federalists were attempting to expand the document into too grand a governmental edifice. If "high-flying Castle-builders," warned the *National Gazette,* overloaded the political structure with turrets and spires, it would collapse like the tower of Babel. America's government might be the world's finest, but there was still possibility of improvement. Changes were needed that would render it impossible to copy Great Britain's despotism. Shorter terms for senators would have blocked approval of Jay's Treaty. The house should share in diplomatic negotiations, and Supreme Court justices should be permitted no other offices.[8]

Some Republicans argued almost from the Constitution's

451

inception that it was a compact between the states. "CIN-CINNATUS" contended man's experience had shown a republican form of government unworkable if spread over too wide a territory or too many people. This did not mean, however, that monarchy was inevitable; a compromise was possible, and the framers of the Constitution had created one. They recognized the commonwealths as the Constitution's basis, and it was a contract among commonwealths rather than between the citizens and the government. He who opposed the idea of a league of thirteen states united for general defense and happiness was "truly an *antifederalist*." [9]

The states, "Brutus" concurred, assuredly did not surrender independence and sovereignty when joining the Union. Consolidation was "that many headed monster of power, that creature of monarchy and oppression." Despite all democratic belief in the people, majority rule could be dangerous. Hence Republicans opposed measures blurring state boundaries or jurisdictions. The Constitution specified that representation should be apportioned among the *states,* and creating excise zones that cut across state lines or establishing federal court districts were attacked as undermining the *"remaining sovereignty and independence of the individual states."* Federalists desired to eliminate state governments as genuine factors in political life; already the administration had "palmed an unconstitutional excise law upon a free people, and has used its best endeavours to dismember a member of itself by attempting to filch two-thirds of its territory, and put it under a guardianship of trustees." [10]

True federalism meant faith in a central government for national purposes, with states retaining their local autonomy, but the party appropriating the name demanded implicit obedience to all dictates of the central authority.[11] Debate over replies to the Virginia and Kentucky Resolutions had evoked some statements that the general government was "national" rather than "federal." This revealed a trend toward consolidation, and made it clear who were actually anti-federalists.[12]

Permitting states to be sued in courts of law was another

blow at state sovereignty. How could a commonwealth possess real authority if individuals could bring charges against it? *The Federalist* papers had denied such a contingency.[13] A "Citizen of the United States" might applaud making fraudulent states amenable to justice as were individuals, but practical men asked what the court would do if the state proved insolvent. Sending legislators to jail would not help, and to pay the judgment from the federal treasury would subvert republican government and the states themselves.[14]

Following the Supreme Court's ruling in *Chisholm* v. *Georgia,* which established that states could be sued, and word of a suit pending against Massachusetts, Governor Hancock called a special session of that state's legislature. He saw the Court's decision as crucial to schemes for absorbing the states as a prelude to monarchy; even England had assumed no such power over any of its colonies. Both Virginia and Massachusetts proposed an amendment voiding suits against states by individuals, and Republicans enthusiastically endorsed the suggestion, which was added to the fundamental law as the Eleventh Amendment in 1798.[15]

To be preserved, state governments must be guarded from all encroachments, however subtle, by national authority. A major argument for the Constitution had been that the states could check a central power's voracious appetite for control. That check evaporated, however, if federal officials could also hold state office—and several sat in legislatures. Likewise, federal courts would soon swallow all jurisdiction unless state attorneys were made equal to federal district attorneys. Massachusetts executive officers could not be legislators, and surely it violated the spirit of the law to seat national officials. The *Herald of Freedom* advocated returning to the old system of having the states pay the salaries of their senators and representatives.[16]

"President" John Sullivan of New Hampshire justified retention of his post after also becoming a Federal District Judge on the ground that when the state acceded to the Constitution she was no longer "sovereign and independent," and her previously drawn state constitution did not apply. Republicans venomously attacked this statement, for if one commonwealth had so lost her sovereignty, the others had lost theirs. Thus a paltry federal appointment could easily warp men's principles and sacrifice states' rights. When, as was inevitable, a conflict occurred between the interests of Congress and the several states, to which authority would men holding office under both give their loyalty? Federal Judge David Sewall was elected to the Massachusetts Senate, but Republicans cried "no man can serve two masters!" and that body refused to seat him. Emoluments from the administration were an effective, if insidious, way of extending national power. Collectors of federal taxes should similarly be denied positions under the state.[17]

Since Democrats of that day held the national charter was designed to place definite limits on governmental authority, they deplored the looseness with which Federalists interpreted the Constitution. After Hamilton's Report on Manufactures (1791) expanded upon the general welfare and "necessary and proper" clauses, the *National Gazette* asked if *anything* could be excluded from the purview of Congress. Before the Constitution was adopted, Hamilton had assured men that construction by implication was impossible, since it would lead to dictatorship and elimination of the states.[18]

The Invalid Pensions Act of 1792 instructed federal Circuit Courts to receive and report on applications for disability pensions for Revolutionary veterans. Pennsylvania circuit judges refused to entertain the claim of William Hayburn on the ground Congress could assign the courts judicial duties only, and Hayburn's succeeding petition regarding this first challenge to the constitutionality of a law attracted wide attention. Republicans generally applauded the judges' action and expressed hope the National Bank might encounter a similar fate. Federalists talked of impeachment, as though (sniffed the *General Advertiser*) "forsooth Congress were wrapped up in the cloak of papal infallibility, which has been torn from the shoulders of the Pope; and that it was damnable heresy . . .

to doubt the constitutional orthodoxy of any decision of theirs. . . ." Northern judges agreed to act as "commissioners" in pensions cases, but the *National Gazette* noted even this diplomatically indicated the unconstitutionality of the law. Despite the talk, no motion was made to impeach.[19]

Another administrative weapon was abuse of the treaty-making power—as Jay's compact, from inception to the required appropriations, proved. If the Executive were not here limited by the specific grants of power to other branches of the government, nothing in the Constitution would restrain him. Any inadequacy of authority should be remedied by amendment, not construction; if one department could absorb the others, government became one of men rather than laws and verged on despotism. Even Adams' peace moves in 1800 were suspect to some. Treaties often provoked a third nation to war, and the administration had expanded the covenanting authority alarmingly, in both foreign relations and domestic aggrandizement.[20]

If any agency had power to construe the Constitution, it was the several states, which were parties to the contract. Should Congress exceed its authority, was "there any alternative between an abandonment of the Constitution and resistance?" Did not state officers violate their oath to support the fundamental law if they enforced unconstitutional legislation? Congress, to be within its rights, must have been vested with positive power to pass any specific act, yet Federalist Judge Iredell told a Pennsylvania Grand Jury the grant of enumerated powers did not preclude the national legislature from having others. This European concept that the administration could do anything not expressly forbidden undermined the fundamental concept of American government. "A Constitutionalist" insisted the expediency of the measures was irrelevant; the key issue was their legality. If Congress could dictate where the Constitution was silent, America was a consolidated government indeed.[21]

Opponents of the administration dreaded adding to the authority of any branch of the federal government; this could be

455

done only by violating the principle of separation of powers or by weakening the states. In either event popular rights were endangered. The Judiciary Bill of 1800 exemplified another Federalist effort toward centralized authority, for federal districts crossing state lines might invalidate the elementary principle that parties should be tried in the state where the crime was committed. Which state's civil law should be applied when the district contained parts of two commonwealths? The world would marvel that Congress wasted even a day considering a measure so obviously unconstitutional. A Senate that advised the President, held the *Independent Chronicle* earlier, was no fit court for his impeachment trial. Checks were needed "against the designs of self[ish] interests." Other Republicans objected to Theodore Sedgwick's urgings that ambassadors should frequently be given almost unqualified discretion; this would deny the concept of limited national sovereignty.[22]

Some thought rendering Supreme Court judges ineligible for any other state or federal office would curtail undue executive influence over the judiciary. New York and Rhode Island had advocated this suggestion when adopting the Constitution. Appointment of Chief Justice Oliver Ellsworth as a commissioner to Paris in 1799 revived the proposal, and Congressman Edward Livingston urged banning judges from any federal post within six months after leaving office. Republicans grumbled that Federalist judges' charges to grand juries implied public servants could do no wrong. The Constitution separated executive and judicial powers; perhaps other nations did forbid aliens to come and stay at will, but America was unique—and to give the President sole authority to decide which aliens should be deported was unconstitutional. Associate Justice Iredell had noted publication of falsehoods was not one of the rights of man, but passing unlawful acts was no right of government.[23]

Separation of powers was vital, and particularly suspect was the growing might of the Chief Executive. That government was best that afforded the least opportunity for venality,

456

but the President could use patronage and funds to move toward omnipotence:

> Americans! . . . Recollect, upwards of *two millions* of dollars [are] annually at the disposal of the Executive! Reflect on this circumstance, and you must hold in execration the men who would advocate an increase of presidential influence: But there are such men; they call themselves Federalists!

Leasing of iron foundries during the crisis with France was similarly opposed. Supplies should be obtained by contract, which provided fewer chances for manipulation and surrendered far less power to the President.[24]

Already Adams was more puissant than George III. He had his own ministers, his presidential messages were not so subject to attack as a premier's speeches, and with his patronage went virtually unlimited power of removal. A king professing religion would never have invited an adulterer to dinner with his wife; if Jefferson *had* written the letter to Phillip Mazzei, his prophecies had come to pass.[25] Adams called on Americans to draw the sword and at first would have denied Congress access to the commissioners' report from Paris. If he had the exclusive right to decide on war or peace, America was even now a monarchy. The Alien and Sedition Laws, the "standing" army, and Ross's proposed electoral commission of 1800, were all unconstitutional efforts to strengthen the Executive.[26]

Publicity was at least a partial safeguard against infringements upon the rights of the populace and the reserved powers of the states. Americans were interested in their new government, the *Federal Gazette* noted, commenting proudly on the avidity with which subscribers read its accounts of the First Congress. Widespread information through newspapers had improved the government "by bringing it home to the door of every citizen." Full publicity focused on principles and characters and prevented impositions from lies and misrepresentations. True Americans would insist on their right to read all the facts, domestic and foreign. Only monarchists, or newcomers afraid of freedom, favored restricting knowledge.[27]

As Republican editor Thomas Cooper pointed out, bad governments undertook to shield themselves from investigation by preventing information and discussion. Tyranny fattened on ignorance. A good Republican editor, descanted "Democritus," should be impartial and lucid and should furnish the public with news as soon as he was convinced of its reliability. The merits of Republicanism rendered it unnecessary to delete information, print wild reports or use turgid rhetoric as did Federalist journalists. Yet since Democrats had no "loaves or fishes" to distribute and since innocence once corrupted was rarely restored, Jeffersonian printers had to remain firm against all blandishments. True Republicans deplored restrictions upon the press even in France, though they twitted Federalists who criticized that policy there and favored it in America. Officials in a republic possessed only those powers bestowed on them for the good of all; the people granting this authority possessed the right to limit it. Defamation of private citizens was punishable at law, and thus adequate protection was provided for public figures in their personal capacities. Even if unrestrained investigation hurt their reputations, they would at most only lose government offices in which they had no vested right. Administrators with the best of principles could still err; without a free press they might remain in office without censure. It was better to run the risk of some individuals' lost prestige than have a whole people deprived of their rights without their consent or knowledge.[28]

Secrecy in political matters, then, was always suspect, presumably inimical to the popular interest, and consistently opposed. From the first, Republicans viewed secret Senate sessions as an affront to American citizens. At the outset of Washington's presidency, opposition to titles was so effective on the floor of the House that representatives joined the public in reprobating them. Why were not the Senate doors open in order that people could identify the friends of liberty in that body? There was no valid reason for admitting the public to one chamber and excluding it from the other. Several state legislatures urged publication of debates and ordered their senators to work for open sessions. Bache slyly apologized for an error in his columns—"The Frontier Bill, is not lost in the Senate as was reported a few days since. Part only was rejected in the committee of the whole. Mistakes of this kind would not so often happen, were the doors of the Senate kept open." [29]

The public was kept ignorant even of the arguments favoring closed sessions. This was as dark as the mysteries of freemasonry; where people had to obey blindly, they were in effect slaves. Senators who might be tempted to court popular favor by disguising their sentiments from gallery visitors were unworthy of their posts, and only publicity could show citizens which of their delegates truly represented them. Some of the opposition to Adams' reelection as Vice President was attributed to his presiding so long over a clandestine body without altering the situation. Closed doors hinted at conduct that might not be upright and indicated contempt for the people.[30]

In 1793 Senate debates were held publicly, and two years later reporters were admitted,[31] but the Republican campaign against other instances of governmental secrecy continued. Congressmen sending lengthy letters to their constituents might find them reproduced, as an example for others to report on their actions, in newspapers far from their homes. Other writers denied the President's right to withhold documents from Congress, or even to present them to that body as confidential. Such procedure made Congress a mere puppet of the Executive. When Washington indicated he was sending only part of Gouverneur Morris' correspondence to the Senate, a sarcastic observer congratulated both senators and the people on being relieved of "the necessity of thinking for themselves." [32]

A House resolution in 1796 would have prohibited, until appointment of an official stenographer, publication of any extracts of congressional speeches without permission from the author. Republicans protested this would mean farewell to American liberties. Even England had no such policy; it was as if a clerk refused to permit an employer to examine his own ledger. The proposal to name a stenographer (who would in any event be but a mouthpiece for the body hiring him) had been withdrawn for some weeks. Full intelligence concerning public questions was vital in a country so vast as the United States. The duty of those near the seat of government was "to mark with a diligent eye the measures of Congress . . . and by a timely disclosure, to nip in the bud, the first blossoms of legislative encroachment." While printers sometimes mistook the sentiments of speeches, so also did other congressmen, and even stenographers were not infallible. Philadelphia editors had ever been ready to publish corrections; this resolution indicated either congressmen's shame concerning their own utterances or a desire to put a bridle on their constituents and strike a blow at the press.[33] Such objections presumably helped defeat the motion.

Speaker Jonathan Dayton's duplicate proposal in 1798 was similarly denounced. Bache demanded retention of open sessions and insisted on his duty as editor to print the debates in his *Aurora*. If his reserved seat for reporting were lost by refusal to submit to censorship, he vowed to sit in the gallery and transcribe as accurately as he could. Unintentional errors might thus result, but this move to deprive the public of quick and complete information would not prevent publication of the debates.[34]

Equally sinister were attempts of authorities to restrict dissemination of newspapers. As noted earlier, sizable circulation depended upon cheap mailing rates, and exchange privileges constituted the heart's pulse of most editors' supply of news.[35] Thus postal regulations vitally affected the gazettes. Efforts to raise rates, to tax the papers, or to limit the service in any way might doom anti-administration newssheets.

In early 1790 shrieks of remonstrance greeted the Postmaster-General's plan to tax newspapers for use of the mails. An impost of even one or two cents had "an obvious Tendency to shackle the Press . . . and degrade the Freemen of this country." Timothy Pickering had also requested a general prohibition on private transmission of letters, except for those borne by friends, special messengers, or known public carriers. Since most newspaper postriders often carried mail as well, this request could be interpreted as a further hindrance to wide distribution of printed matter. An amendment would have empowered Pickering to specify certain papers that could be mailed at reduced rates; critical editors applauded the defeat of this obvious attempt to foster a "court press." [36]

As agitation for some tax continued, resisting printers resorted to sarcasm. Pickering's request had earned him Americans' gratitude for promoting peace and order. Everyone realized that newspapers had fomented all the commotions that had plagued the country for the past twenty years. Their cheapness had enabled every ignorant plebeian to inform himself on political affairs, and then to take the liberty to criticize his superiors and to oppose the law of the land. A tax of only a penny per paper would so check circulation that none but citizens of the "rich and BETTER SORT"—whose good sense would not allow abuse of the government that gave them exclusive privileges—could buy them. So much capital might also be required for publishing that editors would be forced either to suspend printing or to accept bribes from the administration.[37]

The New York *Daily Advertiser* waxed poetic, in Freneau's style:

'Tis time to tax the news (old Gripus *cries*)
  Subjects were never good that were too wise:

. . . . . . .

[Papers at one time had been useful, in arousing
  the people against England.]
Those times are past; (my sentiments excuse)
  The well-born sort alone, should read the news,
No common horde intrude behind the scene
  To view the movements of the state machine:
One paper only, fill'd with pompous stuff,
  One paper for this country is enough.
That fill'd with gifts, from chaplains, 'squires, and quacks,
  *Shall have the merit to escape a tax.*' [38]

461

If the federal government "must stand or tumble" according to public opinion, a tax on newspapers was most unwise. It would generate suspicion, disturb the popular mind, and possibly lead to the horrors of anarchy.[39]

In reality "tax" was an emotional term applied by the press to an increase in postal rates. Papers had earlier been carried with the mails, at the will of the local postmasters, who were under no obligation to forward them. The act of 1792 charged a cent per paper for the first hundred miles, and a cent and a half beyond that.[40] Printers contended a blanket rate of a half cent would amply cover the cost of transporting the gazettes; any additional fee was an intolerable burden. Twenty to seventy dollars postage a week was more than most publishers could pay, and if they raised subscription prices circulation would drop. These new rates permitted London papers to be sent to Philadelphia more cheaply than could those of Savannah or Portland; was the administration trying to secure internal peace through ignorance? It rested with "the People themselves, who are the fountain of government, to *demand* the free circulation of political information. . . ."[41]

More intemperate writers considered the post office bill "a thousand times worse than the British Stamp-Act," and groups of newspaper subscribers met to protest the rates. Philadelphia editors, whose papers had a large national circulation, were especially interested, and some believed the postage charges (like closed Senate sessions) were designed to prevent diffusion of information concerning congressional proceedings.[42]

Thanks to Senate obduracy, the rates were finally adopted. Editors grumbled that the act contravened the First Amendment and showed the upper chamber foiled the popular will. Federalists claimed the charge was needed to cover expenses, but apparently no survey of costs was made until after passage of the law. Virginians thought the new rate bore out Patrick Henry's lugubrious prophecy—"When oppressions take place, our Representatives may tell us, we contended to your interests, but we could not carry our point, because the Representatives from New-Hampshire, Massachusetts, Connecticut, &c., were against us." Washington had advised Congress to cultivate enlightenment of its constituents, since public confidence was the soundest foundation for any laws enacted; printers noted this advice was at odds with postal charges that had "materially cramped the circulation of those truly valuable publications," the newspapers. Wistfully they hoped for a speedy repeal of the law.[43]

Many Federalist journals found the post office regulations disagreeable and joined Republicans in attacking them. Yet others emphasized that the law in no way violated freedom of the press, but only the right to transport papers by mail without cost. And the *Columbian Centinel* noted that giving newspapers postal status, and requiring postmasters to forward them immediately, made the circulation of news more speedy and effective than ever before.[44]

Whether Democrats agreed efficient mail service had been achieved or not, it was greatly needed. Editors frequently complained of irregularities in deliveries, and some suspected political motives produced them. Irrespective of the cause, printers who believed themselves guardians of the public weal were obliged to sound an alarm "whenever this sacred key to freedom and independence receives abuse."[45] Pickering had pledged to end the confusion even before the law of 1792,[46] but murmurs continued for years afterward. Oftentimes speculators in distant towns had later information than was available to reputable merchants.[47]

The epithet of "LIAR" was bestowed on the Postmaster-General for requesting an additional "tax" on newspapers in 1794 on the ground that they overburdened the mails and pre-empted space wanted for more valuable material. If mails were crowded, charged the Norwich *Weekly Register,* it was with privileged letters and packages from officials to their henchmen. "How much more authentic such communications are than the idle stories, and mutilated extracts which appear in a country printer's paper, where the Editor prints what he pleases. . . ." Another increase in rates was proposed in

463

1796, along with the suggestion that postmasters be empowered to refuse all papers on which the ink was not dry. Republicans were positive that copies of the *Aurora* and similar gazettes would be found slightly damp; they consequently applauded when the Senate dropped the bill.[48]

Accusations that Federalists tampered with the mails to handicap opposition publications or to benefit their own increased as the century neared its close. An early issue of the Baltimore *American* referred to the *"post-office persecution"* suffered by Republican printers. Editors of independent sentiments too often found themselves deprived of incoming mails, and their papers were delivered much more irregularly than if they had "abounded in federal fals[e]hoods, calumny and superstition." Even private letters to or from them were allegedly opened or destroyed, and many copies (chiefly "in those counties where the Post-Masters were *aristocrats*") of Callender's *Prospect Before Us* never reached subscribers to whom they had been addressed.[49]

When the local post office reportedly threatened to refuse handling the *Wilmington Gazette,* editor Hall made plans to get his papers circulated by private means, if need be. In Newark, Federalist postal officers had frequently damned the *Centinel of Freedom* to hell, and to judge from the irregular service had been sending mailed copies in that direction. Also, through "carelessness," at times newspapers were sent at the letter rate. English jurists held private correspondence inviolate even in times of greatest religious or political feeling, but Federalists unctuously published and republished the reputed letter of Jefferson "to the betraying Mazzei." The Massachusetts Essex Junto was probably behind the temporary refusal of the Salem stage to carry the *Constitutional Telegraphe,* and in New London Charles Holt offered a reward for the offenders who had destroyed or delayed copies of his *Bee* in the mails. Significantly, Federalist gazettes were rarely troubled with such problems.[50]

The loudest outcry, however, was reserved for the most direct attack upon freedom of the press—the Alien and Sedition

Acts. As the two measures have been linked in history texts, so were they in journalistic parlance of the time. A number of aliens had entered the publishing field, and many leading Republican editors had come from outside the country.[51] Democrats considered both acts as directed at the newspaper profession.

Federalists regarded foreign-born residents as potentially, if not actually, subversive. The danger from them and Americans of French sympathies was considered fully as menacing as that from abroad, and this xenophobia became an obsession as tension with Paris mounted. Also, restless Ireland had for years been attempting to throw off British rule, and the Society of United Irishmen had branches in America as early as 1794. Pro-Irish articles appeared frequently in Republican papers, and the outbreak of the Irish revolt in 1798 added British Minister Liston's influential voice to those calling Adams' attention to the threat from aliens in the United States. Federalist "conspiracy" tales aided this campaign, and Federalist editors opposed restricting the law to aliens of a nation with which America was engaged in actual hostilities.[52]

Satire was the chief weapon of the Republican press while the Alien Law was still pending. Since harboring known aliens without notifying a federal judge was forbidden, one hospitable Virginian bemoaned being required to send a courier 130 miles to the seat of government before he could offer dinner to a European guest. The New York *Argus*, in *"The Compliments of the Season"* portrayed the astonishment of two citizens upon seeing each other out of prison after passage of the act. In Philadelphia it was sarcastically rumored that English-born William Cobbett was so worried about the law he had consulted a lawyer about its application in his case.[53]

There was, of course, no danger to Cobbett when the law was finally passed. The President was empowered to deport without trial any alien he deemed dangerous. Jeffersonians stressed the obvious opportunities for harshness and injustice, stating that jurisdiction over friendly aliens was a prerogative of the states.[54] Federalists, who had previously proposed a

465

hundred dollar tax on naturalization, detested the tradition of providing political asylum. This law, a throwback to the Inquisition, was part of a plot to establish a military government that would aid British aristocrats when England crumbled.[55] America possessed ample means of dealing with unruly individuals, and did not the Constitution entitle aliens to equal protection as long as they were law-abiding? Liberty was in far more danger internally than it was from any foreign foe; a Congress that could overstep constitutional bounds and disregard the right of jury trial in one instance would "have little difficulty in doing it again." The number of aliens was so small that any idea they could threaten America's government was preposterous, but their departure could hurt economically. Over $2,000,000 was withdrawn from Philadelphia banks alone shortly after the introduction of the Alien Law, and the indicated loss of eight times that much to the nation as a whole would be but a fraction of the cost of the impending French war.[56]

Even more abhorrent was the Sedition Act, which Republicans saw as designed to secure "the insolence of office." Many Federalists associated freedom of the press with embarrassment in foreign relations and the scurrility and abuse heaped upon the administration by the opposition prints. Moderate ones cited English common law to the effect that this liberty meant freedom from prior censorship but not from libel suits, and Republicans charged Federalist eagerness to invoke the libel code. Some prosecutions for sedition were actually commenced before passage of the "gag bill," and Judge Peters (*United States* v. *Worrall*, April, 1798) had argued that there was a United States common law in addition to federal statutes.[57]

While the measure was still under consideration, the *Independent Chronicle* reprinted the First Amendment as a "COMMENTARY" on the Sedition bill. Tories were warned that the same restrictions might one day be turned against them. Rights granted to the people by the Constitution were not revokable by any legislative body.[58] This bill was clearly aimed at Republicans. A Federalist reportedly stated that once it became law they would *"begin first with* JEFFERSON *and* GALLATIN, *banish* them and then . . . take the others *one by one."* Violations of the spirit of the Constitution, acidly commented the New York *Argus,* had become a matter of course; this bill flagrantly contravened the letter as well. To laugh at the cut of a congressmen's coat would become treason, and Senator Uriah Tracy was commencing his "war of extinguishment" by starving the aliens among Americans. This bill, forecast the *Chronicle,* was the last gasp of an "expiring Aristocracy"; independence would "eventually arise with renovated lustre." Free nations permitted citizens to speak openly of their government; an administration that restricted public observations on its proceedings was of dubious integrity.[59]

Nonetheless, the bill passed. Anyone printing or uttering statements designed to bring Congress or the administration into disrepute was liable to a fine of not over $2,000 and imprisonment for not more than two years. Hamilton contended that the truth could be used as a defense, but Federalist judges insisted that it be proved to the full. Jefferson, who had predicted such earlier, was convinced the law was intended to suppress "the Whig presses." [60]

Eager Federalists could scarcely wait. Almost two weeks before enactment of the law, Benjamin Bache was arrested for libeling the President in connection with the published letters from Talleyrand. This made it difficult, according to the *Independent Chronicle,* "to determine *whether there is more safety and liberty to be enjoyed at Constantinople or at Philadelphia,"* and popular contributions were called for to assist Bache "in his struggle with power." Charges were also preferred against John D. Burk of the *Time Piece,* but it seems probable Bache's case led to introduction of the Sedition bill in the form that was finally adopted.[61]

With the statute now on the books, citizens were advised to hold their tongues and to make tooth-picks out of their pens. Mere mention of Congress by an allegedly unfriendly newssheet might be construed as bringing that body into contempt.

Again people were reminded that the act directly defied the Constitution, threatened liberty of opinion, and screened from scrutiny the conduct of their own government.[62] Since the law would not only "muzzle the press, but prevent the verbal communication of political truths" if some spy should overhear them, one wag suggested forming a "THINKING CLUB." The group could meet at 7:30 and begin to think precisely at 8:00 p.m. Men

> who may not have had the good fortune to be born *deaf & dumb,* and who consequently may have the treasonable infirmity of exercising the faculty of speech, in order to obviate every possibility of danger, may be accommodated with *Constitutional muzzles* at the door.
>
> The first question to be thought of is—How long shall we be permitted to think? Dumb waiters are provided.[63]

Forthcoming libel trials would determine whether the press could be the sentinel of liberty, or merely a "vehicle of *madrigals, rebuses,* and *lampoons* on the people—the *register* of deaths, births, and marriages." Federalists allegedly had caucused over outlawing thinking, but apparently Republicans would be able to exercise their cerebral processes a little longer. Some physicians, however, had predicted "from the silence which must shortly be observed, that the next generation will be born dumb!" And the defiant *Aurora* squibbed *"Something like treason, by the new bill":*

> Some time ago there were people so wicked as to think America could not have a worse man for President, than gen. Washington; but we learn that they have since, from the most complete conviction, acknowledged the error of their opinion.[64]

More seriously, was not a libel now whatever the President and a Federalist judge and grand jury chose to make it? The Executive ordered the prosecution, appointed the marshal, and named the judges. Noah Webster had called the Sedition Law "the fruit of opposition," but he would have been more accurate had he said "the fruit of *ambition.*" Whispers suggesting nullification began to appear. The *Centinel of Freedom* reasoned Federalists pretended the need for an unconstitutional measure to keep people in submission, yet if it were criminal to flout constitutional laws it should be equally so to obey unconstitutional ones. Unless the fundamental document were inviolable it served no purpose. Together with a record of the congressional vote, underneath a copy of the hated act, the *Palladium* printed a declaration by George Nicholas flatly branding it unconstitutional.[65]

Numerous popular gatherings in Kentucky, Virginia, Tennessee, and New York condemned the law and called on state legislatures to devise remedies against it.[66] Reports of a special session of the Virginia legislature were accompanied by predictions that that body of "true Americans" would promptly find the Alien and Sedition Acts oppressive and unlawful. Federalists were challenged to distinguish between the licentiousness they claimed to be eliminating, and a healthy freedom of the press required to acquaint people with their government. The line had never been clearly drawn. Actually the Sedition Law would encourage dishonesty, for it was an effort to make printers submissive to the will of a jealous administration. Even when the defendant proved the truth of an alleged libel, he still underwent the discomfort of a trial. Delaware Federalists seemed able to find little to say for the act, provoking the comment that "It must be a rotten measure, indeed, to defend which its friends cannot find a single plausible argument." If a Jeffersonian gazette carried a letter favorable to the law, this evidenced its support of free discussion, in contrast to the position of the government.[67]

Some boasted the aristocratic faction was "amazed and paralyzed" at the hardiness with which Republicans defied oppression and congressional denunciation to maintain an unshackled press. Demand for the *Aurora* had increased since Bache's persecution. Threats and stupid Federalist stormings of collusion with France only proved an unconstitutional law could not repress the rights of free men. The people of the nation would "teach their SERVANTS that their liberties are not to be parted with, with impunity." [68]

Trials under the act were termed travesties. As was natural

in presidential appointees, judges were partial.[69] Juries were packed; that in the case of Congressman Matthew Lyon had been deliberately chosen from towns known to be hostile to him.[70] In any event, libel and slander were common law offenses, over which federal courts had no jurisdiction; the Constitution gave them criminal authority only over treason and piracy.[71] Moreover, virtually every federal judge had pronounced the act constitutional in preliminary charges to grand juries before any case had actually occurred. While the truth was supposed to constitute a valid defense, judges allegedly misconstrued the law to require proof for opinion as well as fact and rendered this provision no protection for the accused.[72]

Stories sympathetic to defendants crowded Jeffersonian gazettes. The *Guardian of Freedom* cynically contrasted the fine speech of America's commissioners to France with actual practice in this country. The commissioners had informed Talleyrand that "In the United States no individual fears to utter what judgment or his passions dictate, and an unrestrained press conveys alike to the public eye the labors of virtue and the efforts of particular interests." Underneath was the word that Benjamin Bache, of the *Aurora,* and John D. Burk and James Smith, editors of *Time Piece,* had been arrested for publishing libels against the government. Burk was never brought to trial, although even after a rift between him and Smith the *Time Piece* portrayed the editors as persecuted for suggesting the letter Adams sent to Congress as Elbridge Gerry's was a forgery.[73] The arrest of William Durrell, editor of the Mount Pleasant, N.Y., *Register,* for reprinting a "libel" on Adams from the *New-Windsor Gazette,* was widely heralded as another instance of administrative oppression.[74]

On October 25, 1798, the *Independent Chronicle* announced that its editor, Thomas Adams, had been arraigned before the Federal Circuit Court for seditious publications. Promising continued support of the Constitution and popular rights, the paper stated it would not endeavor to prejudice the public mind by pre-trial comments. Nevertheless, four days later it contended a construction never intended by their authors had been placed on its articles, while vilification in the Federalist press passed unnoticed.[75]

Matthew Lyon, tried and convicted some two weeks earlier, was given a martyr's role. At first denied writing materials in his cell, the Vermont congressman later sent out letters on the unfairness of the trial and the inhumane treatment accorded him. He had been prosecuted for stating he could not support Adams when men of merit were dismissed from office for independent thinking and public welfare was subordinated to pomp and avarice. He had also published Joel Barlow's letter from Paris calling Adams' accusations of dishonesty and piracy against that nation insane. His fine of $1,000 was unduly heavy, and Lyon held the jail sentence further disclosed the court's vindictiveness. The marshal in whose custody he was placed was a personal foe who had unnecessarily paraded him through the town of Vergennes under guard. His prison had little light and no heat, but he vowed if he lived to make the runoff race for congressman to which his plurality had entitled him. Probably it was fortunate that Bache had died of yellow fever before he too was tortured with the Sedition Law.[76] "The place of *victim Lyon's* confinement is without shelter from a freezing northern climate, or fire-place to dispell the chilling damps—" shrieked the *Aurora*. "If he should be frozen to death, *could an honest* jury bring in a verdict?—MURDER!" [77]

John Marshall, newly returned from France, was quoted as deeming the Alien and Sedition Acts inadvisable and unnecessary. Republicans opposing him for Congress regarded this as tantamount to holding them constitutional; otherwise he would have stressed their illegality as the strongest argument against them. Yet in France he had clearly indicated liberty of the press was constitutionally protected in America. At best he sought election to a body he had openly condemned as acting unwisely.[78]

One Jerseyman, overheard expressing the wish Adams were dead, was immediately arrested. Democrats admitted the sentiment was improper, but argued that prosecution for it showed American liberty had nearly vanished. Federalist animosity toward civil rights, they charged, could be traced as far back as the defamation against the Democratic Societies. Americans had possessed more freedom under Britain. Then one could criticize King George, "But *John Adams* is not to be censured; he is immaculate!" The President's own memory was conveniently short—in earlier writings he had exhorted the press to *"be not intimidated . . . from publishing with the utmost freedom, whatever can be warranted by your country. . . ."* [79]

Charles Holt mordantly summarized the "Creed of a Federalist Editor." Convinced that offices and emoluments were the exclusive prerogative of Federalists, and poverty and persecution the lot of Republicans, the "editor" determined to side with the former. He repented earlier attempts to inform the people with candor and objectivity, and to cast doubt on the wisdom of the faultless administration. Though the nation was united and ready to defend its rights, the government was in danger of being overthrown by seditious aliens and others and in its sagacity had freed the press on one side and rendered those printing anything on the other liable to fine and imprisonment. Therefore it had been resolved "to make the politics of our paper in the future *strictly federal;* which is to say, we will publish, every thing that can be said (whether true or false) to serve the cause of England, aristocracy and despotism, against France, democracy and liberty." [80]

Republicans utilized political pressure as well as ridicule and invective. Massachusetts voters desiring a land tax and spies enforcing a Sedition Law were enjoined to elect Harrison Gray Otis, who had favored those measures. A liberty pole was raised in Dedham against the acts, and the ringleaders were tried for sedition.[81] Jefferson regarded the Alien and Sedition Laws as tests to see if the people would endure even greater infractions of the Constitution. Next step would be to make Adams President for life. He drew up a set of resolves, which were presented to the Kentucky legislature in November, protesting the unconstitutionality of the statutes. Inasmuch as Governor Garrard of that state had already uttered similar opinions, the famous Kentucky Resolutions passed in short order.[82]

These received wide attention. In brief, they defined the Constitution as a compact between the states, which could judge for themselves when the agreement had been violated. Congress possessed power to punish only a few specified crimes, such as treason and violations of international law; moreover, the First Amendment expressly forbade interference with freedom of speech or press. Control over aliens was reserved to the states, and the article temporarily prohibiting federal interference with the slave trade had stated: ". . . the migration . . . of such persons as any of the *States* . . . shall think proper." Loose construction of the Constitution destroyed all limitations prescribed by that document; since the Alien and Sedition Acts were unconstitutional, Kentucky called on her sister states for concerted action to declare them void and to secure their repeal.[83]

Federalists immediately pilloried the resolves. Pickering's abusive reply affronted Westerners, and others referred to Kentucky Attorney General George Nicholas' inflammatory style and "the disorganizing legislature of Kentucky." Publisher Beaumont (of the *Palladium* and the Washington, Ky., *Mirror*) was accused of organizing popular support for the legislative action.[84]

Democratic gazettes either ridiculed their opponents' rage and threats, or called on other legislatures to follow suit. The *Centinel of Freedom* applauded, and asked New Jersey citizens if they would stand idle while the Constitution was trampled under foot.[85] Pennsylvanians were similarly adjured, and the Virginia Assembly did adopt John Taylor's and Madison's similar resolutions late in December, 1798. Virginia lawyer George Hay called on Adams to admit the doubtful constitutionality of the Acts. Elected officials possessed only the authority expressly granted to carry out their duties. Yet history showed that individuals so selected sometimes endeavored to usurp power, and one abuse by persons or state legislatures did not justify another by the national government. Constitutional decisions should be affected only by the immutable principles of reason and truth.[86]

Federalists retorted that Virginia in 1792 had enacted an alien law more arbitrary than the federal one she reprobated; they blamed the press for the agitation and asserted that most of the population even in Kentucky did not oppose the ordinances.[87] The resolutions were the work of blackguards and showed the extent of disruptive French influence. Virginia wanted to dissolve the Union, though loyal citizens feared nothing from the operation of the laws. Administration supporters asked state legislatures to reject the resolutions, or better still to dismiss them without discussion.[88]

Despite numerous petitions, the legislatures refused to endorse the protests.[89] "A snapped decision," snarled the *Centinel of Freedom,* when New Jersey's legislature declined to debate the resolves. At least the question merited serious consideration; a fair study would have discredited the noisome laws. Fearful Massachusetts Federalists, resorting to belittling and slander rather than reason, rammed through that state's rejection of the resolutions before nearly three-fourths of the House members had arrived at the seat of government. Republicans challenged opponents to explain a sovereignty that afforded the sovereign no right to define invasions of its constitutional rights. Failing this, most persons would think legislators who took an oath of allegiance to Massachusetts and still opposed the Resolutions were forsworn.[90]

The *Aurora* publicized remonstrances against the Sedition Act, the "tyrannical and degrading effects" of which were bringing the nation ever closer to monarchy. It printed the Virginia and Kentucky Resolutions, but had remarkably little to say about them as such.[91] Since the resolves were unpopular in many parts of the country, Republican newspapers generally reprinted them and approved their determining the Alien and Sedition Laws unconstitutional, but hesitated to accept the doctrine that a state could decide for itself whether or not to obey a federal law. The South, however, was more inclined to regard the states fully as competent as the federal courts to interpret the national compact.[92] Ugly rumors circulated that Virginia planned armed resistance to the detested statutes, but that state's press vigorously denied the accusation. The Old Dominion, said "VIRGINIUS," had never refused submission to any law, "however oppressive or unconstitutional." Criticism of the administration and demands that it return to the Constitution were very different from defiance of the government.[93] Madison's Report of 1799, defending the Resolutions, demonstrated the Constitution was ratified by states rather than by the people as a whole. While the Resolutions were not in themselves a campaign issue in 1800, they admirably served the same purpose as do issues in modern political platforms.[94]

Certainly opposition to the laws *per se* continued apace. Arrests for sedition were invariably condemned in Republican columns. A series by "Hortensius" denounced the Sedition Act as dangerous, calling it an illegal "attack on the liberty of the press." [95] Matthew Lyon, reelected to Congress, wrote from jail that the vote corroborated the splendid sentiments of the Virginia and Kentucky Resolutions.[96] Twenty years earlier, noted the *Bee,* a flagstaff with the American standard was called a liberty-pole and cherished accordingly. Now it was a "Sedition-Pole," subject to destruction by the federal government, as by the British in '75. True, the British were tyrants, but American administrators were not, "for the Sedition Law forbids our calling them so." [97] Judge Alexander Addison, of the Pennsylvania Supreme Court, was castigated for attempting to undo the Zenger case in restricting juries to a mere determination of whether or not the alleged libel had actually been printed. Obviously, this would render trial by jury meaningless; moreover, Addison's view that even some truths were not "proper for publication" evinced desire to court the smiles of power rather than to promote patriotism, truth, or the rights of man.[98]

Continued strictures against the measures brought legal action against the *Independent Chronicle*. Feared and hated by Boston Federalists, who had publicly burned copies on Independence Day and had expelled its editor from a local fire company, it was too prominent to escape application of the Sedition Act.[99] As noted, Editor Thomas Adams was arraigned in October, 1798, and scheduled to stand trial the following June. His accusation that Massachusetts assemblymen who rejected the Virginia and Kentucky Resolutions thus violated their oaths of office brought proceedings in earnest.[100]

In a second action, Thomas Adams and his younger brother Abijah were both indicted. Since physicians' statements attested the seriousness of the former's illness (he died in May), only Abijah was actually arrested. He was merely the bookkeeper, but the Federalists' intent was clear. "THE CHRONICLE is destined for persecution," cried the paper, reaffirming an intention to support popular liberties without wavering. It pledged later details of the indictment and trial, but in the meantime scorned to bias its "numerous readers on this subject." No more appeared until Abijah was found guilty of publishing (through aiding to distribute) the objectionable statements that the court, following English common law, held libelous. Young Adams received thirty days, with quarters at first so miserable friends prevailed upon the jailer to give him decent accommodations.[101] Six issues of the paper carried the entire trial, and (since Judge Francis Dana had called English common law Americans' "birthright") Adams' completion of his sentence was hailed as indicating he had partaken "of an *adequate proportion* of his '*birth-right.*' " [102]

Of such stuff is martyrdom made, and Jeffersonians utilized the opportunities. The co-editors of the *Harrisburger Morgenröthe* were arrested in August and placed under excessive bail for alleged sedition.[103] Pickering sought prosecution of Jacob Schneider when the *Readinger Adler* advocated voting against Senator Ross as one of the "political murderers of our liberty." [104] Newark's Luther Baldwin undoubtedly used poor taste in expressing hope that a saluting cannon would find its target in President Adams' posterior. But did that justify a companion turning informer and warrant a $150 fine? Jefferson was an officer of the government, also, and order-loving Federalists said worse things about him by the hour.[105] Charles Holt's *Bee* had only to comment unfavorably on the standing army to be indicted for sedition discouraging recruiting. Democrats considered Holt an obvious victim. Connecticut was full of lawyers ready to prostitute their talents, and the *Bee* was almost the only paper in which that state's citizens could express their honest opinions of men and events.[106]

Recently widowed Ann Greenleaf was already under indictment for articles advocating liberty-poles and attacking the Alien and Sedition Laws when her *Argus* carried a letter accusing Hamilton of an effort to buy out the *Aurora*. Suit for libel was commenced at once, even though the letter had earlier been published elsewhere; the zeal of the *Argus* in the cause of republicanism had marked it for destruction.[107] Jersey Democrats were warned to refrain from "talking truths that *hate the light*," lest they be gagged. Sedition trials had lost their novelty, but some persons were low enough to be bribed to inform on their neighbors "for a thoughtless expression." Charges filed against the *Aurora* were not immediately pressed; exultant Jeffersonians saw the Pennsylvania Republican victory of 1799 as retribution for the authors of the Sedition Act. Even Federalists saw the unwisdom of bringing Duane to trial.[108]

In some instances repression appeared to succeed. Thomas Adams died, and the *Independent Chronicle* was cowed for some time after Abijah's imprisonment.[109] Mrs. Greenleaf was forced to sell the *Argus* two months before the New York elections of 1800.[110] But for the most part the laws backfired, and protests against them as tyrannical continued to appear.[111] English-born philosopher Thomas Cooper outlined the process by which, were he so inclined, he could overthrow American democracy. Undermining the Constitution by implied powers and stifling liberty through a sedition law were the first two steps. Next in order came deriding of the rights of man, excluding immigrants who might spread ideas of free-

477

dom, keeping only sycophants in office, securing clerical support by a show of religion, favoring moneyed classes over farmers, and raising a large army and navy. All these the Federalists had achieved, with their siren song of "confidence in the executive." [112]

Kentucky's legislature reiterated its protest, denying it was the only dissatisfied state. True friends of the Constitution tried to preserve it from destruction.[113] The administration showed further discrimination when Duane was held for $4,000 bail (a fortune to one not a speculator or without the money-making opportunities of public office) after a half-dozen armed ruffians had been freed on a twentieth of that sum.[114] Federalists belittled the Vice President and part of the House and openly threatened Virginia's legislature with the vengeance of national power. Yet those who were "for enslaving the people" were warned no government long endured after it had lost public confidence, as "the people are the Government." The number of Republican prints had "considerably increased" since passage of the laws, showing the breath of persecution only fanned the embers of liberty into flame.[115]

Irish immigrants petitioned for repeal of the Alien Act, which discouraged industry and wealth from coming to America. And those who had forfeited their rights as human beings by leaving their native lands were counselled to remain inconspicuous in America and certainly not to enlist in the army of the nation that proscribed them.[116] Kentucky aliens seeking naturalization were told they could take advantage of the old five-year residence requirement until June 18, 1799, and the steps to be followed were outlined.[117]

Virginia's legislature also reinsisted that the laws were dangerous and unconstitutional. If it were impossible for a President and Congress to betray their trust there would be no provision for impeachment. Yet the only ground for impeachment lay in public examination of official conduct, and the Sedition Act outlawed the procedure. This could eventually either destroy the governmental system or provoke "a convulsion that might prove equally fatal to it," although Virginia again denied any intent to rebel. Vermonters conceded the importance of national rights, but a happy and prosperous Union depended also upon those of the states. With, in Fenno's homely simile, the old sow now ready to swallow up her pigs, even some Federalists allegedly believed the state assemblies possessed authority to investigate the constitutionality of federal laws.[118]

Other Republican writers tautologized that many administration men had deliberately voted for a law they knew to be unconstitutional. North Carolina's Senator Alexander Martin had clearly shown the bill illegal in 1798—and then said "aye" immediately afterward, reportedly feeling "the *damn'd printers*" had become so abusive they had to be checked, irrespective of the Constitution. Now his remarks prior to the vote would constitute ground for imprisonment.[119] South Carolina seemed less violently opposed than other Southern states, but allegedly had its Assembly session been longer the Virginia and Kentucky Resolutions would have received another endorsement.[120]

Additional trials demonstrated Federalist ruthlessness. With Mrs. Greenleaf already scheduled to be tried, David Frothingham, journeyman printer on the New York *Argus,* had admitted setting the type for the letter about Hamilton. As a result he languished in the New York Bridewell. The affair demonstrated Hamilton's "gentle, forgiving spirit and magnanimity"; the letter's truth was not allowed to be proved, it had been printed in three papers before the *Argus,* and the decision made liable every apprentice concerned in publishing the piece. Frothingham had a large family dependent upon him, and the whole matter revealed

> the little, vindictive spirit of a pretender to importance[,] and the generosity of a man, unknown to fame, at least of a bad kind, who voluntarily stepped forward to shield his employer from the revenge of a spiteful prosecutor. The mighty commander in this business *out generalled* himself.[121]

Nearly three months before Holt's own trial, readers of the *Bee* were informed publication would be suspended on April 2,

1800, "for a length of time not to be determined by the Editor." Subscribers were requested to settle their accounts and to trust the paper would "not die, but only SLUMBER." The printer had concluded an equal number of enemy troops would produce less damage and uneasiness than the disorderly soldiers of the army (which he called "standing," rather than "provisional") he had observed.[122] Republicans wanted to know why the term "standing army" was seditious; England's mutiny bill was passed annually for a military establishment regarded as permanent. But maybe "provisional" was a better term for men who did nothing but eat provisions. "Standing" implied the troops would stand and face the enemy. So many attended the trial that court was moved to a church, but Holt was sentenced to three months and a $200 fine.[123]

Connecticut Federalists regretted the punishment was not heavier, but Republicans snorted at the "land of liberty" and unctuously sympathized at Holt's fate. After completing his term, the printer promised to enlarge the revived *Bee* and to serve the public with equal zeal and more prudence, having learned to appreciate freedom more than ever.[124]

Almost simultaneously occurred the more famous trial of Thomas Cooper in Philadelphia. Though for some time his *Sunbury and Northumberland Gazette* had maintained a running fire against the administration, the actual charges against Cooper were based on handbills refuting the accusation his attacks originated in resentment at not receiving a federal appointment. Widely reprinted in Republican papers, these bills branded Adams an incompetent who created a permanent army and navy as personal tools and arbitrarily interfered with federal courts by ordering the surrender of Jonathan Robbins to the British.[125]

During the trial, Cooper argued his remarks dealt only with the President's public actions—constitutionally legitimate subjects for observation. Refused certified copies of Adams' speeches, he read newspaper extracts to support his statements. He also asked that Adams be summoned as a witness, but this too was denied. "An Enquirer" pretended bewilderment at the denial; surely the President's high office did not exempt him the obligations of justice and humanity. If every partisan judge could decide what witnesses should be admitted, popular liberty was indeed at an end. And why were authenticated copies of presidential answers to laudatory addresses during the XYZ crisis withheld? If Adams wrote such answers they could not be libelous; if he did not they could be openly disavowed. Slyly, "An Enquirer" noted administration foes would ask who would ever be acquitted if the Executive disavowed his own acts, prejudged testimony, and rejected witnesses? Owning he could not answer this, he hoped someone could.[126]

The trial won considerable space in Jeffersonian columns. Convicted, Cooper was fined $400 and sentenced to six months in prison. While he was incarcerated, some Federalist friends in Northumberland petitioned Adams for his pardon. Cooper thanked them by a letter to the *Aurora,* but said he preferred to stay in jail until Adams had publicly apologized for the treatment accorded Joseph Priestley and himself. Otherwise a pardon would be merely a campaign trick, and he wanted to be no "cats-paw of electioneering clemency." [127]

The defendant served his full term, and his release in October, 1800, proved that prison had not dampened his republicanism. When Hamilton's notorious "confidential" letter against Adams reached the press, Cooper obtained a copy and announced plans to prosecute him for sedition. Calling on Hamilton to acknowledge his authorship, he averred the letter damned the President more completely than ever had any Republican. Though the press of business kept Cooper from pushing the matter, exultant Jeffersonians felt the incident further discredited the Federalists and their odious laws.[128]

Securing contributions for imprisoned printers was one method of demonstrating Republican solidarity, but it also landed the *Vermont Gazette*'s Anthony Haswell in jail himself. The paper had criticized the treatment of Matthew Lyon, had pilloried "Old Tories" in public posts, and had advertised for a lottery to raise Lyon's fine. For this Haswell

481

paid $200 and served two months, but he insisted his conscience was clear and he would not exchange his cell for a palace in Washington. If his friends would only aid his family and visit him occasionally he would be happy.[129]

Publicized almost as much as the Cooper trial was the contempt charge against William Duane. The *Aurora* had bitterly damned James Ross's bill for creating an electoral commission to count the votes in the coming election of 1800. Duane called it a barefaced attempt, in conjunction with a scheme to divide Pennsylvania into electoral districts, to win by fair means or foul. He also decried the system of secret caucuses by which the bill was framed as a vicious means of enabling an actual minority of the Senate, by binding all members of the caucus, to dominate the lawmaking body. Furious Federalists haled him before the Senate for violating its privileges.[130]

Apparently the case was a shrewd Republican seizure of a chance to manufacture favorable public opinion. Vice President Jefferson sat in the Senate chair, and letters show Duane had discussed the course of action with him, Thomas Cooper, and Alexander J. Dallas. The editor challenged senatorial jurisdiction and requested counsel, which was allowed him with the understanding it would be limited to cross-examination. Duane, as planned, asked Cooper and Dallas to serve, and they answered that the Senate had prejudged the case and the limitation imposed upon them would be equivalent to a gag. Publishing these replies, the *Aurora*'s editor thereupon declined to appear again without a lawyer; the Senate voted him in contempt and issued a warrant for his arrest. Duane eluded the sergeant-at-arms until a monster petition (arguing that the condemnation violated both freedom of press and the right of jury trial) on his behalf was presented to the Senate. It was read before that body, and the case was then dropped, but the feeling engendered may have partly accounted for the viciousness of the prosecution against Cooper.[131]

Last of the important sedition trials [132] was that of James Thomson Callender of the Richmond *Examiner*. Of all the defendants he merited the least sympathy, yet his trial was probably the most unfair. He had printed a vulgar, scurrilous pamphlet, *The Prospect Before Us,* but witnesses could not testify as to its accuracy until after the questions asked them had been approved by Justice Samuel Chase. A fanatically partisan Federalist, Chase finally imposed his will on the court. He contemptuously disparaged Callender throughout the trial and expressed his pleasure at the verdict of guilty. Callender was fined $200, sentenced to nine months, and placed under bond for two years' good behavior.[133]

The *Examiner*'s editor continued writing from the Richmond jail. Though he described it as one of the most loathsome in the world, his enemies opposed letting him out for a breath of air. He advised them to indulge their hatred while they might, for March 4 next would end their opportunities. His letters, contending that Hamilton's pamphlet against Adams confirmed many of the statements for which Callender had been indicted, were published in the local papers and attracted more attention than had they been composed in a conventional office. Virginia had expressly reserved freedom of the press in adopting the Constitution; she was now urged to exercise her sovereignty and free the prisoner.[134]

Democrats insisted the bias so evident in Callender's case was typical; intolerance and favoritism were Federalist characteristics. No Democratic mobs had ever molested administration printers or threatened congressmen for their opinions, while a New Jersey colonel said if a *"staunch jury"* did not soon suppress the *Centinel of Freedom* his troops would.[135] The records of Adams, Jefferson, and Pinckney should be equally open to investigation in 1800, but those who libeled Jefferson went unpunished while Republicans who said half as much against Adams were jailed. "Porcupine" and Fenno, noted the *Independent Chronicle* (reverting to form as Jefferson's victory appeared more likely), criticized the President, but it was noticeable *they* had not been indicted for sedition. Unfair judges were warned they were accountable in the next world even if they escaped retribution in this one.[136]

483

Justice Chase was held to be only the ringleader in a gigantic witch hunt. Printers of the chief Republican newspapers were singled out as targets, for most states above North Carolina had their sedition cases.[137] Chase's gross unfairness in the Cooper trial had been followed by attempts to coerce grand juries to indict the editors of the Baltimore *American* and the Wilmington *Mirror of the Times;* against Callender in Virginia he had succeeded. The judges generally were Federalist partisans.[138]

Republicans stressed the pernicious consequences of both iniquitous laws. During the summer of 1800 a Canadian paper purportedly blamed America's controlled press and illiberal legislation for the moving of four hundred families within a month north across the border. The Lancaster *Intelligencer* stormed, "It may very well be called a Revolution, when the *British colonists* of Canada, point at the *Republican Freemen* of the United States . . . and, laughing with scorn, compare their condition with ours." [139]

Expiration of the Alien Act was greeted with joy. Federalists said Republicans reviled it owing to fear for their favorite, Gallatin, and asserted no native Americans had been prosecuted for sedition, but Jeffersonians gave them the lie direct.[140] Though the Alien Law had never been enforced— through clemency, Federalists assured everyone—Democrats celebrated its demise. If never used, it had been obviously unnecessary, but as part of a system of terror contrived to keep the governing faction in power its memory would serve "to perpetuate a merited sentence of condemnation" on Adams' policies. Immigrants could now rejoice that America for them was no longer convertible into "a mere bastile of executive discretion"; the only regret was that so "cruel and unconstitutional" a law should have existed for its full two-year lifetime.[141] Several writers now called for encouragement of immigration; Americans had all been aliens at one time, and naturalization should again be facilitated. This would please thousands who had fled to America for asylum from the "oppression of our good ally George III." A poem, "ON THE

ALIEN LAW," related how Ireland wept at her lost liberty until she found it in America. After 1798 she was forced to weep again, for affliction confronted her where she had hoped to find redress:

> Reflect Columbians! on the ungenerous part;
> Let indignation kindle in each heart;
> Strong on your memories impress the fact,
> *Elect not him, who sanctioned this* act.[142]

The Sedition Law, however, also exclusively for Republicans, remained in force somewhat longer. John Ward Fenno could publish a pamphlet on how the growing power of the central government was destroying the Union; punning on the name of the detested jurist, the *Virginia Argus* noted his statements would make "excellent game to *Chase,* if it were not that the sedition law was made for a particular party." In the coming election Adams' conduct remained screened behind the unconstitutional statute, while Jefferson's was exposed to full examination and the extremes of slander.[143]

Tench Coxe, dismissed over two years previously as Commissioner of Revenue, in 1800 published a letter claiming Adams was a monarchist at heart. Republicans praised Coxe, whose charge Adams denied, though they warned he was exposing himself to persecution for sedition. Coxe claimed Benjamin Rush had informed him of the monarchical wishes of several prominent figures in and out of public life; when Rush declined to support his allegation against Adams, Coxe accused him of fear or being bribed by a federal appointment. From his cell Callender gloated, but wistfully wished this evidence had been available for his own trial.[144]

By this time Hamilton's afore-mentioned attack on Adams had appeared, through the courtesy of Aaron Burr. Jeffersonians reveled in this assault and in Webster's riposte at Hamilton in defense of the President. The public was now treated to pictures of Federalist leaders as painted by themselves. But the Sedition Act should be applied without respect for persons; Hamilton, at least, should be prosecuted.[145] Accordingly, Cooper made his gesture of threatening suit.

485

Indisputably, the Sedition Law was a key issue in the 1800 campaign. Federalists continued to cry that undoubted Democratic falsehoods (such as claiming their property was assessed more heavily than that of administration supporters) proved need for the measure, but popular sentiment against it was too high. Were there no other reason for compelling Adams and his adherents to leave public office, pronounced "A REPUBLICAN" in South Carolina, the Sedition Act would be more than sufficient. There should be no risk of even seeming to approve so clear an attack on the Constitution and the rights of man.[146]

The election returns proclaimed, exulted the Georgetown *Cabinet*, that Americans were "A Seditious People!" The majority had decided Adams was unfit for the Presidency. For saying much less than this, many Republicans had "been immersed in fines or immured in prisons. Where are now the advocates of the Sedition Law? . . . Shall the PEOPLE go unpunished?" Thomas Cooper insisted the statute had been unfair to the last; it had not been applied to Hamilton after all. But Jefferson had become President-elect, so no charges would be brought, for his administration would not be stained by any such persecutions.[147] A Jeffersonian toast relative to the ordinances deemed so contrary to the Constitution proved more than prophetic: "The Alien and Sedition acts—May they remain only like ornamental marble over the memory of the party that erected them. . . ."[148]

# XIII
## REPUBLICAN POLITICAL STRATEGY

In the warfare of politics the successful force, believing the best defense is a good offense, sometimes creates issues instead of waiting for such to develop naturally. And at nearly all times it has some techniques, standing operating procedures, to apply respecting questions of almost every sort. In the absence of more favorable opportunities these techniques come to constitute campaign material in themselves.

A most popular weapon in the political arsenal of both Republicans and Federalists was what later analysts have designated "name-calling." It appealed to fear or hate rather than to reason. If the labels newspapers applied to opponents and their policies gained currency, the labels would produce, without supporting evidence, unthinking popular rejection of the groups and ideas under attack.

Though there exists no evidence of definite Federalist plans to establish a monarchy during that party's control of the government,[1] for twelve years either "aristocrat" or "monarchist" was Republican publishers' favorite epithet for their adversaries. The recent war against George III and the contemporary class struggle in Europe aided their efforts. A known desire of some Americans for stronger government, and above all the constant reiteration of the monarchical charge, convinced many sincere citizens there was grave danger that a throne might be established in the United States.[2]

The cry of "monarchist" was early raised and long maintained. Most Americans trusted Washington when he assumed the Presidency; had he lusted for power he could have taken it before disbanding the Revolutionary army. In the absence of precedents, possibly some of his ceremony was justified. But in itself ceremony was distrusted, even by many with faith in the motives of the man; a show of reverence for any human being was un-American. Washington might endorse congressional measures, yet "a greater than he, i.e. the PEOPLE, do not 'approve' of all the Acts of Congress." [3] It was only a step from other high-sounding titles "to the appellation of *Majesty;* so that some of us may *yet live* to behold another *George* wielding the sceptre of the western world." [4]

Moreover, if Washington were above suspicion, his advisers were not. Hamilton had urged a near-monarchy at the Constitutional Convention.[5] Within four months of the first inaugural, a macaronic verse entitled *"The Dangerous \*\*\*\*\*\*\*\*\*"* was circulating. It called Adams *"Ye wou'd-be Titled,"* said he had been clothed with authority in an evil hour, and warned that if he attempted to gain a crown Columbia's God would hurl him down to his "native *Dunghills."* Supporters of the administration protested, but a correspondent noted the injustice of the poem's sentiments was not proved.[6]

A federal mint, and Washington's head on coins, were opposed as monarchical practices. Even official celebrations of the President's birthday smacked of royalty. While Americans were grateful for what he had done, they wanted this "farce" to set no precedent.[7] Though Federalists branded those who opposed their program as "Jacobins" and "Disorganizers," surely an enlightened people could distinguish between speculating monarchy-jobbers and genuine friends of the Constitution.[8]

Early leader of this press campaign to tar Federalists with the stick of royalism was Freneau. His *National Gazette,* quoting Madison, identified opponents of speculation and trends toward hereditary government as the true lovers of the

Union. In a studied design to render Hamilton odious, he interpreted the Secretary's every move as a stroke toward fastening a crown upon America. Veneration of the Chief Executive, loose construction of the Constitution, a perpetual public debt, interesting legislators in speculation and speculators in legislation, charging the opposition with enmity to all government, and following England as a model—all were recommended "rules" for converting a republic into a despotism, and Hamilton had approved every one.[9]

A popular pastime was quoting Adams' writings to show his monarchical leanings. His own words allegedly showed him unfit for reelection to the Vice-Presidency in 1792; to make him President would put America on the highroad to hereditary government. After the 1797 inauguration, an "Aristocratic Song" used the tune of "Yankee Doodle" to recount the desire of Federalists for titles and of this "principled Royalist" for a crown.[10]

When Washington's administration resented Genêt's and Adet's appeals to the people, "A native of Pennsylvania" felt America had reached "the threshold of monarchy," if the Executive was above accounting to the citizenry. The Virginian supposedly had hand-picked his successor, which to Bache's *Aurora* was as bad as the hereditary principle that would have operated had he children of his own. At his brief emergence from retirement to take command of the army of 1798 the acidulous Callender nicknamed him the "monarch of Mount Vernon." [11]

Republicans, rather than "openly avowed aristocrats," were the authentic patriots. By 1799, Independence Day reportedly produced from Federalists only groans and harangues "on the blessings of monarchical forms of governments." The *Aurora* maintained Federalists thought "a limited monarchy more tolerable than was heretofore supposed," and predicted that after France fell British arms would place an English prince upon an American throne.[12]

Hack journalists such as "Peter Porcupine" would be unworthy of notice, claimed Jeffersonian printers, if they sought only places and pensions. But the "exclusive Federalists" really wanted power, titles, and a king. Congressman Robert G. Harper had publicly asserted mankind was *"incapable of remaining under a republican form of government"*; a Delaware ex-governor reputedly had spent but *"few happy hours since our separation from Britain."* Although Hamilton's only conquests had been over women like Maria Reynolds, he had a Napoleonic complex, and there were those ready to support him. A country that had swallowed a stamp tax and excise might not gag at Alexander I once he were enthroned.[13]

Adams was supposed to be invariably yearning for a scepter. His attitude toward Congress showed a trend to "despotism," and John Langdon, Tench Coxe, or others were cited as overhearing him affirm Americans would never be happy without a king and hereditary Senate.[14] Feasts and demonstrations in his honor promoted the "idolatry" which a "detestable and nefarious conspiracy in this country" was using "to bring about—monarchy." Adams' penchant for hereditary rulers purportedly led Jefferson to dryly observe that at one German university the chemistry professor had gained his chair by inheritance, *"and a precious chemist he was!"* Disorderly Federalists were termed "Aristocratic banditti," striving for the same goal of enthroning a king. Fortunately, said Republicans, the people had detected this gigantic plot, and the election of 1800 saved America from a monarchical fate.[15]

Almost as pleasant as "monarchist" or "speculator" for Democratic tongues was the name "Tory" when applied to their political foes. The term of course had great emotional connotations, associating Federalists with England and intimating that Jeffersonians were lineal descendants of the valiant patriots of '75. Consequently, "Tory faction," or "American Tories," were expressions frequently in print. Federalists showed "all the venom, and ARISTOCRATIC insolence of a Royalist" in trying to forestall a French-language paper in Baltimore. James Rivington, notorious Loyalist printer during the Revolution, was said to be writing for New York Federalist gazettes, and Benedict Arnold would have approved both Federalist goals and practices.[16] The New York *Argus* disgustedly commented that half the celebrants at Washington's birthday ball in 1797 would only a few years previously have gladly borne his head on a pole. "Old South" decried Federalist expertise at invective and called for elimination of confusion by returning to the good old party names of Whig and Tory.[17]

Undeniably, much as with "liberal" and "conservative" today, there was fogginess in nomenclature. Republicans protested when called "Antifederalist," for that term had become discredited since the struggle over adoption of the Constitution. Freneau's paper, warning against the label, well described the name-calling technique:

> . . . *antifederal* will be artfully used (in the ensuing elections . . .) to prejudice the uninformed. Be it known that no such party as the antifederal exists in the United States. It is a word without a representative in society, and only to be found in the mouths of interested persons. . . .

Other editors claimed administration proponents were the true anti-federalists, for they constantly strove to destroy the federal nature of the Union.[18]

"Jacobin" was comparable. Habitually hurled at Republicans, the epithet meant those who stirred up international strife, but the *Independent Chronicle* insisted it properly belonged to the aristocratic, British-sympathizing Federalists.[19] Since definitions varied so widely, "An Enquirer after Truth" sarcastically requested genuine information about the title. One person called the Jacobin an enemy to all government, another a foe of federal government. A third insisted he supported the Constitution; others stated he favored France and opposed England, while still others viewed him as a descendant of the Jacobites of James II's reign. The *Chronicle* snorted that real American Jacobins were those neglecting work to attend Adams' train "of mock royalty" on his tour from Massachusetts to Philadelphia, or those who imposed on their fellow citizens and profited by their distress. Other characteristics were "seducing married women and then publishing

491

their disgrace [an obvious reference to Hamilton], provoking the resentment of France and courting an alliance with the English." Thus the designation came to be used by both parties in an effort to render it meaningless. "Disorganizers" and (as has been noted) "Illuminati" likewise became common shuttlecocks of political conversation.[20]

So eager were Federalists to portray their opponents as promoters of anarchy and violence that Republicans relished every opportunity for countercharges. Some supporters of appropriations for Jay's Treaty talked of turning the House of Representatives out by armed force, a proposal that might be expected from such "*men of order* and friends to the Constitution.*" The beating of Bache while he watched work on the frigate *United States* proved Federalists were more unruly than the party they vilified. It was "the *self-created* 'friends to order and good government' " who had stolen liberty-caps from town flagstaffs, had insulted Congressman Matthew Lyon, had disrupted a Baltimore church service, and had attacked several Democratic editors. Had Republicans similarly taken the law into their own hands, "*the fate of Fries would be nothing to it.*" [21]

With tongue in cheek, one "HELLEBORE" reported a "scientific experiment" he had conducted to determine the cause and cure for the disease of Federalism. For four days and nights in 1798 he made a patient wear a black cockade, and observed the reaction. On the first day the subject sang "Hail Columbia," and paraded the streets at night with a bludgeon. The second day he damned the French and praised the English; the third he talked of an established church and was in transports at being a native American (born in Connecticut, rather than Pennsylvania or Virginia). At the fourth day he seemed "to have lost his reason; he consistently muttered curses against Frenchmen, jacobins, and democrats; he stabbed one of my servants and three times attempted to set my house on fire." Removing the cockade and placing the victim in an oven at 288° F. liberated a vapor, which proved to be "federo" gas when it combined instantly with gold dust thrown into the air. Moreover, the recovered patient deserted the army. Clearly, "federo gas" harmfully affected the human system. Joseph Thomas' mob which tried to pull down Bache's house, those men who ignored Sunday but carefully observed fast days "for worshipping [A d a ms]," and the intended murderers of Callender had obviously been charged with the noxious vapor—which could produce all sort of disorders.[22]

Every means of intimidation was utilized by the alleged respecters of peace, person, and property. In Lancaster, Pennsylvania, they broke into a stable to shave the tails of horses for the cavalcade designed to welcome Governor McKean. There were plots against the lives of Duane and John Randolph, Congressman Lyon had been beaten, and George Logan was attacked in the Pennsylvania legislature. Federalists scoffed at Democratic parades, but their own in Richmond insulted gentlemen and "affrighted [ladies] to a serious degree"; in Philadelphia they threatened a resort to arms if Jefferson were elected, and in Maryland drunken "advocates of RELIGION" nearly rioted in disappointment over a local election loss. The grafting Dayton and immoral Hamilton were typical, revealing the hypocrisy of the party they led.[23]

In contrast, Republicans, following their Maryland victory, indulged in no "whooping or hallowing, no blackguarding, or beating the rogue's march—all decency and decorum." This was a lesson in manners from which "Aristocrats" could profit in the unlikely event they should ever again be in the majority.[24] Thus Jeffersonians coupled accusations of disorder and disloyalty against their rivals with the propaganda device of "glittering generalities." If they could convincingly portray themselves as reasonable, well-behaved and loyal, acceptance for their program and candidates would be more easily obtained. Thus they signed their letters "WHIG" or "SPIRIT OF '76," and called for a return to the party names of Revolutionary days. At times they tried to arrogate to themselves the title of "Federal Republicans." [25] Labels are often more important and effective than most men realize, and Democrats hoped to acquire more than their share of the most favorable.

Still another standard weapon in the Republican newspaper campaign was the blanket indictment. This covered virtually all phases of the Federalist program, reaching into the past, warning of present moves, and at times dourly predicting the future. It was used to analyze administration leaders, means, and goals—and to condemn them all. It was always applicable and ever-growing, for each year added new offenses to the list of charges.

Generally speaking, these arraignments appeared in one of three forms. The first was a summary, more often than not presented as a "creed" of one party or the other. If printed as a Federalist doctrine, the Republican answer might be given, in order that the reader could contrast evil with good. Since most of the specific arguments used have already been noted, a sample or two should illustrate:

### The Political Creed of 1795

1. I believe in God Almighty as the only Being infallible.

2. I believe that a system of excise must of itself, if continued, infallibly destroy the liberty of any country under Heaven.

3. I believe that national Banks are equally dangerous to a free country.

4. I believe that a man who holds his fellow citizens at an awful distance in private life, will hold them in contempt if by accident he finds himself for a time placed above them.

5. I believe that man wants to be king who chooses the advocates of kingly government to be his first councillers and advisers.

6. I believe that a little smiling, flattering adventurer was once placed at the head of a national Treasury, because he had contended for a monarchy over a free people.

7. I believe the man who was sent as ambassador to a great nation, and at a very critical moment, was sent because he contended for the same thing.

8. I believe that a man wishes to be a despot, who makes alliances with despots in preference to freemen and republicans.

9. I believe proclamations are no better than Pope's Bulls; that as far as they respect religious ceremonies, they are contrary to freedom of conscience; that as they respect government, they either counteract the force of law, or . . . pretend a superior skill as to its meaning.

10. I believe there is something more designed than fair govern-

ment, when the people are too frequently ordered to fast or give thanks to God.

11. I believe that honest government requires no secrets. . . .

12. I believe that all honest men in a government, wish their conduct and principles made known to the governed.

13. I believe it is the duty of every freeman to watch over the conduct of every man who is entrusted with his freedom.

14. I believe that a blind confidence in any men who have been of service to their country, has enslaved, and will ever enslave, all the nations of the earth.

15. I believe that a good joiner may be a chancy watch maker; that an able carpenter may be a blundering taylor; and that a good general may be a most miserable politician.[26]

The "Letter of a Republican" presented the alleged articles of Federalist faith, together with Democratic replies to some of them:

23. I believe Blount's conspiracy with Liston would have been a good thing had it not exploded too soon.

23. No answer

24. Hamburg Tubs shows a masterly stroke of Timothy Pickering's diplomatic talents.

24. Like the X Y Z, Harper's clues, and the alarm about Logan, this is another fake.

25. To rebaptize any measurer of windows with hot or cold water is an act of high treason, and subjects the county in which it happened, and the two adjoining counties to military vengeance.

26. The Irish have a moral duty to pay their taxes despite lack of representation.

26. Taxation without representation is tyranny.

27. 'Twould be a shame if Napoleon were to destroy in Egypt the excellent government of the Mamelukes.

28. If Congress passes any law—, no matter how destructive and unconstitutional, as long as the judges don't pronounce it such, the people are obligated to obey, for they have no way to redress their wrongs.

28. When governors break the solemn pact between themselves and the governed, the latter may do likewise.

29. A new and triumphant combination is arising against France.

29. No comment

495

30. I believe (like St. Austin—even against probability) in the military endowments of *Alexander* the *little*.

30. I say of such generals, as Fabricius did of the doctrines of Epicurus, *may the enemies of the Republic never have better.*

And lastly, I believe in any absurdity, whether of fact or opinion, that the cabinet in their wisdom may think proper to prescribe.[27]

The second form of an over-all denunciation was also a synopsis, but usually as a letter examining the record of the Federalist party, or in answer to some question. For instance, "Brutus," in the *Sun of Liberty*, reviewed Federalist performances to see if their politicians were entitled to confidence. They had tried to increase the standing army as early as 1793. They had negotiated the damnable British treaty, with its extension of contraband, surrender on debts, invitation to impressments, and abrogation of the French alliance. They had given the President unconstitutional powers through the Alien and Sedition Acts, raised a "provisional" army while discouraging the militia, created a navy, multiplied public offices, and piled expense upon expense. Attempting to control the election of 1800, they had tried to establish a committee that would frustrate the popular will. They had postponed the census to deprive faster-growing states of "their due weight in the ensuing election." They had proscribed from office all who dared question them, persecuted opposition printers, and abused political rivals with scurrilous language. Their silence condoned British depredations, for they emitted but a "hollow murmur" at the grossest outrages. Yet they magnified French excesses and then sent ministers to treat while they vilified France at home. Their leading editor had called republicanism "the highest note in the gamut of folly." And still this party was requesting popular approval! [28]

Best, perhaps (even though sometimes prolix), of these barrage arguments was the third type—a series of letters or essays. More and more of these appeared as the century closed. Though his *National Gazette* expired earlier, no writer was more effective in this method than Philip Freneau. The *Aurora* was his medium and satire, his weapon.

His ironical communication signed "A Monarchist" set the stage. To avoid accusation of being libelous, Freneau apparently in all seriousness attacked the "erroneous principle" that rulers should always act openly and fairly. Ancient scholars had generally contended those in authority were subject only to laws they themselves made. Money was needed to assure the supremacy of a prince or President, and sedition laws to protect them from criticism. Lyon's trial had beneficially inculcated respect for the government; cutting off his head, though wrong in itself, might have been even better for the nation. That which was *"profitable* can never be *unlawful"*; if Presidents were bound by laws, one might as well be a drayman. Only enemies of order opposed the Alien Law, as was proved by the discontent with the *"temperate, humane,* and *just"* government of Ireland.[29]

With this prologue, Freneau launched his series of some two dozen letters written by a supposed yokel, "Robert Slender," to the *Aurora.* Dedicated to the *people,* rather than presumptuously to Adams or Pickering, they supposedly solicited further information from "A Monarchist." Frequently "Slender" added the initials "O.S.M." to his signature to show that (in good Federalist terminology) he was "One of the Swinish Multitude." Thus Freneau used the "plain folks" technique,[30] identifying himself with the nation's commonality.

Naively, "Slender" was amazed at "A Monarchist's" facts. He was also surprised the *Aurora,* which he had always considered a *"French* paper" and had picked up only through curiosity, had printed the letter. He had discontinued his former subscription to *Porcupine's Gazette* because it "taught the children to *curse* and speak bawdy." Although neighbors called him turncoat, the *Aurora* seemed so fair "Slender" couldn't help reading it. Dull-witted himself, he had shown the article by "A Monarchist" to a friend; surely only heathen princes would violate their word and exceed their legal authority. The friend disillusioned him. So-called Christian rulers were often worse than pagans, but the church never excommunicated *anyone* of wealth and influence. When "Slender" wondered to whom the people could turn for help, his friend told him American farmers were truly virtuous and would preserve the nation and the Constitution.[31]

As revealed by his letters, "Robert Slender" was a simple little man, fearful of all the unintelligible (to him) happenings around him. He hated controversy and had been convinced Americans were insane when they opposed the might of George III. So he had hidden during the Revolution—but at its close, with Washington's unbelievable triumph, he emerged from his retreat and began to prate "about Liberty, Independence, Freedom and such like things, just as the rest of my neighbours did, who had hid as well as I."

Since then he had been perpetually puzzled. Could someone explain why the poor soldiers had been tricked out of their hard-earned pay by getting only twelve cents on the dollar, and old Tories were given places of power and trust? What meant those awesome terms, "funding system," "assumption," and a "national bank"? How could a public debt be "a public blessing"? In what way was he influenced by French ideas, when even some English words (in the only language he knew) were difficult? When France overturned Antichrist, an event for which Protestants had long prayed, why did Federalists now resent anyone's thanking God for it? [32]

Soon "Slender" was bewildered by the Federalist campaign letter of "A Maryland Clergyman." The letter was so long he was certain he could never understand it, but since it was written by a pastor it would be sacrilegious not to read it. Its praise of Adams pleased "Slender"; he was gratified the President was virtuous. But he failed to comprehend why France wished to make a "perfect Bedlam" out of America. Had she helped America gain independence only to convert it into a madhouse? And why did all those preachers who so loved the

498

Gospel not go to France, where apparently the Word was sorely needed?

News heard in the tavern while perusing his newspaper terrified "Slender." All "men of the *first rank,* and all friends of order and good government," spoke of war, and he believed them. Cobbett had told of an army of United Irishmen and a plot to burn Philadelphia. Now word of the XYZ affair gave "Slender" nightmares of a French invasion, so he started barring the door and went to bed quaking every night. He prayed for a strong navy and a British alliance, until Gerry's account showed the alarm had been *"for some special purpose,* only a voice." [33]

As a "weakly little fellow, . . . not very fool-hardy," "Slender" had always supported good government. Yet the law was being defied, apparently because people had "too much *freedom*—our chief magistrate has *too little* power, and therefore is not sufficiently respected." However, the behavior of the army made him wish Congress had specified whether or not being a volunteer under the President conferred exclusive privileges. "It has somehow or other popt into my head that it does," like an acquaintance who, once made constable, announced he could thereafter kick, beat, or kill any man he chose. "Slender" did not object if this were so with "the men whom the President delighteth to honour"; the public welfare was unquestionably safe in their wise and humane hands. But it should be publicized in order that people would not run the risk of offending such men. Lacking information, he was ready to leave Philadelphia and hide where he "was during the last war." [34]

There were many of these letters, and most are amusing even today. Undoubtedly they tickled the risibilities of delighted Republicans, and their pointed irony made Federalists squirm. "Slender" had firmly believed all the tales of plots and thought Bache's packet from Talleyrand would verify them. But Bache had opened the parcel before witnesses, "and lo! the important communication proved to be two pamphlets—

My neighbours laughed at me . . . whilst I stood in the middle, as still as a mouse, and as sheepish as Hamilton when he wrote the story about Reynold's [*sic*] wife." [35]

Religion, British outrages, the standing army, Jonathan Robbins, the Alien and Sedition Laws—"Slender" had questions, misinformation, or ridiculous comments on them all. The army needed a graduated scale of punishment for various offenses, and placing men in an oven (at 70° for five minutes for abusing a Democrat, to 200° for desertion) was suggested.[36] Small wonder George III and Robert Liston associated with the horsethief Isaac Sweezy. A king's record— "bribery, spies, secret service money, assassinations, open violations of . . . justice"—would convince anyone horsethievery was the more honorable profession.[37] Though American law forbade trade with the French, it was only sensible to use the ship taking the minister to St. Domingo to carry cargo. Anyway, Federalists did not have to obey the law—did not Scripture say "the LAW was not made for the righteous, but for sinners and the rebellious?" Perhaps it was a mistake, and the goods aboard were all designed for Hamburg, but the mishap went undiscovered until ten days after the ship sailed. Every man was subject to error; the only perplexing thing was why the Federalists kept making so many.[38]

Anything but subtle, the letters were so shrewdly phrased that a prosecuting attorney would have appeared ridiculous trying to prove them seditious. "Slender's" wide-eyed queries and observations constituted a clever exposé of Federalist foibles and policies. Part of their effectiveness arose from the humor Freneau so frequently used. During the campaign for the adoption of the Constitution it had been noted that "pointed ridicule is . . . of more efficiency than serious argumentation," [39] and Republicans remembered the lesson. Earlier the *National Gazette* belittled Federalist claims of vast blessings derived from the new government. Freneau noted that poverty still existed, but people should be impressed by the fact that ships were sailing on the Delaware and crops had been sown and harvested.[40]

Other correspondents derided Federalist claims to piety. They prayed consistently: "God preserve our Constitution from wild Democratic storms." True patriots, however, called on the Father somewhat differently:

> Send, O Lord, regeneration
> Purify our Morbid air
> Purify our sickly nation!
> Abrogate our Musty laws!
> Send, O lord, regeneration!
> Succor, Lord, a righteous cause! . . .[41]

Appealing to superstition, "A Prognosticating Old Soldier" humorously noted that the new copper cents depicted a man from whose head the liberty cap had been blown off, apparently by "an *aristocratical blast of easterly wind.*" He hoped in the future the coiners would "be careful to fix the Cap firmly on the Head of the *Image.*" Often such symbolism had meaning; during the Revolution he had seen paper money bearing a snake with its tail in its mouth, which prophesied bad luck for the common soldiers. Sure enough, they got *"bit"* and received but 2 *s. 6d.* per pound on their notes.[42]

Political caucuses were caricatured by other writers. In them U.S. District Court Judge Richard Peters (well-read in the humorist Joe Miller) was said to pursue a pun as eagerly as Georgia Senator James Gunn and the ci-devant Congressman Harper did "a black beauty." Imaginary conversations pictured the Federalists as much more concerned with pleasure, witty phrases, or persecuting their opponents, than with the true business of state.[43]

Duane's *Aurora* pretended to philosophize. Human beings were of all sorts; some fled from the very scent of liberty, as some dogs do from game. Hogs reveled in filth, and there were men who resembled them. A Georgetown paper had applauded the adequate filling of governmental posts, but a glance at Adams' Cabinet in 1800 would disabuse observers. Secretary of the Treasury Wolcott was "scarcely qualified to hold the second desk in a Mercantile Counting House." Attorney-General Lee was a cipher lacking both talent and ex-

perience. Secretary of the Navy Stoddert was a tobacco merchant and cunning small town politician. Secretary of State
Marshall was a sophist and rhetorician, pliant enough to succeed in a corrupt court. Samuel Dexter, new Secretary of War,
himself had said the office could with equal propriety have
been bestowed upon his mother. Adams may have tried to improve his Cabinet, but only a blind man would call the appointees satisfactory.[44]

As is true today, political partisans of the 1790s relished
jokes on their adversaries or the government. When Congress
moved to Philadelphia some wit urged a glass dome for its
meeting hall, to *"throw a better light on their proceedings."*
Somewhat later the term "Federalist" was said to resemble
charity, for it covered a multitude of sins. A Republican favorite was the tale of an Irishman who had heard "Porcupine's" story that as an indentured servant Matthew Lyon had
been traded for a couple of Connecticut bullocks. Pat visited
Congress in Philadelphia, but was unable to identify Lyon,
though he heard Congressmen Allen and Griswold speak in
the House. At dinner that evening he was asked, " 'Did you
see Mr. Lyon?' *'No, by J—,'* cried Pat, *'but I saw the two
Conn. Bullocks he was traded for!' "* [45]

Much of the ridicule concentrated on Federalists' love of
titles and ostentation. Recognized as indicating desire for
monarchy, these appeals to vanity were also jeered for themselves. Titles smelled "of the corruptions of European government"; un-American and imitative, they were calculated
only to please children and simpletons. Charles II had well
said that the *'net'* added to 'baron' "was only contrived to
catch fools with." [46]

Were not the names given offices by the Constitution sufficiently honorific? It would be more rational "to present our
Chief Magistrates with a piece of gingerbread, or a rattle,
when we address them, than with a high sounding title." That
giving such titles was a "universal custom" meant nothing; it
affronted the intelligence of free citizens who had broken away

from Europe to be rid of its follies. Yet if titles were so potent, Americans should give Washington a good one, something like

'The Most Illustrious, Powerful, Majestic, Magnificent and Sublime the President of the United States'—and as mankind are so apt to be caught by mere sound, it would not be amiss to add *Terrific*, in order to keep the Spaniards in awe, and drive the English forever from Novascotia and Canada.[47]

Some saw the presidential tour of New England in 1789 as equivalent to a state procession. They blamed pro-administration prints for near-hysteria leading Americans to bestow encomiums and adoration rightfully accorded solely to the Deity. Well it was that Washington was so poised; another mortal would have been "converted into a perfect—*devil.*" The "farcical insignificance of set levees," and Mrs. Washington's parties, did not show republican simplicity, although one writer felt a concerted effort to dazzle the public was "perfectly consistent with the spirit of the new Constitution, in which there is a strong aristocratical tendency." [48]

Certain titles were reproaches to their bearers. What could be more cutting to a diminutive, deformed wretch than to be saluted as *Majesty*, or to one writhing on a sickbed, as *Serene Highness?* Scoundrels deserving the gallows were called *Right Honorable*, and men abasing themselves before royal puppets, *Lords;* "Goddess of Liberty! kick down these gewgaws." The Connecticut legislature was praised for following France's example and abolishing honorifics. Where used to be Colonels, Honorables, and Esquires, "Now none are more than simple *Masters.*" Had God deemed a class of nobles necessary to administer governments, doubtless He would have created a distinct species for that purpose.[49]

In every country ambitious men had at times striven to introduce distinctions invidious to merit and the rights of man. Fortunately, the overthrow of nobility in France had operated "like an early frost toward killing it in America." Now little was heard of titles such as "Most honourable", "which a year or two ago disgraced one or two of our public Papers.—Our correspondent ventures to predict—that 'Publicola' will never be king of America nor his son Prince of B[raintre]e." [50]

Republicans consequently disliked celebrating Washington's birthday as a public feast day. Admitting the President's greatness, Bache's *General Advertiser* almost from the beginning thought "this mode of expressing our gratitude for the services of any individual . . . possessed too strong a tincture of monarchy. . . ." Independence Day merited rejoicing by Americans, "but let the Birth-Days of Presidents be blotted from the Calendar of Feasts." In 1793 Bache ran a mock advertisement "To the *Noblesse* and *Courtiers* of the United States," calling for a "Poet Laureat" by February 21. Since the occupation was rather new in America, aspirants should write to England for lessons. The individual selected to "render this essential service" of composing "birthday odes . . . will be well provided for by government. . . ." [51]

"A SUBSCRIBER," miffed because the Philadelphia (dancing) assembly had been postponed until February 22, wrote no man ever deserved better of his country than Franklin. Yet Poor Richard's laurels had been given to another no more than his equal in fame and talents. Succeeding Presidents would expect a continuance of such marks of worship, and to call out the militia for these affairs converted that body "into a *pretorian* band" for an "abject monarchical parade . . . dishonorable to Freemen." [52] As party feeling heightened, Washington was berated for signing letters "your obedient" and omitting the word "servant." No wonder, when the birthday of this "American Caesar" was observed with such pomp, he behaved "with all the insolence of an emperor of Rome." To some, the ultimate was reached when a Boston paper referred to the occasion as America's "POLITICAL CHRISTMAS"; surely it was sacrilegious to rank the President with Christ. [53]

Extolling governments and rulers, however unworthy, was called a stale device to keep people quiescent. Turkey and Brit-

ain were notorious for it, "and there are other governments
. . . coming on tolerably well in the same line." An independent America should have legal decisions rendered without "that Harlequin dress" affected by the Supreme Court.
"Sidney" argued presidential levees revitalized the deplorable
residue of unreasoning British servility in America. Washington could readily set aside a day each week for informal gatherings if he genuinely wished to meet the people. Another correspondent saw these exclusive gatherings as creating a new
order of citizens. Largely confined to governmental officials,
and sharing in the $25,000 annually allowed for the Presiden-
tial table, this group could be styled *the most noble order of
the goose.*" Members should have a knife and fork as coat of
arms, and wear a ribbon, with a rattle attached, around the
waist in imitation of a child's sash.[54]

Republicans saw titles as not inconsequential, but as the beginnings of evil distinctions in a society already replete with
differences in wealth and condition. Soon officials would be
tempted to "carry the joke further" and would emulate Europe in tryanny also. The respect accorded any office should
depend upon the ability of its incumbent. One of Genêt's
predecessors in America had detected aristocratic leanings in
some personages, and had predicted to Versailles that French
titles of nobility would shortly be in vogue in America. "G—l
K.[nox] was to be a Count, Mr. H[amilton] a Marquis, Mr.
John Jay a Baron, and half a dozen whose names remained *in
petto,* were to be knighted." With the French Revolution,
however, "titles [were] abolished in France. It is very probable Mr. William Willcocks, was to be one of the Cheva-
liers." [55]

Significantly, the administration and its kept press desired
no criticism; they raised a "hue and cry . . . against every
man who writes on the measures of government without dip-
ping his pen in molasses." Republican editors derided the fulsome flattery and pretentiousness of the "Federal Court." One
"dreamed" a typical social column ten years hence:

On Monday last arrived in this city in perfect health, His Most Serene Highness the protector of the United States, who on Wednesday next will review the regular troops which compose the garrison.

Yesterday came on before the circuit court of the Protector, the trial of James Barefoot, laborer, for carelessly treading on the great toe of My Lord Ohio. The defendant was found guilty, but as the offense appeared quite accidental, and his lordship had already inflicted on him fifty lashes, the court fined him only 100 pounds and ordered him to be imprisoned six months. Considering the blood and rank of the prosecutor, the humanity of the sentence cannot be too highly extolled. His lordship's toe is in a fair way of recovery, although one of the physicians thinks the nail is in danger.

Yesterday was capitally convicted by a majority of the jury, John Misprison, for high treason, for lying with the mistress of the Protector's second son, the Duke of Erie. Great efforts will be made to obtain a pardon, but it is feared that the enormity of the offense, with a suspicion of its being the third or fourth time he has taken this liberty with his Grace, will prevent this desired effect.

Sunday last, being the birthday of the Protector's lady, was celebrated in this city with becoming attention. No divine service was performed. The levee of her Highness was remarkably crowded. She looked uncommonly cheerful considering it is the ninth month of her pregnancy. In the evening the theatre was unusually brilliant in expectation of her Highness's company, who for the reason just mentioned, was obliged to forego the pleasure. . . .

To remedy the inconvenience attending the election on the death of every protector, a bill will be brought in at the next session of Congress to make the office hereditary, and to increase his annual revenue from five hundred thousand to one million of dollars. It is certainly impossible for his Highness to support this dignity of his high station upon his present small allowance. . . .

The hereditary council will meet in the future at the new palace in Philadelphia. This superb edifice cost the moderate sum of six hundred thousand dollars, ten cents and 5 mills. . . .

A few copies of the act to restrain the freedom of the press may be had at this office.[56]

"RIGADOON" compared already-existing ceremony to a congregation of beasts celebrating "the birthday of an Orang-Outang." A Charleston newspaper shrewdly combined ridicule and name-calling, offering ten bank shares and a contract to build a frigate to anyone furnishing two political party labels enduring so long as a single year. If the label naming Republicans could contain an allusion to French influence it would be "sweet and politic"; any veil covering enough shortcomings would do for the aristocratic, ci-devant Federalists. *"Enquire of Mr. Alexander Lovetitle, in Aristocracy street, at the corner, just as your [sic] are turning into Monarchy Alley."* [57]

If "composing panegyricks" instead of law-making was to be the chief business of legislative bodies, sniffed the New York *Argus,* Americans should build a eulogy factory. And portentously, after 1796 Federalist admiration seemed immediately transferred to the President-elect; an executive whose term was ending was considered a nobody. Noah Webster, for instance, ignored Paine's attack on Washington but desperately defended Adams. As predicted, the new Chief Executive's birthday began to be widely commemorated. Republicans called Federalists monarchists when they observed it, and twitted them for their oversight when they didn't. The *Independent Chronicle* quoted Franklin, "Time is money," and estimated Boston lost 15,000 workdays "imitating the pageant of Royalty." Baltimoreans commented on the wine consumed, cigars smoked, and the public auction held upon the occasion, whereas patriotic Republicans celebrated only the nation's birthdate.[58]

Adams' vanity and love of display were called notorious. Boston gave him parades when he should have remained in Philadelphia *"minding his business."* As things were in 1797, America's pilot should not be "on the top-gallant yard, airing himself, and cutting capers. . . ." Washington at least had military successes to partially justify the slavish shows in his honor, but would it not be wise to wait until Adams' term was over to see whether or not he merited public gratitude? [59]

To Democrats "An exact adherence to precedent, is of all absurdities the most absurd," but "aping of British customs" continued. Simply because the British Commons had one, Harper demanded a wool sack as a seat for the House Speaker.

Bache contended the new song, "Hail Columbia," sung in Philadelphia's theater to the tune of the "President's March," had a royalist flavor. It was "full of the most ridiculous bombast and the vilest adulation of the Anglo-Monarchical party." [60]

During the Franco-American crisis Federalists encouraged resolutions supporting the administration. Republicans scolded these as showing servile subservience to the will of the President and as ignoring other branches of the government. Group letters, they charged, dishonestly claimed to represent the unanimous sentiment of their membership, and to state that Adams deserved ALL the *"admiration, gratitude* and *love"* of his countrymen was blasphemous. Toasts to presidential prerogatives and the privileges of freemen were more than the *Aurora* could endure. Public officials had no "prerogatives," but only duties—and the "privileges" of freemen had always been termed *rights*.[61] Now a naval vessel was named for the President, and doubtless before the squadron was complete others would have to be christened for Lady Adams, Squire Quincy, and Squire Charley. Federalists in lesser positions seemed equally avid for pomposity.[62]

Annoyed Federalist writers called attention to the rich dress of French officers and the bodyguard for the Directory. They sang Pickering's praises when his son entered naval service as a mere midshipman, but the Baltimore *American* scoffed at such "magnanimous humility." Surely it tarnished the *"splendor of our national character,"* for young Mr. Pickering should have been given at least an Admiral's commission.[63]

Washington's return from retirement to command the American army against France was marked by more of the acclaim so sickening to Republicans. Federalist papers, they said, approached idolatry in their rhapsodies. The Cincinnati had declared the General *"adored* as a God!" Russell's *Centinel* was cautioned that Adams was President now, and continued prattle about "god-like" Washington could lead a jealous Executive to relieve its editor of his profitable public printing.[64]

Republicans joined in the national sorrow when the first President died, but they soon contended the eulogies were being carried too far. Almost every sermon, play, or oration ended with an ode to the departed. No human being should be so venerated. An expensive statue for him would be folly, for great men lived longest in the affections of their country-men.[65]

Federalists used other means than synthetic veneration for their leaders to help them win elections. Some were technicalities, others clever stratagems; the Republican press found most unethical and many actually illegal. Accusations centered around charges of tricks, intimidation, and irregularities at the polls. In Boston it was said Benjamin Austin, Jr., lost fifty votes in a close congressional election because voters had failed to add the "Jr." onto his name. "Electioneering caitiffs" harangued the voters in Georgia when they supposedly were gathered together for militia drill, though any citizen so influenced would be selling *"the noblest birthright of a freeman, for a mess of pottage."* Adams' two electoral votes from Pennsylvania in 1796 were exactly two more than he would have received, said Democrats, if the new doctrine on citizenship had been revealed prior to the election, if printed ballots had been legalized sufficiently in advance for Jeffersonians to obtain them, if returns from certain counties had not been burned or delayed, or if Federalists had not been hypocritically meticulous in throwing out improperly marked ballots.[66]

Republicans themselves added interesting touches to campaigns at times. Since Federalist foreign policy was popular in 1798, their opponents practiced what has been more recently classified as "card-stacking." [67] They said very little about international affairs and ran candidates under a "Constitutional Federalist" or "Federal Republican" slate, as opposed to the "Federal Aristocratic Ticket." Intending to confuse voters by concealing their list under another name, they also avoided distasteful issues.[68]

But Federalists were no tyros in manipulation. They put up candidates with no intention to support them, in order to split the Republican vote. At times they pretended until the last possible moment to have no nominees, thereby inducing two Republicans to compete against each other. They printed and circulated their handbills on the Sabbath in an effort to outstrip their rivals. And they used secret caucuses to name candidates, while Democrats favored the more open correspondence method or else state nominating conventions. Virginia required election judges to be sworn in before a magistrate, but in a barefaced attempt to rob freemen of their franchise Federalist magistrates in Democratic York County had refused to administer the oath. A New York caucus in 1800 tried to keep state senators away from the legislature in order that no quorum could certify the state's electoral vote.[69]

"Friends of law and order" also resorted to intimidation or economic pressure. Boston tradesmen were supposedly menaced with loss of business unless they followed the dictates of influential Federalists. Pennsylvania voters in 1798 were allegedly bribed or threatened at the polls, and Norfolk merchants refused to employ those failing to support the Federalist ticket.[70]

As tension grew in 1799 and 1800, and administration supporters saw their cause weakening, charges of sharp practices increased. The *Chronicle* exhorted Bostonians to stand firm at the polling places and to refuse to be cowed. Resolution was needed in New York, where *"Cockade Clubs"* tore Republican ballots out of voters' hands and substituted "Royal ones" by force. Prisoners from the Bridewell and Negroes off the streets were said to be imported to vote for the candidates of ambitious faction. At Connecticut town meetings, a nod or wink from an influential businessman or landowner often dictated nominations for office.[71]

Actual frauds at the polls accompanied these methods. Accusations to this effect had appeared in print almost from the inception of the federal government. In a Massachusetts congressional election of 1790 all the aristocrats and "Brito-Americans" voted for Fisher Ames; many of the Boston "electorate" purportedly had been forced "to *enquire the way to* Faneuil Hall," and one man was caught putting in six ballots. The *Carlisle Gazette* suggested an efficiency award for citizens of Mifflin County, Pennsylvania, where Federalists polled 2,065 votes when the area had but 1,100 qualified electors. Boston papers warned "certain high flying unprincipled Aristocrats" they would be under close surveillance against attempts to slip "more than *one vote* (unknown to the Selectmen)" in the ballot box. Ames was again elected to Congress in 1794, but Republicans claimed many voters had been brought in; Boston, with 2,132 persons eligible, had recorded 2,811 votes. The *Chronicle* demanded "a serious investigation" of this "most daring violation of the rights of the People . . . ever practiced in this country. . . ." For years Boston Republicans asserted only "negroes and foreigners" produced Federalist victories in that community.[72]

Complaints of dishonesty were rife in the extremely close Pennsylvania vote in the presidential election of 1796. Reportedly one Allegheny County district went solidly for Jefferson, but the election judge turned over the ballots to an aristocrat who destroyed them. Lancaster County returns showed no votes for Democrat William Brown, candidate for presidential elector, but when the governor demanded the ballot boxes election judges revised the figure to 618. A postmaster withheld returns from the strongly-Democratic western counties until the Philadelphia poll had closed. It was singular that all these "mistakes" happened to favor the Federalists. Though Jefferson obtained 13 of Pennsylvania's electoral votes, Republicans were still resentful—and contended only imported voters from neighboring states had enabled Federalists to overcome a Jeffersonian majority in western Maryland.[73]

To forestall such tactics in 1800, Boston Republicans offered $20 reward for an exact count of British pensioners and other illegal voters in that city. Many in New Jersey also believed Federalists gained office by fraudulent votes and held it without concern for the popular interest. Only Jefferson's accession to the Presidency would rectify the situation, for Federalist rascality was not limited to elections. Politics on the bench by administration-appointed judges was sufficiently notorious that the Baltimore *American* could refer to the "Federal Judge, (or in other words Federal Prosecutor)" in one story it reprinted.[74]

Favoritism—or nepotism, which was worse—allegedly permeated the executive branch also. "Spoils system" may not have become a current expression until later, but the practice was well known in the eighteenth century. While at elections Republicans advocated rotation in office, they questioned its benefits if Democratic underlings were ousted or new partisan Federalist appointments made. "An ESSAY on PUPPYISM" did not deal with respectable bulldogs or spaniels. Of the two-legged variety, most insidious was "a puppy in Office; fawning, like a Spaniel, upon those on whom his advancement or continuance in office depends, but ever snarling at, and endeavoring to prey upon the vitals of all who may be in his power." Judged by his appointments to high office (Knox, Jay, Morris, Hamilton, *et al.*), Washington's record might not be so illustrious after all.[75]

By 1798 seemingly the most essential criterion for public office was a record of consistent support for Adams' administration. "Mr. Adams turns out of office every man who differs from his opinion and gives an office to no man who differs from it; as if probity and merit were confined to those who think exactly as he does." Republicans hastened to reassure worried officeholders that rumors of the President's dangerous illness were unfounded. According to the tenets of presidential infallibility, federal employees (facing probable loss of their jobs) must have felt

> It would indeed be melancholy in the extreme, to have any fatal accident happen to the president. All good men pity his political insanity and pray for his long life and conversion; but however melancholy such a mishap might be, it is to be feared the wags would laugh intolerably to see the monstrous numbers of vicars of Bray that would, on such an occasion, be exhibited to the public view.[76]

A Federalist partisan too old for eligibility for state office was given a federal judgeship in New York, probably to provide for his dotage. When Adams' reply to a body of Jersey militia men asserted the government "was not a party," the *Aurora* retorted:

> He certainly must have forgotten that he was elected by a party, that he is supported by a party, and that he supports none but a party. Who are the persons delegated to public office[?] None but men of a particular mode of thinking. Who nominates to public office? Mr. Adams. How then can he intimate that the administration is not a party? The degree of party feeling is the highest recommendation to favour and the question is not, who is best qualified by virtue and talents; but who will be most steadfast in the support of certain policies. Let this be denied by those who dare.[77]

The *Albany Register* cited a British king who claimed as long as he appointed judges and bishops he would have the law and gospel he pleased. Numerous New Englanders dismissed for Republicanism, or for failing to sign a fawning testimonial for the President, demonstrated Adams' adherence to this policy. Lust for office seemed the sole motivation for some Federalists, and repudiation of such men at the polls meant little when they could be rewarded with appointive berths.[78]

Of course Republicans behaved similarly when they achieved power. Thomas McKean turned out many Federalist officeholders after he became Pennsylvania's governor. Replacements were his political adherents exclusively, and several were relatives. Jeffersonian editors, noting McKean merely exercised rights claimed so often by his opponents, derived considerable satisfaction from Federalist rage. In 1800, however, they inconsistently derided the claim that Pinckney made political appointments strictly on merit and never preferred his relatives. This intimated none of Pinckney's numerous kinfolk was qualified for office—which might be correct, "but we cannot see in this any additional reason why he should be chosen President of the U. S." [79]

Yet most Republicans firmly believed nepotism and family influence were no laughing matter in the Adams administration. Even Abigail was a political force with which to be reckoned. One senator, hearing that envoys had been appointed to reopen negotiations with France, was "certain the business originated with the Old Woman; as the President would not dare to make a nomination without her approbation." [80] Colonel William S. Smith, Adams' son-in-law, reportedly had gone to Detroit to speculate in the lands of persons moving to Canada, and (concealing his true mission) told people the President had sent him there on affairs of state. Adams nominated him for Adjutant-General of the army, but some senators considered Smith a Republican and refused confirmation. The President clearly regarded all the government as his personal estate; after heaping offices on his "*booby son,*" he planned to care for his daughter's husband. But even to please Adams, the Senate had refused to break the rule against appointing non-Federalists to high army posts. This, ironically observed the *Aurora,* was wrong. The President should be able to provide for *all* his family, however reprehensible a portion of it might be. [81]

Fully aware of the criticism, Adams wrote Smith later of his embarrassment because generals had re-submitted Smith's name for a colonelcy. Senatorial confirmation for any higher post was now impossible, and the man's ostentation had excited such envy that the President feared approval of this appointment was uncertain. [82] Another rejection would be a bitter blow, but this time (sneered the *Aurora*) the Senate felt the "old gentleman must be indulged," and made Smith colonel of the first regiment. Later Adams appointed Smith surveyor and inspector for the port of New York, although he wrote, "I anticipate criticism in everything which relates to Colonel Smith." But he praised his son-in-law's war record and diplomatic assistance and added: "I see no reason or justice in excluding him from all service, while his comrades are all ambassadors or generals, merely because he married my daughter." [83]

Additional buffets came because of his eldest son. Republican editors noted that John Quincy Adams became minister plenipotentiary to Berlin as the first appointment of his father's administration, whereas Washington had refrained from selecting even distant relatives for office.[84] The *Independent Chronicle* held "the American Prince of Wales" had been sent abroad with a salary "to prosecute his studies," enjoy free travel, or be married with splendor in London. Presumably the President intended to provide comparable junkets to other members of his family. It acidly commented that

> This young man, from an obscure practitioner of the law, has been mounted on the political ladder with an uncommon celerity. His *Excellency* has given his *papa* many communications, and on their contents it seems he [the President] has in some measure founded his high-toned language on the conduct of the French.

News of the wedding brought the jeer that "Young JOHN [Q.] ADAMS' Negociations, have terminated in a Marriage Treaty with an English lady—. . . . It is a happy circumstance that he has made no other Treaty." Here was a tyro who might unwittingly bring on international complications in an effort to achieve fame; and a family income of some $150,000 for the next four years indicated the Adamses were doing well for themselves at public expense.[85]

The opposition press insisted downright dishonesty was used to line other Federalist pockets. Some of the accusations concerned speculation and malfeasance in high places [86] that was petty graft, but there were ugly charges of fraud in construction of the new Capitol building, and the sums allegedly missing from the "tribute" intended (as noted earlier) for Indian chiefs or Algerian corsairs were quite significant. Duane's columns captioned "Public Plunder," *"Anglo Federalist Politics* Illustrated by FEDERALIST CHARACTERS," and "PUBLIC MONEY *versus* PUBLIC LOANS," all devoted to instances of Federalist peculation, ran for weeks in 1800.[87]

Nor was all the villainy limited to graft in office. The would-be assassin of Bache received but a fifty-dollar fine, which was paid for him anonymously; later he was commissioned to carry dispatches to Paris. Surely the next plotter against the editor's life could not complain for lack of encouragement. Joseph Thomas, Federalist congressional candidate, provided a Republican journalistic carnival when he was charged with swindling and forgery in Philadelphia. Report had it this example of Federalist honesty and respect for law had suddenly left town, and the *Chronicle,* noting three hangings for forgery at Newgate Prison, commented "Our Federal Thomas's manage these affairs better." [88]

In addition to discrediting the Federalist party Jeffersonian papers did their utmost to produce disunity within it. An amusing short-lived effort attempted to divide Washington's followers from those of Adams; perhaps momentarily they even hoped to induce Adams to adopt some portions of the Republican program. At any rate, immediately after his election several printers commenced wooing him; even Bache noted that although Adams was an aristocrat, he was a patriot. He possessed both talents and integrity, added the *Washington Gazette,* commenting on the good fortune of the nation to have such men as Adams and Jefferson at its helm in "this hour of difficulty and danger." [89]

Adams' inaugural address was praised for its acknowledgement that all power was derived from the people, and its belittling the trappings of royalty. He pledged respect for the Constitution and for state governments. Anti-republicans would gnash their teeth over his determination "not to attempt or support any amendment to the Constitution . . . but in the mode prescribed therein!" He would be no tool of party, but promised to "love virtuous men of all . . . denominations"; despite his book, *Defence of the American Constitutions,* he practiced a refreshing simplicity in office.[90]

This honeymoon period lasted only until Adams' "war whoop" against French conduct, in May, 1797. After that Republican editors attacked the new President even more bitterly than they had the old. Sporadic attempts were made later to excite Adams' jealousy of Washington, especially when the later was called from Mount Vernon to command the army in 1798,[91] but prospects of exploiting any rift here came to be regarded as less fruitful than the one between the President and Hamilton.

Determined to weaken or eliminate the influence in government of their *bête noire,* Republican papers told of Hamilton's
intrigue to have Thomas Pinckney elected President in 1796 instead of Adams. Had New England states not detected Hamilton's scheme and scattered their second-choice votes, Adams
might have been relegated to the vice-presidency for another
four years. His Federalism was unquestioned, but Hamilton
feared he would not be pliable.[92]

The real split, however, developed late in 1799, after
Adams had resolved to make peace with France. At first in-
credulous, Federalists themselves began to attack the President
—an admission, smugly observed "JUNIUS BRUTUS," that
he was capable of error. Stories spread that Hamilton, determined to defeat Adams for reelection, contemplated supporting Pickering. In truth the party was inimical to Adams, but
had no other candidate with even his chances against Jefferson.
The *Aurora* now talked of three parties—Republicans,
Friends of the President, and Followers of Hamilton. Both
the latter groups were "Aristocrats," but were classified as
"Adamites" and "Pickeroons" respectively. The extreme Federalists ("Pickeroons") had castigated Adams in the *Gazette
of the United States* for sending William Vans Murray to
treat with France. Though the President then deprived Fenno
of printing rights for his *Discourses of Davila,* the editor still
published officially for the Senate and State Department. Some
Adamite leaders possessed ability, but most were little better
than the dominant Pickeroons, who had pushed through the
more odious measures of 1798–1800.[93]

What factors caused Hamilton to write his pamphlet "concerning the public conduct and character of JOHN ADAMS"
are still something of a mystery, but this amazing production
was custom-made for use as a Republican campaign document.
Intended only for the eyes of leading Federalists, it fell into
opposition hands, and Jeffersonians reveled in its references to
Adams' "unfortunate character," explanations of his "unfitness" for the Presidency, and accusations of leniency in the
Fries Rebellion and of jealousy toward Washington.[94]

517

The *American Citizen* believed the work "intended to gratify party resentment and promote monarchical views." If C. C. Pinckney were elected President, Hamilton might be returned to the preeminence that once had been his; actually, the pamphlet showed neither Hamilton, Adams, nor Pinckney was to be trusted. Through freedom of the press, pronounced the *Republican Watch Tower,* a vigilant people could ever detect unscrupulous individuals' base designs. Both Adams and Hamilton had advocated monarchy; their schemes were disclosed and the two had a falling out. John charged Alexander with immorality and British influence, whereupon Alexander called John incompetent and vain. Timothy [Pickering] wept and howled at being dismissed, and the revelation of each other's secrets had rendered all of them "objects of public contempt and disgrace." The *Aurora* and other papers contended the pretensions of Adams, Hamilton, and the Pinckneys to public confidence were "now fairly before the public," exhibited by themselves. Hamilton was mute concerning charges of monarchism against him, and the danger of selecting a President controlled by him was self-evident. Yet Adams favored a hereditary Senate and ruler, and he had knowingly placed Hamilton at the head of an army four times as large as that with which Cromwell had conquered all England. The Constitution could not be safe under *any* of these men.[95]

"A Voter" asserted every Federalist elector would mark his ballot for Pinckney, but not all would for Adams. If Pinckney were made "the *nominal* President, Mr. Hamilton will be the real one." The only choice was between Hamilton's intrigue for a huge army, gigantic debt, British dominance, war with France and "establishment of a monarchy," and Jefferson— "for Mr. Adams is out of the question." Jeering southern Republicans noted thoughtful Federalists deplored the imprudence of the pamphlet. Hamilton's dubious political and moral principles made him suspect to New Englanders; now that he had violated all bounds of decorum, they would probably refuse to vote for Pinckney.[96]

Even earlier, Jeffersonians had played upon the possibility

of Pinckney's election and had striven to alienate him and Adams. The *Independent Chronicle* proclaimed "The CAT out of the BAG," with *"British Federalists"* intending to trick Adams out of the Presidency."ORTHODOX FEDERAL-ISTS" would vote for Adams and Jefferson. Were Adams to expose Pinckney as freely as Hamilton had exposed Adams, other editors predicted both men would be found unfit for the high office they sought. As it was, the evidence these individuals furnished against one another rendered all other information comparatively insignificant. Adams' letter to Tench Coxe, on "British influence" as related to Pinckney, was reprinted; despite the President's explanation, it contributed to party disharmony, and in some eyes marked Pinckney undesirable to hold a constable's post.[97]

New Englanders were slyly informed that Democrats had long believed Federalists in their region could not be dictated to by Anglophile Hamilton. Surely they would not abandon their chieftain for those who now thought it "federal" to undermine popular confidence in the chief Executive, or support the favorite of the man who had labeled him too inept to be President. Meanwhile, "A Friend to Peace" warned South Carolinians that Hamilton's publication made Massachusetts unlikely to vote for Pinckney since Southerners now were not expected to support Adams.[98] These divisive tactics did not in themselves win the election for Jefferson, but they increased the confusion among already-demoralized Federalists.

Years before 1800 Republicans had developed another technique to help discredit the party in power. Personal abuse is as old as time itself, but political writers of that day indulged in it to an almost unbelievable extent. "Patience herself" cried the *Pennsylvania Herald,* "would fret if she was obliged to repeat the numerous invectives by which the President is bespattered every morning in that mirror of freedom the Aurora."[99] Even Washington, hero though he was, was not exempt. Before leaving office he was branded a despot, a tool of faction, an Anglophile, an embezzler, a traitor, and a murderer.

At the outset there had been uniform approval for the Virginian. Almost no one questioned his fitness to lead the nation, and some papers later most bitter against the Federalists praised him highly.[100] During his first term almost the only criticism centered around his aloofness and alleged liking for display. He had forgotten the old soldiers in the matter of redeeming their certificates. Celebration of his birthday was another example of "royal manners"; it was a kingly custom that fed his self-esteem. If he tried to avoid crowds in Philadelphia or on his travels, he was "distant"; if he welcomed a reception or speeches, the affair was a "monarchical parade." [101]

All this, however, was comparatively mild. Much of it was directed against the custom rather than the individual. But three events in his second term—the Genêt affair, the Whiskey Rebellion, and the Jay Treaty—made Washington the object of as concentrated a campaign of vilification as has been known in American political life. Republicans had opposed the President on some aspect of all these incidents, and in each they had suffered defeat. To recapitulate, Genêt was recalled and the nation had supported the Neutrality Proclamation. The Whiskey Rebellion was suppressed, and the Executive's remark about "self-created societies" had seriously hurt the Democratic Clubs. And Jay's covenant, despite popular disapproval, had been both ratified and accepted. Republicans agreed with French minister Fauchet that nothing could "make any impression upon the Government which his [Washington's] name protects"; without him the Federalists would be powerless. Since Jefferson and Randolph had failed to convert him, the only alternative was to force him into retirement. This was a primary purpose of the poison pen campaign launched against him.[102]

Attacks upon the President's character began in earnest in 1793. An editorial vanguard asserted he had started out auspiciously, but was debauching the country. The Neutrality Proclamation flouted both treaty obligations and the popular will. He desired a crown, and his treatment of Genêt showed he regarded himself as no servant of the people. His show of honesty and patriotism was mere sham. Unduly sensitive to press reaction, Washington was showing the effect of these slanders as early as June, 1793. "The publications in Freneau's and Bache's papers," he wrote, "are outrages on common decency." [103]

Nor were these assaults confined to Philadelphia. The *New York Journal* printed a purported letter by a Virginian replying to queries about the President. Using blanks as a gesture toward concealment, it averred people had a complete ignorance of, and excessive confidence in, his character. His neighbors knew "that aristocratical blood flows in [Washington's] veins"; gambling, "reveling, horse racing and *horse whipping*" constituted the essentials of his education. "Accustomed to be *obeyed from the cradle,* _____ will, did not, and could not brook restraint." Luck enabled him to gain notoriety at Braddock's defeat, but failed to obtain him preferment from the crown. "From this moment, and from this *wound to* [Washington's] *pride,* we may date [his] apparent attachment to liberty—revenge the principle, and pride the stimulus." A tyrant in personal affairs, he was friendly to France only as long as that nation had a king. "Infamously niggardly" in private transactions, he was a "most horrid swearer and blasphemer." His pretense of religion, and of serving for nothing while taking what was given him, were "To entrap the generous and unsuspecting affections of the p[eopl]e of A[meric]a." By 1794 Federalists commented that every measure of the Executive had been denounced as a "most abominable stretch of power." [104]

But it took the English treaty to produce the extremes of Democratic vituperation. While there had been much animadversion on America's British policy and howls of protest at Jay's nomination for the mission there was—perhaps in hope he would reject the detested agreement—a brief respite in the attacks on Washington himself. When he finally affixed his signature, the opposition made up for its ephemeral restraint. Washington was described as a pawn of England and was denied any statesmanlike attributes.[105]

"Hancock" fired the opening gun. A ruinous treaty had been arbitrarily promulgated and the people treated contemptuously. Washington's reply to the citizens of Philadelphia who asked him to withhold his signature was worthy of an Oriental despot. Only the evidence of his own letter could make its superciliousness credible. He had referred the petitioners to his answer to similar resolutions from Boston, when he should have given them the courtesy of specific attention. He had acted unconstitutionally in naming Jay and in the provisions of the treaty itself. Obviously the happiness and the Constitution of his nation meant nothing to the Executive. In Letters II and III "Hancock" upbraided Washington for finding time to write an individual reply to a small group of merchants *approving* his treaty stand. This action contradicted his assertion he had no partiality for his own opinion and actions. Certainly the style of *this* answer was quite different from that addressed to the people.[106]

The President had condemned self-created societies as "full of mischief," but he welcomed messages of approbation from self-created Chambers of Commerce. Clinton, Jefferson, Dickinson, Madison and other able patriots opposed the treaty; merely invoking Washington's name could not suppress their reasoning. Implication that his mind was superior to theirs was absurd. Everyone knew "his modesty is conformable to his abilities"; the fortunate outcome of the Revolution afforded him a military reputation, but he never claimed political talents, and he possessed no literary ones. "It matters not to those seven-eighths of the people, whether their petitions have been despised by GEORGE GWELPH or by GEORGE WASHINGTON."[107]

"Valerius" thought the people had misjudged their chief. As long as Washington's signature had been withheld from the treaty, America's liberties and interests were supposed secure, though they hung on the whim of a single man. To argue that war with England meant disaster was unworthy of the victor of Yorktown; Britain depended upon America for foodstuffs, and this sophistry was only a blind to implement a policy of utter submission to her insults. Weighed "in the scales of unerring truth," Washington's character was deficient. "Your voice may have been heard when it called to virtue and glory, but it will be lost in the tempest of popular fury whenever it speaks the language of lawless ambition." Any doctrine setting up one man against the will and welfare of his countrymen was treasonable.[108]

Still more impassioned was the series by "Belisarius." The treaty had awakened Americans from their delusions of gratitude. They demanded to know the source of an influence so destructive of free representative government. Washington's mantle of infallibility, begotten by "the pride of fancied dignity," probably prohibited an answer, but "Belisarius" charged he had "pursued the advice of wicked counsellors." Once the President had stated he could never hear the voice of the people without veneration and love, but his view had changed now that that voice was critical.

America's prosperity had resulted from formation of the Union, European wars, a general impost and citizens' industry, independently of the President. The administration's malevolent policies had sanctioned plunder by speculators on war-worn veterans, produced an $80,000,000 debt, mortgaged the public funds, set up a Bank, and erected a moneyed aristocracy. Fear of a war endangering its debt led this aristocracy to insist on servile submission to British outrages. Indian hostilities costing $7,000,000 and several thousand lives had led to a standing army. A vile excise caused a costly insurrection and a vain attempt to muzzle freedom of opinion (by denouncing the Democratic Societies). The neutrality proclamation had encroached on the powers of Congress and initiated a policy of marked enmity toward France. Jay's Treaty had been undertaken on Washington's authority alone; its terms violated congressional prerogatives and endangered both domestic tranquility and peace with an ally. So ran the record of an administration "trumpeted to the world by your idolatrous worshippers, as unequalled in wisdom and unparalleled in the history of nations." Truth was that along with the awful sentence of execration which awaits that ambitious Catiline, who has been the principal adviser and chief promoter of all your measures, the name of Washington will descend with his to oblivion. Gratitude may yield a falling tear at the recollection of your military services; but gratitude, sir, is a living virtue, and the stern, tho unerring voice of posterity, will not fail to render the just sentence of condemnation on the man who has entailed upon his country deep and incurable public evils.[109]

Presidential infallibility was a mirage. At one time Washington had decided not to sign the treaty; then he quickly reversed himself, proving his judgment was not unerring. He had ordered the treaty published after the Senate had adjourned and had delayed signing to muster support from the British faction. His reply to the Boston petition said he had not signed and would not until further communication with England, yet on August 14 (the day he did affix his signature) he told the people of Wilmington the answer to Boston applied also to them. This was at best a double evasion, and it punctured the myth of Washington's honesty; it also disclosed his haste and passion and the unreliability of form letters as answers to resolutions.[110]

The whole series of "Belisarius" was equalled in vituperation by letters from the pen of "Pittachus." If a once-honest man should escape censure for turning rogue, Benedict Arnold had a claim on American affections for his early services in the Revolution. The people had failed to find any new virtues in the treaty merely because of Washington's signature, and Federalists could not use it to cram the covenant down their throats. "Pittachus" ridiculed word that the public receptions of the President were still well attended. Surely the public needed to be informed that its resentment had not yet been evidenced to "Saint Washington by so cruel an expression of utter contempt for the mock pageantry of royalty, as absence from a presidential levee." Other writers demanded to be shown a single act of Washington to prove him a friend to America, or they sardonically tendered him a crown. To lull the people, his military achievements had been decked out in all their charms; in fact he had fought for power and glory rather than for the nation's liberties and had conducted himself as though he alone were entitled to the fruits of independence. The American people had "spoiled their President, as a too indulgent parent spoils a child." By November "Pittachus" and others were calling for impeachment.[111]

For some eighteen months maledictions of this temper and quality persisted, actually growing in violence until Washington left office. Even then rumblings continued, some of them after his death. Frequently stressed, and perhaps expanded from criticism of his "monarchical manners" was the accusation that he desired to become a despot. "Valerius" incessantly decried Washington's "dark schemes of ambition," and warned him the American people would "look to death, the man who assumes the character of an usurper." Caesar also had twice refused a crown, but at last had accepted it. Perhaps Washington had rejected an office at the close of the Revolution (as "Portius" had also noted) because no post was big enough for his ambition, or he feared to risk further a reputation so precariously built. Surely his refusing a salary had been a "solemn farce," for his expenses more than matched one.[112]

The Virginian hoped to further his own tyrannical ends by "advancing the greatest good of the least number possessing the greatest wealth." He was warned to cease "further anathema at the expression of popular opinion," for his fellow citizens would not regard him as a demi-god, whatever his ceremonies. They saw him as a "frail mortal, whose passions and weakness are like those of other men," and soon opposition to him would be a passport to popular favor.[113]

Hypocritically pretending to be a republican and friend of the people, said critics, Washington when elevated to power betrayed the trust reposed in him and thus forfeited all claim upon public indulgence. Drunk with ideas of his own omniscience, he now disregarded the popular voice as the breath of faction. Federalists under the Articles had labored to exaggerate national distress and to discredit democracy; with strengthened central authority, the President now maintained "the seclusion of a monk and the supercilious distance of a tyrant." [114]

"A TRUE BLOODED YANKEE" mourned that if Washington ever were an ardent patriot he had since changed. Yet —doubtless perturbed that the fury of the attacks was disgusting many independent citizens—this same writer asked for more moderation in criticizing "the worthy old General." [115] But other Republicans insisted past performances did not exempt present conduct from investigation, and New Yorkers noted the loudest protests came from those who had led in vilifying Governor George Clinton. [116]

Not that Washington had comparable ability. "Valerius" held his military reputation purely fortuitous; he had been named Revolutionary commander because of his very colorlessness. His titular post brought him credit due the entire army, despite "a cloud of proofs" of his incapacity as a general. But, the contention ran, judicious observers kept silent, and others were led by all the praise to feel that he who had won the war could frame a Constitution and guide a nation equally well. Actually his great virtue lay in his "insipid uniformity of mind, which had been happy in proportion to the contracted sphere of its operations." America had not made him President because she felt him the wisest of her sons. "She knew . . . nature had played the miser when she gave you birth; and that education had not been lavish in her favours." Yet she had trusted his modesty and thought sound judgment without great talents would reduce the danger of ambition. That confidence had been misplaced, for evil advisers had taken advantage of the fact that a weak mind yields to suggestion. Jefferson, the apparent exception to the President's reliance on foes of republicanism, was victim of the sinister plan. Jefferson was already famous. Jealous of him, fearing he might block moves for a monarchy, Washington had called him from France to be consistently outvoted in the Cabinet. [117]

On the Independence Day following Jay's Treaty, "An Old Soldier" remarked only the President had anything to celebrate; he had triumphed over the Constitution. How long would Americans "suffer themselves to be *awed* by *one* man?" Despite all France had done for him, Washington's arbitrary foreign policy had treacherously betrayed her. His questions submitted to the Cabinet at Genêt's arrival revealed ignorance, and his conduct thereafter showed partiality and the influence of British emissaries. "Tricks, subterfuges and abominations" had been used to ally America with England and to provoke hostilities with France. People might blame Hamilton for the "foulest projects," but every circumstance stamped Washington as the instrument, if not the principal. Even his Farewell Address evinced animosity and was silent on British seizures. The *Boston Gazette* demanded an investigation of his conduct to determine how far he merited French censure.[118]

It was upon foreign affairs and British influence that Jefferson's famous letter to Philip Mazzei was written. While the communication dealt with other items as well, the storm of controversy it evoked centered around its criticism of Washington. After charging both executive and judiciary (along with speculators, timid men, and British merchants) with enmity to Republicans, the writer told of the apostates who had embraced this heresy and practiced "ingratitude and injustice toward France." Included were men who had been "Solomons in council and Sampsons in combat," but who had been shorn "by the harlot, England." [119]

Perhaps no letter of Jefferson's career caused him more difficulty. Obviously, "Solomons . . . and Sampsons" referred to Washington. Surprised Democrats recoiling under Federalist counterblasts did not at first admit Jefferson's authorship. Whoever did make the analysis, they said, had given a picture "substantially correct." Later they claimed the American translation had subtly altered certain of Jefferson's meanings, but insisted the existence of British influence in America was undeniable. Considering that the letter had been penned before the open breach with France, it seemed positively prophetic.[120]

The attacks of "Paulding," "Juno," "Sidney," and "A Calm Observer" equalled "Belisarius" or "Pittachus" in bitterness. Those who yet shrank from direct recrimination called Washington the puppet of deceitful ministers.[121] The people were not ungrateful; Washington was the one who had shown ingratitude. Never had a man been more honored by his country, and yet he had rammed through the British treaty in defiance of the known will and interests of his countrymen.[122]

The cry of "ingrate" was echoed by the most popular pamphleteer of the age. Tom Paine had gone to France, and was imprisoned as a moderate in the National Convention when Robespierre rose to power. He then appealed to Washington, saying he had entered France solely to help establish a government—and therefore retained his American citizenship. Gouverneur Morris, American minister to Paris, was hostile, and Washington declined to interfere in French internal affairs. Paine was freed at the end of the Terror, but he never forgave his former General. He vented his spleen in a lengthy letter to the President, and excerpts appeared in the Republican press. Once Washington was in office, Paine asserted, he assumed all credit to himself:

> You commenced your presidential career by encouraging and swallowing the grossest adulation, and you travelled America from one end to the other to put yourself in the way of receiving it. You may have as many addresses in your chest as James I. . . . And . . . treacherous in private friendship (for so you have been to me, and that in the day of danger), and a hypocrite in public life, the world will be puzzled to decide whether you are an apostate or an imposter: whether you have abandoned good principles or whether you ever had any.[123]

"Would to God," the *Independent Chronicle* cried to the long-suffering President, "you had retired . . . four years ago, while your public conduct threw a veil of sanctity round you. . . ."[124]

Now Washington's very honesty was being questioned. "A Calm Observer" commenced a series in the *Aurora* bluntly insisting the President was overdrawing his lawful compensation of $25,000 annually. In view of repeated assertions of his disinterestedness and earlier refusals to accept a salary, this public accusation was most embarrassing.[125]

Replying immediately, Treasury Secretary Wolcott conceded it was common practice to advance sums to the President's private secretary solely for household expenses. At times these might have exceeded the regular quarterly division of the salary, but never had advances been made without a legislative appropriation. Account books showing this procedure had always been presented to Congress, and if the practice were evil the fault lay with that body and with the Treasury Department. Wolcott hinted at an investigation of Bache's paper and correctly surmised a concerted effort existed to discredit the administration. Bache retorted any inquiry would be welcome and denied his paper was controlled by men in or out of power.[126]

"A Calm Observer" called Wolcott's evasions "a complete acknowledgement of guilt." If Washington had received more than $6,250 in any one quarter, or $25,000 in any year, he had violated the Constitution and the law that ordered payment of officials at the end of a quarter rather than the beginning. Since he was fully as responsible for this condition as had been his secretaries or the Treasury Department, impeachment was called for. "ONE OF THE PEOPLE" cited figures to show Treasury books supported the charges against the President. Was not Washington overdrawn by $5,150 by April 30, 1791, still $4,150 in arrears a year later, and $1,037 short at the end of his first term? Had he not received $4,750 more than his authorized quarterly salary in the three months following his second inauguration, and was he not still overdrawn? Wolcott's reply that these sums had been spent on the President's household may have been intended to reflect upon his private secretaries, but Washington was known to keep careful accounts. In any event, he was not entitled to draw as much as he pleased, no matter where the excess went. Had he died or resigned, who would then have been responsible for repaying the indebtedness? There was no virtue in publishing the Treasury reports; this was required by law. Talk of investigating Bache sounded like a threat, and the public would not be satisfied with the Secretary's mere assertion that *"it is his belief,* that nothing in the least contrary to the law has been practiced."[127]

These charges were reprinted in all sections of the nation,[128] and others joined in the outcry. What would posterity say of him who was guilty of this? Federalists claimed the attacks came from Washington's Revolutionary War enemies, but the *Aurora* countered that Jay's Treaty and the President's own appointments had converted all *these* men into fast friends. At any rate, criticizing the source did not answer the accusations. "Pittachus" felt Wolcott's efforts had only worsened matters. Under his theory, the moment an appropriation was made any official could dip his hand in the Treasury and take out his annual salary. Washington had even anticipated a second term! Surely he could no longer boast of disinterestedness and sacrifice, if he grabbed like a miser for every penny before it came due. "Scipio" professed a desire to clear Washington's reputation, but admitted his inability to refute the evidence.[129]

Hamilton taxed Republicans with seeking to eliminate Washington as the big obstacle in their drive for political power. The Treasury Department, he noted, issued money only for objects previously authorized by specific legislation. Following passage of such a law, disbursements were frequently made (as in the case of contractors for supplies, and the War Department for the pay of troops) in advance if it appeared both advantageous and safe. Governmental officers had no right to demand advance payment (and Washington had not requested it), but it was perfectly proper for them to accept it. Washington had received no additional money beyond that which had been voted him. The Treasury had never advanced him more than a quarter's salary, and still owed him $846 at the end of the last quarter.[130]

Democrats refused to accept this interpretation of the law. Hamilton had confessed Washington had received payments before they were due, even though "performance of the service must precede the right to demand payment." If the *Aurora*'s accusation of "a common defaulter" were untrue, "the authors, printers and publishers of it ought to be shipped for Botany Bay, but if true the officers of government will merit a gentle *reprimand.*" Moderate men might conclude that the President appeared to have received only authorized advances, and that the accusations "were prompted more by ill nature, than by any love for the . . . people," yet Jeffersonians regarded their case as proved. Certainly the fable that Washington served the nation without compensation had been exploded. Men could now regard him as paid in full, and often before recompense was due. "Thus the veil is taken off the eyes of the people in this particular." [131]

More serious crimes still were also laid at Washington's door. His past record was exhumed, and several ancient libels revived. There was the old French and Indian War atrocity tale that he had killed Captain Jumonville while the latter was under a flag of truce.[132] He was alleged to have similarly fired on white flags during the Revolution. As if murder charges were not sufficient, Washington was also labeled a traitor. Callender asked if there was any logical reason for believing he would be more faithful to the present government than he had been to King or Confederation. Naturally these two "treasonable" acts were well known, but he was accused of actually favoring Britain at the very time he was leading America's armies. In 1776 he allegedly had written privately, *"I love my King, you know I do; a soldier and a good man cannot but love him."* [133]

Even the "Lund Washington letters" were dusted off and used. These British forgeries during the Revolution, purportedly seized with Washington's body-servant at Fort Lee, pictured the General as considering the American cause hopeless and as betraying some of his own troops to their death. In wartime the fabrication had been laughed to scorn as an obvious English blow at patriot morale, but now the slander was repeated nineteen years later. Immediately after Adams' inauguration Washington issued a public denial that any of these letters were authentic. Some Republicans approved this declaration, but the New York *Argus* cynically asked why it had been so delayed. If Washington were waiting until he left office, he had also "retired" in 1783—and should have disavowed the communications then. During the war, the paper claimed, they had been deemed genuine by friends and enemies alike.[134]

Most of this abuse was primarily intended to drive Washington from public life. And, while historians have sometimes moralized on the ineffectiveness of scurrility *per se,* indisputably this ever-recurring obloquy made the Virginian miserable and heightened his determination to retire. Shortly after his signing of the English treaty there were reports he would offer his resignation to Congress and hints this would be desirable.[135]

At Hamilton's insistence, Washington postponed announcing his decision not to run again, but by late spring, 1796, Republican leaders knew such was his plan. Perhaps fearful of a change of mind, however, their editors expressed doubts of his willingness to relinquish power. "Paul Pindar" wrote poems "To the GREAT W——N," indicating disbelief he was weary "of the court"; all rulers in history had "lov'd dominion to the very last." Even after Washington's public refusal to be a candidate, "WATCHMAN" reminded readers the British faction had persuaded him to run in 1792 and was circulating petitions "praying him not to quit" now; it knew it could elect no one else.[136]

Jeffersonians saw the Farewell Address as a campaign document, concocted by Hamilton. Yet they tried to forestall any alteration of Washington's decision. All sorts of evils were ironically predicted if the "Perpetual Dictator of the U. S." left office; British merchants and protection against all-devouring France still required an infallible Executive. French minister Adet thought the address both insolent and dishonest, and Bache felt only enemies of popular freedom could accept it. How could a man owning five hundred slaves pretend to defend Christianity and liberty?[137]

Even after Adams' election, the *Aurora* asserted Washington had not run through fear of defeat. The paper's editorial Christmas present to the departing President has become famous:

> If ever a nation was debauched by a man, the American Nation has been debauched by Washington. If ever a nation has suffered from the improper influence of a man, the American Nation has suffered from the influence of Washington. If ever a nation was deceived by a man, the American Nation has been deceived by Washington. Let his conduct, then, be an example to future ages. Let it serve to be a warning that no man may be an idol, and that a people may confide in themselves rather than in an individual. Let the history of the Federal Government instruct mankind, that the masque of patriotism may be worn to conceal the foulest designs against the liberties of a people.[138]

Never, said the *Argus* in 1797, had Washington's birthday been celebrated so unanimously; Tories pretended to rejoice at their beloved leader's anniversary, and "real whigs" could not conceal their satisfaction at soon being rid of a President who had brought his country to the verge of destruction. An elder statesman reportedly said he cared not who occupied the Executive office "if W. does but go *out,* because there is not another man in America who can ruin the U.S." And Bache printed a pamphlet "*to destroy undue impressions in favor of Mr. W.*" It reiterated the Jumonville "assassination" tale, painting Washington as an inferior general, a mediocre politician, and a rather ordinary planter. Desiring only money and glory, he had insidiously accustomed America to speculation, corruption, and monarchy. Since his character had "been founded on false appearance," it could "only command respect while it remains unknown." [139]

The day after Adams' inauguration the *Aurora* called for rejoicing:

> 'Lord, now lettest thou thy servant depart in peace, for mine eyes have seen thy salvation,' was the pious ejaculation of a pious man who beheld a flood of happiness rushing in upon mankind. If ever there was a time that would license the reiteration of the ejaculation, that time is now arrived, for the man who is the

533

source of all the misfortunes of our country is this day reduced to a level with his fellow-citizens, and is no longer possessed of power to multiply evils upon the United States. If ever there was a period for rejoicing, this is the moment. Every heart, in unison with the freedom and happiness of the people, ought to beat high with exultation that the name of Washington ceases from this day to give currency to political iniquity and to legalize corruption. A new era is now opening upon us, an era which promises much to the people, for public measures must now stand upon their own merits, and nefarious projects can no longer be supported by a name. When a retrospect is taken of the Washingtonian administration for eight years, it is a subject of the greatest astonishment that a single individual should have cankered the principles of republicanism in an enlightened people just emerged from the gulf of despotism, and should have carried his designs so far as to have put in jeopardy its very existence. Such, however, are the facts, and, with these staring us in the face, the day ought to be a JUBILEE in the United States.[140]

Even death did not end criticism. In 1800 a writer called for legislation prohibiting friends of monarchy or England from occupying the presidential chair. Another branded Washington hypocrite and sponsor of stock jobbers. Kentucky Republicans toasted "The memory of gen. Washington . . . down to the year of 1787, but no further." Fisher Ames had said in his eulogy that to the enemies of the government its very merits became offenses, so Federalists found it logical "that as soon as party found the virtue and glory of WASHINGTON were obstacles, the attempt was made, by calumny, to surmount them both. [141]

What so infuriated Republicans was the secure hold Washington had on the affections of the people. "Veritas" almost from the first had warned him to "Remember thou art a man," and cautioned him against sycophants. "WILLIAM TELL" reminded Americans that the Jews of old had adored men rather than God, and "were deservedly left a prey to their enemies." Now Washington, like Nebuchadnezzar, "greedily received unhallowed praise"—but (also like the Babylonian ruler) he was falling into contempt and should be driven from among men. Distrusting Washington's supporters, "CASCA" pronounced: "When the first magistrate of a free people becomes the idol of the enemies of liberty, it is certain that he has apostatized; it is necessary that he should be removed." Others attacked the *"exaggerated encomiums and fulsome flattery"* designed to produce "a state of abject vassalage" in the people. The Virginian was referred to Dean [Jonathan] Swift's comparison of praise to ambergris—"a little whiff of it . . . is very agreeable, but when a man holds a whole lump of it to your nose, it is a *stink* and strikes you down." [142]

Most Democratic-Republicans mourned the passing of Washington, and the press almost uniformly observed the amenities at word of his death. But some felt America was going to extremes in her veneration. "SEWALL" thought it blasphemous to talk of the master of Mount Vernon returning to the bosom of God and interceding for America there. More likely heaven had taken him "to check our profaneness, and teach us not to put our trust in MAN." A Christian people should at least preserve the proprieties, and principles instead of individuals should be the objects of attachment in republics. If Washington's character were as great as believed, erection of a monument to him was "useless and pernicious." Viewing his name and fame as the Federalists' greatest asset, to the end Republicans editors resisted adulation of the First President.[143]

Washington, therefore, was far from receiving universal approbation, and John Adams was an infinitely more vulnerable target. Critics had delightedly ridiculed his parsimoniousness, corpulence, partiality for British "principles," vanity, and love of ostentation as Vice-President even in those days when restraint had been felt advisable respecting the Virginian. On one of Adams' countless journeys home from Philadelphia, ran a popular story, his liberality was disclosed when he donated a half-dozen workmen "ONE QUARTER OF A DOLLAR" for an hour's extra labor to repair a bridge so his coach could cross. Doubtless the "Duke of Braintree" had even favored them with a condescending smile. He was known to have more money with him, for he had withheld a number of coins shortly before this incident when making a donation to employees at a woolen factory. Men of this stamp endangered society more than highway robbers; they deprived people of money merely to gratify a malicious heart.[144]

Although Adams denied authorship of "Publicola" (actually the production of his son John Quincy), virtually everyone assumed he had written this tribute to the British governmental system. Hence Jefferson's comment on "heresies" in endorsing Paine's *Rights of Man* was considered a thrust at the "squire of Quincy" and his desire for an American king and nobility. Adams' own efforts to deny a "passion for titles" and a distaste for republics failed to convince Republicans. An earlier "VALERIUS" found the Vice-President both monarchical and dishonest; he had indicated that in case of an equal division in the Senate he felt obliged to approve bills that had already passed the House, yet on the representation bill he flouted popular desire and voted against it.[145]

During the campaign of 1796 charges were rife that Adams was attached to the British cause, and Bostonians were informed that sentiments and character counted for more than a man's birthplace; believers in America and democracy would vote for Jefferson. Other writers pointed to his love of titles and belief in heredity. "Safety" commented he had "the confidence of but few, and I may say the friendship of none." He had sons in high offices, whereas Jefferson was for freedom and had no one to succeed him. The latter had pledged promotion of commerce and agriculture as primary objectives, but Adams had indicated no knowledge of either.[146]

Some questioned both Adams' ability and patriotism. Tom Paine stamped him one of those "disguised traitors" who had assumed the name of Federalist. He had defended the British soldiers involved in the Boston Massacre for one hundred guineas, and then turned patriot to erase the stain. Jefferson was his superior in every respect—philosophy, consistency, talents and republicanism. In France Adams' diplomacy had been made sport of; whatever Revolutionary contributions he had made were outweighed by his corruption in favor of monarchy during his stay in England. While presiding over the Senate he had voted down the embargo, approved titles and secret sessions, and "supported every measure which the patriot condemns." If the cry of "war" were not merely Federalist electioneering, Jefferson would surely fight England with fully as much resolution as Adams. Washington never recommended Adams to succeed him, or considered him as a true administrator. Adams had not participated in Cabinet meetings and his office had "been kept in a perfectly dormant state in an executive sense." A Baltimore versifier asked heaven to keep the seat Washington had so gloriously occupied free from the New Englander's "pamper'd pride," and Mrs. Adams dreaded the expected calumny, with "near half the country opposed to his election." [147]

As President, little that Adams said or did or refrained from doing escaped scathing denunciations. He was attacked for neglect of governmental affairs and for frequent trips from the capital. His public papers and speeches were illogical or ambiguous. Only dotage could explain his assertion that it was needful to put America "into a *posture of defense*" against France, and raise 80,000 militia to protect "commerce *on the high seas*." Did his reference to the French in 1798 as "our enemies" mean that he had arrogated to himself the power of declaring war? Had "the delirium of vanity" produced by high-sounding addresses from bellicose partisans "unhinged his mind, already enfeebled by age, that such monstrous absurdities issue from him?" Others also questioned his sanity and said he was "cast of God as polluted water out at the back door." [148]

When he declined an invitation to a "popular" ball commemorating Washington's birthday, the promoters were sarcastically labeled "presumptuous" to suppose Adams would demean his station and mingle with shopkeepers. The *Centinel of Freedom* applauded the "downright democratism" of William and Mary students who burned the President in effigy; this contrasted favorably with the eulogies and displays for him and Washington. Like the latter, Adams had established a

537

"praise manufactory" at Philadelphia which by then must have nearly surfeited him with encomiums. Doubtless the "ear-ticklers" in the servile Pennsylvania legislature would be rewarded by posts and profits. "DEMOCRITUS" ironically berated Clinton, Madison, and Jefferson for perfidy and disloyalty in opposing "*you* . . . the oracle of all wisdom, and the fountain of all patriotism," who had "been deputed specially from Heaven to unite the American people . . . in opposition to foreign usurpation." Adams was making genuine progress toward monarchy, and his replies to congratulatory Federalist addresses were superior to the orations of Demosthenes.[149]

More directly, the *Aurora* enraged the First Lady by describing her spouse as "old, querulous, bald, blind, crippled, toothless Adams." He drove to Washington City with raised curtains in his coach in order that people could see him, but was mortified when the army, critical of Pickering's removal, failed to parade for him. His partisanship even influenced his religion; in Philadelphia he regularly attended Presbyterian services, but in Baltimore, where the Presbyterian clergyman "is an avowed REPUBLICAN," he went to the Episcopalian church.[150]

Again during the campaign of 1800 his writings were cited to prove his predilection for England and monarchy. His pardon of Fries and disbanding the army might show a recent change in political conduct, but his opinions had not varied. He had publicly said that "republican government may be interpreted to mean anything or nothing," and an old communication (which he had branded a forgery) showed the ruthlessness of his nature when he advocated fining, jailing, or hanging all those inimical to the American Revolutionary cause. Jefferson's conciliatory inaugural in 1801 was termed "a pleasing contrast to the exterminating war-whoops of John Adams," that "infuriated partisan." [151]

Alexander Hamilton was an even more delectable morsel for Republican scandalmongers. Opponents believed him the brains of the Federalist party, more dangerous than Adams and, gratifyingly, still more vulnerable. As Secretary of the Treasury Hamilton frequently clashed with Jefferson, charging the latter and Freneau with collusion in the *National Gazette*'s indictment of the administration's program. Supporters of Jefferson (who denied the allegation) charged Hamilton had cravenly waited to commence his attack until the Secretary of State had left Philadelphia. They briefly noted the appeal to Congress of Andrew G. Fraunces—which was to have later repercussions—that Hamilton had been guilty of misconduct in connection with a demand for payment of Treasury warrants. Fraunces was unable to prove Hamilton had cleared $30,000 speculating with Duer, but he led John Beckley and Monroe eventually to James Reynolds. At the time Hamilton simply stigmatized the plaintiff as a "despicable calumniator," and there seems to have been no organized press effort to impugn seriously the Secretary's honesty while in office.[152]

His resignation produced flights of sarcasm. What would become of the United States? It should weep as did Rachel for her lost child. Lost would be those "darling brats, that we have nursed with so much care and tenderness, the excise and funding systems, now their parents have abandoned them to other hands!" "*Ham* and his *chickens,* however abundantly rich from the funding system, appear . . . to have really got the *pip,*" said another writer when Jay's Treaty was investigated and its unpopularity made evident. The "*virtual President of the United States*" might be driven "to despair" by denunciations of the covenant. Federalists had excoriated Gallatin as a foreigner and fomenter of the Whiskey Rebellion, but Democrats retorted that Hamilton was also a foreigner, an obvious Anglophile whose excise had produced the revolt, and that he got into office through influence. Callender's *Prospect Before Us* slurringly referred to him as "the son of a campgirl" in the West Indies.[153]

Juiciest tidbit for Jeffersonian publishers was, as noted, the well-known Maria Reynolds story. Suspicions of Treasury Department irregularities and charges that Hamilton himself had speculated in securities were partly based on the revelation, growing out of Fraunces' claims, that the Secretary had paid James Reynolds $1,415 for mysterious "services rendered." Investigation by Monroe, Muhlenberg, and Venable at the time elicited from Hamilton the confession that he had had an affair with Reynolds' wife, and that the payments were a form of blackmail. Since the Secretary's official probity seemed uninvolved, the investigators had dropped the matter, but Callender's *History of the United States for 1796* had unearthed the old hints of corruption and aired them to the world. Hamilton then published a pamphlet asserting his financial integrity, but disclosing his relations with Mrs. Reynolds.[154]

Here was grist for the mills of scandal. The *Aurora* immediately sneered that "a treatise in favour of adultery" was a novel way for the Secretary to "screen his *immaculate* character from the imputation of speculation," and hoped "liberality towards his mistress" did not explain a missing book of public accounts. Republicans had long squirmed under taunts of "disorderly Jacobins"; now, they cried, what did Hamilton's turpitude reveal about Federalist morals? This systematic sensualist who afterward published the shame of his victim had struck a blow at the very basis of society. If Hamilton would so treat his own family and would cuckold Reynolds, what faith could be had in "his fidelity in any other transaction?" A wit speculated obscenely on the *"national business"* Alexander and Maria had transacted in Mrs. Hamilton's absence. Hopefully the "father of the funding system" had not contaminated "the whole progeny of 6 per cents, 3 per cents, and deferred stock." The chief mourner of the degeneracy of French morals was guilty of "KISS and TELL"; "Evalina" thought at very least he could have preserved silence concerning the woman he had seduced. The fact that he was a rake did not preclude the possibility of being a swindler also.[155]

From that time on, "adulterer" almost invariably accompanied any mention of Hamilton's name in the Republican press. It placed him on the level of British generals Howe and Burgoyne, and should have disqualified him for army command. Adams might pretend piety, but the morality of his associates produced serious doubts. The *Independent Chronicle* even suggested Hamilton's epitaph, as an acrostic:

A SK—who lies here beneath this monument?
L o!—'tis a self created MONSTER, who
E mbraced all vice. His arrogance was like
X erxes, who flogg'd the disobedient sea,
A dultery his smallest crime; when he
N obility affected. This privilege
D ecreed by Monarchs, was to that annext.
E nticing and entic'd to ev'ry *fraud,*
R enounced virtue, liberty and God.

H aunted by whores—he haunted them in turn:
A ristocratic, was this noble *Goat.*
M onster of monsters, in pollution skill'd:
I mmers'd in mischief, brothels, funds, & banks.
L ewd slave to lust,—afforded consolation;
T o mourning whores, and tory—lamentation.
O utdid all fools, tainted with royal name;
N one but fools, their wickedness proclaim.[156]

If Hamilton ever entertained hopes of high elective office the Reynolds affair destroyed them. Other evils—notably desire for a centralized government, conceit, love of England, and the baleful effects of his financial system—were charged against him, but inevitably detractors returned to his immorality. Foes said his military tour through New England had been planned to promote disaffection against Adams among the troops; instead Hamilton learned Americans would not follow a profligate, and that his "descent from a dubious father, in an English island" made him an unacceptable Presidential candidate. Tales of attempted dalliance, once with the wife of an absent host on this very eastern trip, made him appear a confirmed lecher. Federalists called Thomas Cooper's proposed libel suit against Hamilton "impudent," but was it not equally impudent for the New Yorker "to publish an account of his amours with the *wife* of Reynolds," as well as to declare Adams unfit for the Executive chair? [157]

Other efforts were made to discredit lesser Federalists, but these were not so spectacular. Robert Goodloe Harper was viciously berated, probably because he had once belonged to a French Jacobin society in Charleston, and was considered an apostate. Republicans gibed at his formal, lengthy, and immoderate speeches, and Freneau wrote a poem: "When HARPER a harping doth tune up his harp, for fear of a harpy look sharp. . . ." In one session of the House he had wasted some $6,000 worth of public time, "by making superfluous motions for the sake of making superfluous speeches about them. . . . He has a very pretty delivery, if any obliging friend could supply him with a suitable stock of ideas." [158]

The Charleston French society records showed "Goody Harper" had been an officer for a time, despite his assertion he had attended but two meetings. Already notorious as a demagogue and *"servile tool of administration,"* this (Jeffersonians said) convicted him of falsehood as well. Predominantly Federalist Staunton, Virginia, had given him a dinner in 1798, but he was warned other portions of that state would welcome his insolence with tar and feathers. A leader in spreading tales of French "atrocities," in 1799 Harper moved to Baltimore (perhaps because he no longer represented the sentiments of his constituents), but he retained his congressional seat from South Carolina until his term expired in 1801. Meanwhile the *Aurora* accused him of fraudulent land claims in the Palmetto State, failure to pay a Philadelphia firm for wine he purchased and then sold, and tax evasion. On hearing a Mr. Harper had opened a theater in Providence, it wanted to know

> Whether this is the celebrated Hocus Pocus performer, who exhibited so many tricks with clues—tubs with false bottoms—forged letters—Liston's surprising shoulder clapping alarm traps; the wonderful sword and scales balancer, who performed so many feats with the black art, and who performed such surprising gambols in the hot water war? Is it the same Harper, or is it another conjurer of the same name? [159]

Vilification of John Jay has already been noted; his treaty sufficiently prejudiced most minds against him. But it was also alleged he had opposed religious freedom and admission of foreigners in New York State, and that his sole contribution during the Revolution had been to weaken public faith in Continental currency by forcing his debtors to pay in specie. At Paris he dishonorably began negotiations with England despite America's pledge to France, and as Governor of New York he was accused of urging legislation violating the state constitution and of favoring old Tories in his appointments.[160]

To Republicans, William Wilcocks (who wrote against Genêt and in favor of Jay's Treaty) was "an idiot" and "squalling brat" whose tales signified nothing.[161] John Marshall had deserted his country's "true interests" in France, and was unworthy of the confidence of fellow Virginians.[162] Timothy Pickering, tardy at the Revolutionary battle of Concord, had exceeded his authority as Secretary of State; he was Hamilton's puppet, had been in the pay of the British minister, and had (so ran the indictment) embezzled thousands from the Federal Treasury.[163] Pickering's fellow secretary, Oliver Wolcott, also Hamilton's creature, was likewise accused of financial irregularities.[164]

Boston papers castigated Fisher Ames as an extremist who had obtained office dishonestly; Harrison Gray Otis' speeches were fit accompaniment for a lullaby; Rufus King neglected his duty and American mercantile claims to tour the English countryside.[165] Patrick Henry was an apostate from freedom's cause, but his death should wipe out all save the memory of his early efforts for America's liberties.[166] Secretary of War McHenry was utterly incompetent; Hamilton's tool, portions of his official reports were admittedly translations from foreign magazines.[167] Republican opinion of Justice Samuel Chase was summed up in the *Aurora*'s vicious little couplet: "Cursed of thy father, scum of all that's base, / Thy sight is odious and thy name is [Chase]."[168] Fisher Ames reported that even the daughters of Federalist leaders were "newspapered."[169]

Abuse, ridicule, slander—rare indeed was the Republican paper which did not indulge in personalities. As the Federalist press correctly but ineffectually pointed out, the "most un-wearied pains had been taken" to render the highest officials contemptible to the people. In some instances "the insults . . . of the democratic scunks" produced disgust and retire-ment from office. In others they begot a counter-virulence equally extreme. In most cases they accomplished the object of weakening whatever veneration for those in power that might have prevented the overthrow of the Federalist party in 1800.[170]

Though Federalists also pursued a program of invective against individuals, the Democrats (out of power during much of the period) were far less vulnerable to criticism. Even so, Republican editors utilized considerable space defending their leaders from attack. They branded Federalist accusations false and motivated by enmity for popular liberties. The calumny against "tried and true" George Clinton demon-strated the attempts to destroy citizens' confidence in their real friends. Clinton's record showed his detractors could not be inspired by desire for the public weal; if they did not hate him as a man, unquestionably they hoped to gain power by weakening safeguards for popular rights.[171]

Abuse of Tom Paine was countered by recalling his pam-phleteering for independence. Those reading *The Rights of Man* would not be misled by attempts to injure its author, and Jefferson's endorsement of the volume was approved: Politi-cal heresies *were* abroad in America. Paine's deistical *Age of Reason* somewhat muted the expostulations in his defense, but his move to France and work in the National Convention showed his sincere attachment to liberty. No living mortal had done more for freedom.[172]

Albert Gallatin was a notable Federalist target. Adminis-tration supporters sneered at his accent and foreign birth, im-pugning his loyalty and implication in the Whiskey Rebellion. Jeffersonians heatedly asked if being a native of Geneva con-stituted a felony. Many who now boasted of their native American citizenship would still be British subjects but for the exertions "of those whom they now affect to contemn." Otis had derided Gallatin as a vagrant arriving in America "without a second shirt to his back," and there were unruly Federalist demonstrations against him as his political influence grew. Republican newspapers jeered Otis (who later apologized) and ridiculed the mobs as samples of "law and order." Laudatory biographical sketches stressed Gallatin's abilities. Federalists sought to destroy his reputation to forestall exposure of their own perfidy. "To enumerate all the measures which have been adopted to sacrifice him, would fill a volume." Actually, unlike those of that other foreigner, Hamilton, his morals were *"exemplary and . . . his political principles are sound."* His extensive knowledge of public finance enabled him to foil some of the most "invidious" administration schemes. His entire life was a consistent record of opposition to tyranny, both foreign and domestic; national interest demanded his retention in office.[173]

Although Anglophiles also censured James Madison, Republicans considered him among the nation's leading luminaries. Instrumental in achieving the Constitution, he had ever shown himself true to the ideals of popular government. Even New Englanders had deplored the retirement of Jefferson's fellow Virginian from Congress in 1799, praising his elocution and unassailable logic, and surmising his decision sprang from disgust at the administration's stupidity and folly. Under Federalist officials, "probably at this time the post of honor is in the private station." [174]

Similar sentiments were expressed when Monroe was recalled from France. His behavior at Paris had been that of any honorable man and lover of freedom. Those abusing him only reflected on Washington, who had appointed him. Extracts from his *View* furnished *"incontrovertible* evidence" of Monroe's patriotism, damning secret diplomacy, and the government's deliberate misleading of France. Monroe merited national gratitude rather than Federalist scorn.[175]

Republicans dismissed any reflections upon Franklin as absurd, though criticisms doubtless irritated his grandson Bache.[176] Signed receipts or vouchers for over $300,000 were printed to refute Fenno's claim that Alexander J. Dallas had mishandled funds entrusted him to pay the Pennsylvania militia during the Whiskey Rebellion.[177] Aspersions against Tench Coxe could not discredit his letters; both Washington and Hamilton had honored him and found him assiduous and honest. If he were an ex-Tory, he had "abjured the sins of his youth"; in any event, the charge was a peculiar one to come from the party that had appointed countless others to posts of trust. Coxe's domestic life was without blemish, and his conduct in office had been good. The whole outcry was raised to divert attention from his exposure of the monarchical sympathies of Adams and Pinckney.[178] Virginia politician John Taylor was described as "one of the ablest political disputants either in the new world or the old one. His private life is as irreproachable, and useful, as his literary publications are instructive and admirable." The animadversions on his writings in William Rind's *Virginia Federalist* were compared to a "cur barking at the moon." [179] Dr. Benjamin Rush, Stevens T. Mason, Benjamin Austin and others were similarly defended from "political persecution" by the "enemies of republicanism." [180]

The recognized leader of American democracy, however, much as he remained in the background for a time,[181] was Thomas Jefferson. Commencing with Hamilton's assault on him as Freneau's patron, the administration press subjected him to especial attention. Republicans vigorously rallied to his support, though items in his behalf were not commonplace until shortly before Washington's retirement. As early as 1792 they professed pleasure the then Secretary of State was being censured, for

> it will have a happy tendency to open the eyes of the people, to the strides of certain men in power, who are wishing to turn every staunch Republican out of office, who has the discerning to ken their arbitrary measures and honesty sufficient to reveal them.

And despite Hamilton's displeasure, the State Department had every right to negotiate a loan from France rather than

Holland if it seemed to America's advantage. The calumny was merely "convincing proof of the badness of the cause behind it"—besmirching another tribune of popular rights.[182]

Rumors in 1793 of Jefferson's prospective retirement from the State Department pleased Federalists, but "MIRABEAU" beseeched him not to quit; "At present you appear to be the colossus of opposition to *monarchical deportment, monarchical arrogance, and monarchical splendor;* but were you withdrawn, monarchy and aristocracy like an inundation, would overflow our country." When retirement did come nearly a year later, Republicans extolled Jefferson's services and lamented his decision. His correspondence over Genêt had been in shining contrast to the slovenly double-talk so common in European diplomatic reports. Every patriot regretted the loss of the able Secretary, but his office had often compelled him "to lend his name to measures which militated against his well known principles," and such a situation was too disagreeable to be long continued.[183]

During the Revolution Jefferson's foes had made ugly charges that as Virginia's governor he had shown neglect of his office, military inefficiency, and even cowardice, but an Assembly investigation exonerated him completely.[184] Nevertheless unscrupulous Federalists in the campaign of 1796 revived the old canards. Did the nation, they asked, want a President who had twice (once as governor and once as Secretary of State) deserted his post in time of need? Republican journalists pointed out that on the occasion in question Jefferson's gubernatorial term had expired, and they reviewed in detail the Virginia Assembly's resolutions so fully clearing him. Since he had announced his intent to resign almost a year earlier, his relinquishment of the State Department was also in no sense a "desertion." Republicans were convinced that Patrick Henry's name had only been put up in Virginia as a blind for electors planning to vote for Adams.[185] A Federalist resurrection in 1800 of the false charges about Jefferson's conduct as governor was met with a letter by Judge John Tyler, testifying that herculean efforts by Jefferson had raised fewer than half enough men to defend Richmond, and that the Governor had been one of the very last to leave that city as the British entered it. In reality, Tyler continued, he had conscientiously remained at his post when many "blustering self-stiled federalists" would have cowered from danger or surrendered to British demands. Jefferson's war record, the letter held, had been excellent—and where could Americans' liberties be safer than with the author of the Declaration of Independence? The very behavior as Virginia's executive for which he had been upbraided showed his careful observance of popular rights and his opposition to centralized government.[186]

The *Centinel of Freedom* printed a song—"Jefferson and Liberty"—to counteract the "ADAMS and LIBERTY" shouted by Federalists; a part of it ran:

'Tis the wretches who wait
To unite Church and State
The name of MUNROE [*sic*], BURR and JEFFERSON hate.[187]

Far from overthrowing the Constitution, his partisans claimed the Virginian would strengthen that document. From Paris in 1788 he had allegedly rejoiced at its adoption, stating the addition of a Bill of Rights was all that was wanting. The *Independent Chronicle* even committed the schoolboy error of calling him "one of the framers of the Constitution"; more accurate writers simply demanded proof of his "plot" to destroy America's system of government. Jefferson had never evinced ambition for office, whereas Adams' writings applauded the British system of government.[188]

The two candidates differed in other respects. Adams, continued Republicans, held human beings incorrigible; the iron hand needed to keep them orderly would mean an ever more authoritarian government. Jefferson, they wrote, believed man could improve his lot if he were not regimented. Thus he inclined toward preserving the republican principles with which America's career began. Both men were honorable individuals, but it was held Jefferson had consistent political views whereas Adams' entire career showed no fixed beliefs. Jefferson considered morality essential to good government; Adams' appointments indicated he did not. In religion Jefferson deemed each person accountable solely to his Maker, while Adams was supported by the country's outstanding bigots. Jefferson's writing was described as clear and concise, and Adams' as prolix and ambiguous.[189]

Martinsville, North Carolina, publicly banned a pamphlet on *The Pretensions of Thomas Jefferson to the Presidency examined* . . . as the sort of lying publication coming to influence elections unduly. Boston's "Americanus" assured Federalists Jefferson would not dismiss them all from office nor destroy the funding system if elected. He argued that the Virginian would retain capable men at their posts, and clemency would help Republicans to remain in power. For Jefferson to destroy public credit, now dependent upon the deplorable funding, would undermine his own authority as President.[190]

Federalists again cited the Mazzei letter to "prove" Jefferson's ingratitude and animosity toward Washington. Republicans countered that Federalists employed Washington's memory "as an engine of election"; Americans could show true reverence for that memory "by declaring, that even his name shall not prevent the full use of your own understandings." Jefferson's own eulogy (to the effect that Washington's name would triumph over time and be adored as long as liberty had votaries) directly refuted those who claimed he calumniated the First President.[191]

For Federalists to complain about "scurrility" was like teaching fishes to swim. Though Jefferson drafted the document making America a separate nation and occupied the second highest office in the land, he was subjected to the malice of scriveners such as Cobbett. This malignity, Republicans claimed, really only insulted the people of those states that had given him their suffrages. Administration hirelings should examine their own columns to see if they did not contain abuse of Jefferson, who was also a governmental figure, at least equal to that which they protested in opposition papers.[192]

Among the libels against the Vice-President were some impugning his business honesty. To an allegation in 1800 that he had not paid certain debts to British merchants the *Examiner* elatedly expressed astonishment that his enemies attacked him on a score which could only add luster to his reputation. In 1774, it stated, Jefferson had sold 5,000 acres to pay Farrel and Jones in England, offering the purchasers' notes to his creditors' agent. The agent instead preferred to renew Jefferson's own note; during the Revolution the purchasers redeemed their obligations in Virginia's depreciated currency, which Jefferson (as required by law for debts due Englishmen) deposited in the state treasury. When the state failed to compensate British creditors after the war, Jefferson—instead of claiming the debt had been legally discharged in good faith —paid the sum a second time. His only other debt was to Kipper and Company, whose agent he saw immediately upon returning from France. That agent was on record, affirmed the paper, commending Jefferson's conduct as "strictly honourable." Thus could genuine virtue so stir malice that base fabrications were circulated as campaign weapons.[193]

Another issue was Jefferson's personal position respecting slavery. He never fully approved of the institution, as shown by a publicized letter to Benjamin Banneker on the desirability of elevating the Negro's condition. Yet Federalists still dwelled on the fact that the apostle of freedom owned over a hundred slaves. Southern Democrats found in this reassurance that he was not hostile to that species of property; word was that he considered slavery a question for the states themselves to handle. The *Examiner* admitted he wished to improve the black men's lot, but with due respect for society and the safety of their masters. It denied he favored immediate emancipation and scoffed at the thought his doctrines had inspired the Haitian massacres. Republicans saw the matter as purely an election trick; in the South Federalists accused Jefferson of plotting abolition, and in the North they charged him with favoring either banishment or perpetual slavery for Negroes. Besides, Washington, "as a GOD ador'd," had owned several times as many. "And likewise, how many hundreds, nay thousands and millions of human beings, the Sedition and Alien laws, & Hamilton's army were intended to hold in slavery." There were other forms of bondage than that distinguishable by color.[194] Slurring Federalist references to Jefferson's "Congo harem" were apparently considered beneath notice by Republican editors.[195]

Foes sneered at Jefferson's "pretensions to learning," but "An American" held him equal in political knowledge, thought, and literary ability to Washington himself. When the *Philadelphia Gazette,* reporting a postmaster's theft of a banknote, gibed that the culprit no doubt got his "extraordinary fondness for *Notes*" from following Jefferson, the replies were bitter. The aristocratic party, insisted Republicans, must be near its demise when it stooped to such miserable shifts as feeble witticisms at the expense of such a truly valuable contribution to scientific knowledge as the *Notes on Virginia.* For political reasons "Decius" might call Jefferson the "calumniator of Cresap" in asserting he had killed the relatives of a friendly Indian leader, but "A Friend of the People" retorted that the Maryland frontiersman had been definitely proved guilty of slaying Chief Logan's family at the outset of Lord Dunmore's War back in 1774.[196] Except from those favoring an established religion, the volume deserved rhapsodies. It breathed "a pure spirit of morality," and combined "the sweetness of Xenophon with the force of Polybius, information without parade, and eloquence without effort." Anyone should prize the opportunity to vote for such an author! [197]

Federalists alleged Jefferson's reports on weights and measures (to Congress under the Confederation) had been based on a British work, but the New York *Argus* challenged Professor John Kemp of Columbia College to satisfy the world on assertions he had furnished Jefferson the necessary calculations in the reports. Possibly he did so, for "Philo," four years later, contended the originality of the reports was unimportant. It required ability and judgment to recognize and apply earlier discoveries, and Jefferson—despite this "gothic age" of barbarism—would go down in history as a genuine scientist

and philosopher. Perhaps the most effective answer to deroga-
tions of Jefferson's scientific standing appeared in the *Carolina
Gazette*. It listed all the other officers of the American Philosophical Society for 1799 in lower case type, but heading the
roll was "THOMAS JEFFERSON, President." [198]

Other instances of praise signified the Virginian's popularity, kept his name favorably before the public, and stressed his
undeniable abilities. Accounts of banquet toasts to "the Virtuous and Patriotic THOMAS JEFFERSON" were frequent, and resolutions and letters lauding him found their way
into print. By 1800 he was the man "most like the immortal
George Washington." [199] His letters as Secretary of State to
Genêt proved he would be no puppet of France if elected. His
record showed him "one of the most enlightened and honorable statesmen who ever lived." Laudatory biographical accounts, usually entitled "The Character of Thomas Jefferson,"
appeared in numerous papers. The most popular version ran
about five newspaper columns, telling how fame had pursued
him and his "superior distinction . . . was founded on the alliance of virtue and fortune." Slow to anger, he was "invulner-
able to the shafts of malignity which fall everywhere around
him." [200] Only a false return in one state and the suppression
of votes in another had denied him the Presidency in 1796. "A
Friend of Truth" listed the high posts he had held, and tren-
chantly queried; "If Mr. Jefferson is so bad a man, what are
all those who had so highly confided in him?" [201]

Republicans found every aspect of Jefferson's life "an ornament to human nature," and argued people were beginning to
esteem public personages in direct proportion to the dirt flung
at them by groups such as the "Essex Junto." The *Aurora* cynically summarized the mudslinging with a list of "IMPERI-
OUS REASONS why THOMAS JEFFERSON SHOULD
NOT BE ELECTED PRESIDENT"—and included his
authorship of the Declaration of Independence and the statute
for religious toleration in Virginia. Even after a Republican
victory was assured his magnanimous letters disclosed he

would not make the executive branch of government preponderant, and would try to reconcile the differences which had "been artificially excited" between the parties.[202]

Religion, or the lack of it, produced perhaps the bitterest contumely of the entire campaign. Jefferson's inclination toward rationalism indicated he favored a mild form of deism; after Franklin's death and Paine's removal to Europe, he was America's best known man of that leaning. To bigots or Federalists with political ends in view this was at one with atheism, and he was pilloried as a man without religion.[203]

Some of this abuse cropped out in 1796, when "ALGERNON SIDNEY" in rebuttal stressed the silence of the Constitution on the religious beliefs of the President. Presumably his doctrinal opinions were not a public concern; in any event, Article II restricted the powers of any Executive who might be disposed to interfere. If a charge of irreligion were intended to imply immorality, it backfired; unlike some of his hypocritical opponents, Jefferson's private life was spotless. The devil sometimes used religion as a screen for wicked designs, and such seemed Federalist policy. Hamilton, their chief, was

> well known for his many moral qualities. Glowing from the incestuous embraces of some deluded wife, or perhaps running from some public brothel, he flies to the anti-chamber of his office, in a moment he conjures back assumption, and excise laws, entrusts them to his faithful myrmidons, who with zeal only equalled by the faithful crew of fallen spirits, sanction by their authoritative voice, these edicts of injustice, robbery and oppression.[204]

Pro-British scribblers labeled Jefferson deist because he opposed an established hierarchy. Whatever his personal creed, he possessed the true spirit of Christianity, advocating toleration and resisting governmental interference between a man and his God. Why did Federalists remain silent concerning Adams' communications with the Socinians? Surely a person who denied the divinity of Christ was no more to be relied upon than a deist. In reality, honest investigation showed conclusively that Jefferson believed in Providence. His writings stated bluntly: *"We are answerable* for them [rights of conscience] to our GOD." [205]

The election year of 1800 witnessed the full flood of abuse. The *Chronicle* said Jefferson was censured for urging repeal of Virginia's laws against deism and atheism. But if these beliefs were criminal, then "why not Arians and Socinians, as their sentiments lead to the same fountain?" If elected Jefferson would occupy the presidential chair with as much orthodoxy as Washington and more purity than Hamilton. From all the pother, one might think the man a candidate for the papacy rather than the Presidency.[206]

His opposition to religious tests and the mandates of a dictatorial clergy entitled him "to equal honor with the immortal Luther." A man's fitness for office should rest on his *moral* conduct rather than profession of any particular religious dogma. Jefferson's opposition to persecution and his belief that every man should worship God according to the dictates of his conscience proved him a champion of "the WHOLE CHURCH," and not just a fractional part of it. Were he an atheist, said the Baltimore *American,* he no more deserved to "be president than [judge] Sam Chase," but countless instances existed of his true reverence. No honest man could read the preamble to his statute for religious freedom and discover any sentiments other than those of the highest Christianity therein. Cries of "Sabbath-breaking" and "infidelity" came well from the party which had profaned the Apostle's Creed by publishing a travesty on it to deride Pennsylvania's Governor McKean, which had a Luther Martin, Maryland's Attorney-General, reeling drunkenly down Baltimore streets after Sunday dinners, and which prated of the Decalogue (including the injunction against adultery) when it was proficient "only in the study of *'Hoyle on Gaming.'* " [207]

If Jefferson favored irreligion and immorality, he would favor *"a standing army"* as one of the most effective means of forwarding such ideas. Since he did not, accusations of promoting these evils were groundless. Voltaire had noted that in

Europe "atheism" was commonly charged to discredit persons whose political views were disapproved.[208] The *Notes on Virginia* were utilized both for and against their author. Federalists cited the passage, "What matters it if my neighbor believes there to be twenty Gods or no God? It neither picks my pocket nor breaks my leg." They usually gave just enough of it to make it appear *Jefferson* felt it unimportant whether there were twenty Gods or none—and damned him as an atheist. Republicans railed at this lifting of words out of context; Jefferson's accusers, frantic at approaching defeat, had converted his "reasoning against *religious establishments,* into a blasphemous argument against religion itself." The *Notes* (which should have been read in their entirety) called slavery a moral evil, and liberty a gift from God; only a hypocrite could say an atheist wrote such words. Such use of incomplete statements would give an entirely erroneous impression of even the Bible—witness Galatians 3:13 ("Christ being made a curse for us").[209]

Federalist politicians who deserted righteousness for money and power were the real promoters of atheism and deism. Clerical support for Adams resembled "papism," and the adoration shown the President was actually irreverent. Such clergymen forgot Washington's dictum (here Republicans were using the "transfer" appeal) that "the path of true piety is so plain as to require but little political direction." His opponents might preach religion, but Jefferson *practiced* it. Soon someone would accuse him directly of being a Christian, "or what is perhaps still worse, of being an honest man, a crime which some people can never forgive." [210]

Another ugly Federalist tale ran that Jefferson, riding past a neglected church with Mazzei, had remarked it was *"good enough for him that was born in a Manger."* Republicans felt this shrewdly perfidious; Mazzei had returned to Europe and could not deny the story before election time, and Dr. John B. Smith (to whom he supposedly related the incident) was dead. The *Vermont Gazette* printed Dr. Smith's "true version" of what had actually happened: Mazzei, commenting on the run-down appearance of the building, stated Italian priests would refuse to enter such a place. Jefferson had replied, "And yet *meaner places were deemed grand enough to dispense truth in, by* HIM *who was born in a manger."* Surely this was at least as credible as any tale with a "Porcupine" foundation.[211]

A truly Christian people, said Jeffersonians, would keep church separate from state, if only to preserve the clergy from corruption. The instant rulers united politics and religion America would be under a religious tyranny. Jefferson was a philosopher who lived his faith and was *known* to be attached to the Constitution; these facts were said to "irresistably demand" his election.[212] A change in national politics was desperately needed, lest America follow England's path and find all liberties undermined. Thus considerable interdenominational support had developed for Jefferson; nine of New York City's thirteen newly chosen legislators were said to be "elders or principals of different religious congregations." In an effort to counteract this support, bigots such as Parson Linn had branded Jefferson a deist whose election would endanger religion. Fortunately, the age of delusion was passing; well-known Christians had completely refuted Linn and had shown Jefferson's views coincided with those of the great divines. His election would be a justified rebuke to "the strong predilection of ambitious and dictatorial priests" for meddling in temporal affairs. The false alarm of "religion is in danger" had been too often prostituted.[213]

In some respects climaxing the campaign, though it proved poorly timed, was what conceivably may have been the most daring hoax in American politics. Whether Federalists deliberately originated the story, or capitalized on a misunderstanding enabling them to practice "psychological warfare" seems impossible to prove. Since the tale apparently first saw print in a Jeffersonian paper, the latter is more probable. But Federalists circulated it, and seldom troubled to deny it even after it had been exploded. Republican reaction was instantaneous and illuminating, yet had the "news" been postponed three months it might possibly have won the election for Adams.

The story was that Jefferson had suddenly died. *"P. S.— MELANCHOLY"* was the heading in the Baltimore *American.* Two men from Winchester, said the editor, had the sad report via horseback rider from Charlottesville; Thomas Jefferson had succumbed "after an indisposition of 48 hours." Prayers were offered to the Deity that the information might be untrue. The Philadelphia *True American* picked up the story next day, and the day afterward (without quite so much evidence of regret) the New York *Commercial Advertiser* carried it. Simultaneously the *Gazette of the United States* noted "the report of Mr. Jefferson's death appears to be entitled to some credit." [214]

Democratic printers questioned the information almost from the start. The day after its announcement, the *American* stated mail from Charlottesville gave no indication of Jefferson's illness or demise. In New York the skeptical *American Citizen* observed that no other Philadelphia paper mentioned the item, that names of the news bearers (here given as being from Fredericktown) could not be ascertained, and that nothing was said about the nature of the illness. First to brand the tale "A Federal Bone" was the *Aurora,* claiming Federalists had spread it to dampen Republican spirits on the Fourth of July. On that Independence Day, when a correspondent from Alexandria told of seeing two letters in the statesman's own handwriting, the *American* gleefully proclaimed "JEFFERSON lives," and congratulated citizens that the author of the Declaration would in all probability be at the head of the government for the next birthday of the nation.[215]

Best explanation for the story was that a Negro near Monticello named Tom, who had once lived with Jefferson's family, had died and someone had jumped to the conclusion it was the Democratic leader.[216] Yet—accident or design—the report was widely spread and caused Democrats no little concern. It was "a *federal trick*" and "*absolutely false,*" stormed the *Centinel of Freedom*. The editor of the *Constitutional Telegraphe* named it a "FAKE RUMOUR," and marked "the grim horrible, and ghastly smiles of *a few well known old tories, refugees and apostate whigs*" when the original story reached Boston. After carefully attempting to trace the report, he concluded "it must have originated with a deranged or lying aristocratic federalist." The *Newport Mercury,* though not strongly Republican, also carried an article denouncing the tale as one of Federalist invention and circulation. The *Gazette of the United States* did note the erroneousness of the news, and twitted Democrats for their alarm, but most Federalist papers simply dropped the matter. Republican editors sensed "malignant motives" behind the affair, but rejoiced in its failure and in the added fillip given to their party's sentiments: "The upright, the patriotic and the virtuous Thomas Jefferson still lives, the ornament of his country, and worthy of universal suffrage." [217]

# XIV ELECTIONEERING TACTICS

Like its military counterpart, political campaigning faces many uncertainties. Ability to capitalize on the accidental or unexpected may at times spell the difference between success and disaster. Republican editors quickly comprehended that unforeseen occurrences frequently might be turned to their advantage. Such incidents might be fitted into preconceived long-range strategic planning; more often they were exploited as the occasion arose. Sometimes an attack from the administration could be neatly converted into a telling counter-thrust.

Clearly, as already noted, certain Federalist "name-calling" fell into this latter category. Accusations of "disorder" frequently backfired, for Republicans delightedly gloated over any departures from strict decorum by their opponents. They also worked to convince the public their own loyalty to the Constitution and representative government was (despite contrary assertions) infinitely more genuine than that of the Federalists. In 1800 they argued the Constitution's very life depended on Jefferson's election, even though he was undoubtedly backed by most of those who had opposed adoption of the fundamental law—along with many who had favored it. Experience had convinced these earlier critics that there was scant danger of despotism under a just construction of the document, and yet "mischiefs have arisen, not from the constitution but from the abuse of it." After being briefly tutored by the notorious Duer, asserted Republicans, Hamilton had inaugurated the funding system and had set in motion countless violations of the charter. Federalists from the outset had employed their favorite trick of confusing opposition to the administration with disloyalty to the Constitution and government itself, even though in reality Republican principles coincided with both national welfare and the concepts of the Founding Fathers.[1]

So it was with national unity. While Federalists had long belabored the opposition as "disorganizers," evidence after Washington's retirement indicated not all administration followers considered the Union inviolate. Republicans deplored war with France as needless and unwise, but they normally expressed willingness to defend their country and disclaimed plans for actual secession. Contrariwise, some Federalists murmured of a separation if Adams were defeated in 1796, and the "High Federalist" war party of 1799 questioned the wisdom of remaining within a nation pusillanimous enough to consider peace with the Directory. Jeffersonian printers saw these as maleficent effects of an intense partisanship that preferred national dissolution to political disappointment:

> The happy continuation of our union has not only been threatened by a series of untoward measures but its very *expedience* has been openly questioned. How consistent is this with an affected attachment to *order* and the exclusive character of federalism let the people be the judge![2]

Several Republican papers either published or cited "Burleigh's" diatribes against Jefferson during the campaign of 1800. The New England writer suggested that if "Jacobins" took over and toppled the Constitution, "the northern states, being much more generally Federal, will be more united, and better able to form a government for themselves, than the southern." Democrats retorted that this paragon of loyalty (former Congressman John Allen of Connecticut) was "one of those peculators or speculators, who voted in the last year of Mr. *Adams's* stewardship, to run the country eight millions of dollars in debt; a sum sufficient to load two hundred thirty-five waggons." Neighbors of "Burleigh" hinted that "while he assisted to run the country in debt, he managed to . . . improve his own circumstances." Apparently he was "rather more attached to his own interest than to that of the community" and feared an accounting might be required if Jefferson triumphed. Assuredly his talk of a northern confederacy was in itself all-sufficient comment upon Federalist loyalty to the United States as such.[3]

Printed epithets came into their own during the American Revolution,[4] were utilized in the struggle over adoption of the Constitution, and continued essentially unabated. Inasmuch as the terms "ARISTOCRAT" and "DEMOCRAT" were so bandied about, the *Independent Chronicle* undertook to define them in an acrostic:

| | | |
|---|---|---|
| Ambitious | : | Decent |
| Robber, an | : | Enticing |
| Impudent | : | Modest |
| Slovenly | : | Obliging |
| Treacherous | : | Careful |
| Outrageous | : | Religious and |
| Crafty | : | Amiable |
| Rigorous | : | Tradesman. |
| Artful | : | |
| Turk | : | |
| or one who wants an Arbitrary Government, and a share in the administration thereof. | : | or other good citizen, who wishes a government founded on the Rights of the People, or one who endeavors to support such a one when established.[5] |

When Federalists, relieved at Adams' narrow victory in 1796, expressed hope that he and Jefferson by their offices would be able to end discord and unite the people, Republicans swiftly exposed the hypocrisy. While the result was in doubt writers in the *Columbian Centinel* had represented Jefferson as a disorganizer and anarchist—"in short, as a thorn in the government! Let these British tools reconcile these inconsistent cries if they can."[6] A prominent pro-administration paper might be denominated a "COMMON SEWER of the Tory faction," and correspondence committees formed to generate sentiment favoring House appropriations for Jay's covenant were compared to terrorist groups in the bloodiest days of the French Revolution. These American organizations had been formed secretly, persuaded clergymen to laud men plotting the country's ruin, and were inimical to free deliberations in Congress. "What think ye now of 'self-created Societies,' ye TREATY TERRORISTS?"[7]

Democrats held they had the nation's true interests at heart. Unanimous approval of Pinckney's and Wayne's treaties proved Democrats acknowledged merit and did not, as Federalists claimed, reprobate every act of the administration. Despite insinuations, they were not tarred with foreign influence. Gallic ideas had not corrupted America's public characters; honest men opposed many measures of the federal government simply because such measures were obnoxious in themselves— but Federalists accused "every republican channel of information" of being in French pay. Many administration leaders had never wanted the Revolution to affect anything other than political ties with Britain, and some were beginning to regret even that. A "staunch Federalist" was reputedly overheard declaiming that

> Mr. Adams was right for the people were originally deceived into the revolution, they would never have taken up arms in the beginning, had they supposed that it would have gone the length that it since had arrived at; things have now [under Adams] taken the right turn, they are going back to their proper state again.[8]

The "Ministerialists of *America*" had accepted the Constitution only because it provided the maximum of centralization obtainable; they had ridiculed the Bill of Rights and had acquiesced in it reluctantly. The *Chronicle* cynically queried, "What is FEDERALISM?" When the administration's program suited Federalist editors any criticism of officials was undermining the entire structure of government, but they freely censured Adams' moves toward peace. Truth was that in the "Anglo-Federalist Vocabulary" the Constitution was "a mere substitute . . . a form of government *made* to produce traitors." Adams as Vice-President had readily surrendered such senatorial rights as being truly consulted on executive appointments because he confidently expected to succeed to the Executive chair. The Federalist-sponsored Ross's election bill, which would have virtually permitted the President to appoint an "Upper House," and machinations with Burr in the House balloting showed complete disregard for the fundamental law.[9]

Was it not significant that Federalist newspapers frequently failed to publish the Declaration of Independence when July rolled around, though Republican organs consistently commemorated that anniversary? The principles in that immortal document were the basis for all subsequent just policies; it and the Constitution were the foundation of America's true government. "Either the Declaration . . . is wrong, or those who look to it are still right." In reality the "New Tories" were worse than the old. Frequently confidence was reposed in them, and they would lead America "through the channel of dreadful deception, headlong to a state of political ruin."[10]

As already noted, one of the most potent Federalist artifices was the cry to "stand by Washington." Insofar as he directly endorsed certain policies, this was the technique later categorized as "testimonial." If an attempt were made to indirectly support a policy through association with his name, the device could be denominated "transfer."[11] In either case the effect was noteworthy.

Republicans asserted the Senate had not been "consulted" in the naming of Gouverneur Morris as minister to France; consent was gained "through terror of a name." Even though Bache considered seven-eighths of them under British influence, he was amazed "with what insolence the courtly junto throw the President [Washington] into the foreground of all their dirty pasquinades, to give them a currency."[12] During the furor over the Jay Treaty, when critics contended Washington was selling his country, an old soldier retorted the General had made and raised the nation and could be trusted with it in any market. Pleading for implementation of the treaty, Federalists asked whether people intended to support Washington or that instigator of the Whiskey Rebellion, Albert Gallatin. Randolph's dismissal, expostulated Democrats, showed a certain party had "unfortunately gotten the president's confidence," and also that it was dangerous to express an opinion contrary to any partisan view he had openly adopted. In 1800 a concerted Federalist effort was made to show Adams had followed Washington's policies. On Washington's birthday the *Columbian Mirror* used two pages to reprint the Farewell Address—"The legacy of the Father of his Country." American readers would prefer this state paper to any foreign news items: "From it the misguided will find a clue to the path of Patriotism, and the wavering be able to decide; while the Federalist may exult on his great example." [13]

At times, though, "transfer" could also be used by the opposition. However much they affected to despise it as a Federalist device, Republican editors were quick to employ it when practicable. In 1796 some Massachusetts Federalist legislators attacked naming Presidential electors by popular vote. The *Independent Chronicle* termed these men enemies of Washington, casting aspersions on past electors so chosen who had voted for the First President. By 1799 certain Republican writers were praying for prolongation of his life—notwithstanding the "many errors into which he has been led . . . by the easiness of his nature," Washington's "bare existence is a control upon a daring and ambitious spirit [Hamilton] that would lead us to monarchy." Next spring Gerry was supported for governor of Massachusetts because he had "acted in every situation agreeable to the recommendation of Washington in his Legacy," and "Sidney" blatantly denied any similarity between the conduct of the first President and that of the second. The latter had approved the Sedition Act, whereas the former never during his public life wished to gag the mouths of his fellow citizens or prevent any inquiry into his conduct. . . . The integrity of his own heart and the testimony of a breast filled with love of his country, was to him a sufficient shield against all the darts of malevolence.[14]

Republicans claimed (now that denial was impossible) that Washington had died just as he was awakening to the hideous errors of Federalist foreign policy. The *Bee* felt him chiefly responsible for sending a new mission to France and stated he had been heard to express himself more severely against Britain "for the last two months of his life than for several years past." Had Hamilton not so long deceived him, he would have on all occasions acted with Jefferson, Madison, and other staunch Democrats.[15]

Jeffersonians also appealed to the Farewell Address. "Old South" said its stress on economy, love of the Union, and dislike for large military establishments thoroughly confounded Federalist sophists. Ames's "funeral oration" had been wilfully misleading, and criticism rather than eulogy, when it implied Washington had opposed the French Revolution. The tragedy was that public officials had not followed the policies outlined in the First President's valedictory. The program they had actually pursued had been very nearly disastrous, and in the eyes of the world America had lost the moral leadership that had been its possession in 1783.[16]

If Federalists claimed credit for the nation's material well-being they must concede that at least a "portion of the miseries with which a people become afflicted" was attributable to bad government. Adams may have tried to alleviate the troubles of the country, but he in fact devoted his "abilities such as they are . . . to measures whose tendency is to aggravate and increase them." Bank statements, the crowded dockets of American courts, and the millions due in private notes or for British importations afforded "a true picture of the internal prosperity" of the nation.[17]

The whiplash of criticism flicked many another wound. St.

Clair's defeat by Western Indians embarrassed the administration in divers ways. It produced charges of graft and incompetence,[18] lamentations about the cost and ineffectiveness of the Indian policy generally, and accusations of official persecution in a vain effort to uncover a scapegoat. St. Clair had testified that General Richard Butler (killed in the battle) had not passed on to him information received from Captain Jacob Slough of an Indian concentration before the engagement. Butler's brigade major, Ensign John Morgan, defending his fallen chief, asserted no such report was made to Butler and that St. Clair himself had ordered Slough's reconnaissance. This Slough denied, and Secretary of War Knox called Morgan in for questioning. When, at the request of Butler's widow, Morgan turned the correspondence in the case over to the newspapers for publication, St. Clair arrested him for mutiny.[19]

Republican editors chose to regard Butler as a conveniently silent victim of administration blunders and Morgan as a brave and honest subordinate risking his future to defend his superior's memory. Refused an immediate trial where fellow officers might have testified on his behalf, after months of confinement Morgan was summoned to Cincinnati from South Carolina to answer the charges against him. Anti-administration columns labeled this order to stand trial at a frontier post, where neither accusers nor evidence were available, *"tyranny and despotism"* on the part of Knox and St. Clair. Those who had wanted Cabinet members to appear personally before Congress were reminded "circumstances alter cases." Knox had denied

> the heroic MORGAN . . . trial on the spot, where he could produce substantial evidence of the truths he asserted, and . . . ordered [him] hundreds of miles into the wilderness for the purpose. Let not then the Secretary of War complain of 'ex parte evidence.'[20]

The viciousness shown against Morgan argued something more than private pique. St. Clair had implied his cowardice, though volunteer witnesses had sworn to his courage. The only question remaining was "whether it is an act of mutiny in an inferior officer, to write and point out to the . . . executive of the United States, the misconduct and official misrepresentation of his commanding general." After acquittal seemed likely, the unrelenting St. Clair induced the court to reopen the case, renewing charges of mutiny, though correspondents felt Morgan had proved the accuracy of his assertions.[21]

In truth, the affair was drawn out unconscionably. New Year's Day, 1794, saw reports that the verdict of the court-martial had finally reached the President, but despite rumors the ensign had been acquitted he did not for six weeks officially learn his fate. It was eventually revealed he had been cleared of falsehood and cowardice, but found guilty of appealing to Knox over his commander's head. Notwithstanding some talk of dismissal, he was let off with a reprimand from the Secretary. Administration critics snorted at this "leniency"; this had been an attempt to victimize a junior officer and make him a whipping boy for incompetence in high places. Intimidation was to be the order of the day against all who dared question Federalist measures.[22]

Another presumably unrehearsed incident of which Republicans were able to make partisan capital centered around Matthew Lyon, Vermont's stormy petrel of politics. A fire-eating patriot with a flair for histrionics and crude oratory, Lyon possessed a war record about which there had been some question. As a lieutenant commanding a detachment in advance of Gates's army, Lyon was court-martialled after his men (apparently against his will) retreated without orders. He was cashiered, and an unfounded story developed that Gates had forced him to don a wooden sword and had drummed him out of camp. Though accusations of cowardice were probably groundless—Vermonters elected him to civil posts during the war—the high-strung Lyon was understandably sensitive concerning the matter.[23]

Some years after the Revolution, Lyon established a printing press at Fair Haven, where he and his paper soon became noted for outstanding Republicanism. After three narrow defeats, he was finally elected to Congress in 1796 from the Western District of Vermont, and he vigorously resisted measures leading toward war or increased federal expenditures. His bumptiousness and extreme Jeffersonianism speedily made him a target for Federalist "lies and shafts of malice poured forth from a set of parasites." Democrats compared these attacks to stones thrown by children at the stars and urged Lyon to continue his efforts until America truly learned economy.[24]

Clearly Lyon had stamped himself as a man for Federalists to eliminate from public life if possible, and Representative Roger Griswold of Connecticut taunted him on the floor of Congress about the wooden sword episode. The infuriated Vermonter thereupon spat in Griswold's face, and Federalists haled him before the House Committee on Privilege for expulsion proceedings. The *Independent Chronicle* wanted Griswold expelled for his insult. With a French war imminent:

> It is time good manners should take the place of the Grub-street trash which the *Royalists* celebrate for their wit. Connecticut wit, is proverbial; but it has not often met its just punishment before. Mr. Griswold, we presume, as he has had the *prudence* not to strike, will in the future be more cautious than to indulge his tongue in *language* which he does not choose to *support*.[25]

Philadelphia society was indignant at the incident, and Cobbett sneered the "Spitting Lyon" sadly needed taming. Hard-pressed Republican printers felt compelled to defend the ill-mannered congressman in order to prevent his imprisonment. They charged Griswold with the cowardice he mocked in Lyon, and then inconsistently noted that violation of the House injunction (after a scuffle between the two men) against further conflict would be a clear breach of privilege. Lyon was a representative of the people, and Congress should protect its members from infamous attacks. Moreover, Lyon's foes called him coward in one breath, and in the next accused him of constantly seeking a fight![26]

The Committee on Privilege recommended expulsion, but a vote closely following party lines permitted Lyon to retain his seat. The *Aurora,* gloating that several Federalist *"Hot-bloods"* had declared seats in Congress disgraceful if Lyon remained, suggested a half-dozen choice resignations to speed up the public business that had been neglected over questions of privilege. The whole affair was silly when war threatened with France and insults from England abounded.[27] Low puns were made concerning the importance Federalists attached to punishing the "American Lyon" for expectorating while they crouched "like Spaniels" to receive much greater indignities from "the British Lion," and a scatological letter from a spurious "BRITISH AGENT" ordered 1,200 chamber pots *"with the likeness* of SIR ROGER SPITTLE *at the bottom thereof."* [28]

One account had Lyon sending Griswold a challenge, but so pusillanimous was the latter that he had the bearer of the note thrown in jail. Had Griswold agreed to a duel "instead of muttering and wiping the spittle from his chops," the nation would have been saved a "Jockey Wrangle" and several thousand dollars' worth of wasted time. Federalists obviously sought to eliminate Lyon's vote and refused to consider lesser penalties. Speaker Dayton had permitted Griswold to mouth further insults while quickly calling Lyon to order, but considered a mere reprimand ineffectual because he lacked "words of thunder" to "BLAST" the Vermonter. The *Bee* stated Federalist barking against "the *Lyon"* was echoed by *"curs"* throughout America, but the king of beasts laughed "their vain attempts to scorn, and though gored by every cowardly *bullock* [29] in the land will rise superior to all their malice." [30]

Certainly the Federalist press seethed with accounts of Lyon's "barbarism," and applauded the caning Griswold gave him shortly afterward. Republicans called this surprise attack vicious, cited other Federalist insults, and referred sarcastically to that party's "respect for law and order." Lyon himself wrote widely reprinted open letters to his constituents, attacking discretionary powers that would make the President a "Monarch," urging that ministers' stations and pay be fixed, and giving his side of the dispute with Griswold. He pledged himself to resign if defeated in the forthcoming election, but said those who objected to his behavior toward the Connecticut congressman would almost certainly cavil at any course he took.[31]

Although foes vowed that if Lyon ever started a newspaper in Connecticut he would get more kicks than customers, correspondents reported his economic and political views were highly popular there as well as in Vermont. Pro-administration gazettes demanded his repudiation in 1798, but Lyon gained a plurality in the congressional election despite his imprisonment for sedition. With Democratic journals exploiting his persecution, he managed to win the run-off and return to Philadelphia. Thus, partly through Jeffersonian press efforts and partly because of his own bluff popularity, Lyon became a national figure and a symbol of resistance to administration abuse.[32] When the brother of a Federalist Connecticut congressman spat in the face of his legal antagonist during a court trial, many Republicans felt even the stigma upon their party for indecent behavior had been somewhat relieved.[33]

Political martyrs are an asset to any party and doubly so when it is in the process of formation, but Republicans strove in many other ways to build up an organization and gain adherents for their cause. Clinton, Madison, and Jefferson were so interested in forming groups among the agricultural and laboring classes that Federalist papers early in the decade began protesting over these "conspiracies" against the "government."[34] Electioneering notices for candidates of differing views appeared in the press almost from the start. Some of these were informal if emphatic:

> Mr. PRINTER,
> At our town-meeting which our warrant says is to be on the last Monday of this month, I and all my *neighbours* intend to vote for Judge WHITE, Mr. JAMES SHEAFE, and Mr. WILLIAM PLUMER [for Congress], and we don't care who knows it.
> A COUNTRY-MAN.[35]

Others were more elaborate. "BRUTUS" appealed to inhabitants of the County of Philadelphia (as distinguished from residents of the city itself) to pick a Representative who would bring Pennsylvania the prestige to which her position in the Union entitled her:

> Panegyric would be fruitless, after informing you that your eye would be properly directed to the late speaker of the Federal House of Representatives, FREDERICK AUGUSTUS MUHL-ENBERG. This gentleman's character needs no eulogium. . . . The dignified rank he held as Speaker . . . —the high estimation he was held in by the different delegations, which raised him to this station—the general satisfaction which he gave—and the eclat with which he vacated the chair, all solicit your interest and regard:—His habits of political life—his intimate acquaintance with the interests of this State, and of the Union—his education and information—his spotless integrity, all point him out as the most eligible character which is offered to your consideration. It would be a misfortune to the State of Pennsylvania to lose this Gentleman's abilities and influence, and lost they will be unless the citizens of this district should adopt him; for the Philadelphians necessarily require a commercial character, or FREDERICK AUGUSTUS MUHLENBERG would be the man of their choice.[36]

A Virginia paper reported certain candidates soliciting support as presidential electors from that state in 1792 were "decidedly in favor of Republican men for the high offices of President and Vice-President." The "Gentleman who has offered his services" to the Norfolk district "declares to the voters his determination to vote *only for such persons as are of known Republican principles.*" [37]

Thomas McKean, Alexander J. Dallas, and other Pennsylvania Democrats formed a Committee of Correspondence in 1792. Initially professing non-partisanship, it sent out questionnaires to candidates and then list_d the men it deemed fit to serve. Thus it hoped to "dispel dark clouds of ignorance and tyranny"; of course most of the names approved were Republican. This committee, or one descending from it, still functioned near the century's close. In the gubernatorial race of 1799 its published address exhibited "in strong colors the personal merits and public services of Mr. McKean," whose friends printed letters to voters in various papers throughout Pennsylvania and organized committees for him in a number of counties.[38]

The *National Gazette* again supported Muhlenberg, as an experienced and firm Republican, in 1793. Several notices that year blamed Governor Mifflin for non-enforcement of certain laws, appointments for purely personal reasons, and followers' threats of physical violence against those who chose to vote against him. Farther north, "An Independent Tradesman" exhorted Bostonians to bestir themselves from the torpor into which "Tories' fair speeches" had lulled them. Unless liberty's supporters were firm and united its friends might be turned out of the Massachusetts legislature.[39]

Old Tories made constant reiteration of democratic principles necessary everywhere if the blessings of those principles were to be preserved. In 1794 the *Independent Chronicle* toiled manfully to defeat Fisher Ames for Congress from the Boston district. "Almost every Tory" was said to be supporting this Anglophile. When Federalists printed a list of prominent men for Ames, The *Chronicle* sarcastically singled out reactionaries Stephen Higginson and Eben Parsons as "particular friends to the Tradesmen and Manufacturers of this town." [40]

"AN ALARM" warned Philadelphians that Adams, a monarchist and proponent of hereditary government might be elected President in 1796, "unless you will turn out on Friday the fourth day of November, & by your votes call forth Thomas Jefferson, the friend of the people, a republican in principle and manners, whose talents will bear a comparison with those of any man of the United States." [41] A North Carolina candidate for elector pledged his vote for Jefferson and advertised a criticism of Adams' aristocatic views. That state's citizens had been denied an opportunity to vote for presidential electors in 1792, and the *North Carolina Journal* wanted all candidates to similarly announce their intention in order that the vote would truly reflect the will of the commonwealth. More and more electoral candidates were indicating for whom they would vote, but the practice was yet far from universal.[42] Up-state New Yorkers formed nominating tickets and committees of correspondence early in the year. That most of these early campaigners were of the party desiring to cram British policies down American throats was significant, Republicans said. It showed the royalists regarded the election of 1796 as crucial; lovers of freedom should take heed.[43]

Democratic electioneering of the 1790s generally consisted of candidates' announcements for political posts, assertions of the necessity of choosing Jeffersonians, and repeated assurances that if the people only roused themselves the forces of reaction could be suppressed. Alleged Federalist ruses, such as warnings of war or claims that changes in the state legislature would displace Washington from the Presidency, were exposed and ridiculed. Federalists were pictured as alarmed and fearful of Republican strength; their offers of coalition tickets were mere expedients, by which they hoped to elect at least a few of their candidates through Jeffersonian votes. In New York City, where Republicans needed a clean sweep of the city delegation to achieve a majority in the legislature, Federalists could well afford to do this, and had they the power to carry a ticket of their own they would have proposed no coalition.[44]

Each "ensuing election" was "of primary concern" and would determine "the political complexion of affairs" for some time to come. The situation in the state or nation hinged upon Republican success in the local balloting, and a Federalist victory might bring a drastically curtailed franchise. "These are surely motives strong enough to induce every freeman, who feels the least interest in the welfare of his country to step forward." Writers warned somnolent Democrats that election of a Federalist governor or congressman might entail a base surrender of popular rights, or flayed "hesitators" who secretly approved Republican efforts but took no active part in the contest.[45]

New Jersey committees of delegates from township organizations in Essex and Morris counties certified that town meetings had picked identical Republican tickets for state offices in 1799, and urged signing petitions for popular choice of presidential electors. "BOB SHORT" in Boston observed "Republicans of the Southern States 'work it right,' " and urged their

573

Massachusetts colleagues to quickly select their gubernatorial candidate and get his name before the public. Committess of correspondence should be established throughout the state.[46]

Newspaper campaigning reached new heights in 1800, for this most important contest would "fix our national character" and possibly decide the fate of liberty the world over. In March the *Raleigh Register* notified readers that Messrs. Alston and Rogers, "both good Republicans," were candidates for electors. "Friends of the Federal Republican interest" in New York were asked to meet at the City Tavern Hotel "to take measures respecting the APPROACHING ELECTION." The *American Citizen* stressed New York's importance nationally and the gravity of the issues; an article "to the citizens of the United States" accented the urgency of choosing Republican candidates, and there were predictions headed "Republican and Federal Calculations and Designs." Vermonters were reminded of the time of their congressional election, and Virginians were implored to save America from the domestic tyranny of an "Easterner" as they had once saved her from a foreign yoke. New Jersey's "JACK OAKUM" told all the crew of the Federal ship that when they were piped on deck to elect a commander for the next voyage he'd not vote for Adams. Adams had not used the Constitution as a compass and had threatened old sailors who showed him the ship was endangered. Jefferson, on the other hand, was a courageous, loyal, and able seaman who had been a good first mate under Washington.[47]

These campaign notices reiterated, or presented in condensed form, many of the issues. "AN AMERICAN" called "caucus influence" worse than that of either England or France. Americans could meet European pressures—"we can read, and Newspapers, those eminently useful vehicles of information, are in almost every man's hand"—but against secret control there was no defense. Both political parties tended to use "Republican" as a term of approbation; Elbridge Gerry and Federalist Caleb Strong were each so called in Massachusetts, and Levi Lincoln (running for Congress) was hailed as "no Frenchman" but "a Republican whig in 1775 and a Republican federalist today." [48]

Republican meetings and the candidates they chose to support were dutifully recorded. Oftentimes these meetings called for publication of their proceedings in specified papers sympathetic to their cause. To draw voters to the polls, the *New Jersey Journal* invoked "that spirit which compelled you to resist . . . the British tyrant" to "clip the aspiring wings of any domestic usurper." "Freedom of choice and the citizen voting," expounded one Kentuckian, "is the . . . GREAT PALLADIUM OF LIBERTY." He saw public treats for voters, and candidates' bows and "thank you, sirs" every time citizens announced them as their choice, as insidious steps to undermine legal prohibitions on open bribery. No man of independence would bow and scrape; if he were the better candidate, the voters were doing *themselves* a favor. Men extremely anxious for votes probably had more than the public interest at heart. Occasionally Federalist arguments were converted into appeals to Democratic partisans. The *New Hampshire Gazette* noted that counter attractions or inclement weather reduced the Federalist vote while nothing hindered "the jacobins" from turning out full force. This fact, commented the Baltimore *American,* disclosed Federalist preoccupation with trifles and revealed Republicans as firm, active, and vigilant.[49]

"Dialogs" between purported Federalists and Republicans, with the latter inevitably possessing the better case, appeared in pre-election periods. "ELECTION DAY IS FREEMAN'S DAY," reminded "WASHINGTON." On this occasion men of spirit could express their reprobation for high taxes, sedition laws, alien acts, and hostility toward France. "Lycurgus" insisted the popular will was for Jefferson. Adams, if by some subterfuge elected, would face a Republican House and a weakened Senate; he should refuse the Presidency in any case, for the people had lost confidence in him and only Jefferson could preserve the Union. Voters who failed to turn out would forfeit their share in the glorious "VICTORY

OF REASON AND TRUTH over error"; even where victory seemed a foregone conclusion, Republicans should not be lulled into overconfidence.[50]

Republican press comments and editorials to some extent attempted to "get out the vote." Ostensibly non-partisan, these appeals may have been in keeping with Jeffersonian philosophy or based on the conviction that the greater the balloting the better the prospects of Democratic success. Invoking state pride in early 1793, the *Chronicle* noted Pennsylvania's sizable vote as reason why Massachusetts citizens must rouse themselves to raise their state in the estimation of the others and "convince Congress that we are attentive to our rights and liberties." The *Aurora* asserted no duty in a representative government was more important than the casting of one's ballot. At times even a single vote could be decisive; Jay's Treaty would not have been adopted had there been just "ONE MORE upright Senator." Other writers emphasized the tremendous powers of the Presidency to show the importance of elections, or bemoaned that in 1799 18,000 eligible Massachusetts freemen had failed to vote. Jerseymen were again reminded that exercise of the franchise was one privilege as yet not denied them, though its retention was in danger. Upon that state's legislature depended the possibility of choosing presidential electors by popular vote.

> Electors of New-Jersey, UNITE in support of Republican characters, be unanimous in your ticket and success will attend you. . . . Be firm, be vigilant, be enterprising, and you will maintain the ground you have acquired. By your fortitude and unanimity at this crisis, the rights and freedom of your country may be preserved and handed down to posterity; therefore remember, UNITED YOU STAND, DIVIDED YOU FALL.

Virginia Republicans should be early to the polls; only their own negligence could cost them success. Administration officeholders were said to run "up and down the streets to gull the people," while Democrats busily denied passing out election tickets in a Charleston, South Carolina, synagogue. That an aged Washington could ride eighteen miles to the polling place in bad weather was held up as an example to all true patriots of both parties.[51]

Most frequent of electioneering appeals was what is classified today as the "bandwagon idea," based on inculcating the belief that the trend strongly favored Republican candidates and that one might waste his vote, or be regarded as eccentric, by voting for the opposing party. The presumed effectiveness of this as a campaign weapon was augmented by the fact that not all state and congressional elections were held simultaneously, and that state legislatures usually selected the presidential electors. Even if these electors were popularly chosen,[52] they might be selected at different dates, since the sole constitutional requirement was that the electoral vote be cast on the same day throughout the nation.

Essentially this technique consisted of four procedures, reiterated *ad infinitum* (and for Federalists, *ad nauseam*). These were boastful predictions of Republican success, gleeful accounts of Federalist forebodings, gloating items about actual Democratic triumphs and concomitant Federalist chagrin, and descriptions of Jeffersonian victory celebrations. Right would always triumph, it was prophesied; disconsolate administration supporters were ready to desert their party; local and national returns showing Republican gains were carefully published; and the triumphal songs, parades, and banquets were always examples of "decent hilarity"—joyous but orderly.[53]

This practice began at least as early as May, 1792, when the *National Gazette* hailed the burgeoning signs of democracy in Congress and the country. Soon the *Gazette of the United States* deplored the appearance of a party opposed to the administration, and Freneau was admitting his sheet was supported by a party, if by that term Fenno meant "a very respectable number of anti-aristocratic, and anti-monarchical people of the United States." [54] Even the foreign-language press publicized Republican congressional tickets and noted their victories. The *New-York Journal* in October predicted

Adams would be hard pressed for the Vice-Presidency, and this estimate (or urgings for Republicans to unite on one candidate) was widely disseminated.[55]

For a party just being formed, Republicans made a remarkable fight in 1792. Hamilton's financial agenda, Washington's alleged monarchical behavior, St. Clair's defeat, apportionment, and the speculative crash all figured as issues aiding the opposition in America's first true campaign. When anxious Federalists persuaded Washington (who had not desired a second term) to run again, Republicans concentrated on the Vice-Presidency. They won a majority in the House, garnered fifty votes for Clinton against seventy-seven for Adams, and after the election found themselves with a potent political organization. Virginia, New York, North Carolina, and Georgia all went for Washington and Clinton, and partisan writers thanked the electors in the name of liberty.[56]

The Massachusetts state election of 1793 saw a Republican slate presented for which "a number of respectable citizens" were "determined to give in their suffrages"; the *Chronicle* asserted "as an undeniable fact . . . that BENJAMIN AUSTIN, jun. will have a very large majority of votes" for congressman from Boston, irrespective of any comments to the contrary in the *Centinel* or elsewhere.[57] Federalists there were said to be only feigning willingness a year later for the runoff election needed to send Ames to Congress. Gains of several congressional seats in New York and Pennsylvania showed Americans thought highly of those men branded as "Jacobins." In New York Republicanism did not mean "anything or nothing" (as Adams had phrased it), but a margin of eight seats to two. A similar triumph in the balloting for Massachusetts legislators brought an optimistic prophecy of the early disintegration of "the force of the *tory party*." [58]

There was rejoicing at Sam Adams' "vast majority" for re-election to the governorship of Massachusetts in 1796. This Adams had been under fire as *"the enemy of Washington,"* but his two-to-one margin must have convinced "the *British faction* . . . that the name of the President will no longer shield them from the just indignation of an insulted and injured people!" Republicans had played up the Governor's war record, and after his victory "British desperadoes" were told they might as well attempt moving mountains as to lower him in the esteem of all true Americans. Representatives who had opposed Jay's Treaty were returned from both the city and county of Philadelphia though every Federalist "engine was set in motion" against them. Surely this indicated a trend; administration supporters "should hide their diminished heads." [59]

Tennesseans, proud of their new statehood, regretted Washington's decision to retire, but welcomed Jefferson, enlightened statesman and friend to the rights of man, as his probable successor. Choices of Jeffersonian electors in various states in November were greeted as indicating a popular trend. Fredericksburg's *Republican Citizen* noted *"with inexpressible satisfaction . . . that both of the successful Candidates"* there were *"friends of Mr. Jefferson,"* and Vermonters were congratulated over a similar result in that state.[60] Prospect of a Democratic triumph in Pennsylvania led the *Independent Chronicle* to say the likelihood of the Virginian's election might disappoint a few who desired a "Yankee President," but Jefferson was "truly *Yankee"* in principles, while Adams was "compleatly *British."* The press publicized Kentucky's electoral unanimity for Jefferson and Burr, and also favorable preliminary national returns. As late as December 12 the *Aurora* claimed victory, even though the contest might go to the House, and in the absence of the Georgia and South Carolina returns the *Kentucky Gazette* professed hopefulness until mid-January.[61]

Boston "Real Republicans" exulted in the success of their fellow Jeffersonians in the New York legislative election of 1797, and "General DEARBORNE's [*sic*]" probable return to Congress from the Maine district demonstrated the people were "recovering a just sense of their true interest." Yellow fever drove many common citizens away from the Philadelphia area while the well-to-do retired only to nearby estates, but the Republican ticket there was barely defeated, and Israel Israel (vice-president of the Democratic Society) was victorious. Other parts of Pennsylvania were reported going Republican, and the votes of seventy-five women in Elizabeth speeded the success of the party's cause in New Jersey.[62]

Naturally Jeffersonian tactics compelled denials that any comparable "bandwagon" inclination toward the Federalists existed. The attempt of Messrs. Albright and Lahn to imitate Cobbett by starting a *"German Porcupine"* in Lancaster cost them the public German-language printing of the legislative journals for Pennsylvania. Though such an action against a Republican paper would have been roundly condemned, the *Aurora* interpreted this to prove Federalist influence was waning, instead of increasing as administration supporters boasted.[63]

Prognostications of a Democratic victory in the New York state and congressional election of 1798 gained considerable currency. Manhattan reports were that

> Notwithstanding the influx of wealth and power, in defiance of all exertion and of every art that could be practiced, Republican virtue and firmness are triumphant. Edward Livingston and all the Republican members are beyond doubt the Republican representatives of this great city.

Final gubernatorial results were not yet in, but if the city was any criterion Jay was defeated. There his "influence has so far declined, that he will scarcely have one-fifth of the majority he had before." However they might be gagged by Sedition laws, the people would make themselves heard at elections—and would refute Federalist assertions that administrative measures were publicly supported. Other states should follow this example.[64]

Despite pressures from seacoast merchants, and postponement of executive appointments until after elections to then reward friends of administration candidates, voters were said to be recording Republican preferences. A Marylander denied that the men in his town raised an Independence Day toast "to the virtuous [Federalist] *majority* of Congress" as reported;

instead, one *was* drunk to Jefferson. Autumnal congressional victories in various quarters were recorded with delight, and the Federalist Charleston *State Gazette* allegedly printed returns of the South Carolina assembly race within a black border. The *Centinel of Freedom* wrote surely these accumulated verdicts would exhilarate the people and depress "lawyers, place-hunters, and pensioners, and the whole horde of court-sycophants." [65]

With tongue in cheek the Frankfort *Palladium* bemoaned the "melancholy truth" that "Jacobinism, alias Democratic principles" had become epidemic. For protection from this dread malady it offered a "receipt": A "good dose of *implicit obedience,* mixed with some pills of ground *Porcupine quills,* diluted with a syrup of *liquid favour* from government; This, taken inwardly, will secure from all contagion whatever." "WILL HONEYCOMB" affected similar concern over the spread of Republicanism. The arch-traitor George Logan had been returned to office in Pennsylvania, and the seditious Lyon, in Vermont. Even with probable French financial support, "what a hardened set of fellows" were Vermont mountaineers "to fly, as it were in the face of authority! We could not have done worse in Kentucky!" [66]

The "Royalists" were said to be concerned about the 1799 and 1800 elections, for all their devices would prove inadequate. Although some administration newssheets reveled in favorable toasts and continued to print articles on the growth of Federalism, Republicans cited Fenno's dying remarks to the effect that *"the sun of Federalism was rapidly declining."* Re-election of Dr. Aaron Hill to the Massachusetts legislature showed that, notwithstanding the "efforts of official influence," the "independent yeomenry" were "determined to maintain their 'birthright.' " [67]

McKean's triumph over Ross in the Pennsylvania gubernatorial contest of 1799 generated tremendous Jeffersonian enthusiasm. Thomas Cooper had strongly urged Northumberland County to support the victor, and the *Aurora* began campaigning for him as early as April. Amid intense excitement papers had posed questions on Ross's stand respecting Jay's Treaty and the standing army, or brought charges of deism to counteract assertions McKean was Catholic. Mid-August saw assertions that 17,000 of the state's anticipated 30,000 voters had signified preference for the Republican candidate, and Federalists were refusing bets his majority would exceed 4,000. The *German Porcupine* was said to have openly asked ex-Tories to oppose McKean, who had helped confiscate their property in the Revolution, but Republicans claimed "every dirty artifice" of his opponents would not defeat him. The count of the ballots was heralded from Boston to Baltimore and further. "Republicans rejoice!" announced the *Constitutional Telegraphe*. "I KNEW IT!" added the *American,* when Democrats won the Maryland state election and the Pennsylvania returns were known. Victories in northern New Jersey, and impressive gains in strongly Federalist Connecticut, seemed to show an irresistible Republican tide was setting in.[68]

A rapidly expanding subscription for the newly formed *National Magazine* reinforced this belief. Fifty subscribers signed in Georgia almost immediately, and sixty-six, in Connecticut. The latter feat was miraculous, for that state sent to Congress "seven of the most bullying servile satellites of Adams or those who'd lick the dust at Liston's feet," not to mention "war of extinguishment" Senator Tracy. "This looks as if the people of Connecticut were beginning to think for themselves." [69]

Monroe's election as governor of the most populous state and Gerry's gains in Massachusetts underlined the trend. Now a Bay State yeoman could openly state he was a Jacobin, though not long since such an admission was nearly as dangerous as to confess Christianity in the early days of the Church. No tyro in vilification, the Lancaster *Intelligencer* solemnly observed the very scurrility of the Federalist press had reacted against the league of "Traitors, Tories, Refugees and British agents." Already the *Gazette of the United States* and *Porcupine's Gazette* had folded, and other leading organs were fast sinking into oblivion. Wise Federalists "would do well to retire into that obscurity, which alone can save them from the contempt of the Citizens of America." [70]

Possibly even more than McKean's victory the autumn before, the New York spring election of 1800 presaged a Republican triumph. The two parties were so evenly matched in the legislature that control of that body—and the state's electoral vote—hinged on the vote in New York City. With indefatigable effort, Burr fashioned an unusually strong Republican ticket there which was not publicly announced until after the Federalists had named their candidates. Offering rewards for detection of Federalist bribery, and assiduously marshalling their own voters, Democrats swept their slate into office. The elated *American Citizen* shouted "The *Friends* of *Liberty* in this Country have much reason to rejoice," and swore the contest had been unmarked by Republican falsehood, personal abuse, plots, or disorder. Federalists who resorted to wild tales of shipboard massacres as in the last election should now be convinced truth had more effect than prevarication. In Goshen the *Orange Patrol* quoted the *Republican Watch Tower*:

> The Goddess of Liberty has put to flight the demon of Aristocracy. . . . You had to contend with powerful and insidious foes —a host encompassed you on every side.—Federal, State and Corporation officers, took the field against you— . . . Major General Hamilton, COMMANDER IN CHIEF OF THE ARMY, paraded on horseback at every poll. . . . Every Tory, Every British Factor and runner came forward to browbeat and abuse. . . . But all would not do—The independent Electors rallied round the Constitution—They spurned at the infamous menaces, and still more infamous promises of the Aristocrats. . . . They obtained a glorious, honorable, and complete VICTORY. Huzza for *Liberty*—Huzza for the *Constitution*—Huzza for *Jefferson!* [71]

Since New York state's electoral votes seemed destined for Jefferson, New Jersey citizens were urged to follow this example:

> No apology is now left for you to remain inactive—your exertions are loudly called for by every principle of policy—you who have

583

been waiting to join the *strong side,* are now assured that you may come forward with security, and afford your suffrages for men who are the friends of Mr. Jefferson—whose election to the Presidential chair involves in it the completion of our political prosperity, and whose conciliatory disposition will no doubt tend to disseminate harmony and concord between parties, alleviate the burthen of taxes, and lay open to you a field of enjoyment, which the concentrated efforts of a sordid aristocracy has been endeavoring to deprive you of.[72]

Virginia and Pennsylvania saw predictions of a Democratic landslide in November, and Federalists whistled in the dark to claim an Adams victory while conceding votes in Pennsylvania and elsewhere.[73] Though Gerry was edged out again in Massachusetts, the margin was so narrow Republicanism was clearly on the upswing. Even Eastern areas were perceiving there was "something rotten in the state of Denmark," and not all the "hypocritical arts of the hierarchy" could smother the republican spirit. In June Adams passed through New York without a parade; such a "wonderful change" was the result of the late election.[74]

Virginians foresaw eradication of senatorial tyranny, and soon the powers of government would no longer exceed the Constitution. Jefferson's election—ever more probable— would tend to remove the internal evils and dangerous principles of which the people complained. Mounting criticism of an expensive, burdensome, warlike, and inefficient administration was each day adding new members to the opposition party. "Changes are about to be made. . . ." trumpeted the *Vermont Gazette.* The political complexion of papers in the last mail was the most favorable yet, and the news augured fair.[75]

The "increasing spirit of republicanism" was a source of extreme satisfaction to real friends of the nation, announced the *American Citizen.* Any doubters should peruse the newspapers from all parts of the country. Republican sheets were exuberant over the inevitability of approaching triumph, and administration gazettes were filled with apprehension. Some Virginia Federalist electoral candidates were alleged to "have unequivocally declared their preference for Mr. Jefferson"; the New Jersey House appeared likely to join that state's Senate in Republican columns, and even Connecticut was said to be in grave danger of "catching the Democratic fever" as thrifty peace-loving New Englanders began to see through the pomp and trickery of the administration. Federalists were in "glorious confusion." They detested and abused Adams, but dared not abandon him.[76]

All this occurred because the administration "attempted too much, and pushed its designs with too great force." American sentiment had changed for the better; "Now those . . . attached to wicked schemes of government . . . want to know what they should do to be saved." Failure of Ross's election bill marked the end of a last-gasp attempt, and Georgians heard a minimum of six new Republican seats in the United States Senate was certain. A Boston Jacobin saw carriage breakdowns on Middle Street for Adams and Hamilton within a few days of each other as symbolic of their imminent reduction "to a level with their *respectable* fellow citizens." "Daniel" compared the public banquets accorded these two worthies on their travels to Belshazzar's feast, and *"Dick Moonlight"* felt the futile attempts of aristocrats to check Republicanism were like the old woman who tried to sweep the sunshine out of her house with a goose wing.[77]

The usual electoral predictions appeared rather early in the year. In May the German-language *Lancaster Correspondent* forecast 87 votes for Jefferson and only 47 for Adams. Federalists of course had their own prognostications, which Republican columns discounted as so exaggerated they were patently foolish and thereby ineffectual. Administration supporters were warned that possibly they could carry New Jersey, as prophesied, but considering the way the state had suffered during the Revolution and been deceived by designing leaders, the result was certainly doubtful. Maryland Federalists had consoled themselves thinking that state's assembly would choose its electors, but Democrats insisted the legislature would not convene prior to the election and electors (with Jefferson receiving five or six votes) would be chosen from districts as usual.[78]

More and more Federalists, however, were recognizing the reality of Democratic hopes. With relish the *Mirror of the Times* itemized the signs since the New York vote had rendered Jefferson's election likely. Fries had been pardoned and the Provisional Army disbanded. Pickering and McHenry had left the Cabinet. Cobbett and Dr. Nicholas Romayne had departed for England, and J. W. Fenno had relinquished the *Gazette of the United States*. Harper, Sedgwick, and other Federalist figures had announced their retirement from Congress, and the *Aurora* talked of "THE HYDRA DYING." Even Britain, sensing the trend, was stepping up her seizures.[79] Adams was unpopular, Ellsworth a known monarchist with violent ways, Pinckney's pretended negotiations with French envoys (one "a lady, to whom, for aught we know he might have been more cordially attached than to any political object whatever") would not be forgotten, and Pickering was a *"Forlorn Hope"* indeed. The Federalist party was virtually destitute of leaders.[80]

Duane began comparing administration personages who resigned to rats deserting a sinking ship. The practice was copied extensively, with stories of retiring Federalists captioned "ANOTHER RAT." A few leaders, such as Senator John Lawrence of New York and Congressman Jeremiah Wadsworth of Connecticut, rated "A GREAT BIG RAT." Actually, sneered the *Virgina Argus,* Wadsworth was far more interested in his party's health than his own. Soon "resignations" were so numerous that individual instances received little attention. The *Aurora*'s "Ship news" deduced the vessel *"Administration"* had encountered unusually rough weather. It was so near foundering the ship had to be lightened. First Ross's "iron machine" and most of the army were jettisoned.

> The whole ocean for a league round was covered with regimentals. . . . It was thought advisable to throw over the sailing master *Timothy Pickering,* and *M'Henry,* captain of marines. These remonstrated . . . but as they had been the means it was thought,

of causing a great leakage, and taking so many troops on board, captain Adams ordered them over.[81]

Early election indications all favored the Republicans—or so that party claimed. Their candidates for assessor and election inspector were successful in Pittsburgh. First returns showed them leading in Maryland, Joseph Badger was regarded a certainty to replace "[William] *Gordon,* one of the *rats,"* in Congress from New Hampshire, and in New Jersey "a Republican Legislature is anticipated with confidence." Levi Lincoln and Jacob Crowninshield received pluralities over noted Massachusetts Federalists, and Crowninshield's backers predicted a three to one majority in the runoff, while an "anglo-federalist" in the *Columbian Centinel* was alleged to have sadly acknowledged it was also three to one Jefferson would become President. No longer was it a disgrace to be called a Democrat in Connecticut; Jeffersonians there circulated printed lists of candidates, electioneered vigorously all summer, and professed majorities in many towns hitherto uniformly Federalist. In Hartford the *American Mercury,* long a target for priestly attacks, had gained so many subscribers at the expense of the rival *Courant* that it was commencing to be concerned about its supply of paper. Pretended Federalist "NATHAN SLEEK" stressed in the *Bee* the party's mistakes and lamented the evil days on which it had fallen.[82]

Thanks to "Anglo-Federalist" misconduct, converts to Republicanism were rapidly increasing. Adams had asserted if Hamilton had headed the provisional army for two full years America would have required another army to disband it. If Pinckney failed to achieve the Presidency, Hamilton declared he would lose his head or be commanding a victorious army in three years. Senator Tracy had endorsed a hereditary Executive and Senate, saying it was "liberty enough for the people to chuse their representatives." Fenno's pamphlets, plus Pickering's and Dayton's defalcations, had taken the scales from the eyes of deluded men. Even Rhode Island had rejected "Imlay the duellist" and incumbent Congressman John Brown, the "friend to Human Slavery." Ross and Addison were losing all

587

influence in Pennsylvania, where in the western counties Republicans elected all their ticket "from Coroner to Congressman." Meanwhile the press noted "MORE RATS!" who were retiring rather than face certain defeat at the polls. And the Adams-Hamilton dispute caused the *Independent Chronicle* to dryly note that where "the 'federal *rats*' are not quitting the political ship, it appears that the *Commercial Gazette,* and the *Centinel* are letting the CAT out of the bag to pursue them." [83]

Prophecies of Jefferson's triumph crowded news columns as the final vote drew near and early contests went favorably. As "Comfort for the Anglo-Federalists" the *Aurora* compiled three sets of figures to show the virtual certainty of Adams' defeat:

|  | Jefferson | Adams |
|---|---|---|
| The Anglo Federalist WISHES | 60 | 63 |
| The Simple Federalist FEARS | 69 | 54 |
| Republicans *Expect* | 92 | 46 |

On election day the same paper contrasted for Philadelphians Federalist performance, or "Things As They Have Been," with "Things As They Will Be" under a Republican administration.[84] Borrowing from the title of Callender's history, the *American* had a table, headed "The Prospect before Us," giving Jefferson ninety electoral votes to Adams' fifty-two. Reports from North Carolina, Pennsylvania, and Maryland county balloting indicated a Republican sweep. In Georgia it was said "not one of the few aristocrats . . . cared to offer himself as a candidate." Early Democratic victories were heralded by such headlines as *"Republicanism Triumphant,"* while preliminary Federalist successes in South Carolina and New Jersey received little attention.[85]

"From the complexion of the southern votes," ran a letter to a Boston paper, "it is ascertained that Mr. JEFFERSON will be the next President. . . ." The imprisoned Callender exhorted Democrats to go to the polls, even appealing to trimmers—"no man of reflection will be so silly as to cast away his vote upon the *losing side;* when it amounts to a mathematical demonstration that THOMAS JEFFERSON *must and shall be President!"* As pilot, Adams had "veered to every point in the compass of guilt and absurdity." He was noted for stinginess, but had erased three-fourths of the market price on Virginians' tobacco. With Rhode Island and Maryland going Republican, his "kingdom has departed from him. . . . Now is the time, when the head of federal robbers shall be hunted from their den; when public indignation shall overtake them in their race of infamy. . . . Hurraw!" [86]

The *American Citizen* attempted to analyze the situation. Georgia, Kentucky, and Tennessee were safe for Jefferson. South Carolina would give him eight votes, and North Carolina nine (or more "if British influence is not spread over the country"). Virginia's twenty-one would go for her native son, and about seven Maryland electors would favor him also. New Jersey and Delaware were doubtful, but only a handful of state senators could deprive Jefferson of Pennsylvania's fifteen votes. New York's twelve would be cast for "Jefferson and liberty." Vermont was probably Republican; presumably the rest of New England would go to Adams. Jefferson could thus expect at least eighty-three votes out of 138.[87] For the superstitious there was the story of a hen near Winchester, Virginia, which laid an egg on which *"Thomas Jefferson shall be the* SAVIOUR *of his Country"* was visible. Some derided this as the work of a farmer's wife who had written on the shell to influence her husband's vote, but one gentleman was said to have "found it to be a natural egg. Thus the Hens declare war against the presidency of Mr. Adams!" [88]

By November 1, Democrats claimed both parties conceded Jefferson's election. Many of his most violent opponents were said, after discovering the falsehoods of "Burleigh" and similar writers, to have become his warm admirers. Most of the early ballots apparently were cast and counted in Republican states, for the *Examiner* of November 11, on the basis of allegedly actual returns, claimed a five-to-one lead for Jefferson in the electoral college. "Tom Bowling" was screaming "Rats,

Rats, Rats!," and there were warnings the day was "not far off when every unrighteous judge will be brought to judgment." Newspapers elatedly reported Republican successes in Virginia, Massachusetts, New York, North Carolina, and Pennsylvania. Rhode Island had broken "the phalanx of toryism and priestcraft"; Maryland was "regenerated"; even with Pennsylvania's votes uncast (because of the deadlocked legislature), Adams could retire.[89] Federalists were accused of adopting the bandwagon technique to the extent of falsely reporting a victory in South Carolina. In truth, Republicans had (they claimed) a majority there, and they called their opponents' effort "a new federal mode of carrying" an election. As it in fact turned out, the situation in the state was not definitely known until the legislature actually selected Jeffersonian electors December 2.[90]

In Pennsylvania the circumstances were most dramatic and critical. The commonwealth's voters obviously favored Jefferson, but holdovers enabled Federalists to retain a two-vote margin in the state Senate. Republicans, commanding a majority of thirty-two in the House, wished to choose the electors by a joint ballot, but the Senate proved obdurate, and for some time it appeared the state's fifteen votes would be lost. Interest was intense the country over. The *Aurora* condemned the Federalist call for a compromise method of choosing electors (based on the percentage of party votes in the previous election) as "the last shift of a struggling dying faction!," and asked why this method was not applied in New Jersey and Massachusetts, where Republicans had sizable minorities or had elected Congressmen but failed to gain seats in the electoral college.[91]

Three methods of selecting presidential electors were then used: selection by the state legislature, popular election by the voters in districts, or popular election on a state-wide basis. Whichever device was actually used for a particular state usually depended upon what seemed most advantageous for the party controlling the state at that moment. Virginia seems to have been the first commonwealth to change its method for political expediency. Its electors had formerly been chosen by district, but early in 1800 John Taylor, Madison, and others pushed through the legislature a measure for choosing them by a statewide ticket. The avowed object was to prevent a choice for President that was contrary to the will of the American people, but the measure made virtually impossible the selection of any Federalist electors from the state. Republicans claimed, replying to agonized Federalist protests, that most states chose delegates either at large or by the state legislature. Yet, as long as all three methods were used, a minority party possibly could have named the President by capturing those states with general tickets and also obtaining some electors in the states that selected by districts. Such had occurred in 1796 when New York, with six Republican congressmen out of ten, gave its entire electoral vote to Adams. "FRANKLIN" added that the district method often divided a state's vote and thus deprived Virginia of her real power in national affairs. The general ticket reflected the will of *all* the people, as it should. To those professing fear that these electors (many of whom could not be known to individual voters) might prove false to their trust, it was stressed that the men were long-standing friends of Jefferson, and that the election was based on the sound foundation of principle and character.[92]

Virginia's action naturally triggered retaliations elsewhere. Maryland's "exclusive modern Federalists" tried to change from the district method to selection of electors by the legislature. One writer claimed this effort so aroused the people they chose a Republican House as soon as possible. If Federalists had only wished to counteract Virginia they should have adopted that state's mode of naming electors from the state at large.[93] In Massachusetts and New Hampshire the legislatures took over the appointment of electors. Republicans remonstrated that while the Constitution gave that body power to direct how the state should select them, doing it itself usurped the people's most important right. The legislatures of Pennsylvania and New Jersey, which had performed this function in 1796, delayed for a time taking any action concerning the matter. In Pennsylvania, especially, this was considered part of the obstructionist tactics of Federalists disappointed after Ross's defeat.[94]

During the XYZ affair the Federalist resurgence in New York was so great that many realists had felt the Democrats would probably lose the state in 1800. Consequently, Burr's friend Assemblyman John Swartwout in 1799 had sponsored a bill to divide the state into electoral districts, so that (irrespective of the result of the April election of 1800) Jefferson would be assured of at least some electoral votes in the state. The proposal was rejected, and Republicans in 1800 used the legislature's "lack of confidence in the people" as a campaign argument. After the spring voting Federalists were, of course, anxious to adopt the district system. Much criticism has been directed at Hamilton's efforts to secure a change to that effect, but it is difficult to see how his motives differed appreciably from those of his opponents.[95]

Meanwhile the struggle continued in Maryland, where "Civis" called on Federalists to convene the legislature and pass an ordinance for the selection of electors by that body. Administration supporters would not suffer Virginia to nullify all the Federalist votes in that state and retain all the Republican votes in Maryland, when Federalists had the power to ensure Adams' reelection. Other Federalists argued a uniform system of district choice of electors the nation over would be fairest and would give Jefferson only sixty-three votes, but Virginia had shifted to the general ticket method to deprive Adams of from six to eight votes there. Now Maryland Republicans were laboring for the very system their partisans had abolished in Virginia. Republicans retorted that the right of district voting had been eliminated in many regions the Federalists controlled, and the way a state voted was the prerogative of each individual commonwealth. They told citizens men who would deprive the people of their suffrage were unworthy of confidence. "A Virginian" denied his state would have ever given Adams six votes under any system and added that since Virginia made no attempt to govern Maryland's choice of electors people of the latter state should be in no wise concerned by any desire to counteract Virginia's ballots.[96]

The Maryland legislature had already achieved considerable unpopularity the previous year by requiring a property qualification for voting. The *American* had then screamed "No taxation without representation," and predicted further "innovations" would follow this first step toward tyranny; now the cry was raised again. The *Baltimore Telegraphe* sarcastically added it was obvious that the four state representatives from each county had far more sense than its entire population. If Marylanders could be persuaded they should have no part in selecting Presidential electors, they might soon be induced into surrendering their franchises altogether. "Q" averred the state Senate in reality opposed Adams; the Federalist leaders wished to elect Pinckney, and therefore all true men would vote for those favoring the right of popular suffrage. Republican editors applauded the "foiling" of the Federalist effort when the newly elected legislature proved unfriendly to a shift from the district method.[97]

In Pennsylvania the majority of two state senators opposing the will of the House, governor, and people was compared to a pistol ball's trying to stop the movement of the earth. Adams might as well withdraw to the Duchy of Braintree and "chaunt requiems to the manes of Jonathan Robbins." Appealing to sectional feeling and state pride, Republicans noted that, save for one New Jersey judge, the states along the Delaware had no federal executive or judicial posts. Voters prayed the legislature might select electors expressing the evident will of Pennsylvania and secure for the commonwealth the legitimate weight in federal proceedings "of which she has been so long and so clearly deprived." Only a joint vote of both houses would "truly express the will of the people"; what if the Constitution had permitted Pennsylvania only a single vote? Countless petitions were circulated to reinforce the argument. Pleased at the deadlock, administration supporters, with their thirteen votes against the Republicans' eleven in the Senate, insisted each house should act separately and jeered at Jeffersonian inconsistency in striving *for* legislative choice of electors in Pennsylvania and *against* it in Maryland.⁹⁸

Never, sputtered Republicans, had so flagrant an outrage been perpetrated upon a free people. Federalist leaders were betraying their constituents, deliberately discrediting democratic processes in the eyes of the people, and reducing "Pennsylvania to a cypher in the Union." A majority of 18,000 votes faced virtual disfranchisement, whereas in neighboring New Jersey a much smaller aristocratic margin produced a unanimous electoral vote. The fault lay not in the Constitution but in the enemies of liberty. "Of what use is the Senate?" came an incensed cry from Northumberland, Pennsylvania. Hamilton or British bribery was blamed for the impasse, and the contumacious "THIRTEEN" were held up to execration or were burned in effigy (even after the election) in all parts of the state. Even so, resentful Republicans were finally compelled to accept an arrangement that permitted the Senate to name seven electors and the House eight, practically nullifying the commonwealth's vote.⁹⁹

Elsewhere, however, Democrats were exultant. Kentucky was *"a dead shot for Jefferson."* So too were Georgia and Tennessee, despite aristocratic attempts to mislead voters in the former state. Virginia's light vote still gave her native son a better than three to one margin. Jeffersonians jeered at the *Columbian Centinel*'s forecast that Adams would be reelected, 72–66. They wanted to know where that paper got its "best information from all the states," and retorted "it would be utterly ridiculous to treat this shameless *political diagram* as a thing rational." ¹⁰⁰

Tasting victory, Republican newspapers began to amplify their tables and jubilation with analyses of their success. "What had produced this political upheaval?" asked one. Its answer amounted to a detailed indictment of Federalist policies. Raising 75,000 volunteers instead of relying on militia, and creating a hired army, had played a part. So had spending eighty-seven and one-third million dollars, and upping expenses to $12,800,000 for 1800. Also included were Jay's Treaty; forcing through a naturalization law "twice as long as that which . . . Great Britain imposed upon us"; attempts to deprive Pennsylvania and New Jersey of their right to choose presidential electors; and Ross's scheme to commit congressional power in elections to a committee of six Senators, six Representatives, and the Chief Justice. To these could be added the failure to prosecute William Blount for treason, and John Ward Fenno and others for advocating presidential power to appoint Senators and the abolition of state governments; the sad but complete vindication of the facts in Jefferson's Mazzei letter; increasing proof that Pickering was attached to the British interest, and that Federalist leaders had monarchical leanings; evidence of Jefferson's belief in religious liberty; and "The manifest wishes of the Republicans to keep peace with all the world, and to keep down the public expenses." [101]

The *Examiner* and *Tree of Liberty* agreed the crudeness with which the administration tried to carry out its program was responsible. The Alien and Sedition Laws, corruption in high places, and attempts to intimidate "where half a dozen constables could have preserved the peace" would inevitably rouse any respectable people from their lethargy. Lastly, there had been "A Republican press which opened the eyes of the misinformed, and gave them the true state of affairs." "Anglo-Feds" were deserting to the Republican cause, "striving to escape the disgrace which their deluders daily experience." Good Jeffersonians would welcome them as brothers "redeemed from the abyss of servile slavery." [102]

That it was some time before the exact totals were known in no way limited the number of "authentic" political box-scores that appeared. Not every chosen elector had openly proclaimed his views, and there was ever the possibility that a vote might be changed. In late November the *Lancaster Correspondent* listed 48 sure Jefferson votes, and but 30 for the "Monarchists." The *American* insisted the Virginian would have 71 votes (to Pinckney's 60, Burr's 59 and Adams' 56) even without Pennsylvania's suffrage. He might lose Rhode Island's four votes and still have five more than enough for election. There was especial doubt over C. C. Pinckney's strength; Adams would receive no southern votes, but even the *Independent Chronicle* feared the possibility that (even with two-thirds of the people for Jefferson) Pinckney might become President. Its table gave Jefferson 73 (his correct total), Pinckney 71, and Adams and Burr 65 each. Apparently the Charleston *Times,* in doubtful South Carolina, had one of the earliest accurate tabulations, and even this was not listed as known fact.[103]

As late as December 12 Federalists were claiming Adams' reelection as "pretty certain." That very day, however, the *American* called the legislature-selected South Carolina slate "A Death Stroke for old Tories and Aristocrats," and the following issue carried an editorial captioned *"The Jigg's Up."* Praising Jefferson, the editor concluded: "Such is the character, who for four years, (I hope for forty) is to guide the helm of state; and let every friend to his country's prosperity, happiness and independence, say LAUS DEO!" "Be glad America!" shouted the *Readinger Adler.* The *Mirror of the Times* congratulated its readers that Jefferson's accession to the presidential chair was now guaranteed "by recent and concurring accounts from South-Carolina, the last hope of expiring Federalism." At long last American Republicans, after patiently enduring severe persecution under an insolent tyranny, had through energy, perseverance, and unanimity realized their hopes. New Yorkers were reminded of the part their city had played in achieving this happy result. Adams and Hamilton were crestfallen, and the latter lacked even the consolation of a good conscience.[104]

"A FRIEND TO EQUAL RIGHTS" assured fellow Republicans that when honorable principles were adorned with virtuous conduct the complete discomfiture of their enemies was inevitable. Final returns on the electoral count were considering news as late as January, 1801, and Democratic gloating continued unabated. Decrying presidential addresses to

Congress (and the concomitant replies), the *American* still felt "President Adams' LAST *speech*" was better than his earlier ones. It had the merit of brevity, as Adams was in an ill humor, though everything of interest it contained might have been said in twenty lines. But its mildness did show the Chief Executive was aware of "the gratification which will result from a moderate, rather than a violent exit from public life." "BOB SHORT," in the same issue, was not even that generous. His doggerel described the second President:

> He had 'twas thought, something more horrid to say,
> When his tongue lost his power, and he fainted away;
> Some say 'twas his conscience that gave him a stroke;
> But those who know him treat that as a joke.[105]

The "Register of Rats" continued in the *Aurora* and the *American*. Jay was *"A great* 'Rat' " when he declined to run again for governor of New York; Wolcott, Pickering, and others were *"Rats* thrown *overboard!"* John Marshall, Samuel Dexter, and "John Steele, Non-Controller of the Treasury," were called rats "ABOUT TO JUMP OVERBOARD," and Oliver Ellsworth allegedly resigned because he was a "sick rat" who expected a foreign appointment.[106]

Some Republicans were concerned about the tie vote between Jefferson and Burr; would the Federalist House be able to frustrate the popular desire? One writer even suggested that Jefferson would be President, but the Senate might have to decide between Burr and Adams for the Vice-Presidency. Anxiety was great while the House balloted throughout February,[107] but Republican festivals were held before that time and broke out anew after Jefferson's victory. There were parades, balls, bonfires, barbecues and feasts—with toasts to the Constitution, freedom of the press, Democratic leaders, and the "Tree of Liberty moistened by the tears of Aristocracy." Inauguration time produced similar festivities, and even the Federalist press was said to have conceded that these celebrations had "been executed with complete success." [108]

Along with predictions of and celebrations for Democratic triumphs, the "bandwagon" technique also required minimizing the party's setbacks. Federalist claims were continually discounted and their successes belittled; Jeffersonian defeats were explained away. Often charges of sharp election practices were used to account for the results. When Fisher Ames carried Boston over Benjamin Austin, 371–330, in 1792 for Congress, the *Boston Gazette* compiled a table to show that almost every vote for Ames had been an interested one:

Votes for A——.

| | |
|---|---:|
| Custom-house officers and Runners | 35 |
| Excise Officers and Runners | 12 |
| Branch Bank Officers, Directors and Runners | 22 |
| Loan-Officers and Clerks | 6 |
| Speculators, Brokers and Runners | 67 |
| Lawyers and Clerks | 31 |
| Persons interested deeply in the Funds, alias Paper-Men | 177 |
| Merchants | 8 |
| Mechanicks | 12 |
| A noted, idle stroller, who has *been too fat* to engage in any Business but Speculation! | 1 |
| Whole Number, | 371 |

Notwithstanding this, and the fact that "the Poll was artfully closed at Half past Twelve o'Clock (which precluded a very *respectable* and *industrious* Class of Citizens giving in their Votes) yet Honestus [Austin's *nom de plume*] had a very handsome support without benefit of CLERGY." [109]

Adams' reelection as Vice-President the same year was not a fair test. No effort had been made to compare his merits with those of Clinton (whose name was presented hopelessly late in the day) before the public. As the incumbent, only an adequate review of his conduct could furnish cause for his removal. People were indifferent; the Pennsylvania vote for electors was less than a tenth of that cast in the congressional election. Thus there was little indication of the popular view, though there was reason to believe that indifference would be less pronounced as policies and events unfolded. [110]

Greenleaf's *Patriotic Register* scoffed at the *American Mi-*

*nerva's* "immense concourse" of people at Jay's departure, in 1794, from New York for London. Other than regular loafers, less than two hundred had witnessed the sailing. The New York gubernatorial election of 1795 was a bitter pill for Republicans, but the *Aurora* claimed the narrowness of Jay's victory showed his treaty was unpopular even in his home state. Had the *freemen* instead of the *freeholders* been allowed to vote for governor, the result would have been different.[111]

Republicans should not have been discouraged at the accession of Adams to the Presidency in '97, nor think aristocrats outnumbered lovers of freedom. If the *people* of the states rather than the legislatures had chosen the electors, Jefferson would have been inaugurated. As it was, only illegalities in Pennsylvania and Maryland, plus the fact that Jeffersonians had "the influence of a certain great character to contend against," prevented that occurrence. Aristocrats would lose influence with Washington's retirement, and Adams' record during the Revolution made it possible that he would yet "disappoint the British Faction." When the suspicious *Minerva* protested against the praise Republicans gave Adams at the commencement of his administration and hinted at French influence over them, the *Argus* retorted that two-thirds of the Adams electors from mercantile states had been chosen in secret caucuses under the immediate influence of Anglophiles.[112]

In 1798 Israel Israel was defeated for Pennsylvania state senator only "by a small majority," and Harrison Gray Otis was reelected to Congress from Boston because of city machine politics. The latter result was regrettable, but actually mattered little since Otis had but slight influence in Congress. Compared to Gallatin he was as tinsel to sterling.[113] Elections following the XYZ Affair generally disappointed Republicans; even in Virginia several Federalist congressmen were chosen. The *Aurora* counselled Federalists not to be too exultant, nor Democrats downcast. "As it is usual in blindness of party zeal, to exaggerate what is wished, so too frequently we are apt to believe what we fear," though it must be confessed "the election of general [John] *Marshall* is a remarkable instance of popular delusion." However, many of his voters were known to be of the Democratic persuasion, he had avowed political sentiments similar to those of his opponent and had danced around bonfires with prospective voters, and he had allegedly spent $6,000 in the campaign.[114]

Even the New York state race of 1800 was sufficiently close so that some Republican papers prepared alibis for a possible defeat. As the polls closed, the *American Citizen* talked of the "weight of property, [and] undue influence"; the Federalist majority of over 900 in the previous election made it none too sanguine. The *Bee* carried a typical example of similar comments on other elections: "We expect the federal party has carried their ticket for Presidential election in R. Island. If they have not, it has not been for the want of intrigue, labor and artifice of every kind." Crowninshield's defeat for Congress in Massachusetts was blamed on "bigoted preachers," but the race had been close and "the good sense of the people will eventually rise superior to all such wicked interference." [115]

Where apologies were unneeded for election results Republican papers offered none. Banquets and toasts for party leaders were the rule in victory or defeat.[116] If deceased members of the community had been Republicans that fact was uniformly noted in their obituaries; perchance it was considered as favorable to them in the next world, or its mention showed the depths to which party spirit permeated men's ideas and actions. More likely it was designed to indicate the prevalence of Republicanism and to encourage others to emulate such worthy examples.[117] Successes often produced editorial gloating. New York Republicans were felicitated on Edward Livingston's reelection to Congress in '98, "notwithstanding the multifarious *intrigues* of your antagonists." McKean's election in Pennsylvania would have a healthy effect on *"the rising* generation" in that state. Young men, sermonized the *Aurora,* could now see the inestimable value of a virtuous life. McKean himself, thanking his supporters, charged "Traitors, refugees, tories, French aristocrats, British agents and British subjects, and their corrupt dependants, together with not a few apostate whigs" had all combined against him in the race. The New York election of 1800 was regarded as a triumph of liberty, and German-language papers constantly repeated their "Hurra für Freyheit und Jefferson." [118]

Western Pennsylvania Federalists had difficulty getting a candidate to run for Congress against Gallatin, and Pittsburgh's *Tree of Liberty* sneeringly offered "A Few Cents Reward" and a handsome number of votes to anyone who would run. It published the "maimed Federal Ticket":

Congress
NOBODY
[State] Senator
NO BODY worth mentioning
Assembly
DUNNING M'NAIR [etc.]

The Republican ticket, printed underneath, "will be supported . . . by the great bulk of the honest and independent yeomanry of the county. . . ." Federalists in New Jersey had provided for choosing congressmen at large to exclude Republicans, but in 1800 there was hope they would fall into the pit they had dug. And Jay had "declined the honor of being defeated by Clinton" in New York the following spring.[119]

Even Jefferson's election did not eliminate the printed barbs. Republican papers were understandably curious about the fire which destroyed many War Department records in November, 1800. Dexter's office had been "locked *for two weeks"*; it was peculiar that his return from the North coincided with the night the fire was discovered. Duane's *Aurora,* especially, hinted Federalists were not at all sorry to see certain accounts go up in smoke. Wolcott, in the Treasury Department, had denied Pickering and McHenry were guilty of peculation, but it was significant that now the records which might have settled the issue were conveniently out of the way. The Secretary of the Treasury had been the first man at the fire and apparently had made great effort to extinguish it. But he had said nothing about the origin of the blaze and resigned from office shortly after its occurrence. More than one writer echoed "Simon Slim" that something was amiss. Federalists raged at these "diabolical" charges, and even implied Duane had started the conflagration. This evoked additional Democratic derision, and the *Aurora* began to talk of the "Federal Bonfire."[120]

Taunts and suspicions doubled when a very similar fire gutted the Treasury Department records in January. Dexter had been moved to fill the Secretary's post, and once again the "Honorable OLIVER WOLCOTT . . . of 'blazing flame' " had been among the earliest on the scene. The Georgetown *Cabinet* openly charged the conflagration was no accident. Paper had been scattered on the floor of the Auditor's office, and three unidentified men had been seen locked in a nearby room. How did it happen that Wolcott got there first and that wagons—almost impossible to obtain even during daytime—were there to cart away trunks and crates of papers so quickly after the alarm? Wolcott supposedly claimed these were purely private papers, but why did he not sacrifice them for the government records? What were his own papers doing there, anyway?

Here was more than mere coincidence. When the funds set aside for the standing army were to be audited, the War Office was consumed. Now that Pickering's accounts and Wolcott's conduct were to be investigated, there was a blaze in the Treasury. Clearly Federalists feared what would be uncovered when Republicans took over; the Treasury fire was obviously intended to operate "as a final settlement of all accounts." Federalist charges that Republicans were the incendiaries here also were preposterous. Assuredly, snorted the New York *Temple of Reason,* these Republican firebugs flew through the keyhole into the Treasury Office. An investigation was demanded, and though the official report minimized the loss as inconsequential, the Republican press utilized fully this opportunity to cast further onus upon the Federalists.[121]

Editors of the now-successful opposition, galled by Adams' "midnight appointments," endeavored to turn popular opinion against them. Several men had been advanced from lower judicial posts to newly created (and irremovable) federal judgeships. In some instances members of Congress were named to fill their old offices. Jeffersonians seethed that this violated the spirit of the Constitutional prohibition on the appointment of congressmen during their terms—and if the present incumbents were for any reason to refuse their promotions, "it would follow that men were *formally appointed* to fill places *not vacant,* which seems to involve an absurdity." [122]

Yet in spite of all resentment, the Republican triumph brought with it a sobering sense of responsibility. Jefferson, printers realized, would be President of the entire nation. In that vein some of them anticipated the conciliatory mood of his inaugural address. The Baltimore *American,* a leader here as it had been in the bitter struggle, noted that "BE UNITED, was the last injunction which trembled from the lips of the departed WASHINGTON." [123]

# XV AN APPRAISAL

Never again were Federalists to regain their lost power. Democratic-Republicans came into complete control of both the legislative and executive branches of the government. Only Lincoln's plurality in 1860 even approached this amazing political exploit of developing a victorious electoral machine from virtually nothing within less than a decade. With all their gifts for leadership, and all the popular topics that arose, Madison, Jefferson, and their companions could not possibly have worked this miracle without the aid of the newspapers.[1] Devoted Republican editors and tireless correspondents, oftentimes more intemperate and enthusiastic than judicious and accurate, acquainted voters with candidates' abilities, aroused citizens to the real or imagined dangers of Federalist policies, and developed the issues and reasoning that came to spell Jefferson's ultimate success.

Just which arguments were most telling may be difficult to evaluate accurately. As recent studies and events have emphasized, the impact and strength of appeals to public opinion are not easily calibrated. Yet there is sufficient evidence—much of it internal—to warrant a number of conclusions.

The Jeffersonian movement was greatly advanced by the emphasis placed on certain charges that had a wide appeal. Reiteration proved the confidence Republican printers possessed in the efficacy of these contentions; they would not have wasted costly space repeating arguments deemed impotent. It seems similarly reasonable to assume that those criticisms producing the greatest reaction in the Federalist press or in the minds of administration leaders were those that were most telling. By these tokens the three deadliest weapons in the Republican arsenal were the accusations that Federalists were aristocrats desirous of a monarchy, that the cost of government was excessive, and that the Washington and Adams administrations were dominated by British interests. Each of these charges was heatedly denied or ridiculed by Federalists, but each was repeated incessantly throughout the period covered by this study. Whether Republican printers fully believed them or not is beside the point. Certainly they expected their readers to accept them.

People of a later day may have difficulty appreciating the fear Americans had of a domestic monarchy during the last decade of the eighteenth century. To us the possibility seems to have been absurdly remote. Yet, as Louise Dunbar in her study on *Monarchical Tendencies* shows,[2] the cry of "aristocrat" or "throne-lover" was so frequently raised that no student of the times can escape being impressed by its very recurrence.

Only recently liberated from England, Americans of that day had a profound disinclination for any return to royal control. It should also be recalled that the ideals of popular sovereignty and individual liberty were for the first time being tested on a national scale—and in a world generally unfriendly. European events appeared to indicate that kings would exert every effort to regain or extend their sway and that monarchy was synonymous with despotism. The Freneaus, Holts, Bradfords, and Baches (perhaps with fingers crossed) pandered to this fear, added to it, and turned it to their purpose. Federalists denounced as calumnious the imputation of absolutism and emphatically disavowed alleged statements by Adams or other leaders that were interpreted as friendly to hereditary power.[3] Yet many citizens believed the indictment, and the royalist proclivities of Hamilton and a few other ranking party members were sufficiently well known to lend color to it. No charge was made more frequently,[4] and there seems little reason to question its efficacy.

The stress placed upon extravagance demonstrated another shrewd selection of accusations. Colonial Americans (as "Poor Richard" showed) had appreciated the value of thrift. Independence did not eliminate this characteristic overnight, and in consequence assaults on supposedly tremendous expenses and wastes of the government received a ready hearing.

From the pay provided the first congressmen to the budget for Adams' military establishment, critics of the administration harped on its prodigality, public debt, and taxes.[5] All the devices then known—spelling out numbers in upper-case type, comparisons with budgets of earlier years, estimates of the number of wagons required to convey the sum in question—were utilized to publicize adversely the various appropriations. The theme was one which Democratic editors refused to let their readers forget. Authorities no less than the *Connecticut Courant* and Webster's *Commercial Advertiser* admitted openly that one of the most potent Jeffersonian arguments was the high cost of the government "and the increasing debt owing to military and naval operations." The charge rankled in Federalist breasts; their journals denied governmental outlays had increased disproportionately, pointed to national prosperity and adequate resources, or noted the need for protection in a chaotic world. A change in administration, they insisted, would not reduce expenditures.[6]

Yet to people of a slow-moving age, who could recall that Washington's first fiscal year cost less than one million dollars, a statement that Adams' four-year term would consume eighty times that sum was overwhelmingly impressive. Concomitant complaints of corruption in official circles and of inordinate profits to speculators added to the weightiness of the indictment. Even Federalists' claims of prosperity aided Republicans' arguments. Newspaper readers were made to feel a truly prosperous country should make great strides toward wiping out its indebtedness and could appreciably lower its taxes.

Under the Federalists the United States had done neither. Logically, to opposition publishers, this simple syllogism appeared to demand a change in government, and so the voters ruled in 1800.

The third great thesis, and in many respects most damning of all, was that the Federalist party was but a tool of Britain and desired to return America to her former colonial status. Interest then in foreign affairs was probably at an all-time high, and Democratic readers avidly perused endless accounts of America's treachery to her wartime ally, the execrable Jay Treaty, English bribes or plots, and official hostility to the French Revolution as proof of Albion's "influence." If anything, the space devoted to foreign affairs in the present study (approximately one-third of the total) would lead to an underestimation of the attention paid to them in the press of that day. Americans feared, hated, and distrusted England, and the mere suggestion that a man was an old Tory or British sympathizer was apt to be an ineradicable, often insuperable, political handicap. After Jefferson's election Fisher Ames acknowledged privately that cries of "British influence" were the greatest single factor in producing the Federalist downfall.[7]

Although these three contentions were most stressed, others were also significant. Insinuations of graft, while reinforcing those of extravagance, in themselves helped produce distrust of the administration. Personal abuse seems to have speeded Washington's retirement from the political arena and may have similarly affected other leaders. The friction engendered and abetted between certain Federalist chieftains doubtless speeded that party's defeat. At specific times and in certain areas, pleas made to a particular class or section had (from the Republican standpoint) a salutary effect. Even the "bandwagon" approach must have been of some worth. Invocations to constitutional principles had some impact but were restricted to accusations that Federalists were not adhering to the fundamental law. After all, the most that can be done under our political system toward realizing a philosophy or set of objectives through an election is to vote one man or party out of office and another in. In the final analysis the Democratic-Republican journals were devoted to that end—and criticisms of monarchism, expense, and an Anglophile policy appeared most effective in achieving the goal.

Surveying the journalistic activity of this period, it is evident that some presses were more valuable than others in forging the Jeffersonian party. Again the criteria for determining relative importance are not absolute, but they appear reasonably adequate. Since quoting from other newspapers was a universal practice of the day, those that were most copied must have possessed the greatest influence. If the Federalist press frequently berated many of these same publications we have another clue to their influence. Surely the majority of papers whose editors underwent prosecution for sedition were especial thorns in the side of the administration. Circulation figures, where available, furnish some indication. And both friendly and inimical remarks, by public men and by other publishers, facilitate the task of selection.

Until its demise in 1793 the foremost Republican journal was Freneau's *National Gazette.* After that time, without real question, the palm passed to the Philadelphia *General Advertiser,* later (and better) known as the *Aurora.* Benjamin Franklin Bache edited it until his death in 1798, when William Duane took over. Duane has been described as the "most effective journalist of his time," [8] and Bache was assuredly very close behind him.

The *Aurora* had a number of advantages that it used effectively in forwarding the Republican cause. Founded as the *General Advertiser* in 1790 (the title was changed November 8, 1794), it was printed in Philadelphia, at that time generally considered "the capital of the new world." [9] Its founding, by the 21-year-old grandson of the renowned Benjamin Franklin, almost coincided with the removal of Congress from New York to the Quaker City for a ten-year period.

At that time, when news bureaus, special correspondents, and instantaneous transmission of information were unknown, a newspaper at the seat of government enjoyed a four-fold superiority: It got the news first (days or even weeks ahead of gazettes in more distant localities), and not infrequently had it in print and to subscribers in those localities as soon as private sources or public mails could convey it there. At the source of information, it was aware of news trends, rumors, and stories about to break; occasionally it could play a part in the origin or development of the latter. It had the opportunity for eye-witness reporting, with all the freshness and vividness that implies. And since its political stories were largely first-hand accounts, it presumably might be more accurate than those journals that received their accounts from sources several times removed, or that conceivably made errors in copying.

Moreover, under both Bache and Duane the *Aurora* had regular reporters transcribing the reports of congressional sessions. Though these summaries of the proceedings were a service not exclusive with the *Aurora,* they circulated widely, and the paper almost automatically attained considerable prestige with hinterland editors and readers alike.[10] After the *National Gazette* expired the *Aurora* was clearly the dominant Republican newspaper in Philadelphia, but significantly its position of national supremacy did not long survive removal of the capital to Washington.[11]

In 1798, the publication boasted a circulation of 1,700 subscribers. While that year saw the Republican cause at low ebb, the figure (if accurate) probably compared favorably with that for any of the nation's other papers except possibly *Porcupine's Gazette* and the *Columbian Centinel* (which was not a daily). At that time Jefferson feared its number of readers was declining, but in May, 1801, Duane wrote Madison that the *Aurora*'s circulation was "more extensive . . . than any other paper in the Union," though "active hostility of the Custom House" had so hurt his advertising the paper was unprofitable.[12] Also, upon several occasions numerous copies were sent for free distribution into areas where Republicanism needed bolstering.[13] Since newspapers then were read in taverns as a sort of library service or loaned much more than at present, circulation figures give only a rough estimate of the number of people who read them. Democrats were generally less wealthy than Federalists, and it may be assumed that each copy of the *Aurora* was perused by more individuals than was true for any administration organ. From 1793 on it was in all likelihood the most influential newssheet in the country.

Bernard Faÿ states that by 1797 Bache was recognized as America's leading journalist and that the *Aurora* had become the nation's foremost journal. Commonly called "the bible of democracy," it set the standard for the Republican press.[14] If anything, Duane—in courage, sheer delight in controversy, sincerity, and trenchant style—proved an even abler editor than his predecessor. He excelled in choler and invective; like Bache, he spoke the language of the people; he possessed wide experience, and his articles made absorbing reading. In Duane's obituary the New York *Star* stated "No man had in his time more influence. . . ."[15]

Leadership, of course, had its penalties. From the first, Federalists believed Bache and later Duane must somehow be rendered impotent. More than any other editors, they were subjected to the choicest pejoratives of administration supporters, who sneered at the *Aurora* as "Anti-American," "slanderous," or "lying."[16] Since Bache had criticized Washington, Cobbett insulted the memory of Franklin, hoping thereby to discredit Bache's paper. Prior to the autumn of 1796 Republicans had comparatively few leaders of stature sufficient to warrant attack; even Jefferson had received relatively little attention from the press. This made it even more imperative for Federalists to weaken the *Aurora*'s effectiveness. For awhile the public was treated to odious comparisons between Washington and Franklin; one would believe that neither could have been great without detracting from the fame of the other.[17]

It was the *Aurora* whose office was destroyed and whose publisher, Bache, was twice beaten by Federalist hoodlums.[18] It was the same gazette, still under "Lightning Rod Junior," whose editor had to defend himself against charges of "treason."[19] Probably only the coming of the dread yellow fever to Philadelphia prevented a suit against him under the Sedition Act. Federalists' elation at Bache's death in the epidemic was unconcealed, for the fighting editor had accused Adams of falsehood on the official status of the French XYZ agents in an article published the very day he died.[20] Any joy was short-lived, however, for Duane proved an equally virile and bitter antagonist. He too was manhandled by Federalist attackers, and he was tried for libel and breach of privilege by the Senate.

Under both men, the paper was berated for "shameless prostitution of the truth." The reactions of Washington and Oliver Wolcott to it are well known. President Adams wished to try the Sedition Law on Duane and asked if there were "anything evil in the regions of actuality or possibility" which the *Aurora* had not suggested concerning him. John Quincy Adams considered Duane the ablest opposition propagandist, and Republican leaders such as Jefferson and Madison esteemed his services highly. Quotations from the publication far outnumbered those from any other in the Republican press. The *Constitutional Telegraphe* related the "villainy, slander, violence, etc." used in efforts to destroy the paper "before and since Bache's death." It added that a leading Federalist (probably Hamilton) had endeavored to buy the *Aurora* in order to suppress it.[21] Probably no greater tribute was ever paid to the significance of the journal.

Federalist press offensives against Democratic newssheets invariably mentioned the *Aurora*. John Wayne's Boston *Federal Gazette* attempted to revive its ailing fortunes with a stream of invective against the *Bee, Carey's United States Recorder,* the Portsmouth, N. H., *Oracle of the Day*—and the *Aurora.*[22] The Massachusetts legislature supposedly justified its move to deprive that state's voters of choosing presidential electors directly because "the *Aurora* and other *Jacobin* papers had plumed themselves on the certainty of two votes for Mr. *Jefferson* in Massachusetts."[23] When Republicans attempted to found a "National Paper," a disgruntled writer queried if the *Constitutional Telegraphe*, the *Bee*, the New York *Argus*, the *Aurora*, "and a host of such like papers" were not "sufficient to emit all the gall of democratic bitterness. . . ." [24] Other pro-administration papers labeled the *Aurora*'s editor "most infamous of the Jacobins," and devoted entire articles to the newspaper's "falsehood and misrepresentation . . . absurdities, contradictions . . . vulgarity and insolence." [25] A "certain federal Senator" allegedly confessed in 1800 that "If the *Aurora* is not blown up soon, Jefferson will be elected in defiance of everything!" Following Adams' defeat, the *Pittsburgh Gazette* commented that the change in office would bring one blessing: "The pages of the *Aurora*, and its little dependant papers, will be no longer stained with calumny and abuse but will for years be filled with eulogies on the administration." [26] But Democrats in the District of Columbia toasted "The radiant precursor of eternal day" whose editor was chiefly responsible for the triumph.[27]

Although the *National Gazette*'s existence was much shorter, its vigor probably lifted it to second place in over-all influence among Republican journals. For the period of its publication it enjoyed a more nearly official status as a party organ than did any other Democratic paper. Jefferson and Madison had been instrumental in its establishment, solicited subscriptions for it, and probably helped direct its policies.[28] In historian John Bach McMaster's eyes its appearance "marked the beginning of a new party." Freneau already possessed standing as the bard of the Revolution. Witty, penetrating, and always interesting, his paper in two years converted the nation's political journalism into a free-for-all. The *National Gazette* was indispensable in helping consolidate the Republican party, and its influence in opposing Federalism was wide and longlasting. It was Freneau who started the song that prosperity was confined to a few wealthy speculators who benefited from the pennies of the poor. He also drummed heavily upon the themes of the national debt, monarchical trends, and domination by Britain.[29]

Ridicule and irony were Freneau's principal stock in trade, though the *National Gazette* struck hammer-blows upon occasion. Semi-authoritative, its lead was followed by most anti-administration papers. Its English and grammar were a step above most of its competitors, and its files indicate more careful proofreading. The publication carried relatively few advertisements, for Freneau was more writer than businessman. Some issues had almost no paid space, and advertisements rarely filled as much as a full page. Though the journal at first claimed to be impartial, it was not (at least for long). In its editor's eyes, the nation was losing those republican principles on which the American Revolution had been based, and the paper dinned continually on the need for reasserting them.[30]

Both Freneau and Bache had command of the French language (the former's State Department post, it will be recalled, was that of translator), and there may have been more than mere coincidence between this fact and the rise of their papers to Republican preeminence. French, Irish, and German immigrants in Philadelphia tended to gather at the office of one editor or the other, a number of their newspaper advertisements were in French, and with the help of such men as Gallatin and Duane the two newssheets could be used to rally the foreign-born to the Democratic cause.[31]

The *National Gazette*'s circulation of nearly 1,700 was nationwide. Only sixteen journals were published south of the Potomac in 1791,[32] and Freneau's was the only newspaper circulating generally in that area. Anti-administration leaders saw to it that copies got to frontier settlements hitherto beyond reach of the press. It boasted readers in every state, and extracts from it appeared in all Republican periodicals as well as in most smaller papers, whatever their leaning. Public opinion had not yet crystallized in 1791, and Freneau's barbs —against funding and the National Bank, aristocracy and England—had a telling effect. His deft irony drove Federalists frantic; the *Gazette of the United States*'s attempts to answer in kind the "stinking rhymes" of this "sink" were completely outclassed.[33]

Even so, the paper was still not a paying proposition. Freneau's only other language was French, and the need to pay for translations of Russian, Dutch, and other documents coming to the State Department led him to resign his official post in October, 1793. Actually, Jefferson erred politically in employing him at the State Department. Freneau had planned to start a paper anyway, it would have crusaded against the administration wherever printed, and Republican leaders could have completely (instead of partially) subsidized it privately. As it was, there was evidence enough to lend color to Federalist charges that Freneau was a hireling. In addition to the translator's job, he had been promised the printing of all Departmental notices and publications. Jefferson several times denied writing for any paper, but he frequently urged others to do so, and he was a past master at achieving the inclusion of those items he wished to appear in print.[34]

Freneau wore no man's collar, but in Federalist eyes the effect was the same as though he did. His readers penned letters to Congress against Hamilton's measures, and the administration sought desperately to discredit him. Thus Hamilton had his own letter (ostensibly by "T. L.") published in the *Gazette of the United States,* hinting that Freneau was being paid to abuse the very government that had hired him. At first Freneau thought John Fenno envied the success of the *National Gazette* and retorted with an "Advertisement Extraordinary" on "T. L.'s" behalf, calling for a public employee whose body and soul would be at the disposal of the administration. Soon Hamilton was openly branding Freneau Jefferson's creature and calling on the Secretary of State to resign if he so opposed every administration measure. The *National Gazette* laughed at its foes, and in verse defied them to silence it.[35] Despite all pressure, Jefferson refused to abandon Freneau; for another year the paper continued its journalistic leadership. Finally, late in 1793, business difficulties accomplished what Hamilton had failed to achieve. The *National Gazette* ceased publication, but not until Jefferson had confided to his private notes (which were the basis for the later-published *Anas*) that it had preserved the Constitution and had done more than any other agency to check the drift toward monarchy. Conceivably it was from Freneau that Bache got much of his fire and boldness.[36]

Third in significance among Republican newspapers was Boston's *Independent Chronicle.* Under the double handicap of being located far from the nation's geographic or political center and being printed in an area generally Federalist, this journal did yeoman service for Jeffersonian interests. Thomas Adams was its publisher, but its ablest writer was Benjamin Austin, Jr., for years familiar to *Chronicle* readers as "Old South" or "Honestus." The paper commenced its career with violent opposition to the Society of Cincinnati, and thus it turned naturally to the Republican cause.[37]

In such a position it met the consistent hostility of Benajmin Russell's *Columbian Centinel,* possibly the most ably edited Federalist newspaper, and the competition of the well-established *Boston Gazette.* The latter enjoyed the enormous prestige of having been Sam Adams' vehicle during the Revolution, and it was rabidly Republican. Perhaps the *Gazette*'s abuse of Federalists was too gross, however; it fell upon evil days financially, and gradually declined in importance.[38] Its place as Democratic spokesman was assumed by what the *Columbian Centinel* dubbed "the lying *Chronicle*," which proved able to hold its own in the rough and tumble of Boston politics. A sedition suit and a change of owners cooled its ardor briefly in 1799,[39] but except for that period New England Democrats consistently imbibed "the truth, and proper sentiments" from this paper. Clippings from it appeared in Jeffersonian columns the nation over, and Fisher Ames—as a leading Federalist qualified to speak—wrote of its influence as "most pestiferous." [40]

By 1799 administration leaders classified three other papers —the New York *Argus,* the Baltimore *American,* and the Richmond *Examiner*—with the *Aurora* and the *Independent Chronicle* as the leading opposition journals against which legal suits should definitely be brought. These party organs were strategically located, capably edited, and circulated considerably beyond the cities of their publication. But the *American* and *Examiner* were comparative latecomers, and even the *Argus* (compared to the *Aurora* and *Chronicle*) was more nearly regional than national in its appeal.[41]

Second to the *Chronicle* in importance for New England, and surpassing it in caustic invective, was Charles Holt's New London *Bee*. Never exceeding a circulation of one thousand, after its establishment in 1797 this was the most incisive Democratic voice in Connecticut. Like the *Independent Chronicle* it was widely quoted, and publisher Holt won for himself a prison term for sedition. Other New England papers with a Republican leaning were less significant, but the Boston *Constitutional Telegraphe,* the Salem, Massachusetts, *Impartial Register,* and the Portsmouth, New Hampshire, *Republican Ledger* exerted considerable influence.[42] Anthony Haswell's *Vermont Gazette* and Matthew Lyon's *Fair Haven Gazette* dispensed Republican doctrine to the voters of the Green Mountain State and were of sufficient consequence to bring sedition suits against their publishers.[43]

In upstate New York Jefferson's mainstay was the *Albany Register,* also fairly frequently cited the country over. Most New York City gazettes had a limited circulation outside the lower Hudson River area, and the *Register* was located at the state capital. Backed by the Clintonian faction, it secured a share of the public printing and allegedly exerted quite an influence on the legislature when that body was in session.[44]

Manhattan's principal Republican printer, throughout his lifetime, was Thomas Greenleaf. His *New-York Journal* was perhaps the first American paper to issue a country edition, and the city version was exceedingly potent until he supplanted it with the daily *Argus* in 1795.[45] Though it relied rather heavily upon the *Aurora,* the *Argus* was the leading Jeffersonian organ in the New York area until Greenleaf's death in 1798. His widow tried to carry on, but a journeyman, David Frothingham, was convicted of sedition, and the paper was eventually sold to James Cheetham. Probably the *Argus* rates

617

close behind the *Independent Chronicle* in over-all significance, but its place in the city was speedily taken over by Cheetham's *American Citizen,* founded in 1800. Cheetham liked to be deemed an American John Wilkes, and his papers (the weekly *Journal* was renamed the *Republican Watchtower*) were among the most extreme in the nation.[46]

Philadelphia had Colonel Eleazer Oswald's *Independent Gazetteer* and [James] *Carey's United States Recorder* in addition to the *Aurora.* Both were influential. Oswald, a Revolutionary War hero and prominent Antifederalist, died in 1795, when the *Aurora* described him as "a firm Republican from nature" who "always espoused the rights of man . . . at all hazards, in spite of party, or courtly arrogance. . . ."[47] Carey was a bookseller who attempted several newspapers. None lived long, but all were strongly Democratic, and the *Recorder,* particularly, earned Federalist hostility.[48] Andrew Brown's *Philadelphia Gazette* considered itself Republican, and possessed some influence, for it too carried reports of congressional proceedings. At one time it hired Callender to transcribe notes at the sessions, and the paper was said to be prospering at the time of Brown's death in 1797.[49] Samuel Harrison Smith's *New World* was also fairly effective. Secretary of the American Philosophical Society when Jefferson was its president, Smith later set up the weekly *Universal Gazette.* This paper did so well that Jefferson persuaded him to move to Washington and establish the *National Intelligencer,* which became the official organ for the Jefferson administration.[50]

Elsewhere in Pennsylvania, Lancaster late in the decade became a center of Democratic papers. Its *Intelligencer,* launched in 1799, was skilled in defamation and was referred to many times by other journals. The same year saw establishment of the *Lancaster Correspondent,* which appears to have succeeded the *Readinger Adler* and Kammerer's *Philadelphische Correspondenz* as Republicans' leading German-language newspaper. Pittsburgh's *Tree of Liberty,* Washington's *Herald of Liberty* and Greensburg's *Farmers' Register* were also actively Democratic and considered important, but they too were not set up until very near the close of the century.[51]

Printed continuously throughout the decade, Shepard Kollock's Elizabethtown *New Jersey Journal* was in some respects the strongest Jeffersonian publication in that state.[52] Its supremacy, though, was seriously challenged by Freneau's Mount Pleasant *Jersey Chronicle* in 1795 and 1796, and even more so by the Newark *Centinel of Freedom* after that time.[53] Each of the latter gazettes was more vehemently Republican than the *New Jersey Journal,* and the *Centinel* (edited by Revolutionary veteran William Pennington) particularly came into prominence. Cited all over the country, by 1800 it had eclipsed the *Journal* in partisan influence and ranked close behind Republicanism's "big five" in that respect.

The Wilmington *Delaware Gazette* was blandly Democratic, but the *Mirror of the Times* was the party's foremost support in that state after 1799. Had Justice Chase's wishes been followed, this newssheet would have been added to the select list of those tested by the Sedition Act. Maryland possessed the *Baltimore Telegraphe,* but that rather temperately Republican paper was completely overshadowed when the *American* appeared. In vehemence and virulence the latter yielded little to any press. Its vigor brought almost immediate recognition as a chief Jeffersonian spokesman in the South, and its first issue boldly proclaimed the intention to give "an energetic and undivided support" to the Republican cause despite all the scurrility and pressure which might be exerted against it. During the crisis with France its unswerving course even gained for it a tribute in the form of a figurehead of a ship built for a partisan merchant of the Maryland seaport.[54]

Despite her lack of sizable cities, Virginia was amply supplied with journals, but nearly all were small and of brief existence. Changes of title and ownership occurred with unusually disturbing frequency. The Richmond *Virginia Argus* functioned valiantly for the Democrats from 1796 on, and selections from it cropped up in columns from New England to

Georgia. In Fredericksburg the *Genius of Liberty* and in Norfolk the *Epitome of the Times* were prominent, though they were latecomers to the field. The *Petersburg Intelligencer* finally took a stand for Jefferson after its predecessor—one of the innumerable *Virginia Gazettes*—had long straddled the fence. So much support was gained by the *Alexandria Times* that Federalists of that city were said to have tried to prevent it from obtaining seafaring news and to have plotted a blacklist for workers who read it.[55]

After 1798, however, the outstanding Democratic spokesman in Virginia was also the most intemperate. Meriwether Jones's Richmond *Examiner*, with the able assistance of Scottish refugee James Thomson Callender, rapidly gained a reputation for abusiveness even in that day. Callender's venom exceeded that of Duane or Holt. He was vulgar and slanderous, but people read what he had to say. Infuriated Federalists concocted at least one scheme to destroy the *Examiner* office, and few events of the period pleased them more than Callender's conviction and prison sentence for sedition. Even so, the contumacious editor penned articles "from the Richmond jail" for publication, and the net effect of the prosecution was probably helpful to Republicans.[56]

Leading Jeffersonian voice in North Carolina was Joseph Gales's *Raleigh Register*. Not established until 1799, it was still the first strongly partisan paper in the state.[57] Since Gales had taken shorthand reports of congressional debates for Oswald's *Independent Gazetteer* (which he purchased about a year after Oswald's death), he was conversant with governmental figures and proceedings. North Carolinians needed a Republican mouthpiece, and the *Raleigh Register* admirably filled the bill. For some decades after Jefferson's election it remained one of the leading liberal newspapers of the Southland.[58]

Charleston, although one of the nation's larger cities, had relatively few periodicals. The Republican viewpoint, however, was rather consistently and on the whole ably presented by the *City Gazette,* especially after Philip Freneau's brother Peter became editor in 1797. It was well written and, though Jeffersonian, not bitterly biased. A share in the state printing enabled it to continue in operation, and eventually the paper became a controlling political force in South Carolina.[59]

Georgia's journals were colorful but not consistent partisans; most of the newspapers west of the mountains, however, leaned toward the Republicans. By all odds the most significant paper beyond Pittsburgh was the first, John Bradford's Lexington *Kentucky Gazette*. Forced by economic necessity into the publishing business, Bradford, purchasing his type from Federalist John Scull of Pittsburgh, soon became an outstanding Democratic printer. He was active in local politics, and for some years the *Kentucky Gazette* enjoyed the state printing.[60] *Stewart's Kentucky Herald*, of Lexington and Paris, the Washington *Mirror* and the Frankfort *Palladium* (the last two jointly operated by William Hunter and William Beaumont) were its chief rivals, and excerpts from each occasionally found their way into Eastern presses. There were papers of at least mildly Jeffersonian persuasion in both Tennessee and the Northwest Territory, but the extent of their influence is difficult to gauge.

The foregoing gazettes, of course, were not the only ones to purvey the Republican party line, but an effort has been made to indicate those with the largest followings in their respective areas. Viewed nationally, those most valuable from the Jeffersonian standpoint were probably the *Aurora, National Gazette, Independent Chronicle,* New York *Argus,* Richmond *Examiner,* Baltimore *American, Centinel of Freedom,* New London *Bee,* the *American Citizen, Virginia Argus, Vermont Gazette, Kentucky Gazette,* the *Time Piece, Constitutional Telegraphe,* and the Charleston *City Gazette,* roughly in that order.[61] These were, however, only the bellwethers of a much larger number that devoted their time and news space to overthrowing the Federalist party. And it must be remembered that there was a fraternity among Republican journals. They advertised for one another, accepted subscriptions for each other, and applauded the establishment of each new Jeffersonian paper.[62] The result made them more formidable than mere numbers might indicate.

Despite statements made then and later, journalistic critics of the administration were no infinitesimal minority. Federalist editors often deliberately cultivated the idea that they were, apparently on the "bandwagon" principle that belittling the opposition might make it seem contemptible. Occasionally even Republican printers confirmed this picture, for some of them had no wish to minimize either the task confronting them or (later) the magnitude of their accomplishment.[63]

Yet it is evident that Republican presses were far from insignificant. Nominally, they were clearly outnumbered during the period covered by this study. Even the *National Gazette* did not openly oppose Washington's reelection in 1792 (although it and a number of other papers favored Clinton for Vice-President), and it has been estimated there were four times as many Federalist as Democratic papers in the campaign of 1796.[64] The journals in commercial areas—perhaps swayed by both advertisers and subscribers—were largely pro-administration. But in the West the preponderance was the other way, and most new gazettes founded after 1796 were Republican. By 1800 the journalistic odds against Jefferson had dropped to no worse than two to one.[65]

This ratio still fails to reflect accurately the true situation. Not only were Republican newssheets being established twice as rapidly as Federalist ones, but most of these, as became new members of the faith, were more zealous and partisan than the older organs of the opposite belief. There have been assertions that journals of this period could be easily classified, but careful investigation proves the need of some qualification. Many papers commonly regarded as Federalist were either lukewarm in their affiliation or sufficiently liberal to permit considerable criticism of the administration. The approximately seventy Democratic gazettes in late 1800 were active in achieving Jefferson's victory; it does not follow that all the others were equally vigorous in Adams' behalf.[66]

Most additions to the Democratic force were newly

founded presses, but despite the infrequency of turncoat editors a few did change their affiliation.[67] In 1799 the *Impartial Journal* scathingly denounced the "amazing changes" in the conduct of a number of editors. Once it became apparent their Federalist doctrines were becoming unpopular, these fair-weather soldiers began calling for the impartiality they had earlier described as treasonous, or actually published Francophile or Republican sentiments:

> If this, Citizens, can be called *good Conduct*, we pray never to practice it,—if no other way can be adopted, for us to gain the good will of you, we are sure of never possessing it. Can you put any dependance on the man who . . . will shift as the wind blows . . . ? I think you will not;—firmness in Printers is necessary . . . to give the readers . . . an opportunity to find out the truth. . . .[68]

Charles Holt professed to note a perceptible difference after completing his prison term for sedition. The number of new Republican papers started by mid-1800, coupled with "the trimming of a great proportion of old federal papers, indicates a great change in public sentiment." [69]

Holt may have been overly optimistic, but many Federalists did deplore the founding of Republican journals all the way from New Hampshire to Savannah.[70] The *Constitutional Telegraphe* refuted the *Columbian Centinel*'s "shameless and violent lie" that only twenty of the nation's more than two hundred papers were Republican. Notwithstanding Federalist denials, over fifty decidedly Democratic gazettes had been founded since the passage of the Alien and Sedition Acts.[71] Since many nominally Federalist newspapers were rather half-heartedly so by 1800, and most of the Democratic ones were enthusiastic, the actual disparity in numbers and influence was far from overpowering. In 1800 the effective proportion was about three to two, and for the entire decade a ratio of approximately two strongly Federalist vehicles for every violently Republican journal seems as accurate a portrayal of the situation with respect to newspapers' impact as possible.[72] It may be, as apparently some assume, that the great majority of

623

those editors whose newspapers are classified in the appendix as politically "impartial" or "uncertain" were Federalists. But their publications failed to reflect clearly this fact (if such it was), and it is misleading to consider them part of an "over-whelmingly Federalist press." Out of 109 papers in November, 1792, only 23 papers could be safely denominated Republican, but even then 36 others showed no decided partisanship. Four years later 162 newspapers existed; while only 34 of them unquestionably supported Jefferson, again 36 were doubtful. By 1800 the 231 papers printed included at least 40 which took no definite stand, and another 68 with positions best described as inclined "moderately" toward one party or the other.[73]

Actually there is reason to modify somewhat the wide-spread impression that the presses of the era were almost invariably violently one-sided.[74] Obviously party spirit was rife, and in numerous instances it was carried to extremes that would not be tolerated today. Many of the most effective Jeffersonian papers were among the most rabid. Yet a considerable number of publishers conscientiously attempted neutrality, some seemed in doubt, and still more were sufficiently independent to print items and letters critical of the cause toward which they leaned.

Admittedly the immoderate publications on each side in great degree set the journalistic tone for the times. In their efforts to discredit the opposition, extremist editors contributed to the picture already outlined for them. Thus Republican printers accused Federalist publishers of supporting the administration because of bribes, public printing contracts, or threatened loss of support by leading advertisers or political figures. Federalists made countercharges that French gold, or disappointments in office-seeking and government printing, helped explain the virulence of Democratic organs.[75] Such choice epithets as "that most infamous of all lying repositories," or "Of all the papers on the continent, none are more unfaithful reporters of intelligence," frequently appeared.[76] "Traitor" and "hypocrite" were only mild pejoratives, and

Mathew Carey could call Cobbett "the most tremendous scourge that hell ever vomited forth to curse a people," but such denunciation was often primarily for popular consumption.[77]

Cobbett himself decried professions of impartiality as useless,[78] but various editors eschewed politics almost altogether, or deplored the intolerance which others practiced. Even Philadelphia had no distinctly partisan press, assert some authorities, until 1791, and the National Gazette printed items defending Hamilton as late as September of the following year.[79] John Bradford's Republican sympathies were undeniable, yet in 1796 his Kentucky Gazette reprinted a Boston notice of Washington's forthcoming retirement and the concomitant need to choose Federalist electors. And John Scull's influential Pittsburgh Gazette was rather liberal, for all its Federalist tinge. Its columns were open to administration adversaries, and it carried lengthy Jeffersonian expositions by Hugh H. Brackenridge and other writers.[80] French Minister Ternant might report to Paris in 1792 that presses teemed with articles defending or attacking the new federal government, but throughout the decade many newspapers deplored the "spirit of party."[81]

So violent were some publishers and correspondents that it is difficult to aviod cynicism at their claims of objectivity. But the protestations of impartiality and denunciations of political intemperance are impressive through volume alone. From Georgia to Massachusetts papers disclaimed calumny and reprobated excess. In Connecticut and Kentucky they inveighed against "the Daemon of contention" which "left no room for reason and common sense," while New York's Columbian Gazette called "a plague on both your houses." When dozens of journals professed themselves open to both sides, and even the Palladium could give nearly three columns to an item from the Gazette of the United States, it is erroneous to categorize all publications of the period as either black or white.[82] The grays may have been a minority, but they were still numerous and of many shades.

While this study is primarily concerned with the partisan press, whatever their political inclination, these newspapers were remarkably modern in their utility. A twentieth-century study assigns six major functions to a newspaper in society: conveying news to its readers, expressing opinions on significant events and policies, furnishing some background for understanding current questions, providing entertainment, serving (through advertising) as a market place, and providing some instruction of an encyclopedic nature.[83] Acknowledging the limitations of the times, anyone who peruses the journals of the 1790s must admit that they admirably performed these services. Though contemporary propaganda methods might be more subtle, the devices used by party organs then were essentially similar to those of today.

Politically, however, Republican presses were handicapped in that prior to 1796 the party had no universally acknowledged standard bearer. As long as Jefferson was in Washington's Cabinet his political activities were circumscribed, and he could not be openly hailed as the leader of the opposition. Much has been assumed about his endeavors to form an anti-administration party then,[84] though more recently scholars have assigned larger roles in early leadership to Madison and John Beckley.[85] Certainly whatever Jefferson did of this nature could not be widely publicized at the time.

Jefferson's intimacy with Madison was known, as was the fact the two visited George Clinton in 1791 while they were on a "botanizing" vacation.[86] Infrequently, the Secretary was mentioned as a person worthy of emulation, and it was said he, Madison, and Sam Adams were untainted by the corrupting funding system.[87] While the opposition press carried little or no criticism of the State Department, absence of animadversion does not constitute a campaign buildup, and there was no flood of favorable comments either. Beyond expressing an occasional hope he would not resign,[88] and defending him against Hamiltonian attacks, Republican journalists paid comparatively little attention to Jefferson before his retirement. As noted, Madison, Clinton, and Gallatin all won more notice in their columns.

Yet none of these men commanded the position the author of the Declaration of Independence came to occupy in Democratic eyes. Gallatin was a foreigner ineligible for the Presidency. Clinton had opposed adoption of the Constitution and had powerful enemies in his own state of New York. Madison, recipient of more widespread acclaim at first, still lacked sufficient nationwide appeal to make him a formidable candidate. Beckley was relatively unknown, and, while Sam Adams and William Branch Giles were sometimes mentioned favorably, neither was ever the focus of a concerted publicity effort.

Jefferson's resignation from the State Department produced publicized regrets. Yet the *General Advertiser* found it no surprise that he should wish to leave office. His opinions had been disregarded in executive councils, though his post compelled him to give the sanction of his name to measures he found repugnant. Southern papers noted Jefferson did not quit because he could no longer hold his place; his recognized ability made Washington reluctant to see him depart. His writing was "copious without prolixity," or "concise without abruptness"; he left "with an unblemished reputation." A significant comment was: "In the United States, though we have, as must always happen among a free people, much difference of opinion, we have hitherto nothing that can in any degree deserve the name of faction." [89]

Even these encomiums did not lead to a full-scale press campaign on Jefferson's behalf. To those who read only the newspapers, his retirement must for a time have seemed tantamount to oblivion. He himself apparently wrote nothing for them [90] (although he urged Madison to do so), and Republican newssheets generally made little mention of him. From behind the scenes he was presumably not uninterested, and a casual reference in 1795 noted Senator Aaron Burr had gone southward to see him and Madison on "business of importance," [91] but not until 1796 did he receive much printed attention. Washington's imminent withdrawal from public life facilitated Jefferson's public entrance upon the political stage, and thereafter the latter's press support was open and unchallenged by other Republicans.

This support demonstrated its value in the election of 1796, which was so close that Jefferson, second-highest candidate in the electoral count, became Vice-President under Adams. Even that exciting contest was eclipsed in color, vehemence, and significance by the one of 1800. Democratic editors accentuated growing encroachment by the central government on the powers of the states. They viewed it as all part of a gigantic plot to undermine the Constitution, to create an autocratic government to benefit speculators or grafters, and to make America an English satellite in foreign relations. Increased taxes, nepotism, a standing army, the Alien and Sedition Acts—each was part of this grand design. Personal invective approached record heights, and Jeffersonians exploited the friction between Adams and Hamilton, and the suspicion between Adams and C. C. Pinckney, in efforts to split the Federalists. They slyly strove to checkmate Hamilton's alleged desire to bring Pinckney to the Presidency by urging Northern Federalist electors to vote for Adams and Jefferson, while informing Southern voters ballots should be withheld from Adams because Massachusetts was unlikely to vote for Pinckney.[92] Margins in New York and South Carolina spelled triumph for Jefferson and Burr, who received seventy-three votes each as against Adams' sixty-five and Pinckney's sixty-four.[93]

Almost to a man Republican electors had intended Jefferson for the first place, but their solid discipline gave Burr an equal number of votes. The tense session of a Federalist-controlled lame duck House that finally elected Jefferson after thirty-six ballots has often been described[94] and extends beyond the scope of this study. So, too does the momentousness of a brief item in January, 1801, noting that "John Marshall, Esq., is appointed by the President, Chief Justice of the U.S."[95] The major political change had already taken place.

So narrow was the Republican electoral majority that on

the basis of these returns the victory scarcely seems a violent overthrow. Outside New York State Jefferson had seven fewer votes than four years earlier. Most of Adams' gains, however, came from Pennsylvania, where a faithful expression of popular sentiment would have added to the Democratic count. While both sides acquired votes through election tricks, Federalists clearly benefited more from such tactics, and only thus was the Jeffersonian margin so slight. More truly indicative was the makeup of the new Congress, where a Federalist edge in the House was converted into an overwhelming superiority for the Democrats.[96] In essence, therefore—particularly considering their party's humble origins less than a decade before—the election of 1800 represented a tremendous victory for Republicans. In that accomplishment the Jeffersonian press had a decisive role.

A final observation stresses the vital contribution of the fourth estate. That it was fundamental in achieving this triumph was a judgment then as well as later. Perhaps at no time in our history have gazettes been more significant. And from Jefferson's famed expression of preference, in 1787, for living with newspapers in the absence of a government to existing under a government without newspapers,[97] this importance was widely recognized.

Freedom of the press and need for diffusion of information have been accented as essential tenets of the Democratic doctrine. Editors protesting proposed postal "taxes" stressed these arguments. Permission to print both sides of political issues was meaningless if through increased costs or restricted circulation "the poor sort of people have it not in their power" to read the journals.[98] Franklin had once agreed, wrote "A. V.," that newspapers were light things—so were feathers, yet they served to show which way the wind blew. Therefore where gazettes were absolutely free they were an infallible guide to "the real temper of the times." Liberty of the press, argued even the *Massachusetts Mercury,* was the surest proof of liberty of the citizenry. Republicans accepted this conclusion, though they questioned Federalist implications that both were continuous realities under Adams' administration. The *American Mercury* held the discovery of printing struck a deathblow at every species of tyranny. In America, descanted "The Observer," presses had multiplied to disseminate intelligence:

> It is from newspapers that the mass of the people derive their knowledge; and the principles of many thousands have been determined in support or opposition of federal measures, by the accidental perusal in youth, of a federal or antifederal paper. Indeed many persons of wealth and reputation in the world, have gotten their knowledge from no other source than that of a newspaper, though by some silly shame none will confess it.[99]

In 1800 *Port Folio* magazine declared the United States had become "a nation of newspaper readers," and a year earlier the novelist Charles Brockden Brown had asserted papers were "more widely read and diffused" in America "than in any other part of the world."[100] Foreign observers uniformly noted the prevalence of gazettes as contrasted with Europe.[101] As Pierre Dupont de Nemours remarked in 1800, while "a large part of the nation reads the Bible, all of it assiduously peruse[s] the newspapers. The fathers read them aloud to their children while the mothers are preparing breakfast. . . ." Another lamented America's lack of literary attainments, but stated its people showed a peculiar propensity for authorship and consumption "of political invectives for a newspaper."[102] Most mature Americans, especially in New England, could read and write, and it was "extremely probable, what has often been asserted by judicious observers, that newspapers were habitually read by every person of a reading age in the country. . . . No vehicles of knowledge . . . more cheap and commodious were ever contrived."[103]

That the influence of these printed pages extended beyond the individual subscribers has already been shown. As in Revolutionary times, many persons scanned the latest information or had it read to them.[104] Freneau's "Robert Slender" slipped out to a nearby typical tavern "where now and then a few neighbours meet to spit, smoke segars, drink apple whiskey . . . and *read the news"* from the papers available there.[105] Very frequently, single newspaper subscriptions represented an association of several families.[106] New publishers confidently relied on the seemingly insatiable American appetite for political intelligence, and they professed a sense of high calling. Printers felt their business had been "chiefly instrumental in bringing mankind from a state of blindness and slavery to their present advancement in knowledge and freedom."[107] James Lyon believed his proposed *Friend of the People* could as a national newspaper "rally, concentrate and nationalize" the efforts of Republicans in all parts of the country toward the election to the Presidency of one "not engulphed in the vortex of British corruption."[108]

It is scarcely surprising that publishers themselves should be convinced of the importance of their efforts. But secondary writers as well have been convinced. According to Hildreth, never did individual papers exert so much power. Their educating influence operated in even the most sparsely settled areas and was more potent than all institutions of higher learning.[109] For the average American, the newspaper was the focus of literary interest; men allegedly regarded it as a duty to keep abreast of governmental affairs.[110] Printers definitely affected community opinion; as Preserved Smith put it, to a great degree the literature of the period was the development of journalism. Cheapness, brevity, timeliness, and readability made gazettes the chief reading matter of general interest.[111] The 1790s witnessed a steady increase in the number of votes cast in elections, though the suffrage was not widened appreciably.[112] Obviously there was growing interest on the part of the electorate, and for much of this the press could claim credit. In molding public opinion, both urban and rural, these four-page sheets were tremendously effective. As Jefferson stated: "Our citizens may be deceived for awhile, and have been deceived; but so long as the presses can be protected, we may trust to them for light."[113]

Against all hindrance—hatred, violence, bankruptcy, imprisonment and (for all they knew) danger to life itself—these editors battled for the overthrow of Federalism.[114] North Carolinians as early as 1792 attributed Adams' loss of their state to Freneau's attacks, and Jefferson and Madison considered the *National Gazette* one of the strongest influences in American politics. Over the nation Democrats looked to Freneau as an oracle, and Adams later traced his eventual overthrow to him.[115] Jefferson had from the start realized that newspapers were indispensable in shaping public opinion, and the *Aurora*—as heir to the mantle of the *Gazette*—has been called the "strongest single factor" from 1793 to 1801 in the publicity which culminated in Jefferson's victory.[116] To Adams, Bache speedily became as dangerous and obnoxious as Freneau, and some later writers accord him first rank among founders of the Republican political organization.[117] Bache was succeeded by Duane, and his biographers bluntly state that Jefferson's election was owing to him.[118]

Even allowing for overenthusiastic claims for individuals, it is evident the Republican press generally was largely responsible for the "revolution" wrought in 1800. Suggestions of anti-administration printers that the French peril was a hoax to promote an American despotism fell on fertile soil and won enough believers to reverse Federalist successes of 1798. Charles Pinckney wrote Jefferson that his letters in the Charleston *City Gazette* had literally rained over the Carolinas and Georgia *"from the mountains to the ocean."* [119] About 1790 American leaders commenced the policy of deliberately securing newspaper support; these gazettes, more than any other agency, achieved the radical change of mind during the following decade. Much of what they printed was distorted, and some deliberately false, but they were effective. Republican strength was mostly in rural areas, where newspapers were the party's chief support. Freedom of the press— both as an issue and a reality—largely accounted for Jefferson's coming to office.[120]

Jeffersonian chieftains fully comprehended their indebtedness. Bache's death in 1798 produced many encomiums as well as Federalist execrations testifying to his importance.[121]

Ever alert to the vital nature of the press in a democratic society, Jefferson feared Federalist papers from the start and helped found and aid ones to present his viewpoint. He appealed for subscriptions to the *Aurora* and *Carey's United States Recorder* at the time of the Alien and Sedition Laws, saying that if those journals failed "republicanism will be entirely browbeaten." [122] One "SIMPLETON" thought it "happy for democracy that it is *Argus*-eyed, expands its views with the rise of *Aurora,* keeps a well ordered *Time-Piece,* is dilligent as the *Bee,* and faithful as the *Chronicle*" to detect the amazing prevalence of administration measures "accidentally" favoring Britain. [123]

In 1799 Jefferson charged Madison and others to set aside some time daily to write for the papers. That summer was the time, he asserted, for Republicans to make their supreme effort: "THE ENGINE IS THE PRESS." [124] Such steps seemed necessary to combat the Federalist newssheets, for Callender claimed *Porcupine's Gazette* was being "sent *gratis,* over the country, to a great number of deputy post-masters," while Pickering had the effrontery to rail at "calumniators" of the administration. [125] When Republican congressmen met in May at a Philadelphia boarding house to confirm the Jefferson-Burr ticket for 1800, it was decided the press would be the primary agency utilized in their endeavor. [126] During and after the campaign of 1800 Jeffersonians repeatedly toasted their press as "the bulwark of liberty" and "the instrument of heaven to instruct mankind." The "Editors of the republican presses throughout the Union" had "deserved well of their country," and publisher Duane was "the Cicero of Anglo-Federal conspiracies." [127] The frequency of such opinions when Jefferson assumed office showed general realization of the indispensable part journals had played in his victory. The *Mirror of the Times* waxed confident over America's future under an administration beaming "with all that renders life desirable." Delaware had not gone completely Republican, but the election results had converted many, and "The diffusion of correct information, among those who are uninformed, by means of Newspapers devoted to the cause of morality and freedom" could be trusted to complete the job so gloriously begun.[128]

Although nearly two years later an embittered Callender charged Jefferson with ingratitude toward the editors who had elected him,[129] in reality the new President seemed fully conscious of his obligation. He disliked billingsgate journalism and encouraged Samuel H. Smith's more urbane *National Intelligencer* as the organ of his administration, but to the end of his life Jefferson gave aid to Duane, particularly, in a number of ways. The publisher became a lieutenant-colonel in the army and obtained governmental stationery contracts, while the President personally purchased volumes from his bookstore and at varying times solicited financial aid for the *Aurora*.[130] After he left the Presidency Jefferson epitomized the contribution of the Democratic press generally in noting that the paper

> has unquestionably rendered incalculable services to republicanism through all its struggles with the federalists, and has been the rallying point for the orthodoxy of the whole Union. It was our comfort in gloomiest days, and is still performing the office of a watchful sentinel. We should be ungrateful to desert him [Duane], and unfaithful to our own interests to lose him.[131]

Near the end of his life Jefferson could—when Duane had apparently turned apostate—still comment:

> Yet the energy of his press, when our cause was laboring, and all but lost, under the overwhelming weight of its powerful adversaries, *its unquestionable effect in the revolution produced on the public mind,* which arrested the rapid march of our government toward monarchy, overweigh in fact the demerit of his desertion.[132]

A more clear cut admission of deep indebtedness could scarcely be made.

Supposedly Washington once told Genêt he did not read the newspapers and little cared what they said of his administration,[133] but most Federalist leaders came eventually to quite another opinion. Like his Republican antagonist, Hamilton immediately recognized the cardinal importance of a favorable press, and he was instrumental in founding at least

three administration papers during this period.[134] Fisher
Ames by 1795 was demanding vindication of Jay's Treaty in
the newspapers.[135] Soon Cobbett was sneering that the typical "Modern Patriot" was compounded of several ingredients
"strained through ten sheets of the *Aurora*," and charging
that

> The Gazettes in this country have done it more real injury than
> all its enemies ever did or can do. They mislead the people at home
> and misrepresent them abroad. . . .
> I shall be told that the people are not obliged to read these
> abominable publications. But they do read them, and thousands
> who read them, read nothing else. To suppress them is impossible;
> they will vomit forth their poison; it is a privilege of their natures,
> that no law can abridge; and therefore the only mode left is, to
> counteract its effects.[136]

Federalist papers lashed out at leading Democratic publications as vehicles "of gall and untruth," and the press generally
was denominated "venal, servile, base and stupid." Yet administrative leaders were counselled to use newspapers to "keep
our friends and regain our deserters."[137] Alarmed, the *New
York Gazette* in 1799 avowed nothing contributed more "towards misleading the good yeomanry of our country" than the
circulation of Republican journals. These "effusions of *disappointed* men" were being distributed everywhere at the expense of designing manipulators, and were "read by a class of
people who never do, or have not the time to investigate their
contents." Such readers swallowed publishers' claims that they
had only the national welfare in view, and the result had been
that many innocent citizens had become "open enemies of our
constitutional government."[138] One irate Federalist believed
Republicans had two methods of making converts, and newspapers played an integral part in both. One consisted of circulating so many anti-government lies that weak minds were convinced; the other in sending "newspapers and pamphlets to a
man, who though totally disregarding them, finds himself suspected, and stigmatized as a *democrat,* till from mortification
and resentment, he actually becomes one."[139]

Residents of Portsmouth, New Hampshire, were warned

Jacobins were so determined to overthrow America's government that they were "not satisfied with spreading all the sedition in their power by their vile tongues," but planned to start a paper in that city to accomplish their end. In Pennsylvania, Harrisburg Republicans reputedly had guaranteed five hundred subscriptions to the local publisher if he would print only news favorable to their party.[140] The *United States Oracle* admonished Federalists to bestir themselves before all was lost. The opposition was fully organized and hard at work:

> In all the states new presses are established, from Portsmouth in New-Hampshire to Savannah in Georgia; through which the orders of the Generals of the faction are transmitted with professional punctuality; which presses serve as sounding boards to the notes that issue through the great *'speaking trumpet of the devil,'* the *Philadelphia Aurora.*—The Conductors of these Presses, have their rations issued to them, and are prompted in proportion to their abuse and defamation of the President, Congress, and the Northern States; and to the number of lies, innuendoes and suggestions they may produce from day to day.

Friends of government took these "hirelings" too lightly and relied on the common sense of the people to discern their falsehoods, but experience had shown this to be a mistake. Men of talents should "assume their pens, and with plain truths and patriotic eloquence confound their enemies, though mailed in tenfold more brass than they now are." [141]

Democratic professions of loyalty to the Constitution were only a ruse, cried the *Litchfield Monitor*. Public office was that party's only aim; for that purpose it had established papers far and wide to denounce the administration. The *Aurora* and its ilk were crammed with untruths, sniffed the *Federalist and New Jersey State Gazette*. "But still this retail of calumny has its use; it puts words into the mouths of stupid and malignant Jacobins, and completely gulls the gaping simplicity of many honest people." [142]

The *Connecticut Courant*'s "Burleigh" denounced the *Aurora* as "the vilest newspaper than ever disgraced a free country," and added one "of the most efficacious modes of destroying governments which the jacobins have pursued in every country where they have existed, has been corrupting the channels of public information, and disseminating falsehood and slander." This created uneasiness and undermined morals to lay the groundwork for anarchy. After prevailing in France, "The same plan has been in a considerable degree, and with no small success, adopted in this country, to destroy our government." Republicans initially got certain papers "to *revile, belie* and *slander*" the administration. Freneau's *National Gazette* was first, followed by the *Aurora, Argus* and *Independent Chronicle;* then subordinate papers, of a "similar spirit of profligacy, were planted in various parts of the U. S." The *Aurora* came to be the nucleus:

> What ever appeared in that [paper] was faithfully copied into the others; and tho' but a few were to be found in many parts of the country who would pay for such papers, they were sent round the country *gratis*. They were read by those few, the main sentiments were repeated to others, and in this way the sentiments were not only scattered, but a perfect union of opinion was established. Whoever has been careful enough to watch the progress of jacobinism in the country, must have observed, that on every important subject, the sentiments to be inculcated among the democrats, has been first put into the Aurora. This was the heart, the seat of life. From thence the blood has flowed to the extremities by a sure and rapid circulation, and the life and strength of the paper have thus been supported and nourished. It is even astonishing to remark, with how much punctuality and rapidity, *the same opinion* has been circulated and repeated by these people, from the highest to the lowest.
>
> *By means like these, the greatest part of the mischief which we now experience has been occasioned.* A constant publication, and repetition of falsehood, which, to a great part of the people, is never contradicted, will eventually produce mischief; because the conclusion which they will draw, will be, that if these things were not true they would be contradicted. . . .[143]

Mocking Democrats printed "resolutions" of a pretended meeting of frightened New England Federalists advocating shackling the press. The considered judgment of these "leaders" was that "we must root out printing, or printing will root

637

out us." [144] Frantically Ames, Dwight, and others attempted to activate newspapers to check the rising whirlwind. Republicans, said Ames, were outmatched by force or logic; "but while they depend on lies" and spread them so industriously, "they will beat us." [145]

Beat them the Republicans did, and best testimony to the paramount contribution of the Jeffersonian press during the campaign of 1800 consists of Federalists' explanations for their defeat. The *Washington Federalist* compared the election to a horse race between the *"Bay Yankey"* and the *"Cotesworth"* against the *"Monticello"* and the *"York."* Some "imported jockies," having "no character to lose," busied themselves during the race throwing

> large quantities of muddy water at the Bay Yankey and the Cotesworth. This was done by means of an invention originally intended for a vast speaking trumpet, but altered by the jockies, into an engine for throwing preparations of mud. . . .
>
> The jockies, in excuse for themselves, pretended it squirted mud for the preservation of the machinery. They said, that pure air would destroy it for a speaking trumpet; but that mud would secure it from being damaged, and was the best thing in the world to make it work freely. . . .
>
> [The Bay Yankey and the Cotesworth were nosed out, owing to the muddy water thrown at them], their rivals, the Monticello and the York, not having such obstacles to encounter.[146]

Seeking recourse in verse, the *Connecticut Courant*'s "The Triumph of Democracy" named many "factious printers" responsible for Jefferson's success.[147] "Leonidas" depicted these gloaters as already "partitioning the booty of slander and calumny, dividing the offices of men, *whom their malicious falsehoods have deprived of subsistence.*" Others compared the "incessant and unremitting calumny" of Jeffersonian presses to perpetual friction which would "at length wear away the hardest substance." Accustomed to detraction, the American people had become convinced "that where so much was said there must be some foundation in fact." [148] While some Federalists berated their party for tardiness in recognizing the value of newspapers, the *New England Palladium* mournfully conceded "a most powerful cause of the rapid decay of our government is a licentious and prostituted press. . . . The effect it has already produced exceeds calculation, and is next to miraculous." [149]

Lamenting Federalists insisted no administration ever deserved more of its country, yet in no nation was liberty so profaned.

> How happens it? Popular prejudice is everywhere an instrument, and popular passion an agent, of innovation and revolution. *The actions of these, however, would be feeble without newspapers. By newspapers, prejudice finds eyes, and passion a tongue. The reason, that ought to be a ruler, turns pimp to faction and enlists as a mercenary soldier. Excellent in their use, intolerable in their abuse, we are forced to ponder about newspapers, whether we can do without them, or endure them. Liberty would be a goddess, and really immortal, if she could be thus dieted on poisons; if she could play unhurt with the forky tongues of the Chronicle and Aurora.*[150]

"Through the successful zeal of the *Aurora* and other pestilential presses," seconded the *Alexandria Advertiser*, public opinion—"poisoned with the most unfounded suspicions of the late administration"—had accepted the view that the government was corrupt and prodigal and sought to erect a monarchy on the ruins of republicanism.[151]

John Adams agreed. Shortly after leaving the Presidency, he wrote his administration had been overthrown by Freneau, Duane, Callender, Cooper, and Lyon. "A group of foreign liars encouraged by a few ambitious native gentlemen" had "discomfited the education, the talents, the virtues and the prosperity of the country." [152] Eight years later he still attributed his defeat to the writings of such as Freneau, Brown, and Callender. Franklin's old dislike for him, he believed, had been transmitted through Bache to the *Aurora*, and that publication had exacted a potent reckoning.[153] In 1813 he wrote Jefferson that the leading Republican editors had been "terrorists." [154] When John Randolph a little later charged, *"The artillery of the press has long been the instrument of our* [Randolph's faction of the Republican party's] *subjugation,"* the venerable ex-President stated he had never expected such a confession from such a penitent, and reminded a friend of the "artillery" directed against his own administration.[155]

Perhaps Fisher Ames put it most succinctly. Just after Jefferson's inauguration he wrote: "The newspapers are an overmatch for any government. They will first overawe and then usurp it. This has been done; and the Jacobins owe their triumph to the unceasing use of this engine. . . ." [156]

When both victor and vanquished concur as to the decisive factor in the outcome of a contest, little remains to be said. Through exploitation of every Federalist weakness, untiring reiteration of Republican principles and foreign dangers, and incessant use—sometimes subtly, often rudely—of all types of appeals, the newspapers had been instrumental in founding a party and bringing it to victory.

Their methods were not always pretty. Many of their arguments pandered to hatred, disgust, loyalty, confidence, envy, or fear. At times some papers relied on invective, falsehood and distortion, doubtless on the time-worn assumption that the end justified the means. Nonetheless the Democratic press succeeded. Jefferson used it, and it presented his views, but he could not have been elected in 1800 without it. Of all groups frequently credited with the triumph of democratic principles —the sturdy artisans and "mechanics" of the towns, the equalitarian frontiersmen, the liberal clergy, or the independent yeomen—none did more than the indefatigable and inkstained editors who fought the Republican cause to a triumphant conclusion.[157] Historians may have given them little attention, but the "Jeffersonian Revolution" is their finest epitaph.

# NOTES

# I NEWSPAPERS AND THEIR ROLE

1. Throughout this study the terms "Democratic" and "Republican" are used interchangeably to denote the Democratic-Republican party that elected Jefferson to the Presidency in 1800.

2. On this, see Chapter 15.

3. Elizabeth C. Cook, *Literary Influences in Colonial Newspapers, 1704–1750,* esp. 2–6, 81.

4. See Arthur M. Schlesinger, Sr., *Prelude to Independence,* particularly 51–84, and citing (p. vii) David Ramsey, *The History of the American Revolution* (Philadelphia, 1789).

5. Roy P. Fairchild, ed., *The Federalist Papers,* xi, ff.

6. For recognition of early sympathy for Federalist ideas among urban dwellers not among the socially elite, see a recent study by William Bruce Wheeler, "Urban Politics in Nature's Republic" (Ph.D. dissertation, University of Virginia, 1967), 406–10.

7. See Julian P. Boyd, *et al.,* eds., *The Papers of Thomas Jefferson,* XVI, 237–41, quoting a letter of Jefferson to his daughter Martha, Apr. 26, 1791. (Hereafter cited as Boyd, *TJ Papers.*)

8. Boyd, *TJ Papers,* XVI, ix.

9. Jefferson to Bache, Apr. 22, 1791, cited in Boyd, *TJ Papers,* XVI, 246.

10. Jefferson's letter of Sept. 17, 1792, to Edmund Randolph said that he had preserved "through life a resolution . . . never to write in a public paper without subscribing my name . . ." and specifically branded as false charges that he wrote for Freneau's paper; Albert E. Bergh, ed., *The Writings of Thomas Jefferson,* VIII, 411. Samuel E. Forman, "The Political Activities of Philip Freneau," *Johns Hopkins University Studies in Historical and Political Science* 20, nos. 9–10,

(Sept.–Oct., 1902), tells of Jefferson's disavowal, 62–63. Freneau swore out an affidavit before the mayor of Philadelphia stating that Jefferson had never influenced him to set up a newspaper, affected his policies, or composed articles for him to print, though portions of this statement seem disingenuous; *ibid.*, 55–56. The affidavit appeared in the Philadelphia *Gazette of the United States*, Aug. 8, 1792; Jacob Axelrad, *Philip Freneau*, 237, reprints it with a commentary and discusses the entire issue at length, 201–08, 235–41. The New York *American Citizen*, Jan. 26, 1801, carried a later similar denial by Freneau. Yet there seems little question about Jefferson's sponsorship of the paper; see Bernard A. Weisberger, *The American Newspaperman*, 41–43; Edwin Emery and Henry Ladd Smith, *The Press and America*, 144; *et al.* Cf. Boyd, *TJ Papers*, XVI, 242–43.

11. Jefferson to George Washington, Sept. 9, 1792, cited in Boyd, *TJ Papers*, XVI, 246.

12. Writing to Thomas Mann Randolph, Nov. 2, 1793, Jefferson held that "want of money" was Freneau's chief problem and hoped subscribers in Virginia would speedily settle their accounts. Paul Leicester Ford, ed., *The Writings of Thomas Jefferson*, VI, 438.

13. Boyd, *TJ Papers*, XVI, 247. The writer wishes here to thank Dr. Boyd for numerous gracious suggestions and for expression of his opinion of Jefferson's relationship with the *National Gazette*.

14. Dumas Malone, *Jefferson and His Time*, II, 424. Cf. however, *ibid.*, III, 249; Weisberger, *American Newspaperman*, 43.

15. E.g., Rufus Griswold, *The Republican Court*, 289, asserts Freneau "confessed" that Jefferson dictated some of the most offensive passages in the *National Gazette*, including attacks on Washington; Meade Minnigerode, *Jefferson—Friend of France*, 172, accuses the Secretary of hypocrisy and of attacking his colleagues "virulently, and anonymously . . . in his *National Gazette.*" George L. Roth, "Verse Satire on 'Faction,' 1790–1815," *William & Mary Quarterly*, series 3, 17 (Oct., 1960), 480, notes several satirists of that day found Jefferson's connection with the *National Gazette* "a perfect example of his lies and intrigue." Cf. Silas Bent, *Newspaper Crusaders*, 99–100, 107. Sources obviously hostile to Jefferson, however, must be viewed dubiously in the absence of positive evidence, which the present writer has been unable to uncover. Philip Marsh, "The Griswold Story of Freneau and Jefferson," *American Historical Review* 51 (Oct., 1945), 68–73, discredits the "confession," but admits (p. 71) "the whole matter is almost as clouded as before."

16. Douglas S. Freeman, *George Washington*, VI, 404. Freeman also (p. 396) challenges the idea that the New York City press was ex-

clusively Federalist, saying that before the *Gazette of the United States* New York had not a single newspaper of truly "pronounced 'Federal' views." Alexander DeConde, *Entangling Alliance,* 58, calls Freneau "more Jeffersonian than Jefferson" and asserts: ". . . his official duties were not to interfere with his newspaper work. They did not."

17. A letter from James Madison to Jefferson, May 1 1791 (cited in Forman, "Political Activities," 61, and Axelrad, *Philip Freneau,* 204), indicates that the latter was fully aware of Freneau's design. Noble E. Cunningham, *The Jeffersonian Republicans,* 13, states the project to establish Freneau's paper—though he doubts it was the *planned* first step in organizing a national party—was "jointly initiated by Madison and Jefferson." See also Edith M. Barstow, *News and These United States,* 85; Irving Brant, *James Madison, Father of the Constitution,* 334–36; Sidney Kobre, *Foundations of American Journalism,* 161–63; Carl E. Prince, *New Jersey's Jeffersonian Republicans,* 16n.; Leonard D. White, "The Hamilton-Jefferson Feud," in *The Gaspar G. Bacon Lectures on the Constitution of the United States, 1940–1950,* 221; Alfred F. Young, *The Democratic Republicans of New York,* 196–97; and Malone, *Jefferson,* II, 425.

18. Letter to Philip Mazzei, Apr. 24, 1796, cited in Malone, *Jefferson,* III, 266–69. Bernard Faÿ, *The Two Franklins,* 150–51; Claude G. Bowers, *Jefferson and Hamilton,* 152; Mary S. Austin, *Philip Freneau, The Poet of the Revolution,* 152–4, 157, 160; William M. Sloane, *Party Government in the United States of America,* 58; S. G. W. Benjamin, "Notable Editors between 1776 and 1800," *Magazine of American History* 17 (Feb., 1887), 125–6; Joseph T. Buckingham, *Specimens of Newspaper Literature,* II, 137–8; William Sullivan, *Familiar Letters on Public Characters and Public Events,* 143; Forman, "Political Activities," 29–33, 48, 52–66, 99–101; and the Philadelphia *National Gazette,* Sept. 19, 26, 1792.

19. Forman, "Political Activities," 65–66; Robert E. Spiller, *et al., Literary History of the United States,* I, 171–72, quotes Jefferson's comment that Freneau saved the Constitution when it was "galloping fast into monarchy."

20. "Q.," in the Boston *Independent Chronicle,* Sept. 6, 1792. Jefferson keenly desired a *general* newspaper—and the name, *National Gazette,* was no accident; Cunningham, *Jeffersonian Republicans,* 15.

21. Lewis Leary, *That Rascal Freneau,* 237–39, notes the poet's courage of his own convictions and points out that he continued to support Genêt after Jefferson became disgusted with the French minister; Axelrad, *Philip Freneau,* stresses (e.g., 237, 269) Freneau's integrity.

22. For Jefferson's relations with the *Aurora*, see Faÿ, *Two Franklins,* 294, 297–98, 312 (though he adds that Bache always assumed full responsibility for anything he published) ; Allan Nevins, *American Press Opinion, Washington to Coolidge,* 4; Sullivan, *Familiar Letters,* 77, 143; Weisberger, *American Newspaperman,* 58.

23. This is conceivable but probably unfounded. Presumably, several Democratic Senators were willing to communicate advantageous information to Bache. Nevertheless, the Newburyport, Mass., *Newburyport Herald,* Aug. 10, 1798, alleged that after the last dispatches from France were sent to Congress, Bache and other leaders were closeted with Jefferson; the Halifax *North Carolina Journal,* Aug. 13, 1798, carried this statement as part of a letter from Philadelphia. A correspondent in the Washington, D. C., *Washington Gazette,* July 22, 1797, stated the Vice-President had asked a friend in Hagerstown, Maryland, to circulate the *Aurora* as widely as possible, calling it the best paper on the continent.

24. Claude G. Bowers, "William Duane," in Allen Johnson and Dumas Malone, eds., *Dictionary of American Biography,* V, 468.

25. Douglas C. McMurtrie, *A History of Printing in the United States,* II, 267. Frank van der Linden, *The Turning Point,* esp. 12–18, 23–27, 81–82, 180–83, 210–11, deals with Smith's publishing efforts in Philadelphia and the establishment of the *National Intelligencer.* Kobre, *Foundations,* 173, says, "At Jefferson's suggestion, Smith moved his print shop to Washington."

26. Jefferson's copies of his own letters for the dates cited by Callender were reported missing from his files. However, he conceded modest donations, saying he contributed toward the fines of all Republican editors punished under the Sedition Act; letters to James Monroe, July 15, 17, 1802, in Bergh, *Writings of Thomas Jefferson,* X, 331–34. Cunningham, *Jeffersonian Republican,* 169–72, notes the difficulty of reconciling Jefferson's later protestations with his behavior around 1800. The libel prosecution in 1804 of Harry Croswell of the Hudson, N. Y., *Wasp,* was occasioned by his reprinting from the New York *Evening Post* the story that Jefferson had hired Callender to slander Washington; Leonard W. Levy, *Freedom of Speech and Press in Early American History,* 297–99; Weisberger, *American Newspaperman,* 61 ; Emery and Smith, *The Press,* 169–71; James M. Smith, "Alexander Hamilton, the Alien Law, and Seditious Libels," *Review of Politics* 16 (July, 1954), 312, Eugene F. Kramer, *The Croswell Libel Case and Freedom of the Press in New York State,* 3–7. Barstow, *op. cit.,* 95, notes Jefferson's "lame explanation"; see also Benjamin Ellis Martin, "Transition Period of the Ameri-

can Press," *Magazine of American History* 17 (April, 1887), 285–86; Nevins, *American Press Opinion,* 4; Sloane, *Party Government,* 58; and George Gibbs, *Memoirs of the Administrations of Washington and John Adams,* II, 293–96. In Volume I, 377, Gibbs also charges Jefferson subsidized Tom Paine, as well as Callender, to abuse Washington, but the present writer discovered no substantiating evidence.

27. A statement to this effect appeared in a letter from Jefferson to Thomas Mann Randolph, cited in Bowers, *Jefferson and Hamilton,* 174.

28. Faÿ, *Two Franklins,* 299; Bernard Faÿ, "Benjamin Franklin Bache, a Democratic Leader of the 18th Century," *Proceedings of the American Antiquarian Society* 40 (Oct., 1930), 279–80. Beckley (Clerk of the House of Representatives) wrote as "A Calm Observer," charging Washington with being a defaulter.

29. Walter R. Fee, *The Transition from Aristocracy to Democracy in New Jersey, 1789–1829,* 103; Frank M. Anderson, "Contemporary Opinion of the Virginia and Kentucky Resolutions," *American Historical Review* 5 (Oct., 1899), 54.

30. Alston G. Field, "The Press in Western Pennsylvania to 1812," *The Western Pennsylvania Historical Magazine* 20 (Dec., 1937), 233; J. Cutler Andrews, *Pittsburgh's Post-Gazette,* 45–46; McMurtrie, *A History of Printing,* II, 92; and Osman Castle Hooper, *History of Ohio Journalism, 1793–1933,* 2. See also the *Pittsburgh Gazette,* Nov. 30, Dec. 7, 1799.

31. Cunningham, *Jeffersonian Republicans* 131–33.

32. *Ibid.,* 173.

33. Letter to Oliver Wolcott, Aug. 7, 1800, in Gibbs, *Memoirs,* II, 399–400.

34. Letter of "G," Philadelphia *National Gazette,* Aug. 15, 1792. Cf. Margaret Woodbury, *Public Opinion in Philadelphia,* 22; and John S. Bassett, *The Federalist System,* 47.

35. Kobre, *Foundations,* 141; James M. Lee, *America's Oldest Daily Newspaper, The New York Globe,* 3, 6; Martin, "Transition Period," 286–87; Kemp Malone, "Noah Webster," in Johnson and Malone, eds., *Dictionary of American Biography* (cited as *DAB*), XIX, 595–96.

36. New York *Columbian Gazette,* June 22, 1799; Boston *Constitutional Telegraphe,* Nov. 23, 1799. Williams was an Englishman who wrote under the pseudonym of "Anthony Pasquin" and later turned Democratic; Charles Warren, ed., *Jacobin and Junto,* 94–95.

37. Kobre, *Foundations,* 145–46.

38. *Philadelphische Correspondenz,* Oct. 13, 1795.

39. Forman, "Political Activities," 80; Columbia, S. C., *State Gazette,* Feb. 27, 1795.

40. Frederic Hudson, *Journalism in the United States,* 145; Frank L. Mott, *American Journalism,* 134.

41. Bernard Faÿ, "Early Party Machinery in the United States: Pennsylvania in the Election of 1796," *Pennsylvania Magazine of History and Biography* 40 (Oct., 1936), 381–83; Faÿ, *Two Franklins,* 152–53.

42. See the list prepared by the author in collaboration with Eugene P. Link, in the latter's *Democratic-Republican Societies, 1790–1800,* 38n. Because of the difficulty of definitely establishing membership in some instances, this tabulation is incomplete but shows some thirty printers almost certainly connected with these societies:

| | |
|---|---|
| *Vermont:* | Prosper Brown, of the Fair Haven *Farmers' Library* |
| | Anthony Haswell, of the Bennington *Vermont Gazette* (see Feb. 28, 1794) |
| *Mass.:* | Possibly Thomas and Abijah Adams, Boston *Independent Chronicle* |
| | John K. Baker, of the Hallowell [Me.] *Tocsin;* Portland *Eastern Herald* |
| *N. Y.:* | David Denniston, later of the New York *American Citizen* |
| | Philip Freneau, of the *National Gazette* and later other papers |
| | Thomas Greenleaf, of the New York *Journal* and the *Argus* |
| | Probably John I. Johnson, later of the New York *Diary* |
| | William Keteltas, who later established the New York *Forlorn Hope* |
| | Elihu Palmer, of the *Temple of Reason* |
| | Elias Winfield, later of the Newburgh *Rights of Man* |
| | John Fellows |
| | Naphtali Judah |
| *New Jersey:* | Aaron Pennington, of the Newark *Centinel of Freedom* |
| *Kentucky:* | John Bradford, of the Lexington *Kentucky Gazette* |
| *Delaware:* | Robert Coram, of the *Delaware Gazette* |
| *Penn.:* | Robert Aitkin, of the Philadelphia *Pelosi's Marine List* |

Benjamin F. Bache, of the *General Advertiser* and *Aurora*

Probably William H. Beaumont, of the Washington *Western Telegraphe*

Robert Cochran, later of the Philadelphia *Independent Whig*

William Dickson of the Lancaster *Intelligencer*

John Israel, of the Washington *Herald of Liberty* and Pittsburgh *Tree of Liberty*

Henry Kammerer of the *Philadelphische Correspondenz*

Eleazer Oswald of the Philadelphia *Independent Gazetteer*

James D. Westcott of the Bridgeton, N. J., *Argus*

*N. Carolina:* Caleb D. Howard of the Fayetteville *North-Carolina Chronicle*

John Sibley of the Fayetteville *Gazette*

*S. Carolina:* Thomas B. Bowen, of the Charleston *Columbian Herald*

John Markland, of the Charleston *City Gazette*

John Miller, who tried to found a paper in the upcountry in 1795 (see the *State Gazette of South Carolina,* Nov. 26, 1795) and did later establish the *Weekly Messenger.*

43. Woodbury, *Public Opinion,* 113; E. Merton Coulter, "The Efforts of the Democratic Societies of the West to open the Navigation of the Mississippi," *Mississippi Valley Historical Review* 11 (Dec., 1924), 377–78.

44. Jefferson is said to have made this statement to Senator Langdon; Lawrence Mayo, *John Langdon of New Hampshire,* 272.

45. Jabez D. Hammond, *History of Political Parties of the State of New-York,* I, 279.

46. J. E. Bonnet, *Etats-Unis de l'Amerique a la Fin du XVIIIᵉ Siecle,* I, 272.

47. Hezekiah Packard, *Federal Republicanism displayed in Two Discourses* . . . (Boston, 1799), 1–35, *passim.* Packard felt that the nation would have been better off if opposition presses, at least, had been suppressed.

48. Peacham, Vt., *Green Mountain Patriot,* Oct. 26, 1798.

49. Emery and Smith, *The Press,* 140.

649

50. Newport, R. I., *Companion*, May 2, 1798. This first issue of the *Companion* was naturally attempting to justify its existence.

51. "Country Correspondent," from the *National Gazette*, cited in the Norwich, Conn., *Weekly Register*, July 3, 1792.

52. New York *American Citizen*, Mar. 19, 1800.

53. Peacham, Vt., *Green Mountain Patriot*, June 1, 1798.

54. New London, Conn., *Bee*, Mar. 26, 1800.

55. Clarence S. Brigham, in his invaluable *History and Bibliography of American Newspapers, 1690–1820*, lists 538 known to have been printed during these twelve years; the present writer has actually examined files of 512.

56. Mott, *American Journalism*, 45, 98, 161; John B. McMaster, *A History of the People of the United States*, II, 63–64. For items illustrative of the paper shortage, see the New Bedford, Mass., *Medley*, Nov. 27, 1792; *Edwards' Baltimore Daily Advertiser*, June 15, 1792; Whitestown, N. Y., *Western Centinel*, Mar. 18, 1795; New Haven *Connecticut Journal*, Jan. 4, 11, 1797; and the York, Pa., *Volks-Berichter*, July 25, 1799, among countless others. The Augusta, Ga., *Augusta Herald*, Feb. 12, 1800, apologized to its readers for temporarily using paper of poor quality.

57. Long primer or small pica (ten or eleven point) was most commonly used (Mott, *American Journalism*, 49), but some papers, such as the Baltimore *Maryland Journal* (e.g., June 12, 1792), were largely printed in type as small as four and one-half point. Modern classified advertising type is usually agate (seven point).

58. The best description of the process seen by this writer is in an unpublished manuscript by Ralph Adams Brown, "The New Hampshire Press, 1775–1789," 24–30; brief accounts are in Milton W. Hamilton, *The Country Printer: New York State, 1785–1830*, 8; George W. Purcell, "A Survey of Early Newspapers in the Middle Western States," *Indiana Magazine of History* 20 (Dec. 1924), 356; Alfred M. Lee, *The Daily Newspaper*, 24–25; Robert Peter, *History of Fayette County, Kentucky*, 364; and Mott, *American Journalism*, 46, 162.

59. Lee, *Daily Newspaper*, Tables II–VII, 712–17. These tables are incomplete and omit "country editions," but the preponderance of weeklies would be even greater if every paper were listed. Cf. Brigham, *Bibliography*, I & II.

60. *Idem*; Boston *Federal Gazette*, Jan. 1, 1798; McMaster, *A History*, II, 63. One newspaper published only on Sunday was briefly attempted.

61. *Boston Gazette,* Oct. 19, 1789.

62. Mott, *American Journalism,* 159; at the time a barrel of flour sold for $9. The Baltimore *Telegraphe,* Mar. 25, 1797, asserted Philadelphia dailies charged $8 or more; the Georgetown, D. C., *Cabinet* (Dec. 30, 1800) was priced at $5 annually.

63. E.g., the Nashville *Tennessee Gazette,* Apr. 30, 1800; Lexington *Kentucky Gazette,* May 16, 1799; Gilmanton, N. H., *Rural Museum,* Feb. 28, 1800.

64. One cent per paper in the case of the Knoxville, Tenn., *Knoxville Gazette* (see the issue of Apr. 17, 1797).

65. Mott, *American Journalism,* 60–61, 159–60; George W. Purcell, "Survey," 357.

66. In 1792 only about 75 American communities had official postal service; Vermont and the whole area west of Pittsburgh had no post offices. The main post road ran from Wiscasset, Me., to Savannah. Wesley E. Rich, *The History of the United States Post Office to the Year 1829,* 69, 71–72.

67. E.g., John Scull, of the *Pittsburgh Gazette,* and George Roulstone, of the *Knoxville Gazette.* See Andrews, *Pittsburgh's Post-Gazette,* 3.

68. See the Savannah, Ga., *Columbian Museum,* July 26, 1796, and the Knoxville, Tenn., *Knoxville Gazette,* Mar. 13, 1797, for two examples among innumerable others. Complaints were particularly prevalent in winter, when roads were especially bad.

69. Bernard Faÿ, *Notes on the American Press at the End of the Eighteenth Century,* 2–3; Mott, *American Journalism,* 160.

70. Howard M. Jones, *America and French Culture,* 29, states there were 103; Brigham, *Bibliography, passim,* lists 104. Lee, *Daily Newspaper,* 711, notes only 92; while William A. Dill, *Growth of Newspapers in the United States,* 79, lists 106 (though mentioning only 103 on p. 28). Both the Winchester *Willis's Virginia Gazette,* June 19, 1790, and the Portland, [Me.], *Cumberland Gazette,* June 28, 1790, carried a Pennsylvania estimate of perhaps 70 papers at that time. In 1791, 85 journals, turning out nearly 4,000,000 copies annually, were said to be published; *Boston Gazette,* Jan. 9, 1791; Exeter *New Hampshire Gazetteer,* Jan. 28, 1791.

71. Isaiah Thomas, *The History of Printing in America,* II, 9, simply estimates "at least" 150 American gazettes in 1800, but Lee, *Daily Newspaper,* 15, 712–17, enumerates 242 (including 7 "country editions"). The following tabulation, based upon Lee's lists but noting variations from Dill or Brigham, gives some idea of the distribution of these papers:

| State | Papers in 1790 | Papers in 1800 |
|---|---|---|
| Maine | 2 | 5 |
| New Hampshire | 6 | 12 |
| Vermont | 2 | 7 |
| Massachusetts | 11[a] | 21 |
| Rhode Island | 4 | 7 |
| Connecticut | 8[b] | 18 |
| New York | 13[c] | 37 |
| Pennsylvania | 17[d] | 44 |
| New Jersey | 3 | 7 |
| Delaware | 1[e] | 2 |
| Maryland | 5[f] | 10 |
| Dist. of Columbia | 1[g] | 7 |
| Virginia | 9 | 23 |
| West Virginia | 1[h] | 3 |
| North Carolina | 2[i] | 8 |
| South Carolina | 4 | 7 |
| Georgia | 2 | 5 |
| Kentucky | 1 | 4 |
| Tennessee | | 2 |
| Ohio | | 4 |
| Mississippi | | 1 |
| Louisiana | | 1[j] |
| | 92 | 242* |

[a] Dill, *Growth of Newspapers,* 79, gives a total of fourteen.
[b] Dill lists ten, although Brigham has but eight.
[c] Fourteen, according to Dill.
[d] Twenty-four are listed by Dill.
[e] Dill says two; Brigham gives one.
[f] Dill records nine.
[g] Brigham lists two.
[h] Part of Virginia until much later; none are given by Dill.
[i] One, in Dill's compilation.
[j] Technically, Louisiana was not yet a part of the United States.
*—Not all these lasted the entire year; see Chapter 15.
72. Martin, "Transition Period," 277.
73. Jones, *America and French Culture,* 29, lists only 24 papers out of 103 in 1790 south of Pennsylvania; cf. Virginius Dabney, *Liberalism in the South,* 86; and Dill, *Growth of Newspapers,* 63. There was a paper for every 26,563 inhabitants in New England, and one for every

25,235 in the North Atlantic region, but the Southern states (presumably because of scattered population and lack of cities) had only one for every 105,213.

74. Benjamin, "Notable Editors," 99; Dover, Del., *Friend of the People,* Sept. 28, 1799.

75. E. Wilder Spaulding, *New York in the Critical Period,* 39, notes only eight papers were published in 1788 in that state outside New York City; Hamilton, *Country Printer . . . , passim,* stresses the rapid spread of country journals following adoption of the Constitution. The Baltimore *Federal Gazette,* Apr. 29, 1797, cites the increasing popularity of dailies.

76. Lee, *Daily Newspaper,* 29. These impressions (McMaster, *A History,* II, 63) presumably meant 200 copies *on one side* per hour; Brown, "New Hampshire Press," 30, says the average New Hampshire pressman turned out fewer than two thousand papers on a single side in a twelve-hour day. On the other hand, Kobre, *Foundations,* 156, calls 260 impressions "the usual work of an hour." However, Mott, *American Journalism,* 105, notes an alleged circulation of eight thousand for the Hartford *Courant,* though conditions were admittedly atypical and his source perhaps not unimpeachable.

77. And there were a number; Samuel H. Smith's Philadelphia *New World,* which tried two editions a day, must have had at least two presses (Mott, *American Journalism,* 116n.). Several printers had "two-press shops" by the Revolution, and Isaiah Thomas and others had three presses afterward; Brown, "New Hampshire Press," 23.

78. The Newark *Centinel of Freedom* (Mar. 18, 1800) professed to blanket northeastern New Jersey, the *Albany Register* (Oct. 16, 1798) made a similar assertion for northwestern New York, and the editor of the Carlisle, Pa., *Telegraphe* (Feb. 16, 1796) boasted his newssheet was distributed over "three counties" in that state.

79. Mott, *American Journalism,* 159.

80. Mary E. Clark, *Peter Porcupine in America,* 95; Faÿ, *Notes . . . ,* 28, estimates its peak at about 3,200. Cf. the Philadelphia *Porcupine's Gazette,* Apr. 22, Aug. 12, Nov. 2, 1797. (It should be noted that Democratic editors charged Federalists gifts enabled Cobbett to send free copies to many who did not order them; New London, Conn., *Bee,* Mar. 7, 1798; Philadelphia *Carey's United States Recorder,* Mar. 17, 1798.) Even after the paper's popularity declined, in 1799 it professed to have over 2,000 readers—as large a circulation as any English daily; Mott, *American Journalism,* 159.

81. Baltimore *Federal Gazette,* Dec. 24, 1800.

82. When it was still the *General Advertiser,* Bache spoke (Jan. 28, 1794) of over 100 names added in two months as a rapid increase in circulation. Near the turn of the century, its subscribers numbered about 1,700.

83. See Lee, *Daily Newspaper,* Table XV, 728, and Table XVII, 730.

84. Hamilton, *Country Printer,* 212. Isaiah Thomas thought 600 customers, with considerable advertising, were needed to maintain the average weekly; Clarence S. Brigham, *Journals and Journeymen,* 20.

85. Brigham, *Journals,* 20–21; the *Boston Gazette,* Oct. 19, 1789, carried a publisher's estimate that 76,438 copies nationally were printed each week; this (including dailies and semi-weeklies) averaged between 500 and 600 per paper. Dill, *Growth of Newspapers,* 11; Brigham, *Journals,* 20; Lee, *Daily Newspaper,* 728; and Mott, *American Journalism,* 159, give approximations for the 1800 figure.

86. Mott, *ibid.,* 159; Freeman, *Washington,* VI, 395; Guion Johnson, *Ante-Bellum North Carolina,* 95–96.

87. See the Alexandria, Va., *Columbian Mirror,* Feb. 9, 1799, criticizing the grumbling against the house tax which occasioned Fries' Rebellion.

88. These were quite prevalent; as early as May 13, 1789, the *Albany Gazette* announced that one of its postriders would ride weekly to Great Barrington, Conn., where he would "meet and exchange papers with the several post riders from Boston, Hartford, New London, Springfield, New Haven and Litchfield." (Quoted in Munsell, *Typographical Miscellany,* 226).

89. Martin, "Transition Period," 277. Ownership of many of these (and others) frequently changed hands; see Brigham, *History and Bibliography,* esp. I, xii.

90. E.g., Allan Nevins, "Freneau," in Edwin R. A. Seligman, ed., *Encyclopedia of the Social Sciences,* VI, 483–84; Hudson, *Journalism,* 144–45 (on the deaths of Bache, John Fenno and Thomas Greenleaf); Newark, N. J., *Centinel of Freedom,* Oct. 1, 1799; John Spargo, *Anthony Haswell,* 37–38.

91. From $200 (Poughkeepsie, N. Y., *Poughkeepsie Journal,* Sept. 18, 1798; cited in Hamilton, *Country Printer,* 11) to $800 (Mott, *American Journalism,* 162).

92. To quote Brigham, *Journals,* 21, "circulation was reflected in cost." In 1798 the weekly expense of printing the Boston *Columbian Centinel* was said to be $120, the *Massachusetts Mercury* $80, and the *Commercial* [Russell's] *Gazette* $50. Proportionately, paper was very high-priced. Benjamin Edes pathetically confessed (*Independent Chronicle,*

Mar. 23, 1795, Jan. 5, 1797) that advertising income did not defray his *Boston Gazette*'s paper bills, and the daily Baltimore *Federal Intelligencer,* July 1, 1795, boasted that its paper for the preceding half year cost $950. Free exchange copies alone cost the New York *Herald* (June 19, 1794) an estimated $500 annually.

93. Brigham, *Journals,* 27, gives advertising as the chief source, and Charles C. Crittenden, *North Carolina Newspapers before 1790,* 21, says subscriptions and advertisements. Except for city mercantile journals, it is difficult to see how advertising could have dominated. The Dedham, Mass., *Columbian Minerva,* Mar. 21, 1799, announced 1,000 subscribers were necessary for a profit at a time when it had fewer than 670.

94. Brigham, *Journals,* 23–25. Some subscribers fell years behind on their payments; Andrews, *Pittsburgh's Post-Gazette,* 4–5.

95. E.g., the *Pittsburgh Gazette,* Mar. 30, 1799.

96. Baltimore *American,* Oct. 20, 1800. In Newark the Democratic *Continel of Freedom,* Mar. 25, 1800, noted that it was not supported by government funds or patronage, and the Dedham, Mass., *Columbian Minerva,* Nov. 21, 1799, put out only a "half-sheet" (two pages) to emphasize the gravity of the situation.

97. Isaiah Thomas, Benjamin Russell, Noah Webster, and John Melcher (of the Portsmouth *New Hampshire Gazette*) were examples, though Melcher probably made much of his money in fields other than printing. Mott, *American Journalism,* 77–78, 128, 131; Annie R. Marble, *From 'Prentice to Patron,* esp. 173–214; Brown, "New Hampshire Press," 54, 62.

98. This, more than the yellow fever epidemic, caused cessation of the paper; Faÿ, *Two Franklins,* 158–59. Jefferson, at the time, shared this opinion—see *supra,* note 9; Kobre, *Foundations,* 166.

99. Duane's figures as to Bache's losses are said to have appeared in the Philadelphia *Aurora,* Apr. 23, 1800, (Willard G. Bleyer, *Main Currents in the History of American Journalism,* 117), although the present writer failed to locate the statement, and it may have appeared in the tri-weekly country edition of that date. Bache certainly admitted (*Aurora,* June 5, 1798) that the paper was not a paying proposition. Federalists asserted the French minister subscribed for 400 copies (which Bache denied, and countered with accusations of Federalist subsidies for Fenno; *Aurora,* May 12, 1798) and that French funds supported other opposition sheets. See the Boston *Columbian Centinel,* cited in the Providence, R. I., *United States Chronicle,* Oct. 15, 1798; and the Philadelphia *Carey's United States Recorder,* June 30, 1798.

100. Mott, *American Journalism,* 123, 130.

101. Some idea, however, can be gained from the fact that Christian Jacob Hutter, editor of the German-language Lancaster, Pa., *Lancaster Correspondent,* lost $5,000 in little over three years. See Daniel Miller, "Early German American Newspapers," *Proceedings, Pennsylvania-German Society* 19 (1910), 47; Carl Wittke, *The German-Language Press in America,* 30.

102. See Spaulding, *New York,* 20; Worcester *Massachusetts Spy,* Apr. 10, 1799; Clark, *Peter Porcupine,* 172 ff.; William Reitzel, "William Cobbett and Philadelphia Journalism, 1794–1800," *Pennsylvania Magazine of History and Biography* 59 (July, 1935), 238–39; Munsell, *Typographical Miscellany,* 96. Stephen B. Weeks, *The Press of North Carolina in the Eighteenth Century,* 38–39, and the Poughkeepsie, N. Y., *Poughkeepsie Journal,* Apr. 30, 1794, give other examples of publishers' activities.

103. Rich, *Post Office,* 75.

104. Ralph L. Rusk, *The Literature of the Middle Western Frontier,* I, 143–44; Faÿ, *Notes,* 4; Purcell, "Survey," 348, 357. John Bradford received $100 annually as public printer for Kentucky, and after the capital was moved to Frankfort he and his son set up a paper there in an effort to retain the income from official publications; William H. Perrin, *The Pioneer Press of Kentucky,* 14–15, 19–20. In Georgia the *Augusta Chronicle* and the *Southern Centinel* competed for the state printing; McMurtrie, *History of Printing,* II, 394–95; Nelson, *History of American Newspapers,* 54; Louis T. Griffith and John E. Talmadge, *Georgia Journalism, 1763–1950,* 18–20. Abraham Hodge's various newspapers vied in North Carolina with Allman Hall's *Wilmington Gazette;* Weeks, *Press of North Carolina,* 41–42. George Roulstone in 1794 was paid $600 for printing the public documents of the territory soon to become Tennessee; Douglas C. McMurtrie, *Early Printing in Tennessee,* 20.

105. E.g., the reference to *"loaves and fishes"* in the Newark, N. J., *Centinel of Freedom,* Mar. 25, 1800.

106. Jefferson's resignation from the State Department, depriving the *National Gazette* of some governmental patronage, may have been a reason why that journal did not resume publication; Forman, "Political Activities," 74. Mott, *American Journalism,* 144, feels that public printing contracts, like post office appointments, were an indirect means of control over the press.

107. And of most other political understanding; a correspondent in the Boston *Argus,* Feb. 21, 1792, wrote that (because of his "retired situa-

tion") virtually all he knew was what he read in the papers. Bassett, *Federalist System,* 165–69, describes the population and economic life of America at this time; cf. Manning Dauer, *The Adams Federalists,* 4–5. See also the Windsor, Vt., *Windsor Federal Gazette,* Mar. 10, 1801.

108. Huntley Dupré, "The *Kentucky Gazette* Reports the French Revolution," *Mississippi Valley Historical Review* 26 (Sept., 1939), 167.

109. Nevins, *American Press Opinion,* 6.

110. See the Richmond *Virginia Argus,* Jan. 21, 1800, announcing James Lyon's new paper, the *Friend of the People.* This bi-weekly, priced at only one dollar a year, was not published for profit but for "only patriotic motives."

111. The Georgetown, S. C., *Georgetown Gazette,* July 5, 1800, charged that 200 *"Frenchified Virginians, alias democrats,"* put up $600 in advance to circulate the above-mentioned Richmond *Friend of the People.* See also Cunningham, *Jeffersonian Republicans,* 173–74.

112. Dupré, *"Kentucky Gazette,"* 167.

113. New York *American Minerva,* Dec. 9, 1793 (see Mott, *American Journalism,* 158–59).

114. Windsor *Vermont Journal,* Jan. 17, 1792. For a similar philosophy, see the first issue of the Newark, N. J., *Woods's Newark Gazette,* May 19, 1791. Nevins, *American Press Opinion,* 5, and Rusk, *Literature of Frontier,* I, 154, comment on this widespread characteristic.

115. Lancaster, Pa., *Intelligencer,* Jan. 15, 1800.

116. Worcester *Massachusetts Spy,* Apr. 3, 1794.

117. Frankfort, Ky., *Palladium,* Aug. 28, 1798.

118. E.g., the Carlisle, Pa., *Telegraphe,* Feb. 16, 1796, pledged secrecy to all contributors desiring it and prompt attention to future communications.

119. Mott, *American Journalism,* 141, describing the *Kentucky Gazette;* the same applied to virtually all Western papers. Often these reports of Indian forays were inaccurate or exaggerated.

120. See the first issue of the Peacham, Vt., *Green Mountain Patriot,* Feb. 23, 1798.

121. Hugh Henry Brackenridge, in the *Pittsburgh Gazette,* July 29, 1786, cited in Leland D. Baldwin, *Pittsburgh: The Story of a City,* 113. See also Dupré, *"Kentucky Gazette,"* 167; and Harry M. Tinkcom, *The Republicans and Federalists in Pennsylvania, 1789–1801,* 75.

122. European news and items from Eastern states made up from one-

half to two-thirds of the news columns of Western papers. The Cincinnati *Freeman's Journal,* Oct. 27, 1798, had almost twelve of its sixteen columns so filled, and this proportion has been called "average"; Rusk, *Literature of Frontier,* I, 147.

123. E.g., the New Bern *North Carolina Gazette,* Oct. 12, 1793; July 4, 1795, etc.; Philadelphia *General Postbothe,* Nov. 27, 1789; Jan. 5, 8, 1790; *et al.* Cf. Dupré, *"Kentucky Gazette,"* 168.

124. See the Norwich, Conn., *Norwich Packet,* 1792–1793, *passim.*

125. There might be as many as eighty or a hundred days since the last news items, although such gaps were unusual. Delano A. Goddard, *Newspapers and Newspaper Writers in New England,* 8, tells of the situation in Massachusetts in March, 1800; the Philadelphia *Neue Philadelphische Correspondenz,* Mar. 22, 1797, reminded readers that the Atlantic crossing was a lengthy one in wintertime. Word from England averaged from six to eight weeks in transit, while reports direct from Europe took considerably longer; Malone, *Jefferson,* III, 40; Brigham, *Journals,* 56.

126. New York *Commercial Advertiser,* Apr. 23, 1800.

127. F. W. Hamilton, *A Brief History of Printing in America,* 24; Albert B. Faust, *The German Element in the United States,* I, 167.

128. Goshen, N. Y. *Goshen Repository,* Oct. 15, Nov. 12, 1793. Jefferson was well aware of the part played by sources of foreign news in shaping the versions available to the American public; see Boyd, *TJ Papers,* XVI, 239–41, 246.

129. Boston *American Herald,* Aug. 30, 1790 (quoted in Mott, *American Journalism,* 155–58).

130. Boston *Independent Chronicle,* Oct. 21, 1790.

131. Faÿ, *Revolutionary Spirit,* 451.

132. Bache's translations in the *General Advertiser* and later the *Aurora* were said to be for a time the only ones in Philadelphia and to have been instrumental in bringing together French sympathizers in that city; Faÿ, "Bache," 291. German and Dutch papers were also occasionally used by Republican printers. Mott, *American Journalism,* 154, ably summarizes the importance of foreign papers.

133. Anson E. Morse, *The Federalist Party in Massachusetts to the Year 1800,* 140. That this was true is essentially the basic thesis of Cunningham, *Jeffersonian Republicans;* see especially 45, 256. Private letters often revealed the close attention paid by many persons to national concerns. E.g., the letter of Oliver Wolcott, Sr., of Litchfield, Conn., to his son Oliver, Jr., Aug. 12, 1793, flayed the state of Virginia for her "levelling" and "negro-driving" citizens, and attacked Ritten-

house of Philadelphia for "forming a Jacobin club to run the United States." Oliver Wolcott Papers, IV, 109.

134. Rich, *History of the Post Office*, 70 ff.; Mott, *American Journalism*, 161. Congress granted the privilege to further understanding and acceptance of federal legislation; it was even suggested that many papers should be sent out under congressional frank to more widely disseminate the news. See Thomas H. Benton, *Abridgment of the Debates of Congress, from 1789–1856*, I, 331–32.

135. Guion Johnson, *Ante-Bellum North Carolina*, 783. This dependence was not quite so great in seaport towns; see the New York *Herald*, June 19, 1794. "Amicus," in the Columbia, S. C., *State Gazette*, Feb. 6, 1795, was typical of complaints about mail service.

136. Quoted in the Norwich, Conn., *Weekly Register*, Apr. 30, 1793.

137. Philadelphia *General Advertiser*, Feb 4, 1794. Even the criticism from the *National Gazette* noted above, which was unique in that it commented on copying Congressional debates, centered chiefly on the lack of proper acknowledgments.

138. Philadelphia *Aurora*, Feb. 1, 1796; see also the Baltimore *Federal Gazette*, Feb. 6, 1796. For some cases in which credit *was* given to Bache's paper, see the Philadelphia *National Gazette*, Mar. 9, 1793; the Boston *Independent Chronicle*, Feb. 24, 1794; and the Baltimore *Federal Gazette*, Feb. 6, 1796.

139. Worthington C. Ford, ed., *Thomas Jefferson & James Thomson Callender*, 4. Callender worked on Brown's paper for a time; there is reason to believe he was hired partly to record the debates.

140. Boston *Independent Chronicle*, June 5, 1797.

141. *Ibid.*, Feb. 24, 1794; Nevins, *American Press Opinion*, 145–46. A similar allegation was made and denied about Otis's remarks in 1797; see note 140.

142. If practiced at all widely, it would seem to have been done by the reporters actually sitting in on the debates, and no evidence has been found that they purposely misrepresented. In the few checks the present writer made with Benton's *Abridgment* (another summary, of course) the sketches seemed impartial enough. It is true that Greenleaf's *New York Journal*, June 20, 1798, did protest against "the banishing from the House of all Stenographers but one."

143. Salem, Mass., *Impartial Register*, July 17, 1800.

144. Probably most of these letters were genuine, but the same correspondent might use different pen names on various occasions. "Americanus," "Tully," "Pacificus," "Titus Manlius," "Civis," "Camillus," "No Jacobin," and "Fact," for example, were all pseudonyms used by

Alexander Hamilton; Lynch, *Party Warfare*, 40, 45, 72; Woodbury, *Public Opinion*, 42–43; Bleyer, *Main Currents*, 114; Nathaniel Weyl, *Treason*, 78. Charles Pinckney styled himself "The Republican Farmer" and "A South Carolina Planter," as well as "The Republican"; Anon., "South Carolina in the Presidential Election of 1800," *American Historical Review* 4 (Oct., 1898), 114. "Veritas" and "Valerius," who both made bitter attacks upon Washington in the *Aurora*, were probably Judge Thomas McKean—although some have charged that these were pen names for Jefferson; Marsh, "Griswold Story," 72; Malone, *Jefferson*, III, 110. "Brutus," "Robert Slender" and "Peter Pindar" were all aliases used by Freneau; Emery and Smith, *Press* and America, 145; Spiller, *et al., Literary History of the United States*, I, 173–74.

145. The most celebrated instance in which this has been suggested was the letters of "Freeholder" (and perhaps "Curtius") questioning John Marshall during his campaign for Congress in 1798; see Albert J. Beveridge, *Life of John Marshall*, II, 388–89, 395–96; Alexandria, Va., *Alexandria Times*, Oct. 11, 1798; Boston *Columbian Centinel*, Oct. 20, 1798. However, a poem in the unfriendly Boston *Independent Chronicle*, Feb. 21, 1799, stated "Curtius" was John Thomson of Petersburg, Va., and Beveridge (II, 396n.) agrees.

146. E.g., the Philadelphia *Aurora*, July, Aug., 1800, *passim*.

147. New London, Conn., *Bee*, Oct. 22, 1800. "Abraham" was Abraham Bishop, who delivered a strongly Republican Phi Beta Kappa address at New Haven that year; Cunningham, *Jeffersonian Republicans*, 208.

148. E.g., Clyde A. Duniway, *The Development of Freedom of the Press in Massachusetts*, 143; Sloane, *Party Government*, 57–58. Hudson, *Journalism*, 141, calls it the era of "The Political Party Press." McMaster, *A History*, II, 397, 497, says papers "teemed" with abusive articles. Malone, *Jefferson*, III, 73, 391, refers to "this time of reckless and irresponsible journalism," and comments that modern readers must inevitably be impressed by the violence of the press.

149. See Sloane, *Party Government*, 58; Delbert H. Gilpatrick, *Jeffersonian Democracy in North Carolina, 1789–1816*, 94.

150. Poughkeepsie, N. Y., *American Farmer*, Oct. 29, 1799. Since this item was captioned "Extract from an eastern paper of Oct. 1," there must have been still another journal desiring objectivity. The Edenton, N. C., *Post Angel*, Sept. 10, 1800, also denounced vituperation.

151. From a letter in the Peacham, Vt., *Green Mountain Patriot*, Apr. 6, 1798.

152. Mott, *American Journalism*, 146. Cf. Lee, *Daily Newspaper*, 3–4, on Noah Webster's pledge to keep his New York *American Minerva* "chaste and impartial."

153. Brattleboro, Vt., *Federal Galaxy*, Jan. 6, 1797.

154. Newark, N. J., *Newark Gazette*, Sept. 4, 1798.

155. Washington, Ky., *Mirror*, July 17, 1799.

156. Baltimore *American*, May 16, 1797; quoted in Cunningham, *Jeffersonian Republicans*, 168.

157. New York *American Citizen*, Mar. 10, 1800.

158. E.g., the (Federalist) Keene, N. H., *Columbian Informer*, Mar. 24, 1795, twitted "Jacobins" over their concern that *"most of the Presses have devoted themselves to the side of government,"* as though it were criminal to support constituted authorities. See also the York, Pa., *Volks-Berichter*, July 26, 1799.

159. Quoted in Martin, "Transition Period," 274; the same general thought may be found in Thomas, *History of Printing*, II, 202–03.

160. These were (1) "Name Calling," or the use of unpopular labels to obtain unthinking condemnation of groups or programs the propagandist wishes rejected; (2) "Glittering Generalities," or uses of terms connoting worthy aims and ideals to gain an uncritical acceptance and approval of a cause; (3) "Transfer," or identifying a stand with some revered individual or institution in order to acquire prestige and sanction that will win acceptance for arguments; (4) the "Testimonial," to persuade readers that leaders in various walks of life support certain measures or condemn those of the opposition; (5) the "Plain Folks" technique, wherein the propagandist or his candidate subtly flatters his audience and convinces them of an identity of interests by trying to appear as common as any of the group to which he is appealing; (6) "Card-Stacking," or deliberate distortion of the evidence, raising of new issues to divert attention from embarrassing facts, and the use of half-truths and falsehoods in order to win adherents; and (7) the "band wagon" means of leading people to believe that their group or section is already overwhelmingly behind the propagandist's program—implying that since "everybody is doing it," opposition is not only futile but might even appear ridiculous. Institute for Propaganda Analysis, "How to Detect Propaganda," *Propaganda Analysis*, 1 (Nov., 1937), 5–7. Malone, *Jefferson*, III, 391, points out that editors indulged in guilt by association (a reversal of "Transfer"), as well as all these other techniques.

161. Thomas, *History of Printing*, II, 202–04.

162. Boston *Columbian Centinel*, Oct. 11, 1800.

163. Quoted from the usually careful Frank L. Mott (*American Journalism*, 121).

164. George D. Luetscher, *Early Political Machinery in the United States*, 1; see also Alexander DeConde, *Entangling Alliance*, 260: "Most newspapers in the Federalist era were Federalist organs."

165. Mott, *American Journalism*, 122, estimates the ratio of Federalist to Democratic papers in 1800 as two to one. If meant to include only those journals whose position was unmistakable, the estimate is substantially correct. It is, however, a very different thing from any implication that two-thirds of *all* the papers were Federalist. Page 121 of the same work indicates there was no electioneering during the campaign of 1792; this is definitely inaccurate unless limited to the Presidential candidate (Washington) alone, as there were numerous articles concerning the Vice Presidency (especially for Clinton against Adams) and other offices.

166. Philadelphia *General Advertiser*, Oct. 23, 1790; cited in Woodbury, *Public Opinion*, 7.

BUSINESSMEN AND SPECULATORS
IN THE SADDLE

1. What went on in Freneau's mind is, of course, conjecture, but his conduct both before and immediately after this event supports this conclusion. His schooner reached New York harbor the day before Washington reached the city, and was decorated in honor of the new President's arrival. See Forman, "Political Activities," 1–15; Axelrad, *Freneau*, 179.

2. Charles A. Beard, *An Economic Interpretation of the Constitution of the United States*, and Charles A. Beard, *Economic Origins of Jeffersonian Democracy;* Orrin Grant Libby, *The Geographical Distribution of the Vote of the Thirteen States on the Federal Constitution, 1787–88, passim;* Hammond Bray, *Banks and Politics*, 191; Jackson Turner Main, *The Anti-Federalists*, esp. 72–118. Cf. Robert E. Brown, *Charles A. Beard and the Constitution*, and Forrest McDonald, *We the People, passim.* There were of course technically but eleven states under the new government at this time.

3. E. g., Beard, *Jeffersonian Democracy, passim;* Harry C. Allen, *The Anglo-American Relationship since 1783,* 213; William N. Chambers, *Political Parties in a New Nation,* 7–44, 76–80. Joseph Charles, *The Origins of the American Party System,* 91–118, argues that parties were extremely nebulous until the Jay Treaty.

4. The mounting attacks upon government expenses are discussed in Chapter 3.

5. Nathan Schachner, *Alexander Hamilton,* 235–36; Broadus Mitchell, *Alexander Hamilton,* II, 19–22.

6. *Boston Gazette,* Aug. 17, 1789; reprinted "from a late Phila. Paper" without comment.

7. E.g., the Richmond *Virginia Independent Chronicle,* Jan. 6, 1790.

8. Boston *Independent Chronicle,* Mar. 4, 1790.

9. "A Farmer," in the Philadelphia *Pennsylvania Gazette,* Feb. 17, 1790.

10. See Beard, *Jeffersonian Democracy,* 113; Andrew C. McLaughlin, *A Constitutional History of the United States,* 226. The New Haven *Connecticut Journal,* Mar. 17, 1790, complained that "aristocratic influence" in Congress would probably fix the interest rate at six per cent. It was finally determined that two-thirds of the new debt was to bear six per cent from the date of issue and the remainder, the same rate from 1801, with any arrears of interest to be funded at three per cent; Bassett, *Federalist System,* 32. For figures on the debt, see Morris Zucker, *Periods in American History,* 326; and Irving Brant, *James Madison, Father of the Constitution,* 290. Beard, *Jeffersonian Democracy,* 133–35, and McMaster, *A History,* I, 568, give slightly higher figures.

11. Item from the Philadelphia *Federal Gazette,* in the *Boston Gazette,* Feb. 1, 1790.

12. McLaughlin, *Constitutional History,* 226; Howard Jones, *America and French Culture,* 34n.; Walter R. Fee, "The Effect of Hamilton's Financial Policy Upon Public Opinion in New Jersey," *Proceedings of the New Jersey Historical Society* 50 (1930), 32–33.

13. Baltimore *Maryland Gazette,* Feb. 19, 1790; Philadelphia *Pennsylvania Gazette,* Mar. 17, 1790.

14. Apparently one of the first uses of this expression, later attributed to Hamilton.

15. "An Independent Observer," in the *New York Daily Gazette,* Feb. 15, 1790; quoted in the *Boston Gazette,* Mar. 1, 1790. Cf. Young, *Democratic Republicans,* 171.

16. Boston *Columbian Centinel*, Mar. 20, 1790; cited in Bowers, *Jefferson and Hamilton*, 57.

17. See the New York *Gazette of the United States*, Jan. 20, 1790.

18. "A War Worn Soldier," in the Boston *Columbian Centinel*, Feb. 24, 1790 (quoted in Bowers, *Jefferson and Hamilton*, 57–58).

19. Boston, *Independent Chronicle*, Mar. 4, 1790.

20. Philadelphia *Pennsylvania Gazette*, Mar. 17, 1790; cited in Woodbury, *Public Opinion*, 44. This was one of the relatively few anti-Semitic references of this entire period, but it was by no means unique; see the *New-York Journal*, Apr. 22, 29, Sept. 9, 1790.

21. Philadelphia *Pennsylvania Gazette*, Apr. 1, 1790; reprinted in the Poughkeepsie, N. Y., *Poughkeepsie Journal*, Apr. 6, 1790.

22. "A FRIEND TO SUBSTANTIAL JUSTICE," in the Richmond *Virginia Independent Chronicle*, Apr. 7, 1790.

23. See an item "From a N. Y. paper," in the Charleston, S. C., *City Gazette*, July 13, 1790. This article, however, did note that the government, as a party to a contract, could not fairly act as a judge in its own cause. See the speech of Congressman Hugh Williamson, Edenton *State Gazette of North Carolina*, Sept. 17, 1790.

24. Portland [Maine], *Cumberland Gazette*, Feb. 15, July 26, 1790; New Haven *Connecticut Journal*, Mar. 17, 1790.

25. Philadelphia *Pennsylvania Gazette*, Jan. 27, Feb. 3, 1790; Baltimore *Maryland Gazette*, Feb. 26, 1790; Woodbury, *Public Opinion*, 45–46. For other fears that specie would flow out of the country, see the Boston *Independent Chronicle*, Aug. 5, 1790; Philadelphia *General Advertiser*, July 20, 1791; Philadelphia *National Gazette*, Oct. 20, 1792.

26. "Uncle Toby," from the Salem, Mass., *Salem Gazette*, in the Boston *Independent Chronicle*, Dec. 16, 23, 1790.

27. Beard, *Jeffersonian Democracy*, 180, 194–95; Woodbury, *Public Opinion*, 50–51; Robert A. East, *Business Enterprise in the American Revolutionary Era*, 269, 280.

28. Elbridge Gerry to Sam Adams, in East, *Business Enterprise*, 274.

29. E.g., see the speeches in Congress on the public debt quoted in the Philadelphia *National Gazette*, Apr. 26, 1792; Beard, *Jeffersonian Democracy*, 136–38.

30. "A Pennsylvanian," in the Philadelphia *Pennsylvania Gazette*, Apr. 21, 1790; quoted in Woodbury, *Public Opinion*, 44–45.

31. "Mercator," cited in Woodbury, 42.

32. See "Cato," and "Fact," in the Philadelphia *National Gazette*, Sept. 5, 11, 1792.

33. *Ibid.*, Sept. 15, 1792; "American Farmer," Mar. 2, 9, 1793, and "Gracchus," Mar. 9, 1793.

34. "A REPUBLICAN CITIZEN," in the Baltimore *Maryland Journal*, Mar. 23, 1790.

35. *New York Daily Advertiser*, Feb. 22, 1790; cited in Bowers, *Jefferson and Hamilton*, 59.

36. Item from the *New York Daily Advertiser*, in the Portland [Maine] *Cumberland Gazette*, Mar. 22, 1790.

37. The plan was given in the Boston *Independent Chronicle*, Dec. 31, 1789; see also "Equity," in the issues of Jan. 14, 28, Feb. 11, 1790; and "One of the People," Aug. 5, 1790.

38. New Haven *Connecticut Journal*, Feb. 2, 1791.

39. Boston *Independent Chronicle*, Mar. 17, 1791.

40. "VERITUS," in the Burlington, N. J., *Burlington Advertiser*, Jan. 25, 1791.

41. "JUNIUS," in the Boston *Independent Chronicle*, Aug. 19, 1790. "A FRIEND TO MODEST MERIT," in the Exeter *Newhampshire Gazetteer*, Aug. 13, 1790, would have classified foreign security holders separately and would have paid them in land.

42. "An Old Soldier," in the Boston *Independent Chronicle*, Mar. 25, 1790; see also the earlier letters of "Equity," in the issues of Apr. 30, May 28, 1789.

43. *Ibid.*, Apr. 15, 1790. Nothing came of these attempts, and it was later hinted (*ibid.*, Feb. 2, 1792) that speculators probably bribed the promoters to abandon them.

44. Item from Hartford, Conn., in the Edenton, N. C., *State Gazette of North Carolina*, Feb. 11, 1791.

45. Boston *Independent Chronicle*, Aug. 12, 1790.

46. "W. O.," in the *New-York Journal*, Mar. 25, 1790.

47. *Ibid.*, Apr. 1, 22, 1790. See letters by "X," "C," "A. B.," and "Z," respectively, *ibid.*, Apr. 15, 19, 29, and May 24, 1790. Hamilton's failure to render clear reports to Congress at regular intervals is regarded by Malone, *Jefferson*, III, 17, as one of the most legitimate criticisms of his conduct as Secretary.

48. Philadelphia *National Gazette*, Jan. 26, Feb. 9, 1792. Other papers (e.g., the *Boston Gazette*, Sept. 5, 1791) had earlier referred approvingly to Mirabeau's "Reflections."

49. New Haven *Connecticut Journal*, Aug. 11, 1790.

50. Boston *Independent Chronicle*, Aug. 19, 1790.

51. New Brunswick, N. J., *Brunswick Gazette*, Oct. 4, 1791.

52. Portsmouth, N. H., *Osborne's New Hampshire Spy*, Mar. 3, 1790; reprinted in the *Boston Gazette*, Mar. 15, 1790. See also the issue of the *Brunswick Gazette* cited in note 51.

53. "Brutus," in the Philadelphia *National Gazette*, Mar. 15, 19, 1792; Forman, "Political Activities," 50; Bowers, *Jefferson and Hamilton*, 163–64; Lynch, *Party Warfare*, 22–23.

54. Philadelphia *National Gazette*, Mar. 22, 26, 29, Apr. 2, 5, 9, 1792.

55. New Brunswick, N. J., *Brunswick Gazette*, Aug. 23, 1791.

56. "BELISARIUS," in the Philadelphia *National Gazette*, Aug. 1, 1792; *Boston Gazette*, Sept. 10, 1792; Augusta, Ga., *Augusta Chronicle*, Sept. 22, 1792.

57. Philadelphia *National Gazette*, May 24, Aug. 8, 1792; the Annapolis *Maryland Gazette*, Sept. 27, 1792, also noted that borrowing abroad would have been cheaper.

58. Letter of Col. J. N. Cumming, of Newark, in the Philadelphia *National Gazette*, Jan. 5, 1793; reprinted in the Norwich, Conn., *Norwich Packet*, Jan. 24, 1793. See also "Cato," in the Newark, N. J., *Woods's Newark Gazette*, Feb. 4, 1795.

59. Item from Boston in the New York *Greenleaf's New York Journal*, Jan. 21, 1795.

60. New York *Argus*, Nov. 11, 1795.

61. Assertions made in Democratic papers were not always accurate, but I did not consider checking the validity of every statement as properly within the province of this study. Fallacious arguments are frequently effective.

62. Norwich, Conn., *Norwich Packet*, Jan. 24, 1793. See also appeals to Washington by "CINCINNATUS," in the Philadelphia *National Gazette*, Jan. 23, 1793; and "Legion," in the Boston *Independent Chronicle*, Jan. 13, 1791.

63. "GRACCHUS," in the Philadelphia *National Gazette*, Jan. 16, 1793; and a similar item (from the Boston *Independent Chronicle*), *ibid.*, Sept. 22, 1793.

64. Philadelphia *National Gazette*, Jan. 12, 1793; Norwich, Conn., *Norwich Packet*, Jan. 24, 1793; Elizabethtown, *New Jersey Journal*, Jan. 30, 1793.

65. "AN OLD SUBSCRIBER," in the Baltimore *Maryland Journal*, Sept. 3, 1794.

66. Philadelphia *General Advertiser*, Feb. 17, 1794.

67. E.g., Newark *Woods's Newark Gazette*, June 14, 1792; Mount Pleasant, N. J., *Jersey Chronicle*, Oct. 10, 1795.

68. Newark *Woods's Newark Gazette,* Apr. 9, 30, Dec. 17, 1794; Fee, *Transition,* 20–26; and Fee, "Effect of Hamilton's Financial Policy," 32–33.

69. Philadelphia *National Gazette,* May 10, 1792; Norwich, Conn., *Norwich Packet,* May 31, 1792. "Loaves and fishes" later became a favorite expression in the *Aurora* and other Republican papers.

70. Beard, *Jeffersonian Democracy,* 112–13.

71. Philadelphia *National Gazette,* Apr. 30, 1792, Mar. 9, 1793. Cf. Edgar E. Robinson, *The Evolution of American Political Parties,* 64; also a letter on the "Origin of Parties in Congress," in the Bennington *Vermont Gazette,* Dec. 26, 1794.

72. Raymond Walters, Jr., "The Origins of the Jeffersonian Party in Pennsylvania," *Pennsylvania Magazine of History and Biography* 66 (Oct., 1942), 444.

73. Newburyport, Mass., *Morning Star,* July 15, 1794.

74. Republican criticisms of Federalist policy towards England are discussed in Chapter 6.

75. Philadelphia *General Advertiser,* Apr. 12, 1794; Norfolk *Virginia Chronicle,* Apr. 24, 1794; item from the *Boston Gazette,* in the Newburyport, Mass., *Morning Star,* Sept. 9, 1794.

76. "VALERIUS, No. III," in the Newark *Woods's Newark Gazette,* Apr. 30, 1794.

77. New York *Gazette Française,* Feb. 1, 1796.

78. New York *Gazette,* July 15, 1796; New Haven, *Connecticut Journal,* Aug. 10, 1796; *Pittsburgh Gazette,* Aug. 6, 1796. (Cf. Young, *Democratic Republicans,* 572.)

79. "An American," Newark, N. J., *Centinel of Freedom,* Dec. 28, 1796; Boston *Independent Chronicle,* Jan. 16, 1797.

80. Figures vary, but apparently only about $21,500,000 was actually assumed; Zucker, *Periods in American History,* 326; Bassett, *Federalist System,* 33–34; Howard Jones, *America and French Culture,* 34n.; Irving Brant, *James Madison, Father of the Constitution,* 306–07.

81. New York *Gazette of the United States,* Dec. 19, 1789; *Boston Gazette,* Jan. 4, 1790.

82. Bassett, *Federalist System,* 34–35. E.g., see the *Boston Gazette,* May 10, Aug. 16, 1790: Boston *Independent Chronicle,* July 1, 1790; Pittsfield, Mass., *Berkshire Chronicle,* June 17, 1790; Richmond *Virginia Independent Chronicle,* Jan. 6, 1790; Hudson, N. Y., *Hudson Weekly Gazette,* Apr. 29, 1790.

83. *Boston Gazette,* Jan. 25, 1790.

84. This argument was advanced in Massachusetts; Morse, *Federalist Party*, 63n.

85. Woodbury, *Public Opinion*, 54–55; Charleston, S. C., *City Gazette*, Jan. 24, 1791.

86. The Boston *Independent Chronicle*, May 13, 1790, gave a rather detailed summary of Madison's arguments in Congress against the proposal.

87. *New-York Journal*, June 11, 1790; Richmond *Virginia Independent Chronicle*, July 7, 1790.

88. E.g., the resolutions of the Virginia House; Edenton *State Gazette of North Carolina*, Nov. 26, 1790. The Constitution made no express grant of the power to assume debts.

89. Beard, *Jeffersonian Democracy*, 178–81; Brant, *Madison*, 306–18.

90. Philadelphia *National Gazette*, Oct. 10, 1792; Beard, *Jeffersonian Democracy*, 167–68; Bowers, *Jefferson and Hamilton*, 61–62.

91. "SYDNEY," Philadelphia *National Gazette*, Apr. 23, 1792; Woodbury, *op. cit.*, 54.

92. Baltimore *Maryland Journal*, July 9, 1790; Richmond *Virginia Independent Chronicle*, July 28, 1790.

93. *New-York Journal*, July 6, 1790.

94. Apparently he had asked that the vote be postponed until constituents' opinions could be ascertained; *New York Packet*, June 1, 1790; cf. Brant, *Madison*, 317–18.

95. "B.K." and "A Citizen of America," *New-York Journal*, July 27, 1790; Baltimore *Maryland Gazette*, Aug. 6, 1790.

96. New York *Gazette of the United States*, Aug. 25, 1790.

97. *New-York Journal*, Aug. 31, 1790; Georgetown, D. C., *Times and Patowmack Packet*, Sept. 22, 1790.

98. "SYDNEY," in the Philadelphia *National Gazette*, Apr. 23, 1792.

99. "Solon, Jun.," in the Philadelphia *National Gazette*, May 17, 1792.

100. Norwich, Conn., *Chelsea Courier*, Feb. 1, 1797; see Bassett, *Federalist System*, 37–38, for Gallatin's rationalization.

101. Beard, *Economic Interpretation*, 33–37, citing James T. Callender, *A History of the United States for 1796*, 224.

102. "An Hartford Observer," *New-York Journal*, May 18, 1790; "A FRIEND TO MODEST MERIT," Exeter *Newhampshire Gazetteer*, Aug. 13, 1790; "SYDNEY," "MERCATOR," and "FRANKLIN," in the Philadelphia *National Gazette*, Apr. 23, Aug. 25, 1792, Feb. 16, 1793.

103. Letter of Congressman John Mercer, Annapolis *Maryland Gazette,* Sept. 16, 1792.

104. McMaster, *A History,* II, 29–31; Hammond, *Banks and Politics,* 54–55, 68. Cf. Joseph J. Spengler, "The Political Economy of Jefferson, Madison and Adams," in David Jackson, ed., *Studies in Honor of William Kenneth Boyd,* 31–32.

105. "Z.," Philadelphia *General Advertiser,* Feb. 21, 1791; Bache's father had been a director in this bank; Hammond, *Banks and Politics,* 63. "Cincinnatus," Philadelphia *Dunlap's American Daily Advertiser,* Feb. 7, 8, 1793.

106. The New Haven *Connecticut Journal,* Mar. 23, 1791, satirized the Bank in an article on shipping (a favorite analogy of the day); "A Pennsylvanian," Philadelphia *American Daily Advertiser,* Feb. 5, 1791; McLaughlin, *Constitutional History,* 229n., 231n.

107. Henry H. Simms, *Life of John Taylor,* 50; see Bowers, *Jefferson and Hamilton,* 76–77, on the House vote.

108. Philadelphia *Pennsylvania Gazette,* May 11, 1791; cited in Bowers, *Jefferson and Hamilton,* 78.

109. McMaster, *A History,* II, 37–38; East, *Business Enterprise,* 297–98; Young, *Democratic Republicans,* 216–17, tells of the eagerness to buy and notes New York State soon purchased 152 shares.

110. Boston *Herald of Freedom,* June 17, 21, 1791.

111. Item from the *Boston Gazette,* Norwich, Conn., *Norwich Packet,* Aug. 25, 1791.

112. "C," Philadelphia *General Advertiser,* Aug. 12, 1791; Norwich, Conn., *Norwich Packet,* Aug. 25, 1791; Exeter *New Hampshire Gazetteer,* Aug. 26, 1791. But "RUSTICUS, jun.," in the Boston *Argus,* Aug. 2, 1791, warned speculators of vigorous retaliation by the people if a land tax eventuated.

113. Newark, *Woods's Newark Gazette,* Sept. 22, 1791, Mar. 22, 1792; New Brunswick, N. J., *Brunswick Gazette,* Mar. 20, 1792; Fee, "Hamilton's Financial Policy," 43.

114. New York *Daily Advertiser,* Jan. 20, 26, 1792, cited in Joseph S. Davis, *Essays in the Earlier History of American Corporations,* II, 84–85; East, *Business Enterprise,* 299.

115. "CAUTION," Philadelphia *National Gazette,* Oct. 10, 1792.

116. "Caius," Philadelphia *National Gazette,* Feb. 6, 1792; see also *ibid.,* July 4, 1792; Woodbury, *Public Opinion,* 60–61 ff.

117. "A LOOKER ON," *Boston Gazette,* Oct. 31, 1791; *ibid.,* Dec. 12, 1791, Mar. 5, 1792, Feb. 25, 1793; Boston *Independent Chronicle,*

Jan. 10, 1792, Apr. 3, ("A CITIZEN"), Apr. 13, 16, 20 ("MER-CATOR"), May 7 ("An Elector"), 1795.

118. Boston *Independent Chronicle,* July 12, Aug. 30, Sept. 6, 1792, Oct. 27, 1794.

119. "Plain Truth," Philadelphia *National Gazette,* Oct. 17, 1792.

120. "PROBATIONARY ODES," "ODE V, To a Truly Great Man," Philadelphia *National Gazette,* June 22, 1793. See Forman, "Political Activities," 64; Mary Austin, *Freneau,* 161.

121. Fee, "Hamilton's Financial Policy," 43–44; Norwich, Conn., *Norwich Packet,* Mar. 6, 1792.

122. E.g., the Newark, N. J., *Woods's Newark Gazette,* Feb. 26, 1794, Jan. 14, Feb. 25, 1795; Elizabethtown, *New Jersey Journal,* Apr. 30, 1794.

123. "YORICK," from the New York *Evening Post,* in the Philadelphia *Independent Gazetteer,* Apr. 25, 1795; Lansingburgh, N. Y., *Lansingburgh Recorder,* Apr. 28, 1795. See also the Philadelphia *Aurora,* Mar. 23, 1795; New Haven *Connecticut Journal,* May 13, 1795. For an earlier prediction that this increase in the circulating medium would give "the glare of increasing wealth without the reality of it," note "Colbert," in the Boston *Independent Chronicle,* Dec. 13, 1791.

124. Louisville, Ga., *State Gazette and Louisville Journal,* Sept. 3, 1799.

125. Philadelphia *National Gazette,* Jan. 12, 1793.

126. Beard, *Jeffersonian Democracy,* 114; Beard, *Economic Interpretation,* 41–46, 48–49.

127. Boston *Independent Chronicle,* June 11, 1789; New Haven *Connecticut Journal,* June 24, 1789.

128. Bassett, *Federalist System,* 15–16.

129. New Haven *Connecticut Journal,* July 15, 1789.

130. Baltimore *Maryland Gazette,* Jan. 8, 1790; an excise on retailing liquor was preferred.

131. *Boston Gazette,* July 12, 1790.

132. Burlington, N. J., *Burlington Advertiser,* Oct. 5, 1790.

133. Cf. the Portland [Maine], *Cumberland Gazette,* Apr. 19, 1790; "RUSTICUS, jun.," in the Boston *Argus,* Aug. 2, 1791; Norwich, Conn., *Norwich Packet,* Aug. 25, 1791.

134. "Colbert," Boston *Independent Chronicle,* Nov. 22, Dec. 13, 1791.

135. See the *National Magazine, 1799,* 391–97, for a summary of the

arguments used. The present study considers opposition to the excise in Chapter 3.

136. From the Philadelphia *Federal Gazette;* Philadelphia *National Gazette,* June 4, 1792.

137. This summary of post-Revolutionary business changes is based on East, *Business Enterprise,* 322–23; and Davis, *American Corporations,* I, 178.

138. See Davis, *American Corporations,* I, 111–338. Schachner, *Hamilton,* 237–39, says Hamilton was probably unaware of Duer's illegal activities.

139. Davis, *American Corporations,* I, 188.

140. "An Independent Observer," New York *Daily Gazette,* Feb. 10, 1790; *Boston Gazette,* Mar. 1, 1790; "A Farmer," Baltimore *Maryland Gazette,* Feb. 26, 1790.

141. "LAMENTATIONS—CHAP. XXXIX," in the *Baltimore Journal,* Mar. 26, 1790.

142. Elizabethtown *New Jersey Journal,* Sept. 1, 1790.

143. Savannah *Georgia Gazette,* Sept. 30, 1790.

144. "Discrimination," *New-York Journal,* Aug. 20, 1791; see also the issue of Aug. 3.

145. *Ibid.,* Aug. 10, 13, 17, 20, 1791; New York *Daily Advertiser,* Aug. 9, 1791; New Haven *Connecticut Journal,* Aug. 17, 1791.

146. Baltimore *Maryland Journal,* Feb. 15, 1791.

147. "Scripomania," New Haven *Connecticut Journal,* Aug. 24, 1791.

148. Philadelphia *General Advertiser,* Aug. 12, 1791. See the New York *Daily Advertiser,* Aug. 8, 9, 13, 15, 1791, for price quotations.

149. Philadelphia *Pennsylvania Gazette,* Sept. 7, 1791.

150. "Square Toes," Philadelphia *General Advertiser,* July 14, 1791; Exeter *New Hampshire Gazetteer,* Aug. 5, 1791; Norwich, Conn., *Norwich Packet,* Aug. 18, 1791.

151. *New-York Journal,* Mar. 30, 1791; Philadelphia *Pennsylvania Gazette,* Aug. 17, 1791; Easton, Md., *Maryland Herald,* Aug. 23, 1791.

152. Philadelphia *Freeman's Journal,* July 27, 1791.

153. New York *Daily Advertiser,* Aug. 8, 1791.

154. *Ibid.,* Aug. 15, 1791; Baltimore *Maryland Journal,* Aug. 24, 1791.

155. Boston *Independent Chronicle,* Sept. 15, 1791.

156. *Ibid.,* Mar. 22, 1792. See also the Norwich, Conn., *Norwich Packet,* Mar. 15, 1792, on interest rates.

157. "An Observer," Boston *Independent Chronicle,* Aug. 18, Sept. 1, 1791; "A Definition of Parties," *National Magazine,* 126–28, later asserted labor was the true source of wealth.

158. *Boston Gazette,* Dec. 26, 1791.

159. Philadelphia *National Gazette,* June 4, 1792 (erroneously cited in Bowers, 165, as Jan. 4); *New-York Journal,* June 9, 1792.

160. *New-York Journal,* June 9, 1792.

161. Fredericktown, Md., *Bartgis's Federal Gazette,* May 22, 1792.

162. Philadelphia *National Gazette,* June 21, 1792.

163. *Ibid.,* June 25, 1792.

164. *Ibid.,* July 14, 1792; the issue of July 4 has an article in similar vein.

165. Norwich, Conn., *Norwich Weekly Register,* Mar. 27, 1792; see also the *Norwich Packet,* Mar. 15, 1792.

166. Philadelphia *National Gazette,* June 4, 1792.

167. Baltimore *Maryland Journal,* Aug. 24, 1792.

168. Philadelphia *National Gazette,* Feb. 27, 1792.

169. *Ibid.,* May 7, 1792. See similar articles in the *Boston Gazette,* June 4, 1792, and the New Brunswick, N. J., *Brunswick Gazette,* Mar. 27, 1792.

170. E. Wilder Spaulding, *His Excellency George Clinton,* 235; Davis, *American Corporations,* I, 281, 297, 302–04.

171. Philadelphia *National Gazette,* Mar. 29, May 10, 1792; Philadelphia *General Advertiser,* Apr. 17, May 10, 1792; Newark, *Woods's Newark Gazette,* May 10, 17, 1792; *New-York Journal,* May 23, 30, 1792. See Davis, *American Corporations,* I, 259–63, 291–302.

172. "The SPECULATOR, No. VIII," Norwich, Conn., *Norwich Weekly Register,* Apr. 3, 1792.

173. Philadelphia *National Gazette,* Apr. 30, 1792; New Haven *Connecticut Journal,* May 9, 1792.

174. Philadelphia *National Gazette,* Apr. 16, 1792.

175. *Boston Gazette,* Apr. 23, 1792. Simsbury was a famed prison of the Revolutionary era.

176. "The Speculator," Philadelphia *National Gazette,* Sept. 19, 1792.

177. *Ibid.,* May 31, 1792; Norwich, Conn., *Norwich Weekly Register,* June 12, 1792.

178. *Boston Gazette,* May 7, 1792.

179. *Ibid.,* May 21, Aug. 13, 1792.

180. Norwich, Conn., *Norwich Packet,* July 5, 1792.

181. Charleston, S. C., *Columbian Herald,* July 25, 1793.

182. "A SUFFERER BY SWINDLERS," New York *Columbian Gazetteer,* Feb. 8, 1794; see also *Greenleaf's New York Journal,* Mar. 11, 1795.

183. Worcester, Mass., *Independent Gazetteer,* Jan. 7, 1800.

184. Savannah, Ga., *Columbian Museum,* June 6, 1797; Washington, D. C., *Washington Gazette,* June 28, 1797. The privateersman's name was given as "Thomas" Whippo, however.

185. Halifax *North Carolina Journal,* Jan. 2, 1797.

186. "A Farmer," Newbury, Vt., *Orange Nightingale,* May 22, 1797.

187. Philadelphia *Aurora,* May 14, 1798; the New York *Diary,* Nov. 8, 1797, told of news-rigging.

188. Baltimore *Federal Intelligencer,* Apr. 7, 1795.

189. East, *Business Enterprise,* 275, 315–22; Beard, *Economic Interpretation,* 49, 82.

190. Boston *Independent Chronicle,* Oct. 28, Nov. 4, 1790; cf. the *National Magazine,* 128–29; Arthur P. Whitaker, *The Spanish-American Frontier,* 126–39; and "INVESTIGATIO[N]," Augusta, Ga., *Augusta Chronicle,* Nov. 27, 1790. Later references are in the Augusta, Ga., *Southern Centinel,* Nov. 27, 1794, Apr. 9, 16, 1795.

191. *Boston Gazette,* Feb. 1, 1790; Baltimore *Maryland Journal,* May 10, 1791.

192. Bennington *Vermont Gazette,* in the Knoxville, Tenn., *Knoxville Gazette,* Dec. 3, 1791.

193. "BRADDOCK," Newark *Woods's Newark Gazette,* Jan. 12, 1792; item from the Dover, N. H., *Phenix,* in the Boston *Argus,* Feb. 26, 1792. Duer's Scioto land venture was probably the target for these comments; see Davis, *American Corporations,* I, 130–39, 143–45, 157, 213–16, 224, 230–31, 244–52.

194. Whitaker, *Spanish-American Frontier,* 214; McMaster, *A History,* II, 479–80; Ulrich B. Phillips, "Georgia and States Rights," *Annual Report of the American Historical Association, 1901,* II, 29–30.

195. See the abstract of Charles B. Haskins, "The Yazoo Land Companies," *Annual Report of the American Historical Association, 1890,* 83. Augusta, Ga., *Southern Centinel,* Feb. 19, 26, 1795; Savannah, Ga., *Columbian Museum,* Mar. 25, 1796.

196. Halifax *North Carolina Journal,* Jan. 12, 1795; Providence, R. I., *United States Chronicle,* Mar. 5, 1795.

197. Philadelphia *Aurora*, Feb. 16, 1795; Charleston, S. C., *Columbian Herald*, Mar. 18, 1795.

198. *Idem.*

199. E.g., the Augusta, Ga., *Southern Centinel*, Jan. 22, Feb. 19, 26, Mar. 19, 26, May 14, Sept. 3, Oct. 1, 10, 28, Nov. 5, 1795; Mar. 17, 1796; *Augusta Chronicle*, Mar. 28, 1795; Savannah *Georgia Gazette*, cited in Charleston, S. C., *Columbian Herald*, Apr. 17, 1795. Charles W. Janson, *The Stranger in America*, 275, erroneously says 1798; see also McMaster, *A History*, II, 480; Phillips, "Georgia and States Rights," 31.

200. Boston *Independent Chronicle*, Jan. 11, 1796.

201. Augusta, Ga., *Southern Centinel*, Feb. 18, 1796; McMaster, *A History*, II, 480.

202. Boston *Independent Chronicle*, Feb. 1, 29, 1796; Richmond, Va., *Richmond and Manchester Advertiser*, Mar. 30, 1796. See also Haskins, "Yazoo Land Companies," 83.

203. Boston *Independent Chronicle*, Feb. 29, Mar. 3, 7, 1796; passage of the Jay Treaty before the Yazoo sale makes the charge of dubious accuracy.

204. E.g., Augusta, Ga., *Southern Centinel*, Feb. 18, 25, Mar. 3, 1796; Savannah, Ga., *Columbian Museum*, Apr. 1, 12, 1796; Janson, *Stranger in America*, 275–76.

205. Richmond, Va., *Richmond and Manchester Advertiser*, Apr. 6, 1796; Savannah, Ga., *Columbian Museum*, Mar. 11, 22, Apr. 5, 8, 26, May 3, 1796. Federalist arguments, even earlier, were in the Augusta, Ga., *Southern Centinel*, Nov. 27, 1794; Jan. 1, 8, Apr. 30, 1795; and later, *ibid.*, Sept. 18, Oct. 27, 1796; *Augusta Chronicle*, Aug. 6, 1796.

206. "A Friend to Honesty," Boston *Independent Chronicle*, Mar. 3, 1796.

207. Savannah, Ga., *Columbian Museum*, July 21, 1797.

208. Philadelphia *Aurora*, Mar. 26, 1798; Philadelphia *Carey's United States Recorder*, Mar. 27, 1798; Augusta, Ga., *Augusta Chronicle*, Nov. 4, 1797; Augusta, Ga., *Augusta Herald*, Sept. 10, 1800; Janson, *Stranger in America*, 276; McMaster, *A History*, II, 458.

209. Beard, *Economic Interpretation*, 49.

210. Halifax *North Carolina Journal*, Nov. 9, Dec. 21, 1795; Jan. 2, 1797; Oliver Wolcott, Sr., to Oliver Wolcott, Jr., Litchfield, Conn., Feb. 15, 1796 (Wolcott Papers, Vol. V).

211. Item from the Philadelphia *Courier Française*, in the Newburyport, Mass., *Newburyport Herald*, Oct. 31, 1797.

212. Charleston *South Carolina State Gazette*, Aug. 10, 1797.

213. New York *Diary,* Oct. 19, 1797.

214. Pittsburgh *Tree of Liberty,* Sept. 6, 20, 1800.

215. *Ibid.,* Oct. 11, Nov. 1, 1800.

216. Beard, *Economic Interpretation,* 85.

217. Bowers, *Jefferson and Hamilton,* 466.

218. New York *American Citizen,* July 17, 22, 26, 1800; Newark *Centinel of Freedom,* July 22, 29, 1800; Philadelphia *Aurora,* July 28, 1800; Baltimore *American,* July 28, 1800; Richmond *Virginia Argus,* Aug. 8, 12, 1800. The New York *Republican Watchtower,* July 19, 1800, also carried the letter (No. III) with the injunction for its destruction.

219. Frankfort, Ky., *Palladium,* Aug. 28, 1800.

220. New York *American Citizen,* July 26, 1800; Richmond *Virginia Argus,* Aug. 8, 12, 1800.

221. John Woods's *Suppressed History of the Administration of John Adams,* cited in Beard, *Economic Interpretation,* 86.

222. Philadelphia *Aurora,* Aug. 9, 11, 13, 15, 1800; Richmond *Virginia Argus,* Aug. 19, 22, 1800; Newark, N. J., *Centinel of Freedom,* July 8, 22, 1800; etc.

223. Philadelphia *Aurora,* Sept. 2, 1800; Frankfort, Ky., *Palladium,* Sept. 25, Oct. 30, 1800.

224. Item from the *Aurora,* in the New York *American Citizen,* July 7, 1800.

225. "A WINDING UP of Jonathan Dayton's public affairs," *ibid.,* July 31, 1800.

226. Pittsburgh *Tree of Liberty,* Sept. 13, 1800.

227. "Brutus," in the Nashville *Tennessee Gazette,* Nov. 26, 1800.

228. Item from the Bennington *Vermont Gazette,* in the Pittsburgh *Tree of Liberty,* Sept. 13, 1800. See Chap. 13, for additional charges of dishonesty in Federalist public officials.

 THE HIGH COST OF GOVERNMENT

1. Letter, from a proclaimed Federalist, Elizabethtown *New Jersey Journal,* July 8, 1789; Winchester *Virginia Gazette,* July 22, 1789.

2. *Boston Gazette,* Sept. 7, 1789.

3. New Brunswick, N. J., *Brunswic Gazette,* July 28, 1789; Boston *Herald of Freedom,* Sept. 15, 1789; Elizabethtown *New Jersey Journal,* Aug. 19, Nov. 4, 1789; "Junius," *Boston Gazette,* Oct. 5, 1789, and Boston *Independent Chronicle,* Oct. 8, 1789.

4. "A CITIZEN," Boston *Herald of Freedom,* Sept. 15, 1789; *Boston Gazette,* Oct. 5, 1789.

5. New Haven *Connecticut Journal,* Sept. 16, 1789; Fairfield, Conn., *Fairfield Gazette,* Sept. 23, 1789; Boston *Independent Chronicle,* Sept. 10, 17, 1789.

6. E.g., Boston *Herald of Freedom,* Sept. 29, 1789; *Boston Gazette,* Oct. 12, 1789.

7. Boston *Independent Chronicle,* Sept. 3, 1789.

8. "D——," *New-York Journal,* Sept. 17, 1790.

9. New Haven *Connecticut Journal,* Sept. 23, 1789; Newburyport, Mass., *Essex Journal,* Oct. 14, 1789.

10. New Haven *Connecticut Journal,* Oct. 14, 1789.

11. *Idem.;* Boston *Herald of Freedom,* Sept. 15, 1789; Bennington *Vermont Gazette,* Nov. 23, 1789; "A GEORGIAN," Augusta, Ga., *Augusta Chronicle,* June 12, 1790.

12. Boston *Independent Chronicle,* July 1, 1790; Edenton, *State Gazette of North Carolina,* Aug. 6, 1790; Charleston *State Gazette of South Carolina,* Aug. 12, 1790.

13. Portland [Maine] *Cumberland Gazette,* May 3, 24, 1790; Albany, N. Y., *Albany Register,* May 3, 1790; *New-York Journal,* Apr. 8, 1790.

14. Elizabethtown, *New Jersey Journal,* June 30, 1790 (from the *Connecticut Journal*); "An Observer," Boston *Independent Chronicle,* May 13, 1790.

15. *Boston Gazette,* May 10, 1790.

16. *Ibid.,* June 21, July 5, 1790; Boston *Independent Chronicle,* Aug. 19, 1790.

17. Richmond *Virginia Independent Chronicle,* July 7, 1790; *Boston Gazette,* June 28, 1790.

18. Item from New York, Nov. 15, in the Boston *American Herald,* Nov. 22, 1790.

19. Philadelphia *General Advertiser,* Feb. 1, 1791 (item from Georgetown).

20. Grand Jury of Greenville County, S. C., Feb. 1792; *Boston Gazette,* May 21, 1792.

21. *Boston Gazette,* Apr. 2, 1792, June 10, 1793.

22. Halifax *North Carolina Journal,* Apr. 30, 1794.

23. Philadelphia *National Gazette,* Jan. 2, 1793.

24. Baltimore *Maryland Journal,* Mar. 15, 1793; Philadelphia *General Advertiser,* Jan. 31, 1794.

25. Philadelphia *General Advertiser,* Jan. 1, 1793; Philadelphia *National Gazette,* Jan. 2, 1793.

26. *Boston Gazette,* June 14, 1790; New Haven *Connecticut Journal,* July 14, 1790; Wilmington *Delaware Gazette,* Aug. 7, 1790; cf. the Burlington, N. J., *Burlington Advertiser,* Aug. 24, 1790, for the other side of the question.

27. Pittsfield, Mass., *Berkshire Chronicle,* Aug. 5, 1790; but cf. *ibid.,* Aug. 12, 1790.

28. Item from the *Aurora,* in the Nashville, Tenn., *Rights of Man,* Mar. 11, 1799.

29. New York *Argus,* Feb. 15, 1797; "A Republican," Boston *Independent Chronicle,* Apr. 12, Oct. 8, 1798. See also the Newark, N. J., *Centinel of Freedom,* Dec. 28, 1796; Richmond *Virginia Argus,* Aug. 19, 1800.

30. Richmond, Va., *Examiner,* Jan. 17, 1800; also the Baltimore *American,* Nov. 5, 1800. However, even Washington found difficulty in obtaining able men for public offices.

31. Elizabethtown *New Jersey Journal,* Feb. 11, 1800; Richmond, Va., *Examiner,* Feb. 18, 1800; New London, Conn., *Bee,* Feb. 19, 1800; Raleigh, N. C., *Raleigh Register,* Feb. 25, 1800.

32. Richmond, Va., *Examiner,* Feb. 18, 21, 1800; Charleston, S. C., *City Gazette,* Mar. 7, 1800; Stonington, Conn., *Impartial Journal,* Apr. 15, 1800. The Philadelphia *Aurora* congratulated the public "on the effect of our remarks"; Richmond, Va., *Examiner,* Feb. 28, 1800.

33. Philadelphia *Aurora,* Feb. 27, 1797; Boston *Independent Chronicle,* Mar. 9, 1797, Aug. 13, 1798; Elizabethtown *New Jersey Journal,* June 21, 1797.

34. Richmond, Va., *Examiner,* Feb. 14, 1800; Baltimore *American,* Aug. 25, Nov. 5, 1800; Pittsburgh *Tree of Liberty,* Nov. 1, 1800.

35. Boston *Independent Chronicle,* May 12, 16, 1796; *Albany Register,* May 13, 1796.

36. Charleston *South Carolina State Gazette,* June 4, 1796.

37. Charleston, S. C., *Columbian Herald,* June 6, 1796.

38. Philadelphia *Daily Advertiser,* Feb. 18, 1797; "Aristides," Philadelphia *Aurora,* Jan. 4, 1797; Boston *Independent Chronicle,* Jan. 16, 1797.

39. Philadelphia *Aurora,* June 12, 1800; Baltimore *American,* June 16, 1800.

40. New York *Argus,* Jan. 25, 1797; Elizabethtown *New Jersey Journal,* Dec. 12, 1797; Washington, D. C., *Washington Gazette,* May 3, 1797; Pittsfield, Mass., *Sun,* Oct. 7, 1800.

41. New York *Argus,* Jan. 25, 1797; Philadelphia *Daily Advertiser,* Feb. 10, 18, 1797.

42. Richmond, Va., *Examiner,* Dec. 6, 1798; Richmond *Friend of the People,* July 5, 1800.

43. Boston *Independent Chronicle,* Dec. 7, 1797; the issue of Jan. 17, 1799, cited figures to show England could acquire eight naval guns for what it cost America to buy or build only five.

44. Baltimore *American,* July 16, 1800.

45. Boston *Independent Chronicle,* Jan. 8, 1798.

46. Philadelphia *Daily Advertiser,* Jan. 25, Feb. 10, 1797.

47. Chambersburg, Pa., *Farmers' Register,* May 9, 1798.

48. Nine thousand laborers, idle, at $1 a day, plus $3,000 "tavern expense"; Philadelphia *Carey's United States Recorder,* May 19, 1798.

49. Item from the *Aurora,* Boston *Independent Chronicle,* July 30, 1798; Knoxville, Tenn., *Genius of Liberty,* Aug. 21, 1798; and Frankfort, Ky., *Palladium,* Dec. 18, 1798.

50. Hartford, Conn., *American Mercury,* Mar. 28, 1799.

51. Boston *Columbian Centinel,* Apr. 17, 1799 (cited in Morse, *Federalist Party,* 177).

52. Philadelphia *Aurora,* June 10, 1799; Boston *Independent Chronicle,* June 27, 1799. See also the Richmond, Va., *Examiner,* Jan. 7, 1800; Richmond *Virginia Argus,* Feb. 11, 1800.

53. In North Carolina alone assessors spent nearly $40,000; Baltimore *American,* Aug. 11, 1800.

54. *Greenleaf's New York Journal,* Apr. 13, 1799; Richmond *Virginia Argus,* Mar. 17, 1800.

55. "OLD SOUTH," Boston *Independent Chronicle,* Jan. 16, 1800; Boston *Constitutional Telegraphe,* Jan. 18, 1800.

56. Spengler, "Political Economy," 33–34; Boston *Independent Chronicle,* Apr. 18, 1800. For an example of the way in which the Democratic press hammered upon the topic of governmental expenses, see the

Boston *Independent Chronicle,* Jan. 10, 14, 17, 21, 28, Mar, 26, Aug. 23, 1799.

57. Richmond *Virginia Argus,* May 2, 6, 1800.

58. New London, Conn., *Bee,* Aug. 27, 1800.

59. Fredericksburg *Virginia Herald,* June 20, 1800; Lexington *Kentucky Gazette,* July 3, 1800.

60. See the Hartford *Connecticut Courant,* Jan. 13, 1800.

61. See tables (citing Gallatin) in the Raleigh, N. C., *Raleigh Register,* Sept. 30, 1800; Fredericksburg, Va., *Courier,* Oct. 24, 1800; Pittsburgh *Tree of Liberty,* Sept. 20, 1800.

62. Richmond *Virginia Argus,* Oct. 31, 1800.

63. Baltimore *American,* June 14, 1799; Boston *Constitutional Telegraphe,* Jan. 4, 1800; Richmond *Virginia Argus,* Jan. 7, 1800.

64. "A Pennsylvanian," Pittsburgh *Tree of Liberty,* Oct. 18, 1800. Figures reported in Democratic newspapers for military expenditures varied confusingly; cf. the Alexandria, Va., *Alexandria Times,* Mar. 26, 1800; Richmond *Virginia Argus,* Aug. 26, 1800; Worcester *Massachusetts Spy,* Oct. 15, 1800.

65. "A Scots Correspondent," Richmond *Virginia Argus,* Feb. 11, 1800; see also the Richmond *Examiner,* Feb. 25, 1800.

66. Wilmington, Del., *Mirror of the Times,* Dec. 6, 1800.

67. Philadelphia *Aurora,* Aug. 26, 1800; Pittsburgh *Tree of Liberty,* Sept. 13, 1800.

68. Richmond *Virginia Argus,* Oct. 21, 1800; cf. Richmond, Va., *Friend of the People,* May 16, 1800.

69. Newfield, Conn., *American Telegraphe,* May 21, 1800; Richmond *Virginia Argus,* Nov. 4, 1800. Democratic local administrations also would be less costly, was the claim; New York *Diary,* Jan. 29, 1798; *Albany Register,* Apr. 22, 1800.

70. Newark, N. J., *Centinel of Freedom,* Aug. 19, 1800.

71. New York *American Citizen,* May 1, 1800.

72. Philadelphia *Aurora,* Jan. 13, 1800; Richmond *Examiner,* Jan. 28, 1800.

73. Boston *Herald of Freedom,* May 5, 1789.

74. Letter from Boston, Augusta, Ga., *Augusta Chronicle,* July 10, 1790. Richmond *Virginia Independent Chronicle,* Apr. 14, June 16, 1790.

75. Item from Newbern, N. C., Baltimore *Maryland Journal,* Aug. 20, 1790; Baltimore *Maryland Gazette,* Aug. 27, 1790.

76. *Boston Gazette,* July 12, 1790.

77. Charleston, S. C., *Columbian Herald,* Sept. 16, 1790.

78. E.g., the Philadelphia *General Advertiser,* Jan. 22, Feb. 3, 5, 1791; and one from Pittsburgh (signed "Albert Gallatine, Clerk"), Winchester *Virginia Gazette,* Aug. 27, 1791. For an earlier reaction, Philadelphia *Pennsylvania Packet,* Dec. 27, 1790.

79. Actually the amount varied with the proof of the spirits and the size of the still; see McMaster, *A History,* II, 189n., citing the *Acts of the Second Congress,* May 8, 1792; Link, *Democratic-Republican Societies,* 67.

80. New Brunswick, N. J., *Brunswic Gazette,* Aug. 30, 1791.

81. Baltimore *Maryland Gazette,* Sept. 27, 1791; cf. Philadelphia *Freeman's Journal,* Sept. 28, 1791, for an account of the quarrel between the two counties.

82. "PHILANTHROPUS," Augusta, Ga., *Augusta Chronicle,* Nov. 28, 1791.

83. "CENTINEL," Philadelphia *National Gazette,* May 7, 1792; *Boston Gazette,* June 11, 1792.

84. Philadelphia *National Gazette,* Apr. 23, May 3, 10, 17, 1792.

85. *Ibid.,* May 24, 1792. For other "SYDNEY" letters, see Apr. 30, May 21, 1792.

86. Fayetteville, N. C., *Fayetteville Gazette,* Jan. 2, 1793.

87. "H.B.," Philadelphia *National Gazette,* Aug. 12, 1792.

88. Boston *Argus,* May 25, 1792.

89. Philadelphia *National Gazette,* May 31, June 18, 25, 1792. Cf. the smug remark in Bowers, *Jefferson and Hamilton,* 252, that Federalists "satisfied the moron-minded that a demand for a law's repeal is the same as urging its violation."

90. Philadelphia *National Gazette,* Nov. 28, Dec. 1, 5, 1792; and Leland D. Baldwin, *Whiskey Rebels,* 87, citing the *Pittsburgh Gazette.*

91. Baldwin, *Whiskey Rebels,* 69–73, gives an excellent summary of the resentment. See also *Woods's Newark Gazette,* June 11, 1794; *Pittsburgh Gazette,* Jan. 24, 1795.

92. The region was largely anti-Federalist, but dominated by a few Federalist families; Baldwin, *Pittsburgh,* 172; E. Bruce Thomas, *Political Tendencies in Pennsylvania, 1783–1794,* 192–93; Harry M. Tinkcom, *The Republicans and Federalists in Pennsylvania, 1790–1801,* 54–55.

93. Link, *Democratic-Republican Societies,* 50, 147; *Philadelphia Gazette,* Aug. 7, 1794; Tinkcom, *Republicans and Federalists,* 91–96.

94. Baldwin, *Whiskey Rebels,* 102–03; McMaster, *A History,* II, 189–

90. The New Haven *Connecticut Journal*, Aug. 20, 1794, gives a typical "Tom the Tinker" letter. See MS. by Link, "The Democratic Societies in the Carolinas," 17, citing a letter to Hamilton on the influence of the *National Gazette*.

95. Philadelphia *Dunlap's American Daily Advertiser*, July 8, Aug. 28, 1794.

96. *Pittsburgh Gazette*, Apr. 26, June 23, 1794; Baldwin, *Whiskey Rebels*, 97–99.

97. Philadelphia *General Advertiser*, July 26, 1794; *Baltimore Daily Intelligencer*, July 31, 1794. Actually the administration *had* moved slowly in enforcement.

98. Philadelphia *General Advertiser*, Aug. 2, 1794; *Baltimore Daily Intelligencer*, Aug. 6, 1794; Philadelphia *American Daily Advertiser*, July 31, Aug. 9, 28, Sept. 11, Oct. 6, 1794 (cited in Luetscher, *Early Political Machinery*, 50); Norfolk *Virginia Chronicle*, Sept. 22, 1794; Newark *Woods's Newark Gazette*, Sept. 24, 1794; Canaan, N. Y., *Columbian Mercury*, Oct. 1, 1794.

99. *Baltimore Daily Intelligencer*, Aug. 25, Sept. 2, 6, 1794; *Pittsburgh Gazette*, Aug. 30, Sept. 6, 1794; Halifax *North Carolina Journal*, Sept. 10, 17, 24, 1794; Lexington *Kentucky Gazette*, Sept. 20, 1794; Baldwin, *Whiskey Rebels*, 172–74, 180.

100. Halifax *North Carolina Journal*, Sept. 24, 1794; Norwich, Conn., *Norwich Weekly Register*, Oct. 14, 1794. A letter in the Lexington *Kentucky Gazette*, Nov. 1, 1794, attacked frontiersmen for talk of returning to their British allegiance.

101. Letter to Philadelphia *General Advertiser*, Aug. 21, 1794; see Baldwin, *Whiskey Rebels*, 108–09, 221; Fee, *Transition*, 46. Boston *Columbian Centinel*, cited in the Boston *Independent Chronicle*, Aug. 18, 21, 1794.

102. Boston *Independent Chronicle*, Aug. 28, 1794.

103. *Baltimore Daily Intelligencer*, Sept. 10, 1794. Reference to the rebellious French (monarchist) province was in the *Hartford Gazette*, Sept. 11, 1794.

104. Philadelphia *American Daily Advertiser*, Sept. 10, 15, 24, 1794; *New York Journal*, Sept. 13, 1794. See Bowers, *Jefferson and Hamilton*, 253; Luetscher, *Early Political Machinery*, 50; John C. Miller, *The Federalist Era*, 161. The Philadelphia *General Advertiser*, Sept. 5, 1794, contrasted the administration's firmness here with its supineness toward British Governor Simcoe's warning against settling the Genesee country.

105. Philadelphia *General Advertiser,* Sept. 15, 1794; Easton, Pa., *Neuer Unpartheyischer Eastoner Bothe,* Oct. 8, 1794.

106. Boston *Independent Chronicle,* Oct. 6, 1794; Philadelphia *General Advertiser,* Nov. 10, 1794; McLaughlin, *Constitutional History,* 257; Link, *Democratic-Republican Societies,* 180n.

107. The New York *American Minerva* labeled this charge ridiculous, for Westerners still resented British retention of fur-trading posts; Charleston, S. C., *Columbian Herald,* Oct. 17, 1794.

108. Easton, Pa., *Neuer Unpartheyischer Eastoner Bothe,* Nov. 5, 1794; Philadelphia *American Daily Advertiser,* Oct. 25, Nov. 6, 1794; "An Old Soldier," Lexington *Kentucky Gazette,* Oct. 18, 1794; Miller, *Federalist Era,* 155.

109. Philadelphia *General Advertiser,* Oct. 11, 15, 1794; Charleston *South Carolina State Gazette,* Oct. 29, 1794.

110. Philadelphia *General Advertiser,* Nov. 3, 6, 8, 10, 1794. Secretary Knox was in Maine on personal business.

111. McMaster, *A History,* II, 202–03; *Pittsburgh Gazette,* Nov. 7, 1795; Tinckom, *Republicans and Federalists,* 101–06.

112. E.g., see the Providence, R. I., *United States Chronicle,* Sept. 11, 1794; Miller, *Federalist Era,* 159.

113. Boston *Independent Chronicle,* Nov. 3, 6, 1794; Bowers, *Jefferson and Hamilton,* 257–58; Miller, "First Fruits," 118–43; Baldwin, *Whiskey Rebels,* esp. 110–12, 259; Young, *Democratic Republicans,* 419–20.

114. Philadelphia *Aurora,* Nov. 24, 29, Dec. 22, 27, 1794; James D. Richardson, ed., *A Compilation of the Messages and Papers of the Presidents,* I, 155, 158; *New-York Journal,* Dec. 12, 1794.

115. *Baltimore Daily Intelligencer,* July 31, 1794; Augusta, Ga., *Augusta Chronicle,* Dec. 20, 1794; Philadelphia *General Advertiser,* Aug. 16, Sept. 6, 1794; Easton, Pa., *Neuer Unpartheyischer Eastoner Bothe,* Oct. 8, 1794; Elizabethtown, Md., *Washington Spy,* Sept. 22, 1795; Baltimore *Federal Gazette,* Dec. 20, 1796.

116. *Philadelphia Gazette,* Dec. 13, 1794; Halifax *North Carolina Journal,* June 1, 1795.

117. Philadelphia *National Gazette,* July 11, 1792; Trenton, *New Jersey State Gazette,* May 21, 1794; "Hancock," Philadelphia *General Advertiser,* June 9, 1794; Philadelphia *Independent Gazetteer,* Jan. 24, 1795.

118. Philadelphia *National Gazette,* June 18, Aug. 4, 22, 1792; "A CORRESPONDENT," Newark *Centinel of Freedom,* Dec. 7, 1796; Boston *Independent Chronicle,* June 1, 1797.

119. New York *Argus,* Jan. 24, Mar. 2, 9, 1797; Boston *Independent Chronicle,* Feb. 9, Mar. 13, 1797.

120. Sag Harbor, L. I., *Frothingham's Long Island Herald,* July 2, 1798. See Fredericktown, Md., *Bartgis's Federal Gazette,* Oct. 4, 1797; Bennington *Vermont Gazette,* Jan. 9, 1798; New York *Argus,* Mar. 18, 1799. Cf. the Hartford *Connecticut Courant,* Jan. 17, 1797; Rutland, Vt., *Rutland Herald,* Apr. 1, 1799.

121. Philadelphia *Gales' Independent Gazetteer,* Jan. 17, 1797.

122. Boston *Independent Chronicle,* Jan. 8, Mar. 15, Apr. 5, 1798.

123. E.g., "A QUIET CITIZEN," from the *Connecticut Courant,* Newport, R. I., *Companion,* Nov. 24, 1798; Alexandria, Va., *Columbian Mirror,* Nov. 15, 1798, Feb. 9, 1799.

124. Hartford, Conn., *American Mercury,* Mar. 22, 1798.

125. Item from the *Albany Register,* Philadelphia *Aurora,* Nov. 19, 1798; Boston *Independent Chronicle,* Mar. 28, 1798.

126. Philadelphia *Carey's United States Recorder,* May 31, 1798.

127. Boston *Independent Chronicle,* Aug. 2, 23, Oct. 22, Nov. 1, 1798.

128. "Is this sedition?"—Stonington, Conn., *Journal of the Times,* Nov. 28, 1798.

129. "An Essex Dutchman," Newark *Centinel of Freedom,* Oct. 23, 1798; Boston *Independent Chronicle,* Nov. 1, Dec. 17, 1798; Frankfort, Ky., *Guardian of Freedom,* Dec. 13, 1798.

130. Boston *Independent Chronicle,* Mar. 7, 1799.

131. New London, Conn., *Bee,* Feb. 5, 1800.

132. Frank M. Eastman, "The Fries Rebellion," *Americana* 16 (Jan. 1922), 71–74, has the best account. See also McMaster, *A History,* II, 434–38; Bennett M. Rich, *The Presidents and Civil Disorder,* 21–30; and Miller, *Federalist Era,* 247–48.

133. Norwich, Conn., *Courier,* Mar. 27, 1799; Portsmouth, N. H., *Federal Observer,* Apr. 11, 1799.

134. E.g., Stonington, Conn., *Journal of the Times,* Apr. 2, 1799.

135. Bennington *Vermont Gazette,* Apr. 4, 1799; Boston *Independent Chronicle,* Apr. 4, 1799.

136. Boston *Independent Chronicle,* Mar. 21, 1799; Suffield, Conn., *Impartial Herald,* Apr. 23, 1799.

137. Bennington *Vermont Gazette,* Apr. 4, 1799; Newark *Centinel of Freedom,* May 7, 1799; New York *Argus,* Apr. 8, 1799.

138. New York *Greenleaf's New York Journal,* Mar. 27, 1799; Boston *Independent Chronicle,* Apr. 1799, *passim* (esp. Apr. 11, 15, 18);

Frankfort, Ky., *Palladium,* May 23, 1799; Eastman, "Fries Rebellion," 75.

139. *Readinger Adler,* Apr. 23, 1799; Philadelphia *Aurora,* Apr. 24, 1799; Newark, N. J., *Centinel of Freedom,* Apr. 30, 1799; Alexandria, Va., *Alexandria Times,* Apr. 29, 1799; Georgetown, D. C., *Centinel of Liberty,* May 3, 1799; Richmond, *Virginia Argus,* May 10, 24, 1799; Frankfort, Ky., *Palladium,* May 30, 1799. Cf. the Georgetown, S. C., *Georgetown Gazette,* June 12, 1800, for the Federalist version.

140. Phildelphia *Aurora,* July 1, 1799; Lancaster, Pa., *Lancaster Journal,* July 6, 1799. Another example of military intimidation is given in the Philadelphia *Universal Gazette,* May 23, 1799.

141. Frankfort, Ky., *Palladium,* June 6, 20, 1799, May 22, 1800; Richmond, Va., *Examiner,* June 20, 1800; Lexington *Kentucky Gazette,* July 24, 1800; Eastman, "Fries Rebellion," 80–81.

142. Philadelphia *Aurora,* May 22, 1800; New York *American Citizen,* May 26, 1800; Tinkcom, *Republicans and Federalists,* 238–40, 246–47; Howard M. Jenkins, ed., *Pennsylvania, Colonial and Federal,* II, 167, 172; William M. Meigs, "Pennsylvania Politics Early in This Century," *Pennsylvania Magazine of History and Biography* 17 (1893), 462n. Tales of further unrest in York County were denied; Richmond *Virginia Argus,* Jan. 28, 1800.

143. E.g., see Robinson, *Jeffersonian Democracy,* 25–26, on New England's reaction.

144. "A Republican," Boston *Independent Chronicle,* Dec. 12, 1793.

145. Letter in the (Federalist) Providence, R. I., *United States Chronicle,* Aug. 4, 1791; Philadelphia *National Gazette,* Oct. 16, 1793.

146. *Baltimore Daily Repository,* June 13, 1792.

147. "AN ENGLISHMAN," Philadelphia *Aurora,* July 16, 1798.

148. Richmond *Virginia Independent Chronicle,* Mar. 10, 1790.

149. Providence, R. I., *United States Chronicle,* Aug. 4, 1791.

150. Bassett, *Federalist System,* 33; Anonymous, "Party Violence, 1790–1800," *Virginia Magazine of History and Biography* 29 (Apr. 1921), 177.

151. Philadelphia *National Gazette,* May 3, 1792; cited in Forman, "Political Activities," 50.

152. *Boston Gazette,* June 18, 1792; Philadelphia *National Gazette,* June 18, 1792; see Washington's address of Oct. 25, 1791, Richardson, *Messages . . ,* I, 100.

153. Philadelphia *National Gazette,* June 7, 28, Oct. 10, 20, 1792; New Haven *Connecticut Journal,* June 13, 1792; *Baltimore Daily Re-*

*pository,* June 12, 1792; Georgetown *South-Carolina Independent Gazette,* Sept. 15, 1792.

154. Philadelphia *National Gazette,* Mar. 9, June 1 (quotation), 1793.

155. Boston *Columbian Centinel,* Feb. 16, 20, 1793; Philadelphia *Gazette of the United States,* Feb. 23, Mar. 9, 1793; cited in Bowers, *Jefferson and Hamilton,* 197–99. Philadelphia *National Gazette,* Feb. 27, 1793; Faÿ, *Two Franklins,* 165; McMaster, *A History,* II, 116–17; Malone, *Jefferson* (hereafter cited as *TJ*), III, 20–34.

156. Philadelphia *National Gazette,* Feb. 20 ("Franklin"), 27 ("Decius"), Mar. 9, 1793; Norwich, Conn., *Weekly Register,* Mar. 5, 1793. Bowers, *Jefferson and Hamilton,* 199–200, states Jefferson inspired and planned this entire congressional attack; Faÿ, *Two Franklins,* 165, agrees, but Malone, *TJ,* III, 21, 25–31, qualifies this somewhat.

157. Malone, *TJ,* III, 26.

158. Philadelphia *National Gazette,* Mar. 27, 1793; see "TIMON," *idem,* and Beard, *Jeffersonian Democracy,* 21.

159. "Knoxville," Boston *Independent Chronicle,* Mar. 6, 1794.

160. Trenton *New Jersey State Gazette,* Jan. 20, 1795; Richardson, ed., *Messages and Papers,* I, 159.

161. Philadelphia *General Advertiser,* Feb. 11, 1794; Charleston, S. C., *Columbian Herald,* Mar. 17, 1794.

162. Philadelphia *Independent Gazetteer,* Jan. 28, 1795; reprinted from the Stockbridge, Mass., *Western Star,* Boston *Independent Chronicle,* Feb. 20, 1795; Charleston, S. C., *Columbian Herald,* Oct. 7, 1795.

163. "Citizens of America," Charleston, S. C., *Columbian Herald,* May 2, 1796; New York *Diary,* Jan. 11, Feb. 7, 1797.

164. Philadelphia *Aurora,* Aug. 2, 1798; Boston *Independent Chronicle,* Oct. 11, 1798.

165. Richmond, Va., *Examiner,* Feb. 21, 1800. For a Federalist answer, see the Providence, R. I., *Providence Journal,* Mar. 9, 1800; Nashville *Tennessee Gazette,* Apr. 30, 1800. On Gallatin, Bowers, *Jefferson and Hamilton,* 70, 293–94; and Raymond Walters, Jr., *Albert Gallatin,* 88–93.

166. "A Scots Correspondent," Richmond, Va., *Examiner,* Jan. 14, 1800.

167. *Ibid.,* Mar. 21, 1800.

168. "Colbert," Boston *Independent Chronicle,* Oct. 23, 1800. This was probably deliberately misleading. The figure for the original funding

685

was too low, and amounts for assumption and the foreign debt were apparently not included in it.

169. Richmond *Virginia Argus,* Sept. 19, 1800; New York *American Citizen,* Sept. 9, 1800.

170. Richmond *Virginia Argus,* Sept. 30, 1800.

171. Item from the New York *Republican Watch Tower,* Providence, R. I., *Impartial Observer,* Sept. 8, 1800. See also Richmond *Virginia Argus,* Sept. 2, 1800; Philadelphia *Aurora,* Sept. 20, 1800; Morristown, N. J., *Genius of Liberty,* Oct. 9, 1800; Worcester *Massachusetts Spy,* Nov. 4, 1800.

172. E.g., see references in Boston *Independent Chronicle,* Oct. 13, 1800; Georgetown, D. C., *Washington Federalist,* Dec. 1, 1800; Zucker, *Periods in American History,* 326.

173. Philadelphia *National Gazette,* Oct. 17, 1792, Jan. 9, Mar. 27, 1793. Portions of the material on the following pages first appeared in Donald H. Stewart, "The Press and Political Corruption during the Federalist Administrations," *Political Science Quarterly* 67, No. 3, (Sept. 1952), 526–46. Used with permission of *Political Science Quarterly.*

174. Edenton, N. C., *State Gazette of North Carolina,* Mar. 24, 1795.

175. E.g., see these and replies (from the *Aurora*), Carlisle, Pa., *Telegraphe,* Nov. 17, 1795. The present study discusses the charges in Chap. 13, *infra.*

176. Bridgeton, N. J., *Argus,* Nov. 27, 1795.

177. Nathan Schachner, *Aaron Burr,* 146; Bowers, *Jefferson and Hamilton,* 187–90; Mitchell, *Alexander Hamilton,* II, 403–21. Callender's charges as late as 1797 were based on this incident; see Chap. 13; McMaster, *A History,* 336–38; Brant, *Madison,* III, 365–66.

178. Baltimore *City Gazette,* Mar. 16, 1797.

179. New York *Time Piece,* Oct. 31, 1797; Boston *Independent Chronicle,* Nov. 9, 1797.

180. Boston *Independent Chronicle,* Nov. 27, 1797, Jan. 29, 1798; Philadelphia *Aurora,* Jan. 18, 1797.

181. From the Richmond *Virginia Argus* (Apr. 1798), in the *National Magazine,* 103.

182. Philadelphia *Aurora,* Nov. 8, 1798.

183. *Ibid.,* June 24, 1798. Cf. Federalist denials of the tale, with affidavits, Newburyport, Mass., *Newburyport Herald,* Feb. 6, 1798; see also Chap. 14.

184. Item from the *National Magazine,* New London, Conn., *Bee,* Feb. 19, 1800.

185. Philadelphia *Aurora,* May 23, 1800; Newark *Centinel of Freedom,* May 27, 1800.

186. Newark, N. J., *Centinel of Freedom,* May 27, 1800; see also Chap. 2.

187. E.g., Philadelphia *Aurora,* June 17, 18, 19, 21, 22, 1800; New York *American Citizen,* June 19, 1800; Petersburg, Va., *Petersburg Intelligencer,* June 27, 1800; Raleigh, N. C., *Raleigh Register,* July 1, 1800; New York *Republican Watchtower,* Aug. 13, 1800.

188. Philadelphia *Aurora,* June 30, July 2, 1800; Baltimore *American,* July 9, 1800.

189. Philadelphia *Aurora,* July 9, 14, 1800; Baltimore *American,* July 12, 17, 1800.

190. "A Development of the Anglo-Federal System," Philadelphia *Aurora,* June 18, 1800; New York *American Citizen,* June 20, 1800; Baltimore *American,* June 21, 1800.

191. Philadelphia *Aurora,* June 17, 21, 23, 1800; Baltimore *American,* June 20, 26, 1800; New York *American Citizen,* June 24, 25, 1800; Newark *Centinel of Freedom,* July 1, 1800; Stonington, Conn., *Impartial Journal,* July 1, 8, 1800; Lexington *Kentucky Gazette,* July 17, 1800.

192. "AGENT," Baltimore *American,* July 7, 1800.

193. Philadelphia *Aurora,* June 24, July 15, 1800; Baltimore *American,* June 27, July 18, 1800; New York *American Citizen,* July 26, 1800.

194. Philadelphia *Aurora,* June 19, July 14, 1800; Petersburg, Va., *Petersburg Intelligencer,* June 27, 1800; Baltimore *American,* July 17, 1800.

195. Philadelphia *Aurora,* June 25, 1800; Baltimore *American,* June 28, 1800; Wilmington, Del., *Mirror of the Times,* June 28, 1800; Boston *Constitutional Telegraphe,* July 2, 1800; Salem, Mass., *Impartial Register,* July 3, 1800; New York *Forlorn Hope,* July 5, 1800.

196. Philadelphia *Aurora,* June 25, 1800; New York *Forlorn Hope,* July 5, 1800. Federalists stressed the official practice of entrusting monies to agents on account; this naturally made for heavy debits against certain individuals. See items from the *Philadelphia Gazette* and *Claypoole's Americn Daily Advertiser,* in the *Raleigh Register,* July 8, 1800; but cf. "THE CONFESSION OF OLIVER WOLCOTT," New York *American Citizen,* June 27, 1800; Lexington *Kentucky Gazette,* July 17, 1800.

197. New York *American Citizen,* June 30, 1800.

198. Philadelphia *Aurora*, July 3, 1800; Baltimore *American*, July 9, 1800.

199. Baltimore *American*, July 24, 1800. See also "LOAN OFFICE versus 8% loans," Philadelphia *Aurora*, July 12, 1800; New York *American Citizen*, July 15, 1800; New York *Republican Watchtower*, July 16, 1800.

200. Wilmington, Del., *Mirror of the Times*, July 12, 1800; Philadelphia *Aurora*, July 15, 1800; Baltimore *American*, July 18, 1800.

201. Philadelphia *Aurora*, July 18, 1800; Baltimore *American*, July 24, 1800.

202. New editor of the *Gazette of the United States*, replacing John Ward Fenno, was Caleb Wayne.

203. Philadelphia *Aurora*, Aug. 5, 1800; Baltimore *American*, Aug. 8, 1800.

204. Philadelphia *Aurora*, Aug. 7, 1800; Baltimore *American*, Aug. 11, 1800.

205. Baltimore *American*, June 28, 1800; New York *American Citizen*, July 5, 1800; New York *Forlorn Hope*, July 5, 1800; Newark *Centinel of Freedom*, July 8, 1800; Stonington, Conn., *Impartial Journal*, July 22, 1800. Robert (not "Billy") Liston was the British minister to America.

206. Philadelphia *Aurora*, June 6, 1800; Richmond *Virginia Argus*, June 13, 1800.

207. See the Newark *Centinel of Freedom*, July 1, 1800; Lexington *Kentucky Gazette*, July 24, 1800.

208. Wilmington, Del., *Mirror of the Times*, June 21, 1800.

209. Newark *Centinel of Freedom*, July 1, 8, 1800.

210. These refer to issues discussed later in this study, especially Chap. 8.

211. Newark *Centinel of Freedom*, July 8, 1800.

212. "JONATHAN CHEATALL," *ibid.*, July 22, 1800.

213. Morristown, N. J., *Genius of Liberty*, June 26, 1800.

214. Wilmington, Del., *Mirror of the Times*, June 28, 1800; Baltimore *American*, July 4, 1800; Lexington *Kentucky Gazette*, July 24, 1800.

215. Portsmouth, N. H., *Republican Ledger*, Aug. 19, 1800.

216. Baltimore *American*, Aug. 7, 1800; Pittsburgh *Tree of Liberty*, Aug. 30, Sept. 30 (with a correction), 1800. See, earlier, Philadelphia *Aurora*, June 17, 1800; Lexington *Kentucky Gazette*, July 10, 1800; on Pickering and Chase.

217. Alexandria, Va., *Alexandria Times,* Jan. 10, 1800.

218. Augusta, Ga., *Augusta Chronicle,* Oct. 4, 1800.

219. Newark *Centinel of Fredom,* Sept. 23, 1800.

220. Philadelphia *Aurora,* Aug. 5, 1800; Richmond *Virginia Argus,* Aug. 19, 1800. Cf. *supra,* note 50.

221. The nickname came from Senator Uriah Tracy's expressed desire for a "war of extermination" with France; see Chap. 7. Philadelphia *Aurora,* Aug. 12, 1800; Pittsburgh *Tree of Liberty,* Aug. 20, 1800.

222. New London, Conn., *Bee,* Sept. 17, 1800; Boston *Constitutional Telegraphe,* Oct. 1, 1800.

223. "A PLAIN QUESTION," Richmond *Virginia Argus,* Sept. 19, 1800.

224. *Idem.*

225. These were similar to (but more venomous than) the *New Yorker* "profiles" of a century and a half later. Philadelphia *Aurora,* Oct. 13, 1800; Richmond *Virginia Argus,* Sept. 2, Oct. 21, 1800.

226. Richmond *Virginia Argus,* Sept. 2, 1800.

227. *Ibid.,* Sept. 16, 1800.

228. *Idem.*

229. Wilmington, Del., *Mirror of the Times,* Jan. 28, 1801.

IV EUROPEAN NEWS THROUGH AMERICAN EYES

1. In Chap. 1.

2. My notes on press reactions to American foreign relations equal the total on all other topics combined—and perforce I omitted many pertinent items. In the words of Julian K. Boyd (*Number 7: Alexander Hamilton's Secret Attempts to Control American Foreign Policy,* x) "during these early years the gravest threats to the existence of the United States were external in origin," though historians have largely ignored them.

3. Howard M. Jones, *America and French Culture,* 507, blames this on the Indian warfare in colonial days, the French reputation for profligacy, and religious bigotry.

4. Childs, *French Refugee Life,* 16–19; Bernard Faÿ, *The Revolutionary Spirit in France and America at the end of the Eighteenth Century,* 206–09, 215, 222–25; and Jones, *America and French Culture,* 507–08, 525–27, tell of the increasing friendship for, and influence of, France in America. Cf. Morton Borden, *Parties and Politics in the Early Republic, 1789–1815,* 47–48.

5. *Boston Gazette,* Sept. 21, 1789, and almost any issue for two or three years thereafter (that of Nov. 23, 1789, has little other news); Dupré, *"Kentucky Gazette,"* 169–80; and the Lexington *Kentucky Gazette,* Nov. 21, 1789, ff.; Edenton *State Gazette of North Carolina,* Sept. 1789, ff.; and the Charleston, S. C., *City Gazette,* 1789–90, *passim;* Jones, *America* . . . , 534–35.

6. *Boston Gazette,* Sept. 7, 1789.

7. Lexington *Kentucky Gazette,* Nov. 21, 1789; Winchester *Virginia Gazette,* Oct. 28, 1789; New York *Gazette of the United States,* Oct. 10, 1789.

8. Wilmington *Delaware Gazette,* July 16, 1792; Boston *Columbian Centinel,* Jan. 9, 1793; Jones, *America* . . . , 531–34; Bowers, *Jefferson and Hamilton,* 207–08.

9. E.g., the Philadelphia *National Gazette,* July 18, 1792; Easton *Maryland Herald,* July 24, 1792; *Boston Gazette,* Dec. 10, 17, 1792; Charleston *South Carolina State Gazette,* July 24, 1793; a summary in the Lexington *Kentucky Gazette* as late as Apr. 17, 1800; and countless others.

10. Norwich, Conn., *Norwich Packet,* Dec. 29, 1791–Jan. 26, 1792; Concord, N. H., *Mirrour,* May 6, 1793; Trenton *New Jersey State Gazette,* Sept. 18, 25, 1793; Danbury, Conn., *Republican Journal,* Sept. 23, 1793; Lexington *Kentucky Gazette,* Nov. 16, 23, 1793; Philadelphia *Aurora,* Aug. 27, 1795; Richmond, Va., *Richmond and Manchester Advertiser,* Sept. 10, 12, 17, 19, 1795; Cincinnati, [Ohio], *Centinel of the Northwest Territory,* Oct. 17, 24, 1795; Frankfort, Ky., *Palladium,* Apr. 17, 24, 1800; are but samples.

11. Wilmington *Delaware Gazette,* July 16, 1791; Philadelphia *Dunlap's American Daily Advertiser,* Jan. 3, 1793; *Boston Gazette,* Jan. 14, 1793; Charles Warren, *Jacobin and Junto,* 46–47; Charles D. Hazen, *Contemporary American Opinion of the French Revolution,* 281–83; serve to illustrate this point.

12. Poughkeepsie, N. Y., *Poughkeepsie Journal,* May 29, 1793, citing the Boston *Independent Chronicle.*

13. Norwich, Conn., *Norwich Packet,* June 28, 1792, crediting a letter to the staunchly Federalist *Columbian Centinel* (showing how univer-

sal was pro-French feeling) ; Windsor, Vt., *Morning Ray*, July 10, 1792; Philadelphia *National Gazette*, Aug. 15, 1792; Norfolk *Virginia Chronicle*, Aug. 18, 1792; Augusta, Ga., *Augusta Chronicle*, Aug. 18, 1792.

14. Philadelphia *National Gazette*, Feb. 9, 1793; see also Hazen, *Contemporary American Opinion*, 164.

15. *Boston Gazette*, Jan. 21, 24, 28, 1793; Boston *Columbian Centinel*, Jan. 26, 30, 1793; Boston *Independent Chronicle*, Jan. 24, 31, 1793; Boston *Massachusetts Mercury*, Jan. 30, 1793; Norwich, Conn., *Norwich Packet*, Jan. 31, 1793; Philadelphia *National Gazette*, Feb. 2, 1793.

16. Philadelphia *National Gazette*, Dec. 26, 29, 1792; Savannah *Georgia Gazette*, Jan. 24, 1793; *Boston Gazette*, Jan. 28, 1793; Philadelphia *American Daily Advertiser*, Jan. 3, Feb. 5, 18, 1793; Philadelphia *Gazette of the United States*, Feb. 6, 1793; Ellis Paxon Oberholtzer, *The Literary History of Philadelphia*, 125–26. See Hazen, *Contemporary American Opinion*, II, 89–96; and Bowers, *Jefferson and Hamilton*, 207–08; for other instances.

17. Dover, N. H., *Phenix*, Mar. 2, 1793; Philadelphia *National Gazette*, Feb. 2, 1793; Trenton *New Jersey State Gazette*, Feb. 13, 1793; Halifax *North Carolina Journal*, Feb. 27, 1793.

18. E.g., Wilmington *Delaware Gazette*, June 15, 1793; Augusta, Ga., *Southern Centinel*, July 24, 1794.

19. Item from the Philadelphia *American Daily Advertiser;* Trenton *New-Jersey State Gazette*, Mar. 27, 1793.

20. *Boston Gazette*, Jan. 21–Feb. 4, 1793; Boston *Independent Chronicle*, Jan. 17, 24, 1793; Philadelphia *National Gazette*, Jan. 30, Mar. 23, 1793; Charleston, S. C., *Columbian Herald*, Sept. 19, 1793; cf. Hazen, *Contemporary American Opinion*, 211–14; Philadelphia *General Advertiser*, May 23, 1793; Philadelphia *Independent Gazeteer*, June 30, 1792.

21. Charleston, S. C., *Columbian Herald*, Sept. 19, 1793.

22. Wilmington *Delaware Gazette*, July 16, 1791; Philadelphia *General Advertiser*, June 22, 1792; Philadelphia *National Gazette*, May 4, 1793; Norwich, Conn., *Norwich Packet*, May 16, 1793.

23. Bennington *Vermont Gazette*, Nov. 15, 1793; Philadelphia *Aurora*, Aug. 27, 1795; Boston *Independent Chronicle*, Sept. 3, 1795.

24. Boston *Independent Chronicle*, Apr. 27, May 12, July 7, 1791; Providence, R. I., *United States Chronicle*, Dec. 29, 1791.

25. Philadelphia *General Advertiser*, May 3, 1791. Adams' series, "Dis-

courses on Davila," ran in the Philadelphia *Gazette of the United States* during much of 1790.

26. Charleston *South Carolina State Gazette,* July 24, 1793; Concord, N. H., *Mirrour,* Nov. 26, 1793; New Haven *Connecticut Journal,* Jan. 2, 1793.

27. See Bowers, *Jefferson & Hamilton,* 207–11; Edenton *State Gazette of North Carolina* in 1790, cited in Jones, *America and French Culture,* 534–35n.; and the New York *Gazette of the United States,* Jan. 13, 1790, reprinting a letter from the Boston *Massachusetts Centinel.* But such instances were rare before 1793.

28. See the New Haven *Connecticut Journal,* Nov. 14, 1792 ff. (esp. Mar. 28, 1793); Hartford *Connecticut Courant,* cited in Philadelphia *National Gazette,* Jan. 16, 1793; Concord, N. H., *Mirrour,* Apr. 22, 1793; New York *Daily Advertiser,* Dec. 8, 1798; Morse, *Federalist Party,* 57–77. Even the Boston *Independent Chronicle,* Mar. 28, 1793, talked of "Louis the Unfortunate."

29. Columbia, S. C., *Columbia Gazette,* Jan. 14, 1794; Boston *Independent Chronicle,* Mar. 6, July 24, 1794; Vernon Stauffer, *New England and the Bavarian Illuminati,* 84n. On seizures, see Chap. 8.

30. Philadelphia *National Gazette,* Apr. 20, 1793; Bowers, *Jefferson & Hamilton,* 211, states the pun first appeared in the *Pittsburgh Gazette.*

31. Bowers, *Jefferson & Hamilton,* 211.

32. *Boston Gazette,* Nov. 19, 1792.

33. Philadelphia *National Gazette,* Feb. 20, Apr. 10, May 4, 1793; Chestertown, Md., *Apollo,* May 10, 1793; Boston *Independent Chronicle,* Apr. 18, 1793; New York *Diary,* Apr. 13, 1793; Augusta, Ga., *Augusta Chronicle,* May 4, 1793; Norwich, Conn., *Norwich Packet,* Apr. 4, 1793; Boston *American Apollo,* Mar. 22, 1793; Kingston, N. Y., *Farmer's Register,* May 11, 1793; Richmond *Virginia Gazette & Manchester Advertiser,* Apr. 29, 1793.

34. Augusta, Ga., *Southern Centinel,* July 25, 1793; Norwich, Conn., *Norwich Packet,* Feb. 14, 1793; "A Member of the French Republican Society," Charleston *South Carolina State Gazette,* Sept. 3, 1793; Danbury, Conn., *Republican Journal,* Aug. 5, 1793; "From a Virginia paper," Philadelphia *National Gazette,* May 25, 1793.

35. Norwich, Conn., *Norwich Packet,* Jan. 23, 1794; but cf. the New Haven *Connecticut Journal,* Jan. 16, 1794.

36. *Boston Gazette,* Oct. 8, 1792; Boston *Independent Chronicle,* July 25, 1793; Concord, N. H., *Hough's Concord Herald,* Nov. 14, 1793.

37. Carl Becker, *The Declaration of Independence,* 256; Jones, *Amer-*

*ica and French Culture,* 391–92; Hazen, *Contemporary American Opinion,* 269–71.

38. New Haven *Connecticut Journal,* July 6, 1791; Newark, N. J., *Centinel of Freedom,* Aug. 21, 1798.

39. Philadelphia *National Gazette,* Mar. 27, 1793; Boston *Independent Chronicle,* Jan. 30, 1794; Philadelphia *General Advertiser,* Feb. 18, 1794; Columbia, S. C., *Columbia Gazette,* June 20, 1794.

40. *New York Journal,* Jan. 13, 1798; Boston *Independent Chronicle,* Apr. 26, 1798; earlier, see the *Boston Gazette,* Apr. 29, 1793.

41. Boston *Independent Chronicle,* Mar. 6, July 24, 1794; Philadelphia *General Advertiser,* July 31, Sept. 4, 1794; *Aurora,* Feb. 18, 1795; Stauffer, *New England and Bavarian Illuminati,* 84n.

42. Edenton *State Gazette of North Carolina,* June 1, 1793.

43. Boston *Independent Chronicle,* Nov. 24, 1794.

44. New York *Greenleaf's New York Journal,* Mar. 11, 1796; New London, Conn., *Bee,* Nov. 8, 1797.

45. Boston *Independent Chronicle,* Nov. 16, 1797; Elizabethtown, *New Jersey Journal,* Nov. 15, 1797; Dedham, Mass., *Minerva,* cited in the Boston *Independent Chronicle,* Mar. 17, 1800.

46. Boston *Independent Chronicle,* July 11, 1796, Aug. 8, 1799, Mar. 31, 1800.

47. *Ibid.,* Aug. 6, 1798.

48. Newark *Centinel of Freedom,* Feb. 4, 1800.

49. Baltimore *American,* June 8, Sept. 28, Dec. 6, 1799; Boston *Independent Chronicle,* June 24, July 8, Dec. 20, 1799.

50. Only in Austria had the record been tarnished; item from the Philadelphia *Aurora,* New York *Diary,* Jan. 18, 1798. Cf. the *Aurora,* July 16, 1798; Boston *Independent Chronicle,* July 23, 1798, Sept. 16, 1799.

51. For early Federalist accounts, see the New Haven *Connecticut Journal,* Mar. 13, 1794, May 27, 1795. Many administration papers reprinted Pickering's later report of French spoilations; e.g., Wilmington, N. C., *Hall's Wilmington Gazette,* Apr. 6, 1797.

52. Boston *Independent Chronicle,* Apr. 16, 1798.

53. Augusta, Ga., *Augusta Chronicle,* Oct. 18, 1800.

54. See early letters concerning the *Droit d'Aubaine,* Philadelphia *General Advertiser,* Mar. 18, 1791; *Boston Gazette,* Apr. 18, 1791; Edenton *State Gazette of North Carolina,* Apr. 22, 1791.

55. *Baltimore Daily Intelligencer,* Oct. 31, 1793; New London, Conn., *Bee,* Oct. 18, 1797.

56. The French privateer apologized for his error; *Independent Chronicle,* July 27, 1797.

57. Savannah, Ga., *Columbian Museum,* May 24, 1799; Boston *Independent Chronicle,* July 24, 1800. See also the Charleston, S. C., *Columbian Herald,* Aug. 8, 1793; and the Federalist Wilmington, N. C., *Hall's Wilmington Gazette,* Apr. 4, 1799.

58. E.g., Philadelphia *Dunlap's American Daily Advertiser,* Aug. 12, 1793; *New York Weekly Museum,* Jan. 17, 1795; Boston *Independent Chronicle,* May 9, 1799.

59. Boston *Independent Chronicle,* Mar. 20, 23, 1796; Philadelphia *Aurora,* June 14, 30, 1796; Baltimore *Federal Gazette,* June 18, 1796; New London, Conn., *Bee,* July 6, 1797; Philadelphia *Carey's United States Recorder,* Mar. 1, 1798.

60. New London, Conn., *Bee,* July 6, 1797; "AN AMERICAN MERCHANT," Philadelphia *Carey's United States Recorder,* Mar. 8, 10, 1798.

61. "G.," New York *Time Piece,* Oct 13, 1797; Boston *Independent Chronicle,* Oct. 26, 1797.

62. Edenton, N. C., *State Gazette of North Carolina,* July 14, 1796; New York *Time Piece,* Oct. 13, 1797; Boston *Independent Chronicle,* May 14, 1798.

63. Philadelphia *National Gazette,* Jan. 12, Feb. 6, 1793; earlier, see "HUMPHREY," Boston *Herald of Freedom,* May 1, 1789.

64. *Albany Register,* Apr. 15, 1793; Boston *Independent Chronicle,* Aug. 26, 1793.

65. "AN OLD FRENCH SOLDIER," Philadelphia *General Advertiser,* Aug. 27, 1793. See items from this paper in the Boston *Independent Chronicle,* Jan. 20, 27, 1794; and from the New York *Diary,* Augusta, Ga., *Augusta Chronicle,* Feb. 15, 1794.

66. Harrisburg, Pa., *Oracle of Dauphin,* July 25, 1796.

67. From the *Virginia Gazette,* in the Norwich, Conn., *Norwich Packet,* Jan. 10, 1793.

68. Item from the Philadelphia *Aurora;* Boston *Independent Chronicle,* Dec. 25, 1797.

69. Boston *Independent Chronicle,* Jan. 8, 1798; New York *Journal and Patriotic Register,* Jan. 20, 1798.

70. Philadelphia *Aurora,* Dec. 22, 1796, citing a letter from Washington to Gen. Israel Putnam.

71. Edenton *State Gazette of North Carolina,* Dec. 16, 1796; surprisingly, this was captioned "From the [Boston] Columbian Centinel."

72. Norwich, Conn., *Norwich Packet,* Jan. 23, 1794; see also the Norfolk *Virginia Chronicle,* July 24, 1794.

73. E.g., Halifax *North Carolina Journal,* Apr. 27, 1795; Boston *Federal Orrery,* June 15, 1795, Oct. 20, 1796; Hazen, *Contemporary American Opinion,* 118, 283.

74. Mount Pleasant, N. J., *Jersey Chronicle,* May 2, 1795; Sag Harbor, N. Y., *Frothingham's Long Island Herald,* Sept. 13, 1797. Earlier, see the Alexandria, Va., *Columbian Mirror,* Aug. 21, 1793, ff.; Baltimore *Maryland Journal,* Aug. 30, 1793.

75. Boston *Independent Chronicle,* Aug. 5, 1799. Other toasts were too frequent to catalog; e.g., Dover, N. H., *Phenix,* Jan. 26, 1793; Philadelphia *National Gazette,* Feb. 2, 1793; Columbia, S. C., *Columbia Gazette,* Aug. 1, 1794; Philadelphia *Gazette of the United States,* Nov. 1, 1794; Philadelphia *Courier Français,* Jan. 13, Feb. 24, Apr. 3, 8, 1795; New York *Journal and Patriotic Register,* Jan. 6, 1798, etc.

76. Boston *Independent Chronicle,* Nov. 14, 18, 1793; *Baltimore Daily Intelligencer,* Nov. 27, 1793; Edenton *State Gazette of North Carolina,* Dec. 14, 1793.

77. Beverly W. Bond, Jr., "The Monroe Mission to France," *Johns Hopkins University Studies in Historical and Political Science,* series 25 (Feb.–Mar., 1907), 28–29; Philadelphia *Aurora,* Jan. 5, 13, 1796; New York *Gazette Française,* Jan. 11, 13, 1796; Richmond, Va., *Richmond and Manchester Advertiser,* Jan. 16, 1796; Faÿ, *Two Franklins,* 292–93.

78. New York *Journal and Patriotic Register,* Jan. 13, 1798.

79. Item from the Elizabethtown *New Jersey Journal,* Edenton *State Gazette of North Carolina,* June 1, 1793; Stauffer, *New England and Bavarian Illuminati,* 83; Link, *Democratic-Republican Societies,* 125.

80. Burlington, Vt., *Burlington Mercury,* Apr. 1, 1796; New York *Argus,* Dec. 1, 1795; Edenton *State Gazette of North Carolina,* Dec. 17, 1795; Boston *Independent Chronicle,* Oct. 5, 1797.

81. New York *Journal and Patriotic Register,* Jan. 6, 1798; Boston *Independent Chronicle,* Aug. 9, 1798.

82. Boston *Independent Chronicle,* Sept. 13, 1798.

83. Providence, R. I., *United States Chronicle,* Oct. 2, 1794.

84. Philadelphia *National Gazette,* Nov. 17, 1791; Philadelphia *Courier Française,* Dec. 7, 1797; Boston *Independent Chronicle,* Dec. 30, 1799.

85. Philadelphia *National Gazette,* June 21, 1792; the prayer was reprinted in the Philadelphia *Federal Gazette,* Sept. 23, 1793.

86. "John Bull," Philadelphia *National Gazette,* June 15, 1793; "PAETUS THRAESAE," Boston *Independent Chronicle,* July 11, Aug. 12, 1799.

87. Boston *Independent Chronicle,* Sept. 16, 1799; John Quincy Adams, *Parties in the United States,* 15, attests to the popularity of such sentiments.

88. Baltimore *American,* Sept. 9, 1799; Faÿ, *Two Franklins,* 162.

89. *Boston Gazette,* Jan. 28, 1793; Morton Borden, *Parties and Politics,* 47–48, stresses this feeling.

90. Boston *Independent Chronicle,* Dec. 16, 1793; Columbia, S. C., *Columbia Gazette,* Jan. 14, 1794; table by "Russell," Philadelphia *Aurora,* Dec. 12, 1795.

91. See Chap. 8.

92. Link, *Democratic-Republican Societies,* 9, 126; item from the Charleston, S. C., *Columbian Herald,* in the Boston *Independent Chronicle,* Sept. 5, 1793.

93. *Baltimore Daily Intelligencer,* Nov. 27, 1793; Edenton *State Gazette of North Carolina,* Dec. 14, 1793; *Pittsburgh Gazette,* Dec. 14, 1793.

94. Philadelphia *National Gazette,* Dec. 12, 1791; Knoxville, Tenn., *Knoxville Gazette,* Nov. 20, 1795. See, for example, Philadelphia *General Advertiser,* Jan. 28, 1793; Chestertown, Md., *Chestertown Appollo,* May 10, 1793; *Baltimore Daily Repository,* Sept. 18, 1793; New York *Columbian Gazetteer,* Oct. 7, 1793.

95. Resolutions of the Charleston Republican Society, *Baltimore Daily Repository,* Sept. 18, 1793.

96. "G.," New York *Time Piece,* Oct. 13, 1797; Boston *Independent Chronicle,* Oct. 26, 1797.

97. Philadelphia *General Advertiser,* Jan. 1, 1794.

98. Boston *Independent Chronicle,* May 19, 1796.

99. Philadelphia *National Gazette,* May 8, 1793; New York *Argus,* June 9, 1795; "An Orthodox Federalist," Boston *Independent Chronicle,* Feb. 16, 1797; Reading, Pa., *Readinger Adler,* Nov. 27, 1798.

100. Boston *Independent Chronicle,* May 8, 15, 1797, and "Heraclitus," Sept. 9, 1799; Baltimore *American,* May 27, 1799.

101. "Letter No. X," Philadelphia *Independent Gazetteer,* May 17, 1795; Charleston, S. C., *State Gazette,* June 22, 1795.

102. Alexandria, Va., *Alexandria Times,* Jan. 13, 1800.

103. E.g., the Charleston, S. C., *City Gazette*, June 30, 1790; Reading, Pa., *Readinger Adler*, Oct. 16, 1798, Apr. 15, 1800.

104. New York *Gazette of the United States*, July 22, 1789; Boston *Herald of Freedom*, Aug. 7, 1789.

105. E.g., the Philadelphia *General Advertiser*, May 23, 1793.

106. Boston *Independent Chronicle*, Oct. 6, 1794; *Baltimore Daily Intelligencer*, Apr. 30, May 2, 1794; Philadelphia *General Advertiser*, May 28, 1793; Augusta, Ga., *Southern Centinel*, June 27, 1793; Edenton *State Gazette of North Carolina*, Feb. 4, 1794.

107. Winchester *Virginia Gazette*, Sept. 2, 1789; Augusta, Ga., *Augusta Chronicle*, June 5, 1790; Bennington *Vermont Gazette*, May 17, 1790; Danbury, Conn., *Republican Journal*, Aug. 5, 1793.

108. *New-York Journal*, May 4, 1790; Bennington *Vermont Gazette*, May 17, 1790; Edenton *State Gazette of North Carolina*, Nov. 26, 1790; Philadelphia *National Gazette*, May 11, 1793. See Bradford Perkins, *The First Rapprochement*, 2–5.

109. Augusta, Ga., *Augusta Chronicle*, Jan. 1, 1791; cf. the Philadelphia *National Gazette*, June 8, 15, 1793.

110. Boston *Massachusetts Centinel*, cited in the *New-York Journal*, Apr. 15, 1790.

111. Philadelphia *General Advertiser*, June 14, 1793, Mar. 21, 1794; Norwich, Conn., July 2, 1793.

112. Miller, *Federalist Era*, 152–53; Bassett, *Federalist System*, 66; Perkins, *First Rapprochement*, 105; Boston *Independent Chronicle*, Sept. 22, 1794; see Chap. 6.

113. E.g., Boston *Herald of Freedom*, June 30, 1789.

114. Item from New York, *Baltimore Daily Intelligencer*, Mar. 25, 1794.

115. *Boston Gazette*, Sept. 19, 1791; Philadelphia *National Gazette*, June 4, 1792; *New York Weekly Museum*, July 18, 1795; item from the Boston *Independent Chronicle*, Dumfries, Va., *Republican Journal*, Aug. 18, 1796.

116. Edenton *State Gazette of North Carolina*, Feb. 7, 1794.

117. *Baltimore Daily Repository*, Oct. 29, 1791; Rutland, Vt., *Farmers' Library*, Aug. 26, 1793; "Orthodoxus," Boston *Independent Chronicle*, Mar. 26, 1798; Philadelphia *National Gazette*, Feb. 2, 1793.

118. "SYPHAX," Boston *Independent Chronicle*, May 20, 1799.

119. Easton *Maryland Herald*, Aug. 30, 1791; Philadelphia *Freeman's Journal*, Aug. 17, 1791; Philadelphia *National Gazette*, Nov. 17, 1791; Wilmington *Delaware and Eastern Shore Advertiser*, Jan. 31, 1795;

Baltimore *Maryland Journal,* Sept. 15, 1796; Boston *Independent Chronicle,* Oct. 23, 1797.

120. Philadelphia *General Advertiser,* July 10, 1794. For similar opinions, see the Exeter, N. H., *Lamson's Weekly Visitor,* May 26, 1795, June 20, 1795; Baltimore *American,* July 4, 1799.

121. Philadelphia *Aurora,* Aug. 21, 1798.

122. Augusta, Ga., *Southern Centinel,* Nov. 14, 1793.

123. Richmond *Virginia Argus,* Apr. 5, 1799. See also the Lexington *Kentucky Gazette,* May 13, 1797; Reading, Pa., *Readinger Adler,* Dec. 3, 1798; Raleigh, N. C., *Raleigh Register,* Sept. 30, 1800.

124. Boston *Independent Chronicle,* Oct. 23, 1797; Frankfort, Ky., *Palladium,* Sept. 5, 1799; Philadelphia *Aurora,* Mar. 12, 1799; Richmond *Virginia Argus,* Mar. 26, 1799.

125. Georgetown, D. C., *Columbian Chronicle,* Mar. 6, 1795; Georgetown, D. C., *Centinel of Liberty,* Feb. 18, 1800.

126. Newark *Centinel of Freedom,* May 5, 1797; the Boston *Independent Chronicle,* July 29, 1799, denied even a community of interest with England.

127. Augusta, Ga., *Augusta Chronicle,* June 18, 1791; "AMERICANUS," Philadelphia *National Gazette,* Dec. 8, 1791; "The LIAR," Norwich, Conn., *Weekly Register,* Apr. 22, 1794.

128. *New-York Journal,* June 25, 1790; Boston *Independent Chronicle,* Dec. 16, 1793, Apr. 7, 1794; Columbia, S. C., *Columbia Gazette,* Jan. 14, 1794; item in the Edenton *State Gazette of North Carolina,* May 2, 1794.

129. See Chaps. 5 and 7.

130. Boston *Independent Chronicle,* Apr. 24, May 5, 1794; see also an item from the New York *Commercial Advertiser,* Savannah, Ga., *Columbian Museum,* Oct. 15, 1799.

131. E.g., "CYMON," Providence, R. I., *United States Chronicle,* Apr. 3, 1794.

132. *Baltimore Daily Intelligencer,* Apr. 24, 1794; item in the Boston *Independent Chronicle,* May 12, 1794; "A WHIG OF 1775," Norwich, Conn., *Weekly Register,* Mar. 18, 1794; Charleston *South Carolina State Gazette,* Feb. 6, 1794.

133. Philadelphia *General Advertiser,* May 19, 1794; Boston *Independent Chronicle,* May 29, 1794.

134. "Worcester," Boston *Independent Chronicle,* June 5, 1794.

135. E.g., *ibid.,* Feb. 10, Oct. 9, 1794, Feb. 16, 1797.

136. *Ibid.,* Oct. 27, 1796, Aug. 9, 1798; Raleigh, N. C., *Raleigh Regis-*

*ter,* Nov. 12, 1799; Lexington *Kentucky Gazette,* Jan. 2, 1796. Cf. Boyd, *Number 7,* xiii, 84–85.

137. "Foresight," Boston *Independent Chronicle,* Apr. 7, 1794.

138. Charleston, S. C., *City Gazette,* May 9, 1799; Philadelphia *Aurora,* Feb. 9, 1799; Richmond *Virginia Argus,* Feb. 15, Nov. 12, 1799.

TARGET: AMERICAN FOREIGN POLICY

1. Philadelphia *Aurora,* May 16, 1795; Frederick J. Turner, "The Policy of France toward the Mississippi Valley in the Period of Washington and Adams," *American Historical Review* 10 (Jan., 1905), 256; Harry C. Allen, *Great Britain and the United States,* 274–75; also *supra,* Chap. 4.

2. "THE CATERER," Letter "No. III," *New-York Journal,* Mar. 14, 1791; *Boston Gazette,* July 18, 1791. See also Young, *Democratic Republicans,* 268, for uneasiness on the New York frontier.

3. Item from Albany, New Brunswick, N. J., *Brunswick Gazette,* Feb. 28, 1792.

4. *Boston Gazette,* July 18, 1791.

5. Newark, N. J., *Woods's Newark Gazette,* Jan. 12, 1792; Baltimore *Maryland Journal,* Jan. 25, 1792; Philadelphia *National Gazette,* Jan. 9, 1792, Oct. 5, 1793.

6. E.g., the New Haven *Connecticut Journal,* Dec. 29, 1790; *New-York Journal,* Mar. 7, 1791; *infra,* Chap. 9.

7. Letter from Pittsburgh, Concord, N. H., Hough's *Concord Herald,* Feb. 14, 1793; Dover, N. H., *Phenix,* Mar. 2, 1793. See Chap. 9, on the Treaty of New York.

8. Boston *Independent Chronicle,* May 16, 1793; *Boston Gazette,* June 24, 1793; Philadelphia *National Gazette,* Jan. 9, 1792; Rutland, Vt., *Farmers' Library,* Apr. 15, 1793; Andrews, *Pittsburgh's Post-Gazette,* 42.

9. Philadelphia *General Advertiser,* Dec. 14, 1791; *Boston Gazette,* Jan. 2, 9, 30, 1792; Philadelphia *National Gazette,* Jan. 9, 1792.

10. Boston *Independent Chronicle,* Oct. 9, 1794.

11. E.g., the open letter of the New York City Democratic Society, Charleston *South Carolina State Gazette*, July 11, 1794; New London *Connecticut Gazette*, Apr. 3, 1794; Halifax *North Carolina Journal*, Apr. 30, 1794; Trenton *New Jersey State Gazette*, July 16, 1794; *Baltimore Daily Intelligencer*, July 19, Sept. 9, 1794. See *supra*, Chap. 4; Link, *Democratic-Republican Societies*, 142–43.

12. Portland [Maine] *Cumberland Gazette*, Mar. 29, 1790; Baltimore *Maryland Journal*, Apr. 6, 1790.

13. Lexington *Kentucky Gazette*, May 17, 1794; Miller, *Federalist Era*, 187; Bassett, *Federalist System*, 78–79.

14. *Boston Gazette*, Dec. 17, 1792; Dover, N. H., *Phenix*, Dec. 26, 1792; Philadelphia *National Gazette*, Feb. 2, 1793.

15. Charles M. Thomas, *American Neutrality in 1793*, 14; Bowers, *Jefferson and Hamilton*, 215–16; Bassett, *Federalist System*, 86.

16. The document was widely republished; e.g., the Germantown, Pa., *Germantauner Zeitung*, Apr. 30, 1793, and other foreign language newspapers; Knoxville, Tenn., *Knoxville Gazette*, June 15, 1793; Kingston, N. Y., *Farmer's Register*, May 4, 1793; *Boston Gazette*, May 6, 1793; etc.

17. The treaties are summarized in Bassett, *Federalist System*, 84, 119. See Thomas, *American Neutrality*, 126–27; Samuel Flagg Bemis, *Jay's Treaty*, 137; S. F. Bemis, "Washington's Farewell Address: A Foreign Policy of Independence," *American Historical Review* 39 (Jan., 1932), 250.

18. Bemis, "Washington's Farewell Address," 250.

19. Jefferson to Madison, June 23, 1793, Jefferson's *Works* (federal edition), VII, 407–08. Cf. Madison to Jefferson, June 10, 1793, Gaillard Hunt, ed., *Writings of James Madison*, VI, 127; Bemis, *Jay's Treaty*, 140, 145; Malone, *TJ*, III, 69–71, McLaughlin, *Constitutional History*, 252.

20. Philadelphia *National Gazette*, May 15, 1793; also the issues of Apr. 27, May 4, 18, 1793. But most eschewed any idea of war with Britain at this time; see the Boston *Independent Chronicle*, Aug. 26, 1793; *New-York Journal*, June 19, 1793.

21. Forman, "Political Activities," 68; Minnigerode, *Jefferson*, 181; Marsh, "The Griswold Story," 72; Leary, *That Rascal Freneau*, 235–36; Axelrad, *Philip Freneau*, 255–57.

22. Philadelphia *National Gazette*, June 1, 1793; Woodbury, *Public Opinion*, 64–65. See also Philadelphia *General Advertiser*, July 15, 22, 1793, on the probability of war with France.

23. Philadelphia *National Gazette*, June 5, 8, 1793; Columbia *South*

*Carolina Gazette*, July 16, 1793; Forman, "Political Activities," 68; Woodbury, *Public Opinion*, 65–66.

24. Elizabethtown *New Jersey Journal*, May 15, June 12, 1793. Fee, *Transition*, 36, however, states most of New Jersey seemed to approve the proclamation; cf. Prince, *New Jersey's Jeffersonian Republicans*, 13–14.

25. *Boston Gazette*, May 13, 20, 1793.

26. Philadelphia *National Gazette*, July 24, 1793; "A Republican," Philadelphia *General Advertiser*, July 15, 1793; Boston *Independent Chronicle*, May 7, 16, 23, 1793; Hartford *Connecticut Courant*, July 29, Aug. 5, 26, 1793; Hazen, *Contemporary American Opinion*, 180; Luetscher, *Early Political Machinery*, 32; Stauffer, *New England and Bavarian Illuminati*, 104.

27. *New-York Journal*, June 15, 1793; Charleston, S. C., *Columbian Herald*, July 25, 1793; Philadelphia *National Gazette*, May 15, 18, 22, Aug. 3, 1793.

28. Philadelphia *National Gazette*, Sept. 21, 1793; Richmond, Va., *Richmond & Manchester Advertiser*, Sept. 12, 1793; Charleston, S. C., *Columbian Herald*, July 25, 1793; *Baltimore Daily Intelligencer*, Dec. 10, 1793.

29. Boston *Columbian Centinel*, May 18, July 31, Aug. 14, 24, 1793; Feb. 26, 1794; see Morse, *Federalist Party*, 71n.

30. Philadelphia *National Gazette*, July 24, 1793.

31. Rutland, Vt., *Farmers' Library*, May 27, 1794.

32. Chestertown, Md., *Apollo*, May 10, 1793; *New-York Journal*, June 15, 1793; Philadelphia *National Gazette*, July 24, 31, 1793; resolutions from Amelia and Shenandoah counties, Virginia, *Baltimore Daily Intelligencer*, Nov. 11, Dec. 10, 1793; Charleston, S. C., *City Gazette*, Mar. 17, 1794; Boston *Independent Chronicle*, Apr. 18, 1794; Philadelphia *American Daily Advertiser*, July 29, 1794.

33. "VERITAS," Philadelphia *National Gazette*, June 1, 1793, *et seq.;* July 24, 1793; "Z," *Richmond Chronicle* (cited *ibid.*, May 22, 1793).

34. Letter in the Charleston, S. C., *Star and Charleston Daily Advertiser*, July 12, 1793; Louis B. Dunbar, "A Study of 'Monarchical' Tendencies in the United States, from 1776 to 1801," 116.

35. Philadelphia *Gazette of the United States*, June 8, 29–July 20, 1793; McMaster, *A History*, II, 114, 119–20; Malone, *TJ*, III, 110–11; Bowers, *Jefferson & Hamilton*, 225–26; Woodbury, *Public Opinion*, 73.

36. Philadelphia *National Gazette*, Aug. 24–Sept. 18, 1793; Mc-

Master, *A History,* II, 114; Malone, *TJ,* III, 110; McLaughlin, *Constitutional History,* 253, 255–56; Bowers, *Jefferson & Hamilton,* 226.

37. Philadelphia *National Gazette,* June 15, 1793.

38. *New York Daily Advertiser,* July 13, 1793.

39. E.g., Philadelphia *American Daily Advertiser,* Mar. 15, July 29, 1794; Boston *Independent Chronicle,* Apr. 18, 1794; Woodbury, *Public Opinion,* 70–71; Luetscher, *Early Political Machinery,* 43–44; Link, *Democratic-Republican Societies,* 127–30.

40. Bassett, *Federalist System,* 118; Miller, *Federalist Era,* 141; Allen, *Great Britain,* 284; Charleston, S. C., *Columbian Herald,* July 25, 1793.

41. Philadelphia *National Gazette,* June 5, 8, 1793; Norwich, Conn., *Norwich Weekly Register,* June 25, 1793; Charleston, S. C., *Star,* July 12, 1793; Salem, Mass., *Salem Gazette,* June 18, 1793.

42. "Brutus," Philadelphia *National Gazette,* June 8, 1793.

43. Philadelphia *General Advertiser,* Aug. 3, 1793; Philadelphia *National Gazette,* Aug. 3, 28, 31, 1793; Charleston, S. C., *Star,* July 12, 1793; Salem, Mass., *Salem Gazette,* Aug. 13, 1793, cited in James D. Phillips, "Salem's Part in the Naval War with France," *New England Quarterly* 16 (Dec., 1943), 546–47.

44. "ARCHY SIMPLE," and "CENTINEL," Charleston, S. C., *Columbian Herald,* Aug. 29, 31, 1793, replying to the Charleston *City Gazette,* Aug. 15, 1793.

45. "JUBA," Philadelphia *General Advertiser,* July 22, 1793.

46. Charleston, S. C., *Star,* Aug. 27, 1793; Jefferson to Madison, Ford, ed., *The Writings of Thomas Jefferson,* IX, 211–15; Jefferson, *Anas,* in Bergh, ed., *The Writings of Thomas Jefferson,* I, 363–65, 373; Jefferson to G. Morris, Aug. 16, 1793; *ibid.,* IX, 202–09; Malone, *TJ,* III, 114–19.

47. Augusta, Ga., *Southern Centinel,* July 11, 1793.

48. Augusta, Ga., *Augusta Chronicle,* July 20, 27 ("A REPUBLICAN"), 1793; Staunton, Va., *Staunton Spy,* Feb. 1, 1794.

49. Boston *Columbian Centinel,* Aug. 24, 1793; the Constitutional Society of Boston, *ibid.,* Nov. 6, 16, Dec. 18, 1793; Boston *Independent Chronicle,* Oct. 10, 14, 1793; Thomas, *American Neutrality,* 212–13; Link, *Democratic-Republican Societies,* 149; cf. Jefferson to Madison, Sept. 1, 1793, Bergh, ed., *Writings of Thomas Jefferson,* IX, 212.

50. "Brutus," *Greenleaf's New York Argus,* May 7, 1794; "GRACCHUS," Philadelphia *General Advertiser,* Feb. 10, 1794; Philadelphia *American Star,* Feb. 13, 1794; Norfolk, Va., *Norfolk Chronicle,* Mar.

1, 1794; Charleston, S. C., *Columbian Herald,* Mar. 17, 1794. See Genêt's earlier protest, *Baltimore Daily Intelligencer,* Nov. 5, 1793.

51. Boston *Columbian Centinel,* Nov. 13, 1793; Boston *Independent Chronicle,* Nov. 25, 1793, Jan. 20, 1794; Augusta, Ga., *Southern Centinel,* Nov. 21, 1793. Cf. Thomas, *American Neutrality,* 216–19; and Morse, *Federalist Party,* 72–74 (the best secondary account).

52. Philadelphia *National Gazette,* May 22, 25, 1793; Charleston, S. C., *Columbian Herald,* Aug. 15, 1793; Philadelphia *American Daily Advertiser,* Aug. 27, 1793.

53. Boston *Independent Chronicle,* Mar. 13, 1794.

54. *Boston Gazette,* May 20, 1793; Charleston, S. C., *Columbian Herald,* July 25, 1793; Petersburg *Virginia Gazette,* July 26, 1796; Bemis, *Jay's Treaty,* 137. But cf. "No Jacobin," Charleston, S. C., *Telegraphe,* Aug. 31, 1793 (contending the right was not granted France, but only forbidden to her opponents); Charleston *Columbian Herald,* Aug. 8, 10, 1793.

55. Charleston, S. C., *Columbian Herald,* Sept. 7, 1793.

56. This is challenged in Frank Monaghan, *John Jay,* 412; see Joseph Charles, "The Jay Treaty: The Origins of the American Party System," *William and Mary Quarterly,* series 3, 12 (Oct. 1955), 590n. For the period prior to 1795, however, the statement seems substantially correct. Cf. Miller, *Federalist Era,* 140–41; Young, *Democratic Republicans,* 366–67.

57. Bemis, "Washington's Farewell Address," 250; McMaster, *A History,* II, 167.

58. Excerpt from the New Brunswick, N. J., *Advertiser,* Philadelphia *National Gazette,* Sept. 28, 1793.

59. Maude Howlett Woodfin, "Citizen Genêt and His Mission" (University of Chicago doctoral dissertation, 1928), 585–92; Philadelphia *National Gazette,* Aug. 7, 17, 24, 1793; Philadelphia *Dunlap's American Daily Advertiser,* July 31, Aug. 1, 13, 27, 1793; Winchester *Virginia Centinel,* Aug. 12, 19, 20, 1793; Portsmouth *New Hampshire Gazette,* Aug. 20, 1793; Newport, R. I., *Newport Mercury,* Aug. 20, 1793; Charleston, S. C., *Star,* Aug. 24, 1793; *New-York Journal,* June 19, July 4, 6, 18, 21, 1793.

60. Item from the *New-York Journal,* Philadelphia *National Gazette,* July 31, 1795.

61. Miller, *Federalist Era,* 141; Bassett, *Federalist System,* 119–20.

62. Woodbury, *Public Opinion,* 67; Charleston, S. C., *Patriotic Français,* May 19, 1796; Philadelphia *Aurora,* May 16, July 1, 1796; Norfolk, Va., *American Gazette and General Advertiser,* July 12, 1796.

63. E.g., Minnigerode, *Jefferson, passim;* Bowers, *Jefferson & Hamilton,* 214–20, 224–25, 227–31. The best account is Woodfin, "Citizen Genêt," yet even this leaves one uncertain as to whether Genêt was made a scapegoat by Jefferson or merely the victim of his own blunders; cf. Axelrad, *Philip Freneau,* 253–61.

64. Cf. Woodfin, "Citizen Genêt," 564; and Jefferson to Gouverneur Morris, Aug. 16, 1793, Bergh, ed., *Writings of Thomas Jefferson,* IX, 182.

65. Philadelphia *Dunlap's American Daily Advertiser,* Apr. 22, May 21, 24, 30, 1793; *Baltimore Daily Repository,* May 15, 20, 1793; Winchester *Virginia Centinel,* May 20, 1793; Germantown, Pa., *Germantauner Zeitung,* May 28, 1793; Bowers, *Jefferson & Hamilton,* 217–18; Minnigerode, *Jefferson,* 193; Woodfin, "Citizen Genêt," 118; Jefferson to Monroe, May 5, 1793, Ford, ed., *Writings of Thomas Jefferson,* II, 75–78.

66. Philadelphia *National Gazette,* Apr. 24, 27 ("AN OLD SOLDIER"), May 1, 4, 15, 1793; Concord, N. H., *Hough's Concord Herald,* May 9, 1793; Philadelphia *Dunlap's American Daily Advertiser,* May 14, 1793; Philadelphia *General Advertiser,* May 17[?], 1793; Faÿ, *Two Franklins,* 176; Thomas, *American Neutrality,* 83; Minnigerode, *Jefferson,* 196–97.

67. Philadelphia *National Gazette,* May 18, 22, 25, 1793; Philadelphia *Dunlap's American Daily Advertiser,* May 23, 1793; Boston *Independent Chronicle,* May 30, 1793; Richmond *Virginia Gazette,* June 3, 1793; *Boston Gazette,* May 27, 1793; Philadelphia *General Advertiser,* June 4, 7, 1793; Halifax *North Carolina Journal,* June 5, 1793; Augusta, Ga., *Southern Centinel,* June 13, 1793; Malone, *TJ,* III, 93–95; Thomas, *American Neutrality,* 84; Faÿ, *Two Franklins,* 177; Bowers, *Jefferson & Hamilton,* 219–20; Minnigerode, *Jefferson,* 196–97.

68. Charleston, S. C., *Star,* July 12, 1793; Faÿ, *Two Franklins,* 177–78; Bassett, *Federalist System,* 91–92. Jefferson's part in the treatment accorded the French minister has never been made completely clear. Genêt himself contended the Secretary of State led him on, pretending friendship for France, to betray him as a scapegoat for party purposes; Minnigerode, *Jefferson,* agrees. Malone, *TJ,* III, 90–139, discounts such a possibility; most authorities feel Genêt's downfall resulted from his own conduct, though Woodfin, "Citizen Genêt," esp. 338–39, is not absolutely certain he was not used as a cat's paw.

69. *Boston Gazette,* Apr. 29, 1793.

70. Boston *Independent Chronicle,* May 16, 1793 (supplement); "AN OLD SOLDIER," Philadelphia *General Advertiser,* June 7, 1793.

71. Richmond *Virginia Gazette and Richmond and Manchester Advertiser,* June 27, 1793; Charleston, S. C., *Star,* July 12, 1793.

72. Ellis P. Oberholtzer, *Literary History of Philadelphia,* 126–27; McMaster, *A History,* II, 104. Cf. Woodfin, "Citizen Genêt," 237.

73. Democrats in many areas praised the pronouncement; e.g., Boston *Independent Chronicle,* May 30, 1793.

74. On privateers, see, e.g., Philadelphia *Dunlap's American Daily Advertiser,* May 13, 1793; Norfolk *Virginia Chronicle,* July 6, 1793; *Norfolk and Portsmouth General Advertiser,* July 6, 1793; Woodfin, "Citizen Genêt," 367–70, 598–602, 614–17. Among the many items on recruiting, Portsmouth *New Hampshire Gazette,* May 14, 1793; Salem, Mass., *Salem Gazette,* May 14, 1793; Charleston, S.C., *Star,* Aug. 29, 1793; Richmond *Virginia Gazette and Richmond Chronicle,* Jan. 24, 1794; Norwich, Conn., *Weekly Register,* July 1, 1794. The most damning indictment of Genêt's conduct is found in Jefferson's letter to Gouverneur Morris, Aug. 16, 1793, Bergh, ed., *Writings of Thomas Jefferson,* IX, esp. 193–94, 201–04; see Malone, *TJ,* III, 126–28; Bassett, *Federalist System,* 92–95.

75. Turner, "Policy of France," 261–62; John H. Wolfe, *Jeffersonian Democracy in South Carolina,* 73–75. On Genêt's schemes to conquer Louisiana, see Link, *Democratic-Republican Societies,* 133–41; Woodfin, "Citizen Genêt," 433–35, 446–55; Thomas, *American Neutrality,* 177–86; Bassett, *Federalist System,* 79–83; Turner, "Policy," 260–63; John Bakeless, *Background to Glory,* 339–45; Charleston, S. C., *Star,* Aug. 27, 1793.

76. Augusta, Ga., *Southern Centinel,* Jan. 30, 1794. See Genêt's letter of July 4, 1797, to Jefferson; Woodfin, "Citizen Genêt," 564–65; and also Minnigerode, *Jefferson,* 172, 188–89, 211–13, on this subject.

77. Charleston, S. C., *Star,* Aug. 29, 1793; Concord, N. H., *Hough's Concord Herald,* Jan. 2, 9, 16, 1794; New Haven *Connecticut Journal,* Jan. 16, 1794; Hazen, *Contemporary American Opinion,* 184–85; Bassett, *Federal System,* 98.

78. Jones, *America and French Culture,* 132–34; for a sample of notice in the American press at this time see the Philadelphia *Dunlap's American Daily Advertiser,* Feb. 23, 1793.

79. Philadelphia *National Gazette,* June 29, 1793; Philadelphia *Dunlap's American Daily Advertiser,* July 14, Aug. 6, 7, 1793; Philadelphia *Courier Politique,* Dec. 10, 1793; *Edwards' Baltimore Daily Advertiser,* Dec. 21, 1793.

80. Philadelphia *Dunlap's American Daily Advertiser,* July 31, 1793; Augusta, Ga., *Southern Centinel,* Sept. 19, 1793; *Edwards' Baltimore*

*Daily Advertiser,* Jan. 2, 1794; New Haven *Connecticut Journal,* Jan. 9, 1794; for later comments on French governmental relief, the Boston *Independent Chronicle,* Sept. 19, 1796. The most coherent account of this involved affair is in Woodfin, "Citizen Genêt," 415–21.

81. Faÿ, *Two Franklins,* 182–83; the *General Advertiser* is said to have gained 300 subscribers within two months after Genêt's arrival.

82. Boston *Independent Chronicle,* June 13, July 25, 1793; *Baltimore Daily Repository,* Sept. 17, Oct. 1, 1793; Philadelphia *Dunlap's American Daily Advertiser,* July 31, Dec. 22, 1793; *Baltimore Daily Intelligencer,* Nov. 17, Dec. 30, 1793; New Haven *Connecticut Journal,* Jan. 2, 1794; Halifax *North Carolina Journal,* Jan. 1, Feb. 19, 1794; Augusta, Ga., *Southern Centinel,* Jan. 30, 1794; Salem, Mass., *Salem Gazette,* Jan. 7, 1794; Woodfin, "Citizen Genêt," 417–18, 440, 585–86; "A Mechanic," *New-York Journal,* Aug. 10, 1793.

83. Philadelphia *Dunlap's American Daily Advertiser,* Aug. 15, 1793 (citing the letter of Aug. 5, 1793); Petersburg *Virginia Gazette and Petersburg Intelligencer,* Aug. 23, 1793. Wilcocks continued his criticism of Genêt for months; see the letter from the New York *Daily Advertiser* in the Edenton *State Gazette of North Carolina,* Dec. 14, 1793. The name was frequently spelled "Willcocks."

84. Philadelphia *Dunlap's American Daily Advertiser,* Aug. 15, 1793; Boston *Independent Chronicle,* Nov. 14, 1793.

85. Charleston, S. C., *Columbian Herald,* Dec. 5, 14, 1793; *Edwards' Baltimore Daily Advertiser,* Nov. 25, 1793; *New-York Journal,* Nov. 27, 1793; Boston *Independent Chronicle,* Dec. 9, 1793.

86. Philadelphia *Aurora,* Sept. 5, 1795; Charleston, S. C., *Columbian Herald,* Oct. 5, 1795.

87. Genêt charged Washington with arbitrary and unconstitutional action in depriving Duplaine of his exequatur; *Baltimore Daily Intelligencer,* Nov. 5, 1793.

88. Philadelphia *Federal Gazette,* Nov. 9, 1793; Edenton *State Gazette of North Carolina,* Dec. 14, 1793.

89. Charleston, S. C., *City Gazette,* in the Charleston *State Gazette,* Feb. 14, 1794; "A Friend to Liberty and Equality," Newark, N. J., *Woods's Newark Gazette,* Aug. 14, 1795.

90. See his letter to the *Albany Argus,* Sept. 29, 1823, quoted in Woodfin, "Citizen Genêt," 574. Earlier disavowals were frequent; e.g., *New-York Journal,* Aug. 24, Dec. 28, 1793; Hartford *Connecticut Courant,* Aug. 26, 1793; Trenton *New Jersey State Gazette,* Oct. 30, 1793; Staunton, Va., *Staunton Spy,* Nov. 9, 1793; Norwich, Conn., *Weekly*

*Register,* Jan. 7, 14, 1794; Providence, R. I., *United States Chronicle,* Jan. 16, 1794; Concord, N. H., *Hough's Concord Herald,* Jan. 23, 1794; (various letters from Genêt to Washington, Jefferson, Moultrie, and Randolph). See Malone, *TJ,* III, 135–36, Monaghan, *John Jay,* 355–59.

91. Jefferson wrote Madison, Sept. 1, 1793; "I can assure you it is a fact." (Bergh, ed., *Writings of Thomas Jefferson,* IX, 213. Bemis, *Jay's Treaty,* 149, holds that Jefferson had hoped to keep Genêt's threat a secret. See also Thomas, *American Neutrality,* 225–26; Woodfin, "Citizen Genêt," 367, 382n.; and Leary, *That Rascal Freneau,* 238, on the subject.

92. Woodfin, "Citizen Genêt," 334, 373; reprint, from the New York *Diary,* in the Charleston S. C., *Columbian Herald,* Aug. 27, 1793; "A Citizen," *New-York Journal,* Aug. 14, 1793; Charleston, S. C., *Columbian Herald,* Aug. 27, 1793. For sample Federalist comments, see "Henry," from the Hartford *Connecticut Courant,* Worcester *Massachusetts Spy,* Nov. 28, 1793; New Brunswick, N. J., *Arnett's Brunswick Advertiser,* Nov. 12, 1793; *Hartford Gazette,* Jan. 16, 1794; Philadelphia *American Star,* Feb. 18, 1794. Two years later, the Boston *Columbian Centinel,* Mar. 9, Dec. 28, 1796, referred to the "insidious conduct of Genêt."

93. Philadelphia *Dunlap's American Daily Advertiser,* Aug. 21, 1793.

94. *New-York Journal,* Aug 21, 1793; Norwich, Conn., *Weekly Register,* Sept. 3, 1793; "An Inquirer," from the *New-York Journal,* Boston *Independent Chronicle,* Sept. 2, 1793.

95. *New-York Journal,* Aug. 14, 21, 22, 31, Sept. 7, 1793; Philadelphia *Dunlap's American Daily Advertiser,* Aug. 21, 1793; Charleston, S. C., *Columbian Herald,* Aug. 27, 1793; Newburyport, Mass., *Impartial Herald,* Aug. 31, 1793.

96. "A FRENCH DESCENDANT," Charleston, S. C., *Star,* Aug. 31, 1793; "BOLD JUSTICE," Boston *Independent Charonicle,* July 25, 1793; "Hamlet," Winchester *Virginia Centinel,* Sept. 16, 1793; "JUBA," Philadelphia *National Gazette,* July 10, Aug. 17, 21, 1793.

97. *Baltimore Daily Repository,* June 14, 1793; "GRACCHUS," Philadelphia *General Advertiser,* Feb. 10, 1794; Philadelphia *American Star,* Feb. 13, 1794; Norfolk, Va., *Norfolk Chronicle,* Mar. 1, 1794; Charleston, S. C., *Columbian Herald,* Mar. 17, 1794.

98. Concord, N. H., *Hough's Concord Herald,* Jan. 2, 1794; Woodfin, "Citizen Genêt," 208.

99. E.g., Philadelphia *General Advertiser,* Dec. 10, 1793; Charleston *South Carolina State Gazette,* Dec. 31, 1793; Edenton *State Gazette*

of *North Carolina,* Jan. 4, 1794; Norwich, Conn., *Weekly Register,* Dec. 24, 1793; Boston *Independent Chronicle,* Dec. 23, 26, 1793.

100. "Mentor," Rutland, Vt., *Farmers' Library,* reprinted in the Boston *Independent Chronicle,* Dec. 12, 1793.

101. Dumfries *Virginia Gazette and Agricultural Repository,* Dec. 19, 1793; Edenton *State Gazette of North Carolina,* Jan. 4, 1794; Lynchburg, Va., *Union Gazette* Jan. 18, 1794; "CATO," Kingston, N. Y., *Rising Sun,* Dec. 28, 1793; *Edwards' Baltimore Daily Advertiser,* Dec. 21, 24, 1793; "A FRENCH DESCENDANT," Charleston, S. C., *Columbian Herald,* Dec. 24, 1793.

102. Boston *Independent Chronicle,* Aug. 26, Nov. 21 ("Junius"), 1793; Philadelphia *National Gazette,* Oct. 26, 1793; *Baltimore Daily Intelligencer,* Oct. 30, 1793.

103. Boston *Independent Chronicle,* Sept. 2, 1793; New Brunswick, N. J., *Guardian,* Nov. 19, 1793; "Brutus," *Greenleaf's New-York Journal,* May 7, 1794.

104. Boston *Independent Chronicle,* Aug. 22, 1793; see also Jefferson to Madison, Sept. 1, 1793, Bergh, ed., *Writings of Thomas Jefferson,* IX, 213.

105. Boston *Independent Chronicle,* Oct. 7, 1793; Philadelphia *National Gazette,* Sept. 28, 1793.

106. Charleston, S. C., *Columbian Herald,* Oct. 3, 1793. See also the Boston *Independent Chronicle,* Aug. 22, 1793; Augusta, Ga., *Southern Centinel,* Aug. 22, 1793; Kingston, N. Y., *Farmer's Register,* Aug. 10, 1793; *Baltimore Daily Repository,* Sept. 5, 1793; "A FRIEND TO THE PEOPLE," Alexandria, Va., *Columbian Mirror,* Oct. 2, 1793; Philadelphia *National Gazette,* Oct. 5, 9, 1793.

107. "JUNIUS AMERICANUS," New York *Argus,* June 9, 1795.

108. *Edwards' Baltimore Daily Advertiser,* Nov. 25, 1793; Hartford, Conn., *Hartford Gazette,* Feb. 17, 1794.

109. Startlingly enough, a Federalist report to this effect was actually circulated; Concord, N. H., *Mirrour,* Dec. 16, 1793.

110. *Baltimore Daily Intelligencer,* Dec. 2, 30, 1793; Norwich, Conn., *Weekly Register,* Jan. 28, 1794.

111. E.g., Augusta, Ga., *Southern Centinel,* Jan. 30, 1794; earlier, "A PLEBEIAN," Newark, N. J., *Woods's Newark Gazette,* Aug. 14, 1793. Cf. Woodfin, "Citizen Genêt," 321; Link, *Democratic-Republican Societies,* 130.

112. Boston *Independent Chronicle,* Oct. 10. 1793; Richmond *Virginia Gazette and Richmond and Manchester Advertiser,* Oct. 17, 1793; Winchester *Virginia Centinel,* Nov. 11, 1793; Philadelphia *Dunlap's*

*American Daily Advertiser,* Dec. 3, 1793; Savannah *Georgia Journal,* Dec. 7, 1793. See also Woodfin, "Citizen Genêt," 321, 350–51; Bowers, *Jefferson & Hamilton,* 229; McMaster, *A History,* II, 140; Brant, *Madison,* III, 383.

113. E.g., Boston *Independent Chronicle,* Oct. 17, 1793.

114. *Ibid.,* Jan. 23, 1794; but cf. below, note 120.

115. Philadelphia *General Advertiser,* Dec. 21, 1793; "BRUTUS," *Greenleaf's New York Journal,* May 7, 1794.

116. Charleston, S. C., *Columbian Herald,* Mar. 10, 1794; Woodfin, "Citizen Genêt," *passim.*

117. Boston *Independent Chronicle,* Feb. 3, 1794.

118. The expression is Jefferson's, in his letter to G. Morris, Aug. 16, 1793; Bergh, ed., *Writings of Thomas Jefferson,* IX, 203–04.

119. Boston *Independent Chronicle,* Apr. 27, 1795; New York *Argus,* May 14, 1795; Lexington *Kentucky Gazette,* Apr. 30, 1796.

120. *New-York Journal,* Dec. 25, 1793, Jan. 11, 1794; Philadelphia *Dunlap's American Daily Advertiser,* June 6, 1794; Winchester *Virginia Centinel,* June 16, 1794.

121. Charleston, S. C., *City Gazette,* June 25, 30, 1794; *Baltimore Daily Intelligencer,* Aug. 11, 12, 13, 14, 1794; *New-York Journal,* Mar. 5, 1794; Ulrich B. Phillips, "The South Carolina Federalists," *American Historical Review* 14 (July, 1909), 733–34; Woodfin, "Citizen Genêt," 440.

122. Cincinnati [Ohio] *Centinel of the Northwest Territory,* Jan. 25, 1794; Lexington *Kentucky Gazette,* Feb. 8, 1794; Coulter, "The Efforts," 389; Bakeless, *Background to Glory,* 342; American Historical Association *Reports,* 1896, 952 ff.; McMaster, *A History,* II, 142; Dale Van Every, *Ark of Empire,* 293–95.

123. Link, *Democratic-Republican Societies,* 139–141; *Pittsburgh Gazette,* Apr. 5, 1794. But see Eastern criticism in the Boston *Independent Chronicle,* Mar. 20, 1794.

124. Woodfin, "Citizen Genêt," 446–55; Bond, "The Monroe Mission," 26; Minnigerode, *Jefferson,* 358. For samples of newspaper interest, see Winchester *Virginia Centinel,* Feb. 3, 24, 1794; Haverhill, Mass., *Guardian of Freedom,* Feb. 13, 1794; Richmond *Virginia Gazette and Richmond Chronicle,* Mar. 14, 1794; Philadelphia *American Daily Advertiser,* Mar. 28, Apr. 5, 14, May 21, June 3, 4, 1794.

125. Link, *Democratic-Republican Societies,* esp. 6–15, 19–40, 125–28, 130–229, gives an excellent account of the factors leading to the formation of the societies. See also Childs, *French Refugee Life,* 146–48.

126. Philadelphia *Gazette of the United States,* June 15, 1793; Philadelphia *National Gazette,* June 8, July 17, 1793; Philadelphia *Federal Gazette,* July 15, 1793.

127. See the Lexington *Kentucky Gazette,* Aug. 31, 1793; Bowers, *Jefferson & Hamilton,* 224; cf. Malone, *TJ,* III, 121–22.

128. Philadelphia *American Daily Advertiser,* Mar. 27, May 15, 1794; *New-York Daily Gazette,* Apr. 21, 1794. See Chap. 12, for more on the Democratic Societies, and p. 183, on this incident.

129. Philadelphia *Gazette of the United States,* May 5, 1794; Philadelphia *American Daily Advertiser,* Aug 2, 1794.

130. Philadelphia *General Advertiser,* Feb. 25, 1794.

131. Washington refused to extradite Genêt, as Fauchet had requested. See Jones, *America and French Culture,* 546; Van Every, *Ark of Empire,* 295n.

132. E.g., he officially disapproved of Genêt's expeditions against Louisiana and Florida; Link, *Democratic-Republican Societies,* 141; Van Every, *Ark of Empire,* 294.

133. Jones, *America and French Culture,* 547; Bemis, "Washington's Farewell Address," 256–57.

134. Fauchet's "Dispatch No. 10," dated Oct. 31, 1794; see Boston *Columbian Centinel,* Jan. 2, 1796; New Haven *Connecticut Journal,* Jan. 7, 1796; Alexandria, Va., *Columbian Mirror & Alexandria Gazette,* Apr. 26, 1796; Martinsburg, [W.]Va., *Potowmack Guardian,* May 12, 19, 1796; etc. Also Baldwin, *Whiskey Rebels,* 266–67; Mc-Master, *A History,* II, 230–33.

135. Miller, *Federalist Era,* 169–170; Bassett, *Federalist System,* 131–32; McMaster, *A History,* 234; Faÿ, *Two Franklins,* 258.

136. Brant, *Madison,* III, 426–29; Bassett, *Federalist System,* 131–33; Edmund Randolph, *Interesting State Papers, etc.,* 1–4; Edmund Randolph, *A Vindication of Mr. Randolph's Resignation,* 5–8.

137. Providence, R. I., *Providence Gazette,* Aug. 8, 1795; *Boston Gazette,* Aug. 10, 1795; Randolph, *A Vindication,* esp. 8–11; Randolph, *Interesting State Papers,* 9; McMaster, *A History,* II, 234–35.

138. Item from the New York *Argus,* Newport, R. I., *Newport Mercury,* Oct. 13, 1795; Lexington *Stewart's Kentucky Herald,* Dec. 1, 1795.

139. Richmond, Va., *Richmond and Manchester Advertiser,* Sept. 26, Oct. 31, Nov. 7, 1795; Boston *Independent Chronicle,* Nov. 2, 1795; Lexington *Stewart's Kentucky Herald,* Nov. 17, 1795; Lexington *Kentucky Gazette,* Dec. 5, 1795.

140. Boston *Columbian Centinel,* Jan. 2, 1796; New Haven *Connecticut Journal,* Jan. 7, 1796.

141. This last was a mangled version from a London paper, but reprinted in the United State; Alexandria, Va., *Columbian Mirror,* Apr. 26, 1796.

142. Boston *Independent Chronicle,* Oct. 5, 1795; see also Baldwin, *Whiskey Rebels,* 269, for this viewpoint.

143. "A REAL REPUBLICAN," Newport, R. I., *Newport Mercury,* Mar. 1, 1796; see also the Boston *Independent Chronicle,* Jan. 11, 14 ("Candor"), 1796.

144. Boston *Independent Chronicle,* Nov. 16, Dec. 7, 1795.

145. *Ibid.,* Dec. 7, 1795; *Baltimore Telegraphe,* Feb. 18, 1796; Richmond, Va., *Richmond and Manchester Advertiser,* Feb. 27, 1796.

146. E.g., Boston *Independent Chronicle,* Jan., 1796, *passim;* Charleston *South Carolina State Gazette,* May 26, 27, 31, June 3, 4, 6, 7, 1796.

147. Randolph, *A Vindication,* 23–26; Washington later gave him permission to look at the letter in question.

148. *Ibid.,* 15–17; Randolph, *Interesting State Papers,* esp. 1–4, 11–17, 77–124; Randolph, *Political Truths,* 4–31, 38–39, 43; Clark, *Peter Porcupine,* 49–50; *New York Herald,* Jan. 2, 1796 (a supposedly impartial abstract) ; Boston *Independent Chronicle,* Jan., 1796, *passim;* Charleston *South Carolina State Gazette,* May 26–June 7, 1796; Richmond, Va., *Richmond & Manchester Advertiser,* Jan. 6, 10, 13, 1796; Amherst, N. H., *Village Messinger,* Jan. 26, Feb. 2, 1796.

149. Boston *Independent Chronicle,* Jan. 11, 14, 1796; item from the New York *Diary,* in the Richmond, Va., *Richmond and Manchester Advertiser,* Jan. 6, 1796.

150. New York *Argus,* Dec. 25, 1795; Philadelphia *Aurora,* Jan. 6, 1796.

151. New York *Herald,* Jan. 2, 1796.

152. E.g., one Girard was described as "a real democrat" who "fulfills all his *wheat contracts,"* Alexandria, Va., *Columbian Mirror,* July 7, 1796.

153. "Must not every true American be struck with horror . . ." at this infamy in high place?—Brookfield, Mass., *Moral and Political Telegraphe,* Dec. 30, 1795 (also Oct. 28, Nov. 25, 1795) ; New York *Daily Gazette,* Dec. 25, 1795; Faÿ, *Revolutionary Spirit,* 370.

154. Boston *Independent Chronicle,* Jan. 29, Feb. 1, 1798.

155. Faÿ, *Two Franklins,* 263.

# VI JUSTICE JAY AND HIS TREATY

1. "CAUTION," from the Georgetown, D. C., *Times and Potowmack Packet*, Oct. 20, 1790, cited in the New Haven *Connecticut Journal*, Nov. 3, 1790; Charleston, S. C., *City Gazette*, Sept. 17, 1790.

2. Miller, *Federalist Era*, 16, 143–44n.; Curtis P. Nettels, *The Emergence of a National Economy, 1775–1815*, 230.

3. McMaster, *A History*, II, 165–66; Young, *Democratic Republicans*, 349, 366.

4. Edenton *State Gazette of North Carolina*, Dec. 14, 1793; Morse, *Federalist Party*, 74n.; James Alton James, "French Diplomacy and American Politics, 1794–1795," *Annual Report of the American Historical Association, 1911*, 155.

5. Fredericktown, Md., *Bartgis' Federal Gazette*, Aug. 1, 1793. This paper, favoring peace, was pleased to note talk of retaliation had not yet developed.

6. Boston *Independent Chronicle*, June 27, 1793; Leominster, Mass., *Rural Repository*, July 5, 1793; Charleston, S. C., *Columbian Herald*, Aug. 22, 1793; Philadelphia *American Daily Advertiser*, Jan. 4, 1794.

7. Charleston, S. C., *Columbian Herald*, Aug. 22, 1793; Bennington *Vermont Gazette*, Oct. 4, 1793; Richmond *Virginia Gazette*, Oct. 18, Dec. 6, 1793; Philadelphia *American Daily Advertiser*, Jan. 4, 1794.

8. *New-York Journal*, Mar. 15, 22, 29, 1794; "A True American," Philadelphia *Merchants' Advertiser*, Feb. 20, 1798, cited in the Savannah, Ga., *Columbian Museum*, Mar. 16, 1798. Young, *Democratic Republicans*, 366–67, 375, says 307 in two "waves."

9. Philadelphia *American Daily Advertiser*, Jan. 4, 1794; letter from London in the Alexandria, Va., *Virginia Gazette and Alexandria Advertiser*, Sept. 19, 1793; letter from Liverpool, *Pittsburgh Gazette*, Oct. 19, 1793. Since the last-named paper leaned Federalist, these letters were presumably genuine.

10. William Miller, "First Fruits of Republican Organization: Political Aspects of the Congressional Election of 1794," *Pennsylvania Magazine of History and Biography* 63 (Apr., 1939), 130; Boston *Indepen-*

*dent Chronicle,* June 27, Oct. 2, 1793; New York *Columbian Gazetteer,* cited in the Norwich, Conn., *Norwich Packet,* Oct. 31, 1793.

11. Bennington *Vermont Gazette,* Oct. 4, 1793; Concord, N. H., *Hough's Concord Herald,* Oct. 24, 1793. See also an item from the Philadelphia *General Advertiser,* in the Newburyport, Mass., *Morning Star,* May 6, 1794.

12. For complaints on the secrecy concerning the November 6, 1793, orders, see the Hartford, Conn., *Hartford Gazette,* Mar. 24, 1794; the Newburyport, Mass., *Morning Star,* May 6, 1794, stated British agents in Philadelphia knew about these instructions some weeks before they were made public and that Tories benefited from that knowledge. Comment on the orders of Jan. 8, 1794, may be found in the Trenton *New Jersey State Gazette,* Apr. 9, 1794. As a result of these instructions English men-of-war were allegedly stationed in Chesapeake Bay to follow out to sea and capture any ship carrying food; Boston *Independent Chronicle,* Sept. 11, 1794.

13. Trenton *New Jersey State Gazette,* Mar. 19, 1794; Charleston, S. C., *City Gazette,* Mar. 20, 1794; *New York Journal,* Mar. 29, 1794.

14. E.g., see the *Hartford Gazette,* Oct. 30, Dec. 1, 1794; Norwich, Conn., *Weekly Register,* Mar. 18, Apr. 22, 1794; and almost any issue of the Boston *Independent Chronicle* or *Boston Gazette* from late 1793 throughout 1794, in addition to specific citations already made.

15. E.g., *Philadelphische Correspondenz,* June 20, July 18, 1794; speech at Pittsburgh, July 4, 1794, of H. H. Brackenridge, cited in the *Baltimore Daily Intelligencer,* July 28, 1794; Augusta, Ga., *Southern Centinel,* May 28, 1795; New York *Argus,* June 8, 1795.

16. "The Crisis," from the *Independent Chronicle,* Rutland, Vt., *Farmers' Library,* June 24, 1793; see also "Philo Solon," from the Philadelphia *Independent Gazetteer,* in the Winchester, Va., *Virginia Centinel,* Aug. 3, 1795.

17. Boston *Independent Chronicle,* Feb. 20, 1794; Norwich, Conn., *Weekly Register,* Mar. 18, 1794; Miller, *Federalist Era,* 145.

18. See the *Boston Gazette,* Mar. 28, 1794; Norfolk, Va., *Virginia Chronicle,* Aug. 21, 1794.

19. Providence, R. I., *United States Chronicle,* Mar. 27, 1794; Boston *Independent Chronicle,* Apr. 3, 1794.

20. Richmond *Virginia Gazette and Richmond Chronicle,* Feb. 21, 1794; Norfolk *Virginia Chronicle,* June 16, 1794.

21. Philadelphia *General Advertiser,* Mar. 17, 1794; Boston *Independent Chronicle,* Mar. 27, 1794; *Baltimore Daily Intelligencer,* Mar. 31, 1794.

22. *Idem.;* Norwich Conn., *Weekly Register,* Mar. 25, 1794.

23. Boston *Independent Chronicle,* Dec. 23, 1793, Jan. 20, Feb. 20, 1794.

24. Philadelphia *American Star,* Apr. 17, 1794; reprinted in the Edenton *State Gazette of North Carolina,* May 2, 1794.

25. Providence, R. I., *United States Chronicle,* Mar. 27, 1794.

26. Note a letter from the *London Morning Chronicle,* saying America desired peace but was being forced into war by British policies, *Baltimore Daily Intelligencer,* Apr. 11, 1794; also *ibid.,* Mar. 21, 1794.

27. Norwich, Conn., *Weekly Register,* Mar. 18, 1794; Charleston, S. C., *Columbian Herald,* Apr. 28 ("A CITIZEN"), May 2, 1794; Leominster, Mass., *Rural Repository,* June 2, 1794. Even earlier, see "Cato," *New-York Journal,* Dec. 11, 18, 1793, Jan. 8, 18, 1794.

28. Philadelphia *American Daily Advertiser,* Jan. 16, Mar. 21, 1794; *Baltimore Daily Intelligencer,* Mar. 12, 1794 (merchants and citizens of New York pledged themselves to pay extra taxes to help pay for defense preparations) ; Hanover, N. H., *Eagle,* Apr. 7, 1794; *Boston Gazette,* Mar. 24, 1794; Halifax *North Carolina Journal,* Mar. 19, 26, 1794.

29. Norwich, Conn., *Weekly Packet,* Apr. 22, 1794. See McMaster, *A History,* II, 170–71. A number of congressmen were said to have voted for a navy at public expense in order to protect commerce in which they were interested and to lower insurance rates.

30. Letter in the *New-York Journal,* cited in the Newburyport, Mass., *Morning Star,* Apr. 15, 1794.

31. Charleston, S. C., *Columbian Herald,* Mar. 12, 1794; Boston *Independent Chronicle,* May 12, 1794; Halifax *North Carolina Journal,* Apr. 16, 1794.

32. E.g., *New-York Journal,* Apr. 26, June 8, 18, 1794; Philadelphia *American Daily Advertiser,* Mar. 21, May 3, June 21, 1794; *New York Daily Gazette,* May 9, 1794; Allen, *Great Britain,* 285; Young, *Democratic Republicans,* 386–87.

33. McMaster, *A History,* II, 179–81, summarizes Madison's resolutions; see also Lawrence S. Mayo, *John Langdon of New Hampshire,* 246–47; Miller, *Federalist Era,* 143; Samuel Flagg Bemis, "The United States and the Abortive Armed Neutrality of 1794," *American Historical Review* 24 (Oct., 1918), 34; Boston *Independent Chronicle,* Feb. 17, 20, 1794; Philadelphia *General Advertiser,* Mar. 26, 1794.

34. Philadelphia *General Advertiser,* Mar. 26, 1794; Norfolk *Virginia Chronicle,* Apr. 5, 1794. Bowers, *Jefferson and Hamilton,* 244, indicates Parker opposed the resolutions, but this contradicts the press of

the day; moreover the *Dictionary of American Biography*, XIV, 234, calls him an "Anti-Federalist." See, however, p. 414.

35. Boston *Independent Chronicle*, Feb. 17, 1794; Lynch, *Fifty Years of Party Warfare*, 40.

36. New York *Columbian Gazetteer*, Mar. 6, 1794. Cf. the *New-York Journal*, Mar. 1, 1794; *New York Daily Advertiser*, Mar. 6, 1794; Augusta, Ga., *Southern Centinel*, Apr. 17, 24, 1794.

37. Miller, "First Fruits," 124. See Bemis, *Jay's Treaty*, 189–91, for comments on the debates in Congress; Young, *Democratic Republicans*, 373–75, notes fervor in New York state.

38. "CATO," in the New York *Diary*, reprinted in the *Hartford Gazette*, Feb. 10, 1794; Bemis, "Abortive Armed Neutrality," 39.

39. Philadelphia *General Advertiser*, Apr. 14, 1794.

40. "CATO," Hartford, Conn., *Hartford Gazette*, Jan. 23, 27, Feb. 6, 10, 1794.

41. Philadelphia *General Advertiser*, Feb. 11, 1794; Boston *Independent Chronicle*, Feb. 24, 1794.

42. Norfolk *Virginia Chronicle*, July 17, 1794.

43. Augusta, Ga., *Southern Centinel*, Apr. 24, May 8, 1794; Norfolk *Virginia Chronicle*, May 12, 1794 (resolutions of Fayetteville, N. C.).

44. "CYMON," in the Providence, R. I., *United States Chronicle*, Mar. 6, 20, 1794; the latter letter is also in the Norwich, Conn., *Norwich Packet*, Mar. 27, 1794.

45. "CATO," No. V, from the New York *Diary*, in the *Baltimore Daily Intelligencer*, Jan. 13, 1794.

46. From a summary of communications on the subject to the *Pittsburgh Gazette*, in Andrews, *Pittsburgh's Post-Gazette*, 42; and a vulgar letter by "Hector," from the Wilmington *Delaware Gazette*, in the Newburyport, Mass., *Morning Star*, June 10, 1794.

47. Boston *Independent Chronicle*, Sept. 18, 1794; "Pacificus" was Alexander Hamilton, writing earnestly in defense of neutrality.

48. "A True Whig" and "A Friend to Mankind," in the *Baltimore Daily Intelligencer*, May 1, 7, 1794.

49. Philadelphia *General Advertiser*, Apr. 19, 1794; Boston *Independent Chronicle*, Apr. 28, 1794.

50. Philadelphia *General Advertiser*, Feb. 5, Apr. 13, 1794. See "The LIAR," in the Norwich, Conn., *Weekly Register*, Apr. 22, 1794, to the effect that members of Congress might be interested in the public funds and feared a war would depreciate their holdings; therefore they would have the government bow to England.

51. Newburyport, Mass., *Morning Star,* Apr. 15, 1794; Norfolk *Virginia Chronicle,* May 1, 1794.

52. McMaster, *A History,* II, 173, quoting a Boston item in the Philadelphia *American Daily Advertiser,* Mar. 22, 1794; Charleston *South Carolina State Gazette,* Apr. 5, 1794.

53. Philadelphia *General Advertiser,* Mar. 26, 1794; also the Norfolk *Virginia Chronicle,* Apr. 5, 1794.

54. James, "French Diplomacy," 176; Bemis, "Abortive Armed Neutrality," 35.

55. *Baltimore Daily Intelligencer,* Mar. 29, 1794.

56. Philadelphia *American Daily Advertiser,* Apr. 1, 1794; McMaster, *A History,* II, 174, citing the *American Daily Advertiser,* May 8, 1794, and the *New York Daily Gazette,* May 9, 1794.

57. Bemis, "Abortive Armed Neutrality," 35–36; Miller, *Federalist Era,* 154.

58. E.g., the resolutions of the Boston town meeting, in the Halifax *North Carolina Journal,* June 4, 1794. The Boston *Independent Chronicle,* Apr. 21, 1794, vehemently attacked a petition of Boston merchants requesting the lifting of the embargo, in that it misrepresented the sentiment of the town.

59. "A Consistent Republican," Boston *Independent Chronicle,* Sept. 25, 1794; see also the issue of Sept. 29, 1794.

60. *Ibid.,* May 26, 1794; Newburyport, Mass., *Morning Star,* May 27, 1794.

61. *Baltimore Daily Intelligencer,* May 23, 24, 26, 27, 1794; *Boston Gazette,* June 2, 1794.

62. *Baltimore Daily Intelligencer,* May 21, 24, 1794; Newark, N. J., *Woods's Newark Gazette,* May 28, 1794.

63. *Baltimore Daily Intelligencer,* May 28, 1794.

64. *Ibid.,* June 5, 1794; for reports of frontier plans to stop river trade with the British or Spanish see an item from Whitestown, Pa., in the Newburyport, Mass., *Morning Star,* June 3, 1794. Young, *Democratic Republicans,* 388, describes New York's reaction.

65. Providence, R. I., *United States Chronicle,* Apr. 4, 1794; Charles, *Origins,* 101; Bowers, *Jefferson and Hamilton,* 244; McMaster, *A History,* II, 186–87.

66. Brant, *Madison,* III, 395; Bowers, *Jefferson and Hamilton,* 244.

67. The first mention noticed by the present writer of this term—some years before it became famous (prior to the War of 1812) in American history.

68. Boston *Independent Chronicle,* Mar. 24, 1794.

69. Philadelphia *General Advertiser,* Apr. 8, 14, 1794; Norwich, Conn., *Weekly Register,* May 20, 1794; Bassett, *Federalist System,* 123, 125; McMaster, *A History,* II, 187; Mayo, *John Langdon,* 246–47; Charles, *Origins,* 101.

70. E.g., Boston *Independent Chronicle,* May 5, 1794; Norfolk *Virginia Chronicle,* June 16, 1794; *Baltimore Daily Intelligencer,* June 26, 1794; *Hartford Gazette,* Sept. 4, 1794; Philadelphia *General Advertiser,* Oct. 31, 1794.

71. A series in the *Albany Register,* reprinted in the Newburyport, Mass., *Morning Star;* see the issue of May 6, 1794.

72. Letter of "ARISTOCRAT," Norfolk *Virginia Chronicle,* Apr. 18, 1794.

73. A. L. Burt, *The United States, Great Britain, and British North America,* 142; McMaster, *A History,* II, 187–88; Edgar E. Robinson, *The Evolution of American Political Parties,* 65–66; Monaghan, *John Jay,* 364–67.

74. *New York Journal,* Aug. 10, 1793; Philadelphia *National Gazette,* Aug. 14, 1793.

75. See Allan Nevins, *The American States During and After the Revolution,* 346; Bassett, *Federalist System,* 70; Bond, *Monroe Mission,* 23–24; Andrews, *Pittsburgh's Post-Gazette,* 42; Lexington *Kentucky Gazette,* Sept. 19, 26, 1794 (cited in Luetscher, *Early Political Machinery,* 44–45).

76. Philadelphia *General Advertiser,* Apr. 8, 1794.

77. *Ibid.,* Apr. 28, 1794; Robinson, *American Political Parties,* 65–66; Burt, *United States,* 142.

78. Resolutions of the Democratic Society of Pennsylvania, approved by the German-Republican Society of Philadelphia and the Newark Republican Society, Charleston *South Carolina State Gazette,* July 26, Oct. 9, 1794; Newark, N. J., *Woods's Newark Gazette,* June 18, 1794; Charleston, S. C., *Columbian Herald,* July 28, 1794; *Philadelphia Gazette,* Nov. 29, 1794; Newburyport, Mass., *Morning Star,* Nov. 19, 1794; resolutions of the Democratic Society of the "District of Pinckney," S. C., in Eugene P. Link, "Democratic Societies in the Carolinas," 18; Link, *Democratic-Republican Societies,* 130.

79. Augusta, Ga., *Southern Centinel,* June 12, 1794; *New-York Journal,* Nov. 5, 1794.

80. Philadelphia *General Advertiser,* Apr. 28, 29, 1794; Boston *Independent Chronicle,* May 12, 1794; Philadelphia *American Daily Advertiser,* May 12, July 29, Aug. 2, 1794; Philadelphia *Aurora,* Mar.

17, 1795; "Franklin" No. IX, Philadelphia *Independent Gazetteer,* Apr. 22, 1795.

81. Boston *Independent Chronicle,* Apr. 28, 1794.

82. Philadelphia *General Advertiser,* May 14, 1794; Luetscher, *Early Political Machinery,* 44–45.

83. *Baltimore Daily Intelligencer,* May 27, 1794; Bemis, *Jay's Treaty,* 224–25, 231, 246–51. Cf. Miller, *Federalist Era,* 164–65; Monaghan, *John Jay,* 380. Boyd, *Number 7,* esp. 11, 29–30, 59, notes that Hamilton in 1790–91 had been in secret communication with British agents.

84. "A True Whig," *Baltimore Daily Intelligencer,* May 1, 1794. The Boston *Independent Chronicle,* May 5, 1794, envisaged England gulling Jay with fair promises while she did as she pleased and then ridiculed America.

85. "Mirror," Norfolk *Virginia Chronicle,* May 26, 1794; Charleston, S. C., *City Gazette,* June 14, 1794.

86. E.g., *Baltimore Daily Intelligencer,* June 27, 1794. McMaster, *A History,* II, 213–14, has a suspiciously similar account of a ceremony which he says occurred in Philadelphia, from the *New-York Journal,* Aug. 2, 1794. Conceivably this was a story of the same Kentucky affair which the *Journal* merely copied from a Philadelphia paper.

87. Charleston, S. C., *Daily Evening Gazette,* Feb. 14, 1795; Richmond, Va., *Richmond and Manchester Advertiser* ("More British Depredations"), Mar. 30, Apr. 2, May 23, 1795; Philadelphia *Aurora,* Apr. 13, 1795; Mt. Pleasant, N. J., *Jersey Chronicle,* May 2, 1795; Boston *Independent Chronicle,* Apr. 20, 23, 1795; Augusta, Ga., *Augusta Chronicle,* June 13, 1795; Trenton *New Jersey State Gazette,* June 16, 1795; etc.

88. The titular phrase is from Frank Mott, *A History of American Magazines,* 188–89. E.g., see the *Hartford Gazette,* Sept. 4, 1794; Mt. Pleasant, N. J., *Jersey Chronicle,* May 2, 1795; Philadelphia *Aurora,* Apr. 13, 29, 1795; Boston *Independent Chronicle,* Aug. 27, Nov. 3, 1795.

89. Philadelphia *General Advertiser,* Aug. 29, 1794; Frederick Austin Ogg, "Jay's Treaty and the Slavery Interests of the United States," *Annual Report of the American Historical Association, 1901,* I; 284.

90. Newburyport, Mass., *Morning Star,* Nov. 19, 1794. Cf. McMaster, *A History,* II, 213; Portsmouth, N. H., *Oracle of the Day,* Nov. 25, 1794.

91. Philadelphia *General Advertiser,* Sept. 5, 1794; Norfolk *Virginia Chronicle,* Sept. 18, 1794; Charleston *South Carolina State Gazette,* Sept. 22, 1794.

92. Charleston *South Carolina State Gazette,* Jan. 19, 1795.

93. Perhaps London was rowing one way and looking the other; Norfolk *Virginia Chronicle,* Oct. 6, 1794; *Greenleaf's New York Journal,* Sept. 20, Oct. 18, 1794.

94. Boston *Independent Chronicle,* Nov. 3, 1794; Norfolk *Virginia Chronicle,* Nov. 20, 1794.

95. Philadelphia *Aurora,* Dec. 5, 1794; Boston *Independent Chronicle,* Dec. 18, 1794; Hallowell, [Maine], *Eastern Star,* Feb. 17, 1795.

96. "A.," *Greenleaf's New York Journal,* Oct. 29, 1794; Boston *Independent Chronicle,* Nov. 10, 17, 1794; and the Elizabethtown, Md., *Washington Spy,* Nov. 27, 1794. See similar opinion in the Norfolk *Virginia Chronicle,* Nov. 17, 1794. We almost certainly would not get the posts if Jay said nothing about them, cried the Philadelphia *Aurora,* Dec. 5, 1794.

97. "Tom the Tinker" (a Federalist using that name to remind readers of the Whiskey Rebellion), Halifax *North Carolina Journal,* Nov. 10, 1794; and the Providence, R. I., *United States Chronicle,* Dec. 18, 1794, give samples of this mordancy.

98. Boston *Independent Chronicle,* Nov. 13, 1794. See also *Greenleaf's New York Journal,* Dec. 20, 1794.

99. Boston *Independent Chronicle,* Dec. 18, 1794, Feb. 12, 1795; *Greenleaf's New York Journal,* Dec. 20, 1794, Feb. 14, 1795; Philadelphia *Aurora,* Feb. 2, 1795.

100. Letter of Ames, Feb. 3, 1795, cited in Seth Ames, ed., *Works of Fisher Ames,* I, 166. See the Halifax *North Carolina Journal,* Jan. 4, 12, 1795; *Hartford Gazette,* Feb. 5, 9, 1795; Philadelphia *Aurora,* Feb. 2, 6, 1795.

101. Baltimore *Federal Intelligencer,* June 5, 1795; Newbern *North Carolina Gazette,* June 6, 1795. See Young, *Democratic Republicans,* 441, on Jay's return.

102. E.g., the *Baltimore Telegraphe,* Mar. 25, 1795; "Franklin," Nos. XI, XII, Philadelphia *Independent Gazetteer,* May 20, 26, 1795. Some writers held the secrecy unconstitutional; New York *Argus,* June 18, 20, 1795.

103. Boston *Independent Chronicle,* Apr. 23, 1795; see also, earlier, *Greenleaf's New York Journal,* Jan. 7, 1795 (referring to an item in the *Albany Gazette,* Dec. 22, 1794). Wheeler, "Urban Politics," 265, notes Republicans were drafting anti-treaty arguments in 1794.

104. Providence, R. I., *United States Chronicle,* Mar. 26, July 2, 1795; Philadelphia *Gazette of the United States,* cited in the Richmond, Va., *Richmond and Manchester Advertiser,* July 2, 1795.

105. Philadelphia *Aurora,* June 18, 1795; Baltimore *Federal Intelligencer,* June 23, 1795.

106. Washington, D. C., *Impartial Observer and Washington Advertiser,* July 3, 1795. See also the Philadelphia *Aurora,* June 16, 22, 23, 1795; Richmond, Va., *Richmond and Manchester Advertiser,* July 2, 1795; New York *Argus,* July 2, 1795; Washington, D. C., *Impartial Observer,* July 3, 1795; Augusta, Ga., *Augusta Chronicle,* July 11, 1795.

107. Boston *Columbian Centinel,* Feb. 18, 1795.

108. Philadelphia *Aurora,* Feb. 10, 1795; "A FARMER," Carlisle, Pa., *Telegraphe,* Feb. 17, 1795; "Montgomery," Nos. I–III, *Greenleaf's New York Journal,* Apr. 8, 11, 15, 1795; Boston *Independent Chronicle,* Apr. 23, 1795; Mt. Pleasant, N. J., *Jersey Chronicle,* May 9, 1795.

109. McMaster, *A History,* II, 214, lists them as appearing in May and June, but letters appeared as early as March 11, 1795. So popular was the series that 300 subscribers to the Danbury, Mass., *Danbury Chronicle* were said to have petitioned for its republication in that paper.

110. "Franklin," Philadelphia *Independent Gazetter,* Mar. 11, 1795; New York *Mott & Hustin's New York Weekly Chronicle,* Mar. 19, 1795; Carlisle, Pa., *Telegraphe,* Mar. 24, 1795; McMaster, *A History,* II, 214.

111. "Franklin," Philadelphia *Independent Gazetteer,* Mar. 18, 1795; Charles, "Jay Treaty," in *Origins of the American Party System,* 101–03, agrees on the motive for Jay's appointment—the Federalists wanted to take the matter out of the Republican House, where they feared adoption of effective measures against England.

112. "Franklin," Letter No. VI, Philadelphia *Independent Gazetteer,* Apr. 4, 1795.

113. "Franklin," Letter No. II, *ibid.,* Mar. 14, 1795; Exeter, N. H., *Weekly Visitor,* May 5, 1795; Boston *Independent Chronicle,* May 11, 1795; Charleston *South Carolina State Gazette,* June 24, 1795.

114. "Franklin," Letter No. V, Philadelphia *Independent Gazetteer,* Apr. 1, 1795.

115. "Franklin," Letter No. VIII, *ibid.,* Apr. 18, 1795; Baltimore *Federal Intelligencer,* Apr. 24, 1795; Charleston *South Carolina State Gazette,* May 27, 1795.

116. "Franklin," Letter No. X, from the Philadelphia *Independent Gazetteer* (probably May 17, 1795) in the New York *Argus,* May 21, 1795; Carlisle, Pa., *Telegraphe,* June 2, 1795; Elizabethtown, Md., *Washington Spy,* June 16, 1795; Charleston *South Carolina State Ga-*

*zette,* June 22, 1795. Some Canadian militia (unauthorized) had fought with the Indians at Fallen Timbers; Burt, *United States,* 139; Van Every, *Ark of Empire,* 342.

117. "Franklin," Letter No. XI, Philadelphia *Independent Gazetteer,* May 20, 1795; New York *Argus,* May 26, 1795; No. XII, Carlisle, Pa., *Telegraphe,* June 16, 1795; New York *Argus,* June 2, 1795. Washington held the treaty four months before submitting it to the Senate. See Woodbury, *Public Opinion,* 83–85, for a summary of "Franklin's" arguments; Letters No. XIII and No. XIV appeared in the New York *Argus,* June 12, 17, 1795.

118. New York *Argus,* May 19, 1795; Baltimore *Federal Intelligencer,* June 25, 1795; see also the Georgetown, D. C., *Columbian Chronicle,* June 27, 1795.

119. New York *Argus,* May 22, 1795. Incomplete returns in New York did not indicate Jay's election until May 28; see the *Argus,* May 28, June 6, 1795.

120. *Ibid.,* May 29, June 9, 1795; see also the Philadelphia *Aurora,* May 27, 1795; Richmond, Va., *Richmond and Manchester Advertiser,* June 6, 1795.

121. "Sidney," II, III, Philadelphia *Aurora,* June 19, 22, 1795; the New York *Argus* carried Nos. I, II, and III, June 19, 22, 24, 1795.

122. Mt. Pleasant, N. J., *Jersey Chronicle,* May 16, June 6, 13, 1795.

123. Philadelphia *Aurora,* June 26, 1795. The extent to which this was reprinted was indicative both of the wide interest in the treaty and of the fury with which it was to be condemned; e.g., the Baltimore *Telegraphe,* June 29, 1795; Georgetown, D. C., *Columbian Chronicle,* June 30, 1795; New Haven, Conn., [mildly Federalist] *Connecticut Journal,* July 1, 1795; Lynchburg, Va., *Lynchburg and Farmers' Gazette,* July 11, 1795.

124. "A CITIZEN," Philadelphia *Aurora,* June 29, 1795; reprinted in the Philadelphia *American Daily Advertiser,* June 30, 1795; New York *American Minerva,* June 30, 1795; Philadelphia *Courier Français,* July 2, 1795; Portsmouth *New Hampshire Gazette,* July 7, 1795; Trenton *New Jersey State Gazette,* July 7, 1795; Newfield, Conn., *American Telegraphe,* July 8, 1795; Brookfield, Mass., *Moral and Political Telegraphe,* July 8, 1795; Richmond, Va., *Richmond and Manchester Advertiser,* July 4, 1795; Providence, R. I., *United States Chronicle,* July 11, 1795; Lynchburg, Va., *Lynchburg and Farmers' Gazette,* July 18, 1795; *et al.*

125. McMaster, *A History,* II, 216, accepts (at least by implication) Mason's story that someone else first gave Bache the information for

his abstract. Bowers, *Jefferson and Hamilton*, 273; Sullivan, *Familiar Letters*, 62; and Faÿ, *Two Franklins*, 239–40, name Mason as that individual, while an anonymous article, "Thomas Paine's Second Appearance in the United States," *Atlantic Monthly* 4 (July, 1859), 5, refers to Mason's "near treason." According to John Harold Wolfe, *Jeffersonian Democracy in South Carolina*, 83, Senator Pierce Butler, of S. C., sent a copy of the treaty to Madison while it was still supposedly "secret." See the Philadelphia *Aurora*, July 1, 1795, for notices of the pamphlet; the treaty text did not appear in that paper, but was reprinted in almost countless gazettes: Philadelphia *American Daily Advertiser*, July 3, 1795; New York *Argus*, July 4, 1795; New Haven *Connecticut Journal*, July 8, 15, 1795; Richmond, Va., *Richmond and Manchester Advertiser*, July 9, 11, 1795; Boston *Independent Chronicle*, July 9, 13, 1795; Portsmouth *New Hampshire Gazette*, July 14, 1795; Hudson, N. Y., *Hudson Gazette*, July 16, 23, 1795; York *Pennsylvania Herald*, July 22, 29, Aug. 5, 1795; Hanover, N. H., *Eagle*, July 27, 1795; Lynchburg, Va., *Lynchburg and Farmers' Gazette*, July 25, 1795; Fayetteville *North Carolina Centinel*, July 25, 1795; Halifax *North Carolina Journal*, July 13, 20, 1795; etc. Note also Malone, *TJ*, III, 245n.

126. Who presumably had one, or soon would; Philadelphia *Aurora*, Dec. 12, 1795; Boston *Independent Chronicle*, Dec. 21, 31, 1795. King, incidentally, denied the charge; Boston *Independent Chronicle*, Dec. 31, 1795. See the Dumfries, Va., *Republican Journal*, July 17, 1795 (item originally from the *Maryland Journal*), for a spirited defense of Mason's alleged act.

127. Philadelphia *Aurora*, June 27, 1795; New York *American Minerva* (where the retort was made that if slaves were deducted, as virtual cattle without votes, over two-thirds of the people approved), July 8, 1795; Trenton *New Jersey State Gazette*, July 7, 1795; Lynchburg, Va., *Lynchburg and Farmers' Gazette*, July 11, 1795; etc. Winfred E. A. Bernhard, *Fisher Ames*, 258–59, notes that the treaty dispute represented a basic cleavage "over the direction of American foreign policy," and that Ames felt public opinion was so frenzied "our federal ship is near foundering."

128. New York *Argus*, July 2, 1795, which blamed the funding system for the treaty vote.

129. Anon., "Second Visit of Tom Paine," 5.

130. Philadelphia *Independent Gazetteer*, quoted in the *Baltimore Federal Intelligencer*, July 8, 1795; Trenton *New Jersey State Gazette*, July 7, 1795; Lynchburg, Va., *Lynchburg and Farmers' Gazette*, July 25, 1795; New York *Argus*, July 8, 1795; Norwich, Conn., *Weekly Register*, July 22, 1795.

131. Made at Frankford Creek, Pa., Philadelphia *Aurora*, July 7, 1795; Edenton *State Gazette of North Carolina*, July 23, 1795. At the same dinner Mason was lauded for "manly patriotism." For other toasts, see the Baltimore *Telegraphe*, July 11, 1795; Philadelphia *Aurora*, July 13, 1795; *Greenleaf's New York Journal*, July 15, 1795; *Boston Gazette*, July 27, 1795; New York *Argus*, July 7, 1795.

132. Baltimore *Telegraphe*, July 11, 1795; Exeter, N. H., *Weekly Visitor*, July 28, 1795.

133. Philadelphia *Aurora*, July 3, 1795.

134. Philadelphia *Independent Gazetteer*, July 8, 1795; Philadelphia *Aurora*, July 9, 1795; Philadelphia *Gazette of the United States*, July 7, 17, 1795; New York *Argus*, July 15, 1795; Lynchburg, Va., *Lynchburg and Farmers' Gazette*, July 25, 1795; Martinsburg, [W.] Va., *Potomak Guardian*, July 18, 1795; *Pittsburgh Gazette*, July 25, 1795.

135. Bowers, *Jefferson and Hamilton*, 275; Malone, *TJ*, III, 248.

136. See the *New York Weekly Museum*, July 4, 1795, for an intimation that popular feeling might determine whether or not Washington would sign. The *Aurora* (cited in the *New York Weekly Museum*, Aug. 8, 1795) wrote that since the President had not yet affixed his signature, "expressions of popular opinion are not only proper but desirable." Possibility that England might reject the modified treaty was to be hoped for, said "MARIUS," Augusta, Ga., *Augusta Chronicle*, Aug. 1, 1795—but even this should not spare Jay and his supporters from "the detestation they deserve." See also an article in the Trenton *New Jersey State Gazette*, Sept. 15, 1795.

137. Boston *Independent Chronicle*, July 16, 1795; Boston *Columbian Centinel*, July 15, 1795; McMaster, *A History*, II, 217–18; Wheeler, "Urban Politics," 368.

138. Brookfield, Mass., *Moral and Political Telegraphe*, July 29, 1795; Norfolk *Virginia Herald*, July 29, 1795; Savannah *Georgia Gazette*, Aug. 20, 1795; *New York Weekly Museum*, July 18, 1795; Richmond, Va., *Richmond and Manchester Advertiser*, July 23, 1795; Bennington *Vermont Gazette*, Aug. 7, 1795.

139. Boston *Federal Orrery*, in the *New York Daily Gazette*, July 17, 1795; New Haven *Connecticut Journal*, July 22, 1795; York *Pennsylvania Herald*, Aug. 5, 1795; Brookfield, Mass., *Moral and Political Telegraphe*, July 22, Aug. 5, 1795; McMaster, *A History*, II, 218.

140. *New York Weekly Museum*, July 4, 1795.

141. New York *Herald*, July 22, 1795, cited in McMaster, *A History*, II, 218–20. See the New York *Argus*, July 20, 1795; Baltimore *Federal Intelligencer*, July 24, 1795. Young, *Democratic Republicans*, 447–54, describes the meeting, but doubts Hamilton was stoned.

142. Richmond, Va., *Richmond and Manchester Advertiser,* July 23, 1795; Boston *Independent Chronicle,* July 27, 1795.

143. Elizabethtown *New Jersey Journal,* July 15, 1795; New York *Gazette Française,* July 17, 1795; Baltimore *Federal Intelligencer,* July 21, 1795; Exeter, N. H., *Weekly Visitor,* July 28, Aug. 11, 18, 25, 1795; Newfield, Conn., *American Telegraphe,* July 29, 1795; Trenton *New Jersey State Gazette,* July 28, Aug. 4, 1795; Richmond, Va., *Richmond and Manchester Advertiser,* July 30, Aug. 15, 1795; Halifax *North Carolina Journal,* Aug. 3, 1795; New Haven *Connecticut Journal,* Aug. 5, 1795; Savannah *Georgia Gazette,* Aug. 6, 20, 1795; Georgetown, D. C., *Columbian Chronicle,* Aug. 4, 1795; Dumfries, Va., *Republican Journal,* July 31, 1795; Washington, D. C., *Impartial Observer,* Aug. 7, 1795; Greenfield, Mass., *Greenfield Gazette,* July 30, 1795; Boston *Independent Chronicle,* Aug. 6, 13, 17, 24, 1795; Amherst, Mass., *Amherst Journal,* Aug. 14, 1795; Dice Robins Anderson, *William Branch Giles,* 38; Prince, *New Jersey's Jeffersonian Republicans,* 16–17; etc.

144. E.g., Richmond, Va., *Richmond and Manchester Advertiser,* July 23, 1795; Baltimore *Federal Intelligencer,* July 25, 1795; Carlisle, Pa., *Kline's Carlisle Gazette,* July 29, 1795; Boston *Independent Chronicle,* July 20, 1795; Alexandria, Va., *Columbian Mirror,* July 28, 1795; Lynchburg, Va., *Lynchburg and Farmers' Gazette,* Aug. 8, 1795; McMaster, *A History,* II, 225–26. The Edenton *State Gazette of North Carolina,* July 30, 1795, reported the local petition was at the newspaper office for the convenience of prospective signers.

145. "A REPUBLICAN," Trenton *New Jersey State Gazette,* Aug. 4, 1795.

146. New York *Argus,* July 1, 23, 1795; Savannah, Ga., *Southern Centinel,* Sept. 10, 1795; Boston *Independent Chronicle,* July 23, Oct. 26, 1795.

147. Portsmouth *New Hampshire Gazette,* July 28, 1795.

148. Boston *Independent Chronicle,* July 30, Aug. 3 (poem), 1795.

149. Trenton *New Jersey State Gazette,* Aug. 18, 1795; Dover, N. H., *Sun,* Sept. 12, 1795.

150. Wilmington *Delaware and Eastern Shore Advertiser,* Aug. 1, 1795; Savannah, Ga., *Southern Centinel,* Sept. 10, 1795.

151. Elizabethtown *New Jersey Journal,* July 15, 1795; Richmond, Va., *Richmond and Manchester Advertiser,* July 23, 1795; Exeter, N. H., *Weekly Visitor,* July 28, 1795.

152. One of the first writers to use this technique, and certainly one of the most influential, was "Decius," in the New York *Argus,* July

10, 11, 13, 14 ff., 1795; *Baltimore Telegraphe,* July 16–23, 1795; Boston *Independent Chronicle,* July 20–23, 1795. Almost as effective was "Cato," also from the *Argus,* cited in the *Baltimore Telegraphe,* July 23, 27, 31, 1795. Young, *Democratic Republicans,* 448, identifies "Decius" as Brockholst Livingston, and "Cato" as Chancellor Robert R. Livingston.

153. Boston *Independent Chronicle,* July 20, 1795; see also the *Edenton State Gazette of North Carolina,* Apr. 28, 1796.

154. See the report of the Charleston, S. C., committee on the treaty; Augusta, Ga., *Southern Centinel,* Aug. 13, 1795; "Decius," New York *Argus,* July 10, 1795 ff.; etc.

155. "AN AMERICAN," from the *Independent Chronicle,* in the Hartford *American Mercury,* July 20, 1795; Augusta, Ga., *Augusta Chronicle,* Aug. 22, 1795. See also the Boston *Independent Chronicle,* July 9, 15, 1795; Washington, D. C., *Impartial Observer and Washington Advertiser,* July 31, 1795; Alexandria, Va., *Columbian Mirror,* July 21, 1795; Baltimore *Federal Intelligencer,* Aug. 1, 1795.

156. Delbert H. Gilpatrick, *Jeffersonian Democracy in North Carolina,* 71–72; New York *Argus,* July 11, 1795.

157. New York *Argus,* July 13, 16, 1795 ("Decius" was Brockholst Livingston, according to McMaster, *A History,* II, 245); Augusta, Ga., *Southern Centinel,* Aug. 13, 1795.

158. Baltimore *Federal Intelligencer,* June 30, 1795; cf. Miller, *Federalist Era,* 167, suggesting that Jay wanted to promote domestic textile manufacture. Augusta, Ga., *Augusta Chronicle,* Aug. 8, 1795; Augusta, Ga., *Southern Centinel,* Aug. 13, 1795; Albany, N. Y., *Albany Register,* Aug. 3, 1795.

159. Only by a stretch of the imagination could it be called reciprocity; see the Charleston, S. C., *Columbian Herald,* Oct. 12, 1795. The New York *Argus,* July 7, 1795, claimed this article was the key to the whole treaty; by it Britain succeeded in having America surrender a valuable trade and hurt the French. Cf. the Boston *Independent Chronicle,* Aug. 3, 1795; "A Merchant," (from the *Salem Gazette*), Exeter, N. H., *Weekly Visitor,* Aug. 11, 1795; and an "ADVERTISEMENT EXTRA" in the Richmond, Va., *Richmond Chronicle,* July 25, 1795— "Wanted to purchase or charter. One Thousand Vessels: burthen from 70 tons down to nothing. Enquire at No. 12 [12th Article], Treaty Lane."

160. Washington, D. C., *Impartial Observer,* July 31, 1795.

161. *Idem.;* Haverhill, Mass., *Guardian of Freedom,* Aug. 13, 1795; Trenton *New Jersey State Gazette,* Sept. 8, 1795.

162. Boston *Independent Chronicle*, July 9, 1795; "Decius," from the New York *Argus*, in the Albany, N. Y., *Albany Register* (which gives credit to the New York *Journal*), Aug. 3, 1795; New Brunswick, N. J., *Genius of Liberty*, Aug. 10, 1795.

163. "JURICOLA," from the *Philadelphia Gazette*, in the Charleston, S. C., *Columbian Herald*, Oct. 12, 1795; similarly, see the Baltimore *Telegraphe*, July 23–25, 1795; Mt. Pleasant, N. J., *Jersey Chronicle*, July 25, 1795; Exeter, N. H., *Weekly Visitor*, July 28, 1795; Washington, D. C., *Impartial Observer*, Aug. 7, 1795; Fayetteville *North Carolina Centinel*, Aug. 8, 1795; Lexington *Stewart's Kentucky Herald*, Nov. 24, 1795; McMaster, *A History*, II, 229. Someone, said "Impartial," in the New York *Argus*, July 4, 1795 (reprinted in the Washington, D. C., *Impartial Observer*, July 27, 1795), should have provided Jay with a copy of the Constitution to remind him of the powers of Congress.

164. "A Republican," Boston *Independent Chronicle*, July 9, 15, 1795, reprinted in the Washington, D. C., *Impartial Observer*, July 31, 1795. The New York *Argus*, July 8, 1795, held the agreement fastened "FETTERS upon the trade" of America; cf. the Baltimore *Federal Intelligencer*, June 26, 1795; "ATTICUS," Martinsburg, [W.] Va., *Potomak Guardian*, July 25, 1795. England was jealous of America's carrying trade and hoped to destroy it, added the Exeter, N. H., *Weekly Visitor*, July 28, 1795.

165. Resolution adopted in Petersburg, Va., Aug. 4, 1795; Fayetteville *North Carolina Centinel*, Aug. 8, 1795; "Mercator," from the *Boston Mercury*, Richmond, Va., *Richmond and Manchester Advertiser*, July 23, 1795; Exeter, N. H., *Weekly Visitor*, July 28, 1795; Newark, N. J., *Woods's Newark Gazette*, Sept. 9, 1795.

166. Newfield, Conn., *American Telegraphe*, Aug. 12, 1795.

167. Mount Pleasant, N. J., *Jersey Chronicle*, Aug. 29, 1795; Newark, N. J., *Woods's Newark Gazette*, Sept. 9, 30, 1795.

168. Augusta, Ga., *Augusta Chronicle*, Aug. 1, 1795; New York *American Minerva*, Aug. 5, 1795; Baltimore *Telegraphe*, July 23–25, Aug. 1, 1795; Washington, Pa., *Western Telegraphe and Washington Advertiser*, Aug. 17, 1795; Savannah *Georgia Gazette*, Aug. 20, 1795; Ogg, "Jay's Treaty," 286–87; McMaster, *A History*, II, 245–47; Gilpatrick, *Jeffersonian Democracy*, 67–73.

169. Exeter, N. H., *Weekly Visitor*, July 28, 1795; Fayetteville *North Carolina Centinel*, Aug. 8, 1795.

170. "Lucius," Boston *Independent Chronicle*, July 20, 1795; Hammond, *Political Parties in N.Y.*, I, 93; see also the Kingston, N. Y., *Rising Sun*, Feb. 27, 1795, on British insincerity.

171. "WHACUM," from the *Newport Mercury*, in the Exeter, N. H., *Weekly Visitor*, Aug. 18, 1795; Trenton *New Jersey State Gazette*, Oct. 13, 1795.

172. New York *Argus*, cited in Fairhaven, Vt., *Farmers' Library*, Aug. 3, 1795; Carlisle, Pa., *Carlisle Telegraphe*, July 28, 1795.

173. Fairhaven, Vt., *Farmers' Library*, Aug. 3, 1795.

174. Fayetteville *North Carolina Centinel*, Aug. 8, 1795; Jones, *America and French Culture*, 534n.

175. New York *Argus*, June 18, 1795; Washington, D. C., *Impartial Observer*, June 26, 1795; resolutions from Philadelphia, Baltimore *Federal Intelligencer*, Aug. 1, 1795; see also the Sag Harbor, L. I., *Frothingham's Long Island Herald*, Oct. 26, 1795.

176. E.g., Philadelphia *General Advertiser*, June 7, 1794.

177. Newburyport, Mass., *Morning Star*, Nov. 19, 1794.

178. Bond, "Monroe Mission," 9–10, 12–36, 51–53. This condition was true when only the "more excusable" sections of the treaty had as yet been made known to the Directory; Chambersburg, Pa., *Chambersburg Gazette*, Sept. 3, 1795; Boston *Independent Chronicle*, Aug. 6, 1795; Troy, N. Y., *Recorder*, Aug. 18, 1795; Washington, D. C., *Impartial Observer*, Sept. 5, 1795. See also the Boston *Independent Chronicle*, Jan. 21, 1796; Lancaster, Pa., *Lancaster Journal*, July 15, 1796.

179. Philadelphia *Dunlap and Claypoole's American Daily Advertiser*, Aug. 6, 1795; Baltimore *Federal Intelligencer*, Aug. 15, 1795; Alexandria, Va., *Columbian Mirror*, Aug. 15, 1795; Chambersburg, Pa., *Chambersburg Gazette*, Aug. 20, 1795.

180. Boston *Independent Chronicle*, July 20, 1795; Portsmouth *New Hampshire Gazette* ("Benevolus"), July 21, 1795; Philadelphia *Aurora*, Aug. 3, 1795; Newfield, Conn., *American Telegraphe*, Aug. 12, 1795.

181. Mt. Pleasant, N. J., *Jersey Chronicle*, Aug. 22, 29, 1795; Lexington *Kentucky Gazette*, Oct. 24, Dec. 5, 1795. The Philadelphia *Aurora*, Oct. 6, 1795, claimed that out of 50,000 Philadelphia residents only 408 petitioners in favor of the treaty could be found.

182. Faÿ, *Two Franklins*, 250.

183. Boston *Independent Chronicle*, Aug. 13, 1795.

184. From the Wilmington *Delaware Gazette*, in the Georgetown, D. C., *Columbian Chronicle*, Sept. 8, 1795; Richmond, Va., *Richmond and Manchester Advertiser*, Sept. 12, 1795. The address was reprinted in the Fredericktown, Md., *Rights of Man*, Sept. 2, 1795.

185. Lexington *Kentucky Gazette*, Sept. 26, 1795. See Marshall's let-

ters, *ibid.,* Oct. 3, 17, 24, 31, Nov. 7, 1795, after he had been refused space in the Lexington *Stewart's Kentucky Herald.*

186. Philadelphia *Aurora,* Nov. 14, 1795; Boston *Independent Chronicle,* Dec. 14, 1795. John C. Miller, *Alexander Hamilton,* 427–30.

187. Letter from Pittsburgh, in the Baltimore *Federal Intelligencer,* Aug. 28, 1795.

188. Lexington *Kentucky Gazette,* Oct. 24, 1795.

189. "BRUTUS," Lexington *Stewart's Kentucky Herald,* Aug. 18, 1795; Lexington *Kentucky Gazette,* Sept. 19, Oct. 24, 1795, ff. See also the Fayetteville *North Carolina Centinel,* Aug. 8, 1795.

190. New York *Argus,* July 2, 1795.

191. Portsmouth *New Hampshire Gazette,* July 21, 1798; reprinted in the Exeter, N. H., *Weekly Visitor,* July 28, 1798.

192. Mt. Pleasant, N. J., *Jersey Chronicle,* Sept. 15, 1795; also the Lexington *Stewart's Kentucky Herald,* Nov. 17, 1795.

193. New York *Diary,* cited in the Fayetteville *North Carolina Centinel,* July 25, 1795; see also the Boston *Independent Chronicle,* Sept. 5, 1795.

194. Newburyport, Mass., *Impartial Herald,* Aug. 11, 1795. An earlier similar item was in the Wilmington, N. C., *Wilmington Chronicle,* July 31, 1795.

195. *New York Gazette Française* (which waited until the adverse reaction of the French minister before printing much on the treaty), July 27, 1795.

196. The New York *Argus* is a good illustration of the regularity with which these letters were printed. "Hancock," Nos. I–IV, was in the issues of Aug. 24, 29, Sept. 7, 11, 1795, respectively; "Valerius," Nos. I–XI, appeared Aug. 25, Sept. 4, 14, 21, 29, Oct. 15, 24, Nov. 2, 13, 23, Dec. 1, 1795; and "Belisarius," Nos. I–V, was in Sept. 26, 28, 30, Oct. 7, 17, 1795. The Mt. Pleasant, N. J., *Jersey Chronicle* carried "Valerius" at weekly intervals (with one exception) from Sept. 5–Dec. 5, 1796. Bernhard, *Fisher Ames,* 262, comments on the effectiveness with which Washington's name was used to quiet popular opposition; a letter from Madison to Edmund Pendleton (Feb. 7, 1796), is cited as stating that "No where has this policy been exerted with so much effect as in New England."

197. Philadelphia *Aurora,* Aug. 21, 1795; New York *Argus,* Aug. 24, 1795; Boston *Independent Chronicle,* Sept. 10, 1795.

198. Philadelphia *Aurora,* Sept. 9, 15, 1795; Baltimore *Telegraphe,* Sept. 14, 1795; Boston *Independent Chronicle,* Sept. 24, 1795.

199. Philadelphia *Aurora,* Sept. 9, 25, 1795; Baltimore *Telegraphe,* Sept. 14, 1795; Boston *Independent Chronicle,* Sept. 14, 24, 28, 1795; New York *Argus,* Sept. 29, 1795.

200. Mt. Pleasant, N. J., *Jersey Chronicle,* Oct. 17, 1795; *Greenleaf's New York Journal,* Oct. 28, 1795.

201. "Sydney," Boston *Independent Chronicle,* May 12, 1795; "Marcus" (reprinted *ibid.*), July 30, 1795.

202. *Ibid.,* Sept. 12, 1795.

203. From the Wilmington *Delaware Gazette,* Baltimore *Telegraphe,* Sept. 16, 21, 1795.

204. Reprinted in New York *Greenleaf's New York Journal,* Oct. 28, Nov. 11, 25, 1795.

205. Philadelphia *Aurora,* Jan. 4, 1796.

206. Mt. Pleasant, N. J., *Jersey Chronicle,* Nov. 7, 14, 21, 1795; Baltimore *Telegraphe,* Nov. 11, 1795; *Greenleaf's New York Journal,* Nov. 28, 1795. For more detail about the personal attacks on Washington, see Chap. 13.

207. From the Philadelphia *Aurora,* in the Mt. Pleasant, N. J., *Jersey Chronicle,* Aug. 1, 1795. See the item headed "Interesting Fact" in the Newfield, Conn., *American Telegraphe,* July 29, 1795; also accounts in the Halifax *North Carolina Journal,* Aug. 10, 1795; Alexandria, Va., *Columbian Mirror,* July 28, 1795; New York *American Minerva,* July 22, 1795; Dumfries, Va., *Republican Journal,* July 31, 1795; Lexington *Stewart's Kentucky Herald,* Aug. 18, 1795; Wilmington, N. C., *Wilmington Chronicle,* Aug. 20, 1795.

208. The *New York Daily Gazette* carried "Camillus" from July 30, Aug. 3, 10, 14, 22, 29, Sept. 3, etc., up to Dec. 15, 16, 21, 29, 1795. Perhaps 75,000 slaves were taken by the British during the Revolution. Many of these were behind enemy lines at the time the treaty was signed, and Americans had hoped to restore them to their former masters by having it specified that the English troops should be withdrawn without them; Ogg, "Jay's Treaty," 275–76.

209. "JURICOLA," Washington, D. C., *Impartial Observer,* Sept. 14, 1798; the Wilmington, N. C., *Wilmington Chronicle,* July 31, 1795, had earlier emphasized this same point. See also Ogg, "Jay's Treaty," 288–92.

210. Philadelphia *Aurora,* Dec. 10, 1795.

211. *Ibid.,* Aug. 15, 1795, Jan. 6, 1796; *New York Journal,* Oct. 24, Dec. 25, 1795; New York *Argus,* Dec. 25, 1795. "ONEIROPHILUS," in the Baltimore *Telegraphe,* Feb. 10, 1796, alleged "Camillus"

put him to sleep, but he nevertheless asked 39 questions about the advisability of union again with Britain.

212. Georgetown, D. C., *Columbian Chronicle,* Aug. 21, 1795.

213. Wilmington, N. C., *Wilmington Chronicle,* July 31, 1795; Richmond, Va., *Richmond and Manchester Advertiser,* Nov. 21, 1795; Lynch, *Party Warfare,* 53.

214. See "HORATIUS," Charleston, S. C., *Columbian Herald,* Nov. 12, 1795; *Albany Gazette,* Nov. 23, 1795; Mary Elizabeth Clark, *Peter Porcupine in America,* 48.

215. "Atticus," Philadelphia *Independent Gazetteer,* July 15, 1795; "CA IRA," Philadelphia *Aurora,* July 21, 1795; Lexington *Stewart's Kentucky Herald,* Aug. 18, 1795.

216. Richmond, Va., *Richmond Chronicle,* Oct. 24, 1795.

217. Lynchburg, Va., *Lynchburg and Farmers' Gazette,* Aug. 8, 1795; the Exeter, N. H., *Weekly Visitor,* Aug. 25, 1795, tells of burnings in Savannah and Charleston. These and other instances may be found in the Bennington *Vermont Gazette,* Sept. 18, 1795; *Boston Gazette,* Sept. 14, 1795 (for Portsmouth, N. H.); Fayettesville *North Carolina Centinel,* July 25, 1795; Baltimore *Federal Intelligencer,* July 22, 1795 (for Norfolk); Wilmington *Delaware and Eastern Shore Advertiser,* Aug. 1, 1795.

218. Exeter, N. H., *Weekly Visitor,* Sept. 8, 1795; Dover, N. H., *Sun,* Sept. 12, 1795.

219. Fayetteville *North Carolina Centinel,* July 25, 1795; *Boston Gazette,* Aug. 25, 1795.

220. Hallowell, [Maine], *Tocsin,* Oct. 2, 1795.

221. New York *American Minerva,* Nov. 10, 1795; Martinsburg, [W.] Va., *Potomak Guardian,* Nov. 16, 1795. (In the latter paper the letter was unsigned.)

222. *Pittsburgh Gazette,* Aug. 15, 1795; but cf. *ibid.,* Nov. 14, 1795, approving surrender of the western posts.

223. Resolves of the Franklin Society, Charleston, S. C., *City Gazette,* Oct. 28, 1795; Brookfield, Mass., *Moral and Political Telegraphe,* Sept. 23, 1795; John C. Miller, *Sam Adams, Pioneer in Propaganda,* 395–99.

224. *Boston Gazette,* Aug. 25, 1795; Newfield, Conn., *American Telegraphe,* Aug. 26, 1795. This drew sharp Federalist retorts from the Hartford *Connecticut Courant;* see the Newfield, Conn., *American Telegraphe,* Sept. 16, 1795; New York *American Minerva,* Aug. 17, 1795.

225. Wilmington *Delaware Gazette,* Aug. 22, 1795.

226. Fayetteville *North Carolina Centinel,* July 25, 1795; McMaster, *A History,* II, 217–18, has an account of the Boston incident concerning the privateer.

227. Exeter, N. H., *Weekly Visitor,* Aug. 25, 1795. The issue of Sept. 8, 1795, condemned the demonstration at Rye, N. H. (*supra*), as "contemptible."

228. Greenleaf's *New York Journal,* Aug. 29, 1795; reprinted in the Elizabethtown Md., *Washington Spy,* Sept. 22, 1795.

229. New York *Argus,* Sept. 4, 1795; also in the Boston *Independent Chronicle,* Sept. 21, 1795.

230. Newfield, Conn., *American Telegraphe,* Aug. 19, 1795; *New York Weekly Museum,* Aug. 8, 1795; Halifax *North Carolina Journal,* Sept. 14, 1795.

231. Richmond, Va., *Richmond and Manchester Advertiser,* July 11, 1795; Augusta, Ga., *Southern Centinel,* Aug. 27, 1795.

232. The present writer was unable to locate this in the paper credited with its origin, but see the Washington, D. C., *Impartial Observer,* Aug. 7, 1795; and the Knoxville, [Tenn.], *Knoxville Gazette,* Oct. 2, 1795. McMaster, *A History,* II, refers to it on p. 254.

233. Lexington *Kentucky Gazette,* Sept. 26, 1795; Elizabethtown, Md., *Washington Spy,* Nov. 5, 1795.

234. From the Lexington *Stewart's Kentucky Herald,* in the Charleston *South Carolina State Gazette,* Nov. 11, 1795.

235. Richmond, Va., *Richmond and Manchester Advertiser,* July 30, 1795.

236. Charleston, S. C., *City Gazette,* July 14, 17, Sept. 5, 1795; Philadelphia *Aurora,* July 25, 1795; Exeter, N. H., *Weekly Visitor,* Sept. 1, 1795.

237. E.g., see an account of the big dinner at Portsmouth, N. H., for Senator John Langdon; Lexington *Stewart's Kentucky Herald,* Aug. 18, 1795; or the story of a similar banquet at Lexington, Va., in honor of Senator John Brown, in the Richmond, Va., *Richmond Chronicle,* Oct. 27, 1795.

238. See the Mt. Pleasant, N. J. *Jersey Chronicle,* Feb. 6, 1796; Randolph, *Vindication,* 28–35, 40, 53.

239. Faÿ, *Two Franklins,* 247–48.

240. E.g., "Hancock," No. II, from the Philadelphia *Aurora,* Bennington *Vermont Gazette,* Sept. 18, 1795; and see the *New York Journal,* Sept. 2, 1795.

241. Boston *Independent Chronicle,* Oct. 26, 29, 1795; Faÿ, *Revolutionary Spirit,* 359.

242. Boston *Independent Chronicle*, Aug. 17, 1795; Boston *Columbian Centinel*, Aug. 26, 1795; Wolfe, *Jeffersonian Democracy*, 90–91.

243. Philadelphia *Aurora*, Jan. 2, 1796; Richmond, Va., *Richmond Chronicle*, Jan. 22, 1796.

244. Thomas Jefferson to W. B. Giles, Dec. 31, 1795; Ford, ed., *Writings*, VII, 44.

245. Philadelphia *Aurora*, Jan. 21, 1796; Alexandria, Va., *Columbian Museum & Alexandria Gazette*, Mar. 8, 1796; Wolfe, *Jeffersonian Democracy*, 92.

246. Baltimore *Federal Intelligencer*, Aug. 17, 20, 1795; Providence, R. I., *United States Chronicle*, Aug. 27, 1795. See also the New York *Argus*, Aug. 13, 1795; and the Wilmington *Delaware Gazette*, Aug. 22, 1795.

247. Wolfe, *Jeffersonian Democracy*, 92–93. See Samuel F. Bemis, *Pinckney's Treaty*, 283–84; Pinckney *did* write Randolph, commending Jay's work as accomplishing about all that was possible under the circumstances. Later, after the wave of vicious American opposition, he partially recanted, writing Jefferson (Feb. 26, 1796) that while Jay had consulted him, he had not been present at the actual negotiations and could not share in the merits or demerits of the treaty.

248. Philadelphia *Aurora*, Apr. 1, 1796; Boston *Independent Chronicle*, Apr. 7, 1796. Rarely has there been a greater contrast between two treaties—Jay's was essentially "a humiliating document," and compared to it Pinckney's "was a paean of triumph"; Bemis, *Pinckney's Treaty*, ix.

249. Philadelphia *Aurora*, Apr. 1, 1796; Norfolk, Va., *American Gazette, and Norfolk & Portsmouth Public Advertiser*, Apr. 8, 1796; Boston *Independent Chronicle*, Apr. 14, 1796.

250. "An American," Charleston, S. C., *City Gazette*, Apr. 2, 1796; "Philo-Paulding," Philadelphia *Aurora*, Aug. 1, 1796; Boston *Independent Chronicle*, Aug. 18, 1796.

251. "A READER," Carlisle, Pa., *Telegraphe*, Aug. 18, 1795.

252. From the Bennington *Vermont Gazette*, Aug. 28, 1795, in the Trenton *New Jersey State Gazette*, Sept. 15, 1795.

253. Boston *Independent Chronicle*, Aug. 10, 1795.

254. Baltimore *Federal Intelligencer*, Dec. 12, 1795; Augusta, Ga., *Southern Centinel*, Dec. 17, 1795; Philadelphia *Aurora*, Feb. 10, 1796.

255. Charleston, S. C., *Columbian Herald*, Mar. 1, 3, 1796.

256. Philadelphia *Aurora*, Feb. 2, 23, 1796; see the Richmond, Va., *Richmond and Manchester* Advertiser, Jan. 13, 1796, for an answer to the Federalist argument that this was but a *copy* of the ratification.

257. The New Haven *Connecticut Journal,* Apr. 27, May 4, 1796, carried resolutions both for and against the treaty appropriations.

258. Philadelphia *Aurora,* Mar. 3, 4, 1796; Boston *Independent Chronicle,* Mar. 21, 1796. The latter promised to give both sides of the House debate, but it printed the speeches of Madison, Giles, Lyman, Livingston and Gallatin—and of no Federalists—in its issues of Mar. 24, 28, Apr. 1, 4, 7, 1796.

259. Philadelphia *Aurora,* Mar. 5, 1796; Boston *Independent Chronicle,* Mar. 14, 1796; Norfolk, Va., *American Gazette,* Mar. 25, 1796.

260. Boston *Independent Chronicle,* Mar. 24, 1796; see the Norfolk, Va., *Norfolk and Portsmouth Public Advertiser,* Apr. 22, 1796, for a similar view. Bowers, *Jefferson and Hamilton,* 294–97.

261. Martinsburg, [W.] Va., *Potomak Guardian,* Apr. 7, 1796.

262. Bowers, *Jefferson and Hamilton,* 298; Perkins, *First Rapprochement,* 39–40.

263. Boston *Independent Chronicle,* Apr. 11, 1796; Charleston *South Carolina State Gazette,* Apr. 16, 1796.

264. *DAB,* II, 68–70; Boston *Independent Chronicle,* Apr. 14, 1796; Charleston *South Carolina State Gazette,* May 16, 1796.

265. Cited in Bowers, *Jefferson and Hamilton,* 299.

266. *Boston Gazette,* Apr. 25, 1796. See also the Philadelphia *Aurora,* Mar. 14, 1796; Mt. Pleasant, N. J., *Jersey Chronicle,* Apr. 16, 1796; Richmond, Va., *Richmond and Manchester Advertiser,* Apr. 27, 1796; McLaughlin, *Constitutional History,* 259.

267. Washington, Pa., *Western Telegraphe and Washington Advertiser,* Apr. 5, 1796.

268. Savannah, Ga., *Columbian Museum,* May 13, 17, 1796; Fredricksburg, Va., *Republican Citizen,* June 22, 1796.

269. Boston *Independent Chronicle,* Apr. 25, May 2, 1796; Baltimore *Telegraphe,* Apr. 26, 1796; *Philadelphische Correspondenz,* Apr. 29, 1796; Bowers, *Jefferson and Hamilton,* 300–01.

270. Philadelphia *Aurora,* Apr. 26, 29, 1796; Boston *Independent Chronicle,* Apr. 28, 1796; Carlisle, Pa., *Telegraphe,* May 3, 1796; *Boston Gazette,* May 2, 1796. Cf. the Brookfield, Mass., *Moral and Political Telegraphe,* May 4, 1796; and Miller, *Federalist Era,* 174.

271. Philadelphia *Aurora,* Apr. 15, 1796; *Greenleaf's New York Journal,* Apr. 19, 1796; Boston *Independent Chronicle,* Apr. 25, 1796; Savannah *Georgia Gazette,* May 5, 1796. See Perkins, *First Rapprochement,* 40–41.

272. Bennington *Vermont Gazette,* May 4, 1796; see also the Albany, N. Y., *Albany Register,* Apr. 29, 1796; *Boston Gazette,* May 5, 1796;

Dumfries, Va., *Republican Journal*, May 10, 1796; Savannah, Ga., *Columbian Museum*, May 17, 1796; McMaster, *A History*, II, 283.

273. E.g., *Baltimore Telegraphe*, Oct. 22, 1795; Mt. Pleasant, N. J., *Jersey Chronicle*, Dec. 12, 1795.

274. Baltimore *Federal Gazette and Baltimore Daily Advertiser*, Mar. 19, 21, 31, 1796; Boston *Independent Chronicle*, Mar. 17, 1796; Richmond, Va., *Richmond and Manchester Advertiser*, Mar. 30, Apr. 2, 1796; Richmond, Va., *Richmond Chronicle*, Apr. 1, 1796; even the New York *American Minerva*, Mar. 16, 1796, considered such conduct unauthorized. For other difficulties of the *Eliza*, see the *Philadelphische Correspondenz*, Sept. 29, 1795; Baltimore *Federal Gazette*, June 9, 13, 1796; Savannah, Ga., *Columbian Museum*, May 6, 1796; Martinsburg, [W.] Va., *Potomak Guardian*, June 23, 1796; New York *Argus*, Sept. 2, 1796; Edenton *State Gazette of North Carolina*, Sept. 22, 1796.

275. Baltimore *Federal Gazette*, May 14, 1796; Savannah, Ga., *Columbian Museum*, June 7, 1796.

276. E.g., the Boston *Independent Chronicle*, Apr. 7, 1796; Newbern *North Carolina Gazette*, Apr. 30, 1796; Charleston *South Carolina State Gazette*, May 23, 1796; Edenton *State Gazette of North Carolina*, May 19, 1796.

277. Cincinnati, [Ohio], *Centinel of the North West Territory*, May 7, 1796; New York *Argus*, Aug. 4, 1796; Albany, N. Y., *Albany Gazette*, Aug. 5, 1796; New York *American Minerva*, Aug. 9, 1796; Brookfield, Mass., *Moral and Political Telegraphe*, Aug. 17, 1796; all tell of Pigot's savagery. For conditions under impressment, see the Boston *Independent Chronicle*, Apr. 7, 1796; Boston *Price Current*, Apr. 11, 1796; letter of James Bond (aboard the *Thetis*), Charleston *South Carolina State Gazette*, Aug. 24, 1796; Burlington, Vt., *Burlington Mercury*, June 3, 1796; Philadelphia *Aurora*, Aug. 11, 1796; Baltimore *Federal Gazette*, Apr. 19, Aug. 16, 1796; Savannah, Ga., *Columbian Museum*, Aug. 30, 1796.

278. Carlisle, Pa., *Telegraphe*, May 3, 1796; Burlington, Vt., *Burlington Mercury*, June 10, 1796.

279. Elizabethtown, Md., *Washington Spy*, June 29, 1796.

280. Philadelphia *Aurora*, Apr. 30, 1796; Boston *Independent Chronicle*, May 9, 1796; Bennington *Vermont Gazette*, May 4, 1796; Norfolk, Va., *American Gazette*, May 27, 1796; Poughkeepsie, N. Y., *Republican Journal*, June 1, 1796.

281. Halifax *North Carolina Journal*, May 2, 1796; Boston *Independent Chronicle*, May 2, 1796. A similar line of reasoning had been

advanced some months before by the Sag Harbor, N. Y., *Frothingham's Long Island Herald*, Oct. 26, 1795.

282. Boston *Independent Chronicle*, Apr. 21, 1796.

283. *Ibid.*, May 2, 1796; Fairhaven, Vt., *Farmers' Library*, May 30, 1796.

284. Philadelphia *Aurora*, May 11, 1796; Boston *Independent Chronicle*, Jan. 5, May 2, 5, 1796; Bennington *Vermont Gazette*, May 4, 1796; Joseph Francis Thorning, *Religious Liberty in Transition*, 47.

285. Miller, *Federalist Era*, 174–75; Perkins, *First Rapprochement*, 41–42; Bowers, *Jefferson and Hamilton*, 305–07. Lynch, *Party Warfare*, 57, doubts that this speech was as influential as has been pictured, but cf. Ames, *Works*, II, 44–45, 50–51, 55; and Bernhard, *Fisher Ames*, 267–73.

286. Boston *Independent Chronicle*, May 9, 1796.

287. Fayetteville *North Carolina Minerva*, June 9, 1796; see also Faÿ, *Two Franklins*, 294–95; *New York Weekly Museum*, May 7, 1796.

288. Norfolk, Va., *Norfolk and Portsmouth Public Advertiser*, May 13, 16, 1796. See the *Pittsburgh Gazette*, May 21, 1796; Bowers, *Jefferson and Hamilton*, 306–07; and "SYDNEY," in the Boston *Independent Chronicle*, May 12, 1796. The *Boston Gazette*, May 9, 1796, carried a poem on the treaty vote, ending in the lines:

> Ye tories now lift up your heads,
> And raise your triumphs high
> The whigs to quick destruction tread,
> Till their remembrance die.

289. E.g., Norfolk, Va., *Norfolk and Portsmouth Public Advertiser*, May 13, 1796; Washington, Pa., *Western Telegraphe*, May 31, 1796; Fredericktown, Md., *Bartgis's Federal Gazette*, June 30, 1796; letter of Thomas Claiborne (from the *Petersburg Gazette*), in the Baltimore *Federal Gazette*, June 28, 1796.

290. "Paulding," Nos. XII, XIII, Philadelphia *Aurora*, July 25, Aug. 2, 1796; Boston *Independent Chronicle*, Aug. 4, 11, 1796.

291. "Paulding," No. XIV, Philadelphia *Aurora*, Aug. 11, 1796; Boston *Independent Chronicle*, Aug. 22, 1796. An earlier "Paulding" letter on the treaty may be found in the Norfolk, Va., *American Gazette*, June 15, 1796.

292. Boston *Independent Chronicle*, Jan. 21, 1796; see also "Pittachus," Philadelphia *Aurora*, Jan. 13, 1796.

293. "Paulding," No. XV, in the Philadelphia *Aurora*, Aug. 24, 1796;

Boston *Independent Chronicle,* Sept. 12, 1796; Dumfries, Va., *Republican Journal,* Sept. 2, 1796.

294. Editorial in the Boston *Independent Chronicle,* Apr. 4, 1796. See also *ibid.,* Oct. 20, 1796; Dumfries, Va., *Republican Journal,* June 23, 1796; Providence, R. I., *State Gazette,* June 25, 1796; Haverhill, N. H., *Grafton Minerva,* July 14, 1796; Lancaster, Pa., *Lancaster Journal,* July 15, 1795; James Austin, *Life of Elbridge Gerry,* II, 177–79, 182–83.

295. "Portius," Philadelphia *Aurora,* Oct. 11, 1796; Boston *Independent Chronicle,* Oct. 24, 1796; "Gracchus," from the Dedham, Mass., *Minerva,* in the Boston *Independent Chronicle,* Feb. 17, 1798.

296. "Cato," Philadelphia *Aurora,* July 28, 1797; Boston *Independent Chronicle,* June 11, Aug. 7, Nov. 27, 1797; similar condemnations of the agreement as a *casus belli* appeared in the New York *Diary,* Jan. 26, 1797; Charleston, S. C., *City Gazette,* June 29, 1797; Wiscasset, [Me.], *Wiscasset Argus,* June 30, 1797; Newark, N. J., *Centinel of Freedom,* Mar. 27, 1798; Ballston Spa, N. Y., *Saratoga Register,* Nov. 21, 1798. On the *Rédacteur* story, see the Georgetown, D. C., *Centinel of Liberty,* Jan. 16, 1796; Edenton *State Gazette of North Carolina,* Feb. 1, 1798; Philadelphia *Gazette Français,* Feb. 28, Mar. 1, 1798. The treaty, exploded the Lexington *Kentucky Gazette,* Apr. 26, 1797, ". . . instead of proving the author a Solomon . . . proves him an Ass. . . . Our misfortunes have multiplied from the moment of its acceptance." For a reasoned discussion of France's position, see Bemis, "Washington's Farewell Address," 251–55.

297. Washington, D. C., *Impartial Observer,* Aug. 14, 1795; Dumfries, Va., *Republican Journal,* Aug. 14, 1795; Carlisle, Pa., *Telegraphe,* Aug. 18, 1795; Fair Haven, Vt., (headed "Ca Ira"), *Farmers' Library,* Aug. 3, 1795; Exeter, N. H. (*"So much for British Amity"*), *Weekly Visitor,* Sept. 8, 1795.

298. Boston *Independent Chronicle,* Feb. 15, Aug. 27, Sept. 29, 1796; Bennington *Vermont Gazette,* Mar. 2, 1796.

299. Boston *Independent Chronicle,* Mar. 15, 1798; see also *ibid.,* Feb. 25, Aug. 27, Sept. 29, 1796, and the Lexington *Kentucky Gazette,* May 13, 1797, for earlier gloomy predictions.

300. "BLESSED EFFECTS OF JAY'S TREATY," Lexington *Kentucky Gazette,* Sept. 10, 1795.

301. Boston *Independent Chronicle,* Feb. 13, 1797.

302. Philadelphia *Gazette of the United States,* Apr. 19, 1796; Martinsburg, [W.] Va., *Potomak Guardian,* July 14, 1796; Boston *Independent Chronicle,* May 15, July 17, 1797.

303. Boston *Independent Chronicle,* Oct. 10, 19, 1797.

304. New London, Conn., *Bee,* Mar. 21, 1798. See the Boston *Independent Chronicle,* Oct. 7, 1797; Philadelphia *Merchants' Advertiser,* Feb. 20, 1798; Savannah, Ga., *Columbian Museum,* Mar. 16, 1798, for other, but proportionately comparable, statistics.

305. Boston *Independent Chronicle,* Oct. 19, 22, 1795; *Philadelphische Correspondenz,* Sept. 29, 1795; Richmond, Va., *Richmond Chronicle,* Oct. 24, 1795; Elizabethtown, Md., *Washington Spy,* Nov. 5, 1795.

306. New York *Argus,* Oct. 14, 1795; Elizabethtown, Md., *Washington Spy,* Oct. 27, 1795; Lexington *Stewart's Kentucky Herald* (including the "ha, ha, ha," which did not appear in all the others), Nov. 24 1795. On the *Africa* incident, see Chap. 7.

307. Portland, [Me.], *Gazette of Maine,* Jan. 7, 1796.

308. Boston *Independent Chronicle,* Nov. 27, 1797; Richmond *Virginia Argus,* Aug. 26, Oct. 10, 1800.

309. Letter of "David Jones," from the *Salem Gazette,* Washington, D. C., *Washington Gazette,* Aug. 13, 1796. See the Chambersburg, Pa., *Farmers' Register,* Aug. 29, 1795; Boston *Independent Chronicle,* July 11, 1796; Charleston *South Carolina State Gazette,* Dec. 23, 1796; Annapolis *Maryland Gazette,* Jan. 18, 1798, for other instances of impressment.

310. Fredericksburg, Va., *Republican Citizen,* Aug. 3, 1796.

311. "A Republican," Boston *Independent Chronicle,* Aug. 18, 29, 1796; see also *ibid.,* Aug. 22, Sept. 1, 12, Oct. 3, 1796.

312. Letter of "HUMBUG," Philadelphia *Aurora,* Mar. 1, 1798.

313. New London, Conn., *Bee,* Sept. 5, 1798. See also the Boston *Independent Chronicle,* Aug. 22, Oct. 10, 24, 28, 1799; Philadelphia *Aurora,* Sept. 27, 1799; Augusta, Ga., *Augusta Chronicle,* Sept. 9, 1799; Dedham, Mass., *Columbian Minerva,* Oct. 3, 1799; Lexington *Kentucky Gazette,* Oct. 31, 1799.

314. Article from the *Examiner,* Richmond *Virginia Argus,* Oct. 1, 1799.

315. New York *Argus,* Feb. 8, 1800.

316. Baltimore *American and Daily Advertiser,* Nov. 22, 1800; see also the Boston *Constitutional Telegraph,* Oct. 5, 1799; Lexington *Kentucky Gazette,* Jan. 16, 1800.

317. See Chap. 7.

318. Baltimore *American,* Sept. 7, 1799. For additional instances of British outrages, see the stories of Williams, Jessup, Giles and Carter, Boston *Constitutional Telegraph,* Oct. 9, 1799; Newburyport, Mass.,

*Newburyport Herald,* Sept. 10, Oct. 8, 1799; Northampton, Mass., *Patriotic Gazette,* Oct. 11, 1799; Greenfield, Mass., *Greenfield Gazette,* Oct. 26, 1799.

319. See Brant, *Madison,* IV, 425; Axelrad, *Freneau,* 277; and Malone, *TJ,* III, 249 (citing Jefferson to Edward Rutledge, Nov. 30, 1795). Charles, *Origins,* 166, asserts it was the Treaty above all else which transformed Jefferson into an active party leader, and Anon., "Tom Paine's Second Appearance," 5, refers to an alleged letter from Jefferson to John Rutledge which within a short space utilized a whole battery of adjectives such as "unnecessary, impolitic, dangerous, dishonorable, disadvantageous, humiliating, disgraceful, improper, monarchical, and impeachable" respecting the covenant. Julian P. Boyd, editor of *The Jefferson Papers,* informs the writer that no evidence exists that this letter was written, but it seems evident Jefferson would find little to quarrel with in its sentiments.

320. Philadelphia *Aurora,* Mar. 29, 1800; Richmond *Virginia Argus,* Apr. 11, 1800.

# VII

PERFIDIOUS ALBION

1. See Chapter 5; *Boston Gazette,* Aug. 10, 1795; New Haven *Connecticut Journal,* Aug. 12, 1795; Providence, R. I., *United States Chronicle,* Aug. 20, 1795; Washington, D. C., *Impartial Observer,* Aug. 21, 1795; Newfield, Conn., *American Telegraphe,* Aug. 19, 1795; etc. Most of these papers headed the story "British Conduct."

2. New Haven *Connecticut Journal,* Aug. 12, 19, 1795; Haverhill, Mass., *Guardian of Freedom,* Aug. 13, 1795; Philadelphia *Courier Français* (from the *New York Journal*), Aug. 15, 1795.

3. New Haven *Connecticut Journal,* Aug. 26, 1795; Providence, R. I., *United States Chronicle,* Sept. 3, 1795; Philadelphia *Aurora,* Sept. 3, 1795; Brookfield, Mass., *Moral and Political Telegraphe,* Aug. 26, Sept. 9, 1795; Bennington *Vermont Gazette,* Sept. 11, 1795; New York *Argus,* Oct. 14, 1795; Lexington *Stewart's Kentucky Herald,* Nov. 24, 1795. British sailors had been subjected to abuse in several seaport towns since the treaty; see Wheeler, "Urban Politics," 97.

4. Baltimore *Federal Intelligencer,* Sept. 24, 1795; *Philadelphische Correspondenz,* Sept. 29, 1795; New York *Argus,* Oct. 14, 1795; Cincinnati, [Ohio], *Centinel of the North West Territory,* Oct. 24, 1795.

5. "Paulding," No. XV, Philadelphia *Aurora,* Aug. 24, 1796; Boston *Independent Chronicle,* Sept. 12, 1796.

6. New York *Argus,* cited in the Augusta, Ga., *Southern Centinel,* Aug. 11, 1796.

7. Augusta, Ga., *Southern Centinel,* Dec. 10, 1795; Norfolk, Va., *Norfolk and Portsmouth Public Advertiser,* Apr. 15, 19, 1796.

8. Annapolis *Maryland Gazette,* Sept. 3, 1795.

9. Savannah, Ga., *Columbian Museum,* Jan. 28, Aug. 12, 1796; Boston *Independent Chronicle,* Aug. 8, 1796.

10. Elizabethtown *New Jersey Journal,* June 29, 1796; New York *American Minerva* (a Federalist paper), Nov. 28, 1796; Philadelphia *Gales' Independent Gazetteer,* Dec. 2, 1796. Note also the Philadelphia *Aurora,* July 29, 1796, and the Newark, N. J., *Centinel of Freedom,* July 16, 1799, on the folly of relying on protections.

11. Item from the Philadelphia *Finlay's American Commercial Register,* in the Fair Haven, Vt., *Farmers' Library,* July 18, 1798.

12. Baltimore *Maryland Journal,* in the Richmond, Va., *Richmond and Manchester Advertiser,* June 18, 1796.

13. E.g., Concord, N. H., *Federal Mirror,* Sept. 4, 1795; Norfolk, Va., *Norfolk Herald,* Nov. 14, 1795; Alexandria, Va., *Columbian Mirror,* Mar. 8, 1796; Georgetown, D. C., *Columbian Chronicle,* May 10, 1796; Boston *Independent Chronicle,* May 26, 1796; New York *Herald* (wherein Federalists attempted to belittle seizures), June 8, 1796; Elizabethtown, Md., *Washington Spy,* June 29, 1796; Chambersburg, Pa., *Franklin Repository,* Aug. 4, 1796; Fredericksburg, Va., *Republican Citizen,* Sept. 21, 1796; Washington, D. C., *Washington Gazette,* Sept. 21, 1796; New Haven *Connecticut Journal,* Sept. 21, 1796; Elizabethtown *Jersey Journal,* Sept. 27, 1796; West Springfield, Mass., *American Intelligencer,* Oct. 11, 1796; etc.

14. Boston *Independent Chronicle,* Aug. 8, 1796.

15. Burlington, Vt., *Burlington Mercury,* June 3, 1796; Annapolis *Maryland Gazette,* Jan. 12, 1797.

16. Reading, Pa., *Readinger Adler,* Dec. 19, 1797; cf. the Sag Harbor, N. Y., *Frothingham's Long Island Herald,* May 24, 1797; Boston *Independent Chronicle,* Dec. 25, 1797.

17. Boston *Independent Chronicle,* Aug. 28, 1797.

18. Savannah, Ga., *Columbian Museum,* July 6, 1798.

19. Article from the Philadelphia *Aurora,* Lancaster, Pa., *Intelligencer,* Nov. 20, 1797.

20. Washington, Ky., *Mirror,* May 19, 1798; the Philadelphia *Carey's United States Recorder,* Apr. 19, 1798, with the same article, suggested that for an out-and-out alliance England would possibly mitigate her orders. Cf. the Boston *Independent Chronicle,* May 7, 1798.

21. "AURELIUS" believed banks, wars and speculators also played a part; New York *Diary,* Oct. 17, 1797. On the slump of 1796–97 see Wheeler, "Urban Politics," 112–13.

22. The orders were in response to the impressment of five sailors from the U. S. S. *Baltimore;* Boston *Independent Chronicle,* Jan. 31, 1799; Frankfort, Ky., *Palladium,* Feb. 12, 1799; Miller, *Federalist Era,* 224–25.

23. New York *Argus,* June 13, 1798; Boston *Independent Chronicle,* June 21, 1798. For samples of added outrages, see the *Chronicle,* Nov. 9, 1797, Jan. 18, May 3, July 23, 1798; Annapolis *Maryland Gazette,* June 22, 1797; New York *Tablet,* June 27, 1798; Savannah, Ga., *Columbian Museum,* July 6, 1798; Augusta, Ga., *Augusta Chronicle,* Nov. 24, 1798.

24. Boston *Independent Chronicle,* June 11, 14, 1798.

25. Frankfort, Ky., *Palladium,* Feb. 12, Nov. 21, 1799; Greensburg, Pa., *Farmers' Register,* May 24, 1799. For other such "fruits of the British Treaty" see the New London, Conn., *Bee,* Jan. 2, 1799; Lexington *Stewart's Kentucky Herald,* Feb. 5, 1799; Baltimore *American,* July 13, Oct. 5, 1799; Newark, N. J., *Centinel of Freedom,* July 16, 1799; Norfolk, Va., *Epitome of the Times,* July 25, 1799; Savannah, Ga., *Columbian Museum,* May 24, 1799; Boston *Constitutional Telegraphe,* Oct. 5, 1799; Richmond *Virginia Federalist* (which had long refrained from publishing such stories, deeming them false), Oct. 12, 1799; Raleigh, N. C., *Raleigh Register,* Oct. 29, 1799; Augusta, Ga., *Augusta Chronicle,* Nov. 23, 1799; *et al.*

26. Philadelphia *Aurora,* Feb. 1, 1799; Savannah, Ga., *Columbian Museum,* Feb. 26, 1799. Actually, in 1796–1797, losses to France were probably greater; see the insurance figures cited in Wheeler, "Urban Politics" 15n. For a sample of French seizures, see New Bedford, Mass., *Columbian Courier,* July 10, Oct. 9, 1799; but, said the Charleston, S. C., *City Gazette,* June 12, 1799, Englishmen had started this practice; cf. "PAETUS THRASEA," Boston *Independent Chronicle,* Aug. 26, 1799.

27. Newburyport, Mass., *Newburyport Herald,* Sept. 10, 1799; Boston *Constitutional Telegraphe,* Oct. 9, 1799; Northampton, Mass., *Pa-*

*triotic Gazette,* Oct. 11, 1799; Richmond *Virginia Federalist,* Oct. 12, 1799; Greenfield, Mass., *Greenfield Gazette,* Oct. 26, 1799; Newark, N. J., *Centinel of Freedom,* Oct. 22, 1799; Richmond *Virginia Argus,* Nov. 8, 1799.

28. Dedham, Mass., *Dedham Minerva,* Nov. 14, 1799.

29. *Albany Register,* cited in the Morristown, N. J., *Genius of Liberty,* Nov. 28, 1799.

30. Boston *Independent Chronicle,* Oct. 31, 1799; see the Richmond *Virginia Federalist,* Oct. 12, 1799.

31. Washington, Pa., *Herald of Liberty,* in the Richmond, Va., *Examiner,* Jan. 14, 1800. See the affidavit of Thomas Coats, Newburgh, N. Y., *Rights of Man,* Nov. 3, 1800; and an earlier comment on Federalist silence regarding British insults, Boston *Independent Chronicle,* Nov. 8, 1798.

32. Letter of H. H. Kennedy, Philadelphia *True American,* Mar. 29, 1800.

33. Stonington, Conn., *Impartial Journal,* Apr. 1, 1800; Boston *Independent Chronicle,* Apr. 28, 1800.

34. Augusta, Ga., *Augusta Herald,* Aug. 13, 1800.

35. Augusta, Ga., *Augusta Chronicle,* Aug. 9, 23, 30, 1800; Castine, [Me.], *Castine Journal,* Aug. 29, 1800; Pittsburgh *Tree of Liberty,* Aug. 30, 1800; Stonington, Conn., *Impartial Journal,* Apr. 29, 1800; Boston *Independent Chronicle,* Aug. 7, 1800; Philadelphia *Aurora,* Oct. 11, 1800; Richmond, Va., *Examiner,* Oct. 24, 1800.

36. E.g., the Raleigh, N. C., *Raleigh Register,* Aug. 12, 1800; Lexington *Kentucky Gazette,* Aug. 14, 1800; Washington, D. C., *National Intelligencer,* Nov. 12, 1800.

37. This summary is taken from the Raleigh, N. C., *Raleigh Register,* Oct. 22, 1800; cf. the brief account in McMaster, *A History,* II, 448.

38. "MUTIUS," Richmond *Virginia Argus,* Oct. 22, 25, 1799; "Aristogiton," Richmond, Va., *Examiner,* Oct. 22, 1799; Newark, N. J., *Centinel of Freedom,* Nov. 12, 19, 1799; Baltimore *American,* Oct. 28, 30, 1799. For similar sentiments, see the Boston *Constitutional Telegraphe,* Nov. 13, 1799. Reports of Williams' later capture and hanging produced a fourth wave of animadversions.

39. Miller *Federalist Era,* 221–22; Alexander DeConde, *The Quasi-War,* 200–01.

40. Philadelphia *Aurora,* Mar. 16, 1799; Baltimore *American,* July 2, 1799.

41. Boston *Constitutional Telegraphe* (Ebenezer Giles incident), Oct.

9, 1799; Newburyport, Mass., *Newburyport Herald,* Oct. 8, 1799; Philadelphia *Aurora* (beating of W. Gamble), Oct. 11, 1800; Richmond *Examiner,* Oct. 24, 1800; Newburgh, N. Y., *Rights of Man* (letter of Thomas Coats on the surrender of four Americans), Nov. 3, 1800.

42. Reading, Pa., *Readinger Adler,* Sept. 30, 1800; Philadelphia *Aurora* in the Boston *Constitutional Telegraphe,* Sept. 27, 1800; New London, Conn., *Bee,* Oct. 1, 1800; Pittsburgh *Tree of Liberty,* Oct. 11, 1800.

43. Adams himself had initiated an investigation; Pickering's letter to Bee was dated June 3, 1799. For accounts of the trial, judgment and surrender, see the Charleston *South Carolina State Gazette,* Aug. 1, 1799; Boston *Independent Chronicle,* Aug. 19, 1799; Richmond *Virginia Argus,* Aug. 19, 1799. Cf. Samuel E. Morison, *Life and Letters of Harrison Gray Otis,* I, 180; DeConde, *Quasi-War,* 204–05; Page Smith, *John Adams,* II, 1024–25; and Perkins, *First Rapprochement,* 124–25 (although newspaper evidence challenges Perkins' conclusion that the public was never greatly aroused).

44. Philadelphia *Aurora,* Aug. 12, 1799; Stonington, Conn., *Journal of the Times,* Sept. 17, 1799. The murdered Capt. Pigot, noted for brutality, was said to have met his just desserts; Boston *Constitutional Telegraphe,* Oct. 12, 1799.

45. Baltimore *American,* Oct. 5, 1799.

46. New London, Conn., *Bee,* Sept. 4, 1799; Boston *Constitutional Telegraphe,* Nov. 9, 16, 1799; McMaster, *A History,* II, 446; Wolfe, *Jeffersonian Democracy,* 127–28.

47. From the Charleston, S. C., *City Gazette,* in the Boston *Constitutional Telegraphe,* Oct. 23, 1799; Richmond *Virginia Argus,* Nov. 5, 1799; Newark, N. J., *Centinel of Freedom,* Nov. 5, 1799; Lancaster, Pa., *Intelligencer,* Nov. 6, 13, 1799; Reading, Pa., *Readinger Adler,* Nov. 5, 12, 19, Dec. 3, 1799; Frankfort, Ky., *Palladium,* Nov. 14, 21, 1799; Pittsfield, Mass., *Berkshire Gazette,* Jan. 14, 1800; Wolfe, *Jeffersonian Democracy,* 128.

48. "Robert Slender," Philadelphia *Aurora,* Aug. 22, 24, Sept. 3, 1799; Baltimore *American,* Sept. 7, 1799.

49. "THE PEOPLE," Newark, N. J., *Centinel of Freedom,* Oct. 22, 1799; Elizabethtown, N. J., *Jersey Journal,* Oct. 29, 1799; Richmond *Virginia Argus,* Nov. 8, 1799; Lancester, Pa., *Intelligencer,* Nov. 20, 1799.

50. "Last letter of J. Robbins," Philadelphia *Aurora,* Oct. 5, 1799; Baltimore *American,* Oct. 10, 1799; Newark, N. J., *Centinel of Free-*

*dom,* Oct. 22, 1799; Lancaster, Pa., *Intelligencer,* Oct. 23, 1799; Frankfort, Ky., *Palladium,* Oct. 31, 1799.

51. Baltimore *American,* Oct. 5, 10, 1799.

52. Philadelphia *Aurora,* Oct. 5, 1799; cited in McMaster, *A History,* II, 447–48.

53. McMaster, *A History,* II, 447; Miller, *Federalist Era,* 223–24; Morison, *Harrison G. Otis,* I, 180; Philip M. Marsh, "Philip Freneau and His Circle," *Pennsylvania Magazine of History and Biography* 63 (Jan. 1939), 55n.; Smith, *Adams,* II, 1025.

54. Lancaster, Pa., *Intelligencer,* Oct. 9, 1799; Baltimore *American,* Oct. 25, Nov. 4, 1799; Newark, N. J., *Centinel of Freedom,* Nov. 5, 1799; Boston *Constitutional Telegraphe* (citing an Albany paper), Nov. 6, 1799; Raleigh, N. C., *Raleigh Register,* Nov. 12, 1799; Morristown, N. J., *Genius of Liberty,* Nov. 28, 1799.

55. E.g., Lancaster, Pa., *Intelligencer,* Oct. 30, Nov. 13, 1799; Newark, N. J., *Centinel of Freedom,* July 22, 1800.

56. *Gazette of the United States,* in the Newark, N. J., *Centinel of Freedom,* Dec. 3, 1799; Concord, N. H., *Courier of New Hampshire,* Dec. 7, 1799; see also the Charleston *South Carolina State Gazette,* Nov. 15, 22, 1799; Georgetown, S. C., *Georgetown Gazette,* Dec. 18, 1799. Pinckney's letters continued to run after word of Robbins' death; Newark, N. J., *Centinel of Freedom,* Oct. 29, 1799; Northumberland, Pa., *Sunbury and Northumberland Gazette,* Dec. 28, 1799; etc.

57. New Haven *Connecticut Journal,* Nov. 28, 1799; Frankfort, Ky., *Palladium,* Jan. 2, 1800; Nashville *Tennessee Gazette,* Apr. 1, 1800; Pittsburgh *Gazette,* May 3, 1800.

58. New London, Conn., *Bee,* Nov. 27, 1799; Newark, N. J., *Centinel of Freedom,* Dec. 3, 10, 1799; Lancaster, Pa., *Intelligencer,* Dec. 25, 1799.

59. Philadelphia *True American,* Feb. 11, 1800; Peacham, Vt., *Green Mountain Patriot,* Mar. 5, 1800; Morristown, N. J., *Genius of Liberty,* Mar. 6, 1800; *Albany Register,* Mar. 7, 1800; Lexington *Kentucky Gazette,* Mar. 20, 1800; Nashville *Tennessee Gazette,* Apr. 1, 1800; Wolfe, *Jeffersonian Democracy,* 123. Perkins, *First Rapprochement,* 124–25, states that Republicans were quite willing to drop the issue without House debate, but that Federalists insisted upon the vote (which they won, 61–35).

60. Petersburg *Virginia Gazette,* Apr. 1, 1800; Warren, *Making of the Constitution,* 150.

61. Richmond *Virginia Argus,* Mar. 17, 1800; Richmond, Va., *Examiner,* Mar. 25, 1800.

62. Newark, N. J., *Centinel of Freedom*, Apr. 22, 1800.

63. Morristown, N. J., *Genius of Liberty*, June 26, 1800; Raleigh, N. C., *Raleigh Register*, July 1, 1800; Lexington *Kentucky Gazette*, July 10, 1800; Baltimore *American*, Aug. 20, 1800; Richmond *Virginia Argus*, Sept. 2, 1800. Federalists countered with an item from the Danbury, Conn., *Sun of Liberty*, Aug. 20, 1800, wherein Samuel Morse, editor, who had earlier believed Robbins to be an American, retracted and announced his conviction that Robbins had never lived in Danbury; Philadelphia *Gazette of the United States*, Sept. 27, 1800; Providence, R. I., *Providence Journal*, Oct. 15, 1800; Augusta, Ga., *Georgia Herald*, Oct. 22, 1800. See accounts of the Maryland pre-election arguments between Dewall (Dem.-Rep.) and Key (Fed.) in the Newark, N. J., *Centinel of Freedom*, Sept. 16, 1800.

64. Boston *Independent Chronicle*, Feb. 6, 1797, Mar. 27 ("The Honest Watchman"), 30, May 31 ("A Republican"), 1798; Richmond *Virginia Argus*, Feb. 12, 1799.

65. Philadelphia *Aurora*, in the Lexington *Kentucky Gazette*, Jan. 28, 1797; Boston *Independent Chronicle*, Feb. 1, 5, 1798; Newark, N. J., *Centinel of Freedom*, Apr. 3, 1798.

66. Philadelphia *Carey's United States Recorder*, Mar. 29, 1798; see also the Boston *Independent Chronicle*, Apr. 2, 5, Oct. 25, 1798.

67. Philadelphia *Aurora*, Nov. 20, 1799; Lancaster, Pa., *Intelligencer*, Nov. 27, 1799; Lexington *Kentucky Gazette*, Dec. 12, 1799; Frankfort, Ky., *Palladium*, Dec. 19, 1799.

68. New British duties in 1797 charged 19 shillings additional for each hogshead of tobacco brought in an American ship, 3s 9d per tierce of rice, etc.; Philadelphia *Aurora*, Apr. 26, 1798; Boston *Independent Chronicle*, May 7, 1798. The Halifax *North Carolina Journal*, May 22, 1797, gave without comment Chief Justice Ellsworth's ruling that these unsettled debts were bona fide obligations; see the Philadelphia *Aurora*, Apr. 11, 1799; Boston *Independent Chronicle*, Apr. 22, 1799; and the Charleston, S. C., *City Gazette*, Apr. 25, 1799, on the unwisdom of food shipments.

69. Reading, Pa., *Readinger Zeitung*, Mar. 22, 1797; *Readinger Adler*, Apr. 22, 1800; New York *American Citizen*, July 19, 1800; Raleigh, N. C., *Raleigh Register*, Sept. 23, 1800; *Baltimore Telegraphe*, Oct. 31, 1800; Augusta, Ga., *Augusta Chronicle*, Dec. 20, 1800.

70. Philadelphia *Daily Advertiser*, Feb. 10, 1797; Boston *Independent Chronicle*, Aug. 10, 1797, Mar. 12, July 9, 26, 1798.

71. Presumably the Ussher chronology was used; Elizabethtown, Md., *Washington Spy*, Aug. 24, 1796. The Providence, R. I., *Impartial*

*Observer,* Sept. 8, 1800, cited the *Aurora's* comparisons of British governmental revenue and expenditures.

72. E.g., Baltimore *Maryland Journal,* Aug. 13, 1796; Lexington *Kentucky Gazette,* Jan. 7, 1797; New York *Time Piece,* Aug. 16, 1797; Louisville, Ga., *State Gazette and Louisville Journal,* Dec. 17, 1799.

73. E.g., the Philadelphia *National Gazette,* Aug. 29, 1792, Apr. 27, 1793; Philadelphia papers of July 20, 23, 1795, in the Lexington *Stewart's Kentucky Herald,* Aug. 18, 1795; *ibid.,* June 30, 1795.

74. Newburyport, Mass., *Political Gazette,* Feb. 16, 1796. See references for the preceding note, and Donald H. Stewart, "Irish Immigration to New York City, 1790–1840," (Columbia University, 1938), 3, 24.

75. Philadelphia *Carey's Daily Advertiser,* July 8, 25, 31, 1797; Boston *Independent Chronicle,* July 24, 27, 31, Aug. 3, 7, 1797; Washington, D. C., *Washington Gazette,* Sept. 23, 1797.

76. "A Philanthropist," Boston *Independent Chronicle,* Oct. 16, 1797.

77. Philadelphia *Carey's United States Recorder,* Apr. 19, May 3, 1798; Augusta, Ga., *Augusta Chronicle,* Dec. 15, 1798.

78. Philadelphia *Carey's United States Recorder,* May 17, 19 ("Montgomery"), Aug. 14, 1798; *Baltimore Telegraphe,* June 13, 1798, *et seq.;* Boston *Independent Chronicle,* June 7, Aug. 6, Sept. 3, 1798.

79. Philadelphia *Aurora,* Aug. 27, 1798.

80. Newport, R. I., *Companion,* June 6, 1798; Boston *Independent Chronicle,* Aug. 23, Oct. 11, 1798; Savannah, Ga., *Columbian Museum,* Sept. 4, 1798; Newburyport, Mass., *Newburyport Herald,* Sept. 4, 1798; Frankfort, Ky., *Guardian of Freedom,* Sept. 25, 1798, Feb. 14, 1799; Chambersburg, Pa., *Farmers' Register,* Jan. 2, Apr. 10, 1799; Philadelphia *Aurora,* Mar. 23, 1799.

81. Georgetown, D. C., *Centinel of Liberty,* Jan. 22, 1799; Washington, Ky., *Mirror,* Mar. 1, 1799; Lexington *Kentucky Gazette,* Nov. 28, 1799; Boston *Independent Chronicle,* June 12, 1800; Richmond *Virginia Argus,* Sept. 26, 1800.

82. Philadelphia *Freeman's Journal,* Dec. 7, 1791; Norfolk *Virginia Chronicle,* Sept. 22, 1792; Dover, N. H., *Phenix,* Mar. 2, 1793; Augusta, Ga., *Southern Centinel,* Mar. 27, 1794. See Elisha P. Douglass, "The Adventurer Bowles," *William and Mary Quarterly* 6 (Jan. 1949), 3–29; Van Every, *Ark of Empire,* 121–25.

83. Georgetown, S. C., *Georgetown Gazette,* Jan. 22, Feb. 15, 1800;

Charleston, S. C., *City Gazette*, Mar. 11, 1800; Fredericksburg *Virginia Herald*, Mar. 21, 1800.

84. Item from Savannah in the Charleston, S. C., *City Gazette*, Apr. 5, 1800; Newark, N. J., *Centinel of Freedom*, Apr. 29, 1800. Bowles was later captured by a hostile Creek faction and imprisoned by the Spaniards; Van Every, *Ark of Empire*, 125.

85. Philadelphia *Aurora*, Sept. 19, 1800; Richmond *Virginia Argus*, Sept. 26, 1800.

86. "AMERICANUS," Boston *Independent Chronicle*, Aug. 7, 1800.

87. See the Brooklyn, N. Y., *Long Island Courier*, Oct. 15, 1791.

88. Boston *Independent Chronicle*, Sept. 23, 1793; "FARMERS," *Edwards' Baltimore Daily Advertiser*, Feb. 8, 1794; Baltimore *Federal Intelligencer*, June 25, 1795.

89. Richmond, Va., *Richmond and Manchester Advertiser*, July 4, 1795; Boston *Independent Chronicle*, Jan. 8, 1798.

90. Rutland, Vt., *Farmers' Library*, Feb. 17, 1794.

91. New York *Argus* ("Warren"), July 27, 1796; Philadelphia *Aurora*, July 28, 1796; Boston *Independent Chronicle*, Aug. 8, 11, 15, 1796.

92. Boston *Independent Chronicle*, May 14, 1798.

93. Baltimore *American*, Nov. 4, 1799; Boston *Constitutional Telegraphe*, Nov. 13, 1799; Newark, N. J., *Centinel of Freedom*, Nov. 19, 1799; "Reflection," Boston *Independent Chronicle*, Oct. 9, 1800.

94. McMaster, *A History*, II, 170–71; Alexander DeConde, *A History of American Foreign Policy*, 84–85; Bassett, *Federalist System*, 113–14; Samuel F. Bemis, *A Diplomatic History of the United States*, 150; Exeter, N. H., *Weekly Visitor*, July 14, 1795.

95. Newburyport, Mass., *Morning Star*, Nov. 12, 1794.

96. See the *Baltimore Daily Intelligencer*, Jan. 1, 1794; Augusta, Ga., *Southern Centinel*, Jan. 9, 23, 1794; Newburyport, Mass., *Morning Star*, Apr. 15, May 20, 1794; *Hartford Gazette*, Feb. 2, 1795; Trenton *State Gazette of New Jersey*, Feb. 17, 1795.

97. Alexandria, Va., *Columbian Mirror*, Mar. 8, 1796; *New York Weekly Museum*, May 7, 1796; McMaster, *A History*, II, 588–93.

98. Sag Harbor, N. Y., *Frothingham's Long Island Herald*, Feb. 8, 1797.

99. Letter of William Blount, Apr. 17, 1797, Knoxville, Tenn., *Knoxville Gazette*, May 1, 1797.

100. Boston *Independent Chronicle*, Nov. 15, 1798.

101. Philadelphia *Aurora*, Jan. 24, July 23, 1800; Boston *Independent*

*Chronicle,* Feb. 3, 1800; Baltimore *American,* July 26, 1800; Danbury, Conn., *Sun of Liberty,* Aug 14, 1800.

102. Ames, *Fisher Ames,* II, 287.

103. Philadelphia *National Gazette,* May 11, June 8, 1793.

104. Philadelphia *Pennsylvania Journal,* May 15, 1793; *New-York Journal,* July 24, 1793; New Brunswick, N. J., *Guardian of Freedom,* July 31, 1793.

105. Norwich, Conn., *Weekly Register,* Apr. 22, 1794.

106. Philadelphia *National Gazette,* July 13, 1793; Forman, *"Political Activities,"* 51–52. See the Philadelphia *General Advertiser,* Apr. 4, 1793; Boston *Columbian Centinel,* May 15, 1793; New Brunswick, N. J., *Guardian of Freedom,* June 26, 1793. The Fredericksburg, Md., *Bartgis's Federal Gazette,* Apr. 4, 1798, noted roistering Federalists and British naval officers singing "God Save the King." Baltimore and Philadelphia Federalists were alleged to have toasted George III before President Adams; New York *American Citizen,* May 12, 1800. Federalists supposedly opposed celebrating Independence Day, ostensibly because it revived old animosities, but actually because it exhibited republican sentiment; Baltimore *American,* Aug. 3, 1799; New York *American Citizen,* July 5, 1800.

107. Boston *Independent Chronicle,* Apr. 28, 1794. See also the Philadelphia *General Advertiser,* Feb. 4, 1794; Charleston, S. C., *Columbian Herald,* Mar. 12, 1794: and the Norwich, Conn., *Weekly Register* (on British "bribery" in Philadelphia), Apr. 22, 1794, for similar opinions.

108. *Edwards' Baltimore Daily Advertiser,* Apr. 2, 1794; Boston *Independent Chronicle,* Apr. 18, 1794; Norwich, Conn., *Weekly Register,* Apr. 22, 1794.

109. Faÿ, *Revolutionary Spirit,* 361; Cobbett was cited as an example.

110. Newburyport, Mass., *Morning Star,* June 10, 1794.

111. Halifax *North Carolina Journal,* Feb. 8, 1796; Philadelphia *Aurora,* Feb. 12, 1796.

112. Philadelphia *Aurora,* Apr. 18, 1795, Sept. 2, 1796 ("Paulding," No. XVI); Boston *Independent Chronicle,* Sept. 15, 1796.

113. *"A Real Federalist,"* Newark, N. J., *Centinel of Freedom,* Jan. 11, 1797; reprinted in the Boston *Independent Chronicle,* Jan. 30, 1797.

114. Boston *Independent Chronicle,* Feb. 1, 1797.

115. Philadelphia *Aurora,* May 20, 1797; New London, Conn., *Bee,* June 14, 1797.

116. "Cato," from the Philadelphia *Aurora,* quoted in the Boston *Independent Chronicle,* July 24, 1797.

117. *Albany Register,* Oct. 16, 1797; Newton, N. J., *Farmers Journal,* Nov. 1, 1797.

118. Wiscasset, [Me.], *Wiscasset Argus,* Dec. 8, 1797.

119. Richmond, Va., *Richmond and Manchester Advertiser,* Jan. 30, 1796; Philadelphia *Aurora,* June 9, 1796; Boston *Polar Star,* Jan. 20, 1797; Charleston, S. C., *City Gazette,* June 1, 1797; Boston *Independent Chronicle,* June 22, 1797; Wolfe, *Jeffersonian Democracy,* 106–07.

120. Philadelphia *Aurora,* Jan. 26, 1797; Philadelphia *Daily Advertiser,* Feb. 10, 1797; Boston *Independent Chronicle,* Aug. 3, 24, 31, 1797.

121. Philadelphia *Aurora,* Apr. 7, 1797; Boston *Independent Chronicle,* Apr. 20, 1797.

122. "Aristides, I," from the *Kentucky Gazette,* in the Washington, D. C., *Washington Gazette,* Oct. 21, 1797. See also the Philadelphia *Aurora,* Nov. 30, 1796; Lexington *Kentucky Gazette,* Jan. 14, 1797; Boston *Independent Chronicle,* May 15, 1797.

123. Philadelphia *Aurora,* May 29, 1797; reprinted in the Charleston *South Carolina State Gazette,* June 9, 1797. The Charleston *City Gazette,* July 26, 1797, saw the Liston-Harper relationship as a visible indication of the operation of "British gold . . . among us."

124. Boston *Independent Chronicle,* July 27, 1797; New Haven *Connecticut Journal,* Aug. 7, 1797.

125. Richmond *Virginia Argus,* April, 1798, cited in the *National Magazine,* 103–105.

126. Reading, Pa., *Readinger Adler,* Oct. 2, 1798; Morristown, N. J., *Morris County Gazette,* Feb. 6, 1798.

127. Boston *Independent Chronicle,* Feb. 4, 7, 1799; New London, Conn., *Bee.,* Feb. 27, 1799.

128. Lexington, Ky., *Stewart's Kentucky Herald,* Mar. 12, 1799.

129. Boston *Independent Chronicle,* Apr. 25, 29, 1799; Philadelphia *Aurora,* June 18, 1799.

130. Philadelphia *Aurora,* Feb. 9, 1799; Boston *Independent Chronicle,* Feb. 21, 1799; Richmond *Virginia Argus* (on the alleged purpose of Maitland's visit), Apr. 19, 1799.

131. Described later in this chapter.

132. Baltimore *American,* July 30, 1799. See also the New York *Argus,* July 25, 1799.

133. Newark, N. J., *Centinel of Freedom,* Mar. 25, 1800.

134. New London, Conn., *Bee,* Mar. 19, 1800; Morristown, N. J.,

*Genius of Liberty,* Mar. 13, 1800. The Alexandria, Va., *Alexandria Times,* Mar. 12, 1800, called this discriminating in favor of the British against native sons; see also an item from the New York *Argus* in the Lexington *Kentucky Gazette,* Apr. 3, 1800.

135. "A CENTINEL," Boston *Constitutional Telegraphe,* Jan. 15, 1800.

136. "JACOBIN," *idem;* "Hancock," *ibid.,* Jan. 25, 1800; Newark, N. J., *Centinel of Freedom,* Mar. 11, 1800; Richmond, Va., *Examiner,* Mar. 25, 1800; item from the *Petersburg Republican,* Richmond, Va., *Friend of the People,* May 16, 1800; "Mr. LISTON, Keeps moving," Pittsburgh *Tree of Liberty,* Aug. 30, 1800; Baltimore *American,* Nov. 4, 1800; Wilmington, Del., *Mirror of the Times,* Nov. 26, 1800. See also an item from the Wilmington *Delaware and Eastern Shore Advertiser* in the Alexandria, Va., *Alexandria Times,* Jan. 31, 1800; *National Magazine,* 112; and a comment on the *Connecticut Courant,* Hartford *American Mercury,* Oct. 10, 1799. The Richmond, Va., *Examiner's* list (from the Philadelphia *Aurora*) was in the issue of Oct. 7, 1800.

137. Perhaps first mentioned at the time of Pickering's, Wolcott's and McHenry's opposition to sending new envoys to France in 1799; Meade Minnigerode, *Presidential Years,* 93–94.

138. Philadelphia *Aurora,* Feb. 6, 1800; Natchez, [Miss.], *Green's Impartial Observer,* June 2, 1800; Newark, N. J., *Centinel of Freedom,* Sept. 9, 1800; Pittsburgh *Tree of Liberty,* Sept. 27, 1800; Richmond *Virginia Argus,* Sept. 26, Oct. 3, 1800; Richmond, Va., *Examiner,* Nov. 7, 1800. See also (on Adams' own stay in England) the Elizabethtown *New Jersey Journal,* Oct. 7, 1800.

139. Richmond *Virginia Argus,* Sept. 16, 1800; Portsmouth, N. H., *Republican Ledger,* Sept. 23, 1800.

140. Timothy Pickering to Adams, Philadelphia, July 24, 1799; Adams, *Works,* IX, 3.

141. John Adams to Timothy Pickering, Aug. 1, 1799; *ibid.,* IX, 3.

142. Danbury, Conn., *Sun of Liberty,* Aug. 13, 1800.

143. Baltimore *American,* Sept. 27, 1799.

144. New York *American Citizen,* May 26, 1800; see the *London Morning Chronicle,* June 25, 1800, as quoted in the Pittsburgh *Tree of Liberty,* Aug. 30, 1800.

145. Morristown, N. J., *Genius of Liberty,* Aug. 14, 1800. See *supra,* Chap. 3.

146. Quotation allegedly from the *London Evening Post,* July 29, 1800, Newark, N. J., *Centinel of Freedom* (citing the Boston *Constitu-*

*tional Telegraphe*), Sept. 16, 1800. On Adams' writings, see the New York *American Citizen,* Oct. 17, 1800; Richmond *Virginia Argus,* Oct. 28, 1800; Raleigh, N. C., *Raleigh Register,* Nov. 4, 1800; Richmond, Va., *Examiner,* Nov. 7, 1800.

147. New London, Conn., *Bee,* Oct. 29, 1800.

148. E.g., Fredericktown, Md., *Rights of Man,* July 20, 1796; Richmond, Va., *Virginia Federalist,* June 1, 8, 1799.

149. Philadelphia *Aurora,* Jan. 6, 1795; Philadelphia *Daily Advertiser,* May 30, June 3, 1797; "A YANKEE," Newark, N. J., *Centinel of Freedom,* May 1, 1798.

150. Hartford, Conn., *American Mercury* (professing to print both sides of the question), Oct. 3, 1799; New York *Argus,* Jan. 7, 1799.

151. "FOURTH of JULY, 1776," Elizabethtown *Maryland Herald,* Nov. 15, 1798; "A Potowmac Planter," Richmond, Va., *Examiner,* June 10, 1800; "Curtius," Richmond *Virginia Argus* (quoted in the Boston *Independent Chronicle,* Jan. 3, 1799); "Aristocratic Hilarity," Reading, Pa., *Readinger Adler,* Nov. 20, 1799; Portsmouth, N. H., *Republican Ledger,* cited in the Boston *Constitutional Telegraphe,* Jan. 25, 1800.

152. Geneva, N. Y., *Impartial American,* Jan. 6, 1801.

153. Philadelphia *Aurora,* May 27, July 6, 1797. See McMaster, *A History,* II, 339–41; Van Every, *Ark of Empire,* 341–42; Miller, *Federalist Era,* 189–91; James R. Jacobs, *Tarnished Warrior,* 173; Faÿ, *Two Franklins,* 325; and Beard, *Economic Interpretation,* 78.

154. Blount's letter to Carey (Apr. 21, 1797), Pickering's to Liston, and Liston's reply were all in the Philadelphia *Gales' Independent Gazetteer,* July 7, 1797. See also the Philadelphia *Courier Français,* July 8, 1797; Boston *Independent Chronicle,* July 13, 1797; Reading, Pa., *Readinger Adler,* July 18, 1797; Edenton *State Gazette of North Carolina,* July 27, 1797, et al.

155. E.g., the Washington, D. C., *Washington Gazette,* quoted in the Newburn *North Carolina Gazette,* Aug. 5, 1797. A similar argument was used by the Boston *Columbian Centinel;* see the Boston *Independent Chronicle,* July 13, 1797.

156. Philadelphia *Aurora,* July 6, 1797; Boston *Independent Chronicle,* July 13, 1797.

157. Boston *Independent Chronicle, idem;* Russell edited the Federalist *Columbian Centinel.*

158. *Ibid.,* July 17, 31, 1797.

159. *Ibid.,* July 13, 1797; cf. the Fredericktown, Md., *Bartgis's Federal Gazette,* July 26, 1797; and a lengthy Federalist reply (insisting Blount was a Democrat), Worcester *Massachusetts Spy,* July 19, 1797.

160. Philadelphia *Aurora,* July 10, 1797; Philadelphia *Gales' Independent Gazetteer,* July 11, 1797; Philadelphia *Courier Français,* July 12, 1797; Edenton *State Gazette of North Carolina,* July 27, 1797; Beard, *Economic Interpretation,* 79. See also the Danbury, Conn., *Republican Journal,* July 19, 1797; Boston *Independent Chronicle,* July 13, 17, 24, Sept. 4, 1797; Kenneth W. Colgrove, "The Attitude of Congress Toward the Pioneers of the West from 1789 to 1820," *Iowa Journal of History and Politics* 8 (Jan. 1910), 37, citing a letter of Jefferson from Ford, *Writings of Thomas Jefferson,* VII, 190.

161. "MUSTARD," Boston *Independent Chronicle,* Aug. 14, 1797; see also *ibid.,* July 24 ("Cato," from the Philadelphia *Aurora*), 27 ("Marcus"), 1797.

162. Philadelphia *Courier Français,* July 16, 1797; Boston *Independent Chronicle,* July 17, 20, 24, 31, 1797; Charleston, S. C., *City Gazette,* Aug. 18, 1797. The name was frequently spelled "Romayne."

163. Sag Harbor, N. Y., *Frothingham's Long Island Herald,* July 15 (see also July 8, 26), 1797; Boston *Independent Chronicle,* July 24, 1797; item from the New London, Conn., *Bee,* Charleston, S. C., *City Gazette,* Aug. 18, 1797.

164. Philadelphia *Aurora,* July 12, 1797.

165. Boston *Independent Chronicle,* July 20, 27, Aug. 10, 1797, Jan. 8, 1798. See also the New London, Conn., *Bee,* July 26, 1797.

166. E.g., Philadelphia *Merchant's Daily Advertiser,* Dec. 18–21, 1797; *Baltimore Telegraphe,* esp. Dec. 21, also Dec. 22, 23, 25, 27–30, 1797, Jan. 1, 1798; Philadelphia *Courier Français,* Dec. 20–29, 1797, Jan. 2–4, 1798.

167. See the Philadelphia *Aurora,* July 10, 12, 1797; Philadelphia *Merchant's Daily Advertiser,* Dec. 21, 1797, *et seq.;* Boston *Independent Chronicle,* Dec. 28, 1797, Jan. 8, 1798.

168. New London, Conn., *Bee,* Dec. 20, 1797; "JONATHAN," Morristown, N. J., *Morris County Gazette,* Jan. 9, 1798. Cf. the New London *Connecticut Gazette,* Jan. 17, 1798.

169. *Greenleaf's New York Journal,* Jan. 24, Feb. 3, 1798 (making invidious comparisons with the conduct of the French Directory, which had unearthed a somewhat similar plot at Paris, Sept. 4, 1797); Philadelphia *Aurora,* Jan. 1, Feb. 6, 1798.

170. Boston *Independent Chronicle,* Jan. 10, 1799 (see also Jan. 17, 1799).

171. *Ibid.,* Jan. 21, Feb. 4, 1799; Chambersburg, Pa., *Farmers' Register,* Jan. 23, 1799; Frankfort, Ky., *Palladium,* Feb. 19, 1799.

172. Philadelphia *Aurora,* July 13, 15, 1799; Norfolk, Va., *Epitome of the Times,* July 25, 1799; Charleston *South Carolina State Gazette,*

July 31, Aug. 3, 1799; Washington, Ky., *Mirror,* Aug. 7, 1799; Georgetown, S. C., *Georgetown Gazette,* Aug. 14, 21, 1799; Frankfort, Ky., *Palladium,* Aug. 8, 1799. The last-named spelled the name "Sweeny," but most papers used the "z".

173. Philadelphia *Aurora,* Aug. 28, 1800; New York *Forlorn Hope,* Sept. 6, 1800.

174. Reading, Pa., *Readinger Adler,* Oct. 21, 1800; Pittsburgh *Tree of Liberty,* Oct. 25, 1800; Fredericksburg, Va., *Courier,* Nov. 7, 1800; Raleigh, N. C., *Raleigh Register,* Nov. 18, 1800. See also the *Raleigh Register,* Sept. 30, 1800; Charleston, S. C., *City Gazette,* Sept. 16, 1800; Charleston, S. C., *Federal Carolina Gazette,* Nov. 13, 1800. Leonard D. White, *The Federalists,* 288–90, suggests Coxe switched his political allegiance as early as 1791, and this caused his removal later.

175. Richmond, Va., *Examiner,* Oct. 24, Nov. 4, 7, 1800. Adams' letter to Thomas Pinckney intimated that whatever he had written to Coxe had probably been garbled. He could not be certain without seeing the eight-year-old original letter, but he had not personally known all the Pinckneys in 1792 and had been told the British government had intimated one of them as more acceptable than Adams himself. He now praised both Thomas and Charles Cotesworth Pinckney highly, assuring them he did *not* believe they were under British influence, and criticizing the dragging of every old private letter, years later, into newspapers for purposes of revenge. See the Philadelphia *Poulson's American Daily Advertiser,* Oct. 27, 1800; Fredericktown, Md., *Rights of Man,* Nov. 5, 1800.

176. Richmond *Virginia Argus,* Aug 29, 1800. For examples of the other charges, see the Philadelphia *Aurora,* Mar. 28, 1797; Lexington *Kentucky Gazette,* Apr. 26, 1797; Baltimore *American,* Sept. 26, 1799.

177. Boston *Independent Chronicle,* June 12, 1800; Philadelphia *Aurora,* June 28, July 10, 1800 ("anglo-federal party" was a favorite expression with this paper in 1800); Richmond *Virginia Argus,* Oct. 10, 1800.

178. Philadelphia *Aurora,* Sept. 19, 1800; reprinted in the Richmond *Virginia Argus,* Sept. 26, 1800.

179. Philadelphia *Aurora,* Sept. 15, 1800; Richmond *Virginia Argus,* Sept. 23, 1800.

180. Boston *Independent Chronicle,* June 12, 1800; also the Philadelphia *Aurora,* July 10, 1800. The New York *American Citizen,* July 19, 1800, was another paper emphasizing the need of closer ties with France.

 GALLIA AGGRIEVED

1. *New York Journal,* Mar. 4, 1795; Philadelphia *Independent Gazetteer,* Mar. 7, 1795.

2. New York *Herald,* Jan. 2, 1796. The Philadelphia *Aurora,* Apr. 3, 1795; Lexington *Kentucky Gazette,* Apr. 25, 1795; Richmond, Va., *Richmond Chronicle,* July 19, 1796; "Fabius," Nos. I, II, III, in the Philadelphia *New World,* commencing Apr. 17, 1797. For Federalist expressions of approval, see the Baltimore *Federal Gazette,* Sept. 8, Nov. 8, 15 (citing the *American Minerva*), 1796.

3. Sag Harbor, N. Y., *Frothingham's Long Island Herald,* Feb. 8, 1797.

4. Boston *Independent Chronicle,* Feb. 23, June 19, 1797.

5. Baltimore *Maryland Journal,* Apr. 17, 1797; Boston *Independent Chronicle,* June 22 (citing the Charleston, S. C., *City Gazette*), Oct. 9, 16, 23, 1797, Jan. 14, 1799; Philadelphia *Courier Français,* Oct. 10, 1797; Philadelphia *Aurora,* Oct. 12, 1797.

6. E.g., the Chambersburg, Pa., *Farmers' Register,* Nov. 28, 1798; Boston *Independent Chronicle,* Jan. 14, 1799; Washington, Ky., *Mirror,* Apr. 26, 1799; the quotation is from the Boston *Constitutional Telegraphe,* Nov. 6, 1799. For a Federalist report see the New Haven *Connecticut Journal,* Mar. 7, 1799.

7. Philadelphia *Aurora,* Nov. 7, 1798; Boston *Independent Chronicle,* Feb. 18, 1799.

8. Petersburg *Virginia Gazette,* Apr. 1, 1800.

9. See Merle E. Curti, *Peace or War,* 26; DeConde, *American Foreign Policy,* 56–58, 69.

10. Philadelphia *Aurora,* Dec. 26, 1797; reprinted in the Boston *Independent Chronicle,* Jan. 8, 1798.

11. E.g., the Paris, Ky., *Rights of Man,* Oct. 11, 1797; Norfolk, Va., *American Gazette,* July 22, 1796; Frankfort, Ky., *Palladium,* June 27, 1799; Boston *Independent Chronicle,* Apr. 22, Dec. 26, 1799; Salisbury *North Carolina Mercury and Salisbury Advertiser,* June 27, 1799; Boston *Constitutional Telegraphe,* Dec. 21, 1799, Jan. 15, 1800; Goshen, N. Y., *Orange Patrol,* Jan. 7, 1800.

12. Some 300 sail were alleged to have been taken by the French in the year ending June 1, 1797; Stauffer, *New England and the Bavarian Illuminati*, 124. Earlier, Pickering reported 316 American ships lost to French cruisers in 1795; DeConde, *Quasi-War*, 9.

13. Philadelphia *Aurora*, June 14, 1796; Baltimore *Federal Gazette*, June 18, 1796; Boston *Independent Chronicle*, June 27, 30, 1796; Richmond, Va., *Richmond Chronicle*, July 23, 1796. Cf. an item from Philadelphia in the Halifax *North Carolina Journal*, July 25, 1796, suggesting American "Jacobins" had arranged the capture of the *Mount Vernon* to produce a prophesied rupture with France.

14. Dumfries, Va., *Republican Journal*, July 7, 1796; Boston *Independent Chronicle*, July 11, 1796.

15. E.g., the New London, Conn., *Bee*, July 6, 1797; Savannah, Ga., *Columbian Museum*, May 24, 1799.

16. See "An American Merchant," Philadelphia *Aurora*, Feb. 6, 7, 1798.

17. Boston *Independent Chronicle*, Mar. 22, 1796, Feb. 13, 1797; Philadelphia *Aurora*, Aug. 8, 1796, Jan. 31, 1797; Savannah, Ga., *Columbian Museum*, Oct. 11, 1796; Charleston, S. C., *City Gazette*, Apr. 21, 1797; New York *Argus*, Apr. 2, 1799.

18. The structure should be commenced immediately, to afford relief to Mantua without delay; Philadelphia *Aurora*, Apr. 3, 1797; Philadelphia *Daily Advertiser*, Apr. 3, 1797; Charleston, S. C., *City Gazette*, Apr. 21, 1797.

19. Bemis, "Washington's Farewell Address," 257–59, 264.

20. Letter in the Boston *Independent Chronicle*, July 24, 1797.

21. Philadelphia *Aurora*, Oct. 31, 1796; Clark, *Peter Porcupine*, 85–86. See also Meade Minnigerode, *Presidential Years*, 57–58; and the letters of William L. Smith to Ralph Izard, Philadelphia, Nov. 3, 8, 1796, reprinted in the *American Historical Review*, 14 (July, 1909), 781–82, 784–85.

22. Philadelphia *Aurora*, Nov. 4, 1796; Hazen, *Contemporary American Opinion*, 285–86.

23. Philadelphia *Aurora*, Nov. 18, 1796; New Haven *Connecticut Journal*, Nov. 23, 1796; Bemis, "Washington's Farewell Address," 264–65; Clark, *Peter Porcupine*, 85–86; Faÿ, *Revolutionary Spirit*, 372; "Bache," *DAB*, I, 463; Hazen, *Contemporary American Opinion*, 285–87.

24. Minnigerode, *Presidential Years*, 57–60; Clark, *Peter Porcupine*, 86; Jones, *America and French Culture*, 547; Miller, *Federalist Era*, 200; Morison, ed., *Life and Letters of H. G. Otis*, I, 71; see also the

*Annual Report of the American Historical Association, 1903,* II, 912–1081, *passim.* Boston *Independent Chronicle,* Nov. 14, 17, 1796; "AN AMERICAN," from the Hartford *Connecticut Courant,* Danbury, Conn., *Republican Journal,* Nov. 28, 1796; Knoxville, Tenn., *Knoxville Gazette,* Dec. 19, 1796 (Adet's note was reprinted, Dec. 26, 1796, Jan. 2, 9, 16, 1797); Lancaster, Pa., *Lancaster Journal,* Nov. 25, 1796.

25. Letter in the Philadelphia *Aurora,* Jan. 5, 1797; reprinted in the Boston *Independent Chronicle,* Jan. 16, 1797; E. Wilson Lyon, "The Directory and the United States," *American Historical Review* 43 (Apr., 1938), 517. See also the *Aurora,* Apr. 19, 1798; Hazen, *Contemporary American Opinion,* 287.

26. Boston *Independent Chronicle,* Nov. 17, 24, Dec. 1796, Feb. 9, 1797; Washington, D. C., *Washington Gazette,* Mar. 4, 1797; Bemis, "Washington's Farewell Address," 265–66; McMaster, *A History,* II, 313.

27. Boston *Independent Chronicle,* Dec. 29, 1796; Charleston, S. C., *City Gazette,* Mar. 2, 1797; "A Frenchman," Philadelphia *Aurora,* May 20, 1797; McMaster, *A History,* II, 313–14.

28. Philadelphia *Aurora,* Jan. 2, May 17, 1797; Augusta, Ga., *Southern Centinel,* Feb. 2, 1797; Philadelphia *New World,* Feb. 6, 1797; McMaster, *A History,* II, 314–16.

29. *Le Rédacteur,* Dec. 20, 1796, in the Augusta, Ga., *Southern Centinel,* Mar. 16, 1797.

30. Jones, *America and French Culture,* 547; McMaster, *A History,* II, 319; Wolfe, *Jeffersonian Democracy,* 100–02; Bond, "Monroe Mission," esp. 30–31, 33–36, 44–47, 51–53, 59–62, 71–74, 80–83.

31. Boston *Independent Chronicle,* Aug. 3, 1797.

32. *Ibid.,* Dec. 29, 1796 (from the Washington, D. C. *Washington Gazette*), Jan. 2, 9, 23, Feb. 2, 13, 1797; Philadelphia *Aurora,* Dec. 21, 24, 1796, Feb. 4, 14, 17, Mar. 15, 1797; Philadelphia *New World,* Jan. 18, 1797; Philadelphia *Daily Advertiser,* Feb. 20, 1797; New York *Argus,* Mar. 13, 1797; Wolfe, *Jeffersonian Democracy,* 108–09. See the Norfolk, Va., *American Gazette and General Advertiser,* July 15, 1796, on Thomas Pinckney's displacement at the Court of St. James.

33. "AN EXAMINATION OF THE LATE LETTER FROM MR. PICKERING TO MR. PINCKNEY," in the Philadelphia *Daily Advertiser,* Feb. 7, 8, 9, 1797; Norwich, Conn., *Chelsea Courier,* Mar. 15, 22, 29, Apr. 5, 1797; Charleston *South Carolina State Gazette,* Mar. 22, 23, 1797. See also the last-named, Feb. 17, Mar. 28, 1797; Philadelphia *Aurora,* Jan. 24, 1797; Lexington *Kentucky Ga-*

*zette,* Mar. 11, 1797; and the Staunton *Virginia Gazette,* Mar. 29, 1797; on Pickering's animosity toward France.

34. On Pinckney abroad, see the letter of Delacroix to Adet, Jan. 3, 1797, in Lyon, "The Directory," 517; McMaster, *A History,* II, 320–21; Wolfe, *Jeffersonian Democracy,* 102. The Philadelphia *Aurora,* Mar. 27, 1797, carried Adams's call for a special session; see also Wolfe, *Jeffersonian Democracy,* 104.

35. Philadelphia *Aurora,* Mar. 14, 16, 20, 1797; Staunton *Virginia Gazette,* Mar. 29, 1797; McMaster, *A History,* II, 310; see also De-Conde, *Quasi-War,* 12.

36. Philadelphia *Aurora,* Mar. 31, 1797; reprinted in the Charleston, S. C., *City Gazette,* Apr. 25, 1797. See also the Boston *Independent Chronicle,* May 1, 1797.

37. Philadelphia *Aurora,* May 19, 1797; Philadelphia *Daily Advertiser,* May 19, 1797; Wolfe, *Jeffersonian Democracy,* 104; DeConde, *Quasi-War,* 25–26; Richardson, *Messages and Papers,* I, 223–29.

38. Philadelphia *Aurora,* May 19, June 6, 1797; Boston *Independent Chronicle,* May 25, 29, 1797; Sag Harbor, N. Y., *Frothingham's Long Island Herald,* June 7, 1797; Faÿ, *Two Franklins,* 323–25.

39. Philadelphia *Aurora,* Mar. 15, May 19, 20, 25, 1797; New York *Argus,* Apr. 6, 1797; Boston *Independent Chronicle,* May 18, 29, Aug. 14, 1797; Philadelphia *Daily Advertiser,* May 19, 1797; Wolfe, *Jeffersonian Democracy,* 104–05.

40. Philadelphia *Aurora,* May 22, 23, 27, 1797; Boston *Independent Chronicle,* Aug. 14, 1797.

41. Boston *Independent Chronicle,* May 1, June 12, 15, 22, 26, 1797; on a meeting in Caroline County, Va., see the Portland, [Maine], *Eastern Herald* (letter of Edmund Pendleton to Congressman Anthony New), May 10, 1797.

42. New York *Time Piece,* June 9, 1797, cited in Nevins, *American Press Opinion,* 23–24; Boston *Independent Chronicle,* May 1, July 17, 1797.

43. Boston *Independent Chronicle,* Apr. 6, May 8, Nov. 20, 1797, Mar. 22, 1798; Washington, D. C., *Washington Gazette,* Feb. 1, 1797; Philadelphia *Aurora,* Mar. 22, 1798.

44. Wolfe, *Jeffersonian Democracy,* 104–05; Bowers, *Jefferson and Hamilton,* 348–49; Bond, "Monroe Mission," 87–88.

45. Philadelphia *Aurora,* May 31, June 1, 17, 1797; Boston *Independent Chronicle,* Aug. 3, 1797.

46. Bond, "Monroe Mission," 80–83, 88–93, 96; Philadelphia *Gales' Independent Gazetteer,* Aug. 4, 1797; Bennington, Vt., *Tablet of the*

*Times,* Aug. 24, 1797. See Philip Freneau, *Letters on Various Interesting and Important Subjects,* p. iii, for the belief that Federalists were determined to provoke war with France; also Philadelphia *Aurora,* Jan. 27 ("FIAT JUSTICIA"), Mar. 12, 1798; New York *Journal and Patriotic Register,* Jan. 10, Feb. 14, 1798; Boston *Independent Chronicle,* Feb. 8, 1798 ("A. Z."); "Junius," in the mildly Federalist Lancaster, Pa., *Lancaster Journal,* June 2, 1798; and DeConde, *Quasi-War,* 103–06.

47. Bowers, *Jefferson and Hamilton,* 342–44, 350–51; Wolfe, *Jeffersonian Democracy,* 107–08; McMaster, *A History,* II, 329; see the Philadelphia *Daily Advertiser,* June 27, 1797, deriding the work of Congress in an *"Advertisement Extraordinary."*

48. A nickname for Otis, from a remark in his speech against the "wild Irish."

49. Samuel Sitgreaves, who had expressed willingness to "die in the last ditch" to defend his country.

50. Philadelphia *Aurora,* June 17, 1797. See the Boston *Independent Chronicle,* June 15, July 10, 13, 1797; and James T. Austin, *The Life of Elbridge Gerry,* II, 149–50.

51. New York *Argus,* Mar. 31, 1797; Philadelphia *Daily Advertiser,* Apr. 25, 1797; Boston *Independent Chronicle,* July 6, 27, 1797, August 31, 1798.

52. Philadelphia *Aurora,* Jan. 22, 1798; Boston *Independent Chronicle,* Feb. 1, 1798.

53. Morison, *Otis,* I, 74; Philadelphia *Gazette of the United States,* Apr. 13, 25, 26, 1796; Philadelphia *Aurora,* May 5, Sept. 28, 1797; Philadelphia *Daily Advertiser,* May 2, 1797; Boston *Independent Chronicle,* May 15, June 22, 1797; Newbury, Vt., *Orange Nightingale,* Sept. 4, 1797.

54. Boston *Independent Chronicle,* Nov. 20, Dec. 4, 7, 1797.

55. New York *Diary,* Nov. 7, 1797.

56. Philadelphia *Porcupine's Gazette,* Nov. 22, 1797; Boston *Independent Chronicle,* Nov. 30, Dec. 4, 1797.

57. Philadelphia *Aurora,* Jan. 12, 27, 1798 (cited in Woodbury, *Public Opinion,* 90–91); New York *Diary,* Feb. 3, 1798; *Baltimore Intelligencer,* Mar. 14, 1798; *Greenleaf's New York Journal,* Jan. 10, Mar. 14, 1798; Newark, N. J., *Centinel of Freedom,* Jan. 16, 1798. See also "An American Merchant," in the Philadelphia *Carey's United States Recorder,* Mar. 24, 27, 29, 1798; and "FIAT JUSTICIA," in the *Aurora,* Jan. 27, 1798, and Boston *Independent Chronicle,* Feb. 5, 1798.

757

58. New York *Time Piece*, Jan. 17, 1798; Philadelphia *Aurora*, Mar. 14, 1798; Woodbury, *Public Opinion*, 92.

59. "Junius," Nos. I and II, Boston *Independent Chronicle*, Jan. 29, Feb. 1, 1798; reprinted in the Newburyport, Mass., *Newburyport Herald*, Feb. 2, 6, 1798.

60. Boston *Independent Chronicle*, Mar. 19, 26, 1798; see also the issues of Jan. 15 and Apr. 9 ("Veritas"), 1798.

61. Philadelphia *Carey's United States Recorder*, Feb. 3, 1798. For an earlier similar opinion see the Philadelphia *Daily Advertiser*, Apr. 25, 1797.

62. Boston *Independent Chronicle*, Apr. 10, 13, 17, 27, 1797, *et seq.*, Feb. 26, 1798.

63. Philadelphia *Aurora*, Mar. 2, 1798; Boston *Independent Chronicle*, Mar. 12, 1798.

64. Boston *Independent Chronicle*, Mar. 26, 1798.

65. *Ibid.*, Nov. 20, 1797, Feb. 1, Mar. 19, 26, 1798.

66. E.g., *ibid.*, Mar. 22 (from Roxbury, Mass.), Mar. 26 (Milton, Mass.), Apr. 5 (Dorchester and Cambridge, Mass.), Apr. 9, 16 (other Mass. towns), and Apr. 16 (Richmond, Va., and Newark, N. J.), 1798; McMaster, *A History*, II, 374–75.

67. *Ibid.*, Feb. 1, 19, Mar. 29, 1798; *Greenleaf's New York Journal*, Feb. 3, 1798; New York *Argus*, Feb. 10, 17, 1798.

68. Philadelphia *Aurora*, Mar. 20, 21, May 26, 1798; Philadelphia *Carey's United States Recorder*, Mar. 20, 22, May 26, 1798; Boston *Independent Chronicle*, Mar. 29 ("A Roxbury Man"), Apr. 2, 6, 1798.

69. Philadelphia *Aurora*, Mar. 21, Apr. 24, 1798; Philadelphia *Carey's United States Recorder*, Mar. 22, 1798.

70. Frankfort, Ky., *Guardian of Freedom*, July 3, 1798.

71. Letter of "M." in the New York *Argus*, Feb. 17, 1798.

72. Boston *Independent Chronicle*, Jan. 25 ("A REPUBLICAN"), Feb. 7 ("CAUTION"), 1798; Philadelphia *Aurora*, Feb. 13, 1798; Philadelphia *Carey's United States Recorder*, Mar. 22, 1798; *Baltimore Intelligencer*, Mar. 28, 1798; "A Sincere Lover of Peace," New York *Argus*, Apr. 5, 1798.

73. "An Advocate for Neutrality," from the Salem, Mass., *Salem Gazette*, in the Newburyport, Mass., *Newburyport Herald*, Feb. 9, 1798; Boston *Independent Chronicle*, Mar. 29, 1798.

74. Boston *Independent Chronicle*, Feb. 15, 1798; Sag Harbor, N. Y., *Frothingham's Long Island Herald*, Mar. 19, 1798.

75. Boston *Independent Chronicle*, Feb. 12, Apr. 2, 1798.

76. *Baltimore Intelligencer,* Mar. 26, 1798; Newark, N. J., *Centinel of Freedom,* Apr. 3, 10, 1798; Savannah, Ga., *Columbian Museum,* Apr. 24, 1798; "One of Your Constituents," to H. G. Otis, in the Boston *Independent Chronicle,* May 3, 1798.

77. Boston *Independent Chronicle,* May 25, 1798.

78. Sag Harbor, N. Y., *Frothingham's Long Island Herald,* May 7, 1798; Boston *Independent Chronicle,* Apr. 9, 1798. Various petitions were noted in the latter paper, Apr. 23, (Newark), Apr. 26, 30 (Caroline County, Va.), May 17 (James City, Va.), May 28, (Portsmouth, Va.), 1798; Philadelphia *Carey's United States Recorder,* Mar. 27, 1798; *Baltimore Intelligencer,* Apr. 11, 1798; Troy, N. Y., *Farmers' Oracle,* Apr. 3, 1798; Savannah, Ga., *Columbian Museum,* Apr. 10, 1798.

79. *Boston Gazette,* Apr. 2, 1798. The *Independent Chronicle* of the same date compared Adams to "the Emperor of Germany"; for the quotation, see the Philadelphia *Aurora,* Mar. 20, 1798; reprinted in the Augusta, Ga., *Augusta Chronicle,* Apr. 21, 1798.

80. New York *Argus,* Feb. 24, 1798.

81. Charleston *South Carolina State Gazette,* Mar. 29, 1798 (cited in Wolfe, *Jeffersonian Democracy,* 119). This paper later changed to condemnation of France after the XYZ affair.

82. "BLESSED ARE THE PEACEMAKERS. *Porcupine in all his glory!,"* in the Philadelphia *Carey's United States Recorder,* Mar. 22, 1798.

83. New York *Greenleaf's New York Journal,* Mar. 24, 1798.

84. Philadelphia *Carey's United States Recorder,* Mar. 27, 1798.

85. Boston *Independent Chronicle,* Feb. 15 ("Plain Truth"), 19 ("Nestor"), Mar. 26, Apr. 2, 1798. As late as Apr. 6, 1798, the New York *Time Piece* was thankful the House existed to block the probable desire of the Senate for arming and war.

86. Philadelphia *Aurora,* Mar. 14, 1798.

87. *Ibid.,* Apr. 3, 1798. Adams sent the papers to the House this same day.

88. Item from the *Albany Register,* Troy, N. Y., *Farmers' Oracle,* Apr. 3, 1798.

89. Boston *Independent Chronicle,* Apr. 12, 1798; see also the Philadelphia *Aurora,* Apr. 4, 5, 1798, praising Adams for acceding to the Republican-inspired House demand; the issue of Apr. 9, and the New York *Diary,* Apr. 11, 1798, printed the papers.

90. Pickering, not the envoys, used these letters in transmitting the

papers to Congress; the real names were Hottinguer, Bellamy, and Hauteval. Summaries of the XYZ affair are in Wolfe, *Jefferson Democracy*, 108–12; Miller, *Federalist Era*, 210–12; Bowers, *Jefferson and Hamilton*, 365–66; Austin, *Gerry*, II, 279; Samuel E. Morison and Henry S. Commager, *Growth of the American Republic*, I, 268–69; McMaster, *A History*, II, 368–74; DeConde, *Quasi-War*, 46–52.

91. E.g., Philadelphia *Carey's United States Recorder*, Apr. 5, 1798; and an item from Philadelphia in the Boston *Independent Chronicle*, Apr. 19, 1798.

92. See the New York *Diary*, Apr. 9, 11, 1798; Edenton *State Gazette of North Carolina*, May 10, 1798. The Philadelphia *Carey's United States Recorder*, Apr. 9, 10, 1798, had in addition some comments from the *Aurora;* the Frankfort, Ky., *Guardian of Freedom*, May 8, 1798, summarized the incident with the assessment that any break was not irreparable.

93. Philadelphia *Aurora*, Apr. 9, 1798; Philadelphia *Carey's United States Recorder*, Apr. 10, 1798; New York *Time Piece*, Apr. 13, 1798.

94. Boston *Independent Chronicle*, Apr. 16, 23, May 7, 1798; Philadelphia *Aurora*, Apr. 28, May 10, 1798.

95. Boston *Independent Chronicle*, Apr. 30, 1798.

96. *Ibid.*, Apr. 16, 1798.

97. *Baltimore Intelligencer*, Apr. 11, 1798; "Harrington," in the New York *Diary*, May 7, 1798; "Lysander," from the New York *Time Piece*, in the Newark, N. J., *Centinel of Freedom*, May 1, 1798; Boston *Independent Chronicle*, Apr. 16 (item from the New York *Argus*), May 31, Aug. 27 ("Caution"), 1798.

98. "ANTI-MACHIAVEL," Philadelphia *Aurora*, May 4, 1798; Philadelphia *Carey's United States Recorder* (which remained comparatively quiet on the XYZ question), May 5, 1798. See also 'A Republican,' Boston *Independent Chronicle*, May 10, 1798.

99. Boston *Independent Chronicle*, Apr. 19, 23, 1798; see also the Charleston, S. C., *City Gazette*, May 5, 1798.

100. "Cato," Newark, N.J., *Centinel of Freedom*, Apr. 24, May 1, 1798; Boston *Independent Chronicle*, May 17, 1798. See also the latter paper, Apr. 12, 1798.

101. Now editor of the New York *Time Piece;* replaced by John D. Burk late in Mar., 1798.

102. New York *Time Piece*, May 11, 1798; New York *Argus*, May 12, 1798. See also the Frankfort, Ky., *Guardian of Freedom*, June 12, 1798; Faÿ, *Revolutionary Spirit*, 414; and the letter of Representative Abraham Baldwin to the Governor of Georgia, in the Savannah, Ga.,

*Columbian Museum,* June 26, 1798. Mention of "Wiskovitch" may be found in the Wilmington, N. C., *Hall's Wilmington Gazette,* May 31, 1798; and the New York *Diary,* May 7, 1798.

103. Stauffer, *New England and Bavarian Illuminati,* 129; Faÿ, *Two Franklins,* 342–43; Miller, *Federalist Era,* 212–13. See the letter of Stephen Jacob to Oliver Wolcott, Windsor, Vt., May 21, 1798 (Wolcott Papers, Vol. XIV, No. 100), noting that even the sinners in western Vermont whom Matthew Lyon had seduced were now eager to enter the national service against France.

104. *Baltimore Telegraphe,* May 26, 1798; "A TRUE LOVER OF LIBERTY," Boston *Independent Chronicle,* June 18, 1798.

105. Philadelphia *Aurora,* July 11, 1798.

106. New York *Argus,* July 6, 1798.

107. Reading, Pa., *Readinger Adler,* May 6, 1800; a similar view (respecting the tribute to Algiers) was expressed by "OLD MAN OF THE MOUNTAIN," Newark, N. J., *Centinel of Freedom,* June 17, 1800.

108. Boston *Independent Chronicle,* May 7, July 14, 26, 1798.

109. E.g., Newark, N. J., *Woods's Newark Gazette,* May 29, 1798; Trenton *New-Jersey State Gazette* (cited in Fee, *Transition,* 79–80), Apr. 24, May 1, 8, 15, July 24, 1798; DeConde, *Quasi-War,* 81.

110. Philadelphia *Aurora,* Apr. 17, 1798; Philadelphia *Carey's United States Recorder,* Apr. 18, 1798; Boston *Independent Chronicle,* Apr. 26, 1798.

111. Boston *Independent Chronicle,* Apr. 30, 1798; New York *Argus,* May 18, 1798.

112. Elizabethtown, N. J., *New Jersey Journal,* June 12, 1798. See also the Newark, N. J., *Centinel of Freedom,* July 17, 24, Aug. 14, 1798; Trenton *New Jersey State Gazette,* July 17, 1798 (cited in Fee, *Transition,* 84); Morristown, N. J., *Genius of Liberty,* July 19, 1798; Richmond, Va., *Observatory,* July 23, 1798.

113. E.g., resolutions of Scott County, Ky., Frankfort, Ky., *Guardian of Freedom,* July 3, 1798; Savannah, Ga., *Columbian Museum,* Aug. 24, 1798. It was emphasized that the Mississippi would automatically be closed, and that the West especially would suffer in such a conflict; cf. Humphrey Marshall, *The History of Kentucky,* II, 278–79. The Philadelphia *Carey's United States Recorder,* Apr. 12, 14, 1798, carried resolutions from Richmond, Va., and Cambridge and Dorchester, Mass., against war and arming merchant ships; see also the Boston *Independent Chronicle,* Apr. 23, May 14, 17, 1798.

114. Philadelphia *Aurora*, July 20, Aug. 4, 1798; Savannah, Ga., *Columbian Museum*, Aug. 24, 1798. College authorities later reprobated the deed, and presumably only a few students had helped "country boys" to do it.

115. Item from New London, Conn., in the Philadelphia *Aurora*, May 19, 1798.

116. Boston *Independent Chronicle*, May 28 (resolutions of Fredericksburg, Va.), June 7 (from Bennington, Vt.), 1798; see the Frankfort, Ky., *Guardian of Freedom*, May 8, 1798.

117. Boston *Independent Chronicle*, May 18, 21, 24, 28, 31, June 4, 7, 1798. Extracts were in the first two issues; then the entire memorial was printed.

118. New York *Argus*, May 21, 1798; Newark, N. J., *Centinel of Freedom*, May 22, 1798; Boston *Independent Chronicle*, May 28, 1798.

119. New York *Argus*, June 23, 1798.

120. Chambersburg, Pa., *Farmers' Register*, June 13, July 4, 1798.

121. Philadelphia *Aurora*, May 19, 1798; "An Old and Uniform Whig," New York *Argus*, May 21, 1798.

122. Philadelphia *Gazette of the United States*, Apr. 6, 17, 18, 23, 26, 1798; McMaster, *A History*, II, 376–77; Philadelphia *Aurora*, Apr. 29, 1798; DeConde, *Quasi-War*, 82.

123. New London, Conn., *Bee*, May 28, 1798.

124. Boston *Independent Chronicle*, June 14, 1798; Allen, *Our Naval War with France*, 58–59.

125. Boston *Independent Chronicle*, June 7, 1798.

126. Nathan Schachner, *Aaron Burr*, 150; Wolfe, *Jeffersonian Democracy*, 121–22; Georgetown, S. C., *Georgetown Gazette*, Sept. 18, 1798.

127. Philadelphia *Carey's United States Recorder*, Apr. 7, 18, 1798; Philadelphia *Aurora*, Apr. 17, 1798.

128. Newark, N. J., *Centinel of Freedom*, May 8, 1798; see the Philadelphia *Aurora*, Apr. 18, 1798.

129. Hudson, N. Y., *Hudson Gazette*, Apr. 24, 1798; Boston *Independent Chronicle*, May 24, 1798.

130. Philadelphia *Aurora*, July 4, 1798; Boston *Independent Chronicle*, May 14, 17, 28, July 12, 1798; New York *Argus*, June 21, 1798.

131. New London, Conn., *Bee*, May 30, 1798; Georgetown, S. C., *Georgetown Gazette*, July 3, 1798.

132. "AMERICANUS," Chambersburg, Pa., *Farmers' Register*, May

23, 1798; "PACIFICUS," Boston *Independent Chronicle,* Apr. 26, 1798.

133. Philadelphia *Country Porcupine,* May 4, 1798; Philadelphia *Porcupine's Gazette,* May 15, 1798; McMaster, *A History,* II, 380–81.

134. Philadelphia *Porcupine's Gazette,* May 8, 1798 (cited in McMaster, *A History,* II, 381); see also the Boston *Independent Chronicle,* July 9, 1798 (seconding Noah Webster's suggestion that cockade-wearers should now volunteer their services); Savannah, Ga., *Columbian Museum,* July 31, 1798 (citing the Charleston, S. C., *City Gazette*).

135. Philadelphia *Carey's United States Recorder,* May 10, 1798 (cited in Clark, *Peter Porcupine,* 128); Philadelphia *Aurora,* May 12, 1798. See also the Boston *Independent Chronicle,* July 2, 1798, advising Democrats not to wear the cockade.

136. Philadelphia *Porcupine's Gazette,* May 15, 1798; Robert W. Jones, *Journalism in the United States,* 159–60.

137. "Another Youth," *Baltimore Telegraphe,* May 23, 1798; cf. "Youth," Baltimore *Federal Gazette,* May 19, 1798.

138. Philadelphia *Carey's United States Recorder,* May 26, June 28, 1798; Boston *Independent Chronicle,* July 5, 1798.

139. Warren, *Jacobin and Junto,* 83–84; Boston *Independent Chronicle,* Aug. 20, 1798.

140. New York *Argus,* May 14, June 30, 1798; Philadelphia *Carey's United States Recorder,* July 3, 5, 14, 1798. The Federalist New York *Commercial Advertiser* was quoted as condemning the practice; Boston *Independent Chronicle,* July 30, 1798.

141. Boston *Independent Chronicle,* July 9, 1798; Philadelphia *Carey's United States Recorder,* July 14, 28, Aug. 18, 1798; Philadelphia *Aurora,* July 19, 1798; New London, Conn., *Bee,* Sept. 5, 1798; Goshen, N. Y., *Goshen Repository,* Oct. 30, 1798.

142. Boston *Independent Chronicle,* Nov. 12, 1798.

143. Goshen, N. Y., *Goshen Repository,* Nov. 20, 1798; Boston *Constitutional Telegraphe,* Nov. 13, 1799. As late as June 16, 1800, the Philadelphia *Aurora* carried a lengthy article derogating the cockade.

144. The Alien and Sedition Acts are discussed in Chap. 12.

145. Philadelphia *Aurora,* June 16, 1798 (cited in Faÿ, *Two Franklins,* 347–48); the letter was reprinted in the Boston *Independent Chronicle,* June 25, 1798. See Faÿ, *Revolutionary Spirit,* 405; Lyon, "The Directory," 523–24.

146. New York *Argus,* June 21, 1798; Worcester *Massachusetts Spy,* June 27, 1798; cf. the Boston *Independent Chronicle,* June 28, 1798.

147. Philadelphia *Aurora,* June 19, 21, 1798; New York *Argus,* June 21, 22, 23, 1798; Philadelphia *Carey's United States Recorder,* June 19, 21, 23, 30, 1798; *Boston Gazette,* July 2, 1798; Clark, *Peter Porcupine,* 132; Faÿ, *Two Franklins,* 348–49. Bache died of yellow fever before he could be tried.

148. Though an independent one; Lynch, *Party Warfare,* 67–68, 93; Austin, *Gerry,* II, 111–18, 133–35, 154; DeConde, *Quasi-War,* 13, 28–30.

149. Boston *Independent Chronicle,* June 11, 18, 28, 1798; New York *Argus,* June 21, 26, 1798; Philadelphia *Aurora,* June 9, 1798; Sag Harbor, N. Y., *Frothingham's Long Island Herald,* July 2, 1798.

150. Albany, N. Y., *Albany Register,* June 29, 1798; see also the Boston *Independent Chronicle,* June 28, 1798; and James M. Smith, *Freedom's Fetters,* 3–4, on Marshall's reception.

151. See Gerry's letters of Apr. 4, 16, 1798 (to Talleyrand and to Adams) in the Fredericksburg, Va., *Genius of Liberty;* the (Federalist) Worcester *Massachusetts Spy,* July 4, 1798; Lynch, *Party Warfare,* 73; Clark, *Peter Porcupine,* 130; Austin, *Gerry,* II, 232–34, 262; DeConde, *Quasi-War,* 177.

152. Virtually the entire correspondence was reprinted in the Worcester *Massachusetts Spy,* July 4, 1798, Feb. 6, 13, 20 (together with an *"Extra"* of Pickering's report on the affair), 1799; see the Boston *Independent Chronicle,* Aug. 27, Oct. 4, 1798; Frankfort, Ky., *Palladium,* Sept. 25, Oct. 2, 1798. Lyon, "The Directory," 523–25, says Talleyrand had instructed Létombe (French *charge d'affaires* here, to whom Jefferson had allegedly indicated a policy of protraction in negotiations would eventually win France virtually all she asked) to give this letter the widest publicity. See Faÿ, *Revolutionary Spirit,* 405; Austin, *Gerry,* II, 223–24; McMaster, *A History,* II 405–09, gives an account unfriendly to Gerry.

153. Boston *Independent Chronicle,* Aug. 27, 1798; Philadelphia *Aurora,* Sept. 4, 1798 (noting the translation came from the Salem, Mass., *Salem Gazette,* but seemed at least semi-official).

154. Boston *Independent Chronicle,* Aug. 27, 1798; Frankfort, Ky., *Palladium,* Oct. 2, 1798; "Timoleon," Lexington *Kentucky Gazette,* Nov.–Dec., 1798 (cited in Faÿ, *Revolutionary Spirit,* 414).

155. Philadelphia *Aurora,* Sept. 3, 1798; the "pestilence" reference was to the yellow fever epidemic of 1798, which in a few days was to kill Bache himself.

156. Richmond *Virginia Gazette and General Advertiser*, July 31, 1798; Philadelphia *Aurora*, Aug. 31, Sept. 1, 1798; Boston *Independent Chronicle*, Sept. 10, 1798.

157. Boston *Independent Chronicle*, Sept. 20, Oct. 1, 8, 1798; Reading, Pa., *Readinger Adler*, Oct. 16, 1798; Page Smith, *John Adams*, II, 984; Austin, *Gerry*, II, 234; McMaster, *A History*, II, 408; Lyon, "The Directory," 527–28.

158. E.g., Lexington *Kentucky Gazette*, June 27, 1798; Boston *Independent Chronicle*, June 28 ("Phocion"), July 30, 1798; Savannah, Ga., *Columbian Museum*, July 6, 1798.

159. New London, Conn., *Bee* (probably July 4, 1798), cited in the Savannah, Ga., *Columbian Museum*, Aug. 10, 1798. See also the New York *Argus*, June 30, 1798; Newark, N. J., *Centinel of Freedom*, July 31, 1798.

160. Boston *Independent Chronicle*, July 26, 1798.

161. Philadelphia *Aurora*, June 1, 1798.

162. *Greenleaf's New York Journal*, Apr. 28, 1798.

163. "A CITIZEN OF THE WORLD," Savannah, Ga., *Columbian Museum*, Jan. 26, 1798; see also Feb. 6, 23, 1798.

164. E.g., the Augusta, Ga., *Augusta Chronicle*, Jan. 7, 1797; Boston *Independent Chronicle*, Aug. 31, 1797; Paris, Ky., *Rights of Man*, Sept. 27, 1797; New London, Conn., *Bee*, Sept. 27, 1797; Danbury, Conn., *Republican Journal*, Oct. 2, 1797; New York *Argus*, May 22, 1798; Philadelphia *Aurora*, Aug. 21, 1798.

165. Item from New London, Conn., in the New York *Argus*, June 5, 1798.

166. Boston *Independent Chronicle*, May 21, 1798.

167. Philadelphia *Aurora*, Sept. 1, 5, 1798; Boston *Independent Chronicle*, Sept. 17, 24, 1798.

168. Trenton *New Jersey State Gazette*, Oct. 23, 1798; Worcester *Massachusetts Spy*, Feb. 6, 13, 20, 1799; Frankfort, Ky., *Palladium*, Mar. 7, 28, 1799. The letters were laid before Congress Jan. 5, 1799, together with unfavorable comments by Pickering, who may have felt they would hurt the administration if read by themselves; Austin, *Gerry*, II, 237 (see also, 152, 301); John Adams, *Correspondence*, 63; Philadelphia *Aurora*, Jan. 23, 1799; New York *Argus*, Jan. 28, 1799; Boston *Independent Chronicle*, Feb. 18, Mar. 7, 1799; Frankfort, Ky., *Guardian of Freedom*, Feb. 21, 1799; Washington, Ky., *Mirror*, Mar. 8, 1799.

169. Frederick B. Tolles, *George Logan of Philadelphia*, 152–57; War-

ren, *Making of the Constitution*, 121; Malone, *TJ*, III, 377–78; De-Conde, *Quasi-War*, 155–57.

170. New York *Argus*, June 22, Nov. 17, 1798; Philadelphia *Aurora*, Nov. 10, 1798; Boston *Independent Chronicle*, Nov. 29, 1798; Tolles, *George Logan*, Chap. 8; Curti, *Peace or War*, 26–27; Faÿ, *Two Franklins*, 341–42; Allen, *Naval War with France*, 246; McMaster, *A History*, II, 409–10.

171. Philadelphia *Aurora*, Nov. 21, 1798; Suffield, Conn., *Impartial Herald*, Nov. 27, 1798; Portsmouth, N. H., *Federal Observer*, Nov. 29, 1798; Scipio, N. Y., *Levana Gazette*, Dec. 5, 1798; Augusta, Ga., *Augusta Chronicle*, Dec. 29, 1798; Boston *Independent Chronicle*, Jan. 3, 1799.

172. New York *Daily Advertiser*, Dec. 22, 1798; Portsmouth, N. H., *Federal Observer*, Nov. 22, 1798; New Haven *Connecticut Journal*, Nov. 22, 1798; Lynchburg, Va., *Lynchburg Weekly Gazette*, Dec. 8, 1798; Suffield, Conn., *Impartial Herald*, Jan. 1, 1799; Litchfield, Conn., *Litchfield Monitor*, Jan. 9, 1799.

173. Philadelphia *Aurora*, Dec. 21, 24, 1798, Jan. 3, 1799; New York *Argus*, Dec. 29, 1798, Jan. 5, 1799; Newport, R. I., *Newport Mercury*, Jan. 15, 1799; Middletown, Conn., *Middlesex Gazette*, Jan. 18, 1799; New Haven *Connecticut Journal*, Jan. 19, 1799; Norwich, Conn., *Norwich Packet*, Jan. 16, 1799; Litchfield, Conn., *Litchfield Monitor*, Jan. 23, 1799; Lexington *Stewart's Kentucky Herald*, Feb. 19, 1799; Frankfort, Ky., *Palladium*, Feb. 19, 1799.

174. Boston *Independent Chronicle*, Jan. 7, 1799; Chambersburg, Pa., *Farmers' Register*, Jan. 9, 1799.

175. Curti, *Peace or War*, 27; Malone, *TJ*, III, 430–31; Frankfort, Ky., *Palladium*, Feb. 12, 19, 1799. While the United States has no such legislation against selling arms to other countries, this "Logan Law" is still in effect; Morison and Commager, *Growth*, I, 377; DeConde, *American Foreign Policy*, 70, 73. Philadelphia *Aurora*, June 1, 10, 1799, Aug. 9, 1800; Boston *Independent Chronicle*, Jan. 14, 24, June 27, 1799; Frankfort, Ky., *Guardian of Freedom*, Jan. 3, 1799; Hartford, Conn., *American Mercury*, Jan. 24, 1799; Georgetown, D. C., *Centinel of Liberty*, June 14, 1799.

176. Newark, N. J., *Centinel of Freedom*, May 29, June 5, 1798; Boston *Columbian Centinel*, July 14, 1798; Boston *Independent Chronicle*, July 16, 1798; Allen, *Naval War*, 64–65.

177. Boston *Independent Chronicle*, Aug. 2, Sept. 17, 1798; Philadelphia *Aurora*, Aug. 29, 1798.

178. Philadelphia *Carey's United States Recorder,* June 21, 26, 1798; Philadelphia *Aurora,* Nov. 20, 1798.

179. New York *Argus,* June 5, 6, 1798; Newark, N. J., *Centinel of Freedom,* July 3, 10 ("Brutus"), 1798.

180. Edmund K. Alden, "Bache," *Dictionary of American Biography,* I, 463.

181. Newark, N. J., *Centinel of Freedom,* July 17, 1798; Frankfort, Ky., *Palladium,* Aug. 9, 1798; Savannah, Ga., *Columbian Museum,* Mar. 22, 1799.

182. "Decius," cited in the New Haven *Connecticut Journal,* May 15, 1799.

183. Philadelphia *Aurora,* Nov. 20, 21, Dec. 10, 1798; Newark N. J., *Centinel of Freedom,* Dec. 11, 1798; Boston *Independent Chronicle,* Dec. 17, 1798; Marshall, *History of Kentucky,* II, 279.

184. E.g., Pickering replied to the resolutions of Prince Edward County, Va., that it was not his province to forward addresses to the Executive; the Philadelphia *Aurora,* Nov. 6, 10, 21, 1798, called this "worse than Richelieu." See also the issue of Nov. 14, 1798; and the Boston *Independent Chronicle,* Nov. 22, 1798.

185. New York *Argus,* May 29, 1798; Philadelphia *Carey's United States Recorder,* May 31, 1798; Boston *Independent Chronicle,* Dec. 6, 1798, Feb. 4, 1799, Jan. 6, Apr. 21, May 5, 1800; Reading, Pa., *Readinger Adler,* May 6, 1800.

186. Georgetown, S. C., *Georgetown Gazette,* Sept. 18, 1798; Lexington *Kentucky Gazette,* Oct. 10, Nov. 14, 1799; Philadelphia *Aurora,* June 5, 1800; Augusta, Ga., *Augusta Chronicle,* June 28, 1800; Stauffer, *New England and Bavarian Illuminati,* 125–26.

187. Washington, Ky., *Mirror,* Mar. 1, 1799; Boston *Independent Chronicle,* Feb. 4, 1799; Stonington, Conn., *Impartial Journal,* Oct. 8, 1799.

188. See the Philadelphia *Carey's United States Recorder,* Mar. 1, 1798; Ballston Spa, N. Y., *Saratoga Register,* Nov. 21, 1798; Boston *Independent Chronicle,* Jan. 28, Feb. 18, 1799, Apr. 28, 1800 (item from the Baltimore *Federal Gazette*); Philadelphia *Aurora,* Aug. 7, 1799; Savannah, Ga., *Columbian Museum,* Sept. 13, 1799; and the Raleigh, N. C., *Raleigh Register,* Dec. 14, 1799; for comments on these negotiations.

189. Philadelphia *Aurora,* Feb. 22, 1799; Augusta, Ga., *Augusta Chronicle,* Mar. 30, 1799; Miller, *Crisis in Freedom,* 78, tells of the sentiments of Francis Dana of Massachusetts (see also p. 105), so that the possibility of some confusion of sources exists. Note "A TRUE AMER-

ICAN YANKEE," Providence, R. I., *Providence Journal*, Jan. 30, 1799, on the needlessness of a war with France.

190. New York *Argus*, Jan. 24, 1799; Portsmouth, N. H., *Republican Ledger*, Sept. 19, 1799.

191. E.g., Suffield, Conn., *Impartial Herald*, Nov. 27, 1798, Jan. 8, 1799; Portsmouth, N. H., *Federal Observer*, Nov. 29, 1798; Providence, R. I., *Providence Journal*, May 29, 1799; Baltimore *American*, June 13, 1799.

192. Fredericktown, Md., *Bartgis's Federal Gazette*, Aug. 9, 1797 ("FARMER"); Boston *Independent Chronicle*, Nov. 27, 1797; "A Virginian," Richmond *Virginia Argus*, Mar. 5, 1799.

193. See the Boston *Independent Chronicle*, Dec. 16, 1799 ("DECENCY"); Mar. 13 ("HANCOCK"), May 5 ("THE PEOPLE"), 1800. The *Centinel* was quoted in the New London, Conn., *Bee*, Oct. 8, 1800; the present writer did not see the original.

194. From the Washington, Ky., *Mirror;* Frankfort, Ky., *Palladium*, Jan. 1, 1799.

195. Richmond, Va., *Examiner*, Jan. 14, 1800; Lancaster, Pa., *Intelligencer*, Mar. 12, 1800. See Chap. 7, on Cramond's prophesy of a simulated rupture between Adams and Liston; Philadelphia *Aurora*, Nov. 21, 1799; Newark, N. J., *Centinel of Freedom*, Nov. 26, Dec. 3, 1799; Litchfield, Conn., *Litchfield Monitor*, Dec. 11, 1799.

196. Savannah, Ga., *Columbian Museum*, Mar. 22, 1799; Greensburg, Pa., *Farmers' Register*, Aug. 2, 1799. See *"Remarks* on LISTON'S LETTERS," Newark, N. J., *Centinel of Freedom*, July 23, 30, 1799; Morristown, N. J., *Genius of Liberty*, Aug. 1, 1799. McKee was the British Indian agent.

197. Philadelphia *Aurora*, Feb. 20, 1799; Charleston, S. C., *City Gazette*, Mar. 16, 1799; Baltimore *American*, Sept. 23, 1799.

198. The French secret service spent annually (presumably in 1798) only 200,000 livres (roughly $42,000), while the British disbursed over £180,000; Boston *Independent Chronicle*, May 6, 1799.

199. Philadelphia *Aurora*, Aug. 24, 1799; Savannah, Ga., *Columbian Museum*, Sept. 13, 1799.

200. Chambersburg, Pa., *Farmers' Register*, Jan. 9, 1799; see also the letter of Edmund Pendleton, Frankfort, Ky., *Palladium*, June 13, 1799.

201. *Greenleaf's New York Journal*, July 7, 1798; Boston *Independent Chronicle*, Jan. 28, 31, Mar. 14, 1799; Philadelphia *Aurora*, Aug. 26, 1800; Baltimore *American*, Aug. 29, 1800.

202. Newark, N. J., *Centinel of Freedom*, Apr. 29, 1800.

203. Baltimore *American,* July 25, 1799; see also the New London, Conn., *Bee,* Apr. 24, 1799; Philadelphia *Aurora,* June 10, 1799; Boston *Independent Chronicle,* June 27, 1799.

204. Boston *Independent Chronicle,* Dec. 31, 1798 ("Honestus"), Feb. 25, Nov. 7 ("OLD SOUTH"), 1799; Raleigh, N. C., *Raleigh Register,* Oct. 21, Dec. 16, 1800, Feb. 3, Mar. 3, 1801; Portsmouth, N. H., *Republican Ledger,* Dec. 16, 1800; Gilpatrick, *Jeffersonian Democracy,* 91–92, 120.

205. Philadelphia *Aurora,* Feb. 25, 1799; Chambersburg, Pa., *Farmers' Register,* Mar. 13, 1799; Richmond, Va., *Examiner,* in the Bennington *Vermont Gazette,* Apr. 4, 1799; Frankfort, Ky., *Palladium,* June 13, 1799. A letter by "Nestor," in the Philadelphia *Aurora,* May 17, 1798, was reprinted (as still timely) in the Richmond *Virginia Argus,* Aug. 26, 1800.

206. Newton, N. J., *Farmers Journal,* Nov. 1, 1797; "American," Boston *Independent Chronicle,* May 16, 1799; Baltimore *American,* Oct. 1, 1799.

207. Philadelphia *Aurora,* June 5, 1799; Petersburg, Va., *Virginia Gazette and Petersburg Intelligencer,* June 18, 1799; "THE AMERICAN" (from the New York *Argus*), Morristown, N. J., *Genius of Liberty,* Sept. 12, 1799; Baltimore *American,* Oct. 23, 1799; Richmond, Va., *Examiner,* Dec. 6, 1799; Natchez, [Miss.], *Green's Impartial Observer,* June 2, 1800; Richmond *Virginia Argus,* Sept. 23, 1800.

208. Charleston, S. C., *Carolina Gazette,* May 9, 1799; Philadelphia *Aurora,* June 5, 1799; Petersburg *Virginia Gazette and Petersburg Intelligencer,* June 18, 1799.

209. Major Benjamin Russell, of the Boston *Columbian Centinel.*

210. Boston *Independent Chronicle,* Sept. 21, 1797; Washington, D. C., *Washington Gazette,* Sept. 30, 1797.

211. Boston *Independent Chronicle,* Sept. 25, 1797; Washington, D. C., *Washington Gazette,* Oct. 7, 1797.

212. Boston *Independent Chronicle,* Sept. 21, 1797.

213. *Ibid.,* Sept. 25, 1797.

214. Georgetown, S. C., *Georgetown Gazette,* Oct. 16, 1799; Newark, N. J., *Centinel of Freedom,* Nov. 19, 1799; Allen, *Our Naval War,* 120–21.

215. Boston *Independent Chronicle,* Aug. 20, 23, 1798.

216. Baltimore *American,* July 19, 1799; item from the Washington, Pa., *Tree of Liberty,* in the Litchfield, Conn., *Farmers' Monitor,* Nov. 12, 1800.

217. Boston *Independent Chronicle,* June 11, 1798; New York *Time Piece,* July 18, 1798.

218. Boston *Independent Chronicle,* Sept. 29, 1800.

219. *Ibid.,* May 23, 1799; Philadelphia *Aurora,* Apr. 23, 1799; Richmond *Virginia Argus,* July 2, 1799.

220. Newport, R. I., *Newport Mercury,* Sept. 20, 1796; see also the Philadelphia *Gazette of the United States* ("A CITIZEN"), in the Providence, R. I., *United States Chronicle,* June 30, 1796; Baltimore *Federal Gazette,* Aug. 2, 1796; and the Edenton *State Gazette of North Carolina,* Apr. 20, 1797.

221. The article concluded with a poem stressing the long hours of writing, the poor clothes and starvation diets of such editors; Boston *Independent Chronicle,* Oct. 2, 1797.

222. New York *Argus,* June 9 (citing the *Time Piece*), 16, 1798; Newport, R. I., *Companion,* June 9, 1798.

223. E.g., "NO FRENCHMAN," Newark, N. J., *Centinel of Freedom,* July 17, 1798; Bennington *Vermont Gazette,* Mar. 21, 1799; Boston *Independent Chronicle,* May 16, 1799.

224. Boston *Independent Chronicle,* Jan. 14, 1799; Allen, *Our Naval War,* 72–74.

225. Philadelphia *Aurora,* Aug. 25, 1800; Richmond *Virginia Argus,* Sept. 2, 1800; New London, Conn., *Bee,* Sept. 17, 1800.

226. Boston *Independent Chronicle,* Apr. 8, 11, 18, 1799; see Allen, *Our Naval War,* 93–100.

227. Washington, Ky., *Mirror,* June 7, 1799; "Consistency," from the Wilmington, Del., *Mirror of the Times,* in the Lancaster, Pa., *Intelligencer,* Mar. 12, 1800; "N.," in the Augusta, Ga., *Augusta Chronicle,* June 21, 1800; Allen, *Our Naval War,* 182–85.

228. Augusta, Ga., *Southern Centinel,* Feb. 28, 1799; Newport, R. I., *Newport Mercury,* Mar. 5, 1799. Cf. McMaster, *A History,* II, 441; Wolfe, *Jeffersonian Democracy,* 126; and DeConde, *Quasi-War,* 189–90.

229. Item from Albany, in the Boston *Independent Chronicle,* Mar. 18, 1799; "Important Detection," Brattleboro, Vt., *Federal Galaxy,* Mar. 19, 1799; Bennington *Vermont Gazette,* Mar. 21, 1799; Stonington, Conn., *Journal of the Times,* Apr. 2, 1799.

230. Philadelphia *Aurora,* Mar. 7, 1799; Charleston, S. C., *City Gazette,* Mar. 23, 25, 1799; Boston *Independent Chronicle,* Apr. 15, May 2, 1799 (the quotation is from the latter date); Alexandria, Va., *Alexandria Times,* May 17, 1799; Charleston, S. C., *Carolina Gazette,* May 23, 1799.

231. Philadelphia *Aurora,* Apr. 30, May 1, 1799; "Taylor plot," Alexandria, Va., *Alexandria Times,* May 3, 1799; Frankfort, Ky., *Palladium,* May 30, 1799. The Warren, R. I., *Herald of the United States,* May 11, 1799, gave a Federalist account, with no mention of Toussaint. Cf. Wheeler, "Urban Politics," 122.

232. *New-York Gazette,* Apr. 19, 1799; Boston *Independent Chronicle,* May 2, 1799; Charleston, S. C., *Carolina Gazette,* May 16, 1799 (with a lengthy quotation on this "electioneering manoeuvre" from *Greenleaf's New York Journal,* and a correspondent's report that the *Ocean* had arrived safely in Vera Cruz); Stonington, Conn., *Journal of the Times,* May 21, 1799; Danbury, Conn., *Republican Journal,* May 27, 1799.

233. See the (independent Federalist) Annapolis *Maryland Gazette,* May 9, 1799; Philadelphia *Aurora,* June 6, 1799; Baltimore *American,* June 10, 1799; McMaster, *A History,* II, 442–43. Morse's political role is discussed in Chap. 10.

234. E.g., see the Dedham, Mass., *Columbian Minerva,* May 16, 1799.

235. Boston *Independent Chronicle,* Sept. 8, 1800.

236. New London, Conn., *Bee,* Oct. 1, 1800. See the Augusta, Ga., *Augusta Chronicle,* Sept. 27, 1800; and "P.A." Boston *Independent Chronicle,* Oct. 13, 1800 (retorting that one Negro confessed a leading Henrico County *Federalist* had promised to advance money for the plot!). For the *"Illuminati"* reference see Chap. 10; on earlier alleged Haitian emissaries to the slaves, see the Boston *Independent Chronicle,* Nov. 7, 1793; *Baltimore Daily Intelligencer,* Dec. 4, 1793.

237. Richmond, Va., *Examiner,* Oct. 10, 1800; Norfolk, Va., *Epitome of the Times,* Oct. 13, 1800. Cf. the Federalist Portsmouth, N. H., *United States Oracle,* Oct. 25, 1800.

238. Charleston, S. C., *City Gazette,* Mar. 20, 1799.

239. Baltimore *American,* June 5, 1799; the device was said to be that of Harper.

240. Boston *Independent Chronicle,* Apr. 18, 1799; Philadelphia *Aurora,* June 5, 6, 1799; Hartford *American Mercury,* June 6, 1799; "A CRAFTSMAN," Norristown, Pa., *Norristown Gazette,* Sept. 6, 1799; Boston *Constitutional Telegraphe,* Oct. 2, 1799; Stauffer, *New England,* 345–46.

241. "Old South," Boston *Independent Chronicle,* Sept. 8, 1800.

242. Philadelphia *Aurora,* Oct. 4, 1800; Pittsburgh *Tree of Liberty,* Oct. 18, 1800. James Abercrombie was a Philadelphia Episcopalian preacher noted for Federalist sermons; see Chap. 10.

243. Philadelphia *Aurora,* Dec. 10, 1798; "Honestus," Boston *Independent Chronicle,* Dec. 24, 1798; Smith, *John Adams,* II, 994–96, 999;

Bowers, *Jefferson and Hamilton*, 428–29; Louis Kurtz, *The Presidency of John Adams*, 348–49, 371; McMaster, *A History*, II, 498–99.

244. Philadelphia *Aurora*, Feb. 19, 1799.

245. Philadelphia *Porcupine's Gazette*, Feb. 19, 20, 21, 1799.

246. Philadelphia *Aurora*, Feb. 21, 22, 1799.

247. Boston *Independent Chronicle*, Feb. 28, Mar. 4, 1799; Charleston, S. C., *City Gazette*, Mar. 18, 1799.

248. Boston *Independent Chronicle*, Feb. 28, Mar. 18, 1799; Richmond, Va., *Examiner*, Feb. 28, 1800.

249. Boston *Independent Chronicle*, Mar. 7, Oct. 24 ('Old South'), 1799; Richmond *Virginia Argus*, Mar. 8, 1799.

250. Boston *Independent Chronicle*, May 2, June 3, July 22, Sept. 11, 1799 (see also the issue of Jan. 8, 1798, on Lafayette); Philadelphia *Aurora*, June 12, 1799; Washington, Ky., *Mirror*, July 5, 17, 1799.

251. E.g., an item from the Richmond, Va., *Examiner*, in the Lexington *Kentucky Gazette*, Oct. 10, 1799.

252. Lexington *Kentucky Gazette*, Nov. 14, 1799; Richmond, Va., *Examiner*, Feb. 28, 1800; Kurtz, *Presidency of John Adams*, 348, 371–72, 376; Smith, *John Adams*, II, 1002–1003; Allen, *Our Naval War*, 110; DeConde, *Quasi-War*, 178–80, 184–85.

253. Miller, *Federalist Era*, 245; Smith, *John Adams*, II, 1003.

254. The present writer found not a single mention of this fact.

255. Boston *Constitutional Telegraphe*, Nov. 9, Dec. 21, 1799.

256. Portsmouth, N. H., *Republican Ledger*, Nov. 27, 1799; the mildly Federalist Louisville, Ga., *State Gazette and Louisville Journal*, Dec. 17, 1799. When Adams attended church in Fredericktown, Md., the Augusta, Ga., *Augusta Chronicle*, June 21, 1800, noted that the text for the sermon (*"Blessed are the peace makers"*) was "happily adapted to the occasion, while a negociation is pending"; the Boston *Constitutional Telegraphe*, Sept. 3, 1800, cried that every successive trick of the "Anglo-Federalists" only involved them in further disgrace—they were trying to foredoom the talks to failure, when Gerry and Logan had already done most of the commissioners' work for them.

257. Philadelphia *Aurora*, Oct. 18, 1800; Pittsburgh *Tree of Liberty*, Nov. 8, 1800; see "A Spectator," from the *Albany Centinel*, Portsmouth, N. H., *Federal Observer*, Dec. 13, 1799. Morison, *Otis*, I, 164n., states all but two Federalist papers backed Adams in his decision for conciliation. This seems extreme if consistent support of the President's peace overtures is meant, but a number did. Both the Boston *Columbian Centinel* and *Massachusetts Mercury* favored the attempt; Kurtz, *Presidency of John Adams*, 377.

258. Georgetown, D. C., *Washington Federalist,* Nov. 25, 1800; and (earlier, and somewhat ambiguously) "JUNIUS AMERICANUS," in the Salem, Mass., *Impartial Register,* July 24, 1800. The quotation is from the Pittsfield, Mass., *Sun,* Oct. 14, 1800.

259. Portsmouth, N. H., *Republican Ledger,* Aug. 19, 1800; see the Boston *Independent Chronicle,* Aug. 25, 28, Sept. 29, 1800, denying that France demanded an offensive-defensive alliance, and noting that a fair treaty could be made with her as readily as with an Indian tribe; "A REPUBLICAN of '76," Charleston, S. C., *City Gazette,* Nov. 13, 14, 15, 1800.

260. Pittsfield, Mass., *Sun,* Oct. 14, Nov. 25, 1800; Lexington *Kentucky Gazette,* Oct. 27, Dec. 1, 1800; Georgetown, D. C., *Washington Federalist,* Nov. 25, 1800.

261. Article from the Boston *Independent Chronicle,* in the Washington, D. C., *National Intelligencer,* Nov. 28, 1800.

262. Reported Republicans; see accounts of Adams' alleged conversations with Gideon Granger, Portsmouth, N. H. *Republican Ledger,* Sept. 23, 1800. Note also Chapters 7 and 13.

263. See the Pittsburgh *Tree of Liberty,* Sept. 13, 1800; Boston *Columbian Centinel,* Oct. 8, 11, 1800; Tench Coxe's letter in the New London, Conn., *Bee,* Nov. 19, 1800; and Gilbert Chinard, *Honest John Adams,* 303–04.

264. Raleigh, N. C., *Raleigh Register,* Nov. 4, 1800; Chinard, *Honest John Adams,* 304–05.

265. E.g., Adams' speech to Congress in late 1800 was described as breathing "more temper and moderation, and we are glad to see it, than any since his elevation to the Presidential chair—It is a good omen of peace and amity, that the French Jacobins . . . in the *royal* cant of St. James', are no longer *denounced* and *re-echoed* at this side of the Atlantic. . . ."; New York *Temple of Reason,* Nov. 29, 1800.

## IX ISSUES SECTIONAL AND PAROCHIAL

1. E.g., the *New York Packet,* June 12, 1790; Georgetown, D. C., *Times and Patowmack Packet,* June 23, 1790; Baltimore *Maryland Gazette,* July 20, 30 (quoting a Boston paper), Aug. 10 ("A REPUBLI-

CAN," from the New Haven *Connecticut Journal*), 1790. Baltimore's merchants pledged over $100,000 in an effort to convince Congress the capital should be located in that city; Wheeler, "Urban Politics," 155. See also Constance McLaughlin Green, *Washington, Village and Capital, 1800–1878*, I, 7–11.

2. On Baltimore, Wheeler, "Urban Politics," 154–55. The quotation (italics added) is from the Philadelphia *Pennsylvania Mercury*, June 19, 1790. See also "A TRAVELLER," Philadelphia *Federal Gazette*, Aug. 17, 1789; Woodbury, *Public Opinion*, 106–11; Bowers, *Jefferson and Hamilton*, 141.

3. *New York Packet*, June 12, 1790, Jan. 18, 1791; see also the Edenton *State Gazette of North Carolina*, Sept. 13, 1790; Miller, *Federalist Era*, 49.

4. Richmond *Virginia Independent Chronicle*, July 21, 1790.

5. Georgetown, D. C., *Times and Patowmack Packet*, June 23, 1790.

6. E.g., the Baltimore *Maryland Gazette*, Aug. 31, 1790. Baltimoreans were outraged by the assumption vote, and for the fall election of Maryland's congressmen (all chosen at large) organized a "Chesapeake Ticket," which successfully ousted those who had approved the Potomac site; Annapolis *Maryland Gazette*, Oct. 28, 1790; Wheeler, "Urban Politics," 156.

7. "A CUSTOMER," Fredericktown, Md., *Bartgis's Federal Gazette*, Oct. 27, 1796.

8. Herman Ames, "The Proposed Amendments to the Constitution . . . during the First Century of Its History," *Annual Report of the American Historical Association, 1896*, II, 43–45; Boston *Independent Chronicle*, Aug. 27, Sept. 3, 1789; *Boston Gazette*, Sept. 7, 14, 1789.

9. Philadelphia *National Gazette*, Dec. 1, 1791; New Brunswick, N. J., *Brunswic Gazette*, Apr. 3, 1792; Bassett, *Federalist System*, 49–50; McMaster, *A History*, II, 53, 57.

10. Richmond, Va., *Examiner*, Jan. 28, 1800 (though admitting that the approaching election would not be affected by any change, and there was little public excitement on the question); cf. "A VIRGINIAN," Boston *Constitutional Telegraphe*, Nov. 23, 1799; Newark, N. J., *Centinel of Freedom*, Aug. 5, 1800; Pittsburgh *Tree of Liberty*, Aug. 30 (citing the *Centinel of Freedom* and the *Lancaster Intelligencer*), Oct. 11, 1800.

11. New Brunswick, N. J., *Brunswick Gazette*, Feb. 28, 1792. (The paper dropped the "k" in its title two issues later; Brigham, *History and Bibliography*, I, 505.) Rutland, Vt., *Farmers' Library*, Aug. 5, 1793; Philadelphia *National Gazette*, Oct. 9, 1793; the Vermont salaries

included 4 senators and representatives, $4,800; a district judge, $800; clerk's and marshal's fees, postoffice salaries, inspector of revenue, etc., $2,600.

12. Washington, Ky., *Mirror,* Sept. 8, 1798.

13. Philadelphia *Aurora,* June 12, 1800.

14. "A REPUBLICAN *of St. Bartholomews,"* reprinted in the Federalist Charleston *South Carolina State Gazette,* Oct. 16, 1800, as a sample of Democratic divisive tactics; Nashville *Tennessee Gazette,* Nov. 12, 1800.

15. New London, Conn., *Bee,* Feb. 12, 1800.

16. Richmond, Va., *Richmond and Manchester Advertiser,* Oct. 22, 1796; Philadelphia *New World,* Nov. 3, 1796; Halifax *North Carolina Journal* (citing the New York *Argus*), Aug. 7, 1797.

17. Philadelphia *Aurora,* May 12, 1798. There were sixteen states in all at the time.

18. New London, Conn., *Bee,* Jan. 30, 1799.

19. *Ibid.,* Aug. 27, 1800; "A REPUBLICAN *of St. Bartholomews,"* Charleston *South Carolina State Gazette,* Oct. 16, 1800 (see note 14 above) ; cf. the New York *American Citizen,* Apr. 22, 1800.

20. See Chap. 3.

21. Item from the Greensburg, Pa., *Farmers' Register,* in the Pittsburgh *Tree of Liberty,* Oct. 18, 1800; note Cunningham, *Jeffersonian Republicans,* 219–20.

22. Newark, N. J., *Centinel of Freedom,* Aug. 5, Nov. 4 (citing the *Aurora*), 1800; "A Friend to the Federal Constitution," Richmond *Virginia Argus,* Nov. 4, 1800.

23. E.g., see the Providence, R. I., *United States Chronicle,* Jan. 15, 1795; Boston *Columbian Centinel,* Mar. 9, 1796. Beard, *Jeffersonian Democracy,* 236–37, and Miller, *Federalist Era,* 107–08, indicate fairly wide use of such arguments.

24. Boston *Independent Chronicle,* Jan. 26, 1795.

25. *Ibid.,* Dec. 21, 1795; New York *Gazette Française,* Feb. 10, 1796; "FRANKLIN" (replying to 'Gustavus' of the Hartford *Connecticut Courant*), New London, Conn., *Bee,* Sept. 6, 1797.

26. *New-York Journal,* Mar. 18, 1790; Augusta, Ga., *Augusta Chronicle,* July 3, 1790.

27. Boston *Columbian Centinel,* Dec. 16, 1795; Norfolk, Va., *Norfolk Herald,* Jan. 4, 1796.

28. Newburgh, N. Y., *Mirror,* Oct. 15, 1798.

29. Jefferson's views on slavery had long been known; see Becker,

NOTES TO CHAPTER IX

*Declaration of Independence,* 180–81. Federalists circulated a letter, allegedly by him urging liberation of the blacks; Washington, D. C., *Washington Gazette,* June 7, 1797; Georgtown, D. C., *Centinel of Liberty,* Sept. 23, 1800; Charleston, S. C., *City Gazette,* Oct. 3, 1800 ("A Republican," cited in Beard, *Jeffersonian Democracy,* 215, 373, 375); Charleston *South Carolina State Gazette,* Oct. 16, 1800.

30. Nicholas opposed amending the state constitution to require emancipation and also to require property qualifications for voting; Frankfort, Ky., *Palladium,* Apr. 11, 1799.

31. *Philadelphia Gazette,* Oct. 7, 1800; cited in Anon., "Party Violence," 177.

32. Philadelphia *Aurora,* Jan. 9, 1800; Alexandria, Va., *Alexandria Times,* Jan. 16, 1800.

33. "ARISTIDES," in the *Boston Gazette,* Jan. 11, 1790.

34. Boston *Independent Chronicle,* Nov. 1, 1792, Jan. 25, Feb. 11, 1796.

35. Charleston, S. C., *Columbian Herald,* May 16, 20, 1796; Haverhill, N. H., *Grafton Minerva,* June 2, 1796.

36. "Pelham," from the Hartford Connecticut Courant, Nov. 21, 1796, in the Philadelphia *New World,* Nov. 30, 1796; Charles R. Brown, *The Northern Confederacy,* 14. See Hervey P. Prentiss, *Timothy Pickering as the Leader of New England Federalism,* 23, where, however, it is mistakenly asserted that talk of disunion was not revived in 1800.

37. Philadelphia *New World,* Nov. 30, 1796; Boston *Independent Chronicle,* Jan. 2, 1797.

38. Philadelphia *New World,* Dec. 23, 1796, Jan. 3, 1797.

39. Boston *Independent Chronicle,* July 6, 1797.

40. Philadelphia *Carey's United States Recorder,* Feb. 27, 1798.

41. Boston *Independent Chronicle,* Apr. 22, July 4, 1799, Jan. 2 ("OLD SOUTH"), 1800.

42. Item from a Philadelphia paper, Richmond *Virginia Argus,* Mar. 11, 1800; Lexington *Kentucky Gazette,* Mar. 27, 1800.

43. Washington, D. C., *National Intelligencer,* Nov. 10, 1800.

44. "Burleigh" (said to be John Allen, ex-Congressman from Connecticut), No. XIII, in the Hartford *Connecticut Courant,* Sept. 15, 22, 1800; Letter No. VIII, attacking Freneau, was reprinted in the *Pittsburgh Gazette,* Sept. 12, 1800. The "Burleigh" series ran in the *Courant* from June 30–Oct. 6, 1800; J. Eugene Smith, *One Hundred Years of Hartford's Courant,* 76–78, 285.

45. Richmond, Va., *Examiner*, Oct. 17, 1800; New London, Conn., *Bee*, Oct. 22, 1800; Newburgh, N. Y., *Rights of Man*, Nov. 3, 1800. On Virginia's arming, see McMaster, *A History*, II, 495; Miller, *Federalist Era*, 241, mentions moves toward possible separation as early as 1799.

46. Item from the *Virginia Gazette and General Advertiser*, in the Hartford, Conn., *American Mercury*, Mar. 28, 1799; Boston *Independent Chronicle*, Apr. 4, 1799; see also the New London, Conn., *Bee*, Oct. 8, 15, 1800.

47. "A Consistent Republican," Boston *Independent Chronicle*, Oct. 2, 1800.

48. A letter from "Racoun Creek" (apparently in either Kentucky or the Northwest Territory), reprinted in the Newburyport, Mass., *Essex Journal*, June 22, 1791.

49. "THE CORRESPONDENT," Savannah *Georgia Gazette*, Aug. 22, 1793.

50. The thirty taciturn "kings" who accompanied McGillivray to New York made a great impression on the populace there. Freneau wrote several essays, supposedly by "OPAY MICO," "one of the chiefs"; Leary, *That Rascal Freneau*, 174–75. On the Georgia border question, see Frederick J. Turner, "English Policy toward America in 1790–1791," *American Historical Review* 7 (July, 1902), 707; Whitaker, *Spanish-American Frontier*, 36–37, 61–62, 68–69; Freeman, *Washington*, VI, 272–73; Bassett, *Federalist System*, 72, 74–76; Randolph C. Downes, "Creek-American Relations, 1790–1795," *Journal of Southern History* 8 (Aug., 1942), 350–54; Van Every, *Ark of Empire*, 64–74, 212–14.

51. "AMERICANUS," Charleston, S. C., *City Gazette*, Sept. 29, 1790; "METELLUS," Augusta, Ga., *Augusta Chronicle*, Oct. 16, 30 (see also "A Sentinel"), 1790; Phillips, "Georgia and States Rights," 41–43.

52. Augusta, Ga., *Augusta Chronicle*, May 28 ("DANIEL GAINES"), Oct. 15, Nov. 5 ("THE SOUTHERN CENTINEL"), Dec. 3 ("ATTICUS"), 24 ("MARIUS"), 1791; Bassett, *Federalist System*, 72, indicates the Cherokees apparently broke up the frontier settlements.

53. Philadelphia *National Gazette*, Apr. 16, June 14, 1792. Jackson later became senator, then governor; *DAB*, IX, 544–45.

54. Downes, "Creek-American Relations," 356–58, 360; John A. Carroll & Mary W. Ashworth, *George Washington: First in Peace*, VII, 54–55, 82–84, 174, 246; Savannah *Georgia Gazette*, June 13, 1793

("OCONEE-ENSIS"); Augusta, Ga., *Southern Centinel,* June 13, 1793; Augusta, Ga., *Augusta Chronicle,* July 6, 1793; Norwich, Conn., *Norwich Packet,* July 25, 1793.

55. Phillips, "Georgia and States Rights," 44; Downes, "Creek-American Relations," 363–66; Van Every, *Ark of Empire,* 255–56, 259, 267–68.

56. Augusta, Ga., *Augusta Chronicle,* May 11, 1793 ("To the Printer of the *Baltimore Daily Repository"*); Augusta, Ga., *Southern Centinel,* June 20, 1793.

57. Savannah *Georgia Gazette,* June 13 ("OCONEE-ENSIS"), 27, Aug. 8, 1793; Augusta, Ga., *Southern Centinel,* July 4 (esp. "VASA"), Aug. 8, 1793; Augusta, Ga., *Augusta Chronicle,* July 6, 1793; Philadelphia *National Gazette,* Sept. 14, 1793. See Downes, "Creek-American Relations," 367.

58. Augusta, Ga., *Southern Centinel,* Sept. 12 ("Manlius"), Oct. 24, 1793; Augusta, Ga., *Augusta Chronicle,* Oct. 5, 1793 ("MENTOR").

59. Carroll and Ashworth, *George Washington,* VII, 240; Bassett, *Federalist System,* 77; Downes, "Creek-American Relations," 369–70. The (Republican) House called for 10,000 militia; the Senate cut this figure nearly ninety per cent and the measure was never passed.

60. Augusta, Ga., *Southern Centinel,* Dec. 19, 26 ("Zolius"), 1793, Aug. 14, 28, Sept. 11 ("Manlius" No. II.), 1794; Augusta, Ga., *Augusta Chronicle,* Nov. 8, 1794 ("OCONEE").

61. Charleston, S. C., *Columbian Herald,* Mar. 3, 1796; Savannah, Ga., *Columbian Museum,* Mar. 18, 1796; Downes, "Creek-American Relations," 369–70, 372–73; Carroll and Ashworth, *George Washington,* VII, 396n.; Phillips, "Georgia and States Rights," 45. See Chap. 2 for the Yazoo story.

62. Augusta, Ga., *Augusta Chronicle,* Jan. 10, 1795; Baltimore, Md., *Federal Gazette,* Sept. 13, 14, Oct. 1, 1796; Phillips, "Georgia and States Rights," 46.

63. Winchester *Virginia Centinel,* Dec. 1, 1789.

64. Item from Philadelphia, New Haven *Connecticut Journal,* Dec. 29, 1790; Philadelphia *Freeman's Journal,* Feb. 9, 1791. The *New-York Journal,* Mar. 7, 1791, sardonically mentioned a rumor that Harmar would be superseded because *"his diction* is far from elegant!" Cf. North Callahan, *Henry Knox,* 317–19.

65. Philadelphia *Freeman's Journal,* Aug. 10, 17 ("A Constant Reader"), 1791.

66. Letter from Marietta, Ohio, *ibid,* Feb. 2, 1791.

67. E.g., the *Boston Gazette,* Nov., 1791–Mar., 1792, *passim* (esp.

"Anti Pizar[r]o," Jan. 2, 1792), July 8, 15, 1793; Philadelphia *General Advertiser*, Dec. 14, 1791; New Brunswick, N. J., *Brunswick Gazette*, Jan. 31, 1792.

68. Windsor, Vt., *Morning Ray*, Nov. 22, 1791; item from the Philadelphia *American Daily Advertiser*, in the Norwich, Conn., *Norwich Weekly Register*, Feb. 14, 1792; *Boston Gazette*, July 2, Dec. 3, 1792.

69. Philadelphia *General Advertiser*, Jan. 7, 28, 1792; Windsor *Vermont Journal*, Feb. 21, 1792; Concord, N. H., *Concord Herald*, Mar. 21, 1792; *Boston Gazette*, Apr. 30, June 11 (letter from the Baltimore *Maryland Journal*), 1792; Philadelphia *National Gazette*, Oct. 10, 1792.

70. *New-York Journal*, Dec. 31, 1791; Philadelphia *General Advertiser*, Jan. 2, 10, 1792; Hartford, Conn., *American Mercury*, Feb. 14, 1792; Windsor, Vt., *Morning Ray*, Feb. 21, 1792; Windsor *Vermont Journal*, Feb. 21, 1792; "POLYBIUS," from the Boston *American Apollo*, in the Philadelphia *National Gazette*, Mar. 1, 1792.

71. Philadelphia *National Gazette*, Feb. 9, 1792; Boston *Independent Chronicle*, May 2, 1792; Norwich, Conn., *Norwich Packet*, Aug. 23, 1792. The Halifax *North Carolina Journal*, Feb. 20, 1793, even asserted the post of Secretary of War would be abolished and Knox, brought to answer for expending millions in disgraceful contracts without security. See Bassett, *Federalist System*, 53–54; Bowers, *Jefferson and Hamilton*, 163, 175; Colgrove, "Attitude of Congress," 93; Callahan, *Henry Knox*, 319–21; McMaster, *A History* 44–47; Leonard D. White, *The Federalists*, 71. As shown in Chap. 2, Duer of the Treasury Department was involved.

72. Colgrove, "Attitude of Congress," 93–95; "Julius," Halifax *North Carolina Journal*, Jan. 23, 1792, called for economy and a boundary at the Ohio River; John Steele in the House (cited in the *Boston Gazette*, Jan. 28, 1793) gave figures showing that military expenses had jumped about nine hundred per cent between 1790 and 1793.

73. Letters in the Philadelphia *National Gazette*, Feb. 1, 1792; Philadelphia *General Advertiser*, Feb. 2, 1792; Concord, N. H., *Concord Herald*, Mar. 21, 28, 1792; Lexington *Kentucky Gazette*, May 12, 19, 1792; item from the *Pittsburgh Gazette*, Trenton *New Jersey State Gazette*, Dec. 26, 1792; Halifax *North Carolina Journal*, Jan. 23, 1793.

74. "ARISTIDES," Lexington *Kentucky Gazette*, Jan. 4, 11, 1794; Trenton *New Jersey State Gazette*, July 23, 1794; Halifax *North Carolina Journal*, Aug. 6, 1794; letter of William Blount to Brigadier General White (Apr. 17, 1797), advising petitioning Congress for reimbursement for payments to redeem relatives from the Indians, Knoxville, Tenn., *Knoxville Gazette*, May 1, 1797.

75. Halifax *North Carolina Journal,* Jan. 12, 1795; "An Elector of Electors" (from Pittsburgh), Baltimore *Maryland Journal,* Nov. 12, 1796.

76. E.g., Jones, *American and French Culture,* 488–90.

77. Beard, *Jeffersonian Democracy,* 24; see the Fayetteville *North Carolina Minerva,* June 9, 1796.

78. Note the reference to the Lexington *Kentucky Gazette,* Boston *Independent Chronicle,* Oct. 26, 1797; Nashville *Tennessee Gazette,* Nov. 12, 1800 (protesting limitations on immigration as harmful to the West); cf. Jones, *America and French Culture,* 491.

79. From the Philadelphia *Porcupine's Gazette,* Sept. 21, 1798, with a reply (by "A SUBSCRIBER"), Frankfort, Ky., *Palladium,* Oct. 23, 1798.

80. Frankfort, Ky., *Guardian of Freedom,* Nov. 29, 1798; item from the Washington, Pa., *Herald of Liberty,* in the Frankfort, Ky., *Palladium,* Jan. 29, 1799; Washington, Ky., *Mirror,* Feb. 8, 1799.

81. "One of the Unenlightened Mass," Frankfort, Ky., *Palladium,* Dec. 4, 1798.

82. Lexington *Stewart's Kentucky Herald,* Mar. 12, 1799.

83. Frankfort, Ky., *Palladium,* Apr. 4, 1799 (from the Washington, Pa., *Herald of Liberty*); Washington, Ky., *Mirror,* Apr. 19, 1799; Pittsburgh *Tree of Liberty,* Oct. 11, 25, 1800.

84. Philadelphia *National Gazette,* July 18, 1792.

85. *New-York Journal,* June 23, 1792; Philadelphia *National Gazette,* July 4, 1792. Apparently not every Republican newspaper would grant universal suffrage.

86. Dover, N. H., *Phenix,* Dec. 26, 1792; New York *Time Piece,* Oct. 23, 25, 31, Nov. 1, 10, 13, 1797 (cited in Leary, *That Rascal Freneau,* 297–98); Axelrad, *Philip Freneau,* 313.

87. Halifax *North Carolina Journal,* June 12, 1793.

88. E.g., see the Philadelphia *General Advertiser,* Jan. 23, 24, 1792; Boston *Independent Chronicle,* Feb. 2, 1792; Philadelphia *National Gazette,* Mar. 1, June 18, Aug. 25, 29, Sept. 1, 8, Nov. 7, 24, 1792; *Boston Gazette,* June 13, 1796.

89. Boston *Independent Chronicle,* Oct. 30, 1792; the issue of Oct. 26, 1795, also charged almost constant abuse of Southerners.

90. Hartford, Conn., *Hartford Gazette,* Mar. 31, 1794; Boston *Independent Chronicle,* Apr. 16, 1795; Albany, N. Y., *Albany Register,* Oct. 24, 1796.

91. Morison, *Otis,* I, 177n.; Beard, *Jeffersonian Democracy,* 154, 392–

93; Orin Grant Libby, "The Geographical Distribution of the Vote of the Thirteen States on the Federal Constitution, 1787–8," *Bulletin of the University of Wisconsin* 1 (1894) v–vi; Curtis P. Nettels, *The Emergence of a National Economy,* 114, 122.

92. New York *American Minerva,* Feb. 9, 11 (cited in the *Baltimore Telegraphe*), 1796; Richmond, Va., *Richmond and Manchester Advertiser,* Feb. 27, 1796.

93. Philadelphia *Aurora,* Jan. 26, 1798.

94. Democrats believed the big reason for expelling Lyon was to eliminate his vote; see the New York *Journal and Patriotic Register,* Feb. 14, 17, 28, 1798, with citations from various papers. On the spitting incident, see Chap. 14.

95. New York *Argus,* Feb. 24, 1798; cf. an item from the *Petersburg Republican,* in the Richmond, Va., *Friend of the People,* May 16, 1800, calling Webster a "British pensioner" and resenting his labeling Virginia irreligious and rebellious.

96. Philadelphia *Carey's United States Recorder,* June 28, 1798; "Aristides," Washington, Ky., *Mirror,* July 21, 1798.

97. Boston *Independent Chronicle,* Nov. 22, 1798; Philadelphia *Aurora,* Feb. 12, 1800; Alexandria, Va., *Alexandria Times,* Feb. 20, 1800.

98. Richmond, Va., *Examiner,* Mar. 14, 1800.

99. Prentiss, *Timothy Pickering,* 7 (the expression about Virginia was actually used a little later, in the Massachusetts election of 1802); New York *American Citizen,* June 16, 1800; "An ENEMY to PERSECUTION," Providence, R. I., *Impartial Observer,* Aug. 11, 1800.

100. New York *American Citizen,* Apr. 15, 1800.

# X CLASS AGAINST CLASS

1. "Humble Republican," Charleston, S. C., *Columbian Herald,* Sept. 28, 1793; see Charlotte M. and Benjamin E. Martin, "The New York Press and Its Makers in the Eighteenth Century," *Half-Moon Series* 2 (Apr., 1898), 156; writings of William Manning (cited in Link, *Democratic-Republican Societies,* 49n.).

2. Charleston, S. C., *Columbian Herald,* Sept. 28, 1793.

3. Philadelphia *General Advertiser,* Feb. 22, 1794.

4. New York *American Citizen,* in the Baltimore *American,* Sept. 18, 1800; Philadelphia *Aurora,* quoted in the Pittsburgh *Tree of Liberty,* Oct. 4, 1800. Cf. the Richmond, Va., *Examiner* (citing the *Albany Register*), Oct. 21, 1800.

5. Keene *New Hampshire Recorder,* Feb. 26, 1789; a Philadelphia pamphlet entitled *"A Plea* for the Poor Soldiers," *New-York Packet,* Jan. 19, 1790; Philadelphia *National Gazette,* quoted in the Norwich, Conn., *Norwich Packet,* Jan. 24, 1793.

6. Reprinted (from the Philadelphia *American Daily Advertiser*) in the Burlington, N. J., *Burlington Advertiser,* Feb. 8, 1791; Charleston *State Gazette of South Carolina,* Mar. 14, 1791.

7. "CINCINNATUS," Philadelphia *General Advertiser,* Jan. 8, 11, 1793; Philadelphia *National Gazette,* Jan. 19, 1793; the quatrain is from *"The Soldier's Complaint,"* Concord, N. H., *Hough's Concord Herald,* June 20, 1793.

8. Philadelphia *Dunlap's American Daily Advertiser,* Jan. 16, 1793; "A CONTINENTAL SOLDIER," Philadelphia *National Gazette,* June 2, 1793; Elizabethtown *New Jersey Journal,* Oct. 23, 1793; "No Matter Who," Augusta, Ga., *Southern Centinel,* Apr. 10, 1794; Philadelphia *Aurora,* Aug. 12, 1796; Washington, D. C., *Washington Gazette,* Aug. 24, 27, 1796.

9. "Cincinnatus," Hanover, N. H., *Eagle,* July 13, 1795; earlier, see "A MECHANIC" (from the Philadelphia *Pennsylvania Mercury*), Winchester *Virginia Gazette,* Apr. 3, 1790 (cf. the issues of May 8, 22, 1790); Elizabethtown *New Jersey Journal,* Apr. 14, 1790; Philadelphia *Pennsylvania Mercury,* Dec. 23, 1790.

10. Philadelphia *General Advertiser,* Dec. 20, 1790; Hudson, N. Y., *Hudson Weekly Gazette,* Feb. 17, 1791; letter from Philadelphia, in the Edenton *State Gazette of North Carolina,* Feb. 25, 1791; White, *The Federalists,* 397; Callahan, *Knox,* 281.

11. "Poem" by Georgia Inspector-General, Augusta, Ga., *Augusta Chronicle,* Nov. 20, 1790; Norwich, Conn., *Norwich Packet,* Oct. 17, 1793; "A FRIEND TO TRUTH," Newark, N. J., *Centinel of Freedom,* Oct. 1, 1799.

12. "A MILITIA OFFICER," Philadelphia *Aurora,* May 30, 1795; Knoxville, Tenn., *Knoxville Gazette,* Feb. 6, 13, Mar. 6, 1797; Nashville *Tennessee Gazette,* Apr. 9, 1800; New London, *Bee,* Oct. 8, 1800.

13. E.g., see Beard, *Jeffersonian Democracy,* 415–30 (esp. 427–28, 430), 432, 435; Merrill D. Peterson, *The Jeffersonian Image in the*

*American Mind,* 43–44, 364–66; Wilfred E. Binkley, *American Political Parties,* 78; Malone, *TJ,* III, 194.

14. Hamilton's attempt to show agriculture indirectly benefited in higher land prices and easier loans failed to convince most farmers; Beard, *Jeffersonian Democracy,* 124–27, 131, 148–50; cf. "An American Farmer," in a pamphlet, *Letter Addressed to the Yeomanry of the United States* (Philadelphia, 1793); Gibbs, *Memoirs,* I, 39 (citing James Jackson of Georgia).

15. Windsor, Vt., *Spooner's Vermont Journal,* Aug. 7, 1792 (cited in Bowers, *Jefferson and Hamilton,* 179).

16. E.g., the appeal of Jacob Weygandt and Son, Easton, Pa., *Neuer Unpartheyischer Eastoner Bothe,* Nov. 25, 1794; Philadelphia *Philadelphische Correspondenz,* Oct. 13, 1795; Fredericksburg, Va., *Republican Citizen and Planter's Chronicle,* June 15, 1796.

17. Beard, *Jeffersonian Democracy,* 213–14, 249, 252–53.

18. Philadelphia *General Advertiser,* June 14, 1793, Jan. 2, 1794 ("A Farmer of the Back Settlements"); Norwich, Conn., *Weekly Register,* July 2, 1793.

19. Philadelphia *General Advertiser,* May 14, 1794; see Chap. 6.

20. "A FARMER," Carlisle, Pa., *Telegraphe,* Feb. 17, 1795.

21. Here, apparently, is one of the first instances of the popular fallacy that the phrase "all men are created free and equal" came from the Constitution rather than the Declaration of Independence.

22. "CLEON," Philadelphia *Aurora,* Oct. 24, 1795.

23. Philadelphia *Daily Advertiser,* Feb. 18, 1797 (comments on Washington's speech to Congress); "A CITIZEN," Lexington *Kentucky Gazette,* Jan. 16, 1800.

24. Fredericktown, Md., *Bartgis's Federal Gazette,* Apr. 23, 1800.

25. Reading, Pa., *Readinger Adler,* Sept. 4, Oct. 23, 1798.

26. "A REPUBLICAN," Boston *Independent Chronicle,* Aug. 1, 1799; Albany, N. Y., *Albany Register,* Apr. 8, 1800 (cited in Beard, *Jeffersonian Democracy,* 367–68).

27. Philadelphia *Aurora,* Aug. 1, 2, 1800; Boston *Constitutional Telegraphe,* Oct. 1, 1800.

28. "A Republican," Charleston, S. C., *City Gazette,* Oct. 3, 1800 (quoted in Beard, *Jeffersonian Democracy,* 215, 373–74).

29. Richmond, Va., *Examiner,* Jan. 10 ("A Scots Correspondent"), Feb. 21 ("BRITISH AMITY"), 1800; for an earlier example, the Carlisle, Pa., *Telegraphe,* Nov. 17, 1795.

30. Annapolis *Maryland Gazette,* Apr. 11, 1799; Richmond *Virginia*

*Argus,* Apr. 26, 1799, Sept. 30, 1800 (the quotation is from the latter issue) ; Philadelphia *Aurora,* May 17, Aug. 29, 1800; Charleston, S. C., *City Gazette,* June 21, 1800; New York *American Citizen,* July 2, 1800; Augusta, Ga., *Augusta Chronicle,* July 19, 1800; Baltimore *American,* Sept. 2, 1800.

31. "FACTS SPEAK LOUDER THAN WORDS," Philadelphia *National Gazette,* Oct. 20, 1792.

32. Boston *Independent Chronicle,* cited in the Norwich, Conn., *Norwich Packet,* Aug. 23, 1792.

33. Boston *Independent Chronicle,* Jan. 9, 1794; Edenton *State Gazette of North Carolina,* Feb. 7, 1794 (giving the exact figure with Britain as $5,922,012 in her favor) ; Philadelphia *General Advertiser,* Jan. 15, 1794; Charleston, S. C., *Columbian Herald,* Feb. 10, 12, 14, 1794.

34. "Manlius" and Congressman Dexter had talked of the insignificance of American trade; see the Boston *Independent Chronicle,* Oct. 9, 20, 1794, also the issues of Jan. 25, July 9, 1795; Exeter, N. H., *Weekly Visitor,* July 14, 1795.

35. Boston *Independent Chronicle,* Feb. 24, Mar. 3, 6, 10, 20, 24, June 19, 24, 1794. The opening of these ports was dictated by economic necessity, but it permitted Republicans to claim French friendship; see Beard, *Jeffersonian Democracy,* 269, 272–73.

36. Halifax *North Carolina Journal,* Apr. 6, 1795, Feb. 29, 1796; Windsor, Vt., *Spooner's Vermont Journal,* Feb. 22, 1796.

37. Reprinted in the Boston *Independent Chronicle,* July 6, 1795; see *ibid.,* Feb. 2, 1797.

38. Philadelphia *Daily Advertiser,* June 21, 1797; New York *Time Piece,* July 5, 1797; Boston *Independent Chronicle,* July 20, 1797.

39. Richmond, Va., *Richmond and Manchester Advertiser,* Apr. 20, 1796; Philadelphia *Aurora,* Jan. 21, 1797. Washington's message of Dec. 9, 1795, had stressed economic progress; Richardson, *Messages and Papers,* I, 174–81.

40. E.g., Georgetown, S. C., *Georgetown Gazette,* Sept. 18, 1799; Portsmouth *New Hampshire Gazette,* Feb. 26, 1800.

41. Boston *Independent Chronicle,* Nov. 8, 1798 (comment on Gov. Tickenor's speech to the Vermont legislature), Feb. 21, 1799; Baltimore *American,* June 17, Sept. 10, 1800; Philadelphia *Aurora,* Aug. 29, 1800.

42. E.g., the New York *Gazette Française; Courier de Boston;* Easton, Pa., *Neuer Unpartheyischer Eastoner Bothe;* Philadelphia *Gemeinnützige Philadelphische Correspondenz;* Philadelphia *Journal des Revo-*

*lutions;* and the York, Pa., *Unpartheyische York Gazette.* Carl Wittke, *The German Language Press in America,* 29, mentions the Baltimore *Neue Unpartheyische Baltimore Bote.*

43. Walters, "Origins," 442; John J. Stoudt, book review in the *Pennsylvania Magazine of History and Biography* 66 (July, 1942), 376; Tench Coxe, *A View of the United States of America,* 161; George C. Keidel, *The Earliest German Newspapers of Baltimore,* 3–4; Wittke, *German Language Press,* 26, 29. It must be reiterated, however, that a brief existence was also common for English-language newspapers; see Chap. 1.

44. Philadelphia *Pennsylvania Packet,* Nov. 19, 1788 (cited in Thomas, "Political Tendencies," 161; see also Robert L. Brunhouse, *The Counter-Revolution in Pennsylvania, 1776–1790,* 217–18.

45. Faÿ, "Bache," 279–80, 291. Wheeler, "Urban Politics," 115, tells of Republican friendliness to immigrant groups, though p. 131 questions German voting as a bloc.

46. See the Philadelphia *Gazette of the United States,* June 9, 1792; Philadelphia *National Gazette,* June 11, 15, 1792 (cited in Leary, *That Rascal Freneau,* 203–04).

47. Richmond *Virginia Gazette and Richmond Chronicle,* Oct. 7, 1794.

48. E.g., Easton, Pa., *Neuer Unpartheyischer Eastoner Bothe,* Mar. 18, 1795; *Philadelphische Correspondenz,* Sept. 29, 1795; "A GERMAN FARMER," Chambersburg, Pa., *Farmers' Register,* Oct. 3, 1798; Reading, Pa., *Readinger Adler,* Oct. 16, Dec. 3, 1798, Apr. 22, 1800.

49. Newburyport, Mass., *Newburyport Herald,* Jan. 15, 1797; item addressed "To German farmers," Reading, Pa., *Readinger Adler,* Oct. 23, 1798.

50. Reading, Pa., *Readinger Adler,* Sept. 18, 1798.

51. *Ibid.,* Oct. 2, 9, 1798.

52. Reading, Pa., *Readinger Zeitung,* Mar. 20, 27, 1799 (for Federalist comments); *Readinger Adler,* Feb. 26, 1799 (cited in Clark, *Peter Porcupine,* 138); Lancaster Pa., *Lancaster Correspondent,* Aug. 24, Sept. 7, 28, Oct. 5, 12, Dec. 22, 1799. The Lancaster, Pa., *Intelligencer,* Nov. 13, 1799, carried samples of victory toasts to the German and Irish voters.

53. New York *American Citizen,* Apr. 21, 1800; Charles H. Ambler, *Sectionalism in Virginia from 1776–1861,* 79 (citing the *Calendar of Virginia State Papers,* IX, 121, 131); Newark, N. J., *Centinel of Freedom,* Oct. 7, 1800; Philadelphia *Aurora,* Aug. 13, Sept. 27, 1800; Charleston, S. C., *City Gazette,* Sept. 3, 1800. Wheeler, "Urban Politics," 125n., mentions Federalist efforts in Philadelphia to whip up

feeling against Israel Israel and Moses Levy (though neither was a Jew). Anti-semitism was comparatively rare, but instances did occur; see the Richmond *Virginia Argus,* Aug. 19, 1800, and Link, *Democratic-Republican Societies,* 51, for samples in Republican literature.

54. Philadelphia *Gazette of the United States,* Dec. 29, 1790, Sept. 5, 23, 29, Oct. 10, 1792; cited in Beard, *Jeffersonian Democracy,* 221–22, 225–27, 229–33.

55. At this time "mechanic" was applied chiefly to carpenters, black-smiths and other village workmen; "artisan" was usually used for the mass of workers in the cities (Beard, *Jeffersonian Democracy,* 435n.).

56. "Lucius," Hartford, Conn., *American Mercury,* Apr. 11, 1791; Norwich, Conn., *Norwich Packet,* May 10, 1792. Articles in the last-named paper (Apr. 5, 12, 19, 26, June 28, Oct. 4, 1792, and 1793, *passim*), plus similar items elsewhere and studies such as Wheeler, "Urban Politics," (e.g., p. 140), call for modification of Beard's asser-tion (*Jeffersonian Democracy,* 246n.) that not much attention was paid to capturing the votes of workingmen in the towns. Robinson, *Jeffersonian Democracy,* 101, calls Arthur Fenner the gubernatorial candidate of the Rhode Island anti-commercial group in 1791; Wheeler, "Urban Politics," 151, 158–59, notes the Maryland rivalry between Baltimore city and the planting aristocracy of the state. See also the New York *Diary,* Jan. 18, 1793 (cited in Luetscher, *Early Political Machinery,* 58); 'A Mechanic,' *Baltimore Daily Intelligencer,* Jan. 22, 1794; 'A CITIZEN,' *Edwards' Baltimore Daily Advertiser,* Dec. 4, 1793; Baltimore *Federal Intelligencer,* Nov. 18, 1794.

57. Lexington *Kentucky Gazette,* Oct. 15, 1791.

58. Carlisle, Pa., *Telegraphe,* Feb. 10, 1795; Philadelphia *Aurora,* Oct. 15, 1795; Wilmington *Delaware and Eastern Shore Advertiser,* Oct. 17, 1795; Boston *Independent Chronicle,* Oct. 31, Nov. 3, 7, 1796, Oct. 8, 1798.

59. *Greenleaf's New York Journal,* Feb. 18, Mar. 22, 1797; New York *Time Piece,* Oct. 16, 1797; Boston *Independent Chronicle,* Oct. 26, 1797.

60. Middletown, Conn., *Middlesex Gazette,* Mar. 16, 1798 (cited in the Boston *Independent Chronicle,* Apr. 12, 1798).

61. Newark, N. J., *Centinel of Freedom,* May 8, 1798; Philadelphia *Carey's United States Recorder,* June 28, 1798; Baltimore *American,* Sept. 28, 1799 (cited in Luetscher, *Early Political Machinery,* 21).

62. Boston *Independent Chronicle,* May 23, 1799, *et seq.*

63. John A. Krout and Dixon Ryan Fox, *The Completion of Independence,* 279; Morison, *Otis,* I, 42. Many Federalists—in New York the

Samuel Joneses, Jr. and Sr., Richard Harison, Josiah Ogden Hoffman, and Cadwallader Colden—had been Tories during the Revolution; Dixon Ryan Fox, *The Decline of the Aristocracy in the Politics of New York*, 12–14; Fee, *Transition*, 107; Wheeler, "Urban Politics," *passim* (esp. 221–22); Robinson, *Jeffersonian Democracy*, 114–15. The Boston *Independent Chronicle*, Mar. 19, 1795, urged voters to defeat Samuel Dexter (lawyer from Middlesex) for reelection to Congress, because nine lawyers from one state were sufficient, and Massachusetts had yet to send a real farmer to Congress.

64. "A Lawyer's Prayer," Bennington *Vermont Gazette*, Mar. 31, 1788; *Boston Gazette*, Jan. 25, 1790; Boston *Independent Chronicle*, Jan. 20, 1791, Mar. 19, 1795; Philadelphia *General Advertiser*, Apr. 18, 1791; "A.B.," Philadelphia *Aurora*, Mar. 10, 1795.

65. New Haven *Connecticut Journal*, May 26, 1790; Boston *Independent Chronicle*, June 10, 1790.

66. Boston *Independent Chronicle*, Jan. 27, 1790 (the reference to the Catholic Church showed that New England was still bigoted). For other charges of undue influence by the bar, see the *New-Haven Gazette*, June 29, 1791; "A Mechanic not yet a Free-Man," Norwich, Conn., *Norwich Packet*, Sept. 8, 1791; Lexington *Kentucky Gazette*, Oct. 15, 1791; *Boston Gazette*, Oct. 15, 1792; Boston *Independent Chronicle*, Oct. 30, 1794, Nov. 1, 1798; and Luetscher, *Early Political Machinery*, 138 (citing the *New Jersey Gazette*).

67. Rutland *Herald of Vermont*, Aug. 13, 1792; *Boston Gazette*, Jan. 14, 1793; the figures for Massachusetts were cited in the Philadelphia *National Gazette*, Jan. 26, 1793; and the Halifax *North Carolina Journal*, Feb. 20, 1793.

68. Norwich, Conn., *Weekly Register*, Mar. 13, 1792; Norwich, Conn., *Norwich Packet*, Sept. 20, 1792; Rutland *Herald of Vermont*, Aug. 13, Sept. 3, 1792; Keene, N. H., *Columbian Informer*, July 10, 1793; Alexandria, Va., *Columbian Mirror*, Aug. 13, 1795 (the statement was almost certainly incorrect as regards the Stamp Act). For other samples of anti-lawyer feeling, see the *Baltimore Evening Post*, Sept. 17, 1793; Trenton *New Jersey State Gazette*, Feb. 5, 1792; Savannah, Ga., *Columbian Museum*, Aug. 22, 1797; Boston *Independent Chronicle*, Jan. 18, June 18, Nov. 19, 1798; Reading, Pa., *Readinger Adler*, Sept. 4, 1798; etc.

69. Augusta, Ga., *Southern Centinel*, July 4, 1793; *New-York Journal*, Nov. 27, 1793; Boston *Independent Chronicle*, Dec. 9, 1793; Trenton *New Jersey State Gazette*, Jan. 15 ("Brutus," from the New York *Journal*), Feb. 19 ("Hambden"), 1794; Providence, R. I., *United*

*States Chronicle,* Mar. 6, 1794; Norwich, Conn., *Weekly Register,* Apr. 22, 1794 ("The LIAR").

70. Philadelphia *General Advertiser,* Apr. 12, 1794; Charleston *South Carolina State Gazette,* Apr. 30, 1794, Jan. 9, 1795 (noting the bar's resistance to any reforms); New York *Journal,* Oct. 4, 1794 (mentioned in Luetscher, *Early Political Machinery* 45–46, quoting resolutions of the Democratic Society of Canaan, New York); Boston *Independent Chronicle,* Feb. 5 ("Observer"), Oct. 15, 1795.

71. Boston *Independent Chronicle,* Mar. 12, 1795, May 30, June 6, 1796; the series by "HONESTUS" [Benjamin F. Austin, Jr.] written in 1786 was reprinted in 1798 when an attempt to revise the Circuit Court Bill was defeated—*ibid.,* Feb. 12, 15, 1798, Mar. 31, 1800.

72. Savannah, Ga., *Columbian Museum,* Apr. 28, 1797; Boston *Independent Chronicle,* Dec. 11, 1797 (on dismissal of the French minister's charges against Porcupine, contrasted with the English minister's successful suit against Democratic editor Thomas Greenleaf), Feb. 12 (Freneau's poem, "A Slap at Lawyers"), Nov. 1, 5, 1798; Philadelphia *Aurora,* Nov. 9, 1798; Baltimore *American,* Nov. 11, 1799; Alexandria, Va., *Alexandria Times,* Jan. 28, 1800.

73. Pittsfield, Mass., *Sun,* Sept. 23, 1800.

74. New London, Conn., *Bee,* Nov. 26, 1800.

75. Augusta, Ga., *Southern Centinel,* Sept. 4, 1794; Augusta, Ga., *Augusta Chronicle,* Sept. 6, 1794.

76. Charles R. Keller, *The Second Great Awakening in Connecticut,* 12; see also Jones, *America and French Culture,* 392.

77. The best summary of this situation is in Stauffer, *New England and the Bavarian Illuminati,* 86–89, 96–102; see also Robinson, *Jeffersonian Democracy,* 110, 145; Keller, *Second Great Awakening,* 4–5, 12–17, 25; Krout and Fox, *Completion of Independence,* 164–65; Jones, *America and French Culture,* 377.

78. Merle E. Curti, "The Great Mr. Locke, America's Philosopher, 1783–1861" *Huntington Library Bulletin,* No. 11 (Apr., 1937), 114–15; I. Woodbridge Riley, *American Thought,* 4, 6, 54–55, 66; Faÿ, *Revolutionary Spirit,* 228; Jones, *America and French Culture,* 542n.; David M. Ludlum, *Social Ferment in Vermont, 1791–1850,* 28–31.

79. Riley, *American Thought,* 12–18.

80. *Ibid.,* 87–89; Stauffer, *New England and Bavarian Illuminati,* 72–74; Ludlum, *Social Ferment,* 29–30; Krout and Fox, *Completion of Independence,* 165.

81. Stauffer, *New England and Bavarian Illuminati,* 13–14, 47; Robinson, *Jeffersonian Democracy,* 129–30, 132–35, 141; Krout and Fox,

*Completion of Independence,* 165–66, 170; Fox, *Decline of the Aristocracy,* 25, 27. Most New England preachers had endorsed the Revolution and the Constitution; those who had suffered under Shays' Rebellion favored the Federalists. Ludlum, *Social Ferment,* 94–95, 98, 100, 103–04; Faÿ, *Revolutionary Spirit,* 364–65; Rich, *U.S. Post Office* 34.

82. Ludlum, *Social Ferment,* 30; Stauffer, *New England and Bavarian Illuminati,* 47–48, 59–62.

83. Boston *Columbian Centinel,* Sept. 12, 1792; Philadelphia *National Gazette,* Sept. 26, 1792 (Leary, *That Rascal Freneau,* 216–17).

84. Philadelphia *National Gazette,* Jan. 16, 1793; Keller, *Second Great Awakening,* 15.

85. Norwich, Conn., *Weekly Register,* Sept. 10, Nov. 5, 1793; Hartford, Conn., *American Mercury,* May 16, 1793 (cited in Robinson, *Jeffersonian Democracy,* 145); New Haven *Connecticut Journal,* Oct. 23, 1793, Jan. 23, Mar. 13, 1794; Newfield, Conn., *American Telegraphe,* Apr. 8, 29, 1795; see also the *American Mercury,* Aug. 14, 1794, for a burlesque on the subject from the Hartford *Connecticut Courant,* Aug. 11, 1794; and Joseph F. Thorning, *Religious Liberty in Transition,* 102.

86. Walpole, N. H., *Farmer's Weekly Museum,* Oct. 10, 1794; Stockbridge, Mass., *Western Star,* Nov. 18, 1794, Mar. 1, 1796; Boston *Massachusetts Mercury,* Mar. 13, 17, 20, 1795; Morse, *Federalist Party,* 107–09, 217.

87. Boston *Independent Chronicle,* Jan. 30, Mar. 6, Apr. 14, July 24, Aug. 4, 7, 11, 14, 1794.

88. Stauffer, *New England and Bavarian Illuminati,* 89–95; Thorning, *Religious Liberty,* 42–43; Faÿ, *Revolutionary Spirit,* 366–67, 417–19; Morse, *Federalist Party,* 126–27. The New York *American Minerva,* Jan. 6, 1795, reprinted Osgood's sermon.

89. Boston *Independent Chronicle,* Nov. 27, Dec. 11, 22, 25, 29, 1794, Jan. 5, 8, 12, 15, 1795; see also Stauffer, *New England and Bavarian Illuminati,* 111–12.

90. Boston *Independent Chronicle,* Jan. 15, Mar. 30, 1795; Salem, Mass., *Salem Gazette,* Jan. 20, 1795; Morse, *Federalist Party,* 131–33; Stauffer, *New England and Bavarian Illuminati,* 91–93; Thorning, *Religious Liberty,* 44.

91. Keene, N. H., *Columbian Informer,* Feb. 17, 1795; "Observator," Boston *Independent Chronicle,* Feb. 23, 1795.

92. Boston *Independent Chronicle,* July 20, Oct. 5, 1795, Feb. 16, 27, 1797; Salem, Mass., *Salem Gazette,* Aug. 25, 1795.

93. Boston *Independent Chronicle,* e.g., Mar. 2, 19, 23, 26, Apr. 3 (esp. letters by "URBANUS"), July 23, 27, Dec. 3, 1795, June 24, Dec. 6, 31, 1798, Apr. 18, 28, 1799, Sept. 22, 1800 ("Philanthropus").

94. Morse, *Federalist Party,* 149, 169, 187–88; Thorning, *Religious Liberty,* 48, quotes the Boston *Columbian Centinel,* Feb. 13, 1796, praising the clergy for the "unadulterated Federalism" of the substantial yeomanry of Massachusetts and New Hampshire.

95. Philadelphia *Independent Gazetteer,* Mar. 12, 1795; Richmond, Va., *Richmond Chronicle,* Nov. 24, 1795; Richmond, Va., *Richmond and Manchester Advertiser,* Nov. 28, 1795. On Abercrombie, see Clark, *Peter Porcupine,* 24, 100.

96. Boston *Independent Chronicle,* Aug. 6, 13, Sept. 3, Oct. 5, Nov. 26, 1795, May 12, Oct. 5, 1796.

97. *Ibid.,* Jan. 5, May 2, 5, 26, June 30, 1796; Jan. 5, Sept. 7, 1797, Feb. 5, 1798; Philadelphia *Aurora,* May 11, 1796; Morse, *Federalist Party,* 122–23.

98. Boston *Independent Chronicle,* Feb. 25, July 25, Nov. 24, 1796, Oct. 26, Nov. 2, 1797 (cited in Morse, *Federalist Party,* 112–14); see also "A sincere Christian," New London, Conn., *Bee,* June 5, 1799.

99. Item from Philadelphia, Hartford, Conn., *American Mercury,* Apr. 11, 1797. For other anti-clerical items see the Boston *Independent Chronicle,* Feb. 16, Apr. 13, 20, May 1, Nov. 6, 1797, Jan. 4, Apr. 12, May 3, June 21, July 30, Nov. 1, Dec. 3, 6, 10, 17, 23, 1798, April 1, 15, 1799, Apr. 14, 21, 1800; New London, Conn., *Bee,* Apr. 10, 1799.

100. Lancaster, Pa., *Lancaster Correspondent,* Sept. 7, 1797; Boston *Independent Chronicle,* Sept. 11 ("Piso"), Oct. 16 ("A Friend to the Clergy"), Oct. 30, Nov. 2, 20, 27, 1797; New York *Time Piece,* Nov. 15, 1797; Boston *Constitutional Telegraphe,* Oct. 5, 1799.

101. Philadelphia *Carey's United States Recorder,* Mar. 27, 1798; Boston *Independent Chronicle,* Apr. 2, June 7, 1798.

102. Boston *Independent Chronicle,* Apr. 30, 1798; Philadelphia *Aurora,* May 2, 9, 1798.

103. Boston *Independent Chronicle,* Jan. 11, Aug. 20, Sept. 27, Nov. 5, 1798, Jan. 7, 1799. (The quotation is from the last-named date.)

104. Philadelphia *Aurora,* Aug. 14, 17, 21, 1798.

105. Reading, Pa., *Readinger Adler,* Sept. 18, Oct. 9 ("George Well-informed"), 1798.

106. Boston *Independent Chronicle,* Jan. 10, 24, Feb. 18, Apr. 18, May 2, Oct. 21, 1799; Hartford, Conn., *American Mercury,* Mar. 28, 1799; Boston *Constitutional Telegraphe,* Oct. 30, 1799.

107. Boston *Independent Chronicle,* Apr. 1, 1799.

108. Philadelphia *Aurora,* Apr. 23, May 7, Aug. 8, 13, 1799; see Freneau, *Letters,* iv–v. For more on "Robert Slender," see Chap. 13.

109. Baltimore *American,* June 4, 1799.

110. Philadelphia *Aurora,* Sept. 23, 1799; Lancaster, Pa., *Intelligencer,* Oct. 2, 1799. For Federalist opinion, see several items in the Philadelphia *Universal Gazette,* Sept. 19, 1799.

111. New York *Argus,* June 7, 1798; Boston *Independent Chronicle,* Oct. 11, 1798 ("Faith, Hope, and Charity").

112. Georgetown, D. C., *Centinel of Liberty,* Oct. 1, 1799.

113. Baltimore *American,* Dec. 10, 17, 1799.

114. "A Maryland Clergyman," Lancaster, Pa., *Intelligencer,* Mar. 12, 1800; Wilmington, Del., *Mirror of the Times,* Aug. 30, 1800.

115. New York *Argus,* Jan. 15, 1800; Boston *Independent Chronicle,* Apr. 21, 1800 ("JUSTICE").

116. Newark, N. J., *Centinel of Freedom,* Feb. 25, 1800.

117. Philadelphia *Aurora,* June 12, 1800.

118. E.g., see the York, Pa., *Der Volks Berichter,* July 17, Aug. 14, 21, 1800.

119. Charleston, S. C., *City Gazette,* July 12, 1800.

120. Frankfort, Ky., *Palladium,* July 17, 31, 1800; Lexington *Kentucky Gazette,* Aug. 7, 1800. "A Republican" had earlier made similar statements; see Niels H. Sonne, *Liberal Kentucky, 1780–1828,* 43–45.

121. Boston *Independent Chronicle,* Aug. 25, Sept. 1, 1800; see the retorts, *ibid.,* Aug. 28, Sept. 11, 1800.

122. Philadelphia *Gazette of the United States,* Sept. 27, Oct. 9, 1800.

123. "Robert Slender," Philadelphia *Aurora,* Oct. 9, 1800; Richmond *Virginia Argus,* Oct. 21, 1800.

124. Northampton, Mass., *Hampshire Gazette,* Oct. 28, 1800; New York *Temple of Reason,* Nov. 8, Dec. 6, 1800. Personal observation confirms the conclusions of Morse, *Federalist Party,* 116–17, and Hazen, *Contemporary American Opinion,* 270, concerning New England Republicans' reluctance to appear critical of religion *per se.*

125. Stauffer, *New England and Bavarian Illuminati,* 142–85, *passim* (particularly 158–60 and 180–83, where data from the Bavarian government seemed, in 1786, to confirm this hypothesis), also 199–208. Jones, *America and French Culture,* 397–98, gives a summary.

126. Robison's full title was *The Proofs of a Conspiracy against all Religions and Governments of Europe carried on in the secret meetings*

*of the Free Masons, Illuminati, and Reading Societies* (Edinburgh, 1797); Barruel's was *Memoires pour servir a l'histoire du Jacobinisme, 1797–1798* (Hartford, Conn., 1799); Faÿ, *Revolutionary Spirit,* 365; Stauffer, *New England and Bavarian Illuminati,* 199–204, 209, 212–28; Faÿ, *Notes on the American Press,* 26.

127. Stauffer, *New England and Bavarian Illuminati,* 128, 228–36; Jones, *America and French Culture,* 398–99; John C. Miller, *Crisis in Freedom,* 145–46; James K. Morse, *Jedidiah Morse, A Champion of New England Orthodoxy,* 51–52, 55–56; Keller, *Second Great Awakening,* 19–20; G. Adolf Koch, *Republican Religion,* 253–54.

128. Morse, *Jedidiah Morse,* 45; Boston *Independent Chronicle,* May 24, 1798.

129. Boston *Independent Chronicle,* May 31, June 14, 1798; Stauffer, *New England and Bavarian Illuminati,* 244–52; Morse, *Jedidiah Morse,* 53–54.

130. Philadelphia *Aurora,* Aug. 3, 10, 1798; Hartford, Conn., *American Mercury,* Sept. 26, Oct. 4, Nov. 7, 14, 1799; see Stauffer, *New England and Bavarian Illuminati,* 281–82, 287.

131. Boston *Massachusetts Mercury,* July 27, Aug. 3, 10, 14, 17, 21, 28, 31, Sept. 7, 14, 18, 21, Nov. 13, 30, 1798; Boston *Columbian Centinel,* Aug. 11, Sept. 8, 12, 1798, Jan. 5, 1799, *et seq.;* see Stauffer, *New England and Bavarian Illuminati,* 255–56, 276–80.

132. Stauffer, *New England and Bavarian Illuminati,* 282–85.

133. *Ibid.,* 264–71; Boston *Independent Chronicle,* Jan. 7, 1799.

134. Stauffer, *New England and Bavarian Illuminati,* 348–52; Koch, *Republican Religion,* 259–60; Faÿ, *Revolutionary Spirit,* 423–24.

135. E.g., the New London, Conn., *Bee,* May 22, 1799, charged that Timothy Dwight (president of Yale) headed the list of true Illuminati in America.

136. Jones, *America and French Culture,* 399–400.

137. Boston *Independent Chronicle,* May 9 ("Bunker Hill"), 20 ("Credulity"), 30 ("A Friend to a *Real* Clergyman, and an Enemy to Bigotry"), June 3, 13, 1799; see also the issues of *ibid.,* May 13, 16, 20, 27, 30, June 6, 10, 1799; the Hartford, Conn., *American Mercury,* June 6, Aug. 29, 1799; and the New London, Conn., *Bee,* Aug. 21, 1799.

138. Philadelphia *Aurora,* Nov. 16, 1799, Sept. 12, 1800; Baltimore *American,* Sept. 16, 1800; Jones, *America and French Culture,* 339–400; Stauffer, *New England and Bavarian Illuminati,* 319–24.

139. Stauffer, *New England Bavarian Illuminati,* 319–20. Cf. p. 182.

140. *Ibid.,* 313–14; Faÿ, *Revolutionary Spirit,* 423.

141. Hartford, Conn., *American Mercury,* Sept. 26, 1799.

142. New London, Conn., *Bee,* Nov. 20, 27, Dec. 4, 1799, Jan. 15, Feb. 5, 1800; Boston *Constitutional Telegraphe,* Nov. 16, 1799; Philadelphia *Aurora,* Nov. 16, 25, Dec. 6, 9, 1799; Hartford *American Mercury,* Nov. 1, 4, 1799; Norwich, Conn., *Packet,* Jan. 2, 1800. Stauffer, *New England and Bavarian Illuminati,* 317–19, is authority for the statement that the printed letter from Ebeling was actually the one to Bentley. See Adam Weishaupt's letter, from the *Gotha Gazette,* in the Worcester *Massachusetts Spy,* Jan. 8, 1800; New London, Conn., *Bee,* Jan. 22, 1800; Faÿ, *Notes on the American Press,* 26.

143. For Federalist arguments, see the Northampton, Mass., *Hampshire Gazette,* Jan. 8, Apr. 2, 1800; Boston *Massachusetts Mercury,* Dec. 27, 1799; Hartford *Connecticut Courant,* Nov. 30, 1799, May 19, Sept. 22, Oct. 8, 1800. The Republican quotation is from the Richmond *Virginia Argus,* Jan. 7, 1800; the counterattack continued with publication of Ogden's pamphlet, *A View of the New England Illuminati.* Jeffersonian printers lauded this disclosure of "tyranny at the northward"; Philadelphia *Aurora,* Feb. 14, 1800; Alexandria, Va., *Alexandria Times,* Feb. 20, 1800; Charleston, S. C., *City Gazette,* Mar. 5, 1800; Baltimore *American,* Sept. 16, 1800, *et al.* Stauffer, *New England and Bavarian Illuminati,* 355–59, tells of the anti-Illuminist orations of Abraham Baldwin, refused a place to speak for a Phi Beta Kappa address at New Haven.

144. Philadelphia *Aurora,* Sept. 1, 1800.

145. Newark, N. J., *Centinel of Freedom,* July 29, 1800; Baltimore *American,* Aug. 1, 1800.

146. "Bunker Hill" (from the Boston *Independent Chronicle*), Baltimore *American,* Oct. 23, 1800; Newark, N. J., *Centinel of Freedom,* Oct. 28, 1800; Raleigh, N. C., *Raleigh Register,* Nov. 18, 1800; Dedham, Mass., *Columbian Minerva,* Nov. 11 ("Clericus"—against Jefferson), 18 ("CONFUCIUS"), 1800; Thorning, *Religious Liberty,* 167; Koch, *Republican Religion,* 275.

147. Philadelphia *Constitutional Diary,* Dec. 19, 1800; Philadelphia *Aurora,* Feb. 13, 15, 1798, Feb. 13, 1799.

148. Richmond *Virginia Argus,* Sept. 26, 1800; Philadelphia *Aurora,* Sept. 27, 1800.

149. Newark, N. J. *Centinel of Freedom,* Sept. 17, 1799; Baltimore *American,* Sept. 27, 1799, Aug. 11, 1800.

150. This was, of course, questioned in New England.

151. "A REPUBLICAN," Charleston, S. C., *Charleston City Gazette,* Nov. 18, 1800.

 REPUBLICANISM AND THE
NATURE OF SOCIETY

1. Carl L. Becker, *The Declaration of Independence,* 24–26, 76–79. See also Curti, "Great Mr. Locke," 117, 135. While Clinton Rossiter, *Seedtime of the Republic,* 358–59, discounts any idea of an exclusive reliance on Locke, he calls him "the most popular source of Revolutionary ideas."

2. See Merrill Jensen, "Democracy and the American Revolution," in John C. Wahlke (ed.), *The Causes of the American Revolution,* 74; Ola Winslow, *Master Roger Williams,* 188, 239.

3. Becker, *Declaration,* 52–72; George P. Fisher, "Jefferson and the Social Compact Theory," *Annual Report of the American Historical Association, 1893,* 165–66, 172; P. Emory Aldrich, article concerning Locke's effect on America, in the *Proceedings of the American Antiquarian Society, 1879,* 27; Curti, "Great Mr. Locke," 107; Rossiter, *Seedtime,* 439.

4. For testimony as to the prevalence of Locke's ideas, see Aldrich, *Proceedings,* 30–35; Leon Howard, *The Connecticut Wits,* 8, 235; Bernhard Knollenberg, *Origin of the American Revolution,* 66, 160, 198; Schlesinger, *Prelude,* 34; John M. Blum *et al., The National Experience,* 65, 87, 89, 101; John A. Garraty, *The American Nation,* 79, 120. Curti, "Great Mr. Locke," 136–37, discusses implications of Locke's thinking; on his faith in posterity and the future, see Carl L. Becker, *The Heavenly City of the Eighteenth Century Philosophers,* esp. 118, 131.

5. Several of the British utilitarians (notably Barwis and Bentham) accepted and stressed this view. See Henry V. S. Ogden, "The State of Nature and the Decline of Lockian Political Theory in England, 1760–1800," *American Historical Review* 46 (Oct., 1940), 22–23, 29–31; John H. Randall, Jr., *Making of the Modern Mind,* 359–61. The influence of English political ideas is pointed out by Faÿ, *Revolutionary Spirit,* 307–08; and by William Seal Carpenter, *The Development of American Political Thought,* 72.

6. Jones, *America and French Culture,* 402–05; Link, *Democratic-Republican Societies,* 100–06; Becker, *Declaration,* 34–47. For news-

paper examples, see the Philadelphia *National Gazette,* Dec. 5, 1792, Feb. 6, 9, 20, 1793; Halifax *North Carolina Journal,* July 10, 1793; Philadelphia *Aurora,* Jan. 26, 1795; etc.

7. Faÿ, *Revolutionary Spirit,* 224–25, 340; Paul M. Spurlin, *Montesquieu in America, 1760–1801,* esp. 6–13, 30–39, 50–51, 227, 246–53. Cf. the Philadelphia *General Advertiser,* June 28–Sept. 1, 1791, Dec. 7, 19, 1792; Philadelphia *Aurora,* Jan. 26, 1795, Feb. 27, 1796, Aug. 14, 1797.

8. Mary-Margaret H. Barr, *Voltaire in America, 1744–1800,* esp. 100–04, 109, 112–20; Link, *Democratic-Republican Societies,* 100–06. Julian P. Boyd, *Between the Spur and the Bridle,* 22, suggests the distinction between the European *philosophes* and the Enlightenment in America.

9. The *Baltimore Telegraphe,* Apr. 21, 1795, astutely and accurately noted that those French principles causing Federalists and Englishmen so much concern were actually largely English in origin.

10. Herbert M. Morais, *Deism in Eighteenth Century America,* 37–48; G. Adolf Koch, *Republican Religion,* 28–50, 208–20. For samples of American deist writers see the Philadelphia *National Gazette,* July 7, 14, Aug. 4, 15, Sept. 1, 1792; Newburgh, N. Y., *Mirror,* Oct. 22, 1798, July 9, 1799.

11. Philadelphia *General Advertiser,* June 30, July 1, 2, 1791, *et seq.;* Koch, *Republican Religion,* 21–22.

12. Howard, *Connecticut Wits,* 212–13, 278–79; Faÿ, *Revolutionary Spirit,* 420–21; Raymond G. Gettell, *History of Political Thought,* 363–64.

13. Boston *Independent Chronicle,* July 16, 1789, reprinted Oct. 8, 1798.

14. *Ibid.;* see also the New York *American Citizen,* Feb. 14, 1801.

15. Philadelphia *General Advertiser,* May 19, 1791.

16. Lexington *Kentucky Gazette,* Jan. 16, 1800; see also, e.g., the Boston *Independent Chronicle,* Nov. 16, 1797; Newark, N. J., *Centinel of Freedom,* Aug. 19, 1800.

17. The quotation is from the Philadelphia *National Gazette,* Aug. 29, 1792; see also the Baltimore *American,* Nov. 4, 1800.

18. For the quotation, Philadelphia *American Daily Advertiser,* Jan. 15, 1795 (cited in Luetscher, *Early Political Machinery,* 61); on the Democrats as old Whigs, Philadelphia *National Gazette,* Sept. 26, 1792; Wilmington, Del., *Mirror of the Times,* Feb. 19, 1800.

19. Philadelphia *Aurora,* Nov. 24, 1798.

20. "Mr. Paine's opinion on the nature of government," in the Boston *Independent Chronicle,* June 21, 1792; Philadelphia *National Gazette,* Dec. 22, 1792.

21. Charleston, S. C., *Columbian Herald,* Aug. 15, 1793. See also the Savannah, Ga., *Columbian Museum,* Mar. 18, 1796; and the New York *Diary,* Mar. 1, 1797.

22. New York, *Greenleaf's New York Journal,* Mar. 16, 1799; Baltimore *American,* Oct. 6, 1799.

23. Albany, N. Y., *Albany Register,* May 20, 1800 (on Webster); Pittsfield, Mass., *Sun,* Oct. 7, Nov. 4, 1800; Philadelphia *Aurora,* Jan. 28, 1800; Alexandria, Va., *Alexandria Times,* Feb. 5, 1800.

24. Quotation from the Boston *Independent Chronicle,* July 3, 1800; New London, Conn., *Bee,* Sept. 24, 1800.

25. Washington, D. C., *Washington Gazette,* May 19, 1797.

26. Boston *Independent Chronicle,* Oct. 21, 28, 1790 (citing Adams); Elizabethtown, Md., *Washington Spy,* Dec. 9, 1794; Philadelphia *General Advertiser,* Jan. 27, 1794; Newark, N. J., *Centinel of Freedom,* May 3, 1797.

27. Providence, R. I., *United States Chronicle,* Jan. 23, 1794; cf. the Richmond, Va., *Examiner,* Mar. 29, 1799.

28. E.g., see the letter of Congressman John Fowler to his Kentucky constituents, Washington, Ky., *Mirror,* Apr. 12, 1799; cf. Roy F. Nichols, *The Invention of the American Political Parties,* 190.

29. The quotation is from the Newark, N. J., *Centinel of Freedom,* June 3, 1800. On salaries, see the Haverhill, Mass., *Guardian of Freedom,* Nov. 6, 1794.

30. *Baltimore Daily Intelligencer,* May 24, 1794.

31. Edenton, N. C., *State Gazette of North-Carolina,* Oct. 15, 1790; Philadelphia *General Advertiser,* Mar. 31, 1791.

32. Boston *American Herald,* Nov. 1, 1790. This item seems to support Charles A. Beard's contention that American political parties evolved at least in part out of the struggle over adoption of the Constitution. For a similar view, see also the Philadelphia *National Gazette,* Sept. 26, 1792. Yet it has been noted (see Chaps. 2–3) that much of the early organized resistance to Federalism coalesced around opposition to the administration's financial program—and a number of scholars contend that true parties did not really exist prior to the Jay Treaty dispute. See Cunningham, *Jeffersonian Republicans,* 23; Wheeler, "Urban Politics," 97, 171, 264, 367; and Charles, *Origins,* 95–96, 116–17. Nichols, *Invention,* xi–xii, 1, argues that institutionalized parties as such did not develop until about 1848, and that elites actually controlled state govern-

ments in the 1790s (p. 183). To Nichols most voters in this period were influenced by geographical considerations, although he notes steps toward a genuine political campaign in 1796 (pp. 193–94), and true efforts respecting a national organization by Republicans after passage of the Alien and Sedition Acts (p. 202).

33. New York *Argus,* May 11, 1795.

34. *Boston Gazette,* Feb. 8, 1790; Boston *Independent Chronicle,* July 15, 1790.

35. Boston *Independent Chronicle,* Dec. 6, 1790; Philadelphia *National Gazette,* Mar. 26, 1792; Philadelphia *American Daily Advertiser,* Dec. 29, 1794.

36. Bennington *Vermont Gazette,* Mar. 2, 1796.

37. Boston *Independent Chronicle,* Mar. 29, 1798; Lexington *Kentucky Gazette,* Jan. 16, 1800.

38. Pittsfield, Mass., *Sun,* Oct. 7, 1800.

39. Washington, Ky., *Mirror,* Apr. 5, May 3, 1799; Raleigh, N. C., *Raleigh Register,* Sept. 9, 1800. This seems, however, to have been merely what Fenno thought should be done, rather than an avowed Federalist program (as some Republican papers suggested). Fenno, son of the John Fenno who founded the *Gazette of the United States* and who died in 1798, apparently resolved to sell out in 1799 when Adams sent Murray to make peace with France; he finally did so in 1800. See Brigham, *History and Bibliography,* II, 913.

40. Boston *Constitutional Telegraphe,* Oct. 9, 1799.

41. Norwich, Conn., *Weekly Register,* Jan. 21, 1794.

42. Philadelphia *National Gazette,* Dec. 5, 1791; Lexington *Kentucky Gazette,* Jan. 16, 1800; Philadelphia *Aurora,* Apr. 2, 1796; Northumberland, Pa., *Sunbury and Northumberland Gazette,* June 29, 1799; "A Democrat," in the Fairhaven, Vt., *Farmers' Library,* July 11, 1796; Boston *Independent Chronicle,* Sept. 18, 1797.

43. E.g., the Trenton *New Jersey State Gazette,* Oct. 3, 1792; Philadelphia *Carey's United States Recorder,* May 19, 1798; New York *Argus,* Jan. 21, 1799.

44. Savannah, Ga., *Columbian Museum,* Apr. 26, May 6, 1796; Philadelphia *Aurora,* Nov. 17, 1798; Boston *Independent Chronicle,* Aug. 26, 1799; Newark, N. J., *Centinel of Freedom,* Mar. 11, 18, 1800; "A Republican," in the Washington, D. C., *National Intelligencer,* Oct. 31, 1800.

45. *Albany Register,* July 29, 1793; Elizabethtown, N. J., *Jersey Journal,* Mar. 27, 1798.

46. E.g., Wheeler,"Urban Politics," 140 *et al.;* see Link, *Democratic-Republican Societies,* 76–78, 86–91, 93–94, on urban membership in the "democratic clubs" of that day.

47. Philadelphia *General Postbothe,* Feb. 12, 1790; Philadelphia *Level of Europe,* Feb. 9, 1795; Joseph Dorfman, "The Economic Philosophy of Thomas Jefferson," *Political Science Quarterly* 55 (1940), 98–102, 107; New York *Diary,* Sept. 22, 1791.

48. Cited in the Boston *Independent Chronicle,* Apr. 13, 1798.

49. Joseph J. Spengler, "The Political Economy of Jefferson, Madison and Adams," in David K. Jackson (ed.), *Studies in Honor of William Kenneth Boyd,* 38–42; see also Eugene T. Mudge, *The Social Philosophy of John Taylor of Caroline,* 5–6, for Taylor's generally coincidental views. James Truslow Adams, *The Living Jefferson,* 166–67, emphasizes that American democracy was considered unique and possible only because of the abundance of free land. Donald Davidson, *Attack on Leviathan,* 328–30, suggests Jefferson may have foreseen some of our modern dilemmas and attempted to avoid them by setting up a form of government based on an agricultural society.

50. Savannah, Ga., *Columbian Museum,* May 17, 1796. The Washington, Ky., *Mirror,* Aug. 14, 1799, asserted that in the cities British influence was rampant, and "the *worst of everything is uppermost."*

51. New York *Time Piece,* Apr. 21, 1797; see also the Newfield, Conn., *American Telegraphe,* May 6, 1795. Lynton K. Caldwell, *The Administrative Theories of Hamilton and Jefferson,* esp. 112, has citations showing Jefferson's faith in the power of ideas and his confidence that the people would ultimately right public wrongs.

52. *Greenleaf's New York Journal,* Apr. 4, 1798; Boston *Constitutional Telegraphe,* Oct. 9, 1799; New York *American Citizen,* Apr. 26, 1800; Richmond *Virginia Argus,* Sept. 5, 1800.

53. Philadelphia *National Gazette,* Dec. 19, 1792; see also the issues of May 7, July 21, 1792. Cf. the Boston *American Herald,* Oct. 25, 1790; Halifax *North Carolina Journal,* Sept. 19, 1792; Fairhaven, Vt., *Farmers' Library,* Aug. 8, 1796.

54. Philadelphia *National Gazette,* July 25, 1792; Dumfries, Va., *Republican Journal,* July 17, 1795 (for the quotation); Fredericktown, Md., *Bartgis's Federal Gazette,* Apr. 14, 1796; Chambersburg, Pa., *Farmers' Register,* June 27, 1798.

55. See the resolutions of the Republican Society of Newark, in the Charleston *South Carolina State Gazette,* July 26, 1794; Charleston, S. C., *Columbian Herald,* July 28, 1794. Note also "Real Friend of his Country," in the latter paper, Oct. 13, 1795; "CATO," in the Newark,

N. J., *Woods's Newark Gazette* (which had not yet turned Federalist), Dec. 10, 1794; and "Some of the Principles of American Republicanism," Washington, D. C., *Washington Gazette,* May 17, 1797.

56. The quotation is from the Fredericktown, Md., *Bartgis's Federal Gazette,* Apr. 14, 1796; see also "A Citizen of the North Western Territory," Chillicothe [Ohio] *Scioto Gazette,* Nov. 27, 1800. The New York *Diary,* Feb. 25, 1797, warned, "Beware of those who cry out 'There is no danger—there is no danger!' for 'Broad is the road' to despotism." Only the people as a whole, echoed the Philadelphia *Aurora,* Dec. 6, 1797, calling on them to *"Watch and oppose,"* could be consistently desirous of the general welfare.

57. Philadelphia *National Gazette,* July 25, 1792; Norwich, Conn., *Norwich Packet,* Aug. 9, 1792.

58. *Philadelphische Correspondenz,* Apr. 9, 1793; Philadelphia *National Gazette,* Apr. 13, 1793.

59. Link, *Democratic-Republican Societies,* 13–15. For expressions of this philosophy see, e.g., the *Baltimore Daily Repository,* June 26, 1793; Lexington *Kentucky Gazette,* Aug. 24, 31, 1793; Boston *Independent Chronicle,* Jan. 16, Aug. 28, 1794. The quotation is from the *Baltimore Daily Intelligencer,* May 24, 1794.

60. E.g., the New Haven *Connecticut Journal,* Oct. 9, 1793; Charleston, S. C., *City Gazette,* Mar. 18, 1794; *Baltimore Daily Intelligencer,* May 8, 1794, *et al.*

61. See, for examples, the Newark, N. J., *Woods's Newark Gazette,* Mar. 26, 1794; Windsor, Vt., *Spooner's Vermont Journal,* Apr. 21, 1794; Portland, [Mass.], *Gazette of Maine,* Aug. 23, 1794.

62. Philadelphia *National Gazette,* Sept. 28, 1793; New York *Daily Gazette* (on Charleston), Apr. 21, 1794; Philadelphia *American Daily Advertiser,* Aug. 2, 1794; Baltimore *Federal Intelligencer,* Nov. 14, 1794.

63. Wheeler, "Urban Politics," e.g., 164, 260, 361; *Baltimore Daily Intelligencer,* Oct. 16, 1794; Baltimore *Federal Intelligencer,* Nov. 14, 18, 1794; Lancaster, Pa., *Lancaster Journal,* Sept. 9, 1795; etc.

64. See the excerpt from the New York *American Minerva,* in the Worcester *Massachusetts Spy,* June 5, 1794; New Haven *Connecticut Journal,* June 25, 1794.

65. An added inducement would be that they could thus more easily carry out the wishes of the British minister to this country; Philadelphia *General Advertiser,* Apr. 16, 1794.

66. *Baltimore Daily Intelligencer,* June 14, 1794; New York *Herald,* Oct. 30, 1794.

67. E.g., see the Boston *Columbian Centinel*, Oct. 4, 1794; Worcester, Mass., *Worcester County Intelligencer*, Dec. 2, 1794; William Miller, "The Democratic Societies and the Whiskey Insurrection," *Pennsylvania Magazine of History and Biography* 62 (July, 1938), 324–26.

68. For samples of the resolutions see the Newark, N. J., *Woods's Newark Gazette*, Sept. 24, 1794; Philadelphia *American Daily Advertiser*, Aug. 14, Sept. 8, Oct. 6, 1794; Charleston *South Carolina State Gazette*, Oct. 20, 1794; Philadelphia *Gazette of the United States*, Sept. 1, 1794; New York *Herald*, Sept. 4, 1794; Philadelphia *Aurora*, Sept. 23, 1794.

69. Baltimore *Federal Intelligencer*, Dec. 2, 1794; Norwich, Conn., *Norwich Weekly Register*, Jan. 13, 1795; "A QUAKER," Boston *Independent Chronicle*, Dec. 15, 1794.

70. Boston *Independent Chronicle*, Dec. 11, 1794; Philadelphia *Aurora*, Dec. 22, 1794; New Haven *Connecticut Journal* (address of the German Republican Society), Jan. 15, 1795; Philadelphia *Independent Gazetteer*, Jan. 17, 28, 31, 1795.

71. E.g., Boston *Independent Chronicle*, Jan. 12, 26, Feb. 26, Mar. 2, 16, 1795; Philadelphia *Aurora*, Jan. 19, 22, Feb. 10, 1795; *Greenleaf's New York Journal*, Jan. 28, Mar. 25, 1795; *et al.*

72. Link, *Democratic-Republican Societies*, 13–15. Cf. the Charleston *South Carolina State Gazette* (increasingly Federalist), Apr. 22, 1795; Philadelphia *Gazette of the United States*, Sept. 1, 1796; Dumfries, Va., *Republican Journal*, Sept. 9, 1796; Boston *Independent Chronicle*, Jan. 21, 1796, Jan. 30, 1797; Fairhaven, Vt., *Farmers' Library*, July 1, 1796; New York *Argus*, July 6, 1798; Philadelphia *Aurora*, Dec. 22, 1798; Danbury, Conn., *Republican Journal*, Mar. 26, 1798; Newark, N. J., *Centinel of Freedom*, Aug. 12, 1800.

73. Boston *Independent Chronicle*, May 4, 1797, as well as earlier issues.

74. Baltimore *Maryland Journal*, May 21, 1790, Oct. 3, 1792; the quotation is from the Philadelphia *Freeman's Journal*, Feb. 16, 1791; see also the Philadelphia *National Gazette*, Dec. 19, 1791.

75. Washington, Ky., *Mirror*, Mar. 8, 1798; for the quotation, see the Charleston *South Carolina State Gazette*, Nov. 26, 1795.

76. Bennington *Vermont Gazette*, Mar. 2, 1796.

77. Boston *Independent Chronicle*, Jan. 21, 25, 1796, Mar. 4, 1799; Richmond, Va., *Examiner*, Dec. 6, 1798; Frankfort, Ky., *Palladium*, May 15, 1800; though modern beauty contests were unknown, the idea (essentially) of this sort of judgment was presented by "Lycurgus," Richmond *Virginia Argus*, Aug. 26, 29, 1800.

78. "A True American," in the Boston *Independent Chronicle,* Mar. 4, 1799; see also "PAETUS," *ibid.,* Aug. 22, 1799; Richmond *Virginia Argus,* Aug. 29, 1800. The quoted injunction is from the Frankfort, Ky., *Palladium,* May 15, 1800.

79. Philadelphia *National Gazette,* May 3, 1792; Rutland *Herald of Vermont,* July 9, 1792.

80. Faÿ, *Notes on the American Press,* 6; Wheeler, "Urban Politics," 114–15, 142, 257, 407–08; Philadelphia *Aurora,* Mar. 15, 1797; Richmond, Va., *Examiner,* Oct. 22, 1799.

81. *Boston Gazette* (for the quotation), Sept. 13, 1790; Philadelphia *General Advertiser,* Feb. 28, 1793.

82. *Boston Gazette, ibid.;* see also the Washington, D. C., *Washington Gazette,* May 17, 1797.

83. See Ames, "Proposed Amendments," 66, 240; Philadelphia *National Gazette,* May 1, 1793; Boston *Independent Chronicle,* Oct. 28, 1800; Washington, D. C., *National Intelligencer,* Jan. 12, 1801; for examples of this sentiment. When Republican John Beckley was dismissed as clerk of the House of Representatives, however, Jeffersonians condemned the step as the unnecessary removal of a man with valuable experience; Boston *Independent Chronicle,* May 22, 1797.

84. Albany, N. Y., *Albany Register,* July 18, 1791; Baltimore *American,* July 17, 26, 1800; *Baltimore Telegraphe,* Nov. 8, 1800. The quotation is from "Aristogiton," in the Richmond, Va., *Examiner,* Oct. 22, 1799.

85. Wilmington *Delaware Gazette,* July 16, 1791; Philadelphia *National Gazette,* July 7, 1792; Norwich, Conn., *Weekly Register,* Aug. 21, 1792; Boston *Independent Chronicle,* Dec. 3, 1798; Boston *Constitutional Telegraphe,* Oct. 9, 1799; Pittsburgh *Tree of Liberty,* Nov. 15, 1800.

86. Philadelphia *General Advertiser,* Feb. 13, 1794; Charleston, S. C., *Columbian Herald,* Mar. 19, 1794; J. Mark Jacobson, *The Development of American Political Thought,* 252; Beard, *Jeffersonian Democracy,* 323–27, 331.

87. Philadelphia *Daily Advertiser,* June 20, 1797; New York *Time Piece,* Sept. 1, 1797.

88. Fredericktown, Md., *Bartgis's Federal Gazette,* Sept. 16, 1799.

89. Philadelphia *National Gazette,* May 1, 1793; "Rags," in the *Baltimore Daily Intelligencer,* Feb. 10, 1794; Fredericktown, Md., *Bartgis's Federal Gazette,* Feb. 25, 1799; Greensburg, Pa., *Farmers' Register,* Sept. 14, 1799.

90. Philadelphia *National Gazette,* Feb. 27, 1792, Mar. 30, 1793;

Caldwell, *Administrative Theories,* (citing Jefferson's letter of Oct. 28, 1795, to Madison), 169; Washington, D. C., May 17, 1797; Washington, Ky., *Mirror,* Aug. 14, 1799; Richmond, Va., *Examiner,* Mar. 29, 1800. For Freneau's comparison, see the New York *Time Piece,* Sept. 21, 1797.

91. This is noted, for instance, in Wheeler, "Urban Politics," e.g., 140–41.

92. E.g., Haverhill, Mass., *Guardian of Freedom,* Nov. 6, 1794; Elizabethtown, Md., *Washington Spy,* Dec. 9, 1794; White, *The Federalists,* 293; Caldwell, *Administrative Theories,* 124, 133–34. See Chap. 3 on Democratic concern for economy in government.

93. "PHILOLENTHEROG," Boston *Independent Chronicle,* Mar. 13, 1800; the New York *American Citizen,* Mar. 17, 1800; and the Albany, N. Y., *Albany Register,* May 20, 1800, developed similar reasoning.

94. Philadelphia *General Postbothe,* Feb. 12, 1790; Boston *American Herald,* Nov. 15, 1790; Trenton *New Jersey State Gazette,* Feb. 20, 1793; Charleston, *State Gazette of South Carolina,* Mar. 21, 1793; New Haven *Connecticut Journal,* Nov. 6, 1794; Norfolk *Virginia Chronicle,* Nov. 17, 1794; New York *Argus,* June 2, 1795.

95. Trenton *New Jersey State Gazette,* Feb. 20, 1793; New Haven *Connecticut Journal,* Nov. 6, 1794; Washington, Ky., *Mirror,* Apr. 12, 1798; Norfolk, Va., *Epitome of the Times,* June 28, 1798; Newark, N. J., *Centinel of Freedom,* May 7, 1799; Richmond *Virginia Argus,* Jan. 7, 1800. The quotation is from the Philadelphia *Aurora,* Aug. 15, 1798.

96. *New-York Journal,* Jan. 24, 1791; Philadelphia *General Advertiser,* May 21, 22, 1794; Boston *Independent Chronicle,* June 5, 1794; "A Calm Observer," New York *Argus,* May 12, 1795; see also the issue of June 2, 1795. For views on the navy, see the Bridgetown, N. J., *Bridgetown Argus,* Nov. 19, 1795; *New York Weekly Museum,* Mar. 5, 1796; Philadelphia *Aurora,* Aug. 29, 1798; Boston *Independent Chronicle,* Nov. 26, 1798; Lexington *Kentucky Gazette,* July 24, 1800; Richmond, Va., *Examiner,* Oct. 24, 1800. Cf., however, "A Friend of the People," Morristown, N. J., *Genius of Liberty,* Oct. 9, 1800, denying that Jefferson opposed an "adequate" navy, or that he would abandon American sea-borne commerce.

97. Boston *Independent Chronicle,* Mar. 4, 1798; cf. Senator Mason of Virginia, in the Philadelphia *Gazette of the United States,* June 27, 1798; Augusta, Ga., *Augusta Chronicle,* Jan. 26, 1799. See also Morison, *Otis,* I, 66, 102–03; and DeConde, *Quasi-War,* 99.

98. Norfolk, Va., *Epitome of the Times,* June 28, 1798; Philadelphia *Aurora,* July 11, 1798; Boston *Constitutional Telegraphe,* Nov. 6, 1799; Raleigh, N. C., *Raleigh Register,* Dec. 31, 1799; Richmond *Virginia Argus,* Jan. 7, 1800; New London, Conn., *Bee,* Jan. 15, 1800.

99. Boston *Independent Chronicle,* Jan. 14, 17, 1799; Elizabethtown, N. J., *Jersey Journal,* Jan. 22, 1799; Chambersburg, Pa., *Farmers' Register,* Mar. 6, 1799; Morristown, N. J., *Genius of Liberty,* Nov. 7, 1799. The Newark, N. J., *Newark Gazette,* Nov. 11, 1800; and the Washington, D. C., *National Intelligencer,* Nov. 28, 1800, expressed similar views. Even President Adams had allegedly earlier given thanks that the United States had no standing army; Boston *Constitutional Telegraphe,* Oct. 5, Nov. 13, 1799; Richmond, Va., *Examiner,* Feb. 28, 1800; Wilmington, N. C., *Wilmington Gazette,* Mar. 20, 1800.

100. Philadelphia *Aurora,* Feb. 20, May 16, 24, 1799; Boston *Independent Chronicle,* Aug. 20, 1798, Jan. 17, 1799; Dedham, Mass., *Minerva,* Aug. 15, 1799; Boston *Constitutional Telegraphe,* Nov. 6, 1799; Salisbury, N. C., *North Carolina Mercury,* Mar. 20, 1800.

101. Baltimore *American,* June 25, 1799. For an account of the beating, see *ibid.,* May 29, 1799; and the Philadelphia *Aurora,* May 16, 24, 1799. The *American,* June 24, 27, Sept. 2, 7, 1799, cited other instances of disorderliness on the part of the troops; cf. the Boston *Independent Chronicle,* Aug. 20, 1798; New London, Conn., *Bee,* June 5, 1799; New York *Argus,* Jan. 18, 1800; Newark, N. J., *Centinel of Freedom,* Feb. 18, 1800; Richmond, Va., *Examiner,* Mar. 4, 11, 1800; Anon., "Party Violence, 1790–1800," 177.

102. Philadelphia *Aurora,* Feb. 11, 20, 1799; Boston *Independent Chronicle,* Mar. 4, 28, 1799; Albany, N. Y., *Albany Register,* Feb. 21, 1799; Windsor, Vt., *Spooner's Vermont Journal,* Apr. 2, 1799; New London, Conn., *Bee,* June 5, 1799; Baltimore *American,* June 17, 1799.

103. Boston *Independent Chronicle,* Oct. 31, 1799 (quoted in Warren, *Making of the Constitution,* 122, where the date is erroneously given as 1798) ; Philadelphia *Aurora,* Jan. 27, 1800.

104. Frankfort, Ky., *Palladium,* Feb. 13, 1800; a Federalist version may be found in the New York *Commercial Advertiser,* Feb. 1, 1800. See also Janson, *Stranger in America,* 145–46, 166n.

105. Philadelphia *Aurora,* Jan. 16, 1800; Alexandria, Va., *Alexandria Times,* Jan. 20, 23, 1800; see Miller, *Crisis in Freedom,* 127–30, on Holt.

106. New London, Conn., *Bee,* Feb. 5, 1800; the Newark, N. J., *Centinel of Freedom,* Mar. 18, 1800, gives Adams' quotation. See the

Raleigh, N. C., *Raleigh Register,* Feb.–Mar., *passim,* 1800; and the Reading, Pa., *Readinger Adler,* Mar. 4, 1800; the Richmond, Va., *Friend of the People,* May 16, 1800, made the association with Senator Ross's proposal.

107. Goshen, N. Y., *Orange Patrol,* June 10, 1800. See also the Newark, N. J., *Centinel of Freedom,* June 17, 1800; Philadelphia *Aurora,* June 19, 23, 1800; Lexington *Kentucky Gazette,* July 10, 1800; Baltimore *American,* Nov. 6, 1800; Lynchburg, Va., *Lynchburg Weekly Gazette,* Nov. 15, 1800.

108. *New-York Journal,* Jan. 28, 1790; New York *Time Piece,* Mar. 13, 1797.

109. Lexington *Kentucky Gazette,* Oct. 15, 1791.

110. Portsmouth, N. H., *Osborne's New Hampshire Spy,* Feb. 19, 1791; Philadelphia *National Gazette,* June 18, 1792; Boston *Independent Chronicle,* Dec. 14, 1795; Reading, Pa., *Readinger Adler,* Oct. 3, 1798; Washington, D. C. *National Intelligencer,* Dec. 19, 1800.

111. *New-York Journal,* Nov. 16, 1791.

112. Newark, N. J., *Newark Gazette,* May 10, 1792; Philadelphia *General Advertiser,* May 15, 1792; Edenton *State Gazette of North Carolina,* Feb. 7, 1794 (citing a public toast); Baltimore *Federal Intelligencer,* Dec. 6, 1794; *Greenleaf's New York Journal,* Jan. 3, 1795; Bennington, Vt., *Tablet of the Times,* May 4, 1797; Boston *Independent Chronicle,* Jan. 8, 1798; Newark, N. J., *Centinel of Freedom,* May 13, 1800.

113. Knoxville, Tenn., *Knoxville Register,* Oct. 9, 1798. See also the Philadelphia *Aurora,* Nov. 7, 1798; Baltimore *American,* Sept. 4, 9, 1800.

114. Baltimore *American,* June 30, 1800; in addition, note the New York *Republican Watchtower,* Oct. 29, 1800. See Chap. 12 for discussion of the Alien and Sedition Acts.

115. Boston *Independent Chronicle,* Jan. 8, 1798.

116. Washington, D. C., *Washington Gazette,* May 17, 1797. Beard, *Jeffersonian Democracy,* 463, however, points out that Jefferson and many Republican leaders did not regard universal manhood suffrage as an essential article of their political faith, and that Virginia and North Carolina were among the last states to grant such suffrage.

117. Philadelphia *General Advertiser,* Mar. 15, 1792.

118. E.g., the Wilmington *Delaware Gazette,* Mar. 20, 1790, Nov. 12, 1791; Wilmington *Delaware and Eastern Shore Advertiser,* Dec. 27, 1794. See John A. Munroe, *Federalist Delaware, 1775–1815,* 175–76, 191–92; H. R. Good, *A History of American Education,* 81–82, 93–

95. The *Albany Register,* Nov. 20, 1795; and Young, *Democratic Republicans,* 524–26, tell of the press and efforts for public schools in New York state.

119. Philadelphia *American Daily Advertiser,* Dec. 25, 1794 (for the quotation); see also the Philadelphia *General Advertiser,* May 28, 1792; and the Mt. Pleasant, N. J., *Jersey Chronicle,* June 6, 13, 20, 27, July 4, 1795.

120. New London, Conn., *Bee,* Mar. 26, 1800.

121. Philadelphia *General Advertiser,* Mar. 15, 1792; Washington, D. C., *Washington Gazette,* Dec. 9, 1797; Robert Coram, *Political Inquiries, to Which is Added a Plan for the General Establishment of Schools throughout the United States* (Wilmington, Del., 1791), esp. 78–79 (quotation), 93, 97–101. Samuel H. Smith, editor of the Philadelphia *New World,* and later of the Washington *National Intelligencer,* was convinced of the desirability of such a system of schools; see Krout and Fox, *Completion of Independence,* 178. A summary of Jefferson's own views respecting public education can be found in Gettell, *A History of Political Thought,* 363–64. The importance of posterity in the thinking of the times is emphasized in Becker, *Heavenly City,* esp. 140–42.

CONSTITUTIONAL
GOVERNMENT: REPUBLICAN
INTERPRETATION

1. "An Independent Federal Elector," Philadelphia *National Gazette,* Aug. 15, 1792; "PARADOX," Norwich, Conn., *Norwich Packet,* Oct. 25, 1792.

2. "PAULDING, No. I," Philadelphia *Independent Gazetteer,* May 21, 1796.

3. Washington, D. C., *Washington Gazette,* Jan. 7, 1797.

4. Philadelphia *Aurora,* Nov. 29, 1798.

5. New York *Argus,* Apr. 24, 1799; Newark, N. J., *Centinel of Freedom,* Aug. 19, 1800; Morristown, N. J., *Genius of Liberty,* Aug. 28, 1800; Richmond *Virginia Argus,* Oct. 31, 1800.

6. Baltimore *American,* Oct. 24, 1800; "One of the People," Savannah, Ga., *Columbian Museum,* Nov. 25, 1800.

7. Portsmouth, N. H., *Republican Ledger,* July 29, 1800.

8. Philadelphia *National Gazette,* Apr. 30, 1792; Norfolk, Va., *American Gazette,* Mar. 22, 1796.

9. Boston *Herald of Freedom,* Oct. 16, 1789.

10. Boston *Independent Chronicle,* Feb. 18, 1790; Augusta, Ga., *Augusta Chronicle,* May 28, 1791 (probably referring to the Treaty of New York with the Creeks); Philadelphia *National Gazette,* Apr. 2, 1792; Poughkeepsie, N. Y., *Poughkeepsie Journal,* Aug. 21, 1793, July 9, 1794; Baldwin, *Whiskey Rebels,* 67. See the Goshen, N. Y., *Goshen Repository,* Nov. 18, 1794, and the Baltimore *Fell's Point Telegraphe,* Apr. 17, 1795, for the opinion that the federal government was a wall of defense, but the states were the "repositories of civil liberty."

11. From the *Columbian Centinel*[!], Worcester *Massachusetts Spy,* Apr. 26, 1797.

12. Albany, N. Y., *Albany Register,* Mar. 4, 1800.

13. Poughkeepsie, N. Y., *Poughkeepsie Journal,* Sept. 4, 1792; Philadelphia *National Gazette,* Sept. 18, 1793; Boston *Independent Chronicle,* Sept. 16, 19, 1793. The reference here is presumably to *The Federalist,* No. 81. (See Roy P. Fairfield, ed., *The Federalist Papers,* 248; but cf. No. 80, *ibid.,* 239.)

14. *New-York Journal,* Aug. 10, 1793; Philadelphia *National Gazette,* Aug. 10, 14, 1793; Boston *Independent Chronicle,* Mar. 31, 1794, Mar. 2, 6, 1797; Fair Haven, Vt., *Farmers' Library,* Oct. 5, 1796.

15. On the proposed amendment, see the Philadelphia *National Gazette,* Apr. 30, July 24, 1793; *Boston Gazette,* Aug. 5, 1793; Norwich, Conn., *Norwich Weekly Register,* Feb. 11, 1794; Alfred H. Kelly and Winfred A. Harbison, *The American Constitution,* 191–93.

16. *Boston Gazette,* Jan. 18, Feb. 1, 1790; Boston *Herald of Freedom,* Jan. 22, 29, Mar. 12, June 8, 1790; Boston *Independent Chronicle,* Jan. 28, 1790 (but cf. also Apr. 5, 1790).

17. Boston *Independent Chronicle,* Feb. 4, 1790; Jan. 17, Mar. 25, 1799; Salem, Mass., *Impartial Register,* June 8, 1790; *Boston Gazette,* Jan. 31, 1791.

18. Philadelphia *National Gazette,* Jan. 12, 1792; cited in Woodbury, *Public Opinion,* 100–01, Forman, "Political Activities," 45–46. See the *New-York Journal,* Jan. 25, 1792; Washington, Ky., *Mirror,* Sept. 8, 1798 ("An Old American"); Richmond *Virginia Argus,* Mar. 15, 1799 ("VIRGINIUS"); on the dangers of implied powers.

19. Philadelphia *Claypoole's Daily Advertiser,* Apr. 16, 1792; Philadelphia *National Gazette,* Apr. 16, 19, 23, 1792; Philadelphia *General*

*Advertiser,* Apr. 20, 1792; Norwich, Conn., *Norwich Packet,* May 3, 1792; Kelly and Harbison, *American Constitution,* 190. A description of the entire question may be found in Max Farrand, "The First Hayburn Case," *American Historical Review* 13 (Jan., 1908), 281–85.

20. "Federalist," Boston *Independent Chronicle,* Mar. 9, 13, 16, 1797; Washington, D. C., *National Intelligencer,* Nov. 7, 1800.

21. Philadelphia *Carey's United States Recorder,* July 3, 1798 (cited in Woodbury, *Public Opinion,* 103–04) ; Pittsfield, Mass., *Sun,* Sept. 30, 1800.

22. Boston *Independent Chronicle,* Jan. 25, Feb. 1, 1796, Nov. 3, 1800 ("Cato Americanus") ; Charleston *South Carolina State Gazette,* Mar. 21, 1797; Nashville *Tennessee Gazette,* Apr. 16, 1800.

23. Ames, *Works,* 147–48; "A Citizen," Boston *Independent Chronicle,* June 17, 1799; Richmond, Va., *Examiner,* Mar. 18, 1800.

24. Boston *Independent Chronicle,* Mar. 29, 1798; see also "CAUTION," *ibid.,* Apr. 5, 1798, and (earlier) "Q," in the Philadelphia *National Gazette,* Nov. 17, 1792.

25. Item from the Philadelphia *Aurora,* Boston *Independent Chronicle,* Apr. 5, 1798. For the letter to Philip Mazzei, see Chap. 13.

26. Charleston, S. C., *Carolina Gazette,* Apr. 12, 1798; Morristown, N. J., *Genius of Liberty,* Oct. 23, 1800 ("Brutus," from the Danbury, Conn., *Sun of Liberty*) ; Charleston, S. C., *Times,* Oct. 10, 20, 1800 ("Jonathan Foster").

27. Philadelphia *Federal Gazette,* Oct. 3, 1789; Philadelphia *General Advertiser,* Sept. 24, 1791.

28. Northumberland, Pa., *Sunbury and Northumberland Gazette,* cited in Malone, "First Years of Thomas Cooper," 145–46; Boston *Constitutional Telegraphe,* Oct. 2, 1799; New York *American Citizen,* May 9, 1800; Dedham, Mass., *Columbian Minerva,* May 22, 1800; New London, Conn., *Bee,* Aug. 23, 1800.

29. Philadelphia *General Advertiser,* Feb. 13, 1792; Norwich, Conn., *Norwich Packet,* Feb. 23, 1792. See also the *Boston Gazette,* Aug. 10, 1789; and items noting that the states of S. C., N. C., Va., Pa., Md., and N. Y. all urged open sessions—Fayetteville *North Carolina Chronicle,* Dec. 20, 1790; Charleston, S. C., *City Gazette,* Jan. 14, 1791; Philadelphia *Gazette of the United States,* Jan. 19, 1791; New Haven *Connecticut Journal,* Feb. 2, 1791; Elizabeth G. McPherson, "The Southern States and the Reporting of Senate Debates, 1789–1802," *Journal of Southern History* 13 (May, 1946), 223–35.

30. Norwich, Conn., *Norwich Packet,* Aug. 23, 1792; Augusta, Ga., *Augusta Chronicle,* Sept. 1, 1792; Halifax *North Carolina Journal,*

Dec. 5, 19, 1792, Feb. 20, 1793; Baltimore *Maryland Journal*, Jan. 18, 1793; "CONDORCET," Norwich, Conn., *Weekly Register*, Jan. 1, 1793; Philadelphia *National Gazette*, Feb. 13, 16, 1793; Boston *Independent Chronicle*, Feb. 28, 1793.

31. Philadelpha *General Advertiser*, Mar. 5, 1794; McPherson, "Southern States," 238–40; Schachner, *Burr*, 133.

32. Philadelphia *General Advertiser*, Jan. 1, Mar. 5, 1794; for an example of these communications of congressmen, see John Fowler's letter to his Kentucky constituents, reprinted in the Boston *Independent Chronicle*, Sept. 20, 1798; cf. McPherson, "Southern States," 245.

33. Martinsburg, [W.] Va., *Potowmac Guardian*, Mar. 10, 1796.

34. Philadelphia *Aurora*, Feb. 14, 1798; Boston *Independent Chronicle*, Feb. 22, 1798.

35. See Chap. 1.

36. Baltimore *Maryland Journal*, Feb. 23, 1790; Pittsfield, Mass., *Berkshire Chronicle*, Mar. 25, 1790; Edenton *State Gazette of North Carolina*, Aug. 6, 1790.

37. Baltimore *Maryland Journal*, Feb. 22, 1791; Edenton *State Gazette of North Carolina*, Mar. 11, 1791.

38. New York *Daily Advertiser*, Feb. 17, 1791; Philadelphia *Freeman's Journal*, Mar. 9, 1791; Georgetown, D. C., *Georgetown Weekly Ledger*, Mar. 19, 1791; Edenton *State Gazette of North Carolina*, Mar. 25, 1791.

39. Portland *Gazette of Maine*, Mar. 10, 1791; Baltimore *Maryland Journal*, Jan. 10, 1792; Elizabethtown *New Jersey Journal*, Jan. 11, 1792.

40. *Boston Gazette*, Mar. 12, 1792. See also Frank L. Mott, *American Magazines*, 120n.; McMaster, *A History*, II, 59–62. Benjamin, "Notable Editors," 120–21, says one-half cent additional for *each* hundred miles beyond the first.

41. *Baltimore Daily Repository*, Jan. 5, 1792; Baltimore *Maryland Journal*, Jan. 10, Feb. 7, 1792.

42. Philadelphia *National Gazette*, Dec. 26, 1791 (for debate on the bill), May 28, July 9, 14, 1792; Philadelphia *Federal Gazette*, Feb. 7, 1792.

43. *Boston Gazette*, July 9, 1792; Dover, N. H., *Phenix*, Dec. 21, 1792. The former, Feb. 11, 1793, and the Norwich, Conn., *Weekly Register*, Feb. 12, 1793, reported that two leading papers had already folded.

44. Concord, N. H., *Concord Herald*, July 18, 1792; Boston *Colum-*

*bian Centinel,* Sept. 12, 1792 (cited in Mott, *American Journalism,* 161).

45. Edenton *State Gazette of North Carolina,* Apr. 15, 1791.

46. New Brunswick, N. J., *Brunswick Gazette,* Feb. 7, 1792.

47. E.g., see the Wilmington, N. C., *Wilmington Chronicle,* July 31, 1795.

48. Norwich, Conn., *Weekly Register,* Mar. 4, 1794; Philadelphia *Aurora,* May 19, 1796; *Baltimore Telegraphe,* May 23, 1796; Dumfries, Va., *Republican Journal,* May 26, 1796.

49. Baltimore *American,* May 20, 22, 25, 1799; New London, Conn., *Bee,* July 3, 1799; Philadelphia *Aurora,* Jan. 8, 1799; Boston *Constitutional Telegraphe,* Nov. 27, 1799; Richmond, Va., *Examiner,* Dec. 10, 1799. See also Anon., "Party Violence," 173–74.

50. Wilmington, N. C., *Wilmington Gazette,* Oct. 31, 1799; Newark, N. J., *Centinel of Freedom,* Oct. 8, 22, 1799, July 8, 1800, Jan. 13, 1801; Richmond, Va., *Examiner,* June 10, 1800; Raleigh, N. C., *Raleigh Register,* Aug. 12, 1800; *Constitutional Telegraphe,* Oct. 18, 1800; New London, Conn., *Bee,* Aug. 27, 1800; Salem, Mass., *Impartial Register,* Dec. 1, 1800.

51. Burk, Callender, Cooper, Duane (though born in America), Lyon, Mathew Carey, and Joseph Gales immediately come to mind.

52. See Wolfe, *Jeffersonian Democracy,* 116; Paul J. Foik, *Pioneer Catholic Journalism,* 7–9; Mary Clark, *Peter Porcupine,* 104–05; Smith, *Freedom's Fetters,* 23–26.

53. Philadelphia *Carey's United States Recorder,* May 10, June 21, 1798; New York *Argus,* May 17, 1798. Smith, *Freedom's Fetters,* 47, tells of the harboring provision.

54. McLaughlin, *Constitutional History,* 268; Savannah, Ga., *Columbian Museum,* Aug. 24, 1798; Frankfort, Ky., *Palladium,* Oct. 16, 1798 (this last carried the text of the statute, captioned: "INSERTED BY REQUEST. LAW OF THE UNION.").

55. Philadelphia *Carey's United States Recorder,* May 12, 1798; New York *Argus,* June 21, 22, 1798; Philadelphia *Aurora,* July 2, 3, 4, 7, 12, 25, 1798. Smith, *Freedom's Fetters,* 23, says the proposed tax was $20.

56. Savannah, Ga., *Columbian Museum,* Aug. 24, 1799 (item from the Bennington *Vermont Gazette*); Fredericktown, Md., *Bartgis's Federal Gazette,* Sept. 5, 1798. "D.B.," Pittsburgh *Tree of Liberty,* Aug. 30, 1800, also stressed that treatment of aliens lay within the police power of the states; the United States had only concurrent power, and even in England only enemy aliens (in time of actual war) could

be deported without jury trial. See also the Washington, Ky., *Mirror*, Sept. 8, 1798, Feb. 22, 1799; Philadelphia *Carey's United States Recorder*, June 16, 1798; Boston *Independent Chronicle*, June 25, 1798. Frank M. Anderson, "The Enforcement of the Alien and Sedition Laws," *Annual Report of the American Historical Association, 1912*, 115–16, tells how the measure drove John D. Burk into hiding. Burk had agreed to leave the country in an out-of-court settlement for a case of seditious libel; Leonard W. Levy, *Freedom of Speech and Press in Early American History*, 241. Actually he went to Virginia under an assumed name; Joseph I. Shulim, *John Daly Burk*, 25–26, 30, 33, 35–36.

57. Levy; *Freedom of Speech*, Duniway, *Freedom of Press in Mass.*, 141–43; Morison, *Otis*, I, 120; Lucy M. Salmon, *The Newspaper and Authority*, 113. See the Baltimore *Fell's Point Telegraphe*, Apr. 20, 1795 (citing the *New York Journal*); Anderson, "Enforcement," 118–19 (citing the Charleston *Carolina Gazette*, May 16, 1799); New York *Greenleaf's Daily Advertiser*, Nov. 2, 4, 1799; and Smith, *Freedom's Fetters*, 201–02.

58. Philadelphia *Carey's United States Recorder*, June 7, 1798; Boston *Independent Chronicle*, June 14, 18, 1798; New London, Conn., *Bee*, June 20, 1798.

59. Philadelphia *Carey's United States Recorder*, June 19, 1798; Philadelphia *Aurora*, June 29, July 3, 6, 1798; New York *Argus*, June 29, 1798; Boston *Independent Chronicle*, July 5, 1798.

60. Bergh, ed., *Writings of Thomas Jefferson*, X, 32 (Jefferson to Madison, Apr. 26, 1798); Mott, *Jefferson and the Press*, 28–30. See also Smith, *Freedom's Fetters*, 153–55, 421–22; Salmon, *Newspaper and Authority*, 113; and Frank L. Mott and Ralph D. Casey, *Interpretations of Journalism*, 58–59. The bill passed July 10, 1798; Payne, *History of Journalism*, 178. For its text, see the Philadelphia *Aurora*, June 6, 1798.

61. Boston *Independent Chronicle*, July 5, 9, 1798; Newport, R. I., *Companion*, July 7, 1798; New York *Time Piece*, July 9, 1798; Frankfort, Ky., *Guardian of Freedom*, July 31, 1798; McMaster, *A History*, II, 390–93; Smith, *Freedom's Fetters*, 181, 193–94.

62. Philadelphia *Aurora*, July 11, 12, 1798; Boston *Independent Chronicle*, July 16, 19, 23, 30, 1798; Chambersburg, Pa., *Farmers' Register*, July 18, 1798.

63. Philadelphia *Carey's United States Recorder*, July 12, 1798; Frankfort, Ky., *Guardian of Freedom*, Aug. 7, 1798. Similarly, see the Philadelphia *Aurora*, July 14, 1798; a "poem" on "American Liberty; or

The Sovereign Right of Thinking," New York *Time Piece,* Aug. 8, 1798; and a suggested "Pantomime" code for German voters, in the Reading, Pa., *Readinger Adler,* Oct. 9, 1798.

64. Philadelphia *Aurora,* July 18, 19, 1798; Sag Harbor, N. Y., *Frothingham's Long Island Herald,* Aug. 13, 1798; Frankfort, Ky., *Palladium,* Aug. 21, 1798.

65. Philadelphia *Aurora,* Aug. 4, 1798; Warren, *Jacobin and Junto,* 98; McMaster, *A History,* II, 397–98; Newark, N. J., *Centinel of Freedom,* July 31, 1798; Frankfort, Ky., *Palladium,* Aug. 9, 1798 (also the Knoxville, Tenn., *Knoxville Register,* Sept. 11, 1798; Elizabethtown *Maryland Herald,* Oct. 25, 1798).

66. Frankfort, Ky., *Palladium,* Aug. 9, 21, Sept. 4, 11, 18, Nov. 6, 1798; Lexington *Kentucky Gazette,* Aug. 1, 1798; Richmond, Va., *Observatory,* Aug. 27, Oct. 1, 1798; Boston *Independent Chronicle,* Sept. 3, 13, 27, 1798; Knoxville, Tenn., *Knoxville Register,* Aug. 28, Oct. 2, 16, 1798; Litchfield, Conn., *Monitor,* Sept. 26, 1798 (referring to the "deluded citizens of Kentucky"); Stonington, Conn., *Journal of the Times,* Oct. 17, 1798; Philadelphia *Aurora,* Nov. 20, Dec. 1, 7, 1798; New York *Greenleaf's Daily Advertiser,* Dec. 8, 1798; Anderson, "Virginia and Kentucky Resolutions," 46. Henry M. Wagstaff, *Federalism in North Carolina,* 32, notes that the House of that state's legislature publicly reprobated the Alien and Sedition Acts.

67. Philadelphia *Aurora,* Aug. 1, 22, 1798; Boston *Independent Chronicle,* Aug. 13, 27, 1798; Frankfort, Ky., *Palladium,* Sept. 25, 1798; "Gracchus," Fredericksburg, Va., *Genius of Liberty,* Nov. 13, 1798; cf. the Litchfield, Conn., *Monitor,* Aug. 15, 1798.

68. Newark, N. J., *Centinel of Freedom,* Sept. 18, 1798; Boston *Independent Chronicle,* Oct. 1, 1798; Chambersburg, Pa., *Farmers' Register,* Oct. 3, 1798.

69. See Judge Alexander Addison's charge to a Pennsylvania grand jury, Washington, Pa., *Western Telegraphe,* Oct. 23, 1798.

70. *Albany Gazette,* Oct. 19, 1798; Boston *Independent Chronicle,* Nov. 22, 1798; New London, Conn., *Bee,* Nov. 28, 1798.

71. McLaughlin, *Constitutional History,* 269, 273; Levy, *Freedom of Speech,* 186–88, 233–36; Smith, *Freedom's Fetters,* 133.

72. A summary is in Anderson, "Enforcement," 125–26; New York *Time Piece,* Aug. 25, 1798. For the relevant Anthony Haswell case, see the *Albany Register,* May 21, 1800; cf. Smith, *Freedom's Fetters,* 369–70.

73. New York *Time Piece,* July 2, 4, 9, 1798; New London, Conn., *Bee,* July 18, 1798; Richmond *Virginia Gazette,* July 31, 1798; Frank-

fort, Ky., *Guardian of Freedom*, Aug. 21, 1798; Smith, *Freedom's Fetters*, 214–15, 217.

74. See the New York *Time Piece*, Aug. 8, 1798; Boston *Independent Chronicle*, Aug. 9, 1798; *Albany Gazette*, Aug. 14, 1798; Frankfort, Ky., *Palladium*, Sept. 4, 1798; and Hamilton, *Country Printer*, 270, 315.

75. Boston *Independent Chronicle*, Oct. 25, 29, 1798. There were three objectionable items: a "Communication," and letters by "Y" and "Sydney," in the issues of Aug. 23, Sept. 20, 24, 1798; see the Worcester *Massachusetts Spy*, Oct. 31, 1798; Stauffer, *New England and Bavarian Illuminati*, 133n.

76. Boston *Independent Chronicle*, Oct. 22, 29, Nov. 22, 1798; New Haven *Connecticut Journal*, Nov. 1, 1798; Frankfort, Ky., *Palladium*, Nov. 20, Dec. 11, 1798.

77. Philadelphia *Aurora*, Nov. 10, 1798.

78. Alexandria *Times and Virginia Advertiser*, Oct. 11, 1798; Fredericksburg, Va., *Genius of Liberty* ("Cassius"), Oct. 19, 1798; Boston *Independent Chronicle* ("American Citizen"), Nov. 5, 1798.

79. Newark, N. J., *Centinel of Freedom*, Nov. 6, 1798; Philadelphia *Aurora*, Nov. 9, 1798; Boston *Independent Chronicle*, Nov. 5, 15, 22, 1798; Frankfort, Ky., *Palladium*, Jan. 13, 1799.

80. From the New London, Conn., *Bee*, in the Frankfort, Ky., *Palladium*, Oct. 25, 1798. The Boston *Independent Chronicle*, Nov. 26, 1798, again noted no Federalist printers had been indicted.

81. Boston *Independent Chronicle*, Nov. 5, 8, 1798, June 13–17, 19, 20, 1799 (cited in Anderson, "Enforcement," 122–23); Boston *Columbian Centinel*, Nov. 7, 10, 1798; James M. Smith, "The Federalist 'Saints' versus 'The Devil of Sedition'," *New England Quarterly* 28 (June, 1955), 198–215.

82. See Jefferson to Stevens T. Mason, Oct. 11, 1798, in Bergh, ed., *Writings*, X, 61–62; Anon., "Party Violence," 172; Levy, *Freedom of Speech*, 266–67; Mott, *Jefferson and the Press*, 30; Malone, *TJ*, III, 399–406; Frankfort, Ky., *Guardian of Freedom*, Nov. 13, 1798.

83. McMaster, *A History*, II, 419–22, describes the resolutions in their original form. See also Morison, *Otis*, I, 114; and Malone, *TJ*, III, 405–08; Smith, *Freedom's Fetters*, 71, 79, discusses state control over aliens.

84. Frankfort, Ky., *Palladium* (including an item from the *Reading Weekly Advertiser*), Dec. 4, 1798; *Baltimore Intelligencer*, Dec. 12, 1798; Charleston *Carolina Gazette*, Jan. 10, 1799.

85. See the Frankfort, Ky., *Palladium*, Jan. 22, 1799 ("Listen and

Tremble Ye Kentucky Legislators") ; Lexington *Stewart's Kentucky Herald,* Jan. 30, 1799; Newark, N. J., *Centinel of Freedom,* Dec. 18, 1798; Boston *Independent Chronicle,* Dec. 27, 1798; Washington, Ky., *Mirror,* Feb. 1, 1799.

86. Chambersburg, Pa., *Farmers' Register,* Jan. 9, 1799; letter of Hay, Jan. 5, 1799, in the *National Magazine,* 352–53; cf. Levy, *Freedom of Speech,* 269–71. For a summary of the Virginia Resolutions, see Simms, *John Taylor,* 75–76; and Brant, *Madison,* III, 461–63.

87. E.g., New York *Daily Advertiser,* Dec. 15, 1798; Edenton *State Gazette of North Carolina,* Jan. 2, 1799; Frankfort, Ky., *Palladium,* Jan. 8, 1799.

88. E.g., the Philadelphia *Country Porcupine,* Dec. 12, 1798, Apr. 1, 3, 1799; Trenton, N. J., *Federalist,* Jan. 14, 1799; and other papers cited in Anderson, "Virginia and Kentucky Resolutions," 48–52. Also the Chambersburg, Pa., *Farmers' Register* Jan. 16, 1799; New Brunswick, N. J., *Guardian,* Feb. 5, 1799; Providence, R. I., *Providence Journal,* Feb. 27, 1799.

89. Though some legislators did; see the dissent of 22 Pennsylvania Assembly members, Frankfort, Ky., *Palladium,* Feb. 28, 1799. For petitions, see the Elizabethtown *New Jersey Journal,* Jan. 15, 29, Feb. 5, 1799; Chambersburg, Pa., *Farmers' Journal,* Jan. 9, 16, Feb. 13, 1799; Boston *Independent Chronicle,* Jan. 17, 21, 31, Feb. 28, Mar. 7, 14, 18, 1799; Wilmington *Delaware Gazette,* Feb. 20, 1799, etc. The New London, Conn., *Bee,* Feb. 20, 1799 said remonstrances flooded Congress from all parts of the country *"excepting New England."* In North Carolina the House approved, but an adverse Senate vote prevented action; there was also a report that the Tennessee legislature endorsed the Resolutions (Boston *Independent Chronicle,* Feb. 11, May 6 ,1799).

90. Newark, N. J., *Centinel of Freedom,* Jan. 22, 1799; Philadelphia *Aurora,* Feb. 5, 1799; Washington, Ky., *Mirror,* Feb. 22, 1799; Morristown, N. J., *Genius of Liberty,* Mar. 7, 1799; Boston *Independent Chronicle,* Jan. 31, Feb. 4, 14, 18, 25, Mar. 4, 1799. The statement implying legislative perjury led to the indictment and conviction of Abijah Adams of the *Chronicle;* see Levy, *Freedom of Speech,* 210–12; Payne, *Journalism in the U.S.,* 184; Anderson, "Virginia and Kentucky Resolutions," 58–62; and Smith, *Freedom's Fetters,* 253.

91. Philadelphia *Aurora,* Feb. 7, 21, 22, 1799, cited in Dunbar, "A Study of 'Monarchical' Tendencies," 122–23; Anderson, "Virginia and Kentucky Resolutions," 50.

92. Anderson, *ibid.,* 50–51, 56, 58n.; Richmond *Virginia Argus,* Mar. 5, 1799; Richmond, Va., *Observatory,* Aug. 9, 1799; Anson E. Morse,

"Causes and Consequences of the Party Revolution of 1800," *Annual Report of the American Historical Association, 1894,* 532–33.

93. Richmond *Virginia Argus,* Mar. 15, Apr. 12, 1799; Richmond *Examiner,* Mar. 29, 1799. But cf. Wagstaff, *Federalism in N. C.,* 24, for widespread belief that Virginia would secede.

94. Richmond, Va., *Examiner,* Apr. 29, 1800; Richmond *Press,* Jan. 31, 1800 (cited in Anderson, "Virginia and Kentucky Resolutions," 241, 243–44); see Robinson, *American Political Parties,* 67–68, and Miller, *Federalist Era,* 241–42. Philip G. Davidson, "Virginia and the Alien and Sedition Laws," *American Historical Review* 36 (Jan., 1931), 336–42, however, denies Virginia contemplated forcible opposition to the Federal government.

95. Frankfort, Ky., *Guardian of Freedom,* Jan. 17, 1799; Philadelphia *Aurora* ("Hortensius"), Feb. 2, 7, 8, 11, 1799; New York *Argus,* Feb. 6, 1799; Richmond, *Virginia Argus,* Feb. 26, 1799; Frankfort, Ky., *Palladium,* Apr. 18, 25, 1799.

96. Philadelphia *Aurora,* Feb. 8, 1799; Lexington *Stewart's Kentucky Herald,* Mar. 12, 1799. See also the New York *Argus,* Jan. 2, 1799, on this election.

97. New London, Conn., *Bee,* Feb. 20, 1799; Boston *Independent Chronicle,* Feb. 28, 1799.

98. Lexington *Stewart's Kentucky Herald,* Jan. 30, Feb. 5, 1799; Frankfort, Ky., *Palladium,* Jan. 15, 29, Feb. 5, 1799; Philadelphia *Aurora,* Feb. 19, 1799; New York *Argus,* Feb. 21, 1799; Charleston, S. C., *City Gazette,* Mar. 18, 1799.

99. *Albany Centinel,* Aug. 3, 1798; Wheeler, "Urban Politics," 385.

100. Smith, *Freedom's Fetters,* 252–53; Warren, *Jacobin and Junto,* 103n.

101. Boston *Independent Chronicle,* Feb. 25, 28, Mar. 4, 7, Apr. 4, 8, 1799. See Smith, *Freedom's Fetters,* 251–55; Levy, *Freedom of Speech,* 210–11; Anderson, "Virginia and Kentucky Resolutions," 62–63, 226–27.

102. Boston *Independent Chronicle,* Apr. 11, 15, 18, 22, 25, 29, May 2, 1799; see also Duniway, *Freedom of Press in Mass.,* 144–46; Levy, *Freedom of Speech,* 211–12; and Payne, *Journalism in the U.S.* 185.

103. New London, Conn., *Bee,* Sept. 18, 1799; Frankfort, Ky., *Palladium,* Oct. 3, 1799.

104. Philadelphia *Aurora,* July 30, 1799.

105. New York *Argus,* Oct. 12, 15, Nov. 15, 1799; Newark, N. J., *Centinel of Freedom,* Oct. 15, 1799; Frankfort, Ky., *Palladium,* Oct. 21, 1799; Lancaster, Pa., *Intelligencer,* Oct. 30, 1799; Richmond

*Virginia Argus,* Nov. 5, 1799. See Smith, *Freedom's Fetters,* 270–74.

106. Boston *Independent Chronicle,* Oct. 3, 1799; New York *Argus,* Oct. 4, 1799; Lexington *Kentucky Gazette,* Oct. 24, 1799.

107. New York *Argus,* Nov. 6, 9, 1799; Philadelphia *Aurora,* Nov. 11, 1799; Richmond *Virginia Argus,* Nov. 19, 1799; Charleston *South Carolina State Gazette,* Nov. 27, 1799.

108. Newark *Centinel of Freedom,* Oct. 15, 1799; Lancaster, Pa., *Intelligencer,* Oct. 30, 1799; Richmond, Va., *Examiner,* Oct. 29, 1799.

109. At times the paper seemed almost Federalist. Its June 17, 1799, issue condemned the man who had been convicted for raising a liberty-pole in Dedham.

110. Brigham, *History and Bibliography,* I, 610.

111. E.g., the Louisville, Ga., *State Gazette and Louisville Journal,* Aug. 20, 1799; and the Dedham, Mass., *Columbian Minerva* (cited in Warren, *Jacobin and Junto,* 100).

112. Northumberland, Pa., *Sunbury and Northumberland Gazette,* June 29, 1799; *National Magazine,* 106–11.

113. Richmond, Va., *Examiner,* Dec. 6, 1799; Boston *Independent Chronicle,* Dec. 26, 1799; *National Magazine,* 113–25; Charleston, S. C,. *City Gazette,* Jan. 13, 1800; New London, Conn., *Bee,* Jan. 1, 1800; Boston *Constitutional Telegraphe,* Jan. 16, 1800.

114. Baltimore *American,* Aug. 7, 1799.

115. Lancaster, Pa., *Intelligencer,* Oct. 30, 1799; Newark, N. J., *Centinel of Freedom,* Nov. 12, 1799; Richmond, Va., *Examiner,* Dec. 17, 1799 ("A Scots Correspondent") ; letter of David Brown, cited in Anderson, "Enforcement," 125. See, earlier, the Philadelphia *Aurora,* Feb. 20, 1799; and the Boston *Independent Chronicle,* June 13, 20, 1799.

116. Boston *Independent Chronicle,* Feb. 25, Mar. 7, 1799; Litchfield, Conn., *Monitor,* Feb. 27, 1799; Philadelphia *Aurora* (cited in Lynch, *Party Warfare,* 77) ; New London *Connecticut Gazette,* Apr. 3, 1799; Baltimore *American,* May 16, 25, 1799.

117. Frankfort, Ky., *Palladium,* June 6, 1799.

118. Bennington, *Vermont Gazette,* Apr. 4, 1799; Richmond, Va., *Examiner,* Jan. 7, 17, 1800; Frankfort, Ky., *Palladium,* Feb. 20, 1800; New London, Conn., *Bee,* Jan. 22, 1800; Raleigh, N. C., *Raleigh Register,* Jan. 14, 28, Feb. 11, 18, Apr. 29, 1800; Richmond *Virginia Argus,* Jan. 17, 31, 1800; Lexington *Kentucky Gazette,* Feb. 27, 1800; Peacham, Vt., *Green Mountain Patriot* ("A Moderate Democrat"), Mar. 19, 26, Apr. 2, 9, 16, May 7, 1800.

119. New London, Conn., *Bee*, Feb. 12, 1800.

120. Anderson, "Contemporary Opinion," 236 (citing the Philadelphia *Aurora*, Jan. 30, 1800) ; see also Wolfe, *Jeffersonian Democracy*, 128.

121. New London, Conn., *Bee*, Jan. 1, Feb. 12, 1800. Frothingham was fined $100 and sentenced to four months, despite the jury's recommendation of clemency; see the Lancaster, Pa., *Intelligencer*, Dec. 11, 1799.

122. New London, Conn., *Bee*, Jan. 8, Apr. 2, 1800; Richmond *Virginia Argus*, Apr. 18, 1800; Boston *Independent Chronicle*, Apr. 28, 1800.

123. Newark, N. J., *Centinel of Freedom*, Apr. 29, 1800; Philadelphia *Aurora*, Apr. 25, 29, 1800; Richmond *Virginia Argus*, May 13, 1800; Smith, *Freedom's Fetters*, 375–81.

124. *Albany Register*, Apr. 22, 1800; Newark *Centinel of Freedom*, Apr. 29, 1800; Richmond, Va., *Friend of the People*, May 16, 1800; New London, Conn., *Bee*, Aug. 27, 1800.

125. See Dumas Malone, "The First Years of Thomas Cooper," 147; Lancaster, Pa., *Intelligencer*, Nov. 27, 1799; Savannah *Georgia Gazette*, May 15, 1800; Lexington *Kentucky Gazette*, May 15, 1800; *Albany Register*, May 16, 1800.

126. From the *Poughkeepsie Journal* ("An Enquirer"), Richmond, Va., *Friend of the People*, May 16, 1800; Charleston, S. C., *City Gazette*, June 20, 1800.

127. Reading, Pa., *Readinger Adler*, Apr. 22, 1800; Georgetown, D. C., *Centinel of Liberty*, Apr. 25, 29, 1800; Easton, Pa., *American Eagle*, May 1, 1800; Philadelphia *Aurora*, May 17, 1800; Lancaster, Pa., *Intelligencer*, May 28, 1800; Raleigh, N. C., *Raleigh Register*, June 3, 1800; Frankfort, Ky., *Palladium*, June 19, 1800; Malone, "First Years of Thomas Cooper," 153; Payne, *Journalism in the U.S.*, 182–83; Smith, *Freedom's Fetters*, 307–30.

128. See the Philadelphia *Aurora*, Nov. 5, 7, 20, 25, Dec. 31, 1800 (Hamilton's letter appeared Oct. 25, 27) ; Malone, "First Years of Thomas Cooper," 154–55; Joseph Dorfman, *The Economic Mind in American Civilization, 1606–1865*, II, 530; Dumas Malone, "The Threatened Prosecution of Alexander Hamilton under the Sedition Act by Thomas Cooper," *American Historical Review* 29 (Oct. 1923), 76–81; *Philadelphia Gazette*, Nov. 19, 1800; Frankfort, Ky., *Palladium*, Nov. 25, 1800; Lexington *Kentucky Gazette*, Dec. 1, 1800.

129. See the Bennington *Vermont Gazette*, Jan. 3, 1799, May 19, 26, 1800; Philadelphia *Aurora*, Oct. 24, 1799; New London, Conn., *Bee*, Oct. 30, 1799; Vergennes, Vt., *Vergennes Gazette*, May 15, 1800; *Albany Register*, May 22, 30, 1800; Anderson, "Enforcement," 119;

Smith, *Freedom's Fetters*, 359–73; Lee, *American Journalism*, 102–03. For another example of contributions, see the Charleston, S. C., *City Gazette*, May 20, 1800.

130. This account is largely a condensation of McMaster, *A History*, II, 462–64.

131. Smith, *Freedom's Fetters*, 277–303; McMaster, *A History*, II, 464–65; Philadelphia *Aurora*, Mar. 27, May 13, 1800; Boston *Constitutional Telegraphe*, Apr. 9, 12, 1800; Georgetown, D. C., *Centinel of Liberty*, Mar. 28, 1800; Lancaster, Pa., *Intelligencer*, Apr. 19, 1800; Malone, "First Years of Thomas Cooper," 148–49. The petition as it circulated in Philadelphia was reprinted in the Frankfort, Ky., *Palladium*, Apr. 27, 1800.

132. Mott, *Jefferson and the Press*, 31, states there were 25 arrests in all under the Act, with 10 convictions. There were 5 additional convictions under common law for seditious libel. Eight men out of 15— Adams, Callender, Duane, Frothingham, Holt, Durrell, Haswell and Lyon—were convicted for newspaper statements; Cooper and Mackay Crosswell, of the *Wasp* and Catskill, N. Y., *Catskill Packet* (Lee, *American Journalism*, 102–03), were other editors punished. Warren, *Jacobin and Junto*, 112–13, says 11 convictions were sustained under the Sedition Act; Smith, *Freedom's Fetters*, 185, mentions "at least seventeen verifiable indictments," three of which were returned under common law.

133. Georgetown, D. C., *Centinel of Liberty*, June 3, 1800; Richmond, Va., *Examiner*, June 4, 6, 1800; Baltimore *American*, June 12, 17, 1800; Petersburg, Va., *Petersburg Intelligencer*, June 20, 1800; Simms, *John Taylor*, 98; Smith, *Freedom's Fetters*, 334–58; Payne, *Journalism in the U.S.*, 194.

134. Richmond, Va., *Examiner*, Oct. 10, Nov. 18, 1800; Richmond *Virginia Argus*, Nov. 11, 1800.

135. See the Richmond, Va., *Examiner*, Feb. 18 (telling of an assault on the Staunton *Scourge of Aristocracy*, and threats against congressmen), Apr. 1, 1800; Newark, N. J., *Centinel of Freedom*, Mar. 18, 1800.

136. New London, Conn., *Bee*, Mar. 19, 1800; Boston *Independent Chronicle* ('IMPARTIALIS'), Apr. 28, 1800; Newark *Centinel of Freedom*, Sept. 24, 1799, Apr. 29, 1800; Baltimore *American*, Oct. 23, 1800.

137. Anderson, "Enforcement," 120; Smith, *Freedom's Fetters*, 186–87.

138. Baltimore *American*, June 4, 1800; Charleston, S. C., *City Gazette*, June 20, 1800; Richmond, Va., *Friend of the People*, July 5, 1800; Philadelphia *Aurora*, July 7, 1800; Raleigh, N. C., *Raleigh*

*Register,* July 22, 1800; Newark *Centinel of Freedom,* July 29, 1800; Lancaster, Pa., *Correspondent,* July 26, 1800; Anderson, "Enforcement," 119–20.

139. Lancaster, Pa., *Intelligencer,* May 14, 1800; New London, Conn., *Bee,* Oct. 1, 1800.

140. Cf. the New York *Daily Advertiser,* Dec. 10, 1798; and the New London, Conn., *Bee,* Oct. 1, 1800. Holt, Haswell, Adams, Durrell, and Greenleaf, among others, were natives.

141. Baltimore *American,* June 28, 1800; Portsmouth *New Hampshire Gazette,* July 8, 1800; Lexington *Kentucky Gazette,* July 24, 1800; Richmond *Virginia Argus,* Sept. 20, 1800.

142. Pittsburgh *Tree of Liberty,* Aug. 30, 1800 ("HOSPES") ; Boston *Constitutional Telegraphe,* Sept. 27, 1800 ("Sidney") ; Pittsfield, Mass., *Sun,* Dec. 30, 1800; Lewistown, Pa., *Western Star,* Feb. 19, 1801. The poem is from the Charleston, S. C., *City Gazette,* Oct. 2, 1800.

143. Richmond *Virginia Argus,* Aug. 15, 1800; see the Augusta, Ga., *Augusta Herald,* Aug. 6 ("Zenos"), Oct. 8 ("EMELIUS"), 15, 29, 1800; Annapolis *Maryland Gazette,* June 23, 1800 (letter of Gabriel Duval, cited in the Newark *Centinel of Freedom,* Aug. 19, 26, Sept. 2, 1800).

144. See the Boston *Independent Chronicle,* Jan. 8, 1798; Philadelphia *Aurora,* Oct. 5, 1800; Richmond, Va., *Examiner,* Oct. 21, 28, 1800; Frankfort, Ky., *Palladium,* Oct. 31, 1800.

145. Nathan Schachner, *Alexander Hamilton,* 396–97; Broadus Mitchell, *Alexander Hamilton: The National Adventure,* II, 485–86; Pittsfield, Mass., *Sun,* Nov. 18, 25, Dec. 9, 1800.

146. Baltimore *Federal Gazette,* Sept. 18, 1800; Charleston *Carolina Gazette,* Sept. 11, 1800.

147. Georgetown, D. C., *Cabinet,* Dec. 30, 1800; Philadelphia *Aurora,* Dec. 31, 1800.

148. Morristown, N. J., *Genius of Liberty,* July 17, 1800.

XIII    REPUBLICAN POLITICAL
STRATEGY

1. See Dunbar, " 'Monarchical' Tendencies," 115, citing A. J. Beveridge and S. E. Morison.

2. *Ibid.*, 115–16, 126. The European wars were ones "between Republicanism and monarchy, or liberty and bondage!" Boston *Constitutional Telegraphe,* Oct. 19, 1799.

3. *Boston Gazette,* Sept. 6, 1790 ("Homo") ; *New York Packet,* Apr. 28, 1791.

4. Boston *Herald of Freedom,* July 31, 1789.

5. Extract from James T. Callender, *Sketches of the History of America* in the Boston *Constitutional Telegraphe,* Oct. 19, 1799 ; see also the Lancaster, Pa., *Intelligencer,* Dec. 4, 1799.

6. See advertisement and comment, Boston *Independent Chronicle,* Aug. 27, 1789.

7. Philadelphia *National Gazette,* Mar. 29, 1792 ; Charleston *State Gazette of South Carolina,* Feb. 11, 1793. See McMaster, *A History,* II, 72–73 ; and a quotation from the *National Gazette* in Minnigerode, *Jefferson—Friend of France,* 167.

8. *New-York Journal,* June 13, 1792.

9. Philadelphia *National Gazette,* Mar. 29, July 4, 7, 1792 ; summary in Forman, "Political Activities," 49–50.

10. McMaster, *A History,* II, 88 ; see the Baltimore *Maryland Journal,* Oct. 16, 1792 ; Georgetown, D. C., *Centinel of Liberty,* Oct. 14, 1796 ; Philadelphia *New World,* Oct. 26, 1796 ; Boston *Independent Chronicle,* Dec. 7, 1797 ; Newark *Centinel of Freedom,* May 29, 1798.

11. Philadelphia *Aurora,* Jan. 5, 6, 7, 9, 23, 26, 1797 ; Callender, *Prospect Before Us,* 18, cited in Dunbar, " 'Monarchical' Tendencies," 118.

12. Reading, Pa., *Readinger Adler,* Sept. 14, 1798, suggesting also that Federalists may have inspired the Whiskey Revolt ; Philadelphia *Aurora,* July 4, Aug. 17, 18, 1799.

13. Philadelphia *Aurora,* July 27, 1798, Mar. 2, 1799, Aug. 11, 1800 ; Portsmouth, N. H., *Republican Ledger,* Dec. 18, 1799 ("THE EXAMINER, No. 3") ; Alexandria, Va., *Alexandria Times,* Feb. 20, 1800 (from the *Mirror of the Times*) ; Baltimore *American,* Aug. 14, 1800.

14. Philadelphia *Aurora* (cited in Dunbar, " 'Monarchical' Tendencies," 120–21), July 8, 14, Aug. 14, Sept. 27, 29, 1797, Feb. 27, Mar. 30, 1798 ; Raleigh, N. C., *Raleigh Register,* Aug. 12, 1800 ; Richmond *Virginia Argus,* Oct. 10, 21, 1800 ; New York *American Citizen,* Oct. 13, 1800 ; Washington, D. C., *National Intelligencer,* Nov. 18, 1800.

15. Norfolk, Va., *Epitome of the Times,* Sept. 25, 1800 ; Savannah, Ga., *Columbian Museum,* Oct. 10, 1800 ; New London, Conn., *Bee,* Oct. 22, 1800 ; Nevins, *American Press Opinion,* 25–26 (citing the

*Aurora*) ; Anon., "Party Violence," 173; Dunbar, " 'Monarchical' Tendencies," 125–27.

16. Raymond Walters, Jr., "The Origins of the Jeffersonian Party in Pennsylvania," *Pennsylvania Magazine of History and Biography* 66 (Oct., 1942), 453, has an interesting discussion on name-calling. See the *Baltimore Evening Post,* Sept. 18, 1793; *New York Journal,* Mar. 18, 1795; Boston *Independent Chronicle,* Mar. 30, 1795, Oct. 4, 1798 ("Democritus," quoting a "letter" from Arnold).

17. E.g., the New York *Argus,* Feb. 27, 1797; New London, Conn., *Weekly Oracle,* Mar. 18, 1799; Boston *Constitutional Telegraphe,* Jan. 18, 1800 (noting the mourning of "British agents" at Washington's death) ; Boston *Independent Chronicle,* Aug. 18, 1800.

18. "L," in the Philadelphia *National Gazette,* Aug. 8, 1792; "A Fair Statement," in the Charleston, S. C., *City Gazette,* May 18, 1798.

19. Boston *Independent Chronicle,* June 15, 1795 ("A Republican") ; Aug. 27, Sept. 27, 1798.

20. See Chap. 10; see Ames, *Works,* II, 109, 121–23, for various Federalist usages; and the Boston *Independent Chronicle,* Nov. 27, 1797; Dedham, Mass., *Columbian Minerva,* Oct. 10, 1799.

21. Charleston *South Carolina State Gazette,* May 7, 1796; for Bache's own story of his beating, see the Philadelphia *Aurora,* Apr. 6, 1797; Boston *Independent Chronicle,* Apr. 20, 1797. See also the Newark *Centinel of Freedom,* Apr. 17, Aug. 13, Sept. 4, 1798, May 21, July 30, 1799; Philadelphia *Aurora,* May 9, July 20, Aug. 2, 1798, May 16, 1799; Baltimore *American,* May 21, July 12, Aug. 14, 20, 1799; Chambersburg, Pa., *Farmers' Register,* Feb. 20, 1799; Frankfort, Ky., *Palladium,* June 13, 20, 1799; New York *Argus,* July 1, 1799; Richmond *Virginia Argus,* July 12, 1799; Anon., "Party Violence," 175.

22. Philadelphia *Constitutional Diary,* Jan. 1, 1800.

23. Raleigh, N. C., *Raleigh Register,* Jan. 7, Apr. 1, 1800; Richmond, Va., *Examiner,* Feb. 11, 1800 (also an item cited in Anon., "Party Violence," 176) ; Newark *Centinel of Freedom,* Mar. 4, 1800; Baltimore *American,* Sept. 3, Oct. 22, 1800; New London, Conn., *Bee,* Sept. 10, 17, Nov. 26, 1800; Richmond *Virginia Gazette,* Sept. 30, 1800.

24. Baltimore *American,* Nov. 3, 1800. Cf. the Richmond *Virginia Argus,* Nov. 5, 1799, for a similar account of an earlier Republican celebration in Philadelphia.

25. See the Institute for Propaganda Analysis, "How to Detect Propaganda," *Propaganda Analysis* 1 (Nov., 1937), 5–6; Boston *Constitutional Telegraphe,* Oct. 2, 1799; Raleigh, N. C., *Raleigh Register,* Aug. 12, 1800; Boston *Independent Chronicle,* Aug. 18, 1800.

26. Lexington *Stewart's Kentucky Herald*, Dec. 29, 1795 (from the Philadelphia *Aurora*). Somewhat similar "creeds" appeared, for example, in the Norwich, Conn., *Weekly Register*, May 6, 1794; and the Richmond, Va., *Observatory*, Aug. 27, 1798.

27. *National Magazine*, 349–52. (The excerpt is not verbatim, but the original form and meaning have been retained.)

28. "Brutus," reprinted in the Morristown, N. J., *Genius of Liberty*, Oct. 23, 1800. See the comparable "What are the fruits of John Adam's [*sic*] Administration?", Newark *Centinel of Freedom*, Mar. 25, 1800; Frankfort, Ky., *Palladium*, Apr. 24, 1800.

29. "A Monarchist," Philadelphia *Aurora*, Mar. 25, 1799. Leary, *That Rascal Freneau*, 308, has a competent summary, and the entire series is reprinted in Freneau, *Letters*, 5–133.

30. As categorized by the Institute for Propaganda Analysis, "How to Detect Propaganda," 6, 7.

31. Philadelphia *Aurora*, Mar. 29, 1799.

32. *Ibid.*, Apr. 23, 1799; see Freneau, *Letters*, 19–22.

33. Philadelphia *Aurora*, May 6, 16, 1799.

34. *Ibid.*, May 20, 1799.

35. *Ibid.*, June 11, 1799.

36. *Ibid.*, Aug. 20, 1799; the penalty for abusing a Federalist would be 2 hours 50 min. at 100°.

37. *Ibid.*, Aug. 17, 1799.

38. *Ibid.*, Aug. 16, 1799. Other "Slender" letters appeared in the issues of May 3, June 18, Aug. 1, 8, 9, 23, 24, Sept. 3, 11, Oct. 2, Dec. 4, 1799.

39. Letter of David Humphreys to George Washington in 1787, quoted in Spurlin, *Montesquieu*, 192.

40. Philadelphia *National Gazette*, Jan. 12, 1793; see Leary, *That Rascal Freneau*, 225.

41. "A Democrat," Nashville, Tenn., *Rights of Man*, Mar. 11, 1799.

42. Lancaster, Pa., *Intelligencer*, Mar. 19, 1800.

43. Philadelphia *Aurora*, June 3, 1800; Baltimore *American*, June 6, 1800.

44. Philadelphia *Aurora*, June 12, 1800.

45. *Boston Gazette*, Oct. 18, 1790; Boston *Independent Chronicle*, Sept. 4, 1797; Philadelphia *Carey's United States Recorder*, Feb. 8, 1798.

46. Boston *Independent Chronicle*, July 9, 1789, Apr. 29, 1800; Philadelphia *Federal Gazette*, May 11, 1789. The *Boston Gazette*, May 25,

June 22, July 27, Aug. 3, 17, Oct. 12, 1789, maintained a running fire of ironic comment from the outset of Washington's administration; see Hazen, *Contemporary American Opinion*, 211, 277–78, for the prevalence of attacks on dress and display.

47. The quotations are from the Boston *Herald of Freedom*, June 19, Aug. 7, 1789; see also the Winchester *Virginia Gazette*, May 27, June 24, 1789; Boston *Courier de Boston*, July 2, 1789; Boston *Independent Chronicle*, July 16, 1789; Winchester *Virginia Centinel*, July 29, 1789.

48. Lansingburgh, N. Y., *Federal Herald*, Nov. 2, 1789; Sullivan, *Familiar Letters*, 17–18; Edenton *State Gazette of North Carolina*, Oct. 15, 1790; Austin, *Philip Freneau*, 163.

49. Philadelphia *General Advertiser*, May 16, June 7, 10, 1791; Elizabethtown, Md., *Washington Spy*, June 1, 1791; *Albany Register*, June 13, 1791; Bennington *Vermont Gazette*, June 13, 1791; Dover, N. H., *Political Repository*, June 23, 1791.

50. See the Baltimore *Maryland Journal*, Sept. 20, 1791 ("NO TITLES"); Philadelphia *National Gazette*, Jan. 19, 1792; Philadelphia *Freeman's Journal*, Oct. 5, 1791; Dumfries, Va., *Virginia Gazette*, Oct. 13, 1791; Charleston *State Gazette of South Carolina*, Nov. 10, 1791. (Republicans believed "Publicola," to be John Adams, whereas it was actually the sobriquet of John Quincy Adams.)

51. Philadelphia *General Advertiser*, Mar. 4, 1791, Jan. 2, 1793; Philadelphia *National Gazette*, Jan. 5, 1793; Boston *Independent Chronicle*, Jan. 24, 1793. See also the protests in the Philadelphia *Independent Gazetteer*, Mar. 7, 1795 ("Aristides"), and the Boston *Independent Chronicle*, Mar. 26, 1795, against poems reminiscent of British poets laureate.

52. Philadelphia *General Advertiser*, Feb. 16, 1793 (since Bache was Franklin's grandson, "A SUBSCRIBER" may have been the editor), Feb. 5, 1794; Philadelphia *National Gazette*, Feb. 27, 1793; Elizabethtown *New Jersey Journal*, Apr. 30, 1794; Philadelphia *Aurora*, Feb. 21, 1795.

53. Charleston *South Carolina State Gazette*, Oct. 15, 1795; Philadelphia *Aurora*, Feb. 20, Mar. 7, 1796; New York *Argus*, Mar. 6, 1797.

54. Philadelphia *General Advertiser*, Jan. 26, 29, Feb. 4, 12 ("MIRABEAU"), 1793; Philadelphia *National Gazette*, Jan. 30, Feb. 20, 1793; Baltimore *Maryland Journal*, Feb. 8, 1793; Philadelphia *Dunlap's American Daily Advertiser*, Feb. 9, 1793 ("A.B.C."); Norwich, Conn., *Norwich Packet*, Feb. 21, 1793.

55. Newark, N. J., *Woods's Newark Gazette*, Feb. 7 ("American Citizen"), July 10, 24 ("CATO"), 1793; Petersburg *Virginia Ga-*

*zette,* Mar. 29, 1793; Trenton *New Jersey State Gazette,* Aug. 28, 1793; Augusta, Ga., *Southern Centinel,* Oct. 3, 1793; New London, Conn., *Bee,* Oct. 25, 1797; Baltimore *Edwards' Baltimore Daily Advertiser,* Nov. 25, 1793. (Wilcocks was the writer who labored so hard to discredit Genêt.)

56. Philadelphia *National Gazette,* May 10, Aug. 28, 1792; the lengthy quotation is from the latter issue. Forman, "Political Activities," 44–45, credits Freneau with the authorship, but the item specifically states "From the New York Journal." The last paragraph is of interest as in a sense prophesying the Sedition Act.

57. Charleston, S. C., *Columbian Herald,* Mar. 19, 1794; Augusta, Ga., *Southern Centinel* ("RIGADOON"), Dec. 24, 1795.

58. New York *Argus,* Dec. 27, 1796; Philadelphia *Aurora,* Jan. 10, 1797, Jan. 10, 1797, Jan. 16, 1798; for the Federalist side, see the New York *Diary,* Mar. 7, 1797. The Boston *Independent Chronicle* estimated 20,000 persons spent a half day each walking in streets and staring out of windows, 1,000 days lost from headaches, etc., Nov. 1, 1798; Baltimore *American,* Nov. 5, 1799; New York *American Citizen,* Nov. 8, 1800; Richmond *Virginia Argus,* Nov. 21, 1800.

59. Philadelphia *Daily Advertiser,* Aug. 24, 1797; Newark *Centinel of Freedom,* Aug. 30, 1797; Georgetown, D. C., *Centinel of Liberty,* Sept. 12, 1797 ("Aristides").

60. New York *Time Piece,* Nov. 29, 1797; Boston *Independent Chronicle,* Dec. 14, 1797; Philadelphia *Aurora,* Apr. 27, 1798; Scharf and Wescott, *History of Philadelphia,* I, 493; Clark, *Peter Porcupine,* 127; Payne, *History of Journalism,* 171.

61. E.g., the Newark *Centinel of Freedom,* May 22, June 12, 1798; Philadelphia *Aurora,* July 13, 1798; Trenton *New Jersey State Gazette,* July 24, 1798; Boston *Independent Chronicle,* Mar. 14, 1799 ("A Friend to Christianity").

62. New York *Diary,* Oct. 23, 1797, Feb. 9, 1798; Philadelphia *Daily Advertiser,* July 19, 1797; Charleston, S. C., *City Gazette,* Aug. 10, 1797 (poem on titles in Congress); Bennington *Vermont Gazette,* Nov. 28, 1797 (address to the Governor of Massachusetts); New York *Argus,* June 21, 1799; Richmond *Virginia Argus,* July 23, 1799.

63. E.g., the New York *American Minerva,* Jan. 27, 1796; Providence, R. I., *United States Chronicle,* Feb. 18, 1796; cf. the Baltimore *American,* Sept. 5, 1799.

64. Philadelphia *Carey's United States Recorder,* Aug. 4, 14, 1798.

65. New London, Conn., *Bee,* Feb. 12, 1800; New York *American Citizen,* May 13, 1800.

66. Boston *Independent Chronicle,* Jan. 3, 1792; Augusta, Ga., *Southern Centinel* ("An Observer"), Aug. 29, 1793; Philadelphia *Aurora,* July 20, 1797.

67. In this, all arts of deception (half-truths, falsehoods, over-emphasis and under-emphasis) distract attention from potentially embarrassing items; *Propaganda Analysis,* I, 7.

68. Boston *Independent Chronicle,* Oct. 22, Nov. 5, 1798; Morison, *Otis,* I, 155.

69. Boston *Independent Chronicle,* Mar. 28, 1799; Philadelphia *Aurora,* Feb. 15, 1800; Richmond, Va., *Examiner,* Feb. 28, Nov. 11, 1800; New London, Conn., *Bee,* May 22, 1800; Richmond *Virginia Argus,* Sept. 19, 1800; also Luetscher, *Early Political Machinery,* 125–32, 136–37.

70. Philadelphia *Aurora,* Mar. 1, 1798; Philadelphia *Carey's United States Recorder,* Mar. 3, 1798; Boston *Independent Chronicle,* May 7, Oct. 25, 1798.

71. Boston *Independent Chronicle,* Apr. 1, 1799; New York *Argus,* May 3, 1799; Hartford, Conn., *American Mercury,* Sept. 11, 1800 (cited in Robinson, *Jeffersonian Democracy,* 113).

72. Boston *Independent Chronicle,* Oct. 7, 1790; *Boston Gazette,* Oct. 11, 1790; Carlisle, Pa., *Carlisle Gazette,* Dec. 19, 1792 (citing the *Pittsburgh Gazette,* claiming then to be non-partisan); Boston *Independent Chronicle,* Nov. 4, 6, 13, 27, Dec. 22, 1794, May 14, 21, 25, 28, 1795, Nov. 10, 14, 17, Dec. 8, 1796, Nov. 5, 8, 1798, Oct. 9, 1800; also Warren, *Jacobin and Junto,* 72n. The Boston *Columbian Centinel,* however, noted (Nov. 8, 1794, cited in Morse, *Federalist Party,* 149) that in the gubernatorial election of 1794, Republicans had said nothing when their victorious candidate received 2,301 votes in Boston; cf. Wheeler, "Urban Politics," 351, 362, on voting in that city.

73. Philadelphia *Aurora,* Nov. 25, 29, Dec. 2, 6, 1796; Fredericktown, Md., *Bartgis's Federal Gazette,* Dec. 8, 1796; Baltimore *Federal Gazette,* Dec. 14, 1796; McMaster, *A History,* II, 299. See also the Philadelphia *Aurora,* Nov. 6, 1797, Oct. 25, 1799; and Russell Ferguson, *Early Western Pennsylvania Politics,* 153.

74. Baltimore *American,* July 4, 1800; Boston *Independent Chronicle,* Nov. 3, 1800; Morristown, N. J., *Genius of Liberty,* Dec. 18, 1800 (cited in Fee, *Transition,* 109).

75. E.g., Baltimore *Maryland Journal,* Aug. 27, 1790; Boston *American Herald,* Aug. 30, 1790; Philadelphia *Independent Gazetteer,* May 23, 1795 ("I. H.," "An ESSAY on PUPPYISM"); New York *Greenleaf's New York Journal,* June 21, 1796. For Federalist ridicule

of rotation, see the Burlington, N. J., *Burlington Advertiser* ("Marcus"), Dec. 21, 28, 1790, Jan. 4, 11, 18, 1791.

76. Philadelphia *Aurora,* Feb. 27, 1798; Boston *Independent Chronicle,* Mar. 15, 1798; Philadelphia *Carey's United States Recorder,* Apr. 5, 1798. (The Vicar of Bray was an English cleric noted for changing religious beliefs to hold his post, 1640–1688.)

77. New York, *Greenleaf's New York Journal,* Apr. 25, 1798; for the quotation, see the Philadelphia *Aurora,* July 11, 1798.

78. Philadelphia *Carey's United States Recorder* (citing the Portsmouth, N. H., *Oracle of the Day*), July 24, 28, 1798; Boston *Independent Chronicle,* July 26, 1798; Philadelphia *Aurora,* Nov. 7, 1798 (quoting the *Albany Register*), June 9, 1800; Richmond, Va., *Examiner,* Dec. 3, 1799; Richmond *Virginia Argus,* Nov. 12, 1799; New London, Conn., *Bee,* Jan. 8, 1800.

79. Richmond, Va., *Examiner* ("A Scots Correspondent"), Jan. 3, 1800; New York *Argus,* Jan. 31, 1800; Raleigh, N. C., *Raleigh Register,* Feb. 25, 1800; Jenkins, *Pennsylvania,* II, 163–64, 172; Wheeler, "Urban Politics," 129. Even Duane did not break with McKean over nepotism until later; Allen Clark, *Duane,* 19. The New York *American Citizen,* Oct. 17, 1800; and Raleigh, N. C., *Raleigh Register,* Oct. 17, 1800, comment on Pinckney.

80. Charleston, S. C., *City Gazette,* Mar. 5, 1800; the President allegedly later used the expression "Old Woman" to this senator at a dinner when Mrs. Adams' name arose. For evidence that Abigail Adams was concerned (and wrote frequently to her friends) about political matters, see Smith, J. M., *Freedom's Fetters,* 15–16, 96–97, 191, 212, 248, 315, 341; Smith, Page, *Adams,* 131–32, 839, 908, 932, 1000, 1060–61, *et al.*

81. "IMPORTANT FACTS," Philadelphia *Aurora,* Nov. 5, 1798. See also the Philadelphia *Carey's United States Recorder,* July 24, 1798.

82. Adams to Smith, Dec. 19, 1798 (Adams, ed., *The Works of John Adams,* VIII, 617–18.

83. Philadelphia *Aurora,* Jan. 8, 1799 (the letter noted just above calls the post a lieutenant-colonelcy); see Adams to Alexander Hamilton, June 20, 1800 (Adams, ed., *Works of John Adams,* IX, 61–63 and notes).

84. Philadelphia *Aurora,* May 22, 1797; Philadelphia *Daily Advertiser,* May 22, 1797; Charleston *South Carolina State Gazette,* June 9, 1797 (which noted Washington had earlier named J. Q. Adams to a ministerial post at Lisbon).

85. Boston *Independent Chronicle,* May 29, June 1, July 24, Sept. 18,

1797, Mar. 26, 29, 1798. For reference to the wedding see James Truslow Adams, *The Adams Family*, 120 (where the news item is erroneously dated Sept. 14, 1797); the lady, Louisa Johnson, was actually the daughter of the American consul in London.

86. See Chap. 2.

87. Newark, N. J., *Centinel of Freedom*, June 10, 24, July 1, 1800; Philadelphia *Aurora*, June 17, 1800, *et seq.;* New York *American Citizen*, July 26, 31, Aug. 23, 1800, *et al.* On the Capitol, see the Georgetown, D. C., *Centinel of Liberty*, Apr. 9, 1799.

88. Philadelphia *Carey's United States Recorder*, Apr. 26, 1798; New York *Greenleaf's New York Journal*, Aug. 11, 1798; Boston *Independent Chronicle*, Aug. 13, 20, 23, 1798 (the issue of Aug. 20 said Thomas had "been detected in counterfeiting").

89. Faÿ, *Two Franklins*, 308–11; Washington, D. C., *Washington Gazette*, Feb. 25, 1797.

90. New York *Argus*, Mar. 8, 1797; Charleston *South Carolina State Gazette*, Mar. 28, 1797; Philadelphia *Aurora*, Mar. 14, 16, 20, 1797.

91. Philadelphia *Carey's United States Recorder*, Aug. 14, 1798.

92. Boston *Independent Chronicle*, Dec. 12, 29, 1796; New York *Argus*, Feb. 3, 1797; Philadelphia *Daily Advertiser*, Feb. 17, 1797.

93. Philadelphia *Constitutional Diary*, Dec. 11, 1799; Frankfort, Ky., *Palladium*, Apr. 10, 1800; Philadelphia *Aurora*, May 19, 1800.

94. Frankfort, Ky., *Palladium*, Nov. 18, 1800; New York *Republican Watch Tower*, Nov. 8, 1800; Augusta [Me.], *Kennebec Gazette*, Nov. 14, 1800; see also the Portsmouth *New Hampshire Gazette*, Dec. 9, 1800, belittling the letter. Cf. Mitchell, *Hamilton*, II, 471–84; Smith, Page, *Adams*, II, 1043–45.

95. New York *American Citizen*, Oct. 24, 1800; Richmond *Virginia Argus*, Nov. 4, 1800; Salem, Mass., *Salem Impartial Register*, Nov. 13, 1800; New York *Republican Watch Tower*, Oct. 29, 1800; Norfolk, Va., *Epitome of the Times* ("BRIEF ANIMADVERSIONS," from the Philadelphia *Aurora*), Nov. 6, 1800; Morristown, N. J., *Genius of Liberty*, Nov. 13, 1800.

96. Washington, D. C. *National Intelligencer*, Nov. 7, 1800; Augusta, Ga., *Augusta Chronicle*, Nov. 15, 1800.

97. Boston *Independent Chronicle*, Aug. 18, Sept. 8, 1800; Pittsburgh *Tree of Liberty*, Sept. 13, 1800; Georgetown, D. C., *Centinel of Liberty*, Oct. 3 ("Q"), 28, Nov. 7, 1800; New York *American Citizen*, Oct. 7, 24, 1800; Georgetown, D. C., *Washington Federalist*, Nov. 4, 1800; New London, Conn., *Bee*, Nov. 5, 1800; Washington, D. C.,

*Universal Gazette,* Nov. 6, 1800; Richmond, Va., *Examiner,* Nov. 7, 1800. Cf. Chap. 7; Leonard D. White, *The Federalists,* 225; and Smith, Page, *John Adams,* II, 1046–47.

98. Pittsfield, Mass., *Sun,* Nov. 25, Dec. 16, 1800; Washington, D. C., *National Intelligencer,* Nov. 12, 1800; New York *American Citizen,* Dec. 12, 1800. Cf. Chap. 9.

99. York *Pennsylvania Herald* (citing the Philadelphia *Gazette of the United States*), June 29, 1796; Freeman, *Washington,* VI, 411–13; Carroll & Ashworth, *Washington,* VII, 5–7, 86, 97–98, 116–17, etc.

100. E.g., the Boston *Independent Chronicle,* May 8, 1789, Nov. 10, 1791.

101. Griswold, *Republican Court,* 289; Coley Taylor and Samuel Middlebrook, *The Eagle Screams,* 39–41.

102. E.g., see James, "French Diplomacy," 161; Faÿ, *Two Franklins,* 267–68; Freeman, *Washington,* VI, 411; Carroll & Ashworth, *Washington,* VII, 5–7, 85–86.

103. McMaster, *A History,* II, 110–11; see "Veritas," and the Philadelphia *Gazette of the United States,* June 1, 5, 1793, *et seq.;* also Leary, *That Rascal Freneau,* 234–35; Buckingham, *Specimens,* II, 140; Carroll & Ashworth, *Washington,* VII, 85.

104. *New-York Journal,* Dec. 7, 1793; Philadelphia *Gazette of the United States,* Sept. 6, 1794. See Chap. 3.

105. Sullivan, *Familiar Letters,* 62; see French minister Adet, in Dunbar, " 'Monarchical' Tendencies," 116.

106. "Hancock," in the Philadelphia *Aurora,* Aug. 21, Sept. 3, 8, 1795; New York *Greenleaf's New York Journal,* Aug. 25, 29, Sept. 9, 1795; Boston *Independent Chronicle,* Sept. 10, 17, 1795.

107. Boston *Independent Chronicle* ("Truth" and "MILLIONS"), Sept. 7, 1795.

108. "Valerius," in the Philadelphia *Aurora,* Aug. 22, Sept. 1, 9, 17, 25, 1795, *et seq.;* New York *Greenleaf's New York Journal,* Aug. 25, Sept. 5, 16, 23, 30, Oct. 17, 24, Nov. 4, 14, 25, 1795; Boston *Independent Chronicle,* Sept. 14, 28, 1795. For a Federalist retort, see the Wilmington *Delaware and Eastern Shore Advertiser,* Oct. 17, 1795.

109. "BELISARIUS," in the Philadelphia *Aurora,* Sept. 11, 1795; New York *Greenleaf's New York Journal,* Sept. 26, 1795; Mt. Pleasant, N. J., *Jersey Chronicle,* Oct. 10, 1795.

110. "BELISARIUS," Philadelphia *Aurora,* Sept. 22, 1795; New York *Greenleaf's New York Journal,* Sept. 30, Oct. 3, 10, 17, 1795.

111. Philadelphia *Aurora,* Aug. 22, Sept. 9, 21 ("ATTICUS"), Sept.

23, 25, 27, Oct. 14, 1795; Boston *Independent Chronicle,* Sept. 24, Oct. 5, 15, Nov. 2, 23, 1795; Elizabethtown, N. J., *New Jersey Journal* (whose editor, Kollock, disapproved of this virulence), Sept. 30, 1795; cf. the *Richmond Chronicle,* Nov. 24, 1795; *Greenleaf's New York Journal,* Nov. 28, 1795.

112. Philadelphia *Aurora,* Sept. 30, 1795; New York *Greenleaf's New York Journal* ("PORTIUS"), Oct. 28, 1795; Bridgeton, N. J., *Argus* ("Cincinnatus"), Nov. 19, 1795.

113. "BELISARIUS," Philadelphia *Aurora,* Sept. 15, 1795; Boston *Independent Chronicle,* Oct. 5, 1795; "Pittachus," New York *Greenleaf's New York Journal,* Oct. 24, 1795.

114. Philadelphia *Aurora,* Sept. 27 ("PITTACHUS"), 30 ("PIT-TACHUS"), Oct. 21 ("VALERIUS"), 1795; New York *Greenleaf's New York Journal,* Oct. 24, 1795.

115. New York *Argus,* Nov. 12, 1795; Philadelphia *Independent Gazetteer,* Nov. 14, 1795. Note also the Elizabethtown *New Jersey Journal,* Sept. 30, 1795; Trenton *New Jersey State Gazette,* Oct. 6, 1795.

116. New York *Greenleaf's New York Journal,* Dec. 2, 1795.

117. "VALERIUS," Philadelphia *Aurora,* Oct. 21, Nov. 11, 1795.

118. Philadelphia *Aurora,* June 30, 1796 ("An Old Soldier"), Mar. 3, 1797; *Boston Gazette,* Dec. 16, 1796, Feb. 13, 1797; Boston *Independent Chronicle,* Mar. 16, 1797; New York *Argus* (cited in McMaster, *A History,* II, 305); Buckingham, *Specimens,* II, 141–42. Federalists countered charges of Washington's "ignorance" by saying he was no lawyer and used common sense; New York *Herald,* June 15, 1796; Washington, D. C., *Washington Gazette,* June 22, 1796.

119. Philadelphia *Aurora,* Mar. 15, 1797. Reportedly the letter first appeared in the Paris *Moniteur,* Jan. 25, 1797. See Chap. 1, for its effect.

120. Boston *Independent Chronicle,* May 18, 22, 1797; Charleston, S. C., *City Gazette* ("CRITO"), Apr. 5, 1800; Newark, N. J., *Centinel of Freedom,* May 27, 1800; Richmond *Virginia Argus* ("Greene"), Sept. 16, 1800; Baltimore *Federal Gazette,* Aug. 1, 1800.

121. See the Boston *Independent Chronicle,* Apr. 27, 1795. "Paulding" was reprinted in the New York *Argus,* July 25, 29, Aug. 5, 15, 30, Sept. 6, 1796; "Sidney" in *ibid.,* Oct. 24, 28, 31, 1796.

122. Philadelphia *Aurora* ("PITTACHUS"), Sept. 26, 1795; Bridgeton, N. J., *Argus* ("CINCINNATUS"), Nov. 19, 1795.

123. Alexandria, Va., *Alexandria Gazette,* Feb. 18, 1797; McMaster, *A History,* II, 303; Channing, *History of the U. S.,* IV, 175; Bond,

"Monroe Mission," 27; Bassett, *Federalist System,* 142–43. Bache printed the entire pamphlet and advertised it in the Philadelphia *Aurora* (e.g., Feb. 27, 1798). See Clark, *Peter Porcupine,* 77–78; Federalists were extremely denunciatory of Paine and Bache (e.g., the Baltimore *Federal Gazette,* Jan. 4, 1797).

124. Extract from Jasper Dwight's [Duane's?] "Strictures" on the Farewell Address; Boston *Independent Chronicle,* Jan. 12, 1797.

125. "A Calm Observer"; the first letter was in the Philadelphia *Aurora,* Oct. 23, 1795. The "Observer" was John Beckley, Clerk of the House of Representatives; Newark *Centinel of Freedom,* Apr. 15, 1800. See Chap. 3; Clark, *Peter Porcupine,* 88–89; Faÿ, *Two Franklins,* 271–72.

126. Philadelphia *Aurora,* Oct. 26, 1795; Boston *Independent Chronicle,* Nov. 5, 1795.

127. Philadelphia *Aurora,* Oct. 27, 28, Nov. 5, 1795; New York *Greenleaf's New York Journal,* Oct. 31, 1795; Boston *Independent Chronicle,* Nov. 9, 16, 19, 1795; Mt. Pleasant, N. J., *Jersey Chronicle,* Nov. 14, 1795.

128. E.g., *Greenleaf's New York Journal,* Oct. 28, 31, Nov. 4, 7, 1795; Wilmington *Delaware Gazette,* Oct. 30, 1795; Mt. Pleasant, N. J., *Jersey Chronicle,* Nov. 7, 14, 21, 1795; Poughkeepsie, N. Y., *Republican Journal,* Nov. 18, 1795; Edenton *State Gazette of North Carolina,* Dec. 17, 1795.

129. Philadelphia *Aurora,* Nov. 3 ("PITTACHUS"), 26, 1795; Keene, N. H., *Rising Sun* ("Scipio"), Dec. 22, 1795.

130. New York *Greenleaf's New York Journal,* Nov. 21, 25, 1795; Boston *Independent Chronicle,* Nov. 26, 30, 1795 (from the New York *Daily Advertiser,* Nov. 11, 1795).

131. Newfield, Conn., *American Telegraphe,* Nov. 18, Dec. 2, 1795; New York *Argus* ("LONGINUS"), Nov. 26, 1795; Boston *Independent Chronicle,* Nov. 30, Dec. 3 ("Observator"), 1795; Mt. Pleasant, N. J., *Jersey Chronicle,* Dec. 26, 1795; Charleston *South Carolina State Gazette,* Dec. 31, 1795.

132. Philadelphia *Gazette of the United States,* Mar. 12, 1797; Wilmington *Delaware Gazette,* Mar. 15, 1797; Philadelphia *Aurora,* Mar. 13, 1797; New York *Diary,* Mar. 18, 1797; Bleyer, *Main Currents,* 117; Faÿ, *Two Franklins,* 273–74.

133. Boston *Independent Chronicle,* Feb. 13, 1797; see the Portsmouth, N. H., *Federal Observer,* May 30, 1799, telling of the charge by Duane (as "Jasper Dwight") that Washington had fired on a white flag; and *"The Prospect Before Us,"* cited in Beard, *Jeffersonian Democracy,* 81.

134. *New York Daily Gazette*, Nov. 17, 1795; Philadelphia *Gazette of the United States*, Mar. 10, 1797; New York *Argus*, Mar. 18, 1797; Boston *Independent Chronicle*, Mar. 20, 1797; McMaster, *A History*, II, 302–03; Taylor & Middlebrook, *The Eagle Screams*, 62–63; Freeman, *Washington*, IV, 582; Carroll and Ashworth, *Washington*, VII, 321; Bassett, *Federalist System*, 142; Sloane, *Party Government*, 68.

135. Carlisle, Pa., *Carlisle Telegraphe*, Nov. 17, 1795; see Carroll and Ashworth, *Washington*, VII, 321, 398; Ford, ed., *The Writings of Thomas Jefferson*, XIII, 266, 366, 378, 427; Bassett, *Federalist System*, 142; Griswold, *Republican Court*, 357–58. For the moralizing, see Sloane, *Party Government*, 60; but Washington wrote Hamilton, June 26, 1796, of his "disinclination to be longer buffeted in the public prints by a set of infamous scribblers"; Robert W. Jones, *Journalism in the United States*, 170.

136. Ulrich B. Phillips, ed., "South Carolina Federalist Correspondence, 1789–1796," *American Historical Review* 14 (July, 1909), 780; Lynch, *Party Warfare*, 58–60; Charleston *South Carolina State Gazette* ("Paul Pindar"), Aug. 3, 1796; *Boston Gazette* ("WATCHMAN"), Sept. 26, 1796.

137. Charleston *South Carolina State Gazette* ("Paul Pindar"), Oct. 3, 1796; Minnigerode, *Presidential Years*, 36–38. Clark, *Peter Porcupine*, 95–96, sees all this as part of a deliberate plan (which did not cease after Adams' election) to discredit Washington; Dr. Leib, Dr. Reynolds, Beckley, Bache and Duane were the prime movers. Faÿ, *Two Franklins*, 270–71, adds these charges were spread from Maine to Carolina, and "Through [John] Beckley Jefferson was in communication with Bache. Monroe in France sent items for anonymous publication, and Paine also wrote for the *Aurora.*"

138. Philadelphia *Aurora*, Dec. 21, 23, 1796 (see also the issue of July 18, 1797); Carroll and Ashworth, *Washington*, VII, 410; Clark, *Peter Porcupine*, 89; Warren, *Jacobin and Junto*, 67; Bleyer, *Main Currents*, 116.

139. *Boston Gazette*, Dec. 26, 1796, Jan. 16, Feb. 13, 1797 (cited in Payne, *History of Journalism*, 174); New York *Argus*, Feb. 27, 1797; Philadelphia *Aurora*, Feb. 17, 1797; Faÿ, *Two Franklins*, 315; Warren, *Jacobin and Junto*, 68.

140. Philadelphia *Aurora*, Mar. 5, 1797. McMaster, *A History*, II, 306, Bleyer, *Main Currents*, 116–17, and Faÿ, *Two Franklins*, 315–16, all say March 6. See also the New York *Daily Gazette*, Mar. 10, 1797.

141. Alexandria, Va., *Alexandria Times*, Jan. 8, 1800; Lexington *Ken-*

*tucky Gazette,* Jan. 30, 1800; Portsmouth, N. H., *United States Oracle,* Mar. 22, 1800 (quoting disapprovingly from Callender's *Prospect Before Us*).

142. Philadelphia *National Gazette,* June 12, 1793 ("Veritas"); Goshen, N. Y., *Goshen Repository* ("WILLIAM TELL"), Sept. 15, 1795; Petersburg, Va., *Petersburg Intelligencer* ("CASCA," cited in the Philadelphia *Aurora,* Jan. 27, 1796); Halifax *North Carolina Journal* ("CITIZEN"), July 4, 1796; Boston *Independent Chronicle,* July 23, 1798.

143. "SEWALL," from the Boston *Constitutional Telegraphe* (in the Lancaster, Pa., *Intelligencer,* Jan. 15, 1800); Charleston, S. C., *City Gazette,* Jan. 25, 1800; Portland, [Me.], *Eastern Herald* ("DECENCY"), Feb. 3, 1800; Alexandria, Va., *Alexandria Times,* Feb. 21, 1800; Newport, R. I., *Newport Mercury,* Feb. 25, 1800; New York *Republican Watch Tower,* May 13, 1800; New London, Conn., *Bee,* Dec. 31, 1800. For a Federalist retort, stressing the sincerity of popular grief, see the Charleston, S. C., *Federal Carolina Gazette,* Feb. 6, 1800.

144. New Haven, Conn., *New Haven Gazette,* May 18, 1791; Newark, N. J., *Woods's Newark Gazette,* June 2, 1791; Edenton *State Gazette of North Carolina,* June 24, 1791; Philadelphia *General Advertiser,* June 27, 28, 1791 (quoting ("PHILANTHROPOS," from the Hartford, Conn., *American Mercury*); New Brunswick, N. J., *Brunswick Gazette,* June 28, 1791; Baltimore *Maryland Journal,* July 1, 1791; Wilmington *Delaware Gazette,* July 16, 1791. Adams was quite aware of these newspaper criticism—see Adams, ed., *Works,* VIII, 503.

145. John Adams to TJ, July 21, 1791. Jefferson's recommendation had been "reprinted with great care in the newspapers"; Adams, ed., *Works,* VIII, 506–09. See also *ibid.,* VIII 511–13, and Jefferson's letter of May 8, 1791; Dan E. Mowry, "Political Verse Satires of the Factional Period of American History, 1789–1806," *Americana* 5 (Feb., 1910), 217–18; Philadelphia *National Gazette* ("VALERIUS"), Mar. 29, 1792.

146. Philadelphia *Aurora,* Oct. 18, 1796; Boston *Independent Chronicle,* Oct. 24, 27, 31 ("Safety," and "A Farmer"), 1796; Richmond, Va., *Richmond and Manchester Advertiser,* Oct. 22, 1796; Philadelphia *New World,* Nov. 3, 1796; Lancaster, Pa., *Lancaster Journal,* Nov. 4, 1796.

147. Newark, N. J., *Centinel of Freedom,* Oct. 26, Nov. 2, 1796; Fee, *Transition,* 75–76; Philadelphia *Aurora,* Oct. 29, 1796; New York *Argus,* Nov. 1, 1796 (cited in McMaster, *A History,* II, 291–92); Philadelphia *New World* ("Cassius"), Oct. 28, 1796 (cf. the Boston

*Independent Chronicle* ["Senex"], Aug. 6, 1798); Lancaster, Pa., *Lancaster Journal*, Nov. 4, 1796; Woodbury, *Public Opinion*, 127 (citing the Philadelphia *New World*); Boston *Independent Chronicle*, Nov. 24, 1796 (poem from the *Baltimore Telegraphe*); Abigail Adams to Elbridge Gerry, Dec. 31, 1796, in Austin, *Gerry*, II, 143. See the *Baltimore Federal Gazette*, Oct. 6, 1800, for a Federalist claim that Washington had faith in Adams.

148. On Adams' trips, see the Boston *Independent Chronicle*, Aug. 17, 1797; Lynch, *Party Warfare*, 89, notes he spent over six months in Quincy in 1799. For other criticisms, see the New York *Time Piece*, Nov. 24, 1797; Philadelphia *Aurora*, Nov. 28, 1797, May 23, 1798; Koch, *Republican Religion*, 129–30; S. E. Morison, *Oxford History*, 347.

149. Fredericktown, Md., *Bartgis's Federal Gazette*, Mar. 7, 1798; Philadelphia *Carey's United States Recorder*, ("DEMOCRITUS"), June 5, 1798; Newark, N. J., *Centinel of Freedom*, July 31, 1798; Baltimore *Intelligencer*, Dec. 26, 1798.

150. Abigail Adams to Mary Cranch, Apr. 26, 1798 (cited in Smith, Page, *John Adams*, II, 961); Philadelphia *Aurora*, June 7, 24, 1800; Baltimore *American*, June 11, 27, 1800; Petersburg, Va., *Petersburg Intelligencer*, June 17, 1800.

151. Staunton, Va., *Political Mirror*, June 3, 1800; Boston *Constitutional Telegraphe*, June 11, 1800; Philadelphia *Aurora*, Aug. 13, 1800; Wilmington, N. C., *Wilmington Gazette*, Aug. 24, 1800; Richmond *Virginia Argus*, Aug. 29, Sept. 19 (quoting the Philadelphia *Aurora*, May 22, 1798), 1800; Richmond, Va., *Examiner*, Oct. 17, 1800; New London, *Connecticut Gazette*, Mar. 4, 1801; Washington, Pa., *Herald of Liberty*, Mar. 23, 1801.

152. Philadelphia *Gazette of the United States*, Sept. 8, 1792; Boston *Independent Chronicle*, Oct. 17, 1793; Lynch, *Party Warfare*, 26–27; Schachner, *Alexander Hamilton*, 364–72.

153. Wilmington *Delaware Gazette*, Feb. 21, 1795; New York, *Greenleaf's New York Journal*, Oct. 31, 1795; Boston *Independent Chronicle*, Apr. 21, 1796; Schachner, *Hamilton*, 388.

154. Mitchell, *Alexander Hamilton*, II, 400–21; Faÿ, *Two Franklins*, 325–26.

155. Philadelphia *Daily Advertiser*, July 17, 1797; Philadelphia *Aurora*, July 28, 1797; Boston *Independent Chronicle*, Sept. 14, 25, 28, Oct. 2, 5, 1797; *National Magazine*, 87–94, 156–64.

156. Boston *Independent Chronicle*, Oct. 16, 1797. See *ibid.*, Feb. 26, Mar. 1, July 30, Dec. 20, 1798; Philadelphia *Aurora*, July 23, 1798,

May 4, 1799; Philadelphia *Carey's United States Recorder,* July 24, 1798.

157. E.g., Morristown, N. J., *Morris County Gazette* ("MENIPPUS"), Oct. 18, 1797; Boston *Independent Chronicle,* Jan. 25, 1798, July 31, 1800 ("MANLIUS"); Salem, Mass., *Impartial Register,* Aug. 4, 1800; New York *American Citizen,* Oct. 29, 1800; Baltimore *American,* Nov. 1, 1800; Norfolk, Va., *Epitome of the Times,* Dec. 1, 1800.

158. Philadelphia *Aurora,* Feb. 27, 1797; Charleston *South Carolina State Gazette,* Mar. 18, 1797; New York *Time Piece,* Dec. 1, 1797; Wolfe, *Jeffersonian Democracy,* 87n.

159. Philadelphia *Carey's United States Recorder,* June 16, 1798; Richmond, Va., *Observatory,* Sept. 13, 1798; Knoxville, Tenn., *Knoxville Register,* Oct. 2, 1798; Baltimore *American,* Aug. 5, 1799; Wolfe, *Jeffersonian Democracy,* 129; Morristown, N. J., *Genius of Liberty* (citing the *Aurora*), Sept. 18, 1800; Philadelphia *Aurora,* Nov. 3, 1800; Baltimore *American,* Nov. 6, 1800. Federalists denied the charges against Harper; see the Baltimore *Federal Gazette,* Nov. 6, 1800.

160. See the broadside of "AN ELECTOR," *PLAIN FACTS* (New York: 1798).

161. Philadelphia *Aurora,* Feb. 2, 21, 1795.

162. See the Litchfield, Conn., *Monitor,* Dec. 26, 1798; Boston *Independent Chronicle,* Dec. 31, 1798.

163. Boston *Independent Chronicle,* Aug. 31, 1797; Philadelphia *Aurora,* May 23, 1800; New Haven *Connecticut Journal,* June 25, 1800; Prentiss, *Timothy Pickering,* 7.

164. Boston *Independent Chronicle,* Dec. 7, 1795; Harrisburg, Pa., *Oracle of Dauphin,* Mar. 9, 1801.

165. Ames to Thomas Dwight, July 3, 24, Aug. 8, 1794, Ames, ed., *Works of Fisher Ames,* I, 145–47; Boston *Independent Chronicle,* Jan. 8, Feb. 26, 1798.

166. Frankfort, Ky., *Palladium,* July 4, 1799.

167. Philadelphia *Aurora,* May 23, Nov. 17, 1800; Baltimore *Federal Gazette,* Nov. 29, 1800.

168. Philadelphia *Aurora,* Aug. 8, 1800.

169. Ames, ed., *Works of Fisher Ames,* I, 168–69, referring to the daughters of a Col. Worthington (apparently of Vermont).

170. For discussion of personal abuse as a policy, see the Fredericktown, Md., *Rights of Man,* Sept. 2, 1795 (the "democratic scunks" quotation); Augusta, Ga., *Augusta Herald,* Sept. 17, 1800; Anon., "Party

Violence," 175. Note also Albert J. Beveridge, *Life of John Marshall,* I, 147n., concerning Washington's difficulty in finding someone to replace Randolph.

171. Philadelphia *National Gazette,* Dec. 8, 1792.

172. *New-York Packet,* May 26, 1791; Philadelphia *General Advertiser,* Aug. 5, 1791; Baltimore *Maryland Journal,* Aug. 24, 1791; Richmond, Va., *Examiner* ("A Scots Correspondent"), Nov. 21, 1800.

173. Dumfries, Va., *Republican Journal,* May 5, 1796; Edenton *State Gazette of North Carolina,* Aug. 5, 1796 (biographical sketch); Boston *Independent Chronicle,* July 27, Aug. 3, 1797, Mar. 29, Oct. 8, 1798, Sept. 11, 1800; Philadelphia *Aurora,* Nov. 5, 1798; Nashville, Tenn., *Nashville Intelligencer,* Aug. 28, 1799; Pittsburgh *Tree of Liberty,* Sept. 27, 1800; Morison, *Otis,* I, 56–57.

174. Philadelphia *Aurora,* Apr. 24, 1798; Boston *Independent Chronicle,* Apr. 4, 1799.

175. Boston *Independent Chronicle,* Feb. 9, Apr. 20, 1797, Feb. 1, 5, 12, 19, Mar. 1, 1798; Washington, D. C., *Washington Gazette,* May 3, 1797.

176. New London, Conn., *Weekly Oracle,* Jan. 21, 1797.

177. Lancaster, Pa., *Intelligencer,* Jan. 1, 1800.

178. *Ibid.,* Jan. 22, 1800; Baltimore *American,* Nov. 7, 1800; Richmond, Va., *Examiner,* Nov. 7, 1800; see also White, *Federalists,* esp. p. 225.

179. Richmond, Va., *Examiner,* Mar. 21, 26, 1800 (cited in Simms, *John Taylor,* 98–99).

180. Philadelphia *Aurora,* June 4, 1795; Boston *Independent Chronicle,* Aug. 14, Oct. 17, 1797, May 21, Aug. 9, Sept. 3, 1798; Philadelphia *Merchant's Daily Advertiser,* Oct. 11, 1797; New York *Argus,* May 2, 1798. See Koch, *Republican Religion,* 132–33, on the suit of Rush vs. Cobbett.

181. Cunningham, *Jeffersonian Republicans,* esp. 85–86, 257–58; Malone, *TJ,* III, 180–93, 273–76; Chambers, *Political Parties,* 82–83.

182. Philadelphia *National Gazette,* Sept. 19, Dec. 12, 1792; Taylor and Middlebrook, *The Eagle Screams,* 68–70, have a popularized account of the attacks made on Jefferson. Boston *Independent Chronicle,* Oct. 18, 1792 (cited in Bowers, *Jefferson and Hamilton,* 174); see also Charles O. Lerche, Jr., "Jefferson and the Election of 1800: A Case Study in the Political Smear," *William and Mary Quarterly,* 3rd Ser., 5 (Oct., 1948), 467–69.

183. Philadelphia *National Gazette* ("MIRABEAU"), Jan. 12, 1793;

Concord, N. H., *Hough's Concord Herald,* Jan. 16, 1794; Edenton *State Gazette of North Carolina,* Jan. 31, 1794; Boston *Independent Chronicle* ("An American"), July 3, 1798. The Philadelphia *General Advertiser,* Jan. 12, 1793, printed a Federalist sneer at the difficulty of finding a fit successor for Jefferson.

184. Maude H. Woodfin, "Contemporary Opinion in Virginia of Thomas Jefferson," in Avery Craven, ed., *Essays in Honor of William E. Dodd,* 39–42. Jefferson's executive competence might be open to debate in certain respects, but he was hampered by constitutional restrictions upon the governor's power and he never claimed to be a military expert. His personal courage and devotion to office seem fully vindicated. For the best account of this period in his life see Malone, *TJ,* I, 330–69, though Marie Kimball, *Jefferson in War and Peace,* 125–358, furnishes more detail.

185. Georgetown, D. C., *Centinel of Liberty,* Oct. 21, 1796 ("Voter"); Washington, D. C., *Washington Gazette,* Oct. 26 (Gerard Banks, from the Fredericksburg *Virginia Herald*), Nov. 9 (Letter of John Mayo), 1796; Richmond *Virginia Gazette,* Oct. 26, 1796; Fredericktown, Md., *Bartgis's Federal Gazette,* Oct. 27, Nov. 3, 1796; Annapolis *Maryland Gazette* ("CUSTOMER"), Nov. 3, 1796; Elizabethtown, Md., *Washington Spy,* Nov. 30, 1796.

186. Fredericktown, Md., *Rights of Man,* June 18, 1800 (Tyler's letter); see also *ibid.* ("Scaevola"), Sept. 12, 1798; Boston *Polar Star,* Oct. 18, 1796; Alexandria, Va., *Columbian Mirror,* Oct. 20, Nov. 1, 1796; Newark, N. J., *Centinel of Freedom* ("JOHN HOMESPUN"), Aug. 26, 1800; In the Charleston, S. C., *City Gazette,* July 4, 1800, "Americanus" (John Beckley—see Bernard Faÿ, "Early Party Machinery in the United States," 382), inaccurately states that Jefferson exactly 24 years earlier had proposed the Declaration in Congress; Augusta, Ga., *Augusta Herald,* Oct. 15, 1800; New York *Republican Watch Tower,* Apr. 5, 1800; Boston *Independent Chronicle,* July 21, Sept. 11, 1800; Boston *Constitutional Telegraphe,* Dec. 3, 1800; James T. Adams, *The Living Jefferson,* 192–93.

187. Newark, N. J., *Centinel of Freedom,* Aug. 12, 1800.

188. Letter dated July 31, 1788 (Philadelphia *National Gazette,* Sept. 29, 1792; Charleston *Carolina Gazette,* Jan. 10, 1799); Alexandria, Va., *Columbian Mirror,* Oct. 20, 1796; Boston *Independent Chronicle,* May 15, 19 ("Honestus"), Aug. 11, 1800; Charleston, S. C., *City Gazette,* July 17, 1800; Boston *Constitutional Telegraphe,* Dec. 3, 1800. For a Federalist version, see the Fredericksburg *Virginia Herald,* May 9, 1800; for Jefferson's reaction to newspaper vilification, see Mott, *Jefferson and The Press,* 38–40.

189. *Greenleaf's New York Journal,* Dec. 9, 1796; Raleigh, N. C., *Raleigh Register* ("A REPUBLICAN"), Oct. 21, 1800.

190. Halifax *North Carolina Journal,* Dec. 12, 1796; Boston *Independent Chronicle* ("Americanus"), Sept. 8, 1800.

191. Augusta, Ga., *Augusta Chronicle* ("BRUTUS"), July 13, 1799. See also the Frankfort, Ky., *Palladium,* June 19, 1800; New York *American Citizen,* July 10, 1800; Boston *Independent Chronicle,* Sept. 11, 1800; Richmond *Virginia Argus,* Oct. 14, 1800.

192. Philadelphia *Daily Advertiser,* May 3, 1797; Salem, Mass., *Impartial Register,* June 30, 1800.

193. Richmond, Va., *Examiner* (in the Richmond *Virginia Argus,* Mar. 14, 1800); Elizabethtown *Maryland Herald,* Sept. 11, 1800; Raleigh, N. C., *Raleigh Register,* Sept. 30, 1800. Malone, *TJ,* II, 259–60, 441–46, would indicate this version is substantially correct.

194. Jefferson to Benjamin Banneker, Oct. 30, 1791 (reprinted in the Philadelphia *General Advertiser,* Oct. 16, 1792); Charleston *South Carolina State Gazette,* Oct. 16, 1800; Providence, R. I., *Providence Journal,* Nov. 5, 1800; Richmond, Va., *Examiner,* Nov. 18, 1800; Norwalk, Conn., *Sun of Liberty,* Nov. 18, 1800; Taylor and Middlebrook, *The Eagle Screams,* 73–74.

195. Taylor and Middlebrook, *The Eagle Screams,* 85; W. Edward Farrison, "The Origin of Brown's *Clotel,*" *Phylon* 15 (Dec. 1954), 350–54.

196. The *Gazette's* sneer, of course, was a gibe at Jefferson's volume; Newark, N. J., *Centinel of Freedom* ("An American"), Nov. 2, 1796; *Philadelphia Gazette,* May 22, 1800; Lancaster, Pa., *Intelligencer,* June 4, 1800; Lexington *Kentucky Gazette,* June 26, 1800; Boston *Independent Chronicle,* Aug. 18, 1800. Marylander Michael Cresap was blamed by Mingo chieftain Logan (hitherto friendly to whites) for the brutal and unprovoked murder of the Indian's mother, sister, brother and several cousins; the affair led to retaliations and to Lord Dunmore's War. Jefferson's *Notes* reprinted Logan's famed "oration"; since Cresap was related to leading Maryland's Federalists, the charge seemed to have political overtones. Modern scholars are convinced one Daniel Greathouse (rather than Cresap) wiped out the Indian family. See Malone, *TJ,* I, 386–87n.; Dale Van Every, *Forth to the Wilderness,* 342; and John Bakeless, *Background to Glory,* 25–28.

197. New York *American Citizen,* July 10, 1800; Richmond *Virginia Argus,* Oct. 28, 1800.

198. Charleston *Carolina Gazette,* Jan. 31, 1799; New York *Argus,* Aug. 5, 1796; New London, Conn., *Bee,* Sept. 24, 1800.

199. E.g., Fredericksburg, Va., *Genius of Liberty*, July 3, 1798; Charleston *Carolina Gazette* ("AMYNTAS"), Aug. 21, 1800; Richmond, Va., *Examiner*, Oct. 14, 1800 (resolutions from Burlington, N. J.); Pittsfield, Mass., *Sun*, Dec. 30, 1800.

200. Augusta, Ga., *Augusta Chronicle* ("A FARMER"), Sept. 28, 1799; Augusta, Ga., *Southern Centinel*, Nov. 7, 1799. The five-column article appeared in the Lexington *Kentucky Gazette*, May 29, 1800; Frankfort, Ky., *Palladium*, June 5, 1800; Boston *Independent Chronicle*, June 30, 1800; Baltimore *American*, July 3, 1800; New York *American Citizen*, July 12, 14, 1800; Raleigh, N. C., *Raleigh Register*, Aug. 5, 1800; Pittsburgh *Tree of Liberty*, Sept. 27, 1800. Similar histories of Jefferson's past accomplishments appeared in the Providence, R. I., *Impartial Observer*, Sept. 22, 1800; Newark *Centinel of Freedom*, Aug. 12, 1800; etc.

201. Philadelphia *Aurora*, Aug. 22, 1800; Baltimore *American*, Sept. 1, 1800; Elizabethtown *Maryland Herald*, Sept. 4, 1800; Pittsburgh *Tree of Liberty*, Sept. 6, 1800; Frankfort, Ky., *Palladium*, Sept. 18, 1800; Easton, Md., *Republican Star*, Dec. 23, 1800; Salem, Mass., *Impartial Register*, May 29 ("A Friend of Truth"), Dec. 4, 1800.

202. Boston *Independent Chronicle* ("OLD SOUTH"), July 31, 1800; New York *American Citizen* (citing the Philadelphia *Aurora*), Sept. 16, 1800; Pittsburgh *Tree of Liberty*, Oct. 4, 1800; Richmond, Va., *Examiner*, Nov. 11, 1800 ("A Scots Correspondent"), Jan. 27, 1801; Washington, D. C., *National Intelligencer*, Feb. 2, 1801.

203. Jones, *America and French Culture*, 395–96.

204. Richmond, Va., *Richmond and Manchester Advertiser* ("ALGERNON SYDNEY"), Nov. 8, 1796.

205. Philadelphia *Aurora*, Nov. 17, 1796, Sept. 5, 1798; Litchfield, Conn., *Monitor* ("Censor Morum"), Aug. 15, 1798; Augusta, Ga., *Southern Centinel* ("ANTI SABATICUS"), Sept. 16, 1798; Boston *Independent Chronicle* ("M.R."), July 24, 1800. Riley, *American Thought*, 85, suggests Jefferson himself believed the clergy opposed him for his work for religious freedom in Virginia.

206. Boston *Independent Chronicle*, May 8, 12, 1800; New York *American Citizen*, May 21, Aug. 18, 1800; Newark, N. J., *Centinel of Freedom*, July 8, 1800; Charleston, S. C., *City Gazette*, Aug. 18, 20, 1800; Richmond *Virginia Argus*, Sept. 9, 1800.

207. Newark, N. J., *Centinel of Freedom*, July 8, 1800; Baltimore *American*, July 14, 24, 25, Aug. 6, Oct. 24, 1800; Boston *Independent Chronicle*, July 21, 24, Aug. 18, 1800; Raleigh, N. C., *Raleigh Register*,

July 22, 29, 1800; Danbury, Conn., *Sun of Liberty*, Aug. 13, 1800; New London, Conn., *Bee*, Sept. 10, 1800.

208. Baltimore *American*, Aug. 6, 1800; Boston *Independent Chronicle*, Sept. 18, 1800.

209. Boston *Independent Chronicle*, May 12, 1800; Baltimore *Federal Gazette* ("A Voter"), July 25, 1800; Baltimore *American*, Aug 6, Sept. 12, 1800; Newark, N. J., *Centinel of Freedom*, Aug. 12 ("JOHN HOMESPUN"), Sept. 23, 1800; Charleston, S. C., *City Gazette* ("No Friend to Religious Establishments"), Aug. 20, Sept. 15, 1800; Georgetown, D. C., *Centinel of Liberty* ("NO SLANDERER"), Sept. 5, 1800; Raleigh, N. C., *Raleigh Register* ("HERMIT OF WAKE"), Oct. 7, 1800; Richmond, Va., *Examiner*, Nov. 21, 1800. Federalists hit Jefferson's "irreligion" hard among the Germans; see the York, Pa., *Der Volks Berichter*, July 17, Aug. 14, 21, 1800.

210. Newark, N. Y., *Centinel of Freedom*, Aug. 26, Sept. 2, 1800; Philadelphia *Aurora*, Sept. 20, 1800; Elizabethtown *Maryland Herald* Sept. 25, 1800; Savannah, Ga., *Columbian Museum*, Oct. 17, 1800; Providence, R. I., *Providence Journal*, Nov. 5, 1800; Norwalk, Conn., *Sun of Liberty*, Nov. 18, 1800.

211. Boston *Independent Chronicle*, Sept. 4, 25, 1800; Raleigh, N. C., *Raleigh Register*, Sept. 30, 1800.

212. Newport, R. I., *Newport Mercury* ("PARODY OF BION"), Sept. 9, 1800; Newark, N. J., *Centinel of Freedom* ("Timoleon," and others), Sept. 30, Oct. 7, 1800; Wilmington, N. C., *Wilmington Gazette* ("JACK CARELESS"), Oct. 23, 1800.

213. New London, Conn., *Bee*, Sept. 17, 1800.

214. Baltimore *American*, June 30, 1800; New York *Commercial Advertiser*, July 2, 1800; Philadelphia *Gazette of the United States* (no longer so ardently Federalist), July 2, 1800; New York *American Citizen*, July 3, 1800.

215. Baltimore *American*, July 1, 4, 1800; New York *American Citizen*, July 3, 5 (citing the Philadelphia *Aurora*), 1800. See the New York *Prisoner of Hope*, July 5, 1800; Augusta, Ga., *Augusta Chronicle*, July 12, 1800; Savannah, Ga., *Columbian Museum*, July 22, 1800.

216. Philadelphia *Gazette of the United States*, July 3, 1800; New York *Prisoner of Hope*, July 9, 1800; Mt. Pleasant, N. Y., *Impartial Gazette*, July 22, 1800. Mention of this false rumor is made in Lerche, "Jefferson and the Election of 1800," 489.

217. New York *American Citizen*, July 7, 1800; Philadelphia *Gazette of the United States*, July 5, 16, 1800; Newark, N. J., *Centinel of Freedom*, July 8, 1800; Gilmanton, N. H., *Gilmanton Gazette*, July 8,

15, 1800; Boston *Constitutional Telegraphe,* July 9, 1800; Savannah, Ga., *Columbian Museum,* July 15, 1800; Easton, Pa., *American Eagle,* July 17, 1800; Lexington *Kentucky Gazette,* July 24, 1800; Newport, R. I., *Newport Mercury,* Sept. 9, 1800; Taylor and Middlebrook, *The Eagle Screams,* 80.

# XIV

## ELECTIONEERING TACTICS

1. Philadelphia *National Gazette,* May 3, 1792; Boston *Independent Chronicle,* Mar. 28, 1793; Pittsburgh *Tree of Liberty* ("A JEFFERSONIAN"), Sept. 20, 1800. See the New York *Commercial Advertiser,* Apr. 29, 1800; for charges Republicans were enemies to the Constitution, and Apr. 30, 1800, that they now appealed to Washington.

2. "Considerations on the temper, views and consequences of *Party* in the United States," Boston *Independent Chronicle,* Aug. 20, 1798.

3. Savannah, Ga., *Columbian Museum,* Sept. 19, 23, 1800; see also the Hartford, Conn., *Courant,* June 25, 1800.

4. E.g., Schlesinger, *Prelude to Independence,* 218, 225, 239, and *passim.*

5. Boston *Independent Chronicle,* Sept. 24, 1795.

6. *Ibid.,* Jan. 16, 1797; Washington, D. C., *Washington Gazette,* Jan. 28, 1797.

7. Boston *Independent Chronicle,* Jan. 12, 1795 (referring to the Boston *Columbian Centinel*), Sept. 1, 1796.

8. Martinsburg, [W.] Va., *Potowmac Guardian,* May 5, 1796; Boston *Independent Chronicle,* June 19, *et seq.* ("Marcus"), 1797; July 5, 1798 (the "staunch Federalist").

9. Boston *Independent Chronicle,* Aug. 14, 21 ("TULLY"), Dec. 11, 1797; Washington, Ky., *Mirror,* Apr. 19, 1799 (the "vocabulary" called liberty "a magnificent nothing," and *"A bad Constitution. . . . One . . .* calculated only for peace"); Natchez, [Miss.] *Green's Impartial Observer,* Dec. 13, 1800; Frankfort, Ky., *Palladium,* Mar. 3, 1801. See the Philadelphia *Federal Gazette* ("PETER PREJUDICE, Junior"), Sept. 5, 1798, for an amusing Federalist article bemoaning the passing of knee breeches, and talk of "amendments" in the new trousers

before they were even tried on—alterations which the tailors insisted upon even after it had been decided they were no longer needed.

10. New York *American Citizen,* Mar. 14, July 9, 1800.

11. Institute for Propaganda Analysis, *Propaganda Analysis,* I, 6.

12. Boston *Independent Chronicle* ("TULLY"), Aug. 14, 1797; Philadelphia *General Advertiser,* Feb. 20, 1794. Anthony Pasquin (John M. Williams) was an English immigrant Federalist editor, noted for scurrility; see the Richmond *Virginia Argus,* Apr. 26, 1799.

13. Lexington, Ky., *Stewart's Kentucky Herald,* Nov. 17, 1795; Boston *Columbian Centinel,* Apr. 30, 1796; Brookfield, Mass., *Moral and Political Telegraphe,* May 11, 1796; Alexandria, Va., *Columbian Mirror,* Feb. 22, 1800; Newark, N. J., *Centinel of Freedom,* Sept. 16, 1800.

14. Boston *Independent Chronicle,* June 9, 1796, Jan. 21, 1799; Mar. 13, 1800 ("HANCOCK"); Newark, N. J., *Centinel of Freedom* ("Sidney"), Aug. 12, 1800; Georgetown, D. C., *Centinel of Liberty* (speech of Col. Mercer at Elk Ridge, Md.), Aug. 15, 1800.

15. New London, Conn., *Bee,* Jan. 8, 1800; Boston *Constitutional Telegraphe,* Dec. 8, 1800.

16. Boston *Independent Chronicle,* Sept. 17, 1798, Jan. 9 ("X"), Mar. 10, 13, 17, 1800; Newark, N. J., *Centinel of Freedom,* Jan. 14, 21, 1800; New London, Conn., *Bee,* Jan. 22, Feb. 5, 1800 (from the *Independent Chronicle*).

17. Boston *Independent Chronicle,* Aug. 10 ("TULLY"), Dec. 25, 1797.

18. See Duer's answer to Congress's report on contractors, Concord, N. H., *Concord Herald,* June 20, 1792. Chap. 2 tells of Duer's involvement.

19. Philadelphia *National Gazette,* Mar. 12, 1792; Norwich, Conn., *Norwich Packet,* Mar. 29, 1792; Janson, *Stranger,* 406–07; Van Every, *Ark of Empire,* 223–24; Callahan, *Knox,* 320.

20. Philadelphia *National Gazette,* Dec. 17, 1792, Feb. 20, 1793; Norwich, Conn., *Norwich Packet,* Mar. 7, 1793. The letters of Morgan and St. Clair, and the testimony of Slough and one Edward Butler found their way into many columns. E.g., see the Norwich, Conn., *Norwich Weekly Register,* Apr. 17, 1792; Concord, N. H., *Concord Herald,* Apr. 18, 25, May 23, 30, 1792; Lexington *Kentucky Gazette,* May 5, 1792.

21. Norwich, Conn., *Norwich Weekly Register,* May 1, 1792, Norwich, Conn., *Norwich Packet,* Oct. 24, 1793.

22. *Baltimore Daily Intelligencer,* Mar. 17, 1793; Halifax *North Carolina Journal,* Jan. 1, 1794.

23. J. Fairfax McLaughlin, *Matthew Lyon—The Hampden of Congress,* 121–30.

24. See Brigham, *Bibliography,* II, 1083–1084, 1091; McLaughlin, *Lyon,* 204–05; Troy, N. Y., *Farmer's Oracle,* Dec. 7, 1797.

25. Boston *Independent Chronicle,* Feb. 8, 1798. See also the New York *Diary,* Feb. 1, 1798; Philadelphia *Carey's United States Recorder,* Feb. 3, 8, 1798; *Baltimore Telegraphe,* Feb. 8, 1798; Troy, N. Y., *Farmer's Oracle,* Feb. 20, 1798.

26. Foresighted, Harper was said to have prevented examination of "evidence" supporting the latter argument; New York *Time Piece,* Feb. 12, 1798; Philadelphia *Aurora,* Feb. 14, 16, 1798. See the Boston *Independent Chronicle,* Feb. 12, 26, 1798; Faÿ, *Two Franklins,* 335; Page Smith, *John Adams,* II, 949–50.

27. Boston *Independent Chronicle,* Feb. 12, 22, 1798; Philadelphia *Aurora,* Feb. 14, 1798; Philadelphia *Carey's United States Recorder* ("CONNECTICUTENSIS"), Feb. 24, 1798.

28. Philadelphia *Carey's United States Recorder,* Feb. 15, 19, 22, 27, 1798.

29. See the tale of the two Connecticut bullocks in Chap. 13, p. 502.

30. New London, Conn., *Bee,* Mar. 14, 1798. Cf. *ibid.,* Feb. 21, 1798; New York *Time Piece,* Feb. 9, 1798; *Boston Gazette,* Feb. 19, 1798; Troy, N. Y., *Farmer's Oracle* ("Federal Cowardice"), Feb. 27, 1798; Boston *Independent Chronicle,* Feb. 26, Mar. 1, 1798; Philadelphia *Aurora,* Feb. 16, Mar. 9, 1798. McLaughlin, *Lyon,* 307, states Lyon's friends contended this failure to oust him roused Adams' ire and resulted in invoking the Sedition Law.

31. Boston *Independent Chronicle,* Mar. 15, 1798; Charleston, S. C., *Charleston City Gazette,* Mar. 26, 1798. For Federalist reactions see the New Haven *Connecticut Journal,* Feb. 8, 15, 22, 1798; Danbury, Conn., *Republican Journal,* Feb. 19, 26, 1798; Lansingburgh, N. Y., *American Spy,* Feb. 27, 1798; Edenton *State Gazette of North Carolina,* Mar. 1, 1798; Savannah *Georgia Gazette,* Mar. 9, 1798; Augusta, Ga., *Augusta Chronicle,* Mar. 10, 1798; Concord, N. H., *Mirror,* Feb.–Mar., 1798, on the canings; even the mildly Federalist Washington, Pa., *Western Telegraphe,* Feb. 27, 1798, made Griswold the aggressor here.

32. New York *Greenleaf's New York Journal,* Mar. 20, 1798; Peacham, Vt., *Green Mountain Patriot,* Sept. 21, 1798; Boston *Independent Chronicle,* Nov. 1, 1798; Scipio, N. Y., *Levana Gazette,* Dec. 5, 1798; Elizabethtown, N. J., *Jersey Journal,* Jan. 15, 1799; Frank-

fort, Ky., *Guardian of Freedom,* Jan. 31, 1799; Lexington *Stewart's Kentucky Herald,* Mar. 13, 1799; McLaughlin, *Lyon,* 225–305, 337–39. For Federalist disgust at Lyon's reelection, see the Litchfield, Conn., *Monitor,* Jan. 30, Mar. 5, 1799.

33. The culprit was Stephen Hoffmer, who was fined $15; New York *Argus,* Jan. 12, 1799.

34. E.g., see the Boston *Columbian Centinel,* Aug. 22, 1792.

35. Exeter, N. H., *Newhampshire Gazetteer,* Aug. 13, 1790.

36. Philadelphia *General Advertiser,* Sept. 9, 1791.

37. Norfolk *Virginia Chronicle,* Oct. 20, 1792.

38. Philadelphia *National Gazette,* Sept. 19, 29, 1792; Georgetown, D. C., *Centinel of Liberty,* Apr. 23, 1799; Lancaster, Pa., *Lancaster Journal,* Aug. 28, 1799; Lancaster, Pa., *Intelligencer,* Aug. 28, Sept. 4, Oct. 5, 1799; Greensburg, Pa., *Farmers' Register,* Sept. 28, 1799. See Wheeler, "Urban Politics," 71–74, on this group in 1792.

39. Philadelphia *National Gazette* ("A Farmer"), Apr. 17, 1793; *Boston Gazette* ("An Independent Tradesman"), May 6, 1793; Philadelphia *General Advertiser,* Aug. 10, 21, 1793.

40. Boston *Independent Chronicle,* Jan. 9 ("X"), Nov. 3, 1794; Ames won the race by a narrow margin.

41. Philadelphia *Aurora,* Oct. 29, 1796.

42. Edenton *State Gazette of North Carolina,* Oct. 20, 27, Nov. 3, 1796 (noted in Gilpatrick, *Jeffersonian Democracy,* 74–75); Halifax *North Carolina Journal,* Sept. 5, 1796; Baltimore *Federal Gazette,* Oct. 4, 20, 25, Nov. 3, 1796; Cunningham, *Jeffersonian Republicans,* 94–95.

43. New York *Greenleaf's New York Journal,* Apr. 8, 1796.

44. Baltimore *Maryland Journal,* Sept. 5, 1796; Fredericktown, Md., *Bartgis's Federal Gazette,* Dec. 22, 1796; New York *Argus,* Apr. 25, 1797.

45. Philadelphia *Aurora,* Oct. 9, 1797. E.g., see also electioneering articles in the Hudson, N. Y., *Hudson Gazette,* Apr. 24, 1798; Elizabeth *Maryland Herald* ("An Old Soldier of '76"), Aug. 30, 1798; Boston *Independent Chronicle,* Sept. 24 ("Democritus"), Nov. 5, 1798; Stonington, Conn., *Journal of the Times,* May 21, 1799.

46. Newark, N. J., *Centinel of Freedom,* Oct. 8, 1799; Boston *Constitutional Telegraphe,* Jan. 8, 1800.

47. Raleigh, N. C., *Raleigh Register,* Mar. 11, 1800; New York *Commercial Advertiser,* Mar. 24, 1800; New York *American Citizen,* Apr. 2, 3, 5, 1800; Newark, N. J., *Centinel of Freedom,* May 6, June 24,

Aug. 19, 1800; Peacham, Vt., *Green Mountain Patriot,* Aug. 13, 1800; Newark *New Jersey Journal,* Aug. 19, 1800 (cited in Fee, *Transition,* 100); Richmond *Virginia Argus,* Sept. 2, 1800; Richmond, Va., *Examiner,* Oct. 31, 1800.

48. See the (mildly Federalist) Worcester *Massachusetts Spy,* Mar. 12 ("AN AMERICAN"), 26, July 30, Aug. 13, Oct. 1, 1800.

49. E.g., the Lexington *Kentucky Gazette,* May 1, 1800; Portsmouth *New Hampshire Gazette,* July 29, 1800; Baltimore *American,* June 11, Aug. 11, 1800; Elizabethtown *New Jersey Journal,* Aug. 19, 1800; Reading, Pa., *Readinger Adler,* Aug. 7, 26, 1800; Pittsburgh *Tree of Liberty,* Aug. 30, Dec. 25, 1800; Newark, N. J., *Centinel of Freedom* (in which the "REPUBLICAN TICKET" was starred), Sept. 23, 1800; Wilmington, Del., *Mirror of the Times,* Dec. 25, 1800.

50. E.g., the Edenton *State Gazette of North Carolina,* Oct. 20, 1796; Boston *Polar Star,* Nov. 1, 3, 1796; Charleston, S. C., *Charleston City Gazette,* Aug. 11, 1800; Newark, N. J., *Centinel of Freedom,* Sept. 23, 1800; Pittsburgh *Tree of Liberty,* Sept. 27, 1800; Lexington *Kentucky Gazette,* Oct. 13, 27, 1800; Richmond, Va., *Examiner,* Oct. 17, 1800; Washington, D. C., *National Intelligencer* ("LYCURGUS"), Nov. 3, 1800; Baltimore *American,* Nov. 10, 1800.

51. Boston *Independent Chronicle,* Jan. 3, 1793, Mar. 21, 1799; Philadelphia *Aurora,* Oct. 13, 1795; Philadelphia *New World* ("CASSIUS"), Oct. 28, 1796; Newark, N. J., *Centinel of Freedom,* Oct. 8, 1799 (the quoted appeal to the "Electors of New-Jersey"); Richmond, Va., *Examiner,* Nov. 1, 1799; Alexandria, Va., *Times,* Nov. 2, 1799 (on Washington); Charleston, S. C., *Times* (on the synagogue controversy), Oct. 13, 16, 18, 21, 1800.

52. As was the case in eight states in 1796, and five in 1800; Cunningham, *Jeffersonian Republicans,* 94n., 176n.

53. Luetscher, *Early Political Machinery,* 24n.; Minnigerode, *Presidential Years,* 118.

54. Philadelphia *National Gazette,* May 10, June 21, 1792; Philadelphia *Gazette of the United States,* June 6, 1792; Bowers, *Jefferson and Hamilton,* 166–67.

55. *New-York Journal,* Oct. 3, 1792; Philadelphia *National Gazette,* July 7, 11, Oct. 10, 1792; Germantown, Pa., *Germantauner Zeitung,* Oct. 9, Nov. 6, 1792; Halifax *North Carolina Journal,* Oct. 24, Dec. 19, 1792; Norwich, Conn., *Norwich Packet,* Nov. 22, 1792.

56. Fayetteville, N. C., *Fayetteville Gazette* ("Henrico"), Jan. 2, 1793; Bassett, *Federalist System,* 45–55; Chambers, *Political Parties,* 72–73. Cunningham, *Jeffersonian Republicans,* 33–49, suggests real

party organization had not yet been attained; Nichols, *Invention*, 181–82, concurs.

57. Boston *Independent Chronicle*, Mar. 28, Apr. 4 (Austin carried Boston, but failed to win the district as a whole), 1793; *Boston Gazette*, Apr. 1, 1793.

58. Baltimore *Edwards' Daily Advertiser*, Nov. 20, 1794; Philadelphia *Aurora*, Feb. 10, 1795; Boston *Independent Chronicle*, Feb. 23, May 18, 1795; Amherst, N. H., *Amherst Journal*, Mar. 13, 1795.

59. Philadelphia *Aurora*, Apr. 15 (reprinted in the Mt. Pleasant, N. J., *Jersey Chronicle*, Apr. 30, 1796), Oct. 19, 1796; Morse, *Federalist Party*, 161. See Schachner, *Aaron Burr*, 142, for comments on widespread discontent among the artisans and mechanics.

60. Lexington *Kentucky Gazette*, Nov. 5, 1796; Fredericksburg, Va., *Republican Citizen*, Nov. 9, 1796; Bennington *Vermont Gazette*, Nov. 11, 1796.

61. Boston Independent Chronicle, Nov. 14, 17, 1796 (Pennsylvania went for Jefferson, fourteen electoral votes to one; Tinkcom, *Republicans and Federalists*, 172); Philadelphia *Philadelphische Correspondenz*, Nov. 15, 1796; Philadelphia *Aurora*, Nov. 29, Dec. 12, 1796; Lexington *Kentucky Gazette*, Dec. 10, 1796, Jan. 18, 1797.

62. Boston *Independent Chronicle*, May 11, 25, Oct. 26, 1797; Philadelphia *Aurora*, Oct. 16, 1797; New London, Conn., *Bee*, Oct. 25, 1797; Tinkcom, *Republicans and Federalists*, 176–77.

63. Philadelphia *Aurora*, Dec. 11, 1797; New York *Diary*, Dec. 2, 1797; Boston *Independent Chronicle*, Dec. 25, 1797.

64. Philadelphia *Carey's United States Recorder*, May 1 (quotation from the New York *Time Piece*), June 28, 1798; Philadelphia *Aurora*, June 22, 1798. Jay was reelected, but six out of New York's ten congressmen, in "a state long celebrated as the last refuge of Tories . . . are the 'true friends of their country,' "; Boston *Independent Chronicle* ("SIDNEY"), Sept. 24, 1798.

65. Fredericktown, Md., *Bartgis's Federal Gazette*, Sept. 5, 1798; Boston *Independent Chronicle*, Sept. 20 (N. C.), Nov. 5 (on the black-bordered Federalist paper), Nov. 8 (Mass.), 1798; Newark, N. J., *Newark Gazette*, Sept. 11, 25, 1798; Elizabethtown *New Jersey Journal*, Sept. 4, 18, Oct. 2, 9, 16, 23, 1798; Trenton *New-Jersey State Gazette*, Sept. 11, 1798; Reading Pa., *Readinger Adler*, Oct. 16, 1798; Newark, N. J., *Centinel of Freedom*, Oct. 30, 1798. The shift in New Jersey from electing congressmen at large to choosing them by districts enabled Republicans to gain control of the United States House; see Fee, *Transition*, 88, 93–96.

66. Frankfort, Ky., *Palladium,* Jan. 1 (from the *Herald of Liberty*), Feb. 12, 19, 1799.

67. Richmond *Virginia Argus,* Apr. 16, 1799 ("From a N. Y. paper") ; Boston *Independent Chronicle,* May, 9, 1799; Baltimore *American,* May 14, 1799; cf. the Hartford *Connecticut Courant,* July 12, 1799.

68. Philadelphia *Aurora,* Apr. 12, Aug. 15, 17, 20, 21, Sept. 11 (cited in Malone, "First Years of Thomas Cooper," 146–47), Oct. 1, 1799; Lancaster, Pa., *Intelligencer,* Aug. 14, 21, Sept. 25, Nov. 13, 1799; (cf. the German-language Federalist account in the York, Pa., *Unpartheyische York Gazette,* July 25, Aug. 8, 1799) ; Greensburg, Pa., *Farmers' Register,* Aug. 16, Sept. 28, 1799; Baltimore *American,* Oct. 11, 23, 28, 1799; Boston *Constitutional Telegraphe,* Oct. 23, 26, Nov. 2, 27, 1799; Newark, N. J., *Centinel of Freedom,* Oct. 15, 22, 1799; Richmond, Va., *Examiner,* Oct. 22, 29, 1799; Raleigh, N. C., *Raleigh Register,* Nov. 5, 1799; Reading, Pa., *Readinger Adler,* Nov. 12, 19, 1799; McMaster, *A History,* II, 449.

69. *National Magazine,* I (1799), 101.

70. Boston *Constitutional Telegraphe,* Jan. 1, 22, Apr. 9, 16, 1800; Frankfort, Ky., *Palladium,* Jan. 2, 1800; Lancaster, Pa., *Intelligencer,* Jan. 15, 1800; Reading, Pa., *Readinger Adler,* Mar. 11, 1800; New York *American Citizen,* Apr. 14, 1800; Boston *Independent Chronicle,* Apr. 17, 1800.

71. Goshen, N. Y., *Orange Patrol* (from the New York *Republican Watch Tower*), May 13, 1800. See the New York *American Citizen,* Apr. 30, May 3, 5, 1800; New York *Forlorn Hope,* May 10, 1800; Baltimore *American,* June 16, 1800; Frankfort, Ky., *Palladium,* June 19, 1800; Minnigerode, *Presidential Years,* 92–93; Cunningham, *Jeffersonian Republicans,* 177–183. The state's presidential electors were selected by a joint ballot of both houses of the legislature.

72. Newark, N. J., *Centinel of Freedom,* May 6, 1800.

73. Lancaster, Pa., *Americanische Staatbothe,* Apr. 30, 1800; Lancaster, Pa., *Lancaster Correspondent,* May 3, 10, 1800; Richmond *Virginia Argus,* May 13, 27, 1800; Lancaster, Pa., *Intelligencer,* May 14, 1800.

74. New York *American Citizen,* May 15, June 28, 1800; Lancaster, Pa., *Intelligencer,* May 21, 1800; Richmond *Virginia Argus,* May 27, 1800. A letter from Timothy Pickering to John Adams (May 12, 1800) suggests even Adams believed Jefferson's election was assured after the New York vote; see Adams, *Works of John Adams,* IX, 54–55.

75. Lexington *Kentucky Gazette* (item from the Richmond *Examiner*),

May 15, 1800; Bennington *Vermont Gazette,* May 19, 1800 (reprinted in the Newfield, Conn., *American Telegraphe*).

76. New York *American Citizen,* Apr. 14, June 2, 1800; Charleston, S. C., *City Gazette* (letter of Meriwether Jones), May 20, 1800; Frankfort, Ky., *Palladium,* June 19, 1800.

77. Baltimore *American,* June 12, July 7 ("Simon Slim"), 15, 16 (*"Dick Moonlight"*), 1800; Philadelphia *Aurora,* Apr. 28 (asserting rejection of Ross's bill demonstrated the value of a free press), July 11, 1800; Augusta, Ga., *Augusta Chronicle,* July 5, 1800; Boston *Constitutional Telegraphe,* July 9, 1800.

78. Lancaster, Pa., *Lancaster Correspondent,* May 3, 1800; New York *American Citizen,* July 14, 1800 (reprinted in the Baltimore *American,* July 17, 1800); Newark, N.J., *Centinel of Freedom,* Aug. 12, 1800; Richmond *Virginia Argus,* Aug. 29, 1800; Frankfort, Ky., *Palladium,* Sept. 25, 1800. When polled, Republicans controlled the Maryland legislature, and the old system of selection was followed; Richmond, Va., *Examiner,* Oct. 17, 1800.

79. Wilmington, Del., *Mirror of the Times,* July 19, 1800; see also the Newark, N.J., *Centinel of Freedom,* May 13, 20, 1800, on Thomas Cooper's refusal of a presidential pardon as "electioneering clemency."

80. Richmond *Virginia Argus,* June 13, 1800.

81. New London, Conn., *Bee,* Aug. 27, Sept. 3 (from the *Aurora*), 1800; Baltimore *American,* July 23, 25, Aug. 12, 23, 25, 1800; Philadelphia *Aurora,* July 23, 1800; Morristown, N.J., *Genius of Liberty,* Aug. 14, 1800; Richmond *Virginia Argus,* Aug. 26, 1800.

82. Pittsburgh *Tree of Liberty,* Sept. 20, Oct. 11, 1800; Richmond *Virginia Argus,* Sept. 19, 26, 1800; Hartford *Connecticut Courant,* Sept. 1, 8, 29, 1800; Hartford, Conn., *American Mercury,* Sept. 11, 25, 1800; New London, Conn., *Bee,* Sept. 17, 24, Oct. 15, 1800; Boston *Independent Chronicle,* Aug. 28, Sept. 4, 8, 1800; Boston *Constitutional Telegraphe,* Oct. 1, 1800; Richmond, Va., *Examiner,* Oct. 10, 1800; Georgetown, D. C., *Centinel of Liberty,* Oct. 14, 1800.

83. Baltimore *American,* Sept. 1, Oct. 20, 21, 1800; Richmond *Virginia Argus,* Sept. 16, 1800; Boston *Independent Chronicle,* Oct. 16, 1800; Pittsburgh *Tree of Liberty,* Oct. 18, 25, 1800; Lancaster, Pa., *Lancaster Correspondent,* Nov. 1, 1800.

84. Philadelphia *Aurora,* Sept. 27, Oct. 14, 1800; Frankfort, Ky., *Palladium,* Oct. 23, 1800. Pennsylvania's fifteen votes were in considerable doubt, which accounts for the discrepancy in the totals tabulated.

85. Baltimore *American,* Oct. 21, 1800; Newark, N.J., *Centinel of Freedom,* Oct. 21, Nov. 4, 1800; Boston *Independent Chronicle,* Oct.

23, 27, 1800; Richmond, Va., *Examiner,* Oct. 24, Nov. 4, 1800; Augusta, Ga., *Augusta Chronicle,* Oct. 25, 1800; Raleigh, N. C., *Raleigh Register* (from the Savannah Ga., *Columbian Museum*), Oct. 28, 1800; Richmond *Virginia Argus,* Oct. 31, 1800. "Hurrah for Freedom, Constitution and Jefferson!" cried the Lancaster, Pa., *Lancaster Correspondent,* Oct. 18, 1800; a campaign biography of Jefferson appeared Sept. 6, 20, 1800.

86. Boston *Independent Chronicle,* Oct. 30, 1800; Richmond, Va., *Examiner,* Oct. 31, 1800.

87. New York *American Citizen,* in the New London, Conn., *Bee,* Oct. 29, 1800.

88. The mildly Federalist Savannah, Ga., *Columbian Museum,* Nov. 7, 1800, printed this tale without comment.

89. Baltimore *American,* Nov. 1, 1800; Philadelphia *Aurora,* Nov. 1, 1800; Richmond *Virginia Argus,* Nov. 4, 11, 25, 1800; Richmond, Va., *Examiner,* Nov. 7, 11, 1800; Newark, N. J., *Centinel of Freedom* ("Tom Bowling," from the Boston *Independent Chronicle*), Nov. 11, 1800; Charleston, S. C., *City Gazette,* Nov. 13, 15, 17, 1800; Augusta, Ga., *Augusta Chronicle,* Nov. 15, 1800; Pittsburgh *Tree of Liberty,* Nov. 22, 1800; Newport, R. I., *Guardian of Liberty,* Nov. 22, 1800.

90. Richmond *Virginia Argus,* Nov. 14, 1800; see Cunningham, *Jefferson Republicans,* 231–36.

91. Philadelphia *Aurora,* Nov. 1, 5, 1800; Richmond, Va., *Examiner,* Nov. 14, 1800; Tinkcom, *Republicans and Federalists,* 247–52.

92. New London, Conn., *Bee,* Feb. 5, 1800; Richmond *Virginia Argus,* Jan. 31, Mar. 11, 14, 1800; Simms, *John Taylor,* 96.

93. Richmond, Va., *Examiner,* Oct. 14, 1800; Pittsfield, Mass., *Sun,* Dec. 9, 1800.

94. New York *Argus,* Feb. 6, 1800; Wilmington, Del., *Mirror of the Times,* June 28, 1800; Boston *Constitutional Telegraphe,* July 2, 1800; Providence, R. I., *Impartial Observer,* Oct. 27, 1800; Pittsfield, Mass., *Sun,* Oct. 28, 1800; Boston *Independent Chronicle,* Oct. 30, 1800. Minnigerode, *Presidential Years,* 105–06, and Miller, *Federalist Era,* 257–58, 267–68, summarize the question. The New Jersey legislature finally picked Federalist electors; Prince, *Jeffersonian Republicans,* 60–61; Newark *Centinel of Freedom,* Nov. 11, 1800.

95. Albany, N. Y., *Albany Register,* Apr. 22, 25, 1800; Jabez D. Hammond, *The History of Political Parties in the State of New York,* I, 122–23; Spaulding, *George Clinton,* 240n.; Mitchell, *Hamilton,* II, 467–68.

96. Baltimore *American,* June 17 ("A Virginian"), 25, Aug. 23, 1800;

NOTES TO CHAPTER XIV

Charleston *South Carolina State Gazette*, July 2, 1800; Baltimore *Federal Gazette*, July 3 ("Civis"), 31 ("BYSTANDER"), Aug. 5 ("Voter"), 1800; Georgetown, D. C., *Centinel of Liberty*, Aug. 5, 26, 1800; see Joseph Gurn, *Charles Carroll of Carrollton, 1737–1832*, 172; Robinson, *Jeffersonian Democracy*, 34–35.

97. Baltimore *American*, Oct. 10, 16, 17, 1799; Georgetown, D. C., *Centinel of Liberty*, Aug. 12 (from the *Baltimore Telegraphe*), Sept. 23, 26, 30, Oct. 3, 7, 1800; Washington, D. C., *National Intelligencer*, Oct. 31, 1800.

98. Philadelphia *Aurora*, Oct. 25, Nov. 1, 1800; Washington, D. C., *Universal Gazette*, Nov. 6, 1800; Pittsburgh *Tree of Liberty*, Nov. 6, 8, 1800; Georgetown, D. C., *Washington Federalist*, Nov. 8, 24, 1800; Litchfield, Conn., *Farmer's Monitor* (from the New York *Republican Watch Tower* [on requiems to Robbins, as a horrible example]), Dec. 3, 1800.

99. Newark, N. J., *Centinel of Freedom*, Nov. 18, 1800; Richmond, Va., *Examiner*, Nov. 21, 1800; Washington, D. C., *Universal Gazette*, Nov. 20, 27, Dec. 4, 11, 1800; Pittsburgh *Tree of Liberty*, Nov. 22, Dec. 27, 1800; Baltimore *American*, Nov. 26, Dec. 2, 1800; New York *American Citizen*, Nov. 29, 1800; *Baltimore Telegraphe*, Dec. 3, 1800; Lexington *Kentucky Gazette*, Dec. 8, 1800; Pittsfield, Mass., *Sun*, Dec. 9, 1800; Northumberland, Pa., *Sunbury and Northumberland Gazette*, Dec. 20, 1800; Norristown, Pa., *True Republican*, Jan. 2, 1801; Minnigerode, *Presidential Years*, 106. See Wheeler, "Urban Politics," 135–38, on this arrangement.

100. Nashville *Tennessee Gazette*, Aug. 27, Oct. 22, 1800; Richmond, Va., *Examiner*, Nov. 21, 1800; Chillicothe, [Ohio], *Scioto Gazette*, Nov. 27, 1800. See the claims for Tennessee and Maryland in the Fincastle, Va., *Herald of Virginia*, Dec. 5, 1800.

101. Richmond *Virginia Argus* (from "a Philadelphia paper"), Nov. 4, 1800.

102. Pittsburgh *Tree of Liberty*, Nov. 1, 1800; Richmond, Va., *Examiner*, Nov. 14, 1800; Baltimore *American*, Nov. 26, 1800.

103. Lancaster, Pa., *Lancaster Correspondent*, Nov. 22, 1800; Baltimore *American*, Nov. 20, 27, 1800; New York *American Citizen*, Dec. 1, 1800; Boston *Independent Chronicle*, Dec. 4, 15, 1800; New London, Conn., *Bee*, Dec. 10, 1800; Boston *Constitutional Telegraphe*, Dec. 6, 1800; Charleston, S. C., *Times*, Dec. 5, 1800.

104. Baltimore *Federal Gazette*, Dec. 12, 1800; see also the Hartford *Connecticut Courant*, Dec. 8, 1800 ("the non-election of Jefferson is now certain. . . ."); Baltimore *American*, Dec. 12, 13, 1800; Newark,

N. J., *Centinel of Freedom*, Dec. 16, 1800; Wilmington, Del., *Mirror of the Times*, Dec. 17, 1800; New York *American Citizen*, Dec. 18, 20, 1800; Reading, Pa., *Readinger Adler*, Dec. 23, 1800. Cunningham, *Jeffersonian Republicans*, 232–37, tells how Democrat Charles Pinckney won the South Carolina state legislature for Jefferson.

105. Baltimore *American*, Dec. 1, 1800; Norfolk, Va., *Epitome of the Times*, Dec. 30, 1800; Augusta, Ga., *Augusta Chronicle*, Jan. 1, 1801; Lancaster, Pa., *Lancaster Correspondent*, Jan. 3, 1801. Adams' address was delivered Nov. 22, 1800.

106. Baltimore *American*, Dec. 4, 5, 20, 25, 1800.

107. Frankfort, Ky., *Palladium*, Dec. 30, 1800; Washington, D. C., *National Intelligencer*, Dec. 24, 1800, Jan. 5, 7, 12, Feb. 13, 18, 1800; van der Linden, *Turning Point*, 282–314.

108. Raleigh, N. C., *Raleigh Register*, Feb. 3, Mar. 10, 31, 1801; Washington, D. C., *National Intelligencer*, Feb. 9, 20, 27, 1801; Morristown, N. J., *Genius of Liberty*, Feb. 26, 1801; Elizabethtown *New Jersey Journal*, Mar. 10, 17, 1801; Augusta, Ga., *Augusta Chronicle*, Mar. 7, 14, 28, 1801; Newark, N. J., *Centinel of Freedom*, Mar. 17, 1801.

109. *Boston Gazette*, Nov. 5, 1792. The figures are for Boston alone, not the entire district.

110. Philadelphia *National Gazette*, Dec. 12, 1792.

111. New York *Greenleaf's Patriotic Register*, May 17, 1794; Boston *Independent Chronicle*, May 26, 1794; Philadelphia *Aurora*, June 9, 1795 (New York's "freemen" had elected six Republicans out of ten congressmen).

112. Wilmington *Delaware Gazette*, Mar. 1, 1797 (reprinted in the Philadelphia *Aurora*, Mar. 3, 1797); New York *Argus*, Mar. 15, 1797.

113. Albany, N. Y., *Albany Register*, Mar. 2, 1798; Boston *Independent Chronicle*, Nov. 8, 1798.

114. Philadelphia *Aurora*, May 6, 1799; Boston *Independent Chronicle*, May 13, 1799; Baltimore *American*, May 16, 1799; *Anonymous*, "Party Violence," 177.

115. New York *American Citizen*, May 2, 1800; Boston *Independent Chronicle*, Oct. 27, 1800; New London, Conn., *Bee*, Nov. 26, 1800.

116. See Chap. 13. For other examples, see the Baltimore *Federal Gazette*, July 6, 1797 (Philadelphia dinner for Monroe on his return from France); Independence Day celebrations and toasts in such papers as the Frankfort, Ky., *Guardian of Freedom*, July 10, 1798, and the Georgetown, D. C., *Centinel of Liberty*, July 16, 1799; and Christmas

toasts for Monroe, Taylor, Giles, etc., Richmond *Virginia Argus,* Jan. 3, 1800.

117. Richmond, Va., *Examiner,* Oct. 24, 1800 (cited in Anonymous, "Party Violence," 178–79) ; Gilpatrick, *Jeffersonian Democracy,* 114n.

118. Philadelphia *New World,* Dec. 19, 1796; New York *Time Piece,* Apr. 28, 1797; Philadelphia *Aurora,* Oct. 17, 1799; Raleigh, N. C., *Raleigh Register,* Nov. 26, 1799; Reading, Pa., *Readinger Adler,* Nov. 19, 1799, July 1, 1800.

119. Pittsburgh *Tree of Liberty,* Aug. 30, 1800; New London, Conn., *Bee,* Nov. 26, 1800.

120. Baltimore *Federal Gazette,* Nov. 10, 1800; Norwalk, Conn., *Sun of Liberty,* Nov. 25, 1800; Providence, R. I., *Providence Journal,* Nov. 26, 1800 (suggesting Duane's complicity) ; Baltimore *American* ("Simon Slim"), Jan. 3, 1801; McMaster, *A History,* II, 517–18.

121. Baltimore *American,* Jan. 31, Feb. 4, 1801; Georgetown, D. C., *Cabinet,* cited in the Philadelphia *Aurora,* Jan. 25, 27, 29, Feb. 2, 1801; Newark, N. J., *Centinel of Freedom,* Feb. 3, 1801; Savannah, Ga., *Columbian Museum,* Feb. 13, 1801. See also the New York *Temple of Reason,* Jan. 31, 1801; Washington, D. C., *National Intelligencer,* Jan. 30, Mar. 4, 1801; and McMaster, *A History,* II, 518.

122. Washington, D. C., *National Intelligencer,* Feb. 20, 1801.

123. Baltimore *American,* Jan. 7, 1801.

 AN APPRAISAL

1. Chambers, *Political Parties,* 152. There was certainly no true nation-wide political organization, or any real attempt to form one, before 1791 or 1792; one could reasonably advance the claim that not until 1796 did the Republicans attempt a truly national ticket. See *ibid.,* 70, 86; Cunningham, *Jeffersonian Republicans,* 13, 23, 35, 49, 94; and (for New York and New Jersey) Young, *Democratic Republicans of N. Y.,* 566, 575–78; Prince, *New Jersey's Jeffersonian Republicans,* 19.

2. Dunbar, " 'Monarchical' Tendecies," 2–164.

3. E.g., the Keene *New Hampshire Sentinel* (quoting the Boston *Massachusetts Mercury*), Dec. 6, 1800.

4. See Chap. 13.

5. E.g., Chaps. 2, 3.

6. Hartford *Connecticut Courant,* Jan. 13, 1800 (from the New York *Commercial Advertiser*) ; Pittsfield, Mass., *Sun,* Oct. 28, 1800; New Haven *Connecticut Journal,* Dec. 4, 1800.

7. This charge was the "hardest thing for Federalists to bear"; Ames to Christopher Gore, Dec. 28, 1800; Seth Ames, ed., *Works of Fisher Ames,* I, 287.

8. Glenn Leroy Bushey, "William Duane, Crusader for Judicial Reform,"*Pennsylvania History* 5 (July, 1938), 156; Philip Marsh, "Philip Freneau and His Circle," *Pennsylvania Magazine of History and Biography* 63 (Jan., 1939), 56; Mott, *American Journalism,* 129; Smith, *Freedom's Fetters,* 188–90, 278.

9. Link, *Democratic-Republican Societies,* 10; see also Anderson, "Virginia and Kentucky Resolutions," 47–48.

10. For examples of this type of coverage (usually reasonably objective), see the Federalist Providence, R. I., *United States Chronicle,* Dec. 1, 1796; Litchfield, Conn., *Monitor,* Mar. 13, 1799 (this latter gives no credit, but the congressional session of Mar. 2, 1799, is remarkably similar to the *Aurora's* accounts). Federalist papers frequently copied non-political or foreign news from the *Aurora;* e.g., the New Haven *Connecticut Journal,* July 25, 1798, Mar. 14, 1799; Faÿ, *Two Franklins,* 157–58. Dunlap and Claypoole's *American Daily Advertiser* and Brown's *Federal Gazette* also carried summaries, but the *Aurora's* accounts seemed most influential. Thomas, *History of Printing in America,* I, 139–40; Scharf & Westcott, *History of Philadelphia,* III, 1977; Lee, *Daily Newspaper,* 59.

11. Mott, *American Journalism,* 127, 129.

12. See Allen C. Clark, *William Duane,* 56; Smith, *Freedom's Fetters,* 192; Chambers, *Political Parties,* 83; and the claim (Philadelphia *Aurora,* June 5, 1798) that it circulated as widely as the *Gazette of the United States.* Federalist papers (e.g., the Harrisburg, Pa., *Oracle of Dauphin,* Feb. 23, 1801) reluctantly conceded the *Aurora's* extensive circulation, but on lack of profits, see William Duane to James Madison, May 10, 1801; C. Worthington Ford, ed., "Letters of William Duane," *Proceedings of the Massachusetts Historical Society,* second series, 20 (May, 1906), 263.

13. The Boston *Columbian Centinel,* Jan. 24, 1798, charged Matthew Lyon had franked hundreds of copies of "that Pandora box of anarchy" to his Vermont constituents; the Litchfield, Conn., *Monitor,* Nov. 21, 1798, noted another occasion of allegedly gratuitous circulation.

14. Faÿ, *Two Franklins,* 305, 310; Clark, *William Duane,* 15; Smith, *Freedom's Fetters,* 188–90; Kurtz, *Presidency of John Adams,* 136–37.

15. Mott, *American Journalism,* 129; Ford, "Letters of William Duane," 257; Woodbury, *Public Opinion,* 26–27; Scharf and Westcott, *History of Philadelphia,* III, 1977–1978; Clark, *Duane,* 7.

16. E.g., the Georgetown, D. C., *Washington Federalist* (which never-the-less frequently quoted the *Aurora* that year), Dec. 2, 1800; Harrisburg, Pa., *Oracle of Dauphin* (item from the Philadelphia *Gazette of the United States*), Feb. 23, 1801.

17. Philadelphia *General Advertiser,* Feb. 16, 1793; Faÿ, *Two Franklins,* 282–85, 287–88.

18. Freneau, *Letters,* iv; *DAB,* I, 463; Hudson, *Journalism in the United States,* 210; Smith, *Freedom's Fetters,* 192–93.

19. At the time of Jay's Treaty, and again in 1798; Philadelphia *Aurora,* Jan. 25, 1798. Bache's nickname came from his grandfather's discovery; *DAB,* I, 462.

20. Philadelphia *Aurora,* Sept. 10, 1798; Faÿ, *Two Franklins,* 356–57. Mott, *American Journalism,* 146, cites the Boston *Russell's Gazette:* "The memory of this scoundrel cannot be too highly execrated." The Boston *Independent Chronicle,* Sept. 24, 1798, noted the "inhuman re-marks . . . of unprincipled Editors" on Bache's demise.

21. Boston *Constitutional Telegraphe,* Nov. 23, 1799; this was essentially the same story that produced a libel suit by Hamilton against *Greenleaf's New York Argus.* See the *Pittsburgh Gazette,* July 12, 1800, on "prostitution of the truth"; John Adams to Timothy Pickering, Aug. 1, 1799 (along with other citations, Woodbury, *Public Opinion,* 28–29).

22. Philadelphia *Carey's United States Recorder,* Mar. 13, 1798.

23. Boston *Constitutional Telegraphe* (quoting the Albany, N. Y., *Albany Register*), July 2, 1800.

24. Dan Harrison, Georgetown, S. C., *Georgetown Gazette,* July 5, 1800. The proposed paper was the Richmond, Va., *Press;* only two issues have been located (see Brigham, *Bibliography,* II, 1141).

25. E.g., the Philadelphia *Porcupine's Gazette,* Mar. 12, 1798; York, Pa., *York Recorder* ("OF THE *AURORA*"), July 9, 1800. For a sample of ridicule (in a misspelled item about "the *rory*"), see the Peacham, Vt., *Green Mountain Patriot* (from the New Haven, Conn., *Messenger*), Aug. 27, 1800.

26. Frankfort, Ky., *Palladium,* Apr. 10, 1800; *Pittsburgh Gazette,* Jan. 23, 1801. The latter paper felt praise of a bad administration was better than condemnation of a *good* one.

27. Washington, D. C., *National Intelligencer*, Feb. 25, 1801.

28. Bent, *Newspaper Crusaders*, 99–100, flatly asserts Jefferson wrote anonymously for Freneau and other editors, charging some of Freneau's editorials agreed almost verbatim with Jefferson's statements. The matter is still debated (cf. Cunningham, *Jeffersonian Republicans*, 26–27; Leary, *That Rascal Freneau*, 359; and *supra*, Chap. I), but evidence to support the accusation has not been found.

29. Mott, *American Journalism*, 124–25; Allan Nevins, "Freneau," *Encyclopedia of the Social Sciences*, VI, 483–84; Benjamin, "Notable Editors," 122–23; Austin, *Philip Freneau*, 160; Sullivan, *Familiar Letters*, 79; Don Ensminger Mowry, "Political Verse Satires of the Factional Period of American History, 1789–1806." *Americana* 5 (Feb., 1910), 217; McMaster, *A History*, II, 49.

30. Philadelphia *National Gazette*, Oct. 31, 1791, May 7, June 21, 1792, July 3, 1793; Leary, *That Rascal Freneau*, 203–36; Axelrad, *Freneau*, 223–24.

31. Faÿ, "Benjamin Franklin Bache," 279–80, 291.

32. Nine in Virginia, two in North Carolina, three in South Carolina and two in Georgia; see Dabney, *Liberalism in the South*, 87.

33. E.g., see the Philadelphia *Gazette of the United States*, Sept. 7, 1793; Forman, "Political Activities," 65–66. Marsh, "Philip Freneau and His Circle," 47, comments on the paper's nationwide circulation.

34. Cf. n. 28; Leary, *That Rascal Freneau*, 190–91, 244–45; Mott, *Jefferson and the Press*, 23–26; John Tebbel, *The Compact History of the American Newspaper*, 59–63.

35. Philadelphia *National Gazette*, July 28, Sept. 22, 1792; Leary, *That Rascal Freneau*, 208–13; Miller, *Federalist Era*, 91–92; Malone, *TJ*, II, 426–28, 459–63; Mitchell, *Hamilton*, II, 208–12.

36. Bowers, *Jefferson and Hamilton*, 156; Mott, *Jefferson and the Press*, 16–25 (esp. p. 21).

37. Benjamin, "Notable Editors," 109–11; Delano A. Goddard, *Newspapers and Newspaper Writers in New England, 1787–1815*, 17–20.

38. Douglas C. McMurtrie, *The Beginnings of the American Newspaper*, 25–28; Mott, *American Journalism*, 75–76; Nelson, *Notes*, 268; Goddard, *Newspapers*, 14–15; Thomas, *History of Printing*, I, 136–39, II, 56.

39. E.g., the Boston *Independent Chronicle*, May 9, 13, 1799; see Chap. 12.

40. Letter published, *ibid.*, Oct. 30, 1794; see Fisher Ames to Oliver Wolcott, Nov. 14, 1796 (cited in Warren, *Jacobin and Junto*,

67); Abigail Adams (classifying it with the *Aurora*) to Mary Cranch, Apr. 26, 1798 (noted in Smith, *Freedom's Fetters*, 97).

41. J. M. Smith, *Freedom's Fetters*, 186.

42. See Benjamin, "Notable Editors," 114–16 (on the *Impartial Register*); Robinson, *Jeffersonian Democracy in N. E.*, 53–54 (on the *Republican Ledger* and the *Constitutional Telegraphe*); Goddard, *Newspapers*, 24 (stressing the *Telegraphe*). Miller, *Crisis in Freedom*, 126–27, confirms the *Bee's* significance.

43. Spargo, *Haswell*, 41–44, and the Philadelphia *Porcupine's Gazette*, Oct. 19, 1798, attest to the *Vermont Gazette's* significance; McLaughlin *Lyon*, 199, 206–08, tells of Lyons' publication. See also Smith, *Freedom's Fetters*, 227–29, 359.

44. Charles H. Levermore, "The Rise of Metropolitan Journalism, 1800–1840," *American Historical Review* 6 (Apr., 1901), 449; Miller, *Crisis in Freedom*, 30.

45. The *Journal* was called the only Democratic paper in New York in 1794; William Miller, "First Fruits of Republican Organization: Political Aspects of the Congressional Elections of 1794," *Pennsylvania Magazine of History and Biography* 63 (Apr. 1939), 124n. After the *Argus* appeared, the *Journal* was continued as a semi-weekly; Martin, "Transition Period," 283; Brigham, *Bibliography*, I, 610, 647. It claimed a circulation of two thousand by the end of 1794; Young, *Democratic Republicans*, 425.

46. Mott, *American Journalism*, 134, 150, 183; E. Wilder Sapulding, *His Excellency George Clinton*, 225; Levermore, "Metropolitan Journalism," 447–48.

47. Philadelphia *Aurora*, Oct. 15, 1795; see the New Haven *Connecticut Journal*, Oct. 7, 29, 1795.

48. Faÿ, *Notes on the American Press*, 13–14; W. C. Ford, "Jefferson and the Newspaper," 89 (on the *Recorder's* significance).

49. Baltimore *Federal Gazette*, Feb. 11, 1797; Scharf and Westcott, *History of Philadelphia*, III, 1977; Faÿ, *Two Franklins*, 156. The paper was the Philadelphia *Federal Gazette* until 1793; Brigham, *Bibliography*, II, 905.

50. Nelson, *Notes*, 78; van der Linden, *Turning Point*, 23, 81–82, 91, 133–34, 179–81, 210–11; Mott, *Jefferson and the Press*, 47; Douglas C. McMurtrie, *A History of Printing in the United States*, II, 267–68. James Lyon's Georgetown *Cabinet* came to share Jeffersonian predominance in the District of Columbia with the *Centinel of Liberty*, but its first issue did not appear until late in 1800; see McMurtrie, *History*, II, 265.

51. See the *Pittsburgh Gazette*, Sept. 7, Nov. 9, 1799.

52. B. H. Goldsmith, "The Press," in Irving S. Kull, ed., *New Jersey; A History*, IV, 1327; Fee, *Transition*, 34; McMurtrie, *History*, II, 236–37. Elmer T. Hutchinson, "A Pioneer New Jersey Printer," *Proceedings of the New Jersey Historical Society* 55 (Apr. 1937), esp. pp. 134–35, 139, gives a sketch of Kollock's life.

53. Leary, *That Rascal Freneau*, 254–55; Fee, *Transition*, 66, 78; Prince, *Jeffersonian Republicans*, 38–39, 56, 72, 79, 80, 89.

54. Baltimore *American*, Mar. 14, Oct. 7, 1799; the paper commented sarcastically about those editors who followed "the fashion of changing sides."

55. Alexandria, Va., *Alexandria Times*, Jan. 18, 1800; Robinson, *Jeffersonian Democracy in N. E.*, 54.

56. Smith, *Freedom's Fetters*, 335–45, 358; and Mott, *American Journalism*, 135, give a bit on the *Examiner*. See the Richmond, Va., *Examiner*, June 10, 1800; Richmond *Virginia Federalist*, July 30, 1800, ff.

57. The Edenton *State Gazette of North Carolina* and the *Fayetteville Gazette* (whose editor belonged to the Democratic Society) were inclined toward Republicanism, but not ardently so.

58. Martin, "Transition Period," 266; Dabney, *Liberalism in the South*, 87–88.

59. The *Carolina Gazette* was the weekly edition; Brigham, *Bibliography*, II, 1024; William L. King, *The Newspaper Press of Charleston, South Carolina*, 37–38; Mott, *American Journalism*, 135; Austin, *Philip Freneau*, 140–42.

60. Douglas C. McMurtrie, *John Bradford, Pioneer Printer of Kentucky*, 3–4, 8, 11; Perrin, "First Newspaper," 124, 127.

61. Inevitably, this is a somewhat subjective listing, but there are several compilations (some by editors of the day, others by secondary writers) confirming many of the names in this highly select group. E.g., see the Georgetown, D. C., *Cabinet*, Dec. 30, 1800; Portsmouth, N. H., *Republican Ledger*, Dec. 25, 1799; Newark, N. J., *Centinel of Freedom*, Oct. 8, 1799; Leary, *That Rascal Freneau*, 254–55; Koch, *Republican Religion*, 251; and Warren, *Making of the Constitution*, 93–94. Smith, *Freedom's Fetters*, 188, 207, calls the New York *Time Piece* the most rapidly growing Democratic paper in the country in 1798.

62. See the advertisement for the proposed Georgetown, D. C., *National Cabinet*, in the Baltimore *American*, Aug. 6, 1800; or the comment in the Georgetown, D. C., *Cabinet*, Dec. 30, 1800.

63. See Ford, ed., *Writings of TJ*, VII, 48—though Jefferson said (late in 1795) that while Republicans far outnumbered Federalists, the

latter controlled most of the newspapers. Cf. the Boston *Independent Chronicle,* Nov. 19, 1798, quoting Charles Holt (of the New London *Bee*) that nine-tenths of Connecticut's papers were Federalist. But that year was the nadir of Republican fortunes, and Connecticut the most Federal of all states. At least three more Democratic papers were founded there by 1800, and even if Holts' dismal estimate were accurate (for the area where Jeffersonianism was weakest), for the nation over by the last of the decade Republican papers must have constituted a very respectable minority in numbers.

64. Frank L. Mott, "Newspapers in Presidential Campaigns," *Public Opinion Quarterly* 8 (Fall, 1944), 349–50.

65. *Ibid.,* 362–63. David Lord, in Morristown, N. J., wrote Alexander Hamilton, Apr. 11, 1798, "9 tenths of the Presses out of the great towns in America south of the Hudson are Democratic. . . ." (quoted in Mott, *American Journalism,* 196n.) ; Philadelphia *Aurora,* Nov. 23, 1799 (on the frequency with which Jeffersonian presses were being established) ; cf. Young, *Democratic Republicans,* 426, 576; and *infra,* note 72.

66. There were approximately 231 papers printed at this time. The estimate of Republican ones is from Mott, "Newspapers in Presidential Campaigns"; cf. the present writer's estimates in the Appendix.

67. Mott, *ibid.,* 351, states "For an established paper to change political faith would have marked it as a Judas." But cf. *supra,* note 54.

68. Stonington, Conn., *Impartial Journal,* Oct. 15, 1799.

69. New London, Conn., *Bee,* Aug. 27, 1800.

70. Muzzey, *Jefferson,* 182.

71. Boston *Constitutional Telegraphe,* cited in the New London, Conn., *Bee,* Jan. 15, 1800. This exaggeration was perhaps not a great one; the (Federalist) Castine, [Me.], *Castine Journal,* Jan. 14, 1800, noted this claim and also one that a rapid spread of Republican principles had resulted.

72. Of the papers noted in the Appendix (which is nearly complete, and lists all those personally examined by the writer), 231 existed in the fall of 1800. Of these, 67 were adjudged Republican, 49 decidedly so. Forty were doubtful or impartial; of the 124 remaining, only 74 could be clearly classed as "decidedly" Federalist. In this writer's estimate, 74 to 49 comes fairly close to truly portraying the comparative newspaper strength of the two parties at this time. Infallibility is not claimed in classifying these gazettes; frequently party affiliation was difficult or impossible to determine from the issues actually examined. Of the 512 papers personally consulted, however, the writer classified 123 as

impartial or doubtful, 260 as Federalist (139 unquestionably so), and 129 as Republican. Seventy-two of the latter were decidedly Jeffersonian, and 57 independently Democratic. See Appendix, *infra,* for bibliographical comment on these papers.

73. Cf. notes 65 and 72, *supra;* Brigham, *Bibliography,* I, II, *passim.*

74. E.g., North, *Newspapers and Periodical Press,* 31, states the neutral and colorless journal "virtually disappeared" in this period; Tebbel, *Compact History,* 75, says "the press was entirely in the hands of politicians." Cf. Mott, *American Journalism,* 168–69.

75. E.g., the *Boston Gazette,* June 4, 1792; Chambersburg, Pa., *Farmers' Register,* June 27, 1798; Smith, *Freedom's Fetters,* 360n. (on Haswell's *Vermont Gazette)* ; New London, Conn., *Bee,* Apr. 18, 1798; Richmond *Virginia Argus,* Sept. 9, 1800 (suggesting a small fixed sum be paid *all* gazettes publishing federal laws).

76. Boston *Independent Chronicle,* July 13, 1797 (on the *Columbian Centinel)* ; Philadelphia *Aurora,* Sept. 18, 1797 (concerning the Boston *Mercury)* ; cf. the Philadelphia *Porcupine's Gazette,* June 7, 1798.

77. Much of this seems to have been taken for granted; Carey and Cobbett were said to have later become good friends. See Mott, *A History of American Magazines,* I, 159–60.

78. Philadelphia *Porcupine's Gazette,* Mar. 4, 1797 (cited in Jones, *Journalism in the United States,* 165.)

79. Woodbury, *Public Opinion,* 7; e.g., "FACT," "CIVIS," and "AMICUS," in the Philadelphia *National Gazette,* Sept. 12, 1792. See note 30 above.

80. Lexington *Kentucky Gazette,* July 9, 1796; Reuben Gold Thwaites, "The Ohio Valley Press before the War of 1812–15," *Proceedings of the American Antiquarian Society* 19 (Apr., 1909), 311, 315–16; Payne, *History of Journalism,* 203.

81. Boston *Independent Chronicle,* July 26, Oct. 11, 1798; Frank W. Scott, "Newspapers, 1775–1860," in William P. Trent, *et al.* (eds.), *The Cambridge History of American Literature,* I, 249. Ternant, who preceded Genêt, regularly sent the Philadelphia *General Advertiser* and *National Gazette* to the French government. For sample criticisms of partisanship see the Georgetown, D. C., *Times,* Apr. 6, 1791; Newark *Centinel of Freedom,* Sept. 17, 1799; Philadelphia *Poulson's American Daily Advertiser,* Oct. 1, 10, 1800.

82. Hartford, Conn., *Hartford Gazette,* Jan. 13, 1794; Savannah, Ga., *Columbian Museum,* Mar. 11, 1796, May 16, 1797; Washington, Ky., *Mirror,* June 2, 1798; New York *Columbian Gazette,* May 11, 1799; Frankfort, Ky., *Palladium,* Feb. 12, 1799 ("BY PARTICULAR

DESIRE"); Wilmington, Del., *Mirror of the Times,* Dec. 7 ("A MODERATE"), 1799; Pittsfield, Mass., *Sun,* Sept. 23, 1800.

83. Malcolm M. Willey, "The Functions of the Newspapers," *Annals of the American Academy,* 219 (Jan., 1942), 19.

84. E.g., Morison, *Otis,* I, 46, fixes March, 1790 (when Jefferson assumed office as Secretary of State) as the beginning of the two national parties. Nathan Schachner, *Thomas Jefferson: A Biography,* I, 436, notes Jefferson was regarded as "the head of a party" in 1791.

85. Charles, *Origins,* 80–85; Chambers, *Political Parties,* 59–60; Cunningham, *Jeffersonian Republicans,* esp. 86–87, talks of "Madison's Party"; Malone, *TJ,* III, 180–93, 273.

86. Bowers, *Jefferson and Hamilton,* 79–82, tells of the trip to New York and New England, though he minimizes its importance in the actual formation of the party. Cf. Schachner, *Jefferson,* I, 437–38; Wilfred E. Binkley, *American Political Parties,* 78; Cunningham, *Jeffersonian Republicans,* 11–12.

87. Baltimore *Maryland Journal,* Mar. 22, 1791; Philadelphia *National Gazette* (citing the Boston *Independent Chronicle*), Sept. 22, 1792.

88. Philadelphia *National Gazette,* Mar. 6, 1793; see Chap. 10.

89. Philadelphia *General Advertiser,* Jan. 6, 1794; Halifax *North Carolina Journal,* Jan. 29, 1794 (the quotation is "from a late Philadelphia paper"), Augusta, Ga., *Southern Centinel,* Feb. 6, 1794.

90. E.g., see Bergh, ed., *Writings of Thomas Jefferson,* IX, 340; X, 56, 172–73.

91. Lexington *Stewart's Kentucky Herald,* Dec. 1, 1795.

92. E.g., the Boston *Independent Chronicle,* Aug. 18, Sept. 8, 1800; Washington, D. C., Nov. 12, 1800.

93. Wishing to avoid any risk of Pinckney's gaining the Presidency over Adams, some suspicious Rhode Islander voted for Jay; Chambers, *Political Parties,* 161.

94. Chambers, *Political Parties,* 165–68; Cunningham, *Jeffersonian Republicans,* 239–45; Miller, *Federalist Era,* 268–73; van der Linden, *Turning Point,* 246–313; Schachner, *Jefferson,* II, 656–58.

95. Brooklyn, N. Y., *Long Island Courier,* Jan. 28, 1801.

96. Edward Stanwood, *A History of the Presidency,* 57, 63; Schachner, *Jefferson,* II, 679; Edward Channing, *A History of the United States,* IV, 211n.; Cunningham, *Jeffersonian Republicans,* 247–48.

97. Thomas Jefferson to Edward Carrington, Jan. 16, 1797; Bergh, ed., *Writings of Thomas Jefferson,* VI, 57–58.

98. Philadelphia *National Gazette,* Apr. 6, 1793 ("Cato," from the Richmond[?] *Virginia Gazette*).

99. Peacham, Vt., *Green Mountain Patriot,* Feb. 17, 1801. See also the Harrisburg, Pa., *Oracle of Dauphin* ("A. V."), Feb. 3, 1794; Boston *Independent Chronicle,* July 30, 1798; Lancaster, Pa., *Intelligencer* ("NEWSPAPERS *The Enemies of Despotism*"), Mar. 26, 1800.

100. Mott, *History of American Magazines,* I, 160. The Philadelphia *Gazette of the United States,* Mar. 4, 1799, stated that papers accounted for nine-tenths of America's reading matter. Brown's quotation is from the *Monthly Magazine,* I (1799), 13–14.

101. It was noted most Americans took the newspaper of their locality; in 1791 J. P. Brissot and J. E. Bonnet felt such journals served as a good guide to public opinion and explained widespread popular interest in politics. See Scott, "Newspapers," 247–49, 253–54; François La Rochefoucauld-Liancourt, *Travels through the United States of North America,* II, 666.

102. Scott, "Newspapers," 248; irrespective of quality, the *quantity* of such "invectives" was stupendous, said "CANDIDUS" [Jacques Brissot de Warville?], "On American Literature," *Monthly Magazine and American Review,* I (1799), 342.

103. "FRANCISCO," "Parallel between New-England and Great-Britain," *Monthly Magazine and American Review,* I (1799), 13–14.

104. See Chap. 1; Carl Bridenbaugh, *Rebels and Gentlemen,* 76.

105. Philadelphia *Aurora,* Sept. 11, 1799 (italics added). See also *ibid.,* May 16, 1799; Freneau, *Letters,* 43, 128.

106. "FRANCISCO," *Monthly Magazine,* I, 13–14.

107. Bleyer, *Main Currents,* 123–24; La Rochefoucauld, *Travels,* II, 666, noted that despite their numbers, the supply of newspapers still fell short of the demand. The quotation, by the owner of an early Kentucky paper, is from Lawrence C. Wroth, "The First Press in Providence," *Proceedings of the American Antiquarian Society,* 51 (new series) [Oct. 1941], 354.

108. Richmond *Virginia Argus,* Jan. 21, 1800. The cheapness of the projected paper was stressed, and Republican printers were asked to print Lyon's announcement free of charge.

109. North, *Newspaper and Periodical Press,* 31 (citing Hildreth); Scott, "Newspapers," 247, 251.

110. Jane Louise Mesick, *The English Traveller in America, 1785–1835,* 227–28.

111. Wroth, "First Press," 365–68, gives the Cincinnati, [Ohio], *Western Spy,* Dec. 24, 1799, as an illustration of editorially answering

correspondents' letters; Preserved Smith, *History of Modern Culture*, II, 279–80 (cited in Helen O. Mahin, *The Development and Significance of the Newspaper Headline*, 10.)

112. Chambers, *Political Parties*, 124, 164; Edgar E. Robinson, *The Evolution of American Political Parties*, 65, gives much of the credit to the Democratic Societies.

113. Bridenbaugh, *Rebels and Gentlemen*, 76; Woodbury, *Public Opinion*, 7; Thomas Jefferson to Archibald Stuart, May 14, 1799 (Ford, ed., *The Writings of Thomas Jefferson*, VII, 378).

114. Faÿ, *Two Franklins*, esp. 336, 338.

115. Forman, "Political Activities," 38, 76–77, 102; Payne, *History of Journalism*, 152, 163; Leary, *That Rascal Freneau*, 220–21 (quoting the *Letters of John Adams*, II, 119); Smith, *John Adams*, II, 1053.

116. Channing, *History of the U. S.*, IV, 165; Jefferson to Elbridge Gerry, May 13, 1797 (quoted in Austin, *Gerry*, II, 140); Marsh, "Philip Freneau and His Circle," 56; Bushey, "William Duane," 156; Mott, *Jefferson and the Press*, 47.

117. *Letters of John Adams, Addressed to His Wife* (C. F. Adams, ed.), II, 134 (cited in Leary, *That Rascal Freneau*, 220); Faÿ, *Two Franklins*, 359–61; Faÿ, "Bache," 295, 304; Woodbury, *Public Opinion*, 29 ff.

118. Clark, *Duane*, 7; Bushey, "William Duane," 151, 156; Mott, *American Journalism*, 129; McMaster, *A History*, II, 439. Woodbury, *Public Opinion*, 27, more conservatively calls him "one of the chief factors" in discrediting Adams' administration.

119. Charles Pinckney to Jefferson, Oct. 12, 1800, *American Historical Review*, 4 (1898), 114 (quoted in Beard, *Jeffersonian Democracy*, 376, and Cunningham, *Jeffersonian Republicans*, 188).

120. Chambers, *Political Parties*, 152; Faÿ, *Notes* . . . , 14; Beard, *Jeffersonian Democracy*, 198n.; Mott, *Jefferson and the Press*, 37. Jones, *Journalism in the United States*, 178, comments on the falsehoods in the press.

121. E.g., the Savannah, Ga., *Columbian Museum*, Sept. 28, Oct. 2, 1798; Faÿ, *Two Franklins*, 360.

122. Mott, *Jefferson and the Press*, 3, 5, 15–16. Jefferson wrote Thomas Mann Randolph, May 12, 1791, about efforts to persuade Freneau to start a paper, and commenting on Bache's improved *General Advertiser*. He wanted Bache to print all his advertisements on one sheet, so the news page could be mailed cheaply, "& be as generally taken instead of Fenno's"; Jefferson, *Writings* (Ford, ed.), V, 336–37. On Nov. 2, 1793, he wrote Randolph of the need to revive the *National Gazette; ibid.*, VI 438.

123. Bennington *Vermont Gazette,* Jan. 30, 1798 (italics added).

124. Jefferson to James Madison, Feb. 5, 1799; Jefferson, *Writings* (Lipscomb, ed.), X, 96 (upper case letters mine).

125. From "The Prospect Before Us," Richmond, Va., *Examiner,* Jan. 17, 1800.

126. Nichols, *Invention,* 207.

127. E.g., the Morristown, N. J., *Genius of Liberty,* July 17, 1800 (toasts at Stanhope, N. J.); New York *American Citizen,* Nov. 3, 1800; Baltimore *American,* Nov. 7, 1800; Newport, R. I., *Guardian of Liberty* (celebrating Jefferson's inaugural), Mar. 7, 1801; Elizabethtown, N. J., *New Jersey Journal,* Mar. 17, 1801.

128. Wilmington, Del., *Mirror of the Times,* Dec. 31, 1800.

129. Quoted in the Halifax *North Carolina Journal,* Sept. 13, 1802.

130. Mott, *Jefferson and the Press,* 47–50.

131. Jefferson to William Wirt, Mar. 30, 1811; Jefferson, *Writings* (Ford, ed.), IX, 316–17.

132. Jefferson to James Monroe, Oct. 19, 1823; *ibid.* (Ford, ed.), X, 275.

133. Edmond Genêt to Thomas Jefferson, July 4, 1797 (cited in Woodfin, "Citizen Genêt," 548).

134. Fenno's *Gazette of the United States,* Webster's *American Minerva,* and Cobbett's *Porcupine's Gazette;* Frank L. Mott and Ralph D. Casey, *Interpretations of Journalism,* 420–21.

135. Ames to Oliver Wolcott, July 9, 1795; A. E. Morse, *Federalist Party in Massachusetts,* 130n

136. McMaster, *A History,* II, 253; Washington, D. C., *Washington Gazette,* Feb. 4, 1797. Cobbett blamed the Democratic press for the Whiskey Rebellion, agitation against Britain and Jay's Treaty, and paving the way for French outrages.

137. Litchfield, Conn., *Monitor,* Mar. 20, 1799; Fisher Ames to Timothy Pickering, Nov. 5, 1799 (in Ames, ed., *Works,* I, 264–65; see also pp. 269, 274–76, 290, for other letters indicating Ames's awareness of the importance of newspapers and their part in the developing opposition to Adams).

138. Reprinted in the Vergennes, Vt., *Vergennes Gazette,* June 20, 1799; cf. (earlier) the Wilmington *Delaware and Eastern Shore Advertiser* ("Real Friend of his Country"), Nov. 7, 1795. The *Argus, Aurora* and *Independent Chronicle* were most frequently mentioned as this type of paper; Boston *Federal Gazette,* Jan. 16, 1798; Hartford *Connecticut Courant,* Mar. 31, 1800. The Portsmouth, N. H., *Oracle of the Day,* June 22, 1799, noted the *Bee* as well; the Danbury, Conn.,

*Farmers Journal*, July 2, 1800, listed "Cooper, Duane and Callander" [*sic*] as the great sources "of political calumny."

139. Hartford *Connecticut Courant*, Mar. 31, 1800 (item from the Litchfield, Conn., *Monitor*).

140. Portsmouth, N. H., *Federal Observer*, May 16, Oct. 17, 1799.

141. Portsmouth, N. H., *United States Oracle*, Mar. 22, 1800.

142. Hartford *Connecticut Courant*, Aug. 18 (from the Litchfield, Conn., *Monitor*), Sept. 1 (from the Trenton, N. J., *Federalist*), 1800.

143. Hartford *Connecticut Courant*, July 21 ("Burleigh," No. IV), Aug. 18 ("Burleigh," No. VIII, source of the lengthy quotation. The last set of italics is added), 1800; Baltimore *Federal Gazette*, Aug. 29, 1800.

144. New London, Conn., *Bee* (from the Hartford, Conn., *American Mercury*), Oct. 29, 1800.

145. Ames, ed., *Works of Fisher Ames*, II, 116. See also *ibid.*, 120, 126; and the letter of George Cabot to Alexander Hamilton, Oct. 11, 1800 (cited in Goddard, *Newspapers*, 20).

146. Savannah, Ga., *Columbian Museum* (from the Georgetown, D. C., *Washington Federalist*), Feb. 24, 1801. The names of the horses, of course, represented Adams, Pinckney, Jefferson, and Burr.

147. Duane, Haswell, Holt, Thomas Adams [of the *Independent Chronicle*], David Denniston [*American Citizen*], Samuel Parker [*Constitutional Telegraphe*], Ebenezer Rhoades [who took over the *Independent Chronicle*], and Elisha Babcock [*American Mercury*] were named. Hartford *Connecticut Courant*, Jan. 5, 1801; Savannah, Ga., *Columbian Museum*, Feb. 10, 1801.

148. Georgetown, D. C., *Washington Federalist*, Dec. 19, 1800; Portsmouth, N. H., *United States Oracle* ("Leonidas," from the Boston *Columbian Centinel*), Jan. 17, 1801.

149. Hanover, N. H., *Dartmouth Gazette* (quoting the New York *Spectator*), Feb. 7, 1801; Boston *New England Palladium*, June 9, 1801 (cited in Robinson, *Jeffersonian Democracy in New England*, 69–70); Muzzey, *Thomas Jefferson*, 162.

150. Hanover, N. H., *Dartmouth Gazette* (from the Boston *New England Palladium*), Feb. 7, 1801.

151. Alexandria, Va., *Alexandria Advertiser*, Mar. 20, 1801.

152. John Adams to Benjamin Stoddert, Mar. 31, 1801; Adams, *Works*, IX, 582. Cf. Scott, "Newspapers," 181, and Chinard, *Honest John Adams*, 317. Adams found Jefferson's pardon of Callender, vilest of the slanderers, almost unforgivable (Chinard, *John Adams*, 321); for

remarks on Duane, see a letter to Thomas B. Adams, Sept. 15, 1801 (cited in Smith, *John Adams,* II, 1071).

153. John Adams to Mercy Otis Warren, July 20, Aug. 15, 1807 (cited in Smith, *John Adams,* II, 1068, 1088); John Adams to Skelton Jones, Mar. 11, 1809 (Adams, *Works,* IX, 612). The writings of Cobbett and Hamilton, and the widely republished circular letters from congressmen, also contributed (he felt) to his downfall.

154. C. F. Adams, ed., *Works of John Adams,* X, 48.

155. John Adams to James Lloyd, Feb. 6, 1815; *ibid.,* X, 118.

156. Fisher Ames to Theodore Dwight, Mar. 19, 1801; Ames, *Works of Fisher Ames,* I, 294–95 (also cited in Goddard, *Newspapers,* 21).

157. Significantly, a similar conclusion has been reached as to the role of the press during the Revolutionary era in Wroth, "First Press," 383, and Schlesinger, *Prelude to Independence,* 281, 284–85.

# APPENDIX

# Annotated List of Newspapers

## KEY TO ABBREVIATIONS FOR LIBRARIES CONSULTED

The writer wishes to acknowledge his indebtedness to the personnel of the libraries listed below for their generous help and the use of those library facilities in connection with the research for this study. The abbreviations serve as a guide to identify the newspaper files actually examined.

| | |
|---|---|
| A.A.S. | American Antiquarian Society, Worcester, Massachusetts. |
| B.A. | Boston Athenaeum, Boston, Massachusetts. |
| B.P.L. | Boston Public Library, Boston, Massachusetts. |
| C.C.L. | Charleston College Library, Charleston, South Carolina. |
| C.L. | Carnegie Museum Library, Pittsburgh, Pennsylvania. |
| C.L.S. | Charleston Library Society, Charleston, South Carolina. |
| C.U. | Columbia University Library, New York, New York. |
| Conn.H.S. | Connecticut Historical Society, Hartford, Connecticut. |
| Conn.S.L. | Connecticut State Library, Hartford, Connecticut. |
| D.C. | Dartmouth College Library, Hanover, New Hampshire. |
| D.M.P.L. | Des Moines Public Library, Des Moines, Iowa. |
| D.U. | Duke University Library, Durham, North Carolina. |
| Dr.U. | Drake University Library, Des Moines, Iowa. |
| Ga.H.S. | Georgia Historical Society, Savannah, Georgia. |
| H.L. | Handley Library, Winchester, Virginia. |
| H.U. | Harvard University Library, Cambridge, Massachusetts. |
| Hu.L. | Huntington Library, San Marino, California. |
| J.C.B. | John Carter Brown Library, Providence, Rhode Island. |
| K.P.L. | Lawson-McGhee Library (Knoxville Public Library), Knoxville, Tennessee. |
| L.C. | Library of Congress, Washington, D. C. |

L.I.H.S.   Long Island Historical Society, Brooklyn, New York.
L.P.L.   Lexington Public Library, Lexington, Kentucky.
M.H.S.   Massachusetts Historical Society, Boston, Massachusetts.
Md.H.S.   Maryland Historical Society, Baltimore, Maryland.
N.C.H.C.   North Carolina Historical Commission, Raleigh, North Carolina.
N.C.S.L.   North Carolina State Library, Raleigh, North Carolina.
N.H.H.S.   New Hampshire Historical Society, Concord, New Hampshire.
N.J.H.S.   New Jersey Historical Society, Newark, New Jersey.
N.L.H.S.   New London County Historical Society, New London, Connecticut.
N.Y.H.S.   New York Historical Society, New York, New York.
N.Y.P.L.   New York Public Library, New York, New York.
P.L.   Peabody Institute Library, Baltimore, Maryland.
P.L.C.   Philadelphia Library Company (Ridgeway Branch), Philadelphia, Pennsylvania.
Pa.H.S.   Historical Society of Pennsylvania, Philadelphia, Pennsylvania.
U.of C.   University of Chicago Library, Chicago, Illinois.
U.C.L.A.   University of California at Los Angeles Library, Los Angeles, California.
U.Ga.   University of Georgia Library, Athens, Georgia.
U.N.C.   University of North Carolina Library, Chapel Hill, North Carolina.
U.P.   University of Pittsburgh Library, Pittsburgh, Pennsylvania.
U.W.   University of Wisconsin Library, Madison, Wisconsin.
Va.S.L.   Virginia State Library, Richmond, Virgina.
Vt.S.L.   Vermont State Library, Montpelier, Vermont.
W.&L.   Washington and Lee Library, Lexington, Virginia.
W.L.   Watkinson Library, Hartford, Connecticut.
W.H.S.   Wisconsin Historical Society, Madison, Wisconsin.


NEWSPAPERS (arranged alphabetically by state and place of publication).

The entire name of the paper (such as *"Fairfield Gazette, and Independent Intelligencer"*) is not given if it can be clearly identified without the subtitle, as the latter parts of these names were frequently changed by those papers which used them. Occasional variations in the spelling of names are not noted if the paper can be easily distinguished without them; the text, however, follows the spelling for the particular issue in question. Inasmuch as full details as to publishers and changes in subtitles are available in Clarence S. Brigham, *History and Bibliography of American Newspapers* (Worcester, Mass.: American Antiquarian Society, 1947), vols. I and II, that information is normally not repeated here.

Unless otherwise indicated, papers are weeklies. An asterisk (*) denotes that every known extant issue of that particular paper was examined. On the basis of copies consulted, the present writer has attempted to classify the political leanings of the various newspapers. Abbreviations at the end of the brief descriptions signify the libraries in which he consulted issues of the paper concerned for the years given.

### CONNECTICUT

Bridgeport, *American Telegraphe,* 1800.* A continuation of the paper of the same name published at Newfield, which was incorporated as Bridgeport in Oct., 1800. Independently Federalist. Conn.S.L.

Danbury, *Farmers Chronicle,* 1793–1796. Doubtful, perhaps gradually growing more Federalist. H.U., L.C., P.L.C.

Danbury, *Farmer's Journal,* 1790–1793. By Nathan Douglas and Edwards Ely. Almost no politics; doubtful. A.A.S., L.C., H.U.

Danbury, *Farmers Journal,* July 2, 1800. By Stiles Nichols. This issue seems Federalist. Conn.H.S.

Danbury, *Republican Journal,* 1793.* By Nathan Douglàs. The few extant issues are doubtful; perhaps independently Democratic. A.A.S.

Danbury, *Republican Journal,* 1796–1800. By Nathan Douglas and Stiles Nichols. New numbering; distinct from the paper published three years earlier. Appears mildly Federalist in 1796–1797, but should be classed as doubtful; little politics. A.A.S., H.U.

Danbury, *Sun of Liberty,* Aug. 13, Oct. 8, 1800. Democratic. A.A.S.

Fairfield, *Fairfield Gazette,* Feb. 25, June 17, Sept. 23, 1789. Little politics; impartial. A.A.S.

Hartford, *American Mercury,* 1787–1799. Democratic, though somewhat independently so at times. A.A.S., H.U.

Hartford, *Connecticut Courant,* 1794–1795, 1799–1801. Federalist. A.A.S., Conn. H.S.

Hartford, *Hartford Gazette,* 1794–1795. Semi-weekly. Probably independently Federalist; certainly not strongly so. L.C., W.L.

Hartford, *New Star,* Feb. 2, 1796.* Doubtful, since this single issue gives no clue as to the political leaning of the paper. A.A.S.

Litchfield, *Farmer's Monitor,* 1800. A continuation of the *Litchfield Monitor.* Federalist. H.U.

Litchfield, *Litchfield Monitor,* 1798–1800. Federalist. Conn.H.S., H.U., L.C.

Middletown, *Middlesex Gazette,* 1787–1788, 1793–1801. Federalist. A.A.S., H.U.

New Haven, *Connecticut Journal,* 1789–1800. Independently Federalist, gradually growing more partisan in the latter part of this period. L.C.

New Haven, *Federal Gazetteer,* Feb. 22, 1797. No indication of partisanship from this issue. H.U.

New Haven, *Messenger,* 1800–1801. Little politics, but seems Independently Federalist. H.U.

New Haven, *New Haven Gazette,* 1791. Doubtful; not much politics, possibly leans Federalist. A.A.S.

New London, *Bee,* 1797–1801. Strongly Democratic. N.Y.H.S., A.A.S.

New London, *Connecticut Gazette,* 1791, 1794–1795, 1797–1801. Federalist. H.U.

New London, *New London Advertiser,* 1795. No indication as to political leaning. H.U., L.C.

New London, *Weekly Oracle,* 1797–1801. Appears Federalist. H.U.

Newfield, *American Telegraphe,* 1795–1798. Independently Federalist, H.U., L.C.

Norwalk, *Sun of Liberty,* Nov. 18, 25, 1800, Mar. 10, 1801. A continuation of the Danbury *Sun of Liberty,* Democratic. N.Y.H.S., L.I.H.S.

Norwich, *Chelsea Courier,* 1796–1798. Doubtful; perhaps independently Federalist. H.U.

Norwich, *Courier,* 1798–1801. A continuation of the above paper. Seems mildly Federalist in 1799, but rather impartial in the last half of 1800; apparently tried to present both sides. H.U.

Norwich, *Norwich Packet,* 1792–1798, 1800. Seems impartial, or perhaps even mildly Democratic, until 1794; Federalist, though not bitterly so, after the later part of that year. L.C., H.U.

Norwich, *Weekly Register,* 1792–1795. Seems to be impartial, or perhaps independently Democratic. H.U., L.C., N.Y.H.S.

Sharon, *Rural Gazette,* 1800–1801. Federalist. H.U., Conn.H.S.

Stonington, *Impartial Journal,* 1799–1800. A continuation of the *Journal of the Times.* Probably independently Democratic. A.A.S., Conn. H.S., H.U.

Stonington, *Journal of the Times,* 1798–1799. Probably independently Democratic. Conn.H.S., H.U.

Suffield, *Impartial Herald,* 1797–1799. Federalist; later independent. H.U.

Windham, *Phenix; or Windham Herald,* 1797–1798. Seems independently Federalist. H.U.

Windham, *Windham Herald,* 1798–1799. A continuation of the *Phenix;* or *Windham Herald.* The few issues consulted appear to lean Federalist. H.U.

Dover, *Friend of the People,* Sept. 28, 1799. Semi-weekly. Political leaning of the paper is doubtful from this lone issue; perhaps independently Federalist. H.U.

Wilmington, *Delaware and Eastern-Shore Advertiser,* 1794–1799. Semi-weekly. Independently Federalist, mildly so at first. L.C., H.U., Phila.L.C., A.A.S.

Wilmington, *Delaware Gazette,* 1787–1793, 1795–1799. Weekly, semi-weekly, and tri-weekly. Political character of the paper varied; claimed impartiality, but in the main seems to lean Democratic. L.C., A.A.S., H.U., Phila.L.C.

Wilmington, *Mirror of the Times,* 1800–1801. Semi-weekly. Democratic. H.U.

Wilmington, *Monitor,* 1800. Weekly and semi-weekly. Federalist. H.U.

Georgetown, *Cabinet,* Dec. 30, 1800; Feb. 4, Mar. 4, 1801. Daily. Democratic. A.A.S.

Georgetown, *Centinel, and Country Gazette,* 1797–1798. A country edition of the *Centinel of Liberty.* Probably impartial. A.A.S., H.U.

Georgetown, *Centinel of Liberty,* 1796–1800. Semi-weekly. Claimed impartiality, and seems nearly impartial; perhaps a slight leaning toward the Federalists. Phila. L.C., H.U., A.A.S., L.C.

Georgetown, *Columbian Chronicle,* 1795–1796. Semi-weekly. Independently Federalist. H.U.

Georgetown, *Museum,* 1800. Daily, for a time. Really a continuation of the *Centinel of Liberty.* Doubtful; may have leaned slightly Federalist. L.C.

Georgetown, *Times, and Patowmack Packet,* 1789–1791. Doubtful; perhaps mildly Federalist. L.C.

Georgetown, *Washington Federalist,* 1800. Daily (during sessions of Congress) and tri-weekly. Federalist. L.C.

Georgetown, *Georgetown Weekly Ledger,* 1790–1793. Doubtful. H.U., A.A.S.

Washington, *Advertiser,* 1796. Semi-weekly. Doubtful; rather impartial. H.U., A.A.S.

Washington, *Advertiser,* Nov. 20, 1800. Daily. Federalist. A.A.S.

Washington, *Washington Gazette,* 1796–1798. Semi-weekly and weekly. Professed impartiality, but seems mildly Democratic. A.A.S., L.C.

Washington, *Impartial Observer, and Washington Advertiser,* 1795. Doubtful; material from both sides, possibly a bit more from the Democratic viewpoint. H.U., L.C.

Washington, *National Intelligencer,* 1800. Tri-weekly. Democratic. L.C.

Washington, *Universal Gazette,* 1800. A continuation of the Philadelphia paper of the same name and virtually a weekly edition of the *National Intelligencer.* Not as partisan as the *National Intelligencer,* but leans toward the Democratic party. L.C.

GEORGIA

Augusta, *Augusta Chronicle,* 1790–1800. Weekly, semi-weekly, and tri-weekly. Seems impartial, though it was referred to as "Jacobin." Ga.H.S.

Augusta, *Augusta Herald,* 1799–1801. Weekly and semi-weekly. Federalist. U.Ga.

Augusta, *Southern Centinel,* 1793–1799. Impartial at first; gradually gets more Federalist. L.C., Ga.H.S.

Louisville, *State Gazette and Louisville Journal,* 1799. Little politics, but seems mildly Federalist. U.Ga.

Savannah, *Columbian Museum,* 1796–1801. Semi-weekly. Independent at first, gradually becoming mildly Federalist. Ga.Hist.Soc.

Savannah, *Georgia Gazette,* 1789–1801. Little politics, but seems to lean Federalist. Ga.H.S.

Savannah, *Georgia Journal,* 1793–1794. Semi-weekly. Appears mildly Democratic, though far more concerned with foreign news. Ga.H.S.

KENTUCKY

Frankfort, *Guardian of Freedom,* 1798–1799. Really a Frankfort edition of the *Kentucky Gazette,* established in an attempt to secure the public printing. Independently Democratic. U. of C., L.C.

Frankfort, *Kentucky Journal,* Dec. 5, 1795.* This single issue has only non-political news. P.L.C.

Frankfort, *Palladium,* 1798–1801. Democratic. U.of C.

Lexington, *Kentucky Gazette,* 1793–1799. Weekly and semi-weekly. Democratic. H.U., U.of C.

Lexington (later Paris), *Stewart's Kentucky Herald,* 1795–1799. Democratic. U.of C., L.C.

Paris, *Rights of Man,* 1797–1798.\* Doubtful; perhaps impartial. H.U.
Washington, *Mirror,* 1797–1799. Democratic. U. of C., L.C.

MAINE (then part of Massachusetts)

Augusta, *Kennebec Gazette,* 1800. A continuation of the *Kennebeck Intelligencer.* Federalist. H.U.
Augusta, *Kennebeck Intelligencer,* 1797–1798. Federalist. H.U.
Castine, *Castine Journal,* 1799–1800. Federalist. H.U., L.C.
Fryeburg, *Russel's Echo,* 1798–1799. Appears to be Federalist. H.U.
Hallowell, *Eastern Star,* 1795. (Hallowell was the early name for Augusta.) Seems impartial, with material from both sides. H.U., W.H.S.
Hallowell, *Tocsin,* 1795–1797. Independently Federalist. H.U., L.C.
Portland, *Cumberland Gazette,* 1787–1788, 1790–1791. Doubtful; probably leaned Federalist. N.Y.H.S., A.A.S.
Portland, *Eastern Herald,* 1792, 1795, 1797, 1799–1800. Not a lot of politics, but after being sold by Thomas Wait it came to be Federalist. H.U., B.A.
Portland, *Gazette,* also known as *Jenk's Portland Gazette,* 1798–1799. Federalist. P.L.C., M.H.S.
Portland, *Gazette of Maine,* 1790, 1793, 1795–1796. Seems Federalist, though not a lot of politics. H.U., N.Y.H.S., P.L.C., A.A.S.
Portland, *Oriental Trumpet,* 1797–1800. Federalist. N.Y.H.S., H.U.
Wiscasset, *Wiscasset Argus,* 1797 (Dec. 30)–1798 (Jan. 6, 13).\* Political leaning not apparent. A.A.S., H.U.
Wiscasset, *Wiscasset Telegraph,* 1797–1798. Federalist; mildly so at first, but increasing in partisanship during 1798. H.U.

MARYLAND

Annapolis, *Maryland Gazette,* 1787, 1790–1793, 1795–1799. Not much political news; independently Federalist. H.U., L.C., Md.H.S.
Baltimore, *American,* 1799–1801. Daily. Decidedly Democratic. Md.H.S.
Baltimore, *Baltimore Daily Intelligencer,* 1793. Daily. Impartial; perhaps leaning Democratic. L.C.
Baltimore, *Baltimore Evening Post,* 1792, 1793. Daily. Later became *Edward's Baltimore Daily Advertiser.* Doubtful; perhaps independently Democratic. P.L.C.
Baltimore, *Baltimore Intelligencer,* 1798, 1799. Tri-weekly. Independently Democratic. Md.H.S., H.U.

Baltimore, *Baltimore Telegraphe,* 1795–1801. Daily. Gradually became independently Democratic. Md.H.S., P.L., H.U., A.A.S.

Baltimore, *City Gazette,* 1797.* Daily. A continuation of the *Baltimore Telegraphe;* name later changed back again. Very little politics; apparently tried to be impartial. A.A.S., H.U.

Baltimore, *Daily Repository,* 1792, 1793. Daily. Rather doubtful; possibly independent Federalist. L.C.

Baltimore, *Eagle of Freedom,* 1796.* Tri-weekly. No indication of political affiliation. P.L.C.

Baltimore, *Edward's Baltimore Daily Advertiser,* 1793, 1794. Daily. Independently Democratic. Md.H.S.

Baltimore, *Federal Gazette and Baltimore Daily Advertiser,* 1796, 1798, 1800. Daily. A continuation of the *Federal Intelligencer.* Professed impartiality, but seems independently Federalist. H.U., L.C., Md.H.S.

Baltimore, *Federal Intelligencer,* 1794, 1795. Daily. A continuation of the *Baltimore Daily Intelligencer.* Doubtful; perhaps leaning slightly Federalist. L.C., Md.H.S.

Baltimore, *Fell's-Point Telegraphe,* 1795. Tri-weekly. Seems impartial. A.A.S., H.U.

Baltimore, *Maryland Gazette; or the Baltimore Advertiser,* 1790, 1791. Doubtful; perhaps independently Federalist. Md.H.S.

Baltimore, *Maryland Journal,* 1787, 1790–1793, 1795–1797. Weekly, semi-weekly, tri-weekly, daily. Independently Federalist. A.A.S., H.U., Md.H.S.

Baltimore, *Sunday Monitor,* Dec. 18, 1796.* Impartial. Md.H.S.

Baltimore, *Weekly Museum,* 1797.* Doubtful. H.U.

Chestertown, *Apollo,* 1793. Semi-weekly. Apparently independently Democratic. A.A.S., H.U.

Easton, *Maryland Herald and Eastern Shore Intelligencer,* 1791–1794, 1796, 1798–1801. Independently Federalist. H.U., L.C., Md.H.S.

Easton, *Republican Star,* 1800. Democratic. L.C.

Elizabethtown, *Maryland Herald,* 1797–1801. Doubtful; perhaps leans slightly Federalist. Md.H.S.

Elizabethtown, *Washington Spy,* 1790–1797. Doubtful; gradually became mildly Federalist. Md.H.S.

Fredericktown, *Bartgis's Federal Gazette,* 1792–1796, 1798–1800. Came to be independently Democratic. H.U., L.C., Md.H.S.

Fredericktown, *Maryland Gazette,* 1791. No indication as to political leaning. H.U.

Fredericktown, *Rights of Man,* 1794–1798, 1800. Appears Federalist. H.U., Md.H.S.

Boston, *American Apollo,* 1792–1794. Almost like a literary magazine; impartial. B.A., B.P.L.

Boston, *Argus,* 1791–1792. Semi-weekly and weekly. A continuation of the *Herald of Freedom.* Democratic. H.U., M.H.S.

Boston, *Boston Gazette,* 1789–1793, 1796–1798. By Benjamin Edes and son. Democratic. N.Y.P.L., H.U., L.C.

Boston, *Boston Gazette,* 1800–1801. Semi-weekly. A continuation of *Russell's Gazette;* not to be confused with Benjamin Edes' earlier *Boston Gazette.* Federalist. B.A.

Boston, *Boston Price Current and Marine Intelligencer,* 1795–1798. Weekly and semi-weekly. After June 1798, it was changed to *Russell's Gazette.* Not much politics; became Federalist. P.L.C., B.A., H.U.

Boston, *Columbian Centinel,* 1791, 1795–1796. Semi-weekly. Federalist. N.Y.H.S., H.U.

Boston, *Constitutional Telegraph,* 1799–1800. Semi-weekly. Democratic. H.U., B.P.L., B.A.

Boston, *Courier and General Advertiser,* 1795–1796. Semi-weekly. Federalist. H.U., B.P.L., B.A.

Boston, *Courier de Boston,* 1789.* French-language. No indication of partisanship. A.A.S.

Boston, *Federal Gazette,* 1798. Daily and semi-weekly. Federalist. H.U., B.A.

Boston, *Federal Orrery,* 1796. Semi-weekly. Probably Federalist. H.U.

Boston, *Herald of Freedom,* 1789–1791. Semi-weekly. Probably independently Democratic, despite professions of impartiality. H.U., A.A.S.

Boston, *Independent Chronicle,* 1789–1800. Weekly and semi-weekly. Democratic. L.C.

Boston, *Massachusetts Centinel,* 1787, 1789, 1790. Semi-weekly. Federalist. H.U., N.Y.H.S.

Boston, *Massachusetts Mercury,* 1795–1798. Tri-weekly and semi-weekly. Federalist. H.U.

Boston, *Polar Star,* 1796–1797. Daily. Doubtful, though the editor was a Democrat. B.A., N.Y.H.S.

Boston, *Russell's Gazette,* 1798–1800. Semi-weekly. A continuation of the *Boston Price Current.* Federalist. H.U., L.C.

Boston, *Saturday Evening Herald* (later the *American Herald*), 1790. Impartial. A.A.S.

Boston, *Times,* 1794.* Tri-weekly. Claimed to be non-partisan, but probably independent Federalist. N.Y.P.L., A.A.S.
Brookfield, *Moral and Political Telegraphe,* 1795–1796. A continuation of the *Worcester Intelligencer.* Independently Federalist, though not much politics. A.A.S., H.U.
Brookfield, *Political Repository,* 1798, 1800. Federalist. H.U.
Brookfield, *Worcester Intelligencer,* 1794–1795. Independently Federalist. A.A.S.
Conway, *Farmer's Register,* 1798. Federalist. A.A.S., H.U., P.L.C.
Dedham, *Columbian Minerva,* 1798–1800. A continuation of the *Minerva.* Impartial at first; became independently Democratic. B.A., H.U.
Dedham, *Minerva,* 1796–1798. Doubtful; seemed undecided. H.U.
Greenfield, *Greenfield Gazette,* 1795–1800. Federalist. H.U., W.H.S.
Greenfield, *Impartial Intelligencer,* Feb. 1, 1792. No information from this issue; perhaps Federalist. A.A.S.
Haverhill, *Guardian of Freedom,* 1793–1795. Became Democratic. A.A.S., H.U., L.C.
Haverhill, *Haverhill Federal Gazette,* 1798. Federalist. H.U., M.H.S.
Haverhill, *Impartial Herald,* 1798. Federalist. H.U., L.C.
Haverhill, *Observer,* Dec. 19, 1800. Federalist, apparently. H.U.
Leominster, *Political Focus,* 1798–1799. Apparently impartial. H.U.
Leominster, *Rural Repository,* 1795–1797. Apparently impartial. H.U.
Leominster, *Telescope,* 1800. Federalist, though not much politics. H.U.
New Bedford, *Columbian Courier,* 1798–1801. Probably Federalist. N.Y.H.S.
New Bedford, *Medley,* 1792–1799. Doubtful at first, becoming independently Federalist. H.U., N.Y.H.S.
Newburyport, *Essex Journal,* 1787, 1789–1794. Non-partisan; virtually no politics. A.A.S., H.U.
Newburyport, *Impartial Herald,* 1793–1797. Weekly and semi-weekly. Mildly Federalist. H.U., L.C
Newburyport, *Morning Star,* 1794. Seems independently Democratic. A.A.S.
Newburyport, *Newburyport Herald and Country Gazette,* 1795, 1797–1799. Semi-weekly. Independently Federalist. L.C., H.U.
Newburyport, *Political Gazette,* 1795–1797. Federalist. H.U., L.C.
Northampton, *Hampshire Gazette,* 1789–1798. Federalist. A.A.S., H.U.
Northampton, *Patriotic Gazette,* 1799–1800. Federalist. H.U.
Pittsfield, *Berkshire Chronicle,* 1788–1790. Doubtful; claimed impartiality. A.A.S.
Pittsfield, *Berkshire Gazette,* 1799–1800. Federalist. H.U.

Pittsfield, *Pittsfield Sun,* 1800–1801. Independently Democratic. N.Y.H.S.

Salem, *Impartial Register,* 1800–1801. Semi-weekly. Independently Democratic. A.A.S.

Salem, *Salem Gazette,* 1791, 1795–1796, 1799. Weekly and semiweekly. Independently Federalist. H.U.

Springfield, *Federal Spy,* 1795–1799. Little politics; perhaps Federalist. H.U.

Springfield, *Hampshire Chronicle,* 1787–1789, 1791, 1795–1796. Probably Federalist. A.A.S., H.U., W.H.S.

Stockbridge, *Western Star,* 1795–1798. Federalist. H.U.

West Springfield, *American Intelligencer,* 1795–1797. Believed to be Democratic. N.Y.P.L., H.U.

Worcester, *Independent Gazetteer,* Jan. 7, 1800. Impartial (?). H.U.

Worcester, *Massachusetts Spy,* 1791–1793, 1795–1800. Federalist, though not bitterly so. A.A.S., H.U.

MISSISSIPPI

Natchez, *Green's Impartial Observer,* 1800. Federalist. U. of C.

NEW HAMPSHIRE

Amherst, *Amherst Journal,* 1795–1796. Doubtful. D.C., H.U., N.Y.H.S.

Amherst, *Village Messenger,* 1796–1800. Federalist, though not much politics. B.P.L., H.U., N.Y.H.S.

Concord, *Concord Herald,* 1790–1794. Mildly Federalist. L.C., N.H.H.S.

Concord, *Courier of New Hampshire,* 1795, 1797–1798. A continuation of *Hough's Concord Herald.* Federalist. B.P.L., H.U.

Concord, *Mirrour,* 1792–1796, 1798–1799. Not much politics; perhaps mildly Federalist. D.C., H.U., L.C.

Concord, *New Star,* 1797. Primarily literary; doubtful in politics. H.U.

Concord, *Republican Gazetteer,* 1796–1797. Not much politics; seems independently Federalist. A.A.S.

Dover, *Phenix* (sometimes spelled *Phoenix*), 1792–1794. A continuation of the *Political Repository.* Gradually became independently Federal. A.A.S., N.H.H.S., W.H.S.

Dover, *Political Repository, or Strafford Recorder,* 1790–1791. Doubtful; probably independently Federalist. B.A., H.U.

Dover, *Sun,* 1795–1799. Independently Federalist. H.U., N.Y.H.S., P.L.C.

Exeter, *American Herald of Liberty*, 1793–1796. Federalist. B.A., N.H.H.S., N.Y.H.S.

Exeter, *Freeman's Oracle*, 1789. Probably Federalist. N.Y.H.S.

Exeter, *Lamson's Weekly Visitor*, 1795. Strove to be impartial. H.U., L.C.

Exeter, *New Hampshire Gazetteer*, 1789–1793. Independently Federalist. B.A., N.H.H.S., N.Y.H.S.

Exeter, *New Hampshire Spy*, 1796–1797. Federalist. A.A.S., N.H.H.S.

Exeter, *Ranlet's Federal Miscellany*, 1799. Had several changes of title. Federalist. L.C., N.Y.H.S.

Gilmanton, *Gilmanton Gazette*, Dec. 13, 1800. Seems Federalist. L.C.

Gilmanton, *Gilmanton Rural Museum*, 1799–1800. Federalist. H.U., N.Y.H.S.

Hanover, *Dartmouth Gazette*, 1799–1801. Federalist. D.C., H.U.

Hanover, *Eagle, or Darthmouth Centinel*, 1793–1798. Pledged impartiality, but became rather Federalist. D.C., H.U.

Haverhill, *Grafton Minerva*, 1796. Seems Federalist. P.L.C.

Keene, *Cheshire Advertiser*, 1792. Doubtful. A.A.S.

Keene, *Columbian Informer*, 1793–1795. Not much politics, but independently Federalist. D.C., N.Y.P.L.

Keene, *New Hampshire Recorder*, 1789. Mildly Federalist. L.C.

Keene, *New Hampshire Sentinel*, 1799–1801. Federalist. D.C., H.U.

Keene, *Rising Sun*, 1795–1798. Federalist. N.Y.H.S.

Portsmouth, *Federal Observer*, 1798–1800. Federalist. B.A.

Portsmouth, *New Hampshire Gazette*, 1791, 1795–1800. Federalist. H.U., N.H.H.S.

Portsmouth, *Oracle of the Day*, 1795, 1797–1799. Semi-weekly and weekly. Independently Federalist. B.A., H.U.

Portsmouth, *Osborne's New-Hampshire Spy*, Feb. 19, 1791. Doubtful. W.H.S.

Portsmouth, *Republican Ledger*, 1799–1801. Democratic. A.A.S., D.C., H.U.

Portsmouth, *United States Oracle of the Day*, 1800–1801. A continuation of the *Oracle of the Day*. Federalist. B.A.

Walpole, *Farmer's Weekly Museum*, 1797, 1799–1800. Federalist. H.U.

Walpole, *New Hampshire and Vermont Journal*, 1795–1797. Federalist. A.A.S.

NEW JERSEY

Bridgeton, *Argus*, 1795–1796. Independently Democratic. H.U.

Burlington, *Advertiser*, or *Agricultural and Political Intelligencer*, 1790–1791. Doubtful. N.Y.P.L.

Elizabeth Town, *New Jersey Journal,* 1787, 1789, 1790–1801. Democratic. N.J.H.S.

Morristown, *Genius of Liberty,* 1795, 1798–1801. Democratic. A.A.S., H.U., P.L.C.

Morristown, *Morris County Gazette,* 1797–1798. Probably independently Federalist. A.A.S., H.U.

Mount Pleasant, *Jersey Chronicle,* 1795–1796. Democratic. N.Y.H.S.

New Brunswick, *Arnett's Brunswick Advertiser,* 1793. Federalist. H.U.

New Brunswick, *Arnett's New Jersey Federalist,* 1795. Independently Federalist. H.U.

New Brunswick, *Brunswick Gazette (Brunswic Gazette* some of this time), 1787–1789, 1791–1792. Doubtful. H.U., L.C., N.J.H.S.

New Brunswick, *Genius of Liberty,* 1795. Appears to lean Federalist. A.A.S.

New Brunswick, *Guardian,* 1792–1794, 1799–1800. Federalist. H.U., L.C., Pa.H.S.

New Brunswick, *New Jersey Federalist,* 1795. Claimed impartiality; probably Federalist. A.A.S., H.U.

Newark, *Centinel of Freedom,* 1796–1801. Democratic. N.J.H.S.

Newark, *Newark Gazette,* 1797–1801. A continuation of *Woods's Newark Gazette.* Federalist. N.J.H.S.

Newark, *Woods's Newark Gazette,* 1791–1797. Federalist. N.J.H.S.

Newton, *Farmers Journal,* 1796–1798. Doubtful. H.U.

Trenton, *Federalist; New Jersey Gazette,* 1798–1801. Federalist. H. U., N.Y.H.S.

Trenton, *New-Jersey State Gazette,* 1792–1796. Gradually became independently Federalist. N.J.H.S.

Trenton, *New Jersey State Gazette,* 1799–1800. Not to be confused with the earlier one of the same name. Federalist. H.U., L.C.

Trenton, *State Gazette,* 1796–1798. Federalist. N.J.H.S., P.L.C.


NEW YORK

Albany, *Albany Centinel,* 1797–1801. Semi-weekly. Federalist. N.Y.H.S.

Albany, *Albany Chronicle,* 1797–1798. Federalist. H.U.

Albany, *Albany Gazette,* 1789–1791, 1795–1797. Semi-weekly. Independently Federalist. A.A.S., H.U., P.L.C.

Albany, *Albany Register,* 1790–1800. Semi-weekly. Democratic. A.A.S., H.U.

Ballston Spa, *Saratoga Register,* 1798.* Impartial, judging from the few copies available. A.A.S.

Bath, *Bath Gazette,* 1797. Probably independently Federalist. H.U.

Brooklyn, *Long Island Courier,* 1800–1801.* Doubtful. L.I.H.S.

Canaan, *Columbian Mercury,* 1794. Doubtful; perhaps Federalist. A.A.S.

Catskill, *Catskill Packet,* 1795–1796. Doubtful; possibly independently Democratic. H.U., N.Y.P.L.

Catskill, *Western Constellation,* Dec. 29, 1800. Possibly Democratic. H.U.

Cooperstown, *Otsego Herald, or Western Advertiser,* 1795–1797. Appears Federalist. H.U., N.Y.P.L.

Geneva, *Impartial American,* Jan. 6, 1801.* Independently Democratic. Conn.H.S.

Geneva, *Ontario Gazette,* Sept. 8, 1797.* Doubtful. A.A.S.

Goshen, *Goshen Repository, and Weekly Intelligencer,* 1789–1799. Doubtful. H.U., N.Y.H.S.

Goshen, *Orange Patrol,* 1800–1801. Democratic, apparently. A.A.S., L.I.H.S., N.Y.H.S.

Hudson, *Hudson Gazette,* 1792–1798. A continuation of the *Hudson Weekly Gazette.* Probably independently Federalist. A.A.S., H.U., N.Y.P.L., W.H.S.

Hudson, *Hudson Weekly Gazette,* 1787–1791. Independently Federalist. A.A.S., H.U.

Johnstown, *Johnstown Gazette,* 1795, 1797–1798. Federalist. H.U., N.Y.P.L.

Kingston, *Farmer's Register,* 1793. Doubtful; perhaps leans Democratic. N.Y.H.S.

Kingston, *Rising Sun,* 1793–1795, 1798. Doubtful; possibly Democratic. N.J.H.S.

Kingston, *Ulster County Gazette,* 1799, 1800. Succeeded the *Rising Sun.* Doubtful; possibly Federalist. N.Y.H.S., W. & L.

Lansingburgh, *American Spy,* 1792, 1795–1798. Federalist. H.U., P.L.C.

Lansingburgh, *Farmer's Oracle,* 1796. Federalist. H.U.

Lansingburgh, *Federal Herald,* 1789, 1790. Not much politics; seems Federalist. A.A.S.

Lansingburgh, *Lansingburgh Gazette,* 1798, 1799. Succeeded the *American Spy.* Federalist. A.A.S., H.U.

Lansingburgh, *Lansingburgh Recorder,* 1794, 1795. Semi-weekly and weekly. Doubtful; perhaps independently Federalist. A.A.S., N.Y.P.L.

Lansingburgh, *Northern Budget,* 1797, 1798. Independently Federalist. A.A.S., H.U.

Lansingburgh, *Tiffany's Recorder,* 1793–1794. Doubtful. A.A.S., N.Y.P.L.

Mount Pleasant, *Impartial Gazette,* July 22, 1800.* Professed impartiality. Conn.H.S.

New York, *American Citizen and General Advertiser,* 1800–1801. Daily. Democratic. N.Y.H.S.
New York, *American Minerva,* 1795, 1796. Daily. Federalist. H.U., N.Y.H.S.
New York, *Argus,* 1795–1800. Daily. Democratic. N.Y.H.S.
New York, *Columbian Gazette,* 1799. Federalist, gradually becoming more independent. B.A., L.C.
New York, *Columbian Gazetteer,* 1793–1794. Semi-weekly. Apparently impartial. N.Y.H.S.
New York, *Commercial Advertiser,* 1800–1801. Daily. Federalist, though not extremely so. N.Y.H.S.
New York, *Daily Advertiser,* 1788, 1791–1792, 1796–1798. Daily. Very little politics, but is Federalist. A.A.S., H.U.
New York, *Diary,* 1796–1798. Daily. Perhaps impartial. H.U., L.C., N.Y.P.L.
New York, *Evening Mercury,* Jan. 1, 3, 1793.* Daily. No politics in these two issues. A.A.S.
New York, *Forlorn Hope,* 1800. Democratic, but little political news. L.C.
New York, *Gazette Française et Americaine,* 1795–1796, 1799. Tri-weekly. Doubtful; chiefly European news. H.U., N.Y.H.S.
New York, *Gazette of the United States,* 1789–1790. Semi-weekly. Federalist. N.Y.H.S.
New York, *Greenleaf's New York Journal,* 1794–1800. Semi-weekly. Democratic. N.Y.P.L.
New York, *Herald,* 1794–1796. Semi-weekly. Mildly Federalist. N.Y.P.L.
New York, *Mercantile Advertiser,* 1798–1800. Daily. Little politics; seems Federalist. A.A.S.
New York, *Minerva,* 1796. Daily. A continuation of the *American Minerva.* Federalist. N.Y.H.S.
New York, *Mott & Hurtin's New-York Weekly Chronicle,* 1795. Doubtful; possibly Democratic. A.A.S., W.H.S.
New York, *New-York Daily Gazette,* 1791, 1795, 1796. Daily. Federalist. H.U., N.Y.H.S.
New York, *New-York Evening Post,* 1794–1795.* Tri-weekly. Leans Federalist. N.Y.H.S.
New York, *New-York Gazette,* 1795–1800. Daily. Probably Federalist. H.U., L.C., N.Y.H.S.
New York, *New-York Journal,* 1787–1793. Semi-weekly and weekly. Democratic. N.Y.H.S.
New York, *New-York Morning Post,* 1787, 1789–1791. Daily. No indication as to partisan allegiance. A.A.S., L.C., H.U.
New York, *New-York Packet,* 1788, 1790–1792. Doubtful. N.Y.H.S.

New York, *New-York Price Current,* 1800, 1801. Commercial news; no politics. A.A.S.

New York, *New-York Weekly Chronicle,* 1795. A continuation of *Mott & Hurtin's New-York Weekly Chronicle.* Doubtful. A.A.S.

New York, *New-York Weekly Museum,* 1791, 1795–1798. Not much politics; perhaps independently Democratic. H.U., N.Y.H.S.

New York, *Porcupine's Gazette,* Jan. 3, 1800.* A single issue; Federalist. N.Y.P.L.

New York, *Prisoner of Hope,* 1800. Weekly and semi-weekly. Impartial. N.Y.P.L.

New York, *Republican Watch-Tower,* 1800–1801. Semi-weekly. Democratic. N.Y.H.S., N.Y.P.L.

New York, *Spectator,* 1800. Semi-weekly. Federalist. N.Y.P.L.

New York, *Tablet,* 1797–1798. Impartial; no politics. L.I.H.S.

New York, *Temple of Reason,* 1800–1801. Not much politics, but leans Democratic. A.A.S.

New York, *Time Piece,* 1797–1798. Tri-weekly. Democratic. N.Y.H.S.

New York, *Youth's News Paper,* 1797. No politics; designed for adolescents. N.Y.P.L.

New Windsor, *New-Windsor Gazette,* 1798. Federalist. H.U.

Newburgh, *Mirror,* 1798. Little political news; perhaps Democratic. A.A.S.

Newburgh, *Orange County Gazette,* 1799. Uncertain; probably Federalist. N.Y.P.L.

Newburgh, *Rights of Man,* 1800. Democratic. N.Y.P.L.

Poughkeepsie, *American Farmer,* 1799–1800. Impartial. A.A.S.

Poughkeepsie, *Poughkeepsie Journal,* 1790, 1793–1795, 1797, 1799. Doubtful; possibly Democratic. B.P.L., H.U., W.H.S.

Poughkeepsie, *Republican Journal,* 1795–1796. Not much politics; probably Democratic. A.A.S., H.U., N.Y.P.L., P.L.C.

Rome, *Columbian Patriotic Gazette,* 1800. Possibly Federalist. A.A.S., L.I.H.S.

Sag Harbor, *Frothingham's Long-Island Herald,* 1791–1798. Independently Democratic. H.U., L.I.H.S., N.Y.H.S., P.L.C.

Salem, *Northern Centinel,* 1798, 1799. Federalist. A.A.S.

Salem, *Times; or Nat'l Courier,* 1794.* Probably independently Democratic. N.Y.P.L.

Salem, *Washington Patrol,* 1795. Federalist. H.U., L.C.

Schenectady, *Mohawk Mercury,* 1795–1797. Not much politics; leans Federalist. H.U., W.H.S.

Schenectady, *Schenectady Gazette,* Oct. 7, 1800. Doubtful. N.Y.H.S.

Scipio, *Levana Gazette or Onondaga Advertiser,* 1798. Affiliation unknown; perhaps independently Federalist. N.Y.P.L.

Troy, *Farmer's Oracle,* 1797–1798. Doubtful; perhaps independently Democratic. H.U.

Troy, *Northern Budget,* 1798–1800. Seems impartial. N.Y.H.S., P.L.C.

Troy, *Recorder,* 1795. Doubtful; perhaps independently Federalist. H.U., L.C., N.Y.P.L.

Upton, *Columbian Courier,* 1794. Inadequate data; possibly Federalist. A.A.S.

Utica, *Whitestown Gazette,* 1796–1798, 1800, 1801. Probably Federalist. N.Y.H.S.

Whitestown, *Western Centinel,* 1794–1797. Independently Federalist. H.U., N.Y.P.L., W.H.S.

Whitestown, *Whitestown Gazette,* 1796–1798. Seems Federalist. H.U.

NORTH CAROLINA

Edenton, *Edenton Gazette,* 1800. Doubtful. U.N.C.

Edenton, *Encyclopedian Instructor,* 1800.* No politics; impartial. A.A.S.

Edenton, *Herald of Freedom,* 1799. A continuation of the *State Gazette of North Carolina.* Mildly Federalist. N.C.H.C.

Edenton, *Post-Angel,* 1800. Impartial? U.N.C.

Edenton, *State Gazette of North Carolina,* 1790–1799. Gradually became Independently Democratic. L.C.

Fayetteville, *Fayetteville Gazette,* 1792–1793. Mildly Democratic. N.C.H.C.

Fayetteville, *North-Carolina Centinel,* 1795. Doubtful. N.C.H.C.

Fayetteville, *North-Carolina Chronicle,* 1790–1791. Doubtful. U.N.C.

Fayetteville, *North-Carolina Minerva,* 1796–1799.* Federalist. N.C.H.C.

Halifax, *North Carolina Journal,* 1792–1800, 1802. Doubtful at first; gradually became Federalist. N.C.H.C., U.N.C.

New Bern, *Newbern Gazette,* 1798–1800. Leans Federalist. H.U., L.C.

New Bern, *North-Carolina Gazette,* 1790, 1791, 1793–1797. Not much politics; possibly mildly Federalist. L.C., U.N.C.

Raleigh, *North Carolina Minerva,* 1796–1800. Federalist. N.C.H.C., U.N.C.

Raleigh, *Raleigh Register,* 1799–1801. Democratic. N.C.S.L.

Salisbury, *North-Carolina Mercury,* 1799–1801. Apparently Federalist. D.U., N.C.H.C.

Wilmington, *Hall's Wilmington Gazette,* 1797–1799. Independently Federalist. U.N.C.

Wilmington, *Wilmington Chronicle,* 1795–1796. Doubtful; perhaps slightly Federalist. H.U., P.L.C.

Wilmington, *Wilmington Gazette,* 1799–1800. A continuation of *Hall's Wilmington Gazette.* Independently Federalist. H.U.

OHIO

Chillicothe, *Scioto Gazette,* 1800.* Seems Democratic. A.A.S.
Cincinnati, *Centinel of the North-Western Territory,* 1793, 1795, 1796. Little politics; perhaps impartial. A.A.S., H.U., P.L.C.
Cincinnati, *Freeman's Journal,* 1796, 1799. Impartial(?). H.U., P.L.C.
Cincinnati, *Western Spy,* 1800–1801. Doubtful. H.U., L.C.

PENNSYLVANIA

Carlisle, *Carlisle Gazette,* 1791–1795. Not much politics; impartial. H.U., N.Y.H.S., P.L.C.
Carlisle, *Eagle,* Sept. 10, 1800. Federalist. A.A.S.
Carlisle, *Telegraphe,* 1795–1796. Independently Democratic. H.U., L.C.
Chambersburg, *Chambersburg Gazette,* 1793, 1795, 1796. Doubtful. H.U., P.L.C.
Chambersburg, *Farmers' Register,* 1798–1799. Independently Democratic. Pa.H.S.
Chambersburg, *Franklin Repository,* 1796, 1799, 1800. Doubtful; perhaps Federalist. H.U., N.Y.H.S., L.C.
Chestnut Hill, *Chestnuthiller Wochenscrift,* 1793. Doubtful; perhaps Democratic. A.A.S.
Doylestown, *Farmer's Weekly Journal,* 1800. No indication of political leaning. L.C.
Easton, *American Eagle,* 1799–1800. Doubtful; perhaps impartial. H.U.
Easton, *Never Unpartheyischer Eastoner Bothe,* 1794, 1795.* Not much politics. A.A.S.
Germantown, *Germantauner Zeitung,* 1792–1793. Semi-weekly and weekly. Democratic. L.C.
Greensburg, *Farmers' Register,* 1799–1800. Democratic. Pa.H.S.
Harrisburg, *Oracle of Dauphin,* 1793–1798, 1801. Independently Federalist; almost Democratic by 1800. H.U., L.C., N.Y.H.S., P.L.C.
Huntingdon, *Guardian of Liberty,* Aug. 14, 1800.* No indication from this one issue. A.A.S.
Huntingdon, *Huntingdon Courier and Weekly Advertiser,* Aug. 8, 1797.* Probably Federalist. A.A.S.
Lancaster, *Americanische Staatbothe,* 1800. A continuation of *Der Deutsche Porcupein.* Federalist. A.A.S.
Lancaster, *Deutsche Porcupein,* 1798. Federalist. L.C.

Lancaster, *The Hive*, 1797. Doubtful. A.A.S.
Lancaster, *Intelligencer*, 1799–1800. Democratic. Pa.H.S.
Lancaster, *Lancaster Correspondent*, 1799. German-language. Definitely Democratic. Pa.H.S.
Lancaster, *Lancaster Journal*, 1795–1799. Independently Federalist. H.U., L.C., P.L.C., U.P.
Lancaster, *Neue Unpartheyische Lancaster Zeitung*, 1793. Seems Federalist. H.U.
Lewistown, *The Monitor of Mifflin & Huntington*, 1798. Perhaps impartial. A.A.S.
Lewistown, *Western Star*, 1801. Appears Democratic. A.A.S.
Norristown, *Norristown Gazette*, 1799–1800. Independently Federalist. A.A.S.
Norristown, *Norristown Herald*, 1800–1801. Federalist. Pa.H.S.
Norristown, *True Republican*, 1801. Democratic. Pa.H.S.
Northumberland, *Sunbury and Northumberland Gazette*, 1796, 1799, 1800. Democratic. H.U., L.C.
Philadelphia, *American Star*, 1794. Tri-weekly. French-language. Seems Federalist. Pa.H.S.
Philadelphia, *Aurora*, 1794–1801. Daily. A continuation of the *General Advertiser*. Democratic. P.L.C.
Philadelphia, *Carey's United States Recorder*, 1798. Tri-weekly. Democratic. P.L.C.
Philadelphia, *Claypoole's American Daily Advertiser*, 1800. Daily. Mildly Federalist. P.L.C.
Philadelphia, *Constitutional Diary*, 1799–1800. Daily. Democratic. H.U., N.Y.H.S., N.Y.P.L.
Philadelphia, *Country Porcupine*, 1798–1799. Tri-weekly. A tri-weekly edition of *Porcupine's Gazette*. Federalist. L.C., M.H.S.
Philadelphia, *Courrier Français*, 1794–1798. Daily and tri-weekly. French-language. Not much politics at first, but came to lean Democratic. J.C.B., N.Y.P.L.
Philadelphia, *Courrier Politique*, 1793–1794. Tri-weekly. French-language. Virtually no domestic news. Impartial. J.C.B., Pa.H.S.
Philadelphia, *Daily Advertiser*, 1797. Daily. Democratic. P.L.C.
Philadelphia, *Dunlap's American Daily Advertiser*, 1791, 1793–1795. Daily. Doubtful; much material from both sides, but perhaps leans a bit Federalist. H.U., Pa.H.S.
Philadelphia, *Federal Gazette*, 1788, 1789, 1791, 1793. Daily. Doubtful. A.A.S., H.U., P.L.C.
Philadelphia, *Finlay's American Naval and Commercial Register*, 1795, 1797. Semi-weekly. Almost no politics; may lean Federalist. P.L.C.
Philadelphia, *Freeman's Journal*, 1791. Possibly mildly Democratic. H.U., L.C.

Philadelphia, *Gales' Independent Gazetteer,* 1796. Semi-weekly. Doubtful. P.L.C.

Philadelphia, *Gazette of the United States,* 1797, 1800, 1801. Semi-weekly and daily. Federalist. H.U., N.Y.H.S.

Philadelphia, *Gemeinnutzige Philadelphische Correspondenz,* Jan. 19, 1790. Political affiliation unknown. A.A.S.

Philadelphia, *General Advertiser,* 1790–1794. Daily. Later called the *Aurora.* Democratic. P.L.C.

Philadelphia, *General Postbothe und die Deutsche Nation in Amerika,* 1789–1790. Semi-weekly. Magazine-like; probably impartial. L.C.

Philadelphia, *Independent Gazetteer,* 1791, 1795, 1796. Daily, weekly, and semi-weekly. Democratic. H.U., P.L.C.

Philadelphia, *Journal des Revolutions,* 1793.\* Tri-weekly. French-language. Impartial. J.C.B.

Philadelphia, *Level of Europe,* 1795–1796.\* French-language. Impartial. B.A.

Philadelphia, *Mail,* 1791, 1793. Daily. Not much politics; possibly independently Federalist. H.U.

Philadelphia, *Merchant's Daily Advertiser,* 1797, 1798. Daily. Doubtful; apparently tried to be impartial. H.U., Pa.H.S.

Philadelphia, *Minerva,* 1795–1796. Possibly Democratic. H.U., L.C.

Philadelphia, *National Gazette,* 1791. Semi-weekly. Democratic. L.C.

Philadelphia, *Neue Philadelphische Correspondenz,* 1790–1792, 1794–1797, 1800. (The *"Neue"* was omitted in the name for several years.) Semi-weekly and weekly. Democratic over most of this period. A.A.S., H.U.

Philadelphia, *New World,* 1796–1797. Twice daily and daily. Professed impartiality, but seems Democratic. L.C.

Philadelphia, *Pelosi's Marine List,* 1791–1792. No politics; impartial. A.A.S., H.U.

Philadelphia, *Pennsylvania Gazette,* 1791, 1795, 1797, 1798, 1800. Federalist. H.U., P.L.C.

Philadelphia, *Pennsylvania Journal,* 1791–1793. Weekly and semi-weekly. Doubtful. H.U., Pa.H.S.

Philadelphia, *Pennsylvania Mercury,* 1790–1791. Tri-weekly and weekly. Not much politics; perhaps mildly Federalist. H.U., Pa.H.S.

Philadelphia, *Pennsylvania Packet,* 1789–1790. Daily. Doubtful; perhaps mildly Federalist. N.Y.H.S.

Philadelphia, *Pensylvanische Correspondenz,* Apr. 24, 1798.\* Semi-weekly. Doubtful. A.A.S.

Philadelphia, *Philadelphia Gazette,* 1800. Daily. Federalist. H.U.

Philadelphia, *Philadelphia Repository,* 1800, 1801. Weekly. Not much news; impartial. A.A.S.

Philadelphia, *Porcupine's Gazette*, 1797–1799. Daily and weekly. Federalist. A.A.S.

Philadelphia, *Poulson's American Daily Advertiser*, 1800. Deplored partisanship; perhaps mildly Federalist. P.L.C.

Philadelphia, *Le Radoteur*, July 16, 1793. Semi-weekly. French-language. Probably impartial. A.A.S.

Philadelphia, *Southwark Gazette*, 1797.* Tri-weekly. Impartial. A.A.S.

Philadelphia, *Supporter*, 1800. Daily and weekly. No indication as to partisanship. H.U.

Philadelphia, *True American*, 1800, 1801. Daily. Attempted to maintain impartiality; perhaps independently Federalist. H.U., Pa.H.S.

Philadelphia, *Universal Gazette*, 1799. Doubtful; perhaps independently Democratic. L.C.

Pittsburgh, *Pittsburgh Gazette*, 1793, 1795–1796, 1798–1801. Weekly and semi-weekly. Independently Federalist. C.L., H.U., P.L.C., U. of C.

Pittsburgh, *Tree of Liberty*, 1800–1801. Democratic. C.L., L.C.

Reading, *Neue Unpartheyische Readinger Zeitung*, 1799–1800. German-language. Seems Federalist. L.C.

Reading, *Readinger Adler*, 1796–1800. German-language. Democratic. A.A.S.

Reading, *Weekly Advertiser*, 1798–1799. Federalist. Pa.H.S.

Uniontown, *Fayette Gazette*, Feb. 10, 1798. Probably Federalist. N.Y.P.L.

Washington, *Herald of Liberty*, Mar. 23, 1801. Democratic. A.A.S.

Washington, *Western Telegraphe*, 1795–1798. Seems Federalist. H.U., P.L.C., U.of C.

West-Chester, *West-Chester Gazette*, Jan. 8, 1794.* Doubtful; perhaps Federalist. Pa.H.S.

Wilkesbarre, *Herald of the Times*, 1796–1797. Independently Federalist. H.U., N.Y.P.L.

Wilkesbarre, *Luzerne County Federalist*, Mar. 9, 1801. Federalist. A.A.S.

York, *Pennsylvania Herald*, 1789, 1790, 1793, 1795, 1796, 1798. Independently Federalist. H.U., P.L.C.

York, *Unpartheyische York Gazette*, 1797. German-language. Doubtful. H.U.

York, *Volks-Berichter ein Yorker Wochenblatt*, 1799–1801. Seems Federalist. A.A.S.

York, *York Recorder*, 1800–1801. Federalist. A.A.S.

Newport, *Companion*, 1798–1799. Independently Federalist. A.A.S.
Newport, *Guardian of Liberty*, 1800–1801. Democratic. H.U.
Newport, *Newport Herald*, 1789–1791. Probably Federalist. A.A.S.,
H.U.
Newport, *Newport Mercury*, 1787, 1788, 1791, 1795–1797, 1799,
1800. Federalist. A.A.S., H.U., L.C.
Newport, *Rhode-Island Museum*, Sept. 29, 1794. Probably Federalist.
A.A.S.
Providence, *Impartial Observer*, 1800, 1801. Democratic. A.A.S.,
N.Y.P.L.
Providence, *Providence Gazette and Country Journal*, 1794, 1795,
1799. Federalist. H.U.
Providence, *Providence Journal*, 1799–1800. Independently Federalist.
L.C.
Providence, *State Gazette*, 1796. Semi-weekly. Claimed impartiality,
but probably independently Federalist. A.A.S., H.U.
Providence, *United States Chronicle*, 1787–1789, 1791, 1794–1796,
1799. Federalist, though not extreme. A.A.S., H.U., L.C.
Warren, *Herald of the United States*, 1793–1795, 1797–1799. Probably
Federalist. H.U., W.H.S.

Charleston, *Carolina Gazette*, 1798–1800. Probably independently
Democratic. H.U.
Charleston, *City Gazette*, 1790, 1791, 1794, 1795, 1798–1800. Daily.
Independently Democratic. C.C.L., C.L.S., H.U., L.C.
Charleston, *Columbian Herald*, 1790, 1793–1796. Semi-weekly, tri-
weekly and daily. Doubtful, growing mildly Federalist. C.C.L.,
C.L.S., HU., P.L.C.
Charleston, *Daily Evening Gazette and Charleston Tea-Table Com-
panion*, 1795.* Daily. Impartial. P.L.C.
Charleston, *Evening Courier*, 1798.* Semi-weekly. Doubtful. H.U.
Charleston, *Federal Carolina Gazette*, 1800. Federalist. H.U., L.C.
Charleston, *South-Carolina State Gazette*, 1794–1797. Daily. A con-
tinuation of the *State Gazette of South Carolina*. Impartial at first;
becomes increasingly Federalist. C.C.L., C.L.S.
Charleston, *Star*, 1793.* Daily and tri-weekly. Seems impartial. A.A.S.
Charleston, *State Gazette of South Carolina*, 1790–1794. Semi-weekly
and tri-weekly. Mostly advertisements, but leans Federalist. C.C.L.

Charleston, *Telegraphe,* 1795.* Daily. Doubtful; perhaps mildly Federalist. A.A.S.

Charleston, *The Times,* 1800–1801. Daily. Nearly impartial; perhaps independently Democratic. C.L.S.

Columbia, *Columbia Gazette,* 1794.* Doubtful; possibly independently Democratic. A.A.S.

Columbia, *South Carolina Gazette,* 1792–1793. Little politics; seems Federalist. A.A.S., P.L.C.

Columbia, *State Gazette,* 1795, 1797, 1798, 1800. A continuation of the *Columbia Gazette.* Doubtful; might be slightly Federalist. H.U.

Georgetown, *Georgetown Chronicle,* 1796, 1797. Weekly and semiweekly. A continuation of the *South-Carolina Independent Gazette.* Doubtful; perhaps Democratic. A.A.S., H.U.

Georgetown, *Georgetown Gazette,* 1798–1800. Weekly and semiweekly. Independently Federalist. C.L.S.

Georgetown, *South-Carolina Independent Gazette,* 1791, 1792. Doubtful; probably Democratic. A.A.S., H.U.

TENNESSEE

Knoxville, *Impartial Observer,* 1800. Mildly Federalist. U.of C.

Knoxville, *Knoxville Gazette,* 1791–1797, 1799, 1801. Bi-weekly and weekly. Seems gradually to lean Federalist. H.U., L.C., P.L.C., U.of C.

Knoxville, *Knoxville Register,* 1798. Doubtful; perhaps Federalist. A.A.S.

Nashville, *Nashville Intelligencer,* 1799.* Mildly Democratic. U.of C.

Nashville, *Rights of Man,* Mar. 11, 1799.* Leans Democratic. U.of C.

Nashville, *Tennessee Gazette,* 1800. Doubtful; perhaps independently Democratic. L.C.

VERMONT

Bennington, *Tablet of the Times,* 1797. Little politics; probably independently Democratic. H.U., Vt.S.L.

Bennington, *Vermont Gazette,* 1787–1791, 1793–1798. Democratic. H.U., L.C., Vt.S.L., W.H.S.

Brattleboro, *Federal Galaxy,* 1797–1799. Federalist. H.U.

Burlington, *Burlington Mercury,* 1796–1797. Doubtful; seems independently Federalist. H.U., P.L.C.

Fair Haven, *Farmers' Library,* 1795–1797. Democratic, though not much politics. H.U.

Newbury, *Orange Nightingale,* 1796–1797. Probably independently Federalist. H.U.

Peacham, *Green Mountain Patriot,* 1798–1801. Claimed impartiality; but seems independently Federalist. A.A.S., H.U.

Putney, *Argus,* 1796–1799. Independently Federalist. H.U., L.C.

Randolph, *Weekly Wanderer,* 1801. Doubtful; perhaps Federalist. A.A.S., Vt.S.L.

Rutland, *Farmers' Library,* 1793–1794. Democratic. A.A.S., Vt.S.L.

Rutland, *Herald of Vermont,* or *Rutland Courier,* 1792. Leans Democratic. H.U., Vt.SL.

Rutland, *Rutland Herald,* 1795–1799. Independently Federalist. H.U.

Vergennes, *Vergennes Gazette,* 1798–1801. Somewhat Federalist. C.H.S., H.U., L.C., P.L.C.

Westminster, *Vermont Chronicle and Windham Advertiser,* 1796. Doubtful; perhaps Federalist. H.U.

Windsor, *Morning Ray,* 1791–1792. Doubtful; perhaps independently Democratic. A.A.S., H.U.

Windsor, *Spooner's Vermont Journal,* 1792–1800. Independently Federalist. A.A.S., H.U., Vt.S.L.

Windsor, *Vermont Journal,* 1790–1792. Doubtful; almost no politics. A.A.S.

Windsor, *Windsor Federal Gazette,* Mar. 10, 1801. Federalist. A.A.S.

VIRGINIA

Alexandria, *Alexandria Advertiser and Commercial Intelligencer,* 1800–1801. Daily. Federalist. A.A.S.

Alexandria, *Alexandria Times,* 1797, 1798, 1800. Daily. Democratic. H.U., L.C., W.H.S.

Alexandria, *Columbian Mirror,* 1793, 1795–1799. Semi-weekly and tri-weekly. Independently Federalist. H.U., L.C., U.of C.

Alexandria, *Virginia Gazette and Alexandria Advertiser,* 1791, 1793. Doubtful; probably Democratic. H.U., L.C., P.L.C.

Dumfries, *Republican Journal,* 1795–1796.* Democratic. H.U., P.L.C.

Dumfries, *Virginia Gazette and Agricultural Repository,* 1791–1793. Doubtful. A.A.S., H.U.

Fincastle, *Herald of Virginia,* Dec. 5, 1800.* Doubtful. L.C.

Fredericksburg, *Courier,* 1800. Semi-weekly. Democratic. A.A.S.

Fredericksburg, *Genius of Liberty,* 1798–1799.* Democratic. A.A.S., L.C., W.H.S.

Fredericksburg, *Republican Citizen,* 1796–1797. Weekly. Independently Democratic. H.U.

Fredericksburg, *Virginia Herald and Fredericksburg and Falmouth Ad-*

*vertiser,* 1787, 1791, 1797–1798, 1800. Weekly and semi-weekly. Federalist. A.A.S., H.U.

Leesburg, *True American,* Dec. 30, 1800. Doubtful. L.C.

Lynchburg, *Lynchburg and Farmer's Gazette,* 1795. A continuation of the *Union Gazette.* Probably Democratic. H.U.

Lynchburg, *Lynchburg Weekly Gazette,* 1798–1799. Seems Federalist. A.A.S., U.of C.

Lynchburg, *Lynchburg Weekly Museum,* 1797. Impartial. H.U.

Lynchburg, *Union Gazette,* 1794.* Doubtful; possibly leans Federalist. A.A.S.

Norfolk, *American Gazette,* 1793–1797. Weekly and semi-weekly. Gradually became independently Democratic. H.U., L.C., P.L.C.

Norfolk, *Epitome of the Times,* 1798–1800. Semi-weekly. Democratic. H.U., L.C.

Norfolk, *Norfolk and Portsmouth Chronicle,* 1791. Impartial. H.U.

Norfolk, *Norfolk and Portsmouth Gazette,* 1789.* Little information; possibly Federalist. L.C.

Norfolk, *Norfolk Herald and Norfolk and Portsmouth Advertiser,* 1795–1797, 1799, 1800. Federalist. H.U., L.C.

Norfolk, *Virginia Chronicle,* 1792, 1794. Weekly and semi-weekly. A continuation of the *Norfolk and Portsmouth Chronicle.* Came to be Democratic. L.C.

Petersburg, *Independent Ledger,* May 8, 1793.* Doubtful. L.C.

Petersburg, *Petersburg Intelligencer,* 1800. Semi-weekly. A continuation of the *Virginia Gazette, and Petersburg Intelligencer.* Probably Democratic. L.C., N.Y.H.S., N.Y.P.L.

Petersburg, *Virginia Gazette and Petersburg Intelligencer,* 1787, 1788, 1793, 1795–1800. Weekly and semi-weekly. Doubtful. A.A.S., H.U., N.Y.P.L., P.L.C., Va.S.L., W.H.S.

Petersburg, *Virginia Star,* 1795. Probably Federalist. H.U.

Richmond, *Examiner,* 1799–1801. Semi-weekly. Democratic. H.U., L.C., N.Y.H.S., Va.S.L.

Richmond, *Friend of the People,* 1800. Fortnightly. Democratic. A.A.S., L.C.

Richmond, *Observatory,* 1798. Semi-weekly. Democratic. H.U.

Richmond, *Richmond and Manchester Advertiser,* 1795–1796. Semi-weekly. Independently Democratic. H.U., L.C.

Richmond, *Richmond Chronicle,* 1795–1796. Semi-weekly. Not much politics, but Democratic. H.U., P.L.C.

Richmond, *Virginia Argus,* 1797–1799. Semi-weekly. A continuation of the *Richmond and Manchester Advertiser.* Democratic. L.C., P.L.C.

Richmond, *Virginia Federalist,* 1799–1800. Semi-weekly. Federalist. H.U.

Richmond, *Virginia Gazette and General Advertiser,* 1790–1799. Weekly and semi-weekly. A continuation of the *Virginia Independent Chronicle.* Doubtful. A.A.S., H.U., N.Y.H.S.

Richmond, *Virginia Gazette and Public Advertiser,* 1791. A continuation of the *Virginia Gazette and Independent Chronicle.* Seems Federalist. H.U.

Richmond, *Virginia Gazette and Richmond and Manchester Advertiser,* 1793–1794. Semi-weekly. Seems independently Democratic. A.A.S., P.L.C., Va.S.L.

Richmond, *Virginia Gazette and Richmond Chronicle,* 1794–1795. Semi-weekly. Doubtful; publisher later Democratic. N.Y.P.L.

Richmond, *Virginia Gazette and Richmond Daily Advertiser,* 1792. Daily. Pledged impartiality, but was slightly Democratic. A.A.S., Va.S.L.

Richmond, *Virginia Gazette and Weekly Advertiser,* 1787–1789, 1791, 1793–1796. Probably mildly Federalist. A.A.S., H.U., Md.H.S., W.H.S.

Richmond, *Virginia Independent Chronicle,* 1790. Doubtful; may lean independently Democratic. L.C.

Staunton, *Phenix,* 1798–1799. Doubtful; seems Federalist. A.A.S., H.U., U.of C.

Staunton, *Political Mirror* or, *The Scourge of Aristocracy,* June 3, 1800.* Democratic. A.A.S.

Staunton, *Staunton Spy,* 1793–1794. Doubtful. A.A.S., P.L.C.

Staunton, *Virginia Gazette,* 1796–1797. Weekly. A continuation of the *Staunton Spy.* Mildly Democratic. H.U., Va.S.L.

Winchester, *Bartgis's Virginia Gazette,* 1789–1791. Probably Federalist. H.L.

Winchester, *Triumph of Liberty,* 1801. Democratic. L.C.

Winchester, *Virginia Centinel* (underwent various name changes, but the name *Centinel* consistently appeared), 1789–1792, 1795, 1798–1801. Seems Federalist. H.L., H.U., L.C., U.of C.

Winchester, *Willis's Virginia Gazette,* 1790. Appears mildly Federalist. H.L.


WEST VIRGINIA (then part of Virginia)

Martinsburg, *Berkeley Intelligencer,* 1790–1800. Indpendently Federalist. B.A., L.C.

Martinsburg, *Potowmac Guardian* (spelled *Potomak* in 1795–1796), 1793, 1795–1797. Probably independently Democratic. H.U., P.L.C., W.H.S.

Martinsburg, *Republican Atlas,* 1801. Democratic. L.C.

Sheperdstown, *Impartial Observer,* 1797. No indication of partisan affiliation. H.U.

Sheperdstown, *Potowmac Guardian,* 1791. Doubtful; editor later became Democratic. H.U.

# BIBLIOGRAPHY

# I. PRIMARY SOURCES

## Manuscripts

Barlow, Joel. Papers. Harvard University Library
Wolcott, Oliver. Papers. New York Public Library

## Books and Articles

A.Z. [pseud.], "Continuation of the Narrative of Newspapers Published in New-England. . . ," *Collections of the Massachusetts Historical Society for the Year 1799,* 64–77.

Adams, John, *The Works of John Adams,* edited by Charles Francis Adams, 10 vols. (Boston: Little, Brown & Co., 1854).

Adams, John Quincy, *Parties in the United States* (New York: Greenburg, 1941).

Ames, Fisher, *The Works of Fisher Ames,* edited by Seth Ames, 2 vols. (Boston: Little, Brown & Co., 1854).

Bentley, William, *Diary of William Bentley, D. D.,* 4 vols. (Salem, Mass.: The Essex Institute, 1907).

Benton, Thomas Hart, *Abridgment of the Debates of Congress, from 1789 to 1856,* 16 vols. (New York: D. Appleton & Co., 1857).

Bonnet, J. E., *Etats-Unis de l'Amerique a la Fin du XVIIIᵉ Siecle,* 2 vols. (Paris: Maradan, 1802 [?]).

CANDIDUS [pseud.], "On American Literature," *Monthly Magazine and American Review* 1 (1799), 338–42.

Chinard, Gilbert, ed., "Correspondence of Jefferson and DuPont de Nemours," *American Historical Review* 37 (Jan. 1932), 358–71.

Coxe, Tench, *A View of the United States of America* (London: J. Johnson, 1795).

Ford, Worthington C., ed., "Letters of William Duane," *Proceedings of the Massachusetts Historical Society* (second ser.), 20 (May, 1906), 257–394.

BIBLIOGRAPHY

————, *Thomas Jefferson and James Thomson Callender* (Brooklyn: Historical Printing Club, 1897).

Foster, Theodore, *Theodore Foster's Minutes of the Rhode Island Convention of March, 1790,* edited by Robert C. Cotner and Verner W. Crane (Providence: Rhode Island Historical Society, 1929).

FRANCISCO [pseud. (Brissot de Warville?)], "Parallel between New-England and Great-Britain," *Monthly Magazine and American Review,* 1 (1799), 12–15.

Freneau, Philip M., *Letters on Various Interesting and Important Subjects* (New York: Scholars' Facsimiles and Reprints, 1943).

Hunt, Gaillard, ed., "Office-Seeking during the Administration of John Adams," *American Historical Review,* 2 (Jan., 1897), 241–61.

Jefferson, Thomas, *The Papers of Thomas Jefferson,* edited by Julian P. Boyd, Vol. 16 (Princeton, N. J.: Princeton Univ. Press, 1961).

Jefferson, Thomas, *The Writings of Thomas Jefferson,* edited by Albert Ellery Bergh, 20 vols. (Washington: The Thomas Jefferson Memorial Association of the United States, 1907).

Jefferson, Thomas, *The Writings of Thomas Jefferson,* edited by Paul Leicester Ford, 10 vols. (New York: G. P. Putnam's Sons, 1895).

Madison, James, *The Writings of James Madison, Comprising His Public Papers and Private Correspondence* . . . , edited by Gaillard Hunt, 9 vols. (New York: G. P. Putnam's Sons, 1900–1910).

Marshall, Humphrey, *The History of Kentucky,* 2 vols. (Frankfort, Ky.: George S. Robinson, 1824).

*National Magazine* (1799).

Otis, Harrison G., *The Life and Letters of Harrison Gray Otis,* edited by Samuel Eliot Morison, 2 vols. (Boston: Houghton Mifflin, 1913).

Phillips, Ulrich B., ed., "The South Carolina Federalists," *American Historical Review* 14 (April–July, 1909), 529–43, 731–43.

————, "South Carolina Federalist Correspondence, 1789–1797," *American Historical Review* 14 (July, 1909), 776–90.

Richardson, James D., ed., *A Compilation of the Messages and Papers of the Presidents,* 20 vols. (New York: Bureau of National Literature, 1897).

Rochefoucauld-Liancourt, Duke de la, *Travels through the United States of North America in 1795–1797,* 2 vols. (London: R. Phillips, 1799).

"South Carolina in the Presidential Election of 1800," *American Historical Review* 4 (Oct., 1898), 111–29.

Thomas, Isaiah, *The History of Printing in America,* 2 vols. (Albany, N.Y.: Joel Munsell, 1874). (*Transactions of the American Antiquarian Society,* 5, 6.)

Turner, Frederick J., ed., "Correspondence of the French Ministers to the United States, 1791–1797," *Annual Report of the American Historical Association, 1903,* II, 7–1110.

Warren, Charles, ed., *Jacobin and Junto, or Early American Politics as Viewed in the Diary of Dr. Nathaniel Ames, 1758–1822* (Cambridge, Mass.: Harvard Univ. Press, 1931).

Wood, John, *A Full Exposition of the Clintonian Faction, and the Society of the Columbian Illuminati* (Newark, N. J.: Printed for the Author, 1802).

*Pamphlets*

AN ELECTOR [pseud.], *PLAIN FACTS, Addressed to every INDEPENDENT ELECTOR in the STATE* [of New York] (New York [?]: 1798 [?]).

Coram, Robert, *Political Inquiries, to Which is Added a Plan for the General Establishment of Schools throughout the United States* (Wilmington, Del.: 1791).

Dwight, Timothy, *A Discourse on Some Events of the Last Century, delivered in the Brick Church in New Haven on Wednesday, Jan. 7, 1801* (New Haven, Conn.: Ezra Read, 1801).

Packard, Hezekiah, *Federal Republicanism displayed in Two Discourses preached on the day of the state fast at Chelmsford, and on the day of the national fast at Concord in April, 1799* (Boston: 1799).

Randolph, Edmund, *A Vindication of Mr. Randolph's Resignation* (Philadelphia: Samuel H. Smith, 1795).

————, *Interesting State Papers, etc.* (London: J. Owen & W. Richardson, 1796).

————, *POLITICAL TRUTH: or Animadversions on the Past and Present State of Public Affairs with an Inquiry into the truth of the charges preferred against Mr. Randolph* (Philadelphia: Samuel Harrison Smith, 1796).

## II. SECONDARY SOURCES

Adams, James Truslow, *The Adams Family* (New York: Blue Ribbon Books, 1933).

————, *The Living Jefferson* (New York: Charles Scribner's Sons, 1936).

Aldrich, P. Emory, "Report of the Council of the American Antiquarian Society" (untitled article on John Locke and His Effect on America), *Proceedings of the American Antiquarian Society, 1879,* 22–39.

Allen, Gardner W., *Our Naval War with France* (Boston: Houghton Mifflin, 1909).

Allen, Harry C., *The Anglo-American Relationship since 1783* (London: Ames & Charles Black, 1959).

———, *Great Britain and the United States* (New York: St. Martin's Press, 1955).

Ambler, Charles Henry, *Sectionalism in Virginia from 1776–1861* (Chicago: Univ. of Chicago Press, 1910).

Ames, Herman V., "The Proposed Amendments to the Constitution of the United States during the First Century of Its History," *Annual Report of the American Historical Association, 1896*, 2: 3–442.

Anderson, Dice Robins, *William Branch Giles: A Study in the Politics of Virginia and the Nation from 1790 to 1830* (Menasha, Wis.: George Banta, 1914).

Anderson, Frank Maloy, "Contemporary Opinion of the Virginia and Kentucky Resolutions," *American Historical Review* 5 (Oct. 1899–Jan. 1900), 45–63, 225–52.

———, "The Enforcement of the Alien and Sedition Laws," *Annual Report of the American Historical Association, 1912*, 115–26.

Andrews, J. Cutler, *Pittsburgh's Post-Gazette* (Boston: Chapman & Grimes, 1936).

Anonymous, "Party Violence, 1790–1800," *Virginia Magazine of History and Biography* 29 (April, 1921), 171–9.

———, "Thomas Paine's Second Appearance in the United States," *Atlantic Monthly* 4 (July, 1859), 1–17.

Austin, James T., *The Life of Elbridge Gerry*, 2 vols. (Boston: Wells & Lilly, 1829).

Austin, Mary S., *Philip Freneau, The Poet of the Revolution* (New York: A. Wessels Co., 1901).

Axelrad, Jacob, *Philip Freneau: Champion of Democracy* (Austin: Univ. of Texas Press, 1967).

Bacot, D. Huger, "Constitutional Progress and the Struggle for Democracy in South Carolina following the Revolution," *South Atlantic Quarterly* 24 (Jan., 1925), 61–72.

Bakeless, John, *Background to Glory: The Life of George Rogers Clark* (Philadelphia: J. B. Lippincott Co., 1957).

Baldwin, Leland D., *Whiskey Rebels: The Story of a Frontier Uprising* (Pittsburgh: Univ. of Pittsburgh Press, 1939).

———, *Pittsburgh: The Story of a City* (Pittsburgh: Univ. of Pittsburgh Press, 1937).

Barker, Howard F., "National Stocks in the Population of the United States as indicated by surnames in the census of 1790," *Annual Report of the American Historical Association, 1931*, I, 107–408.

Barr, Mary-Margaret H., *Voltaire in America, 1744–1800* (Baltimore: Johns Hopkins Press, 1941).

Barstow, Edith M., *News and These United States* (New York: Funk & Wagnalls, 1952).

Bassett, John S., *The Federalist System, 1789–1801* (New York: Harper Bros., 1906).

Baumgartner, Apollinaris W., *Catholic Journalism: A Study of its Development in the United States, 1789–1930* (New York: Columbia Univ. Press, 1931).

Bates, Frank Greene, *Rhode Island and the Formation of the Union* (New York: Macmillan Company, 1898).

Beard, Charles A., *An Economic Interpretation of the Constitution of the United States* (New York: Macmillan Company, 1935).

———, *Economic Origins of Jeffersonian Democracy* (New York: Macmillan Company, 1915).

Becker, Carl L., *The Declaration of Independence* (New York: Harcourt, Brace & Company, 1922).

———, *The Heavenly City of the Eighteenth-Century Philosophers* (New Haven, Conn.: Yale Univ. Press, 1932).

Beer, William, *Checklist of American Periodicals, 1740–1800* (Reprinted from the *Proceedings of the American Antiquarian Society*, Worcester, Mass., 1923).

Bemis, Samuel Flagg, *A Diplomatic History of the United States* (New York: Henry Holt & Co., 3rd ed., 1950).

———, *Jay's Treaty: A Study in Commerce and Diplomacy* (New York: Macmillan Company, 1924).

———, *Pinckney's Treaty: A Study of America's Advantage from Europe's Distress, 1783–1800* (Baltimore: Johns Hopkins Press, 1926).

———, "Thomas Jefferson," in S. F. Bemis, ed., *The American Secretaries of State and their Diplomacy*, 10 vols. (New York: Alfred A. Knopf, 1927), II, 3–93.

———, "The United States and the Abortive Armed Neutrality of 1794," *American Historical Review* 24 (Oct., 1918), 26–47.

———, "Washington's Farewell Address: A Foreign Policy of Independence," *American Historical Review* 39 (Jan., 1934), 250–68.

Benjamin, S. G. W., "Notable Editors between 1776 and 1800," *Magazine of American History* 17 (Feb., 1887), 97–127.

Bent, Silas, *Newspaper Crusaders: A Neglected Story* (New York: Whittlesey House, 1939).

Bernays, Edward L., *Propaganda* (New York: Horace Liveright, 1928).

Bernhard, Winfred E. A., *Fisher Ames: Federalist and Statesman, 1758–1808* (Chapel Hill: Univ. of North Carolina Press, 1965).

Bevan, Wilson Lloyd, ed., *History of Delaware, Past and Present*, 4 vols. (New York: Lewis Historical Publishing Company, Inc., 1929).

Beveridge, Albert J., *The Life of John Marshall,* 4 vols. (Boston: Houghton Mifflin Company, 1916).

Binkley, Wilfred E., *American Political Parties.* 3rd ed. (New York: Alfred A. Knopf, 1958).

Bleyer, Willard Grosvenor, *Main Currents in the History of American Journalism* (Boston: Houghton Mifflin Company, 1927).

Blum, John L., *et al., The National Experience* (New York; Harcourt, Brace & World, 1963).

Bond, Beverly Waugh, Jr., "The Monroe Mission to France, 1794–1796," *Johns Hopkins University Studies in Historical and Political Science,* series 25, Nos. 2–3 (Feb.–Mar., 1907), 9–103.

Borden, Morton, *Parties and Politics in the Early Republic, 1789–1815* (New York: Thomas Y. Crowell Co., 1967).

Bowers, Claude G., *Jefferson and Hamilton* (Boston: Houghton Mifflin Co., 1927).

Bowman, Albert H., "Jefferson, Hamilton, and American Foreign Policy," *Political Science Quarterly* 71 (Mar., 1956), 18–41.

Boyd, Julian P., *Between the Spur and the Bridle* (New York: The Association of American University Presses, 1968).

———, *Number 7, Alexander Hamilton's Secret Attempts to Control American Foreign Policy* (Princeton, N. J.: Princeton Univ. Press, 1964).

Brant, Irving, *James Madison, Father of the Constitution: 1787–1800* (Indianapolis: Bobbs-Merrill Company, 1950).

Bridenbaugh, Carl, "The Press and the Book in Eighteenth Century Philadelphia," *Pennsylvania Magazine of History and Biography* 65 (Jan., 1941), 1–30.

———, and Bridenbaugh, Jessica, *Rebels and Gentlemen: Philadelphia in the Age of Franklin* (New York: Reynal & Hitchcock, 1942).

Brigham, Clarence S., *History and Bibliography of American Newspapers, 1690–1820,* 2 vols. (Worcester, Mass.: American Antiquarian Society, 1947).

———, *Journals and Journeymen* (Philadelphia: Univ. of Pennsylvania Press, 1950).

———, "William McCulloch's Additions to Thomas's History of Printing," *Proceedings of the American Antiquarian Society* 31 (n.s.), (April, 1921), 89–247.

Brown, Charles R., *The Northern Confederacy: New England and the "Essex Junto," 1795–1800* (Princeton, N. J.: Princeton Univ. Press, 1916).

Brown, Philip Anthony, *The French Revolution in English History* (New York: E. P. Dutton & Company, 1924).

Brown, Ralph Adams, "The New Hampshire Press, 1775–1789" (unpublished MS., n.d.).

Brown, Stuart Gerry, *The First Republicans* (Syracuse, N. Y.: Syracuse Univ. Press, 1954).

Brunhouse, Robert L., *The Counter-Revolution in Pennsylvania, 1776–1790* (Harrisburg: Pennsylvania Historical Commission, 1942).

Buckingham, Joseph T., *Specimens of Newspaper Literature* (Boston: Redding & Company, 1852).

Burt, A. L., *The United States, Great Britain and British North America* (New York: Russell & Russell, 1961).

Bushey, Glenn Leroy, "William Duane, Crusader for Judicial Reform," *Pennsylvania History* 5 (July, 1938), 141–56.

Caldwell, Lynton Keith, *The Administrative Theories of Hamilton and Jefferson* (Chicago: Univ. of Chicago Press, 1944).

Callahan, North, *Henry Knox: George Washington's General* (New York: Rinehart & Co., 1958).

Carpenter, William Seal, *The Development of American Political Thought* (Princeton, N. J.: Princeton Univ. Press, 1930).

Carroll, John A., and Ashworth, Mary W., *George Washington: First in Peace* (Vol. VII of Freeman, Douglas, *George Washington*) (New York: Charles Scribner's Sons, 1957).

Chambers, William Nisbet, *Political Parties in a New Nation: The American Experience, 1776–1809* (New York: Oxford Univ. Press, 1963).

Channing, Edward, *A History of the United States*, 6 vols. (New York: Macmillan Company, 1927).

Charles, Joseph, *The Origins of the American Party System* (New York: Harper & Row, 1956).

Childs, Frances Sergeant, *French Refugee Life in the United States, 1790–1800* (Baltimore: Johns Hopkins Univ. Press, 1940).

Chinard, Gilbert, *Honest John Adams* (Boston: Little, Brown & Co., 1933).

Clancy, Herbert J., *The Democratic Party: Jefferson to Jackson* (New York: Fordham Univ. Press, 1962).

Clark, Allen Cullen, *William Duane* (Washington: Privately Printed, 1905).

Clark, Harry Hayden, "Toward a Reinterpretation of Thomas Paine," *American Literature* 5 (May, 1933), 133–45.

Clark, Mary Elizabeth, *Peter Porcupine in America: The Career of William Cobbett, 1792–1800* (Philadelphia: Univ. of Pennsylvania Press, 1939).

Colgrove, Kenneth W., "The Attitude of Congress Toward the Pioneers of the West from 1789 to 1820," *Iowa Journal of History and Politics* 8 (Jan. 1910), 3–129.

Cook, Elizabeth C., *Literary Influences in Colonial Newspapers, 1704–1750* (Port Washington, N. Y.: Kennikat Press, 2nd ed., 1966).

BIBLIOGRAPHY

Coulter, E. Merton, "The Efforts of the Democratic Societies of the West to Open the Navigation of the Mississippi," *Mississippi Valley Historical Review* 11 (Dec., 1924), 376–89.

Crittenden, Charles Christopher, *North Carolina Newspapers before 1790* (Chapel Hill: Univ. of North Carolina Press, 1928).

Cunningham, Noble E., Jr., *The Jeffersonian Republicans* (Chapel Hill: Univ. of North Carolina Press, 1957).

———, "John Beckley: An Early American Party Manager," *William and Mary Quarterly* 13 (Jan., 1956), 40–52.

Curti, Merle Eugene, "The Great Mr. Locke, America's Philosopher, 1783–1861," *Huntington Library Bulletin,* No. 11 (April, 1937), 107–51.

———, *The Growth of American Thought* (New York: Harper & Brothers, 1943).

———, *Peace or War* (New York: W. W. Norton & Company, 1936).

Dabney, Virginius, *Liberalism in the South* (Chapel Hill: Univ. of North Carolina Press, 1932).

Dauer, Manning J., *The Adams Federalists* (Baltimore: Johns Hopkins Univ. Press, 1953).

Davidson, Donald, *The Attack on Leviathan* (Chapel Hill: Univ. of North Carolina Press, 1938).

Davidson, Philip G., *Propaganda and the American Revolution, 1763–1783* (Chapel Hill: Univ. of North Carolina Press, 1941).

———, "Virginia and the Alien and Sedition Laws," *American Historical Review* 36 (Jan., 1931), 336–42.

———, "Whig Propagandists of the American Revolution," *American Historical Review* 39 (April, 1934), 442–53.

Davis, Joseph, *Essays in the Earlier History of American Corporations,* 2 vols. (Cambridge, Mass.: Harvard Univ. Press, 1917).

DeConde, Alexander, *Entangling Alliance* (Durham, N. C.: Duke Univ. Press, 1958).

———, *A History of American Foreign Policy* (New York: Charles Scribner's Sons, 1963).

———, *The Quasi-War* (New York: Charles Scribner's Sons, 1966).

———, "Washington's Farewell, the French Alliance, and the Election of 1796," *Mississippi Valley Historical Review* 43 (Mar., 1957), 641–58.

Diffenderffer, F. R., "Early German Printers of Lancaster and the Issues of Their Press," *Historical Papers and Addresses of the Lancaster County Historical Society* 8 (Jan., 1904), 53–83.

Dill, William A., *Growth of Newpapers in the United States* (Lawrence, Kansas: Univ. of Kansas, April, 1928).

Doob, Leonard W., *Propaganda: Its Psychology and Technique* (New York: Henry Holt & Company, 1935).

904

Dorfman, Joseph, *The Economic Mind in American Civilization, 1606–1865,* 2 vols. (New York: The Viking Press, 1946).
———, "The Economic Philosophy of Thomas Jefferson," *Political Science Quarterly* 55 (1940), 98–121.
Douglass, Elisha P., "The Adventurer Bowles," *William and Mary Quarterly* 6 (Jan., 1949), 3–29.
Downes, Randolph C., *Council Fires on the Upper Ohio* (Pittsburgh: Univ. of Pittsburgh Press, 1940).
———, "Creek-American Relations, 1790–1795," *Journal of Southern History* 8 (Aug., 1942), 350–73.
Dumbauld, Edward, "Thomas Jefferson and Pennsylvania," *Pennsylvania History* 5 (July, 1938), 157–65.
Dunbar, Louise Burnham, "A Study of 'Monarchical' Tendencies in the United States, from 1776 to 1801," *University of Illinois Studies in the Social Sciences* 10 (Mar., 1922), 2–164.
Duniway, Clyde Augustus, *The Development of Freedom of the Press in Massachusetts* (New York: Longmans, Green & Company, 1906).
Dupré, Huntley, "The *Kentucky Gazette* Reports the French Revolution," *Mississippi Valley Historical Review* 26 (Sept., 1939), 163–80.
Dutcher, George M., "The Rise of Republican Government in the United States," *Political Science Quarterly* 55 (June, 1940), 199–216.
East, Robert A., *Business Enterprise in the American Revolutionary Era* (New York: Columbia Univ. Press, 1938).
Eastman, Frank M., "The Fries Rebellion," *Americana* 16 (Jan., 1922), 71–82.
Eiseman, Nathaniel Joseph, "The Ratification of the Federal Constitution by the State of New Hampshire" (unpublished Master's Essay, Columbia Univ., 1936).
Eliot, Thomas D., "The Relations Between Adam Smith and Benjamin Franklin Before 1776," *Political Science Quarterly* 39 (Mar., 1924), 67–96.
Emery, Edwin, and Henry Ladd Smith, *The Press and America* (Englewood Cliffs, N. J.: Prentice-Hall, 1954).
Fairchild, Roy P., ed., *The Federalist Papers* (Garden City, N. Y.: Doubleday & Co. [Anchor Books], 1961).
Farrand, Max, "The First Hayburn Case, 1792," *American Historical Review* 8 (Jan., 1908), 281–85.
Farrison, W. Edward, "The Origin of Brown's *Clotel,*" *Phylon* 15 (Dec., 1954), 347–54.
Fassett, Frederick Gardiner, Jr., *A History of the Newspapers in the District of Maine, 1785–1820* (Orono, Me.: University Press, 1932).
Faust, Albert Bernhardt, *The German Element in the United States,* 2 vols. (Boston: Houghton Mifflin Company, 1909).

Faÿ, Bernard, "Benjamin Franklin Bache, a Democratic Leader of the Eighteenth Century," *Proceedings of the American Antiquarian Society* 40 (Oct., 1930), 277–304.

———, "Early Party Machinery in the United States; Pennsylvania in the Election of 1796," *Pennsylvania Magazine of History and Biography* 60 (Oct., 1936), 375–90.

———, *Notes on the American Press at the End of the Eighteenth Century* (New York: The Grolier Club, 1927).

———, *The Revolutionary Spirit in France and America at the End of the Eighteenth Century* (New York: Harcourt, Brace and Company, 1927).

———, *The Two Franklins: Fathers of American Democracy* (Boston: Little, Brown & Company, 1933).

Fee, Walter R., "The Effect of Hamilton's Financial Policy upon Public Opinion in New Jersey," *Proceedings of the New Jersey Historical Society* 50 (1930), 32–44.

———, *The Transition from Aristocracy to Democracy in New Jersey, 1789–1829* (Somerville, N. J.: Somerset Press, Inc., 1933).

Ferguson, Russell J., "Albert Gallatin, Western Pennsylvania Politician," *Western Pennsylvania Historical Magazine* 16 (Aug., 1933), 183–95.

———, *Early Western Pennsylvania Politics* (Pittsburgh: Univ. of Pittsburgh Press, 1938).

Field, Alston G., "The Press in Western Pennsylvania to 1812," *Western Pennsylvania Historical Magazine* 20 (Dec., 1937), 231–64.

Fisher, George P., "Jefferson and the Social Compact Theory," *Annual Report of the American Historical Association, 1893,* 165–77.

Foik, Paul J., *Pioneer Catholic Journalism* (New York: U. S. Catholic Historical Society, 1930).

Follett, Frederick, *History of the Press in Western New York* (New York: Charles F. Heartman, 1920).

Ford, Worthington C., "Jefferson and the Newspaper," *Records of the Columbia Historical Society* 8 (1905), 78–111.

Forman, Samuel E., "The Political Activities of Philip Freneau," *Johns Hopkins University Studies in Historical and Political Science, 20,* nos. 9–10 (Sept.–Oct., 1902), 465–570.

Fowler, Ila Earle, *Captain John Fowler of Virginia and Kentucky* (Cynthiana, Ky.: The Hobson Press, 1942).

Fox, Dixon Ryan, *The Decline of the Aristocracy in the Politics of New York* (New York: Columbia Univ. Press, 1918).

Franklin, F. G., "The Legislative History of Naturalization in the United States, 1776–1795," *Annual Report of the American Historical Association, 1901,* I, 301–17.

Freeman, Douglas S., *George Washington,* 6 vols. (New York: Charles Scribner's Sons, 1948–1954).

French, Alvah P., "Early History of Westchester County Newspapers," *Americana* 18 (April, 1924), 102–04.

Garraty, John A., *The American Nation: A History of the United States* (New York: Harper & Row, 1966).

Gettell, Raymond G., *History of Political Thought* (New York: The Century Company, 1924).

Gibbs, George, *Memoirs of the Administrations of Washington and John Adams,* 2 vols. (New York: William Van Norden, Printer, 1846).

Gilpatrick, Delbert Harold, *Jeffersonian Democracy in North Carolina, 1789–1816* (New York: Columbia Univ. Press, 1931).

Goddard, Delano A., *Newspapers and Newspaper Writers in New England, 1787–1815* (Boston: A. Williams & Company, 1880).

Good, Harry G., *A History of American Education* (New York: Macmillan, 1956).

Green, Constance McLaughlin, *Washington, Village and Capital, 1800–1878,* vol. 1 (Princeton, N. J.: Princeton Univ. Press, 1962).

Greene, M. Louise, *The Development of Religious Liberty in Connecticut* (Boston: Houghton, Mifflin & Company, 1905).

Griffin, Joseph, *History of the Press of Maine* (Brunswick, Me.: The Press, 1872).

Griffith, Louis T., and Talmadge, John E., *Georgia Journalism, 1763–1950* (Athens, Ga.: Univ. of Georgia Press, 1951).

Griswold, Rufus Wilmot, *The Republican Court, or American Society in the Days of Washington* (New York: D. Appleton & Company, 1856).

Gurn, Joseph, *Charles Carroll of Carrollton, 1737–1832* (New York: P. J. Kenedy & Sons, 1932).

Hall, William Phelps, *British Radicalism, 1791–1797* (New York: Columbia Univ. Press, 1912).

Hamilton, Frederick W., *A Brief History of Printing in America* (Chicago: United Typothetae of America, 1918).

Hamilton, Milton W., *The Country Printer: New York State, 1785–1830* (New York: Columbia Univ. Press, 1936).

Hammond, Bray, *Banks and Politics in America from the Revolution to the Civil War* (Princeton, N. J.: Princeton Univ. Press, 1957).

Hammond, Jabez D., *The History of Political Parties in the State of New-York,* 2 vols. (Cooperstown, N. Y.: H. & E. Phinney, 1845).

Harding, Samuel B., *The Contest over the Ratification of the Federal Constitution in the State of Massachusetts* (New York: Longmans, Green & Co., 1896).

Hart, Freeman H., *The Valley of Virginia in the American Revolution, 1763–1789* (Chapel Hill: Univ. of North Carolina Press, 1942).

Hart, James, *The American Presidency in Action, 1789* (New York: Macmillan Company, 1948).

Harvey, Oscar J., "Wilkes-Barre's Earliest Newspapers," *Proceedings . . . of the Wyoming Historical and Genealogical Society* 18 (1922), 59–98.

Harvey, Ray Forest, *Jean Jacques Burlamaqui* (Chapel Hill: Univ. of North Carolina Press, 1937).

Haskins, Charles B., "The Yazoo Land Companies" (Abstract), *Annual Report of the American Historical Association, 1890,* 83.

Hazen, Charles Downer, *Contemporary American Opinion of the French Revolution* (Baltimore: Johns Hopkins Press, 1897).

Hofstadter, Richard, "Parrington and the Jeffersonian Tradition," *Journal of the History of Ideas* 2 (Oct., 1941), 391–400.

Hooper, Osman Castle, *History of Ohio Journalism, 1793–1933* (Columbus, Ohio: The Spahr & Glenn Company, 1933).

Howard, Leon, *The Connecticut Wits* (Chicago: Univ. of Chicago Press, 1943).

Hudson, Frederic, *Journalism in the United States* (New York: Harper & Brothers, 1873).

Hunt, Gaillard, "Office Hunting during Jefferson's Administration," *American Historical Review* 3 (Jan., 1898), 270–91.

Hutchinson, Elmer T., "A Pioneer New Jersey Printer," *Proceedings of the New Jersey Historical Society* 55 (April, 1937), 133–48.

Institute for Propaganda Analysis, Inc., *Propaganda Analysis,* I (1937–1938).

Jacobs, James Ripley, *The Beginning of the U. S. Army, 1783–1812* (Princeton, N. J.: Princeton Univ. Press, 1947).

———, *Tarnished Warrior* (New York: Macmillan Company, 1938).

Jacobson, J. Mark, *The Development of American Political Thought* (New York: The Century Company, 1932).

James, James Alton, "French Diplomacy and American Politics, 1794–1795," *Annual Report of the American Historical Association, 1911,* I, 153–63.

Janson, Charles William, *The Stranger in America, 1793–1806* (New York: The Press of the Pioneers, Inc., 1935).

Jenkins, Howard M., ed., *Pennsylvania, Colonial and Federal,* 3 vols. (Philadelphia: Pennsylvania Historical Publishing Association, 1903).

Jensen, Merrill, "Democracy and the American Revolution," in Wahlke, John C., ed., *The Causes of the American Revolution* (Boston: D. C. Heath & Co., 1962), 71–85.

Johnson, Allen and Malone, Dumas, eds., *Dictionary of American Biography* 20 vols. (New York: Charles Scribner's Sons, 1928–1936).

Johnson, Guion Griffis, *Ante-Bellum North Carolina* (Chapel Hill: Univ. of North Carolina Press, 1937).

Johnston, Elma Lawson, *Trenton's Newspapers, 1778–1932* (Trenton, N. J.: Trenton Times Newspapers, 1932).

Jones, Howard Mumford, *America and French Culture, 1750–1848* (Chapel Hill: Univ. of North Carolina Press, 1927).

Jones, Robert W., *Journalism in the United States* (New York: E. P. Dutton & Company, 1947).

Keidel, George C., *The Earliest German Newspapers of Baltimore* (Washington: Privately Printed, 1927).

Keller, Charles Roy, *The Second Great Awakening in Connecticut* (New Haven, Conn.: Yale Univ. Press, 1942).

Kelly, Alfred H., and Winfred A. Harbison, *The American Constitution: Its Origins and Development* (New York: W. W. Norton & Co., 1948).

Kimball, Marie, *Jefferson: War and Peace* (New York: Coward-Mc-Cann, 1947).

King, William L., *The Newspaper Press of Charleston, South Carolina* (Charleston, S. C.: Edward Perry, 1872).

Klein, Philip Shriver, *Pennsylvania Politics, 1817–1832, A Game Without Rules* (Philadelphia: Historical Society of Pennsylvania, 1940).

———, "Senator William Maclay," *Pennsylvania History,* X (April, 1943), 83–93.

Knollenberg, Bernhard, *The Origin of the American Revolution* (New York: Macmillan, 1960).

Kobre, Sidney, *Foundations of American Journalism* (Tallahassee, Fla: Institute of Media Research, 1958).

Koch, Adrienne, *The Philosophy of Thomas Jefferson* (New York: Columbia Univ. Press, 1943).

———, and Ammon, Harry, "The Virginia and Kentucky Resolutions: An Episode in Jefferson's and Madison's Defense of Civil Liberties," *William and Mary Quarterly* 5 (April, 1948), 145–76.

Koch, G. Adolf, *Republican Religion: The American Revolution and the Cult of Reason* (New York: Henry Holt & Company, 1933).

Konkle, Burton Alva, *Thomas Willing and the First American Financial System* (Philadelphia: Univ. of Pennsylvania, 1937).

Kramer, Eugene F., *The Creswell Libel Case and Freedom of the Press in New York State* (Albany: Univ. of the State of New York, 1968).

Krout, John A., and Fox, Dixon Ryan, *The Completion of Independence* (New York: Macmillan Company, 1944).

Kull, Irving S., ed., *New Jersey: A History,* 4 vols. (New York: American Historical Society, Inc., 1930).

Kurtz, Louis, *The Presidency of John Adams: The Collapse of Federalism, 1795–1800* (Philadelphia: Univ. of Pennsylvania Press, 1957).
Lasswell, Harold; Casey, Ralph D.; and Smith, Bruce L., *Propaganda and Promotional Activities (an Annotated Bibliography)* (Minneapolis: Univ. of Minnesota Press, 1935).
Leary, Lewis G., *That Rascal Freneau* (New Brunswick, N. J.: Rutgers Univ. Press, 1941).
Lee, Alfred McClung, *The Daily Newspaper in America* (New York: MacMillan Company, 1937).
Lee, James M., *America's Oldest Newspaper, The New York Globe* (New York: The Globe, 1918).
——, *History of American Journalism* (Garden City, N. Y.: Garden City Publishing Company, 1923).
Lerche, Charles O., Jr., "Jefferson and the Election of 1800: A Case Study in the Political Smear," *William and Mary Quarterly* 5 (Oct., 1948), 467–91.
Levermore, Charles H., "The Rise of Metropolitan Journalism, 1800–1840," *American Historical Review* 6 (April, 1901), 446–65.
Levy, Leonard W., *Freedom of Speech and Press in Early American History: The Legacy of Suppression* (New York: Harper & Row, 1963).
Lewin, William, *A Story of New Jersey Journalism* (Newark, N. J.: Newark Printing Company, 1928).
Libby, Orin Grant, "The Geographical Distribution of the Vote of the Thirteen States on the Federal Constitution, 1787–1788," *Bulletin of the University of Wisconsin* 1 (1894), 1–116.
——, "Political Factions in Washington's Administrations," *Quarterly Journal of the University of North Dakota* 3 (July, 1913), 293–318.
——, "A Sketch of the Early Political Parties in the United States," *Quarterly Journal of the University of North Dakota* 2 (April, 1912), 205–42.
Link, Eugene Perry, "The Democratic Societies of the Carolinas" (Unpublished MS., c. 1940).
——, *Democratic-Republican Societies, 1790–1800* (New York: Columbia Univ. Press, 1942).
Ludlum, David M., *Social Ferment in Vermont, 1791–1850* (New York: Columbia Univ. Press, 1939).
Luetscher, George D., *Early Political Machinery in the United States* (Philadelphia: Unknown, 1903).
Lynch, William O., *Fifty Years of Party Warfare (1789–1837)* (Indianapolis: Bobbs-Merrill Company, 1931).

910

Lyon, E. Wilson, "The Directory and the United States," *American Historical Review* 43 (April, 1938), 514–32.

McGuire, James K., ed., *The Democratic Party of the State of New York,* 3 vols. (New York[?]: United States History Company, 1905).

McLaughlin, Andrew C., *A Constitutional History of the United States* (New York: D. Appleton-Century Company, 1935).

McLaughlin, J. Fairfax, *Matthew Lyon—The Hampden of Congress* (New York: Wynkoop Hallenbeck Crawford Company, 1900).

McMaster, John Bach, *A History of the People of the United States, from the Revolution to the Civil War,* 5 vols. (New York: D. Appleton & Company, 1885).

———, and Stone, Frederick D., eds., *Pennsylvania and the Federal Constitution, 1787–1788* (Philadelphia: Historical Society of Pennsylvania, 1888).

McMurtrie, Douglas Crawford, *The Beginnings of the American Newspaper* (Chicago: The Black Cat Press, 1935).

———, *Early Printing in Tennessee* (Chicago: Chicago Club of Printing House Craftsmen, 1933).

———, *A History of Printing in the United States (Middle and South Atlantic States),* (New York: R. R. Bowker Company, 1936).

———, *John Bradford, Pioneer Printer of Kentucky* (Springfield, Ill.: Privately Printed, 1931).

McPherson, Elizabeth G., "The Southern States and the Reporting of Senate Debates, 1789–1802," *Journal of Southern History* 12 (May, 1946), 223–46.

McWilliams, Elizabeth, "Political Activities in Western Pennsylvania, 1800–1816," *Western Pennsylvania Historical Magazine* 7 (Oct., 1924), 225–34.

Mahin, Helen Ogden, *The Development and Significance of the Newspaper Headline* (Ann Arbor, Mich.: George Wahr, 1924).

Main, Jackson Turner, *The Anti-Federalists* (Chapel Hill: Univ. of North Carolina Press, 1961).

Malone, Dumas, "The First Years of Thomas Cooper in America, 1794–1801," *South Atlantic Quarterly* 22 (April, 1923), 139–56.

———, *Jefferson and His Time,* 5 vols. (Boston: Little, Brown & Co., 1948–  ).

———, "The Threatened Prosecution of Alexander Hamilton under the Sedition Act by Thomas Cooper," *American Historical Review* 29 (Oct., 1923), 76–81.

Marble, Annie Russell, *From 'Prentice to Patron: The Life Story of Isaiah Thomas* (New York: D. Appleton-Century Company, 1935).

Marsh, Philip M., "Freneau and Jefferson: The Poet Editor Speaks for Himself about the *National Gazette* Episode," *American Literature* 8 (May, 1936), 180–89.

———, "The Griswold Story of Freneau and Jefferson," *American Historical Review* 51 (Oct., 1945), 68–73.

———, "Maine's First Newspaper Editor: Thomas Wait," *New England Quarterly* 28 (Dec., 1955), 519–34.

———, "Philip Freneau and His Circle," *Pennsylvania Magazine of History and Biography* 63 (Jan., 1939), 37–59.

Martin, Benjamin Ellis, "Transition Period of the American Press," *Magazine of American History* 17 (April, 1887), 273–94.

Martin, Charlotte M., and Martin, Benjamin Ellis, "The New York Press and Its Makers in the Eighteenth Century," *Half Moon Series* 2 (April, 1898), 121–62.

Masterson, William H., *William Blount* (Baton Rouge, La.: Louisiana State Univ. Press, 1954).

Mayes, Martin, *An Historical–Sociological Inquiry into Certain Phases of the Development of the Press in the United States* (Richmond, Mo.: Missourian Press, 1935).

Mayo, Lawrence Shaw, *John Langdon of New Hampshire* (Concord, N. H.: Rumford Press, 1937).

Meigs, William M., "Pennsylvania Politics Early in this Century," *Pennsylvania Magazine of History and Biography* 17 (1893), 462–90.

Mesick, Jane Louise, *The English Traveller in America, 1785–1835* (New York: Columbia Univ. Press, 1922).

Miller, Daniel, "Early German American Newspapers," *Proceedings of the Pennsylvania-German Society* 19 (1910), 1–107.

Miller, John C., *Alexander Hamilton: Portrait in Paradox* (New York: Harper and Row, 1959).

———, *Crisis in Freedom, The Alien and Sedition Acts* (Boston: Little, Brown and Company, 1952).

———, *The Federalist Era, 1789–1801* (New York: Harper & Row, 1960).

———, Sam Adams, *Pioneer in Propaganda* (Boston: Little, Brown and Company, 1936).

Miller, William, "The Democratic Societies and the Whiskey Insurrection," *Pennsylvania Magazine of History and Biography* 62 (July, 1938), 324–49.

———, "First Fruits of Republican Organization: Political Aspects of the Congressional Election of 1794," *Pennsylvania Magazine of History and Biography* 63 (April, 1939), 118–43.

Minnigerode, Meade, *Jefferson—Friend of France* (New York: G. P. Putnam's Sons, 1928).

———, *Presidential Years, 1787–1860* (New York: G. P. Putnam's Sons, 1928).

Mitchell, Broadus, *Alexander Hamilton*, 2 vols. (New York: Macmillan, 1957–1962).

Monaghan, Frank, *John Jay: Defender of Liberty* (New York & Indianapolis: Bobbs-Merrill Company, 1935).

Moore, Jacob B., "History of Newspapers Published in New Hampshire, from 1756 to 1840," *American Quarterly Register* 13 (Nov., 1840), 170–81.

Moore, John W., *Moore's Historical . . . Notes, Relative to Printers, Printing, Publishing, and Editing . . .* (Concord, N. H.: Republican Press Association, 1886).

Morais, Herbert M., *Deism in Eighteenth Century America* (New York: Columbia Univ. Press, 1934).

Morison, Samuel Eliot, *The Oxford History of the American People* (New York: Oxford Univ. Press, 1965).

———, and Commager, Henry S., *Growth of the American Republic*, 2 vols. (New York: Oxford Univ. Press, 1942).

Morse, Anson E., "Causes and Consequences of the Party Revolution of 1800," *Annual Report of the American Historical Association, 1894*, 531–39.

———, *The Federalist Party in Massachusetts to the Year 1800* (Princeton, N. J.: University Library, 1909).

Morse, James King, *Jedidiah Morse, A Champion of New England Orthodoxy* (New York: Columbia Univ. Press, 1939).

Mott, Frank Luther, *American Journalism* (New York: Macmillan Company, 1941).

———, *A History of American Magazines*, 3 vols. (New York: D. Appleton & Company, 1930).

———, *Jefferson and the Press* (Baton Rouge, La.: Louisiana State Univ. Press, 1943).

———, "Newspapers in Presidential Campaigns," *Public Opinion Quarterly* 8 (Fall, 1944), 348–67.

———, and Casey, Ralph D., *Interpretations of Journalism* (New York: F. S. Crofts & Company, 1937).

Mowry, Don Ensminger, "Political Verse Satires of the Factional Period of American History, 1789–1806," *Americana* 5 (Feb., 1910), 211–21.

Mudge, Eugene Tenbroeck, *The Social Philosophy of John Taylor of Caroline* (New York: Columbia Univ. Press, 1939).

Mullett, Charles F., Review of *Jean Jacques Burlamaqui*, by Ray F. Harvey, *American Historical Review* 44 (Jan., 1939), 402–03.

Munroe, John A., *Federalist Delaware, 1775–1815* (New Brunswick, N. J.: Rutgers Univ. Press, 1954).

Munsell, Joel, *The Typographical Miscellany* (Albany, N. Y.: Joel Munsell, 1850).

Muzzey, David S., *Thomas Jefferson* (New York: Charles Scribner's Sons, 1918).

Nelson, William, *Notes toward a History of the American Newspaper* (New York: Charles F. Heartman, 1918).

———, "Some New Jersey Printers and Printing in the Eighteenth Century," *Proceedings of the American Antiquarian Society* 21 (Apr., 1916), 15–56.

Nettels, Curtis P., *The Emergence of a National Economy, 1775–1815* (New York: Holt, Rinehart & Winston, 1962).

Nevins, Allan, *American Press Opinion, Washington to Coolidge* (Boston: D. C. Heath & Company, 1928).

———, *The American States during and after the Revolution, 1775–1789* (New York: Macmillan Company, 1924).

Nichols, Roy F., *The Invention of the American Political Parties* (New York: Macmillan, 1967).

North, S. N. D., *The Newspaper and Periodical Press* (Washington: Government Printing Office, 1884).

Oberholtzer, Ellis Paxson, *The Literary History of Philadelphia* (Philadelphia: George W. Jacobs & Company, 1906).

Ogden, Henry V. S., "The State of Nature and the Decline of Lockian Political Theory in England, 1760–1800," *American Historical Review* 46 (Oct., 1940), 21–44.

Ogg, Frederic Austin, "Jay's Treaty and the Slavery Interests of the United States," *Annual Report of the American Historical Association, 1901*, I, 275–98.

Parrington, Vernon Louis, *Main Currents in American Thought*, 3 vols. (New York: Harcourt, Brace & Company, 1930).

Parsons, Henry S., *A Check List of American Eighteenth Century Newspapers in the Library of Congress* (Washington: Government Printing Office, 1936).

———, "The First American Newspapers," *Antiques* 29 (Feb., 1936), 62–64.

Payne, George Henry, *History of Journalism in the United States* (New York: D. Appleton & Company, 1920).

Penniman, Thomas D., "The Early History of the *Baltimore American*," *Maryland Historical Magazine* 28 (Sept., 1933), 272–78.

Perkins, Bradford, *The First Rapprochement: England and the United States, 1795–1805* (Philadelphia: Univ. of Pennsylvania Press, 1955).

914

Perrin, William Henry, "The First Newspaper West of the Alleghenies," *Magazine of American History* 18 (Aug., 1887), 121–27.

———, *The Pioneer Press of Kentucky* (Louisville, Ky.: John P. Morton & Company, 1888).

Peter, Robert, *History of Fayette County, Kentucky* (Chicago: O. L. Baskin & Company, 1882).

Peterson, Merrill D., *The Jeffersonian Image in the American Mind* (New York: Oxford Univ. Press, 1960).

Phillips, James D., "Salem's Part in the Naval War with France," *New England Quarterly* 16 (Dec., 1943), 543–66.

Phillips, Ulrich B., "Georgia and State Rights," *Annual Report of the American Historical Association, 1901,* II, 3–224.

Pollard, James E., *The Presidents and the Press* (New York: Macmillan Company, 1947).

Prentiss, Hervey Putnam, *Timothy Pickering as the Leader of New England Federalism, 1800–1815* (Evanston, Ill.: Northwestern Univ. Press, 1932).

Presbrey, Frank, *The History and Development of Advertising* (Garden City, N. Y.: Doubleday, Doran & Company, Inc., 1929).

Prince, Carl E., *New Jersey's Jeffersonian Republicans* (Chapel Hill: Univ. of North Carolina Press, 1967).

Purcell, George W., "A Survey of Early Newspapers in the Middle Western States," *Indiana Magazine of History* 20 (Dec., 1924), 347–63.

Purcell, Richard J., *Connecticut in Transition, 1775–1818* (Washington: American Historical Association, 1918).

Randall, John H., Jr., *Making of the Modern Mind* (Boston: Houghton Mifflin, 1940).

Read, Conyers, ed., *The Constitution Reconsidered* (New York: Columbia Univ. Press, 1938).

Reitzel, William, "William Cobbett and Philadelphia Journalism: 1794–1800," *Pennsylvania Magazine of History and Biography* 59 (July, 1935), 223–44.

Rich, Bennett Milton, *The Presidents and Civil Disorder* (Washington: The Brookings Institution, 1941).

Rich, Wesley Everett, *The History of the United States Post Office to the Year 1829* (Cambridge, Mass.: Harvard Univ. Press, 1924).

Riley, Isaac Woodbridge, *American Philosophy: The Early Schools* (New York: Dodd, Mead & Company, 1907).

———, *American Thought, from Puritanism to Pragmatism and Beyond* (New York: Henry Holt & Company, 1915).

Ritenour, John S., "Early Newspapers of Southwestern Pennsylvania," *Inland Printer* 51 (June, 1913), 427–30.

Robinson, Edgar E., *The Evolution of American Political Parties* (New York: Harcourt, Brace & Company, 1924).

Robinson, Elwyn Burns, "The Dynamics of American Journalism from 1787 to 1865," *Pennsylvania Magazine of History and Biography* 61 (Oct. 1937), 435–45.

Robinson, William A., *Jeffersonian Democracy in New England* (New Haven, Conn.: Yale University Press, 1916).

Rossiter, Clinton, *Seedtime of the Republic* (New York: Harcourt, Brace & Co., 1953).

Roth, George L., "Verse Satire on 'Faction,' 1790–1815," *William and Mary Quarterly* s. 3, 17 (Oct., 1960), 473–85.

Rusk, Ralph Leslie, *The Literature of the Middle Western Frontier*, 2 vols. (New York: Columbia Univ. Press, 1926).

Ryden, George H., *Delaware—The First State in the Union* (Wilmington, Del.: Delaware Tercentenary Commission, 1938).

Salmon, Lucy M., *The Newspaper and Authority* (New York: Oxford Univ. Press, 1923).

——, *The Newspaper and the Historian* (New York: Oxford Univ. Press, 1923)

Schachner, Nathan, *Aaron Burr* (New York: Frederick A. Stokes Company, 1937).

——, *Alexander Hamilton* (New York: D. Appleton-Century, Inc., 1946).

Scharf, John T., *A History of Delaware*, 2 vols. (Philadelphia: L. J. Richards & Company, 1888).

——, and Westcott, Thompson, *History of Philadelphia, 1609–1884*, 3 vols. (Philadelphia[?]: Unknown, 1884).

Schlesinger, Arthur M., "Colonial Newspapers and the Stamp Act," *New England Quarterly* 8 (Mar., 1935), 63–89.

——, *Prelude to Independence: The Newspaper War on Britain, 1764–1776* (New York: Alfred A. Knopf, Inc., 1957).

Scott, Frank W., "Newspapers, 1775–1860," in Trent, William P., *et al.,* eds., *Cambridge History of American Literature,* 3 vols. (New York: Macmillan Company, 1933), II, 176–95.

Sears, Louis Martin, *George Washington and the French Revolution* (Detroit: Wayne State Univ. Press, 1960).

Seidensticker, Oswald, *The First Century of German Printing in America, 1728–1830* (Philadelphia: Schaefer & Koradi, 1893).

Seligman, Edwin R. A., ed., *Encyclopedia of the Social Sciences,* 15 vols. (New York: Macmillan Company, 1935).

Sherrill, Charles H., *French Memories of Eighteenth-Century America* (New York: Charles Scribner's Sons, 1915).

Shulim, Joseph I., *John Daly Burk: Irish Revolutionist and American*

*Patriot* (Philadelphia: American Philosophical Society, *Transactions,* n. s., vol. 54, part 6, Oct., 1964).

Simms, Henry H., *Life of John Taylor* (Richmond, Va.: William Byrd Press, 1932).

Sloane, William Milligan, *Party Government in the United States of America* (New York: Harper and Row, 1914).

Smelser, Marshall, "George Washington and the Alien and Sedition Acts," *American Historical Review* 59 (Jan., 1954), 322–34.

———, "The Jacobin Phrenzy: Federalism and the Menace of Liberty, Equality and Fraternity," *Review of Politics* 13 (Oct., 1951), 457–82).

Smith, J. Eugene, *One Hundred Years of Hartford's Courant* (New Haven, Conn.: Yale Univ. Press, 1949).

Smith, James Morton, "Alexander Hamilton, the Alien Law, and Seditious Libels," *Review of Politics* 16 (July, 1954), 305–33.

———, "The Federalist 'Saints' versus 'The Devil of Sedition': The Liberty Pole Cases of Dedham, Massachusetts, 1798–1799," *New England Quarterly* 28 (June, 1955), 198–215.

———, *Freedom's Fetters* (Ithaca, N. Y.: Cornell Univ. Press, 1956).

Smith, Page, *John Adams,* 2 vols. (Garden City, N. Y.: Doubleday & Co., 1962).

Sonne, Niels Henry, *Liberal Kentucky, 1780–1828* (New York: Columbia Univ. Press, 1939).

Spargo, John, *Anthony Haswell, Printer—Patriot—Ballader* (Rutland, Vt.: The Tuttle Company, 1925).

Spaulding, E. Wilder, "The *Connecticut Courant,* a Representative Newspaper in the Eighteenth Century," *New England Quarterly* 3 (July, 1930), 443–63.

———, *His Excellency George Clinton, Critic of the Constitution* (New York: Macmillan Company, 1938).

———, *New York in the Critical Period, 1783–1789* (New York: Columbia Univ. Press, 1932).

Speicher, Ruth, "The Federal Constitution as Viewed by the Newspapers of 1787," *Social Studies* 28 (Oct., 1937), 265–69.

Spengler, Joseph J., "The Political Economy of Jefferson, Madison and Adams," in Jackson, David K., ed., *Studies in Honor of William Kenneth Boyd* (Durham, N. C.: Duke University Press, 1940), 3–59.

Spiller, Robert E.; Thorp, Willard; Johnson, Thomas H.; and Canby, Henry S.; eds., *Literary History of the United States,* 3 vols. (New York: Macmillan Company, 1949).

Spurlin, Paul Merrill, *Montesquieu in America, 1760–1801* (Baton Rouge: Louisiana State Univ. Press, 1940).

Stanwood, Edward, *A History of the Presidency* (Boston: Houghton Mifflin, 1904).

Stauffer, Vernon, *New England and the Bavarian Illuminati* (New York: Columbia Univ. Press, 1918).

Steiner, Bernard C., "Connecticut's Ratification of the Federal Constitution," *Proceedings of the American Antiquarian Society* 25 (1915), 70–127.

————, "Maryland's Adoption of the Federal Constitution," *American Historical Review* 5 (Oct., 1899–Jan., 1900), 22–44, 207–24.

Stewart, Donald H., "Irish Immigration to New York City, 1790–1840" (unpublished seminar MS., Columbia Univ., 1938).

————, "The Press and Political Corruption During the Federalist Administrations" (portions reprinted with permission from the *Political Science Quarterly* 47, No. 3 [Sept., 1952], 426–46).

Sullivan, William, *Familiar Letters on Public Characters and Public Events* (Boston: Russell, Odiorne, & Metcalf, 1834).

Talmadge, John E., *Georgia Journalism, 1763–1950* (Athens, Ga.: Univ. of Georgia Press, 1951).

Tapley, Harriet S., *Salem Imprints, 1768–1825* (Salem, Mass.: Essex Institute, 1927).

Taylor, Coley, and Middlebrook, Samuel, *The Eagle Screams* (New York: Macaulay Company, 1936).

Tebbel, John, *The Compact History of the American Newspaper* (New York: Hawthorn Books, 1963).

Thomas, Charles M., *American Neutrality in 1793* (New York: Columbia Univ. Press, 1931).

Thomas, E. Bruce, *Political Tendencies in Pennsylvania, 1783–1794* (Philadelphia: Temple University, 1938).

Thomas, Elbert D., *Thomas Jefferson, World Citizen* (New York: Modern Age Books, 1942).

Thorning, Joseph Francis, *Religious Liberty in Transition* (Washington: Catholic University of America, 1931).

Thorpe, Francis Newton, *The Constitutional History of the United States,* 3 vols. (Chicago: Callaghan & Company, 1901).

Thwaites, Reuben Gold, "The Ohio Valley Press before the War of 1812–15," *Proceedings of the American Antiquarian Society* 19 (Apr., 1909), 309–68.

Tinkcom, Harry M., *The Republicans and Federalists in Pennsylvania, 1790–1801* (Harrisburg, Pa.: Pennsylvania Historical and Museum Commission, 1950).

Tolles, Frederick B., *George Logan of Philadelphia* (New York: Oxford Univ. Press, 1953).

Turner, Frederick J., "English Policy toward America in 1790–1791," *American Historical Review* 7 (July, 1902), 706–35.

———, "The Policy of France toward the Mississippi Valley in the Period of Washington and Adams," *American Historical Review* 10 (Jan., 1905), 249–79.

Vail, R. W. G., "The *Ulster County Gazette* Found at Last," *Bulletin of the New York Public Library* 35 (April, 1931), 207.

———, "The *Ulster County Gazette* and Its Illegitimate Offspring," *Bulletin of the New York Public Library* 34 (April, 1930), 207–38.

van der Linden, Frank, *The Turning Point* (Washington: Robert Luce, 1962).

Van Every, Dale, *Ark of Empire: The American Frontier, 1784–1803* (New York: William Morrow & Co., 1963).

———, *Forth to the Wilderness* (New York: William Morrow & Co., 1961).

Wagstaff, Henry McGilbert, *Federalism in North Carolina, James Sprunt Historical Publications,* 9, No. 2 (Chapel Hill: Univ. of North Carolina Press, 1910).

Walters, Raymond, Jr., *Albert Gallatin: Jeffersonian Financier and Diplomat* (New York: Macmillan Company, 1957).

———, "The Origins of the Jeffersonian Party in Pennsylvania," *Pennsylvania Magazine of History and Biography* 66 (Oct., 1942), 440–58.

Walton, Joseph S., "Nominating Conventions in Pennsylvania," *American Historical Review* 2 (Jan., 1897), 262–78.

Warren, Charles, *The Making of the Constitution* (Boston: Little, Brown and Co., 1928).

Weeks, Stephen Beauregard, *The Press of North Carolina in the Eighteenth Century* (Brooklyn: Historical Printing Club, 1891).

Weisberger, Bernard A., *The American Newspaperman* (Chicago: Univ. of Chicago Press, 1961).

Weyl, Nathaniel, *Treason* (Washington: Public Affairs Press, 1950).

Wheeler, Joseph Towne, *The Maryland Press, 1779–1790* (Baltimore: Maryland Historical Society, 1938).

Wheeler, William Bruce, "Urban Politics in Nature's Republic: The Development of Political Parties in the Seaport Cities in the Federalist Era" (Ph.D. dissertation, Univ. of Virginia, 1967).

Whitaker, Arthur Preston, ed., "Harry Innes and the Spanish Intrigue: 1794–1795," *Mississippi Valley Historical Review* 15 (Sept., 1928), 236–48.

———, *The Spanish-American Frontier: 1783–1795* (Boston: Houghton Mifflin Company, 1927).

White, Leonard D., *The Federalists: A Study in Administrative History* (New York: Macmillan Company, 1948).

——, "The Hamilton-Jefferson Feud," in *The Gaspard G. Bacon Lectures on the Constitution of the United States, 1940–1950* (Boston: Boston Univ. Press, 1953), 213–31.

Willey, Malcolm M., "The Functions of the Newspaper," *Annals of the American Academy* 219 (Jan., 1942), 18–24.

Williams, Chauncey K., *History of Rutland Newspapers* (Pamphlet: Date and Place unknown, c. 1880).

Winship, George Parker, "French Newspapers in the United States from 1790–1800," *Papers of the Bibliographical Society of America* 14 (1920), 82–126.

——, "Two or Three Boston Papers," *Papers of the Bibliographical Society of America* 14 (1920), 57–81.

Winslow, Ola Elizabeth, *Master Roger Williams* (New York: Macmillan, 1957).

Winsor, Justin, ed., *Memorial History of Boston,* 4 vols. (Boston: James R. Osgood & Company, 1881).

Wittke, Carl, *The German-Language Press in America* (Lexington, Ky.: Univ. of Kentucky Press, 1957).

Wolfe, John Harold, *Jeffersonian Democracy in South Carolina* (Chapel Hill: Univ. of North Carolina Press, 1940).

Woodbury, Margaret, *Public Opinion in Philadelphia, 1789–1801* (Northampton, Mass.: Smith College, 1919–1920).

Woodfin, Maude Howlett, "Citizen Genêt and His Mission" (Ph.D. dissertation, Univ. of Chicago, 1928).

——, "Contemporary Opinion in Virginia of Thomas Jefferson," in Craven, Avery, ed., *Essays in Honor of William E. Dodd* (Chicago: Univ. of Chicago Press, 1935), 30–85.

Wroth, Lawrence C., "The First Press in Providence; A Study in Social Development," *Proceedings of the American Antiquarian Society* 51 (n. s.), (Oct., 1941), 351–83.

Young, Alfred F., *The Democratic Republicans of New York: The Origins, 1763–1797* (Chapel Hill: Univ. of North Carolina Press, 1967).

Zucker, Morris, *Periods in American History* (New York: Arnold-Howard Publishing Company, Inc., 1945).

# INDEX

Abercrombie, James, 330, 401, 410, 416

Abolition, proposals of, 43, 550

Abuse, 449, 543. *See also* Slander

Adams, Abigal, 508, 513, 537-38

Adams, Abijah, 412, 476-77

Adams, John, absences from Capitol, 76-78, 93, 259-60, 536-37; administration of, 323, 339, 367-68, 386, 390, 406, 408-09, 424-25, 428, 444, 465, 470-73, 476, 480-481, 497-98, 513, 548-49, 563, 565; British interests of, 187, 606-07; Cabinet of, 292, 501-02; and Congress, 76, 81, 240, 289-93, 308, 330, 490; elections participated in, 273, 278, 334, 443, 459, 531, 533, 535, 560-61, 591, 598, 613; expenses of government, 75, 81, 607; Federalist viewpoints of, 5, 18, 67, 92-94, 109-13, 124, 233, 253, 265, 267, 269; and France, 119, 282, 387, 516; Fries' Rebellion, 92, 94; and Holland, 307; messages and papers of, 76, 190, 256, 282, 284-85, 291-93, 299, 306, 330, 450, 488-89, 537; midnight court appointments of, 602; mon-

archical tendencies of, 490-93, 508-09, 546, 572; and New England, 589; newspapers support, 3, 31, 570; peace efforts of, 109, 333, 455, 457; personality of, 105, 119, 244, 246, 281, 314, 331, 333, 343, 485-86, 507, 596; political contemporaries of, 247, 261-63, 303, 311, 316, 344, 384, 472, 483, 516-17; religious activities of, 79, 295, 344, 403, 417, 555; unpopularity of, 10, 246, 256, 294, 486, 537, 541-42, 585-86, 599, 639

Adams, John Quincy, 514-15, 536, 612

Adams, Samuel, 10, 153, 165, 399-400, 578, 616

Adams, Thomas, 133, 297, 470, 476-77, 616

Addison, Alexander, 68-69, 475, 587

Adet, Pierre, 129, 172, 207, 277-80, 286-87, 489, 532

Admiralty Courts, 178-79, 192, 232, 238

Adultery, 298, 540

Advertisements, 18, 21, 61, 66, 73, 158, 258, 610, 614

933

935

elections in, 582, 589, 593, 599; frontiersmen in, 551; government of, 87, 366, 368, 435, 493, 511, 580; newspapers in, 58; paper money in, 57, 87, 391; politics in, 587-92

*Maryland Gazette,* 238

Mason, John T., 346

Mason, Stevens T., 198, 546

Masonic Order, 210, 411-13, 459

Massachusetts, 63-64, 116, 123, 182, 339-45, 349, 363-67, 371-73, 380, 391, 404, 463, 491, 510, 564, 591; Democrats in, 157; elections in, 316, 472, 578; Federalists in, 395, 474, 564, 587; legislature of, 48, 51, 63, 74, 91, 347, 453, 476, 572, 581, 612; Republicans in, 590

*Massachusetts Mercury,* 118

Materialism, 396

Mather, Samuel, 131

Mathews, George, 358

Maumee River, 136

Mayflower Compact, 419

Mazzei, Philip, 9, 457, 464, 527, 549, 555, 595

McClenachan, Blair, 214

McClusky, D., 356

McGillivray, Alexander, 141, 144, 250, 353-56

McHenry, James, 93, 109, 272, 543, 586, 601

McHenry, Fort, 318

McKean, Thomas, 311, 388, 407, 493, 513, 554, 571, 581-83

McKee, Alexander, 317

McLean, Canadian rebel, 248

McMaster, John B., 613

McPherson, General, 76

Mechanics, 6-7, 63, 118, 184, 231, 375, 389, 392, 430, 640

Medford, Bishop of, 400-01

Medford, Massachusetts, 399

Mediterranean Sea, 180, 251, 253

"Mentor," 357

Mercantile interests, 113, 362, 377-78, 501-02, 543

Merchantmen, armed, 178, 185, 234, 240-01, 247, 288-91, 308-10, 322, 325

Merchants, 43, 53-55, 63, 83, 99, 119, 139, 156, 185-88, 194-96, 209, 228-32, 258, 278, 299, 315, 319, 328, 341, 345, 354, 369, 376, 381-82, 390-92, 463, 510, 537, 580

Meredith, Samuel, 107-08

Mess of pottage, 48. *See also* Assumption

Methodist Sect, 408, 416

Metropolitan areas, discriminated against, 91

Mexico, 290

Miami Indians, 359

"Michael Servetus," 407

Middle Atlantic States, 48, 340, 342

*Middlesex Gazette,* 431

Mifflin, Thomas, 163-65, 303, 511, 572

Militia and military establishment, 34, 68, 74, 84-88, 91-92, 132, 153, 248, 251, 299, 351, 356, 361, 371, 374-75, 386, 441-44, 513, 537, 546, 594, 607

Miller, Joe, 501

Milton, John, Political writings of, 420

*Minerva* (New York), 20, 367, 599

Minister of Peace called for, 98

Mint, the, 78

Mirabeau, Honoré, 41, 410, 547

*Mirror* (Washington, Ky.), 473

*Mirror of the Times* (Wilmington, Del.), 109, 111, 484, 586, 596

Mississippi River, 145, 168-69, 184,

Necker, Jacques, 41
Negroes, 206, 326, 338, 344-45, 352, 510, 557. *See also* Slaves and slavery
Nepotism, 76, 104, 512-13, 536
"Nestor," 297
Neutral nations, 126, 178-79, 195, 197, 233, 278-79
Neutrality, principles of, 29-30, 46, 87, 120, 134, 147-48, 152-54, 201, 221, 256, 264-66, 275-76, 334, 363, 383
Neutrality Proclamation, 145, 154-55, 183, 243, 253, 279, 520, 523
New England, 16, 28, 48, 90, 258, 342, 360, 365, 368, 391, 397, 401, 410, 503, 517; citizens of, 72-76, 79-81, 85, 90, 111-12, 117, 250, 291, 337-38, 343-44, 349, 363-66, 375, 383-84, 393, 416, 537, 545, 560, 585; clergy in, 80-81, 395-96, 399, 405-06, 410; and Democrats, 367, 616; education in, 369; and Federalists, 76, 342-44, 369, 399, 589, 637; fisheries, 340-41; and Illuminati, 413; merchants in, 369; newspapers, 36, 87, 180, 186, 352; and Republicans, 394, 413; tours of, 374, 541
New England *Palladium,* 638
New Hampshire, 81, 211, 215, 255, 343, 375, 413, 427, 453, 463, 587, 591
*New Hampshire Gazette,* 575
New Haven, Conn., 394
New Jersey, 10, 16, 202, 246, 345, 511, 513, 582-83, 587; citizens of, 375, 393, 471, 576; legislature of, 364, 474, 585, 588-94; newspapers in, 45, 52, 154; politicians in, 39-40, 74, 90, 340, 477, 595, 601

New Jersey College, 417
*New Jersey Journal* (Elizabethtown), 57, 147, 575
*New Jersey State Gazette,* 180
New Jerusalem, 412
New London, Conn., 304, 309, 464
New Orleans, La., 264
"New Tories," 563
*New Windsor Gazette,* 470
New York City, 49, 61, 74, 88, 390, 556, 573, 583, 617
*New York Evening Post,* 10-11
*New York Herald,* 175, 273, 435
*New York Journal,* 12, 30, 48, 50, 59, 162, 191, 212, 292, 365, 368, 521, 577, 617
New York *Star,* 611
New York State, 49, 51, 68, 91, 135, 182, 223, 237, 324, 337-40, 353, 366-67, 391, 393, 456, 469, 514, 589; Democrats in, 301, 580; demonstrations in, 118; elections, 261, 477, 583, 586, 599-600; Federalists, 346, 592; government, 91, 234, 356, 510, 543, 578, 609; harbors in, 61, 155; Illuminati in, 417; mariners of, 187; merchants in, 209; newspapers in, 257, 348, 379; Republicans, 578, 590-91, 600; speculators in, 36; up-state, 572, 617
New York *Temple of Reason,* 401, 602
New York Treaty with the Creeks, 144, 202, 250, 355, 358
New York Trespass Act, 214
Newark, N.J., 291, 435, 464, 476
Newark *Gazette,* 29
Newburport, Mass., 46
Newgate Prison, 516
Newport, R. I., 127, 131, 172, 232, 237, 241, 332
Newport *Companion,* 324

*Petite Démocrate,* French ship, 152
Petitions and petitioners, 40, 84;
133, 184-85, 522
Pettifoggers, 391
Philadelphia, 26, 49-51, 79, 87-88,
92, 111, 135, 152, 157, 185-87,
193, 199, 202, 212, 220, 309-11,
326-30, 337-38, 368, 375, 378,
385-86, 416, 462, 465-67, 480,
491, 499, 502, 506-07, 521-22,
535, 538, 542, 568; Congress removed to, 609; customs collector,
105; Democrats in, 12, 156; Federalists in, 364, 389, 588; harbor,
61; immigrants, 614; merchants,
209; newspapers, 10, 46, 347-48,
416, 551, 610, 618; public square,
118; Republicans in, 11, 610;
theater, 120, 301; town meeting,
214; war hawks in, 291; yellow
fever in, 137, 158, 579, 612
Philadelphia County, 378, 570
*Philadelphia Gazette,* 347, 551, 618
Philadelphia *New World,* 10, 12,
348, 618
*Philadelphische Correspondenz,* 12,
433, 618
"Philanthropus," 401, 409
"Philolentherog," 441, 551
Philosophy and philosophers, 388
*Phoenix,* 179
Physicians, 377
Physiocrats, 377
Pickering, Timothy, 240, 243-44,
247, 253, 256-58, 261, 264, 267-
68, 278-79, 284, 287, 290, 293-
95, 305, 314, 332-35, 363, 460-
63, 476, 497, 508, 517-19, 586,
595, 597; contemporaries of, 70,
174, 280, 543, 601; corruption of,
104-13, 287, 330, 543, 601-02;
dismissal of, 262; and England,
262; and France, 334; Fries Rebellion, 93; as land speculator,

67-70; and newspapers, 111, 246,
473; as Secretary of State, 446,
543
"Pickeroons," 517
Pigot, Captain Hugh, 227
Pinckney, Charles, 6, 632
Pinckney, Charles C., 261-63, 270,
277-81, 292, 296, 302, 306, 311,
334-35, 344-46, 370, 417, 483,
518, 546, 562, 586-87, 593, 596,
628
Pinckney, Thomas, 211, 221-22,
269-70, 344, 517; Treaty nego-
tiated by, 66, 75, 220, 250, 357
Pinckney, Clan, 270, 513
Pioneers, southern, 357
Piracy and pirates, 38, 81-82, 103,
155, 175-77, 195, 191, 210, 246,
251-55, 291, 300, 386, 470
Pitt, William (the Younger), 95,
169, 206, 211, 251, 257-60, 289,
296
"Pittachus," 213, 524-25, 530
Pittsburgh, Pa., 87, 362, 587
*Pittsburgh Gazette,* 11, 216, 613
Pittsburgh *Tree of Liberty,* 11, 329,
364, 595, 601, 613
Pittsfield *Sun,* 410, 428
Plagiarism, 25
"Plain argument," 95
"Plan for the General Establish-
ment of Schools throughout the
United States," 447
Plantations and planters of the
South, 6, 375, 381
Plots, 161-62, 328, 330, 347, 352,
466, 548
Plumer, William, 570
Plunder, 104-05, 109, 515, 523
Plutocracy and plutocrats, 43
Poetry and poets, 20, 52, 61-62, 95-
96, 504
Poison pen campaign, 420
Poland, 132

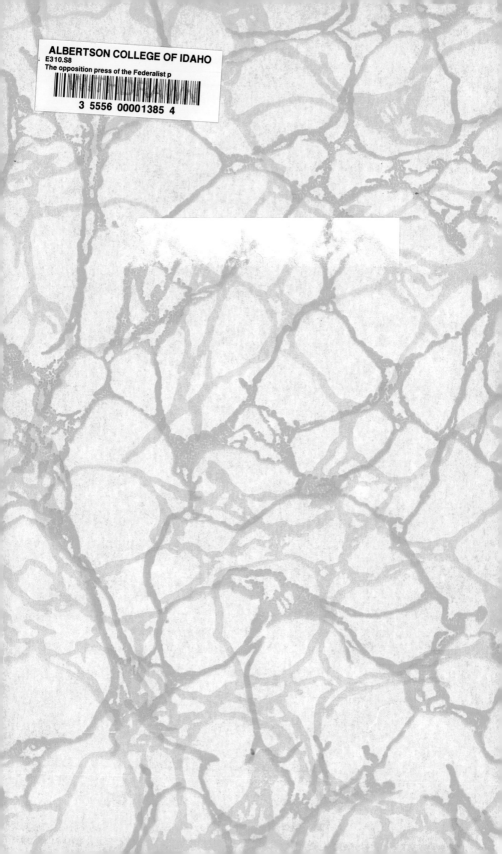